T0396041

The Oxford Annotated Mishnah

The Oxford Annotated Mishnah

*A New Translation of the Mishnah
With Introductions and Notes*

Volume I

EDITED BY
Shaye J. D. Cohen
Robert Goldenberg
Hayim Lapin

OXFORD
UNIVERSITY PRESS

OXFORD
UNIVERSITY PRESS

Great Clarendon Street, Oxford, OX2 6DP,
United Kingdom

Oxford University Press is a department of the University of Oxford.
It furthers the University's objective of excellence in research, scholarship,
and education by publishing worldwide. Oxford is a registered trade mark of
Oxford University Press in the UK and in certain other countries

© Oxford University Press 2022

The moral rights of the authors have been asserted

First Edition published in 2022

All rights reserved. No part of this publication may be reproduced, stored in
a retrieval system, or transmitted, in any form or by any means, without the
prior permission in writing of Oxford University Press, or as expressly permitted
by law, by licence or under terms agreed with the appropriate reprographics
rights organization. Enquiries concerning reproduction outside the scope of the
above should be sent to the Rights Department, Oxford University Press, at the
address above

You must not circulate this work in any other form
and you must impose this same condition on any acquirer

Published in the United States of America by Oxford University Press
198 Madison Avenue, New York, NY 10016, United States of America

British Library Cataloguing in Publication Data

Data available

Library of Congress Control Number: 2020946217

ISBN 978-0-19-284614-3 (Pack)
ISBN 978-0-19-923970-2 (Vol I)
ISBN 978-0-19-284612-9 (Vol II)
ISBN 978-0-19-284613-6 (Vol III)

Printed and bound by
CPI Group (UK) Ltd, Croydon, CR0 4YY

Links to third party websites are provided by Oxford in good faith and
for information only. Oxford disclaims any responsibility for the materials
contained in any third party website referenced in this work.

*Dedicated to the memory of
Robert Goldenberg (1942–2021), Scholar and Friend*

Acknowledgements

This is the work of many years and many hands. Shaye Cohen began it, thinking he could translate and annotate the Mishnah single-handedly. When he realized that the completion of that task would exceed the divinely mandated limit of 120 years, he recruited two others to join him as editors, Robert Goldenberg and Hayim Lapin. Even with the dedicated efforts of all three editors, the project seemed to go on without end; now that the project is finally done, our gratitude is due most of all to our contributors, whose names are listed collectively in the table of contents and individually in the introductions to each tractate.

The editors also thank the following for their assistance in proofreading some early drafts, saving them from numerous errors and suggesting numerous improvements: Gregory Fain, Will Friedman, Rabbi Leonard Gordon, Deborah Klapper, Tzipporah Machlah Klapper, Micah Newberger, and Avram Schwartz. The glossary is the work of Robert Goldenberg and Rabbi Leonard Gordon. Special thanks to Oxford University Press and its editor Tom Perridge for their patience.

Contents

VOLUME I

List of Figures   xiii

List of Contributors   xv

INTRODUCTION   1

THE MISHNAH

ORDER OF ZERA'IM   11

Tractate Berakhot   *Richard S. Sarason*   13

Tractate Pe'ah   *Gregg E. Gardner*   39

Tractate Demai   *Richard S. Sarason*   76

Tractate Kilayim   *Michael Rosenberg*   105

Tractate Shevi'it   *Yair Furstenberg*   144

Tractate Terumot   *William Friedman and Matthew Hass*   195

Tractate Ma'aserot   *Joshua Kulp*   253

Tractate Ma'aser Sheni   *Joshua Kulp*   276

Tractate Hallah   *Joshua Kulp*   309

Tractate Orlah   *Joshua Kulp*   330

Tractate Bikkurim   *Naftali S. Cohn*   345

ORDER OF MO'ED   365

Tractate Shabbat   *Shaye J. D. Cohen*   367

Tractate Eruvin   *Charlotte Elisheva Fonrobert*   438

Tractate Pesahim   *Jonathan Klawans*   494

Tractate Sheqalim   *Miriam-Simma Walfish*   557

Tractate Yoma   *Yonatan S. Miller*   589

Tractate Sukkah   *Jeffrey L. Rubenstein*   628

Tractate Betsah   *Judith Hauptman*   658

Tractate Rosh Hashanah   *Steven D. Fraade*   678

Tractate Ta'anit   *David Levine*   697

Tractate Megillah   *Alyssa Gray*   720

Tractate Mo'ed Qatan   *Gail Labovitz*   741

Tractate Hagigah   *Michal Bar-Asher Siegal*   753

VOLUME II

Contents   iii

List of Figures   v

ORDER OF NASHIM   3

Tractate Yevamot   *Tal Ilan*   5

Tractate Ketubbot   *Robert Brody*   81

Tractate Nedarim   *Robert Goldenberg*   128

Tractate Nazir   *Robert Goldenberg*   181

Tractate Sotah   *Ishay Rosen-Zvi and Orr Scharf*   222

Tractate Gittin   *David Brodsky*   259

Tractate Qiddushin   *Gail Labovitz*   304

ORDER OF NEZIQIN   333

Tractate Bava Qamma   *Hayim Lapin*   335

Tractate Bava Metsi'a   *Hayim Lapin*   382

Tractate Bava Batra   *Hayim Lapin*   439

Tractate Sanhedrin   *Beth Berkowitz*   490

Tractate Makkot   *David C. Flatto*   557

Tractate Shevu'ot   *Elizabeth Shanks Alexander*   584

Tractate Eduyot   *Shaye J. D. Cohen*   628

Tractate Avodah Zarah   *Christine Hayes*   678

Tractate Avot   *Martin S. Jaffee*   710

Tractate Horayot   *Alyssa Gray*   759

VOLUME III

Contents   iii

List of Figures   v

CONTENTS

ORDER OF QODASHIM 3

Tractate Zevahim   *Aryeh Cohen*   5
Tractate Menahot   *Dvora Weisberg*   62
Tractate Hullin   *Jordan D. Rosenblum*   120
Tractate Bekhorot   *Chaya Halberstam*   168
Tractate Arakhin   *Jonah Steinberg*   213
Tractate Temurah   *Tzvi Novick*   244
Tractate Keritot   *Moulie Vidas*   271
Tractate Me'ilah   *Sarra Lev*   305
Tractate Tamid   *Naftali S. Cohn*   331
Tractate Middot   *Naftali S. Cohn*   361
Tractate Qinnim   *Dalia Marx*   387

ORDER OF TOHOROT 401

Tractate Kelim   *Michael Chernick*   403
Tractate Oholot   *Yehudah Cohn*   534
Tractate Nega'im   *Mira Balberg*   610
Tractate Parah   *Marcus Mordecai Schwartz*   675
Tractate Tohorot   *Yair Furstenberg*   718
Tractate Miqva'ot   *Yonatan Adler*   768
Tractate Niddah   *Charlotte Elisheva Fonrobert*   825
Tractate Makhshirin   *Hannah Harrington*   869
Tractate Zavim   *Shlomo Zuckier*   898
Tractate Tevul Yom   *David Levine*   919
Tractate Yadayim   *Leib Moscovitz*   937
Tractate Uqtsin   *Richard Hidary*   957

Appendix: Money, Weights, and Measures   973
Glossary of Untranslated Hebrew Terms   975
Index of Biblical Passages   985
Index of Names and Subjects   989

List of Figures

1A Women in *Yevamot* 1:1   Volume II, 8
1B Women in *Yevamot* 1:3   Volume II, 8
2   The Temple in Jerusalem   Volume III, 366

List of Contributors

Yonatan Adler
Ariel University

Elizabeth Shanks Alexander
University of Virginia

Mira Balberg
University of California San Diego

Beth Berkowitz
Barnard College

David Brodsky
Brooklyn College

Robert Brody
Hebrew University of Jerusalem

Michael Chernick
Hebrew Union College-
Jewish Institute of Religion

Aryeh Cohen
American Jewish University

Shaye J. D. Cohen
Harvard University

Naftali S. Cohn
Concordia University

Yehudah Cohn
New York University

David C. Flatto
Hebrew University of Jerusalem

Charlotte Elisheva Fonrobert
Stanford University

Steven D. Fraade
Yale University

William Friedman
Harvard University

Yair Furstenberg
Hebrew University of Jerusalem

Gregg E. Gardner
University of British Columbia

Robert Goldenberg
Stony Brook University (emeritus)

Leonard Gordon
B'nai Tikvah, Canton, MA

Alyssa Gray
Hebrew Union College-
Jewish Institute of Religion

Chaya Halberstam
Western University, Canada

Hannah Harrington
Patten University

Matthew Hass
Harvard University

Judith Hauptman
Jewish Theological Seminary

Christine Hayes
Yale University

Richard Hidary
Yeshiva University

Tal Ilan
Freie Universität Berlin

Martin S. Jaffee
University of Washington

Jonathan Klawans
Boston University

Joshua Kulp
Conservative Yeshiva

Gail Labovitz
American Jewish University

Hayim Lapin
University of Maryland

Sarra Lev
Reconstructionist Rabbinical College

David Levine
Hebrew Union College-
Jewish Institute of Religion

Dalia Marx
Hebrew Union College-
Jewish Institute of Religion

Yonatan S. Miller
University of Toledo

Leib Moscovitz
Bar-Ilan University

Tzvi Novick
University of Notre Dame

Michael Rosenberg
Hadar Institute

Jordan D. Rosenblum
University of Wisconsin-Madison

Ishay Rosen-Zvi
Tel Aviv University

Jeffrey L. Rubenstein
New York University

Richard S. Sarason
Hebrew Union College-
Jewish Institute of Religion

Orr Scharf
University of Haifa

Marcus Mordecai Schwartz
Jewish Theological Seminary

Michal Bar-Asher Siegal
Ben-Gurion University of the Negev

Jonah Steinberg
Harvard University

Moulie Vidas
Princeton University

Miriam-Simma Walfish
Harvard University

Dvora Weisberg
Hebrew Union College-
Jewish Institute of Religion

Shlomo Zuckier
McGill University

Introduction

Shaye J. D. Cohen and Hayim Lapin

What Is the Mishnah?

The Mishnah ("repetition" or "teaching"), the first rabbinic book, composed in Hebrew in the Land of Israel and edited around 200 CE, is an anthology primarily about matters of Jewish practice, ritual, and law. In addition to statements, whether anonymous or attributed to named individuals, the Mishnah contains other literary forms as well, notably lists, disputes, anecdotes, maxims, Scriptural exegesis, and descriptions of the rituals of the Jerusalem Temple. The Sages named in the Mishnah (called collectively *tanna'im*, "teachers," sing. *tanna*) are customarily assigned by modern scholars to distinct generations; the bulk of the named mishnaic Sages belong to either the generation of Yavneh (ca. 80–120 CE) or the generation of Usha (ca. 140–180 CE). (Yavneh and Usha are the names of towns in the Land of Israel, Yavneh in the south not far from Jerusalem, Usha in the north in Galilee, in which the Sages are said to have gathered.) R. Eliezer, R. Joshua, R. Aqiva, and Rabban Gamaliel are some of the prominent Sages of the Yavneh period, R. Meir, R. Judah, R. Simeon, and R. Yose are some of the prominent Sages of the Usha period. Relatively little material is ascribed to named figures who lived before the destruction of the Jerusalem Temple in 70 CE. By convention we call the Sages "rabbis" and their work "rabbinic," because the title "Rabbi" (abbreviated "R.") regularly appears in their literature.

The Mishnah covers a broad range of topics and is divided into six sections known as "orders" (pl. *sedarim*, sing. *seder*); each order in turn is divided into "tractates" (pl. *massekhtot*, sing. *massekhet*). There are sixty-three tractates in all. The six orders are: *Zera'im* ("Seeds"), on the disposition of the agricultural products of the Land of Israel; *Mo'ed* ("Festivals" or "Set Times"), on Sabbath, festivals, and pilgrimage to the Temple; *Nashim* ("Women"), on marriage, divorce, and family law; *Neziqin* ("Damages"), on civil and criminal law and judicial procedure; *Qodashim* ("Holy Things"), on Temple sacrifices and rituals; and *Tohorot* ("Purities"), on the maintenance of ritual purity and the removal of ritual impurity. Each of the sixty-three tractates, with exceptions, of course, is devoted to a single topic or cluster of topics. Perhaps the greatest exceptions to the overall pattern are tractate *Avot*, which has neither legal content nor thematic unity, and tractate *Eduyot*, a topical miscellany.

The Mishnah is full of legal material but is not a law code, or at least is not obviously a law code. It contains numerous disputes and unresolved arguments; it does not usually state the penalty for the violation of its prescriptions; its coverage is not complete, omitting many vital aspects of its subjects; at no point, except perhaps for the opening chapter of *Avot* which depicts a chain of tradition linking Moses at Mount Sinai to the mishnaic Sages, does the Mishnah advance a global claim for its authority. If the Mishnah is a law code, it is an odd one.

Another remarkable feature of the Mishnah is its seeming obliviousness to its time and place. It seldom mentions the destruction of the Temple in 70 CE (or, for that matter, the defeat of Bar Kokhba in 135 CE); in fact, the Mishnah seems to be in denial of these events. A student of the Mishnah could be forgiven for not realizing that the Mishnah was composed in Roman Palaestina, a province of the Roman Empire. The Mishnah treats at great length the rituals of the Temple, although the Temple is no longer standing; priests and their prerogatives figure prominently, rabbis and their prerogatives hardly at all; it sets out in great detail the requirements of ritual purity, the sources of impurity, and the modes of purification, even though most of the purity system was falling into desuetude after the destruction of the Temple, and even though purification from the most severe forms of impurity was impossible without the Temple system being in place. The replacements that Jewish society was developing for the Temple, its rituals, and its personnel (e.g. synagogues, prayer, rabbis), are of little interest to the Mishnah. The Mishnah is not living in real time and does not seem interested in the affairs of its own time.

If the Mishnah is not a law code, and is not interested in the events of its own time, what is it? What kind of book is the Mishnah? Who created it, why, and for whom? The answers to these questions are elusive and no consensus has been reached. Three points, however, seem certain. First, whatever other purpose it may have been designed to serve, the Mishnah certainly was intended to be studied actively, and indeed it was studied actively: the Mishnah soon became the primary object of study for generations of Sages. The result of their work is the Talmud of Babylonia (the Bavli) and the Talmud of the Land of Israel (the Yerushalmi). Second, the Mishnah is a highly stylized summary of the opinions of Sages over a period of more than a century. The Mishnah is anthological, produced by a "school" or movement. Third, although the Mishnah is anonymous, nowhere identifying its authors/editors, both Talmudim—and virtually all modern scholars—assume that R. Judah the Patriarch, also known simply as Rabbi, was its editor-in-chief. There is an unstated connection between the promulgation of the Mishnah and the administration of the autonomous Jewish community of Palaestina, especially its head, the patriarch.

What is the origin of the Mishnah's laws? One obvious source is Scripture. Large portions of the Mishnah are based on Scripture, specifically the Torah. The rabbinic Sages looked to the Torah for knowledge of religious law and practice. Other Jews did the same: prerabbinic writings of the Second Temple period, such as *Jubilees*, the *Temple Scroll*, the *Damascus Document*, and the essays of Philo of Alexandria, all relate to the Torah in different ways for different purposes but all use the Torah, whether explicitly or implicitly, as the basis for their presentations of Jewish law. So it is no surprise that the Mishnah is tightly bound to the Torah. Some sections of the Mishnah stand in such close relationship with the Torah that barely a line of the former can be understood without knowledge of the relevant verses of the latter. These verses, although essential to understanding the text, are not always quoted; the editor of the Mishnah assumes that the reader[1] will supply what is missing.

What is striking about the Mishnah in this regard, however, is not its dependence on the Torah, but its relative independence from the Torah. The Mishnah is neither a commentary on, nor a paraphrase of, the Torah. It does not belong to the genre of the rewritten Torah. As a rule it does not cite the Torah or speak in biblical Hebrew. Nor is it organized along the lines of the Torah. And yet every so often, for reasons that are not clear, the Mishnah departs from its usual practice and explicitly adduces Scripture,

---

[1] "Reader" is used advisedly, since we are not sure when the Mishnah became a written text. In its earliest stages it was studied orally.

usually the Torah, in order to buttress a legal ruling or to make a homiletical point. Why the Mishnah quotes Scripture where it does is an open question. The Talmudim regularly attach the Mishnah's laws to scriptural verses, since the Mishnah itself usually failed to do so.

The Mishnah drew on other sources beyond Scripture. Some mishnaic laws seem to be of "sectarian" provenance, while others are part of the "common Judaism" of all Jews; some laws seem to derive from the priesthood, others from the scribes. Reflecting the fact that the rabbinic movement itself derived from various groups, the Mishnah too derived its laws from various sources. The common scholarly view that mishnaic law is somehow Pharisaic is not baseless but cannot be sustained. Gamaliel the Pharisee is mentioned by the New Testament (Acts 5:34, 22:3), Simon ben Gamaliel the Pharisee by Josephus (*Vita* 191–192). The Rabban Gamaliel who became the leader of the rabbis of the Yavneh generation surely is a scion of this line; R. Judah the Patriarch, the putative editor of the Mishnah, is his grandson. So there is an important link between the Pharisees of the Second Temple period and the leadership of the Sages of the post-70 period, but this hardly means that all Pharisees became rabbis or that all rabbis were latter-day Pharisees. It is significant that the Mishnah in various passages sees the Sadducees as Other (e.g. *Parah* 3:7), and that in the mishnaic debates between Pharisees and Sadducees (e.g. *Yadayim* 4:6–7) the winners are always the Pharisees, as seen from the fact that mishnaic law always agrees with them against the Sadducees. Hence we may say that the Mishnah is anti-Saducean (*Sanhedrin* 10:1), but otherwise the Mishnah has no Pharisaic self-consciousness. No doubt some of the laws of the Mishnah derive from the Pharisees of the Second Temple period, but the Mishnah itself has little interest in identifying the age or origin of its laws; in any case mishnaic law cannot be regarded *tout court* as Pharisaic.

Some of the Mishnah, then, is old, that is, some of the Mishnah's laws, terminology, and ideas derive from Second Temple times. This is not surprising, since we may be sure that R. Judah the Patriarch did not create the Mishnah out of whole cloth but drew on already existing legal traditions. However, this does not necessarily mean that the Mishnah incorporates previously existing documents, and even if it does (as the Talmudim and most modern scholars assume) it does not necessarily mean that these documents were composed as literary units in Second Temple times. Some scholars have suggested that some of the Mishnah's material, notably the paragraphs dealing with the rituals of the Temple, had achieved documentary status in Second Temple times, but this suggestion seems unlikely. No composition of Second Temple times resembles the Mishnah in structure or content. (One of the Qumran scrolls, *Miqtsat Ma'asei ha Torah*, variously intersects with mishnaic law and somewhat resembles the Mishnah in format, but that is just one relatively brief document.)

The Talmudim would have us believe that the bulk of the Mishnah's rulings, if not its actual words, were revealed to Moses at Mount Sinai. The Mishnah, the Talmud says, is the oral Torah, the essential accompaniment to the written Torah. In this conception, which is more theological than historical, the Mishnah is as old and as authoritative as the Torah. The Mishnah itself hardly supports this conception. The phrase "oral Torah" nowhere appears in the Mishnah and only a few mishnaic laws are traced back to Moses (*Pe'ah* 2:6, *Eduyot* 8:7, *Yadayim* 4:3). Just as the Mishnah seldom quotes the written Torah, it seldom proclaims itself to be the repository of laws that were revealed to Moses.

What is new in the Mishnah? (1) The Mishnah is the first Jewish book to ascribe conflicting legal opinions to named individuals (and groups), (2) who go by the title "rabbi," (3) and who, in spite of their differences of opinion, remain members of a single social network. (4) Some earlier Hebrew works, like *Jubilees* and the *Temple Scroll*, had departed from the sequence of Scripture in order to arrange legal material thematically; writing in Greek, Philo and Josephus had done the same. But the Mishnah's abandonment of the scriptural sequence is total; its thematic arrangement is pursued on a much grander scale, covering many more topics in much greater detail, than in any earlier text. (5) The Mishnah's laws, like the laws of the Torah, are overwhelmingly casuistic; they state the legal outcome of a given situation or condition. Change the condition and the law will change. What is novel in the Mishnah is the Mishnah's penchant for classification. The Mishnah posits legal categories, analyzes them in detail, contrasts one with another, and connects (or contrasts) one law with another on the basis of their legal details.[2] This is new. (6) The Torah distinguishes murder from manslaughter on the basis of the intention of the assailant (Exodus 21:12–14; Numbers 35). In the Mishnah the intention of the actor is taken into account far more often and in a far wider range of contexts than in any earlier Jewish document.[3]

What the Mishnah Is and What the Mishnah Is Not

The Mishnah is not the Torah. God does not speak in the Mishnah; the Mishnah says little about God (or indeed about most theological matters, like creation, free will, the world to come, the unity of God, divine providence, the covenant between God and Israel, the Messiah). When the Mishnah does deal with theology, it is often at the end of a tractate where the homiletical material marks the transition from one tractate to another.[4] The Mishnah never commands as the Torah does; it never says "Thou shalt" or "Thou shalt not." The typical Mishnaic language to indicate obligation or prohibition is "one does x" or "one does not do y." The mishnaic Sages are not prophets or saints; their authority does not derive from direct revelation or from control over the miraculous. When they seek to support their positions, as they sometimes do, they do so by invoking logic or engaging in scriptural interpretation. They do not say "thus spoke the Lord" or "an angel of the Lord came to me."

On the macro level the Mishnah seldom refers to itself. The text is anonymous, never stating who composed it, why, for whom, and using what sources. As noted above the Talmudim assume that R. Judah the Patriarch is the editor of the Mishnah; we have no basis to reject this claim and little evidence from the Mishnah itself to support it. The identity of those who composed the Mishnah is well hidden behind the text. No authorial self-consciousness is evident.[5]

On the micro level the Mishnah frequently refers to itself. One of the standard rhetorical forms in the Mishnah is for the text to introduce a technical term x and then to ask "what is x?" or to introduce a law and then to ask "under what conditions does the law apply?" or to introduce a debate between two authorities about y and then to add the comment "the authorities did not debate y, because on y they agree; no, they debated z."[6] Indeed, the Mishnah has many locutions by which it seems to modify or qualify or interpret its own prior statement.

---

[2] See e.g. *Menahot* 4:1–4 and 9:9; *Bikkurim* chapter 2.
[3] See for example the discussions of *piggul* in *Zevahim* and *Menahot*.
[4] See for example the close of tractates *Sotah, Makkot, Sanhedrin*.
[5] Two exceptions are *Hagigah* 1:8 and *Eduyot* 1:4–6.   [6] e.g. *Keritot* 4:2.

The Mishnah displays astonishing literary uniformity. Across six *sedarim*, sixty-three tractates, (approximately) 524 chapters,[7] and several thousand paragraphs, the Mishnah's style never wavers. It is overwhelmingly casuistic, that is, its home turf is case law. Even when the Mishnah claims "this is the general rule" (e.g. *Berakhot* 6:7), and even when it claims "this is a great general rule" (e.g. *Shabbat* 7:1), what emerges is not philosophical conceptualization or thematic systematization of law so much as a summary of casuistic rules. The Mishnah, when it wishes to, can sort laws into various categories, notably "from the Torah," "from the Sages (or Scribes)," "custom," "a severity," "*halakhah*," "the laws of humanity vs. the laws of Heaven," "an enactment," "an enactment to improve the world," and many others. The Mishnah, when it wishes to, can reveal which opinion among feuding Sages it regards as correct, notably "the *halakhah* follows his words," or as incorrect, notably "against the will of the Sages." But as a rule the Mishnah from one end to the other is not interested in reflecting on the origins or rectitude of its rulings. Instead it is engaged in list making, usually to demonstrate how *x* is like *y* but unlike *z*. The lists can be long or short, numbered or not. Sometimes the Mishnah for no obvious reason will adopt an antiquarian stance, claiming that its laws apply (or applied) to the Israelites in the wilderness or to the Judaeans upon their return from Babylonia.[8] The Mishnah from one end to the other describes, often using present participles, the rituals of the Temple and the judicial procedures of the Sanhedrin, rituals and procedures that were not practiced in the time of the Mishnah, and perhaps that had never been practiced in the manner in which the Mishnah describes them.

In sum: for all of its varied content, the Mishnah is remarkably uniform and remarkably unlike the Torah. The Mishnah represents not just a new literary form in the history of Judaism but also a new way of thinking and ultimately a new religiosity. The Mishnah is the foundational document of the rabbinic Judaism that would emerge in late antiquity, that would become normative in the Jewish communities of the middle ages, and that in traditionalist communities is normative still.

How to Read the Mishnah

Readers encountering the Mishnah for the first time will probably feel that they are stepping into a conversation already in progress. This is a fundamental feature of the work. Wherever one stands in the Mishnah one is in the middle of something. There is no beginning and no end, only middle. For example, the opening line of the Mishnah, "From what time in the evening may one recite the *Shema*?" seems to come out of nowhere: what is the *Shema*? why should it be recited? what is the connection between the evening and the recitation of the *Shema*? The Talmud asks, "where does the teacher stand?" so that acquaintance with the *Shema* is assumed. Like Homer the Mishnah begins *in medias res*.

Another example: tractate *Shabbat* consists of twenty-four chapters devoted almost exclusively to the explication of the labors that are prohibited on the Sabbath. Chapter 7 paragraph 2, a listing of thirty-nine archetypal prohibited labors, would have made a fine introduction to the tractate. Instead, for reasons that are not clear, the opening

---

[7] In printed editions, followed here, *Bikkurim* has four chapters (not three) and *Avot* has six (not five).
[8] *Menahot* 7:2, *Qiddushin* 4:1. *Zevahim* 14:4–10, *Bekhorot* 1:1, *Orlah* 1:2.

paragraph is a well-nigh incomprehensible statement about "two which are four."⁹ The Mishnah, both at the beginning of the tractate and in the body of the tractate, seems to be a hodgepodge of Sabbath rules. The commentators struggle valiantly to find a logical hierarchical structure, but without success. It is all middle.

In this edition we transliterate (and place in italics) rather than translate some of the Mishnah's legal terms; these are explained in the glossary. Some of these terms and concepts derive from the Torah, others are rabbinic innovations. "Private domain" and "public domain," for instance, are nonbiblical terms that play an important role in the laws of damages and the laws of the Sabbath. Even a "biblical" concept, like *piggul* or *terefah*, may take on a specialized meaning in the Mishnah that differs considerably from its meaning in the Torah.

As noted, the Mishnah is organized by topic, but within a given tractate the organization is not always clear. Particularly interesting are those passages in which the Mishnah preserves traces of an atypical organizational principle, such as formal traits (e.g. the series of traditions organized around the expression "the only difference between *a* and *b* is *x*," *Megillah* 1:4–11) or associative logic (e.g. *Qiddushin* chapter 1; *Temurah* 1:4–5), common legal rulings (e.g. *Eduyot* 1:12–14), or the order of Scripture (e.g. *Bava Metsiʿa* 2:9–10). These passages may be evidence of preexisting sources (documents?) used by the editor of the Mishnah.

The historicity of statements attributed to named individual rabbis is a matter of considerable debate among scholars. But historical or not, the attributions may show the kinds of legal issues disputed by members of the different generations. For instance the earliest figures (Hillel, Shammai, and their "Houses") appear primarily in connection with matters of purity, tithes, and personal status, suggesting that the rabbinic legal tradition began in those areas and not, say, with civil law. The attributions to later mishnaic Sages may provide some indication of legal development, or at least show how the Mishnah presents that development.

How to Read This Translation

The goal of this translation is to make the Mishnah accessible to the Hebrew-less reader. Towards that end this translation incorporates the following features: each tractate is accompanied by an introduction, which discusses the tractate's name, organization, major ideas, and relationship with the Torah. The body of the translation is punctuated by descriptive headings, so the reader gets a sense of the themes addressed by the tractate and the organization of the tractate. Sentences are divided into short lines (as if they were poetry) to aid comprehension. Footnotes on the translation signal obscure passages, variant readings, or alternative interpretations. Last and not least are the annotations. The goal of the annotations, as we frequently reminded our contributors, is to provide enough information to the reader so the text makes sense. Too much information will overwhelm the reader; too little leaves the reader confronting a difficult text unaided. The translators were given free rein in their annotations, whether to follow the lead of a single classical commentator, or to flit about from one commentator to another, or to avoid them all. We the editors have tried, and no doubt failed, to maintain consistency in the translation of technical terms and rhetorical patterns; we have

---

⁹ Many Mishnah tractates open with a number or an enumeration. In the case of *Shabbat* this stylistic feature could have been met either by what is now 7:2 or by what is now 1:1. See too *Shevuʿo*t 1:1.

consoled ourselves with the argument that the reader may benefit in noting divergence in the translation of parallel terms and passages.

The text translated here is that of the standard printed edition which, with minor variations, has been reprinted many times from the sixteenth century till now. Most of our translators used the classic edition with traditional commentaries published in Vilna by the Romm publishing house (13 volumes, 1908–1909, frequently reprinted) or the edition with brief academic commentary by Hanokh Albeck published in Jerusalem by Dvir (6 volumes, 1952–1958, frequently reprinted) or the edition with commentary by Pinhas Kehati (Jerusalem, 1998), or all three.

There is yet no modern critical edition of the Mishnah, nor is there consensus among scholars on what a critical edition of the Mishnah would look like. For one thing, the earliest surviving manuscripts were written eight centuries or more after the composition of the Mishnah. In the intervening period (and later), the Mishnah had been subject to intensive study, and "corrections" based on such study were incorporated into the text. The Talmudim, our earliest commentaries, are already aware of differing versions of specific passages, and in many instances propose alterations to the text to solve interpretative problems.

In order to show the reader some of the instability in the transmission of the Mishnah's text our contributors were asked to present variants from two of our main Mishnah manuscripts, variants which affect the meaning of the text. Both manuscripts preserve ancient linguistic forms and a text relatively free from interference from the Talmudic tradition. These manuscripts are thought to reflect the "Palestinian" (more precisely "Byzantine") text tradition and are generally dated to the tenth to the twelfth century CE. The scribes who vocalized these manuscripts were not the ones who copied out the main text. The two manuscripts are:

- **K**: Kaufmann A50, now in the Library of the Hungarian Academy of Sciences. High-resolution images are available at a website of that library, http://kaufmann.mtak.hu/index-en.html.
- **P**: Palatine Library of Parma 3173 (formerly known as de Rossi 138). High-resolution images are available through "KTIV: The International Collection of Digitized Hebrew Manuscripts," a project of the National Library of Israel at https://web.nli.org.il/sites/nlis/en/manuscript/.

Some of our contributors were not satisfied with collecting variants just from **K** and **P**; several collected variants from other manuscripts as well.

- MS Add 470.1 of the Cambridge University Library. William H. Lowe in 1883 published a transcription of this manuscript, hence it is referred to by contributors as **C** (for Cambridge) or **L** (for Lowe). Images of this manuscript are available at https://cudl.lib.cam.ac.uk/view/MS-ADD-00470-00001.
- Readings from a second Parma manuscript (Palatine Library 2596, formerly de Rossi 497), this one containing all the tractates of *Seder Tohorot*, are cited as P_2. Images are available through the "KTIV" website.
- Readings from the Cairo Genizah are cited collectively as **G**.
- Many translators of tractates from *Seder Zera'im* were aided by Nissan Sacks (ed.), *The Mishnah…Order Zera'im* (Jerusalem: Institute for the Complete Israeli Talmud, 1975, two volumes), which collects variant readings from all sources for the tractates in that order.

Information about all these and other manuscripts is most conveniently available in Michael Krupp, "Manuscripts of the Mishna," in *The Literature of the Sages: First Part:*

Oral Tora, ed. Shmuel Safrai (Assen: Van Gorcum, 1987; Philadelphia: Fortress, 1987), 252–262; Hermann L. Strack, *Introduction to Talmud and Midrash*, revised by Günter Stemberger, translated into English by Markus Bockmuehl (Edinburgh: T. & T. Clark, 1996); Eyal Ben-Eliyahu, Yehudah Cohn, and Fergus Millar, *Handbook of Jewish Literature from Late Antiquity 135–700 CE* (Oxford: Oxford University Press for the British Academy, 2012).

Readers interested in consulting images of manuscripts might begin with a National Library of Israel project on Talmudic manuscripts (with only a Hebrew interface), https://web.nli.org.il/sites/nli/Hebrew/collections/jewish-collection/Talmud/Pages/default.aspx. This site includes images of select manuscripts and Cairo Genizah fragments. The "KTIV" portal will provide links to digital images even when that site does not host pictures. Digital critical editions under the direction of Hayim Lapin and Daniel Stökl ben Ezra are underway at http://editions.eRabbinica.org (with a development version at erabbinica.org:8080/exist/apps/digitalmishnah/).

The Rev. Herbert Danby

In 1933, the Clarendon Press of Oxford University published *The Mishnah Translated from the Hebrew with Introduction and Brief Explanatory Notes*, by Herbert Danby, a volume of some 900 pages. It is a mark of the quality of Danby's work that it remains in print almost ninety years later. Our translation is completely independent of his, but we are aware that we are walking in his footsteps. For the Hebrew-less reader, unaccustomed to Mishnaic rhetoric and technical terminology, Danby's translation, while excellent in itself, remains a closed book. Danby was a master translator, but the modern reader demands more from a translation than Danby provides. The goal of our Mishnah translation is to equal Danby's in quality and to surpass it in utility. In tribute to Herbert Danby, a philo-Semitic Christian Hebraist, we have retained almost unchanged his index of biblical passages and his table of weights, measures, and currency. We would have liked to retain his subject index, but we reluctantly came to the conclusion that it is too closely keyed to Danby's own translation and notes for it to be usable in a new setting. For biographical information about the Rev. Danby and an appreciation of his work, see the excellent article by Shalom Goldman in the journal *Modern Judaism* ("The Rev. Herbert Danby (1889–1953): Hebrew Scholar, Zionist, Christian Missionary," *Modern Judaism—A Journal of Jewish Ideas and Experience*, 27:2 (May 2007), pp. 219–245).

THE MISHNAH

ORDER OF ZERA'IM
and
ORDER OF MO'ED

ORDER OF ZERA'IM

Tractate Berakhot   13
Richard S. Sarason

Tractate Pe'ah   39
Gregg E. Gardner

Tractate Demai   76
Richard S. Sarason

Tractate Kilayim   105
Michael Rosenberg

Tractate Shevi'it   144
Yair Furstenberg

Tractate Terumot   195
William Friedman and Matthew Hass

Tractate Ma'aserot   253
Joshua Kulp

Tractate Ma'aser Sheni   276
Joshua Kulp

Tractate Hallah   309
Joshua Kulp

Tractate Orlah   330
Joshua Kulp

Tractate Bikkurim   345
Naftali S. Cohn

Tractate Berakhot

Richard S. Sarason

Introduction

Overview

Tractate *Berakhot* ("Blessings") derives its name from the biblical term *berakhah*, which, when directed toward God, is an expression of praise, gratitude, and acknowledgment of a divine benefaction. The standard rabbinic blessing formula *Barukh attah Adonai*, taken over from Psalms 119:12 and 1 Chronicles 29:10, is often rendered as "Praised (or Blessed) are You, O Lord." *Berakhot* deals with various categories of blessings and prayers that are to be recited in a variety of contexts, both daily and occasional.

Structure and Organization of the Tractate

The tractate lays out rabbinic Judaism's earliest liturgical structures: the twice-daily recitation of *Shema* and its surrounding blessings (chapters 1–3); the thrice-daily petitionary prayer (*Tefillah*, "The Prayer"; chapters 4–5); and blessings of praise, thanks, and acknowledgment (chapters 6–9). The latter are divided into two categories: blessings recited before and after eating (chapters 6–8), and blessings recited over manifestations of divine power and providence (chapter 9).

Relationship to Scripture

Only two of the tractate's topics are based on biblical law. The recitation of *Shema*, which consists of the three paragraphs Deuteronomy 6:4–9, 11:13–21, and Numbers 15:37–41, derives from rabbinic interpretation of Deuteronomy 6:7 and 11:19 (*Recite them when you stay at home and when you are away, when you lie down and when you get up*). The antecedent of *them* is understood to be the scriptural words of these paragraphs, while the Numbers paragraph is associated with the other two on account of the shared theme of physical reminders (*tefillin* in Deuteronomy, fringes in Numbers) to observe God's commandments. The blessing after meals (chapter 7) derives from Deuteronomy 8:10 (*When you have eaten your fill, give thanks to the Lord your God for the good land which he has given you*). The rabbinic obligation to pray three times a day is anticipated in Psalm 55:18 (*Evening, morning, and noon, I complain and moan, and he hears my voice*) and Daniel 6:11 (*Three times a day he knelt down, prayed, and made confession to his God*).

Main Ideas

The recitation of the three scriptural paragraphs of the *Shema* ("hear;" so named from the first word of the first paragraph, *Hear, O Israel!*), is surrounded by rabbinically ordained blessings. The tractate takes these obligations and liturgical structures for granted and deals with the precise times when these verses must be recited, evening and morning (chapter 1), the degree of attentiveness and intentionality that their recitation requires (chapter 2), and the limits of the obligation to recite them (chapter 3).

The *Tefillah* is a petitionary prayer that takes the form (on weekdays) of eighteen blessings—in fact, later rabbinic texts sometimes call it simply "The Eighteen," based on 4:3. In the wake of the Temple's destruction in 70 CE, it comprises the main expression of Israelite worship, corporate and individual (this connection is barely articulated in Tractate *Berakhot* but is stated much more forthrightly in the corresponding tractates of Tosefta and Talmud). Chapter 4 deals with the times for the Prayer and various rules for its recitation, including the extent of attentiveness required. The latter issue continues in chapter 5, along with rules dealing with fluency, error, and confusion in reciting the sequence of blessings.

The rest of the tractate lays out rules governing occasional blessings. Chapter 6 deals with the appropriate blessings to be recited before eating different kinds of agricultural produce and other foods. Distinctions are made between generic categories and items such as wine and bread that are deemed sufficiently important to require their own specific blessings. Chapter 7 deals with the blessings recited after eating a meal. Since meals are often social activities, three people or more who eat together are to recite these blessings as a group. The rules for summoning such a group are given here. Chapter 8 is a series of disputes between the Houses of Shammai and Hillel about various aspects of proper behavior at communal meals, especially the order of the blessings at the beginning and the end of the Sabbath. Chapter 9 details the blessings to be recited upon experiencing natural wonders and acts of divine providence, both for good and for ill.

While Tractate *Berakhot* is placed at the beginning of the Order of *Zera'im*, its thematic connection to that order is somewhat tenuous. The order deals with the various agricultural offerings required by the Torah. The tractate's association with this order derives from its treatment of blessings occasioned by the eating of agricultural produce (chapters 6–7). Theologically relevant to this association is the statement in the Tosefta and Talmud that "it is forbidden for a person to enjoy anything of this world without [reciting] a blessing; if anyone enjoys anything of this world without a blessing, he has committed sacrilege"—that is, he has made improper use of something that belongs to God. Just as separating the required offerings from agricultural produce releases it for human use, so reciting a blessing before partaking of food accomplishes the same thing.

Special Notes for the Reader

Manuscript readings cited in the footnotes have been culled from Nissan Zacks (ed.), *The Mishnah with Variant Readings: Order Zera'im*, vol. 1 (Jerusalem: Institute for the Complete Israeli Talmud, 1972).

Tractate Berakhot

Chapter One

1:1–3 *The Proper Time and Posture for the Recitation of the Shema*

1 From what time may one recite the *Shema* in the evening?
From the hour when the priests enter to eat their *terumah*,
until the end of the first watch—
the words of R. Eliezer.
But the Sages say:
Until midnight.
Rabban Gamaliel says:
Until the rise of dawn.[1]
It once happened that his sons came [home late] from a [wedding] celebration.
They said to him:
We have not recited the *Shema*.
He said to them:
If the dawn has not yet risen, you are [still] obligated[2] to recite.

---

[1] Lit. "until the pillar of dawn rises." [2] **K**, **P**, and many other manuscripts: "permitted."

1:1 *From what time … in the evening?*: The three scriptural paragraphs, Deuteronomy 6:4–9, 11:13–21, and Numbers 15:37–41, which comprise the *Shema*, are to be recited *when you lie down and when you arise* (Deuteronomy 6:7, 11:19).

From the hour when the priests enter their homes.

terumah: Agricultural produce given to the priests (Numbers 18:8–9 and *Terumot*), to be eaten by them only in a state of purity. Priests who have come into contact with a source of impurity must immerse themselves in water and then await nightfall (Leviticus 22:4–7 and *Tevul Yom*). Sunset, then, is when the priests can enter their homes (or, possibly, the Temple) to eat their *terumah*. Why the time for the recitation of the *Shema* should be derived from the time for the consumption of *terumah* the Mishnah does not explain.

until the end of the first watch: The night is divided into three watches of equal duration. Assuming twelve hours of darkness, the first watch would extend from sunset until approximately 10 p.m.

until the rise of dawn: The "pillar of dawn" is the first line of pink light on the horizon before sunrise.

It once happened: Throughout the Mishnah, many of the rulings of Rabban Gamaliel are expressed, as here, through narrative precedents (cf. 2:5–7).

And not only in this case,
but in all cases in which the Sages have ruled "until midnight,"
the obligation extends until the rise of dawn:
The burning of the fatty pieces and limbs[3]—
their obligation extends until the rise of dawn.
And all those [sacrifices] that must be eaten on the same day—
their obligation extends until the dawn rises.
If so, why did the Sages say, "Until midnight?"
In order to keep a person far from transgression.

2 From what time may one recite the *Shema* in the morning?
From the time that one can distinguish between blue and white.
R. Eliezer says:
Between blue and green.
And one must finish it by sunrise.[4]
R. Joshua says:
By the third hour,
for such is the way of the sons of kings to arise at the third hour.
One who recites [the *Shema*] after this time has not lost anything—
he is like a person who is reciting the Torah.

3 The House of Shammai say:
In the evening, every person must recline in order to[5] recite;
and in the morning, they must stand,
as it is said, *when you lie down and when you arise.*

[3] K adds "and the eating of the paschal lambs."
[4] K, P, and most other manuscripts lack: "And ... finish"
[5] Lit. "and."

The burning of the fatty pieces and limbs: Leviticus 1:9, 3:3–5.

until the rise of dawn: Tamid 2:1, 5; Megillah 2:6.

all those [sacrifices] ... same day: Zevahim 5:3, 5–6.

In order to keep a person far from transgression: The logic here is that of the rabbinic dictum to "make a hedge around the Torah" (*Avot* 1:1).

1:2 *between blue and white*: Commentators suggest that this refers to distinguishing between the blue and white threads of the prescribed fringes (*tsitsit*) on one's garment.

Between blue and green: R. Eliezer holds that, for purposes of reciting the *Shema*, "morning" begins only when there is sufficient light to make fine distinctions between close colors.

And one must finish it by sunrise: This is not part of R. Eliezer's dictum, but the anonymous editorial voice.

By the third hour of daylight: Hours, in the Mishnah, are not temporally standardized year-round, but divide the available daylight into twelve equal portions, as does a sundial. Since royalty arises from bed relatively late in the morning, this additional three-hour period may still be considered *when you rise up* for purposes of reciting the *Shema*.

1:3 *The House of Shammai say...the House of Hillel say*: The dispute is over the interpretation of Deuteronomy 6:7, *when you lie down and when you arise*—whether this mandates a precise physical posture for the recitation of the *Shema* (Shammaites) or only the prescribed time for recitation (Hillelites).

But the House of Hillel say:
Every person may recite it in his own way,
as it is said, *and when you are walking in the way*.
If this be so, why is it stated, *when you lie down and when you arise*?
[This means,] at the hour when people lie down and at the hour when people arise.[6]
Said R. Tarfon:
I was [once] walking on the road,
and I reclined to recite [the *Shema*] in accordance with the ruling of the House of Shammai,
and I put myself in danger from brigands.
The Sages[7] said to him:
You deserved to die,[8] because you transgressed the words of the House of Hillel.

1:4–5 *Blessings before and after the Shema*

4 In the morning one recites two blessings before it and one after it;
and in the evening, two before it and two after it, one long and one short.
Where the Sages[9] ruled [to recite a] long [blessing]—
one is not allowed [to recite a] short [blessing];
to [recite a] short [blessing]—
one is not allowed [to recite a] long [blessing];
to seal [with a concluding benedictory formula]—one is not allowed not to seal;
not to seal—one is not allowed to seal.

5 One must mention the exodus from Egypt in the evening.
Said R. Eleazar b. Azariah:
Now, I am almost seventy years old,
and I never merited [learning] that[10] the exodus from Egypt
be said in the evening,
until Ben Zoma expounded it:
As it is said, *so that you may remember the day of your departure from the land of Egypt all the days of your life*:
the days of your life—the days;

---

[6] P, K add "are accustomed to lie down…accustomed to arise."
[7] Lit. "they."   [8] Lit. "You deserved to have made yourself liable [for mortal punishment]."
[9] Lit. "they."   [10] Or, possibly, "I never merited understanding why…"

Every person may recite it in his own way: In whatever physical posture he may wish. The House of Hillel understand the word *way* of *walking in the way* as referring to manner rather than road.

You deserved to die…the House of Hillel: The response takes for granted that the law follows the House of Hillel (cf. *Eduyot* 1:12–14, 4:1–5:5).

1:4 *to seal [with a concluding benedictory formula]*: Sometimes, especially if a benediction is long, containing multiple phrases and ideas, the Sages ordained that it conclude with a brief recapitulation, known as a "seal," itself formulated as a benediction (e.g. " Blessed are You, O Lord, Creator of the luminaries"). Cf. 9:5.

1:5 *One must mention the exodus from Egypt*, the third paragraph of the *Shema*, Numbers 15:37–41.

in the evening: Contrast 2:2.

As it is said: Deuteronomy 16:3.

all the days of your life—[to include] the evenings.
But the Sages say:
The days of your life—this world;
all the days of your life—to include the days of the Messiah.

Chapter Two

2:1–4 *Intention and Attention Required for the Recitation of the Shema*

2 If one was reciting the Torah, and the time for the recitation [of the *Shema*] arrived—
if he focused his mind[11] [to fulfill his obligation], he has fulfilled it;
but if not, he has not fulfilled it.
In the breaks [between sections], one may greet out of respect and respond,
but in the middle [of each section], one may greet [only] out of fear and respond—
the words of R. Meir.
R. Judah says:
In the middle one may greet out of fear and respond out of respect;
in the breaks [between sections] one may greet out of respect and respond to anyone's greeting.

2 These are [the breaks] between the sections:
between the first benediction and the second,
between the second and *Hear*,
between *Hear* and *If you surely hearken*,
between *If you surely hearken* and *And the Lord said*,
between *And the Lord said* and "True and certain."
R. Judah says:
Between *And the Lord said* and "True and certain" one may not stop.
Said R. Joshua b. Qorhah:
Why does *Hear* precede *If you surely hearken*?

[11] Lit. "directed his heart."

2:1 *if he focused his mind*: Throughout the Mishnah, the legal consequence of an action is frequently determined by the actor's intent.

In the breaks…In the middle: The recitation of the *Shema* is not to be interrupted by any activity that compromises a person's attentiveness, such as offering or returning greetings to someone else. Only in the case of severe social pressure or potential danger may a greeting be offered or returned, and then preferably during the breaks between the sections rather than in the middle of the sections themselves.

2:2 *Why does Hear precede…*: The order of the *Shema* paragraphs is deemed to be logical: one must first acknowledge the authority of the legislator before accepting his legislation. Additionally, that which is regularly recited precedes that which is recited less frequently. This paragraph presumes that Numbers 15:37–41 was not recited in the evening (cf. 1:5).

In order that one may first accept upon himself the yoke of[12] the kingdom of heaven,[13] and afterwards accept upon himself the yoke of the commandments.
[Why does] *If you surely hearken* precede *And the Lord said*?
Because *If you surely hearken* is observed both during the day and during the night, while *And the Lord said* is observed only during the day.

3 One who recites the *Shema* but did not do so aloud[14] has [nonetheless] fulfilled his obligation.[15]
R. Yose says:
He has not fulfilled his obligation.
If one recited [the *Shema*] and was not careful with [the correct pronunciation of] its letters—
R. Yose says:
He has [nonetheless] fulfilled his obligation.
R. Judah says:
He has not fulfilled his obligation.
One who recites [the three paragraphs] out of order has not fulfilled his obligation.
If he recited and erred, he must return to the place [in the recitation] where he erred.

4 Skilled workers may recite [the *Shema*] at the top of a tree
or on top of a course of stones,[16]—
what they are not permitted to do with the Prayer.

2:5–8 *Exemptions from the Requirement to Recite the Shema*

5 A bridegroom is exempt from reciting the *Shema*
on the first night [of his marriage]
until the end of the [coming] Sabbath,
if he has not yet consummated the marriage.[17]
It once happened that Rabban Gamaliel recited [the *Shema*] on the first[18] night after he married.
His students[19] said to him:

[12] **K**, **P**, and a number of other manuscripts lack "yoke of."
[13] Or "the kingship" or "sovereignty" of Heaven." "Heaven" is an epithet for God.
[14] Lit. "did not make it heard to his ears."
[15] Some readings attribute this ruling to R. Judah.
[16] Or "wall," "scaffolding."
[17] Lit. "if he has not [yet] performed the act."
[18] **K** lacks "first."
[19] **K**, **P**, and most other manuscripts lack "his students."

2:3 The three rulings in this paragraph concern proper articulation and attentiveness when reciting the *Shema*.

R. Yose says: He has not fulfilled his obligation: Since Scripture says *Hear*, the words must be audible.

2:4 *Skilled workers* who are accustomed to working at great heights will not be distracted from reciting the *Shema* by their physical position, but the Prayer requires a greater degree of concentration.

2:5 *It once happened*: Three precedents articulating the seemingly irregular practices of Rabban Gamaliel (cf. 1:1). Only the first is thematically relevant, as is further indicated by the resumption of the case of the bridegroom on his wedding night at the beginning of 2:8.

Have you not taught us, our Master,[20]
that a bridegroom is exempt from reciting the *Shema*
on the first night [of his marriage]?
He said to them:
I will not heed you to remove from myself the kingdom of Heaven for even a moment.

   6 He washed himself[21] on the first night after his wife died.
His students[22] said to him:
Have you not taught us, our Master,[23]
that a mourner is forbidden to wash himself?[24]
He said to them:
I am not like everyone else; I am delicate.

   7 And when his slave Tevi[25] died, he accepted condolences [for his loss].
His students[26] said to him:
Have you not taught us, our Master,[27]
that we do not accept condolences for [the loss of] slaves?
He said to them:
My slave Tevi was not like all the other slaves; he was a worthy person.

   8 If a bridegroom wishes to recite the *Shema* on the first night [of his marriage],
he may recite.
Rabban Simeon b. Gamaliel says:
Not everyone who wishes to assume a reputation[28] [for piety] may do so.

Chapter Three

3:1–3   *Exemptions from the Obligation to Recite the Shema*

3   One whose dead relative is laid out before him
is exempt from the recitation of the *Shema*, from the Prayer,[29] and from *tefillin*.
Those who carry the bier, their replacements,

[20] **K**, **P**, and most other manuscripts lack "our Master."   [21] Or "bathed."
[22] **K**, **P**, and most other manuscripts lack "his students."
[23] **K**, **P** (added in the margin), and most other manuscripts lack "our Master."   [24] Or "bathe."
[25] Usually vocalized "Tavi."   [26] **K**, **P**, and most other manuscripts lack "His students."
[27] **K**, **P**, and most other manuscripts lack "our Master."
[28] Or, possibly, "take up [i.e. utter] the Name [of God]" (by reciting the *Shema*).
[29] **K**, **P**, and most other manuscripts lack "from the Prayer."

3:1 The topic of mourning practices has already been introduced tangentially in 2:6–7.

Prayer: See 2:4.

tefillin, usually translated phylacteries (Greek for "amulets"), are small leather boxes worn by men on the arm and the forehead; the boxes contain pieces of parchment on which are written the first two paragraphs of the *Shema* and two excerpts from Exodus 13, in accordance with a literal understanding of Deuteronomy 6:8 and 11:18.

and the replacements of their replacements,
whether [they walk] in front of the bier or behind the bier—
those who are needed for [carrying] the bier[30] are exempt [from the recitation of the *Shema*];
those who are not needed for [carrying] the bier[31] are obligated.
These and those [alike] are exempt from the Prayer.

2 When they have buried the corpse and returned—
if they [see that they] will be able to begin and to finish [the recitation of the *Shema*]
before they arrive at the row [of comforters],
they begin; but if not, they do not begin.
Those who are standing in the row [to comfort the mourners]—
those on the inside are exempt [from the recitation of the *Shema*],
but those on the outside are obligated.

3 Women, slaves, and minors are exempt from the recitation of the *Shema* and from *tefillin*,
but are obligated in the Prayer, *mezuzah*, and the Blessing after Meals.

3:4–6 *Exemptions Caused by Seminal Emission*

4 One who has had a seminal emission
may rehearse [the *Shema*] in his mind[32]

---

[30] Lit. "those whom the bier needs." **K** reads here "those who walk in front of the bier are needed"; the reading of the printed text is given in the margin as "another version."

[31] **K** gives in the margin, as "another version", "those who walk behind the bier."

[32] Lit. "think in his heart."

3:2 *standing in the row*: After the burial, the comforters form two rows through which the mourners pass. Those on the inside, closest to the mourners, must focus their attention on comforting them, and not on the recitation of the *Shema*.

3:3 *Women, slaves, and minors*, because of their subordinate social status, are not obligated to perform certain commandments (e.g. *Sukkah* 2:8, *Hagigah* 1:1), described as time-bound (*Kiddushin* 1:7), and cannot serve as agents to exempt others from their obligations (*Sukkah* 3:10, *Rosh Hashanah* 3:8; cf. *Pesahim* 8:7; *Sheqalim* 1:3, 5, 6). Women and slaves are also not obligated to engage in the study of Torah (see *Sotah* 3:4). Regarding the blessing after meals see below, 7:2.

mezuzah: Lit. "doorpost," a container affixed to a doorpost in accordance with a literal understanding of Deuteronomy 6:9 and 11:20. It contains the first two paragraphs of the *Shema*.

3:4 *One who has had a seminal emission* is impure (Leviticus 15:16, Deuteronomy 23:11), and must purify himself through immersion in a ritual bath before studying Torah or praying. He may rehearse the *Shema* in his mind but must not sound out the words as one would normally do (see 2:3). For the blessings before and after the *Shema*, see above, 1:4. The commentators explain that the blessings associated with the *Shema* were understood to have been instituted by the rabbis, hence not to be recited in a state of impurity, but the blessing after meals (see below, chapter 7) was deemed to be biblically mandated (Deuteronomy 8:10), hence to be recited under all conditions.

but may not recite any blessing, either before it or after it.
Over a meal, he may recite the blessings after it but not before it.
R. Judah says:
He may recite the blessings both before them and after them.

5 If one was standing [and reciting] the Prayer
when he remembered that he had had a seminal emission—
he does not stop but shortens [his Prayer].
If one went down [into a pool of water] to immerse himself—
if he can emerge [from the water] and cover himself [with clothing]
and recite [the *Shema*] before the sun rises,
he emerges and covers himself and recites;
but if not, he covers himself with water and recites.
But he may not cover himself with foul-smelling waters or with water used for soaking flax, unless he puts [fresh] water into them.
How far must he distance himself from them and from excrement?
Four cubits.

6 A *zav* who experienced[33] a seminal discharge;
a menstruant who discharged semen;
[and] a woman who, after having sexual intercourse, became a menstruant[34]—
[all these] require immersion.
But R. Judah exempts them.

[33] Lit. "saw." [34] Lit. "saw [or experienced] menstruation."

R. Judah: i.e. he draws no distinction among the blessings and allows all of them to be recited.

both before them and after them: The *Shema* or a meal.

3:5 *shortens [his Prayer]*: Cf. 4:3.

before the sun rises: Cf. 1:2.

he covers himself with water: In order to maintain modesty and a dignified, respectful stance before God.

from them: The foul-smelling waters.

3:6 This paragraph, which has nothing to do with the recitation of the *Shema*, is placed here by association with the previous ones.

A zav: A man who experiences abnormal (nonseminal) genital oozing; see Leviticus 15:1–15. In this mishnah's case, a *zav* has also experienced a normal seminal ejaculation.

a menstruant who discharged semen from a sexual act that took place within the previous three days (*Shabbat* 9:3). The distinction between this case and the following one is the timing of seeing the semen vis-à-vis the onset of menstruation: here, the menstruation preceded seeing the semen, whereas in the following case, the semen was seen before menstruation.

[all these] require immersion: To remove the impurity of the semen (Leviticus 15:15–18), despite the fact that they remain impure as a *zav* or menstruant.

But R. Judah exempts them, since they remain impure in any event.

Chapter Four

4:1–7 *The Recitation of the Prayer*

4 The morning Prayer—until midday.
R. Judah says:
Until the fourth hour.
The afternoon Prayer—until evening.
R. Judah says:
Until the midpoint of the afternoon.
The evening Prayer has no fixed time.
And the additional [Prayer]—the entire day.
R. Judah says:
Until the seventh hour.[35]

2 R. Nehuniah b. ha-Qanah would pray a short prayer
upon entering the house of study and upon departing.
[The Sages] said to him:
What is the nature of this prayer?[36]
He said to them:
Upon entering I pray that no mishap may occur through me,[37]
and upon departing I give thanks for my lot.[38]

---

[35] **K** (added in margin), **P**, and most manuscripts lack "R. Judah says: Until the seventh hour."
[36] Or "What is the reason for this prayer?"; "What is the occasion for this prayer?"
[37] Or "on my account."   [38] Lit. "my portion."

4:1 Paralleling 1:1–2, the prescribed time frames for reciting the thrice-daily Prayer are now delineated.

Until the fourth hour, the end of the first third of daylight. The Tosefta indicates that this dispute is about the latest permissible time for offering the daily morning sacrifice in the Temple, to which the morning Prayer is likened. The dispute over the time for the afternoon Prayer has the same basis.

The evening Prayer has no fixed time, as it does not correspond to a daily Temple sacrifice.

the additional [Prayer] corresponds to the additional offering that was made in the Temple on Sabbaths and Festivals (Numbers 28-29), for which there was no set time.

Until the seventh hour: Here, too, R. Judah takes a more restrictive view, requiring the additional Prayer to be recited by the first hour after midday, assuming that the additional Temple sacrifice would have been offered by that time.

4:2 Here begins a series of disparate rulings on "short" or abbreviated prayers of various sorts. Most of these refer to recitations of the Prayer, but 4:2 refers instead to an instance of personal piety (hence the inquiry of the onlookers, "What is the nature of this prayer?").

Upon entering I pray that no mishap may occur through me: Mistakes in matters of interpretation and determining the law.

3 Rabban Gamaliel says:
Every day a person prays eighteen [benedictions].
R. Joshua says:
A summary of the eighteen.
R. Aqiva says:
If he can pray fluently,[39] he prays eighteen;
if not, a summary of the eighteen.

4 R. Eliezer says:
One who makes his Prayer fixed—
his Prayer is no supplication.
R. Joshua says:
One who is walking in a place of danger may recite a brief prayer,[40] saying:
"Save, O Lord, your people, the remnant of[41] Israel.
At every crossroad[42] may their needs be before you.
Blessed be You, O Lord, who hearkens to prayer."

5 If one was riding on a donkey [when the time arrived to recite the Prayer],
he dismounts;
if he cannot dismount,
he turns his face [toward the Temple];
if he cannot turn his face,
he directs his heart toward the Holy of Holies.

6 If one was sitting in a boat or in a wagon[43] or in a raft,
he directs his heart toward the Holy of Holies.

7 R. Eleazar b. Azariah says:
The additional Prayer [is recited] only in the town assembly;
but the Sages say:
[The additional Prayer is recited]

[39] Lit. "if his prayer is fluent in his mouth."
[40] K (deleted in margin), P, and many manuscripts add "summarizing the eighteen."
[41] K, P, and a number of manuscripts lack "remnant."
[42] The manuscripts provide various readings for this difficult phrase; text and meaning are uncertain.
[43] K (added in margin), P, and many manuscripts lack "or in a wagon."

4:3 *eighteen*: A series of eighteen benedictions with fixed topics (cf. *Rosh Hashanah* 4:5 for a partial list) are prescribed for daily prayer. Here the issue is whether each of them must be recited separately or whether they may be strung together into a single summary benediction; the determining factor is the worshipper's fluency in reciting prayers.

4:4 *One who makes his Prayer fixed—his Prayer is no supplication*: In the context of the surrounding rulings here, all of which deal with alternative formulations of the Prayer, "fixed" must refer to the actual wording of the Prayer, not merely to the worshipper's attitude. The concern is that one's daily recitation of the Prayer must not become routine, lest it lose its intentional focus and direct emotive force as prayer. (This interpretation of the mishnaic ruling is discussed by both Talmuds, as the practical need for fixed wordings of the prayers came to predominate.)

One who is walking in a place of danger: Another situation that calls for abbreviated prayer, regardless of one's fluency.

At every crossroad: A place of danger, but also, by extension, any "liminal" situation. The meaning of the phrase is obscure.

4:7 A pendant, returning to the subject of 4:1.

in the town assembly and not in the town assembly.
R. Judah says in his name:
Wherever there is a town assembly,
the individual is exempt from the additional Prayer.

Chapter Five

5:1   *Proper Concentration in Prayer*

5 One may stand up to pray [the Prayer] only in a serious state of mind.[44]
The pious ones of earlier days would wait an hour before praying,
in order to focus their minds on[45] God.
Even if a king greets him,
he must not respond [while he is praying];
even if a snake is wound around his heel,
he must not interrupt [the Prayer].

5:2   *Occasional Insertions in the Prayer*

2 One mentions [God's] power [to bring] rainfall in "Resurrection of the Dead,"
and petitions for rainfall in "The Blessing of the Years,"
and [recites] "Separation" in "Gracious Bestower of Knowledge."
R. Aqiva says:
One recites it as a separate, fourth blessing.

---

[44] Lit. "heaviness of the head."   [45] Lit. "direct their hearts to."

---

town assembly: A gathering of the local male Jewish citizenry.

5:1 *focus their minds on God*: Lit. "the place," *Hamaqom*, a standard rabbinic epithet for God, likely a metonym for "the God Who dwells in this place," i.e. the Jerusalem Temple, on the basis of Deuteronomy 14:23 and similar verses.

Even if a king greets him: Cf. 2:1.

5:2 *[God's] power [to bring] rainfall*: This is an insertion during the rainy season in the land of Israel, which begins around the time of the autumnal equinox and continues until the time of the spring equinox; the insertion is made from "the last Festival day of Sukkot" through the first day of Passover (cf. *Ta'anit* 1:1–2).

"Resurrection of the Dead": The second blessing of the Prayer, also known as *Gevurot*, "God's Might" (*Rosh Hashanah* 4:5).

"The Blessing of the Years": The tenth blessing of the daily Prayer, into which a petition for rainfall is inserted during the rainy season (*Ta'anit* 1:2–3).

"Gracious Bestower of Knowledge": The fourth blessing of the daily Prayer, and the first of the petitions. "Separation" (*havdalah*) at the end of the Sabbath and Festivals is to be marked here in conjunction with God's gift of knowledge and discernment.

R. Eliezer says:
[One recites it] in "Gratitude."

5:3–5 *Fluency vs. Error or Confusion in The Prayer*

3 One who says, "May Your mercies extend to the bird's nest,"
or "May Your name be invoked over the good,"
or "We give thanks; we give thanks!"—
he is to be silenced.[46]
One who passes before the ark [to lead the Prayer] and errs—
another takes his place,
and one may not be of a mind to refuse at that moment.
From where does he begin?
From the beginning of the blessing in which [the prior prayer leader] had erred.

4 One who passes before the ark [to lead the Prayer]
may not respond "Amen" to the priests
[when they bless the congregation],
because of confusion.
And if there is no other priest there beside himself,
he may not raise his hands [to bless the congregation].
But if he is confident that he can raise his hands [to bless the congregation]
and resume his Prayer [without getting confused],
he is allowed to do so.

5 One who prays and errs—
this is a bad omen for him.

[46] Lit. "they silence him."

"*Gratitude*": The penultimate blessing of the Prayer. In R. Eliezer's opinion, Separation is to be included here, presumably out of gratitude for the divine gift of the Sabbath and Festivals or for the ability to distinguish between sacred and profane time.

5:3 Parallel to *Megillah* 4:9. What is wrong with each of these prayer formulas is not entirely clear. Many scholars have suggested that the problem is dualism (cf. *Megillah* 4:9, which adds at the outset: "One who says, 'May the Good Ones bless you'—this is the way of heresy"). "May Your mercies extend to the bird's nest" (alluding to Deuteronomy 22:6) may suggest that God is *only* merciful, and that a separate deity is responsible for justice or punishment. "May Your name be invoked over the good" (implying, "and not over the bad"), suggests that there is a separate deity responsible for evil in the world. "We give thanks, we give thanks!" suggests that the worshipper is acknowledging two deities.

One who passes before the ark: To lead the congregation in prayer. Cf. *Ta'anit* 2:2, *Megillah* 4:3–6.

From where does he begin? Cf. 2:3.

5:4 *to the priests*: At the conclusion of the Prayer, the priests bless the congregation by reciting the biblical priestly blessing (Numbers 6:24–26); this practice was carried over from the rites of the Temple (so *Tamid* 5:1). The congregation responds "Amen" to each of the three priestly invocations, then the prayer leader continues with the final blessing of the Prayer. The concern here is that if the prayer leader also responds "Amen" to the priests' blessings, he may get confused when resuming the Prayer.

he may not raise his hands: He may not join the priests in blessing the congregation.

5:5 *If the prayer is fluent in my mouth*: Same phrase in 4:3.

And if he is the prayer leader[47] of the congregation—
it is a bad omen for those who have sent him,
because a person's agent is like himself.
The story is told[48] about R. Hanina b. Dosa
that whenever he would pray for sick people,
he would say, "This one will live" or "This one will die."
They said to him:
How do you know?
He said to them:
If the prayer is fluent in my mouth,
I know that he[49] has been accepted [by God];
but if not, I know that he has been rejected.

Chapter Six

6:1–7 *Blessings over Food*

6 How does one recite a blessing over produce?
Over produce of the tree, one says:
"[Blessed are You, O Lord, our God,] Creator of the fruit of the tree";
except for wine, for over wine one says:
"Creator of the fruit of the vine."
And over produce of the earth, one says:
"Creator of the fruit of the earth";
except for bread, for over bread one says:
"Who brings forth bread from the earth."
And over green vegetables, one says:
"Creator of the fruit of the earth."
R. Judah says:
"Creator of diverse kinds of herbs."
  2 If over produce of the tree one recited the blessing "Creator of the fruit of the earth,"
he has fulfilled his obligation;
but if over produce of the earth, [one recited] "Creator of the fruit of the tree,"
he has not fulfilled his obligation;
if over any of these he said, "By whose word[50] everything came into being,"
he has fulfilled his obligation.

---

[47] Lit. "representative, agent."   [48] Lit. "they told."   [49] i.e. the sick person.
[50] Lacking in printed editions, but present in most manuscripts.

5:5 If the prayer is fluent in my mouth: Same phrase in 4:3.

6:2–3 The rule here is that a generic blessing covers all subsets of the genus, while the reverse is not true.

"By whose word everything came into being": The most generic of blessings over food; it covers everything.

3 Over anything that does not grow from the earth,
one says, "[By whose word] everything [came into being]."[51]
Over vinegar, unripe fruit, and locusts,
one says, "[By whose word] everything [came into being]."[52]
Over milk, cheese, and eggs,
one says, "[By whose word] everything [came into being]."[53]
R. Judah says:
One may not recite a blessing over anything that is a kind of curse.

4 If one had before him many different kinds [of produce]—
R. Judah says:
If any of the seven species is among them, he recites the blessing over it;
but the Sages say:
He recites the blessing over whichever of them he wishes.

5 If one recited the blessing over wine before the meal,
he has exempted the wine after the meal.
If one recited the blessing over the appetizer before the meal,
he has exempted the dessert after the meal.
If one recited the blessing over the bread,
he has exempted the appetizer;[54]
if he recited the blessing over the appetizer,[55]
he has not exempted the bread.
The House of Shammai say:
Also not whatever was cooked in a pot.

6 If they sat down to eat,[56]
each one recites the blessing [over food] by himself.
If they reclined,

[51] The manuscripts include the bracketed words; the printed editions do not.
[52] The manuscripts include the bracketed words; the printed editions do not.
[53] K, P, and most other manuscripts lack this entire sentence (which interrupts the connection between R. Judah's statement and its target).
[54] K reads "appetizers."   [55] K reads "appetizers."
[56] K, P, and most other manuscripts lack "to eat."

Wine that has turned to *vinegar*, *fruit* that has fallen off the tree while yet *unripe*, and *locusts*—one may eat them but one does not recite a blessing over them according to R. Judah.

6:4 *the seven species*: Listed in Deuteronomy 8:8 (wheat, barley, grape, fig, pomegranate, olive, date).

6:5 *wine after the meal* was drunk to accompany the blessings after the meal (*birkat hamazon*; see the next chapter).

appetizer…dessert: The same word in Hebrew, meaning an accompanying food, whether before the meal (an appetizer) or after it (dessert).

If one recited the blessing over the bread: Because bread constitutes the substance of a meal, a blessing over bread covers all secondary, accompanying foods, but the reverse does not hold true. The Shammaite ruling further extends this principle. See also 6:7.

6:6 *If they reclined*: In the Greco-Roman context, reclining on a couch to eat constitutes the meal as a social gathering (as opposed to simply being seated individually), hence the communal blessing. *See Pesahim* 10:1.

one recites the blessing for all of them.
If wine came to them during the meal,
each one recites the blessing [over wine] by himself;
if after the meal, one recites the blessing for all of them.
And he [also] recites [a blessing] over the incense,
even though incense is not brought[57] [to the table] until after the meal.
   7 If they brought before him a salted dish at the beginning [of the meal]
and there was bread with it,
he recites a blessing over the salted dish and [thereby] exempts the bread,
for the bread is secondary to it.
This is the general rule:
Whenever a main dish is accompanied by a secondary dish,
one recites a blessing over the main dish
and [thereby] exempts the secondary dish.

6:8   *The Three Blessings after a Meal*

   8 One who ate figs, grapes, or pomegranates,
recites the Three Blessings after [eating] them—
the words of Rabban Gamaliel.
But the Sages say:
[He recites] one blessing that summarizes the three.[58]
R. Aqiva says:
Even if one ate [only] boiled vegetables—
if that was his meal,
he recites the Three Blessings after [eating] them.
One who drinks water to satisfy his thirst

---

[57] Lit. "they do not bring incense."
[58] K, P, and most other manuscripts lack "that summarizes the three."

If wine came to them during the meal: Wine during the meal is drunk individually, hence the blessing over wine is to be recited by each individual for himself.

if after the meal: Wine after the meal will be drunk together, hence the communal recitation of the blessing over wine.

incense: Lit after the meal to clear the air of the smell of foods. Since this is considered to be still a part of the dining ritual, the blessing over spices is recited communally.

6:7   *a salted dish*: In this instance, the salted dish is not an appetizer, as at 6:5, but an independent item. The bread serves to mitigate the salty taste and, for this reason, is considered to be secondary to the salted dish. The hierarchy of blessings follows accordingly.

6:8   *figs, grapes, or pomegranates*: Among the seven species (see above 6:4).

Three Blessings: The full series of blessings after the meal (usually called in English "the Grace after Meals"), as opposed to *one blessing that summarizes* them (cf. 4:3).

One who drinks water to satisfy his thirst: Two alternative blessing formulas are offered for this situation: the first is the most generic formula for eating anything (see 6:2); the second, which reads in full, "Creator of

says, "By whose word everything came into being."
R. Tarfon says:
[He says] "Creator of many living things."[59]

Chapter Seven

7:1–5 *The Invitation to Recite the Three Blessings after a Meal*

7 Three who ate together as one
are obligated [to have one of their number] invite[60]
[the other two to recite the Three Blessings after the meal].
If one [of the three] had eaten *demai*,
or first tithe from which the *terumah* had been removed,
or second tithe,
or produce dedicated to the Temple
that had been redeemed,
or [if one was] a servant who had eaten an olive's bulk [of food],

---

[59] **K** lacks "many" although the word is inserted in the margin; **K**, **P**, and other manuscripts read "creator of living things and their needs."

[60] Or "convene," "summon."

(many) living things and their needs," focuses on the divine fulfillment of human needs, of which thirst is an instance. (Later rabbinic law assigns the first blessing to be recited before drinking water and the second to be recited afterward, but the Mishnah here seems to understand the two as alternative formulas before the act of drinking.)

7:1 *Three who ate together*: Three people constitute the smallest quorum for the public recitation of the blessings after meals. Further on, the text distinguishes liturgically among larger and larger groups. The remainder of the paragraph contrasts a series of paired opposites.

demai: Produce which may or may not have been fully tithed (see *Demai*); a blessing may be recited over it because of the possibility that it *has* been fully tithed. Its paired opposite is *untithed* produce the eating of which is prohibited and hence no blessing may be recited over its consumption.

first tithe from which terumah had been removed: While first tithe is supposed to be given to, and eaten by, a Levite, it may in fact be eaten by anyone without incurring a sin as long as the additional *terumah* (which may be eaten *only* by priests) has been removed from it (see *Ma'aserot* and *Terumot*). Hence, a blessing may be recited over it. Its paired opposite is *first tithe from which terumah had not been removed*, which is prohibited for eating by nonpriests.

second tithe...that had been redeemed: Second tithe must be eaten in Jerusalem (see *Ma'aser Sheni*), and dedicated produce belongs to the Temple. Once these items have been redeemed (with their monetary value going to the original purpose), they may be eaten normally; hence, a blessing may be recited over them. This is contrasted with the situation of *second tithe or produce dedicated to the Temple that had not been redeemed*. These items remain devoted to their original purposes.

a servant who had eaten an olive's bulk: While those serving the meal are not usually included in a quorum for communal blessing after meals, they may be included if they have eaten the minimal amount of food that constitutes a meal (an olive's bulk).

or a Samaritan—
one may include them in the invitation.
But if one [of the three] had eaten untithed produce,
or first tithe from which *terumah* had not been removed,
or second tithe,
or produce dedicated to the Temple
that had not been redeemed;
or [if one was] a servant who had eaten less than an olive's bulk [of food],
or a gentile—
one may not include them in the invitation.

2 One may not include women, slaves, and minors in the invitation.
What is the minimum amount of food [one must consume]
in order to be included in the invitation?
As little as an olive's bulk.
R. Judah says:
As little as an egg's bulk.

3 How does one invite?
In the case of three [people who ate together], one is to say, "Let us bless";
In the case of three in addition to himself, one is to say, "Bless!"
In the case of ten [people who ate together], one is to say, "Let us bless our God";
In the case of ten in addition to himself, one is to say, "Bless [our God]!"
It is all one and the same whether there are ten [people who ate together]
or ten times ten thousand.
In the case of a hundred [people who ate together],
one is to say, "Let us bless the Lord our God";
In the case of a hundred in addition to himself,
one is to say, "Bless [the Lord our God]!"
In the case of a thousand [people who ate together],
one is to say, "Let us bless the Lord our God, the God of Israel";
In the case of a thousand in addition to himself,
one is to say, "Bless [the Lord our God, the God of Israel]!"
In the case of ten thousand [people who ate together],
one is to say, "Let us bless the Lord our God, the God of Israel,

---

a Samaritan: Samaritans in the Mishnah form an interstitial category between Jews and gentiles; because they are like both the one and the other in different respects, they are not deemed to be quite either. For purposes of blessing God over food, Samaritans are deemed to be like Jews. *A gentile*, on the other hand, is assumed to be a polytheist and to bless gods other than the God of Israel. Re Samaritans, contrast 8:8.

7:2 *Women, slaves, and minors*: See 3:3.

an egg's bulk: Larger than *an olive's bulk*; cf. the preceding paragraph, where the olive's bulk is the standard measure.

7:3 *It is all one and the same whether there are ten ... or ten times ten thousand*: This determination, which corresponds to post-Mishnaic practice, contradicts the rest of the paragraph where precisely this distinction is made. The Talmud cogently explains that this statement corresponds to the opinion of R. Aqiva below, who takes issue with that of R. Yose the Galilean.

the Lord of hosts enthroned [upon] the cherubim, for the food that we have eaten";[61]
In the case of ten thousand in addition to himself,
one is to say, "Bless [the Lord our God, the God of Israel,
the Lord of hosts enthroned [upon] the cherubim, for the food that we have eaten]!"
According to the formulation by which one invokes the blessing, they are to respond to him:
"Blessed be the Lord our God, the God of Israel,
the Lord of hosts enthroned [upon] the cherubim, for the food that we have eaten."
R. Yose the Galilean says:
They bless [God] according to the size of the assembly,
as it is said, *In assemblies bless God, the Lord, O you who are from the fountain of Israel.*
Said R. Aqiva:
What do we find in the synagogue?
It is all one and the same whether there are many or few:
one says, "Bless the Lord!"
R. Ishmael says:
"Bless the Lord who is worthy of blessing!"

4 Three who ate together are not permitted to separate
[themselves from the others before reciting together the invitation
and the Three Blessings after a meal];
likewise four; and likewise five.
Six [or more] may separate [into groups of three]—until they are ten.
Ten [or more] may not separate—until they are twenty.

5 Two groups that ate in [separate rooms of] a single house—
when some of them can see each other,
in that case they join together for the invitation;
but if not—
these are to invite by themselves and these are to invite by themselves.
One may not recite the blessing over wine until one puts water into it;
the words of R. Eliezer.
But the Sages say:
One may recite the blessing.

[61] **K, P**, and many other manuscripts lack this last phrase, from "enthroned [upon] the cherubim."

In assemblies bless God: Psalms 68:27. R. Yose reads the prefix to mean not "in," but "with respect to [the size of] assemblies."

7:5 *One may not recite the blessing over wine until one puts water into it*: Undiluted wine is thick, heavily intoxicating, and undrinkable. Diluting wine with water renders it drinkable; hence one can recite a blessing over it (cf. 6:3 above, analogous to inferior produce). This ruling is unrelated to the rest of the chapter and might have been inserted here as a transition to the next chapter.

Chapter Eight

8:1–8 *Disputes between the Houses of Shammai and Hillel about Proper Procedure at Meals*

8 These are the [disputed] matters between the House of Shammai and the House of Hillel
with regard to feasts:
the House of Shammai say:
One is to recite the blessing over the day and afterwards recite the blessing over the wine;
but the House of Hillel say:
One is to recite the blessing over the wine and afterwards recite the blessing over the day.

2 The House of Shammai say:
One is to wash the hands and afterwards mix the cup [of wine];
but the House of Hillel say:
One is to mix the cup and afterwards wash the hands.

3[62] The House of Shammai say:
One is to wipe the hands with the napkin and leave it on the table;

---

[62] **K, P**, and many other manuscripts reverse the order of paragraphs 3 and 4.

8:1–8 This chapter comprises eight disputes between the Houses of Hillel and Shammai about the proper order of activities at communal meals: the focus is on reciting various blessings and maintaining the purity of hands and foodstuffs. The first dispute concerns Sabbath and festival meals, when the named blessings are recited. The dispute about cleaning the house (8:4), however, does not refer to Sabbath meals since, according to the Tosefta at least, cleaning the house is forbidden on the Sabbath. 8:6 is interpolated on account of the shared theme with 8:5, blessings over light and spices at the end of Sabbath. The reference of the other disputes is not specified.

8:1 This dispute applies to the meal at the outset of the Sabbath or the Festival (cf. *Pesahim* 10:2), and is explained by the Tosefta as follows: The *blessing over the day* both acknowledges and inaugurates the beginning of the holy day. The Shammaites give it precedence for this reason; it is the day that provides the occasion for the drinking of wine. The Hillelites give precedence to the wine because it is the presence of a cup of wine at the table that provides the occasion for the blessing over the day to be recited.

8:2 The concern here is for maintaining the purity of the hands, so that they will not render the food impure through touch (cf. *Tohorot*). According to the Tosefta, the Shammaites insist that hands be washed before touching the cup of wine lest any liquids on the outer surface of the cup be rendered impure by contact with impure hands and in turn render the contents of the cup impure, while the Hillelites hold that the outer surface of the cup is in any case always deemed to be impure, and insist that hand washing must always immediately precede the meal, since the primary concern is for the purity of the food. See *Yadayim*.

8:3 The concern here is to preserve the purity of the food. The House of Shammai scruple lest any liquid on the napkin, left over from hand washing, become impure through contact with the cushion on which one is reclining and in turn render the hands impure. The House of Hillel do not scruple about the hands, since

but the House of Hillel say:
On the cushion.

4 The House of Shammai say:
One is to clean the house and afterwards wash the hands;
but the House of Hillel say:
One is to wash the hands and afterwards clean the house.

5 The House of Shammai say:
[The order of blessings after the meal at the end of the Sabbath is]
lamp, food, spices, and Separation;
but the House of Hillel say:
Lamp, spices, food, and Separation.
The House of Shammai say:
[The blessing over the lamp is,] "Who created the light of fire";
but the House of Hillel say:
"Creator of the lights of fire."

6 One may not recite a blessing over the lamp or the spices of gentiles,
nor over the lamp or the spices of the dead,
nor over the lamp or the spices which are in front of idolatry.
One may not recite a blessing over the lamp until he benefits from its light.

---

doubts about whether hands have been made impure are always resolved leniently in favor of purity. The Hillelites instead are concerned lest the liquids on the napkin be rendered impure by contact with the table and then in turn render impure the foodstuffs that are on the table.

8:4 *the house*: That is, the dining area. The concern is to preserve the purity of any edible table scraps (defined as the size of an olive's bulk or larger; cf. 7:1 above). The Shammaites want the table and surroundings to be cleared before hands are washed after the meal, lest any liquids drip on the food scraps and render them susceptible to impurity (cf. *Tohorot* and *Makhshirin*). The Hillelites assume that a knowledgeable servant will remove any edible table scraps before the table is cleared.

8:5 Two disputes between the Houses regarding the order and wording of blessings after the evening meal at the end of the Sabbath, when the Separation (*havdalah*) blessings are recited over spices and a lamp, signifying the resumption of the work week. The first dispute concerns where the regular blessing after the meal is to be inserted in this series. Both Houses agree that one must bless over the lamp at the outset, since the kindling of a light is what most defines the moment. The Shammaites view the blessing over food as the next most defining element (particularly since spices are generally lit after a meal in any event, and their blessing always follows the blessing over food; see 6:6). The Hillelites keep the two short blessings over lamp and spices together, followed by food, and then both Houses conclude with the Separation blessing. The Tosefta gives an entirely different version of this dispute.

8:6 A topically motivated insertion into the series of disputes between the Houses.

One may not recite a blessing…of gentiles: The lamp must have been lit afresh after the close of the Sabbath. That *of gentiles*, even if taken up after the Sabbath, may have been lit during the Sabbath.

or the spices of gentiles: They may have been used for idolatrous worship.

nor over the lamp or the spices of the dead: The primary use of both the light and the spices is for something other than marking the end of the Sabbath; they have been used to honor the dead and to fumigate the corpse.

One may not recite a blessing…from its light: The use of fire constitutes the first act of work marking the beginning of the new week.

7 One who ate and forgot to recite the blessings [after the meal]—
the House of Shammai say:
He returns to his place and recites the blessings;
but the House of Hillel say:
He recites the blessings in the place where he remembers.
Until when may he recite the blessings [after the meal]?
Until the point at which the food in his stomach[63] is digested.

8 If wine came to them after the meal, and there is only enough there for one cup—
the House of Shammai say:
He recites the blessing over the wine and afterwards recites the blessings over the food;
but the House of Hillel say:
He recites the blessings over the food and afterwards recites the blessing over the wine.
One responds "Amen" to an Israelite who recites a blessing,
but one does not respond "Amen" to a Samaritan who recites a blessing,
unless he has heard the entire blessing.

Chapter Nine

9:1–4 *Blessings to be Recited upon Special Occasions*

9 One who beholds a place in which miracles had been performed for Israel says, "Blessed…who performed miracles for our forefathers in this place";
[one who beholds] a place from which idolatry had been uprooted, says,
"Blessed…who uprooted idolatry from our land."

2 In response to comets, earthquakes, lightning, thunder, or windstorms, one says,
"Blessed…whose might and power[64] fill the world."
In response to mountains, hills, seas, rivers, or deserts, one says,
"Blessed…who performs the work of[65] creation."

---

[63] Lit. "bowels," "intestines."
[64] K, P, and many other manuscripts and some printed editions lack "and power."
[65] K, P, and most other manuscripts lack "the work of."

8:8 *If wine came to them…for one cup*: Normally one would drink wine with the meal and would recite the wine blessing at the meal's inception. The blessings after the meal were often accompanied by a cup of wine; the wine blessing in that instance would be recited after the food blessings. In the present case, no wine had been drunk during the meal and only enough wine is now available to recite with the blessings after the meal. The Shammaites treat the wine as a newly arrived item and recite the wine blessing first; the Hillelites continue to give precedence to the blessings after meals. For the wine before and after the meal, cf. 6:5 and 6:6.

a Samaritan: Contrast 7:1 above, which has a more inclusive attitude towards Samaritans.

R. Judah says:
One who beholds the Great Sea says,
"Blessed…who made the Great Sea"—
but only if he beholds it intermittently.
In response to rainfall or good tidings, one says,
"Blessed…who is good and bestows goodness";
In response to bad tidings, one says,
"Blessed…the true judge."

3 If one built a new house or acquired new clothing,[66] he says,
"Blessed…who has given us life."[67]
One recites a blessing over the bad just as one recites a blessing over the good;
and one recites a blessing over the good just as one recites a blessing over the bad.
Whoever cries out over something that has already happened—
this is a prayer in vain.
How so?
If one's wife was pregnant
and he said, "May it be God's will that my wife give birth to a son"—
this is a prayer in vain.
If one was coming along the road and heard the sound of wailing in the city
and said, "May it be God's will that these not be members of my household"[68]—
this is a prayer in vain.

4 One who enters a town prays two prayers,
one upon entering and one upon departing.
Ben Azzai says:
Four: two upon entering and two upon departing.
And he gives thanks for that which is past
and cries out [in supplication] for that which may come in the future.

[66] Lit. "utensils."
[67] K, P, and several other manuscripts: "Blessed…who has brought us to this occasion."
[68] K, P, and most manuscripts: "inside my house."

9:2 *the Great Sea*: The Mediterranean Sea.

good tidings are grouped with *rainfall* here because the sense of having experienced providential benevolence is the same.

bad tidings: Cf. 5:3 above. Acts of divine judgment or punishment derive from the same source as acts of divine benevolence; dualism is firmly rejected.

9:3 This paragraph continues the list of occasional blessings from the previous paragraph. 9:5 below effectively repeats the second item here.

a prayer in vain: One that asks for the alteration of something that already has occurred or of an outcome that already has been determined; it is thus counterfactual.

9:5 *Conclusion*

5 A person[69] is obliged to bless [God] over the bad just as he blesses [God] over the good,
as it is said, *You shall love the Lord your God with all your heart,
with all your soul, and with all your might.*
With all your heart—with both of your impulses, the good impulse and the evil impulse.
With all your soul—even if He takes your soul.
And with all your might—with all your wealth.
Another interpretation:
And with all your might—in response to whatever measure he measures out to you, express much gratitude to Him.[70]
A person may not indulge in any levity[71] while facing the eastern gate [of the Temple], because that is directed towards the Holy of Holies.
One may not enter the Temple Mount with his staff, footwear, purse, or with dust on his feet,
nor may one use it as a shortcut,
and all the more so is spitting [prohibited there].
In the conclusions[72] to all benedictions in the Temple they used to say,[73] "from eternity."[74]
Once the heretics went astray[75] and said, "There is only one world,"
they ordained that one say, "from eternity to eternity."[76]
And[77] they ordained that a person greet his fellow using the divine Name,
as it is said, *Presently Boaz arrived from Bethlehem. He greeted the reapers,*

[69] Lacking in **K, P**. [70] **K, P**, and several other manuscripts add twice "in all things."
[71] Lit. "lighten his head." [72] Lit. "seals." See 1:4 above.
[73] **K, P**, and several other manuscripts lack "they used to say."
[74] Or "from the world." [75] Lit. "corrupted, ruined."
[76] Or "from world to world." [77] **K, P**, and other manuscripts lack "And."

9:5 It is fairly common for tractates of the Mishnah to end rhetorically with citations of scriptural verses and their midrashic interpretation. The rule that begins this paragraph is similar to the one in 9:3, but is here accompanied by its midrashic justification, saved for the tractate's conclusion.

You shall love the Lord your God: Deuteronomy 6:5.

with all your heart: The extended form of the noun, *levav* with two *bets* (as opposed to the more common *lev*) suggests two impulses in the heart.

in response to whatever measure...express much gratitude: Measure (*middah*) and gratitude (*modeh*) play on the biblical *me'odekha*, your might.

"from eternity": This passage turns on the shift in the meaning of *olam*. In the Bible its meaning is temporal ("eternity") but in rabbinic texts its usual meaning is spatial ("world").

"There is only one world": These heretics denied the afterlife, just as the heretics in *Sanhedrin* 10:1 deny the resurrection.

that a person greet his fellow using the divine Name: This ruling may also reflect an antidualist polemic; cf. 5:3 and 9:2–3 above.

Boaz arrived from Bethlehem: Ruth 2:4.

"The Lord be with you!" And they responded, "The Lord bless you!"
And it says, "The Lord is with you, valiant warrior!"
And it says, *Do not disdain your mother when she is old.*
And it says, *It is time to act for the Lord; they have violated your Torah.*
R. Nathan says:[78]
They have violated your Torah; [therefore] it is time to act for the Lord.

[78] K (added in margin) and several other manuscripts lack R. Nathan's dictum.

The Lord be with you: Judges 6:12.

Do not disdain your mother: Proverbs 23:22. The logic of this citation in this context is not clear.

It is time to act for the Lord: Psalms 119:126. In context this seems to mean: in response to the heretics, who violated the Torah, the Sages had to enact new practices.

Tractate Pe'ah

Gregg E. Gardner

Introduction

Overview

Pe'ah is the "corner" or "edge" of a field whose produce is left unharvested for the poor to collect. The tractate discusses *pe'ah* alongside other laws and concepts associated with agricultural offerings for the poor. Its inclusion in the Order of *Zera'im* ("Seeds") is due to this focus on agricultural laws; its inclusion also suggests an analogy between offerings for the poor and those for the priests, which are discussed in other tractates of *Zera'im*.

Structure and Organization of the Tractate

The opening section (1:1), which is the best-known portion of Mishnah *Pe'ah* as it would later be incorporated into Jewish liturgy, places *pe'ah* on a par with agricultural offerings for priests and alongside other commandments of a socio-ethical nature. The core of the tractate discusses poor offerings, which are arranged according to the sequence of the harvest. At the outset of the harvest, the householder designates a portion of grain in the rear of his field that will be left unharvested (*pe'ah*). During the reaping, any produce that falls to the ground must be left for the poor (Gleanings). The cut grains are then bound into sheaves—any that are left in the field belong to the poor (Forgotten Things). The sheaves are then carried off to the granary for processing and storage, at which point a portion (known as poor tithe) is given to the poor. The tractate opens with the definition of its main concept and then an exploration of ambiguous cases. It transitions to the next topic by discussing miscellaneous laws that apply to multiple categories of poor offerings (e.g. 4:6–9, 5:4–6, 8:1–4).

Main Ideas

The householder (i.e. landowner)—or his agent—fulfills the obligation to leave *pe'ah* for the poor by designating an area of the crop that will be left unharvested. The amount designated as *pe'ah* must consist of at least one-sixtieth of the harvest's yield (1:2) and (at least according to R. Simeon) be located in the rear of the field (1:3). Gleanings (*leqet*) are grains that fall to the ground during the reaping, which are likewise left for the poor (4:10–5:3). Forgotten Things (*shikhehah*, also commonly referred to as "forgotten sheaves"), are bundles of cut stalks of grain that the householder left or "forgot" in the field when he transported the rest to the granary (5:7–7:2). There are two poor offerings of grapes: Separated Grapes (*peret*) are individual grapes that have fallen to the ground (like Gleanings), while Defective Clusters (*'olelot*) are malformed clusters of grapes (7:3–8). The poor tithe (*ma'aser 'ani*; 8:5–6) is produce allocated to the poor every third and sixth years of the seven-year Sabbatical cycle, when it replaces the second tithe. The topic of almsgiving is given very brief treatment in tractate *Pe'ah* (8:7), which focuses on institutionalized giving. (A fuller treatment of charity is given in the Tosefta.) It is notable that, despite the tractate's interest in forms of support for the poor, the emblematic rabbinic term for "charity"—*tsedaqah*—is entirely absent from tractate *Pe'ah*. The tractate closes by identifying who is eligible to collect these offerings—thus, defining who is poor (8:8–9).

The Mishnah, as usual, does not provide any theological or philosophical rationale for these requirements. But we can speculate. These "gifts to the poor" are not actually gifts from the householder. The householder, in fact, gives nothing of his own as this produce was never his to give. Rather, these are gifts directly from God. The produce assumes the status of poor offerings seemingly by chance—*pe'ah* is that which happens to grow in the rear of a field, *gleanings* are items that happen to fall to the ground, and so on. These are not accidents but rather the product of divine will, as God chooses which grains, grapes, and olives should be allocated to the poor. Tractate *Pe'ah* instructs the householder how to initiate and facilitate this process without interfering in God's direct distribution of produce to the poor (e.g. 4:1–2). In doing so, the householder acknowledges and protects the poor's exclusive claim to these offerings and, in turn, establishes his own claim to the rest of the crop (minus the offerings for priests)—which he cultivated with God's assistance. The rabbinic practice of reciting a benediction before eating has a similar etiology: the earth and all of its bounty belong to the Lord. The recitation of a benediction allows us to partake of that which is God's. See the introduction to *Berakhot*.

Relationship to Scripture

The terminology for the poor offerings—*pe'ah*, Gleanings, Forgotten Things, Separated Grapes, Defective Clusters, and the poor tithe—derives from a handful of biblical verses, Leviticus 19:9–10, 23:22 and Deuteronomy 14:28–29, 24:19–22, 26:12–13. In expanding these terms into legal concepts, tractate *Pe'ah* departs from biblical law in important ways. First, whereas the Hebrew Bible identifies the recipients by legal and social categories—the poor, strangers, orphans, and widows—the Mishnah defines eligibility solely by economic criteria (8:8–9). Second, the Mishnah conflates the passages from Leviticus and Deuteronomy, erasing their distinctive contexts. The passages from Leviticus are embedded in the Holiness Code (Leviticus 17–26), as the fulfillment of these obligations is part of an effort to be holy like God. The laws in Deuteronomy are motivated by the promise of a reward, namely a blessing from God (Deuteronomy 24:19). By contrast, tractate *Pe'ah* instructs that failing to fulfill these obligations is tantamount to theft, equivalent to stealing what rightfully belongs to the poor (5:6, 7:3). The Mishnah also expands the application of these concepts. *Pe'ah*, for example, applies only to grain in the Hebrew Bible but is expanded in the Mishnah to include all classes of crops—legumes and olives, for example. (1:4–5). Similarly, whereas the Forgotten Things in the Hebrew Bible apply only to harvested grain (Deuteronomy 24:19), in the Mishnah the concept includes standing grain (i.e. uncut and still attached to the ground) that the reaper overlooked (6:7) as well as olive trees (7:1–2). Another departure from biblical law is tractate *Pe'ah*'s discussion of institutionalized almsgiving (8:7), which has no precedent in the Hebrew Bible.

Special Notes for the Reader

In my translation and annotations, I have benefitted from Roger Brooks, *Support for the Poor in the Mishnaic Law of Agriculture: Tractate Peah*, Brown Judaic Studies 43 (Chico, Calif.: Scholars Press, 1983).

Tractate Pe'ah

Chapter One

1:1–3 *Laws of Pe'ah: Quantity and Location*

1 These are things that have no statutory amount:
pe'ah, firstfruits, the appearance offering, acts of kindness, and the study of the Torah.
These are things the profits[1] of which a person consumes in this world,
while the principal endures[2] for him in the world to come:
honoring father and mother, acts of kindness, and making peace between a person and his fellow.
But the study of Torah is equal to them all.

2 One may not reduce *pe'ah* to less than one-sixtieth.[3]

---

[1] Or "fruits." **K:** "some of the profits." [2] **K:** "is preserved." [3] Lit. "sixty."

1:1 *have no statutory amount*: In the Torah; 1:2 establishes that *pe'ah* should be no less than one-sixtieth of the yield.

pe'ah: Lit. "corner" or "edge," refers to Leviticus 19:9, 23:22 where one must refrain from reaping corners or edges of a field. This produce should be left standing for the poor to collect.

firstfruits: The commandment to bring the first ripe fruits to the Jerusalem Temple (Exodus 23:19, 34:26, Deuteronomy 18:4, 26:1–11; *Bikkurim*).

appearance offering: The sacrifices that all male Israelites bring when they appear at the Temple for the three annual pilgrimage festivals (Exodus 23:14–17, 34:20, Deuteronomy 16:16; *Hagigah* 1:1–2).

acts of kindness: Heb. *gemilut hasadim*. Otherwise unspecified benevolent deeds performed by one individual for another; see *Avot* 1:2.

profits: Cf. Isaiah 3:10.

person consumes...world to come: Whereas most commandments generate rewards either in this world or the world to come, those listed here are exceptional as they generate rewards in both worlds.

honoring father and mother: Exodus 20:12, Deuteronomy 5:16.

equal to them all: Emphasizes the significance that the rabbis place on Torah study.

1:2 *one-sixtieth*: The householder (or his agent) cannot designate less than one-sixtieth (a small or "miserly" amount in *Terumot* 4:3) of the standing grain as *pe'ah*.

And even though they said:
Pe'ah has no statutory amount,
everything is according to the size of the field,
and according to the number of poor individuals,
and according to the extent[4] of the yield.[5]

3 One designates[6] *pe'ah* from the beginning of the field or from its middle.
R. Simeon says:
Provided that he designates the statutory amount at the rear of the field.
R. Judah says:
If he leaves one stalk, he may rely on it for the sake of *pe'ah*.
If not, he may only designate it as ownerless property.

1:4–6 Laws of Pe'ah: Produce that is Liable and Exempt

4 They stated a general rule for *pe'ah*:
anything that is food,
and is guarded,
and grows from the land,
and is all gathered at once,
and one brings it in for storage,

[4] K, P lack "extent." [5] Or "humility" or "kindness." Meaning uncertain.
[6] Lit. "gives," and so on throughout the tractate.

---

they said: In the previous mishnah (1:1). The Tosefta harmonizes the contradictory statements by positing that *pe'ah* has a minimum (as in 1:2), but no maximum (as in 1:1).

everything is according to…: A second set of criteria for the amount of *pe'ah*.

yield: Which is likewise the sense in 6:7.

1:3 *One designates*: The householder designates an area of the field as *pe'ah*, where the produce will be left unharvested for the poor to collect.

rear: Accords with the literal meaning of *pe'ah* as the very "edge," "corner," or "extremity" (Leviticus 19:9, 19:27).

one stalk: a symbolic amount of produce left in the rear of the field, to fulfill the sense of *pe'ah* as "edge" or "extremity."

ownerless property: Heb. *hefqer/hevqer*. Land that is unclaimed, abandoned, or whose ownership was renounced by the owner. It is exempt from tithes and poor offerings and is available to poor and nonpoor alike (6:1; *Hallah* 1:3). If the farmer fails to leave at least one stalk in the rear portion of the field as *pe'ah*, then the stalks that he had designated as *pe'ah* in the beginning and middle of the field become ownerless and he has failed to leave *pe'ah* for the poor.

1:4 *a general rule*: Similar to what is liable to tithes (*Ma'aserot* 1:1).

guarded: Privately owned produce, in contrast to ownerless property that is exempt from *pe'ah* (1:3).

grows from the land: Excludes mushrooms (*Ma'aserot* 1:1).

gathered at once: Harvested as a crop, in contrast to produce that is picked individually.

for storage: The produce can be preserved, which excludes vegetables.

is liable to *pe'ah*.
Both grain and legumes are included in this general rule.
  5 And among trees:
sumac, and carobs, and walnuts, and almonds, and vines, and pomegranates, and olives, and dates—
are liable to *pe'ah*.
  6 One may always designate [produce] as *pe'ah*,
and it is exempt from tithes,
until he smooths it over.
And he may designate it as ownerless property,
and it is exempt from tithes,
until he smooths it over.
And he may feed [it to] cattle and wild animals and birds,
and it is exempt from tithes,
until he smooths it over.
And he may collect from the granary and sow,
and it is exempt from tithes,
until he smooths it over—
the words of R. Aqiva.
If a priest and[7] a Levite bought [produce in] a granary,
the tithes belong to them,
until he smooths it over.[8]
One who consecrates [produce] and redeems it—
it is liable to tithes,
until the treasurer smooths it over.

[7] Or "or."   [8] P lacks "until he smooths it over."

1:5 *among trees*: These trees are liable to *pe'ah* because their produce is gathered all at once as a crop and they meet the other qualifications in 1:4. All other trees are exempt.

1:6 *always*: Even after the harvest. 4:1 stipulates that produce designated as *pe'ah* must be left unharvested—literally "attached to the ground"—for the poor to collect. If the householder, however, neglected to designate *pe'ah* during the harvest, then he may still designate *pe'ah* from the harvested produce and exempt it from tithes.

until he smooths it over: Harvested produce that is designated as *pe'ah*, declared ownerless (*hefqer*; see 1:3), fed to animals, or sown, is exempt from tithes until the farmer has prepared it for storage by smoothing over or evening out the pile of grain (4:8, *Ma'aserot* 1:6).

tithes, until he smooths it over: If the grain was bought before the seller has smoothed the produce over, then the priests and Levites can keep the tithes for themselves. If, however, the grain was smoothed over, then it was already liable to tithes.

consecrates [produce]: For the Temple's upkeep to its treasury. The householder later *redeems* the consecrated property (*heqdesh*) with money (2:8, 4:7–8; 7:8; *Sheqalim* 4:6–8).

the treasurer who managed the Temple's funds (cf. 4:8; *Sheqalim* 5:2) *smooths it over* thereby asserting the Temple's ownership of the produce and exempting it from tithes (cf. 4:8).

Chapter Two

2:1–4 *Definition of Grain Fields and Orchards Liable to Pe'ah*

2 And[9] these form a partition [in a field] for the purposes of *pe'ah*:
a riverbed, a pond,
a private road, a public road,
a public path, a private path[10] that is permanent in the summer season and the rainy season,
uncultivated land, newly broken land,
or a different seed.
So too[11] one who reaps for the sake of animal fodder forms a partition—
the words of R. Meir.
But the Sages say:
This does not form a partition, unless he had plowed.

2 A water canal[12] [which divides an area of land so that it] cannot be harvested all at once—
R. Judah says:
It forms a partition.
And as for all the hills that are to be hoed with a hoe—
even though an ox cannot pass over [the hills] with its plow,[13]
he designates [a single] *pe'ah* for all of it.

---

[9] **K**: original hand lacks "And"; added by a later scribe.
[10] **P**: "a private path and a public path."   [11] Lit. "and." **K** lacks the conjunction.
[12] Or "irrigation channel."   [13] Lit. "utensils" or "tools."

2:1 *And these form…purposes of pe'ah*: The underlying principle is that a single "field" for the purposes of *pe'ah* consists of an area that is harvested all at once (1:4). Features and changes in the landscape that compel the farmer to interrupt his harvesting define the boundaries of a field. Thus, the farmer must designate *pe'ah* separately for the land on each side of the boundary (1:3).

private road that is four cubits wide (*Bava Batra* 6:7).

public road that is sixteen cubits wide (*Bava Batra* 6:7).

summer…rainy season: The path is used all year round.

newly broken land: Which had been plowed, but not sown.

different seed: E.g. tares that grow amidst wheat create a boundary (*Kilayim* 1:1).

animal fodder: Cf. 6:10; *Menahot* 10:8.

forms a partition: Where the unripe grain was harvested creates a boundary.

unless he had plowed the land on which the unripe grain grew, thus breaking up the earth and creating a boundary.

2:2 *water canal…a partition*: As in 2:1, this is a feature that prevents the land from being harvested continuously (1:4).

hills…hoe: Isaiah 7:25; hills that can be ploughed by hand with a hoe (*Kelim* 13:2).

he designates…all of it: If the hills cannot be plowed by an ox, then one may have thought that the hills partition the land into multiple fields (2:1). Since, however, the hills can still be hoed by hand, then they do not form a partition.

3 All these form[14] a partition for [a field of] seeds,
but only a fence forms a partition for [a field of] trees.
But if the branches are intertwined,
[the fence] does not form a partition
and one is to designate [a single] *pe'ah* for the whole.
   4 And as for carob trees—
[one designates a single *pe'ah*] for all that see one another.
Rabban Gamaliel said:
In my father's house, they used to designate a single *pe'ah*
for the olive trees that they had in each direction,
and for the carob trees that see one another.
R. Eleazar bar Zadok said in his name:
Also for the carob trees that they had in the entire town.

2:5–6   *Ambiguous Cases: Borders of a Field with Mixed Crops*

5 One who sows his field with one kind—
even though he makes of it two [separate] granaries,
he designates one *pe'ah*.
If one sowed it with two kinds—
even though he makes of them one granary,

---

[14] K: "do not form." "Not" deleted by later hand.

2:3 *All these form...seeds*: Grains. The features in 2:1–2 form partitions in fields of grain, but not orchards, for which *only a fence forms a partition*: 1:5 applies the law of *pe'ah* to orchards. However, only a fence forms a partition because trees can be planted at great distances from one another (whereas grain is sown in close proximity), and the area could include several landmarks.

But if the branches from trees on opposite sides of the fence *are intertwined* above the fence, then it *does not form a partition*. Because of their close proximity, these two trees are considered to be part of one single field (cf. *Kilayim* 5:3); thus, the farmer designates *[a single] pe'ah* for all the trees, on both sides of the fence.

2:4 *carob trees*: These have expansive root systems and grow far from one another (cf. *Bava Batra* 2:7), complicating how a carob orchard should be defined for the purposes of *pe'ah*.

see one another: If one carob tree can be seen when one is standing next to another, then they are considered a single orchard for the purposes of *pe'ah* even if they are separated by a fence.

in each direction: They designated *pe'ah* for each grove of olive trees in the north, east, south, and west sides of town, as each is considered a separate orchard.

and a single designation of *pe'ah for the carob trees that see one another*: The tradition regarding Rabban Gamaliel's father's house provides the precedent for the ruling above.

R. Eleazar disputes Rabban Gamaliel's version of the tradition, saying that Rabban Gamaliel's father's house would give a single portion of *pe'ah for all the carob trees that they had in the entire town*, even if one tree could not be seen from another.

2:5 *one kind* of crop.

If one sowed...two kinds of crops in the same field. A change in crop forms a partition, thus a portion of *pe'ah* must be designated for each field (2:1)—even if he *makes of them one granary*.

One who sows...two kinds of wheat: An ambiguous case involving two species of the same genus (wheat); see 2:6.

he designates two [separate areas] of *pe'ah*.
One who sows his field with two kinds of wheat:
if he makes of them one granary—
he designates one *pe'ah*;
two granaries—
he designates two [separate areas] of *pe'ah*.

6 It once happened that R. Simeon a man of Mizpah,
sowed [his field with two kinds of wheat],
[and came] before Rabban Gamaliel,
and they went up[15] to the Chamber of Hewn Stone and asked.[16]
Nahum the Scribe said:
I received [this tradition] from R. Me'asha,
who received it from [his] father,[17]
who received it from the pairs,
who received it from the prophets as a law [given] to Moses at Sinai:
One who sows his field with two kinds of wheat:
if he made of them one granary—
he designates one *pe'ah*;
two granaries—
he designates two [separate areas] of *pe'ah*.

2:7–8 *Ambiguous Cases: A Field Reaped by Others*

7 A field that gentiles reaped,
Or brigands reaped,
ants chewed up,[18]

---

[15] Earlier hand of **K** lacks "they went up," added by later hand.
[16] Earlier hand of **K** lacks "and asked," added by later hand.
[17] The Hebrew *abba* may also be a proper name.   [18] Or "cut" or "nibbled."

2:6 *Mizpah*: A village in Judaea, north of Jerusalem.

Rabban Gamaliel I, the "elder" (died ca. 50 CE); according to Acts the teacher of Paul and a member of the Sanhedrin (Acts 5:34–39, 22:3); grandfather of Gamaliel II of Yavneh (ca. 80–110 CE).

to the Chamber of Hewn Stone: On the Temple Mount where the Sanhedrin sat in session (*Sanhedrin* 11:2; *Eduyot* 7:4; *Tamid* 4:3; *Middot* 5:4).

Nahum the Scribe: Otherwise unknown in Tannaitic texts (though mentioned later in the Bavli).

Me'asha: Otherwise unknown in Tannaitic texts.

who received it: A chain of Torah transmission going back to the revelation at Sinai, establishing the authority of the following ruling; cf. *Yadayim* 4:3, *Eduyot* 8:7, *Avot* 1:1–18.

the pairs: Five successive pairs of Torah authorities who preceded the rabbinic movement (*Avot* 1:4–15; *Hagigah* 2:2).

as a law [given] by God *to Moses at* the revelation at *Sinai*, which is authoritative without requiring further justification (*Yadayim* 4:3; *Eduyot* 8:7).

2:7 *is exempt [from pe'ah]* because it was not reaped by a Jewish householder or his agent (4:6).

or was destroyed by the wind or cattle—
is exempt [from *pe'ah*].
If one reaped half of it,
and brigands reaped [the remaining] half of it,
it is exempt,
for the obligation of *pe'ah*[19] is from standing grain.

8 If brigands reaped half of it,
and he reaped [the remaining] half of it—
he designates *pe'ah* from what he reaped.
If he reaped half of it,
and sold [the remaining] half of it—
the purchaser designates *pe'ah* for the whole.
If he reaped half of it,
and consecrated [the remaining] half of it—
the one who redeems it from the treasurer designates *pe'ah* for the whole.

Chapter Three

3:1–5 *Ambiguous Cases: Fields Harvested Piecemeal*

3 Rectangular-shaped [furrows] of grain between olive trees—
the House of Shammai say:

[19] K, P: "harvest."

---

is from standing grain in the rear corner (1:3; 4:1). By harvesting the second half of the field and the area designated as *pe'ah*, someone other than a Jew obligated in *pe'ah* has completed the reaping, making the field exempt from *pe'ah*.

2:8 *and* the Jewish householder *reaped [the remaining] half of it* where the stalks standing in the rear corner designated as *pe'ah* would be located.

designates pe'ah from what he reaped: That is, he designates *pe'ah* on behalf of the half that he reaped, not for the field as a whole, as the portion of the field harvested by brigands is not subject to *pe'ah* (2:7).

and sold the remaining *half of* the field after he designated *pe'ah* but before the reaping was complete, then *the purchaser*... ensures that the rear corner is left as *pe'ah* for the whole field.

and consecrated [the remaining] half of the field to the Temple treasury.

the one who redeems [the remaining] half of the field *from the treasurer* with money (1:6, 2:8, 4:7-8; 7:8; Sheqalim 4:6-8).

designates one portion of *pe'ah for the whole* because he purchased the portion of the field that included the produce standing in the rear corner. The question remains, however, why in this case and the previous one the obligation devolves on the purchaser/redeemer to give *pe'ah* on the whole field whereas in the brigand case the field-owner was only obligated to give *pe'ah* for the half of the field he actually reaped.

3:1 *Rectangular-shaped*: Cf. 7:2.

Pe'ah from each and every one.
The House of Hillel say:
From one for all.
But they concede that, if the heads of the rows are intermingled,
he designates *pe'ah* from one for all.

2 One who gives a checkered appearance to his field,
and he left unripe[20] stalks—
R. Aqiva says:
He designates[21] *pe'ah* from each and every one.
But the Sages say:
From one for all.
But the Sages agree with R. Aqiva in the case of one who sows dill or mustard in three places,
That he is to designate *pe'ah* [22] from each and every one.

3 One who uproots[23] fresh[24] onions for the market,
and saves [in the ground] the dry ones for the granary,
designates *pe'ah* for these by themselves and for these by themselves.
And likewise in the case of beans and likewise in the case of a vineyard.

---

[20] Lit. "moist," in contrast to ripe stalks that are dry.
[21] **K, P** lack "He designates." [22] Absent in **P, K**.
[23] Lit. "makes [the ground] smooth [by taking]." [24] Lit. "moist."

Pe'ah must be designated *from each and every* rectangle, as the olive tree constitutes a different seed, which forms a partition (2:1–3); cf. 3:4.

From one for all: the small plots should be together considered collectively, as one field, for the purposes of *pe'ah*.

But they, the House of Shammai, *concede* to the position of the House of Hillel *that, if the heads of the rows* of adjacent plots *are intermingled*, touching one another, then the farmer *designates* one portion of *pe'ah from one* plot *for all* plots whose row tops are intermingled. Thus, they are considered to be one continuous field for the purposes of *pe'ah*.

3:2 *checkered appearance to his field* whereby he reaped the ripe stalks and *left unripe stalks* standing in the field. The patches of unharvested grains standing in the otherwise harvested field look like the spots of a leopard (*namer*; cf. 4:5, "House of Namer") or a checkerboard.

R. Aqiva...each patch of produce; cf. 2:1, 3:1, 3:4.

But the Sages say...: At the outset of the harvest, the farmer designates a single portion of *pe'ah* for the entire plot of land, for both the ripe produce that will be reaped immediately and the unripe produce to be reaped later, cf. 2:1, 3:1, 3:4.

dill or mustard in three places within a single area. The Yerushalmi offers two suggestions: that the individual plots would ripen at different times and that dill and mustard are normally cultivated in individual beds.

3:3 *uproots fresh onions*: He levels or evens out the field by uprooting at least three adjacent onions (*Shevi'it* 4:4).

for the market: To be sold immediately, whereas he *saves* or leaves others in the ground until the *dry* husk is formed, at which point they are uprooted and taken *for the granary*.

designates a portion of *pe'ah*... for the fresh and dry onions individually, which follows 2:6 on two kinds of wheat; cf. 1:4 where only storable items are liable to *pe'ah*.

One who thins [a crop],
designates [pe'ah] from the remainder for what is left.
One who uproots[25] them for a single purpose,[26]
designates from the remainder for the whole.

4 Mother onions are liable to *pe'ah*,
but R. Yose exempts.
Rectangular-shaped [furrows] of onions between vegetables—
R. Yose says:
Pe'ah from each and every one.
But the Sages say:
From one for all.

5 Brothers who divided [a field]—
they designate two areas of *pe'ah*.
If they became co-owners again,
they designate one area of *pe'ah*.
If two bought a tree,
they designate one area of *pe'ah*.
If this one bought its north and that one its south—

[25] Lit. "makes [the ground] smooth [by taking]." [26] Lit. "from one hand." Perhaps "all at once."

---

thins: Removes some plants to make room for others to grow better (*Shevi'it* 4:4). Because this is not considered reaping, the plants removed are exempt from *pe'ah* and only the crops remaining in the ground after the thinning are liable to *pe'ah*.

for a single purpose: Both the removed crops and the remaining crops are intended for the same purpose, unlike the first case where fresh onions were for the market and dry onions for storage. Thus, a single portion of *pe'ah* is designated from the crops still in the ground on behalf of all the produce—both that which has been uprooted and that which remains in the ground.

3:4 *Mother onions*: The Yerushalmi understands these as onions that are not eaten, but used only for their seed.

exempts: Because they are neither eaten nor stored (1:4).

vegetables: Other than onions.

Pe'ah must be designated *from each and every* onion bed, as the vegetables (as a different seed) form partitions for the purposes of *pe'ah* (2:1; cf. 3:1, 3:2).

From one for all: The householder designates *pe'ah* from one rectangular plot of onions on behalf of all plots of onions; cf. 3:1–2.

3:5 *Brothers who divided [a field]*: Before they began to reap.

two areas of pe'ah: Each from his own share of the field.

If they became co-owners again: Before they began to reap.

they designate one area: The Bavli interprets *when you* (pl.) *reap the harvest of your* (pl.) *land* in Leviticus 19:9 to imply that a field held jointly by multiple individuals is liable to a single area of *pe'ah*.

If two individuals jointly *bought a tree* that is liable to *pe'ah* (1:5), *they designate one area of pe'ah* as in the case of a jointly owned field.

If this one bought the produce in *its north* side. This is not joint ownership, but rather divided ownership. Thus, it is analogous to the first case where the two brothers divided a field and each gives *pe'ah* from his own share.

this one designates *pe'ah* for himself, and that one designates *pe'ah* for himself.
One who sells tree stems[27] in his field,
designates *pe'ah* from each and every one.
R. Judah said:
When?
When the owner of the field did not leave [over any for himself].
But if the owner of the field did leave [over for himself],
he designates *pe'ah* for all.

3:6–8 Size of a Field Liable to Pe'ah

6 R. Eliezer says:
A piece of land that has the capacity for a quarter [of a *qav* of seed] is liable to *pe'ah*.
R. Joshua says:
That which makes two *se'ah*.
R. Tarfon says:
Six by six handbreadths.
R. Judah[28] b. Betera says:
Sufficient to reap and to repeat.
And the law[29] follows his words.
R. Aqiva says:
Any piece of land whatsoever is liable to *pe'ah*,

[27] Or "stalks" or "branches" or "saplings."   [28] **K**: "Joshua."   [29] "the *halakhah*."

sells tree stems for the buyer to uproot and plant elsewhere. He did not, however, sell the land which would have joined the trees together as one field and make them liable to a single portion of *pe'ah*. Rather, the purchaser *designates pe'ah from each* tree stem separately.

When? Under what circumstances is the purchaser liable to designate *pe'ah*?

did not leave trees in the field for himself, i.e. he did not begin the harvest. Thus, the buyer is obligated to designate *pe'ah* from the trees.

did leave trees for himself, i.e. he began to harvest before selling the stems—then the seller *designates* a single *pe'ah for all*.

3:6 *quarter [of a qav of seed]*: An area of about one hundred square cubits; a *qav* is a measure of volume.

is liable to pe'ah: Cf. *Kilayim* 2:10. The opinions in this pericope are arranged from largest to smallest amount of land.

two se'ah: (A volume) of produce is liable to *pe'ah*. Whereas R. Eliezer's minimum is based on the field's sowing capacity, R. Joshua sets the minimum based on the field's production. His position is analogous to 6:6–7, where the laws of Forgotten Things do not apply to sheaves containing two *se'ah* or more of produce.

Land that is at least *six by six handbreadths* is liable to *pe'ah*; cf. *Kilayim* 3:1.

R. Judah…says a field is liable to *pe'ah* if it has a sufficient amount of produce to allow a farmer to *reap*—by grasping and cutting a handful of standing grain with a sickle (4:10)—*and to repeat* by grasping and cutting a second handful.

Any piece of land whatsoever: No matter how small.

and to firstfruits,
and [allows] a *prozbul* to be written on its account,
and [allows] property that cannot serve as surety to be acquired with it
by means of money, by a writ, or by possession.

7 One who deeds his property [to another as a gift] when he is lying ill—
if he left out [of the deed] any piece of land whatsoever,
then his gift is a gift.[30]
If he did not leave out any piece of land whatsoever,
his gift is not a gift.[31]
One who deeds his property to his sons,
and deeds any piece of land whatsoever to his wife—
she has forfeited her *ketubbah* payment.
R. Yose says:
If she accepted [some land],
even if he did not deed it to her,[32]
she has forfeited her *ketubbah* payment.

8 One who deeds his property to his slave—
[the slave] goes out a free man.

[30] **K, P**: "is valid" instead of "is a gift." [31] **K, P**: "is not valid" instead of "is not a gift."
[32] **K** lacks "to her."

firstfruits: Exodus 23:19, 34:26; Deuteronomy 18:4, 26:1–11; *Bikkurim*; see above 1:1.

prozbul: A legal instrument (*Shevi'it* 10:3–7) to encourage lending that circumvents the biblical precept (Deuteronomy 15:1–9) that cancels loans every seven years. A *prozbul* can only be written if the borrower owns land (here, any land at all), which serves as his pledge for the loan (*Shevi'it* 10:6).

property that cannot serve as surety: Movables or chattel, as opposed to real estate which is "property that has security," as it can secure a loan.

to be acquired with it: Movable goods are acquired by grasping the object and drawing it towards oneself (*Bava Batra* 5:7, 9:7; *Bava Metsia* 4:2). They can also be acquired by money, by a writ, or by possession, if acquired in conjunction with real estate (*Qiddushin* 1:5). Here, R. Aqiva stipulates that any amount of land can be used for these purposes.

3:7 *when he is lying ill*: Cf. *Bava Batra* 9:6; while he is sick in bed, in contemplation of death.

if he left out [of the deed] any piece of land whatsoever: he retains some land for himself, in order to live off its produce, indicating that he did not write over the gift expecting to die, but rather expecting to recover. Thus, *his gift is* indeed *a* valid *gift* and the property is transferred immediately.

If he did not leave out any piece of land for himself, then he did not expect to recover. Thus, if he recovers, he can retain ownership by retracting *his gift*, as it *is not a* valid *gift*.

ketubbah payment: The sum paid out to his wife upon divorce or his death (8:8; *Ketubbot*).

she has forfeited her ketubbah payment: Because the estate contains no other land from which the payment can be made.

3:8 *his property*: Which includes his slave (Leviticus 25:44–46).

goes out a free man: Because the slave now owns himself.

left out any piece of land: The Bavli interprets this law as applying to movables as well, including slaves.

If [the master] left out any piece of land whatsoever,
[the slave] does not go out a free man.
R. Simeon says:
[The slave] is in any case[33] a free man, unless [the master] says,
"All of my property is hereby given to so-and-so, my slave,
except for one ten-thousandth of it."

Chapter Four

4:1–5 *Collection of Pe'ah*

4 Pe'ah is designated from what is still attached to the ground.
In the case of a suspended vine and a palm tree—
the householder takes it down and distributes to the poor.
R. Simeon says:
Also in the case of smooth nut trees.
Even if ninety-nine [poor people] say to distribute,
but one [poor person] says to [allow them to] snatch,
they must listen to him,
for he has spoken correctly.[34]

---

[33] Lit. "always."   [34] Lit. "according to the *halakhah*."

---

whatsoever: Even retaining a small amount of land indicates that he intended to keep the slave, who *does not go out a free man*.

except for one ten-thousandth of it: Indicating that the master intends to keep some of his property, presumably including the slave.

4:1 *attached to the ground*: Standing grain that has not been reaped or otherwise detached from the land (1:3, 2:7).

suspended vine that is trained to a trellis or wood lattice-work *and a palm tree*—which cannot be accessed by some poor individuals (7:8), or collecting it might result in injury to the poor (4:4) or damage to the householder's property (4:2).

R. Simeon says that the householder must also collect and distribute the produce of *smooth nut trees* which are difficult or dangerous to climb.

Even if ninety-nine [poor people] say that the householder should reap the produce from the ground and then *distribute* it to the poor, *but one [poor person] says* that the householder should leave it unharvested so that the poor can *snatch* or grab the produce with their own hands while it is still attached to the ground, then *they must listen to* the one who wants to snatch the produce. The Mishnah uses a hypothetical scenario to emphasize the importance of allowing the poor to snatch produce from the ground with their own hands, even when the vast majority of the poor would prefer otherwise.

for he has spoken correctly, because *pe'ah* is designated from that which is still attached to the land, as discussed in the first statement in this mishnah.

2 In the case of a suspended vine and a palm tree it is not so.
Even if ninety-nine [poor people] say to snatch,
but one [poor person] says to distribute,
they must listen to him,
for he has spoken correctly.³⁵

3 If one [poor person] took a part of the *pe'ah*,
and threw it on the remainder,
he has no right to any of it.
If he fell on it,
or spread his cloak over it,
they remove it from him.³⁶
And likewise in the case of Gleanings,
and likewise in the case of a sheaf of Forgotten Things.

4 *Pe'ah*—one may not reap it with sickles,
or uproot it with spades,³⁷
so that they not strike one another.

5 Three times³⁸ in the day,
in the morning, at midday, and in the afternoon,
[the poor are permitted to enter a field in search of *pe'ah*].
Rabban Gamaliel says:
They said this only as a minimum.
R. Aqiva says:
They said this only as a maximum.

---

³⁵ Lit. "according to the *halakhah*."
³⁶ **K, P**: "they remove him from it." That is, they remove the poor person from the *pe'ah* that he sought to acquire.
³⁷ Or "mattocks." ³⁸ Text and meaning uncertain.

4:2 *Even if ninety-nine…*: This affirms the rule in the second and third statements of 4:1, that the produce growing on a trellis or palm tree must be collected and distributed by the householder.

4:3 *If one [poor person] threw* the portion that he legitimately claimed *on the remainder* of the *pe'ah*, which had not yet been taken by any other poor person. The Yerushalmi interprets this as an attempt by the poor individual to claim the remainder for himself.

he has no right to any of the additional *pe'ah* because it has not been properly acquired by grasping the object and drawing it towards oneself (*Bava Batra* 5:7, 9:7; *Bava Metsi'a* 4:2). Alternatively, *it* refers even to the *pe'ah* that he had legitimately claimed; he is being fined for not acting properly.

If he fell on it to claim it for himself, *or spread his cloak over it* to hide it from other poor people then *they remove* the *pe'ah from him*. (Cf. n. 36.)

4:4 *not strike one another*: Either accidentally, as suggested by the parallel language with Deuteronomy 19:4 (cf. Exodus 21:18), or intentionally, which would continue the preceding mishnah's discussion of intentional foul play among the poor during the collection of *pe'ah*.

4:5 *Three times in the day* the landowner must allow the poor into his field to collect *pe'ah*.

Rabban Gamaliel says: They: The anonymous Sages of the opening statement of this mishnah.

R. Aqiva says: The Yerushalmi interprets that R. Aqiva intends precisely three collections per day.

[The people] of the House of Namer used to gather by the rope,
and would designate *pe'ah* from each and every furrow.

4:6–9 *Miscellaneous Laws on Poor Offerings and Property Ownership*

6 If a gentile reaped his field,
and afterwards converted,
he is exempt from Gleanings and from Forgotten Things and from *pe'ah*.[39]
R. Judah declares him liable regarding Forgotten Things,
because [the obligation of] Forgotten Things [begins] only at the time of the binding of sheaves.

7 If one consecrated standing grain and redeemed standing grain,
he is liable;
[if one consecrated] sheaves and redeemed sheaves,
he is liable;
[if one consecrated] standing grain and redeemed sheaves,
then it is exempt, because at the moment that it could have become liable it was exempt.

[39] P adds "and from the renunciation of ownership of property"; see 1:3.

Namer: Checkered field (see 3:2), or *Beth-nimrah* of Numbers 32:36.

used to gather by the rope: They reaped the field row by row, where each one was marked off with a rope; cf. Bava Batra 7:2–3.

pe'ah…furrow allowing the poor to collect *pe'ah* following the harvest of each row. Thus, they collected *pe'ah* throughout the day, in line with Gamaliel's position.

4:6 *he is exempt* from allocating the following items, because the laws apply only to Israelites at the time of the harvest (Leviticus 19:9, Deuteronomy 24:19).

time of the binding by which point the gentile had converted.

4:7 *If one consecrated* to the Temple (1:6, 2:8, 4:8; 7:8; *Sheqalim* 4:6–8) *standing grain*: grain still attached to the ground. Consecrated produce is exempt from poor offerings, because it belongs to the Temple and not the householder. These laws only apply to produce owned by the householder, as implied by the language of Leviticus 19:9 and Deuteronomy 24:19: *…your field/harvest…* (cf. 2:8).

and redeemed standing grain from the Temple treasury before he began the harvest, then *he is liable* to the laws of *pe'ah*, Gleanings, and Forgotten Things, which apply when the harvest begins (Leviticus 19:9–10; Deuteronomy 24:19–21).

[if one consecrated] sheaves and then later *redeemed* these *sheaves* from the Temple treasury, then *he is liable* to *pe'ah* and Gleanings, which apply at the time of the reaping. For cut or loose sheaves, the law of Forgotten Things applies at the time of the binding (4:6). Both the reaping and the binding took place before he consecrated the produce, thus he is liable to all three laws.

[if one consecrated] standing grain to the Temple, reaped the stalks, and then *redeemed* the produce as *sheaves* from the Temple treasury, then *it is exempt* because the produce belonged to the Temple during the reaping and binding.

8 Likewise, one who consecrates his produce before the season of tithes,
and redeemed them—they are liable;
during the season of tithes,
and redeemed them—they are liable.
If one consecrated them before they were finished,
and the treasurer finished them,
and afterwards he redeemed them—they are exempt,
because at the time that they could have become liable they were exempt.

9 If one gathered *pe'ah*, and said:
"This is for so-and-so, the poor[40] man"—
R. Eliezer says:
He has acquired it for him.
But the Sages say:
He shall give it to the poor person who is found first.
The Gleanings, and the Forgotten Things, and the *pe'ah* of a gentile are liable to tithes,
unless he declares them ownerless property.

4:10–5:3 *Laws of Gleanings*

10 Which are Gleanings?
That which falls during the reaping.
If one was reaping,
[and] reaped a handful,

---

[40] P lacks "poor."

4:8 *one who consecrates his produce* to the Temple (1:6, 2:8, 4:7, 7:8; *Sheqalim* 4:6–8) *before the season of tithes*: Produce becomes subject to tithing when it ripens or when the pile of stalks is "finished" or smoothed over (*Ma'aserot* 1:2–3, 5–7). Cf. *Hallah* 3:4.

and redeemed them before the season of tithes, then *they are liable* because they belonged to the householder when they became subject to tithing.

before they were finished: See above and 1:6; *Ma'aserot* 1:6.

the treasurer finished them: The moment when the Temple treasurer smooths over the pile of stalks, he asserts the Temple's ownership (1:6). Thus, *they are exempt* because consecrated produce is exempt from tithes.

4:9 *If one* who is rich and, thus, not entitled to the poor offerings, perhaps the field's owner.

He, the rich man, *has* legitimately *acquired it for him*, a particular poor man. The Bavli interprets that R. Eliezer envisions a rich man who suddenly declares all of his property to be ownerless (*hefqer*)—making him poor and eligible to acquire *pe'ah* for himself or for another poor man.

But the Sages: They hold that the rich man has not legitimately acquired the *pe'ah*. Thus, he must hand it over to the first poor man that he meets.

The Gleanings...of a gentile are exempt from poor offerings (4:6). Thus, as ordinary produce, they are *liable to tithes* (*Ma'aserot* 1:1) *unless he declares* the produce *ownerless property* which is exempt from tithes (1:6).

4:10 *Which are*: Cf. 7:3–4, where similar language introduces other poor offerings.

Gleanings: Leviticus 19:9–10, 23:22.

[or] plucked a fistful,
[and then] a thorn pricked him
[and] it fell from his hand to the ground—
this belongs to the householder.
From within the hand or within the sickle—
[this belongs] to the poor;
Back of the hand or back of the sickle—
[this belongs] to the householder;
Top of the hand or the top of the sickle—
R. Ishmael says:
[This belongs] to the poor.
R. Aqiva says:
[This belongs] to the householder.
   11 [Grains found in] ant holes in the midst of standing grain—
These belong to the householder;
[Grains found in ant holes] behind the reapers—
the upper ones belong to the poor,
while the lower ones belong to the householder.
R. Meir says:
All belong to the poor,
because doubtful Gleanings are Gleanings.

Chapter Five

5 A heap of sheaves, under which [the Gleanings] had not been collected—
all that touches the ground thereby belongs to the poor.

From within the hand…to the poor: Produce that falls as a result of normal reaping practices has the status of Gleanings and is left for the poor. But produce that falls due to contact with the *back of the hand or back of the sickle* did not fall as a result of normal reaping practices and belongs to the householder.

4:11 Produce found in *ant holes* (cf. *Ma'aserot* 5:7) located *in the midst of standing grain* that has not yet been reaped *belong to the householder* as only produce that fell during the reaping has the status of Gleanings.

the upper ones: stalks found at the top of the ant holes, which likely were deposited there recently and thus as a result of the harvest, have the status of *Gleanings* and *belong to the poor, while the lower ones* likely were deposited into the ant holes before the harvest, and do not have the status of *Gleanings*—they *belong to the householder*.

5:1 In the case of *a heap of sheaves, under which* are located *Gleanings* that *had not been collected* by the poor, *all* the produce on the bottom of the heap *that touches the ground…belongs to the poor*. This upholds the principle in 4:11 that doubtful *Gleanings* have the status of Gleanings. The Yerushalmi interprets this expansive identification of Gleanings as a penalty for the householder for obstructing the poor's rightful access to Gleanings.

If⁴¹ the wind scattered the sheaves—
they estimate⁴² the amount of Gleanings [the field] is likely to yield,
and he gives it to the poor.
Rabban Simeon b. Gamaliel says:
He gives to the poor as much as usually⁴³ falls.

2 An ear of grain that is in the harvest and its top reaches the standing grain:
If it is to be reaped with the standing grain,
it belongs to the householder;
If not, it belongs to the poor.
If an ear of Gleanings was mixed up in a heap—
[the householder] separates tithes for one ear and gives it to him.
Said R. Eliezer:
But how does this poor person exchange something that did not come into his possession?
Rather, one transfers to the poor person the entire heap,
and separates tithes for one ear and gives it to him.

3 One may not turn a waterwheel—
the words of R. Meir.
But the Sages permit, because it is possible.⁴⁴

---

⁴¹ **K**: "But if." ⁴² **K, P**: "they stand."
⁴³ **K, P** lack "as much as usually," though the sense remains unchanged.   ⁴⁴ **K, P**: "impossible."

If the wind scatters the sheaves that have the status of Gleanings, mixing the Gleanings with ordinary sheaves.

5:2 Concerning *an ear that is* left uncut *in the harvest and its top* was bent over and *reaches the standing* unreaped *grain* in an adjacent field.

If it ... standing grain, then it does not have the status of Forgotten Things and *it belongs to the householder*—because the householder intended to reap it with the adjacent field; thus, it was not "forgotten."

If not, then it has the status of Forgotten Things and *it belongs to the poor*. Parallel to *Eduyot* 2:4.

If an ear of Gleanings that is exempt from tithes *was mixed up in a heap* of produce that is otherwise liable to tithes.

exchange: Since the poor person never received his ear of Gleanings, how can he exchange it for another?

Rather the householder *transfers to the poor person the entire heap*, which includes the ear of Gleanings, as a gift on condition that it be returned. Thus, he possesses the lost ear of Gleanings and is entitled to exchange it.

5:3 *One may not turn a waterwheel* that irrigates a field before the Gleanings are collected, as this may damage the Gleanings or impede the poor's access to the field.

it is possible to avoid damaging the Gleanings by placing them on a fence to keep them dry during irrigation (Tosefta). This also allows the householder to avoid losses that he might have incurred if his irrigation methods are restricted. **K** and **P** read "because it is impossible" for the householder to properly cultivate his field without the waterwheel.

5:4–6 Collection of Poor Offerings

4 If a householder was traveling from place to place,
and was in need of taking[45] Gleanings, Forgotten Things, or *pe'ah* or the poor tithe[46]—
he may take;
but when he returns to his home he must pay[47]—
the words of R. Eliezer.
But the Sages say:
He was a poor man at that moment.

5 One who exchanges with the poor—
that which is his is exempt [from poor tithe],
and that which belongs to the poor is liable.
If two individuals received a field in a sharecropping agreement:
this one gives to the other his share of the poor tithe,
and this one gives to that one his share of the poor tithe.
One who receives a field to reap [as a sharecropper]—
he is forbidden with regard to Gleanings and Forgotten Things and *pe'ah* and the poor tithe.

---

[45] K, P: "If a householder was traveling from place to place and was in need, he may take Gleanings etc."
[46] P lacks "poor tithe."   [47] Lit. "make it whole."

5:4 *If a householder* who is not poor when he is at home.

place to place: From one town to another; cf. 8:7.

in need...poor tithe: Because he did not have sufficient food or money with him.

he must pay: One's eligibility to collect poor offerings is dependent upon one's total holdings—not just what he has in hand at the moment (cf. 8:8–9). Therefore, the householder does not have the status of "poor" and he must pay back to the poor from the town in which he took the poor offerings.

He was poor: Even though he is a householder (usually not poor), he was in need at that *moment* and thus entitled to collect poor offerings. He is not required to compensate the poor.

5:5 *One who exchanges with the poor* ordinary produce for produce with the status of poor offerings.

that which is his: The produce that the householder receives from the poor *is exempt* from tithes, like all produce with the status of poor offerings (1:6).

and the ordinary produce *that* was given by the householder and now *belongs to the poor is liable* to tithes.

If two poor *individuals received a field* to reap *in a sharecropping agreement* whereby they receive portions of the crop as compensation for reaping the field.

this one gives: The poor sharecropper cannot keep the poor tithe from his own field, but he is permitted to give it to another poor sharecropper; cf. 4:9.

One poor man *who receives a field to reap* as part of a sharecropping agreement is considered to be an owner and cannot take poor offerings from his own field (Tosefta), as Leviticus 19:9, 23:22 instruct: *you shall not reap to the very edges of your field.*

Said R. Judah:
When?
At the time when he received [the field] from him for a half, a third, or a quarter;
but if he said to him:
A third of what you reap belongs to you—
he is permitted with regard to Gleanings, Forgotten Things, and *pe'ah*,
but forbidden with regard to the poor tithe.

6 One who sells his field—
the seller is permitted and the buyer is forbidden.
One may not hire a laborer on condition that his son will collect after him.
One who does not allow the poor to collect,
or if he allows one person, but not another,
or if he assists one of them—
he indeed is one who steals from the poor;
concerning him it is said:
Do not remove the landmark of those who ascend.[48]

5:7–8 *Laws of Forgotten Things: Definition*

7 The sheaf that laborers forgot,
but that the householder did not forget;
[or] that the householder forgot,

---

[48] Lit. "those who go up," a euphemism for those who have "come down" from their property—i.e. the "poor." Cf. 7:3.

When? The above circumstances apply before the harvest, when the poor harvester was assigned *a half, a third, or a quarter* of the crop—thereby making him an owner of the field. *But if he* the landowner *said to* the poor laborer: *A third of what you reap belongs to you* then the laborer only acquires possession of a portion of the crop *after* the harvest. In which case, he may collect *Gleanings, Forgotten Things, and pe'ah* because these laws take effect at the time of the harvest—when he was not yet an owner.

but forbidden with regard to the poor tithe which is distributed at the granary after the reaping— when he already owned a portion of the crop.

5:6 *One*: A poor householder.

the seller is permitted to take *pe'ah*, Gleanings, and Forgotten Things because he no longer owns the field, *but the buyer* of the field *is forbidden* even if he is poor, because one may not take poor offerings from his own field (5:5).

Do not remove the landmark of those who ascend: The language plays on the wording of Proverbs 22:28, 23:10, changing *olam* ("ancient") to *olim* ("those who ascend")—a euphemism for the poor, as they have declined in their wealth. Thus, do not steal from the poor by encroaching on their property—the poor offerings; cf. 7:3.

5:7 *The sheaf that laborers forgot*, when they collected the bound produce to be taken to the granary. Laborers are treated as agents of the householder and act on his behalf.

but that the laborers did not forget;
[or] if poor people stood before it or covered it with straw—
this is not Forgotten Things.

8 One who binds sheaves for stack covers or for stack bases,
or for temporary stacks[49] or into sheaves—
it is not liable to Forgotten Things.
If [taken] from there to the granary,
it is liable to Forgotten Things.
One who binds sheaves for a heap,
it is liable to Forgotten Things.
If [taken] from there to the granary,
it is not liable to Forgotten Things.
This is the general rule:
Anyone who binds sheaves for [the purpose of taking them] to the place where the work is finished—
it is liable to Forgotten Things,
from there to the granary—
it is not liable to Forgotten Things;
to the place where the work is not finished—
it is not liable to Forgotten Things,
from there to the granary—
it is liable to Forgotten Things.

[49] "Stack covers...stack bases...temporary stacks"—meanings uncertain.

stood before it or covered it with straw to hide it from view so that the laborers and householder would leave it in the field.

this is not Forgotten Things: Produce that is unintentionally left by the householder and his agents, in accordance with Deuteronomy 24:19 (*you forget*). Sheaves that are left for any other reason, including deliberate attempts by the poor to hide them, do not have the status of Forgotten Things.

5:8 *stack covers...not liable to Forgotten Things*, because the law applies only at the end of the binding process, when the sheaves are removed to the granary or threshing floor.

to the granary for final processing and a sheaf is forgotten, then *it is liable to Forgotten Things*.

One who binds sheaves for the purpose of piling them up into *a heap*, on the understanding that it will be threshed there, and leaves a sheaf, then *it is liable to Forgotten Things*.

to the granary: If the farmer changes his mind and now wants to finish the process by threshing at the granary, and he leaves a sheaf, then *it is not liable to Forgotten Things* because it indicates that he did not intend to finish the process at the initial location.

place where the work is finished: Where they are going to be threshed. If he leaves a sheaf there, then *it is liable to Forgotten Things*. But, if they are later taken *from there to the granary* and a sheaf is left, then *it is not liable to Forgotten Things*.

not finished then *it is not liable to Forgotten Things*. But if he takes it *from there to the granary* where the work will be finished, then *it is liable to Forgotten Things*.

Chapter Six

6:1–3 Disputes on Ambiguous Cases

6 The House of Shammai say:
The renunciation of ownership for the poor is a [valid] renunciation of ownership.
But the House of Hillel say:
It is not a [valid] renunciation of ownership unless it is declared ownerless for the rich as well,
like Seventh-Year produce.
If all[50] the sheaves in the field are a *qav* each,
but one is four *qav*,
and he forgot it—
the House of Shammai say:
It is not Forgotten Things;
but the House of Hillel say:
It is Forgotten Things.

2 A sheaf close to a stone fence or a heap of sheaves,
[or][51] to oxen or tools,
and he forgot it—
the House of Shammai say:
It is not Forgotten Things;
but the House of Hillel say:
It is Forgotten Things.

---

[50] K originally lacks "all"; it is inserted in the margin.   [51] K, P have the conjunction.

6:1 Parallel to *Eduyot* 4:3.

renunciation of ownership over produce (1:3) *for the* benefit *of the poor* alone *is a valid renunciation of ownership.*

Seventh-Year produce: Leviticus 25:11–17; *Shevi'it*.

The four-*qav* sheaf *is not* considered to have the status of *Forgotten Things*—because it has distinctive characteristics, it would not have been "forgotten," but rather intentionally left in the field so that it could be retrieved later. The principle is that the householder can only fulfill the law of *Forgotten Things* unintentionally, by "forgetting." The four-*qav* sheaf is also akin to four one-*qav* sheaves bound together, which the House of Shammai exempt from the law of *Forgotten Things* in 6:5.

6:2 Parallel to *Eduyot* 4:4.

not Forgotten Things: Due to its special location near distinctive objects, it is unlikely to have been forgotten (as in 6:1).

It is Forgotten Things: As in 6:1, positing a strict (from the perspective of the landowner) interpretation of Deuteronomy 24:19, that anything left behind in the field has the status of Forgotten Things.

3 The heads of rows—
the sheaf that is opposite it proves [whether it was forgotten or not].
The sheaf that he picked up to bring to town but forgot it—
they agree that it is not Forgotten Things.

6:4   *Biblical Basis*

4 And[52] these are the heads of rows:
If two began [collecting sheaves] from the middle of the row,
this one facing north and this one facing south,
and[53] they forgot [sheaves] in front of them and behind them—
what is in front of them is Forgotten Things,
but what is behind them is not Forgotten Things.
An individual who began [to collect sheaves] from the head of the row,
and forgot [sheaves] in front of him and behind him—
what is in front of him is not Forgotten Things,
but what is behind him is Forgotten Things,
because[54] it is included in[55] *you shall not go back*.

[52] K, P lack "and."   [53] K lacks "and."   [54] P lacks "because."
[55] K lacks "included in," here and below.

6:3 The meaning of this mishnah is much debated by commentators.

If the householder left a sheaf at *the heads of rows*, then the presence of *the sheaf* that is in the row *opposite it proves* that the first sheaf was not forgotten. The meaning of "heads of rows" is explained in the next mishnah.

bring to town to sell *but forgot it* in the field.

not Forgotten Things: By grasping the sheaf, the householder takes full possession of it, indicating his intention to later retrieve it and bring it to town.

6:4 The meaning of this mishnah is much debated by commentators.

And these are the laws that apply to sheaves located at *heads of rows*.

If two harvesters *began [collecting sheaves] from the middle of the row*, and are standing back to back so that *this one is facing* and working down the row towards the *north and this* other *one is facing* and working down the row towards the *south, and* each worker *forgot [sheaves] in front of them* at each end of the rows *and behind* both of *them*, as they both failed to collect the sheaf in the middle of the row, where they started.

in front of them is Forgotten Things, because the harvester passed by but did not take it.

behind them in the middle of the row, between the harvesters—these are *not Forgotten Things* because neither worker passed by them, so they were not left behind unintentionally. Likewise, since the workers started the collection in the middle of the row, this sheaf can be considered to be the "head" or beginning of another row, which does not have the status of *Forgotten Things* (6:3).

An individual who began [to collect sheaves] from the head of the row, and forgot [sheaves] in front of him—he skipped a sheaf, and he forgot one *behind him*—the sheaf *in front of him is not* considered to have the status of *Forgotten Things* because it can be viewed as the head of another row (6:3).

you shall not go back to get it (Deuteronomy 24:19), as the only way to collect it would be for the farmer to retrace his steps.

This is the general rule:
Anything included in *you shall not go back*—is Forgotten Things;
Whatever is not included in *you shall not go back*—is not Forgotten Things.

6:5–11   *Ambiguous Cases: Produce Intentionally Left Behind*

5 Two sheaves are Forgotten Things,
but three sheaves are not Forgotten Things.
Two piles of olives or carobs are Forgotten Things,
but three are not Forgotten Things.
Two stalks of flax are Forgotten Things,
but three are not Forgotten Things.
Two grapes[56] are Separated Grapes,
but three are not Separated Grapes.
Two ears of grain are Gleanings,
but three are not Gleanings.
These are according to the words of the House of Hillel.
But regarding all of them the House of Shammai say:
Three belong to the poor,
but four belong to the householder.
   6 A sheaf that has two *se'ah* and he forgot it,
is not Forgotten Things.
Two sheaves containing two *se'ah*—
Rabban Gamaliel says:
They belong to the householder.
But the Sages say:
They belong to the poor.

[56] Lit. "single berries" or "shriveled olives." The reference to *peret*, however, suggests that "grapes" are intended.

This is the general rule: If one needs to retrace one's steps in order to collect an overlooked sheaf, then this sheaf has the status of *Forgotten Things* and is left for the poor. But those that the farmer can collect without retracing his steps do not have this status and belong to the householder.

6:5 *olives or carobs...stalks of flax*: The law of Forgotten Things applies to certain fruits and a vegetable. Olive and carob trees are also exceptional with regard to the laws of *pe'ah* (2:4).

Separated Grapes: Individual grapes that fall to the ground and are left for the poor (7:3; Leviticus 19:10).

These...House of Hillel: The rules (and disputes) that two measures of produce qualify as poor offerings but three do not, recall 6:1. The House of Hillel hold that these distinctive amounts of produce could not be "forgotten," but rather were left intentionally by the harvester who planned to return for them (6:2).

6:6 *two se'ah* are *not Forgotten Things* because they are large enough to qualify as a heap, which is exempt (5:8, 6:2).

In the case of *two sheaves containing two se'ah* of grain when combined: If they were left in the field, *Rabban Gamaliel says*: like the two *se'ah* mentioned above, these too do not have the status of Forgotten Things, and thus *belong to the householder*.

Said Rabban Gamaliel:
But does a larger number of sheaves strengthen the rights of the householder
or weaken his rights?
They said to him:
It strengthens his rights.
He said to them:
If one sheaf with two *se'ah* was forgotten—
it is not Forgotten Things,
then two sheaves that have two *se'ah*—
does not logic require that it should not be Forgotten Things?
They said to him:
No.
If you say that one sheaf [of two *se'ah* is not Forgotten Things,
that is] because it is like a heap of grain [in its own right];
would you say [the same] for two sheaves, which are [merely] like bundles?
[Of course not.]

7 Standing grain that contains two *se'ah*,
and he forgot it—
it is not Forgotten Things.
If it does not contain two *se'ah*,
but[57] is likely to produce[58] two *se'ah*,
even if it is of vetchlings—
it is to be regarded[59] as if it were a yield[60] of barley.

8 Standing grain saves the sheaf and the standing grain
[from the status of Forgotten Things].
The sheaf does not save either the sheaf or the standing grain

[57] K originally read: "but if"; "but" was erased. [58] Or "capable of producing."
[59] Lit. "they regard it." [60] P: "crop."

strengthen the rights: As discussed in 6:5, the House of Hillel posit that two sheaves found together have the status of Forgotten Things, but three do not and belong to the householder (House of Shammai: three and four sheaves, respectively).

Since *two sheaves are [merely] like* small *bundles* rather than a large heap, even when they contain a combined two *se'ah*, they may certainly have the status of Forgotten Things.

6:7 *Standing grain*: While Deuteronomy 24:19 applies the law of Forgotten Things only to cut stalks of grain, the mishnah also applies it to standing grain—produce that has not yet been reaped.

that contains two se'ah of grain *and he* seemingly *forgot* to reap *it, is not* considered *Forgotten Things*—just as a sheaf with two *se'ah* of grain does not have the status of Forgotten Things (6:6).

If it does not contain two se'ah: Because it has been damaged.

produce two se'ah in a normal year, *even if it is* thin and withered, like the stalks *of vetchlings*, a type of legume.

as if it were a full *yield of barley* that produces two *se'ah* and, thus, does not have the status of Forgotten Things.

6:8 *saves…standing grain* that is next to it and left in the field from the status of *Forgotten Thing*; cf. 5:2, 6:7.

However, *the sheaf* that was not forgotten *does not save either the sheaf* that was forgotten *or the standing grain* that was forgotten from the status of *Forgotten Things*. In the Tosefta this rule is challenged unsuccessfully.

[from the status of Forgotten Things].
Which standing grain saves the sheaf
[from the status of Forgotten Things]?
Any that is not Forgotten Things, even one stalk.

9 A *se'ah* of uprooted grain,
and a *se'ah* that is not uprooted,
and likewise a tree, garlic, and onions—
they do not join together to constitute two *se'ah*.
Rather, they belong to the poor.[61]
R. Yose says:
If something that belongs to the poor comes in between,
they do not join together,
but if not, they do join together.

10 Grain that is given for fodder or for binding sheaves,
and likewise stalks of garlic plants used for binding[62] and bundles of garlic and onions—
the [law of] Forgotten Things does not apply to them.
And anything that is stored in the ground,
such as black calla and garlic and onions—
R. Judah says:
The [law of] Forgotten Things does not apply to them.
But the Sages say:
The [law of] Forgotten Things does apply to them.

11 One who reaps at night,
and one who binds sheaves [at night],

---

[61] K, P lack "to constitute two *se'ah*. Rather, they belong to the poor."
[62] K inserts "bundles of garlic" in the margin.

Which...: Similar language introduces other poor offerings in 4:10, 7:3, 7:4, 7:8.

6:9 *A se'ah of grain that is not uprooted, and likewise* picked and unpicked fruit *from a tree, do not join together* to measure *two se'ah* combined, which would exempt them from Forgotten Things.

belong to the poor: As Forgotten Things, thus expanding the biblical law of Forgotten Things to include fruits and vegetables.

R. Yose says: If something that belongs to the poor such as other poor offerings *comes in between* each *se'ah*, then they cannot be combined.

6:10 *Grain* left in the field and intended *for fodder* (cf. 2:1; *Menahot* 10:8). Stalks that will be used *for binding* other stalks into *sheaves*. Small *bundles of garlic and onions* that will later be bound together into larger bundles. *Forgotten Things does not apply to them* because these items are not intended for human consumption (1:4) or have not been completely bound (5:8).

stored or left *in the ground*, intentionally, such as tubers after they ripen (*Shevi'it* 5:2).

black calla: Solomon's lily, *Arum palaestinum*; *Kilayim* 2:5.

R. Judah...the Sages: The Yerushalmi understands the disagreement as whether *in the field* in Deuteronomy 24:19 includes produce intentionally buried in it.

6:11 *reaps at night*: An inability to see does not exempt produce left in the field from the status of Forgotten Things, because the harvester could plan for this expected scenario.

and one who is blind—
[the law of] Forgotten Things applies.
But if one had intended to take only the large ones—
[the law of] Forgotten Things does not apply.
If one said:
I reap on condition that whatever I forget I may take—
[the law of] Forgotten Things applies.

Chapter Seven

7:1–2 *Olives*

7 Any olive tree that has a name in the field,
even[63] like a Netofah olive tree in its time,
and one forgot it—
[the law of] Forgotten Things does not apply.
When do these words apply?
[When the tree is distinctive] in its name or its production or its location:
Regarding its name—
that it is *shifkhoni*[64] or a *beshani*.
Its production—that it produces a lot.
Its location—that it stands next to the press or next to a breach.
And all other olive trees—
two are Forgotten Things, but three are not Forgotten Things.
R. Yose says:
[The law of] Forgotten Things does not apply to olive trees.

[63] K, P lack "even."   [64] K has "*shafekhani*" or "*shofkhani*."

---

large ones: Because he intended to return for them, they are not "forgotten."

I reap on condition…: Such stipulations are void because they oppose the law of the Torah (*Ketubbot* 9:1; *Bava Metsi'a* 7:11).

7:1 *Netofah*: Either a town in Judaea near Bethlehem (Ezra 2:22; Nehemiah 7:26) or the Bet Netofah Valley in the Galilee (*Shevi'it* 9:5).

Forgotten Things does not apply: Distinctive olive trees are not Forgotten Things, just like distinctive sheaves in 6:1–2.

shifkhoni: A species of olive.

beshani: a species of olive native to Beisan or Bet She'an (Scythopolis), a city on the edge of the Galilee.

breach in a wall; cf. 6:2 on the status of a sheaf left by a stone fence.

two adjacent unharvested olive trees have the status of *Forgotten Things*, but three are not *Forgotten Things*; cf. 6:6.

2 If an olive tree stands between three rows of two rectangles
and one forgot it—
[the law of] Forgotten Things does not apply.
If an olive tree has two *se'ah*
and one forgot it—
[the law of] Forgotten Things does not apply.
When do these words apply?
If they had not started [to gather] it[s olives].
But if they had started it,
even [if it is] like a Netofah olive tree in its time,
and forgot it,
[the law of] Forgotten Things applies.[65]
Whenever [the law of] Forgotten Things applies to the [olives] under [the tree],
it applies to the [olives] at its top.
R. Meir says:
From the time [the worker with] the harvesting rod has gone.

7:3 Poor Offerings from the Vineyard: Separated Grapes

3 Which are Separated Grapes?
That which drops during the grape harvest.
If one was reaping,
[and] cut a cluster,
[and] it[66] became entangled in the leaves,
[and] it fell from his hand to the ground,
and it broke apart[67]—
this[68] belongs to the householder.

[65] **K**: "it is not Forgotten Things." But corrected by the later hand to the text above.
[66] Or "he."   [67] **K**: "separated."   [68] **P** lacks "this."

7:2 *two rectangles*: Garden beds (cf. 3:1). If the harvester seemingly *forgot* to harvest this olive tree, *Forgotten Things does not apply* because of its distinctive location.

two se'ah: See 6:7.

[olives] gathered *under [the tree]* indicates that he has not completed the harvest and, therefore, the olives *at the tree's top* are not Forgotten Things.

[the worker with] the harvesting rod: The Yerushalmi understands this as one who beats the tree to loosen any remaining olives.

has gone past the tree, indicating that the harvest is complete. All the remaining olives are Forgotten Things.

7:3 *Which are*: Cf. 4:10, 6:8, 7:4, 7:8, where similar language introduces other poor offerings.

Separated or individual fallen *Grapes*: See Leviticus 19:10.

drops to the ground *during the grape harvest*, similar to Gleanings in 4:10. In 6:5, two items of produce qualify as poor offerings, but three do not (or three and four, respectively, according to the House of Shammai).

cut a well-formed *cluster* of grapes from the vine and the cluster (or is it the harvester?) *became entangled in the* grape *leaves and it broke apart* into individual grapes, then *this* is not Separated Grapes and *belongs to the householder*, because it did not fall and break apart as part of the normal process of harvesting grapes (cf. 4:10).

One who lays the basket underneath the vine while he reaps grapes—
He indeed is one who steals from the poor;
concerning him it is said:
Do not remove the landmark of those who ascend.

7:4–8 Poor Offerings from the Vineyard: Defective Clusters and Forgotten Grapes

4[69] What is a Defective Cluster?
Anything that does not have a shoulder or a pendant.
If it has a shoulder or a pendant,
it belongs to the householder.[70]
If there is a doubt,
it belongs to the poor.
A Defective Cluster on the "knee" of the vine—
if it is cut off with [a normal] cluster,
it belongs to the householder.
If not,
it[71] belongs to the poor.
An individual grape [that does not grow within a cluster]—
R. Judah says:
A cluster.
But the Sages say:
A Defective Cluster.

[69] K, P reverse the sequence of 7:4 and 7:5.
[70] K, P lack "If it has a shoulder or a pendant, it belongs to the householder."
[71] P lacks "it."

One who lays the basket to ensure that nothing falls and touches the ground, in an effort to intentionally circumvent the commandment of Separated Grapes.

those who ascend: Proverbs 22:28; see annotation to 5:6.

7:4 *What is*: Cf. 4:10, 6:8, 7:3, 7:8, where similar language introduces other poor offerings.

a Defective Cluster of grapes; an expansion of Leviticus 19:10, Deuteronomy 24:21. See also Isaiah 17:6.

shoulder or a pendant: The cluster of grapes lacks a wide top or a cone-shaped lower portion.

belongs to the householder: Because it is a well-formed, normal cluster.

a Defective Cluster growing on the "knee" of the vine: The vine bent like a knee, so that some of it lies on the ground (*Kilayim* 7:1). A cluster growing here cannot hang down, thus appearing to have neither a shoulder nor a pendant.

if it is cut off with [a normal] cluster, then it is considered normal and *belongs to the householder*.

belongs to the poor, just as doubtful Gleanings have the status of Gleanings (4:11).

R. Judah says that it has the status of *a cluster* and belongs to the householder. *But the Sages say* that it is a *Defective Cluster* because it lacks a shoulder and pendant.

5 One who thins vines—
Just as he [may] thin that which belongs to him,
so too [may] he thin that which belongs to the poor—
the words of R. Judah.
R. Meir says:
In that which is his, he is permitted;
but[72] he is not permitted in that which belongs to the poor.
  6[73] A vineyard in its fourth year—
the House of Shammai say:
[The law of] added fifth and [the law of] Removal do not apply.
But the House of Hillel say:
They do.
The House of Shammai say:
[The law of] Separated Grapes and [the law of] Defective Clusters apply,
and the poor redeem them themselves.
But the House of Hillel say:
All of it is for the vat.
  7 A vineyard that is entirely Defective Clusters—
R. Eliezer says:
It belongs to the householder.
R. Aqiva says:
It belongs to the poor.

[72] K, P lack the conjunction.   [73] K, P reverse the sequence of 7:6 and 7:7.

7:5 *thins*: Prunes or removes vines from an otherwise dense vineyard to create more space for the remaining vines to grow, increasing the yield.

Just as he [may] thin vines *which belong to him*, those with well-formed clusters, *so too [may] he thin* out the vines with Defective Clusters that belong to the poor.

7:6 Parallel to *Maʿaser Sheni* 5:3, *Eduyot* 4:5.

fourth year since it was planted. Produce from the fourth year is to be eaten only in Jerusalem (Leviticus 19:23–24; *Maʿaser Sheni* 5:1–4), just like the second tithe (Deuteronomy 14:22–26; *Maʿaser Sheni*). What follows is a dispute on whether the laws of fourth-year grapes and the second tithe are similar in all respects.

[The law of] added fifth: Leviticus 27:31; *Maʿaser Sheni* 4:3, 5:5; *Bava Metsiʿa* 4:8.

[the law of] Removal: Distribution of tithes to the mandated recipients. Deuteronomy 26:12–13; *Maʿaser Sheni* 5:6.

Defective Clusters apply: Unlike the second tithe, the House of Shammai hold that fourth-year grapes are subject to the laws of Separated Grapes and Defective Clusters (7:3–4). Since the poor are the rightful owners, *the poor* would *redeem them themselves* and bring the money to Jerusalem.

House of Hillel…vat for wine pressing. The House of Hillel hold that fourth-year grapes are exempt from poor offerings (by analogy to the second tithe). Thus, the householder processes all of it into wine, including individual fallen grapes and malformed clusters (which have the status of Separated Grapes and Defective Clusters respectively), before redeeming it.

7:7 *R. Eliezer says*: The entire vineyard *belongs to the householder* because malformed clusters are the norm in this particular vineyard.

R. Aqiva says: the entire vineyard is Defective Clusters and *belongs to the poor* because they all lack shoulders or pendants (7:4).

Said R. Eliezer:
When you harvest [the grapes of your vineyard], do not glean what is left;
if there is no harvest, whence Defective Clusters?
R. Aqiva said to him:
You shall not strip your vineyard bare—
even if they are all Defective Clusters.
If so, why is it said:
When you harvest [the grapes of your vineyard], do not glean what is left?
[To teach that] the poor have no share in the Defective Clusters before the grape harvest.

8 One who consecrates his vineyard before Defective Clusters became known—
the Defective Clusters do not belong to the poor.
After[74] the Defective Clusters in it[75] became known—
the Defective Clusters belong to the poor.
R. Yose says:
Let[76] them give the value of the increase to the Temple.[77]
Which are Forgotten Things on the trellis?
Whatever one cannot reach when extending his hand.
And on ground-trained vines?
After one passed it by.

[74] P: "But after."   [75] K, P lack "in it."   [76] K adds "If so."
[77] Lit. "to consecrated property."

do not glean what is left: Deuteronomy 24:21, which differentiates normal clusters that are part of the harvest from Defective Clusters that are left behind. But *if there is no harvest* of normal clusters, *whence Defective Clusters?* In that case Defective Clusters cannot be differentiated and the law does not apply.

not strip: Leviticus 19:10 prohibits the collection of Defective Clusters in all circumstances, as it lacks reference to the harvest, i.e. of well-formed clusters.

If so, why is it said in Deuteronomy 24:21 *When you harvest?* R. Aqiva responds that Scripture says this not to differentiate well-formed from malformed clusters, but rather to indicate that *the poor have no share... before the harvest* because the laws of Defective Clusters take effect when the grape harvest begins.

7:8 *One who consecrates* or dedicates to the Temple (1:6, 2:8, 4:7–8; *Sheqalim* 4:6–8) the yield of *his vineyard before Defective Clusters became known*, then they *do not belong to the poor* because the law of Defective Clusters became effective while the grapes were property of the Temple, which is exempt from poor offerings (1:6; 4:7). But if the householder consecrated his vineyard *after the Defective Clusters in it became known*, at which point the harvest can begin and the laws on Defective Clusters take effect (7:5), then *the Defective Clusters belong to the poor* because the law became effective while the field still belonged to the householder.

R. Yose says: If additional Defective Clusters grew after the householder consecrated his vineyard, then the poor keep the Defective Clusters identified before the consecration, but they must *give the value* of subsequent growths of Defective Clusters that grew since the field was consecrated *to the* Jerusalem *Temple*.

Which are: Cf. 4:10, 6:8, 7:3–4.

Forgotten Things on the trellis: When does a cluster that is left on a trained vine (*Kilayim* 6:1–4) become Forgotten Things?

Whatever one remembered after passing the vine, but *cannot reach when extending his hand* from his current position by reaching behind him. If he can reach it without walking back and retracing his steps (6:4; Deuteronomy 24:19), then it is not Forgotten Things and belongs to the householder.

Chapter Eight

8:1–4 *Miscellaneous Laws on All Poor Offerings*

8 From when is every person permitted to take Gleanings?
After the last of the gleaners leaves.
In the case of Separated Grapes and in the case of Defective Clusters?
After the poor have left the vineyard and have come [back].
And in the case of olives?
After the second rainfall.
Said R. Judah:
And are there not those who pick their olives only after the second rainfall?
Rather, after the poor person goes out but does not bring back the value of[78] four *issar*.

2 [The poor] are deemed reliable
concerning Gleanings, Forgotten Things, and *pe'ah* in their season,
and concerning the poor tithe during its entire year.
But a Levite is deemed reliable always,
although[79] they are deemed reliable only concerning that which people are accustomed to do.

3 [The poor] are deemed reliable concerning wheat,
but are not deemed reliable concerning either flour or bread.

---

[78] K (later hand, above the line) adds "only" (thus, "and only brings back four *issar*").
[79] K, P lack the conjunction.

8:1 *After the second rainfall*: In the fall, during the month of *Marheshvan* (*Ta'anit* 1:1, 3; 3:1; *Nedarim* 8:5); by this point, the poor would have collected their fill.

pick…after the second rainfall? In which case, the olives do not become ownerless after the second rainfall, as the poor must be given ample time and opportunity after the harvest to collect the poor offerings. *Rather*, everyone is permitted to take olives only *after the poor person goes out* to collect the olives left for him but brings back less than *the value of four issar*—Roman coins equivalent to half a *pondion* (8:7; *Qiddushin* 1:1), enough to purchase a day's worth of food (8:7).

8:2 *[The poor] are deemed reliable* when they claim that the produce that they offer for sale has the status of *Gleanings, Forgotten Things, and pe'ah* which are exempt from tithes (1:6; *Hallah* 1:3) *in their season*—only if the poor sell during the harvest season, when they would have acquired these as poor offerings.

Likewise, the poor's claims that their produce has the status of *the poor tithe*—which is exempt from tithes— are believed *during* the *entire year* in which the poor tithe is due, the third and sixth years of the seven-year (Sabbatical) cycle.

But a Levite who claims that the produce he offers has the status of the first tithe (Leviticus 27:30–33; Numbers 18:21–26; *Ma'aserot*) from which *terumah* (Numbers 18:8, 12, 24, 26; *Terumot*) has already been separated *is deemed reliable always* because the first tithe is offered every year.

accustomed to do: Only produce in the form that it is normally given as poor offerings (see further 8:3).

8:3 *deemed reliable* when they claim that the produce that they offer for sale was acquired as—and has the status of poor offerings, which are exempt from tithes, when the produce is allocated to them in the

[The poor] are deemed reliable concerning a cluster[80] of rice,
but they are not deemed reliable concerning it, either raw or cooked.
[The poor] are deemed reliable concerning beans,
but they are not deemed reliable concerning pounded beans, either raw or cooked.
[The poor] are deemed reliable concerning oil,
when they say that "it is of the poor tithe,"
but they are not deemed reliable when they say that "it is of knocked-down olives."

4 [The poor] are deemed reliable concerning a raw vegetable,
but they are not deemed reliable concerning a cooked one,
unless he had[81] a small amount;
for it is the typical manner of the householder to take it out from his pot.

8:5–6 *The Poor Tithe*

5 One may not give to the poor at the granary less than half a *qav* of wheat
or a *qav* of barley;
R. Meir says:
Half a *qav*.
A *qav* and a half of spelt,[82]
and[83] a *qav* of dried figs
or a *maneh* of fig cake;
R. Aqiva says:
Half a *maneh*.
Half a *log* of wine;
R. Aqiva says:
A quarter.

---

[80] Text and precise meaning uncertain.
[81] K lacks "he had," thus the line reads "unless there was only a small amount."
[82] Or "emmer."   [83] K lack the conjunction.

---

customary way (8:2) with little or no processing. Thus, the poor are trusted in their claims *concerning* unprocessed *wheat*, but not *flour or bread*.

reliable concerning a cluster of rice: While still in its husk.

not deemed reliable concerning it: After being removed from its husk, *either raw or cooked* because this is not how the poor were customarily given rice.

knocked-down olives: those at the top of the tree that had to be knocked down after the harvest (cf. Isaiah 17:6), which are not usually used for oil.

8:4 *raw vegetable*: Which is how the poor usually acquire vegetables as poor offerings.

unless he had a small amount of cooked vegetables, in which case the poor person may be trusted that it came from the poor tithe, because householders typically gave the poor small amounts of cooked vegetables.

8:5 *at the granary*: Where the poor tithe is distributed every third and sixth year of the seven-year (Sabbatical) cycle (Deuteronomy 14:28–29, 26:12–13).

less than: Cf. 1:2, 8:7.

A quarter[-*log*] of oil.
R. Aqiva says:
An eighth.
And [as to] any other produce—
Abba Saul said:
[Enough] so that he may sell them and purchase with [the proceeds] food for two meals.

6 This measure is binding[84] for priests, Levites, and Israelites.
If he would reserve [some]—
he takes half and gives half.
If he had a small amount—
he sets it before them,
and they divide it among themselves.

8:7–9 *Who is Poor?*

7 They may not give to a poor person who travels from place to place
less than a loaf of bread worth a *pondion*—
[made] of [wheat valued at] four *se'ah*[85] per *sela*.
If he lodges overnight,
then they must give him maintenance for lodging.
If he stays for the Sabbath—
they must give him food for three meals.
One who has food[86] for two meals,

---

[84] Lit. "is stated with respect to."   [85] K, early hand, lacks *se'ah*; added by later hand.
[86] P lacks "food," though later added in the margins.

---

food for two meals: Which is what a typical person would consume in a day (8:7; *Eruvin* 8:2; *Kelim* 17:11).

8:6 *This measure*: The quantities enumerated in 8:5. The commentators debate whether the mishnah refers to donors or recipients.

reserve [some] of the produce for his own poor relatives (cf. 4:9), then *he takes half* of the produce for the poor tithe for his relatives *and gives* the remaining *half* to the poor at the granary. Unlike the other poor offerings, the poor tithe is distributed directly by the householder to the poor (cf. 4:1–2).

If he had a small amount of produce and cannot meet the minimum quantities in 8:5.

8:7 *They*: Charity supervisors.

place to place: Town to town; cf. 5:4.

pondion: A *dupondius*, a bronze Roman coin. The bread is *[made] of [wheat valued at] four se'ah* (a quantity) *per sela* (a coin worth forty-eight *dupondii*). This amounts to a loaf of bread that would suffice for two meals (8:5; *Eruvin* 8:2; *Kelim* 17:11).

If he stays for the Sabbath then *they must give him food for three meals*—the requisite number of meals eaten during the Sabbath (*Shabbat* 16:2)

One who has enough *food for two meals*: The minimum amount of food needed for one day (8:5; *Eruvin* 8:2; *Kelim* 17:11), then *he may not take from the soup kitchen*. If he has less, he qualifies for provisions from the

may not take from the soup kitchen.[87]
Food for fourteen meals[88]—
one may not take from the charity fund.[89]
And the charity fund is collected by two and distributed by three.

8 Whoever has two hundred *zuz* may not take
Gleanings, Forgotten Things, or *pe'ah* or the poor tithe.
If he had two hundred less one *dinar*,
even if a thousand give him at once—
he may take.
If they were pledged to his creditor or to his wife's *ketubbah* payment,[90]
he may take.
They do not obligate him to sell his house or his tools.

9 Whoever has fifty *zuz*,
and he buys and sells with them—
he may not take [of the offerings for the poor].
And anyone who does not need to take but takes—
he will not depart from the world[91] until he is in need of other people.

[87] Lit. "dish."   [88] K, P lack "meals."   [89] Lit. "basket."
[90] K reverses the order.   [91] K, P: "he will not die from old age."

soup kitchen (*tamhui*). Literally a "dish," here *tamhui* refers to a communal charitable institution that provides for the poor's basic, short-term needs (Tosefta; cf. *Pesahim* 10:1).

If one has *food for fourteen meals* which would suffice for a full week (the second meal on Friday is delayed until the start of the Sabbath so that one eats three meals during the Sabbath but still only fourteen meals for the week), *one may not take from the charity fund*. If he has less, he is eligible for alms from the charity fund (*quppa*). Literally a "basket," here *quppa* refers to a communal charity fund that provides long-term support for the local poor (Tosefta).

two and distributed by three: Parallels the two individuals needed to oversee public finances and the three needed to supervise the Jerusalem Temple's finances as well as adjudicate monetary rewards (*Sanhedrin* 1:1; *Sheqalim* 5:2).

8:8 *two hundred zuz*: A Roman coin, also known as a *dinar* (denarius). The Mishnah understands two hundred *dinar* as enough to support oneself for a full year (*Ketubbot* 5:1). If he has less, he may take poor offerings.

If he had two hundred less one dinar, then he may take the poor offerings *even if a thousand* people later *give him* one *dinar* each, all *at once*, which would seemingly elevate him above the two hundred-*dinar* threshold; nevertheless, *he may take* the poor offerings because he had less than two hundred *dinar* when the allocations became due: at the time of the harvest for *pe'ah*, Gleanings, and Forgotten Things and when the grains were brought to the granary for the poor tithe.

his wife's ketubbah payment: The sum paid to his wife upon divorce or the husband's death (3:7; *Ketubbot*).

he may take because the two hundred *dinar* must be free of liens.

tools: Used for work. The value of his home and tools is not included when assessing whether he qualifies for poor offerings. The two hundred *dinar* must be liquid.

8:9 *buys and sells with them*: Uses them for commercial purposes, implying that he either has disposable income (and, presumably, enough to support his household) or he can support himself from the revenues of his business activities.

And anyone who needs to take but does not take—
he will not die of old age until he supports others from that which is his.
Concerning him Scripture says:
Blessed is he who trusts in the Lord, whose trust is the Lord alone.[92]
And likewise a judge who judges a judgment of truth according to its truth.
And anyone who is not lame in one leg,
or blind,
or lame in both legs,
but makes himself out as if he were one of them—
he will not die of old age until he becomes one of them, as it is said:
Justice, justice shall you pursue.
And every judge[93] who takes a bribe and perverts judgment—
he will not die of old age until his eyes go dim, as it is said:
Do not take bribes, for bribes blind the clear-sighted.

[92] The original text of **K, P** end the tractate here.
[93] **P** and the later hand of **K** skip the entire seven lines (from "And likewise" until "pursue") and begin here: "And likewise a judge who takes a bribe."

Blessed is he...the Lord alone: Jeremiah 17:7.

Justice...shall you pursue: Deuteronomy 16:20.

Do not take bribes...clear-sighted [and upset the pleas of those who are in the right]: Exodus 23:8.

Tractate Demai

Richard S. Sarason

Introduction

Overview

Demai is an Aramaic word meaning "doubtful" or "perhaps." Since, in context, the doubtful matter is whether or not agricultural produce has been properly tithed, the word may be translated as "Produce Suspected of Being Untithed" or "Produce Not Known to be Fully Tithed." Tractate *Demai* deals with the social consequences of lax observance of the biblical tithing laws (Numbers 18:8–13, 19–32; Deuteronomy 14:22–29, 26:12–15; and Leviticus 27:30–33), as understood by the rabbis (see also *Terumot, Ma'aserot,* and *Ma'aser Sheni*). The tractate assumes a social reality in which most Israelites separate *terumah* from their agricultural produce (Numbers 18:12–13, there called *reishit*, the "first" or choicest portion), which must be given to the priests and is proscribed for nonpriestly use, but do not separate the first tithe (Numbers 18:21–24), assigned to the Levites, or the second tithe (Deuteronomy 14:22ff.), which must be eaten in Jerusalem. The tractate further assumes a group of people who faithfully observe these tithing regulations (*ne'emanim*, "trustworthy people") living in the midst of a larger group of people (*amme ha'arets*, "people of the land," "common folk") who do not. The tractate's rulings regulate food-related social and economic interaction between these two groups of people: what sort of, and how much, tithe must be separated by those who scrupulously observe the tithing laws from produce purchased from, given to, or served to them by those whose tithing observance is deemed to be lax. The specific concern is to avoid accidentally eating *terumat ma'aser*, *terumah* from the tithe, that portion of the first, or Levitical, tithe that must be given to the priests and is proscribed for nonpriestly use (Numbers 18:25–29).

Organization and Structure of the Tractate

The first chapter is a series of lists (a stylistic and rhetorical format common to many opening chapters of Mishnah tractates) relating to leniencies in a variety of doubtful situations: whether certain inferior kinds of produce are liable to tithing at all; how second tithe is to be handled when it derives from produce not known to be fully tithed; whether produce normally not used for human food must be tithed; whether produce purchased at the northern border of the Land of Israel is deemed to be domestic and liable to tithing or foreign and not liable; whether produce purchased abroad is liable for tithing (this last item dovetails with chapter 2).

Chapter 2 (after the first paragraph) defines the characteristic behaviors of those who are trustworthy (*ne'emanim*) in the matter of tithing and of those who, while not themselves priests, scrupulously observe the biblical rules of priestly purity (*haverim*, "associates"). The rest of the chapter and the entirety of chapter 3 lay out situations in which those who observe all the tithing rules need not tithe produce that leaves their possession and will be eaten by someone who might not separate tithes from it: those who sell in bulk and those who distribute charity, for example, need not separate tithes from produce that will leave their possession in such circumstances. On the other hand, those who observe the tithing laws must separate tithes from produce previously given for safekeeping to someone deemed untrustworthy, when it is returned to them.

Chapter 4 deals with situations in which those who observe the tithing laws may believe the testimony of those who ordinarily would be deemed untrustworthy in matters relating to tithing: emergencies on the Sabbath, one compelled by a vow to eat with someone who is untrustworthy, food dealers who acknowledge that their produce is untithed while maintaining that another dealer's has been tithed.

Chapter 5 gives details of the actual tithing procedure to be used when separating tithes from produce that may or may not already have been tithed, and examples of the principle that tithes must not be separated from produce liable to tithing for produce that is exempt and vice versa.

The final two chapters present a variety of cases, forming thematic appendices respectively to chapters 2–3 and chapter 5. Chapter 6 responds to 2:2's ruling that one who is scrupulous about tithing must separate tithes from everything that he sells or gives to someone else. It presents a series of more complicated cases involving shared ownership by one who is trustworthy in the matter of tithing and one who is not. Chapter 7, similar to 5:1–2, gives further details of the tithing procedure, this time in unusual situations involving mixtures of produce that is liable to tithing with produce that is exempt.

Relationship to Scripture

The tractate's relationship to biblical law, as noted, consists only in the rabbinic interpretation of the various tithing regulations in Leviticus, Numbers, and Deuteronomy, and the *terumah/reishit* offering of Numbers 18, which are presupposed throughout. The defining topics and legal issues explored in the tractate, however, all derive from a much later social context: either that of the early rabbis themselves or, perhaps, that of their pre-70 CE predecessors as well, whom they imagine retrospectively. The main assumptions of the tractate that have no scriptural support relate to its treatment of punctilious tithing (specifically) as a sign of piety that functions as a social marker: the prohibition of eating untithed food, the obligation to tithe any produce that passes through one's hands, the obsessive concern about doubt over whether produce has been fully tithed, and so on, as articulated in the overview section above.

Special Notes for the Reader

The translation and annotations are based on my previously published work, particularly "Mishnah-Tosefta Demai," in *The History of Agriculture in the Mishnah and the Tosefta: Translation, Commentary, Theology*, ed. Jacob Neusner (3 vols.; Leiden and Boston: Brill, 2005), 2:803–1145. That work began as my 1977 doctoral dissertation at Brown University, under the supervision of Professor Jacob Neusner, whose insightful guidance I again acknowledge here. Manuscript readings in the footnotes have been culled from Nissan Zacks (ed.), *The Mishnah with Variant Readings: Order Zera'im*, vol. 1 (Jerusalem: Institute for the Complete Israeli Talmud, 1972).

Tractate Demai

Chapter One

1:1–2:1 *Leniencies Pertaining to Demai*

1 Leniently treated items[1] with respect to *demai*:[2]
unripe figs, wild jujuba, hawthorn berries, pine cones, sycamore figs, unripe dates,[3] fennel, and caper-fruit;
and in Judaea: sumac berries, vinegar in Judaea,[4] and coriander.
R. Judah says:
All unripe figs are exempt except for those from trees that bear fruit twice a year.
All wild jujuba are exempt except for the wild jujuba of Shiqmonah.[5]
All sycamore figs are exempt except for those that burst open.[6]

2 [Second tithe separated from] *demai*:
is not subject to the added fifth,

---

[1] Or "leniencies." [2] *Demai*, and so throughout.
[3] Or "fruit fallen off the date palm" (so Danby). [4] Manuscripts lack "in Judaea."
[5] K: "*shiqmah*." [6] Or "that are scarified."

1:1 *Leniently treated items with respect to demai*: That is, with respect to the category of *demai*; kinds of produce that need not be tithed at all when it is unclear whether or not they already have been tithed. All are inferior in some way: immature or fallen off the tree (the kinds of figs, dates, and pine cones listed here; Judaean vinegar, made from inferior grapeskin wine); not fully edible (caper-fruit); or not usually cultivated (wild jujuba, hawthorn berries, fennel; Judaean sumac and coriander). Since only edible, cultivated produce is subject to tithing (*Ma'aserot* 1:1), the doubt here actually pertains to whether the items listed are subject to tithing at all, and to whether they are cultivated in any particular locale. R. Judah's exceptions are kinds of figs and wild jujuba that are valued and eaten in certain locales, hence subject to tithing there.

All unripe figs are exempt from tithing even when they are suspected of being untithed.

except for those that burst open on the tree.

1:2 *[Second tithe] . . . demai*: An elliptical reference to second tithe that has been taken from produce suspected of being untithed. "Second tithe" is the rabbinic name for the tithe of Deuteronomy 14:22–26 (see *Ma'aser Sheni*), which must be brought to Jerusalem and eaten there. In order to lighten the farmer's load, the produce may be redeemed for money of equivalent value; the money then is brought to Jerusalem and used to purchase local produce for eating there. Listed here are laws pertaining to the handling of second tithe that are waived when the tithe has been separated only on account of doubt as to whether or not the produce already had been tithed.

is not subject to the added fifth: If second-tithe produce is redeemed for money, the farmer must pay an added fifth above the market value of the produce as a fine (Leviticus 27:30–31).

and is not subject to Removal,
and may be eaten by an *onen*,
and may be brought into Jerusalem and taken out again,[7]
and one may abandon[8] a small quantity of it along the roads [to Jerusalem],
and one may give it to an *am ha'arets*, and[9] eat its equivalent value;
and one may redeem it silver for silver, copper for copper,
silver for copper, and copper for produce,
provided that he again redeem the produce—
the words of R. Meir.
But the Sages say:
One must bring up the produce[10] and it must be eaten in Jerusalem.

[7] Lit. "it enters Jerusalem and leaves." [8] Or "destroy." [9] Or, more likely, "but."
[10] Or "The produce must be brought up."

is not subject to removal: Tithes that may have accumulated in one's possession must be removed and distributed to their proper recipients (the Levite, the poor, the stranger) at the end of the third and sixth years of each Sabbatical cycle (Deuteronomy 14:28, 26:13). Leftover second tithe, which may not be distributed to anyone, normally must be destroyed (*Ma'aser Sheni* 5:6).

An *onen* is a mourner for one of seven close relatives (Leviticus 21:2–3) before their burial (*Berakhot* 3:1). Deuteronomy 26:14 forbids the eating of second tithe by an *onen* (see *Ma'aser Sheni* 5:12; *Bikkurim* 2:2).

may be brought into Jerusalem and taken out again without penalty. Generally, once second tithe produce has been brought into Jerusalem, it may no longer be removed from the city or redeemed with coins; that is, it may not be commodified (*Ma'aser Sheni* 3:5; the leniency regarding *demai* is also recorded at *Ma'aser Sheni* 3:6).

one may abandon a small quantity of it along the roads: This ruling has been variously explained in accordance with the two possible meanings of *me'abdin* (to lose, to abandon): (1) If a small quantity of the doubtful second tithe has been lost on the journey to Jerusalem, there is no need to replace or make monetary compensation for it; (2) If the journey to Jerusalem becomes physically taxing, the farmer may lighten his load by abandoning a small quantity of the doubtful second tithe along the way, but not a large quantity.

one may give it to an am ha'arets: An *am ha'arets* (lit. "person of the land," a common person) is someone who does not observe the rabbinic purity laws; he can be assumed to defile his own food and any food given to him. Normally, second tithe, which needed to be maintained in a state of purity, would not be given to such a person by anyone who is punctilious about purity regulations.

and eat its equivalent value in Jerusalem. This likely should be read as a penalty clause, "*but* he must eat its equivalent value in Jerusalem" (cf. *Ma'aser Sheni* 1:7).

one may redeem it: That is, exchange its redemption money for other coins. This is not allowed in the case of regular second tithe, lest it seem to treat with disrespect coins that have been consecrated as tithe (see *Ma'aser Sheni* 2:6). One may, however, upgrade the specie (exchange copper coins for silver ones, for example). Downgrading the specie is allowed in the case of *demai*, since these coins are only doubtfully consecrated.

copper for produce: Ordinarily this is not allowed, and if it has been done, then the produce must be brought up to Jerusalem and eaten there as second tithe (*Ma'aser Sheni* 1:5), in order not to derive personal benefit from, or appear to treat lightly, that which has been consecrated.

provided that he again redeem the produce for coins. Since the produce was originally redeemed for coins, it must be brought up to Jerusalem in that form.

One must bring up the produce and it must be eaten in Jerusalem: The Sages apply to *demai* the same stricture as to regular second tithe (see *Ma'aser Sheni* 3:4); the leniencies end at this point.

3 One who purchases [grain] for seed or for cattle,
flour for [dressing] hides,
oil for a lamp, oil for greasing utensils—
[the produce] is exempt from the status of *demai*.
[Produce] from Keziv[11] and beyond
is exempt from[12] the status of *demai*.
The dough offering of an *am ha'arets*,
and a *terumah* mixture,
and [produce] that has been purchased with the money of the second tithe,[13]
and the residues of the meal offerings—
are exempt from the status of *demai*.
Spiced oil—
the House of Shammai declare it liable [to be treated as *demai*],
but the House of Hillel declare it exempt [from the status of *demai*].

4 *Demai*:
one may make an *eruv* with it,

[11] K, P: "Gaziv." [12] Several manuscripts read "liable to." [13] All manuscripts lack "second."

1:3 *One who purchases* various kinds of produce from an *am ha'arets*. The items listed here, while edible, are not generally used as human food, so the tithing strictures do not apply in the case of produce suspected of not having been tithed.

for cattle: The grain will be used as fodder.

oil for greasing utensils: This is also a mode of cleaning utensils.

exempt from the status of demai: Meaning that it need not be tithed.

from Keziv and beyond: The tithing laws apply only to produce grown in the Land of Israel. Keziv, although inside the biblical boundaries (Joshua 19:29), marks the northern border of the area resettled after the Babylonian exile. It is therefore doubtful whether the tithing laws apply to the area "from Keziv and beyond." This is the interpretation found in the Yerushalmi. Manuscripts that include Maimonides' commentary on the Mishnah follow his interpretation of the text here: "liable," since this area still falls within the biblical boundaries of the Land of Israel.

The dough offering of an am ha'arets: The four items listed here are, or contain, consecrated produce, and must be consumed in a state of purity. For the dough offering, see *Hallah*.

a terumah mixture: If *terumah* produce mixes with less than one hundred parts nonsacral produce, it cannot be consumed by anyone other than a priest. See *Terumot* 4:7; *Orlah* 2:1; *Bikkurim* 2:1; and *Shabbat* 21:1.

the residues of the meal offerings: The portion of the meal offering not burnt on the altar is eaten by the priests. See *Menahot* 6:1.

Spiced oil: A mixture of edible oil and spices, generally used to anoint the body. The dispute between the Houses centers on whether the oil in the mixture remains edible in principle, hence subject to tithing, or perhaps on whether the mixture is likely to be used for food. It is unclear whether the subject of the ruling is specifically spiced oil that is *demai* or spiced oil in general.

1:4 *one may make an eruv with it*: An *eruv* (lit. "mixture," "combination") is a legal remedy for extending the area in which a person may walk on the Sabbath and for constructing a joint private domain among neighbors in a shared courtyard within which food and other items may be carried on the Sabbath. Only food that can be eaten may be used to construct an *eruv*; untithed food does not qualify in this regard, but doubtfully tithed food does, since it can be eaten in emergencies (3:1, 4:1; *Eruvin* 3:2).

and one may make a partnership with it,
and one may recite the blessing over it,
and one may invite others [to recite the communal blessing after meals] over it,
and one may separate [tithes from] it naked during twilight [on the eve of the Sabbath].
If one separated second tithe before first [tithe], it does not matter.
Oil with which a weaver lubricates his fingers is liable to be treated as *demai*,
but [oil] that a wool-comber puts on wool is exempt from the status of *demai*.

Chapter Two

2 And[14] these items are to be tithed
when they are *demai* in every place:
pressed figs, dates, carobs, rice, and cumin.
Rice that is [grown] outside of the Land—
all who make use of it are exempt [from tithing].

[14] K, P, and most manuscripts lack "and."

one may make a partnership with it: A partnership is a legal remedy for constructing a joint private domain among neighbors in adjoining courtyards (*Eruvin* 7:6). The reason for the leniency here is identical with that in the previous case.

one may recite the blessing over it: A blessing is recited only over food that may be eaten (*Berakhot* 6). Since *demai* might already have been tithed, a blessing may be recited over it.

one may invite others [to recite the communal blessing after meals]: See *Berakhot* 7:1.

one may separate [tithes from] it naked at twilight: Most commentators treat this as two separate rulings: (1) Ordinarily one may not separate tithes while unclothed, because this act is preceded by a blessing mentioning God's name, which it is disrespectful to utter naked. (See *Terumot* 1:6; cf. *Hallah* 2:3.) No blessing need be recited when separating tithes from *demai*, since this separation is done only as a precaution on account of uncertainty. (2) Tithes may not be separated on the Sabbath because this changes the status of the produce (*Demai* 4:1, 7:1–5; *Betsah* 5:2). The prohibition extends to twilight on the eve of the Sabbath, since the holy day might already have begun (*Shabbat* 2:7). This prohibition is relaxed in the case of *demai*, since those tithes are separated only on account of doubt.

second tithe before first [tithe]: Normally first tithe must be separated before second tithe; reversing the order is deemed to violate a scriptural prohibition (*Terumot* 3:6–7) and renders one unable to say the requisite pronouncement (*Ma'aser Sheni* 5:11). The ruling is relaxed here since the tithes may already have been separated.

Oil...weaver...is liable because it is absorbed into his body and he thereby benefits from it (cf. *Shabbat* 9:4).

Oil...wool-comber...is exempt because it is absorbed in the wool (cf. 1:3).

2:1 *in every place*: Both inside and outside the Land of Israel, because they are recognizable as items grown in the Land and exported abroad.

Rice that is [grown] outside of the Land is exempt from tithing because it is imported from abroad.

2:2–3 Paired Social Categories: Trustworthy Tithers and Observers of Purity Laws

2 One who undertakes to be trustworthy
tithes what he eats, what he sells, and what he purchases,
and does not accept the hospitality of an *am ha'arets*.
R. Judah says:
Even[15] one who accepts the hospitality of an *am ha'arets* is [deemed] trustworthy.
They said to him:
[If] he is not trustworthy concerning himself,
how could he be trustworthy concerning that of others?
3 One who undertakes to be a Fellow
does not sell to an *am ha'arets* wet or dry [produce],
does not purchase from him wet [produce],
does not accept the hospitality of an *am ha'arets*,
and does not receive him as his guest
while [the *am ha'arets*] is wearing his own clothes.
R. Judah says:
Also he may not raise small cattle,
be profuse in [making] vows or in levity,
or defile himself for the dead;

[15] K, P, and some other manuscripts lack.

2:2 *who undertakes*: lit. "who accepts upon himself," perhaps implying an oath. Same phrase in 2:3.

According to R. Judah one may trust an *am ha'arets* not to feed him untithed produce and still be deemed trustworthy, since we are concerned only with the food in his own possession that he might share with others, not with the food that he is willing to eat at someone else's table.

[If] he is not trustworthy concerning himself: If he cannot be trusted regarding the food that he is willing to eat under someone else's roof, how can he be trusted regarding the food that he may give or sell to someone else?

2:3 *One who undertakes to be a Fellow*: Someone who scrupulously observes the purity laws outside the Temple precincts (or when the Temple no longer exists).

wet or dry [produce]: "Wet" produce has been rendered susceptible to impurity by contact with liquids; "dry" produce has had no contact with liquids, so is not (yet) susceptible to impurity (Leviticus 11:34, 38; *Makhshirin*). The former will immediately be made impure by the touch of an *am ha'arets*, who is always presumed to be impure (*Tohorot* 7–8); the latter will eventually become wet and rendered impure.

wearing his own clothes: The clothes of an *am ha'arets* are deemed to convey impurity through pressure (*midras*; *Hagigah* 2:7) to anything on which he sits or lies or leans up against.

small cattle, sheep, and goats, denude the landscape, damaging fields and orchards in their pasturing. (*Bava Qamma* 7:7 prohibits the raising of small cattle in the Land of Israel except in wilderness areas.)

he should not be profuse in [making] vows or in levity: Cf. *Avot* 3:13.

or defile himself for the dead: He should observe all of the priestly rules against corpse defilement (Leviticus 21:1–4; Numbers 19:11–22).

and he ministers in the house of study.
They said to him:
These [rules] do not enter the category.

2:4–5 *Tithing Produce When Selling in Bulk*

4 Bakers—
The Sages required them to separate only [an amount] sufficient
for *terumah* from the tithe and
dough offering.
Shopkeepers are not permitted
to sell *demai*.
All[16] who provision in bulk are permitted
to sell *demai*.
Who[17] are they who provision in bulk?
For instance, wholesalers and grain dealers.
  5 R. Meir says:
That which is usually measured out [for sale] in bulk
and one measured it out in a small quantity—
the small quantity is subject to the [rules governing] a bulk quantity.
That which is usually measured out in a small quantity and one measured it out in bulk—
the bulk quantity is subject to the [rules governing] a small quantity.[18]

---

[16] **P** and several other manuscripts: "But all."
[17] **K**, **P**, and several other manuscripts: "And who."
[18] This line is lacking in all manuscripts. **K** reads as follows: "That which is usually measured out [for sale] in a small quantity and one measured it out in bulk, the small quantity is subject to [the rule governing] the bulk quantity." A later hand in the margin corrected the text to make it conform with the first clause of ours. **P** reads "That which is usually measured out [for sale] in a small quantity and one measured it out in bulk; [or] in bulk and one measured it out in a small quantity, the small quantity is subject to [the rule governing] the bulk quantity." The Tosefta and Yerushalmi seem to confirm our text.

---

house of study: J. N. Epstein plausibly suggests that the text be emended to "a banquet-hall," with the negation governing this clause as well as the previous one ("he may not minister in a banquet hall").

These [rules] do not enter the category: They do not deal with matters of food purity.

2:4 *Bakers* need not separate second tithe from doubtfully tithed produce, presumably to spare them the burden of taking up to Jerusalem large quantities of second-tithe dough or coins.

Shopkeepers: Because they sell in small quantities directly to consumers, retailers must take responsibility for tithing everything that they sell (see 2:2 above and 3:1–3 below).

All who provision in bulk: Because bulk sales are not measured out precisely and frequently end up giving more than what would be the exact measure, it devolves upon the purchaser to measure out the exact amount of tithes that are due (cf. *Bava Batra* 5:11).

2:5 *That which is usually measured out*: In order to avoid any confusion on the part of the purchaser, who might think that produce previously tithed by the vendor was untithed or that untithed produce had already been tithed by the vendor, R. Meir requires following customary procedures even if, in the particular instance, the produce had been sold in irregular measure.

What is considered bulk quantity?
With regard to dry [produce]—three *qav*,
and with regard to wet produce—[an amount equaling the value of] a *dinar*.
R. Yose says:
Baskets of figs, and baskets of grapes, and containers of vegetables—
as long as one sells them by the lot,[19]
he is exempt [from tithing them before he sells them].

Chapter Three

3:1–6 *Tithing Produce That Will Be Given to Others*

3 One may feed the poor with *demai*
and[20] guests with *demai*.
Rabban Gamaliel would feed his laborers with *demai*.
Charity collectors—
the House of Shammai say:
They give that which is tithed to the one who does not tithe,
and that which is not tithed to the one who tithes.
As a result everyone is eating [produce that has been] set right.
But the Sages say:
They collect without preconditions and they distribute without preconditions,
and he who wants to set right [the produce he has received], let him set [it] right.
   2 One who wants to trim away leaves of vegetables to lighten his load
may not throw [them] away until he has tithed [them].
One who purchases vegetables from the market and decides to return [them]
may not return [them] until he has tithed [them], for it is missing only a number.[21]

---

[19] Or "by estimation."   [20] **K**, **P**, and several other manuscripts have instead "one may feed."
[21] Translation and meaning of this phrase are uncertain. **K**: "for he tithes only a number" (corrected in the margin to accord with our text). **P**: "he may not return [them] until he has tithed that which is not tithed except [by] number."

---

he is exempt: As at 2:4, above, the issue here is inexact or estimated measuring of quantity or weight by the vendor. Better to let the purchaser tithe the produce at home, where he can measure it exactly and separate the proper amount of tithes.

3:1 *Charity collectors*: The larger issue under dispute here is whether one must take action to prevent a violation of the law by others, or simply do nothing and let a possible violation occur.

3:2 *One who wants to trim away leaves of vegetables*: The discarded items must be tithed, in accordance with the Shammaite reasoning in the preceding paragraph that one must take action to prevent the violation of a law.

for it is missing only a number: The purchaser can return them once he has determined their exact number and separated the correct tithes. With a slightly different punctuation the text might read: *For he [thereby]*

[If] he was contemplating a purchase[22] and saw another bundle[23] better than that one, he is permitted to return [the original item],
since he had not [yet] drawn it [into his possession].

3 One who finds produce in the road and took it to eat it,
and [then] decided to store it—
he may not store it until he has tithed it.
But if from the outset he took it so that it should not go to waste,
he is exempt [from tithing it].
Anything that a person is not permitted to sell while it is *demai*,
he may not send to his friend while it is *demai*.
R. Yose permits in the case of produce known to be untithed, provided that he inform him.

4 One who brings [his tithed] wheat to a Samaritan miller or to an *am ha'arets* miller—
[the wheat remains] in its presumed status with regard to tithes
and with regard to Seventh-Year produce;
[but if] to a gentile miller—
[the wheat] is *demai*
One who deposits [tithed] produce in the safekeeping of a Samaritan or an *am ha'arets*—
[the produce remains] in its presumed status with regard to tithes
and with regard to Seventh-Year produce;
in the safekeeping of a gentile—
[the produce is deemed to be] like [the gentile's] produce.
R. Simeon says:
It is *demai*.

[22] Lit. "standing and purchasing." [23] Lit. "load."

diminishes only [their] number. The produce may be returned because it has not lost any of its resale value (so Albeck, following the Yerushalmi). The meaning is uncertain.

[If] he was contemplating a purchase: Acquisition only occurs when the purchaser has physically drawn to himself the item to be purchased (*Bava Batra* 5:7).

he is permitted to return [the original item] without having first tithed it.

3:3 *One who finds produce in the road*: Again, once produce has been acquired, it may not be discarded until it has been tithed.

R. Yose permits: R. Yose will *even* permit the sending to a friend of certainly untithed produce (let alone produce that may or may not have been tithed), because one can notify the friend of its status and presume that he will tithe it.

3:4 *a Samaritan miller*: The issue is whether those who are not themselves trustworthy regarding the proper tithing of produce will respect the scruples of those who are, so that the tithed produce of the latter that has been delivered over to them for processing or for safekeeping will not be intermingled with the possibly untithed produce of others (other customers or the untrustworthy person's own produce). Jewish *amme ha'arets* and Samaritans are deemed reliable in this regard (cf. *Tohorot* 7:8), while gentiles are not.

R. Simeon says: R. Simeon also holds that the gentile will mix the tithed produce with his own untithed produce. The Tosefta suggests that R. Simeon holds that gentile produce is exempt from tithing obligations, and that a single item of tithed Israelite produce mixed in would suffice to render the whole mixture *demai*.

5 One who gives [tithed produce] to a female innkeeper
tithes that which he gives to her and that which he receives [back] from her,
since she is suspected of exchanging.
Said R. Yose:
We are not responsible for deceivers;
he tithes only that which he receives from her.

6 One who gives [his tithed produce] to his mother-in-law
tithes that which he gives to her and that which he receives from her,
since she is suspected of exchanging that which is spoiled.
Said R. Judah:
She desires the well-being of her daughter and feels shame before her son-in-law.
R. Judah concedes in the case of one who gives Seventh-Year produce to his mother-in-law,
that she is not suspected of exchanging it[24] [and] feeding her daughter Seventh-Year produce.

Chapter Four

4:1–2   *Relying on the Testimony of Untrustworthy Persons*

4 One who purchases produce from someone not trustworthy about tithing, and forgets to tithe it,
and[25] inquires of [the vendor] on the Sabbath—
may[26] eat at his word.
[But] at nightfall at the close of the Sabbath, he may not eat until he has tithed [the produce].
[If] he did not find [the vendor],

[24] **P, K**, most manuscripts lack "of exchanging."   [25] **K, P**, most manuscripts lack "and."
[26] **K** (in margin), **P**, and many manuscripts: "and may."

3:5 *to a female innkeeper*: So that she may prepare it for him to eat.

since she is suspected of exchanging her own doubtfully tithed produce for his tithed produce.

3:6 *to his mother-in-law*: A variant of the preceding case. Here one takes responsibility for tithing the exchanged produce because of the familial relationship.

feels shame before her son-in-law: She is ashamed to feed her son-in-law spoiled food, and so will substitute for it food of better quality, which might possibly be untithed.

R. Judah concedes: The *am ha'arets* mother-in-law, although lax about tithing laws, is sufficiently wary of the prohibition against eating Seventh-Year produce that she is not suspected of violating it.

4:1 *on the Sabbath*, when tithing is forbidden. See 1:4, 7:1–5.

may eat at his word: In extenuating circumstances that prevent one from separating tithes, he may rely on the word of someone who is not otherwise trustworthy in the matter of tithing.

[and] someone who is not deemed trustworthy in the matter of tithing
said to him, "It is tithed,"
he eats at his word.
[But] at nightfall at the close of the Sabbath, he may not eat until he has tithed [the produce].
Terumah from the tithe from *demai* produce that fell back[27] to its place—
R. Simeon of Shezur says:
Even on a weekday he may inquire of [the vendor] and eat at his word.
   2 One who imposes a vow on his fellow that he eat with him,
and [the guest] does not trust him in the matter of tithing—
he may eat with him on the first Sabbath,
even though he does not trust him in the matter of tithing,
provided that [the host] say to him, "This [food] is tithed."
But on the second Sabbath, even if [the host] vowed to withhold any benefit from him,
[the guest] may not eat until he has tithed [the produce].

4:3–4   *Tithing*

   3 R. Eliezer says:
A person need not designate tithe for the poor from produce *demai*.
But the Sages say:
He designates [tithe for the poor] but he need not separate [it].
   4 One who designated *terumah* from the tithe from *demai*[28]

---

[27] Lit. "returned."
[28] **P** and several manuscripts lack "from *demai*."

Terumah from the tithe … that fell back to its place: i.e. that fell back into the now-tithed *demai*-produce from which it originally had been separated, thus rendering the entire mixture forbidden to a nonpriest. See *Orlah* 2:1.

4:2 *One who imposes a vow on his fellow that he eat with him*: For example, "May you not derive any benefit from me unless you eat with me" (cf. *Nedarim* 3:1). Another instance of an extenuating circumstance in which someone may rely on the word of an *am ha'arets* that his produce has been tithed, here for the sake of preserving a friendship—but only on a single occasion. Cf. 7:1 below.

4:3 *R. Eliezer says*: Tithe for the poor is separated during the third and sixth years of the Sabbatical cycle in place of second tithe (Deuteronomy 26:12–15). A leniency pertaining to the treatment of *demai* is that this tithe need not actually be separated and distributed to the poor, since the produce *might* already have been tithed. R. Eliezer rules that, since tithe for the poor need not be separated from *demai*, it also need not be formally designated (that is to say, its specific location need not be verbally marked out) in the produce. The Sages rule, to the contrary, that the tithing procedure with respect to *demai* needs to be uniform throughout the Sabbatical cycle: since one must formally designate the location of second tithe in the produce, one must also designate the location of tithe for the poor in years three and six, even though one need not separate and distribute it.

4:4 *One who designated terumah from the tithe*: *Terumah* from the tithe, even from doubtfully tithed produce, must always be separated and given to a priest; it cannot be eaten by nonpriests. Similarly, tithe for the poor from produce that certainly has not been tithed must also be physically separated and distributed to

or poor tithe from produce known to be untithed,
may not remove them [from the produce] on the Sabbath.
But if a priest or a poor person were accustomed to eat with him,
they may come and eat, provided that he inform them.

4:5–7 Credibility of the Testimony of Untrustworthy and Unknown Persons

5 One who says to someone who is not trustworthy in the matter of tithing,
"Purchase [produce] for me from someone who is trustworthy,
or from someone who separates tithes,"
[the agent] is not believed.
[If the sender says, "Purchase produce for me] from so-and-so,"
then this one is believed.
[If the agent] went to purchase [produce] from him,
and [subsequently returned and] said to [the sender],
"I did not find him, but I purchased [produce] for you from someone else who is trustworthy,"
he is not believed.

6 One who enters a city, and does not know anyone there,
[and] says, "Who here is trustworthy? Who here separates tithes?"
[and] one says to him, "Me"—
he is not believed.
[But if] he said, "So-and-so is trustworthy," then he is believed.
[If] he went to purchase[29] from him, and said to him,
"Who here sells old [produce]?"
[and] he said to him, "The one who sent you to me"—
even though they mutually benefit each other,
they are believed.

[29] K, P, and many manuscripts: "and purchased."

---

the poor (unlike that from *demai*, in 4:3, which need only be verbally marked out in the produce). But these gifts may not be separated and distributed on the Sabbath. If they have been designated, but not separated, before the Sabbath, then the portion in which they have been verbally marked out may be given to a priest or a poor person who is a guest at one's Sabbath meal. These guests, however, must be informed that the portion they are receiving contains *terumah* or tithe and needs to be handled accordingly (particularly in the case of *terumah*).

4:5 *One who says to someone who is not trustworthy*: The issue in this ruling is the credibility of one's agent who is not trustworthy in the matter of tithing.

4:6 *he is not believed...he is believed*: A person who is suspect in a particular matter is not believed to give testimony about himself in that matter, but he is believed to give testimony about someone else, since he gains no advantage by lying about him. (The logic here is the same as that attributed to Simeon b. Gamaliel at *Bekhorot* 5:4.)

old [produce]: From the previous year, which may be eaten before the offering of the first sheaf (*'omer*) from the new crop (cf. Leviticus 23:14 and *Menahot* 10:5).

they are believed: An extreme application of the previous ruling's logic: since each is not testifying about himself, both are to be believed, notwithstanding the appearance of collusion between them.

7 If donkey-drivers entered a city,
[and] one [of them] said, "My [produce] is new but that of my companion is old";
[or] "My [produce] is not fully tithed[30] but that of my companion is fully tithed"—
they are not believed.
R. Judah says:
They are believed.

Chapter Five

5:1–2 *Procedures for Separating Tithes from Produce Suspected of Being Untithed*

5 One who purchases [a loaf of bread] from an [*am ha'arets*] baker, how does he tithe it?
He removes an amount sufficient for *terumah* from the tithe and dough offering, and says,
"One from one hundred of that which is here, at[31] this side [of the loaf], is [made first] tithe,

---

[30] Lit. "set right," here and below. See 3:1, 7:7.
[31] **K**, **P**, and other manuscripts add "this." See 5:2.

4:7 *My [produce] is new*: i.e. this year's produce, which is forbidden to be eaten before the offering of the first sheaf from the new crop (cf. Leviticus 23:14).

old: See note on 4:6.

they are not believed: They are suspected of collusion. Since neither is trustworthy about himself, neither is believed to testify about someone else.

R. Judah says: They are believed, because neither is testifying about himself. This accords with the final ruling at 4:6.

5:1 *baker*: 2:4 obligates bakers to separate *terumah* from the tithe from grain suspected of being untithed, and dough offering from what they bake before selling (see *Hallah* 2:7). This mishnah refers to bakers not living up to these obligations.

terumah from the tithe: First tithe need not be physically separated and given to a Levite from produce which might already be tithed, but *terumah* from the tithe and dough offering, both of which may be eaten only by priests, must be separated from such produce (see e.g. 7:1–3). The procedure prescribed here allows for this to be done without first having to physically separate first tithe. It is, thus, a "shortcut" or a leniency that is applied in the case of produce only suspected of being untithed, without having to go through the full tithing procedure.

One from one hundred: That is, one-hundredth part of the whole loaf, which is the amount required as *terumah* from the tithe (= one-tenth of the first tithe, which itself is one-tenth of the whole).

of that which is here: Now localized in the separated portion of the loaf.

and the remainder of the [first] tithe is adjacent to it.
This [hundredth part] which I have made [first] tithe is [now] made *terumah* from the tithe for it,
and the rest is dough offering.
And second tithe is to the north of it, or to the south of it, and is desacralized with coins."

2 One who wishes to separate *terumah* and *terumah* from the tithe at once
takes one [part] from thirty-three and a third, and says:
"One from one hundred of that which is here, this,[32] at this side [of the produce],
is nonsacral produce,
and the rest is *terumah* for the whole [of the produce],
and [the] one-hundredth [part of] nonsacral produce which is here,
this, at this side, is hereby [made first] tithe,
and the remainder of the [first] tithe is adjacent to it.
That which I made [first] tithe is [now] made *terumah* from the tithe for it
and the rest is dough offering.[33]
And second tithe is to the north of it, or to the south of it, and is desacralized with coins."

[32] Lacking in **K** (after correction) and other manuscripts.
[33] The last phrase is lacking in several manuscripts, including **K**, **P**, but is inserted in the margin.

and the remainder of the [first] tithe: That is, nine-tenths or nine-hundredths of the whole loaf, now localized in that part of the loaf that has not been separated out.

This [hundredth part] which I have made [first] tithe is [now] made terumah from the tithe for it: That is, for the designated, but not separated, remainder of the first tithe.

and the rest of the separated portion of the loaf is now declared to be dough offering.

And second tithe is to the north of it, or to the south of it: That is, of the designated remainder of the first tithe in the loaf.

desacralized with coins: The sanctity of second tithe produce may be transferred to money, which must be brought to Jerusalem and used there. See generally *Ma'aser Sheni*.

5:2 *One who wishes...at once*: in a single act of separation. The produce discussed in this ruling must be fully and definitely untithed rather than doubtfully tithed, since *terumah* is routinely assumed to have been removed from *demai*, the doubt pertaining only to the status of subsequent tithes. As in the preceding paragraph, a portion sufficient for each gift is separated in the proper order.

one [part] from thirty-three and a third, which is three-hundredths of the whole.

One from one hundred of that which is here: That is, one-hundredth part from among the three-hundredths parts separated.

nonsacral produce: Here, untithed produce from which *terumah* alone has been removed, as distinct from the portion which is being designated as consecrated *terumah*.

and the rest of the three-hundredths parts, that is, two-hundredths, or one-fiftieth, which is approximately the amount that must be separated as *terumah* (cf. *Terumot* 4:3).

That which I made [first] tithe: That is, the hundredth part.

terumah from the tithe for it: That is, for the designated remainder of the first tithe.

and the rest is dough offering: The reference to dough offering is inappropriate here. This is a scribal error, lacking in a number of manuscripts, caused by the similarity of the formulary pattern here and at 5:1.

And second tithe is to the north of it, or to the south of it: That is, of the designated remainder of the first tithe.

5:3–11 *Separating Tithes from One Category of Produce for Another*

3 One who purchases [bread] from an [*am ha'arets*] baker
may separate tithes [either] from the warm for the cold,
or from the cold for the warm,
even from many [diverse] molds—
the words of R. Meir.
R. Judah forbids:
For I say,
Yesterday's wheat derived from one person, and today's wheat derives from another.
R. Simeon forbids with regard to *terumah* from the tithe,
and permits with regard to the dough offering.

4 One who purchases from a [bread] merchant
must separate tithes from each and every mold—
the words of R. Meir.
R. Judah says:
[He separates tithes] from one for all.
R. Judah concedes in the case of one who purchases from a monopolist
that he must separate tithes from each and every one.

5:3 The principle underlying these rulings is that it is forbidden to separate tithes from produce that has already been tithed for produce that has yet to be tithed, and vice versa (cf. 7:6 and *Terumot* 1:5), a concern if the baker uses different batches of wheat on subsequent days. R. Meir holds that the concern does not apply in this case because all of the dough derives from the same baker who buys wheat or flour in bulk and therefore uses the same batch from day to day.

Warm ... cold: Fresh bread made today and bread made yesterday, respectively.

many [diverse] molds: i.e. different batches potentially made from different sources of grain, even if made on the same day.

Yesterday's wheat derived from one person: That is, yesterday's grain may have been tithed, while today's has not been, or vice versa; the grain used in the bread is presumed to derive from different sources.

R. Simeon forbids with regard to terumah from the tithe, and permits with regard to the dough offering: R. Simeon appears to mediate between the positions of R. Meir and R. Judah. He holds, with R. Judah, that the grain might derive from different sources, so that the *terumah* from the tithe must not be separated from different items for each other. But he agrees with R. Meir regarding the separation of dough offering because that obligation is only incurred at the time that the dough is made, and the dough here derives from a single baker.

5:4 *One who purchases from a [bread] merchant*: It is not always known whether a merchant obtains his bread from a single baker or from many bakers. R. Meir's ruling presupposes the latter to be the case, requiring the separation of tithes *from each mold* individually. R. Judah, assuming that the bread comes from a single baker, allows tithes to be separated *from one mold for all*. But R. Judah concedes in the case of a *monopolist* (Hebrew uses the Greek term)—one who has obtained the exclusive concession for a particular locale and by definition obtains his bread from many different bakers—that each mold must be tithed separately.

5 One who purchases from a poor person,
and likewise a poor person who received[34] pieces of bread or cakes of pressed fig,
must separate tithes from each and every one.
But with regard to dates or dried figs,
he may mix them [into a mass] and remove [tithes from the whole mass].
Said R. Judah:
When [does this ruling apply]?
When [each] gift is abundant.
But when [each] gift is little,
he must separate tithes from each and every [gift].

6 One who purchases from a wholesale dealer,
and returned and purchased from him a second time,
may not separate tithes from this one for that one,
even [if he purchased again] from the same chest,[35]
even [if he purchased again] from the same type.
The wholesaler is trusted to say that they [derive] from the same [batch].

7 One who purchases from a householder,
and returned and purchased from him a second time,
may separate tithes from the one [portion] for the other,
even [if the produce comes] from two [different] containers,
even [if the produce comes] from two [different] towns.
A householder who was selling vegetables in the marketplace,
if they bring to him [vegetables] from his own gardens—

---

[34] Lit. "to whom they gave." K, P: "to whom were given."   [35] Or "basket."

5:5 *One who purchases from a poor person*: A poor person is assumed to obtain his produce from many diverse donations (see 3:1); thus he must separate tithes from each donation separately, while one who purchases from him must separate tithes from each item separately.

But with regard to dates or dried figs: The individual dates or figs are deemed to be thoroughly mixed together in the mass such that the proportion deriving from the individual sources remains the same throughout. For this reason, tithes may be separated from any portion of the mass for the whole.

But when [each] gift is little: When the quantity of dates or dried figs is small, they remain discrete and must be tithed separately.

5:6 *One who purchases from a wholesale dealer*: Such a dealer turns over large quantities of produce that have been received from many different growers. One cannot assume that produce purchased on two different occasions, even in close temporal proximity, derives from the same lot. Tithes therefore must not be separated from one purchase for the other.

The wholesaler is trusted to say that they [derive] from the same [batch] since he gains nothing by lying.

5:7 *One who purchases from a householder*: This case is the opposite of the one in 5:6. Produce sold by a householder on his own property is assumed to derive from a single source. Thus, items purchased at different times still have the same status as regards the separation of tithes.

if [they bring] from the gardens of others: Even when purchasing from a single householder in the marketplace, if the produce is known to derive from diverse sources, each item must be tithed separately.

[the purchaser] may separate tithes from one for all;
but if [they bring] from the gardens of others—
[the purchaser] must separate tithes from each and every one.

8 One who purchases fully untithed produce from two places
may separate tithes from the one for the other,
although[36] they have said:
A person is not permitted to sell untithed produce except in case of need.

9 One may separate tithes from [produce] of Israelites for [produce] of gentiles,
from [produce] of gentiles for [produce] of Israelites,
from [produce] of Israelites for [produce] of Samaritans,
from [produce] of Samaritans for [produce] of [other] Samaritans.
R. Eleazar[37] prohibits [separating tithes] from [produce] of Samaritans
for [produce] of [other] Samaritans.

10 A perforated pot—
it has the status of earth.
[If one] separated *terumah* from [produce grown in] the ground

---

[36] K: "because."   [37] So K, P, and several manuscripts; other manuscripts and Tosefta: "Eliezer."

5:8 *fully untithed produce*: Produce from which neither tithes nor *terumah* have been taken.

two places: That is, two vendors.

tithes from the one for the other: Since both portions are known to be completely untithed, the potential problem of one being tithed and other not being tithed does not arise.

although the Sages *have said*: According to this version, the mishnah is ruling that despite having violated the law against selling untithed produce, the sellers' claim may still be believed, and the purchaser need not be concerned that one of the batches may have been tithed. **K** reads here "because they have said," implying a context of duress (see next comment) in which case one may believe the seller's testimony that the produce is untithed.

in case of need: In an emergency, such as when someone else's fully tithed produce has accidentally been mixed with fully untithed produce. *Terumah* and tithes must then be separated from other, fully untithed produce for the proportion of untithed produce in the mixture. In such a situation it is permitted to sell untithed produce to the person who needs it for this purpose, and they may believe one's testimony that the produce is indeed fully untithed.

5:9 *Gentiles*: Produce grown by gentiles in the Land of Israel is deemed liable for tithing, but is presumed to be fully untithed (cf. *Terumot* 3:9). One may therefore separate tithes from (untithed) Israelite produce for it and vice versa.

Samaritans: Produce grown by Samaritans in the Land of Israel likewise is deemed liable for tithing. Samaritans are assumed to tithe what they eat but not what they sell, so in this respect Samaritan produce that is being sold is deemed equivalent to gentile produce, and the same rule applies.

R. Eleazar holds that some Samaritans do indeed tithe the produce that they sell, just like some Israelites, so that each item must be tithed separately.

5:10 The background for all of these rulings is the rule that while one may separate *terumah* from one obligated item for another obligated item, if one separates *terumah* from a nonobligated item for an obligated item, or vice versa, the *terumah* so separated is invalid (see *Terumot* 1:5).

A perforated pot—it has the status of earth: A pot with a perforated bottom can allow a single root of the produce grown inside it to sink into the ground underneath; such produce is considered to have been

for [produce grown in] a perforated pot,
or from [produce grown in] a perforated pot
for [produce grown in] the ground—
his *terumah* is [valid] *terumah*.
[If he separated *terumah*] from [produce grown in a pot] that is not perforated
for [produce grown in one] that is perforated,
it is [valid] *terumah* but he must go back and separate *terumah* again.
[If he separated *terumah*] from [produce grown in a pot] that is perforated
for [produce grown in one] that is not perforated,
it is [valid] *terumah*, but it may not be eaten until he separates for it *terumah* and tithes.
   11 If one separated *terumah* from *demai*
for other *demai* [produce]
[or] from *demai*
for other produce known to be fully untithed—
it is [valid] *terumah*, but he must go back and separate *terumah* again.
[If he separated *terumah*] from produce known to be fully untithed
for other *demai* [produce]—
it is [valid] *terumah*, but it may not be eaten until he separates for it *terumah* and tithes.

grown in the ground (cf. *Uqtsin* 2:10). This renders the produce liable to the separation of *terumah* (cf. *Ma'aserot* 1:1, which rules that *terumah* must be separated from all edible produce that grows in the ground).

it is [valid] terumah but he must go back and separate terumah again from the produce grown in the perforated pot. Produce grown in an unperforated pot is not liable to the separation of *terumah* and tithes, since it does not grow in the ground. For this reason, *terumah* must be separated again for the produce grown in the perforated pot, either from the produce itself or from other produce liable to the same requirement. The putative "*terumah*" that has already been separated from the unperforated pot, even though it was not really necessary, must nonetheless be treated as valid and given to a priest, lest others think that it is being improperly handled (cf. *Terumot* 1:8; 3:1, 4:3). The priest may eat it forthwith, since it was never liable to tithing to begin with.

it is [valid] terumah, but it may not be eaten until he separates for it, that is, for the newly designated "*terumah*": Since the "*terumah*" that the priest has received was separated this time from produce grown in a perforated pot (liable) for produce grown in an unperforated pot (exempt), the separated portion itself remains untithed and is liable to have *terumah* separated from it or for it before the priest may consume it.

5:11 *If one separated terumah from demai for other demai* [produce]: Since *terumah* is assumed to have been separated from *demai*, by definition, the reference in this phrase must be *terumah* of the tithe. Since both items are in a state of doubt as to whether *terumah* of the tithe had been removed from them, the possibility exists that one has violated the rule against separating *terumah* from an obligated item for a nonobligated item or *vice versa*.

from demai for produce known to be fully tithed: The logic here is the same as in 5:10. Since *demai* is exempt from the separation of *terumah*, it is analogous to produce grown in an unperforated pot, and the same rulings follow.

Chapter Six

6:1–12 Tithing Produce that will be Given to Others: The Case of Shared Ownership

6 One who receives a field [as a sharecropper] from an Israelite, a gentile, or a Samaritan,
divides [the produce] in [the owner's] presence.
One who leases a field [as a tenant farmer] from an Israelite
must separate *terumah* [from the entire yield] and [then] give him [what he owes].
R. Judah said:
When [does this ruling apply]?
In the case in which [the tenant farmer] gave [the owner produce] of that very field and that very kind.
But if he gave him [produce] of a different field or of a different kind,
he must [also] separate tithes and [then] give him [what he owes].

2 One who leases a field [as a tenant farmer] from a gentile
must separate [*terumah* and] tithes [from the entire yield]
and [then] give him [what he owes].
R. Judah says:
So too, one who receives his ancestral field [as a sharecropper] from a gentile
separates [*terumah* and] tithes [from the entire yield] and [then] gives him [his share].

6:1 *One who receives a field [as a sharecropper]* takes for his work a fixed percentage of the total yield. The field remains in the possession of the landowner, who shares the attendant risks.

divides [the produce] in [the owner's] presence: Since the sharecropper owns only his portion, he is not obligated to separate anything, including *terumah* (see below), from the owner's portion; dividing it in front of them demonstrates that he has not separated anything on their behalf.

One who leases a field [as a tenant farmer] pays the owner a fixed amount of produce, regardless of the total yield. Since the lessee thereby bears all of the risks, he is deemed to own the field during the tenure of the lease.

separate terumah [from the entire yield]: Since *terumah* is routinely separated at the threshing-floor, the lessee must separate it before giving the owner his portion. He does not, however, need to separate any other tithes from the owner's fixed portion, since the owner is deemed to have owned it from the outset.

that very field which the owner leased to the tenant farmer *and that very kind* which the owner expected the leased field to produce.

[produce] of a different field or of a different kind, he must…give to him from the tithed produce *[what he owes]*, i.e. the rental fee. R. Judah qualifies the foregoing ruling by noting that, if the produce paid as rental to the owner is not what was originally contracted for, then it is not deemed to have belonged to the owner from the outset but to the lessee, who must tithe it before he gives it to someone else.

6:2 *One who leases a field [as a tenant farmer]…and then gives him* from the tithed produce *[what he owes]*, i.e. the rental fee. This ruling seems to hold (and see R. Judah in the next paragraph) that gentiles cannot really own property in the Land of Israel; for this reason, the gentile "owner's" share never belonged to him in the first place, but to the Israelite lessee, who routinely must tithe produce that he gives to another.

So, too, one who receives his ancestral field [as a sharecropper]…gives the gentile *his share* from the tithed produce. R. Judah holds that Israelite ownership of property in the Land of Israel can never be alienated, so the field, although "owned" by a gentile, is still deemed to belong to the family of the lessee, who must therefore separate tithes from any of its produce.

3 A priest or a Levite who received a field [as a sharecropper] from an Israelite—
just as they divide [between them] the nonsacral produce,
so they divide [between them] the *terumah* [or first tithe].
R. Eliezer says:
Also[38] the [*terumah* or] tithes belong to them [to the priest or Levite],
since for this purpose did they come [to sharecrop the field].

4 An Israelite who received [a field as a sharecropper] from a priest or a Levite—
the tithes belong to the owners.
R. Ishmael says:
A villager who received a field [as a sharecropper] from a Jerusalemite—
the second tithe belongs to the Jerusalemite.
But the Sages say:
The villager himself is able to go up[39] and eat it in Jerusalem.

5 One who receives olive trees [as a sharecropper] for oil [from a priest or a Levite]—
just as they divide [between them] the nonsacral produce,
so they divide [between them] the *terumah* [and tithes].
R. Judah says:
An Israelite who receives olive trees [as a sharecropper] from a priest or a Levite for oil[40]
for half of the profit [from its sale]—
the [*terumah* or] tithes belong to the owners.

---

[38] Or "indeed." Not present in **K, P**, and many manuscripts. [39] **K**: "to bring it up."
[40] **K, P**, and many manuscripts: "either for oil or for half of the profit."

6:3 *they divide [between them] the terumah [or first tithe]*: As at 6:1, the owner of a sharecropped field shares the risks, and thus owns his portion of the produce. He is therefore entitled to give the *terumah* and first tithe from his portion to whichever priest or Levite he chooses; it does not automatically go to the sharecropper when the latter is a priest or a Levite.

For this purpose did they come [to sharecrop the field]: R. Eliezer disagrees with the anonymous ruling: it is implicitly understood at the outset that a priest or Levite agrees to sharecrop a field in order to receive the *terumah* or tithe from that field.

6:4 *the tithes belong to the owners*: This is the reverse of the previous case. When the owner of a field is a priest or a Levite, he may exact *terumah* or tithe from the sharecropper's portion of the produce; as the field's owner, he has the upper hand over the sharecropper in these circumstances.

second tithe belongs to the Jerusalemite: The logic of R. Ishmael's position here is that of the previous case: since second tithe must in any event be eaten in Jerusalem, the field's owner has the upper hand and can assert his rights to the sharecropper's portion of the tithe. The Sages deny the analogy with the preceding case, for the reason stated: the landowner here does not hold the privileged position of the priestly landowner there, because any Israelite can eat second tithe when it has been brought to Jerusalem.

6:5 *so they divide [between them] the terumah [and tithes]*: Because olive oil is considered to be a secondary product of the olive tree, and not its "produce," the owner of the olive grove who is a priest or Levite cannot claim prior right to the *terumah* or tithe from the olive oil.

tithes belong to the owners: R. Judah rejects the above distinction between produce (olives) and what is manufactured from olives (olive oil), holding that the owner who is a priest or Levite still maintains his prior claim on all *terumah* or tithe, even when the agreement extends past the olive oil to the profits from its sale.

6 The House of Shammai say:
A person may sell his olives only to a Fellow.
The House of Hillel say:
Also to one who separates tithes.
But the more punctilious among the House of Hillel
would act according to the words of the House of Shammai.

7 Two [people] who gathered [the grapes of] their vineyards into a single winepress,
one [of whom] separates tithes and one who does not—
the one who separates tithes must tithe his own and his portion[41] wherever it may be.

8 Two [people] who [jointly] received a field as sharecroppers,
or who inherited [a field], or who became joint owners—
[the one who separates tithes] may say to [the other],
"You take the wheat in such-and-such a place
and I [will take] the wheat in such-and-such a place";
[or] "you [take] the wine in such-and-such a place
and I [will take] the wine in such-and-such a place."
But he may not say to him,
"You take the wheat and I [will take] the barley;
you take the wine and I will take the oil."

[41] Absent in **P**.

6:6 *A person may sell his olives only to a Fellow*: See 2:3 above. Olives are easily made susceptible to impurity, because they exude oil (see *Makhshirin* 6:4; cf. *Terumot* 3:4), and thus should be sold only to someone who will not let them become impure.

The House of Hillel say: Also to one who separates tithes: A distinctly unusual position in the context of this tractate, and marginalized by the next statement. Its logic is unclear: perhaps it is assumed that the olives will be eaten before they become susceptible to impurity. Whatever the logic, this position contradicts the requirement that those who are scrupulous about maintaining the purity of foodstuffs may not sell or give them to anyone who is not equally scrupulous. The Yerushalmi connects this position to *Shevi'it* 5:8, both examples of the House of Hillel undermining laws that create social boundaries between the observant and nonobservant.

6:7 *the one who separates tithes must tithe his own* share of the wine, commensurate with the amount of grapes he contributed.

his portion: The grapes of both owners have been thoroughly intermingled in the winepress, so every portion of wine removed will contain both the tithing owner's tithed wine and the nontithing owner's untithed wine. The owner who is scrupulous about tithing must therefore additionally separate tithes of *demai* even from his portion of the wine. (Alternatively, "his" refers to the nontither, and means that the tither must separate tithes of *demai* for the nontither's portion of untithed wine that has mixed with his tithed wine. The outcome is the same.)

6:8 *"You take the wheat in such-and-such a place…"*: In order to avoid having to separate tithes for the entire crop or giving untithed produce to someone who cannot be trusted subsequently to tithe it, the person who is meticulous about tithing may stipulate that the spatially localized portion that each one takes had belonged to him from the outset.

But he may not say to him, "You take the wheat and I [will take] the barley": This kind of stipulation, unlike the previous one, is not valid because both owners are deemed to share equally in all of the different crops that the field yields.

9 A Fellow and an *am ha'arets* who inherited [from] their father,
[who was] an *am ha'arets*—
[the Fellow] may say to [his brother],
"You take the wheat in such-and-such a place
and I [will take] the wheat in such-and-such a place";
[or] "you [take] the wine in such-and-such a place
and I [will take] the wine in such-and-such a place."
But he may not say to him,
"You take the wheat and I will take the barley;
you take the wet produce and I will take the dry produce."

10 A proselyte and a gentile who inherited [from] their father,
[who was] a gentile—
[the proselyte] may say to [his gentile brother],
"You take the idols and I [will take] the coins;
you [take] the wine and I [will take] the produce."
But if [he said this] after [the property] came into the proselyte's possession,
this is forbidden.

11 One who sells produce in Syria and says, "It is from the Land of Israel"—
[the purchaser] must tithe [the produce].
[But if the vendor said,] "It is tithed,"
he is believed,
for the mouth that forbade is the mouth that permitted.

6:9 *But he may not say to him, "…you take the wet produce*, which is susceptible to impurity (and may already have become impure if handled by the *am ha'arets* brother; see 2:3), *and I will take the dry produce*, which is not susceptible to impurity": Produce that is susceptible to impurity (wet) and that is insusceptible to impurity (dry) are deemed here to be heterogeneous, like different crops; both owners are deemed to share in them equally such that a retrospective division of ownership would be invalid.

6:10 *"You take the idols and I [will take] the coins; you [take] the wine and I [will take] the produce"*: This retrospective division of ownership is deemed valid because a proselyte is deemed to be a new person whose connections to his gentile family have been severed; he therefore has no automatic inheritance rights with respect to that family.

But if [he said this] after [the property] came into the proselyte's possession, this is forbidden: Although a proselyte has no automatic inheritance rights, he may, if he wishes, take possession through a formal act of acquisition. After doing so, he is deemed to share equally in all parts of the inheritance with his gentile siblings; he can no longer stipulate that the idols or libation-wine belong solely to them in exchange for other items, for he would thereby be deriving benefit from them and their value, which is prohibited.

6:11 *It is from the Land of Israel* and for this reason is liable to tithing, whereas produce grown in Syria by gentiles is not liable to tithing.

[the purchaser] must tithe [the produce]: Since the vendor could have said nothing, allowing the impression that the produce was grown in Syria by gentiles and therefore not subject to tithing, but instead has imposed a stringency on the produce, he is believed.

the mouth that forbade is the mouth that permitted: Having already indicated that the produce is subject to the strictures of tithing, when he simply could have kept silent, the vendor is believed further to say that the produce has already been tithed. See 4:6–7, above. For the principle "the mouth that forbade is the mouth that permitted," see *Ketubbot* chapter 2.

[If the vendor said,] "It is from my [field],"
[the purchaser] must tithe [the produce].
[But if the vendor said,] "It is tithed,"
he is believed,
for the mouth that forbade is the mouth that permitted.
But[42] if it was known that [the vendor] owned a field in Syria,
[the purchaser] must tithe [the produce].
  12 An *am ha'arets* who said to a Fellow,
"Buy for me a[43] bunch of vegetables,"
or "Buy for me one loaf of white bread"—
[the Fellow] may buy without specifying, and is exempt.
But if [the Fellow] said, "This one is mine and that one is my fellow's,"
and they became mixed together,
he must tithe, even if [the *am ha'arets*'s items of produce] are a hundred.

Chapter Seven

7:1–5 *Designating Tithes in Advance of the Sabbath*

7 One who invites his fellow to eat with him,
   but [the guest] does not trust him in the matter of tithing—
[the guest] says on the eve of the Sabbath,
"What I am about to separate tomorrow is hereby [first] tithe,

[42] K, P, and several manuscripts lack "But."   [43] K, P, and many manuscripts add "one."

"It is from my [field]": The produce is liable to tithing if the vendor is an Israelite. The fact that the vendor volunteers this information when he could have kept silent renders credible his subsequent statement that the produce already has been tithed.

But if it was known that [the vendor] owned a field in Syria, [the purchaser] must tithe [the produce]: In this circumstance, the vendor's statement that the produce comes from his field in Syria adds nothing to our previous knowledge, so his subsequent statement that the produce already has been tithed is not given credence.

6:12 *[the Fellow] may buy without specifying* which item is for himself and which is for the *am ha'arets, and is exempt* from tithing the item that he gives to the *am ha'arets*, because he may stipulate retrospectively, as in the cases above, that this had belonged to the *am ha'arets* from the outset.

7:1 *One who invites his fellow to eat with him*: On the Sabbath, when tithing is forbidden; see 1:4 and 4:1.

but [the guest] does not trust him: Cf. 4:2 above.

[the guest] says on the eve of the Sabbath: He stipulates before the Sabbath begins his conditional designation of those tithes that must be separated from the produce that he will eat at his host's house on the Sabbath. Then he may perform the physical act of separation at the other's house without having violated the Sabbath prohibitions, since this simply brings to its conclusion a process that had begun before the Sabbath. Regarding the tithing formula and its logic, see 5:1–2 above.

and the remainder of the [first] tithe is adjacent to it.
That which I have made [first] tithe is [now] made *terumah* from the tithe for it,
and second tithe is to the north of it, or to the south of it, and is desacralized with coins."

2 They mixed for him a cup [of wine]—
he says,
"What I am about to leave at the bottom of the cup is hereby [first] tithe,
and the remainder of the [first] tithe is adjacent to it.
That which I have made [first] tithe is [now] made *terumah* from the tithe for it,
and second tithe is at its mouth, and is desacralized with coins."

3 A laborer who does not trust the householder [in the manner of tithing]
removes a single dried fig and says,
"This one and the nine which follow it are made [first] tithe for the ninety that I [shall] eat.
This one is made *terumah* from the tithe for them,
and second tithe is in the last one,[44] and is desacralized with coins."
And he must leave over one dried fig.
R. Simeon b. Gamaliel says:
He must not leave over [a fig],
for he [thereby] lessens the work for the householder.
R. Yose says:
He need not leave over [a fig], for it is a condition imposed by the court.

4 One who purchases wine from among the Samaritans says,
"The two *log* that I shall separate are [hereby] *terumah*,

[44] Or "at the end." **K**, **P**, and some other witnesses read (correctly) "in the last ones."

7:2 *They mixed for him a cup [of wine]*: Continuing the topic of 7:1, what follows is the formula for designating in advance and separating *terumah* from the tithe from a liquid when the proper amount of tithe cannot be measured and separated out in advance of designation.

7:3 *A laborer who does not trust the householder*: That is, his employer, who feeds his laborers while they are at work (*Bava Metsi'a* 7:1–2).

terumah from the tithe for them: For the following nine figs, which are the remainder of the first tithe, and which he may eat.

second tithe is in the last one[s] and is thereby localized. These may be eaten by the worker once they have been desacralized with coins; see *Ma'aser Sheni*.

And he must leave over: For the priest, i.e. refrains from eating one fig from the meal his employer has provided him.

lessens the work: that is, the amount of work he is capable of performing *for the householder* by not eating the full meal that his employer has provided. Rather, the fig should come from the employer's produce instead of the worker's meal.

it is a condition imposed by the court that the employer pays *terumah* from the tithe for food that he provides his employees while on the job.

7:4 *One who purchases wine from among the Samaritans*: This refers to a situation in which the purchaser cannot separate tithes at present (e.g. it is just before the Sabbath), but wishes to drink the wine on the spot (or on the morrow on the Sabbath). The assumption here is that Samaritans do not separate agricultural offerings at all from produce that they sell.

The two log that I shall separate after the Sabbath *are [hereby] terumah*: Standard *terumah* is calculated at one-fiftieth part of the whole (cf. *Terumot* 4:3).

and [the following] ten [*log* are hereby first] tithe,
and [the following] nine [*log* are hereby] second tithe."
He regards [the wine] as nonsacral produce,[45] and drinks it.

5 [If] one had at home fully untithed figs,
and he was in the house of study or in the field,
he may say,
"The two figs that I shall separate are hereby *terumah*,
and [the following] ten are [first] tithe,
and [the following] nine are second tithe."
[If] they were *demai*,
he says,
"What I shall separate tomorrow[46] is hereby [first] tithe,
and the remainder of the [first] tithe is adjacent to it.
That which I made [first] tithe is [now] made *terumah* from the tithe for it,
and second tithe is to the north of it, or to the south of it,
and is desacralized with coins."

7:6–8 *Tithes from One Category of Produce for Another; Mixtures*

6 If there were before him two baskets of fully untithed produce,
and he said,
"The tithes of this one are in that one,"[47]
the first one is tithed.

---

[45] Meaning and translation uncertain.
[46] K originally lacked "tomorrow," which was added in the margin.
[47] K adds "and of this one in that one."

---

nine [log are hereby] second tithe: Only nine *log* are designated second tithe, since this is figured as a tenth of what remains after first tithe (ten *log*) has been separated.

He regards [the wine] as nonsacral produce: Meaning uncertain. As translated here, the clause is to be understood as follows: Because *terumah*, which is forbidden to nonpriests, is still intermingled with the wine that the purchaser is about to drink, he regards that portion of the wine that he will drink as nonsacral produce. Later, when he physically separates the tithes, he will hold retrospectively that all of the *terumah* is located in that part of the wine that remains in the wineskin.

7:5 The two figs that I shall separate: Corresponding to the ruling at 7:4, what follows is the formula for designating both *terumah* and tithes to be separated at some future time from discrete, homogeneous items of dry produce that are fully untithed. Again, two figs out of one hundred (one-fiftieth) are designated as *terumah*, and the rest follows as at 7:4.

[If] they were demai: But from which *terumah* had been separated. The formula that follows corresponds to that at 7:1, since here, too, the tithe will be physically separated in the future.

What I shall separate tomorrow: One fig out of one hundred.

7:6 the first one is tithed: So that he may eat from it and separate tithes for it from the second basket.

the first one is tithed [but not the second]: The first clause takes effect as soon as it has been uttered: the first basket is deemed to be fully tithed, regardless of the speaker's larger intentions. Tithes can no longer be

[If he said, "The tithes] of this one are in that one,
and [the tithes] of that one are in this one,"
the first one is tithed [but not the second].
[If he said,] "Their tithes are [designated such that] the tithes of each basket are in the other,"
he has [validly] designated.[48]

7 [A mixture of] one hundred [parts] of untithed produce
[and] one hundred [parts] of nonsacral[49] produce—
he removes [from the mixture] 101 [parts].
[A mixture of] one hundred [parts] of untithed produce
[and] one hundred [parts] of [first] tithe—
he removes [from the mixture] 101 [parts].[50]
[A mixture of] one hundred [parts] of tithed[51] nonsacral produce
[and] one hundred [parts] of [first] tithe—
he removes [from the mixture] 110 [parts].

[48] K appears to conflate the second and third clause: "[If he said, 'The tithes] belonging to this one are in this one and belonging to this one are in this one,' their tithes are the tithes of each basket in the other; he has validly designated."
[49] i.e. fully tithed.   [50] This whole clause is originally missing in K, but added in the margin.
[51] Lit. "set right." See 3:1; 4:7.

designated for the second basket from the first, for this now is equivalent to separating tithes for produce that is liable to tithing (the second basket) from produce that has already been tithed (the first basket). (See 5:10–11 and *Terumot* 1:5.) The second half of the formula therefore has no effect.

he has [validly] designated tithes for both of them, since the verbal designations are now phrased so that they take place simultaneously.

7:7 *one hundred [parts] of untithed produce*: The continuation of the ruling makes clear that "untithed produce" here refers to produce that has had *terumah* and first tithe separated from it, rather than fully untithed produce (even though the Hebrew term used here, *tevel*, usually refers to the latter).

[A mixture of] one hundred [parts] of untithed produce [and] one hundred [parts] of nonsacral produce from which one wishes to separate *terumah* from the tithe for its untithed portion.

he removes [from the mixture] 101 [parts]: *Terumah* from the tithe is one-hundredth part of the whole. One hundred and one parts are removed and given to the priest to make certain that one of those parts in fact has come from the untithed portion of the mixture, although we do not know which one it is.

[A mixture of] one hundred [parts] of untithed produce [and] one hundred [parts] of [first] tithe, from which one wishes to separate *terumah* from the tithe for both the untithed produce and the first tithe.

he removes [from the mixture] 101 [parts]: The logic is identical to that of the previous case: one of the 101 parts definitely comes from the untithed produce. But since the remaining one hundred parts separated in this case are deemed to be first tithe, ten of those also now will be *terumah* from the tithe (one tenth of the first tithe)—so a total of eleven of the 101 parts have been designated as *terumah* from the tithe, although it is not possible to know which of the separated parts are the eleven.

[A mixture of] one hundred [parts] of tithed nonsacral produce [and] one hundred [parts] of [first] tithe, from which one wishes to separate *terumah* from the tithe for the portion that is first tithe.

he removes [from the mixture] 110 [parts]: Since *terumah* from the tithe is one-tenth of the first tithe, 110 parts are removed, to make certain that the requisite ten parts have come from the first tithe.

[A mixture of] one hundred [parts] of untithed produce
and ninety [parts] of [first] tithe,
[or] ninety [parts] of untithed produce and eighty [parts] of [first] tithe—
he has lost nothing.
This is the general rule:
As long as the untithed produce is [sufficiently] greater in quantity,
he has lost nothing.

8 One who had ten rows, each containing ten jars of wine,
and he said,
"One outside row is [hereby first] tithe,"[52]
but it is not known which one it is—
he removes two jars from diagonally opposite corners.
[If he said,] "A half of one outside row is [hereby first] tithe,"
and it is not known which one it is—
he removes four jars from the four corners.
[If he said,] "One row is [hereby first] tithe,"[53]
and it is not known which one it is—
he removes one row diagonally.
[If he said,] "A half of one row is [hereby first] tithe,"

[52] K vocalizes this phrase as "The outside row is one out of ten" here and below.
[53] Originally vocalized in K as "one row out of ten" and corrected.

[A mixture of] one hundred [parts] of untithed produce and ninety [parts] of [first] tithe, or ninety [parts] of untithed produce and eighty [parts] of [first] tithe, from which one wishes to separate *terumah* from the tithe for both the untithed produce and the first tithe.

he has lost nothing: That is, he needs to separate only those ten parts from the mixture (or eight and nine-tenths parts in the second case) that are actually designated as *terumah* from the tithe and need not forfeit to the priest an additional quantity of produce, as had to be done in each of the preceding cases. Since there is now a sufficiently large excess of untithed produce in the mixture, all the *terumah* from the tithe can be quantitatively attributed to that portion.

7:8 *One who had ten rows, each containing ten jars of wine* from which *terumah* already has been separated. The question here, as in the previous paragraph, is how to account for the *terumah* from the tithe, which may not be eaten by a nonpriest.

One outside row is [hereby first] tithe for the hundred jars.

he removes two jars from diagonally opposite corners, one of which certainly is first tithe and so can be made *terumah* from the tithe for the hundred jars, since the end points of both diagonals are also the end points of the four outside rows.

A half of one outside row is [hereby first] tithe for fifty jars.

he removes four jars from the four corners, one of which certainly is *terumah* from the tithe for the fifty jars, since the end points of the four diagonals are also the end points of all eight of the outside half-rows.

One row is [hereby first] tithe for the hundred jars.

he removes one row diagonally, in which one of the jars certainly is *terumah* from the tithe for the hundred jars, since each of the ten rows includes one point on the diagonal.

A half of one row is [hereby first] tithe for fifty jars.

and it is not known which one it is—
he removes two rows diagonally.
[If he said,] "A single jar is [hereby first] tithe,"
and it is not known which one it is—
he removes [a tenth part] from each and every jar.

he removes two rows diagonally, in which one jar certainly is *terumah* from the tithe for the fifty jars, since each of the twenty half-rows includes one point on one or the other diagonal.

A single jar is [hereby first] tithe for ten jars.

he removes [a tenth part] from each and every jar, that is, from each of the hundred jars, one of these parts certainly being *terumah* from the tithe for the ten jars. All one hundred parts are given to the priest, since it is not known which of them is the actual *terumah* from the tithe. Commentators note that the priest reimburses the value of the ninety-nine parts that are not his due.

Tractate Kilayim

Michael Rosenberg

Introduction

Overview

Tractate *Kilayim* ("Mixed Species") is the fourth tractate in the Order of *Zera'im*. The tractate details and expands upon the prohibitions in the Torah regarding mixing species of plants and animals for various purposes. Leviticus 19:19 states: *You shall observe my laws. You shall not let your cattle mate with a different kind; you shall not sow your field with two kinds of seed; you shall not put on cloth from a mixture of two kinds of material.* Deuteronomy 22:9–11 relates a very similar, but not identical, set of rulings: *You shall not sow your vineyard with a second kind of seed, else the crop—from the seed you have sown—and the yield of the vineyard may not be used* (lit. else the crop…and the yield…be consecrated). *You shall not plow with an ox and an ass together. You shall not wear cloth combining wool and linen.* The name of the tractate is taken from the word used in both of these biblical passages (the only places in which it appears in the Hebrew Bible) and which seems to mean something like "two kinds," here understood to mean "prohibited mixtures." In addition to the unusual word *kilayim*, the biblical verses—both in Leviticus and in Deuteronomy—feature the word *sha'atnez* to describe forbidden mixtures in clothing (see 9:8).

Structure and Organization of the Tractate

The tractate contains nine chapters. Chapter 1 deals primarily with boundary questions regarding species and modes of planting that may or may not constitute a violation of the Torah's prohibition. The end of the chapter transitions to the topic of chapters 2 and 3, which is the mixture of various species in fields of grain and trees. Chapters 4 through 7 deal with the laws of foreign species in vineyards. Chapter 8 discusses the prohibition of yoking together animals of various species, and chapter 9 concludes the tractate with a treatment of the prohibition of clothing containing a mixture of linen and wool.

Main Ideas

Much of the tractate is devoted to determining whether a given mixture (of grains, vegetables, "seeds," vines, animals, or clothing) violates any of the Torah's prohibitions. It also spends much time defining the boundaries of fields and especially of vineyards, in order to establish the distances at which the prohibition of mixed planting is no longer operative. Another recurrent concern is whether certain acts should be prohibited for appearance's sake because they may appear to violate a Torah prohibition even though in reality they do not (see 3:5, 9:2).

In particular, the rabbis understand the Hebrew root *q-d-sh* ("consecrate") in Deuteronomy 22:9 to mean that the prohibition of mixed species in a vineyard is more severe than that in fields; mixed species in a vineyard may not provide any benefit to its owner, whereas the presence of mixed species in a field is permitted to yield some benefit (e.g. it may be sold).

Relationship to Scripture

Much of the law in the tractate can be read as filling in the gaps and harmonizing the differences between the two versions of the prohibition in Leviticus and Deuteronomy. Leviticus 19:19 details three prohibitions: (1) the breeding of different species of animals with each other; (2) the planting of two species in the same field; and (3) the wearing of garments containing two different kinds of material. In Deuteronomy 22, as in Leviticus 19:19, combinations of plant life, animal species, and clothing materials are forbidden; however, several significant differences appear. First, and most obviously, whereas Leviticus prohibits *breeding* different animal species, Deuteronomy forbids plowing with different species yoked together. Second, while Leviticus presents a general prohibition on wearing clothing containing mixtures of any "two kinds of material," Deuteronomy singles out the combination of linen and wool. Of course, while these two materials may simply represent a typical example of such a combination—as may well be the case with the mention of "an ox and an ass" in the prohibition on working two different species together—the rabbis focus on this specification to limit the prohibition to precisely that combination (see 9:1). Similarly, in Deuteronomy 22, the prohibition of mixing agricultural species is discussed in the context of a "vineyard" rather than a "field," as was the case in Leviticus 19:19, which the rabbis interpret to suggest different rules for the different agricultural settings. Finally, Deuteronomy uses the root *q-d-sh* ("consecrate") in connection with mixed seeds in a vineyard, which the rabbis understand to indicate a more severe prohibition than the one which applies to mixed seeds in general.

Special Notes for the Reader

As is the case with all of the Order of *Zera'im* other than Tractate *Berakhot*, there is no Bavli on this tractate, but there is Tosefta and there is Yerushalmi, which have been relied on by both traditional and modern commentators to help make sense of various obscure passages.

Many of the species mentioned in this tractate are difficult to identify with confidence; the translations should be understood as no more than approximations.

Tractate Kilayim

Chapter One

1:1–6 *Mixed Species*

1 Wheat and vetches
do not constitute Mixed Species one with the other.
Barley and oats,
spelt and rye,
beans and *sappir*,
grass pea and red pea,
and white beans and kidney beans
do not constitute Mixed Species one with the other.
   2 Armenian cucumber and muskmelon
do not constitute Mixed Species one with the other.
R. Judah says:
They do constitute Mixed Species.
Lettuce and wild lettuce,
endives and field endives,
leeks and field leeks,
coriander and field coriander,
mustard and Egyptian mustard,
and Egyptian gourd and bitter gourd,
and Egyptian beans and carob
do not constitute Mixed Species one with the other.
   3 Turnip and cabbage-turnip,
and cabbage and cauliflower,
beet [greens] and sorrel
do not constitute Mixed Species one with the other.[1]
R. Aqiva added:
Garlic and wild garlic,
onions and dwarf-onions,

---

[1] A number of manuscripts, including **K** and **P**, lack "do not constitute Mixed Species one with the other."

1:1 *vetches*: A kind of weed that commonly grows with cereal grains.

sappir: Some species of bean, perhaps *Vicia narbonensis*.

and lupines and wild lupine
do not constitute Mixed Species one with the other.

4 And with regard to trees:
pears and Crustuminum pear,
and quinces and hawthorns
do not constitute Mixed Species one with the other.
Apples and crab-apples,
and peaches and almonds,
and plums and lote fruit—
even though they resemble each other,
they constitute Mixed Species one with the other.

5 Radish and cabbage-turnip,
mustard and charlock,
Greek gourd with the Egyptian and bitter gourd—
even though they resemble each other,
they constitute Mixed Species one with the other.

6 The wolf and the dog,
the wild dog and the jackal,
goats and gazelles,
wild goats and sheep,
the horse and the mule,
the mule and the donkey,
the donkey and the wild donkey—
even though they resemble each other,
they constitute Mixed Species one with the other.

1:7–9 *Grafting and Cross-Fertilization of Trees and Vegetables*

7 One may not graft[2] a tree onto a tree,
a vegetable onto a vegetable,
nor a tree onto a vegetable,
nor a vegetable onto a tree.
R. Judah permits [grafting] a vegetable onto a tree.

8 One may not plant vegetables in the trunk of a sycamore.
One may not graft fringed rue onto thorny broom,
because that is a vegetable onto a tree.
One may not plant a fig-shoot in sea squills so that it will cool it.

[2] Lit. "bring."

1:7 *One may not graft*: Combinations of any differing species, whether trees or "vegetables" (which refers to any produce that grows from the ground, thus including, for example, watermelon, as in the next mishnah) are forbidden.

R. Judah permits [grafting] a vegetable onto a tree: Because he believes that fruits and vegetables cannot in fact interbreed, such that the grafting will not yield new species in any case. The Tosefta explains that R. Judah also permits the grafting of fruits onto vegetable-producing plants.

1:8 *trunk of a sycamore*: After the tree has been cut down.

so that it will cool it: Even though the intent is not to interbreed, but rather to cool the fig shoots.

One may not stick a vine-branch into a watermelon so that it will pour its juices into it,
because that is a tree onto a vegetable.
One may not place a gourd-seed into mallows so that it will protect it,
because that is a vegetable onto a vegetable.

9 One who stows turnips or radishes beneath a vine—
if some of its leaves were uncovered,
he need not concern himself about Mixed Species,
or about the Seventh Year,
or about tithes.[3]
And they may be moved on the Sabbath.
One who plants a grain of wheat and a grain of barley as one,
this thereby constitutes Mixed Species.
R. Judah says:
It does not constitute Mixed Species
unless there are two grains of wheat and a grain of barley,
or a grain of wheat and two grains of barley,
or a grain of wheat and a grain of barley and a grain of spelt.

Chapter Two

2:1–2 *Amount of Foreign Species Needed to Create Mixed Species*

2 Any *se'ah* in which there is a quarter[-*qav*][4] of some other species[5]—
one may decrease it.

---

[3] K swaps "Seventh Year" and "tithes." [4] K, P, and many manuscripts add "of seed."
[5] K, P, and several other manuscripts have "of one species."

1:9 *One who stows*: Stowing a vegetable in the ground is not the same as planting it; hence the legal consequences of stowing are not the same as those of planting. See also *Shevi'it* 5:2.

the Seventh Year: The requirement to let the land lie fallow every seventh year (Leviticus 25; *Shevi'it*).

tithes: See *Demai* and *Ma'aserot*.

moved on the Sabbath: Items not intended for use on the Sabbath may not be moved on the Sabbath; see *Shabbat* chapters 17–18. Since the turnip/radishes were stowed, not planted, they may be moved.

One who plants a grain…this constitutes mixed species: This line effectively begins a new section in the tractate (which runs until 3:7), focusing on the mixing of seeds and opening with a discussion about the minimum amounts for mixed species to be considered forbidden.

2:1 *se'ah*: A unit of measurement of volume, approximately twelve liters.

quarter[-qav]: Another unit of measurement of volume. There are six *qavs* in a *se'ah*. Thus, the mishnah is discussing a situation in which a *se'ah* of seeds of one species have seeds of a different species mixed in, where that second species constitutes at least 1/24 of the mixture.

decrease it: That is, one need only take out enough of the second species such that it makes up less than 1/24 of the total volume rather than uprooting all of the other species.

R. Yose says:
One must sort it.
[The law is the same] whether it is of one species or of two species.
R. Simeon says:
They spoke only [where it is] of one species.
But the Sages say:
Anything that constitutes Mixed Species with regard to the *se'ah* counts toward the quarter-[*qav*].

2 When does this apply?
Grains with grains,
and legumes with legumes,
grains with legumes,
and legumes with grains.
Nevertheless[6] they said:[7]
Inedible seeds of garden produce count
at one part out of twenty-four of the amount planted in a *se'ah*-sized field.
R. Simeon says:
Just as they spoke stringently, so too they spoke leniently:
flax [seeds] in grains count
at one part out of twenty-four of the amount planted in a *se'ah*-sized field.

---

[6] Lit. "In truth."   [7] **K, P**, and many manuscripts lack "they said."

---

sort it: The commentaries understand this to mean that one must entirely remove the quarter-*qav* of secondary species; it is not sufficient merely to remove enough of the secondary species to reduce it to less than $\frac{1}{24}$ of the total mixture.

whether it is of one species or of two species: This line seems to be a commentary on the anonymous opening position and also that of R. Yose: It does not matter whether the quarter-*qav* of secondary species is itself composed of only one secondary species, or of two. In other words, any intrusion of species other than that providing the primary identity of the field in an amount greater than $\frac{1}{24}$ of the total amount of seed constitutes prohibited mixed species. This position is restated by the Sages below.

They spoke only: This phrase limits the scope of the initial clause, producing a more lenient interpretation of the Sages' initial intent. According to the version in the manuscripts, the initial clause in fact read "from *one* species" (rather than "from *another* species"), in which case R. Simeon would be emphasizing the initial formulation in order to refute the expansive interpretation just offered, with which he disagrees. The two versions differ by a single letter.

of one species: R. Simeon disagrees with the previous statement, opining that the Sages only intended to rule that a prohibited mixture is created when at least $\frac{1}{24}$ of the total volume of seed comes from a single infiltrating species.

with regard to the se'ah: That is, with regard to the species that provides the dominant identity of the *se'ah* of seeds.

2:2 *When does this apply?* When does the standard of $\frac{1}{24}$ of the total volume apply?

Inedible seeds: That is, seeds that cannot themselves be eaten, but which are planted to produce some other edible part of a plant.

count: Toward the amount of foreign seed to generate a prohibited mixture.

at one part out of twenty-four ... in a se'ah-sized field: A *se'ah*-sized field is one large enough to be sown with a *se'ah*'s worth of grain. Inedible seeds are measured not based on their own volume, but rather, based on the

2:3–5 *Changing the Crop Composition of a Field*

3 If one's field was sown with wheat
and then he reconsidered and decided to sow it with barley instead—
he must wait until it rots[8] and [the soil] is turned,
and then he may sow [again].
If it had sprouted, he may not say:
"I will sow and then I will turn [the soil]";
rather, he must turn [the soil] and then he may sow.
How much must he plow?[9]
Like the furrows of the rainfall.
Abba Saul says:
Enough that there is not a quarter[-*qav*] left in any *se'ah*-sized field.
  4 If it was sown
and then he reconsidered and decided to plant [trees] instead,
he may not say:
"I will plant [trees] and then I will turn the soil";
rather, he must turn the soil and then he may plant [trees].
If it was planted [with trees]
and then he reconsidered and decided to sow it instead,
he may not say:
"I will sow and then I will uproot";

---

[8] Lit. "sprouts worms."   [9] **K, P**: "How much must be plowed?"

---

amount that would be planted in a field of such a size. Since the number of plants in a field does not grow proportionally with the size of the seeds, the volume of the seeds that would plant such a field will be larger or smaller depending on the size of the seed itself. If, for example, a certain species has small seeds such that a mere *qav* of these seeds would fill a *se'ah*-sized field, then for that species, $1/24$ of a *qav* of seeds of that species planted in a *se'ah*-sized field would be sufficient to generate a prohibited mixture.

so too they spoke leniently: If a certain species has very large seeds, such that more than a *se'ah*'s worth of seeds are needed to fill a *se'ah*-sized field, then the measure of that seed to create a prohibited mixture will be more than a quarter-*qav*. Flax, discussed in the next line, is an example of such a (relatively) large seed.

2:3 *If it had sprouted*: One might think that where the seeds had already sprouted, we could allow greater leniency, since the sprouts are visible, and thus the farmer will certainly remove all of the original crop. Some commentators suggest an alternative explanation as follows: when changing a field from one kind of grain to another, one must wait for the roots to rot, but if the original grain had already begun to sprout, then one may turn the soil immediately. The mishnah would thus read: "If one's field was sown…He should wait until the seed in the ground rots. Or, one turns the soil and then resows, in a case where it had already sprouted. One may not say…" This interpretation also has the benefit of creating a better parallel with 2:4.

How much must he plow? In the case where one turns the soil, how much does one need to plow?

furrows of the rainfall: Furrows intended to capture the rainwater, which are not particularly close together.

Enough: In other words, there must be a furrow in at least every quarter-*qav* of land (see above on 2:1).

rather, he must uproot and then he may sow.
If one wants, one may raze [the trees] to less than a handbreadth and sow, and then uproot.

5 If one's field was sown with hemp[10] or arum lilies,
he may not sow [something else] on top of them,[11]
for they produce only after three years.
Grain in which aftergrowths of woad sprang up,
and similarly the place of the threshing-floors,
in which many species sprang up,
and similarly fenugreek which sprouted weeds—
one is not required[12] to weed.
If[13] one weeded or trimmed [it],
they say to him,
"Uproot all of it other than one species."

2:6–3:7 *Prohibited and Permitted Mixed Plantings*

6 One who wants to make his field into distinct rows,
each of a different species—
the House of Shammai say:
Three ridges of a furrowed field,
but the House of Hillel say:
The size of a Sharonite yoke.
And the words of these are close to being like the words of those.

---

[10] K, prior to being corrected: "caraway." [11] Meaning of Hebrew obscure.
[12] Lit. "They do not require him." [13] K and other manuscripts: "but if."

2:4 *raze [the trees] to less than a handbreadth*: Extremely low-to-the-ground trees are too insignificant to be considered tree-plantings, such that one need not remove them prior to sowing grains in one's field, but even the stumps must eventually be uprooted.

2:5 *hemp*: Commentators prefer the reading found in K, "caraway," since the notion that caraway sometimes takes three years to sprout makes more sense than it does for hemp plants.

for they produce only after three years: That is, sometimes these plants do not produce for up to three years, such that the absence of growth is not necessarily an indicator that the field is now free of these original species.

aftergrowths of woad: Unintended growth from crops that had been previously planted in the field.

one is not required to weed: Since these growths are entirely incidental and out of the owner's control, one is not responsible for removing them.

If one weeded or trimmed: By leaving some of the unintended growth, the farmer has revealed a desire to have that which has been left, and therefore it must be removed completely.

2:6 *Three ridges of a furrowed field*: That is, the width of three of the kinds of furrows plowed in a field in order to develop its growing capacity. This refers either to the distance between each row or to the width of the rows themselves, which is significant enough to consider them an independent plot.

The size of a Sharonite yoke: The size of the yoke used to plow in the plains of Sharon.

7 If the corner[14] of [a field of] wheat
protruded[15] into [a field] of barley—
it is permitted,
because it looks like the end of its field.
If one's [field] was wheat and one's fellow's was of another species,
it is permitted to place near to it [a crop] of that species.
If one's [field] was wheat and one's fellow's was wheat,
it is permitted to place near to it a furrow of flax,
but not a furrow of some other species.
R. Simeon says:
[The law is] one and the same,
whether a seeding of flax or [of] any other species.
R. Yose says:
Even[16] in the middle of one's field
it is permitted to test [the land] with a furrow of flax.

8 One may not place mustard or safflower near a field of grain,
but one may place mustard or safflower near a field of vegetables.
And one may place[17] [a second species] near
untilled land,
or a plowed field,
or an uncaulked stone wall,
or a road,
or a fence that is [at least] ten handbreadths tall,
or a ditch that is [at least] ten deep and four wide,
or a tree that hangs over the earth,
or a rock that is [at least] ten high and [at least] four wide.

[14] Lit. "head of a row."   [15] Lit. "entered."   [16] K lacks "even."
[17] K: "One who places," which is corrected by a later scribe to be in line with the other witnesses.

2:7 *If the corner of [a field of] wheat protruded into* or abutted *[a field of] barley*.

because the corner looks like the end of its field: It is clear to onlookers that the abutting corner is the end of the wheat field, and not an imposition of wheat into what is otherwise a barley field.

to place near to it [a crop] of that species: One may plant the species found in one's neighbor's field in the part of one's own field abutting the other's field, since it will simply look like an extension of one's neighbor's field.

it is permitted to place near it a furrow of flax: Since flax was generally not grown in single furrows, a single furrow planted between the wheat fields of two different landowners would be immediately recognized as testing the arability of the land rather than as an act of agriculture.

Even in the middle of one's field: The use of a singular row of flax is so clearly not for agricultural purposes that one may even place it in the middle of one's own field, rather than having to put it on the border between two fields belonging to two different owners.

2:8 *one may place mustard or safflower*: The reason for this ruling is debated by the commentaries.

one may place [a second species] near: This introduces a list of things that serve as a separation between two fields to allow planting two different crops on either side.

hangs over the earth: A tree whose leaves droop down to or almost down to the ground creates a sufficient barrier between two fields.

9 One who wants to make his field into patches,
each of a different species,
may make twenty-four patches in each *se'ah*-sized field,
one patch for every quarter-[*qav*-]sized field,
and may sow in it whatever species he desires.
If there were one or two patches,
one may sow them with mustard.
If three, one may not sow them with mustard,
because it looks like a field of mustard—
the words of R. Meir.
But the Sages say:
Nine patches are permitted; ten are forbidden.
R. Eliezer b. Jacob says:
Even if his whole field is *kor*-sized—
one may not make in it other than one patch.

10 Anything within[18] the quarter-[*qav*-]sized field
counts towards the measurement of the quarter-[*qav*-]sized field.
An infesting vine,
or a grave,

[18] K: "Within" is absent, but it has been added in by a later hand in the margin.

2:9 *make his field into patches*: That is, one wishes to subdivide a larger field into multiple square plots in order to plant different species in them.

If three: Mustard is not generally planted in such large amounts, and thus three patches of mustard make the field look like a mustard field mixed with a wheat field.

But the Sages say: The Sages disagree not on the number of permissible mustard patches, but on the initial position that permitted twenty-four patches in a single *se'ah*-sized field. They only permit a maximum of nine subdivisions, which results in each subdivision being separated from the others by about the size of an entire subdivision.

kor-sized: A *kor* is thirty *se'ah*.

one patch: In other words, R. Eliezer b. Jacob only permits a single species to be planted in one field, no matter how large the field is.

2:10 *Anything within the quarter-[qav-]sized field counts*: That is, even nonarable land within the quarter-*qav*-sized patch counts as being sown with the foreign species.

A grain in a grain: That is, if one wishes to plant a different kind of grain near an already existing field, and similarly throughout.

quarter-[qav-]sized field: Two meanings have been suggested: first, fields large enough to produce a quarter-*qav* of produce are significant enough to be considered independent fields (see 2:9), such that two such fields containing different species may directly abut each other without being considered a prohibited mixture. Alternatively, it may mean that an empty area the size of a quarter-*qav*-sized field must interpose between two fields of different grains. Indeed, these are not contradictory and the mishnah may intend both; gaps are required between fields smaller than those which might produce a quarter-*qav* of produce, but not between those which can produce that amount. Both of these possibilities apply to the remaining lines of this mishnah as well.

or a rock—
all count towards the measurement of the quarter-[*qav*-]sized field.
A grain[19] in a grain—a quarter-[*qav*-]sized field.
A vegetable in a vegetable—six handbreadths.
A grain in a vegetable [or] a vegetable in a grain—a quarter-[*qav*-]sized field.
R. Eliezer says:
A vegetable in a grain—six handbreadths.
  11 A grain extending onto a grain,
or a vegetable extending onto a vegetable,
[or] a grain onto a vegetable,
[or] a vegetable onto a grain—
it is all permitted, other than Greek gourd.
R. Meir[20] says:
Also cucumber and Egyptian beans,
but I approve their words more than my own words.

Chapter Three

3 A six-handbreadth by six-handbreadth garden bed—
one may sow in it [up to] five [kinds of vegetable] seeds:
four in the four directions of the garden bed,
and one in the middle.
If it had a boundary a handbreadth high—
one may sow in it thirteen:

[19] K: "A grain" is absent, a clear mistake.
[20] The manuscripts have here "Rabbi," i.e. R. Judah the Prince.

six handbreadths: Although a handbreadth is usually a measure of distance and not yield, the reference may to be a garden bed six handbreadths square; see 3:1.

2:11 *extending onto*: In other words, a case where one planted in accordance with the law, but as a result of natural growth the produce is now intermingled.

Greek gourd: Which is particularly invasive in its growth and thus is more likely to appear as a prohibited mixture.

3:1 See *Shabbat* 9:2.

seeds: But cf. 3:2, which forbids seeds but permits vegetables.

four in the four directions of the garden bed and one in the middle: A field of 6 × 6 handbreadths is large enough that one can plant a different species on each side of the square-shaped field, as well as another species in the middle, and the five species can be kept separate enough that they will not appear to be mixed species. Alternatively, "four in the four directions" might mean one in each corner (as opposed to along each side).

one may sow in it thirteen: In order to understand how the boundary allows for more species to be sown in the garden bed, both Talmuds claim that the boundary, in addition to being a handbreadth high, as is stated in the mishnah, must also be a handbreadth wide, thus adding two handbreadths to both the width

three on each boundary
and one in the middle.
One may not plant a head of turnip on the boundary,
because it will fill it up.
R. Judah says:
Six in the middle.

2 One may not plant every kind of seed in a garden bed,
but[21] one may plant every kind of vegetable in a garden bed.
Mustard and smooth beans are kinds of seeds.
Camel bean is a kind of a vegetable.
A boundary that was a handbreadth high and became diminished
remains valid, because it was originally valid.
A furrow and a water channel that are a handbreadth deep—
one may plant three [kinds of] seeds inside of them,
one from here, one from here, and one in the middle.

3 If the corner of a vegetable [bed] protruded[22] into a field
of some other kind of vegetable [bed],
it is permitted, because it looks like the end of its field.
If one's field was sown with a vegetable,
and one wants to plant in it a row of another kind of vegetable—
R. Ishmael says:
[It is prohibited] unless the furrow had gone through[23]
from one side of the field to the other.

[21] K and others lack the conjunction.   [22] Lit. "entered."   [23] K, P: "was going through."

and the length of the garden bed. If one actually plants species on top of the boundary itself, as well as on both sides, this extra space allows for more plants to be sown while keeping an appropriate distance between them.

a head of turnip: A turnip root.

because it will fill it up: Turnips have fast-spreading leaves, and it will thus appear to be intermingled with the crops on that side.

Six in the middle: R. Judah argues that it is possible to fit six species in the middle of this bordered garden bed, and eighteen species in the garden bed as a whole; unfortunately he does not explain exactly how this can be done.

3:2 *One may not plant*: One may not take advantage of the previous mishnah's permission to plant.

seed…vegetable: The distinction between "seeds" and other agricultural crops in the tractate is not spelled out explicitly, but this mishnah may provide one criterion for distinction: size of plant. Commentators understand this mishnah as being based on the idea that "seeds" are those things generally planted in fields, while vegetables are often planted in much smaller garden beds.

valid: Even though the boundary no longer meets the parameters set out in 3:1, since it did when the species were planted, there is no need to uproot any of the plants.

3:3 *corner*: This mishnah applies the ruling of 2:7 above from grain fields to vegetable beds.

unless the furrow is open from one side of the field to the other: That is, one is not allowed to introduce the new vegetable unless there is a furrow that completely divides the field, separating the two kinds of vegetables from each other.

R. Aqiva says:
A length of six handbreadths and a width equal to its full width.
R. Judah says:
A width equal to the width of the sole of a foot.

4 One who plants two rows of cucumbers,
two rows of gourds,
[and] two rows of Egyptian beans—
it is permitted.
[One who plants] a row of cucumbers,
a row of gourds,
[and] a row of Egyptian beans—
it is forbidden.
A row of cucumbers,
a row of gourds,
a row of Egyptian beans,
and[24] a row of cucumbers—
R. Eliezer permits,
but the Sages forbid.

5 A person may plant cucumber and gourd in one hollow,
provided that this leans towards this side,
and this leans towards this side.
And the foliage of this one leans in this direction
and the foliage of this one in this direction.
For whatever the Sages forbade,
they decreed only because of appearance's sake.[25]

---

[24] P: "or." "A row of cucumbers...of Egyptian beans" is missing in K but added in the margin.
[25] K, P, and others lack the second half of this mishnah.

A length of six handbreadths: R. Aqiva disagrees and thinks any furrow of six handbreadths in length is long enough to be considered a barrier. Cf. the position of R. Judah in 3:1.

and a width equal to its full width: It is unclear what this phrase means. Some interpret it to mean that the furrow must be as wide at its top as at its bottom, rather than tapering in a pyramid shape. Other possibilities include that the furrow must have width equal to its length, or alternatively, width equal to its depth.

R. Judah: His position accepts R. Aqiva's length requirement, but modifies his width requirement.

3:4 *One who plants two rows*: Two rows of each crop create large enough plots that the species do not appear to be intermingled.

R. Eliezer permits: The fact of the repeated row of cucumbers demonstrates that he is planting in a fixed order rather than intermingling species. Cf. 3:6.

3:5 *And the foliage of this one leans in this direction and the foliage of this one in this direction*: Most likely, this phrase, which does not appear in most manuscripts, should be understood as an explanation of the preceding line.

appearance's sake: See 9:2 below. The phrase also appears in *Shevi'it* 3:4, *Shabbat* 19:6, and *Bekhorot* 7:5.

6 If one's field was sown with onions,
and one wants[26] to plant in it rows of gourds—
R. Ishmael says:
One uproots two rows and plants one row
and leaves a standing crop of onions in the place of two rows,
and uproots two rows[27] and plants one row.
R. Aqiva says:
One uproots two rows and plants two rows,
and leaves a standing crop of onions in the place of two rows,
and uproots two rows and plants two rows.
But the Sages say:
If there are not twelve cubits between a row and its neighbor,
one may not allow the seed in between to remain.

7 [One who wants to plant] a gourd in a vegetable [field]—
[it is treated] like a vegetable.
But[28] in a grain [field]—
one must give it a quarter-[*qav-*]sized field.
If one's field was sown with grain
and one wanted[29] to plant in it a row of gourds—
one must give it for[30] its work six handbreadths.
And[31] if it grew,

[26] P and others: "and wanted."
[27] K: "And uproots two rows" is missing but added in the margin.
[28] A later editor of K deletes the conjunction. [29] K: "wants," parallel to 3:6.
[30] K and others: "give it its work." P: "give [space] for its work." [31] K lacks the conjunction.

3:6 *onions*: "Onions" is likely not intended specifically, but rather is an example, and this would be true of any crop.

One uproots two rows and plants one row: This mishnah is predicated on the assumption that a "row" is four cubits wide. Thus, if one destroys two rows (= eight cubits) of the original crop ("onions"), and plants one row (= four cubits) of gourds in its place—locating the gourds in the middle of the razed former area of onions—then one will have two cubits on either side of this row of gourds. One then leaves two rows (= eight cubits) of onions standing, and begins the process again on the other side, thus creating another occurrence of two empty cubits, four cubits of gourds, and two cubits of empty space. Taken together, this leaves twelve cubits between each and every row of gourds.

R: Aqiva says: One uproots: R. Aqiva is more lenient, permitting one to make full use of the razed former space of onions for the planting of gourds. This then leaves only the space of standing onions—eight cubits—between each and every row of gourds.

If there are not twelve cubits: The Sages, like R. Ishmael, require twelve cubits between each and every row of the new species.

3:7 *In a vegetable…in a grain*: One wishes to plant gourd next to an existing vegetable or grain field.

like a vegetable: It is subject to the rule of vegetables, i.e. six handbreadths; see 2:10.

a quarter-[qav-]sized field: The same standard as for a vegetable in a grain—see above, 2:10.

one must give it for its work six handbreadths: All that is needed is to leave enough unsown space so as to work that row, i.e. six handbreadths. However, more space is not required, since an entire row of gourds is recognizable as a distinct unit in a way that a single gourd, as in the previous situation, simply is not.

And if it grew: If the row of gourds grew and intruded into the six handbreadths of working space.

one must uproot from before it.
R. Yose says:
One must give it its work four cubits.
They said to him:
Would you treat this more stringently than the vine?
He said to them:
We found that this is more stringent than the vine,
since to a single vine one must [only] give its work six handbreadths,
but to a single gourd one must give[32] a quarter-[*qav*-]sized field.
R. Meir says in the name of R. Ishmael:
Wherever there are three gourds within a *se'ah*-sized field,
one may not introduce seed into the *se'ah*-sized field.[33]
R. Yose b. ha-Hotef Efrati said in the name of R. Ishmael:
Wherever there are three gourds within a *kor*-sized field,
one may not introduce seed into the *kor*-sized field.

Chapter Four

4:1–4 *Unused Space in a Vineyard*

4 A patch in a vineyard—
the House of Shammai say:
Twenty-four cubits;

---

[32] **K, P**, and others lack "one must give."
[33] At this point in **K** some phrases are mistakenly duplicated and crossed out by a later hand.

---

four cubits: Which is equivalent to twenty-four handbreadths. In other words, R. Yose thinks that a greater amount of space is necessary in order to perform the necessary maintenance for that row.

Would you treat this more stringently than the vine? The prohibition of mixed seeds in a vineyard is generally held to a higher standard since those mixtures are prohibited even with regard to deriving benefit. See the introduction to the tractate, and below chapters 4–7. The argument is based on the position of the House of Hillel in 4:5, who rule that a single row of vines does not reach the more stringent requirements of a vineyard, and therefore only requires a distance of six handbreadths.

since to a single vine: As opposed to a row of vines; see 6:1.

but to a single gourd one must give a quarter-[qav-]sized field: As in the opening lines of this mishnah, as opposed to the row of gourds currently under discussion.

Wherever there are three gourds: This is a more restrictive view than either the anonymous opinion's six handbreadths or R. Yose's four cubits, and is apparently based on the concern that the leaves of these plants spread significantly; cf. 2:11 and 3:5.

within a kor-sized field: A *kor* is thirty times the size of a *se'ah*. This position is, therefore, even more restrictive, and may share some affinity with R. Eliezer b. Jacob's position in 2:9.

4:1 *A patch in a vineyard*: A space in a vineyard that has been razed of its vines.

Twenty-four cubits…sixteen cubits: The razed space must be at least twenty-four or sixteen square cubits in order to permit planting other kinds of seeds there.

but[34] the House of Hillel say:
Sixteen cubits.
The untilled ground surrounding the vineyard[35]—
the House of Shammai say:
Sixteen cubits;
but[36] the House of Hillel say:
Twelve cubits.
And what is the "patch in the vineyard"?
A vineyard which has been destroyed from its middle.
If there are not sixteen cubits there,
one may not introduce seed there.
If there were sixteen cubits,
one gives it its work,
and one may sow the remainder.
2 What is the "untilled ground surrounding the vineyard"?
Between the vineyard and the fence.
If there are not twelve cubits there,
one may not introduce seed there.
If there were twelve cubits there,
one gives it its work,
and one may sow the remainder.
3 R. Judah says:
This is only the fence of the vineyard.
What[, therefore,] is the "untilled ground surrounding the vineyard"?
Between the two vineyards.
What is a fence?

---

[34] **K** lacks the conjunction.   [35] Lit. "dancing space," here and below; see Judges 21:21.
[36] Conjunction initially absent in **K** and added by a later hand.

---

untilled ground: See 4:2.

destroyed in its middle: Again, an area in the middle of the vineyard that has been razed of its vines.

sixteen cubits: Following the position of the House of Hillel.

one gives it its work: See notes to 3:7.

4:2 *What is the "untilled ground"*: Mentioned in 4:1.

Between the vineyard and the fence: The empty space between the planted ground of the vineyard and the fence surrounding it.

twelve cubits: Following the position of the House of Hillel from 4:1.

4:3 *This is only the fence of the vineyard*: R. Judah disagrees with the definition of "the untilled ground surrounding the vineyard" provided in 4:2; he thinks the area between the vineyard and the fence should be called "the fence of the vineyard." (Commentators disagree over whether he thinks that one may plant other species there.) He proceeds to offer his own definition of the "untilled ground surrounding the vineyard."

Between the two vineyards: The "untilled ground surrounding the vineyard" refers to empty space between two vineyards; if this area is twelve cubits wide (according to the House of Hillel in 4:1), then one may plant a four-cubit row of some other species there.

a fence…a ditch: How high a fence or deep a ditch constitutes a boundary between two vineyards in and of themselves such that one would not need any empty space to begin planting a new species? See 2:8.

That which is ten handbreadths tall.
And a ditch?
That which is ten [handbreadths] deep and four wide.

4 A divider made of reeds—
if there are not three handbreadths between one reed and the next,
such that a goat could enter—
it is thereby like a divider.
And a fence that has been breached up to ten cubits—
it is thereby like a doorway.
Greater than this—
opposite the breach it is forbidden.
If many breaches were opened up in it—
if what [remains] standing is greater than what was breached,
it is permitted;
but[37] if what was breached is greater than what [remains] standing,
opposite the breach[38] is forbidden.

4:5–7 *Definition of a Vineyard*

5 One who plants a row of five vines—
the House of Shammai say:
It is a vineyard;
but[39] the House of Hillel say:
It is not a vineyard
until there are two rows there.[40]

---

[37] K lacks the conjunction.
[38] K originally lacks "opposite the breach", which is added by a later hand in the margin.
[39] K originally lacks the conjunction, which is added by a later hand.
[40] K, P, and many others lack "there."

4:4 *A divider made of reeds*: Which is therefore not perfectly solid.

such that a goat could enter: If the reeds are spaced far enough apart that a goat could plausibly pass through them, then such a divider does not truly serve as a barrier.

it is thereby like a doorway: Such a breach can be thought of as a reasonably sized entrance in a fence, but greater than this size must be considered an actual break in the fence.

opposite the breach it is forbidden: Since there is an actual break in the fence there is no clear boundary here, and thus different species may not be planted on the two sides of the partition parallel to this breach.

if what [remains] standing is greater than what is breached, it is permitted: If the sum total of the remaining portions of the partition is greater than the sum total of the breaches in the partition, then the entire thing is considered one continuous partition, such that one may plant different species anywhere along the partition.

but if what is breached is greater than what [remains] standing: If, however, the sum total of the breaches is greater than the sum total of the remaining portions of the partition.

opposite the breach is forbidden: One must treat each breach as separating two distinct partitions. In such a case, one may not plant different species on opposite sides of the partition parallel to the breaches, even if the breaches are smaller than ten cubits, since there is no meaningful partition there.

Therefore, one who sows four cubits within a vineyard—
the House of Shammai say:
One has "consecrated" one row;
but[41] the House of Hillel say:
One has "consecrated" two rows.

6 One who plants two [vines] opposite two [vines]
and one [vine] extends [like] a tail—
it is thereby a vineyard.
Two [vines] opposite two [vines] and one [vine] in between,
or two [vines] opposite two [vines] and one [vine] in the middle—
it is not a vineyard
until there are two [vines] opposite two [vines]
and one [vine] extends [like] a tail.

7 One who plants one row [of vines] within one's own [vineyard],
and one row within that of one's fellow,
and a private path or a public path is in the middle,
or a fence that is lower than ten handbreadths [is in the middle]—
these thereby combine.
If [the fence] was taller than ten handbreadths,
they do not[42] combine.

[41] K originally lacks the conjunction, which is added by a later hand.
[42] K originally has "they thereby combine"; "do not" is added in the margin.

4:5 *four cubits within a vineyard*: The four cubits that one must leave for the maintenance of a vine in a vineyard.

"consecrated": Rendered forbidden. See Deuteronomy 22:9 and the introduction to this tractate.

one row: The row of vines nearest the forbidden planting is now forbidden, and no benefit may be derived from it. Since the House of Shammai believe one row to constitute a vineyard, then the "vineyard" that becomes forbidden as a result of the intrusion of a foreign species can be understood as referring to the nearest single row.

two rows: Since the House of Hillel believe that a vineyard must contain at least two rows, two rows become forbidden. Parallel in *Eduyot* 5:2, where it is listed as one of the cases where the House of Hillel are stringent and the House of Shammai are lenient.

4:6 *two [vines] opposite two [vines] and one [vine] extends [like] a tail*: A formation of two parallel pairs of vines, with another vine planted alongside two of them but outside the square formed by imagining the first four vines as its corners, such that the additional vine appears like a tail.

in between…in the middle: These are two similar formations in which the fifth vine is planted within the square formed by imagining the four vines as its corners, rather than outside of it ("like a tail"). One appears to refer to a fifth vine planted alongside the edges of the square, "between" or "in the middle" of two of the vines, while the other refers to a fifth vine planted "between" or "in the middle" of the sides of the square, i.e. inside the square itself, but not along the edges of the imagined square. In either case, since we have a square-shaped formation of vines with nothing extending beyond that square, the definition of "vineyard" has not been met.

4:7 *one row…within one's own…and one row within that of one's fellow*: If someone planted one row of vines on his own property and another row on the adjoining property.

these thereby combine: They are counted as two contiguous rows and thus create a vineyard.

R. Judah says:
If one connected them from above, they thereby combine.

4:8–5:4 Appropriate Space between Rows

8 One who plants two rows:
if[43] there are not eight cubits between them,
one may not introduce seed there.
If they were three [rows]:
if there are not[44] between one row and the next sixteen[45] cubits,
one may not introduce seed there.
R. Eliezer b. Jacob says in the name of Hananiah b. Hakhinai:
Even if the middle [row] was destroyed,
and there are not[46] between one row and the next sixteen[47] cubits,
one may not introduce seed there,
whereas if one had originally planted them,
this would thereby be permitted with eight cubits.

9 One who plants one's vineyard with gaps of sixteen cubits,
it is permitted to introduce seed there.
R. Judah said:
It once happened in Tsalmon[48]
that someone planted his vineyard with gaps of sixteen cubits,

---

[43] K has "and" instead of "if."   [44] K: "not" is absent and added above the line.
[45] K: "twelve."   [46] K: "not" is absent and added above the line.
[47] K: "twelve."   [48] K, P, and most manuscripts: "Tsalmin."

If one connected them from above: If one passed the vines from these two rows over the ten-handbreadth-tall boundary, creating an arbor, they are treated as two contiguous rows despite the existence of a meaningful boundary between them.

4:8 *If there are not eight cubits between them, one may not introduce seed there*: A gap of less than this amount implies that these rows were planted together and that they therefore form a vineyard. A gap greater than eight cubits, however, is sufficiently large that one can view these two rows as independent of each other.

If they were three: If one had planted three rows initially.

If there are not between one row and the next sixteen cubits, one may not introduce seed there: Three rows suggest a larger, more spacious vineyard, and thus any gap less than sixteen cubits may reasonably be viewed as merely a gap within a vineyard. Only when the space between rows is greater than sixteen cubits can one reasonably view the rows as independent of each other.

Even if the middle [row] was destroyed, and there are not between one row and the next sixteen cubits: Removing the middle row would leave the landowner with only two rows, but since the area was originally planted with three rows, the standard of the larger vineyard is still in effect, such that the area is subject to the rules of vineyards unless there is a gap of sixteen cubits or more between the remaining rows.

4:9 *it is permitted to introduce seed there*: Presumably the requirement of leaving six handbreadths from each individual vine for space to perform maintenance (see above, 3:7) still applies.

Tsalmon: Likely modern-day Salama, in the lower Galilee.

and[49] he would direct the foliage of two rows to one side
and sow the clear land.
And[50] in the next year he would direct the foliage to another place[51]
and sow the fallow land.
And the case came before the Sages, and they permitted.
R. Meir and R. Simeon say:
So too one who plants one's vineyard with gaps of eight cubits—
it is permitted.

Chapter Five

5 A vineyard that was destroyed—
if there remains enough so as to collect ten vines within a *se'ah*-sized field
and they are planted in their customary way,[52]
this is thereby called an "impoverished" vineyard.
A vineyard that is planted in a motley fashion—
if one can discern two opposite three, this is thereby [deemed] a vineyard;
but if not, it is not [deemed] a vineyard.
R. Meir says:
Since it appears to be in the form of vineyards,
it is thereby [deemed] a vineyard.
2 A vineyard that is planted with gaps of less than four cubits
[between the rows of vines]—
R. Simeon says:
It is not [deemed] a vineyard.
But the Sages say:
It is [deemed] a vineyard,

[49] **K, P** lack the conjunction.
[50] The conjunction is erased by a later hand in **K**.
[51] **K, P**: "to the place of the seeds."
[52] Or "according to their *halakhah*."

he would direct the foliage of two rows to one side: So that the leaves did not hang over the species planted in between the rows.

And in the next year: So as not to overfarm any particular piece of land.

5:1 *to collect ten vines*: That is, to collect grapes *from* ten vines.

they are planted in their customary way: Their formation meets the legal definition of a vineyard described in 4:6: two vines parallel to three.

5:2 *It is not [deemed] a vineyard*: Such gaps are too small to signal the planning of a vineyard. Each vine is therefore viewed as an independent vine, subject only to the requirement of a separation of six handbreadths for its maintenance separating between it and the planting of other crops.

and the middle rows are viewed[53] as if they were not there.

3 A ditch, ten [handbreadths] deep and four wide,
which passes through a vineyard—
R. Eliezer b. Jacob says:
If it had gone through[54] from one side of the vineyard to the other,
it thereby appears as if it is between two vineyards,
and one may sow in it.
But if not, it is thereby like a winepress.
And[55] a winepress in a vineyard that is ten [handbreadths] deep and four wide—
R. Eliezer says:
One may sow in it;
but the Sages forbid.
A watchtower in a vineyard that is ten [handbreadths] tall and four wide—
One may sow in it.[56]
But[57] if the branches became intertwined, it is forbidden.

4 A vine that is[58] planted in a press or in a ravine—
one gives it its work and one may sow the remainder.
R. Yose says:
If there are not four cubits there,
one may not introduce seed there.
And[59] the house that is in the vineyard—
one may sow in it.

[53] Lit. "they view the middle rows."   [54] **K, P**: "was going through."
[55] **K, P**, and many others lack the conjunction.
[56] **K, P**, and most manuscripts: "One may sow its top."
[57] **K** lacks the conjunction.   [58] A scribe of **K** overwrote the word "is" with "was."
[59] **K** lacks the conjunction.

and the middle rows are viewed as if they were not there: Since it is possible to ignore the middle rows and consider only the external rows, between which there are indeed four cubits, the entire collection is considered a vineyard.

5:3 *between two vineyards*: Since the ditch is large enough to divide the surrounding vineyards (see 2:8 and 4:3), it is not itself subject to the laws of vineyards.

it is thereby like a winepress: The laws of which will be explained in the next lines.

watchtower: Some commentaries think this refers to an actual structure, while others think it refers to a tall mound in a field.

if the branches became intertwined: If the vines on either side of the watchtower grew over it, one can no longer view it as dividing the space into two vineyards. Cf. *Pe'ah* 2:3.

5:4 *its work*: See 3:7.

sow the remainder: The remaining space in the press or ravine.

If there are not four cubits there: If the total area of the press or ravine is not at least four square cubits.

house…sow in it: Even if the branches are intertwined; unlike the watchtower (see 5:3), a house always remains a defined structure independent of the surrounding vineyard.

5:5–8 *Consequences of Mixed Species in a Vineyard*

5 One who plants a vegetable in a vineyard or maintains it,
he thereby "consecrates" forty-five vines.
When [does this rule apply]?
When they were planted with gaps of four or five [cubits between the rows].
If they were planted with gaps of six or seven [cubits between the rows]:
he thereby "consecrates" sixteen[60] cubits in every direction—
circular and[61] not squared.

6 One who sees a vegetable in a vineyard and said:
"When I get to it I will collect it"—
it is permitted.
"When I return I will collect it"—
if it grew by one in two hundred, it is forbidden.

---

[60] K: "twelve," with "sixteen" written as a correction in the margin.   [61] K: "but."

5:5 *or maintains it*: Even if one did not plant the foreign species there, the act of maintaining a preexisting foreign species constitutes an act of forbidden agriculture subject to the rules of mixed species.

"consecrates": Renders forbidden; see note on 4:5.

forty-five vines: The end of this mishnah gives the formula for doing the calculation: the forbidden plant introduced into the vineyard forbids a circular area with a radius of sixteen cubits. Therefore, if the vines are planted four cubits apart, forty-five vines will fit inside of the circular area defined by the forbidden plant and a sixteen-cubit radius.

five [cubits]: According to the formula given at the end of the mishnah, only thirty-seven vines would be forbidden if the rows were planted five cubits apart. The structure of the mishnah, however, implies that forty-five vines would still be forbidden in such a case: it groups rows separated by five cubits with rows separated by four cubits under the heading that forty-five vines are forbidden, and only gives the formula for calculating the number of forbidden vines starting with rows separated by six cubits. The prohibition on forty-five vines in such a case can be explained as a rabbinic decree on account of the ease with which one can confuse vines planted four cubits as opposed to five cubits apart. Alternatively, the mishnah here, as in other places, was simply imprecise.

he thereby "consecrates" sixteen cubits in every direction: Despite the appearance of this phrase following the case of vines planted six or seven cubits apart, this is the general formula for calculating the number of vines rendered forbidden by the introduction of a forbidden plant into a vineyard, with the possible exception of rows separated by five cubits as explained above.

circular and not squared: The prohibition generated by the introduction of the foreign plant extends sixteen cubits in all directions, resulting in a circle of prohibited area. One need not extend that to include the area of the square that circumscribes such a circle, which might have been a reasonable extrapolation. (Cf. *Eruvin* 4:8.)

5:6 *it is permitted*: When the person arrives and removes the forbidden vegetable, both the vegetable and the surrounding vines remain permitted.

"When I return I will collect it": If, however, a person was standing near the forbidden vegetable and, rather than remove it immediately, planned on coming back later to remove it.

If it grew by one in two hundred, it is forbidden: That is, if the vegetable, between the time of saying "When I return…" and the actual removal of the vegetable grew in size by one part out of two hundred (i.e. one-half of one percent growth), both the vegetable and the surrounding vines are forbidden.

7 If one was passing through a vineyard and seeds fell from him,
or they came out with the manure
or with water,
[or] one who sows and the wind blew it behind him—
it is permitted.
If the wind blew it[62] in front of him—
R. Aqiva says:
If they are grasses, he must uproot them,
and if [the produce] is in the early stage of ripening,
he must break it off,
and if it has brought forth grain,
it must be set aflame.
8 One who maintains thorns in a vineyard—
R. Eliezer says:
He has "consecrated" it.
But the Sages say:
Only a plant[63] of the sort that people maintain can "consecrate" a vineyard.
Iris, and ivy, and Madonna lily, and all species of seeds[64]
do not constitute a prohibited mixture in a vineyard.
Hemp—
R. Tarfon says:
It does not constitute a prohibited mixture [in a vineyard].[65]
But the Sages say:
It does constitute a prohibited mixture.
And artichoke constitutes a prohibited mixture in a vineyard.

[62] K, P, and several other manuscripts: "If the wind aided him."
[63] Lit. "something."
[64] K, P, and many other manuscripts: "any species of seed."
[65] K has "in a vineyard" in the text.

5:7 *with the manure*: If there were seeds in the manure used to fertilize the land, and the landowner did not realize it.

it is permitted: In all of these cases the farmer was unaware of the presence of foreign seeds which spread against his will, and is therefore not held liable for their existence.

If they are grasses…set aflame: Since the farmer saw the seeds blown in the vineyard, he is obligated to destroy any produce that results. On the methods of destruction, cf. *Temurah* 7:5.

5:8 *the sort that people maintain*: Since thorns are not generally grown intentionally, their presence in a vineyard does not create a problem of Mixed Species.

all species of seeds do not constitute a prohibited mixture in a vineyard: Only grains and vegetables can generate a prohibited mixture in a vineyard; flowering/fruiting plants do not.

Chapter Six

6:1–9 *Arbors and Trellises*

6 What is an arbor?
One who plants a row of five vines next to a fence that is ten handbreadths high, or next to a ditch that is ten handbreadths deep and four wide—
one gives it its work, four cubits.
The House of Shammai say:
One measures four cubits
from the body of the vines to[66] the field.
But the House of Hillel say:
From the fence to[67] the field.
R. Yohanan b. Nuri said:
All who say thus are mistaken!
Rather, if there are four cubits there from the body of the vines and to the fence, one gives it its work and may sow the remainder.
And how much is the work of the vine?[68]
Six handbreadths in every direction.
R. Aqiva says:
Three.

---

[66] **K** (emended) and **P**: "and to."   [67] **K, P**: "and to."   [68] **P**: "work of the vineyard."

6:1 *next to*: After which the vines climb up the fence or down into the ditch.

one gives it its work, four cubits: Other species must be separated from this arbor by at least four cubits. Since no debate is recorded here, it appears that the House of Hillel, who generally opine that two rows are necessary to create the status of a vineyard (see above 4:5), concede that even a single row of vines planted as an arbor have the status of a vineyard and thus must be separated by at least four cubits from other species.

body of the vines: Rather than from the edge of their foliage.

to the field: To the field in which one wants to sow other species. Commentators disagree about whether the debate concerns planting in the field on the vines' side of the partition, or planting on the other side, the partition itself being insignificant as a boundary since the vines ensconce it.

From the fence: On which the vines are growing. If the mishnah is talking about a field on the vine's side, this is a more lenient view than that of the House of Shammai, since the vines themselves will be within the four cubits; if it is talking about a field on the other side of the partition, it will be more stringent, since the four cubits will be farther away from the vines themselves. Since the House of Hillel is generally more lenient, this might suggest that the field one wishes to plant is on the vine's side.

All who say thus are mistaken!: R. Yohanan b. Nuri disagrees with both of these views. Rather, one row of vines, even when they create an arbor, is insufficient to generate the legal status of a vineyard. The only relevant feature of an arbor is the distance between the planted vines and the fence over which they drape. If four cubits or greater, then one may plant other species between the fence and the space for working those vines, despite the fact that the vines are running along the ground to the fence. If, however, the vines are within four cubits of the fence, then that area is too small to plant anything else, as with the press discussed above in 5:4. Either way, however, one needs no more than the space to work the vines before planting another species on the other side of the vines.

2 An arbor that extends from an embankment—
R. Eliezer b. Jacob says:
If one [can] stand on the ground and collect all of it,
this thereby forbids four cubits in the field.
But if not, it forbids only parallel to it.
R. Eliezer[69] says:
So too one who plants one on the ground and one on the embankment:
If it is ten handbreadths high from the ground,[70]
it does not combine with it.
But if not, this thereby combines with it.
   3 One who trains a vine on part of a trellis frame
may not introduce seed beneath the remainder.
If one introduced [seed], one has not "consecrated" it.
But[71] if the new crept [over the seed], it is forbidden.
And so too one who trains [a vine] on part of a barren tree.
   4 One who trains a vine on part of a fruit-bearing tree
is permitted to introduce seed underneath the remainder.
And if the new crept [over the seed], one need only return it.

[69] **K**: "R. Eliezer b. Jacob." **P**: "R. Eleazar."   [70] **K, P** lack "from the ground."
[71] **K** lacks the conjunction.

6:2 *An arbor that extends from an embankment*: Vines that were planted on an embankment, and which extend over beams such that they overhang the ground below.

this thereby forbids four cubits in the field: Since it is close enough to the ground to be harvested, it has the same status as if it were actually on the ground.

parallel to it: If it is higher than a person can reach, only the area directly below the hanging vine is forbidden to be planted with other species.

one on the ground and one on the embankment: In the absence of an arbor, how close, vertically considered, must two parallel rows of vines be in order to generate the status of a vineyard according to the view of the House of Hillel (see 4:5)?

6:3 *beneath the remainder*: Of the trellis frame, even not directly underneath the part covered by the existing vine.

has not "consecrated" it: Even though planting underneath the other parts of the frame is forbidden, it is not a serious enough violation so as to render benefiting from the vines and the produce forbidden. See 7:3.

But if the new crept [over the seed]: That is, if new growths from the original vine now extend and hang over the area in which other species had been illicitly sown.

it is forbidden: The crops located underneath the new vine growth are now prohibited *post facto*.

And so too one who trains [a vine] on part of a barren tree: The non-fruit-bearing tree (see 6:5) is agriculturally insignificant and thus is legally treated like a trellis frame in the context of forbidden mixed planting.

6:4 *fruit-bearing tree... It is permitted*: Unlike the barren tree discussed in the previous mishnah, which was deemed to be like a trellis, fruit-bearing trees have an independent agricultural identity. The ground underneath the tree, therefore, fundamentally belongs to the tree and not to the vine growing on the tree; anything not directly underneath the vine is therefore fair game for planting.

And if the new crept [over the seed], one need only return it: The expansion of the vine does not render what has grown beneath those areas of the tree prohibited, but one may not leave the visual appearance of Mixed Species, and thus the new vine growth must be pruned and/or retrained to its original space.

It once happened that R. Joshua went to [visit] R. Ishmael in Kefar Aziz,
and he showed him a vine trained[72] on part of a fig tree.
He said to him:
May I introduce seed beneath the remainder?
He said to him:
It is permitted.
And he brought him up from there to Bet Hamaganyah.[73]
and showed him a vine that was trained on part of the beam
and[74] the stump of a sycamore tree in which there were many beams.
He said to him:
Underneath this beam is forbidden, but the rest is permitted.

5 What is a barren tree?
Any [tree] that does not produce fruits.
R. Meir says:
All are [considered] barren trees, other than the olive and the fig.
R. Yose says:
Any type of tree with which one would not plant entire fields
is thereby [considered] a barren tree.

6 Gaps in an arbor—
eight cubits and [a little] more.
And[75] all of the measurements stated by the Sages regarding a vineyard
do not include "[a little] more" other than gaps in an arbor.
What are "gaps in an arbor"?

[72] K, P: "that was trained." [73] K: "Magneya." P: "Magnaya."
[74] K may have originally read "on"; that word was erased, apparently by the original scribe, and changed to read: "within the stump."
[75] K and other manuscripts lack the conjunction.

Aziz: South of Hebron.

Maganyah: It is unclear whether this is a personal name (suggested by the versions without the definite article) or a title or a profession (suggested, but not demanded, by the versions with the definite article).

part of the beam and the stump of a sycamore tree in which there were many beams: The branches of the sycamore tree are called "beams" because they are used for construction. The "stump" refers to the trunk of the tree. This should thus be read: "a vine that was trained on part of a branch attached to the trunk of a sycamore tree, on which there were many branches."

6:5 *What is a barren tree?* Mentioned in 6:3. As will become obvious, "barren" is being defined relative to the legal consequences described there and in 6:4, not the botanical reality, and seems to be a stand-in for which trees are agriculturally insignificant.

R. Meir: This position radically expands the number of trees under which, if they are even partially covered with vines, one may not plant any other species. His limitation of agricultural significance to olive and fig trees may be based on Deuteronomy 8:8 (although failure to include the pomegranate tree is hard to explain), or may simply be based on the reality of what fruits were the primary product in the Land of Israel at the time.

plant entire fields: R. Yose takes a middle position: agriculturally significant trees are those which one would plant to produce large amounts of their fruit, presumably for sale.

6:6 *Gaps in an arbor*: A term to be defined below in this mishnah.

An arbor that was razed in its middle,
but there remain five vines in this direction and five vines in this direction:
If there are eight cubits there,
one may not introduce seed there.
Eight cubits and [a little] more—
one gives it its work,
and one may sow the remainder.

7 An arbor that extends from[76] a wall from the corner and then stops—
one gives it its work,
and one may sow the remainder.
R. Yose says:
If there are not four cubits there, one may not introduce seed there.

8 Canes that extend from an arbor
and one refrained[77] from cutting them—
beneath them is permitted.
If one made them so that the new would creep along it,
it is forbidden.

9 The flower that extends from the arbor—
one views it as if a plumb line were hanging from it;
beneath it is forbidden.
And so too with a dangling vine.
One who stretches a vine-shoot from tree to tree—
beneath it is forbidden.

[76] P: "with."   [77] Lit. "pitied them."

An arbor that was razed in its middle: In other words, if a particular arbor had more than ten vines initially, and then some were destroyed such that there were now essentially two arbors of at least five vines each, one may plant in between the two arbors (which had previously both been part of one larger arbor), provided that the gap is at least eight cubits and a little bit.

6:7 *An arbor that extends from a wall from the corner and then stops*: An arbor planted in the space between two adjoining walls, which does not extend into the space occupied by either wall, but remains only in that corner space between them.

one gives it its work, and one may sow the remainder: Since the vines are not trained on a wall, it does not have the status of an arbor, and one may plant another species at a distance of six handbreadths rather than four cubits.

If there are not four cubits there, one may not introduce seed there: If the area between the two walls is not significant, then it is as if the vines are trained on them, and it must be treated as an arbor. See R. Yose's opinion above, 5:4.

6:8 *Canes that extend from an arbor*: That is, beams of the arbor's frame, without vines attached to them, that extend out from the general frame of the arbor.

If one made them such that the new would creep along it: If one leaves these beams with the hope that vine-growth will extend onto them, then they are considered part of the arbor and one may not plant other species beneath them.

6:9 *And so too with a dangling vine*: A flower that projects from a single vine trained on an arbor-frame renders the space beneath it forbidden.

If one extended it with a rope or reed-grass—
beneath the extension is permitted.
If one made it so that the new would creep along it,
it is forbidden.

Chapter Seven

7:1–2: *Extending Vines*

7 One who sinks a vine into the ground—
if there are not three handbreadths of dirt on top of it,
one may not introduce seed upon it,
even if one sank it into a gourd or a pipe.
If one sank it into a [hard] clod [of earth],
even if there are only three fingers of dirt on top of it,
it is permitted to introduce seed upon it.
The joint in the vine—
it is measured only from the second root of the vine.

2 One who sinks three vines and their roots are visible—
R. Eleazar b. R. Zadok[78] says:

---

[78] According to **K**, **P**, and all the manuscripts. The printed editions erroneously have "R. Eliezer b. Zadok."

If one extended it with a rope or reed-grass: If the vine was too short to reach from tree to tree and one attached some kind of rope in order to connect them.

beneath the extension is permitted: The extension is not a natural part of the vine, and so it is permitted to plant a different species there, unless one intended the vine to continue to grow along the extension.

7:1 *sinks*: That is, one who extends a vine runner and plants it into the earth such that it sprouts in a second place as a new, independent plant.

if there are not three handbreadths of dirt on top of it: There must be enough dirt on top of the buried part of the vine that the roots of plants planted on top of it will not reach down to where the vine is.

even if one sank it into a gourd or a pipe: Even if one embedded the buried part of the vine into a gourd or a pipe, these items are permeable such that the roots of other species could penetrate and mix with the buried vine.

If one sank it into a [hard] clod [of earth]: Which is impermeable.

The joint in the vine: If a vine bends back down and then returns to extend upward.

it is measured only from the second root of the vine: That is, the six handbreadths required for the working of a vine (see 6:1) are to be measured from the place where the vine turns upward and actually begins growing, not from the literal root of the vine.

7:2 *One who sinks three vines*: Instead of sinking the top of an existing vine into the ground, one sinks growths from the middle of each of three vines in the earth that then emerge in a new place. Since the original vines and the newly emerged vines form two rows of three vines each, one has effectively created a vineyard according to the House of Hillel (see 4:5).

and their roots are visible: One sank the original vines such that the roots of the newly emerged vines are still visible.

If between them there are four to eight cubits,
these thereby combine.
But if not, they do not combine.
A vine that withered:
It is forbidden, but it does not "consecrate."[79]
R. Meir says:
Even the cotton tree is forbidden, but it does not "consecrate."
R. Eleazar b. R. Zadok says in his name:[80]
Even upon the vine it is forbidden, but it does not "consecrate."

7:3 *A Summary Paragraph*

3 Which forbid[81] but do not "consecrate"?
The remainder of a razed vineyard,
the remainder of the untilled ground surrounding the vineyard,

[79] **K**, according to a later emendation: "is not consecrated."
[80] **K, P**: "in his name" is absent.
[81] **K, P** read "are forbidden" in place of "forbid."

If between them: Between each pair of vines.

four to eight cubits: If they are more than eight cubits apart, they are designated as individual vines rather than a vineyard (see 4:8). That vines planted closer to each other than four cubits do not form a vineyard is not stated in 4:6, but is implied in 5:5.

these thereby combine: To constitute a vineyard which requires a distance of four cubits before planting a new species.

But if not, they do not combine: To constitute a vineyard, and one need leave only six handbreadths from each vine for its maintenance.

It is forbidden, but it does not "consecrate": Since the vine is withered, one should not even need to leave room for its maintenance before planting a new species. However, because of appearances, it is still forbidden to plant within six handbreadths of it. Nonetheless, if one transgressed and did so, the introduced plants are not rendered forbidden on account of their proximity to the withered vine.

Even the cotton tree is forbidden, but it does not "consecrate": Although it is not a grapevine, since it looks similar to vines, one may not plant within six handbreadths of it. Alternatively: it is forbidden to plant a cotton tree in a vineyard, even though it looks like a grapevine, but the planting of such a tree in a vineyard does not render the entire vineyard prohibited.

Even upon the vine it is forbidden, but it does not "consecrate": If one violated the rule of 7:1 and planted a foreign species in the dirt on top of a sunken vine, the produce is not rendered prohibited.

7:3 *Which forbid*: Some manuscripts have "are forbidden" rather than "forbid." This parallels the formulation in 7:2, and suggests an ideal prohibition whose violation incurs no consequences—the produce resulting from planting Mixed Species in the listed areas is permitted to be consumed. The version which reads "forbid" might mean the same thing, and have come about only in order to have two active verbs in tandem ("forbid," "consecrate"). It is possible, however, that the version that reads "forbids" means to forbid eating the produce that results from planting Mixed Species in the listed areas, but does not "consecrate" them such that all benefit—e.g. selling them or feeding them to one's animals—would be forbidden.

razed vineyard…untilled ground surrounding the vineyard: See 4:1–2. If one planted in violation of the rulings there, the produce is not rendered prohibited, even though the planting was forbidden.

the remainder of gaps in an arbor,
the remainder of trellis frames.
But beneath the vine
or [within] the work-space of the vine
or [within] four cubits within a vineyard,
these thereby "consecrate."[82]

7:4–8: *Miscellaneous Rules*

4 One who caused his vine to overshadow another's grain
has thereby "consecrated" it and is liable for it.
R. Yose and R. Simeon say:
A person cannot "consecrate" something that is not his.

5 R. Yose said:
It once happened that someone sowed his [own] vineyard during the Seventh Year,
and the case came before R. Aqiva, and he said:
A person cannot "consecrate" something that is not his.

6 If one seized a vineyard by force and sowed it [with grain]
and then lost possession of it[83]—

---

[82] K: "become consecrated," a difference of only one Hebrew letter, which has been crossed out.
[83] Lit. "it went out before him," that is, it reverted to its original owner.

---

the remainder of gaps in an arbor: See 6:6.

the remainder of trellis frames: See 6:3.

But beneath the vine or in the work-space of the vine: If one planted beneath the vine itself (see 6:3–4) or within the minimum six handbreadths required for its maintenance (see 6:1).

or [within] four cubits within a vineyard: See 4:5.

7:4 *has thereby "consecrated" it and is liable for it*: The vine renders the grain forbidden for any purpose, and the person responsible for the vine must pay the landowner the value of the consecrated grain.

7:5 *someone sowed his [own] vineyard during the Seventh Year*: With a foreign species.

A person cannot "consecrate" something that is not his: Since during the Seventh Year all land is considered ownerless, it is as if the man sowed another's field, and thus the principle invoked by R. Yose and R. Simeon in the previous paragraph is applicable here as well.

7:6 *If one seized a vineyard by force*: Lit. "one who acts violently." In context, the meaning is perhaps not limited solely to the one who acquired the vineyard illicitly, but even to one who acquired it properly following its theft from its original owners. See *Sanhedrin* 3:3; *Gittin* 5:6.

and then lost possession of it: The vineyard was returned to its original owner.

one must harvest [the grain]: Since the introduction of foreign species to the vineyard occurred against the owner's will, the vineyard remains permissible (see 7:4); the owner, however, must remove the mixed produce immediately so as to make clear that he has no desire for the Mixed Species (cf. 5:6).

one must harvest [the grain] even during the intermediate days of a festival.
Up to how much must he give to the workers?
As much as a third.
More than this, one may keep harvesting it in one's normal way,
even after the intermediate days of a festival.
From what time is he called "one who has seized it by force"?
From the time when [the memory of its original ownership] subsides.

7 If a wind[84] blows vines on top of grain,
one must immediately erect a fence.
If[85] something outside of his control happened to him,
it is permitted.
If grain leans underneath a vine, and so too in the case of a vegetable,

[84] **K**: The word "wind" is preceded by the demonstrative "this," which has been crossed out.
[85] **K** and other manuscripts: "But if."

even during the intermediate days of a festival: When nonessential agricultural work is forbidden; see *Mo'ed Qatan* 1:1–3.

Up to how much must he give to the workers? How much over the normal wage must one be willing to pay workers in order to have the grain cut down during the intermediate days of a festival?

As much as a third: More than the normal wage. Since labor is scarcer during a festival—when Jewish workers would prefer to be idle—those willing to work can command a higher wage.

More than this, one may keep harvesting in the normal way, even after the intermediate days of a festival: If the workers demand more than this wage, the vineyard owner may cut the grain down on his own, even if it means that the cutting will take so long that it continues after the festival ends. Alternatively, the phrase "even after the intermediate days of a festival" might mean that the vineyard owner is not obligated to hire workers at more than thirty-three percent over standard wages even following the holiday.

From what time is he called "one who has seized it by force"? After which, if the original owners reacquire it, they will be required to cut the intruding grain as quickly as possible, as long as labor costs are not thirty-three percent higher than usual.

From the time when [the memory of its original ownership] subsides: From the time that people have forgotten to whom the vineyard originally belonged. If a stolen vineyard is reacquired relatively quickly, then the owner would be under no obligation to quickly cut down the intruding grain, since everyone would know that the thieves had acted illicitly against the vineyard owner's will. After the original owners had been forgotten, however, if they fail to cut down the intruding grain quickly, they might be presumed to be new owners who are pleased by the presence of the grain illicitly mixed into the vineyard.

7:7 *one must immediately erect a fence*: That is, one must immediately build some sort of partition between the vines and the grains (see 2:8, 4:3–4). This word is almost graphically identical to the word "cut," leading some commentaries to understand even the word that normally means "fence" to mean "cut." That meaning is difficult to square with the ruling below about "turning back," which seems to be intended as more lenient than this ruling.

something outside of his control: Lit. "compulsion," some unavoidable event that prevents the owner from immediately building a partition.

permitted: Even if additional growth occurs before he erects the fence; see 5:6.

grain leans…so too…a vegetable: If the grain stalk or a vegetable plant, despite being planted the prescribed distance from the vine, bent of its own accord such that it was partially beneath a vine.

one must turn it back, but it does not "consecrate."
From what time [can] grain become "consecrated"?
From the time when it strikes roots.[86]
And grapes?
From the time when they become like white beans.
Grain that dried entirely and grapes that ripened entirely cannot become "consecrated."

8 A perforated planter "consecrates" in a vineyard,
but an unperforated one does not "consecrate."
But[87] R. Simeon says:
Both this and that forbid[88] but do not "consecrate."[89]
One who transports a perforated planter in a vineyard—
if it grew [by one] in two hundred, it is forbidden.

[86] **K** (originally), **P**, and many other manuscripts: "from the time when it is one-third ripe." The two versions differ by a single letter.
[87] **K**, **P**, and most manuscripts lack the conjunction.
[88] **K**, **P**: "are forbidden" instead of "forbid." Cf. 7:3 above.
[89] **K**: "do not become consecrated."

one must turn it back: That is, one must prune or otherwise move the plant such that it is no longer directly beneath the vine (cf. 6:4).

From what time [can] grain become "consecrated"? At what point in its growth does grain illicitly planted in a vineyard become forbidden, but before which one could uproot it and use it?

strikes roots: In the vineyard. The version in most of the manuscripts and the Yerushalmi only prohibits from the time when the grain has grown to a third of its full growth, a much later point.

From the time when they become like white beans: If another species were planted in a vineyard but it or the grapes themselves were removed prior to the grapes on the vines reaching the size of white beans, then the grapes are not consecrated.

Grain that dried entirely and grapes that ripened entirely: If one subsequently planted a vine next to such a grain or a grain next to a vine with such grapes.

cannot become "consecrated": The Mishnah seems to view the central problem of Mixed Species to be one of simultaneous growth; once either the grain or the grapes have completed their growth, their mixture with other species is not significant enough to generate a post facto prohibition.

7:8 *A perforated planter*: If one placed a foreign plant, planted in a pot with holes in it, in a vineyard.

"consecrates" in a vineyard: Since the roots of the foreign plant can reach into the soil of the vineyard through the pot's perforations, it is as if the plant was planted in the vineyard directly.

Both this and that forbid but do not "consecrate": Whether the pot has holes in it or not, placing it in a vineyard renders the grapes forbidden to be eaten but permitted for use otherwise (e.g. for sale, animal feed, etc.). Cf. 7:3.

transports: But does not put down.

if it grew [by one] in two hundred, it is forbidden: If, during the length of time that one walked through the vineyard carrying the perforated planter, the foreign species grew by $1/200$ of its original size (see 5:6), then the foreign plant is now forbidden. The Tosefta adds that the prohibition does not extend to all benefit from the plant, but only to its being eaten.

Chapter Eight

8:1 *Summary of the Different Kinds of Mixed Species*

8 Mixed Species of the vineyard are forbidden to be planted and to be maintained, and are forbidden to provide benefit.
Mixed Species of seeds are forbidden to be planted and to be maintained,[90]
but are permitted to be eaten, and all the more so to provide benefit.[91]
Mixed Species of clothing are permitted in all matters,
and are only forbidden to be worn.
Mixed Species of domesticated animals are permitted to be raised and to be maintained,
and are only forbidden to be mated.
Mixed Species of domesticated animals are forbidden one with the other.[92]

8:2–6 *Mixed Species of Animals*

2 A domesticated animal with a domesticated animal
or a wild animal with a wild animal,
a domesticated animal with a wild animal
or a wild animal with a domesticated animal,
an impure animal with an impure animal

---

[90] P lacks but adds in the margin "and are forbidden to provide any benefit...forbidden to be planted and to be maintained," a clear case of homeoteleuton.
[91] K, P: "and all the more so to provide benefit" is absent.
[92] K has "one with the other" rather than "one in the other" which is found in P and the printed edition.

8:1 *and to be maintained*: That is, even if another planted them, one may not be engaged in their maintenance; see 5:5–6.

and are forbidden to provide benefit: One may neither eat them nor use them as materials, sell them, or make any other use of them.

but are permitted to be eaten, and all the more so to provide benefit: In other words, the violation has no *post facto* consequences.

and are forbidden only to be mated: In other words, the prohibition is specifically regarding the breeding of animals of different species with each other.

Mixed Species of domesticated animals are forbidden one with the other: That is, any animals of species that are forbidden to mate with each other also may not be worked together, as in 8:2. The likelihood of this interpretation is enhanced according to the reading of **K** ("one with another"), rather than the reading of **P** and the printed editions ("one in another").

8:2 *domesticated animal...wild animal*: Categories that will receive some clarification in 8:4 and 6.

impure animal...pure animal: Animals that may not or may be eaten, respectively; see Leviticus 11.

or a pure animal with a pure animal,
an impure animal with a pure animal
or a pure animal with an impure animal—
[all these] are forbidden to plow, to pull, or to be driven [together].

3 One who drives absorbs the forty,
and[93] one who sits in the coach absorbs the forty.
R. Meir exempts.
And [if] a third [animal] is attached to the harness—
it is forbidden.

4 One may tie a horse neither to the sides of the coach,
nor to the back of the coach,
nor the Libyan ass to camels.
R. Judah says:
All born from a [female] horse,
even though their father is a donkey,
are permitted [to work] with each other.
And so too[94] those that are born from a [female] donkey,
even though their father is a horse,
are permitted [to work] with each other.
But those that are born from a [female] horse with those born from a [female] donkey
are forbidden [from working] with each other.

[93] K lacks the conjunction. [94] K, P: "And all" in lieu of "And so too."

to plow, to pull, or to be driven: Deuteronomy 22:10 forbids plowing with an ox and a donkey simultaneously; the rabbis understand that to include all manner of work with any combination of different animals (cf. *Bava Qamma* 5:7).

8:3 *One who drives*: That is, one who drives a coach drawn by animals of different species.

absorbs the forty: Receives the forty lashes mandated by the Torah. Although the Torah does not explicitly prescribe lashes for working two different animals together, the rabbis assume this to be a standard punishment (see *Makkot* 3:1–9), and Deuteronomy 25:2–3 may imply such a ruling.

and one who sits in the coach: Even though such people are not driving the animals themselves, they are directly benefiting from (and, through their weight, contributing to) the violation.

R. Meir exempts: Those who sit in the coach, presumably because they are not actively engaged in the violation.

And [if] a third [animal] is attached to the harness—it is forbidden: Despite the fact that the Torah explicitly prohibits only working with two different animals simultaneously, the rabbis understand this to mean two different species of animal in any combination of numbers. Thus, if one has two animals of one species and attaches a third animal of a different species to the harness, this is considered a violation of working with Mixed Species of animals.

8:4 *One may tie a horse neither to the sides*: If animals of another species are pulling the coach, even though the horse does not appear to be working together with them, the horse will inevitably contribute to the movement of the coach.

nor the Libyan ass to camels: These animals may not do work together, even though they may appear to be similar species.

All born from a [female] horse, even though their father is a donkey: For purposes of the prohibition of Mixed Species, the identity of the dam is the determining factor.

5 Mules of unknown parentage[95] are forbidden,
but the mule born to a female horse is permitted.
People of the field are [considered] a wild animal.
R. Yose says:
They impart impurity in a tent like a person.
The porcupine and bush-weasel are [considered] a wild animal.
The bush-weasel—
R. Yose says [that] the House of Shammai say:
It imparts impurity through carrying in the amount of an olive,
and through contact in the amount of a lentil.
 6 A[96] wild ox is [considered] a species of domesticated animal.
But[97] R. Yose says:
It is [considered] a species of wild animal.
A dog is [considered] a species of wild animal.
R. Meir says:
It is [considered] a species of domesticated animal.
The pig is [considered] a species of domesticated animal.
The wild donkey is [considered] a species of wild animal.
The elephant and the monkey are [considered] a species of wild animal.
And a person is permitted with all of them to pull and to plow and to be driven.[98]

[95] Meaning uncertain.   [96] K: "And a wild ox…"
[97] K and other manuscripts lack the conjunction.
[98] K, P, and others: "to plow and to pull," lacking "and to be driven," presumably reflecting the assumption that human beings are not generally used to draw coaches.

8:5 *but the mule born to a female horse is permitted*: Commentaries disagree about the meaning of the prohibition and the permission. Context suggests that at issue is whether the animal may be yoked to any or all other animals.

People of the field: The meaning of this phrase is unclear; it may refer to nonhuman primates, although monkeys are referenced explicitly below in 8:6.

are [considered] a wild animal: As opposed to being considered human. Thus, it is forbidden for this species to do work with a different animal species (see below, 8:6).

They impart impurity in a tent like a person: Corpses of this species impart impurity to items and people under the same roof as they, a trait unique to human-corpse impurity; see Numbers 19:14ff.

The porcupine and bush-weasel are [considered] a wild animal: As opposed to being considered a species of vermin, whose carcass imparts impurity through contact (see Leviticus 11:29–31). Since they are in the category of wild animal, the rules of Mixed Species apply to them (see 8:2).

the House of Shammai say: The correct categorization of the bush-weasel as a wild animal or vermin is a matter of doubt. They therefore apply the stringencies of both categories to it, as follows.

It imparts impurity through carrying in the amount of an olive: That is, if one carries a piece of flesh of the corpse of this animal, the piece being in volume the size of an olive, even without coming into direct physical contact with the flesh, one becomes impure, because the animal is regarded as a wild animal.

and through contact in the amount of a lentil: If one comes into direct physical contact with a bit of the corpse of this animal, even if there is only a lentil's worth of flesh, one becomes impure, because the animal is regarded as vermin.

8:6 *A wild ox is [considered] a species of domesticated animal*: And therefore is not considered Mixed Species with regard to domesticated oxen.

dog: According to the Tosefta, the categorization of dogs is relevant to the case of a will in which the testator bequeaths his wild or domesticated animals to a particular person.

Chapter Nine

9:1–10 *Mixed Species of Clothing*

9 Only wool and linen are forbidden on account of Mixed Species, and only wool or linen can become impure through "afflictions."
The priests wear only wool and linen to serve in the Temple.
The wool of camels and the wool of sheep that were hackled together—
if the majority is from the camels, it is permitted,
but if the majority is from the sheep, it is forbidden;
if they are in equal parts, it is forbidden.
And so too linen and hemp that were hackled together.

2 Silk and bast-silk are not subject to Mixed Species,
but they are forbidden for appearance's sake.
Mattresses and cushions
are not subject to Mixed Species,[99]
provided that one's flesh does not touch them.
[The category of] "temporary" does not[100] apply to Mixed Species,

---

[99] K: "but they are forbidden" until "Mixed Species" is absent. This is a clear case of homeoteleuton.
[100] K: "does not" is absent and added in the margin.

9:1 *Only wool and linen is forbidden on account of Mixed Species*: According to Deuteronomy 22:11, the only forbidden combination of materials in clothing is a combination of wool and linen.

and only wool and linen can become impure through "afflictions": The only garments whose blemishes generate impurity (as explained in Leviticus 13:47ff.) are those made of wool and/or linen.

The priests wear only wool and linen: Exodus 39:27–29.

permitted…forbidden: The rabbis understand the Torah only to be referring to wool from sheep; camel-hair, therefore, may be mixed with linen. The ratio of camel-hair to sheep-wool determines whether a mixture of the two may be combined with linen.

And so too linen and hemp: Since Mixed Species of clothing does not apply to hemp, if the majority of the mixture is hemp, it may be combined with wool in a garment.

9:2 *but they are forbidden for appearance's sake*: Since one resembles linen and the other looks like wool, it is forbidden to wear a mixture of these fabrics with linen, wool, or each other, because it will appear like a mixture of linen and wool; cf. 3:5.

Mattresses and cushions: Since the Torah specifically prohibits wearing Mixed Species, one may lie down on them as long as they are covered with a permissible fabric.

[The category of] "temporary" does not apply to Mixed Species: Even casual, fleeting wearing of garments containing mixed species is forbidden.

Nor may one wear Mixed Species even on top of ten [layers]: Of other garments, even though it is not touching one's body.

nor[101] may one wear Mixed Species even[102] on top of ten [layers],
even to steal the tax.

3 Hand towels, wrappers for scrolls, and bath towels
are not subject to Mixed Species.
R. Eliezer[103] forbids.
But[104] barbers' towels are forbidden on account of Mixed Species.

4 The shrouds of a corpse and the saddle of a donkey
are not subject to Mixed Species.
One may not place the saddle on one's shoulder,
even[105] to remove manure with it.

5 Clothes dealers may sell in their normal way,
provided that[106] they do not intend [to cover themselves with them]
in the sun because of the sun,
or in the rain because of the rain.
But the more scrupulous ones fasten them to a staff.

6 Those who sew clothes may sew in their normal way,
provided that[107] they do not intend [to cover themselves with them]
in the sun because of the sun,
or in the rain because of the rain.
But the more scrupulous ones sew on the ground.

[101] K, P, and most manuscripts lack the conjunction and thus begin a new sentence here: "One may not."
[102] K, P, and several manuscripts lack "even." [103] K, P: "Eleazar."
[104] K, P lack the conjunction. [105] P lacks "even." [106] K, P lack "provided that."
[107] K, P lack "provided that."

even to steal the tax: The clothes that one was wearing were not subject to Roman imperial taxes and tolls and thus wearing more layers of clothes could be a way of paying less tax. Cf. *Nedarim* 3:4.

9:3 *Hand towels*, etc.: Since the biblical prohibition only applies to wearing Mixed Species, these items, which only incidentally touch the user, are permitted; R. Eliezer, however, forbids even this incidental contact, perhaps extending the view of 9:2 that "temporary" does not apply to Mixed Species.

But barbers' towels are forbidden on account of Mixed Species: Even according to the anonymous first view that permitted hand towels, because these towels are placed on the body during haircuts.

9:4 *One may not place the saddle on one's shoulder*: Although one is permitted to sit on a saddle containing Mixed Species (see 9:2), one may not place it on one's body for any length of time even for a nonclothing purpose (cf. 9:3).

9:5 *Clothes dealers may sell in their normal way*: That is, they may place their wares on their arms and shoulders to display them to potential buyers, even if the clothing contains Mixed Species.

provided that they do not intend…in the sun because of the sun: Intent to wear the items as useful clothing articles, for example to shade from the sun or protect from the rain, renders the act of wearing them forbidden.

the more scrupulous ones: Adapted from the last phrase of Micah 6:8. Cf. *Demai* 6:6 and *Ma'aser Sheni* 5:1.

fasten them to a staff: So as not to place the clothing containing Mixed Species on their own bodies, they would hang them from a staff for display.

9:6 *Those who sew clothes may sew in the normal way*: That is, they may place the garments on their knees to work on them, even if the clothing contains Mixed Species. See above 9:5.

7 The *birris*-cloak and the Brundisian cloak and
Dalmatian undergarments and shoes made of felt—
one may not wear them until one inspects [them].
R. Yose says:
Those that come from the coast or from overseas do not require inspection,
because their presumption is [that they are made] with hemp.
But felt-lined shoes
are not subject to Mixed Species.

8 Only that which is spun and woven is forbidden on account of Mixed Species,
as it says: *Do not wear sha'atnez—*
something that is hackled, spun, and woven.
R. Simeon b. Eleazar says:
He is estranged and estranges his father in heaven from him.

9 Felted stuff is forbidden because it is hackled.
Woolen edging[108] in a linen garment is forbidden,
because they interlace in the[109] woven [garment].
R. Yose says:
Cords of purple-dyed wool are forbidden [to be tied over a linen garment],
because one stitches before one ties.

[108] K, P: "fringe." [109] Other versions: "like a."

9:7 *birris-cloak…Brundisian cloak…Dalmatian undergarments*: Probably kinds of wool garments from those particular regions, which were sometimes sewed with linen and sometimes not.

until one inspects [them]: To ensure that they do not contain any linen.

overseas: Lit. from "the region of the sea," across the Mediterranean.

9:8 *Do not wear sha'atnez*: Deuteronomy 22:11; cf. Leviticus 19:19. The word *sha'atnez*, usually translated contextually as "a cloth made from mixed fabrics," is here understood as an acronym for *shua* (hackled), *tavui* (spun), and *nuz* (woven).

He is estranged and estranges his father in heaven from him: Heb. *naloz umeliz* ("estranged and estranges"). R. Simeon b. Eleazar understands the concluding word of the acronym to allude to the power of the violation to create estrangement between humans and God.

9:9 *is forbidden*: If combined with linen.

because it is hackled: Despite not being spun, which apparently contradicts 9:8's requirement of both spinning and hackling. The Talmud harmonizes them by limiting this prohibition to rabbinic, not biblical, provenance.

because they interlace: Even though the edging and the remainder of the garment are meant to remain separate from each other, they will either inevitably intermix or at least appear to have done so.

Cords of purple-dyed wool: Used as a kind of belt.

because one stitches before one ties: Because they are temporarily stitched to one's garment to hold it in place prior to tying it.

One may not tie a strip of wool to one of linen to gird one's loins,
even though the strap is between them.

10 Weavers' letters and launderers' letters are forbidden on account of Mixed Species.
One who stitches [wool to linen] with one stitch—
it is not a connection,
and it is not subject to Mixed Species,
and one who removes it on the Sabbath is exempt.
If one made the two ends [of the thread to come through] on[110] one side,
it is a connection,
and it is subject to Mixed Species,
and one who removes it on the Sabbath is culpable.
R. Judah says:
[Not] until he [pushed the thread through] three times.
A sack and a basket combine with regard to Mixed Species.

[110] K: "from."

even though the strap is between them: Even if the wool strip is connected to one end of a leather strap and the linen strip to the other such that they are never woven together, they will nevertheless be tied together as part of the girding, which the rabbis forbid, perhaps on account of appearances (cf. 9:2).

9:10 *Weavers' letters and launderers' letters*: Letters that these professionals sew on to garments to identify their owners.

connection: If two garments are connected, and one becomes impure, the other does as well; see *Kelim* 29:2.

and one who removes it on the Sabbath is exempt: Tearing stitches on the Sabbath is punishable only if two stitches are torn; *Shabbat* 7:2 and 13:2.

If one made the two ends [of the thread to come through] on one side: If one drew a single thread through a garment in one place and then back through in another place, such that both ends of the thread emerge on one side of the garment, that is a sufficiently sturdy act of threading to generate a violation of the prohibition of Mixed Species and the prohibition of removing a stitch on the Sabbath.

three times: Only three stitches is considered significant to establish a connection for impurity, to create Mixed Species, and to violate Sabbath law.

A sack and a basket combine with regard to Mixed Species: If a sack was lined with linen and tied to a basket lined with wool, it would be a violation of the prohibition of Mixed Species to carry it in a manner that resembles the wearing of clothing.

Tractate Shevi'it

Yair Furstenberg

Introduction

Overview

Tractate *Shevi'it*, literally the "Seventh Year," or "Sabbatical Year," addresses the biblical law (Leviticus 25:1–7; Exodus 23:10–11) which demands that the Israelites let the land rest and cease all crop production during the Seventh Year. Since sowing is prohibited, grains cannot grow; the production of fruits is significantly limited as well. Only that which grows wild may be consumed. The landowner must abandon his field for that period; he cannot harvest whatever happens to grow, and he must share the yield with all people and creatures. In addition, Deuteronomy 15:1–11 commands the remission of all debts from fellow Israelites. Situated within the Order of *Zera'im* ("Seeds"), the tractate deals primarily with various aspects of agricultural production during the Seventh Year, while the remission of debts occupies only the final chapter.

Relationship to Scripture and Main Ideas

The biblical concern for limiting manual production and for sharing crops growing wild is reshaped in the Mishnah, which applies the laws of the Seventh Year to the social and market realities of its own time. Consequently, the Mishnah hardly addresses the biblical prohibitions of sowing and tending the produce; rather, it turns to nonbiblical issues, and attempts to implement rabbinic principles within nonrabbinic surroundings. Thus, the main sections of the tractate address the following rabbinic principles: prohibition of improving the land and trees (1:1–4:6); sanctity of Seventh-Year produce (4:7–9:1); and elimination (or removal) of Seventh-Year produce (9:2–9). There is temporal progression in these topics, from rules concerning the end of the sixth year (chapters 1 and 2); rules applicable during the Seventh Year (chapters 3 through 8), and rules concerning the elimination of Seventh-Year produce (chapter 9). In addition, the Mishnah returns regularly to the challenge of dealing with others who do not comply with these rabbinic standards (4:1–3; 5:5–9; 6:4; 9:1, 9).

Structure and Organization of the Tractate

Whereas the Torah prohibits actions that directly pertain to the production of crops, namely sowing, harvesting, and pruning, the rabbis prohibit any labor which may be construed as beneficial for the land or trees. Towards that end, they prohibit plowing both tree groves and grain fields during the sixth year that would provide benefit in the seventh. Only labor required for maintaining the trees may be performed until the New Year (1:1–2:5).

Two additional labors are prohibited by the rabbis, who explicitly acknowledge that these prohibitions were not accepted by others. They prohibit fertilizing the field, even for the sake of the eighth year's crops, and thus one may move only limited quantities of manure into the field. The Mishnah suggests practical solutions to bypass this prohibition, but other Jews, whom the Mishnah regards as "transgressors," did in fact continue to fertilize during the Seventh Year (3:1–4). The rabbis also prohibit removing stones embedded in the ground and cleaning out the field for future use (3:5–4:1). Similarly, one may not uproot trees or chop wood in a manner which improves the tree or the plantation (4:4–6). At the same time, knowing that others neglected these prohibitions, the rabbis also determined the status of fields that were cultivated and improved by transgressors (4:2–3).

The second venue of rabbinic innovation, which occupies the second part of the tractate (roughly corresponding to chapters 5 through 8) concerns the special requirements and prohibitions of Seventh-Year produce. The Mishnah lists which fruits, legumes, and vegetables are to be considered as Seventh-Year produce (2:7–10; 5:1–4; chapter 7). These are subject to the following prohibitions: they may not be wasted and may not be consumed prematurely; the trees on which they grow cannot be chopped (4:7–10); they must be consumed according to their most significant purpose (8:1), and they may not be traded (7:3–4; 8:3–5).

Alongside the unique treatment of Seventh-Year produce, the Mishnah occasionally refers to a specific obligation of "Removal" (7:1–2, 5, 7), and this law is dealt with extensively in chapter 9. According to rabbinic interpretation of Leviticus 25:7, Seventh-Year produce may not be stored for future use but must be consumed while it is still available to the animals in the fields. When the period of Removal arrives, the fruits must be distributed to all; otherwise, the preserved produce is prohibited.

Throughout the tractate, the Mishnah assumes that the market is governed by Jewish "transgressors." Thus, at the transitional point between the first two parts of the tractate the Mishnah adds a unit concerning commercial and social contact with such Seventh-Year "transgressors." It opens with the prohibition of selling implements and animals which, the rabbis fear, may be employed for prohibited field labor (5:6–8), and it moves on to limit contact with those who consume prohibited produce on the Seventh Year (5:9). Furthermore, it is assumed that Seventh-Year produce, even that which could have grown wild during that year, may not be bought indiscriminately in the local markets in the land of Israel. One must wait for the eighth-year harvest (5:5; 6:4) or go to the Syrian market, which is deemed permitted (6:1–2).

In addition, at the margins of the final section concerning the consumption of Seventh-Year produce, the Mishnah readdresses the problematic Seventh-Year market. It lists wild plants and aftergrowths, which transgressors are not suspected of growing illegally (9:1). The Mishnah also acknowledges that people continue to hold Seventh-Year produce, even after the period when it was to have been eliminated (9:9).

The last chapter turns to the remission of debts in the Seventh Year. In contrast to the agricultural prohibitions, which are maintained by the Mishnah with full rigor, well beyond what is demanded by the Torah, the Mishnah is consistently lenient with regard to the remission of debts and offers a variety of methods to evade the biblical demand of loan relief. This includes a narrow definition of loans subject to remission

(10:1–2) and the introduction of a new institution by Hillel the Elder, the *prozbul*, through which one may collect a loan in spite of the Seventh Year (10:3–7). Finally, the Mishnah praises those who repay their loans during the Seventh Year, even if they are not obliged to do so.

Special Notes for the Reader

In the identification and translation of various plants and vegetables mentioned in the tractate I regularly followed the commentary of Judah Feliks on Talmud Yerushalmi tractate *Shevi'it* (Jerusalem: Rubin Mass, 2000).

Tractate Shevi'it

Chapter One

1:1–5 *Plowing the Field before the Seventh Year: Trees*

1 Until when may one plow a field of trees before the Seventh Year?
The House of Shammai say:
So long as the plowing benefits the fruit.
But the House of Hillel say:
Until the Festival of Weeks.
And the words of these are close to the words of these.
  2 What is considered a field of trees?
Any three trees growing within a *se'ah*-sized plot.
If [the three trees were fig trees, and together] were capable of producing
a cake of pressed figs the weight of sixty *mina* in Italian measure,
one may plow a whole *se'ah*-sized plot on their account;
if less than this,

1:1 The rabbis prohibit preparing a field for the seventh year during the latter part of the preceding (sixth) year. The midrashic justification for this extension appears in 1:4.

Until when: Time is a major factor in organizing the laws of this tractate. See 2:1, 3:1, 4:10, 5:5, 6:4.

benefits the fruit: Of the sixth year.

the House of Hillel: The House of Hillel tend towards calendrical standardization; cf. the view of R. Simeon in 2:1.

Festival of Weeks: fifty days after Passover (Leviticus 23:15–16). The Mishnah does not use any of the biblical names for this holiday: "harvest festival" (Exodus 23:16), "festival of weeks" (Exodus 34:22, Numbers 28:26, Deuteronomy 16:10), or "day of firstfruits" (Numbers 28:26). Rather, it uses the term *atseret*, a biblical term of uncertain meaning.

And the words of these: Cf. *Kilayim* 2:6.

1:2 *se'ah-sized plot*: A standard measure of a plot in which one can sow a *se'ah* of grain, equivalent to fifty by fifty cubits (see 3:2; cf. *Kilayim* 2:2; *Bava Qamma* 6:2).

the weight of sixty mina in Italian measure: Ancient sources testify to a variety of mina measures. Sixty Italian *mina* are equivalent to one hundred Roman pounds.

on their account: In this case, plowing the whole field is required for the fruits' benefit.

one may plow for them only the space
large enough for the fig-picker and his basket outside of him.

3 The law is one and the same for non-fruit-bearing trees and fruit-bearing trees—
one considers them as if they were fig trees:
if [the trees were fig trees, and together] were capable
of producing a cake of pressed figs the weight of sixty *mina* in Italian measure,
one may plow the whole *se'ah*-sized plot on their account;
if less than this,
one may plow for them only what is necessary for them.

4 If one [tree] can produce a cake of pressed figs, but [the other] two cannot,[1]
or if two [of the trees] can produce and [the other] one cannot,[2]
one may plow for them only what is necessary for them.
[The same law applies] from three trees up to nine trees.
If there were ten or more,[3] whether they can produce or not,
one may plow a whole *se'ah*-sized plot on their account.
For it is said: *In plowing and in harvesting you shall rest.*
[The verse] has no need to mention the plowing and harvesting
of the Seventh Year;
rather, [the verse must be referring to] the plowing of the sixth year[4]
extending into the Seventh Year,
and the harvesting of the Seventh
extending into the following year.
R. Ishmael says:
Just as the plowing [mentioned in the verse] is an optional act,

---

[1] K, P, and many manuscripts lack "and the other two cannot."
[2] K, P, and many manuscripts lack "and the other one cannot."
[3] Lit. "[and] from ten and up."   [4] Lit. "the eve of the Seventh Year," here and below.

---

fig-picker and his basket: Which seems to correspond to the minimum space necessary for each individual tree, as in 1:3–4.

outside of him: i.e. if the fig-picker is holding the basket on the outside of his body, away from the tree, giving a larger space for plowing.

1:3 *one and the same*: This mishnah extrapolates a general rule from the previous case of figs to all other trees.

non-fruit-bearing trees: For a definition of such trees see *Kilayim* 6:5.

1:4 *If there were ten or more*: This comment returns to 1:2, which conditions the plowing of the field on benefit to the fruit. On the number ten, cf. *Kilayim* 2:9.

For it is said: Exodus 34:21. This midrash returns to the beginning of the chapter and justifies the prohibition of plowing in the sixth year, taken for granted by both Houses. The verse in its simple sense refers to the weekly Sabbath, but our mishnah understands the verse to refer to the Sabbatical (Seventh) Year, parallel to the association of the Sabbath and the Seventh Year in Exodus 23:10–12. Interpreted in this manner the verse prohibits plowing in anticipation of the Seventh Year.

R. Ishmael says: R. Ishmael seems to offer an interpretation of the whole verse with respect to the Sabbath. Since plowing is not an obligatory act, the verse must be prohibiting only nonobligatory acts of harvesting.

so too is the harvesting [mentioned in the verse] an optional act—
this excludes the *omer* harvest.[5]

5 Three trees that belong to three people—
they join together,
and one may plow a whole *se'ah*-sized plot on their account.
And[6] how much [space] must there be between them?
Rabban Gamaliel says:[7]
Enough for an ox[8] to pass with its equipment.

1:6–8   *Plowing the Field before the Seventh Year: Saplings*

6 Ten saplings scattered within a *se'ah*-sized plot—
one may plow the whole *se'ah*-sized plot
on their account[9] until the New Year.
If they were planted[10] in a row or surrounded by a barrier,[11]
one may plow for them only what is necessary for them.

7 Saplings and gourds join together [to create] a *se'ah*-sized plot.
Rabban Simeon b. Gamaliel says:
Every[12] ten gourds in a *se'ah*-sized plot—
one may plow the whole *se'ah*-sized plot
until the New Year.

[5] **K, P** are emended to add "which is obligatory."   [6] **K** lacks the conjunction.
[7] **K, P**, and many manuscripts: "R. Simeon b. Gamaliel."   [8] Lit. "[one of] the herd."
[9] **K, P**, and many manuscripts lack "on their account."   [10] Lit. "made."
[11] Lit. "a crown."   [12] **P, K**, and many manuscripts lack "every."

this excludes: Obligatory harvesting acts, however, such as the *omer*, the first sheaf of the harvest brought to the Temple on the day after Passover (Leviticus 23:10), must be undertaken even on the Sabbath (*Menahot* 10:3). This follows the notion that Temple rituals override the Sabbath (see *Pesahim* 6:1-2).

1:5 *they join together*: To be considered a field of trees; if they fulfill the requirements of 1:2–4, then one may plow the entire field.

1:6 *Ten saplings*: Even though they cannot produce the requisite amount of produce and therefore one should only be permitted to plow around each one, saplings require more treatment, which is crucial for their survival. Therefore, the laws pertaining to them are more lenient, and the whole field may be tended up to the New Year, rather than just the Festival of Weeks.

If they were planted: If the saplings are limited to a defined area from which they draw their water, there is no justification to plow the whole plot.

barrier: Lit. "crown." Most probably used for irrigation. Compare *Parah* 5:7.

1:7 *gourds*: Which are planted in the beginning of the summer and mature later in the season. Plowing and hoeing the field after the Festival of Weeks is thus essential for their nurturing.

Rabban Simeon b. Gamaliel: In contrast to the first view, Rabban Simeon b. Gamaliel claims that even if there were only gourds in the field, one may cultivate the whole field.

8 Until when are they called "saplings"?
R. Eleazar b. Azariah says:
Until they become nonsacred.
R. Joshua says:
Seven years old.[13]
R. Aqiva says:
"Sapling," like its name.
A tree which has been cut down[14] which has grown new shoots—
-[if the stump] is one handbreadth [high] or less,
[the shoots are considered] as a sapling;
[if the stump] is one handbreadth [high] or more,
[the shoots are considered] as a tree—
the words of R. Simeon.

Chapter Two

2:1   *Plowing the Field before the Seventh Year: Grain Field*

2 Until when may one plow a grain field[15] before the Seventh Year?
Until the moisture is gone, [that is,]
as long as people are plowing in order to plant cucumber and gourd fields.
R. Simeon says:
You have given the law of each and every [person] into his own hands!

---

[13] K: "Up to ninety years." In the margin: "nine years."
[14] Lit. "which has been axed."   [15] Lit. "white field."

1:8 *Until they become nonsacred*: On the fifth year after planting; see Leviticus 19:23–25.

R. Joshua says: According to the Tosefta, R. Joshua distinguished between different species: vine—five years, figs—six years, and olives—seven years.

like its name: If people call it a sapling, it is deemed a sapling; cf. *Yadayim* 4:1.

one handbreadth [high] or less…or more: If the tree was cut down close to the ground, its new shoots are considered to be new plants, and are considered as saplings. If it was chopped above one handbreadth, the shoots are deemed to be growing from the old tree, whose surrounding field may not be plowed after the Festival of Weeks before the Seventh Year (cf. *Orlah* 1:3–5).

the words of R. Simeon: In Mishnaic style, the formula "the words of" is usually followed by an opposing view (cf. 2:10), but not here.

2:1 *plow a grain field*: The only agricultural labor that may be performed in the sixth year is for the sake of plantings that will grow and be harvested in the sixth year (1:4). Thus tree plantations may be maintained until late in the summer while they continue to give fruit (1:1); grain fields, however, have completed their growth by the end of the rainy season. Cucumber and gourds are planted early on in the summer while the ground is still moist after the rainy season, and are harvested before the end of the year.

R. Simeon: Follows the House of Hillel in setting a fixed date (1:1).

You have given the law: This exceptional statement, unknown from other contexts, seems to respond to the fact of widespread violation of the laws of the Seventh Year (see 3:1 and 4:1); a standard whose application varies from field to field is easily abused by the unscrupulous.

Rather, in the case of a grain field—until Passover,
and in the case of a field of trees—until the Festival of Weeks.

2:2–5 Other Labors before the Seventh Year: Labors Permitted until the New Year

2 One may fertilize and hoe cucumber and gourd fields until the New Year,
and likewise irrigated fields.
One may cut off tree-warts, strip off leaves, dust [the grapes], and fumigate [the tree] until the New Year.
R. Simeon says:
One may even remove leaves[16] from the grape cluster during the Seventh Year.

3 One may clear away stones until the New Year.
One may remove shoots, trim the tree, and sculpt it until the New Year.
R. Joshua says:
Just as trimming and sculpting [are permitted] in the fifth year,
so too in the sixth year.
R. Simeon says:
As long as I am permitted [to engage] in tending[17] the tree,
I am [also] permitted [to engage] in sculpting it.

---

[16] K, before emendation: "what grows."   [17] Lit. "working," here and below.

2:2 *cucumber and gourd fields*: In order to best cultivate these summer vegetables, it is permitted to fertilize the field and uproot weeds all summer long.

irrigated fields: In which other kinds of vegetables were grown.

cut off tree-warts: The Mishnah adds other summer labors, which include four practices for the preservation of vines. The first two concern the leaves and branches, whereas the latter two protect the grapes themselves. The grapes were dusted and fumigated with sulfur, in order to chase off moths.

R. Simeon: The leaves covering the grapes may cause them to rot. It is therefore permitted to remove the leaves even during the Seventh Year, to save the grapes; the other practices, in contrast, are not crucial for the protection of the fruit and are thus prohibited during the Seventh Year itself.

2:3 *clear away stones*: In contrast to the previous mishnah, clearing away stones is not limited to a specific season. The rules governing this practice during the Seventh Year itself appear in 3:5–10.

remove shoots: The labors are presented from the bottom up: the stones are removed from the ground, shoots growing from the roots are removed, twigs are cut off from the trunk, and the treetop is sculpted. Such long-term maintenance of the tree is prohibited during the Seventh Year itself.

R. Joshua: He rejects the blanket permission to do these labors until the end of the sixth year. Rather, whenever one would cease such labors in a normal year, one must cease them in the sixth year.

R. Simeon: What exactly R. Simeon means (here and in 2:5) by "tending the tree" is not clear. He is usually understood to be referring to the plowing of the tree field until the Festival of Weeks (1:1; 2:1), thus suggesting the strictest position: the tree may be trimmed only as long as the cultivation of the tree, such as plowing around it, is permitted. R. Simeon thus attempts to set a fixed time for all aspects of tree cultivation, as in 2:1, while he is more flexible with respect to the preservation of the fruit itself (2:2).

4 One may sully saplings, wrap them, lop them, prepare houses for them, and irrigate them
until the New Year.
R. Eleazer b. Zadok[18] says:
One may even water[19] the foliage during the Seventh Year,
but not the trunk.

5 One may oil unripe figs and pierce them until the New Year.
The unripe figs of the sixth year that entered the Seventh Year,
and those of the Seventh Year that went forth to the following year—
one may neither oil nor pierce them.
R. Judah says:
In a place where it is customary to oil one may not oil,
since it is considered a labor;
in a place where it is not customary to oil, one may oil.
R. Simeon permits in the case of a tree,[20]
since one is permitted [to engage] in tending the tree.

[18] K, P, and all manuscripts: "R. Zadok."
[19] K (before emendation) and other manuscripts add "on."
[20] K, P, and other manuscripts: "in these cases."

2:4 *saplings*: As in the first chapter, the rules of saplings follow those concerning the trees, and again, their laws are more lenient, due to the special care they require. In contrast to the dispute around tending fully grown trees in the previous mishnah, the permission to tend saplings until the New Year is not disputed.

sully…wrap: To anoint with foul-smelling oil and wrap with leaves or cloth, so as to protect them from harmful insects and the ravages of heat and cold.

R. Eleazer b. Zadok: He adds another leniency with regard to saplings, permitting them to be irrigated during the Seventh Year itself, albeit indirectly.

2:5 *oil unripe figs and pierce them*: Figs were oiled and pierced to expedite their development. As in 2:1–2, any labor required for the cultivation of the crops is permitted until the New Year.

The unripe figs: Although figs that grew in the sixth year which remain on the tree into the Seventh Year are not considered Seventh-Year fruits, it is prohibited to cultivate them during the Seventh Year itself. On the other hand, figs that grew but did not ripen during the Seventh Year itself may not be cultivated even in the following year.

R. Judah…R. Simeon: Both attempt to restrict the scope of the absolute prohibition on oiling unripe figs during the Seventh Year, the former referring to sixth-year figs that enter the Seventh Year, and the latter Seventh-Year figs that exit into the eighth year. Since they are referring to different cases, they may very well agree with each other's leniency (although the Tosefta has R. Judah implicitly disagreeing with R. Simeon).

customary: What is considered agricultural labor is defined by local practice; if oiling is a normal labor, it is prohibited during the Seventh Year, but if not, an individual may choose to engage in it. According to the Tosefta, R. Judah is referring only to sixth-year figs that entered the Seventh Year; Seventh-Year figs themselves may not be touched.

since one is permitted [to engage] in tending the tree: R. Simeon must be referring to the year following the Seventh Year, when tending trees again becomes permitted. According to him, unripe Seventh-Year figs are considered part of the tree (see 4:7) and therefore once tending the tree becomes permitted, so too do oiling and piercing the figs ("these cases," according to most textual witnesses).

2:6–10 *Other Labors before the Seventh Year: Sixth-Year Plants Considered Seventh-Year Produce*

6 One may not plant, root a vine-shoot, or graft in the sixth year
less than thirty days before the New Year.
If one has planted, rooted, or grafted,
one must uproot it.
R. Judah says:
Any grafting which does not take root within three days,
will never take root.
R. Yose and R. Simeon say:
Two weeks.

7 Rice, millet, poppyseed, and sesame seeds
which took root before the New Year
are tithed [with the crops] of the previous year,
and are permitted during the Seventh Year.
Otherwise, they are forbidden during the Seventh Year,
and are tithed [with the crops] of the following year.

8 R. Simeon of Shezur says:
Egyptian beans initially sown for the purpose of yielding seed—
the same rule applies to them.
R. Simeon says:
Camel beans—

2:6 *One may not plant*: The prohibition to plant in the Seventh Year is considered part of the biblical prohibition of sowing (Leviticus 25:4). Since the moment of taking root is considered the essence of planting rather than the moment of insertion into the ground (see 2:7 and e.g. *Kilayim* 7:7), planting close enough to the Seventh Year that it might take root during the Seventh Year is forbidden.

root...graft: These are equivalent to planting (see *Sotah* 8:2).

uproot it: Even the doubt as to whether it took root before or during the Seventh Year is insufficient to permit allowing it to remain in the ground; cf. *Terumot* 2:3.

R. Judah...R. Yose and R. Simeon: As in the previous mishnah, these Sages suggest a more lenient law, at least with respect to grafting.

2:7 *Rice, millet, poppyseed, and sesame seeds*: Which are sown during the summer, and therefore might take root before or after the New Year.

took root: As in 2:6, the moment of taking root—as opposed to the moment of harvesting—defines to which year the crop belongs, and therefore which tithes are to be set aside (see chapters 6–9). In contrast to these seeds, fruits are tithed according to when they begin to ripen and vegetables from the moment they are picked (*Ma'aserot* 1:2–4).

Otherwise: If they took root after the New Year, during the Seventh Year.

2:8 *the same rule applies*: Although legumes are usually treated as vegetables and therefore tithed according to when they are picked, beans sown for their seed are to be treated as seeds and judged according to when they took root, as in 2:7.

Camel beans: Probably so called because of their large size. R. Simeon treats them as seeds here; it is unclear whether he intends this to apply across the board, or only if they were planted for the purpose of yielding seeds. Cf. *Kilayim* 3:2, which classifies them as a vegetable.

the same rule applies to them.
R. Eleazar says:
[The same rule only applies to] camel beans
which formed pods before the New Year.

9 Eunuch onions and Egyptian beans
from which one withheld water for thirty days before the New Year
are tithed [with the crops] of the previous year,
and are permitted during the Seventh Year.
Otherwise, they are forbidden during the Seventh Year,
and are tithed [with the crops] of the following year.
But, [in the case of such onions and beans] in a naturally irrigated field,
[only] if one withheld water from them for two [watering] seasons
[are they tithed with the crops of the previous year and permitted during the Seventh Year]—
the words of R. Meir.
But the Sages say:
[Only if one withheld water for] three.

10 Gourds that one is keeping for seed—
if they hardened before the New Year
and are no longer fit for human food,
one is permitted to keep them during the Seventh Year;
otherwise, it is forbidden to keep them during the Seventh Year.

formed pods: Rather than when they take root, like seeds, or when they are picked, like vegetables.

2:9 *Eunuch onions*: Which do not produce seed.

Egyptian beans: In the previous mishnah, R. Simeon of Shezur treated such beans planted for seed as seeds and followed the moment they took root. This mishnah, which treats them as vegetables, might be discussing such beans when planted as vegetables, or, as suggested by the Tosefta, might simply disagree with R. Simeon of Shezur.

withheld water: Normally vegetables are irrigated until they are picked, which determines their tithing year. Cessation of irrigation, however, indicates that one wishes them to stop growing; if ceased sufficiently in advance of the New Year, then even if they are picked during the Seventh Year, they are considered sixth-year produce.

Otherwise: If one did not cease irrigating for thirty days prior to the New Year, and all the more so if one did not withhold water at all.

naturally irrigated field: A field which generally suffices with rainwater, but to which the farmer provides additional water during the summer, when it does not rain in the Land of Israel. Since that water is only provided irregularly, the rabbis dispute how many rounds of supplemental irrigation must be missed before the New Year so as to classify the crop as belonging to the sixth year, even when picked in the Seventh Year.

2:10 *Gourds that one is keeping for seed*: Gourds are considered vegetables, which follow the moment of picking (*Ma'aserot* 1:2). Thus, if they are gathered in the Seventh Year they are subject to its prohibitions. However, if they have already hardened before the Seventh Year begins and are left in the ground solely for the sake of their seeds, they become mere shells for the conservation of the sixth-year seeds, which may be used in future years.

permitted to keep them: Seventh-Year produce may not be preserved beyond its season, and must be removed from the house (see chapter 9). Even the seeds of hardened gourds would have to be eliminated, unless they are classed as sixth-year vegetables.

Their buds are forbidden during the Seventh Year.
One may dampen the dust of a grain field[21] [during the Seventh Year]—
the words of R. Simeon.
R. Eliezer b. Jacob forbids.
One may stir a rice [field with water] during the Seventh Year.
R. Simeon says:[22]
But one may not trim it.

Chapter Three

3:1–4 *Maintenance of Fields and Trees during the Seventh Year: Fertilization*

3 From when may one take out manure to the dung heaps [during the Seventh Year]? After the workers[23] would have ceased to do so—
the words of R. Meir.

---

[21] Lit. "dampen white dust."   [22] **K**, **P**, and other manuscripts: "The words of R. Simeon."
[23] Lit. "workers of work." **K** (before emendation), **P**, and almost all manuscripts read "transgressors," lit. "sinners of sin," which appears to be the original reading. See 4:1, 5:9, 9:1.

Their buds: Even when the gourds became hard and inedible in the sixth, the soft buds that grow in the Seventh Year are edible and therefore subject to Seventh-Year restrictions.

forbidden: To be kept after the time of Removal.

One may dampen the dust of a grain field: As in 2:2, R. Simeon permits some forms of cultivation, or at least maintenance, even during the Seventh Year.

stir a rice field: By stirring a flooded field, the liquids are preserved and enable the proper development of the rice. R. Simeon permits this labor in the Seventh Year, provided that the rice took root during the previous year and is not considered a Seventh-Year crop (2:7).

But one may not trim it: In contrast to removing leaves in order to save vines from rotting (2:2), cutting the leaves off a rice plant is beneficial but not essential and is therefore forbidden.

3:1 *take out manure*: The rabbis prohibit fertilizing fields by spreading manure during the Seventh Year, as it prepares them for planting. However, manure which accumulates may be removed to piles in the fields, provided that it is not directly used for fertilization.

After the workers would have ceased to do so: Fields were fertilized at different points during the year depending on the crop planted in them. After a field's fertilization season is over—i.e. after the point at which the workers would have stopped fertilizing it in an ordinary year—one may remove manure to the field, since no one will suspect that it is intended for fertilization but rather assume that it is for storage. According to the reading of the manuscripts (which appears to have the original version), the mishnah is referring not to regular workers but to transgressors who do not observe the laws of the Seventh Year properly (cf. 4:1) actually spreading manure in the Seventh Year (see introduction). One must publicly distinguish oneself from transgressors.

R. Judah says:
After the sweetness dries out.
R. Yose says:
After it lumps.[24]

2 How much manure does one take out?
Up to three dung heaps per *se'ah*-sized field,
[each] of ten baskets, each [basket] holding a *letekh*.
One may add baskets, but not dung heaps.
R. Simeon[25] says:
Even dung heaps.

3 A person may fill his field[26] with three dung heaps
per *se'ah*-sized field.
More than this,
he must hew [a hole for] it[27]—
the words of R. Simeon.
But the Sages forbid,
unless he lowers [the dung heaps] three [handbreadths beneath the ground],
or elevates them three [handbreadths above the ground].

---

[24] Lit. "ties up." **K, P** have "becomes lumpy," lit. "becomes tied up."
[25] **K**: "Judah."   [26] Lit. "may make his field."
[27] Meaning uncertain. **K, P**, and most manuscripts lack "he must hew it," in which case the previous sentence should be translated "three dung heaps per *se'ah*-sized field, [and] more than that."

---

sweetness dries out: i.e. once the soft moist ground dries (or, according to R. Yose, after the ground is full of lumps), there is no benefit to spreading the manure, and it will be apparent to all that one is removing it only to be stored. Others interpret "sweetness" in reference to the manure itself.

3:2 *How much manure*: This mishnah and the next address how to lay out the storage heaps to avoid the appearance of fertilization by legislating both the number of heaps and their size.

Up to three: But no more; additional heaps, even if they are large, will appear as if one is fertilizing the field.

letekh: A measure of volume of fifteen *se'ah*, about 150 liters.

One may add baskets: According to this view, ten baskets of one *letekh* each is the minimum size for the pile to be clearly intended for storage and not for fertilizing. One may therefore add to the size of the heaps, but not to their number.

R. Simeon: According to R. Simeon, one may also add as many large heaps as he likes without being suspected of fertilizing; the size alone will demonstrate that one is storing rather than fertilizing. This view is further developed in the next mishnah.

3:3 *A person may fill his field*: This is a restatement of R. Simeon's view of 3:2.

he must hew [a hole for] it: He must lower the dung heap by hewing a hole in the ground so that the dung heap does not appear to have the function of fertilizing his field; cf. the view of the Sages and R. Meir. The manuscripts omit this *he must hew*, which entered our text from 3:6 where, with a slightly different vocalization, it is translated "stone quarry"; according to this version, which seems original, R. Simeon is simply permitting one to add as many heaps as one wishes, without any further requirements.

the Sages forbid: Following the first view in the previous mishnah, the Sages forbid piling more than three dung heaps unless one detaches them from the ground.

A person may pile all his manure into a stockpile.
R. Meir forbids,
unless he lowers [the stockpile] three [handbreadths beneath the ground],
or elevates it three [handbreadths above the ground].
If he [only] had a little bit [of manure],
he may add to it continuously.
R. Eleazar b. Azariah forbids,
unless he lowers [the heap] three [handbreadths beneath the ground],
or elevates it three [handbreadths above the ground],
or piles it on a rock.

4 If one uses his field as a sheep pen,
he may enclose[28] a two-*se'ah*-sized plot,
[and after that has been filled with manure]
he may uproot three sides [of the enclosure] and leave the fourth,[29]
with the result that he is using a four-*se'ah*-sized plot as a sheep pen.
Rabban Simeon b. Gamaliel says:
An eight-*se'ah*-sized plot.
If his whole field is only the size of four *se'ah*,
he must leave out some of it, for appearance's sake.
And one may remove [manure] from the enclosure, and put it in the field
in the manner of those who take out manure.

[28] Lit. "makes a crescent." **K**: "If one uses his field as a sheep pen and encloses."
[29] Lit. "the middle one."

stockpile: That is, a single enormous heap. This is implied by the abovementioned permission to add to any individual heap.

R. Meir forbids: Adding to the heaps unless one detaches them from the ground.

a little bit: Even if one does not have the amount of manure designated in 3:2, one may take out smaller amounts of manure and build a pile over time rather than having to wait until one has the requisite amount.

R. Eleazar b. Azariah forbids: Since a small amount will appear like fertilization.

3:4 *sheep pen*: One may indirectly fertilize the ground by enclosing his sheep in the field during the Seventh Year.

he may uproot: The version in **K** takes for granted that one may use a two-*se'ah*-sized plot of one's field as a sheep pen; the Mishnah only explains how to double the fertilized area.

uproot three sides and leave the fourth: One may build a movable fence and encircle another two *se'ah* plot after completing the fertilization of the first area.

four-se'ah-sized plot: But no more.

eight-se'ah-sized plot: It is unclear whether Rabban Simeon b. Gamaliel permits enclosing an eight-*se'ah*-sized plot as a sheep pen from the outset, or whether he permits continuing to enclose two-*se'ah*-sized plots as sheep pens until one has fertilized a total of eight *se'ah* rather than just four.

he must leave out some of it: He must leave part of the field outside the pen, so as to clarify that the fertilization of the field is a side result and not his sole intention.

put it in the field: Even in the part of the field that remained outside the pen.

in the manner of those who take out manure: He may remove manure from the double sized enclosure to the rest of the field following the provisions presented above in 3:1–3.

3:5–10 *Maintenance of Fields and Trees during the Seventh Year: Removing Stones from the Field*

5 A person may not open a new stone quarry in his field
unless there are in it three layers of stones
which are three by three by a height of three,
a quantity of twenty-seven stones.

6 A fence that consists of [at least] ten stones,
each of which can only be carried by two [people]—
they may be removed.
The height[30] of the fence must be [at least] ten handbreadths;
less than that, it is [considered as] a stone quarry.[31]
And he may level it to less than a handbreadth from the ground [but no further].
When does this apply?
[When the stones are taken] from his own field,
but from his fellow's field
he may take what he likes.
When does this apply?
If he had not begun it during the sixth year,
but if he had begun it during the sixth year,
he may take what he likes.

---

[30] Lit. "measure."
[31] According to the vocalization of **K**, **P**. Alternatively "one may hew [the stones, but not remove them]."

3:5 *A person may not open a new stone quarry in his field*: One is not permitted to remove stones from a field in order to prepare the ground for planting, but one is permitted to do so if one wishes to use the stones for a permitted purpose. One may not start removing stones from a stone-covered region of the field unless there a significant quantity of stones remains there, demonstrating that one does not intend to improve the field.

three by three by a height of three: The meaning of this clause is much debated by the commentators. It is generally assumed that the reference here is to cubits and that each stone is one cubic cubit. This may be inferred from the double definition in the mishnah. However, stones are rarely that large, and therefore the mishnah may be referring only to the number of standard-size stones.

3:6 *A fence*: Removing a stone fence from a field raises the same problems as removing stones from a quarry.

can only be carried by two: If the stones are very large, this demonstrates that one clearly wants the stones for a building project rather than to prepare the field.

they may be removed: The large stones may be removed from the fence, but not other, smaller ones.

less than that: If the fence is too short, it must fulfill the requirements of a quarry (see 3:5) before stones may be removed from it.

he may level it: Whether one is removing stones from a fence or from a quarry, one must not level it completely, but must leave a minimal layer of stone (cf. 3:7) so that the ground cannot be planted.

When does this apply?: Both times this refers to all of the previously mentioned restrictions, including that of not razing completely to the ground.

from his fellow's field: In this case, he is clearly interested in using the stones and not in improving the field, and there are, therefore, no restrictions (see, however, 4:1). Cf. 4:4.

if he had begun it during the sixth year: If one began removing rocks from the quarry or the fence in the sixth year, then one may continue to remove them even in the absence of the amounts previously listed. His having started removing the stones previously proves that he is not doing so in order to improve the field.

7 Stones which the plow shook loose,
or which were covered and later exposed—
if among them are two [stones] each of which can only be carried by two [people],
they may be removed.
One who is clearing away stones in his field may remove those on top,
but must leave those which touch the ground.
And likewise a heap of pebbles or a pile of stones[32]—
one may remove those on top,
but must leave those which touch the ground.
If there is a rock or straw underneath them, they may [all] be removed.

8 One may not build terraces upon the valleys
during the sixth year once the rains have stopped,
since he is preparing them for the Seventh Year,
but he may build [them] during the Seventh Year once the rains have stopped,
since he is preparing them for the year after the Seventh Year.
Nor may one support [the terraces] with earth,
but he may build[33] a [stone] barrier.
Any stone that he can stretch out his hand and take
may be taken [for this purpose].

9 "Shoulder stones" may come from anywhere,
and a contractor may bring them from anywhere.
And what are "shoulder stones"?
Any [stone] that cannot be carried with one hand—

[32] K, P, and several other manuscripts lack "a pile of stones."
[33] K and other manuscripts: "One may build it."

3:7 *Stones which the plow shook loose*: In the sixth year. Unlike quarries and fences, these stones are spread throughout the field rather than concentrated in one spot; as in the case of fences, only very large and toilsome stones may be removed.

leave those which touch the ground: As in 3:6, one may not remove the stones completely, but must leave one layer attached to the ground.

rock or straw: Since the removal of stones does not expose the ground, all the stones lying on top may be removed.

3:8 *terraces*: Building and fixing terraces and leveling the ground with soil was essential for preparing the hilly lands of Judaea and Galilee for cultivation, and is therefore prohibited during the Seventh Year. From this mishnah we learn that it was undertaken annually right after the winter, so as to repair rain damage. As in the case of plowing (1:1), it is prohibited to engage in activities in the sixth year that will improve the field in the seventh.

support [the terraces] with earth: Although one is allowed to build the terrace for the following year, he may not yet add earth, which directly improves the field itself and may be used for cultivation.

Any stone: Since he is clearly building a stone structure rather than improving the land, he need not worry about any of the restrictions detailed in 3:7.

3:9 *"Shoulder stones"*: This mishnah turns from the question of removing stones from a field to another issue of bringing stones to a workplace.

from anywhere: Stones that will obviously be used for building may even be taken from one's own field without concern for any of the restrictions of 3:5–7.

a contractor: Who is known to be building rather than improving their field, can similarly ignore those restrictions; some commentators think this applies even to stones smaller than shoulder stones.

the words of R. Meir.
R. Yose says:
"Shoulder stones" are as their name implies:
any [stones] that can be carried, two or three together, on one's shoulder.

10 One who constructs a fence between his [property] and the public domain [during the Seventh Year]
is permitted to dig down to bedrock level.
What is he to do with the earth?
He must pile it in the public domain and repair[34] it—
the words of R. Joshua.
R. Aqiva says:
Just as one may not destroy the public domain,
he may not repair it, either.
What is he to do with the earth?
He must pile it in his field,
in the manner of those who take out manure.
And likewise one who digs a pit, a trench, or a cave.

Chapter Four

4:1–3 *Maintenance of Fields and Trees during the Seventh Year: Mutual Favors*

4 At first [the Sages] taught:[35]
A person may gather sticks and stones[36] and weeds from his own field [in the Seventh Year],

[34] K, P, and many manuscripts: "prepare."
[35] Lit. "they used to say."
[36] P, K, and other manuscripts lack "stones."

3:10 *dig down*: He may dig out the earth, and it is not considered as an improvement of the field.

He must pile it in the public domain: Since it cannot be spread in his own property, which would improve the field, the earth should be used for fixing public roads.

R. Aqiva: A private person has no authority over the public domain, and may not on his own initiative and out of his own interest carry out public work. Noticeably, this dispute between R. Joshua and R. Aqiva does not concern the Seventh Year specifically, although its consequences play out in that context.

manner of those who take out manure: That is, in accordance with the rules spelled out at the beginning of this chapter (3:1–4); cf. 3:4. Although he is not spreading manure but earth, it may nonetheless seem that he is revitalizing the field.

4:1 *At first*: This phrase also appears in *Nedarim* 9:6 and 11:12, *Gittin* 6:5, *Niddah* 10:6, and *Tevul Yom* 4:5.

own field…fellow's field…largest ones: As in the case of removing stones, one must avoid even the appearance of improving one's field when picking up sticks and weeds. One may therefore only gather large ones, useful for non-field-related needs, and not clean the field completely (cf. 3:6–7).

such as he would gather from his fellow's field,
[that is], the largest ones.
After[37] the number of transgressors increased, [the Sages] decreed
that this one must gather from that one's field
and that one must gather from this one's field,[38]
not [in exchange] for a favor,
nor, needless to say, so that he would stipulate food for [the workers].

2 A field that was cleansed of thorns [during the Seventh Year]
may be sown during the eighth year.
[A field] that was improved or that was made into a sheep pen,
may not be sown during the eighth year.
A field that was improved—
the House of Shammai say:
One may not eat its fruits during the Seventh Year.
But the House of Hillel say:
One may eat.
The House of Shammai say:
One may not eat Seventh-Year fruits [in exchange] for a favor.
But the House of Hillel say:
One may eat[39] [in exchange] for a favor or not [in exchange] for a favor.

[37] **P, K**: "But after."
[38] **K** lacks, possibly as a result of a scribal error, but possibly rendering the previous clause: "that one must gather from another's field."
[39] Absent in **K, P**.

such as he would gather from his fellow's field: This statement is redundant and adds no practical information, but is nonetheless stated in contrast to the next stage.

After the number of transgressors increased: Cf. 3:1 above.

this one must gather from that one's field: Since the person gathering has no direct interest in cleaning out the field, but only in the pickings, it is assumed that he will leave the smaller ones in the field. Presumably, the gatherer takes the sticks and weeds for himself.

not [in exchange] for a favor, nor…so that he would stipulate food for [the workers]: Both are methods of payment for the work. The introduction of reciprocity or payment creates an incentive to clear one's fellow's field entirely, and was therefore forbidden. On the reciprocal exchange of favors see the following mishnah and *Avodah Zarah* 4:3.

4:2 *A field that was cleansed of thorns*: The mishnah implies that removing thorns was prohibited during the Seventh Year, but did not constitute a sufficient improvement as to warrant the punishment of not being allowed to seed it the following year.

improved: Persistent plowing of the field removes the weeds and softens the ground so that it is ready to receive rain.

made into a sheep pen: Beyond what was permitted in 3:4, thus fertilizing a significant part of the field.

The House of Shammai: As in the previous section, the Houses discuss the penalty imposed on those who improve the field (by means of plowing) during the Seventh Year. This dispute between the Houses follows their previous discussion of the matter in 1:1.

a favor: The exact details of this arrangement are not clear. According to Exodus 23:11, the fruits of the Seventh Year must be abandoned and are considered ownerless. Although the owner has no legal capacity

R. Judah says:
The opinions are reversed.
This is among [the cases] in which the House of Shammai are lenient and the House of Hillel are stringent.

3 One may lease plowed land from gentiles during the Seventh Year, but not from an Israelite.
And one may encourage[40] gentiles during the Seventh Year, but not an Israelite.
And one may[41] greet them for the sake of peace.

4:4–6 *Maintenance of Fields and Trees during the Seventh Year: Trees and Wood*

4 One who thins a field of olive trees [during the Seventh Year]—
the House of Shammai say:
He may level [the tree] to the ground.
But the House of Hillel say:
He may [even] uproot.
But[42] [the House of Hillel] concede in [the case of] someone smoothing [the field], that he may only level [the trees to the ground].
What[43] is considered "thinning"?
[Removing] one or two trees.

---

[40] Lit. "Strengthen the hands of," here and below.   [41] Or "must."
[42] K lacks the conjunction.   [43] P, K: "And what."

---

to trade with the fruits that grow in his field, the House of Hillel allow the owner to receive future favors in exchange for his fruits.

R. Judah: The parallel in *Eduyot* 5:1 follows R. Judah's version of the debate.

4:3 *plowed land*: That is, land that was plowed during the Seventh Year.

lease…from gentiles: Since gentiles are not obligated to observe Seventh-Year prohibitions, one may lease a field they have plowed and sow it in the following year.

but not from an Israelite: Leasing land that an Israelite plowed in the Seventh Year violates both the injunction on payments that encourage transgression of the Seventh Year (4:1) and on benefiting from agricultural labor done in violation of the Seventh Year (4:2). As in 4:2, one would presumably be forbidden from sowing such leased land in the following year.

one may encourage gentiles: That is, one may praise gentiles who are engaged in agricultural work and wish them success. The same phrase appears below 5:9 and in *Gittin* 5:9 in the context of "the sake of peace."

4:4 *thins a field of olive trees*: As trees grow and require more space the farmer may choose to remove the weaker trees. Although he may do so for the sake of the trees, he may not do so in order to improve the field itself. Thus according to the House of Shammai one must always leave the roots in the ground; if one wants to use the field, he will need to uproot them after the Seventh Year. The House of Hillel allow even removing the roots as part of maintaining the trees.

[What is considered] "smoothing"?
[Removing] three in a row.
When does this apply?
In his own field;
but in his fellow's field,
even someone smoothing may uproot.

5 One who splits an olive tree
may not cover [the tree] with earth,
but he may cover [the tree] with stones or straw.
One who chops sycamore beams,
may not cover [the tree] with earth,
but he may cover [the tree] with stones or straw.
One may not chop a virgin sycamore in the Seventh Year,
for it is [considered] work.
R. Judah says:
In its typical manner, it is forbidden;
rather, he must either leave more than ten handbreadths [above the ground],
or level it to the ground.

6 One who trims the ends[44] of vines or chops reeds—
R. Yose the Galilean says:
He must leave [at least] one handbreadth [to the ground].

[44] Lit. "tails."

smoothing: If the removed trees reveal a substantial area in the field, even the House of Hillel concede that their roots must be left in the ground, since such significant removal is not about helping the other trees, but about clearing space on the ground.

When does this apply: Cf. 3:6. The Mishnah assumes that one would only remove tree roots from one's fellow's field if interested in them for his own purposes and not to improve the field.

4:5 *One who splits an olive tree*: Apparently, cutting away from the trunk where the trunk is hollow. The cut area was normally covered by earth to prevent it from drying out and to form a scab. Because this has a salutary effect on the tree's growth, it is considered a forbidden form of working the field during the Seventh Year, and one may only apply treatments that are solely protective.

sycamore beams: This refers to the branches even while still attached to the tree; they are called beams because they are used for building. The same language appears in *Kilayim* 6:4.

virgin sycamore: Which is being cut for the very first time, in order to stimulate the future growth of solid branches from the stump. In contrast to the chopping of sycamore beams, this is considered beneficial to the tree, and is therefore prohibited during the Seventh Year.

typical manner: Usually a virgin sycamore is cut within ten handbreadths of the ground, which yields the strongest and straightest branches. R. Judah permits cutting even a virgin sycamore during the Seventh Year with an alteration, either cutting above ten handbreadths, or leveling the tree completely.

4:6 *One who trims the ends of vines or chops reeds*: Not for the sake of improving the plant, but in order to burn the dried vine branches for heat or to weave the reeds into mats.

leave...one handbreadth: In order to distinguish this act from the forbidden pruning of vines (Leviticus 25:4), R. Yose requires cutting the branch one handbreadth above the usual spot, so as not to cultivate the plant and encourage its development.

R. Aqiva says:
He may chop in the typical manner,
with a hatchet, a sickle, or a saw,
or with anything he likes.
A cracked [branch of a] tree—
one may tie it during the Seventh Year,
not so that it might heal,[45]
but so that [the crack] not get bigger.[46]

4:7–10   *Development of Seventh-Year Fruits: Stages of Development*

7   From when may one eat tree-fruit during the Seventh Year?
Unripe figs—
after they turn red,
one may eat one's bread with them in the field.
[After] they ripen,
one may gather them into one's house.
And likewise, figs at this stage[47] in other years of the Seven-Year cycle are liable for tithes.

8   Unripe grapes—
after they produce juice,[48]
one may eat one's bread with them in the field.
[After] they ripen,
one may gather them into one's house.
And likewise, grapes at this stage in other years of the Seven-Year cycle are liable for tithes.

---

[45] Lit. "go up."   [46] Lit. "increase."
[47] Lit. "those that are like these," here and in 4:8–9 below.   [48] Lit. "water."

---

in the typical manner: R. Aqiva does not seem to respond directly to R. Yose's restrictions, since he focuses on allowing the use of ordinary tools (cf. the view of the House of Hillel in 5:4, below) rather than the location of the cut. In this context, *typical manner* would include cutting in the normal place, apparently since this action is substantially different from the pruning that was usually undertaken before the harvest.

cracked [branch of a] tree: A broken branch hanging only by its bark (cf. *Uqtsin* 3:8) may be tied to the tree only to support the attached part, to preserve the branch at least partially and prevent further cracking.

heal…get bigger: The same language appears in a very similar context in *Shabbat* 23:5.

4:7   *From when may one eat*: It is prohibited to waste Seventh-Year produce, which includes eating it before it is fit to be eaten. For each of the three main kinds of fruits, figs, grapes (4:8), and olives (4:9; see Deuteronomy 8:8), the Mishnah defines a preliminary stage at which it may be eaten in the field, and a later stage at which it may be gathered into the house. These correspond to the ordinary ways in which such fruits were eaten; at an early stage they were snacked on but not harvested, while at a later stage they were collected and brought to the house for consumption.

9 Olives—
after they[49] are capable of yielding a quarter [of a *log* of oil] per *se'ah* [of olives],
one may crack them open and eat [them] in the field.
[After] they are capable of yielding a half of a *log* [of oil],
one may crush [them] and anoint [oneself] in the field.
[After] they are capable of yielding a third [of what they will ultimately yield],
one may crush [them] in the field, or gather them into one's house.
And likewise, olives at this stage in other years of the Seven-Year cycle are liable for tithes.
And with regard to other tree fruits—
their season for tithing is the same as their season for the Seventh Year.

10 From when may one not chop trees during the Seventh Year?
The House of Shammai say:
Every [kind of] tree, after it produces [fruit].
The[50] House of Hillel say:
Carob trees—after [the branches] drop down;[51]
vines—after [the grapes] swell;
olive trees—after they blossom;

[49] P, K, and other manuscripts have "olives which."
[50] P, K, and others have "But the."
[51] Or "After it begins to bud."

4:9 *a quarter [of a log of oil] per se'ah*: A *se'ah* of olives is twenty-four *log*. At this early stage the olives yield about one percent of oil, whereas at their fullest they produce about 20–25 percent oil.

other years: Tithes are suspended in the Seventh Year.

liable for tithes: In years in which tithes are in effect, once the fully ripened fruits are brought into the house, they may not be eaten without being tithed; see *Ma'aserot* 1:2–3.

crack...and eat: The bitter juice in the barely ripe olives.

crush: Extract some small amount of oil from the ripening olives.

season for tithing: See *Ma'aserot* 1:2–3. At the very same moments in the Seventh Year, one is permitted to begin consuming those fruits.

4:10 *From when may one not chop trees*: Due to the concern raised in the previous mishnayot about wasting growing fruits (4:7–9), the Mishnah also prohibits cutting off branches from fruit-bearing trees (not to mention chopping down the trees themselves) once fruits have begun to grow on the tree.

produces [fruit]: The intended stage of growth is unclear, whether budding, early edibility, or full growth (cf. 4:7–9).

House of Hillel: The dispute between them and the House of Shammai is unclear. They agree that all but carobs, vines, and olives must not be chopped down once they begin to produce some fruit. The specification of vines and olives tracks 4:8–9; the reason for the presence of carobs and absence of figs is unclear.

Carob...drop down: The underlying term can either refer to a branch loaded with carob, a very late stage, or to the initial budding, a very early stage.

swell: With liquid; cf. 4:8.

blossom: It is unclear whether this means the blossoming of the tree, which occurs before any fruit begins to grow, or the blossoming of the olives such that they can produce oil (cf. 4:9).

every other [kind of] tree[52]—after it produces [fruit].
And every [kind of] tree, once the season for tithing arrives—
it is permitted to cut it.
How[53] much must an olive tree produce, [at which point] it may not be cut?
One quarter of a *qav*.
Rabban Simeon b. Gamaliel says:
It all depends on the olive tree.

Chapter Five

5:1 *Development of Seventh-Year Fruits: Fruits that Begin to Grow during the Seventh Year but Ripen after It*

5 White figs—
their Seventh Year is the second year [of the Seven-Year cycle],
for they ripen[54] only after three years.
R. Judah says:
Persian figs—
their Seventh Year is the following year,
for they ripen only after two years.
They said to him:
They said this only with regard to white figs.

[52] K: "all other [kinds of] tree-fruits."
[53] P and others: "And how much."
[54] Lit. "produce," here and below.

once the season for tithing arrives: This stage represents the end of the growing season and the beginning of the gathering season. At that point, the growth is completed, and cutting off branches or chopping down the trees does not destroy any potential Seventh-Year fruit.

How much must an olive tree produce: Fruitful olive trees should not be cut even in other years, following the restriction of the Torah to destroying fruit-bearing trees during a siege (Deuteronomy 20:19). There is no clear definition of this prohibition in the Mishnah outside of this reference (cf. *Bava Qamma* 8:6).

depends on the olive tree: Olive trees of particular distinction (see *Pe'ah* 7:1) might be required to be preserved even if they produce less than a quarter-*qav*.

5:1 *White figs…Persian figs*: Precise identification uncertain.

only after three years: While most fruits bud and ripen in the same year (see 4:10), white figs ripen only after three seasons on the tree. The tree thus carries three different crops, and those which bud in the Seventh Year are subject to Seventh-Year limitations in the second year of the seventh cycle, which is the third year they will have been on the tree. This ruling implies that the Seventh Year for produce is measured from when it buds rather than when it ripens.

5:2–5 *Development of Seventh-Year Fruits: Arum*

2 One who stores arum in the ground during the Seventh Year—
R. Meir says:
One may not [store] less than two *se'ah*,
up to[55] three handbreadths high
and one handbreadth of earth above it.
But the Sages say:
One may not store less than four *qav*,
up to one handbreadth high
and one handbreadth of earth above it.
And one must store it where people step.

3 Arum remaining after the Seventh Year—
R. Eliezer says:
If the poor gathered its leaves, they have gathered [their share];
otherwise, he must make a calculation with the poor.
R. Joshua says:
If the poor gathered its leaves, they have gathered [their share];
otherwise, the poor have no claim on him to make a calculation.

---

[55] Or "at least," here and below; cf. 3:2.

5:2 *One who stores arum in the ground*: Arum (see Pe'ah 6:10, where it is grouped with garlic and onions) is regularly stored underground in large quantities, but in the Seventh Year one must be careful to maintain a substantial amount of it in the ground so it does not look as though one is planting them in the ground. (Cf. 3:2–4, which similarly mandates minimum amounts to avoid the appearance of transgression.)

two se'ah: twelve *qav*, about fifteen to twenty liters.

three handbreadths high: It is unclear from the language of the text whether this a minimum or a maximum; the same word is used to mean both. If a minimum, the Mishnah wishes to constrain the area in which the arum is stored, so that it is not scattered in a large area, which would resemble planting. If a maximum, it is concerned that one not store the arum too deep, lest one appear to be digging for planting.

and one handbreadth of earth above it: So that any new leaves will not pop out of the ground.

four qav…one handbreadth high: The Sages permit storing one-third as much arum as R. Meir.

where people step: Thereby preventing the growth of new leaves.

5:3 *Arum remaining*: This mishnah refers to arum planted in the ground, not stored. Arum is a perennial which continues to develop in the ground over the course of three or more years. This mishnah discusses a case in which the arum was planted before the Seventh Year.

they have gathered: Even if the arum was planted in the sixth year with the intention of harvesting it after the Seventh Year, the poor are eligible to pick the leaves which grow during the Seventh Year; cf. 5:1.

the poor: Cf. Pe'ah 6:1, where the House of Hillel assume that Seventh-Year produce is available for consumption by anyone, not just the poor.

make a calculation: Removing the leaves that grow in the Seventh Year hampers the growth of the arum corm (the large, round underground stem); leaving the leaves intact contributes to its development. If, therefore, the poor leave the leaves intact during the Seventh Year (presumably at the owner's request), they may claim the proportional value of the growth of the corm in the Seventh Year.

no claim: According to R. Joshua, the poor are entitled only to eat the leaves that grow during the Seventh Year, but they have no share in the corm that develops from them, and cannot negotiate its profit with the landowner.

4 Arum of the sixth year, which remained into the Seventh Year,
and likewise summer onions,
and likewise madder from high-quality ground—
the House of Shammai say:
One may dig them up [only] with wooden rakes.
But the House of Hillel say:
[One may dig them up even] with metal spades.
But[56] [the House of Shammai] concede in the case of madder from rocky ground,
that one may dig it up with metal spades.

5 From when may one buy arum after the Seventh Year?
R. Judah says:
Immediately.
But the Sages say:
[Only] after the new [leaves] become dominant.

5:6–9 Items that May Not Be Sold or Lent during the Seventh Year

6 These are the implements that an artisan may not sell during the Seventh Year:
a plow and all its equipment;
a yoke,

---

[56] K lacks the conjunction.

5:4 *Arum of the sixth year*: In each of the three species mentioned, the plant had completed its grown in the sixth year and could have been gathered then, but was left in the ground for the sake of preservation.

One may dig them up: All agree that these plants are not subject to Seventh-Year prohibitions. The House of Shammai, however, require distinguishing their manner of picking from other years, fitting with the concern throughout this tractate for the appearance of transgression.

concede: If digging with an alternative tool is impossible, then one may use the ordinary tool, possibly because the nature of the ground itself will prove to onlookers that one is uprooting a plant rather than working the ground itself.

5:5 *From when may one buy arum*: This mishnah shifts from the field to the market. Most produce grows and must be consumed in the Seventh Year itself; its presence in the market immediately after the end of the Seventh Year would strongly indicate the transgressive sale of Seventh-Year produce. (The Mishnah assumes that a substantial portion of the population transgress the Seventh Year—see 3:1, 4:1, and 5:6–9.) Arum, by contrast, grows over multiple years, can be stored for long periods of time, and can even be licitly harvested in the Seventh Year (5:4); its immediate availability in the market, therefore, is not necessarily an indication of transgression.

Immediately: In contrast to vegetables, for which one must wait until they newly grow in the eighth year (see 6:4), one may assume the arum being sold may have finished growing in the sixth year and was stored during the seventh.

after the new [leaves] become dominant: Just as with regular vegetables, one must assume that immediately available arum was illicitly planted and harvested in the Seventh Year. Alternatively, this refers to arum planted before the Seventh Year which continued to develop during the Seventh Year, whose leaves were not removed by the poor (see 5:3); the appearance of new leaves in the eighth year indicates that the new growth of the corm has surpassed the old growth, a stringency with which R. Judah is not concerned.

5:6 *yoke*: Used to attach draft animals to plows.

a winnowing fan,
a two-pronged fork.[57]
But he may sell a hand-sickle,
a harvest-sickle,
and a wagon and all its equipment.
This is the general rule:
anything whose function is specifically for transgression[58] is forbidden;
[but if it can be used] for forbidden and permitted [purposes], it is permitted.

7 A potter may sell five oil jars and fifteen wine jars,
for such [are the quantities] one typically gathers from ownerless property.
But[59] if one gathered more, it is permitted.
And one may sell to gentiles in the Land of Israel
but to an Israelite outside the Land [only].

8 The House of Shammai say:
One may not sell him a plowing cow during the Seventh Year,
but the House of Hillel permit,
because he can slaughter it.
One[60] may sell him produce even during sowing season,

[57] Or "mattock."   [58] K (before emendation), P, and other manuscripts: "for work."
[59] K, P lack the conjunction.   [60] P and many other manuscripts: "And one may."

winnowing fan: Used to winnow large amounts of grain. All grain from the previous year would have already been processed, and the small amounts of grain that would grow during the Seventh Year could be winnowed by hand. Such a device, therefore, would only be used by transgressors who had illicitly sown their field.

two-pronged fork: Used for turning over the grains in the granary and for winnowing. In *Betsah* 1:2/*Eduyot* 4:2 it is a tool for digging (a mattock), but digging is not necessarily a forbidden labor during the Seventh Year (see e.g. 5:4).

This is the general rule: This rule follows the House of Hillel (5:8), who permit the sale of anything which might be used in a permitted manner, however infrequently.

5:7 *five oil jars and fifteen wine jars*: Each jar held about fifteen to twenty liters. This is roughly equivalent to the annual consumption of wine and oil per family, which is how much one would typically produce from the ownerless grapes and olives gathered during the Seventh Year.

But if one gathered more: After the fact, if what the customer gathered unintentionally produced larger quantities of wine or oil, he may buy more jars. Notice that while the former ruling is addressed to the potter in an attempt to prevent selling vessels to transgressive customers, the latter is addressed to the scrupulous customer who intended to gather only the accepted quantities but erred.

sell to gentiles... to an Israelite: More than the quantities listed here, and possibly referring to the tools listed in 5:6 as well.

5:8 *sell him*: The identity of the "him" is not stated; the Mishnah seems to mean "a Jew suspected of not observing the Seventh-Year restrictions."

the House of Hillel permit, because he can slaughter it: Despite the extremely low likelihood of slaughtering such a strong, productive cow.

produce: i.e. grain, since one may be buying it for consumption rather than sowing.

and[61] one may lend him his *se'ah* measure,
even though he knows that he has a threshing floor.
And[62] one may change coins for him,
even though he knows that he has workers [in his employ].[63]
But [in] all of these, if [stated] explicitly, it is forbidden.

9 A woman may lend another woman
who is suspected [of transgressing] the Seventh Year
a sifter,
a sieve,
a hand mill,
and an oven,
but may not select or grind with her.
The wife of a Fellow may lend the wife of an *am ha'arets*
a sifter and a sieve,
and may select, grind, and sift with her.
But once [the wife of the *am ha'arets*] adds water,
[the wife of a Fellow] may not come into contact with her,
for one may not encourage transgressors.
And they said all of these [leniencies] only for the sake of peace.

[61] **K** lacks the conjunction. [62] **K** lacks the conjunction.
[63] **P** and others: "that there are workers with him."

se'ah measure: Which would ordinarily be used to measure the grain after winnowing (see *Terumot* 1:7) for customers. However, there is a faint chance it is required for measuring something else.

change coins: The Mishnah follows a logical order: plowing, sowing, winnowing, and finally paying the workers.

5:9 Parallel to *Gittin* 5:9, within a longer unit on "for the sake of peace."

a sifter, a sieve, a hand mill, and an oven: The four implements required for turning grain into bread, which is permitted during the Seventh Year since it does not involve working the land. One may, therefore, lend the necessary tools even to suspected transgressors.

select: Remove stones or other refuse from the grain; see *Shabbat* 7:2.

may not select or grind: One cannot directly assist a suspected transgressor turn the grain into flour, since their grain may have been illicitly planted and harvested during the Seventh Year, rather than left over from the previous year.

Fellow…am ha'arets: The former is careful to observe the rules of purity, while the latter is not (see *Demai* 2:3).

adds water: As long as they are dry, grain and flour are not susceptible to impurity; see Leviticus 11:38 and *Makhshirin*. Therefore, the wife of a Fellow (*haver*) may assist the wife of an *am ha'arets* to produce dry flour from dry grain. Once water is added to the grain to make dough, however, it must be kept in a state of purity for the sake of the dough offering (see *Hallah*, esp. 2:3 and 3:2). An *am ha'arets* is presumed to be in a state of impurity and to immediately defile the dough, and the Fellow's wife cannot assist a violation of the purity rules.

for one may not encourage transgressors: This principle explains the limitations set upon personal contact, but presumes and seems untroubled by the existence of social connections with transgressors.

all of these [leniencies]: Regarding lending utensils to potential transgressors.

for the sake of peace: Unlike the previous principle, this statement assumes that the very existence of social connections with transgressors requires justification. The two statements therefore stand in marked tension, and may simply belong to different literary strata.

And[64] one may encourage gentiles during the Seventh Year,
but not an Israelite.
And one may[65] greet them for the sake of peace.

Chapter Six

6:1–2   *Seventh-Year Laws Outside the Land of Israel*

6 There are three regions[66] with regard to the Seventh Year:
(1) All places possessed by those who came up from Babylonia,
from the Land of Israel to Keziv[67]—
[their produce] may not be eaten nor [its land] cultivated [in the Seventh Year].
(2) All places possessed by those who came up from Egypt,
from Keziv to the River and to Amanah[68]—
[their produce] may be eaten but [the land] may not be cultivated.
(3) From the River and from Amanah and inward—
[their produce] may be eaten and [the land] may be cultivated.

[64] K lacks the conjunction.   [65] Or "must."   [66] Lit. "lands."
[67] K, P, and other manuscripts: "Geziv," here and below.   [68] K, P, and others: "Amanam."

encourage gentiles: With words and presumably even by lending them tools; see 4:3 and 5:7.

greet them: This applies to all years, and not specifically to the Seventh Year.

6:1 *three regions*: This mishnah combines two mapping systems. The first (which appears also in *Hallah* 4:8) specifies major border crossings. The second, unique to our mishnah, identifies these areas with groups of settlements of earlier generations. The mishnah assumes that the boundaries of the "Land of Israel" are known; what is at issue here is the boundaries of Syria (see 6:2).

those who came up from Babylonia: During the Persian period following the destruction of the first Temple and the subsequent exile. They settled Judaea, in the south.

Keziv: North of Akko, which is the northern border of the Land of Israel.

those who came up from Egypt: After the Exodus, conquering the Land of Canaan during the time of Joshua. They settled a much larger area than those who returned from the later exile.

Keziv…River…Amanah: Keziv is the southern border of the second territory; the (Euphrates) River is to the northeast, and Amanah refers to the Amanus mountain range in southern Turkey. (Some versions have "Amanus"; the manuscripts have "Amanam," whose last letter in Hebrew is easily transposed with "s.") The area between these points roughly corresponds to Syria during the Roman period.

inward: From the River and Amanah toward the Mediterranean Sea. Beyond that lies "Outside the Land."

may not be eaten: In the "Land of Israel," produce in the market is prohibited since it is assumed that it was grown illegally, and all other produce needs to be treated according to the rules of Seventh-Year produce.

may be eaten…may not be cultivated: Syria is fundamentally considered gentile land, so its produce is free from the strictures of Seventh-Year produce. Nevertheless one may not work the land itself (see 6:2), possibly owing to its liminal status, having once been conquered.

2 One may process produce in Syria
when it is already separated [from the ground],
but not when it is still attached.
One may thresh, winnow, tread, and bind,
but one may not harvest grain, or harvest grapes, or harvest olives.
R. Aqiva stated a general rule:
Whatever is permitted in the Land of Israel,
one may do likewise in Syria.[69]

6:3–4 *More on Vegetables after the Seventh Year*

3 Onions on which rain fell and [which] subsequently sprouted—
if their leaves are black,
they are forbidden;
if [their leaves are] green,
they are permitted.
R. Hanina[70] b. Antigonus says:
If they can be uprooted by their leaves,
they are forbidden.
Accordingly, [onions with such leaves] in the following year are permitted.

[69] Lit. "Anything the likes of which are permitted in the Land of Israel—one may do it in Syria."
[70] K, P, and most manuscripts: "Hananiah."

6:2 *One may process produce in Syria*: This is equivalent to the second territory, conquered in the time of Joshua, specified in the previous mishnah. This mishnah nuances the prohibition on working the land mentioned there, differentiating between harvesting, which the Torah explicitly prohibits (Leviticus 25:5), and other forms of processing grain, which it does not.

thresh…bind: Which are done to grain separated from the ground. This is either an explanation of the first clause, or issues from a different literary source. For the list of labors, cf. *Shabbat* 7:2.

grain…grapes: Following the order of Leviticus 25:5; for the inclusion of olives, see Exodus 23:11.

R. Aqiva stated a general rule: This is an alternative formulation of the distinction between ground labors explicitly forbidden by the Torah, which are also forbidden in Syria, and labors involved in processing harvested grain, which are permitted in Syria. The exact meaning of R. Aqiva's rule is debated by the commentators; it might refer to labors done in an irregular fashion (see 8:6), and therefore be stricter than the mishnah's earlier blanket permission to process already harvested produce.

6:3 This mishnah and the next interrupt the topical unity of this chapter and append the laws of vegetables left in the ground for more than one season (5:3–5).

Onions: That finished growing in the sixth year but were left in the ground during the Seventh Year.

black…green: The color of the leaves indicates the source of nurturing. Dark green leaves indicate that the onion fed from the soil and are therefore considered Seventh-Year growths; faint green leaves grew from the onion itself and are therefore considered sixth-year growths.

uprooted by their leaves: This is a different standard than color for determining whether the leaves grew as a result of feeding from soil. If one can remove the onion from the ground by pulling on them, such fresh, strong leaves are considered as a product of the Seventh Year.

Accordingly: If one can pull the onion from the ground by its leaves in the eighth year, those leaves clearly flourished after the Seventh Year, and are therefore not subject to its restrictions.

4 From when is one permitted to buy vegetables after the Seventh Year?
From when the same kind has ripened.[71]
Once the early crop has ripened,
the later one is permitted as well.
Rabbi permitted purchasing vegetables immediately following the Seventh Year.

6:5–6 Export and Import of Sanctified Produce

5 One may not remove *terumah* oil that must be burnt or Seventh-Year produce from the Land to outside the Land.
R. Simeon says:
I have received an explicit tradition[72] that one may remove them to Syria,
but one may not remove them to outside the Land.
6 One may not bring *terumah* from outside the Land into the Land.
R. Simeon says:
I have received an explicit tradition that one may bring it from Syria,
but one may not bring it from outside the Land.

[71] Lit. "produced," here and below. **K, P**: "newly ripens" (lit. "produces").
[72] Lit. "explicitly heard," here and below.

6:4 *From when is one permitted to buy vegetables*: This is a direct continuation of 5:5. The Mishnah assumes that the market is full of produce grown and harvested by those who transgressed Seventh-Year prohibitions, and such produce remains prohibited in the eighth year. Thus one must wait until the new harvest arrives to display the previous year's produce.

Once the early crop has ripened: In the eighth year. This is a substantial leniency, which permits assuming that all of the vegetables of a particular species belong to the new year as soon as some of it ripens, even though a significant portion is known to grow later.

Rabbi: Rabbi Judah the Patriarch. This ruling is consistent with other lenient rulings of R. Judah the Patriarch about Seventh-Year produce (as discussed in the Tosefta and the Yerushalmi).

immediately: Based on the possibility that the vegetables in the market were imported from outside the Land.

6:5 *One may not remove*: In general, sanctified foods that must be maintained in a state of purity may not be taken outside the Land of Israel because of fear of defilement (see *Oholot* 2:3).

terumah oil that must be burnt: That is, *terumah* oil which became impure and therefore needed to be burnt (see *Shabbat* 2:1 and *Temurah* 7:5). Even already impure oil may not be brought to an impure place, perhaps reflecting a view prohibiting adding impurity to existing impurity (cf. *Pesahim* 1:6) or a view that such oil ought only be burnt in dignified contexts (see *Terumot* 11:10).

Seventh-Year produce: Although such produce did not need to be eaten in a state of purity (as opposed to *terumah* and second tithe), it nevertheless possessed a sanctity intimately connected to the Land of Israel. This prohibition may also have an economic justification in light of the shortage of food in the Land of Israel during the Seventh Year.

remove them to Syria: Which had an intermediate status (see 6:1–2). It is unclear whether R. Simeon is disagreeing with the first opinion or merely explicating it.

6:6 *One may not bring terumah from outside the Land*: In general, commandments dependent on the Land, are not applicable beyond its borders (*Qiddushin* 1:9), but according to *Hallah* 4:10–11, in Second Temple times some Jews brought priestly gifts to the Temple from outside of the Land. According to the Tosefta *terumah* separated outside the Land must be consumed there. The reason for this injunction is nowhere stated explicitly; perhaps the problem is that such *terumah* is considered *prima facie* impure (see 6:5). The Yerushalmi claims that it was designed to discourage priests from leaving the Land.

Chapter Seven

7:1–3 *Seventh-Year Produce and Its Conversion into Money: Crops Whose Monetary Exchange Is Subject to Seventh-Year Prohibition*

7 A great general rule they said concerning the Seventh Year:
Any [kind] of human food,
or of animal food,
or of species used for dyeing,
and which cannot be preserved in the ground—
it is subject to Seventh-Year [restrictions]
and [if converted into money]
its money is subject to Seventh-Year [restrictions];
it is subject to Removal,
and [if converted into money] its money is subject to Removal.
And which [kinds are these]?
These are:[73]
the leaf of wild ginger,
the leaf of mint,[74]
chicory,
leek,
purslane,
and orchid.
And animal foods:[75]
thorns and thistles.
And of species used for dyeing:
aftergrowths of woad and safflower.
[All] these are subject to Seventh-Year [restrictions],
and their money is subject to Seventh-Year [restrictions];
they are subject to Removal,
and their money is subject to Removal.

---

[73] Singular in original. **K** and many manuscripts read "And which is this? This is."
[74] Or Cetarach, rustyback fern.
[75] **K**: "Of animal foods." **P** and many others: "And of animal foods."

7:1 *A great general rule they said concerning*: This formula signifies the beginning of a new literary unit (cf. 8:1; *Shabbat* 7:1; *Tohorot* 8:6, albeit lacking the word "great").

and which cannot be preserved in the ground: i.e. if left in the ground, they would rot.

Seventh-Year [restrictions]: Namely, those detailed in 7:3–4 and chapter 8.

Removal: Seventh-Year crops that would rot if left in the ground cannot be stored past the end of their season; see chapter 9.

which: The plants mentioned here would not normally be eaten, except in times of shortage, such as the Seventh Year. Only the specific parts used as human or animal food or as dye are subject to Seventh-Year restrictions.

2 And another general rule did they say:
Any [kind] that is not[76] human food,
or animal food,
or a species used for dyeing,
and [those] which can be preserved in the ground—
it is subject to Seventh-Year [restrictions],
and its money is subject to Seventh-Year [restrictions].
[But] neither is it subject to Removal,
nor is its money subject to Removal.
Which [kinds] are these?[77]
The[78] root of wild ginger,
the root of mint,[79]
heliotrope,
corm of the orchid,
and hazelwort.
And of species used for dyeing:
madder
and dyer's reseda.
[All] these are subject to the Seventh-Year prohibition,
and their money is subject to the Seventh-Year prohibition.
[But] neither are they subject to Removal,
nor is their money subject to Removal.
R. Meir says:
Their money must be eliminated by the New Year.
The [Sages] replied to him:
[If] they are not subject to Removal,
all the more so their money [ought not be subject to Removal].

[76] **K**, **P**, and many others read: "Any [kind] of human food or of animal food," identically to 7:1.
[77] Lit. "Which is it?" **K**, **P**, and many manuscripts read "And which is this?"
[78] **K** and many manuscripts insert "This is."   [79] Or "cetarach, rustyback fern."

7:2 *another general rule*: This rule is the mirror image of that of the previous mishnah. (This is not always the case; sometimes the additional rule is unrelated, as in *Ma'aserot* 1:1 and *Shabbat* 7:1, 3.)

not human food…and [those] which can be preserved…not subject to Removal: According to this version, this rule is teaching two separate laws: (1) even inedible species not used for dyeing are subject to Seventh-Year restrictions, albeit not Removal; (2) species that will not rot if left in the ground are exempt from Removal. The version of the vast majority of the manuscripts, however, renders this clause entirely parallel to 7:1, the distinction being that edible or usable species that can be preserved in the ground are not subject to Removal.

Which: As above, only certain marginally edible parts of the plant are mentioned here. Taken together with 7:1, the two mishnayot demonstrate that in some cases while the whole plant might be subject to Seventh-Year restrictions, only some of it might be subject to the law of Removal; see *Niddah* 6:8.

R. Meir: Out of fear of forgetting that the money was obtained in exchange for Seventh-Year produce and is therefore subject to various restrictions (see 8:8), R. Meir requires eliminating the money by the end of the Seventh Year.

3 Pomegranate peels and its bud,
nutshells and [fruit-]seeds—
they are subject to Seventh-Year [restrictions],
and their money is subject to Seventh-Year [restrictions].

7:3 cont.–4 *Seventh-Year Produce and Its Conversion into Money: Trade in Seventh-Year and Other Sanctified Produce*

The dyer may dye for his personal use, but[80] may not dye for profit,
for one may not trade in the produce of[81] the Seventh Year,
nor in firstlings,
nor in *terumah*,
nor in carrion,
nor in *terefot*,
nor in vermin,
nor in creeping things.
And one may not purchase vegetables of the field and sell them in the market,
but he may gather and have his son sell for him.

[80] K, P, and many manuscripts lack the conjunction.
[81] K, before emendation, lacked "produce of."

7:3 *Pomegranate peels*: As in the laws of purity (*Uqtsin* 2:2–4), all parts of the fruit, including its peels and seeds, have the same status and are subject to the same laws.

for one may not trade: Although in principle Seventh-Year produce is considered ownerless property (5:7; *Pe'ah* 6:1) that one may gather for one's own purposes, the Torah sets it aside for consumption and use (Leviticus 25:6) by the poor in particular (Exodus 23:11); it is not intended to generate profit except in rare circumstances. (Cf. *Rosh Hashanah* 1:8; *Sanhedrin* 3:3.) The Mishnah spells out other cases in which trade is restricted despite the fact that the items are one's property and one is permitted to benefit from them, because trading in them is either disrespectful or distasteful.

firstlings: firstborn [animals]: A gift to the priest, who is entitled to eat them (Numbers 18:17–18), but from which he ought not profit. Even a blemished firstling, which may be consumed by nonpriests, is not to be sold (*Ma'aser Sheni* 1:2).

terumah: Despite being considered his personal property (*Hallah* 1:9; *Bikkurim* 2:1), a priest ought not excessively trade *terumah* (cf. *Bikkurim* 3:12).

carrion…terefot…vermin…creeping things: Carrion are improperly slaughtered animals; *terefot* are mortally wounded animals (see *Hullin* 2:4; 3:1–5). For vermin and creeping things, see Leviticus 11:24–31. Although the Torah nowhere forbids profiting from these forbidden foods, and explicitly permits profiting from carrion (Deuteronomy 14:21), one should nevertheless not make one's living from these abominations (see Exodus 22:30; Leviticus 11:43–44).

one may not purchase vegetables and sell…but he may gather and have his son sell: The first clause forbids reselling Seventh-Year vegetables, while the latter permits selling produce one gathers via a family member. The connection is unclear; some commentaries emend the word "purchase" to "gather"; others claim that the Mishnah wishes to teach that even reselling Seventh-Year vegetables is forbidden (selling vegetables one picked oneself being obviously forbidden), while selling one's own picked vegetables via a family member is permitted (reselling via a family member being obviously permitted). The rationale for permitting a child to sell purchased or gathered produce is that it indicates that one is only disposing of those vegetables which are unsuitable for the family's needs, rather than trying to turn a profit.

If he purchased for personal use and some of it was left over,
he is permitted to sell it.

4 If one bought a firstborn animal for his son's wedding feast or for a festival,
but did not need[82] it,
he is permitted to sell it.
Trappers of wild animals, birds, and fish who happened to catch impure species
are permitted to sell them.
R. Judah says:
Even if one happens to find [some impure species] along his way
He may take [it] and sell [it],
as long as this is not his profession.
But the Sages forbid.

7:5–7 Seventh-Year Produce and Its Conversion into Money: Other Crops Whose Monetary Exchange Is Subject to Seventh-Year Prohibition

5 The branches of the hawthorn[83] or of carob trees—
they are subject to Seventh-Year [restrictions]
and their money is subject to Seventh-Year [restrictions].
They are subject to Removal,
and their money is subject to Removal.
Branches of the terebinth, of the pistachio, and the boxthorn—
they are subject to Seventh-Year [restrictions]
and their money is subject to Seventh-Year [restrictions].
[But] they are not subject to Removal,
nor is its money subject to Removal.
Their leaves, however, are subject to Removal,
because they fall from their stem.[84]

---

[82] Or "use." [83] Or "wild jujuba"; or "wild bushes." Precise identification uncertain.
[84] Lit. "their father."

---

for personal use ... left over, he is permitted to sell it: One may sell the surplus of any vegetables purchased in small quantities for oneself and need not enlist a family member since the small quantity will indicate that one is selling surplus. (Alternatively, gathered produce must be sold by a child to indicate that it is surplus and not being professionally traded; purchased produce may be sold by oneself, since it is obviously surplus.)

7:4 *did not need it ... happened to catch*: Unplanned trade in animals and foods normally prohibited from such (7:3) is permitted, since it will not become regular behavior.

R. Judah: This is an additional leniency: those who are not professional hunters who come across the opportunity to capture an impure animal may do so and sell it, since that is not and will not become a regular trade.

7:5 *branches*: These refer to soft branches that can be eaten during times of scarcity. Following 7:1–2, the first set of branches can remain on the tree ("in the ground," as in 7:2), and are therefore subject to Removal, while the second cannot, and are therefore not subject to Removal.

Their leaves: Although the leaves may also be eaten, they cannot be preserved on the tree, since they inevitably fall off.

6 Rose, henna, balsam, and rock rose—
they are subject to Seventh-Year [restrictions]
and their money is subject to Seventh-Year [restrictions].
R. Simeon says:
Balsam is not subject to Seventh-Year [restrictions],
because it is not a fruit.

7 A new rose which one preserved in old oil—
one must collect the rose.
An old [rose which one preserved] in new [oil]
is liable for Removal.
New carobs which one preserved in old wine,
or old [carobs which one preserved] in new [wine],
are liable for Removal.
This is the rule:
Whatever is sufficient to impart a flavor, one is obliged to eliminate,
[when] a species [is mixed] with a different species;
but[85] [when] a species [is mixed] with its [own] species
[in] any amount whatsoever [one is liable to eliminate].
Seventh-Year [produce] forbids [in] any amount whatsoever
[when mixed] with its [own] species,
and forbids [when mixed] with a different species
in an amount sufficient to impart flavor.

[85] K lacks the conjunction.

7:6 *Rose, etc.*: These are subject to Seventh-Year restrictions due to their fragrance.

balsam: The most famous perfume produced in the Land of Israel. According to R. Simeon, since balsam is made of a resin extracted from the tree, it should be considered part of the tree itself, which is not subject to Seventh-Year prohibitions, rather than as a separate fruit.

7:7 *new...old*: "New" refers to Seventh-Year produce; "old" refers to sixth-year (or older) produce.

new rose...old oil: The Seventh-Year rose petals do not impart scent to the sixth-year oil in the time before elimination, and therefore removing them is sufficient to permit the oil.

old [rose] in new [oil]: A sixth-year rose immersed in Seventh-Year oil absorbs flavor from the oil, and therefore both the rose and the oil are subject to Removal. According to the Yerushalmi, however, this clause refers to a Seventh-Year rose immersed in eighth-year oil, the more mature rose imparting its scent to the newer oil.

carobs...wine: The assumption is that carobs both impart and absorb flavor, so whether the carobs or the wine are of the Seventh Year, both are subject to Removal. The Tosefta, however, applies the same rules to carobs as to roses.

This is the rule: When two different foods are mixed, the status of the whole mixture is determined by whether the taste imparted by the prohibited food is detectable. If the forbidden and permitted foods are identical, however, such as regular oil mixed with Seventh-Year oil, it is impossible to distinguish the taste of the permitted food from that of the forbidden food, and the mixture as a whole is rendered forbidden. This principle is also found in *Hallah* 3:10 and *Avodah Zarah* 5:8.

Chapter Eight

8:1–2 *Appropriate Use of Seventh-Year Produce: Principles*

8 A great general rule did they say concerning the Seventh Year:
Any [produce] that is solely human food,
one may not make from it a poultice for people,
and needless to say for animals.
Any produce that is not solely human food,
one may make from it a poultice for people,
but not for animals.
Any produce that is neither solely human food nor solely animal food—
if one intended it to be human food and animal food,
the stringencies of both human [food] and animal [food] are placed upon it.
If one intended it for wood,
it is thereby considered as wood,
such as savory, hyssop, and thyme.

2 Seventh-Year [produce] is permitted[86] for eating, drinking, and anointing:
for eating what is typically eaten
and for anointing what is typically used for anointing.
One may not anoint [with] wine or vinegar,
but he may anoint with oil.
The same applies to *terumah* and second tithe.

---

[86] Lit. "is given," here and below.

8:1 *A great general rule*: After specifying the categories of plants to which Seventh-Year restrictions apply (see 7:1–2), this mishnah, and the rest of the chapter, defines the nature of those restrictions. Cf. *Tohorot* 8:6.

human food…one may not make from it a poultice: The Torah requires eating Seventh-Year produce (Exodus 23:11, Leviticus 25:6); using it for other purposes, such as applying it as a bandage, is considered a waste of Seventh-Year fruits, and is thus prohibited.

not solely human food: i.e. animal food. Although such foods may be used for all human purposes, they are restricted to consumption by animals and may not be used for other animal-related purposes.

neither solely human food nor solely animal food: i.e. things which are not regularly used for food by either.

If one intended it: The status of such produce, which has multiple possible uses, is defined by human intention.

stringencies of both: As human food it may not be used for making a poultice, as above, and as animal food it may not be cooked (Yerushalmi), since cooking is unnecessary for animals and reduces the amount of food unnecessarily.

considered as wood: Which is not subject to Seventh-Year restrictions and may be used for any purpose, including burning for heating.

8:2 *eating, drinking and anointing*: Although these are the basic uses of Seventh-Year fruits, this list must not be exhaustive, since the Mishnah also mentions dyeing (7:1–2, restricted to species only used for that purpose) and lamplighting (below).

One may not anoint…The same applies: See *Ma'aser Sheni* 2:1; cf. *Terumot* 11:1.

Seventh-Year [produce] is less severe than these,
inasmuch as it is permitted to be used for lighting a lamp.

8:3–5 *Appropriate Use of Seventh-Year Produce: Selling and Paying with Seventh-Year Produce*

3 One may not sell Seventh-Year produce by measure, weight, or number; nor [may one sell Seventh-Year] figs by number or vegetables by weight.
The House of Shammai say:
Not even by bundles.
But the House of Hillel say:
What one typically ties up in bundles[87] in the house,
one may also tie up in bundles in the market,[88]
such as leeks and orchid.

---

[87] K: "What is typically tied up in bundles."
[88] K (before emendation) and others: "for the house … for the market."

---

lighting a lamp: Terumah oil may be used for a lamp only when rendered impure (*Terumot* 11:10; *Temurah* 7:5). Such oil is termed 'oil that is to be burnt' (see 6:5 and *Shabbat* 2:1). Second tithe may never be used as fuel, even if rendered impure, since it can be redeemed (see *Ma'aser Sheni* 3:9).

8:3 *One may not sell*: The mishnah above specified the limited circumstances under which it is permitted to sell Seventh-Year fruits (7:3–4). Here the Mishnah further limits the manner in which one may perform the sale.

by measure: Volume.

weight, or number: Such precision was the normal method of selling, which is forbidden. This may mean that nothing may be sold in any of these ways, or it may mean that one may not sell something as it is normally sold, but may sell it in other ways (e.g. something normally sold by measure may be sold by weight or number).

figs by number: Figs were apparently sold by number (*Ma'aserot* 2:5–6; *Bava Batra* 6:2), although they were also measured and weighed (*Terumot* 4:6). This is apparently an example of the rule that something may not be sold as it is normally sold, but may be sold in a different fashion. Some claim, however, that it teaches the opposite: figs, which were generally sold by basket (cf. *Ma'aserot* 1:5, 2:4, 4:2), may not be sold in the less usual fashion either.

nor … vegetables by weight: Vegetables were regularly sold by the bundle (*Demai* 3:2, 6:12; *Ma'aserot* 1:5); only post-Mishnaic sources refer to selling vegetables by weight.

Not even by bundles: Since this was the standard manner of selling vegetables (see above), even though it is not one of the three forbidden methods mentioned above, it is forbidden.

the House of Hillel agree that vegetables may not generally be sold in bundles in the Seventh Year. However, since one may sell what is left from his own household supply (7:3), those which one typically bundles for household transport (or use) may be sold that way.

4 If one tells his worker:
"Take this *issar* and pick me vegetables today,"
his wage is permitted.
[But if one said to his worker:] "Go pick me vegetables today with it,"
his wage is forbidden.
If he took from a baker a loaf for a *pundion*, [saying]:
"After picking vegetables from the field, I'll bring [them] to you,"
it is permitted.
[But] if he took it without saying anything,
he may not pay him with Seventh-Year money,
for one may not repay a debt with Seventh-Year money.

5 One may not give [Seventh-Year money as payment] to
a well digger,
a bathhouse keeper,
a barber,
or a sailor.
But one may give it to a well digger to drink [water],
and to all of them he may give [Seventh-Year money] as a free present.

8:4 *If one tells his worker*: Money used to buy Seventh-Year fruits is subject to the same limitations as the Seventh-Year fruits themselves (7:1-2). This mishnah teaches that money acquires the status of the fruits not only when used to pay for the fruits themselves, but also when paying someone to pick them.

issar: One twenty-fourth of a *dinar*.

"Take this issar and pick me vegetables today": In the first case, the payment is not linked explicitly to the vegetable picking, whereas in the second case it is.

forbidden: i.e. subject to Seventh-Year restrictions: it may be consumed only in specific ways, may not be wasted, and requires removal at the end of the season.

took from a baker a loaf: On credit. The loaf was made from sixth-year wheat.

pundion: Two *issar* (one-twelfth of a *dinar*).

permitted: Paying for the loaf with Seventh-Year produce is permitted; the produce remains and the loaf becomes subject to Seventh-Year restrictions (see 8:7).

if he took it without saying anything: If the purchaser does not explicitly say how he is going to pay for the loaf, it becomes a regular debt, and Seventh-Year fruits may not be used to cover debts. This mishnah thus addresses three scenarios involving payment and Seventh-Year fruits: money not directly associated with the produce; payment of Seventh-Year fruits in exchange for ordinary produce; and repaying debts.

8:5 *One may not give*: Like Seventh-Year produce itself, money that has acquired Seventh-Year restrictions must be used exclusively for food and other permitted purposes (8:1), and just as one may not use it for paying debts (8:4), one may not use it to pay service providers.

to drink: A permitted use of Seventh-Year produce (8:1).

free present: There are no limitations on transferring Seventh-Year money from one person to another, provided that it is not in exchange for services.

8:6–7 Appropriate Use of Seventh-Year Produce: Preparation of Seventh-Year Fruits

6 Seventh-Year figs—
one may not dry them in the drying area,
but one may dry them in a deserted space.
One may not tread grapes in the winepress,
but one may tread them in a trough.
One may not prepare olives in an olive press or a small press,
but one may manually crush them and put them in a tiny press.
R. Simeon says:
He may also grind them in the olive press and put them in a tiny press.
 7 One may not cook Seventh-Year vegetables in *terumah* oil,
so as not to render it invalid.
R. Simeon permits.

8:7 cont.–11 Appropriate Use of Seventh-Year Produce: Illicit Use of Seventh-Year Money and Its Consequence

The last thing [exchanged for Seventh-Year produce]
is caught in the Seventh-Year [restrictions],
and the [original] produce itself is forbidden.

8:6 *Seventh-Year figs*: This mishnah specifies alternative processing methods for figs, grapes, and olives, which may be prepared only on a small scale. This mishnah and the first clause of the next abruptly disrupt the surrounding unit concerning Seventh-Year money exchange, although it fits the larger topic of the chapter (restrictions on the use of Seventh-Year produce).

drying area: Designated for processing figs (cf. *Ma'aserot* 3:2; *Ma'aser Sheni* 3:6).

deserted space: This word might refer to dry land, or specifically to open space in a deserted building (cf. *Megillah* 3:3, which lists activities, including spreading ropes and fruits, which may not be done in a destroyed synagogue).

R. Simeon says: The process of oil production includes two main stages: crushing the olives and pressing the oil from them. R. Simeon is only concerned that the amount ultimately produced be small, but does not require changing the earlier stages of preparation.

8:7 *cook*: Once the vegetables absorb the flavor of the oil, they acquire the same legal status (cf. *Terumot* 10:11).

so as not to render it invalid: Seventh-Year vegetables prepared with *terumah* oil must be kept pure, since it is prohibited to eat impure *terumah*. If the vegetables become impure they must be burned (*Temurah* 7:5), which is a waste of Seventh-Year produce. It is therefore preferable to prepare it with nonsacral oil which can be consumed also in a state of impurity.

R. Simeon permits: He does not forbid on account of the mere possibility of Seventh-Year produce becoming impure and wasted. Cf. *Ma'aser Sheni* 3:2 for a similar debate.

The last thing: This comment refers back to the cases of buying and selling Seventh-Year fruits. Money or anything else given or taken in exchange is subject to Seventh-Year restrictions, in addition to the produce itself.

forbidden: As in 8:4, i.e. subject to Seventh-Year restrictions: it may be consumed only in specific ways, may not be wasted, and requires removal at the end of the season.

8 One may not buy slaves, land, or impure animals with Seventh-Year money,
and if one did buy,
one must consume their equivalent value.
One may not bring
bird sacrifices of a *zav*
or bird sacrifices of a *zavah*,
or bird sacrifices of a parturient
from Seventh-Year money,
and if one did bring one of these,
one must consume their equivalent value.
One may not anoint vessels with Seventh-Year oil,
and if one anointed,
one must consume their equivalent value.

9 Leather which one anointed with Seventh-Year oil—
R. Eliezer says:
It must be burnt.
But the Sages say:
One must consume its equivalent value.
They said in front of R. Aqiva:
R. Eliezer would say:
Leather which one anointed with Seventh-Year oil must be burnt.
He said to them:
Be silent!
I will not tell you what R. Eliezer says about this matter.

10 And they further said in front [of R. Aqiva]:
R. Eliezer would say:
One who eats the bread of Samaritans is like one who eats swine flesh.
He said to them:
Be silent!
I will not tell you what R. Eliezer says about this matter.

8:8 *One may not buy*: This mishnah is repeated verbatim with regard to second tithe in *Ma'aser Sheni* 1:7; cf. 8:2. The basic framework of this chapter's laws concerning Seventh-Year money exchange is shared with the laws of second tithe.

one must consume their equivalent value: He must take other fruits of the same value and eat them in accordance with the restrictions of Seventh-Year fruits.

bird sacrifices: These offerings are prescribed in Leviticus 15:14 (*zav*); 15:29 (*zavah*); 12:8 (parturient). This is more appropriate with respect to second tithe, which was brought to Jerusalem; the pilgrims would naturally like to use the money for sacrifices they owed.

One may not anoint vessels: Only people (8:2).

8:9 *It must be burnt*: It is unclear whether this extreme solution was R. Eliezer's general policy regarding illicit use of Seventh-Year produce that he would apply to all of the cases in 8:8, or whether it should be understood as a judgment of the severity of this particular act. The former possibility is strengthened by the following dialogue with R. Aqiva.

Be silent: Presumably, R. Aqiva did not want to openly dispute his teacher's extreme strictness.

8:10 *bread of Samaritans…swine flesh*: This statement reflects the deep enmity towards the Samaritans in some Second Temple and rabbinic sources.

I will not tell you: R. Aqiva is probably attempting to marginalize these earlier views.

11 A bathhouse that was heated with fodder or straw of the Seventh Year—
one may bathe in it.
But if he[89] is honored, this one may not bathe.

Chapter Nine

9:1 *Removal of Seventh-Year Fruit: Ownerless Species and Aftergrowths*

9 Rue, wild amaranth,[90] and purslane,
coriander that is in the mountains, celery that is in the rivers, and white wallrocket
are exempt from tithes
and may be bought from anyone in the Seventh Year,
for [plants] such as these are not guarded.
R. Judah says:
Mustard aftergrowths are permitted,
for transgressors are not suspected of it.

[89] Or "it [i.e. the bathhouse]." Meaning not certain.
[90] Or "Wild rue and amaranth." K, after emendation: "Amaranth and fennel."

8:11 *fodder or straw*: These are considered animal food (see *Shabbat* 7:4, 18:2) and should not be used as fuel (8:1; cf. 9:7).

one may bathe in it: Since one has no control over the management of the public bath one is permitted to use it.

if he is honored: Since the bath operators may add more fuel for an important person, he may not benefit from a violation done for his sake. The commentators debate the meaning of the final clause.

9:1 *Rue*, etc.: Cf. *Ma'aserot* 5:8.

coriander that is in the mountains: Possibly a species of wild coriander (cf. *Kilayim* 1:2) or a different but similar-looking species (*Bifora testiculata*).

celery that is in the rivers: That is, celery which grows wild in moist places.

exempt from tithes…not guarded: Plants that grow wild and are not cultivated by farmers are not subject to tithes; see *Ma'aserot* 1:1. This applies to non-Seventh Years, since tithes are suspended in the Seventh Year.

bought from anyone in the Seventh Year: Most vegetables may not be bought indiscriminately during the Seventh Year (cf. 6:4, 7:3), due to the fear that the seller or his supplier sowed and harvested them in violation of Seventh-Year prohibitions. Since these plants grow wild and are not usually cultivated, one may assume that the seller has gathered them from ownerless property, which is permitted (5:7). At the same time, they are subject to the same Seventh-Year restrictions as other crops.

Mustard aftergrowths are permitted: R. Judah adds mustard aftergrowths to the above list. Although this plant is occasionally cultivated (e.g. *Pe'ah* 3:2, *Kilayim* 2:8), transgressors had no reason to do, since it would spread on its own in the fallow fields (cf. *Kilayim* 2:9).

R. Simeon says:
All aftergrowths are permitted
except for the aftergrowths of kale,
for [plants] such as these are not among the vegetables of the field.
But the Sages say:
All aftergrowths are forbidden.

9:2–3 *Removal of Seventh-Year Fruit: Territories of Removal*

2 There are three territories with regard to Removal:
(1) Judaea, (2) Transjordan, and (3) the Galilee.
And there are three territories in each one.
[In the Galilee:]
(1) Upper Galilee, (2) Lower Galilee, and (3) the Valley.
From Kfar Hananiah upward, where sycamore trees do not grow—Upper Galilee;
From Kfar Hananiah downward, where sycamore tree do grow—Lower Galilee,
and the Tiberias region—the Valley.
And in Judaea:
(1) the Mountain, (2) the Plain, and (3) the Valley,
and the plain of Lydda is deemed as the plain of the South,
and its mountain is deemed as Mountain of the King.
From Bet Horon down to the sea—one territory.

All aftergrowths: Since the seeds of some cultivated plants may have spread naturally and grow wild around the fields, R. Simeon permits purchasing them.

aftergrowths of kale: Since this species does not spread wild on the fields, R. Simeon forbids buying it indiscriminately on the assumption that it was sown and grown in the seller's garden.

forbidden: To buy in the market, lest the seller be a transgressor. One is, however, permitted to pick aftergrowths found in the field and eat them.

9:2 *Removal*: The rest of the chapter prescribes the laws of Removal, also translated "elimination." During the Seventh Year, one may not harvest large quantities of produce, but may bring that which one picks for one's family's consumption into one's home and store it there (cf. 5:7). Once that kind of produce is no longer available to be harvested, however, one may not keep it. At that point, it must be eliminated, i.e. removed, from the house as well. Commentators debate whether "Removal" means renunciation of ownership and removal from the house to a public place (cf. Deuteronomy 26:13–14), or actual elimination.

territories with regard to Removal: Once a specific kind of produce is no longer available to be picked from the fields of a territory, it must be removed from the houses in that territory as well. The different territories are distinguished by different climates, which affects when each kind of produce finishes (9:3).

upward: North toward the higher mountains of the Upper Galilee.

Mountain...Valley: The Tosefta explains that Mountain refers to Mountain of the King, which is another name for the Judaean Mountains. The Tosefta also explains that "Valley" means the territory from Jericho to Ein-Gedi. The Mishnah, written from a Galilean perspective, does not specify any of the Transjordanian territories.

deemed as: In other words, elimination applies to species in the plain of Lydda and the mountain of that plain when those species are finished in the plain of the South and the Mountain of the King, respectively.

3 Why did [the Sages] say "three territories"?
So that one may eat in each one
until the last [produce] has finished in [that territory].
R. Simeon says:
They only said "three territories" with respect to Judaea.
The rest of the territories are deemed as Mountain of the King.
And all of the territories are equal with respect to olives and dates.

9:4–7: *Removal of Seventh-Year Fruit: The Period of Removal*

4 One may eat [one's stored produce] as long as ownerless produce is available,
but not if only guarded produce is available.[91]
R. Yose permits[92] even if they were guarded.
One may eat even as long as red peas or trees that bear fruit twice a year are available,
but not fruits that ripen only by the winter.
R. Judah permits
as long as they have begun to ripen before the summer ends.

5 If one preserves three kinds [of vegetables] in one barrel—
R. Eliezer says:
One may eat them [only] as long as the first is available.

---

[91] Lit. "One may eat on [the basis of] what is ownerless, and not on [the basis of] what is guarded." K: "and not from what is guarded," possibly in error.

[92] K, P, and other manuscripts: "says."

9:3 *"three territories"*: In other words, why did they subdivide each territory into three subterritories?

finished: Once that species has been picked clean by the poor or by animals.

equal with respect to olives and dates: If olives and dates are still available anywhere in the Land, they need not be eliminated, even if they are finished in one's locale.

9:4 *ownerless produce…guarded produce*: Owners of fields are required to provide access to everyone to consume whatever grows there (Exodus 23:11); produce in such fields is "ownerless." Guarded produce refers to produce in the fields of transgressors who protect the produce in their field instead of abandoning it. The dispute between the Sages and R. Yose, therefore, is whether the theoretical but not practical availability of produce delays the time of elimination.

red peas remain in the fields (in the Akko area, according to the Tosefta) for an extended period of time.

trees that bear fruit twice a year: Once during the spring and once during the summer (see *Demai* 1:1). The Mishnah permits storing the figs from the first harvest until the end of the second one later in the summer.

but not fruits that ripen only by the winter: Those fruits, presumably grapes, which ripen the following winter are considered a separate species, and thus do not determine the time by which the earlier harvests must be eliminated.

R. Judah permits: If some of the fruits that only fully ripen in fall begin to ripen before the end of the summer, i.e. during the Seventh Year, then one may wait to eliminate those fruits until the following winter. Since fruits are classified by when they begin to ripen, and not according to when they are harvested (see 4:7–9); all fruits that have ripened during the Seventh Year are considered one species with respect to the season of removal.

9:5 *preserves*: In a brine.

three kinds [of vegetables] in one barrel: Each kind is completely finished at a different period.

first…last: Referring to the species that finishes first and last, respectively.

R. Joshua says:
Even if only the last is available.
Rabban Gamaliel says:
Whatever kind [of vegetable] has finished from the field,
one must eliminate it from the barrel.
And *halakhah* is according to his words.[93]
R. Simeon says:
All vegetables are considered as one with respect to Removal.
One may eat purslane
until the vetches[94] from the valley of Bet Netofah have finished.

6 One who gathers wet grasses [may eat them]
until the sweetness dries out,
but one who piles up dry ones
[may eat them] until the second rainfall.
[One who collects] leaves of reeds or of vines [may eat them]
until they fall from their stem,[95]
but one who piles up dry ones [may eat them]
until the second rainfall.
R. Aqiva[96] says:
In all these cases [one may eat them] until the second rainfall.

7 Similarly, one who rents a house to his fellow "until the rainy season,"
[the rental is in force] until the second rainfall.
One who has vowed that someone will not benefit from him "until the rainy season,"
[the vow is in force] until the second rainfall.

[93] **P** and other manuscripts lack this sentence. [94] Precise identification unknown. [95] Lit. "their father." [96] **K** (margins): "R. Judah."

R. Eliezer: The Yerushalmi explains that he takes into account the fact that the first vegetable imparts taste to all the other vegetables (see 7:7), and therefore all are to be removed once the first finishes.

R. Joshua: Since the vegetables absorb flavor from each other, the mixture is considered as a new entity, and need only follow the last to finish.

Rabban Gamaliel: This is a compromise view that sees each vegetable as retaining its fundamental identity despite whatever flavor absorption occurs.

R. Simeon: As long as one species of vegetable is still available in the field, one may eat all the other vegetables in one's possession, even if they have finished from the field; this extends R. Joshua's leniency far beyond the narrow case of the barrel. This apparently rejects the underlying assumption of the earlier discussion, which was based on each species finishing at different times. It is clear from 9:3 that R. Simeon is interested in narrowing the removal system to a small number of uniform dates; cf. 2:1.

One may eat: This case may demonstrate R. Simeon's view, with purslane standing in for other vegetables, or it may be claiming that purslane and vetches are similar enough that the former may be eaten until the latter finish.

9:6 *sweetness dries out*: Referring either to the moisture in the land evaporating, or to the wet leaves themselves drying out; see 3:1.

second rainfall: Which marks the beginning of the winter (mid-Marheshvan).

9:7 *rents…has vowed*: In both contracts and vows the rabbis follow common parlance in defining terms; see *Nedarim* 8:5.

Until when may the poor enter the orchards?
Until the second rainfall.
From when may one benefit from or burn fodder and straw of the Seventh Year?
From the second rainfall.

9:8–9 *Removal of Seventh-Year Fruit: The Manner of Removal*

8 One who possesses Seventh-Year produce and the time of Removal has arrived must distribute [enough] food for three meals to each and every person.
The poor may eat after Removal, but not the rich,
the words of R. Judah.
R. Yose says:
Both poor and rich may eat after Removal.
9 One who possesses Seventh-Year produce,
which came to him as an inheritance or which were given to him as a gift—
R. Eliezer says:
It must be given to those who eat [Seventh-Year produce].
But the Sages say:
The sinner should not [be allowed to] profit;
rather, it must be sold to those who eat [Seventh-Year produce],

poor enter the orchards: To gather the gleanings and forgotten produce; see *Pe'ah* 8:1.

benefit from or burn fodder and straw: These are animal foods and may not be burned during the Seventh Year (see 8:11). By the following winter, however, whatever is left in the field is no longer suitable for eating, so whatever one had collected in the house may be "eliminated" through kindling.

9:8 *time of Removal*: When a particular species is finished from the field.

three meals: Sufficient for the Sabbath; two meals sufficed for weekdays (*Pe'ah* 8:7; *Shabbat* 16:2).

to each and every person: According to the Tosefta, this means relatives, friends, and neighbors.

R. Judah…R. Yose: The relationship between this debate and the previous clause is unclear. R. Judah and R. Yose might dispute the identity of "each person" who may receive food sufficient for three meals; alternatively, they may be disputing who has the right to eat produce left over after the initial distribution to "each and every person."

9:9 *Seventh-Year produce…inheritance…gift*: This refers to Seventh-Year produce that was preserved by the owner after the time of Removal and is therefore prohibited for consumption. Although the testator or donor was among those who transgress Seventh-Year laws (see e.g. 4:1, 9:1), the recipient wishes to obey the laws of the Seventh Year.

R. Eliezer…Sages: The commentators offer a wide range of possibilities to make sense of the debate between R. Eliezer and the Sages.

given to those who eat: One may give away the produce to others who transgress Seventh-Year restrictions.

The sinner should not [be allowed to] profit: "Sinner" here refers to those who willingly transgress Seventh-Year restrictions; they may not "profit" by receiving forbidden produce for free.

and its money must be distributed to all people.
One who eats from Seventh-Year dough before its dough offering has been separated is liable to death.

Chapter Ten

10:1–2 *Debt Relief in the Seventh Year: Debts That Are Not Released by the Seventh Year*

10 The Seventh Year releases
loans secured by a document
and loans that are not secured by a document.
Shop credit is not released,
but if [the shopkeeper] turned it into a loan,
then it is thereby released.
R. Judah says:
Each preceding deferred payment is released [but not the current one].
An employee's wage is not released;
but if [the employee] turned it into a loan,
then it is thereby released.

its money...distributed to all people: Money that results from the conversion of Seventh-Year produce must, after the time of Removal, be distributed to all, like the produce itself (7:1).

One who eats: Although Seventh-Year produce is not liable to tithing (4:7), since all produce is ownerless, nevertheless one must separate dough offering (Numbers 15:20) from the dough. *Sifre to Numbers* derives this from the word "throughout the ages" in Numbers 15:21.

liable to death: At the hands of heaven; see *Hallah* 1:9.

10:1 *The Seventh Year releases loans*: Deuteronomy 15:1–11.

not secured by a document: A loan conducted orally before two witnesses (cf. *Bava Metsi'a* 5:11).

Shop credit: Buying on credit is not defined as a loan since there is no defined moment when payment is due, and because the shopkeeper did not intend the extension of credit as a formal loan.

turned it into a loan: By writing a deed for the debt, or by filing a claim for it in court.

R. Judah says: When deferring a new shop payment, the customer automatically transforms all previous debts into a loan, and no additional action on the part of the shopkeeper is required. R. Judah assumes that the merchant's willingness to defer the payment through multiple subsequent transactions is based on the transformation of the previous debts into exactable loans.

An employee's wage: The wage owed to a worker by an employer is considered a postponed payment unless the worker explicitly defines it as a loan.

R. Yose says:
[Wages for] any labor which terminates in the Seventh Year,[97]
are released,
but [wages for] labor which does not terminate in the Seventh Year,
are not released.
    2 One who slaughters a cow and distributed it on the New Year—
if the [previous] month was intercalated,
[the debt] is released;
otherwise, it is not released.
[Fines imposed upon] a rapist, a seducer, or a defamer,
and all financial verdicts of a court
are not released.
One who lends money secured by a pledge,
and one who hands over his deeds to a court—
are not released.

[97] K: "for the Seventh Year," here and below.

R. Yose: Ordinarily an employee's wage becomes a loan only if the employee actively declares it as such. With respect to labors prohibited in the Seventh Year, however, the wage for such labors—which have inevitably been completed before that year—are willy-nilly considered as a loan, and must be collected before they are released.

10:2 *slaughters a cow and distributed it on the New Year*: Because of their size, cost, and the difficulty of preserving meat, groups of people would go in on a cow before festivals (see *Betsah* 3:6), with the exact price of each piece determined after the meat was distributed on the festival itself. In this case, the people committed to purchasing the meat during the Seventh Year, but the meat is only distributed on the first day (the New Year) of the eighth year. The promise of payment is converted into a loan only at the moment of distribution, and only loans made in the Seventh Year are subject to release with the onset of the eighth year. The beginning of the New Year, however, can only be determined after the fact (see *Rosh Hashanah* 4:4).

the [previous] month was intercalated: New months were declared on the basis of the testimony of two witnesses (*Rosh Hashanah* 1:6–2:1). If, however, the new month was not declared on that basis, for whatever reason, before nightfall on the day following seeing the new moon, then the day just ended was declared part of the previous month (*intercalated*), and the day just begun declared the beginning of the new month (*Rosh Hashanah* 3:1). In such a case, the actual first day of the New Year festival ends up being considered the last day of the previous year, and the meat was distributed, and its cost turned into a loan during the Seventh Year, which is then released with the onset of the eighth year that night.

otherwise, it is not released: If the new moon was declared on the first day of the New Year festival, then the meat was distributed and its cost turned into a loan during the eighth year, after the moment of release.

rapist…seducer…defamer: According to the rabbis, the former are subject to a fine of fifty silver coins, equivalent to the woman's bride price (Deuteronomy 22:28–29; Exodus 22:15–16), while the latter must pay his wife's father double the value of the bride price, one hundred silver coins (Deuteronomy 22:19). See *Bekhorot* 8:7. These fines, being imposed by the court, are not subject to Seventh-Year release.

all financial verdicts of a court: Only loans between individuals are relieved, not monetary judgments imposed by the court.

secured by a pledge: Although the previous mishnah stated that all loans are released, including those secured by a deed, if the lender received a pledge as security for the loan, it is considered as if he had already collected the loan.

one who hands over his deeds to a court: This transforms personal loans into financial obligations secured through the court's authority which are therefore not released. See below, concerning the *prozbul*.

10:3–5 Debt Relief in the Seventh Year: The Prozbul Document

3 [A debt secured by a] *prozbul* is not released.
This is one of the things Hillel the Elder enacted
when[98] he saw that the people were refraining from lending to each other,
and were transgressing the words of the Torah:
Beware lest there be a wicked thought in your heart.
Hillel the Elder enacted the *prozbul*.

4 This is the body of the *prozbul*:
"I hand over to you so-and-so and so-and-so,
the judges[99] in place so-and-so,
so that I may collect any debt owed to me[100] whenever I wish."
And the judges sign below, or the witnesses.

5 An antedated *prozbul* is valid,
but a postdated one is invalid.
Antedated loan documents are invalid,

[98] K reads instead "Because he saw." [99] K: "and the judges."
[100] Lit. "that any debt that I have, that I can collect it."

10:3 *prozbul*: This Greek term denotes the transfer of loans to the court (*pros boulen*, lit. "in front of the court"), bringing them into the status of monetary obligations imposed by a court, which are not released (10:2). The exact connection of this innovative institution with the handing of one's deeds to the court, mentioned in the previous mishnah, is not clear. At any rate, Hillel's institution offered a standard process for facilitating loan collection through the intervention of a central civic institution.

one of the things Hillel the Elder enacted: A second documented enactment of Hillel appears in *Arakhin* 9:4, concerning the cancellation of a house sale in a city (Leviticus 25:30).

Beware: Deuteronomy 15:9.

Hillel the Elder enacted the prozbul: The repetition may suggest two layers to this mishnah and to the history of the *prozbul*; cf. *Gittin* 4:3.

10:4 *so that I may collect any debt*: According to all manuscripts of the Mishnah, the creditor only informs the court what loans he holds, and does not transfer the deeds themselves to the court. The public announcement confers the court's authority over the loans. Other versions have "I hand over to you…all debts so that I may collect whenever I wish," indicating that the creditor actually transfers the deeds themselves as part of the *prozbul*.

And the judges sign below: When the creditor wishes to collect the money, he must attach this document to the loan deed (*Ketubbot* 9:9).

10:5 *antedated prozbul…postdated one*: The *prozbul* grants the creditor the right to collect all loans issued prior to its being written and signed. Therefore, if the date which appears on the *prozbul* is earlier than the actual date on which it was written and signed, it is valid, since this change only harms the creditor who created the document by allowing him to collect fewer loans. A postdated *prozbul*, however, would add loans issued after the actual date on which the *prozbul* was being signed, and is therefore invalid.

Antedated loan documents are invalid: Written deeds encumber all of the debtor's property from the date of the loan (*Bava Batra* 10:8), and the creditor can collect such loans from others who bought property from the debtor after that date. Therefore, if the date written on the deed is earlier than the actual date of the loan, property sold by the debtor between the two dates could be unjustly collected from purchasers.

but postdated ones are valid.
If one [person] borrows from five,
he[101] must write a *prozbul* for each and every one.
If five [people] borrow from one,
he need only write one *prozbul* for all of them.

10:6–7   *Debt Relief in the Seventh Year: Securing the Prozbul*

6 One may only write a *prozbul* on the basis of [the debtor's] immovable property.[102]
If [the debtor] has none,
[the creditor] may grant him a minimal share in his property.[103]
If [the debtor] owns mortgaged property in the city,
[the creditor] may write a *prozbul* on its basis.
R. Hutspit says:
One may write [a *prozbul*] for a husband on the basis of his wife's property,
and for orphans on the basis of [their] guardians' property.

7 A beehive—
R. Eliezer says:
It has the same status as immovable property,
and one may write a *prozbul* based on it,

---

[101] K, P, and others: "they."   [102] Lit. "land."   [103] Lit. "field," here and below.

---

he must write a prozbul for each and every one: Since the *prozbul* is a legal act of the creditor, he is responsible for writing it.

10:6 *immovable property*: The reason for this condition is unclear. The property may be considered as a symbolic surety, taken by the creditor or the court before the Seventh-Year release. Alternatively, it may represent the debtor's ability to return the debt in the future.

minimal share: See Pe'ah 3:6.

If [the debtor] owns mortgaged property: In contrast to standard sureties, this property serves to secure the loan even if it is already mortgaged to a third party.

in the city: Presumably meaning in the vicinity of a city. The phrase is unlikely to exclude mortgaged fields located elsewhere. It may refer to wealthy individuals whose fields are close to cities—even they may secure a *prozbul* with mortgaged property.

R. Hutspit: In these cases as well the property cannot actually be collected, since it belongs to others. The relationship between the two parties, however, is opposite in each of the cases. The husband manages his wife's property and enjoys its revenues, while the guardian's own property may at times be used for managing the orphans' needs.

10:7 Parallel in *Uqtsin* 3:10.

A beehive: Ancient beehives were made of earthenware jars which were piled and covered by earth; they could, however, be removed and relocated. This raises the question whether beehives have the legal status of movable vessels or immovable property.

it cannot incur impurity while in its place,
and one who scrapes [honey] from it on the Sabbath is liable.
But the Sages say:
It does not have the status of immovable property,
and one may not write a *prozbul* based on it,
it can incur impurity while in place,
and one who scrapes [honey] from it on the Sabbath is exempt.

10:8–9 *Debt Relief in the Seventh Year: Repaying Loans in the Seventh Year and on Other Occasions*

8 One who repays his loan in the Seventh Year—
[the creditor] must say to him: "I release it."
If [the debtor] says, "I insist,"
he may accept it,
for it says: *And this is the word of release.*
In a similar manner,
a killer who has been exiled to a city of refuge
whom the people of the city wish to honor
must say to them "I am a killer."
If they say "We insist,"
he may accept the honor from them,
for it says:
And this is the word of the killer.

---

it cannot incur impurity: Only movables incur impurity, while the ground and whatever is connected to it always remains pure (Leviticus 11:37–38, as interpreted by the rabbis in *Sifra*).

while in its place: R. Eliezer seems to agree that even though beehives should be considered like the ground, if they actually are moved, they should be treated like movables at least with respect to purity.

scrapes honey from it on the Sabbath: Any action of disconnecting from the ground is equivalent to harvesting, which is one of the thirty-nine labors prohibited on the Sabbath (*Shabbat* 7:2).

10:8 *one who repays his loan*: Following the institutional solution of the *prozbul*, the final mishnayot turn here to encourage voluntary repayment of loans. In this case the creditor fulfills the biblical commandment of loan relief only on a verbal level.

And this is the word of release: Deuteronomy 15:2. The Mishnah offers a midrashic rendering of *word*; the verse simply means "this is the rule which concerns the release."

In a similar manner: See *Makkot* 2:8.

killer: Someone who killed unintentionally and must flee to a city of refuge (Numbers 35:9–34; Deuteronomy 19:1–13).

And this is the word of the killer: Deuteronomy 19:4. Here too the Mishnah offers a midrashic rendering of *word*; the straightforward meaning of the verse is "This is the rule concerning the killer who killed unintentionally."

9 One who repays a loan in the Seventh Year,
the spirit of the Sages is pleased with him.
If one borrows from a proselyte whose children converted with him,
[and the proselyte dies,]
[the borrower] does not have to repay his children;
if, however, he does repay them,
the spirit of the Sages is pleased with him.
All movables are acquired by pulling,
but[104] anyone who stands by his word,
the spirit of the Sages is pleased with him.

[104] K lacks the conjunction.

10:9 *spirit of the Sages*: This mishnah lists three cases in which the legal permission falls short of the appropriate ethical action. Compare *Bava Qamma* 6:4 and contrast *Bava Batra* 8:5.

children converted with him: The children are not legally considered to be his children and therefore do not inherit from their father, since the conversion undoes earlier family and biological connections. The property of a deceased convert is the paradigmatic example of ownerless property; see *Bava Batra* 3:3 and 4:9.

All movables are acquired by pulling: In the case of movables, even if one has paid the seller, the actual acquisition takes place only through physically moving the acquired object (*Qiddushin* 1:5). Thus, for example, a seller may receive the money, but change his mind and sell the object to someone else for a higher sum unless and until the purchaser has moved the object; similarly, a buyer can demand his money back if he has not moved the object. Therefore the rabbis encourage both sides to fulfill their agreement even before the actual acquisition takes place; see *Bava Metsi'a* 4:2.

Tractate Terumot

William Friedman and Matthew Hass

Introduction

Overview

Terumot (plural of the singular *terumah*) refers to two agricultural taxes paid to priests: (1) *terumah*, a small portion separated by the Israelite field owner from fully processed produce, and (2) *terumat ma'aser*, lit. "*terumah* of the tithe," one-tenth of the first tithe. The Israelite field owner gives a tenth of his produce to the Levite; this payment is not sacred, it is merely a civil obligation. (See *Ma'aserot*.) The Levite in turn gives to the priest a tenth of the tithe that he has received. That tenth, called "*terumah* of the tithe," is sacred. The word *terumah* itself is biblical in origin (e.g. Numbers 18:8).

Structure and Organization of the Tractate

The tractate is neatly divisible into roughly two halves: the first five chapters deal with the separation of *terumah* and the consequences of *terumah* mixing with nonsacral produce (see below); the final six chapters deal with the treatment of *terumah* itself, including the consequences of misappropriating it and how priests may or may not use it.

The tractate commences with lists of people who are ineligible to separate *terumah* and legal categories of produce from which *terumah* may not be separated. The first chapter is organized around the ideal/after-the-fact distinction, discussed below; 1:1–5 describes *terumah* separations invalid even after the fact, and 1:6–2:1 enumerates those that are ideally to be avoided but nevertheless effective if done.

The first and second chapters introduce a number of limitations on the permission for vicarious *terumah* separation, restricting it to produce of the same species (2:4, 6), at the same stage of growth and processing (1:10), intended for the same purpose (1:8–9), of similar or better quality (2:5–6), of the same purity status (2:1–2), and located in the same vicinity (4:3). Some of these are absolute requirements and others apply only ideally; for *terumah* of the tithe the proximity requirement is waived (see 4:5).

The third chapter deals in the main with agency (appointing someone else to separate *terumah* from one's produce), the designation requirement, and the proper order of tithes. The fourth (through 4:6) engages the possibility of partial tithing and the statutory amount of *terumah* that must be removed. From 4:7 until the end of chapter 5, the tractate transitions into a lengthy discussion of the neutralization ratio for *terumah* that falls into nonsacral produce, providing a variety of examples and qualifications.

Chapters 6 and 7, respectively, discuss the consequences of unintentional and intentional nonpriestly consumption of *terumah*. The unintentional consumer pays the standard biblical fine for unauthorized consumption of sancta: repayment to a priest of the amount consumed plus an additional fifth (Leviticus 22:14). One who intentionally consumes *terumah*, however, pays only compensation but no additional fine, presumably because the additional fifth was understood as atonement for sin, but the intentional sinner was thought not to deserve atonement. The distinction between intentional and unintentional violation also plays a role in chapter 9, which discusses the consequences of planting the seeds of *terumah* or untithed plants.

Chapter 8 deals, in the main, with the proper care and handling of *terumah*, which, as sancta, must not be wasted or destroyed unnecessarily. The Mishnah addresses circumstances, however, where *terumah* must be destroyed, such as being left uncovered overnight (8:4–7), rendering it forbidden for consumption due to danger, or circumstances in which doubts over its purity arise (8:8) or in which breakage of its container will inevitably lead to unavoidable impurification (8:9–11). This discussion is picked up in chapter 11, which discusses instances where *terumah* produce may or may not be changed from its natural state (11:1, 3), and limits the prohibition of consumption by nonpriests to the edible portions of *terumah* produce (11:4–5). Other issues of nonpriestly benefit from *terumah* are handled here as well, culminating in a discussion of nonpriestly benefit from the light generated by burning impure *terumah* oil (11:10).

Chapter 10 introduces the central rabbinic concept that the flavor of *terumah* food can, under certain circumstances, be imparted to nonsacral food, rendering it prohibited to nonpriests (10:1–4). This leads to a discussion of general rules governing the consequences of cooking, stewing, or pickling together permitted and prohibited foods (10:10–12).

Main Ideas

Terumah is sacred, and produce from which *terumah* has not been removed is called *tevel*, "untithed produce." Intentional consumption of *tevel* or impure *terumah* is, in the rabbinic system, punishable by death at the hands of heaven. *Terumah*'s purity must be guarded, and if that fails, impure *terumah* must be destroyed rather than consumed. The punishment for inadvertent consumption of *terumah* by nonpriests or impure priests is payment of the principal and the addition of a fine, derived from Leviticus 22:14.

Separating *terumah* requires advance designation of a particular portion of a pile of produce as well as the subsequent removal of that portion from the rest of the pile. One of the central assumptions of this tractate is that *terumah* may be separated vicariously from one pile of produce for another, subject to certain (sometimes contradictory) rules and limitations spelled out in the first several chapters of the tractate. Which produce is obligated to have *terumah* removed and when is not mentioned in our tractate, but is taken up in the first chapter of *Ma'aserot*.

When ruling on the validity of a particular act of *terumah* separation, the Mishnah uses the phrases "his *terumah* is *terumah*," "his *terumah* is *terumah* but he must return and separate *terumah* again," and "his *terumah* is not *terumah*," which we translate as "what he/they/one separated is/is not *terumah*" in order to avoid redundancy. The first phrase is self-explanatory; the last entails the consequence that all the produce remains untithed and therefore forbidden for consumption until properly tithed. The middle category and its consequences are dealt with in 3:1–2, and seems to be deployed as a punishment for nonideal but ultimately acceptable *terumah* separations (see 1:8). A central distinction in many of these cases—a distinction shot through all of tannaitic law—is between ideal performance (*lekhatehilah*, lit. "at the outset") and after-the-fact validity (the talmudic term is *bedi'avad*, lit. "after it was done"), indicated in our annotations by the terms "ideally" and "after the fact," respectively.

A major concern of this tractate is the consequence of the accidental mixing of sacral *terumah* with nonsacral produce. If the *terumah* part of the mixture is sufficiently small (one part *terumah* to one hundred parts non-*terumah*) the mixture can be "nullified" and treated as regular produce. The term used for mixing derives from the linguistically obscure root *dalet-mem-ayin* (see Exodus 22:28), which we have translated as "creates a *terumah* mixture." Nullification is described by a term that literally means "goes up" (*ayin-lamed-heh*), which we have translated by variations of the word "neutralize."

Relationship to Scripture

The Bible enjoins a number of agricultural and other taxes (or "gifts") to be paid to the priests (see especially Numbers 18, *Ma'aserot*, *Bikkurim*, and *Hallah*); nowhere, however, does it explicitly discuss the institution of *terumah*—the separation of a small portion of every pile of harvested and processed produce—described by our tractate. (One rabbinic figure even calls the institution of *terumah* textually "unclear" or "ambiguous.") This is not to say that the notion is invented whole cloth; Numbers 18:25–32 requires the Levites to give one-tenth of the processed produce they receive from the Israelites to Aaron the priest, which the rabbis call *terumat ma'aser* (*terumah* of the tithe). On the basis of this requirement, the rabbis establish *terumah* as a universal obligation for all Israelites. Furthermore, the Bible itself uses the word "*terumah*" to describe any number of priestly emoluments and other sanctified contributions to the Temple. The resulting literary redundancies (see e.g. Numbers 15:19–20) provided rabbinic exegetes with ample opportunities to ground their institution of *terumah*, which they do in no fewer than five different verses, finding additional details in several more. Unfortunately, evidence from the Second Temple period, both biblical and extrabiblical, fails to confirm the existence of *terumah* prior to its rabbinic elaboration.

Having been established as sanctified by Numbers 18:29, consumption of *terumah* and *terumah* of the tithe fell under the strictures of Leviticus 22:3–16, restricting consumption to priests and their household in a state of purity and imposing repayment and a fine on nonpriests who violate this restriction.

Special Notes for the Reader

Significant textual variants are cited in the footnotes based on the critical edition of Nissan Sacks (ed.), *The Mishnah with Variant Readings: Order Zera'im*, vol. 2 (Jerusalem: Institute for the Complete Israeli Talmud, 1975). Our annotations are based in large part on the Tosefta, the Yerushalmi, and traditional commentaries; we have also benefited from the work of modern scholars, notably the annotations of H. Albeck, the monograph of Alan J. Avery-Peck, *The Priestly Gift in Mishnah: A Study of Tractate Terumot* (Chico, Calif.: Scholars Press, 1981), and the commentary of Shmuel and Ze'ev Safrai, *Mishnat Eretz Israel: Tractate Terumot* (Jerusalem: Lifshitz College, 2012).

Tractate Terumot

Chapter One

1:1–3 *People Whose Separation of Terumah Is Invalid Even After the Fact*

I Five [categories of people] may not separate *terumah*,
and if they separated *terumah*,
what they separated is not *terumah*:[1]
(1) the deaf-mute,
(2) and the legally incompetent,
(3) and the minor,
(4) and the one who separates *terumah* from that which is not his;
(5) a gentile who separated *terumah* from [the produce] of an Israelite, even with permission,
what he separated is not *terumah*.[2]

  2 A deaf person who can speak but cannot hear
may not separate *terumah*,

---

[1] Lit. "their *terumah* is not *terumah*," here and throughout.
[2] **P** and other manuscripts: "what they [= all five categories] separated is not *terumah*."

1:1 *is not terumah*: And therefore a qualified person must separate *terumah* from the produce afresh to permit its use. See 1:6.

deaf-mute...legally incompetent...minor: See *Rosh Hashanah* 3:8 for the exemption of this triad from ritual commandments. The Tosefta explains that they lack mental acuity (cf. *Arakhin* 1:1). Cf. 3:8, which requires mental awareness when separating *terumah*.

deaf-mute: See 1:2.

the legally incompetent: The Tosefta gives four characteristics of such a person: walking alone at night; sleeping in graveyards; tearing one's garments; and destroying (or losing) items given to him or her.

minor: See 1:3.

from that which is not his: Without the permission of the owner of the produce. See 4:4, which assumes that a person can designate someone else to serve as an agent for separating *terumah*. Contrast the gentile, whose *terumah* separation is invalid even with the owner's permission.

a gentile: Cf. 3:9.

1:2 *who can speak but cannot hear*: Cf. 1:6.

but if he separated *terumah*,
what he separated is *terumah*.[3]
[The] deaf person of whom the Sages speak everywhere
is one who can neither hear nor speak.

3 A minor who has not [yet] produced two [pubic] hairs—
R. Judah says:
What he separated is *terumah*;
R. Yose says:
If he has not yet reached the age of vowing,
what he separated is not *terumah*,
but after he has reached the age of vowing,
what he separated is *terumah*.

1:4–5 *Other Invalid Terumah Separations*

4 One may not separate *terumah* from olives for [olive] oil,
nor from grapes for wine,
but if one separated *terumah*—
the House of Shammai say:
Their own *terumah* is in them,
but the House of Hillel say:
What one separated is not *terumah*.

[3] Lit. "their *terumah* is *terumah*," here and throughout.

---

but if he separated terumah: After the fact, the separated *terumah* is sanctified and the remaining produce may be consumed.

everywhere: Throughout the Mishnah and other related texts, including in 1:1 above.

speak: According to the Tosefta, a deaf person capable of speech is legally competent in all matters.

1:3 *produced two [pubic] hairs*: A standard marker of physical maturity. See *Niddah* 6:11.

What he separated is terumah: After the fact. In the Tosefta, R. Judah requires the child's father to be present for the *terumah* separation to be valid.

age of vowing: The age at which a child has developed the mental capacity to understand the nature of a promise or a vow. According to *Niddah* 5:6, a girl reaches this age at eleven (or twelve) and a boy at twelve (or thirteen).

1:4 *olives for [olive] oil…grapes for wine*: One may not separate *terumah* from untithed, as-yet-unprocessed olives or grapes for the untithed product of fully processed olives or grapes. See 1:10.

House of Shammai…House of Hillel: In the parallel passage in *Eduyot* 5:2, the debate concerns permission before the fact rather than after the fact validity.

their own terumah is in them: The formulation is cryptic but the meaning is clear: the *terumah* separated from the original, unprocessed produce (the olives or the grapes) suffices to permit their consumption, but does not serve to permit consumption of the intended oil or wine.

what one separated is not terumah: Both the intended oil or wine as well as the olives or grapes from which the *terumah* was actually separated remain forbidden for consumption.

5 One may not separate *terumah*:
from Gleanings,
nor from Forgotten Sheaves,
nor from *pe'ah*,
nor from ownerless [produce];
nor from first tithe whose *terumah* was removed,[4]
nor from second tithe or consecrated [produce] that were redeemed,[5]
nor from the obligated for the exempt,
nor from the exempt for the obligated,
nor from the plucked [produce] for the [produce still] attached [to the ground],
nor from the [produce still] attached [to the ground] for the plucked [produce],

[4] **K** and other manuscripts: "was not removed."
[5] **K** and other manuscripts: "were not redeemed."

1:5 Gleanings (Leviticus 19:9–10, 23:22)…*Forgotten Sheaves* (Deuteronomy 24:19)…*pe'ah* (Leviticus 19:9, 23:22): Each of these is exempt from all tithes (see *Hallah* 1:3), including *terumah*, both by the owner of the field whence they came and by the poor person who acquires them. Since such produce was never subject to any tithing requirement, a poor person (not to mention the owner of the field) may not separate *terumah* from them for any other produce he or she may have that requires *terumah* separation. See below.

ownerless [produce]: Produce that grew on ownerless land or that was declared ownerless by the field's owner or a court. Such produce is exempt from all tithes according to *Hallah* 1:3.

first tithe (Numbers 18:21–24)…*second tithe* (Deuteronomy 14:22–27)…*consecrated [produce]* (Leviticus 27): This triad appears regularly in the Mishnah. See especially *Berakhot* 7:1, *Hallah* 1:3, and *Shabbat* 18:1.

first tithe whose terumah was removed: The *terumah* referred to here is *terumah* of the tithe (Numbers 18:25–32). This is, therefore, another example of produce exempt from further tithes which cannot be used for produce still obligated to have tithes removed. Alternatively, this mishnah is arguing that first tithe, despite being called *terumah* by Numbers 18:24, lacks sufficient sanctity to be used for further vicarious *terumah* separations once its *terumah* has been removed. Several manuscripts, however, including **K**, read "first tithe whose *terumah* was **not** [yet] removed." According to that version, *terumah* of the tithe and primary *terumah* are incommensurate, and produce obligated in the former cannot be used for produce obligated in the latter.

second tithe or consecrated [produce] that were redeemed: In these cases, such produce reverts to fully non-sacral status, and are, again, examples of produce exempt from further tithes that cannot be used for produce still obligated in tithes. Here, as above, there exists a version that reads "were **not** [yet] redeemed." According to that version, this mishnah rules that despite the fact that the produce is sanctified as second tithe or Temple dedication, that sanctity differs from that of *terumah* such that one cannot separate further produce from it for the sake of other, untithed produce.

obligated…exempt: Produce becomes obligated in tithing only once it reaches a certain stage of growth; see *Hallah* 1:3 and *Ma'aserot* 1:1–4. If produce has not yet reached that stage, it is "exempt" and tithes cannot yet be separated from it or for it. Similarly, once one has fully tithed obligated produce, it is "exempt" and no further tithes can be removed from it for other, still-obligated produce. Other kinds of exempt produce are detailed in the other clauses of this mishnah.

plucked…attached…new…old: See *Ma'aser Sheni* 5:11.

plucked…attached: Produce that has been removed from the soil (i.e. harvested) is obligated to have *terumah* removed, whereas produce still joined to the ground (i.e. not yet harvested) is not yet obligated to have

nor from the new for the old,
nor from the old for the new,
nor from produce of the Land [of Israel] for produce of outside the Land [of Israel],
nor from produce of outside the Land [of Israel] for produce of the Land [of Israel].
And if one separated *terumah* [in one of these ways],
what one separated is not *terumah*.

1:6–2:1 *Terumah Separations Valid After the Fact*

6 Five [categories of people] may not separate *terumah*,
but if they separated *terumah*,
what they separated is *terumah*:
(1) the mute,
(2) the intoxicated,
(3) the naked,
(4) the blind,
(5) the ejaculant.
They may not separate *terumah*,
but if they separated *terumah*,
what they separated is *terumah*.

terumah separated from it. One cannot, therefore, either separate *terumah* from not-yet-harvested produce for harvested produce nor the reverse, under the rule preventing separating the obligated for the exempt and vice versa.

new…old…old…new: The Tosefta explains that this refers to produce harvested in different agricultural years, measured by the cut-off dates listed in *Rosh Hashanah* 1:1: the 1st of Tishre for vegetables and the 1st or 15th of Shevat for fruits. Thus, e.g., one could not separate *terumah* from a fruit picked on the 14th of Shevat for one picked on the 15th of Shevat, and vice versa.

produce of the Land [of Israel]…produce of outside the Land [of Israel]: Whether produce from outside the Land of Israel is subject to tithing is unclear; see *Shevi'it* 6:1, *Hallah* 2:1, and *Yadayim* 4:3.

1:6 *but if they separated terumah*: After the fact, the produce may be consumed; contrast 1:1 above.

the mute: Although mutes are legally competent in all matters (cf. 1:2), the Tosefta explains that they ought to refrain from separating *terumah* because they are unable to recite the requisite blessing.

the intoxicated: The Tosefta explains that despite their incapacity, the intoxicated are legally culpable for their actions, and therefore their *terumah* separation is valid after the fact.

the naked may not recite blessings or come in contact with the sacred. Contrast *Demai* 1:4 and *Hallah* 2:3.

the blind may not ideally separate *terumah* due to their inability to visually distinguish the quality of produce, according to the Tosefta. See 2:4.

the ejaculant who has not yet immersed in an immersion pool and therefore is not to recite blessings or contact the sacred. See *Berakhot* 3:4.

7 One may not separate *terumah*
by measure, by weight, or by count;⁶
but one may separate *terumah*
from the measured and from the weighed and from the counted.
One may not separate *terumah*
in a small basket or large basket of a [known] measure,
but one may separate *terumah*
in them, in their halves or thirds.
One may not separate *terumah*
in half of a *se'ah*[-sized container] whose half is a measure.

8 One may not separate *terumah* from [olive] oil for crushed olives,
nor [from] wine for trodden grapes;
if, however, one separated *terumah* [in such a fashion],
what one separated is *terumah*,
but⁷ one must return and separate *terumah* [again].
The first [*terumah*] can create a *terumah* mixture by itself,

⁶ Some *genizah* fragments add "But if one separated *terumah*, what one separated is *terumah*."
⁷ Manuscripts lack the conjunction.

1:7 *may not*: Ideally, one should not separate the requisite amount of *terumah* (see 4:3) by exact calculation, but should estimate (cf. 4:6). After the fact, however, such *terumah* is valid.

measure: Volume.

count: e.g. of individual pieces of fruit, sheaves, etc.

from the measured and from the weighed and from the counted: If the amount of produce has already been calculated, one may separate *terumah* from that produce, and need not seek to separate *terumah* for that produce from a different pile that has not yet been measured, weighed, or counted.

which are of a [known] measure: That is, if one knows how much the container itself holds when full, one may not, ideally, separate *terumah* from the produce in it.

but one may separate terumah in them, in their halves or thirds: Even ideally. If the container's subdivisions are entirely unmarked (see the next annotation), then filling the container partway is not considered measuring, since doing so will in fact merely result in an estimation.

whose half is a measure: That is, when the container's halfway point is marked in some fashion, and thus filling the container to this point results in a clear measurement.

1:8 *for crushed olives...for trodden grapes*: Olives or grapes which have undergone initial processing (crushing or treading) but whose liquid has not yet been extracted through pressing.

one must return and separate terumah [again]: From the oil or wine eventually extracted from the crushed olives or trodden grapes. Cf. 1:10 below.

the first...but not the second: What was initially separated as *terumah* has full sacral status; the second *terumah* separation, which was imposed as an added punishment for violating the ideal rule, has a lesser legal status. The Tosefta adds that tithes must be removed from this second *terumah*; cf. 4:3.

can create a terumah mixture: If it becomes mixed with less than one hundred times its volume of nonsacral produce, it bestows sacral status on the whole amount, thus restricting it to consumption by priests. See 4:7 and 5:1.

by itself: Since it has full sacral status; cf. 3:1-2.

and one is liable for an additional fifth for [consuming] it,
but not the second [*terumah*].

9 But one may separate *terumah* from [olive] oil for pickled olives,
and from wine for grapes to be made[8] into raisins.
If one separated *terumah*:
from [olive] oil for olives [intended] for eating,
or from olives for olives [intended] for eating,
or from wine for grapes [intended] for eating,
or from grapes for grapes [intended] for eating,
and changed one's mind to tread them,
one need not separate *terumah* [again].

10 One may not separate *terumah*:
from something whose processing has been completed
for something whose processing has not yet been completed,
nor from something whose processing is not yet completed
for something whose processing has been completed,
nor from something whose processing is not yet completed
for something whose processing is not yet completed.
But if one separated *terumah* [in one of these ways],
what one separated is *terumah*.

[8] Lit. "to make them."

one is liable for an additional fifth: The added fifth is measured as a fifth of the total repayment, which is a fourth of the principal. The penalty for a nonpriest consuming *terumah* is the repayment of the amount consumed plus an additional twenty percent. See Leviticus 22:14 and 6:1 below.

1:9 *[olive] oil for pickled olives*: Both olive oil and pickled olives have completed their processing, and *terumah* may be separated from one for the other; see 1:10 below.

from wine for grapes to be made into raisins: Since grapes are not actively processed to be turned into raisins, and are edible in the same general form during the entire dehydration process, they are always considered to have "completed their processing" (see 1:10 below) and therefore *terumah* may be separated for them from wine, which has also completed its processing.

If one separated terumah, Each of these are cases of separating terumah from produce whose processing has been completed for the same kind of produce whose processing has also been completed: oil/wine for olives and grapes that are currently edible, or, even more obviously, edible olives and grapes for other edible olives and grapes.

olives for olives [intended] for eating: The olives initially referred to here may be ordinary olives processed for consumption, or they may be olives particularly rich in oil, which are legally considered like the oil itself. Cf. 2:6.

changed one's mind ... one need not separate terumah [again]: Since the original *terumah* separation was permitted, changing one's mind to further process the olives or grapes for which *terumah* had been separated—in spite of the ruling in 1:10—does not incur a penalty.

1:10 *processing*: See Ma'aserot 1:5–8 for definitions of when processing is considered complete for various items.

what one separated is terumah: According to 1:8 above, if one separates *terumah* from processed produce (oil, wine) for unprocessed (olives, grapes), one is subject to a penalty: the initial *terumah* separation is valid, but *terumah* must be separated a second time. Why 1:10 omits this penalty is not clear.

Chapter Two

2 One may not separate *terumah* from pure [produce] for impure [produce],
but if one separated *terumah*,
what one separated is *terumah*.[9]
Nevertheless,[10] they said:[11]
A cake of pressed figs,
part of which became impure—
one may separate *terumah* from the pure part for the impure part.[12]
And so too a vegetable bundle,
and so too a pile.
[If, however,] there were two cakes [of pressed figs],
two bundles [of vegetables],
[or] two piles,
one impure and one pure[13]—
one may not separate *terumah* from one for the other.[14]
R. Eliezer says:
One may separate *terumah* from the pure for the impure.

---

[9] Lit. "their *terumah* is *terumah*," here and throughout.
[10] Lit. "In truth."   [11] Manuscripts lack "they said."
[12] Lit. "from the pure that is in it for the impure that is in it."
[13] Manuscripts: "one pure and one impure."   [14] Lit. "from this for that."

2:1 *One may not separate...for impure [produce]...is terumah*: Impure *terumah* may not be consumed by a priest (Leviticus 22:1–9), and must be destroyed (*Temurah* 7:5; cf. 5:1–4). The reason for this ideal prohibition is unstated here. See, however, *Hallah* 1:9 and 2:8, which connect this prohibition to the requirement to separate *terumah* only from proximate produce. (See 4:3 below.) The fear, as explained by later commentaries, is that in order to maintain the purity of the *terumah*, one may opt to use distant produce in order to avoid physical contact with the impure produce. This understanding is supported by the continuation of the mishnah, which permits separating *terumah*—even ideally—from the pure part of a single item, bundle, or pile for its impure part, and only forbids doing so from one item or group for another, where the concern for distance is likely to present itself.

Nevertheless, the Sages said: This phrase, literally meaning "in truth, they said," introduces an (often permissive) exception to a general law or principle. Cf. *Kilayim* 2:2; *Shabbat* 1:3, 10:4; *Nazir* 7:3; *Bava Metsi'a* 4:11; *Bava Batra* 2:3.

cake of pressed figs: The word *'igul* literally means "round," the shape in which pressed fig cakes were usually made; see 4:10. 4:8 makes clear, however, that pressed fig cakes were also made in other shapes.

part of which became impure: Liquid is the classic transmitter of impurity (see, generally, *Makhshirin*); the fig cake referred to here must therefore have been made without liquid, for otherwise impurity would have spread throughout it. See *Tevul Yom* 2:3.

vegetable bundle: Although impurity is even less likely to spread through a tied bundle than a pressed fig cake, the very looseness of its connection might have required separating its pure and impure elements.

a pile: Even produce that is merely stacked and otherwise unconnected is considered sufficiently grouped together to allow separating *terumah* from its pure part for its impure part.

one impure and one pure...from one for the other: If the latter clause is meant to mirror the former ("from one" = the impure; "for the other" = the pure), then the Mishnah has switched topics unannounced (see 2:2). Thus in the vast majority of the versions the order is "one pure and one impure," so that "from one for the other" means "from the pure for the impure."

may separate: Even ideally. Cf. *Hallah* 2:8.

2:2–3 *Consequences of Accidental and Purposeful Violation*

2 One may not separate *terumah* from the impure for the pure,
but if one separated *terumah*—
unintentionally, what he separated is *terumah*;
but [if he did so] intentionally, he accomplished nothing.
And so too a Levite who had untithed [impure] tithe,
[who][15] goes on setting aside [*terumah*] from it—
unintentionally, what he did is done;
intentionally,[16] he accomplished nothing.
R. Judah says:
If he knew about it in[17] the beginning,
[then] even though he [did it] unintentionally,
he accomplished nothing.

3 One who immerses vessels on the Sabbath—
unintentionally, he may use them;
intentionally, he may not use them.
One who tithes or cooks on the Sabbath—
unintentionally, he may eat;
intentionally, he may not eat.
One who plants—
on the Sabbath—
unintentionally, he may preserve it;
intentionally, he must uproot.
In the Seventh Year—
whether unintentionally or intentionally, he must uproot.

---

[15] **K** and other manuscripts: "and [who]."
[16] Some manuscripts add "but."
[17] **K, P**, and other manuscripts: "from."

2:2 *And so too...untithed...tithe*: The Levite, upon receiving the tithe (Numbers 18:21–24) must give a tithe of that tithe to the priest (Numbers 18:25–30), which is called *terumah*. All produce that has not had *terumah* removed from it, including untithed tithe, is called *tevel*. This mishnah applies the same rule to *tevel* tithe that it does to all *tevel* produce; cf. *Bikkurim* 2:5.

R. Judah says: If he knew about it: Once the person becomes aware that the produce is impure, R. Judah is unwilling to give credence to any claims of forgetfulness about its status. The commentaries dispute whether his stringency applies to both cases, only the first case, or only the second case.

2:3 *immerses vessels on the Sabbath*: To purify them. Cf. *Shabbat* 2:7 and *Betsah* 2:2.

unintentionally...intentionally: See *Shabbat* 7:1.

tithes: Including separating *terumah*. See *Betsah* 5:2; cf. *Shabbat* 2:7.

cooks: Cf. *Shabbat* 7:2.

plants: *Shabbat* 7:2 forbids placing seeds in the ground.

on the Sabbath: unintentionally, he may preserve it...In the Seventh Year...unintentionally...must uproot: The Tosefta offers two reasons to distinguish between the Sabbath and the Seventh (Sabbatical) Year: first, because one counts the years (but not the Sabbaths) from planting for legal purposes (*orlah* and fourth-year fruits), one will be constantly aware of the violation; second, since violation of the Seventh Year is more common than violation of the Sabbath, greater sanctions must be enacted against all Seventh-Year violations, including accidental ones.

2:4–6 *Terumah Separation from One Species for Another*

4 One may not separate *terumah* from one species for another,
and if one separated *terumah*,
what one separated is not *terumah*.
All species of wheat are [considered] one [species];[18]
all species of fresh figs, dried figs, and pressed figs are [considered] one [species],
and one may separate *terumah* from one for the other.[19]
[In] any locale where there is a priest,
one separates *terumah* from the best [quality produce],
but [in] any locale where there is not a priest,
one separates *terumah* from long-lasting produce.
R. Judah says:
One always separates *terumah* from the best [quality produce].

5 One separates *terumah* from a whole, small onion
[rather than from] half a large onion.
R. Judah says:
Not so!
Rather, [one separates *terumah* from] half a large onion.
And so too R. Judah used to say:
One separates *terumah*
from the onions of the city dwellers for those of the country,
rather than from those of the country for those of the city dwellers,
because it is high-class food.

6 And one may separate *terumah* from oil-producing olives for pickling olives,
but not [from] pickling olives for oil-producing olives.
And nonboiled wine for boiled [wine],

[18] K adds "All species of figs are [considered] one [species]." [19] Lit. "from this for that."

2:4 *from one species for another*: Cf. *Maʿaser Sheni* 5:11.

are [considered] one [species]: For the purposes of separating *terumah*.

pressed figs: Usually molded into a round cake. (See e.g. 2:1 above.)

long-lasting produce: e.g. from dried produce rather than fresh produce, to preserve it until a priest can be found. Cf. *Bikkurim* 3:3.

from the best: Even if it will spoil more quickly.

2:5 *One separates … R. Judah says: Not so! …*: Following 2:4, this mishnah might reflect the debate over the preference for quality vs. preservation (whole onions lasting longer than cut ones, but larger ones being nicer than smaller ones) in the absence of a locally available priest. Alternatively, Maimonides explains the mishnah as a debate over quality, namely, whether even a locally available priest would consider a whole, small onion of higher quality than a larger, cut onion.

city dwellers … country: These refer either to the types of onions generally consumed by city dwellers or country folk, or to onions grown in those areas. If a reference to species, the latter term might be translated as "wild" or Cyprus onions; cf. *Nedarim* 9:8, where such onions are considered to have positive medicinal benefits. R. Judah thinks that the social status of food is a relevant criterion when determining quality.

but not from boiled [wine] for nonboiled [wine].
This is the general rule:
Anything that can constitute [prohibited] Mixed Species with its fellow—
one may not separate *terumah* from one for the other,[20]
even from the good for the bad;
but anything that cannot constitute Mixed Species with its fellow—
one may separate *terumah* from the good for the bad,
but not from the bad for the good.
But if one separated *terumah* from the bad for the good,
what he separated is *terumah*,
except from darnel for wheat, which is not food.
And Armenian cucumber and muskmelon are one species.
R. Judah says:
Two [different] species.

Chapter Three

3:1–2 *Doubtful Terumah*

3 One who separates *terumah* from an Armenian cucumber
and it turns out to be bitter,
[or] from a watermelon
and it turns out to be rotten—
[what one separated is] *terumah*,
but[21] one must return and separate *terumah* [again].
If one separates *terumah* from a jar of wine
and it turns out to be vinegar—
if it was known that it was vinegar before he separated *terumah* from it,
[what he separated] is not *terumah*;

[20] Lit. "from this for that."   [21] P lacks "but."

2:6 *general rule*: That combines both principles from 2:4, that separating *terumah* from one species for another is invalid even after the fact, and that within the same species, one should ideally separate *terumah* from the better-quality produce.

constitute Mixed Species with its fellow: See *Kilayim* 1:1–5.

darnel: A poisonous weed that grows around wheat and resembles it for part of the growing cycle. Cf. *Kilayim* 1:1.

Armenian cucumber: An elongated fruit than can grow three feet long and three inches in diameter. Also known as snake cucumber or snake melon, it is a variety of muskmelon that more closely resembles the modern cucumber.

muskmelon: A species of melon that includes cantaloupes and honeydews.

one species...two species: See *Kilayim* 1:2.

3:1 *Armenian cucumber*: See 2:6.

is not terumah: According to the Tosefta, this follows the position of R. Judah the Patriarch that wine and vinegar are two separate entities (see 2:4).

if it turned into vinegar after he separated *terumah* from it,
in that case it is [valid] *terumah*;
if there is doubt,
[what he separated is] *terumah*,
but he must return and separate *terumah* [again].
The first [*terumah*] cannot create a *terumah* mixture by itself,
nor is one liable for an additional fifth for [consuming] it,
and likewise the second [*terumah*].
  2 If one of them fell into nonsacral produce,
it does not turn it into a mixture subject to *terumah* restrictions.
If the second fell into another [pile of nonsacral produce],[22]
it does not turn it into a mixture subject to *terumah* restrictions.
If both of them fell into the same [pile of nonsacral produce],[23]
they turn it into a mixture subject to *terumah* restrictions
according to the smaller of the two of them.

3:3–4 *Separation of Terumah by Multiple Owners*

  3 Joint owners who separated *terumah* one after the other—
R. Aqiva says:
What both of them separated is *terumah*;[24]

---

[22] Lit. "into another place."   [23] Lit. "into the same place."
[24] Lit. "the *terumah* of both of them is *terumah*," and so throughout.

---

the first … the second: Both separations are only doubtfully valid, and therefore neither by itself triggers the consequences of mixing or consuming actual *terumah*.

cannot create a terumah mixture: Even if it falls into less than one hundred parts of nonsacral produce; see 1:8, 4:7, and 5:1.

by itself: See 3:2.

liable for an additional fifth: The fine for a nonpriest who consumes *terumah*; see 6:1.

3:2 This mishnah continues to discuss the case of two *terumah* separations from a single pile of produce, further explicating the consequences of their mixing with nonsacral produce.

If one … If the second: 3:1 discussed the case where only one of the two piles mixes with nonsacral produce. This mishnah adds that even if both mix with different piles, one needn't be concerned that between the two piles, one has nullified actual *terumah* in less than the required ratio (see 4:7 and 5:1).

another [pile of nonsacral produce]: Different from the one into which the first fell.

If both of them fell, etc.: In this case, one must relate to one of the separated *terumot* as actual and not just doubtful *terumah*. Since we are dealing with a case of doubt, however, this mishnah rules leniently and only requires assuming that the smaller of the two *terumot* was the actual *terumah* when calculating the nullification ratio.

3:3 *one after the other*: The second partner being unaware that the first had already separated *terumah*.

what both of them separated is terumah: The simple meaning is that the full amount that both separate is fully sanctified as *terumah*. Many commentaries, however, following the Yerushalmi, understand that only half of each partner's *terumah* separation is sanctified, and that the other half remains nonsacral produce which the priest must repay.

But the Sages say:
[Only] what the first separated is *terumah*.[25]
R. Yose says:
If the first separated *terumah* in the statutory amount,
what the second separated is not *terumah*,
but if the first did not separate *terumah* in the statutory amount,
what the second separated is [also] *terumah*.

4 When does this apply?
When he did not speak.
But if he authorized a member of his household
or his male servant or his female servant to separate *terumah*,
what [his agent] separated is *terumah*.
[If] he revoked [the authorization]—
if before [the agent] separated *terumah* he revoked,
what [the agent] separated is not *terumah*;
but if after [the agent] separated *terumah* he revoked,
what [the agent] separated is *terumah*.
Workers do not have permission to separate *terumah*,
except for treaders,
for they render the winepress susceptible to impurity immediately.

3:5 *Verbal Designation of Terumah*

5 If one says:
"The *terumah* of this heap is within it,"

---

[25] **K** has instead "What the second separated is not *terumah*."

---

the first separated is terumah: While the second is not, as some manuscripts state explicitly.

the statutory amount: See 4:3 below.

3:4 *When does this apply*: This mishnah contextualizes the debate between R. Aqiva and the Sages in the previous mishnah over the validity of *terumah* separated by the second owner of jointly held produce.

When he did not speak: "Speak" likely means "permit" or "appoint" here. That is, R. Aqiva and the Sages disagree about the status of the second *terumah* separation if the partners did not agree in advance who would separate *terumah*. If, however, they did agree on who should separate *terumah*, presumably R. Aqiva would concede that if the nonappointed partner separated *terumah*, his separation would be invalid.

But: The transition from the first part of this mishnah to the second part is difficult; the partners are replaced by household members.

Workers do not have permission: That is, they do not have implicit permission to separate *terumah*, but must be given explicit permission (cf. 1:1).

treaders, for they render, etc.: The liquid exuded by the first grapes that are crushed makes the winepress susceptible to impurity by touch. That impurity is then spread to the rest of the grapes, rendering the subsequent *terumah* that is separated impure and thus liable to be destroyed (cf. 2:1–2). Thus, we may assume that the owners would want treaders to separate *terumah* immediately before commencing work to avoid creating a situation where *terumah* would have to be separated from an impure substance or from distant wine (see 4:3).

3:5 *If one says*: The owner of the produce must verbalize his intention to separate *terumah* or tithe from a portion of a particular heap of produce, but need not actually remove the *terumah* or tithe before starting

or: "Its tithes are within it,"
[or]:²⁶ "The *terumah* of this tithe is within it"—
R. Simeon says:
He designated it.²⁷
But the Sages say:
[Not] until he says
"in its north[ern part]" or "in its south[ern part]."
R. Eleazar Hisma says:
If²⁸ one says:
"The *terumah* of the heap is from it for it,"
he designated it.
R. Eliezer b. Jacob says:
If²⁹ one says:
"One-tenth of this tithe is to be made *terumah* of the tithe for it,"
he designated it.

3:6–7 *Proper Sequence in the Separation of Terumah*

6 One who [separated] *terumah* before [setting aside] firstfruits,
[or]³⁰ [set aside] first tithe before [separating] *terumah*,
or [set aside] second tithe before first [tithe],³¹
even though he transgresses a prohibition of the Torah,
what he did is done,

---

²⁶ **K**, **P**, and many other manuscripts have "or."
²⁷ Lit. "called its name," and so throughout.
²⁸ Several manuscripts: "Even if."
²⁹ Several manuscripts: "Even if."
³⁰ Several manuscripts have "or."
³¹ **P** inserts the word "tithe."

---

to eat it (cf. *Demai* 7:1–5). One is then no longer able to separate *terumah* or tithes for it from a different pile or for a different pile from it.

in its norther[ern] part…souther[ern] part: The Sages require the owner to designate the precise section of the heap from which the *terumah* or tithes will be removed.

from it for it: That is, the *terumah* for this heap will come from this heap. It appears that R. Eleazar Hisma is even more lenient than R. Simeon, in that he doesn't require the owner to verbally designate any part of the heap itself to be *terumah*; this understanding is supported by the versions that preface his comment with "even," which implies a greater leniency. Some commentaries suggest that R. Eleazar agrees with R. Simeon regarding *terumah* but disagrees regarding tithing, where he would agree with the Sages that a specific location is required for effective verbal designation.

R. Eliezer b. Jacob says, etc.: Either (1) R. Eliezer b. Jacob is simply stating the same law as R. Eleazar Hisma—namely, that one needn't say "within it" to successfully designate *terumah*—in the context of separating *terumah* from the Levitical first tithe; or (2) he is adding that even using the word "one-tenth," which is related to tithing and not *terumah* separation, is sufficient to permit verbal designation of *terumah*; or (3) whereas R. Simeon permits verbally designating *terumah* of first tithe even in a heap that hasn't yet had *terumah* or tithe separated from it, R. Eliezer b. Jacob only permits verbal designation of *terumah* of first tithe from a heap consisting of separated first tithe itself.

3:6 *second tithe before first [tithe]*: See *Ma'aser Sheni* 5:11.

as it says: *Your fullness and your juices you shall not delay.*

7 And whence [in the Torah do we learn]
that [setting aside] firstfruits is to precede [separating] *terumah*?
This one is called "*terumah*" and "first,"
and that one is [also] called "*terumah*" and "first"!
But firstfruits are to precede everything,³² for they are earliest of all;
and *terumah* [is to precede] first [tithe], for it is [called] "first";
and first tithe [is to precede] second [tithe], for there is "first" in it.

3:8 *Improper Verbal Designation*

8 One who intends to say:
"*terumah*" but said "tithe";
"tithe" but said "*terumah*";
"whole burnt offering" but said "offering of well-being";
"offering of well-being" but said "whole burnt offering";
[I vow] that "I will not enter this house" and said "that [house]";
[I vow] that "I will not benefit from this" and said "from that"—
he said nothing,
until his mouth and his heart agree.

3:9 *The Status of Non-Israelites vis-à-vis Terumah*

9 A gentile or a Samaritan—
what they separated [as *terumah*] is *terumah*;

---

³² **K**, **P**, and other manuscripts lack "everything."

---

as it says, etc.: Exodus 22:28. The verse serves as a source for the prohibition of separating agricultural gifts out of order; "fullness" is understood to refer to firstfruits, and "juices" is understood to refer to *terumah*.

3:7 *This one is called "terumah"*: Terumah in Deuteronomy 12:6, 11, and 17 is understood as referring to firstfruits.

and "first": In Exodus 23:19 and 34:26.

and "first": Numbers 18:12 and Deuteronomy 18:4.

earliest: Firstfruits take precedence because they are designated while still attached to the ground (*Bikkurim* 1:3).

there is "first" in it: i.e. the *terumah* of the tithe (Numbers 18:26).

3:8 *until his mouth and his heart agree*: Cf. *Nazir* 5:1.

3:9 The *Samaritans* were treated by the rabbis as a liminal group, straddling Israelite and non-Israelite identities (see *Berakhot* 7:1, 8:8; *Gittin* 1:5; *Qiddushin* 4:3).

what they separated: From their own produce; cf. 1:1.

their tithes are valid,
and their consecrated offerings are valid.
R. Judah says:
A gentile is not subject to the law of fourth-year vineyard;
but the Sages say:
He is.
The *terumah* of a gentile can create a *terumah* mixture,
and one is obligated an additional fifth for [consuming] it;
but R. Simeon exempts.

Chapter Four

4:1–2 *Partial Terumah Separation or Tithing*

4 One who sets aside partial *terumah* or tithes—
he may remove *terumah* [or tithe] from it for it,
but not for[33] another place.
R. Meir says:
He may even remove *terumah* or tithes from[34] another place.
 2 One whose produce is in a storeroom,

---

[33] P and other manuscripts: "from."   [34] Some manuscripts: "for."

---

fourth-year vineyard: See Leviticus 19:23–25 and *Ma'aser Sheni* 5:1–4. The commentaries explain that this mishnah follows the view that land acquisitions in the Land of Israel by non-Jews are legally efficacious. Cf. *Demai* 5:9.

can create a terumah mixture: If it falls into nonsacral produce; see 4:7 and 5:1.

additional fifth: The penalty for inadvertent consumption of *terumah* by a nonpriest; see 6:1.

exempts: From the additional fifth.

4:1 *partial terumah or tithe*: The owner intends to complete tithing, but wishes to consume part of the produce before doing so (compare 4:2).

from it for it but not for another place: After removing the initial, partial *terumah* or tithe, one may continue to remove *terumah* or tithes in stages within a single pile of produce, but not for another pile of untithed produce. Partial tithing leaves each piece of produce in a state of proportional limbo (see 4:2 and 5:5-6), similar to "exempt" (already tithed) produce which cannot be used to tithe fully obligated produce (see 1:5).

R. Meir, etc.: According to this version of the text, R. Meir is discussing a different scenario than the opening clause: whether one can remove *terumah* or tithes from a fully untithed pile for this partially untithed pile. His opinion here coheres with his rejection of proportional limbo in 4:2. The versions that match the language in both clauses (whether "for another place" or "from another place") highlight that this a point of dispute between the anonymous Sages and R. Meir.

4:2 *storeroom*: containing one hundred *se'ah*, a common example in the Mishnah (see e.g. *Demai* 5:1–2).

se'ah to a Levite (Numbers 18:21–24) *and…poor person* (Deuteronomy 14:28–29): After having separated *terumah*. Approximately twenty percent of the storehouse must be removed for these tithes; only two percent—one-tenth of the necessary amount—has been.

and gave a *se'ah* to a Levite
and a *se'ah* to a poor person—
he may set aside an additional eight *se'ah* and consume them—
the words of R. Meir.
But the Sages say:
One may set aside only proportionally.

4:3–6 *Terumah Separation Amounts and Intention*

3 The statutory amount of *terumah*—
generous,[35] one of forty;
The House of Shammai say:
[One of] thirty;
while the intermediate [is] one of fifty,
and the stingy,[36] one of sixty.
If one separated *terumah* and one of sixty came up in his hand,
it is *terumah*,
and he need not separate [any additional] *terumah*.
If he returned and added [*terumah*],
it is obligated in tithes.
If one of sixty-one came up [in his hand], it is *terumah*,
but[37] one must return and separate the amount of *terumah* to which one is accustomed,
[even from already] measured, weighed, or counted [produce].

[35] Lit. "a pleasant eye" or "an eye of pleasantness."
[36] Lit. "the wicked [eye]."   [37] Absent in **K**.

eight se'ah and consume them: R. Meir views the partial tithe that has been removed as sufficient to permit eating an amount corresponding to it. (Maimonides notes that the numbers here are approximate, since the poor tithe is separated from the produce remaining after separating the Levitical tithe, and thus one would be permitted to eat slightly more than eight *se'ah*.)

proportionally: The Sages view each *se'ah* as only partially tithed and require separating another eight percent from any *se'ah* one wishes to eat, or to complete tithing the entire storehouse.

4:3 *generous…intermediate…stingy*: These terms usually describe a person's disposition (cf. *Avot* 2:9, 11, and 5:19); here, however, they might describe the quality of the amount (i.e. "a generous amount is ¹⁄₄₀", rather than "a generous person gives ¹⁄₄₀"); cf. 4:4, where "intermediate" apparently refers to the measure itself, not the disposition of the person.

he need not separate: Although this wording implies that one may separate additional *terumah* if one wishes, the following clause makes clear that such an act is ineffective and might have negative legal ramifications. (Cf. 3:3.)

obligated in tithes: Once *terumah* was separated in the minimally appropriate—even if undesirable—amount, the produce is no longer subject to the obligation to separate *terumah*. Anything subsequently separated as *terumah* does not obtain sanctified status and must not be treated as such; it is, instead, subject to the regular obligations to separate post-*terumah* tithes.

must return and separate: This translation follows the Tosefta, which requires separating additional *terumah* in this case (cf. 3:3). The Mishnah itself, as is often the case, omits the modal verb, rendering unclear whether it permits, encourages, or requires separating additional *terumah* to reach the ¹⁄₆₀ threshold.

measured, weighed, or counted: From which one is ordinarily forbidden to separate *terumah*; see 1:7.

R. Judah says:
Even[38] [from produce] which is not nearby.

4 [If] one says to one's agent:
"Go out and separate *terumah* [on my behalf],"
[the agent] must separate *terumah* according to the intent of the householder.
If he does not know the intent of the householder,
he separates *terumah* as the intermediate, one of fifty.
If he subtracted ten or added ten,
what he separated is *terumah*.
If [the agent] intended to add even one,
what he separated is *terumah*.

5 One who increases [the amount of] *terumah* [beyond the statutory amount]—
R. Eliezer says:
[He may do so up to] one of ten,
like *terumah* from the tithe;
more than that,
he must make it *terumah* from the tithe for elsewhere.[39]
R. Ishmael says:
Half nonsacral produce and half *terumah*.
R. Tarfon and R. Aqiva say:
As long as [some] nonsacral produce remains there.

[38] Absent in **K**.   [39] **K**: "but not from elsewhere"; other manuscripts: "but not for elsewhere."

which is not nearby: According to *Hallah* 1:9 and *Bikkurim* 2:5, *terumah* for any particular pile of produce must be separated, at least ideally, from produce located in the same vicinity. (For a vivid example of this requirement, see *Hallah* 2:8.) No reason is offered in tannaitic literature for this requirement.

4:4 *subtracted ten or added ten*: By accident, the emissary decreased the amount of *terumah* he should have separated (e.g. from 1/50 to 1/60) or increased it (e.g. from 1/50 to 1/40). This applies whether or not he knows the intent of the homeowner. (Some commentaries explain "ten" not to refer to the change in the denominator of the ratio, but as allowing a 10% deviation on the part of the emissary.)

If [the agent] intended to add even one: That is, to intentionally separate more *terumah* than the homeowner instructed, even in the slightest amount (e.g. by separating 1/49 when he was told to separate 1/50). Alternatively, this clause could also refer to the situation in which he does not know the homeowner's intent, and purposefully deviates from the mandated 1/50 ratio in an attempt to predict the homeowner's intent.

4:5 *like terumah from the tithe*: Numbers 18:26.

terumah from the tithe for elsewhere: According to R. Eliezer, full *terumah* status cannot devolve upon more than one-tenth of one's produce. However, the attempt to designate part of the remaining ninety percent of one's produce causes it to attain a partial sacral status, and therefore must be given to a Levite as part of the tithe, which the Levite must then give to a priest as part of the *terumah* he must separate from his agricultural gifts. According to the version preserved in many manuscripts, this partial *terumah* is tied to the pile from which it was separated, and must only be used as *terumah* for the tithe separated from it; cf. 4:1.

Half…half: One can separate up to fifty percent of one's produce as *terumah*.

As long as [some] nonsacral produce remains there: One may separate as much produce for *terumah* as one wishes, provided a token amount of nonsacral produce remains afterwards. Cf. *Hallah* 1:9, which adopts this position.

6 At three seasons one measures the basket:
(1) at the first ripening,
(2) at the final ripening,
(3) and in the middle of the summer.
The one who counts is praiseworthy;
and the one who measures is more praiseworthy than he;
and the one who weighs is the most praiseworthy of the three of them.

4:7 Neutralization of Terumah

7 R. Eliezer says:
Terumah is neutralized in one and a hundred.[40]
R. Joshua says:
In one hundred and a bit more.
This "and a bit more" has no statutory amount.
R. Yose b. Meshullam says:
"And a bit more" is a *qav* per one hundred *se'ah*,
one sixth per [the amount potentially] creating a *terumah* mixture.

[40] K and other manuscripts: "in a hundred and one."

4:6 *At three seasons*: Different kinds of produce ripen at different points in the season; one is required to estimate or measure the amount of each kind of produce at the height of its ripeness, even though doing so will result in separating less *terumah* or tithe than if one waits for the produce to begin to wither. (The term for "basket" used here usually refers to a basket for collecting figs, different species of which ripen at different points in the season.)

measures the basket: i.e. estimates how much produce at each point in the season would actually fit into a basket of known measure, lest one incorrectly extrapolate from the current amount and thereby separate an insufficient amount of *terumah* or tithe.

counts…measures…weighs: Cf. 1:7, which requires that *terumah* be separated, ideally, through estimation and not direct measure, but permits separating *terumah*, even ideally, from produce which was already counted, measured, or weighed. This mishnah might then in fact be praising those who precisely measure their produce before separating *terumah* from it. (A more radical alternative is to understand this mishnah as disagreeing entirely with 1:7, praising separating *terumah* with precision.) Most commentaries, however, assume that this mishnah is referring to separating tithes and *terumah* from the tithe, both of which are fixed at ten percent by the Torah, and should therefore be separated with care; cf. Avot 1:16.

4:7 *neutralized*: Lit. "goes up." This is functionally equivalent to the word "nullify" used in other contexts of mixtures of forbidden and permitted items (see *Zevahim* 8:6, *Hullin* 6:5); its etymology in this sense is uncertain. Once *terumah* is neutralized, the entire mixture is now permitted to nonpriests; *Orlah* 2:1, however, requires removing the amount of *terumah* that fell in.

in one and a hundred: one hundred units of nonsacral produce are required to neutralize one unit of *terumah*, for a total ratio of 1:101, as demonstrated by the examples in 4:9–11 below. See *Shabbat* 21:1.

In one hundred and a bit more: The final ratio need only be slightly greater than 1:100, i.e. 99 plus an infinitesimal amount of nonsacral produce is sufficient to neutralize one unit of *terumah*.

qav per one hundred se'ah, etc.: A *qav* is a volume measure equivalent to one-sixth of a *se'ah*. For every unit of *terumah*, 99⅙ units of nonsacral produce is required to desacralize it.

4:8–13 *Neutralization of Discrete Objects*

8 R. Joshua says:
Black figs neutralize white [figs]
and white [figs] neutralize black [figs].
Cakes of pressed fig—
the large neutralize the small,
and the small neutralize the large;
the round neutralize the rectangular,
and the rectangular neutralize the round.
R. Eliezer forbids.
But R. Aqiva says:
In the case where it is known what fell,
these do not neutralize those;
but when[41] it is not known what fell, these neutralize those.

9 How?
Fifty [nonsacral] black figs and fifty [nonsacral] white [figs]—
if a [*terumah*] black [fig] fell [into the one hundred nonsacral figs],
the black [figs] are forbidden but the white [figs] are permitted.
If a [*terumah*] white [fig] fell [into the one hundred nonsacral figs],
the white [figs] are forbidden but the black [figs] are permitted.
In the case where it is not known what [kind of *terumah* fig] fell [into the one hundred nonsacral figs],
these neutralize those.
And this is the case in which
R. Eliezer is stringent and R. Joshua is lenient.

10 And this is the case in which R. Eliezer is lenient and R. Joshua is stringent.
Regarding one who presses a *litra* of sliced [*terumah*] figs

---

[41] **K, P**, and many manuscripts: "But in the case where."

4:8 *Black...white...large...small...round...rectangular*: Even though the *terumah* fig or cake that fell in is distinguishable by its color, size, or shape from at least some of the nonsacral items into which it fell (see 4:9), R. Joshua permits joining all items of the same species together to effect neutralization, and would apparently permit consumption of the entire mixture, presumably after having removed one fig (see *Orlah* 2:1).

forbids: That is, R. Eliezer does not permit combining like species for purposes of neutralization of visually distinguishable items. It seems that he forbids consumption of the entire mixture, even if one knows the color, size, or shape of what fell in; see 4:9.

4:9 *How?*: This mishnah describes the case from the point of view of R. Aqiva, spelling out that the implication that even when one knows the identity of the intruding *terumah* fig, only the figs that share its identity are forbidden when present in less than a 100:1 ratio.

stringent...lenient: Even when the identity of the *terumah* fig is unknown, R. Eliezer would forbid the entire mixture; and even when the identity of the *terumah* fig is known and there isn't a sufficient number of its own kind to neutralize it, R. Joshua would permit it.

4:10 *presses...sliced [terumah] figs*: To create a round, pressed fig cake.

on top of the jar
and he doesn't know[42] on which one [he pressed them]—
R. Eliezer says:
One may view them as if they are separate,
and the lower ones neutralize the upper ones.
R. Joshua says:
It is not neutralized unless there are one hundred jars there.

11 A *se'ah* of *terumah* that fell onto a storeroom
and remained on top[43]—
R. Eliezer says:
If there is in what remains on top [less than one in] one hundred *se'ah*,[44]
it will be neutralized in one and a hundred.
R. Joshua says:
It will not be neutralized.
If a *se'ah* of *terumah* fell onto a storeroom—
one must skim off the top.
But if so, why did they say:
Terumah is neutralized in one and a hundred?
If [45] it isn't known whether they mixed together,
or to where it fell.

[42] K, P and manuscripts: "And it is not known."   [43] Meaning uncertain.
[44] K, P, and many manuscripts lack "one hundred *se'ah*."
[45] K, P, and many manuscripts: "In the case where."

barrel: Filled with dried, pressed figs (see e.g. *Oholot* 6:2), in a room full of such barrels.

view them...upper ones: Despite the fact that the top layer of *terumah* figs could not have mixed with the dried, pressed figs underneath, R. Eliezer permits neutralizing the upper *terumah* figs as long as sufficient nonsacral figs are present in the lower part of the barrel. It is unclear whether R. Eliezer requires the requisite ratio in each barrel (and would forbid any barrel that lacked such a ratio), or combines the lower layers of figs in *all* the barrels against the amount of *terumah* figs.

unless there are one hundred jars there: As the Tosefta makes clear, R. Joshua refuses to consider the lower part of the fig cake—into which the *terumah* figs certainly did not mix—as relevant for calculating the neutralization ratio; as such, they remain permitted no matter what. Instead, he requires that there be a total of one hundred barrels to neutralize all of the top layers; in their absence, the top layers of all the jars would be forbidden.

4:11 *storeroom*: Often associated with dried figs; see *Ma'aserot* 1:8.

remained on top: According to this translation, R. Eliezer permits neutralization even in cases where the *terumah* was not removed, whereas R. Joshua requires physically removing it whenever possible. (Although this translation makes good sense of the mishnah, it requires attributing two contradictory senses to the same word: "remain on top" here and "skim off the top" below. Translating the verb consistently, however, generates serious interpretive problems.)

But if so: If one is required to physically remove *terumah* that falls onto nonsacral produce, in what situations would neutralization by ratio come into play?

mixed: If the *terumah* and nonsacral produce mix such that removal of the actual *terumah* is impossible, one may rely on neutralization by ratio.

where it fell: See 4:10, 12.

12 Two large baskets or two storerooms
into one of which a *se'ah* of *terumah* fell,
and it is not known into which of them it fell—
this neutralizes that.
R. Simeon says:
Even if they are in two [separate] towns,
this neutralizes that.
13 Said R. Yose:
A case came before R. Aqiva
regarding fifty bundles of a vegetable,
into which fell one of them,[46] half of which was *terumah*;
and I said before him:
Let it be neutralized,
not because *terumah* is neutralized in fifty and one,
but because there were 102 halves there.

Chapter Five

5:1–4 Mixtures of Terumah and Nonsacral Produce

5 A *se'ah* of impure *terumah* that fell
into less than one hundred [*se'ah* of] nonsacral produce,
or into first tithe,
or into second tithe,
or into consecrated [produce]—

---

[46] P and many manuscripts lack "of them."

4:12 *Two large baskets or two storerooms*: Neither of which by itself contains a sufficient ratio to neutralize the amount of *terumah* that fell in, but which, if added together, do create a sufficient ratio.

this neutralizes that: One may mathematically combine the contents of the two storage units for the purposes of neutralization; cf. 4:10.

two [separate] towns: Even if one's storage facilities are quite distant from each other, one may mathematically combine their contents for the purposes of neutralizing lost *terumah*, even if the possibility of it having fallen into one of them is quite small.

4:13 *one of them*: i.e. an additional bundle of the same kind of vegetable.

half of which: Half of the bundle that fell in.

102 halves: Since the bundle that fell in was half-*terumah* and half-nonsacral, one can reframe the mixture as consisting of half-bundles, in which case one has 101 nonsacral half-bundles, and one *terumah* half-bundle, which is neutralized.

5:1 *impure terumah that fell*: Since the 1:101 neutralization threshold (see 4:7) has not been met, the mixture is forbidden for consumption by nonpriests. Priests, however, are forbidden from consuming impure

whether impure or pure,
must [be left to] rot.
If that [original] *se'ah* was pure,
the mixture[47] can be sold to the priests at the price of *terumah*, minus[48] the price of that *se'ah*,
and if it fell into first tithe, one may designate it as *terumah* of tithe,
and if it fell into second tithe or consecrated [produce], the mixture may be redeemed.
But if that [original] nonsacral produce was impure,
the mixture[49] may be eaten:
dried out, or dry-roasted, or kneaded in fruit juice, or divided into dough,
such that there is not an egg's bulk in one loaf.[50]

[47] Lit. "they," here and throughout. [48] Lit. "except for."
[49] Several manuscripts add "is neutralized and." [50] Lit. "place," here and throughout.

terumah (see 2:1). Since nothing may be done with this produce, it must be destroyed. Cf. 10:11 and *Shabbat* 2:1–2, which permit benefiting from the burning of impure *terumah* oil.

must [be left to] rot: *Temurah* 7:5 states that impure *terumah* must be burned or buried. Either multiple methods of destruction were permitted, or impure *terumah* mixtures, despite being forbidden for consumption, need not be removed as completely from view as impure *terumah* itself.

price of terumah: Which, due to high supply (many farmers and Levites separating *terumah*) and low demand (relatively few priests), is lower than the price of nonsacral produce. The farmer is thus economically punished for his mistake.

minus the price of that se'ah: Which was, initially, supposed to be given freely to a priest. Cf. *Orlah* 2:1.

and if it fell into first tithe: Which had not yet had *terumah* removed from it by a Levite.

one may designate it as terumah of tithe: Either for this pile's tithe if *terumah* had not yet been separated from its tithe, or for another pile of tithe elsewhere. The Levite thereby incurs no loss.

redeemed: In both cases the produce reverts to *terumah* status and is given to a priest; the monetary value of the produce is then spent in Jerusalem or given to the Temple, and no monetary loss is incurred.

But if that...nonsacral produce had been impure...may be eaten: This is the reverse of the first case. The *terumah* that fell in is pure, and therefore must be consumed and not destroyed. Since this is a dry mixture, impurity is not automatically transferred to the pure *terumah* (cf. 2:1); the introduction of liquid, however, would cause impurity to spread to the pure *terumah*, which is also forbidden (see 8:11). Therefore, the mixture must be prepared and consumed in one of the ways enumerated in order to preserve the purity of the *terumah* within it. Cf. *Ma'aser Sheni* 2:3–4.

dried out: See Joshua 9:5 and 1 Kings 14:3. The commentaries are divided as to whether this refers to kneading and baking individual loaves smaller than an egg's bulk (in which case this clause is redundant with the final clause of this mishnah) or as a version of dry-roasting to avoid contamination through liquid (in which case it is redundant with the next clause). One commentary suggests, therefore, that it refers to consuming the wheat kernels after they have dried out of their own accord, which are small enough that even were liquid to fall on them, they would not transmit impurity.

dry-roasted: As long as the produce remains dry, the impure produce cannot render the pure *terumah* impure.

kneaded in fruit juice: Which does not render food susceptible to impurity. See *Hallah* 2:2; cf. 11:2 below and *Makhshirin* 6:4.

such that there is not an egg's bulk, etc.: Food in the amount of less than the volume of an egg does not transmit impurity (see *Orlah* 2:4–5, *Me'ilah* 4:5, and *Tohorot* 2:1), due to it being an insignificant amount of food (see *Sukkah* 2:5).

2 A *se'ah* of impure *terumah* that fell into one hundred [*se'ah* of] pure nonsacral produce—
R. Eliezer says:
Let the *terumah* be separated and burnt,
since I say: The *se'ah* that fell in is the *se'ah* that arose.
But the Sages say:
[The *terumah*] is neutralized and may be eaten:
dried out, or dry-roasted, or kneaded in fruit juice, or divided into dough,
such that there is not an egg's bulk in one loaf.

3 A *se'ah* of pure *terumah* that fell into one hundred [*se'ah* of] impure nonsacral produce—
[the *terumah*] is neutralized and [the mixture] may be eaten:
dried out, or dry-roasted, or kneaded in fruit juice, or divided into dough,
such that there is not an egg's bulk in one loaf.

4 A *se'ah* of impure *terumah* that fell into one hundred *se'ah* of pure *terumah*—
the House of Shammai forbid,
but the House of Hillel permit.
The House of Hillel said to the House of Shammai:
Since pure [*terumah*] is forbidden to nonpriests,
and impure [*terumah*] is forbidden [even] to priests,
[therefore] just as pure [*terumah*] is neutralized,
so too impure [*terumah*] is neutralized.
The House of Shammai said to them:
No!
Just because the [more] lenient nonsacral produce, which is permitted to nonpriests,
neutralized the pure [*terumah*],
should the [more] stringent *terumah*,[51] which is forbidden to nonpriests,
neutralize the impure [*terumah*]?
After they conceded, R. Eliezer said:

[51] **K**, **P**, and many manuscripts lack "*terumah*."

5:2 *R. Eliezer*: Cf. 4:11 and 5:4.

burned: As with all impure *terumah*; see 5:4 below and *Temurah* 7:5, but cf. 5:1 above.

arose: i.e. that was separated. This is a legal rather than factual claim.

But the Sages say, etc.: This clause is difficult. The methods described here were used in 5:1 to protect pure *terumah* from becoming impure; here, however, the *terumah* that fell in was already impure and in any case has been neutralized. Perhaps the Sages are concerned to avoid contamination of even nonsacral produce; alternatively, one is tempted to emend the text by deleting the words after "eaten," although such an emendation is not supported by any textual witnesses.

5:3 This mishnah is the inverse of 5:2, and in contrast to 5:1, the pure *terumah* is neutralized by the impure nonsacral produce. The mixture may, therefore, be consumed by a nonpriest, but only in such a way as to avoid transmitting impurity to the pure (albeit neutralized) *terumah*.

5:4 *forbid…permit*: Consumption by priests.

they conceded: Although the discussion ends with the House of Shammai's counterargument, the continuation of the mishnah as well as the Tosefta make it clear that the House of Shammai are the ones to have conceded.

Let the *terumah* be separated and burnt.
But the Sages say:
[The impure *terumah*] was obliterated in its tiny quantity.

5:5–6   Produce Removed from Terumah Mixtures

5 A *se'ah* of *terumah* that fell into one hundred [*se'ah* of pure, nonsacral produce], [if] one lifted it and it fell somewhere else—
R. Eliezer says:
It creates a *terumah* mixture like definite *terumah*.
But the Sages say:
It only creates a *terumah* mixture proportionally.

6 A *se'ah* of *terumah* that fell into less than one hundred [*se'ah* of pure nonsacral produce],
created a *terumah* mixture, and [produce] from this *terumah* mixture fell somewhere else—
R. Eliezer says:
It creates a *terumah* mixture like definite *terumah*.
But the Sages say:
Terumah mixtures only create *terumah* mixtures proportionally,
and the leavened only leavens proportionally,
and drawn water only invalidates an immersion pool proportionally.

separated and burnt: See 5:2. R. Eliezer was a follower of the House of Shammai, and seems to partially retain their concern that impure *terumah* not be consumed.

obliterated in its tiny quantity: Once neutralized, one need not be concerned to remove any portion of the mixture. Whether the priests who consume this mixture need to observe the stringencies described in 5:1–3 to avoid transmitting impurity is unclear.

5:5 *lifted it*: i.e. removed an amount of produce equivalent to the amount of *terumah* that initially fell in; see 5:4.

like definite terumah: Even though the *terumah* that fell in met the neutralization ratio, R. Eliezer treats the amount removed as having all the properties of actual *terumah* (see 5:2).

proportionally: Despite being neutralized, any produce removed from the pile continues to be treated as having 1/101 *terumah* in it. The language is borrowed from 5:6, and it is difficult to understand what practical impact it should have here.

5:6 *Sages say*, etc.: *Temurah* 1:4.

create terumah mixtures proportionally: e.g. if one *se'ah* of *terumah* fell into ten *se'ah* of nonsacral produce, then any *se'ah* that separates from that mixture is one-tenth *terumah*. If it subsequently fell into another pile of nonsacral produce, as long as there were ten or more *se'ah* of nonsacral produce, it would be neutralized.

leavened: If *terumah* sourdough was used to leaven nonsacral dough, any of that mixed dough which falls into another batch of nonsacral dough in sufficient quantity to leaven it can be neutralized if the proportion of *terumah* dough in the amount that fell in to the total amount of nonsacral dough is greater than 1:100. Cf. *Orlah* 2:6.

drawn water only invalidates: See *Miqva'ot* 2:4 and *Eduyot* 1:3. An immersion pool requires forty *se'ah* of natural water and is invalidated by three *log* (= 1/8 of a *se'ah*) of drawn water. If water from such an invalidated immersion pool makes its way to a valid immersion pool, the water is considered as only invalid proportional to the ratio of drawn to natural water it contains.

5:7–8: *Multiple Terumah Mixings*

7 A *se'ah* of *terumah* that fell into one hundred [*se'ah* of pure, nonsacral produce]—
[if] one lifted it and another [*se'ah* of *terumah*] fell [into the one hundred *se'ah* of neutralized produce],
[and] one lifted it and another [*se'ah* of *terumah*] fell [into the one hundred *se'ah* of neutralized produce],
the mixture[52] is permitted,
until *terumah* exceeds the nonsacral produce.

8 A *se'ah* of *terumah* that fell into one hundred [*se'ah* of pure, nonsacral produce],
and he was unable to lift it before another [*se'ah* of *terumah*] fell—
the mixture is forbidden.
But R. Simeon permits.

5:9 *Post Facto Changes*

9 A *se'ah* of *terumah* that fell into one hundred [*se'ah* of pure, nonsacral produce],
and one ground them and they lessened [in volume] —
just as the nonsacral produce lessened [in volume], so too the *terumah* lessened [in volume],
and they are [still] permitted.
A *se'ah* of *terumah* that fell into less than one hundred [*se'ah* of pure, nonsacral produce],
and one ground them and they increased [in volume]—
just as the nonsacral produce increased [in volume], so too the *terumah* increased [in volume],
and they are [still] forbidden.
If it is known that the nonsacral wheat is higher quality[53] than that of the *terumah*,

---

[52] Lit. "it," here and throughout.   [53] Lit. "nicer."

5:7 *permitted*: Presumably upon removal, as with the first two mixings.

exceeds: The commentaries disagree as to whether this means more than half of the original amount of *terumah* has fallen in (i.e. fifty-one *se'ah*), or more than the original amount (i.e. 101 *se'ah*).

5:8 *forbidden*: Removal of the amount that fell in is a desideratum for neutralization.

permits: For R. Simeon, neutralization occurs independently of removal.

5:9 *ground…lessened…increased*: Since grinding does not affect the entire mixture uniformly, one might have thought that changes in volume might have to be assumed to affect the majority of the mixture. The mishnah adopts a proportionality approach, fixing the ratio at whatever it was at the moment of the initial mixing.

permitted…forbidden: for consumption by nonpriests.

higher quality: The assumption is that higher-quality grain gains volume faster than lower-quality grain when ground. Thus, if the nonsacral produce is higher quality than the *terumah* grain, after grinding one can rely on the changed ratio to effect neutralization.

they are permitted.
A *se'ah* of *terumah* that fell into less than one hundred [*se'ah* of pure, nonsacral produce], and afterwards [additional] nonsacral produce fell there—
If [it happened] unintentionally, [the mixture] is permitted;
but if [it happened] intentionally, [the mixture] is forbidden.

Chapter Six

6:1–4 *Unintentional Consumption of Terumah*

6 One who unintentionally consumes *terumah* must pay the principal plus the added fifth.
The law is one and the same for the one
who eats, drinks, or anoints with it;
whether the *terumah* is pure or impure
he must pay its fifth,
and a fifth of that fifth.
He may not pay with [other] *terumah*,
but only with nonsacral produce that has been tithed,
which then becomes *terumah*.
The payments have the status of *terumah*;
if[54] the priest wishes to forgive [the repayment],
he may not do so.
  2 An Israelite woman who [unintentionally] consumed *terumah*
and subsequently was married to a priest

---

[54] Some manuscripts add "and."

6:1 *One*: Specifically a nonpriest.

principal: Meaning the amount of *terumah* that he actually consumed.

added fifth: See Leviticus 22:14. The added fifth is measured as a fifth of the total repayment, which is a fourth of the principal. Thus, if someone consumed *terumah* worth four *dinar*, he must give five *dinar* worth of produce to the priest as restitution.

he must pay its fifth: The added fifth obtains the status of *terumah* just like the principal. Therefore, were one to consume the added fifth, he would have to repay it to the priest along with a fifth of that amount.

The payments . . . he may not do so: See 7:4.

6:2 *Israelite woman who [unintentionally] consumed terumah*: A woman who was born into a nonpriestly family is not permitted to consume *terumah*. Therefore, she is obligated to repay its value plus the added fifth to a priest.

subsequently was married to a priest: A woman who is married to a priest is permitted to consume *terumah* (see Leviticus 22:10–13). At issue in this case is how this new status affects her obligation to pay a priest for the *terumah* she consumed before she was married.

If the *terumah* that she consumed was *terumah* that a priest had not yet acquired,
she pays the principal and the added fifth to herself.
If the *terumah* that she consumed was *terumah* that a priest had acquired,
she pays the principal to the owners and the added fifth to herself,
because they have said:
One who unintentionally consumes *terumah*
pays the principal to the owners
and the added fifth to any [priest] he wants.

3 If one [unintentionally] feeds *terumah* to his workers or his guests,
he pays the principal,
and they pay the added fifth.
These are the words of R. Meir.
But the Sages say:
They pay the principal and the added fifth,
and he pays them the value of their meal.

4 If one steals *terumah* but did not consume it,
he pays the twofold payment at the price of *terumah*.
If he consumed it,
he pays two principals plus the added fifth:
one principal and added fifth from nonsacral produce,
and one principal at the price of *terumah*.
If he stole consecrated *terumah*, and consumed it,
he pays two fifths plus the principal,
because twofold payment does not apply to consecrated property.

to herself: Since the *terumah* she ate did not yet belong to a specific priest, she can repay herself because she is now a member of a priestly family. Thus, she can simply designate some of her family's nonsacral produce as *terumah*.

6:3 *he pays … the added fifth*: It was the host's responsibility to feed his guests nonsacral food. Since he did not do so, it is his responsibility to repay the principal to a priest. Those who actually ate the *terumah* must pay the added fifth.

the value of their meal: The Sages are of the opinion that the person who actually consumes the *terumah* is responsible for paying both the principal and the added fifth. However, since it was the host who actually fed his workers/guests *terumah*, he must compensate them for the principal.

6:4 *twofold payment at the price of terumah*: A thief is obligated to repay the owner double the value of what he stole (see Exodus 22:7). Since in this case the thief stole *terumah*, the compensation is calculated at the price of *terumah*, which is less than that of ordinary produce.

one principal … price of terumah: In this case the thief is under two sets of obligations. Since he consumed *terumah*, he must repay the principal plus the added fifth, and this payment must be made with nonsacral produce (see 6:1). He can repay the second principal at the price of *terumah*, because that is the value of the produce that he actually stole. This second principal can be paid in money because it is compensation for theft.

consecrated terumah: *Terumah* that a priest had dedicated to the Temple.

two fifths plus the principal: He pays the principal plus one fifth because he consumed *terumah*. He pays the additional fifth because he benefited from consecrated property (see Leviticus 5:16).

twofold payment … consecrated property: See *Bava Metsiʿa* 4:9.

6:5–6 *Paying for the Unauthorized Consumption of Terumah*

5 One may not pay from Gleanings, Forgotten Sheaves, *pe'ah*, or ownerless [produce],
nor from first tithe whose *terumah* has been removed,[55]
nor from second tithe or consecrated produce which had been redeemed,[56]
because one consecrated item cannot be used to redeem another consecrated item.
These are the words of R. Meir.
But the Sages permit [payment] with these [items].

6 R. Eliezer says:
One may pay from one species [of produce] for another,
provided that he is paying from the superior for the inferior.
But R. Aqiva says:
One may pay only from the same species.
Thus if one ate muskmelons of the sixth year,
he must wait for muskmelons of the eighth year
and pay with them.
From the same verse[57] from which R. Eliezer derives a leniency,

---

[55] Several manuscripts read "first tithe whose *terumah* has not been removed." This was the original reading of **K** but it was later corrected to the reading in the body of the translation.

[56] Several manuscripts read "second tithe or consecrated produce which have not been redeemed." This was the original reading of **K** but it was later corrected to the reading in the body of the translation.

[57] Lit. "place" [in the Torah].

6:5 *Gleanings...ownerless [produce]*: One may not separate *terumah* from any of these items. See 1:5.

first tithe whose terumah has been removed...which had been redeemed: See 1:5 with annotations, including the discussion of the manuscript variants. What is important for our context is that these are also items from which one may not separate *terumah*.

because...another consecrated item: This statement probably refers to the final two items listed. Its exact meaning, however, changes based on the different manuscript readings. Second tithe and consecrated produce are initially consecrated, but lose this status once they have been redeemed. Thus, according to the version of our mishnah which reads "had been redeemed," the mishnah teaches that the fact that these items were once consecrated means they cannot be used as repayment for the consumption of *terumah*. According to the manuscripts that read "had not been redeemed," the mishnah is simply teaching that one may not repay with these items because they are still consecrated.

But the Sages permit [payment] with these [items]: The Yerushalmi discusses which items in the mishnah constitute "these [items]." However, the parallel to this mishnah in the *Sifra* suggests that the Sages permit payment with all of the items listed in our mishnah.

6:6 From the superior species e.g. wheat for the inferior e.g. barley: see 2:4 and 2:6.

the sixth year: Farmers must let their land lie fallow every Seventh Year, which is also called the Sabbatical year. See Leviticus 25:1–7 and *Shevi'it*.

he must wait...pay with them: According to R. Aqiva, the individual who consumed muskmelons must repay with muskmelons. The Mishnah appears to assume that since the individual consumed muskmelons toward the end of the sixth year, the first muskmelons that will become available to him are those of the Seventh Year. However, one may not repay with produce from the Seventh Year because it is not liable for *terumah*. Therefore, he must wait to pay with muskmelons harvested after the completion of the Seventh Year.

From the same verse: The dispute between R. Eliezer and R. Aqiva is based on their differing interpretations of Leviticus 22:14.

R. Aqiva derives a stringency,
as it says: *And he shall give the priest the consecrated item*
whatever is fit to become[58] consecrated.
These are the words of R. Eliezer.
But R. Aqiva says:
And he shall give the priest the consecrated item,
[the same type of] consecrated item which he consumed.

Chapter Seven

7:1–4 *Cases That Do Not Require the Added Fifth*

7 One who intentionally consumes *terumah*
pays the principal but[59] not the added fifth.
The payments have the status of nonsacral produce,
[and][60] if the priest wishes to forgive [the payment],
he may do so.

   2 If the daughter of a priest was married to an Israelite
and afterward [unintentionally] consumed *terumah*,
she pays the principal, but not the added fifth,

---

[58] K and other manuscripts read "to be made."
[60] Some manuscripts include this conjunction.
[59] K lacks the conjunction.

---

whatever is fit to become consecrated: R. Eliezer interprets the verse to mean that one may repay with anything that has the potential to become *terumah*.

which he consumed: R. Aqiva focuses on the definite article "the." Therefore he requires the individual to repay with the same kind of produce that he consumed.

7:1 *One*: A nonpriest.

not the added fifth: The requirement of the added fifth is mentioned specifically in relation to someone who unintentionally consumes *terumah*, see Leviticus 22:14 and 6:1 above. Therefore, someone who intentionally consumes *terumah* is exempt from this requirement and only repays the principal. Those commentators who suggest that the added fifth serves as a means of atonement in the case of accidental sin explain that one who wantonly disregards the prohibition against consuming *terumah* is not given the opportunity to atone for his actions.

The payments…he may do so: See 7:4.

7:2 *If the daughter of a priest was married to an Israelite*: The daughter of a priest is allowed to consume *terumah*, but she loses that right upon marrying a nonpriest. See Leviticus 22:12 and *Yevamot* 9:6. If, however, she is divorced or widowed without having had any children, she regains the right to consume *terumah*. See Leviticus 22:13.

but not the added fifth: Only a nonpriest is required to pay the added fifth. Although this woman is not currently allowed to consume *terumah*, the fact that she can potentially regain this right means that she does not fall into the category of "nonpriest."

and her execution [for adultery] is by burning.
If she married any one of those who are disqualified,
she pays the principal plus the added fifth,
and her execution [for adultery] is by strangulation.
These are the words of R. Meir.
But the Sages say:
In both cases she pays the principal but not the added fifth,
and her execution is by burning.

3 If one [unintentionally] feeds *terumah* to his minor children
or to his slaves, whether adult or minor;
if one consumes *terumah* from outside of the Land of Israel;
or[61] if one consumes less than an olive's bulk of *terumah*,
he must pay the principal
but not the added fifth.
The payments have the status of nonsacral produce,
[and] if the priest wishes to forgive [the payment],
he may do so.

[61] Some manuscripts lack the conjunction.

burning: Unlike a regular Israelite, the daughter of a priest is executed by burning if she commits adultery; see Leviticus 21:9. The connection between this ruling and the law about *terumah* is that the daughter of a priest retains aspects of her priestly status even after marrying a nonpriest.

disqualified: People whom she may not marry (e.g. a *mamzer*, a gentile) or who disqualify their children from the priesthood (e.g. a *halal*, a disqualified priest). See *Yevamot* 6:2, *Qiddushin* 4:6.

she pays the principal plus the added fifth: If she unintentionally consumes *terumah*. According to R. Meir, having intercourse with a disqualified person removes this woman's priestly status entirely. Since she now falls into the category of nonpriest, she must pay the added fifth.

strangulation: If she commits adultery she is executed by strangulation, which is the punishment for adultery for all nonpriestly women (Leviticus 20:10; *Sanhedrin* 11:1).

But the Sages say: According to the Sages, the daughter of a priest retains her status even if she marries a disqualified person. Therefore, she still need not pay the added fifth if she unintentionally consumes *terumah*, and her execution for committing adultery is by burning.

7:3 *minor children…slaves*: Young children and slaves are exempt from the laws of restitution. See *Bava Qamma* 8:4.

from outside of the Land of Israel: The Torah does not apply the laws of *terumah* to produce from outside of the Land of Israel.

consumes less than an olive's bulk: Consumption of less than an olive's bulk in volume is not considered a legally significant act of eating.

he must…added fifth: In the first two cases, the individual had the responsibility to feed others ordinary produce, and therefore must repay the value. He need not pay the added fifth because he himself did not actually eat the *terumah* (see 6:3). This is so even though those who actually did eat the *terumah* will not be required to pay the added fifth themselves. In the last two cases, he did not actually transgress the biblical prohibition. Therefore, while he must compensate a priest for the *terumah* he consumed, he need not pay the added fifth.

the payments…he may do so: See 7:4.

4 This is the general rule:
Whenever one must pay the principal plus the added fifth,
the payments have the status of *terumah*,
[and] if the priest wishes to forgive [the payment],
he may not do so.
Whenever one must pay the principal but not the added fifth,
the payments have the status of nonsacral produce,
[and][62] if the priest wishes to forgive [the payment],
he may do so.

7:5–7 *Cases of Uncertainty*

5 If there are two baskets,
one of which contains *terumah* and the other nonsacral produce,
and a *se'ah* of *terumah* falls into one of them,
but it is not known into which it fell,
I say:
"It fell into the [basket] of *terumah*."
If[63] it is not known which [basket] contains *terumah*
and which the nonsacral produce—
if one ate [the contents of] one of them, he is exempt;
and as for the second basket
he treats it as *terumah*,

---

[62] Some manuscripts include this conjunction.   [63] Some manuscripts read "and if."

7:4 *general rule*: This general rule has been applied in several of the previous mishnayot (6:1, 7:1, 7:3).

Whenever one must pay the principal plus the added fifth: Which is to say, when one unintentionally consumes *terumah*. See 6:1. As mentioned above, the principal is meant to replace the *terumah* that was consumed, and the added fifth is meant to atone for the act of consumption.

the payments…may not do so: A nonpriest who unintentionally consumes *terumah* is given a second chance to fulfill his obligation. Thus, his payment obtains the status of fully sanctified *terumah*. Therefore, a priest may not forgive the payment.

Whenever one must pay the principal but not the added fifth: That is, when one intentionally consumes *terumah*.

the payments…he may do so: A nonpriest who intentionally consumes *terumah* is not given a second chance to fulfill his obligation, nor is he given the opportunity to atone for his sin. His payment is simply compensation for consuming what was not his, and therefore remains nonsacral produce. Since it is nothing more than compensation, a priest is allowed to forgive this payment.

7:5 If produce that has been designated *terumah* is mixed with ordinary produce, then the entire mixture is considered *terumah* unless the ratio of ordinary produce to *terumah* is 100:1 (see Introduction and 4:7).

I say: One is allowed to assume that the *terumah* fell into the basket of *terumah*. The basket of ordinary produce is therefore still permitted to nonpriests.

if one ate [the contents of] one of them, he is exempt: He is permitted to assume that he ate from the basket containing nonsacral produce and therefore does not need to pay the penalty for consuming *terumah*.

he treats it as terumah: Since one of the two baskets was certainly *terumah*, he must treat the contents of the second basket as *terumah*.

and it is subject to dough offering.
These are the words of R. Meir.
[But]⁶⁴ R. Yose exempts [from dough offering].
If another person ate [the contents of] the second basket,
he is exempt [from *terumah*].
If one person ate [the contents of] both,
he must pay according to the smaller of the two.

6 If one of [the two baskets] fell into nonsacral produce,
it does not create a *terumah* mixture;
and as for the second
he treats it as *terumah*
and it is subject to dough offering.
These are the words of R. Meir.
But R. Yose exempts [from dough offering].
If the second [basket] fell elsewhere [into nonsacral produce],
it does not create a *terumah* mixture.
If both of them fell into one place, they create a *terumah* mixture according to the smaller of the two.

⁶⁴ Some manuscripts include the conjunction.

subject to dough offering: One is only obligated to separate *hallah* (dough offering) from bread made with nonsacral produce. Although one must treat the contents of the second basket as *terumah*, there is still the possibility that it actually contained nonsacral produce. Therefore, according to R. Meir, the dough offering must still be separated. On the dough offering, see *Hallah* and Numbers 15:17–21.

R. Yose exempts: From the dough offering. Since one must treat the contents of the second basket as *terumah*, he need not factor in the possibility that it may have originally contained ordinary produce.

If another person ate [the contents of] the second basket, he is exempt: Although the first individual must treat the contents of the second basket as *terumah*, another individual is allowed to assume that this basket actually contained nonsacral produce.

If one person ate [the contents of] both, he must pay according to the smaller of the two: In this case he certainly ate *terumah* and must pay the principal and added fifth. He is allowed to assume, however, that it was the smaller basket that contained *terumah*.

7:6 *it does not create a terumah mixture*: One may assume the basket that fell was the one that contained nonsacral produce. On the concept of adulteration, see introduction.

he treats it as terumah and it is subject to the law of dough offering: See previous mishnah.

R. Yose exempts: See previous mishnah.

If the second [basket] fell elsewhere… it does not create a terumah mixture: This is parallel to the situation in the previous mishnah of another person eating from the second basket. One is allowed to assume that this second basket contained nonsacral produce.

If both of them fell into one place, they create a terumah mixture according to the smaller of the two: In this case there is certainly a mixture of *terumah* and nonsacral produce. However, one is allowed to assume that it was the smaller basket which contained *terumah*. Therefore, the mixture is prohibited if the ratio of ordinary produce to the contents of the smaller basket is less than 100:1.

7 If he used one of them as seed, he is exempt,
and as for the second—he treats it as *terumah*,
and it is subject to dough offering.
These are the words of R. Meir.
But⁶⁵ R. Yose exempts [from dough offering].
If another person uses the second as seed, he is exempt.
If someone uses both as seed,
if it is of a kind whose seed disintegrates,
it is permitted,
but if it is of a kind whose seed does not disintegrate,
it is prohibited.

Chapter Eight

8:1–3   *Actions That Were Begun Permissibly but Become Prohibited*

8 A woman who was eating *terumah*,
to whom they came and said:
"Your husband has died,"
or "He has divorced you";
and likewise a slave who was eating *terumah*,

---

⁶⁵ Some manuscripts lack the conjunction.

7:7 *one of them*: The contents of one of the two baskets.

as seed…exempt: In this case someone plants the contents of the basket instead of eating them. He is allowed to assume that what he planted was ordinary produce, and he is exempt from the ruling in mishnah 9:1 below. The line of reasoning is the same as in the previous two mishnayot.

the second…then he is exempt: This is identical to the two previous mishnayot, except the issue is whether the resulting plant may be treated as ordinary produce.

If some one uses both as seed: Some of the seed he planted was certainly *terumah*.

if it is of a kind whose seed disintegrates…it is permitted: If the seed disintegrates in the ground, then it is not considered as being part of the new plant. Therefore, the resulting crop is considered nonsacral produce because it was only the seed that may have been *terumah*. See 9:5.

does not disintegrate, it is prohibited: If the seed does not disintegrate it is considered part of the new plant. Since some of the seeds were *terumah*, the crop is prohibited to nonpriests as *terumah*. See 9:5.

8:1 *A woman*: The daughter of a nonpriest who is married to a priest and therefore eligible to consume *terumah*.

"Your husband has died," or "He has divorced you": The Israelite woman loses her right to consume *terumah* if her marriage is terminated by divorce or the death of her husband.

slave: A slave who is owned by a priest is eligible to consume *terumah*. See Leviticus 22:11.

to whom they came and said:
"Your master has died,"
or "He has sold you to a nonpriest,"[66]
or "He has given you as a gift [to a nonpriest],"
or "He has emancipated you";
and likewise a priest who was eating *terumah*
and it became known that he was the son of a divorcee or a *halutsah*,
R. Eliezer obligates [them] to pay the principal plus the added fifth,
but[67] R. Joshua exempts.
If [a priest] was standing and sacrificing on the altar,
and it became known that he was the son of a divorcee or a *halutsah*,
R. Eliezer says:[68]
All the sacrifices that he [ever] offered upon the altar are invalid.
But R. Joshua declares them valid.
If it became known that he had a blemish, his service is invalid.

2 And in any of those [aforementioned cases],
if *terumah* is in their mouth [when they discover they are not eligible to eat *terumah*],
R. Eliezer says:
They may swallow it.

[66] Lit. "Israelite."   [67] K and others lack the conjunction.
[68] K inserts "R. Eliezer obligates [them] to pay the principal plus the added fifth but R. Joshua exempts." This is obviously a scribal error.

Your master has died…emancipated you: In each of these cases the slave is no longer owned by a priest, and is therefore not eligible to consume *terumah*.

it became known that he was the son of a divorcee or a halutsah: A priest is not permitted to marry a divorcee or a *halutsah* (a woman released from levirate marriage by her husband's brothers; see Deuteronomy 25:7–9). See Leviticus 21:14. Any offspring from such a marriage are disqualified from the priesthood, and therefore not eligible to consume *terumah*.

R. Eliezer obligates [them] to pay the principal plus the added fifth: All of the individuals mentioned thought they were eligible to consume *terumah* and subsequently found out that they were not. R. Eliezer categorizes them as unintentional consumers of *terumah* and therefore requires them to make restitution accordingly; see 6:1.

But R. Joshua exempts these individuals from paying the added fifth. According to R. Joshua, since these individuals had every reason to assume that they were permitted to eat *terumah*, and their status changed because of circumstances beyond their control, their action is not a sin and requires no atonement.

All the sacrifices…are invalid: Since it has become known that the individual under discussion is ineligible for the priesthood, R. Eliezer rules that all the sacrifices that he ever performed are retroactively invalid.

But R. Joshua declares them valid: R. Joshua holds that the sacrifices performed by a disqualified priest are still valid after the fact.

If it became known that he had a blemish, his service is invalid: Certain blemishes disqualify a priest from serving in the Temple; see Leviticus 21:16–23. R. Eliezer and R. Joshua agree that if it becomes known that the priest has always had one of these blemishes, his sacrifices are retroactively invalid.

8:2 *if terumah is in their mouth*: When they were informed that they were no longer permitted to eat it.

They may swallow it: R. Eliezer rules that they may swallow it because they believed they were eligible when they began eating. It is unclear how one should reconcile this ruling with R. Eliezer's statement in the

But[69] R. Joshua says:
They must spit it out.
[If] they said to him:
"You have become impure" or[70] "the *terumah* has become impure,"
R. Eliezer says:
He may swallow it.
But R. Joshua says:
He[71] must spit it out.
[If they said to him:] "You were impure" or "The *terumah* was impure,"
or it became known that [the produce] was untithed,
or that it was first tithe whose *terumah* had not been removed,
or that it was second tithe or consecrated [produce] that had not been redeemed,
or if he tasted the taste of a bug in his mouth—
in these cases he must spit it out.
   3 If one was eating a cluster of grapes
and entered from the garden to the courtyard,
R. Eliezer says:
He may finish [eating].
But R. Joshua says:
He may not finish [eating].

[69] **K** and others lack the conjunction.   [70] Some witnesses lack the conjunction.
[71] **K** and others: "they."

previous mishnah that these individuals must pay the principal and added fifth. Some have suggested that since they must pay in any event, it makes no difference if they swallow what is in their mouths.

They must spit it out: R. Joshua says that since they are now ineligible to consume *terumah*, they must spit it out immediately.

[If] they said to him: The subject of our mishnah has now shifted to a priest who is eligible to eat *terumah* and has *terumah* in his mouth.

"You have become impure"…He must spit it out: An impure person cannot consume *terumah*, and impure *terumah* may not be eaten. See Leviticus 22:4–7; Numbers 18:11–12. In this case, while the *terumah* was still in the individual's mouth, someone informed him that he or the *terumah* became impure after he started eating. R. Eliezer and R. Joshua disagree along the same lines as in the previous case.

[If they said to him:] "You were impure" or "The terumah was impure": While the *terumah* is in his mouth, the individual is informed that he was not permitted to eat this *terumah* in the first place.

first tithe…has not been redeemed: For an explanation of these terms see annotations to 1:5.

he must spit it out: In all of these cases the individual was never permitted to eat the produce that he has in his mouth. Therefore R. Eliezer and R. Joshua agree that he must spit it out immediately.

8:3 *courtyard*: An individual is allowed to snack on the produce in his garden before it is tithed, as long as he does not make a meal out of it. However, once he leaves the garden and enters the courtyard, the produce becomes liable to *terumah* separation and tithing and he is no longer allowed to eat it. See *Ma'aserot* 3:5.

R. Eliezer…R. Joshua: R. Eliezer rules that he may finish eating the grapes because, when he began snacking, he was allowed to snack on the produce. R. Joshua rules that since he is now in the courtyard and no longer permitted to eat produce which has not been tithed, he must stop eating.

If night fell on Sabbath eve
R. Eliezer says:[72]
He may finish [eating].
But R. Joshua says:[73]
He may not finish [eating].

8:4–7 *Uncovered Liquids and Snake Venom*

4 *Terumah* wine that was left uncovered must be poured out,
and there is no need to mention nonsacral [wine].
Three liquids are forbidden when left uncovered:
Water, wine, and milk.
[But] all other liquids are permitted.
How long must they remain [uncovered] to become prohibited?
The amount of time it would take a reptile to emerge from a nearby place and drink.
   5 The amount of uncovered water—
the amount in which the venom will disappear.

---

[72] Some manuscripts read "R. Joshua says he may finish eating" and **K** and others read "R. Eliezer says he may not finish eating."
[73] Some manuscripts read "R. Eliezer says he may not finish eating" and **K** and others read "R. Joshua says he may finish eating."

If night fell on Sabbath eve...He may not finish [eating]: On the Sabbath one is not permitted even to snack on produce which has not been tithed. See *Ma'aserot 4:2*. The Mishnah presents a case where an individual began to snack in the garden prior to the Sabbath, but had not yet finished when it became dark. As in the previous case, R. Eliezer permits him to finish because he was allowed to eat the produce when he began snacking, while R. Joshua rules that he must stop eating. There are a number of manuscript variants for this final case in our mishnah. The version presented here seems to be the original text. The changes were perhaps introduced by scribes who were troubled by the fact that the Mishnah would present two cases that were so similar.

8:4 *Terumah wine that was left uncovered must be poured out*: *Terumah* is meant to be consumed by a priest and it is therefore forbidden to destroy or waste it. See *Shevi'it* 8:2. This case is an exception. The traditional explanation is that the Sages fear that a snake might come and drink from the uncovered liquid, and while doing so may excrete venom into it. The danger overrides the prohibition on wasting *terumah*, and this wine must therefore be poured out so that nobody comes to drink from it.

no need to mention nonsacral [wine]: Ordinary wine, which one is permitted to waste if he so chooses, must obviously be poured out if left uncovered.

8:5 *The amount in which the venom will disappear*: Commentators have interpreted this ruling in two ways: according to the first interpretation, the Mishnah is describing the minimum amount of water that will remain permitted if left uncovered. The assumption is that a large enough quantity of water will neutralize the potency of any venom that a snake may have deposited in the water, rendering it safe to drink. According to the second interpretation, the Mishnah describes the minimum amount of water that will become prohibited if left uncovered. The reasoning behind this interpretation is that when water is in a small enough quantity one would normally be able to see if a snake deposited venom. This would not be the case if there were too much water.

R. Yose says:
In vessels, any amount.
In the ground forty *se'ah*.

6 Figs, grapes, Armenian cucumbers, gourds, watermelons, or muskmelons that have bite marks,[74]
even if they are as [numerous as] a talent,[75]
whether large or small,
plucked or joined [to the soil]—
whatever has moisture in it,
it is forbidden.
[And something] bitten by a snake is prohibited on account of the danger to life.[76]

7[77] A wine filter is forbidden if left uncovered—
R. Nehemiah permits.

[74] Lit. "piercings."
[75] **K** and others read "in a jar."
[76] **K**, **P**, and others read "And a snakebite is forbidden on account of the danger to life."
[77] This mishnah is joined to the previous one in **P**, and is in the margins in **K**.

In vessels, any amount: According to the first understanding noted above, R. Yose is of the opinion that water in vessels does not neutralize the potency of venom. According to the second, he thinks that one is unable to discern the presence of venom if the water is in a vessel.

In the ground, forty se'ah: According to the first reading, there must be at least forty *se'ah* of water in the ground for it to remain permitted if left uncovered. According to the second reading, uncovered water in the ground is prohibited in a quantity of forty *se'ah* or more.

8:6 *that have bite marks*: They may have been bitten by a snake.

a talent: Text and translation uncertain. A talent is a large weight of silver or gold. One might have thought that if a large amount of fruit has what appears to be bite marks, one could safely conclude that no snake could have bitten them all and that the holes must have come from another source. The Mishnah indicates that this is not the case. Some manuscripts read "Even if they are in a jar." According to this reading, the Mishnah refers to a case where there are several pieces of fruit in a jar, but one of them has bite marks. While one might assume that he could eat one of the pieces without bite marks, the Mishnah rules that all the fruit in the jar is prohibited.

whether large or small: Whether the fruit is large or small.

plucked or joined: Whether the fruit is still connected to the ground or has been harvested.

whatever has moisture in it: The juice will carry the snake's venom from the location of the bite to the rest of the fruit, rendering it unsafe to eat and therefore prohibited.

danger to life: One may not slaughter and eat an animal that has been bitten by a snake because the venom may have spread from the location of the bite to other parts of the animal. See *Hullin* 3:5.

8:7 *A wine filter*: A cloth that is stretched over the lid of a jug into which wine is poured in order to separate the sediment from the wine. The anonymous opinion rules that the filter is not considered an adequate cover for the wine below, since a snake may have drunk from the sediment caught in the filter, leaving behind venom that dripped into the wine below.

8:8–11 Impure Terumah

8 A jar of *terumah* about which a doubt of impurity has arisen—
R. Eliezer says:
If it had been placed in an exposed place,
one must place it in a hidden place;
and if it had been uncovered,
one must cover it.
But R. Joshua says:
If it had been placed in a hidden place,
one must place it in an exposed place.
And if it had been covered,
one must uncover it.
Rabban Gamaliel says:
He should not do anything new to it.

9 If a jar [of *terumah* wine] broke in an upper winepress,
and [spilled its contents into] the lower which was impure—
R. Eliezer and R. Joshua agree
that if one can save a *revi'it* in [a way that maintains its] purity,
one must save it.
But if not—
R. Eliezer says:
Let it descend and become impure,
but one may not deliberately[78] render it impure.

[78] Lit. "with his hands."

8:8 This mishnah returns to the discussion of not destroying or wasting *terumah* begun in 8:4. One is obligated to keep *terumah* in a state of purity and may not waste it. On the other hand, *terumah* that is impure may not be consumed and must be disposed of.

R. Eliezer says: R. Eliezer rules that the contents of the barrel must still be treated as pure *terumah*.

If it had been placed in an exposed place, one must place it in a hidden place: The assumption is *terumah* is more likely to become impure in an exposed space, where impure persons, liquids, or other items might come in contact with it and render it impure. Since R. Eliezer rules that the contents of the barrel must still be protected, the individual must move it to a protected space where it has greater protection from sources of impurity.

one must cover it: Once again, to protect it from impurity. Cf. 11:5.

R. Joshua says...uncover it: Whereas R. Eliezer demands protecting potentially impure *terumah*, R. Joshua rules that one must render it definitely impure in order to be able to dispose of it. He must, therefore, move it to an exposed space and uncover it so it has a greater chance of becoming impure.

He should not do anything new to it: Meaning one should neither facilitate its impurification nor take added measures to protect it from becoming impure.

8:9 *If a jar [of terumah wine] broke...which was impure*: The upper portion is where the grapes are pressed, and the bottom portion receives the liquid that flows from them. In this case, pure *terumah* wine from the upper portion is about to mix with impure nonsacral wine in the lower portion, which will cause the entire mixture to become impure *terumah*, which may not be drunk by anyone. See 5:1.

if one can save a revi'it...one must save it: If one can quickly obtain a pure vessel which he can use to scoop out at least a *revi'it* of the wine before it all flows to the bottom, then he is obligated to do so.

Let it descend...render it impure: R. Eliezer prioritizes the obligation to keep *terumah* in a state of purity over the possibility of using impure vessels to quickly remove the *terumah* from the upper portion of the

10 And likewise if a jar of [*terumah*] oil spilled—
R. Eliezer and R. Joshua agree
that if one can save a *revi'it* in [a way that maintains its] purity,
one must save it.
But if not—
R. Eliezer says:
Let it descend and be absorbed [by the ground],
but one may not deliberately[79] cause it to be absorbed.
   11 And regarding both of these cases R. Joshua says:
This is not the [type of] *terumah* about which I am warned not to make it impure;
[I am warned only] not to eat it.
The prohibition of rendering it impure—how?[80]
If one was passing from place to place with *terumah* loaves in his possession,
and a gentile said to him:
"Give me one of them so that I will make it impure,
or else I will make all of them impure":
R. Eliezer says:
Let him make all of them impure,
but let [the Israelite] not give him one to make impure.
R. Joshua says:
One should place one of them in front of him on a rock.

---

[79] Lit. "with his hands."
[80] The word "how" is missing in **P** and other manuscripts. It has been crossed out in **K**.

---

winepress in order to save the nonsacral wine in the bottom portion from becoming prohibited by mixing with *terumah*. One is not permitted to render *terumah* deliberately impure.

8:10 *And likewise if a barrel of [terumah] oil spilled*: Onto the ground, where it will be absorbed by the earth.

Let it descend...cause it to be absorbed: Again, R. Eliezer prefers allowing *terumah* to be wasted passively rather than be rendered impure by being gathered in an impure vessel.

8:11 *And regarding both of these cases*: This refers to the two previous mishnayot. In a case where one is not able to save at least a *revi'it* of the wine or oil in purity, R. Joshua permits collecting it in impure vessels.

This is not the [type of] terumah...not to eat it: R. Joshua asserts that the cases in the two previous mishnayot are not instances where one is obligated to preserve the purity of the *terumah*. There is therefore nothing wrong with collecting it in impure vessels and thereby causing it to become impure. His rationale is not made explicit. The best explanation may be that once *terumah* is inevitably going to become impure, and thus forbidden for consumption, there is nothing wrong with an individual actively rendering it impure.

The prohibition of rendering it impure—how?: According to R. Joshua, what is the case in which one is not permitted to take an active role in making *terumah* impure?

Let him make all of them impure: As usual, R. Eliezer prefers passive acquiescence to the defilement of *terumah*, even when doing so results in a greater net loss of *terumah*.

One should place one of them in front of him on a rock: R. Joshua agrees with R. Eliezer that the individual may not hand over one of the loaves directly. Instead he should leave one on a rock and force the non-Jew to pick it up himself. In this way the individual will save one loaf without taking an active role in rendering the others impure.

8:12 *A Group of Women Threatened with Impurity*

12 Likewise, [a group of] women to whom non-Jews said:
"Give us one from among you so that we may make her impure,
and if not, we will make you all impure,"
let them make everyone impure,
and not hand over a single person from Israel.

Chapter Nine

9:1–6 *Terumah That Has Been Planted*

9 One who plants *terumah*—
if unintentionally, he overturns it;
if intentionally, he lets it remain.
If[81] it had already reached a third of its size,
whether [he planted] it intentionally or unintentionally,
he lets it remain.
But regarding flax, [one who planted it] intentionally overturns it.

[81] P and others read "But if."

8:12 *make…impure*: i.e. rape (Genesis 34:5). The fear that gentiles will rape Jewish women is also expressed in *Avodah Zarah* 2:1.

9:1 *plants terumah*: Plants seeds that were *terumah*. The plants which grow from these seeds are *terumah* in the sense that they are forbidden to nonpriests; see 9:3–4.

he overturns it: Destroys it by plowing over it. The commentators debate whether the Mishnah means that he may overturn it or that he must overturn it. According to the former understanding, since the individual under discussion did not know he was planting *terumah*, he is allowed to overturn the soil and uproot the seeds. He will then be able to plant his field with nonsacral produce which is worth more. See annotations to 5:1. According to the latter, he must overturn the *terumah* plants as a penalty for not being careful with *terumah*.

intentionally, he lets it remain: An individual who intentionally plants *terumah* is penalized for his action. He must therefore allow the seeds to remain in the soil, and the resulting plants will have the status of *terumah*. This is considered a penalty because the value of *terumah* is less than that of ordinary produce.

If it had already reached a third of its size…he lets it remain: It seems that once the plants have grown to a third of their size, uprooting them is considered an act of destroying *terumah*. Thus even an individual who planted the seeds unwittingly must allow them to remain.

But regarding flax, [one who planted it] intentionally overturns it: Flax is an exception to the previous regulations. It must be uprooted even if it grows to over a third of its size. The stalks of the flax plant are not sanctified as *terumah* because they are inedible (see 11:4–5 below), and therefore a nonpriest may still derive benefit from them. The individual who intentionally plants *terumah* cannot be allowed to benefit from this action, and for this reason must uproot the flax plant. The commentators debate whether this ruling also applies to someone who unintentionally plants *terumah*.

2 And [the field of planted *terumah*] is liable to Gleanings, Forgotten Sheaves, and *pe'ah*.[82]
And poor Israelites and poor priests may collect them,
but the poor Israelites sell theirs to priests at the price of *terumah*,
and the money belongs to them.
R. Tarfon says:
Only poor priests may collect, lest [poor Israelites] forget and put it in their mouths.
R. Aqiva said to him:
If so, then only those [priests] who are pure may collect.
  3 And [planted *terumah*] is liable to tithes and the poor tithe.
And poor Israelites and poor priests may take them,
but poor Israelites must sell theirs to priests at the price of *terumah*,
and the money belongs to them.
He who beats [the grain] is praiseworthy.
But the one who threshes, how must he act?
He must hang baskets on the necks of the animals
and place the same kind [of produce as is being threshed] inside of them.
The result[83] is that he is neither muzzling the animal, nor feeding [it] *terumah*.
  4 Growths of *terumah* are *terumah*,
but[84] growths of [their] growths are nonsacral.

[82] Some manuscripts add "and poor tithe." This is probably a scribal error.
[83] Lit. "it [or: he] is found."   [84] K lacks the conjunction.

9:2 *And [the field of planted terumah]*: According to 9:4, the produce of *terumah* seeds is *terumah*. Nevertheless, while real *terumah* is exempt from agricultural gifts and tithes (see 1:5), a field of produce grown from *terumah* seeds is obligated in them but, like regular *terumah*, the produce may only be consumed by priests in a state of purity.

Gleanings...pe'ah: For an explanation of these terms see 1:5.

poor Israelites...may collect: Despite not being allowed to consume it.

and the money belongs to them: And can be spent without restriction.

9:3 *tithes and the poor tithe*: *Terumah* produce is liable to all of the standard tithes.

poor tithe: In the third and sixth year of the seven-year cycle, after separating *terumah* and first tithe, farmers must set aside one-tenth of the remaining produce for the poor. See Deuteronomy 26:12–15.

He who beats [the grain] is praiseworthy: One normally threshes grain by having an animal walk on it on a hard surface in order to separate the grain from the chaff. A problem arises in the case of grain that is *terumah*. A nonpriest is not allowed to feed *terumah* to his animal, and would therefore have to prevent the animal from eating the grain. However, the Torah explicitly prohibits muzzling an animal while it is threshing (Deuteronomy 25:4). This mishnah therefore indicates that it is preferable for an individual to manually thresh grain that is *terumah* by beating it.

But the one who threshes, how must he act?: While it is preferable to thresh manually, the Mishnah still provides a method by which one can use an animal.

He must hang baskets on the necks of the animals: The logic is that the animal will not consume the grain that it is threshing if the same type of grain is readily accessible in the baskets.

9:4 *growths of [their] growths are nonsacral*: If someone took seeds from a plant grown from *terumah* and planted them, the resulting plant is considered nonsacral.

But untithed [produce], first tithe, aftergrowths of the Seventh Year, *terumah* from outside the Land of Israel, produce mixed with *terumah*, and firstfruits—
their growths are nonsacral.
The growths of consecrated produce or second tithe are nonsacral,
but one must redeem them at the time of planting.[85]

5 One hundred plant beds of *terumah* and one of nonsacral produce,
they are all permitted if [planted with] a kind whose seed disintegrates.
But if [planted with] a kind whose seed does not disintegrate,
even if one hundred [were planted] with nonsacral produce and one with *terumah*,
they are all prohibited.

6 Untithed produce—
its growths are permitted if they are of a kind whose seed disintegrates.
But if they are of a kind whose seed does not disintegrate,
[even] the growths of [their] growths are prohibited.
Which is a kind whose seed does not disintegrate?
Such as arum, garlic, and onions.
R. Judah says:
Garlic is like barley.

[85] K, P read "as at the time of planting," and still others read "At the value of their seeds."

But untithed... nonsacral: The Sages are more lenient regarding these categories than they are with *terumah*. It would seem, however, that this ruling only applies if the plant is of a type whose seed disintegrates. See 9:6, *Bikkurim* 2:2.

aftergrowths of the Seventh Year: This term refers to plants which grew on their own during the Seventh (or Sabbatical) Year from seeds which fell into the ground during the previous year. The consumption of such plants is prohibited (*Shevi'it* 9:1). If someone planted the seeds contained in such a plant, the resulting plant is considered nonsacral.

at the time of planting: The entire crop resulting from the second tithe/consecrated produce that was planted is redeemed at the price of the original seed. Thus, if one *se'ah* of seed was planted which then yielded a crop of ten *se'ah*, the entire crop may be redeemed at the price of one *se'ah* of seed.

9:5 *one of nonsacral produce*: One bed, among the one hundred that contain *terumah*, is planted with nonsacral produce and it is not known which one.

permitted... seed disintegrates: If the produce is of a kind whose seed disintegrates, then the presence of even the smallest amount of ordinary produce is enough to render the entire crop permitted. This is probably because, with the disintegration of the seed, there is no actual *terumah* remaining in the ground.

does not disintegrate... prohibited: If the produce is of a kind whose seed does not disintegrate, then even the smallest amount of *terumah* is enough to render the entire crop prohibited. The commentators explain that since the seed that was *terumah* still exists, it is considered to be "attached to the ground," and therefore cannot be nullified even in a 100:1 ratio. See 4:7.

9:6 *growths are permitted... disintegrates*: A nearly identical ruling is found above in 9:4. However, the current mishnah specifies that the growths of untithed produce are only permitted if the produce is a kind whose seed disintegrates. It is worth noting that the term "permitted" in this context means that the produce is treated as ordinary produce that has not yet been tithed, and not according to the stringencies of untithed produce. Therefore, one would be allowed to snack on the produce in the field before tithing it. See annotations to 8:3 and *Ma'aserot* 1:5.

But if they are of a kind... growths are prohibited: Meaning that they must be treated according to the stringencies of untithed produce. One cannot snack on such produce in the field before tithing it.

Garlic is like barley: According to R. Judah, garlic, like barley, is a type of produce whose seed disintegrates.

9:7 Weeding with a Non-Jew

7 If one is weeding among allium plants with a gentile,
even though the produce is untithed,
he may snack from it.
Terumah shoots which became impure—
if one replanted them,
they are purified from their impurity.
But they may not be eaten until one cuts the edible part off.
R. Judah says:
Until one cuts a second time.

Chapter Ten

10:1–4 Terumah Which Imparts Its Flavor to Other Foods

10 A [cooked *terumah*] onion that one placed amidst [cooked] lentils
If whole, it is permitted.
But[86] if one chopped it, [it is forbidden if] it imparts flavor.

[86] K and others lack the conjunction.

9:7 *allium plants*: Whose seeds do not disintegrate in the soil. Context dictates that this mishnah is discussing a Jew working in the non-Jew's field.

even though the produce is untithed: All produce in the Land of Israel is liable to tithes, even if it belongs to a non-Jew (see *Demai* 5:9). Therefore, the allium plants in the non-Jew's field presumably grew from the seeds of untithed produce. According to the ruling in the previous mishnah, one would be not be allowed to snack on them while working in the field. This mishnah informs us that the produce of a non-Jew is an exception to this rule, and a Jew may snack on it in the field.

shoots: Small plants that have been uprooted so they can be replanted in another location.

are purified from their impurity: Plants which are attached to the ground cannot become impure. Thus, while the shoots were able to contract impurity when they were detached because they were considered food, they become pure once they are replanted.

But they may not be eaten until one cuts the edible part off: Even priests may not eat the plants right away because the edible portion is still considered to be impure *terumah*. Once one cuts it off, that which subsequently grows will be considered pure *terumah*.

10:1 *A [cooked terumah] onion*: The translation follows the most natural explanation of the mishnah. However some commentators, following the Yerushalmi, interpret this mishnah as referring to a nonsacral onion placed into *terumah* lentils.

If whole, it is permitted: If the onion is whole, then the lentils remain permitted to nonpriests. It is assumed that because lentils are bland, they do not readily absorb flavor. Thus, if the onion is whole, there is no possibility of transfer of flavor between the two items.

if one chopped it: The chopped onion has the potential to impart its flavor to the lentils.

But regarding all other cooked dishes,
whether [the onion] is whole or chopped,
[it is forbidden if] it imparts flavor.
R. Judah permits minced fish [into which a *terumah* onion was placed],
because [the onion's purpose] is only to remove the foul odor.

2 A [*terumah*] apple which one chopped and placed in a dough, causing it to leaven—
it is prohibited.
[*Terumah*] barley which fell into a cistern of water—
even though its waters were spoiled, they are[87] permitted.

3 If one removes hot bread [from an oven]
and places it over the mouth of a jar containing *terumah* wine:
R. Meir prohibits [the bread].
But R. Judah permits.
R. Yose permits if made from wheat, but prohibits if made from barley,
because barley draws [the liquid from the barrel into itself].

4 An oven that one lit with cumin [of *terumah*], in which one baked [bread][88]—
the bread is permitted because it does not taste of cumin, but only smells of cumin.

10:5–6   *The Special Case of Fenugreek*

5 Fenugreek which fell into a vat containing wine[89]—
if [the fenugreek is] *terumah* or second tithe,

[87] K, P, and others: "their waters are permitted."
[88] "Bread" is in the body of the text of K, P, and several other manuscripts.
[89] K and some other manuscripts read "water."

[it is forbidden if] it imparts flavor: This ruling reflects a general rule that applies throughout the present chapter. If a *terumah* item, in our case an onion, has imparted its flavor to a non-*terumah* item, here lentils, then the non-*terumah* item may no longer be consumed by nonpriests.

other cooked dishes: Foods other than lentils, which more readily absorb flavor.

10:2 *leaven....prohibited*: The dough may not be eaten by a nonpriest because the leavening was caused by an item that was *terumah*.

even though its waters were spoiled: By the flavor of the barley. As we saw in the previous mishnah, normally a non-*terumah* item becomes forbidden if it absorbs the flavor of an item that is *terumah*. In this case, however, the flavor of the barley is detrimental to the taste of the water. Therefore, the Tosefta explains, the water may still be drunk by a nonpriest.

10:3 *R. Meir prohibits [the bread]*: He assumes the hot bread will absorb the flavor of the wine, and therefore rules that it may not be consumed by a nonpriest.

R. Judah permits: He assumes the bread will not absorb the flavor of the wine.

10:4 *only smells of cumin*: Since the bread only smells of cumin, it is not considered as having actually absorbed the flavor of the *terumah*. For this reason, the bread remains permitted to nonpriests.

10:5 *if [the fenugreek is] terumah...with the stalk*: Unlike the seeds, the stalk of the fenugreek plant is not considered sanctified as *terumah* or second tithe because it is inedible (see 11:4–5 below). Whatever flavor it imparts

[the wine obtains the status of the fenugreek] if the seeds are able to impart flavor, but not [if they can do so only] with the stalk.
[But if the fenugreek] is Seventh-Year produce, Mixed Species of the vineyard, or consecrated produce,
[the wine obtains the status of the fenugreek] if the seeds with the stalk are able to impart flavor.

6 If one has bundles of fenugreek that are Mixed Species of the vineyard,
they must be burned.
If one has bundles of fenugreek that are untithed,
he must pound them, calculate the amount of seed they contain, and set aside [*terumah*] from the seed.
But he need not set aside from the stalks.
If[90] he set aside [*terumah* from the stalks as well as the seeds],
he may not say "I will pound [the fenugreek], keep the stalks, and give the seeds [as *terumah*]."
Rather he must give the stalks together with the seeds.

10:7–12 *Permitted Foods Combined with Prohibited Foods*

7 Nonsacral olives that one pickled with *terumah* olives;
crushed nonsacral [olives pickled] with crushed *terumah* olives;
[or] crushed nonsacral [olives pickled] with whole *terumah* olives or in *terumah* liquid—
[all these] are prohibited.
But whole nonsacral [olives pickled] with crushed *terumah* [olives] are permitted.

---

[90] Some manuscripts read "But if…"

---

would not render ordinary food prohibited to nonpriests. In the case under discussion, therefore, the wine would only obtain the status of the fenugreek if the seeds alone had the potential to impart flavor to the wine.

Seventh-Year produce…consecrated produce: Unlike the regulations surrounding *terumah*, the laws of Seventh-Year produce, Mixed Species of the vineyard, or consecrated produce apply to the entire fenugreek plant.

[the wine obtains the status of the fenugreek]: That is, it will become liable to the laws of Seventh-Year produce, Mixed Species of the vineyard, or consecrated produce.

10:6 *they must be burned*: See *Temurah* 7:5.

need not set aside from the stalks: The stalks of fenugreek plants are not liable to the laws of *terumah* because they are inedible. Thus, the individual need only separate *terumah* from the edible seeds.

If he set aside [terumah from the stalks as well as the seeds]: In other words, he did not beat the fenugreek to separate out the seeds, and separated *terumah* from the entire plant.

Rather he must give the stalks together with the seeds: Because he declared the entire plant to be *terumah*.

10:7 *crushed nonsacral…prohibited*: The assumption is that if the nonsacral olives are crushed, they will absorb flavor from the *terumah* olives.

terumah liquid: The liquid in which *terumah* olives were pickled (see 10:12 below). Crushed nonsacral olives that are placed in such liquid are assumed to have absorbed flavor that was secreted by the *terumah* olives.

But whole…permitted: The Mishnah assumes that while whole olives may secrete flavor, they do not absorb it. Therefore, whole nonsacral olives will remain permissible to nonpriests.

8 Impure fish that one pickled together with pure fish—
if the entire jug contains two *se'ah* and the unclean fish weighs ten *zuz*[91] in Judaean measure,
which are five *sela* in Galilean measure,
[all of] the fish is impure and the brine is prohibited.
R. Judah says:
[The brine is prohibited] if there is a *revi'it* in two *se'ah*.
R. Yose says:
[The brine is prohibited if the impure fish comprise] one-sixteenth of the [mixture].
9 If impure locusts were pickled together with pure locusts—
they do not render their brine unfit.
R. Zadok testified concerning the brine of impure locusts
that it is pure.
10 All [vegetables] that are pickled together are permitted, except those [pickled] with allium.
[Thus] if nonsacral allium [was pickled] with *terumah* allium,
[or] if a nonsacral vegetable [was pickled] with *terumah* allium[92]
[the nonsacral item] is prohibited.

[91] This word is missing in **K**.
[92] **K** reads "[or] if nonsacral allium [was pickled with] a *terumah* vegetable." This is corrected in the margin.

10:8 *ten zuz in Judaean measure, which are five sela in Galilean measure…the brine is prohibited*: Ten *zuz* in Judaean measure equals five *sela* in Galilean measure, which amounts to twenty Galilean *zuz*. The entire jug contains two *se'ah*, which equals 9,600 Judaean *zuz*. Thus, the brine is prohibited if the nonkosher fish amount to $1/960$ of the mixture.

a revi'it in two se'ah: A *revi'it* is a quarter *log*, which amounts to fifty *zuz*, or $1/192$ of the total mixture. R. Judah holds that this proportion of nonkosher fish will render the brine prohibited.

one-sixteenth of the [mixture]: Six hundred *zuz*.

10:9 This mishnah is parallel to *Eduyot* 7:2.

impure locusts were pickled together with pure locusts: That is, nonkosher locusts, which may not be consumed, were pickled together with kosher locusts.

do not render their brine unfit: The nonkosher locusts are not considered to have secreted their flavor into the brine. It seems, however, that according to the anonymous opinion, this is only true if the brine was produced by a mixture of kosher and nonkosher locusts.

that it is pure: According to R. Zadok, while nonkosher locusts are prohibited, their brine is permitted and may be consumed in all circumstances.

10:10 *All [vegetables] that are pickled together are permitted*: It is assumed that, in general, vegetables do not impart flavor to each other during the pickling process. Thus, if nonsacral vegetables are pickled with *terumah* vegetables, the nonsacral vegetables may still be consumed by a nonpriest.

except those [pickled] with allium: Alliums are particularly pungent, and thus this mishnah assumes that they will impart flavor during the pickling process. The Tosefta lists onions, garlic, and leeks as examples of alliums.

But if nonsacral allium [was pickled] with a *terumah* vegetable—
[the allium] is permitted.[93]

11 R. Yose says:
All [vegetables] that are stewed with beets [of *terumah*] are prohibited,
because they impart flavor.
R. Simeon says:
Cabbage from an irrigated field [stewed with *terumah*] cabbage from a rainfed field is prohibited,
because it absorbs.
R. Aqiva[94] says:
Anything cooked[95] together is permitted, unless [it is cooked with] meat.
R. Yohanan b. Nuri says:
The liver renders [food] prohibited, but does not itself become prohibited,
because it secretes but does not absorb.

12 If an egg is cooked[96] with forbidden spices,
even its yolk is forbidden,
because [the yolk] absorbs.
The water in which *terumah* is stewed or pickled is prohibited to nonpriests.

[93] K reads "But if a nonsacral vegetable [was pickled] with *terumah* allium." This is corrected in the margin.
[94] Some manuscripts read R. Judah.   [95] Or "boiled."
[96] P and others read "spiced." This is also found in the margins of K.

But if nonsacral allium...is permitted: This ruling is based on the assumption that while alliums will impart flavor to other vegetables, they will not absorb flavor.

10:11 *All [vegetables] that are stewed...impart flavor*: R. Yose extends 10:10's leniency regarding pickling—where only alliums are said to impart flavor to other vegetables—to stewing as well. He states that only the particularly strongly flavored spinach beets are assumed to impart their flavor to other vegetables.

Cabbage from an irrigated field...is prohibited because it absorbs: R. Simeon adds another exception to the general rule that stewed vegetables do not impart flavor to one another. He states that a cabbage from an irrigated field absorbs flavor from a cabbage from a field watered by rain when they are stewed together.

Anything...unless [it is cooked with] meat: R. Aqiva states that, in general, foods do not impart flavor to one another through cooking. Thus, a permitted food remains permitted even if it is cooked with something prohibited. The one exception is meat, which will impart its flavor to any food item with which it is cooked. Therefore, if a piece of prohibited meat is cooked with permitted meat or vegetables, the entire dish is prohibited.

The liver renders...does not absorb: This is an exception to the previous ruling. Since a liver does not absorb flavor, it cannot be rendered prohibited by another food with which it is cooked. Thus, unlike other foods, a liver remains permitted even when cooked with prohibited meat.

10:12 *forbidden spices*: These would include, for example, spices that were *terumah*.

even its yolk is forbidden because [the yolk] absorbs: In spite of the presence of the shell.

Chapter Eleven

11:1–3 *Liquids Containing Terumah*

11 One may not place pressed or dried figs of *terumah* into fish brine, because it ruins them.
But one may place [*terumah*] wine into fish brine.
And one may not perfume [*terumah*] oil,
but one may make [*terumah*] wine into honey-wine.
One may not boil *terumah* wine,
because it diminishes it.
But R. Judah permits, because it improves it.

2 Honey from [*terumah*] dates,
cider from [*terumah*] apples,
vinegar from [*terumah*] winter grapes,
or any other juice from *terumah* fruit—
[if a nonpriest unintentionally consumes any of them],

11:1 As mentioned previously, food that is *terumah* must be consumed, and it is therefore forbidden to waste or destroy it. This mishnah enumerates certain uses of *terumah* that violate this rule.

because it ruins them: The commentators explain that it was common practice to steep dried figs in fish brine in order to release their juice into the sauce. These figs would then be discarded as they were no longer edible. The Mishnah teaches that this practice is tantamount to wasting *terumah*, and is therefore prohibited.

But one may place wine into fish brine: Wine was placed into fish brine in order to enhance the latter's flavor; since in consuming the fish brine the *terumah* wine is also consumed, this is not considered wasteful of *terumah*.

And one may not perfume [terumah] oil: One may not place spices and roots into oil that is *terumah*. The commentators offer two different explanations behind this ruling. The first explanation is that while the spices improve the oil by adding flavor, they also absorb some of the oil. Since the spices are not consumed, the oil they absorbed is considered wasted. This practice, therefore, is tantamount to wasting *terumah*. The second explanation is that the Mishnah is referring to spices and roots that are added for medicinal purposes, but in turn render the oil inedible. Since *terumah* is meant to be consumed, this practice is prohibited.

but one may make [terumah] wine into honey-wine: One may add honey and spices to *terumah* wine in order to make the beverage referred to as "honey-wine." According to the first explanation of the previous case, one must assume that the spices put into the honey-wine are consumed along with the wine, and therefore none of the wine is wasted. According to the second explanation, one is allowed to make *terumah* wine into honey-wine for the simple reason that it will still be consumed.

because it diminishes it: The simplest explanation seems to be that some of the wine will be lost through evaporation during the process of boiling, and this is tantamount to destroying *terumah*. The commentators add that boiling the wine also "diminishes" the quality of the wine, as well as the number of people who would want to drink it.

because it improves it: It seems that R. Judah thinks boiling the wine improves its taste. This contradicts other places in rabbinic literature where boiled wine is implied to be of inferior quality (see e.g. BT *Avodah Zarah* 30a). Some commentators have therefore suggested that the "improvement" occasioned by boiling the wine is that it is better preserved after this process.

R. Eliezer obligates him to pay the principal plus the added fifth.
But R. Joshua exempts.
Furthermore,[97] R. Eliezer declares that [these liquids render produce] susceptible to impurity as other liquids.
R. Joshua said:
The Sages did not list seven liquids as spice counters would![98]
Rather they said that [only] seven liquids [are themselves susceptible to impurity and render produce susceptible] to impurity,
while all other liquids do not.[99]

3 One may not make dates into honey,
apples into cider,
winter grapes into vinegar,
or change any other fruits that are *terumah* or second tithe from their natural state,
except olives and grapes.
One does not receive forty [lashes] on account of [fruit juice that is] *orlah*,
unless it comes from olives or grapes.
One may not bring liquid as firstfruits, except for what which comes from olives or grapes.

[97] **K, P**, and others lack this conjunction.   [98] Translation uncertain.   [99] Lit. "are pure."

11:2 *R. Eliezer obligates… R. Joshua exempts*: The debate between R. Eliezer and R. Joshua concerns the status of juice from *terumah* fruit. R. Eliezer grants such juice full *terumah* status, while R. Joshua does not.

R. Eliezer declares that [these liquids render produce] susceptible to impurity as other liquids: Leviticus 11:34 states that for food to become susceptible to impurity it must be moistened by water. R. Eliezer reads the continuation of this verse, "as to any liquid that may be drunk," to extend to all such liquids the potential for rendering food susceptible to impurity.

did not list seven liquids: See *Makhshirin* 6:4. The seven liquids are dew, water, wine, olive oil, blood, milk, and bees' honey.

as spice counters would: The implication seems to be that spice merchants are inexact when counting their merchandise.

11:3 *from their natural state*: That is, change it from a solid into a liquid.

except olives and grapes: Therefore, one may make *terumah* olives into olive oil and may turn *terumah* grapes into wine. The reasoning behind this ruling seems to be that the normal use of grapes and olives is to make wine and oil.

One does not receive forty [lashes]… unless it comes from olives or grapes: *Orlah* is fruit that grows on trees within the first three years of their planting (see tractate *Orlah*). Such fruit may not be consumed (Leviticus 19:23). One who transgresses this prohibition is liable to forty lashes because he has transgressed a negative commandment. This mishnah teaches that the juice of fruit that is *orlah* does not have the same legal status as the fruit itself. While one is not permitted to drink it, he does not transgress the biblical prohibition by doing so and therefore does not receive lashes. Olive oil and wine are an exception, and are considered to be the legal equivalent of the fruit they came from. Therefore, one who consumes these liquids from fruit that is *orlah* transgresses the biblical commandment and is liable to lashes.

one may not bring liquid as firstfruits, except for what which comes from olives or grapes: As above, a mandatory agricultural gift (here, firstfruits) must be brought with the fruit in its natural state, with the exception of wine and oil (cf. *Hallah* 4:11).

And [of all fruit juices] only that which comes from olives or grapes imparts impurity as a liquid.
And [of all fruit juices] one may offer upon the altar only that which comes from olives or grapes.

11:4–5 *Terumah Produce Not Normally Eaten*

4 The stems of figs, dried figs, *klisim*, and carobs that are *terumah* [all these] are forbidden to nonpriests.

5 *Terumah* seeds are prohibited [to a nonpriest] when [a priest] gathers them, but[100] if he discarded them they are permitted.
And likewise the bones of consecrated offerings—
when [a priest] gathers them, they are prohibited,
but if he discarded them they are permitted.

---

[100] K lacks the conjunction.

---

only that which comes from olives or grapes imparts impurity as a liquid: This is the same as R. Joshua's opinion in 11:2 above.

one may offer upon the altar only that which comes from olives or grapes: The Torah mandates the use of olive oil in the preparation of the grain offering (Leviticus 2:1) and wine is used as a libation upon the altar (Numbers 15:1–12).

11:4 The next two mishnayot are based on the notion that only the parts of produce that are eaten are sanctified as *terumah* and thereby prohibited to nonpriests.

stems of figs: The stems of figs are edible, but people often cast them aside when eating figs. For this reason the Mishnah seeks to clarify their status vis-à-vis *terumah* sanctity.

klisim and carobs: The commentators disagree in their identification of *klisim*. Apparently neither *klisim* nor carobs were considered valuable produce, and priests did not generally desire them. Alternatively, it is possible that our mishnah is referring specifically to the stems of *klisim* and carobs.

are forbidden to nonpriests: All of these items, despite the fact that they are often not eaten, are still sanctified as *terumah* and forbidden to nonpriests.

11:5 *Terumah seeds are prohibited [to a nonpriest] when [a priest] gathers them*: As stated above, only the parts of produce that are eaten obtain full *terumah* sanctity. Seeds are an ambiguous case. While they are sometimes edible, people readily discard them and often do not treat them as food. This mishnah teaches that one evaluates the status of *terumah* seeds based on how the priest treats them. If he retains them, one can assume that he intends to consume them later, and they therefore retain full *terumah* sanctity. For this reason, they are forbidden to nonpriests.

but if he discarded them they are permitted: If the priest discards the seeds, then it is clear that he does not regard them as food. Such seeds are therefore permitted to nonpriests.

the bones of consecrated offerings: The commentators debate the exact meaning of this phrase. It probably refers to the bones of animals that were offered as sacrifices and can now be eaten by priests (e.g. a sin offering). Context dictates that the bones under discussion are those that are edible but not always eaten.

Coarse bran is permitted.
Fine bran of new [grain] is forbidden, but that of old [grain] is permitted.
And[101] [a priest] may act with regard to *terumah* as he acts regarding nonsacral [grain].
If one sifts one or two *qav* of fine flour per *se'ah*,
he may not discard the remainder.
Rather he must place it in a hidden place.

11:6–8 *Drips and Spills*

6 If one cleared a storehouse of wheat that was *terumah*,
he is not required to sit and gather [the kernels] one by one.
Instead, he may sweep[102] in his normal fashion[103] and fill it with nonsacral [grain].
7 And likewise if a jar of [*terumah*] oil spills,
one does not require him to sit and collect it with his hands.
Rather, he may treat it as he would treat nonsacral [oil].

[101] K and others lack the conjunction. [102] K reads "gather." This is probably a scribal error.
[103] Lit. "according to his way."

Coarse bran is permitted: The bran is the outer layer of the grain that is removed in order to make flour. Coarse bran is the part of this layer that is separated during the first sifting. It appears that it was not generally eaten. Therefore, the coarse bran of grain that is *terumah* is permitted to nonpriests.

Fine bran of new [grain] is forbidden: The fine bran is the part of the outer layer of the grain that does not immediately separate. The fine bran of new grain is sometimes moist, which causes some of the flour to stick to the bran. Since the flour is *terumah*, the fine bran is prohibited to a nonpriest.

but that of old [grain] is permitted: Flour does not stick to the fine bran from older grain, which is dry. Therefore, since this bran is discarded and does not contain *terumah*, it is permitted to nonpriests.

And [a priest] may act…nonsacral [grain]: While it is normally forbidden to waste or destroy *terumah*, the Mishnah teaches that a priest is nevertheless permitted to discard the parts of the grain kernel that he would normally discard when milling ordinary, nonsacral grain.

If one sifts…in a hidden place: This is a qualification upon the previous ruling. If one sifts one or two *qav* (1 *qav* = ⅙ *se'ah*) of fine flour from a *se'ah* of wheat, one may not discard the remaining coarser flour because, unlike bran, it is still perfectly edible and therefore retains its status as fully sanctified *terumah*. He must therefore treat it as such by placing it in a hidden space where it is protected from loss or sources of impurity (see 8:8).

11:6 *one does not require…one by one*: In other words, one is not obligated to painstakingly make sure that he removed each and every kernel of grain that was *terumah*.

Instead, he may sweep…nonsacral [grain]: One is only required to perform his due diligence by sweeping his storehouse as he normally would. He may then fill it with nonsacral grain. It is implied that he may then treat the contents of the storehouse, including whatever *terumah* grain may have been left over, as nonsacral produce. This is probably based on the assumption that any leftover *terumah* will be nullified in a 100:1 ratio by the nonsacral produce. While it is normally forbidden to intentionally nullify *terumah* (see 5:9 above), the Sages permit it in our case because the primary intent of the owner is not to nullify the *terumah*, but to store the nonsacral grain.

11:7 *Rather, he may treat it as he would treat nonsacral [oil]*: If a barrel of oil spills, the owner does not generally kneel down and try and scoop up the spilled oil with his hands. Therefore, one is not obligated to do so if his barrel of *terumah* oil spills. This is so despite the fact that the oil left on the ground will certainly be lost.

8 If one pours [*terumah* wine or oil] from one jar to another,
and [the original jar has been emptied to the point that] three drops drip from it,
he may place nonsacral [wine or oil] into it.
If he tipped [the original jar] and drained it,
[the liquid] is indeed *terumah*.
And[104] how much *terumah* of the tithe of doubtfully tithed produce must there be for one to take it to a priest?
One eighth of an eighth.

11:9 *Terumah* Vetches

9 One may feed *terumah* vetches to domesticated animals, wild animals, and fowl. An Israelite who hired a cow from a priest may feed it *terumah* vetches.

[104] Some manuscripts lack the conjunction.

11:8 *If one pours…from one jar to another, and…three drops drip, he may place nonsacral [wine or oil] into it*: In this case an individual decides to pour wine or oil that is *terumah* from one jar into another in order to use the first jar to store nonsacral liquid. This mishnah teaches that one need not painstakingly wipe the jar of all traces of *terumah*. Rather, he may pour out the contents of the jar until the stream slows to the point that only drops are coming out. Once three such drops have left the jar any remaining *terumah* is considered insignificant. He may then fill this jar with nonsacral wine or oil, and any remaining *terumah* will be nullified. See annotations to 11:6 above for why it is permitted to intentionally nullify the *terumah* in this instance.

If he tipped [the original jar] and drained it: If someone, after emptying the jar according to the procedure outlined above, tips the jar so that more liquid comes out, that liquid still has the status of *terumah*. In other words, any residue that remains in the jar retains its sanctified status until it is nullified in a majority of nonsacral liquid.

terumah of the tithe of doubtfully tithed produce: Doubtfully tithed produce is produce from which *terumah* has been removed, but which may not have been tithed. If one obtains doubtfully tithed produce, one must designate tithes before consuming it (for more details see tractate *Demai*). However, because this produce may have in fact been tithed, one is not required to actually distribute first tithe to a Levite, but *terumah* of the tithe must still be given to a priest (see Numbers 18:26). The Mishnah asks how much *terumah* of the tithe there must be to require an individual to go through the trouble of bringing it to a priest. Ordinarily one must bring even a minuscule amount of *terumah* to a priest. This is therefore a leniency occasioned by the fact that the produce under discussion is doubtfully tithed as opposed to untithed.

One eighth of an eighth: i.e. $1/64$. The mishnah does not specify a unit of measurement, but many commentators conclude that the measure is $1/64$ of a *log*. If the owner of the produce has less than this amount, then the *terumah* of the tithe need only be separated and set aside.

11:9 *terumah vetches*: Vetches are bitter plants that were consumed by humans in times of starvation but were generally only used as animal fodder.

to domesticated animals, wild animals, and fowl: Because they are normally used as animal feed and are only rarely consumed by humans. Other types of produce, such as grain, that are eaten by both humans and animals could not be used in this manner as this would be tantamount to wasting *terumah*. The animals mentioned must belong to a priest.

An Israelite who hired…may feed it terumah vetches: Because the cow is still the property of the priest.

But a priest who hired a cow from an Israelite,
even though he is responsible for its food, may not feed it *terumah* vetches.
An Israelite who assessed a priest's cow may not feed it *terumah* vetches.
But a priest who assessed an Israelite's cow may feed it *terumah* vetches.

11:10 *Lighting a Lamp with Oil-That-Is-To-Be-Burned*

10 One may light [a lamp] with oil-that-is-to-be-burned
in synagogues, study-houses, dark alleyways, and over those who are ill,
with the permission of a priest.
If an Israelite woman who is married to a priest regularly comes to her father's house,
her father may light [a lamp with oil-that-is to-be-burned] with her permission.
One may light [a lamp with oil-that-is-to-be-burned] at a wedding banquet, but not in
a house of mourning.

But a priest...may not feed it terumah vetches: Someone who rents another's animal is obligated to feed it. While a priest would be allowed to feed his own animal *terumah* vetches, he may not do so in this case because the cow is still the property of the Israelite. He must therefore feed the animal nonsacral food.

An Israelite who assessed...may not feed it terumah vetches: The commentators debate the exact details of this arrangement. A common explanation is that the owner of the cow gives his animal to another party who will serve as a caretaker for the animal. Both parties intend to split any future profits or losses between them. For this reason, the value of the animal is assessed at the outset (see *Bava Mez'ia* 5:5). According to our mishnah, in such an arrangement the animal becomes the property of the caretaker. Thus, if the caretaker is an Israelite, the cow may not be fed *terumah*, whereas the opposite holds true if the caretaker is a priest.

11:10 *Terumah* that becomes impure must be burned (*Temurah* 7:5), and a priest may derive benefit from its burning. Nonpriests, however, are generally not permitted to derive benefit from the burning of impure *terumah*.

oil-that-is-to-be-burned: This is a technical term for impure *terumah* oil that also appears elsewhere in the Mishnah (e.g. *Shabbat* 2:2).

synagogues...dark alleyways: These are all locations where nonpriests will be present and will therefore benefit from the light of the lamp.

over those who are ill: Specifically nonpriests who are ill.

with the permission of a priest: The translation is according to those commentators who understand the Hebrew *reshut* as "permission." Nonpriests may benefit from the burning of impure *terumah* oil as long as a priest gives them permission to burn it. Others, however, understand *reshut* as "presence." According to this understanding, as long as the burning of the *terumah* oil provides some benefit to a priest, nonpriests may benefit from it as well. The Yerushalmi states that the presence/permission of a priest is only required in the case of lighting a lamp for someone who is ill. This is based on the fact that lighting a lamp in a synagogue, study-house, or dark alley serves the public need.

If an Israelite woman...with her permission: The wife of a priest may consume *terumah* and is therefore also allowed to benefit from the burning of impure *terumah*. According to those who understand *reshut* as "permission," the Mishnah teaches that, since the priest's wife regularly visits her father, she may give him permission to burn impure *terumah* oil even when she is not present. This is based on the assumption that since she visits regularly, she may arrive at any moment. Those who understand *reshut* as "presence" explain that the father may light a lamp with impure *terumah* oil for the simple reason that his daughter is present and will likewise benefit from the light.

These are the words of R. Judah

But[105] R. Yose says:

[One may light a lamp with oil-that-is-to-be-burned] in a house of mourning, but not at a wedding banquet.

R. Meir prohibits in both places.

R. Simeon permits in both places.

[105] K and others lack the conjunction.

at a wedding banquet: In the presence/with the permission of a priest. The commentators, following the Yerushalmi, explain that the concern in this situation is that a guest at the banquet will move the lamp to a location where a priest is not present. According to R. Judah, guests at a wedding banquet will not touch an oil lamp for fear of ruining their nice clothes.

but not in a house of mourning: People in a house of mourning do not wear nice clothes, and there is therefore a greater concern that they will move the lamp.

[One may light a lamp with oil-that-is-to-be-burned] in a house of mourning: According to the Yerushalmi, the reasoning behind this opinion is that since people are subdued in a house of mourning, they are less likely to forget that the lamp contains impure *terumah* oil.

but not at a wedding banquet: People at a wedding banquet are so joyous that they might forget the lamp contains impure *terumah* oil and therefore come to use the oil for something else.

Tractate Ma'aserot

Joshua Kulp

Introduction

Overview

Tractate *Ma'aserot*, "tithes," discusses liability of produce to tithes, which include three types: first tithe, which is to be given to a Levite; second tithe, consumed in Jerusalem or redeemed for money elsewhere; and the poor tithe. The tractate also contains rules relevant to *terumah* and *terumah* from the tithe, both of which are given to priests. The tithe of animals is discussed not in this tractate but in tractate *Bekhorot*.

Structure and Organization of the Tractate

The tractate is not tightly organized. It begins with two general rules concerning the types of produce that are liable for *terumah* and tithes (1:1–2). It then lists various types of produce and determines the moment in their development at which they become liable for tithes (1:2–8). Most of the second chapter treats the proposition that certain acts cause produce to become liable for tithes, specifically being brought into one's house (2:1–4) or being purchased (5–6). The end of the second chapter (2:7–8) and the beginning of the third (3:1–3) deal with workers whose wages are paid in produce and the question of whether they must tithe before eating. After one paragraph on the liability to tithes of found produce (3:4), most of the remainder of chapter 3 discusses whether the bringing of produce into other structures such as a courtyard or a hut makes it liable for tithes as does bringing produce into one's house (3:5–10).

Chapter 4 discusses the cooking, pickling, and salting of produce, and how such processing renders the produce liable for tithing (4:1–4). The last two paragraphs (4:5–6) deal with plants that have parts that must be tithed and other parts that need not be tithed. Chapter 5 opens with two paragraphs about saplings (5:1–2) and then discusses rules related to selling untithed produce (5:3–4). As is often the case in the Order of *Zera'im* (see *Hallah* and *Orlah*, for example) the tractate concludes (5:5–8) with a discussion of the liability to tithes for produce grown outside the land of Israel.

Main Ideas

The requirement to give tithes and *terumah* applies only to food intended for human consumption, owned by a particular person(s), and produced from the ground (1:1a).

A prevalent concern throughout the tractate is the moment at which produce becomes liable for tithes. Produce is liable for tithes only once it has grown sufficiently for it to be considered edible by human beings (1:1b–4). Once the produce has become liable for tithes, one may continue to snack on it, i.e. eat it in an informal manner, until its processing has been completed. In 1:5 this is called "the threshing floor for tithes." At the threshing floor the processing of the wheat into grain is completed. So too each type of produce has its own "threshing floor," the point at which its processing is considered complete and after which even informal snacking is prohibited unless the food is tithed.

Intent also plays a role in determining when produce becomes liable for tithes. If one intends to bring the produce back into the house, as opposed to selling it, it is not liable for tithes until it actually enters the house. But if one intends to sell it at the market, it becomes liable for tithes immediately. The tractate discusses whether bringing produce into one's courtyard or onto one's roof is akin to bringing it into the house. Cooking food, or otherwise rendering it edible for human beings, also completes its processing (4:1). Other actions can cause produce to become liable for tithes, for instance, turning grapes into wine (4:4) and peeling barleycorns (4:5). Throughout the tractate considerable attention is devoted to each individual type of foodstuff, making the tractate a rich source of information on botany, agriculture, and diet.

Relationship to Scripture

The Torah provides conflicting information about what is to be done with the tithe. The relevant verses are Numbers 18:21–32, Deuteronomy 14:22–29, and 26:12–15. Modern scholars argue that these texts are inconsistent with each other because they derive from different sources. This mode of interpretation was obviously not available to ancient Jews. Texts of the Second Temple period (e.g. Josephus, Judith, Tobit, Jubilees, Temple Scroll) propose a variety of solutions. The rabbinic solution, assumed by tractate *Ma'aserot* and by many other tractates in the Order of *Zera'im*, is predicated on the assumption that in any given year, except for the Seventh (Sabbatical) Year when no tithes at all are required, Israelites make multiple payments, a point not stated by the Torah. In all years of the Sabbatical cycle, except the seventh, *terumah* is given to the priests (see *Terumot*). Similarly, in all but the Seventh Year, tithes are given to the Levites, a payment the Rabbis call "first tithe," and the Levite gives a tithe of that to the priest, this payment being called "the *terumah* of the tithe." In years one, two, four, and five a second tithe is set aside for consumption in Jerusalem. In years three and six of the seven-year Sabbatical cycle, instead of the second tithe, a tithe is given to the poor, known as the poor tithe. All these payments are in addition to various others: animal tithes, firstborn animals, firstfruits, fourth-year produce, gifts for the poor, and much else. Whether this system was ever actually implemented is not known.

Special Notes for the Reader

There is much debate and much uncertainty about the precise identification of many of the fruits and vegetables mentioned in the tractate.

Tractate Ma'aserot

Chapter One

1:1 *General Rules Concerning Tithes*

1 [The Sages] stated a general rule concerning tithes:
Whatever is food [for humans],
and is guarded,
and grows from the land,
is liable for tithes.
And additionally [the Sages] stated another general rule [concerning tithes]:
Whatever [is considered] food both at the beginning and at the conclusion [of its growth],
even though [the farmer] holds on to it in order to increase [the quantity of] food,
is liable [for tithes],
whether [it is harvested while it is] small or large.
But whatever is not considered food in the early stage [of its growth]
but is [considered food only] in its later stage,
is not liable [for tithes] until it can be considered food.

1:2–3 *Produce That Is Eaten Only in Its Later Stage of Growth*

2 When do fruits become liable for tithes?
Figs—after they begin to ripen.
Grapes and wild grapes—after they begin to ripen.

1:1 *A general rule*: The same principle appears in *Pe'ah* 1:4.

is guarded: The owner finds the produce worthy of harvesting and storing. Cf. 3:9.

another general rule: If a plant can be eaten at an early stage of growth (when small), it is liable for tithes no matter when it is harvested. See 1:4.

But whatever is not considered food: If the produce is not considered edible at its earlier stage of growth, it need not be tithed if eaten then. Illustrations of this principle will be brought in 1:2–3.

1:2 *begin to ripen*: According to *Shevi'it* 4:7, this is the earliest stage in which figs are considered edible by themselves.

wild grapes: See Isaiah 5:2.

Sumac and mulberries—after they become red;
[similarly] all red fruits—after they become red.
Pomegranates—after they become soft.
Dates—after they begin to swell.
Peaches—after [red] veins begin to show.
Walnuts—after they form a container.
R. Judah says:
Walnuts and almonds—after they form inner skins.

3 Carobs—after they form [dark] spots;
[similarly] all black fruits—after they form [dark] spots.
Pears, Crustuminum pears, quinces, and hawthorns—after they become smooth;
[similarly] all white fruits—after they become smooth.
Fenugreek—after it can be transplanted.
Grain and olives—after they are one-third ripe.

1:4 *Produce That Is Eaten at an Early Stage of Growth*

4 Vegetables:[1] cucumbers, gourds, watermelons, melons,
[and fruits:] apples and citrons
are liable [for tithes whether they are] large or small.
R. Simeon exempts citrons when they are small.
When bitter almonds are liable [for tithes], the sweet almonds are exempt;
when sweet are liable [for tithes], the bitter are exempt.

1:5–8 *When Processing Is Complete and Produce Can No Longer Be Snacked on Without Tithing*

5 What is considered a "threshing floor" for tithes?
Cucumbers and gourds [are liable for tithes] once [the farmer] removes the fuzz.

[1] Or "greens."

---

after they begin to swell: Lit. when they begin to expand like leavened bread.

after they form a container: After the shell contains the nut as a container would.

1:3 *black fruits*: Before the fruit becomes completely black, black spots begin to form.

Crustuminum pears: Mentioned also in *Kilayim* 1:4 and *Uqtsin* 1:6, a high-quality pear with golden skin.

1:4 *cucumbers, gourds, etc.*: All of these vegetables and fruits are eaten at both an early stage in their ripening and a later stage. Hence, even if they are harvested at their earlier stage, they are liable for tithes.

bitter almonds: Bitter almonds are eaten in the early stage of their ripening and sweet almonds are eaten in the later stage of their ripening. Therefore, if bitter almonds are harvested at the later stage, they are exempt, and if sweet almonds are harvested in their early stage, they are exempt.

1:5 *"threshing floor"*: At the threshing floor grain becomes liable for tithes. By extension, the mishnah uses the word "threshing floor" to refer to the point at which the processing of produce has reached a certain stage of completion. Before this point, one can snack without tithing, but not eat a "fixed meal," which is more formal; after this point, even snacking without tithing is prohibited.

And if he does not remove it, once he has made a pile.
Watermelons, once he has trimmed them.
And if he does not trim them, once he puts them in storage.
Vegetables which are tied in bundles, once he ties them up in bundles.
If he does not tie them up in bundles, once he fills up a vessel [with them].
And if he does not fill up a vessel [with them], once he has gathered all that he needs.
[Produce packed in] a large basket, once he has covered [the basket].
If he does not cover it, once he fills up a vessel [with it].
And if he does not fill up a vessel, once he has gathered all that he needs.
When does this apply?
When he [intends to] bring [the produce] to the market.
But if he [intends to] bring [the produce] to his own house,
he may snack from it until he reaches his house.

6 Pomegranate seeds, raisins, and carobs—
once he has made a pile.
Onions—once he has peeled them.
If he does not peel them—
once he has made a pile.
Grain—once he has smoothed out the pile.
If he does not smooth out the pile—
once he has made a pile.
Pulses—once he has sifted them.
If he does not sift them—
once he has smoothed out a pile.
Even after he has smoothed out a pile,
he may take from the broken ears,
from the sides of the piles,
or from that which is mixed in with the chaff, and eat [without tithing].

And if he does not remove it: Rather he sells it with the fuzz, or waits for the fuzz to fall off on its own.

in storage: or "place for drying figs." See *Shevi'it* 8:6.

snack: Before produce is liable for tithes one may eat it in an informal manner (cf. 2:5), but one may not make a formal meal of it.

1:6 *Pomegranate seeds*: Sellers of pomegranates would partially dry the fruit and then bring the seeds to the market.

once he has made a pile: This is the end stage of processing for these types of produce.

peeled: The loose skin would be removed before the onion was brought to market.

smoothed out the pile: Smoothing out the pile aided in measuring the volume and allowed for more waste to be removed.

Pulses: Beans and other such produce that grow in shells must be sifted to remove pieces of dirt.

Even after he has smoothed out a pile: After the pile has been smoothed out , one can no longer eat the produce whose processing has been completed and is part of the pile without tithing it. But if the processing was not completed or the produce is not part of the pile, one can continue to eat without tithing.

broken ears: Ears of grain, the kernels of which were not separated during the threshing process.

7 Wine—once it has been skimmed.
Even though it has been skimmed, he may take from the upper winepress,
or from the duct, and drink [without tithing].
Oil—once it has drained into the trough.
But even once it has drained into the trough,
he may still take oil from the pressing bale,
or from the pressing beam, or from the boards between the press [without tithing],
and he may put such oil on a cake, or large plate.
But he may not put the oil in a dish or stewpot while they are boiling.
R. Judah says:
He may put it into anything except that which contains vinegar or brine.

8 A round [cake of pressed figs]—once it has been smoothed out.
One may smooth it out with fully untithed figs or grapes.
R. Judah forbids.
If one smoothed it out with grapes, it has not thereby been rendered susceptible to impurity.
R. Judah says:
It has been rendered susceptible.
Dried figs—once they have been pressed [into a jar];
and a container [of dried figs], once they have been rolled out.

1:7 *Wine*: The wine that is found in the lower part of the winepress must be tithed once the waste material (skins and seeds) has been skimmed off the top in the lower part of the winepress. He can still drink from the wine in the upper parts of the winepress without tithing because its processing has not yet been completed.

trough: From here the oil will be collected.

the pressing bale...beam...boards: These are the upper parts of the olive press. As with the wine, he may take oil from there without tithing because it has not yet drained into the trough, i.e. still has to undergo processing.

cake, or large plate...dish or stewpot: He may use this oil directly on food but he cannot cook it because cooking produce always makes it liable for tithes.

vinegar or brine: Due to their sharpness these speed the cooking process (*Shabbat* 3:5) and thereby make it liable for tithes.

1:8 *A round [cake]*: The final step in processing a cake of pressed figs was to smooth it out using fruit juice.

One may smooth it out: According to the first opinion, one can use the juice of untithed figs or grapes to smooth out the fig cake, because the amount of juice used is negligible and the untithed figs or grapes do not directly come into contact with the fig cake.

R. Judah forbids: Because the juice that flows from the grapes or figs is to be treated like the grapes or figs themselves and therefore must be tithed.

susceptible to impurity: The dispute here is related to the previous dispute. Food becomes susceptible to impurity only upon contact with a liquid (see Leviticus 11:38 and *Makhshirin*). The grape juice does not cause susceptibility to impurity, for the amount is not considered significant. R. Judah holds that any liquid that comes out of grapes causes susceptibility (see *Terumot* 11:3).

Dried figs: Dried figs which will not be made into a cake can no longer be eaten without tithing once they have been pressed into a jar.

container...rolled out: If the dried figs are simply going to be placed into a storage bin, then they are liable for tithes before all eating once the pile has been rolled out.

If one was pressing [the figs] into a jar, or rolling them into a container,
and the jar broke or the container opened,
he may not snack on them.
R. Yose permits.

Chapter Two

2:1–3   Bringing Produce into a "House" Causes It to Be Liable for Tithes

2 If one was passing through the market and said:
"Take for yourselves [from my] figs,"
they may eat them and are exempt [from tithing].
Therefore if they brought [the figs] into their houses,
they must make them legally fit to be eaten [as produce] known to be untithed.
[But if he said]: "Take and bring [them] into your houses,"
they may not snack from them.
Therefore if they brought them into their houses,
they must only make them legally fit to be eaten [as produce] suspected of being untithed.

2 If they were sitting at the gate or a shop,
and one [passing through the market] said [to them]:
"Take figs for yourselves,"

---

and the jar broke or the container opened: The issue at stake is whether produce that has already become liable for tithes before it can be eaten can go back to a state where one can snack from it without tithing. Once the figs were pressed into the jar or storage bin they became liable for tithes before they could be eaten. When the jar broke or the bin was opened, they return to a state of incomplete processing. According to the first opinion, once they have become liable for tithes, they may not be eaten without tithing. R. Yose holds that they revert to their previous status and may be snacked on without tithing.

2:1 *they may eat them and are exempt [from tithing]*: There are two reasons to assume that these figs have not been tithed. First, he was leaving the marketplace, and it is not customary to tithe figs until they have been brought home. Second, he did not tell the person to bring them into his house, because he knew that doing so would make them liable for tithes. The receiver can eat the figs without tithing only until he brings them into his house.

known to be untithed: Once brought home, the tithes that he separates are considered "certain tithes" because we can be certain that the figs were not yet tithed.

Take and bring [them] into your houses: The receiver cannot snack on the figs before they are tithed because the seller is understood to be saying that the figs have already been in his home, which would make them liable for tithes, but that they have not necessarily yet been tithed.

suspected of being untithed: Once in his home, the purchaser must treat them as *demai*, doubtfully tithed produce (see *Demai*), because it is unknown whether the one who gave them to him tithed them.

2:2 *gate*: The entrance to a courtyard.

they may eat them and are exempt [from tithing],
but the owner of the gate, or the owner of the shop, is liable [to tithe them before eating].
R. Judah exempts [the owner from tithing],
unless he turns his face or changes the place where he was sitting.

3 One who brings up [untithed] produce from the Galilee to Judaea,
or one who goes up to Jerusalem,
may eat [of them] until he reaches his destination,
and the same is true when he returns.
R. Meir says:
[He may eat of them] until he reaches the place
where he intends to rest [on the Sabbath].
But[2] peddlers who travel from town to town may eat [of their untithed wares]
until they reach the place where they intend to stay overnight.
R. Judah says:
The first house [a peddler reaches] is considered to be his house.

2:4 *Separating Terumah before Tithes Have Been Removed*

4 Produce from which one has separated *terumah* before its processing was finished—
R. Eliezer prohibits snacking on it,

[2] Absent in **P, K**.

---

they may eat them and are exempt [from tithing]: Produce becomes liable for tithes when brought into one's own house. Therefore anyone sitting at the gate or inside the shop—other than the owner—can eat the figs without tithing them. The owners, however, must tithe before eating because they are eating in their property, which counts as their home.

unless he turns his face or changes the place where he was sitting: R. Judah holds that a gate and a shop do not cause produce to be liable for tithes because it is not considered decent to eat in such places (cf. 3:5). Only if the owner found a place in which he will not be embarrassed to eat must he tithe before he eats the figs.

2:3 *until he reaches his destination*: When one is traveling on the road for business or making a pilgrimage to Jerusalem and enters an inn to spend the night, he can continue to snack on the produce without tithing. He must tithe only when he arrives at the place, meaning the home, to which he intended to go. This is true even if he is not the owner of that house.

until he reaches the place where he intends to rest [on the Sabbath]: When the Sabbath begins all produce must be tithed before it is eaten (see 4:2). R. Meir adds that merely arriving at a place where one will spend the Sabbath already makes the produce liable for tithes (see 4:2) even if the Sabbath is days away.

peddlers: Peddlers do not have one destination to which they are going. Therefore, the arrival at any place where they intend to spend the night causes their produce to become liable for tithes.

The first house [a peddler reaches] is considered to be his house: Even if he does not intend to spend the night in a certain place, just entering any house makes the peddler's produce liable for tithes.

2:4 *R. Eliezer prohibits snacking*: Even though *terumah* was separated before the physical processing of the produce was completed (see 1:5 and *Terumot* 1:10), doing so indicates a certain finality and obligates the produce to further tithes being removed before it may be further consumed.

but the Sages permit,
except for a basket of figs.
A basket of figs from which one separated *terumah*—
R. Simeon permits [snacking on it],
but the Sages forbid [snacking on it].

2:5–8   *Purchasing Produce Causes It to Be Liable for Tithes*

5 One who says to his fellow:
"Here is an *issar*, give me five figs for it"—
he may not eat [any of them] until he tithes—
the words of R. Meir.
R. Judah says:
He may eat them one at a time and is exempt [from tithing],
but if he combined [them], he is liable [to tithe].
R. Judah said:
It once happened in a rose garden in Jerusalem,
that figs were being sold three or four for an *issar*,
and neither *terumah* nor tithe was ever separated from them.
   6 One who says to his fellow:
"Here is an *issar* for ten[3] figs which I will choose for myself"—
he may choose them and eat [without tithing].
"For a cluster of grapes which I will choose for myself"—
he may pick grapes and eat [without tithing].
"For a pomegranate which I will choose for myself"—
he may take apart [the pomegranate] and eat [it one piece at a time without tithing].

[3] **P, K**: "twenty."

---

except for a basket of figs: Albeck tentatively explains that it was common to give figs to several people (as we saw above in 2:1–2); therefore if one separated *terumah* then he has shown that his intention is to eat and give away the figs while they are in the basket and not to press them into a jar or make them into a fig cake. Thus separating *terumah* indicates that their physical processing is complete, making them liable for tithes before they can be further consumed.

R. Simeon permits: R. Simeon does not consider separating *terumah* to indicate a final processing of the figs, and likely does not distinguish between figs and other types of produce.

2:5 *an issar*: A coin, worth one twenty-fourth of a dinar.

he may not eat [any of them] until he tithes: The sale of the figs causes them to become liable for tithes before eating.

rose garden in Jerusalem: The figs in this garden were eaten one at a time by travelers and therefore tithes were never separated.

2:6 *One who says to his fellow*: In all of these cases, the buyer gives the seller money on condition that he may choose which particular piece of fruit he will pick; the fruit is still attached to the ground. The purchase is only complete once he picks the fruit. He can eat the fruit without tithing, but only one piece at a time, for if he were to pick more than one piece and then eat it, he would be considered to have purchased fruit detached from the ground.

"For a watermelon which I choose for myself"—
he may slice and eat [it one piece at a time without tithing].
But if he said to him: "For these twenty figs,"
or "For these two clusters,"
or "For these two watermelons,"
he may eat [them] as he normally does[4] and is exempt [from tithing],
because he bought them while they were still attached to the ground.

7 One who hires a worker to put figs out to dry[5] with him[6]—
[if the worker] said to him: "On condition that I may eat figs"—
he may eat them and is exempt [from tithing].[7]
[If the worker said:] "On condition that I and my son may eat [figs],"
or "that my son may eat [figs] as my wage"—
he may eat and is exempt [from tithing],
but [if] his son eats, he is liable [to tithe].
[If the worker said:] "On condition that I may eat during the time of the fig harvest,
and after the fig harvest"—
during the time of the fig harvest he may eat and is exempt [from tithing],
but after [the time of] the fig harvest, [if] he eats, he is liable [to tithe],
since he is not eating [with permission] from the Torah.
This is the general rule:
One who eats [with permission] from the Torah is exempt [from tithing],
while one who does not eat [with permission] from the Torah is liable [to tithe].

8 If one was working [as a hired worker]—
among poor-quality figs, he may not eat of high-quality figs,
and if among high-quality figs, he may not eat of poor-quality figs,

---

[4] Lit. "in his usual way."
[5] Or "trim" or "slice"; the verb can refer to multiple steps in the process of preparing figs for drying. See 2:8 and 3:1.
[6] P, K lack "with him"; a later hand inserts it in **K**.
[7] **K** adds "but if he combines [them] he is liable [for tithing]." See 2:5.

But if he said to him, "For these twenty figs," etc.: Here he specifies which of the fruit he wants to eat, thereby acquiring the fruit while it is still attached to the ground. Buying produce attached to the ground does not cause it to become liable for tithes, and therefore, he may snack on it before it is tithed.

2:7 *he may eat them and is exempt from tithing*: According to the rabbinic interpretation of Deuteronomy 23:25–26, a worker in a field is allowed to eat from the owner's produce while he is working in the field (see *Bava Metsi'a* 7:2). The produce that he eats is not considered wages and hence it can be eaten without tithing. This is true even if when making a contract with his employer it looks as if the produce is a wage, since the Bible fundamentally established such an arrangement, which human agreement cannot overturn (*Ketubbot* 9:1, *Bava Metsi'a* 7:11, *Bava Batra* 8:5).

but [if] his son eats, he is liable [to tithe]: The figs that the son eats are considered a wage and therefore must be tithed before being eaten.

since he is not eating [with permission] from the Torah: According to the Rabbis the Torah allows the worker to eat while he is harvesting but not after the harvest has been completed. Figs that he eats after the fig harvest has been completed are therefore liable for tithes before being eaten.

2:8 *poor-quality figs…high-quality figs*: These are considered different species and a worker may eat only from the type of produce with which he is working (see *Bava Metsi'a* 7:4). If he wishes to eat the other type of fig he must tithe, because these would be considered part of his wages.

but he may restrain himself until he reaches the place of the better figs,
and eat.
If one exchanges with his fellow
either [figs] for eating for [figs] for eating,
or [figs] to be dried[8] for figs [to be dried],
or figs [for eating] for figs [to be dried][9]—
he is liable [to tithe].
R. Judah says:
One who exchanges [figs for eating for other figs for eating] is liable [to tithe],
but [if for figs] for drying, he is exempt [from tithing].

Chapter Three

3:1–3 *Produce Eaten by Workers*

3 One who moves figs through his courtyard to be dried,[10]
his children and the other members of his household may eat [of them]
and are exempt [from tithing].
The[11] workers [who work] with him,
if he is not obligated to feed them,[12]
may eat and are exempt [from tithing];[13]
but if he is obligated to feed them, they may not eat [without tithing].

---

[8] See 2:7 and 3:1. [9] This clause is absent in **K**, perhaps owing to a scribal error.
[10] Cf. 2:7–8. [11] **K, P** read "and the workers."
[12] Lit. "when they have no claim to food on him," here and throughout.
[13] **K, P** lack "may eat and be exempt."

If one exchanges: These exchanges are considered purchases and neither party can eat of the figs so acquired before they are tithed.

but [if for figs] for drying, he is exempt: According to R. Judah, purchasing causes produce to be liable for tithes only if the produce's manufacturing has been completed. Therefore, if he exchanges for figs that he intends to dry out, he may eat of them before tithing.

3:1 *exempt [from tithing]*: Bringing produce into one's courtyard causes it to be liable for tithes (see 3:5), but only if the processing was complete. Since these figs were being taken to be dried, a further step in their processing, they are not liable for tithes. Furthermore, the members of his family are considered an extension of himself and are not considered his workers; therefore, they, like him, may eat without tithing.

if he is not obligated to feed them: These workers cannot eat the figs by Torah mandate because they are not working on the figs. If the employer did not guarantee to feed them while working, they can eat the figs without tithing because they are considered a gift and not wages.

but if he is obligated to feed them, they may not eat [without tithing]: The figs are treated as wages and are therefore liable for tithes.

2 One who brought his workers into a field—
if he is not[14] obligated to feed them, they may eat and are exempt [from tithing];
but if he is obligated to feed them, they may eat of the figs one at a time,
but not from the basket, nor from the large basket, nor from the storage yard.[15]

3 One who hires a worker to work with olives,
[and the worker] said to him: "On condition that I may eat the olives,"
he may eat them one at a time and is exempt [from tithing];
but if he combined [them], he is liable [to tithe].
[One who hires a worker] to weed out onions,
[and the worker] said to him: "On condition that I may eat the leaves,"[16]
he may pluck leaf by leaf, and eat [without tithing],
but if he combines them together he is liable [for tithing].

3:4   Found Produce

4 One who found cut figs on the road,
even beside a field of cut figs,
and similarly, if a fig tree overhangs the road,
and one found figs beneath it,
they are permitted on account of theft,
and they are exempt from tithes.
[But if they were] olives or carobs,
they are liable [for theft and tithes].

---

[14] K was corrected to read "if he is obligated…if he is not obligated." This reading seems to be an error.
[15] Or "drying area."   [16] Lit. "[the] green [part]."

3:2 *One who brought his workers into a field*: But not to work with the produce (the figs).

they may eat and are exempt: If the employer is not obligated to feed his workers, then the figs that they eat are a present and since they are still out in the field, the workers may eat them without tithing them.

they may eat of the figs one at a time: Since they are wages, in principle the figs must be tithed before being eaten. However, they may be eaten untithed one at a time until their processing is complete by having been put into a place for storage (see 2:5).

3:3 *One who hires a worker to work with olives*: According to rabbinic law, the Torah permits a worker to eat from his employer's produce only when working at the end of the processing of the produce (see *Bava Metsiʿa* 7:2). The worker in this mishnah was working with the olives before the completion of their processing. Therefore, the olives (or onions) that he receives are considered part of his wages and cannot be eaten without being tithed. He can still eat one olive at a time, but if he gathers them together they are liable for tithes (see 3:2).

3:4 *even beside a field of cut figs*: Spread there in order to dry.

they are permitted on account of theft: Taking these figs is not considered theft because we assume that the field owner wouldn't consider it worth his while to retrieve them.

and they are exempt from tithes: Ownerless produce is always exempt from tithes (see 1:1; *Hallah* 1:3).

[but if they were] olives or carobs, they are liable [for theft and tithes]: Since they are of greater value, we must assume that the owner might want to retrieve them. Therefore, they are not considered ownerless.

One who found dried figs—
if the majority of people had already pressed [their figs],
he is liable [to tithe them before eating];
but if not, he is exempt [from tithing them before eating].
If one found slices of a fig cake,
he is liable [to tithe them before eating],
since it is known that they derive from something whose processing had been completed.
As to carobs—
if he had not yet gathered them on the top of the roof,
he may take some down for his animals and is exempt [from tithing],
since he returns that which is left over.

3:5–9 Produce Brought into a Courtyard

5 Which courtyard [makes produce] liable [for tithes]?
R. Ishmael says:
The Tyrian courtyard, because vessels are stored in it.
R. Aqiva says:
Any courtyard which one person may open and another may shut
does not [make produce liable for tithes].[17]
R. Nehemiah says:
Any courtyard in which a man is not ashamed to eat [makes produce] liable [for tithes].
R. Yose says:
Any courtyard into which a person may enter and no one says to him
"What are you looking for?" does not [make produce liable for tithes].

---

[17] Lit. "is exempt," here and below.

---

dried figs: Figs are liable for tithes once they have been pressed into a jar (see 1:8). The found figs have been dried and they look as if they were pressed, but it is unknown if they have already been pressed into a jar or were simply stepped on by passersby. The status of the figs is determined by what the majority of people in that area have done.

fig cake: It is clear that these figs have already pressed into a jar and cannot be eaten without tithing.

carobs: The final stage in the processing of carobs, the step that makes them fit for human consumption, is bringing them up to the roof to dry out and then making them into a pile (see 1:6). Before they are made into a pile, one may bring them down from the roof to feed them to cattle without tithing. Bringing them down to feed the cattle is not considered the completion of their processing because he may bring the remaining carobs back up to his roof to continue to dry out for human consumption.

3:5 Which courtyard [makes produce] liable for tithes?: Produce is liable for tithes once it is brought into a house or into a courtyard, if the courtyard offers protection from theft.

The Tyrian courtyard: The style of yard commonly found in the city of Tyre. According to both Talmuds a guard sits outside of the Tyrian courtyard and protects it.

Any courtyard which one person may open and another may shut does not [make produce liable for tithes]: A courtyard which either of two people can open is not well-protected. Therefore, produce brought into such a courtyard it is not liable for tithes.

in which a man is not ashamed to eat: In mishnaic times it was considered impolite or uncultured to eat in public; see 2:2 above.

R. Judah says:
Two courtyards one within the other,
the inner one [makes produce] liable [for tithes],
and the outer one does not [make produce liable for tithes].

6 Roofs do not [make produce] liable [for tithes],
even if they are part of a courtyard which [does make produce] liable [for tithes].
A gatehouse, portico, or balcony are like the courtyard [of which they are a part];
if [the courtyard makes the produce] liable [for tithes], they do as well.
And if it does not, they do not.

7 Cone-shaped huts, watchtowers, and huts in the field
do not [make produce] liable [for tithes].
A Ginnosar *sukkah*,
even though it has millstones and poultry within,
does not [make produce] liable [for tithes].
The potter's *sukkah*—
the inner part [makes produce] liable [for tithes] but the outer part does not.
R. Yose says:
Whatever is not a dwelling place in both the sunny season and the rainy season
does not [make produce] liable [for tithes].
A *sukkah* on the Festival [of Sukkot]:
R. Judah declares that it [makes produce] liable [for tithes],
but the Sages declare that it does not.

Two courtyards one within the other: The inner courtyard is sufficiently guarded for it to cause produce to be liable for tithes, but the outer one is relatively open and therefore produce brought into it is still exempt.

3:6 *A gatehouse*: A small structure in which a guard would sit.

portico: An open area with pillars holding up a roof.

balcony: Attached to the second floor. Stairs would lead down from the balcony to the courtyard.

3:7 *Cone-shaped huts*: A structure made of branches or reeds, connected at the top, with a broad, circular base on the bottom. Such a structure does not have a roof and the Rabbis define "houses" as structures with roofs. Hence, it does not render the produce liable for tithes.

watchtowers, and huts in the field: Refers to watchtowers found in the field to guard the vineyards. These are not considered "houses" because they are not regarded as living quarters.

A Ginnosar sukkah: Ginnosar, on the northern shores of the Sea of Galilee, was a region known for the high quality of its agricultural land. People would dwell in these huts most of the year in order to guard the produce in the field. They might bring millstones and poultry into the hut in order to have grain, eggs, and perhaps some meat. Nevertheless, since they do not live in these huts all year round, they do not qualify as houses for the purpose of reckoning liability to tithes.

The potter's sukkah: This hut is divided into two parts—the inner part was used by the potter and his family for living quarters, and the outer part was for work. Cf. the view of R. Judah in 3:5 above.

A sukkah on the Festival [of Sukkot]: Leviticus 23:42 mandates dwelling in *sukkot* for seven days during the Festival of Sukkot. According to R. Judah, the mandate to dwell in the *sukkah* for this period causes it to be considered a house which renders produce liable for tithes. The Sages disagree, reasoning that it is not truly a house, since one dwells there for only one week.

8 A fig tree which stands in a courtyard—
one may eat [figs] one at a time and is exempt [from tithing],
but if he combined [them], he is liable [to tithe].
R. Simeon says:
[He may have] one in his right hand and one in his left hand
and one in his mouth,
[and still be exempt].
If he ascended to the top [of the fig tree],
he may fill his bosom and eat.

9 A vine planted in a courtyard—
one may take a whole cluster [and eat it without tithing].
And similarly in the case of a pomegranate, or a watermelon—
the words of R. Tarfon.
R. Aqiva says:
One may pick only single fruit from the cluster,
or split the pomegranate into slices,
or cut slices of the watermelon [and eat without tithing].
Coriander sown in a courtyard—
one may pluck leaf by leaf and eat [without tithing],
but if he combined them together, he is liable [to tithe].
Savory, hyssop, and thyme which are in the courtyard,
if they are regarded as valuable,[18] are liable [for tithes].

3:10 *Miscellaneous Rules about Liability to Tithing*

10 A fig tree which stands in a courtyard,
and hangs over into a garden—

---

[18] Lit. "guarded, watched; preserved." See 1:4.

3:8 *A fig tree which stands in a courtyard*: Since this tree is already in the courtyard, the figs must be tithed before they are eaten. However, one can still eat the figs one at a time without tithing (see 3:3).

one in his right hand, etc.: One in each hand and one in one's mouth are not deemed to be combined.

If he ascended: Because he is still at the top of the tree, the figs are not considered as having been brought into the courtyard and are exempt.

3:9 *one may take a whole cluster*: R. Tarfon treats the cluster of grapes, the pomegranate, and the watermelon as one single unit, and therefore one can eat the whole thing without tithing. One only needs to tithe if one gathers several clusters or whole pieces of fruit.

One may pick only single fruit: R. Aqiva treats these fruits as if they were already individual units gathered together. Therefore, he can eat only pieces thereof without first tithing.

Savory, hyssop, and thyme: These species are liable for tithes only if they are watched over, which implies that they have been cultivated. If they grow wild, they are exempt.

3:10 *A fig tree which stands in a courtyard, and hangs over into a garden*: When it comes to tithes, the status of a tree is determined by its branches, for they contain the fruit. If the tree stands in the courtyard, but the fruit on branches hangs over into the garden, it is not considered to be in the courtyard, and one may snack from it without tithing.

one may eat [the figs] as he normally does and is exempt [from tithing].
If it stands in the garden and hangs over into a courtyard,
one may eat [the figs] one at a time and is exempt [from tithing],
but if one combined [them], one is liable [to tithe].
If it stands in the Land [of Israel]
and hangs over outside the Land,
or if it stands outside the Land,
and hangs over into the Land—
it all depends on the root.
And as regards houses in walled cities—
it all depends on the root.
But as regards cities of refuge,
it all depends on the branches.
And as regards Jerusalem,
it all depends on the branches.

Chapter Four

4:1–5 *Actions That Make Produce Liable for Tithes*

4 One who pickles, boils, or salts [produce],
[even] in a field,
is liable [to tithe].
One who stores [produce] in the ground is exempt [from tithing].

If it stands in the Land [of Israel]: Only fruit that is grown on a tree within the Land of Israel is liable for tithes. The status of a tree regarding liability is determined by its trunk.

houses in walled cities: Leviticus 25:29–31 states that houses sold within a walled city can be redeemed by the seller for one year. If they are not redeemed within the year then permanent title belongs to the purchaser. See *Arakhin*. The Mishnah extends this rule to trees sold within a walled city. Roots determine whether a tree is deemed to be within or outside the city.

cities of refuge: Accidental murderers must flee to one of the cities of refuge (Numbers 35:9–28; Deuteronomy 19:1–10). The Mishnah refers to a tree found partially within one of these cities. In this case the branches determine the location of the tree. If the blood avenger kills the accidental murderer under the branches which are inside the borders of the refuge city, he is guilty of murder, even if the roots are outside of the city. But if the branches are outside the city, he is exempt, even if the roots are within.

And as regards Jerusalem: Second tithe cannot be redeemed and exchanged for money once it is within the walls of Jerusalem; see *Ma'aser Sheni* 3:7.

4:1 *One who pickles, boils, or salts [produce], [even] in a field*: Processing produce to make it edible causes it to become liable for tithes (see 1:7). This is true even if the processing occurs far from the house.

One who stores [produce] in the ground: Storing produce in the ground, it was believed, warms it up a bit but does not cook it. One may snack from such produce without first tithing it.

One who dips [produce while still] in the field is exempt [from tithing].
One who splits olives so that the bitter taste may come out of them is exempt [from tithing].
One who squeezes olives against his skin is exempt [from tithing].
If[19] he squeezed them and put [the oil] into his hand, he is liable [to tithe].
One who makes a viscous liquid [from grapes or olives]—
[if] to put it in a cooked dish, he is exempt [from tithing].
[If] to put it in an [empty] pot, he is liable [to tithe],
for it is like a small vat.

2 Children who hid figs [in a field] for the Sabbath
and forgot to tithe them—
one may not eat them [even] after the Sabbath
until they have been tithed.
A basket of fruits [designated] for the Sabbath—
the House of Shammai exempt it [from tithes];
but the House of Hillel declare it liable [for tithes].
R. Judah says:
Even one who gathered a basket
to send to his fellow
may not eat of it until he tithes.

3 One who took olives from a vat
may dip them one at a time in salt, and eat them [without tithing];

[19] K, P: "but if."

One who dips: Produce is often eaten by dipping it into saltwater, vinegar, oil, or even wine (see e.g. *Pesahim* 10:3). Such eating is not necessarily part of a formal meal and therefore one may continue to eat the produce without tithing it.

One who splits olives: This is not considered processing the olives sufficiently to cause them to be liable for tithes.

One who squeezes olives directly against his skin in order to oil himself, may eat the oil without tithing. However, if he squeezes the olive in order to get the oil out of it and put it in his hand, he must tithe before he eats this oil.

One who makes a viscous liquid is not considered processing them sufficiently for the liquid to be liable for tithes. However, if he puts the liquid into an empty pot, it is as if he put it in a vat to store it, thereby completing its processing. He now can no longer use the liquid without first tithing it.

4:2 *Children who hid figs [in the field] for the Sabbath*: Any eating done on the Sabbath is considered significant and cannot be considered "snacking" which is exempt from tithes. Therefore, produce generally becomes liable for tithes when the Sabbath begins. The intention to eat something on the Sabbath, even the intention of a child, causes the produce to be liable for tithes, even after the Sabbath is over.

A basket of fruits: Set aside before the Sabbath to be eaten on the Sabbath. The House of Hillel hold that merely intending to eat something on the Sabbath causes it to be liable for tithes. The House of Shammai hold that such food is liable for tithes only once the Sabbath has actually begun. Cf. 2:3.

One who gathers a basket to send as a present *to his fellow*: According to R. Judah, making food into a gift gives it significance, just as the Sabbath does. Therefore, one cannot eat of such produce until it is tithed.

4:3 *one at a time in salt*: The salting of individual olives does not make them liable for tithes (cf 4:1).

but if he salted them, and put them in front of him,
he is liable [to tithe them before eating].
R. Eliezer said:
[If he took them] from a pure vat, he is liable [to tithe them],
but if from an impure [vat], he is exempt [from tithing them],
because he can put back the leftovers.

4 One may drink [wine] from the winepress,
whether [it is mixed] with hot or cold water,
[and] be exempt [from tithing]—
the words of R. Meir.
R. Eliezer b. Zadok declares him liable [to tithe].
But the Sages say:
[If the wine is mixed] with hot water, he is liable [to tithe],
but with cold water, he is exempt [from tithing].

5 One who husks barley
may husk one at a time and eat [without tithing];
but if he husked and put them into his hand,
he is liable [to tithe].
One who rubs [ears of] wheat may shake[20] away [the chaff]
from hand to hand,[21]
and eat [without tithing].
But if he shakes the grain and puts it in his bosom, he is liable [to tithe].
Coriander which one sowed for the sake of the seed—
its plant is exempt [from tithes];

[20] Some versions: "blow," here and below.   [21] K originally had "little by little" and was corrected.

and put them in front of him: Salting several olives at once does make them liable for tithes (see 2:5).

from a pure vat: The olives in the vat are susceptible to impurity because they came into contact with the olive oil (*Makhshirin* 6:4). One will not want to return such olives back to the vat because touching them may have rendered them impure, and since he won't put them back, they have completed their processing and are liable for tithes. If the vat was impure, however, then there is no concern about further defilement and he can put the olives back for further processing; they are therefore not considered to be gathered together even when they are salted and can be eaten without tithing. Cf. 3:4.

4:4 *whether [it is mixed] with hot or cold water*: In mishnaic times it was customary to mix wine with water before it was drunk.

with hot water, he is liable: The wine that has been mixed with warm water will not be poured back into the press because it might cause the cool wine in the press to spoil. Since he won't pour any back the Sages consider its processing to have been completed and therefore the wine is liable for tithes. If it was mixed with cold water he might pour the leftover wine back into the winepress and therefore he can drink it without tithing.

4:5 *One who husks barley*: Husking barley and eating the corns one at a time is considered snacking and therefore one can do so without tithing. If he puts several in his hand at the same time, however, their processing is considered completed and he may not eat without first tithing.

Coriander: If coriander (cilantro) was sown in order to eat the seeds then he needs to tithe only the seeds. He can eat the plant without tithing because when he sowed the plant, his intention was to throw these parts away. However, if he sows it in order to use the plant, then both the plant and the seeds must be tithed before they can be eaten. The seeds are assumed to be of use, even if he didn't specifically intend to use them.

[but] if one sowed it for the sake of the plant,
seed and plant are to be tithed.
R. Eliezer says:
Dill—its seed, plant, and pods are to be tithed;
but the Sages say:
Only cress and rocket, no other, are to be tithed,
seed and plant.

4:6 Which Parts of a Plant Must Be Tithed

6 Rabban Simeon b. Gamaliel[22] says:
Shoots of fenugreek, of mustard, and of white beans
are liable for tithes.
R. Eliezer says:
The caper bush is tithed, shoots, berries, and blossoms.
R. Aqiva says:
Only the berries are tithed, since they [alone] are fruit.

Chapter Five

5:1–2 The Tithing of Saplings

5 One who uproots saplings from his own property
and plants them [elsewhere] within his own property
is exempt [from tithing].
If he bought [saplings] attached to the ground,

---

[22] **K, P**: "Rabban Gamaliel."

Dill: According to R. Eliezer, one needs to tithe all of the parts of a dill plant, because we may assume that the one who planted it intended to eat them all.

the Sages disagree with both R. Eliezer and with the rule about coriander.

4:6 *fenugreek…mustard…white beans*: The shoots of these three plants are edible, and therefore they are liable for tithes.

caper bush: R. Eliezer holds that all three parts of a caper bush must be tithed, because all three are edible. R. Aqiva says that only the capers must be tithed because they are the most valuable part of the bush, the part that is primarily eaten.

5:1 *uproots saplings*: Since the saplings have not completed their growth, one can uproot them and replant them elsewhere. This does not count as planting untithed produce, which some Sages implicitly forbid (see *Pe'ah* 1:6).

If he bought [saplings] attached to the ground: The purchase of produce causes it to be liable for tithes. However, if saplings are bought while still attached to the ground, their fruit is not liable for tithes. Had they been bought detached from the ground, the fruit would need to be tithed before it could be eaten. Cf. 2:6.

he is exempt [from tithing].
If he gathered [saplings] in order to send them to his fellow,
he is exempt [from tithing].
R. Eleazar b. Azariah said:
If similar ones were being sold in the market,
then they are liable [for tithes].

2 One who uproots turnips and radishes from within his own property
and plants them [elsewhere] within his own property—
if for the purpose of seed,
he is liable [to tithe],
since for them this is [equivalent to] the threshing floor.
Onions, once they have taken root in an upper story,
become pure from any impurity.
If some debris fell upon them [even though] they are uncovered—
they are regarded as though they were planted in the field.

5:3–4: *Selling Produce That Needs to Be Tithed*

3 A person may not sell produce, after its time for tithing has arrived,
to one who is not trusted concerning tithes,
nor in the Seventh Year [may one sell Seventh-Year produce]
to one suspected of [transgressing] the Seventh Year.

If he gathered [saplings] in order to send them to his fellow: When one gathers produce to send it to someone, it must first be tithed (see 4:2). However, when one gathers saplings and sends them he is still exempt.

if similar ones were being sold in the market: R. Eleazar b. Azariah says that if the fruit hanging on these saplings is similar to fruit being sold in the market, meaning this fruit has ripened enough that it could be sold in the market, then one cannot eat from it until it has been tithed.

5:2 *One who uproots turnips…for the purpose of seed*: The turnips and radishes must be tithed before being replanted because as soon as he uprooted them their processing was completed. The seeds that will subsequently come from the turnips and radishes will be exempt from tithes (see 5:8).

Onions…in an upper story: Onions that took root in debris/dirt found in an upper story of a building are treated as if they were planted in the ground. If they had previously been impure, they now revert to a state of purity. However, their liability for tithes is not renewed.

If some debris fell upon them: If the onions were in the field and some debris fell on them, they are treated as planted in the field and are liable for tithes, even if their leaves are exposed.

5:3 *A person may not sell produce*: Once produce has ripened enough that it is liable for tithes (see 1:2–4), one should not sell it to a person who is not trusted to tithe produce before he eats it. See *Demai* chapter 2.

nor in the Seventh Year: While it is permissible to sell produce that grows during the Seventh (Sabbatical) Year, the Mishnah forbids selling it to a person who is not trusted to observe the laws of the Seventh Year that apply to that fruit. Such sinners are mentioned frequently in *Shevi'it*.

But if [only some] produce ripened, he may take the ripe ones [for himself]
and sell the [unripe] remainder.

4 A person may not sell his straw, or his olive peat, or his grape pulp
to one who is not trusted concerning tithes,
for him to extract the juice from them.
And if he did extract [the juice],
he is liable for tithes, but is exempt from *terumah*,
because when one separates *terumah*
one has in mind [even] fragments [of grain],
whatever is by the sides,
and whatever is inside the straw.

5:5 One Who Purchases Land in Syria

5 One who buys a field of vegetables[23] in Syria—
if the field has not yet reached the season for tithing,
he is liable [to tithe];
if [he bought the field] after the season for tithing,
he is exempt [from tithing],
and may gather [its produce] in his usual manner.
R. Judah says:
He may even hire workers and gather [the produce].
Rabban Simeon b. Gamaliel says:
When does this apply?
When he bought the land.

[23] Or "greens."

---

if [only some] produce ripened: If some of the fruit has ripened and become liable for tithes, but some of it is still unripe, hence not liable for tithes, he may take for himself the ripe fruit and sell the unripe fruit to anyone, even those who are not trusted to tithe.

5:4 *A person may not sell his straw*: Although straw, olive peat, and grape pulp are not edible and therefore are not liable for tithes, they may not be sold to someone who is not trusted to tithe, if the purchaser intends to squeeze the juice out of the olive peat or grape pulp, or to search for the leftover grains within the straw. These products would be liable for tithes, and since the purchaser doesn't tithe, one may not sell to him.

if he did extract [the juice]: If, nevertheless, he did sell these to someone else, the purchaser must separate the tithes. However, he need not separate *terumah* because when the original seller separates *terumah* for the main product he will intend to separate *terumah* on behalf of these byproducts as well. The "fragments" are broken stalks of wheat that were not threshed. Those *by the side* are stalks that fell to the side of the main pile of wheat; those which are *inside the straw* are the kernels of grain that were not separated (see 1:6). However, the purchaser still needs to separate tithes because the original owner separated tithes based on measurements, and these byproducts were not part of that assessment.

5:5 *One who buys a field of vegetables in Syria*: In rabbinic terminology "Syria" refers to the land that borders Israel to the north and east but is not considered fully part of the "Land of Israel." See *Shevi'it* 6:1–2.

R. Judah says: He may hire workers to help him collect the added growth, even though this will cause more people to know that he is not tithing this field.

But if he did not buy the land—
[even] if the field has not yet reached the season for tithing
he is exempt [from tithing].
Rabbi [Judah the Patriarch][24] says:
He must also[25] tithe proportionally.

5:6 *A Drink Made from Used Grape Skins*

6 One who makes wine from grape skins,
and adds a measured amount of water,
and finds [afterward] the same quantity of liquid—
is exempt [from tithing].
R. Judah declares him liable [to tithe].
If he found more than the measured amount [of water],
he must pay [the tithe] for it from another place, proportionally.

5:7 *Grain in Anthills*

7 Anthills which remained a whole night
near a pile of grain which was liable to be tithed,
[the grain in the anthills] is liable [to be tithed],
since it is obvious that [the ants] have been dragging the whole night
from something [whose processing] is complete.

[24] K, P, and most manuscripts: "Meir."   [25] K lacks "also."

he must also tithe proportionally: Even in a case where he is exempt from tithing, he is still liable to tithe on the percentage of growth that the vegetables experienced after the purchase. Thus if he buys the field after the season for tithing has arrived, he is exempt from tithing on the growth that occurred before this season, but he is liable to tithe for the percentage of growth that took place after he bought the field.

5:6 *One who makes wine from grape skins*: by pouring water over grape skins that have already been used to make wine; the grape skins are then filtered out of the just created wine. If, after filtering, the volume of the wine remains the same as the volume of the added water, it is clear that the grape skins have added color and taste but not volume and are therefore exempt from tithes.

If he found more than the measured amount [of water]: If the measure has increased, the Mishnah recommends that he tithe from *another place*, i.e. other untithed produce. When he does so, he gives it according to the proportion of the increase that the grape pulp caused in the water. For instance, if he found a one-liter increase, he separates tithes for one liter of grapes, thereby giving 100ml of tithe from other wine.

5:7 *Anthills*: Cf. Pe'ah 4:11.

something: The pile of grain (see 1:5).

5:8 *Produce from Outside the Land of Israel*

8 Garlic from Ba'albek,
onions from Rikhpa,[26]
Cilician beans and Egyptian lentils—
R. Meir says: *Qirqas*, too;
R. Yose says: *Qotnym*, too—
[all these] are exempt from tithes
and may be bought from any person in the Seventh Year.
The seeds of upper arum pods,
the seeds of leeks,
the seeds of onions,
the seeds of turnips and radishes,
and other seeds of the garden which are not eaten—
[all these] are exempt from tithes,
and may be bought from any person in the Seventh Year;
for[27] even if the plants from which they grew[28] were *terumah*,
they may still be eaten [by nonpriests].

[26] P and several manuscripts: "Dikhpa."   [27] K lacks "for."   [28] Lit. "their father."

5:8 *Garlic from Ba'albek*: Ba'albek is in the Lebanon valley.

Rikhpa: Or Dikhpa, identity unknown.

Cilician beans: From Cilicia in Asia Minor (modern Turkey).

Qirqas…Qotnym: The identification of these two plants is unknown and variant spellings abound in manuscripts.

are exempt from tithes…the Seventh Year: The produce mentioned here may be assumed to come from outside of the Land of Israel. The laws of tithes and the Seventh Year do not apply outside the Land of Israel (*Terumot* 1:5; *Shevi'it* 6:1).

The seeds of upper arum pods, etc.: These seeds are not eaten and therefore they are not liable for tithes. Also, one can buy them from a person who is suspected of selling Seventh-Year produce because the sanctity of Seventh-Year produce does not apply to these seeds, since they are not generally eaten.

for even if…[by nonpriests]: Explains the previous statement. Even if these seeds grew from *terumah* plants, the seeds themselves are not even subject to tithes, because they are generally not edible and the priests do not care about them (see *Terumot* 11:5). This would be all the more true if the parent plants were not grown from *terumah* seeds.

Tractate Ma'aser Sheni

Joshua Kulp

Introduction

Overview

Ma'aser Sheni is the "second tithe." This tithe, derived from the rabbinic interpretation of Deuteronomy 14:22–26 (see introduction to *Ma'aserot*), is to be brought to Jerusalem and consumed inside the city by its owners. Alternatively, the tithe may be redeemed by its owners outside the city and its proceeds brought to Jerusalem, there to be used to purchase food for consumption inside the city. In addition to discussing the second tithe, the tractate also discusses fourth-year fruit (Leviticus 19:23–25) because many of the same rules apply to both.

Structure and Organization of the Tractate

The tractate begins with a discussion of financial transactions involving second tithe or the money used to redeem the second tithe. Second tithe is considered holy, and therefore may not be sold (1:1–2). Food purchased with second-tithe money is sacred (1:3–7).

The second chapter discusses what may be done with second-tithe produce—eating, drinking, and anointing (2:1–4). It continues with a discussion of coins used to redeem second-tithe produce that became mixed up with nonsacred coins (2:5–6). It concludes with rules related to the sanctity of second-tithe coins.

Most of the third chapter relates to the use of second-tithe coins to purchase food in Jerusalem: how should such purchases be made, what may be bought with this money, the status of second-tithe money and produce that go in and out of Jerusalem, the borders of Jerusalem, and a few other topics. The chapter then discusses food or animals bought with second tithe that becomes impure. It concludes with a discussion whether containers of second tithe wine acquire the sanctity of the wine they contain.

The fourth chapter opens with a description of the procedure through which one redeems or desacralizes second-tithe produce outside of Jerusalem: how one evaluates the produce being redeemed (4:1–2), that redemption of second-tithe produce requires an extra fifth in value (4:3–4), how second-tithe produce is desacralized, and how its sanctity is transferred to coins. The chapter concludes with a discussion of produce and coins whose status is doubtful—they may or may not have the sanctity of second tithe.

The opening paragraphs of chapter five discuss fourth-year fruit which must be brought to Jerusalem and consumed there like second tithe. The last section deals with laws of removing one's tithes from the home at the end of the third and sixth years and recitation of the tithe confession (Deuteronomy 26:12–15).

Main Ideas

Many of the rabbinic laws of second tithe are derived from the interpretation of Leviticus 27:30–31 as referring to second tithe. These verses call this tithe "holy" and state that when it is redeemed (a procedure described in Deuteronomy 14:22–26) one must add an extra fifth. Since the tithe is holy, it can only be consumed in a state of ritual purity. This distinguishes it from first tithe, which is not sacred. Second-tithe produce must be treated in the same way that *terumah* is treated.

There are two processes treated at length in the tractate. The first is the desacralization of second-tithe produce. This is the process whereby the second-tithe produce is redeemed for money. The tractate provides certain mechanisms to ease such a process: for instance, one may set aside a certain amount of money in one's home to be used consistently for the redemption of second-tithe produce (4:8).

The second process is the purchase of food, drink, or oil in Jerusalem with second-tithe coins. The Mishnah discusses what is to be done with the nonedible portions of the purchase (e.g. hides of animals, containers of wine).

Finally, since second-tithe coins are sacred, there are rules governing their exchange for other coins (2:7–10).

Relationship to Scripture

Tractate *Ma'aser Sheni* treats the tithes described in Deuteronomy 14:22–26, the confession described in Deuteronomy 26:12–15, and the fourth-year produce of Leviticus 19:23–25. It also reads Leviticus 27:30–31 as referring to the tithe in Deuteronomy 14. It does not refer to the tithe ("first tithe") in Numbers 18. For further details see the introduction to *Ma'aserot*.

According to the Rabbis, second tithe and food bought with second-tithe coins may be eaten anywhere within the city of Jerusalem. This contrasts with Second Temple groups that restricted the consumption of the tithe to the confines of the Temple.

Deuteronomy 14:24 rules that if one "is distant" from the place in which this tithe is to be consumed, it may be redeemed for money. The distance is not defined. The Rabbis read this in a radical way—anyone living outside of Jerusalem may redeem second-tithe produce (3:7). In contrast, other Second Temple groups (for example the Temple Scroll) require a distance of three days' travel.

By reading Leviticus 27:30–31 as referring to second tithe, the Rabbis understood the desacralization of this tithe for those living outside of Jerusalem as a process of redemption. In contrast, other Second Temple groups did not read these verses as related to second tithe and thus allowed a person to sell second-tithe produce outright.

Leviticus 19:24 states that fourth-year fruit of a tree is to be "sacred *hilulim* for the Lord." The meaning of the word *hilulim* is uncertain and was interpreted in different ways by ancient Jews. Some, especially Qumran authors (for example the Temple Scroll), interpreted the word to mean that fourth-year produce belonged to the priest, although it could be redeemed from him. In contrast, our tractate assumes that it, like second tithe, is to be brought to Jerusalem and consumed there.

Tractate Ma'aser Sheni

Chapter One

1:1–2 *The Prohibition of Selling Second-Tithe Produce*

1 Second tithe—
one may not sell it,
nor use it as a pledge,
nor exchange it,
nor weigh [something] against it.
Nor may one say to his fellow [even] in Jerusalem:
"Here is [second-tithe] wine, give me [in exchange] oil,"[1]
and the same with all other produce;
but one may give it to another as a free gift.[2]

2 Cattle tithe—
one may not sell it if unblemished and alive,
nor [may one sell it] blemished, [whether] alive or slaughtered,

---

[1] K adds "or vinegar."   [2] The vocalizer of K and several manuscripts read "as free gifts."

1:1 *one may not sell...pledge...exchange it*: Leviticus 27:30 (as understood by the Rabbis) calls second tithe "holy." Therefore, it is forbidden to perform any of these nonsacred activities with it.

nor weigh [something] against it: i.e. using second tithe whose weight is known as a counterweight on a scale.

Nor may one say to his fellow . . . : One cannot exchange second-tithe products, one for another, even in Jerusalem, where second tithe must be brought and eaten. Exchange is not considered a respectful act.

But one may give it to another as a free gift: Giving second tithe to another person as a present, when one does not expect anything in return, is not disgraceful and is therefore permitted.

1:2 *Cattle tithe*: Newborn domesticated animals must be tithed each year (Leviticus 27:32; *Bekhorot* chapter 9). The animal's fat and blood are offered on the altar and its meat is eaten by the owners (or anyone else) in Jerusalem (*Zevahim* 5:8). When it is blemished it can be eaten anywhere by anybody and none of it is offered on the altar (see *Bekhorot* 5:1).

may not sell it: Leviticus 27:33 says that this tithe *may not be redeemed*, which the Rabbis understood to mean that it also cannot be sold, in contrast to the firstborn animal (Leviticus 27:27).

unblemished and alive: This phrase appears twice in this mishnah, in different connections and yielding different rules. Here, with respect to the cattle tithe, the implication is that a slaughtered unblemished animal may be sold; the *Sifra*, however, followed by the Talmud, prohibits the sale of any cattle tithe.

nor may one betroth a woman with it.
A firstborn animal—
one may sell it unblemished and alive,
and [one may sell it] blemished, [whether] alive or slaughtered,
and one may betroth a woman with it.
One may not desacralize second tithe for unstamped coins,
nor for coins which are not current,
nor for coins which one does not have in his possession.

1:3–7 *The Status of Food Bought with Second-Tithe Money*

3 One who buys a domesticated animal for a sacrifice of well-being
or a wild animal for nonsacrificial eating[3]—
the hide goes out [from the sanctity of second tithe] to nonsacral [status],
even if [the value of] the hide exceeds [the value of] the meat.
Sealed jars of wine—
[if bought in] a place where they are usually sold sealed,
the jars go out [from the sanctity of second tithe] to nonsacral [status].

[3] Lit. "the meat of desire," here and in 1:4; see Deuteronomy 12:20 and 14:26.

betroth a woman: Since the tithed animal cannot be treated as money, it cannot be used to betroth a woman (*Kiddushin* 1:1).

A firstborn animal: Leviticus 27:26–27; Numbers 18:15–18; Deuteronomy 15:19–23; *Bekhorot*. Similar to the cattle tithe, the fat and blood of a firstborn domesticated animal must be offered on the altar (Numbers 18:17). The meat belongs to the priests and when it is unblemished only priests may eat it (*Zevahim* 5:8). When it is blemished, anyone can eat it, and therefore, the priest may sell it or its meat to a nonpriest and anyone can use it to betroth a woman. When it is unblemished the priests may sell it as long as it is still alive. However, after it has been slaughtered it may not be sold because this is considered disgracing a sacrifice.

One may not desacralize second tithe . . . in his possession: Second tithe must be redeemed for usable coins. This would exclude *unstamped coins*, whose value is equivalent only to the value of their metal, *coins which are not current*, stamped by governments that no longer rule, and *coins which one does not have in his possession* or to which one does not have access (e.g. which have fallen down a well).

1:3 *domesticated animal for a sacrifice of well-being or a wild animal for nonsacrificial eating*: Second-tithe money may be used to purchase animals for food (cf. 2:1), but domesticated animals (sheep, goats, oxen) which are eligible must first be sacrificed (see 1:4).

the hide: One may only purchase edible food with second-tithe money (2:1), and someone who purchases inedible or nonfood items with second-tithe money is normally required to purchase permitted items equivalent to the value of the impermissible item (1:5, 7). In this case, however, the inedible hide is an unavoidable byproduct of a permissible purchase, with the sanctity of the second-tithe money transferred entirely to the meat.

Sealed jars of wine: These jars were sold with the wine, as was typical of the place where the wine was bought. Like the animal hide, the jars are secondary to the wine, and therefore, the sanctity of the second-tithe money is entirely transferred to the wine, not the jars, and one need not purchase edible food in the amount of the cost of the jars.

Walnuts and almonds—
their shells go out [from the sanctity of second tithe] to nonsacral [status].
Grape-skin wine—
before it has fermented,
it may not be bought with money of the [second] tithe;
but after it has fermented,
it may be bought with money of the [second] tithe.

4 One who buys a wild animal for a sacrifice of well-being
or a domesticated animal for nonsacrificial eating—
the hide does not go out [from the sanctity of second tithe] to nonsacral [status].
Open or sealed jars of wine—
[if bought in] a place where they are usually sold open,
the containers do not go out [from the sanctity of second tithe] to nonsacral [status].
Baskets of olives or baskets of grapes [bought] together with the vessel—
the value of the vessel does not go out [from the sanctity of second tithe] to nonsacral [status].

5 One who buys [with second-tithe coins] water or salt,
or produce [still] joined to the soil,
or produce which cannot reach Jerusalem—
[what he purchased] does not acquire [the sanctity of second] tithe.

Walnuts and almonds: Like the animal hide and the wine jars, nutshells are secondary and remain nonsacred, because the intent of the purchase was the meat of the nuts.

Grape-skin wine: See *Ma'aserot* 5:6 and *Hullin* 1:7. Before grape-skin wine is fermented it is considered like water, which cannot be purchased with second-tithe money, because water is not considered food (1:5). Once it ferments it becomes wine, which one may buy with second-tithe money.

1:4 *wild animal...domesticated animal*: Wild animals may not be brought to the altar as sacrifices, and while in general domesticated animals may be bought for nonsacrificial purposes, second-tithe money was to be used only for the purchase of well-being sacrifices, which were eaten by those who offered them (Leviticus 7:15). Since in both of these cases the person did not act properly, the hide does not become nonsacred. In order to desanctify the hide he will have to buy food equivalent to its value and treat that food with the sanctity of second tithe (1:5, 7).

Open or sealed jars of wine: In a place where the jar is not normally sold with the wine, it is not considered secondary to the wine (the customer normally provided his own container) and therefore the jar does not become nonsacred. To desanctify the jar he will have to buy food equivalent to its value and treat that food with the sanctity of second tithe.

Baskets of olives or baskets of grapes: Olives and grapes are not typically sold with their baskets. Therefore, the basket is not considered ancillary to the olives or grapes and the basket does not become nonsacred.

1:5 *water or salt...joined to the soil...cannot reach Jerusalem*: Water and salt are not considered food and may not be purchased with second-tithe money (2:1; *Eruvin* 3:1). Produce still attached to the ground is also not considered food. Finally, it is forbidden to buy produce that will rot before it can reach Jerusalem. In all of these cases, the sanctity of second tithe does not transfer to such items. To remedy the situation he will need to use an equivalent amount of money to buy the type of food that he should have bought in the first place and bring that food to Jerusalem and eat there (1:7).

One who buys produce...[if] unintentionally: Without realizing that the money that was spent was second-tithe money. The result should be that he would have to take the produce to Jerusalem and eat it there. However, since he was not aware that he was using second-tithe money, the purchase is considered an accidental purchase whose return the seller is forced to accept.

One who buys produce [with second-tithe coins outside of Jerusalem]—
[if] unintentionally,
the money must be restored to its [former] place;
[but if] intentionally,
[the produce] must be brought up and consumed in the [holy] place.
If there is no Temple, it must be left to rot.

6 One who bought a domesticated animal
[with second-tithe money outside of Jerusalem]—
[if] unwittingly,
its money must be restored to its [former] place;
[but if] intentionally, it must be brought up and eaten in the [holy] place.
If there is no Temple, it must be buried together with its hide.

7 One may not buy male slaves, female slaves,[4] land, or impure animals
with second-tithe money;
and if he did buy [one of these],
he must consume their equivalent value
[as second tithe in Jerusalem].
One may not bring bird sacrifices of a *zav* or *zavah*,
or bird sacrifices of women after childbirth,
purgation offerings, or guilt offerings,
from second-tithe money,
and if he did bring [one of these],
he must consume their equivalent value
[as second tithe in Jerusalem].
This is the general rule:
Any [expenditure] of second-tithe money
not used for eating or drinking or anointing—
one must consume its equivalent value
[as second tithe in Jerusalem].

[4] **P**, **K**, and most manuscripts lack "female slaves."

[but if] intentionally: Second-tithe money may only be used to purchase food in Jerusalem. If someone nevertheless intentionally buys produce with second-tithe money outside of Jerusalem, they have to take that produce all the way to Jerusalem and eat it there. If there is no Temple, then they must let the produce rot. In neither case may they redeem the produce for money.

1:6 *no Temple*: The rule for animals is identical to the rule for produce (1:5). Without the Temple, the animal can never be eaten, nor can it be used for work; it must be left alone until it dies of natural causes. Even the hide, which is not food and which remains nonsacred if the animal had been purchased for a sacrifice inside Jerusalem (see 1:3), is forbidden and must be buried.

1:7 *One may not buy male slaves*, etc.: Second-tithe money may be used only for the purchase of food (2:1) or oil for anointing.

One may not bring: These offerings, unlike sacrifices of well-being, are not consumed by those who bring them. Cf. *Shevi'it* 8:8.

bird sacrifices of a zav or zavah…women after childbirth: The *zav* and *zavah* are a man or woman who have experienced an abnormal genital discharge (Leviticus 15). For their purification they bring an offering consisting of two birds (Leviticus 15:14, 29) as does the woman after childbirth (Leviticus 12:8). See *Qinim*.

Chapter Two

2:1–4 *What May Be Done with Second-Tithe Produce*

2 Second-tithe [money] may be used for eating, drinking, and anointing:
for eating what is usually eaten,
and for anointing with what is usually used for anointing.
One may not anoint oneself with wine or vinegar,
but one may anoint oneself with oil.
One may not spice oil of second tithe,
nor may one buy spiced oil with second tithe money,
but one may spice wine.
If honey or spices fell into [wine] and increased its value,
the increased value [is allotted to second tithe] proportionally.
If fish was cooked with leek of second tithe,
and thus it increased in value,
the increased value [is allotted to second tithe] proportionally.
If dough of second tithe was baked
and thus increased in value,
the increased value is [entirely allotted] to the second [tithe].
This is the general rule:
Whenever the increase is recognizable,

2:1 *for eating, for drinking, and for anointing*: See *Shevi'it* 8:2.

eating what is usually eaten: If one buys food with second-tithe money, and it spoils, he need not eat it, because it is no longer in the category of that which is usually eaten. The same is true for spoiled drink.

wine or vinegar: Which cannot be used for anointing.

One may not spice oil of second tithe: There are a few explanations as to why second-tithe oil may not be spiced. First of all, some of the oil is soaked up by the spices, and that oil will not end up being used. Second, putting spices in the oil lessens its usefulness as food (cf. 3:2 and *Terumot* 11:1).

nor may one buy spiced oil: Only the wealthy use spiced oil as food, and as such one would be spending second-tithe money wastefully.

but one may spice wine: Because the entire mixture will be drunk and all classes of people drink spiced wine.

If honey or spices fell into [wine] and increased its value: The general rule, explained below, is that if nonsacral produce is used to improve second tithe, the added value is divided up according to the percentage of non-sacral and second-tithe produce in the product. For example, if second-tithe wine was worth two *dinar* and the nonsacral spices and honey were worth one *dinar*, and the mixture together was worth four *dinar*, there is a one *dinar* improvement. Two-thirds of the original value was second tithe and therefore, two-thirds of the improvement is second tithe, and one-third is nonsacral. Two and two-thirds of the final mixture is second tithe and one and one-third is nonsacral. The nonsacral part of the mixture can be bought with second-tithe money and the money would become nonsacral.

If dough of second tithe was baked and thus increased in value: Nonsacral sticks were used to light a fire to bake second-tithe dough. Here the nonsacral element is not noticeable in the final second-tithe product and therefore it is not reckoned as part of the value. So if the second-tithe dough was worth two *dinar*, and the baked bread is worth three *dinar*, all three *dinar* are second tithe.

the increased value [is allotted to second tithe] proportionally;
but whenever the increased value is not recognizable,
the increased value is [entirely allotted] to the second [tithe].
  2 R. Simeon says:
One may not anoint oneself with oil of second tithe in Jerusalem,
but the Sages permit it.
They said to R. Simeon:
If [the law] was lenient in the case of the [more] severe *terumah*,
should we not also rule leniently in the case of second tithe, which is a light matter?
He said to them:
No!
If[5] [the law] was lenient in the case of the [more] severe *terumah*,
a place where [the law] was [also] lenient with regard to vetches and fenugreek,
how can we be lenient in the case of second tithe, though it is a light matter,
a place where [the law] was not lenient with regard to vetches and fenugreek?
  3 Fenugreek of second tithe may be eaten when it is still tender.
But [fenugreek] of *terumah*—
the House of Shammai say:
Anything done with it must be done in a state of purity,
except when it is used for scrubbing the head,
but the House of Hillel say:
Anything done with it may be done in a state of impurity,
except soaking it in water.

[5] The text here is corrupt and must be corrected in accordance with 3:2 and 3:10.

2:2 *One may not anoint oneself with oil of second tithe in Jerusalem*: R. Simeon prohibits anointing oneself with second-tithe oil in Jerusalem lest one do so and then leave Jerusalem, which would constitute benefiting from second tithe outside of Jerusalem. R. Simeon disagrees with the anonymous opinion found in 2:1, which follows the view of the Sages here.

If [the law] was lenient in the case of the [more] severe terumah: *Terumah* is more severe than second tithe in a number of ways; see *Bikkurim* 2:1. The Sages argue that just as it is permitted for a priest to anoint himself with *terumah* oil (*Shevi'it* 8:2) and the law is not concerned lest an Israelite touch such a priest and thereby use the oil, so too the law should not be concerned lest an Israelite derive benefit from second-tithe oil outside of Jerusalem.

vetches and fenugreek: The case of vetches and fenugreek (see 2:3–4) demonstrates that *terumah* is not always treated more severely than second tithe. Hence, one cannot deduce that just because a priest may anoint himself with *terumah* oil, an Israelite may also anoint himself with second-tithe oil, for perhaps that, too, is a place where *terumah* might be treated more leniently than second tithe.

2:3 *Fenugreek*: Fenugreek can be eaten only when young and still tender. Hence, it can be purchased with second-tithe money only at that stage of its growth.

of terumah: According to the House of Shammai, *terumah* of fenugreek must always be treated as *terumah* and dealt with in purity until its stalks have become so hard that they will be used only for washing one's hair. Up until this point it is considered food and the laws of *terumah* apply to it.

but the House of Hillel say: That *terumah* of fenugreek is not treated as *terumah* unless it has been soaked in water to soften it to prepare it for food.

4 Vetches of second tithe may be eaten when still tender,
and they may be brought to Jerusalem and taken out again.[6]
If they become impure—
R. Tarfon says:
They must be divided among pieces of dough.
But the Sages say:
They may be redeemed.
But [vetches] of *terumah*—
the House of Shammai say:
One must soak them and rub them in a state of purity,
but may feed them [to animals] in a state of impurity.
But the House of Hillel say:
One must soak them in a state of purity,
but one may rub them and feed them [to animals] in a state of impurity.
Shammai says:
They must be eaten dry.
R. Aqiva says:
Anything done with them may be done in a state of impurity.

[6] Lit. "they may enter Jerusalem and leave [it]."

2:4 This mishnah is parallel to *Eduyot* 1:8.

Vetches: Like fenugreek, vetches are eaten when tender and young. When they grow they can only be used as animal fodder.

and they may be brought to Jerusalem and taken out again: Normally, once second tithe has been brought into Jerusalem, it cannot be taken out (see 3:5). Vetches are exceptional since when they age they become animal food.

divided among pieces of dough: R. Tarfon holds that second-tithe vetches that have become impure can no longer be redeemed for money, because it would be disgraceful to redeem them and then feed them to animals. To remedy the situation, the vetches are divided up and baked into impure loaves of second-tithe bread, which may then be redeemed. Alternatively, they are divided into pure loaves of second-tithe bread in amounts less than that which can transmit impurity (cf. *Terumot* 5:1–3). In these ways the inedible second-tithe vetches become fit for human consumption.

redeemed: The Sages do not share R. Tarfon's scruples about redeeming vetches that will be then be fed to animals; cf. 3:9.

[vetches] of terumah, etc.: Both the Houses agree that soaking must be done in a state of purity, since adding liquid makes them susceptible to impurity (see *Makhshirin*); they also agree that feeding them to animals may be done in a state of impurity, since at that point they are no longer fit for human consumption. They disagree about whether rubbing must be done in a state of purity. The House of Shammai require purity for rubbing because as long as they are not being fed to animals, they might still be consumed by humans and their purity must be guarded. The House of Hillel hold that rubbing is part of preparing them for animal food and therefore purity is not an issue.

Shammai ruled that *terumah* vetches must not be allowed to become susceptible to impurity at all.

R. Aqiva…state of impurity: Since vetches are really only animal food, one need not guard their purity at all.

2:5–10 *Second-Tithe Coins*

5 Nonsacral coins and second-tithe coins which were scattered
[and become intermingled]—
whatever he gathers [one at a time],
he gathers for second tithe until he completes the sum,
and the remainder are nonsacral.
If he mixed them and scooped them up by the handful,
[they are allocated] proportionally.
This is the general rule:
Anything gathered [one at a time] [is first allocated] to second tithe,
but anything mixed [and scooped] [is allocated] proportionally.

6 A second-tithe *sela* [of silver] which was mixed up
with a nonsacral *sela* [of silver]—
one may bring [copper] coins for the *sela* and say:
"Let the second-tithe *sela*, wherever it may be,
be desacralized for these [copper] coins."
And [then] he must select the better of the two *sela*,
and desacralize [the copper coins] for it,
for [the Sages] have said:
One may desacralize silver for copper [only] in case of necessity.
And[7] not that it may be allowed to remain so;[8]
rather, one must go back and desacralize [the copper] for silver.

7 The House of Shammai say:
One may not exchange one's [silver] *sela* for gold *dinar*,
but the House of Hillel permit it.
R. Aqiva said:
I [once] exchanged silver [*sela*] for gold *dinar* for Rabban Gamaliel and R. Joshua.

---

[7] **K, P**, and most manuscripts lack the conjunction.
[8] **K, P**, and most manuscripts: "Not that one may allow it to remain so."

2:6 *wherever it may be*: i.e. whichever of the two *sela* was originally of second tithe.

[then] he must select the better of the two sela: After transferring the sanctity of the silver *sela* to the copper coins, he transfers it back to the better of the two silver *sela*.

for [the Sages] have said: One may desacralize silver for copper [only] in case of necessity: Changing silver to copper is allowed in case of need such as this, but only when there is no other way to solve the problem. Changing silver coins for other silver coins is never allowed (cf. 2:9). Had it been permissible to exchange silver for silver, he could have picked up the better coin and announced that if it is nonsacred, the other coin would be redeemed through it. And even when copper may be exchanged for the silver, he can only do so temporarily—as soon as he has done so he must change the copper back for silver.

2:7 *One may not exchange one's [silver] selas for gold dinars*: The Talmud explains that the House of Shammai do not allow this lest people delay bringing their silver coins to Jerusalem until they gather enough to exchange them for gold *dinar*.

8 One who exchanges [copper] coins of second tithe for a *sela* [of silver]—
the House of Shammai say:
[He may exchange copper] coins [only] for a whole *sela*,
but the House of Hillel say:
[He may exchange copper coins] for a *sheqel* of silver
and a *sheqel*'s worth of copper coins.
R. Meir says:
One may not desacralize silver and produce for silver,
but the Sages permit it.

9 One who exchanges a second-tithe *sela* [of silver] in Jerusalem—
the House of Shammai say:
[He may only exchange] the whole *sela* for copper coins,
but the House of Hillel say:
[He may exchange the *sela*] for a *sheqel* of silver
and a *sheqel*'s worth of copper coins.
Those discussing [this matter] before the Sages say:
[He may even exchange the *sela*] for three *dinar* of silver
and one *dinar* of [copper] coins.
R. Aqiva says:
[One may exchange the *sela*] for three *dinar* of silver

2:8 This mishnah is parallel to *Eduyot* 1:9.

[He may change copper] coins [only] for a whole sela: According to the House of Shammai, if he has enough second-tithe copper coins to equal an entire silver *sela*, he can exchange them. However, if he only has enough coins for half of a *sela*, and for the other half he has a silver *sheqel* (worth half of a *sela*) of second-tithe money, he cannot exchange the copper and the silver *sheqel* for the silver *sela* because silver second-tithe money cannot be exchanged for other silver.

but the House of Hillel say: Although in general it is forbidden to exchange silver second-tithe coins for other silver coins, in this case it is permitted because the core of the exchange is the copper coins for half of the silver *sela*.

One may not desacralize silver and produce on silver: Half of a *sela*'s worth of produce, and half of a *sela*'s worth of silver coins may not be exchanged, according to R. Meir, for a larger silver coin. This is similar to the House of Shammai's opinion above, whereas the Sages are closer to the opinion of the House of Hillel.

2:9 This mishnah is parallel to *Eduyot* 1:10.

One who exchanges a second-tithe sela [of silver] in Jerusalem: Having arrived in Jerusalem with silver coins of second tithe, he wishes to exchange them for copper coins of lesser value in order to facilitate the purchase of small quantities of food.

[He may only exchange] the whole sela for copper coins: According to the House of Shammai, just as one may not exchange copper and silver coins for silver outside of Jerusalem (see 2:8), so too in Jerusalem one may not exchange silver coins for copper and silver.

a sheqel of silver and a sheqel's worth of copper coins: Consistent with their opinion in 2:8, the House of Hillel permit one to exchange half of a silver *sela* for copper coins (one *sheqel*'s worth) and half for silver coins (one *sheqel*'s worth). (Two *sheqel* are one *sela*.)

three dinar of silver and one dinar of copper coins: This anonymous opinion goes a step further than the House of Hillel. Even if one is exchanging only one *dinar*, equivalent to one quarter of a *sela*, for copper coins, the remaining three quarters can consist of silver coins. The House of Hillel required at least one half of the silver *sela* had to be exchanged for copper.

and one-fourth [of the remaining *dinar* of silver] for copper coins.
R. Tarfon says:
[One-fourth of the *sela* for] four *asper* in silver.
Shammai says:
He must leave [the *sela*] in a shop and [gradually] consume what it is worth.

10 If some of one's children were impure and some pure,
he may put down a *sela* [in a shop] and say:
"For what the pure drink,
this *sela* will be [gradually] desacralized."
As a result the pure and the impure may drink from one jar.

Chapter Three

3:1 *Dividing Second Tithe*

3 One may not say to his fellow:
"Carry up this [second-tithe] produce to Jerusalem
in order to divide it [between us]."
Rather he should say to him,

---

three dinar of silver and one-fourth: R. Aqiva is even more lenient and says that there does not even need to be a full *dinar* of copper, but rather only one-quarter of the fourth dinar of silver needs to be exchanged for copper. Thus three dinars can be silver and as long as the fourth dinar of the *sela* is redeemed for one-quarter of a dinar's worth of copper coins, the exchange is valid.

four asper in silver: R. Tarfon says that the fourth dinar of the *sela* (one-quarter of the value of the *sela*) can be exchanged for four *asper* of silver and one *asper* of copper. R. Tarfon is slightly more lenient than R. Aqiva, who said that a full quarter of the last dinar had to be copper. R. Tarfon, R. Aqiva and "those discussing before the Sages" give progressively lenient versions of the House of Hillel.

He must leave [the sela] in a shop and [gradually] consume what it is worth: Shammai provides a solution which avoids any exchange of coins for other coins. He gives the coin to the shopkeeper and eats from his shop until he has consumed the value of the coin. Shammai represents the strictest opinion: once in Jerusalem, it is forbidden to exchange the coin for other coins altogether.

2:10 *If some of one's children were impure and some pure*: He is in Jerusalem and he wants to buy his pure sons wine with second-tithe money, and give regular nonsacral wine to his impure sons who are not allowed to drink second tithe.

"For what the pure drink, this sela will be [gradually] desacralized": In this way, only the wine that the pure sons take from the jug will acquire the sanctity of second tithe, while what the impure sons take remains nonsacral. We may assume that the impure sons are not to touch the wine in the jug.

3:1 *"Carry up this [second-tithe] produce to Jerusalem in order to divide it [between us]"*: The issue here is whether one can offer second-tithe produce as compensation for help in carrying it to Jerusalem. The word "divide" has financial connotations, rendering this arrangement similar to selling second tithe, which is prohibited (1:1).

"Carry up [this second-tithe produce]
so that we may eat and drink of it in Jerusalem."
But one may give it to another as a free gift.

3:2 Buying Terumah with Second-Tithe Coins

2 One may not buy *terumah* with second-tithe money,
because this reduces [the number of those] who can eat it;
but R. Simeon permits it.
R. Simeon said to them:
If [the law] was lenient with regard to [using second-tithe money
to purchase] sacrifices of well-being,
which brings [the offering to possibly] becoming *piggul*, or remnant, or impure,
should we not also be lenient with regard to [using second-tithe money
to purchase] *terumah*?
The [Sages] said to him:
If [the law] was lenient [to permit using second-tithe money
to purchase] sacrifices of well-being,
because they are permitted to nonpriests,
should we therefore be lenient [to permit using second-tithe money
to purchase] *terumah*,
which is forbidden to nonpriests?

"Carry up…so that we may eat and drink of it in Jerusalem": Since he doesn't use the business-related word "divide," this is permitted.

But one may give it to another as a free gift: If someone wants to have another person carry his second tithe for him to Jerusalem, he is allowed to give it to him as a gift. When they arrive in Jerusalem, the one who carried it may give some or all of the second tithe back to its original owner. See also 1:1.

3:2 *because this reduces [the number of those] who can eat it*: *Terumah* can be eaten only by priests whereas second tithe can be eaten by anyone.

If [the law] was lenient with regard to [using second-tithe money to purchase] sacrifices of well-being: Second tithe may be used to buy well-being offerings (1:3), even though these sacrifices might eventually become forbidden for anyone to eat. Therefore, R. Simeon argues, it should be permitted to use second tithe to purchase *terumah*, which can at least be eaten by priests.

piggul: Refers to a sacrifice offered with the wrong intent (see Leviticus 7:18; Zevahim 2:3, 5).

remnant: Sacrificial meat left over beyond the time when it can be eaten (Leviticus 7:17).

impure: See Leviticus 7:19.

because they are permitted to nonpriests: The well-being offering can be eaten by anyone; although it might become prohibited for anyone to eat, it also might not become prohibited. In contrast, *terumah* is always prohibited to nonpriests, so there is a definite reduction in who can eat it.

3:3–6 *Second-Tithe Money and Produce in Jerusalem*

3 One who has [second-tithe] coins in Jerusalem,
and needs them [to purchase something that cannot be purchased
with second-tithe money],
and his fellow has [nonsacral] produce,
may say to his fellow:
"Let these coins be desacralized for your produce."
It turns out that this one [must] eat his produce in purity,
and the other may do what he needs with his money.
But he may not say thus to an *am ha'arets*,
except when [the money was] from [second tithe of] *demai*.

4 If [one had nonsacral] produce in Jerusalem
and [second-tithe coins] in the provinces,
he may say:
"Let those coins be desacralized for this produce."
If [he had second-tithe] coins in Jerusalem
and [nonsacral] produce in the provinces,
he may say:
"Let these coins be desacralized for that produce,"
provided that the produce ascend to Jerusalem and be eaten there.

5 [Second-tithe] coins may enter Jerusalem and go out again;
[second-tithe] produce may enter, but not go out again.
Rabban Simeon b. Gamaliel says:
Produce too may enter and go out.

3:3 *needs them*, etc.: See 1:7–2:1.

"Let these coins be desacralized for your produce": In this case the owner of the produce did not want to sell the produce and the purchaser did not want to buy it. There has been only a fictional transaction—only the sanctity has been transferred.

am ha'arets: Someone considered not scrupulous about observing the laws of purity and tithing. See *Demai* esp. 2:2–3.

except when [the money was] from [second tithe of] demai: However, if the second tithe came from the purchase of *demai*, produce which was itself bought from an *am ha'arets*, then he can make this fictional exchange even with a different *am ha'arets*. See 3:6 and *Demai* 1:2.

3:4 *provinces*: Anywhere outside Jerusalem. (This term is more commonly contrasted with the Temple itself; see e.g. *Sukkah* 3:12, *Rosh Hashanah* 4:1, 3.)

"Let those coins be desacralized for this produce": Even though the produce and the money are not in the same place, he can buy the produce with this second-tithe money.

If [he had second-tithe] coins in Jerusalem: And, as in 3:3, he wishes to use the money to purchase something besides food.

provided that the produce ascend to Jerusalem and be eaten there: He cannot subsequently desacralize that produce for other coins (see 3:10 and *Demai* 1:2).

6 Produce whose processing was completed and passed through Jerusalem—
its second tithe must be brought back and eaten in Jerusalem.
[Produce] whose processing had not been completed [that passed through Jerusalem],
[such as] baskets of grapes [en route] to the winepress,
or baskets of figs [en route] to the drying place—
the House of Shammai say:
Its second tithe must be brought back and be eaten in Jerusalem,
but the House of Hillel say:
It may be redeemed and eaten anywhere.
R. Simeon b. Judah says in the name of R. Yose:[9]
The House of Shammai and the House of Hillel did not disagree
concerning produce whose processing had not been completed,
that its second tithe may be redeemed and be eaten anywhere.
On what did they disagree?
About produce whose processing was completed,
for the House of Shammai say:
Its second tithe must be brought back and eaten in Jerusalem,
but the House of Hillel say:
It may be redeemed and eaten anywhere.
But the [second tithe of] *demai* may [always] enter and go out again and be redeemed.

3:7–9 Inside and Outside Jerusalem

7 A tree which stands within [Jerusalem] and bends outward,
or which stands outside [Jerusalem] and bends inward—
what is opposite the wall and inwards is deemed as being within [Jerusalem],
and what is opposite the wall and outwards is deemed as being outside.
Olive presses whose entrances are within [Jerusalem] and whose cavity is outside,
or whose entrances are outside [Jerusalem] and whose cavity is within—

[9] **K** has "Simeon" in place of "Yose."

3:6 *Produce whose processing was completed and passed through Jerusalem*: Produce becomes liable for tithes once its processing has been completed (*Ma'aserot* 1:5). If its processing has been completed, its tithes are in a sense already in it, they just have not yet been separated. Therefore, once such produce enters Jerusalem, it cannot be brought out.

The House of Shammai and the House of Hillel did not disagree concerning produce whose processing: In this version of the dispute both sides are more lenient than in the previous version and agree that if the processing of the produce had not yet been completed, the second tithe can be redeemed and eaten in any place.

On what did they disagree? About produce whose processing was completed: The House of Hillel hold only actual second-tithe produce cannot be taken out of Jerusalem; produce whose second tithe had not yet been removed can be taken out of Jerusalem. The House of Shammai hold that once its processing has been completed, the tithe is already present in the produce.

the [second tithe of] demai: Since the tithes may have been separated, it might not have been necessary to take out the second tithe at all. Therefore, the law can be lenient. See *Demai* 1:2.

3:7 Compare *Ma'aserot* 3:10.

the House of Shammai say:
The whole is deemed as being within,
but the House of Hillel say:
What is opposite the wall and inwards is deemed as being within,
and what is opposite the wall and outwards is deemed as being outside.

8 The chambers [of the Temple] which were built in the sacred precincts
but were open towards the nonsacred—
their interior is nonsacred but their roofs are sacred.
Those which were built in nonsacred precincts
but were open towards the sacred—
their interior is sacred but their roofs are nonsacred.
Those which were built in precincts that were both sacred and nonsacred,
and were open towards both the sacred and the nonsacred—
their interior and their roofs that were opposite the sacred and inward[10] are sacred,
[but their interior and roofs] that were opposite the nonsacred and outward[11] are nonsacred.

9 Second tithe which entered Jerusalem and became impure,
whether it became impure through [contact with] a primary [source of] impurity
or through [contact with] a reduced-degree [source of] impurity,
whether it became impure within [Jerusalem] or outside [of Jerusalem]—
the House of Shammai say:
It must all be redeemed and eaten within [Jerusalem],
except that which became impure through [contact with] a primary [source of] impurity outside [of Jerusalem],
but the House of Hillel say:
It must all be redeemed and may be eaten outside [Jerusalem],
except that which became impure through [contact with] a reduced-degree [source of] impurity within [Jerusalem].

[10] Lit. "towards the sacred."   [11] Lit. "towards the nonsacred."

3:8 *their interior is nonsacred but their roofs are sacred*: The interior part is judged according to its opening and is considered to be nonsacred. Sacrifices that are most holy may not be eaten there; sacrifices that are of lesser holiness may not be slaughtered there. One who enters there while impure is not liable. The roofs are holy for they lie in holy ground.

3:9 *a primary [source of] impurity*: Such as vermin or carrion (see *Kelim* 1:1).

a reduced-degree [source of] impurity: Something which was itself defiled by contact with a primary source of defilement.

except that which became impure through [contact with] a primary [source of] impurity outside: This produce was defiled in a serious manner even before it came into Jerusalem; therefore, having been brought in to the city, it may be removed. But produce rendered impure to a reduced degree must be redeemed and, like pure second tithe, be consumed in Jerusalem.

except that which became impure through [contact with] a reduced-degree [source of] impurity within: This produce was pure when it was brought into Jerusalem and only contracted a reduced-degree of impurity. Therefore, like pure tithe it must be eaten in Jerusalem. However, if second tithe becomes impure before coming into Jerusalem, or if it contracts serious impurity within Jerusalem, it can be brought out of Jerusalem and eaten there.

3:10–11   Food Purchased with Second-Tithe Money

10   If that which is bought with second-tithe money becomes impure,
it must be redeemed.
R. Judah says:
It must be buried.
They said to R. Judah:
If second tithe itself, when it becomes impure, is to be redeemed,
does not logic require that that which is bought with second-tithe money
and becomes impure,
is also to be redeemed?
He said to them:
No!
If you say this of second tithe itself, it is because it may be redeemed
even when pure,
at a distance from the [holy] place,
shall you say this of that which is bought with second-tithe money,
which cannot be redeemed when pure at a distance from the [holy] place?

11   A deer which one bought with [second-]tithe money [which then] died
must be buried together with its hide.
R. Simeon says:
It may be redeemed.
If one bought it alive and slaughtered it and it then became impure,
it may be redeemed.
R. Yose says:
It must be buried.
If one bought it slaughtered and it became impure,
in that case it is like produce.

3:10 *it must be redeemed*: The money will be treated as second-tithe money and used to buy produce to be eaten as second tithe in Jerusalem.

If second tithe itself, when it becomes impure, is to be redeemed: As stated in 3:9.

it is because it may be redeemed: Deuteronomy 14:24–25.

which cannot be redeemed when pure at a distance from the [holy] place: But must be brought to Jerusalem and eaten there; see 3:4.

3:11 *must be buried together with its hide*: Since the deer died without being properly slaughtered, it cannot be eaten. In addition, its hide must be buried, because it is imbued with second-tithe sanctity that was not redeemed through proper slaughter (cf. 1:3); cf. *Temurah* 7:3.

It may be redeemed: See 3:9.

If one bought it alive and slaughtered it and it then became impure, it may be redeemed: As is the rule with other produce that was bought with second-tithe money and then became impure; see 3:10.

It must be buried: R. Yose treats it as if it died and was not properly slaughtered.

in that case it is like produce: And even R. Yose would agree that it can be redeemed.

3:12–13 *Containers of Second-Tithe Wine*

12 [A wine seller] who lends containers[12] for second-tithe [wine],
even if he sealed them,
they do not acquire [the sanctity of second] tithe.
If he poured [second-tithe] wine into them without specifying
[that the wine was for sale]—
[if he specifies] before he sealed them,
they do not acquire [the sanctity of second] tithe;
[if he specifies] after he sealed them,
they acquire [the sanctity of] second tithe.
Before he sealed them they are neutralized in one and a hundred;
after he sealed them,
they consecrate any quantity.
Before he sealed them, he may separate *terumah* from one for all the others;
after he sealed them, he must separate *terumah* from each and every one.

13 [If a wine seller sealed his containers and does wants them to acquire second-tithe sanctity,]
the House of Shammai say:
He must open [the containers] and empty them into the winepress,
but the House of Hillel say:
He must open them but need not empty them.
When does this apply?
In a place where they are usually sold closed;

---

[12] K, P, and many manuscripts: "his containers."

3:12 *they do not acquire [the sanctity of second] tithe*: Since only the wine was sold; the jars were merely lent. Cf. 1:3–4.

[if he specifies] after he sealed them, they acquire [the sanctity of] second tithe: Because we assume he meant to sell the jars with the wine, and the jars are secondary to the wine. He will now have to sell the jars in Jerusalem, and then use the proceeds to buy food and eat it there.

neutralized in one and a hundred: This part of the mishnah deals with *terumah*, not second tithe, which is not subject to nullification by ratio (see *Bikkurim* 2:1). Before he corked them, they are neutralized in a ratio of one hundred to one: If one hundred jars of nonsacred wine become mixed up with one jar of *terumah* wine, all of the jars can be considered nonsacral, but one jar needs to be given to a priest as *terumah* (*Orlah* 2:1). But if there are fewer than one hundred nonsacred jars of wine, they must all be considered *terumah*. See *Terumot* 4:7 and 5:1.

they consecrate: They render prohibited *any quantity*: Items sold by quantity cannot be neutralized in any amount (see *Orlah* 3:7).

he may separate terumah from one for all the others: Before being corked, the wine is treated as if it still in one vat. Therefore, *terumah* can be taken from one jar to exempt the wine found in other jars.

3:13 This is a continuation of 3:12.

He must open [the containers] and empty them into the winepress: After having corked the jars, the seller changes his mind and decides not to sell the jars but rather to lend them, or now wants to separate *terumah* from one jar on behalf of them all. According to the House of Shammai, he needs to open the jars and pour the wine back into the winepress. After this step, he can put the wine back into the jar and then sell the wine and not the jars and give *terumah* for one on behalf of them all.

but in a place where they are usually sold open,
the container does not go out to nonsacral status.
But if he wishes to be stringent upon himself to sell [only] by measure,
the container goes out to nonsacral status.
R. Simeon says:
Even if one says to his fellow:
"I am selling [the wine in] this jar to you, but not its container,"[13]
the container goes out to nonsacral status.

Chapter Four

4:1–8   *Redeeming Second-Tithe Produce*

4 If one transports produce of second tithe
from a place where it is expensive to a place where it is cheap,
or from a place where it is cheap to a place where it is expensive,
he redeems it according to the market price of his place.
One who brings produce from the threshing floor into the city,
or jars of wine from the winepress into the city,
the increase [in the price is allotted] to second tithe
and [he must cover] the expenses on his own.[14]

2 One may redeem second tithe at the lower market price:
at the price at which the shopkeeper buys and not at which he sells;
at the price at which the moneychanger takes small change

---

[13] Lit. "except for the containers." **K, P**, and many manuscripts: "except for its container."
[14] Lit. "from his household."

---

in a place where they are usually sold closed: The leniency of the House of Hillel applies only if jars of wine are normally sold closed in that place. See 1:3–4.

if he wishes to be stringent upon himself and to sell [only] by measure: If the seller opens the jar and decides to sell it by measure, then the jar won't be sold with the wine and the jar will become nonsacral.

R. Simeon says: The seller does not even need to uncork the jar; as long as he specifically says to the buyer that he is selling just the wine, then the buyer can use the jar and give it back to him when he is done with it.

4:1 *into the city*: Where the produce and the wine can be sold for a higher price.

the increase [in the price is allotted] to second tithe: He will have to redeem the second tithe at the higher price; see 2:1.

and [he must cover] the expenses on his own: He may not deduct the transportation costs from the value of the produce he is redeeming.

4:2 *the price at which the shopkeeer buys*: The wholesale rate.

the moneychanger takes small change…gives small change: The value of small coins to a moneychanger depends on whether he is giving them (they are worth more) or purchasing them (worth less). When a

and not at the price at which he gives small change.
One may not redeem second tithe in an estimated lump.
If its value is known,
it may be redeemed according to [an evaluation made by] one.[15]
But if its value is not known,
it must be redeemed according to [an evaluation made by] three,
as for instance [in the case of] wine which has formed a film,[16]
or produce which has rotted,
or coins which have rusted.

3   If the owner says: "[I will redeem this second tithe] for a *sela*,"
and another person says: "[I will redeem this second tithe] for a *sela*,"
the owner has the first right, because he must add a fifth.
If the owner says: "[I will redeem this second tithe] for a *sela*,"
and another person says: "[I will redeem this second tithe] for a *sela* and an *issar*,"
the one who offered a *sela* and an *issar* has the first right,
because he adds to the principal.
One who redeems his second tithe must add a fifth,
whether it is his own or whether it was given to him as a gift.

4   One may act in a deceptive manner with [redemption of] second tithe.
How?
A person may say to his adult son or daughter,
or to his Hebrew male or female slave,
"Take these coins and redeem this second tithe for yourself."

[15] Corrected according to **K, P**. Standard printed editions: "a single witness," a mistake.
[16] **K, P**, and most manuscripts: "which has just begun to ferment."

person wishes to exchange small second-tithe coins for a large one (as in 2:8), he can estimate the value of the larger coin at the higher rate, so that it counts for more small coins.

One may not redeem second tithe in an estimated lump: When redeeming second-tithe produce, he must either count it (e.g. ten jars of wine) or measure it (e.g. two *se'ah* of wheat).

If its value is known: Normal produce would have a typical market value and therefore its value can be estimated by an individual.

But if its value is not known: The evaluation of produce or coins that are beginning to deteriorate requires three people (see also *Sanhedrin* 1:3), because its value cannot be easily determined.

4:3 *the owner has the first right, because he must add a fifth*: The owner has to add an extra fifth (Leviticus 27:31), but the other person does not (see also *Bava Metsi'a* 4:8; *Arakhin* 8:2).

an issar: A coin worth 1⁄96 of a *sela*.

because he adds to the principal: The other person's evaluation is accepted, even though the total amount of money is less than it would be if the owner redeemed it and added the extra fifth.

4:4 *One may act in a deceptive manner*: In order to avoid paying the added fifth.

adult son or daughter, or to his Hebrew male or female slave: These people can acquire property independent of the father/master (see also *Eruvin* 7:6).

and redeem this second tithe for yourself: Since he says "for yourself," he is giving the coins as a gift to his offspring or Hebrew slave, and even if they return them to the father/master they, not he, are considered the redeemers.

But he may not say so to his minor son or daughter,
or to his Canaanite male or female slave,
because their hand is as his own hand.

5 If one was standing at the threshing floor and did not have any coins,
he may say to his fellow:
"This produce is hereby given to you as a gift,"
and then he may say again: "Let this [produce] hereby be desacralized
for the coins that are in [my] house."

6 If one took possession[17] of [second-]tithe [produce worth] a *sela*
from the owner,
but before he had time to redeem it
it stood at a price of two *sela*,
[the purchaser] may give [the original owner] one *sela*
and make a profit of one *sela*,
and the second tithe remains [the purchaser's].[18]
If one took possession of [second-]tithe [produce worth] two [*sela*]
from the owner,
but before [the purchaser] had time to redeem it
it stood at the price of one *sela*,
the [purchaser] may give [the original owner] one *sela* out of nonsacral [money]

[17] Lit. "pulled," here and below.   [18] K has "[and] a *sela* of second tithe is his."

because their hand is as his own hand: Any property that a minor or non-Jewish slave (called a Canaanite slave) acquires automatically becomes the property of the father/master (see also *Eruvin* 7:6). Therefore, even if he gives them money to redeem second tithe, it is as if he is redeeming it himself, and he still needs to add the extra fifth.

4:5 *and did not have any coins*: If he had coins he could simply give them to his fellow and have his fellow redeem the produce on his behalf and thereby not have to add the fifth.

"This produce is hereby given to you as a gift": The produce now legally belongs to his fellow, even if he intends to give it back.

"Let this produce hereby be desacralized for the coins that are in [my] house": Now that the second-tithe produce belongs to his fellow, the original owner can redeem it by using coins that he has in his house, without adding the extra fifth. Had he simply redeemed them without first giving them to his fellow, he would have had to add the extra fifth.

4:6 *If one took possession of [second-]tithe [produce worth] a sela*: He bought second-tithe produce with the intention that the seller would use the money he would eventually give him to redeem the produce (thus avoiding having to pay the extra fifth), which is currently worth one *sela*.

before he had time to redeem it: Before the purchaser actually paid the seller the *sela* for the latter to redeem it.

[the purchaer] may give [the original owner] one sela and make a profit of one sela and the second tithe remains [the purchaser's]: The purchaser gives the promised *sela* to the seller, who desacralizes the produce for it. The extra *sela* of the appreciated produce is retained by the buyer and must be treated as second tithe, either by bringing it to Jerusalem or redeeming it (paying the extra fifth) and spending that money in Jerusalem.

[the purchaser] may give [the original owner] one sela out of nonsacral [money] and one sela of his second-tithe money: The buyer owes the seller two *sela*, but the produce now only needs to be redeemed for its current, cheaper price of one *sela* (see 4:1–2). He may, therefore, pay the second *sela* with his own second-tithe money, which the seller will then have to bring to Jerusalem.

and one *sela* of his second-tithe money.
If [the original owner] was an *am ha'arets*,
[the purchaser] must give him from [second tithe of] *demai*.[19]

7 One who redeems second tithe but did not designate it [verbally]—
R. Yose says:
It is sufficient.
But R. Judah says:
He must be explicit.
If one was speaking with a woman concerning her divorce or her betrothal,
and gave her a bill of divorce or betrothal money
but was not explicit [about what he was doing]—
R. Yose says:
It is sufficient.
But R. Judah says:
He must be explicit.

8 One who sets aside an *issar* [for the redemption of second tithe]
and on its basis ate half [of an *issar*'s worth of second tithe],
and then went to another place where [an *issar*] was worth a *pondion*,
may eat another *issar*['s worth of second tithe].
One who sets aside a *pondion* [for the redemption of second tithe]

---

[19] K, P, and most manuscripts: "his *demai*."

---

if [the original owner] was an am ha'arets: It is prohibited to give second-tithe money to an *am ha'arets* because he might not take it to Jerusalem or maintain the necessary purity (see 3:3). In the case of devalued produce, therefore, the buyer may only give him second-tithe money whose source was *demai* (see *Demai* 1:2).

4:7 *but did not designate it*: He did not state, "This is in redemption of second tithe."

but was not explicit: He didn't state, "Behold this is your divorce document" or "Behold you are betrothed to me."

4:8 *One who sets aside*: As redemption money for second-tithe produce that he will eat in the future.

an issar: 1/24 of a *dinar*.

and on its basis ate half [of an issar's worth of second tithe]: Having only transferred the sanctity of half an *issar*'s worth of second-tithe produce; the remaining half of the *issar*, however, was still not second-tithe money.

a pondion: Worth two *issar*.

may eat another issar['s worth of second tithe]: The *issar* doubled in value, so the half that was left unredeemed was now worth a full *issar* in the old terms. Therefore, he can redeem another *issar*'s worth of second-tithe produce before the coin becomes fully imbued with second-tithe sanctity.

may eat another half [an issar's worth of second tithe]: Since the *pondion* lost half its value, he can now only redeem another half of an *issar*'s worth of second-tithe produce.

One who sets aside an issar of second tithe, may eat on its basis eleven parts of the value of an issar: This is a very difficult section whose interpretation is much debated by the commentators. The following is Albeck's explanation. The mishnah refers to a person who is in Jerusalem and eating produce as second tithe based on a coin that he has at home. As he eats the produce, the coin will be redeemed and will revert to being nonsacred. The custom in their time was to buy food at one-tenth of an *issar* or one-hundredth of an *issar*. Since the price of an *issar* would rise and fall (as noted above), he would need to eat eleven parts of an *issar*

and on its basis ate half [a *pondion*'s worth of second tithe],
and then went to another place where [a *pondion*] was worth an *issar*,
may eat another half [an *issar*'s worth of second tithe].
One who sets aside an *issar* of second tithe,
may eat on its basis eleven parts of the value of an *issar*,
or [an additional] one-hundredth of an *issar*.
The House of Shammai say:
In all cases one-tenth part [of an *issar*],
but the House of Hillel say:
In the case of certain [second tithe] an eleventh part,
but in the case of *demai* a tenth part.

4:9–12 *Coins and Produce Which Might Be Second Tithe*

9 All found coins are [presumed to be] nonsacral,
even a gold *dinar* [found] with silver [*dinar*] and with copper coins.
If amidst the coins one found a potsherd
on which was written "tithe"—
this [collection of found coins] is [presumed to be second] tithe.

10 One who finds a vessel on which was written *qorban*—
R. Judah says:
If [the vessel] was [made] of clay, it is [presumed to be] nonsacral,
but what is in it is *qorban*.
But if [the vessel] was [made] of metal, it is [presumed to be] *qorban*,
but what is in it is nonsacral.

---

and not ten parts, and only then would the *issar* become nonsacred. Alternatively, if people were buying produce in one-hundredth increments, then he should eat 101 parts of the produce before the *issar* would be completely desacralized. This is a stringency—he needs to buy more produce than the coin may actually be worth.

in all cases one-tenth part [of an issar]: The House of Shammai disagree with the above rule. He does not need to eat the extra eleventh part.

In the case of certain [second tithe] an eleventh part, but in the case of demai a tenth part: If the coin was used to redeem produce that was certain second tithe, he needs to eat the eleventh part, as taught above. But if the produce was used to redeem *demai*, produce that may already have been tithed, all he needs to eat is the first ten parts, the actual value.

4:9 *All found coins*: Even those found in Jerusalem. See *Sheqalim* 7:2.

even a gold dinar [found] with silver [dinar] and with copper coins: Even though these coins are not commonly put together, the finder need not be concerned that a person had gathered together his second-tithe money.

4:10 *qorban*: The Hebrew word for "sacrifice" which by extension means "sacred" or "property of the Temple." See Gospel of Mark 7:6 and *Nedarim* 3:5.

clay: People did not generally dedicate cheap clay vessels to the Temple. Therefore, the clay vessel itself is presumed to be nonsacred, and the word *qorban* is presumed to refer only to the contents of the vessel.

metal: The word *qorban* is assumed to refer the status of the vessel, not its contents.

The [Sages] said to him:
People are not accustomed to gather nonsacral things into a *qorban* [vessel].

11 One who finds a vessel on which was written:
a *qof*, it is *qorban*;
a *mem*, it is *ma'aser*;
a *dalet*, it is *demai*;
a *tet*, it is *tevel*;
a *tav*, it is *terumah*.
For in the time of danger people would write a *tav* instead of *terumah*.
R. Yose says:
All these [letters may] stand for the names of people.
R. Yose said:
Even if one finds a jar which is full of produce and on it is written *terumah*,
[the produce] is considered nonsacral,
because I say: Last year it was [used for] *terumah* [produce]
but [its owner] emptied it.

12 One who says to his son:
"There is second-tithe [produce] in this corner,"
but the son found [produce] in another corner,
[the found produce] is [presumed to be] nonsacral.
[If the father said:] "There were[20] there one hundred [*dinar* of second tithe],"
but the son found two hundred,
the remainder[21] are nonsacral.
[If the father said: "There are there] two hundred,"
but the son found one hundred,
it is all [second] tithe.

[20] K, P, and most manuscripts have "There is."
[21] K, P have "one hundred [*dinar*] are [second] tithe and the remainder."

People are not accustomed to gather nonsacral things into a qorban [vessel]: Therefore, if the vessel is assumed to be sacred, anything found within it must also be treated as such.

4:11 *For in the time of danger people would write a tav instead of terumah*: During times of persecution for observance of the commandments, people would write only the first letter of the substance found in the vessel to conceal their observance from the persecuting authorities. Hence, if one finds a vessel with one of these letters on it, one should presume that the contents are that type of produce.

All these [letters may] stand for the names of people: And therefore the finder need not be concerned that the produce within might fall into these categories.

4:12 *is [presumed to be] nonsacral*: He can assume that the second-tithe produce was removed and that which he finds is something else.

the remainder are nonsacral: He does not need to assume that the father made a mistake and that all two hundred *dinar* are really second tithe.

it is all [second] tithe: He must assume one hundred *dinar* were removed, and that the remainder is second tithe, not that the father was mistaken or that the produce was removed, as in the first clause.

Chapter Five

5:1–5 *The Laws of the Fourth-Year Vineyard*

5 A fourth-year vineyard—
one marks it with clods of earth;
orlah—[one marks it] with potter's clay;
graves—[one marks them] with lime, which he dissolves and pours on.
Rabban Simeon b. Gamaliel said:
When does this apply? In the Seventh Year.
But the more punctilious would [also] put down coins and say:
"[Let] any [fruit] gathered from here
be desacralized for these coins."

2 [The produce of] a fourth-year vineyard used to be brought up[22] to Jerusalem
[if it grew] within a one day's journey in any direction.
And what is the border [of a day's journey on each side]?
Eilat to the south,
Aqrabat on the north,
Lod to the west,

---

[22] Lit. "used to go up." **K**, **P**, and most manuscripts lack "used to," implying "must."

5:1 *A fourth-year vineyard*: See Leviticus 19:24. According to rabbinic interpretation, the wine of such grapes has the same status as second tithe.

one marks it with clods of earth: In order to let people know that its fruit is sanctified for redemption or consumption in Jerusalem.

orlah: Trees during the first three years of growth (see Leviticus 19:23 and *Orlah*), whose fruit may not be consumed.

graves were marked with lime (Gospel of Matthew 23:27) so that priests and *nezirim*, who are prohibited from contact with death impurity (Leviticus 21:1; Numbers 6:6), will know their location.

In the Seventh Year: Seventh-Year produce is considered ownerless (*Pe'ah* 6:1); anyone can enter a field and eat from the trees or vineyard. To let people know that this produce was prohibited during its first four years of growth they would mark it off. During other years of the Sabbatical cycle they need not mark off forbidden trees, perhaps because taking the fruit would be considered theft, and, according to Rabban Shimon b. Gamliel here, people are not commanded to prevent sinners from transgressing.

the more punctilious: Who wished to not only perform all of the commandments, but would even spend their own money to prevent others from unwittingly transgressing (see *Demai* 6:6).

"[Let] any [fruit] gathered from here be desacralized for these coins": Thus the sanctity of any fruit taken by passersby would automatically transfer to the money, allowing consumption of the fruit and requiring the owner to take those coins to spend in Jerusalem.

5:2 *used to be brought up to Jerusalem*: Within a day's walk on each side of Jerusalem, produce from fourth-year vineyards and orchards could not redeemed.

Eilat: Perhaps near Hebron. Probably not the city of that name in the very south on the Red Sea.

Aqrabat: Located near Shechem.

and the Jordan [river] to the east.
When produce increased, [the Sages] decreed that it could be redeemed
[even if the vineyard was] close to the wall.
And there was a stipulation on this matter:
that whenever they so desired,
the practice would be restored as it had been before.
R. Yose says:
The stipulation [was instituted] after the Temple was destroyed,
and the stipulation was that whenever the Temple would be rebuilt,
the practice would be restored as it had been before.

3   A fourth-year vineyard—
the House of Shammai say:
The added fifth and Removal do not apply,
but the House of Hillel say:
They do.
The House of Shammai say:
Separated Grapes and Defective Clusters apply to them,
and the poor must redeem the grapes for themselves,
but the House of Hillel say:
All of it [must go] to the winepress.

When produce increased: When produce was scarce, to encourage people to bring their produce to Jerusalem, people who lived within a day's walk were not allowed to redeem it. Once produce became more plentiful, the law was changed to allow people to redeem the produce even if their vineyard or orchard was just outside the walls of Jerusalem.

And there was a stipulation on this matter: When they allowed people close to the wall to redeem their produce, they specifically stipulated that any subsequent court could change this arrangement.

The stipulation [was instituted] after the Temple was destroyed: According to R. Yose when the Temple was destroyed the law was changed to allow one to redeem produce even right outside the walls of Jerusalem. At that time, they made a stipulation that when the Temple was rebuilt, it would again be forbidden to redeem fourth-year produce (and by extension, second tithe) within one day's journey from Jerusalem.

5:3   Parallel to *Pe'ah* 7:6 and *Eduyot* 4:5.

The added fifth: Leviticus 27:31 mandates adding a fifth to the redemption of tithes (see 4:3), and according to the House of Hillel, fourth-year fruit by extension (5:5; *Bava Metsi'a* 4:8).

Removal: Deuteronomy 14:28 mandates the removal of tithes from one's household every three years.

Separated Grapes: See Leviticus 19:10 and *Pe'ah* 7:3.

Defective Clusters: Leviticus 19:10, Deuteronomy 24:21, and *Pe'ah* 7:4. The House of Shammai hold that the produce of a fourth-year vineyard only shares with second tithe the requirement to be brought to Jerusalem or redeemed, and is otherwise like nonsacral produce and thus liable to the laws of Separated Grapes and Defective Clusters.

All of it [must go] to the winepress: Fourth-year produce is treated completely like second tithe. As they would with second tithe, the owners press the grapes into wine and bring the wine to Jerusalem.

4 How does one redeem fourth-year fruit?
[The owner] puts down the basket [of fruit] in the presence of three [people] and says:
"How many [such baskets] would a person wish to purchase[23] for himself for a *sela*
on condition that the expenses [to produce the fruit] shall be borne by him?"[24]
He then puts down the coins and says:
"Whatever shall be picked from this [tree] is desacralized for these coins at the price of so many baskets for a *sela*."
5 But in the Seventh Year he must redeem it for its full value.
If [in other years] it had all been made ownerless property,
the person [who redeems it] can only claim the cost of picking it.
One who redeems his own fourth-year fruit
must add a fifth of its value,
whether [the fruit] was his own or was given him as a gift.

5:6–9: *The Removal of Tithes*

6 On the eve of the first day of Passover,
in the fourth and in the seventh [years of the Sabbatical cycle],
the Removal was [performed].
How was the Removal [performed]?
One would give *terumah* and *terumah* from the tithe to their owners,
first tithe to its owners,

[23] Lit. "redeem."   [24] Lit. "from his household."

5:4 *fourth-year fruit*: Although the Mishnah has been specifically discussing the fourth-year produce of a vineyard, everything said heretofore applies to tree fruits as well (which is not surprising since Leviticus 19:23 specifically speaks of trees).

of three [people]: Three are needed to estimate the costs of growing the produce. Determining market price would not require three. See above 4:2.

"How many [such baskets]": They estimate how many baskets of this fruit could be bought with a *sela*, assuming that the purchaser would pay the costs of growing the fruit. In other words, the estimate is of the profit margin not the market value.

5:5 *But in the Seventh Year he must redeem it for its full value*: Since it is forbidden to work the land during the Seventh Year (see *Shevi'it*), when redeeming it there are no costs to deduct from the value of the produce. It must, therefore, be redeemed for full market value.

If [in other years] it had all been made ownerless property: If one declares his field to be ownerless, and then someone comes and picks fourth-year fruit, the one who redeems it can deduct from the market price only the costs involved in picking it but not those involved in growing the produce, for he did not pay these costs.

One who redeems his own fourth-year fruit: This follows the opinion of the House of Hillel in 5:3; see also 4:3.

5:6 *On the eve of the first day of Passover*: This is the reading found in most manuscripts. Other textual witnesses read "the last festival-day of Passover." See 5:10.

Removal: Deuteronomy 14:28; 26:12–15.

terumah and terumah from the tithe: By this point, each agricultural gift must be given to its rightful owner. *Terumah* and *terumah* from the tithe are given to the priests, first tithe is given to the Levites, and poor tithe is given to the poor. Second tithe and firstfruits are special cases because they should have been brought to

the poor tithe to its owners,
and second tithe and firstfruits were removed in every place.
R. Simeon says:
Firstfruits are given to priests like *terumah*.
A cooked dish [with second tithe in it]—
the House of Shammai say:
One must remove it,
but the House of Hillel say:
It is to be considered as already removed.

7 One who has produce [of second tithe] at this time,
and the moment of Removal has arrived—
the House of Shammai say:
One must desacralize it for money,
but the House of Hillel say:
It is all one and the same whether it becomes money or it remains fruit.[25]

8 R. Judah said:
In early times[26] they used to send messengers to householders in the provinces [saying]:
"Hasten to set right your produce before the time of Removal arrives,"
until R. Aqiva came and taught:
All produce which has not reached its time for tithing is exempt from Removal.

[25] Lit. "whether it is money or it is fruit."   [26] Lit. "at first."

Jerusalem and eaten there by this point; there is no one to give them to. Therefore, they must be brought outside and left to rot.

Firstfruits are given to priests like terumah: Deuteronomy 26:4; *Bikkurim* 2:1, 3:12. Since firstfruits are given to the priest, they do not need to be destroyed.

It is to be considered as already removed: Since the second tithe can no longer be seen within the dish, it need not be removed.

5:7 *at this time*: After the destruction of the Second Temple.

One must desacralize it for money: The second tithe must be redeemed and the money set aside.

It is all one and the same: Since the second-tithe produce cannot be brought to Jerusalem, it must be removed at the end of the third and sixth year. Since neither the money nor the produce can be used, the latter need not be redeemed, but should be left to rot; see 1:5.

5:8 *"Hasten to set right your produce before the time of Removal arrives"*: In earlier times (i.e. before R. Aqiva) during the fourth year of the Sabbatical cycle when tithes would be removed (5:6), authorities sent reminders throughout the land to separate *terumah* and tithes from the current year's produce before the time of Removal. Failure to separate tithes for that year's crop would prevent the recital of the confession over tithes (Deuteronomy 26:12–15), since one would not have "cleared out the holy from the house" (5:10).

exempt from Removal: See *Ma'aserot* 1:2–4. The innovation of R. Aqiva was that before this moment, the law of Removal does not apply, and therefore anything untithed at that stage does not prevent reciting the confession.

9 One whose produce was far away from him [at the moment of Removal] must designate them.
It once happened that Rabban Gamaliel and the elders were traveling by ship.
Rabban Gamaliel said:
The tithe which I shall measure out in the future is given to Joshua,
and its place is leased to him.
The other tithe which I shall measure out in the future is given to Aqiva b. Joseph
that he may hold it for the poor,
and its place is leased to him.
R. Joshua said:
The tithe which I shall measure out in the future is given to Eleazar b. Azariah,
and its place is leased to him.
And they each received rent one from another.

5:10–15 *The Confession Over Tithes*

10 In the afternoon of the last[27] festival day [of Passover] they would recite the confession.
How was the confession made?
I have removed the holy from the house—
this refers to second tithe and fourth-year fruit.
I have given it to the Levite—

---

[27] Missing in **K**, **P**, and the vast majority of manuscripts.

5:9 *must designate them*: Verbal designation and assignment of tithes to priests and Levites from afar suffices even in the absence of physically distributing them to their recipients.

The tithe: First tithe.

Joshua: R. Joshua b. Hananiah, a Levite.

and its place is leased to him: In this way, R. Joshua can acquire the tithes without being physically present.

The other tithe: The poor tithe.

Aqiva b. Joseph: Apparently, R. Aqiva was a charity collector.

R. Joshua...tithe: This refers to *terumah* from the tithe, which is given by the Levites to the priests. (Eleazar b. Azariah is a priest.) Leviticus 18:26 refers to it as "tithe from the tithe," which it explains its unique designation here as "tithe."

And they each received rent one from another: Rabban Gamaliel received rent from R. Joshua and R. Aqiva, and R. Joshua received rent from R. Eleazar b. Azariah to complete the transactions.

5:10 *last festival day*: The vast majority of manuscripts omit this word, according to which the confessional would take place in the afternoon of the first day of Passover (see 5:6).

How was the confession made?: The actual confession consisted simply of the recitation of the verses from Deuteronomy 26:13–15.

second tithe: Called "holy" in Leviticus 27:30.

fourth-year fruit: This follows the House of Hillel from 5:3.

this refers to the tithe of the Levites.
And I have given it too—
this refers to *terumah* and[28] *terumah* from the tithe.
To the stranger, the orphan, and the widow—
this refers to the poor tithe, Gleanings, Forgotten Sheaves, and *pe'ah*,
even though these do not prevent [one from making] the confession.
Out of the house—
this refers to dough offering.

11 *According to all your commandments which you have commanded me—*
this implies that if [one set aside] second tithe before the first [tithe],
one cannot recite the confession.
I have not transgressed any of your commandments—
I have not set aside [tithes] from one species for another,
nor from plucked [produce] for [produce still] attached [to the ground],
nor from [produce still] attached [to the soil] for plucked [produce],
nor from new [produce] for old [produce],
nor from old [produce] for new [produce].
Neither have I forgotten—
I have not forgotten to bless you, or to mention your name over it.

12 *I have not eaten from it in my mourning—*
this implies that if he had eaten it in the state of being an *onen*,
he cannot recite the confession.
Neither have I removed any of it when impure—
this implies that if he had set it aside in [a state of] impurity,
he cannot make the confession.
And I have not given any of it to the dead—
I have not purchased with any of it a coffin or shrouds for the dead,
nor have I given any of it to other *onen*.

[28] K lacks "*terumah* and."

---

even though these do not prevent [one from making] the confession: Why this should be so is debated by the commentators.

dough offering: Which is separated from the dough in the house. See Ezekiel 44:30 and *Hallah*.

5:11 *According to all your commandments*: Deuteronomy 26:13.

second tithe before the first: See *Terumot* 3:6.

one species for another: *Terumot* 2:4.

nor from plucked... nor from old [produce] for new [produce]: *Terumot* 1:5.

Neither have I forgotten: When separating *terumah*, one must recite a blessing; see *Terumot* 1:6.

5:12 *I have not eaten from it in my mourning*: Deuteronomy 26:14.

in the state of being an onen: The period between the death of an immediate relative (Leviticus 21:2–3) and their burial (see *Berakhot* 3:1), usually lasting a short amount of time (*Berakhot* 2:6). During this period it is forbidden to eat any "holy things" which would include second-tithe and fourth-year produce.

I have listened to the voice of the Lord my God—
I have brought it to the Chosen House.
I have done everything you commanded me—
with it I have rejoiced and made others rejoice.

13 Look down from your holy abode, from heaven—
we have done what you have decreed upon us;
may you, too, do what you have promised us.
Look down from your holy abode, from heaven, and bless your people Israel—
with sons and daughters.
And the land which you have given us—
with dew and rain and with offspring of cattle.
As you swore to our fathers, a land flowing with milk and honey—
that you may bestow good flavor on the produce.

14 On the basis of this verse [the Sages] said:
Israelites and *mamzerim* may recite the confession,
but not proselytes or freed slaves,
since they have no share in the Land.
R. Meir says:
Also not priests or Levites,
since they did not take a share in the Land either.
R. Yose says:
They have the Levitical cities.[29]

15 Yohanan the High Priest did away with the confession of the tithes.

---

[29] Lit. "cities of pasture land."

---

the Chosen House: Refers to all of Jerusalem and not just the Temple (based on Deuteronomy 14:23). This part of the confession refers to second tithe.

I have rejoiced and made others rejoice: See Deuteronomy 14:26–27.

5:13 *Look down from your holy abode, from heaven*: Deuteronomy 26:15.

5:14 *this verse*: Deuteronomy 26:15, *and the land which you have given us*.

mamzerim: The child of either a *mamzer* parent, or the child of a forbidden sexual union (see *Hagigah* 1:7; *Yevamot* 4:12–13; *Qiddushin* 4:1). Although a *mamzer* suffers from legal and social impairment in connection with marriage, there is legal paternity between a *mamzer* and his biological father.

share in the Land: Only members of the twelve tribes received shares in the land when it was allocated by Joshua (Joshua 13:7ff). A *mamzer* has a share in the land through his biological father, but neither proselytes nor freed Canaanite slaves, who occupy a status akin to that of proselytes, who do not have Israelite fathers, have a share in the land.

priests or Levites…did not take a share in the Land: Numbers 18:20, 23–24.

Levitical cities: Numbers 35:1–8.

5:15 *Yohanan the High Priest*: Perhaps John Hyrcanus (reigned 134–104 BCE).

did away with the confession of the tithes: It is not clear whether this is meant as praise or criticism. Commentaries suggest two explanations. Perhaps in his day people stopped separating tithes, separating only *terumah*. Therefore, they could not make the tithes declaration. Or perhaps people were giving the tithes to the priests, and therefore they could no longer say, *And I have given of it to the Levite*.

He also abolished the "wakers" and the "knockers."
Until his days the hammer used to beat in Jerusalem.
And in his days one did not need to ask[30] about *demai*.

[30] Or "one was not obligated to ask."

the "wakers": Levites who were called "wakers" would recite Psalm 44 when the daily Tamid was offered. Yohanan abolished this practice because it gave the impression that God could sleep, or that God was asleep and not listening to their petitions. See Psalm 44:24.

the "knockers": Refers to the priests who would strike a calf about to be sacrificed. Yohanan abolished this practice lest the blow disqualify the act of slaughter which follows.

Until his days the hammer used to beat in Jerusalem: During the intermediate days of the festival (see *Mo'ed Qatan*), loud work used to be performed. Yohanan tried to prevent this out of respect for these days.

ask about demai: Doubtfully tithed produce (see *Demai*). The meaning of this clause is debated by the commentators. One explanation is that prior to Yohanan's enactment every produce seller had to be interrogated about the status of his produce, because the failure to separate any of the obligatory tithes rendered the produce unfit for consumption. In response Yohanan enacted that no interrogation was needed since the purchaser would separate, at minimum cost to himself, *terumah* from the tithe (about one percent of the produce) and second tithe (which he would consume in Jerusalem). The failure to separate first tithe or poor tithe did not render the produce unfit for consumption.

Tractate Hallah

Joshua Kulp

Introduction

Overview

Numbers 15:17–21 mandates the giving of a portion of one's bread/dough to "the Lord." In biblical Hebrew the word *hallah* meant "loaf" (cf. Leviticus 2:4); the Rabbis, however, understood the obligation to fall on the dough, hence the translation of *hallah* in rabbinic parlance as "dough offering." Many of the same rules that apply to *terumah* apply to *hallah*, most importantly that the dough offering be given to a priest.

A batch of dough is liable for the dough offering only if it is made of any of five grains (1:1), is intended to be consumed as human food (1:8), and consists of at least five quarters of a *qav* (2:6). The Rabbis established the minimum amount to be removed for dough offering as ¹⁄₂₄ for a nonprofessional and ¹⁄₄₈ for a professional baker.

Structure and Organization of the Tractate

The tractate begins by listing the five types of grain subject to the dough offering (1:1–2); these five (wheat, barley, spelt, rye, oats; modern scholars debate the precise identification of the grains translated "rye" and "oats") have special status in other contexts as well, as the Mishnah explains. Most of the rest of the first chapter discusses the moments at which dough is liable for dough offering and at which grain is liable for tithes (1:3–8). The final mishnah of the chapter lists common features of dough offering and *terumah*.

The second chapter discusses offerings from grain grown outside the Land of Israel (2:1–2). It then discusses various rules as to how the dough offering is to be separated (2:3–8). The third chapter continues this discussion, focusing on the rolling out of dough (3:1–6). It concludes with a discussion of mixtures of dough offering and other substances (3:7–10).

Chapter 4 discusses cases in which different batches of dough have been combined (4:1–5). The tractate concludes with more discussion of dough offering and other mandated agricultural offerings outside the Land of Israel. At the very end of the tractate some manuscripts add a paragraph, apparently drawn from the Tosefta, summarizing all the emoluments ("gifts") to which a priest in the Land of Israel is entitled under Torah law.

Main Ideas

Dough offering is unlike *terumah* and tithes in that it is not separated from raw produce, but rather from flour after it has been mixed with water and kneaded into dough. Hence the Mishnah devotes some attention to the definition of dough (1:5–6, 8). The dough offering is limited in scope in that only five grains are subject to it. Furthermore, for the dough to be liable for dough offering it must have a minimal amount (2:6). This leads to discussion of how separate batches of dough can combine into one batch to create the requisite minimum (4:1–5).

The Rabbis apply to the dough offering many of the same rules governing *terumah*: it must be given to a priest and its purity must be preserved. Impure dough offering cannot be consumed; the Mishnah discusses how dough should be made by an impure person (2:3).

The rolling out of the dough to make it into loaves is a critical point in its processing. While the woman making the bread (the Mishnah frequently uses feminine verbs in describing baking bread) may remove the dough offering as soon as she adds water to the flour, the dough offering is not considered to be part of the dough until it is rolled out, and thus one can snack on this dough (3:1). Rolling out the dough functions in much the same way as smoothing out the grain pile or bringing produce into one's home does for tithes and *terumah*—it causes the product to become prohibited for consumption until the offering has been made (see *Terumot* and *Ma'aserot*).

In its discussion of the laws of mixtures, tractate *Hallah* is consistent with concepts and terms found elsewhere in the Mishnah. Homogeneous mixtures (e.g. a mixture of sanctified and unsanctified wheat dough) is treated stringently (3:10), while heterogeneous mixtures (e.g. wheat dough and rice dough) are defined by their dominant flavor (3:7, 10; cf. *Orlah* chapter 2; *Avodah Zarah* 5:8).

Dough offering is obligatory only inside the Land of Israel (2:1). Nevertheless, the Rabbis mandated the separation of dough offering from certain lands close to Israel so that the laws of the dough offering would not be forgotten (4:8). The fear that the dough offering, if not observed, would be forgotten, led eventually to the practice of separating a token offering from doughs outside the Land of Israel. By contrast, tithes and *terumah* ultimately fell into complete desuetude outside the Land of Israel.

Relationship to Scripture

In contrast with the dominant opinion in the Mishnah, many texts of the Second Temple period (Nehemiah 10:38; Philo; Josephus) state that the *hallah* offering was separated after the dough had already been baked into loaves of bread.

The Rabbis assume that the dough offering of Numbers 15:17–21 has the same status as *terumah*; therefore, many of the rules found in Numbers 18 and in Leviticus 22:10–14 are applied to the dough offering. The idea that dough offering is to be given to the priests is consistent with Nehemiah 10:38 and Ezekiel 44:30. The latter also explicitly compares *terumah* with the dough offering.

Tractate Hallah

Chapter One

1:1–2 *The Definition of Grain*

1 Five species[1] [of grain] are subject to the dough offering:
(1) wheat,
(2) barley,
(3) spelt,
(4) oats, and
(5) rye.
These are liable for the dough offering,
and are accounted together as one [when formed into a single dough].
And they are prohibited when new prior to Passover,
and may not be reaped prior to the *omer*.
If they took root prior to the *omer*,
the *omer* permits them;
if not,
they are prohibited until the next *omer* comes.

2 One who eats on Passover an olive-sized piece of unleavened bread made of any of them
has fulfilled his obligation.
[One who eats on Passover] an olive-sized of piece of leavened bread
[made of any of these grains]
is liable for *karet*.

[1] Lit. "things."

1:1 *Five species [of grain]*: This would exclude other grains such as rice and millet (1:4).

are accounted together as one: For purposes of determining the size of the dough (2:6); cf. 4:2. Scholars debate the precise identification of the grains translated here as "oats" and "rye."

when new prior to Passover: See Leviticus 23:14, *Terumot* 1:5; *Ma'aser Sheni* 5:11; *Menahot* 8:1 and 10:5.

omer: The first harvest of the barley which occurs following the first day of Passover; see Leviticus 23:9–13.

1:2 *fulfilled his obligation*: See *Pesahim* 2:5.

karet: The biblical penalty of "extirpation." In rabbinic thinking this a penalty meted out by God. See 3:1 and *Keritot*.

If any one of these [grains, having become leavened,]
became mixed with any other species,
one must remove it on Passover.[2]
One who vows [to abstain] from [consuming] bread or "grain" (*tevu'ah*),
is prohibited from consuming [only] these [five species]—
the words of R. Meir.
But the Sages say:
One who vows [to abstain] from [consuming] "grain" (*dagan*)
is prohibited from [consuming] only these [species].
They are liable for the dough offering and tithes.

1:3–8 *Liability to the Dough Offering*

3 The following are liable for the dough offering, but are exempt from tithes:
Gleanings,
the Forgotten Sheaf,
pe'ah,
ownerless produce,
first tithe whose *terumah* has been removed,
second tithe and consecrated [produce] which have been redeemed,
that which remains over from the *omer*,
and produce which is not yet grown one-third.

[2] Or "One thereby violates [the prohibition of leaven on] Passover."

---

one must remove it on Passover: See *Pesahim* 3:1.

One who vows: Cf. *Nedarim* 7:2.

bread or "grain" (tevu'ah): According to R. Meir, these words when used in a vow refer only to the five species of grain. In *Nedarim* 7:2 he argues that the word *dagan* is a broader term that include, for example, pulse.

But the Sages say: They understand even the word *dagan* in a vow to refer only to the five species. They agree with R. Meir that the words bread and *tevu'ah* refer only to the five grains.

1:3 *gleanings, the forgotten sheaf, pe'ah*: See Leviticus 19:9–10; 23:22; Deuteronomy 24:19–21. See the introduction to *Pe'ah*.

first tithe whose terumah has been removed: The separation of *terumah* from the tithe makes the produce fit for use. See Numbers 18:25–32.

second tithe…redeemed: The sanctity of second tithe can be transferred to money, rendering the produce edible outside of Jerusalem in a state of impurity; see Deuteronomy 14:22–27, Leviticus 27:30–31, and *Ma'aser Sheni*.

that which remains over from the omer: Three *se'ah* worth of barley would be harvested for the *omer*, but only the choicest tenth of a *se'ah* would actually be used for the ritual (*Menahot* 6:6). The rest would be desanctified and then available to be eaten by anyone (*Menahot* 10:4). This flour is exempt from tithes, because when its processing was completed (i.e. when it was harvested and made it into a pile of grain) it was holy and exempt from tithes (for this concept, see e.g. 3:3–4). However, liability for the dough offering is determined by when it was made into dough (3:1), and by the time the *omer* flour was made into dough, it was already nonsacred.

R. Eliezer says:
Produce which is not yet grown one-third is [also] exempt from the dough offering.

4 The following are liable for tithes, but exempt from the dough offering:
rice,
millet,
poppyseed,
sesame seeds,
pulse,
and [a dough made from] less than five-fourths [of a *qav*] of grain.[3]
Sponge cakes,
honey cakes,
dumplings,
a cake [cooked] in a pan,
and a mixture of *terumah* and non-*terumah*,
are exempt from the dough offering.

5 Dough which was originally [kneaded for] sponge cakes,
and in the end is [baked as] sponge cake,
is exempt from dough offering.
[But if it was] originally [kneaded as ordinary] dough,
but in the end is [baked as] sponge cakes,
[or if the dough was] originally [kneaded for] sponge cakes,
but in the end is [baked as ordinary] dough,
it is liable for the dough offering.
Similarly, breadcrumbs are liable [for the dough offering].

[3] **K** lacks from "pulse" until "grain," perhaps by mistake.

produce which is not yet grown one-third: See *Ma'aserot* 1:3, which exempts produce at this early stage from the obligation to be tithed. According to the Sages, since such grain can be used to make bread, dough made from it is liable for the dough offering. R. Eliezer disagrees on the basis of the fact that dough offering is analogized to *terumah* (Numbers 15:20); since *terumah* cannot be separated from produce that is only one-third ripe, neither can dough offering from dough made from it.

1:4 *less than five-fourths [of a qav] of grain*: See 2:6.

Sponge cakes, honey-cakes, dumplings, a cake [cooked] in a pan: These are exempt from the dough offering because they are not baked in an oven.

mixture of terumah and non-terumah: A mixture of nonsacred produce and *terumah* in which there is not a sufficient quantity of nonsacred produce to nullify the *terumah* (there are less than one hundred parts nonsacred for each part *terumah*). This mixture is treated like *terumah* and can only be eaten by a priest. See *Terumot* 4:7 and 5:1. It is exempt from dough offering because it is already considered *terumah*.

1:5 *originally [kneaded as] ordinary dough*: Whose consistency is thicker than that used for sponge cakes.

[baked as ordinary] dough: In an oven and not in a pan, as sponge cakes are cooked.

breadcrumbs: These are made from bread dough but are boiled in small pieces in a pan rather than baked. They are liable for the dough offering because they began as bread, even though they were eventually cooked in a manner similar to sponge cakes.

6 Scalded flour (*me'isah*)—
the House of Shammai declare it exempt [from the dough offering],
but the House of Hillel declare it liable [for the dough offering].
Scalded flour (*halitah*)—
the House of Shammai declare it liable [for the dough offering],
but the House of Hillel declare it exempt
The loaves of the thank [offering] and the flat cakes of a *nazir*—
if one made them for oneself, they are exempt [from the dough offering],
[But if one made them] to sell in the market, they are liable.

7 A baker who made leaven to divide it up—
[the dough] is liable for the dough offering.
Women[4] who gave [flour] to a baker to make leaven for them—
if none of them has the [minimum] statutory amount,
it is exempt from the dough offering.

8 Dough for dogs—
if shepherds eat it,
it is liable for the dough offering,
and one may make an *eruv* with it,

[4] **K, P**, and other manuscripts: "But women."

1:6 *me'isah*: Boiling water poured on top of flour. The House of Hillel rule that it is liable because water is normally poured into flour to make dough. Parallel to *Eduyot* 5:2.

halitah: Flour put into boiling water. The House of Hillel rule that it is exempt because adding flour to water is not the usual way to make dough.

the thank [offering] is accompanied by three loaves of unleavened bread (Leviticus 7:12).

flat cakes of a nazir: When the *nazir* completes his vow, he brings loaves and wafers (Numbers 6:15).

for oneself... to sell: If a person makes these for himself, and from the time he begins to make the dough he intends to use them for these purposes, then they are sanctified from the beginning of their existence, and one does not have to separate dough offering from sanctified food. However, if he makes them to sell in the market, they are not sanctified from the outset, and he must therefore separate dough offering from them.

1:7 *leaven*: The baker would make a large batch of dough that would begin to leaven.

to divide it up: The baker intends to divide the leavened dough into small pieces, each of which contains less than the five-fourths of a *qav* measure necessary for dough to be liable for the dough offering (1:4; 2:6). He will sell the smaller pieces of dough to individuals, who will use to it to leaven their own dough and then bake it themselves. This starter dough is liable for the dough offering, because if he can't find people to buy it, he will recombine it and bake it all himself.

Women who gave [flour] to a baker to make leaven for them: Here the small pieces of dough are already owned by different individuals and do not join together to become liable for the dough offering (cf. 4:1).

1:8 *If shepherds eat it*: If this dough was prepared as food for sheepdogs, but in fact could be eaten by the shepherds, then it is treated as human food.

it is liable for the dough offering: Only human food is subject to the dough offering.

and one may make an eruv... partnership: An *eruv* or a partnership is a common meal which allows one to carry on the Sabbath from a house into a courtyard or from a courtyard into the adjoining alleyway. See the introduction to *Eruvin*.

and one may make a partnership with it,
and one must bless over it,
and one invites others to recite over it the communal blessings after meals,
and it may be prepared on a festival,
and one may fulfill his obligation with it on Passover.
[But] if shepherds do not eat it—
it is not liable for the dough offering,
and one may not make an *eruv* with it,
nor may one make a partnership with it,
nor may one bless over it,
nor may one invite others to recite the communal blessings after meals over it,
nor may it be prepared on a festival,
nor does one fulfill his obligation with it on Passover.
In either case it is susceptible to the impurity that affects food.

1:9 *Laws Common to Dough Offering and Terumah*

9 Dough offering and *terumah*—
one is liable on their account
to death [at the hands of heaven, if eaten intentionally]
or to an added fifth [if eaten unintentionally];
and they are forbidden to nonpriests,
and they are the property of the priest,
and they are neutralized at a ratio of one in a hundred,
and they require the washing of hands
and waiting past sundown,

---

invite others: If eaten in a group of at least three. See *Berakhot* 7:1.

and it may be prepared on a festival: Only human food can be made on the festival.

and one may fulfill his obligation with it on Passover: If unleavened, it could be used for *matsah*.

In either case it is susceptible to the impurity that affects food: Even if it was made solely for dogs, shepherds might eat it occasionally. Therefore, in any case, the dough is subject to the rules of food impurity. Only food that cannot be eaten by humans, for instance straw, would not be subject to these rules.

1:9 *death*: Leviticus 22:9–10.

added fifth: Leviticus 22:14.

property of the priest: He may sell them and use the proceeds as he wishes (cf. *Bikkurim* 3:12). This is not the rule with sacrifices.

neutralized: If one hundred parts of nonsacred produce become mixed with one part *terumah* or dough offering, then one can take out one part, give it to the priest as *terumah*/dough offering and the rest reverts to being nonsacred. If there is less than a 100:1 ratio of nonsacred to *terumah*/dough offering, then the whole mixture must be treated like *terumah*/dough offering and only priests can eat it. See *Terumot* 4:7, 5:1.

sundown: See Leviticus 22:7.

and they may not be taken from the pure for the impure;
but rather [are to be taken] from that which is close by,
and from that whose processing is complete.
One who says:
"My entire threshing floor is *terumah*,"
or "All my dough is dough offering,"
has said nothing, unless he has left some over.

Chapter Two

2:1–2 *Produce Grown Outside the Land of Israel*

2 Produce [grown] outside the Land [of Israel] that came into the Land
is liable for the dough offering.
[If it] went out from here to there—
R. Eliezer declares it liable,
but[5] R. Aqiva declares it exempt.

2 [Produce grown in] earth from outside the Land that came into the Land [of Israel] in a boat
is liable for tithes and to the Seventh Year.
R. Judah said:
When does this apply? When the boat is touching [the ground].
Dough kneaded with fruit juice is subject to the dough offering,
but may be eaten with impure hands.

[5] **K** lacks the conjunction.

---

they may not be taken from the pure for the impure: If one has some pure produce/dough and some impure produce/dough, he cannot separate *terumah* or the dough offering from the pure in order to exempt the impure. See *Terumot* 2:1 and cf. 4:6.

from that which is close by: When one comes to separate *terumah* or dough offering, he must take them out of produce or dough that is close by. See 2:8; cf. 4:6 and *Terumot* 4:3.

processing is complete: *Terumot* 1:10.

"My entire threshing floor is terumah": This is derived from Numbers 15:2, *From the first of your dough give to the Lord terumah*: from the first of your dough, but not all of the first of one's dough. Cf. *Terumot* 4:5.

2:1 *is liable for the dough offering*: Numbers 15:19 only requires removing dough offering "from bread of the Land"; imported grain is liable because it was made into dough when it was already within the Land.

2:2 *is subject to tithes and to the [laws relating to] the Seventh Year*: As if the produce was grown in Israel itself.

Dough kneaded with fruit juice: Such dough is not susceptible to impurity because fruit juice is not one of the seven liquids that makes produce susceptible to impurity (*Terumot* 11:2, *Makhshirin* 6:4; cf. *Terumot* 5:1–3).

2:3–8 *Separating the Dough Offering*

3 A woman may sit and separate her dough offering while naked,
since she can cover herself,
but a man may not.
One who is unable to make his dough in purity
let him make it [in separate] *qav*,
but let him not make it in impurity.
But[6] R. Aqiva says:
He may make it in impurity,
but let him not make it [in separate] *qav*,
for just as he designates the pure one,
so too he designates the impure one;
this one he designates "dough offering" with[7] the name [of God],[8]
and the other one he also designates "dough offering" with the name [of God].
But [separate] *qav* have no portion [devoted] to the name [of God].

4 One who makes his dough [in separate] *qav*,
and they touched one another—
they are [nonetheless] exempt from the dough offering,
unless they stick together.
R. Eliezer says:
Even if one takes out [loaves from an oven] and puts [them] into a basket,
the basket joins them together for [liability to] the dough offering.

5 One who separates the dough offering [from] flour—
it is not [a valid] dough offering,
and [if given to a priest] is stolen property in the priest's hand.

---

[6] P, K, and the majority of manuscripts lack the conjunction.
[7] K (pregloss) and several manuscripts: "for the sake [of God]."
[8] Or "designates dough offering by name," here and below.

2:3 *A woman may sit and separate her dough offering while naked*: Separating the dough offering requires the recitation of a blessing and it is forbidden to recite a blessing while naked (cf. *Berakhot* 3:5). A woman can separate the dough offering while sitting naked because she can hide her genitals with her legs. A man, however, cannot hide his genitals while sitting. Cf. *Terumot* 1:6.

[in separate] qav: The impure person making dough should knead it in quantities smaller than 1¼ *qav*, the minimum amount liable for the dough offering (see 2:6), in order to evade the obligation.

Let him make it in impurity: Even when the dough offering is impure and thus inedible, when one separates it from the dough a blessing will be recited using God's name. This is preferable to kneading each *qav* separately for in such a case no blessing would be recited.

2:4 *Even if one takes out [loaves from an oven] and puts [them] into a basket*: Even though *hallah* is usually taken out from the dough, according to R. Eliezer the separate loaves are joined together by the basket even after they have been baked.

2:5 *One who separates his dough offering [from] flour*: Numbers 15:20 requires taking dough offering from the kneading trough, which the Rabbis understand to exclude raw flour.

not [a valid] dough offering: If the flour designated as dough offering is given to the priest, he must return it.

The dough itself is still liable for the dough offering,
and the flour [separated as dough offering],
if there is the statutory amount [when it is made into dough],
is [still] liable for the dough offering.
But it is prohibited to nonpriests—
the words of R. Joshua.
The [Sages] said to him:
It once happened that a nonpriest elder snatched it [and ate it].
He said to them:
He did something damaging to himself, but he benefited others.

6 Five-fourths [of a *qav*] of flour are liable for the dough offering.
If flour, leavening, light bran,[9] and coarse bran [make up the] five-fourths,
they are liable [for the dough offering].
If the coarse bran was removed from them and returned to them,
they are exempt.

7 The [minimum] statutory amount for the dough offering is one twenty-fourth.
One who makes dough for himself,
or one who makes it for his son's [wedding] banquet
[must separate] one twenty-fourth.
A baker who makes [dough] to sell in the market,
and so too a woman who makes [dough] to sell in the market,
[must separate] one forty-eighth.
If her dough became impure
unintentionally or by an unforeseeable circumstance,
[she must separate] one forty-eighth.
If it was made impure intentionally,
[she must separate] one twenty-fourth,
in order that a sinner should not profit.

[9] Absent in **K**, **P**, and many manuscripts.

The dough itself is still liable for the dough offering: Since taking dough offering from flour does not fulfill the requirement, any dough subsequently created from that flour must still have dough offering removed from it.

But it is prohibited to nonpriests: According to R. Joshua, designating the flour as dough offering, despite being invalid, is sufficient to prohibit all bread produced from that improperly designated flour to nonpriests.

He did something damaging to himself, but he benefited others: The elder transgressed by eating that which was prohibited to him. But in a roundabout way, he helped others. Other nonpriests will now eat such bread thinking that it is permitted to them as well. Since they do not know that it is actually prohibited, they will not be considered as transgressing.

2:6 *they are exempt*: Removal of coarse bran was typical in the processing of better-quality flour, but returning the bran was unusual. Therefore, it does not count as part of the flour in order to make it liable for the dough offering.

2:7 *A baker…a woman who makes [dough] to sell in the market*: Since these people tend to make larger quantities (see 1:7), even one forty-eighth will suffice for a substantial gift to the priest.

dough became impure: Since this dough offering may not be eaten anyway, only a minimal measurement is required.

in order that a sinner should not profit: By giving one forty-eighth instead of one twenty-fourth.

8 R. Eliezer says:
[Dough offering] may be taken from [dough] that is pure
on behalf of [dough] that is impure.
How [may this be done]?
[If one has] pure dough and impure dough,
he takes the requisite amount of dough offering [for the two doughs]
from the [pure] dough, whose dough offering had not yet been removed,
and puts less than an egg's bulk [of pure dough] in the middle,
in order that he may take [the dough offering]
from that which what is close by.
But the Sages prohibit.

Chapter Three

3:1–6 *Rolling Out the Dough*

3 One may snack from dough,
until it is rolled,
in [the case of] wheat [flour],
or until it is made into a solid mass,
in [the case of] barley [flour].
[Once] one has rolled it [in the case of] wheat [flour],

2:8 *R. Eliezer says… but the Sages prohibit*: See *Terumot* 2:1.

How [may this be done]?: The problem is how to join the two batches of dough together so that one dough offering can be taken from both without causing the pure dough to become impure through contact. He cannot just take from one to exempt the other because dough offering taken from one batch of dough cannot exempt a separate batch of dough.

he takes the requisite amount of dough offering…from the [pure] dough: He does this at the outset lest the pure dough be made impure—at least he now has enough pure offering to exempt both batches. Then, between the two batches, he puts an amount of dough less than the size of an egg. This serves to attach the two batches, but because it is less than an egg's worth in volume, the impurity is not conveyed across to the pure dough (see *Orlah* 2:4–5). Now the offering that he took from the pure dough can apply also to the impure dough.

close by: See 1:9.

But the Sages prohibit: Lest he unwittingly cause the pure dough to become impure. Rather he should take pure offering from the pure dough and impure offering from the impure dough.

3:1 *snack*: Informal eating. See *Ma'aserot* 2:4.

until it is rolled: Flat, like pita.

in [the case of] wheat [flour]: Wheat flour is finer and is therefore considered dough once it has been kneaded well and rolled out.

or made it into a solid mass, in [the case of] barley [flour],
one who eats it is liable for death [at the hands of heaven].
As soon as she puts in the water,
she may lift out the dough offering,
provided that there are not[10] there five-fourths [of a *qav*] of flour.

2 If her dough became mixed with *terumah* before she rolled it,
it is exempt [from the dough offering],
because a *terumah* mixture is exempt from the dough offering.
If [it became mixed] after she rolled it,
it is liable [for the dough offering].
If there arose concerning it some doubt of impurity—
before she rolled it,
let it be done in impurity;
after she rolled it, let it be done in purity.

3 If she consecrated her dough before rolling it, and then redeemed it,
it is liable [for the dough offering];
and [if she consecrated it] after she rolled it, and then redeemed it,
it is liable [for the dough offering].

[10] K, P, and most manuscripts lack "not."

until it is made into a solid mass, in [the case of] barley [flour]: Barley flour is coarser and therefore is considered dough once it sticks together into a lump.

death [at the hands of heaven]: The same penalty for a nonpriest who eats *terumah* or nontithed produce. See 1:2 above; Leviticus 22:10.

As soon as she puts in the water: The way to avoid this severe penalty is for the woman to remove the dough offering from the dough as soon as she puts water in the flour. Even though one could continue to snack on it until it is rolled or made into a solid mass, this is not advisable because it might lead one to snack on it at a later point. Note that 3:1–3 have feminine verbs.

provided that there are not there five-fourths [of a qav] of flour: If five-fourths of a *qav* of a flour remain in the trough, then this flour has not been exempted from dough offering by the dough that the woman removed, since dough offering may not be removed from flour (see 2:5). According to the manuscripts that omit the word "not," the Mishnah is saying that in the absence of the statutory amount of flour (see 2:6), she may not take out the dough offering, even if she will add more flour later on.

3:2 *mixed with terumah*: At a ratio less than one part *terumah* per one hundred parts nonsacral produce (see *Terumot* 4:7 and 5:1).

before she rolled it, it is exempt [from the dough offering]: Because it was not yet liable for dough offering (see 3:1) before it became a type of dough exempt from the dough offering.

some doubt of impurity: The dough may or may not have been rendered ritually impure.

done in impurity: In any case the priest cannot eat the offering that will be taken out of the dough, for it may be impure, and therefore it does not matter if she makes it certainly impure.

let it be done in purity: It is forbidden to impart certain impurity to dough offering (or *terumah*) that is only doubtfully impure. Since this dough has already been rolled, and thereby made liable for the dough offering (see 3:1), it is treated as stringently as dough offering, and she must make the rest of the dough in a state of purity.

3:3 *if she consecrated it before rolling it and the Temple treasurer rolled it*: Dough that belongs to the Temple at the moment that dough becomes liable for the offering, that is, when it is rolled, is exempt from the dough offering.

[But] if she consecrated it before rolling it,
and the Temple treasurer rolled it,
and after that she redeemed it,
it is exempt,
since at the moment of its obligation it was exempt.

4 Similarly, one who consecrates his produce
before the time for tithing arrived,
and then redeemed it,
it is liable [to be tithed];
and [if he consecrated it]
after the time for tithing arrived,
and then redeemed it,
it is liable [to be tithed].
[But] if he consecrated it before it was finished,
and it finished
while in the possession of the [Temple] treasurer,
and then he redeemed it,
it is exempt,
since at the moment of its obligation it was exempt.

5 If a gentile gave [flour] to an Israelite to make dough for him,
[the dough] is exempt from the dough offering.
If the gentile gave it to him as a gift—
before rolling it, he is liable [for separate dough offering],
but after rolling it, he is exempt [from separating dough offering].
One who makes dough together with a gentile,
if [the portion] belonging to the Israelite
lacks the [minimum] statutory amount [for the dough offering],
it is exempt from the dough offering.

6 A proselyte who converted and possessed dough—
if it was made before he converted,
he is exempt [from separating the dough offering];
if [it was made] after he converted, he is liable [to separate the dough offering].
And if there is doubt, he is liable [to separate the dough offering],
but one is not liable for the additional fifth [for consuming it] on its account.
R. Aqiva says:
It all depends on the [time of the] formation of the light crust in the oven.

3:4 Parallel to *Pe'ah* 4:8.

before time for tithing arrived: Produce becomes liable for tithes once it has been harvested, processed, and made into a pile. See *Ma'aserot*.

3:5 *If a gentile gave [flour] to an Israelite to make dough for him*: Dough owned by a gentile is exempt from the dough offering, even if a Jew kneaded it. Cf. *Terumot* 3:9.

3:6 *And if there is doubt*: Whether he made the dough before he converted or not, then he must give the dough offering. This dough offering is treated as "doubtful," which means it must be eaten by a priest, and if a nonpriest eats it, he must restore to the priests the value of that which he ate, but not the added fifth.

It all depends on the [time of the] formation of the light crust in the oven: R. Aqiva disagrees with all of the above rulings which hold that dough becomes liable for the dough offering once it is rolled. According to

3:7–10 Mixtures

7 One who makes dough from wheat and from rice—
if it has a taste of grain,
it is liable for the dough offering,
and one may fulfill one's obligation with it on Passover;
but if it does not have the taste of grain,
it is not liable for the dough offering,
and one may not fulfill one's obligation with it on Passover.

8 One who takes the leaven out of dough
whose dough offering had not been removed,
and puts it into dough whose dough offering had been removed—
if he has a supply [of dough] from another place,
he may take out dough offering proportionally,
but if he does not, he takes out one [portion of] dough offering for the whole [dough].

9 Similarly, if olives of [the regular] harvest become mixed
with olives [left over] for striking-off [by the poor],
[or] grapes of [the regular] harvest [become mixed]
with grapes [left over] for gleaning [by the poor]—
if one has a supply from another place,

him, the end of the processing for dough, which is the point at which it becomes forbidden to snack on it, is when it forms a light crust in the oven.

3:7 *One who makes dough from wheat and from rice*: Rice is not one of the five grains subject to the dough offering (see 1:1, 4), and one cannot use it to fulfill the commandment of eating *matsah* on Passover.

it is liable for the dough offering: Even if there is not enough wheat flour to constitute the minimum measure required for dough to be liable for the dough offering (see 2:6), as long as the combination of flours reaches the minimum statutory amount, the taste of wheat is sufficient to make the dough liable.

3:8 *if he has a supply [of dough] from another place*: A third batch of dough from which the dough offering had not yet been removed.

he may take out dough offering proportionally: He can use that batch to remove the dough offering to exempt the leaven alone, without taking into consideration the size of the batch into which the leaven has been placed.

he takes out one [portion of] dough offering for the whole [dough]: He removes the dough offering from the batch to which he added the leaven according to the amount of dough in the entire batch, even though he only added a little bit of leaven. Since he can't separate the dough offering for that little bit of leaven from another batch, the entire batch into which it has been placed is now considered to be dough from which the dough offering has not been removed.

3:9 *olives of [the regular] harvest*: These belong to the owner of the field and are liable for tithes and *terumah*.

olives [left over] for striking-off [by the poor]: See Pe'ah 8:3. These olives are not liable for tithes or *terumah*, because they belong to the poor, just like the gleanings (Leviticus 19:10; Deuteronomy 24:21; Pe'ah 7:4).

he can take out [*terumah* and tithes] proportionally.
But if he does not,
he takes out *terumah* and *terumah* from the tithe for all of them.
And as for the rest,
[he takes out] tithe and second tithe proportionally.

10 One who takes leaven from dough of wheat [flour]
and puts [it] into dough of rice [flour]—
if it has the taste of grain, it is liable for the dough offering;
if not, it is exempt [from the dough offering].
If so, why did they say:
"Fully untithed produce of any amount renders [food] prohibited"?
That is [only with regard to a mixture of] the same kind [of produce],[11]
but [with regard to a mixture of] different kinds [of produce],[12]
[the mixture is prohibited only] when [the untithed produce] imparts taste.

Chapter Four

4:1–5 *Different Batches of Dough*

4 Two women who made two [separate batches of dough, each of a] *qav* [of flour],
and the [batches] touched one another,
even if they are of one kind [of grain], they are exempt [from the dough offering].
If they belong to one woman,
if [they are] the same kind [of grain], they are liable [for the dough offering],
but if of different kinds [of grain], they are exempt [from the dough offering].

---

[11] Lit. "a kind with its own kind," here and below, 4:1–2.
[12] Lit. "[a kind] not with its own kind," here and below, 4:1.

---

he takes out terumah and terumah from the tithe for all of them: If he does not have other produce from which to take out the *terumah*, then he must separate *terumah* and the *terumah* that is taken from tithe for the entire amount, even though the produce that was for the poor was exempt.

[he takes out] tithe and second tithe proportionally: He removes tithe and second tithe for the amount of produce that is actually liable for tithes and second tithe. This is the amount of his produce that is in the mixture; it does not include the produce that belongs to the poor. The law is stricter when it comes to *terumah* and the dough offering because a nonpriest who eats *terumah* or the dough offering is liable for death by the hands of heaven.

3:10 *why did they say*: The earlier Sages. This quote is not in our Mishnah.

"Fully untithed produce of any amount renders [food] prohibited": If even a small amount of untithed produce falls into a large amount of tithed produce, then one cannot eat the produce until he removes tithes and *terumah*.

4:1 *two [separate batches of dough, each of a] qav*: An insufficient amount for each to be liable for the dough offering by itself.

they are exempt [from the dough offering]: They do not join together because they are owned by different people.

2   What is the same kind [of grain]?
Wheat is not accounted together with any [kind of grain] other than spelt;
barley is accounted together with all [kinds of grain] except wheat.
R. Johanan b. Nuri says:
All other kinds are accounted together one with another.

3   Two [separate batches of dough, each of a] *qav* [of flour],
and a *qav* of rice [dough] or a *qav* of *terumah* [dough] in the middle,
are not accounted together.
[If there was] dough[13] between them
whose dough offering had already been taken,
they are accounted together,
since it had once been liable for dough offering.

4   A *qav* of [dough made from] new grain and a *qav* of [dough made from] old grain
which stuck to each other—
R. Ishmael says:
Let him take [dough offering] from the middle,
but the Sages prohibit.
One who takes the dough offering from [dough made with only] one *qav*—
R. Aqiva says:
It is [valid] dough offering,
but the Sages say:
It is not [valid] dough offering.

5   Two [separate batches of dough, each of a] *qav* [of flour],
this one having had its dough offering removed on its own,[14]

---

[13] Lit. "a thing."

[14] **K**, **P**, and the majority of manuscripts: "whose dough offering was removed, this one's on its own, and that one's on its own."

4:2 *What is the same kind*: Such that batches of dough would join together. The five species of grain are listed in 1:1.

4:3 *a qav of rice [dough] or a qav of terumah [dough]*: Neither is subject to the dough offering; see 1:4.

in the middle: That is, between them. See 2:8.

are not accounted together: The exempt dough does not serve to join the two batches that are subject to the dough offering.

4:4 *A qav of [dough made from] new grain and a qav of [dough made from] old grain*: The problem is that the dough offering should not be taken from old grain to exempt new grain, or vice versa. See *Terumot* 1:5 and *Ma'aser Sheni* 5:11.

new grain: Grain that took root since the previous *omer* offering. See 1:1.

Let him take [dough offering] from the middle: That is, from where the doughs are touching. In this way he will take from both and exempt the entire batch.

but the Sages prohibit: Instead, he must take from the old dough to exempt the old and from the new to exempt the new.

[dough made from] one qav: Which is not liable for the dough offering; see 2:6.

and this one having had its dough offering removed on its own,
and [then the baker] went back and made them [into] one batch of dough—
R. Aqiva declares it exempt [from the dough offering],
but the Sages declare it liable [for the dough offering].
It turns out that his stringency is his leniency.

4:6 Dough Offering Separated from Doubtfully Tithed Produce

6 A person may take the requisite amount for the dough offering
from [pure] dough whose dough offering had not [previously] been removed,
in order to work it in a state of purity,
in order to go on separating on its account
the dough offering for *demai*,
until [the taken dough] becomes putrid,
since the dough offering for *demai* may be taken
from pure [dough] for impure [dough],
and from [dough] which is not close by.

4:7–11 Dough Offering Outside the Land of Israel

7 Israelites who were sharecroppers of gentiles in Syria,
R. Eliezer declares their produce liable for tithes
and to the Seventh Year,

4:5 *R. Aqiva declares it exempt*: Because he considers both batches as having had their dough offering removed (see 4:4).

but the Sages declare it liable: Because the dough offering removed when they were separate is not considered dough offering.

his stringency: In reference to R. Aqiva in 4:4.

4:6 *A person may take the requisite amount for the dough offering*: He wants to set aside dough in order for it to count as the dough offering for *demai* dough (*demai* is produce whose tithing status is in doubt; see introduction to *Demai*) that he will receive in the future from which he does not want to bother separating the dough offering.

in order to work it in a state of purity: He should set it aside immediately before the dough becomes impure.

in order to go on separating on its account the dough offering for demai: He separates from the original dough he set aside the dough offering for the doubtfully tithed dough that he will receive in the future. Generally, one cannot separate the dough offering from one batch of dough in order to exempt different dough unless the two batches are in close proximity, nor can one separate the dough offering from pure dough in order to exempt impure dough (1:9, 2:8). But when it comes to *demai* both are permitted. The *demai* dough that he receives is assumed to be impure.

until [the taken dough] becomes putrid: After which he cannot separate the dough offering from it.

4:7 *sharecroppers*: Who receive the land in order to give the owner a share of the produce.

Syria: Where the produce is liable for tithes, but certain leniencies apply; see *Demai* 6:11, *Ma'aserot* 5:5.

R. Eliezer declares their produce liable for tithes and to the Seventh Year: As would be the law in such a case in the Land of Israel.

but Rabban Gamaliel declares [their produce] exempt.
Rabban Gamaliel says:
[One must give] two portions of dough offering in Syria,
but R. Eliezer says:
[only] one portion of dough offering.
They adopted the lenient ruling of Rabban Gamaliel
and[15] the lenient ruling of R. Eliezer.
Afterwards they established the practice
in accordance with Rabban Gamaliel in both respects.

8 Rabban Gamaliel says:
There are three territories with regard to [liability to] the dough offering:
(1) From the Land of Israel to Keziv,[16]
one portion of dough offering.
(2) From Keziv to the river and to Amanah,[17]
two portions of dough offering,
one for the fire and one for the priest.
The one for the fire has a [minimum] statutory amount,
and the one for the priest does not have a minimum statutory amount.
(3) From the river and from Amanah and inward:
two portions of dough offering,
one for the fire and one for the priest.
The one for the fire has no minimum statutory amount,

---

[15] K reads "over." [16] K, P, and several manuscripts: "Geziv," here and below.
[17] K, P, and several manuscripts: "Amanam," here and below.

---

but Rabban Gamaliel declares [their produce] exempt: Since the land is in Syria and it belongs to a non-Jew.

two portions of dough offering in Syria: As is the rule outside of the Land of Israel (see 4:8).

[only] one portion of the dough offering: As in the Land of Israel.

4:8 Cf. *Shevi'it* 6:1.

Keziv: The northern border of the Land of Israel.

two portions of the dough offering, one for the fire and one for the priest: According to the Torah, the dough offering is not separated outside of the Land of Israel (Numbers 15:19). However, the Rabbis decreed that Jews should continue to separate the dough offering from dough outside of the Land of Israel so that the laws of the dough offering would not be forgotten. The problem is land outside of Israel was considered to be impure, so that any dough offering separated there would also be impure and would have to be burned. In order to remember that the dough offering was originally given to priests, the Rabbis decreed that a Jew should separate a second portion of the dough offering and give that portion to the priests.

The one for the fire has a [minimum] statutory amount: Since it is biblically mandated. The minimum measure is 1/48 (see 2:7 above).

and the one for the priest does not have a minimum statutory amount: Since it is only rabbinically mandated.

From the river and from Amanah and inward: Where the agricultural laws do not apply. Both dough offerings are only rabbinically mandated there.

The one for the fire has no minimum statutory amount: Since it is separated only because of a rabbinic decree.

and the one for the priest has a [minimum] statutory amount,
although a *tevul yom* [priest] may eat it.
R. Yose says:
He does not require immersion,
but it is forbidden to the male and female *zav*, to menstruants, and to women after childbirth.
It may be eaten with a nonpriest at the [same] table,
and it may be given to any priest.

9 These may be given to any priest:
things devoted [to God];
firstborn animals;
the redemption of the firstborn son;
the redemption of the firstborn of a donkey;
the shoulder, the cheeks, and the stomach;
the first of the fleece;
terumah oil that must be burnt;
offerings for the altar;
and firstfruits.

but the one for the priest has a [minimum] statutory amount: One of the two portions needs to be of minimum measure so that the laws of the dough offering will not be forgotten.

tevul yom: A person who has immersed in order to remove his impurity and is now awaiting nightfall for his purification to be complete. See 1:9.

He does not require immersion: R. Yose explains that dough offering cannot be eaten by anyone whose impurity stems from their own body.

male *zav*: Leviticus 15:2–15.

female *zav*: Leviticus 15:25–28.

menstruants: Leviticus 15:19–23.

women after childbirth: Leviticus 12.

and it may be given to any priest: Even one who does not observe the purity rules.

4:9 *to any priest*: Even a priest who is not scrupulous in matters of purity.

things devoted [to God]: Leviticus 27:28 and Numbers 18:14.

firstborn animals: The firstborn of pure domesticated animals, sheep, cows, and goats; see Exodus 13:2, 11–13; 22:28–29; 34:19–20; Numbers 18:15–18; Deuteronomy 15:19–23.

the redemption of the firstborn son: Numbers 18:15–16.

the redemption of the firstborn of a donkey: Exodus 13:13, 34:20.

the shoulder, the cheeks, and the stomach: Deuteronomy 18:3.

the first of the fleece: Deuteronomy 18:4.

terumah oil that must be burnt: Impure *terumah* must be burned, but *terumah* oil that becomes impure may be used to light lamps (see *Temurah* 7:5, *Terumot* 11:10). Since it is already impure, it may be given to a priest who does not observe the purity rules scrupulously.

offerings for the altar: Which all priests can be assumed to eat in purity.

firstfruits: Which will be brought to the Temple (see *Bikkurim*) where we can assume that all priests will preserve their purity.

R. Judah prohibits firstfruits.
Vetches of *terumah*—
R. Aqiva permits,
but the Sages prohibit.

10 Nittai, a man of Teqo'a, brought dough offerings from Be-Yittur,
but they did not accept them from him.
The people of Alexandria brought dough offerings from Alexandria,
but they did not accept them from them.
The people from Mount Tsevo'im brought their firstfruits prior to the Festival of Weeks,
but they did not accept them from them,
for it is written in the Torah:
And the festival of the harvest, the firstfruits of your labors, which you have sown in the field.

11 Ben Antinus[18] brought up firstborn animals from Babylon,
but they did not accept them from him.
Joseph the Priest brought firstfruits[19] of wine and oil,
but they did not accept them from him.
He also brought up his sons[20] and members of his household
to celebrate the second[21] Passover in Jerusalem,
but they turned him back,
so that the practice[22] should not become established as an obligation.

---

[18] **K, P**, and several other manuscripts have "Atitas."
[19] **K, P**: "his firstfruits." [20] Or "children." [21] Lit. "minor." [22] Lit. "thing."

R. Judah prohibits firstfruits: They may be given only to priests who can be trusted to observe the purity rules; see *Bikkurim* 3:12.

Vetches: Usually animal food, but occasionally eaten by humans. According to R. Aqiva, since they are usually animal food, the laws of purity do not apply (see *Ma'aser Sheni* 2:4).

4:10 *Be-Yittur*: A city somewhere outside of the Land of Israel.

dough offerings… they did not accept them from him… from them: It is forbidden to bring *terumah* or dough offering from outside of Israel into Israel (see *Shevi'it* 6:6).

Mount Tsevo'im: Possibly to be identified with the mountain mentioned in 1 Samuel 13:18 or Nehemiah 11:34.

firstfruits… but they did not accept them from them: See *Bikkurim* 1:3.

And the festival of the harvest, the firstfruits of your labors: Exodus 23:16. The Mishnah reads the verse as indicating that the firstfruits may not be brought until the festival of the harvest.

4:11 *brought up firstborn animals from Babylon*: See *Temurah* 3:5.

firstfruits of wine and oil: Instead of bringing them as grapes or olives (cf. *Terumot* 11:3).

second Passover: Numbers 9:9–14.

Ariston brought his firstfruits from Apamea,
and they accepted them from him, because they said:
One who buys [a field] in Syria
is like one who buys in the outskirts of Jerusalem.[23]

[23] **K, P** (in the margin), and various other sources here add the following paragraph, which appears in slightly different form in the Tosefta: "Twenty-four gifts were given to the priests [by the Torah]: ten in the Temple, four in Jerusalem, and ten within the borders [of the Land of Israel]. These are the ten that were given to them in the Temple: (1) the purgation offering, (2) the purgation offering of birds, (3) the offering for definite guilt, (4) the offering for uncertain guilt, (5) the well-being offerings of the community, (6) the *log* of oil of one with *tsara'at*, (7) the residue of the *omer*, (8) the two loaves, (9) the showbread, and (10) the residue of meal grain offerings. And these are the four [that were given to them] in Jerusalem: (1) the firstborn animals, (2) the firstfruits, (3) that which is raised up from the thank offering and the ram of the *nazir*, and (4) the skins from the sacred offerings. These are the ten that were given to them outside the Temple: (1) *terumah*, (2) *terumah* from the tithe, (3) dough offering, (4) the first of the shearing fleece, (5) the gifts [from animals slaughtered for food], (6) the redemption of a firstborn son, (7) the redemption of a firstborn donkey, (8) the ancestral field, (9) the field that was devoted to God, and (10) that which was stolen from a proselyte. Any priest who is not expert in these things may not receive them as a gift." Cf. 4:9 above.

but they turned him back: One is obligated to bring one's family to Jerusalem only during the first Passover (see Exodus 23:17).

Apamea: In Syria, from which firstfruits are brought.

Tractate Orlah

Joshua Kulp

Introduction

Overview

Orlah (lit. "foreskin") is fruit that grows on a tree during the tree's first three years of growth. Leviticus 19:23 prohibits the eating of such produce. Tractate *Orlah* prohibits the derivation of any benefit from *orlah*, for example, burning it for light or heat or dyeing with it. Leviticus 19:24 mandates that during the fourth year of the tree's growth the fruit is "holy," which is discussed in *Ma'aser Sheni*. Reckoning the years of a tree's growth is discussed in *Rosh Hashanah* 1:1, where it follows the calendar year and not the year of the tree's growth. Thus a tree which takes root before the first of the month of Tishre, the New Year, is considered to be in its second year immediately after this date, even if in reality it is only in its second month.

Structure and Organization of the Tractate

Only a small amount of the material in this tractate is related directly to the laws of *orlah*. Most of this material is contained in the first chapter. The tractate begins by discussing under what conditions the fruit of a tree is prohibited due to *orlah*. If, for instance, one plants a tree in order to serve as a fence, its fruit is not subject to the prohibition (1:1). A tree planted in the Land of Israel by a gentile is subject to *orlah* (1:2). How do the rules of *orlah* apply vis-à-vis trees that have been uprooted (1:3–5)? The first chapter concludes with a discussion of which parts of a tree are prohibited due to *orlah* (1:7–8).

The second and third chapters are only indirectly related to the topic of *orlah*. They discuss mixtures of prohibited substances, including *orlah*, with permitted substances. The rules governing *orlah* are usually the same as those governing Mixed Species of grain that grow in a vineyard (*kilayim*).

The tractate concludes with a brief discussion of the applicability of the prohibitions of *orlah* and *kilayim* outside the Land of Israel (3:9).

Main Ideas

The first chapter is devoted to the laws of *orlah*. The mishnah discusses whether the uprooting and replanting of a tree resets the three-year *orlah* reckoning. If earth is still attached to the tree and is sufficient to sustain the tree, or if one root still remains, the count does not begin again (1:3–4).

The Mishnah deals with various practices employed in the horticulture of vines and their ramifications for the rules of *orlah* (1:5). The Torah prohibits the consumption of the fruit of a tree during the first three years. This spurs a discussion as to what is considered fruit or the derivative of fruit (1:7-9).

The second and third chapters are devoted to the process of "neutralization." The underlying idea is that when a prohibited substance, such as oil made from *terumah* olives, falls into a permitted substance of the same species, such as oil made from non-sacred olives, if there is a sufficient ratio of permitted to forbidden, the forbidden is "neutralized." The amount of prohibited produce in the mixture must be removed and then the remainder can be treated as permitted. Two ratios are mentioned: 100:1—applicable to *terumah*, *terumah* of the tithe, dough offering, and firstfruits; 200:1—applicable to *orlah* and Mixed Species of grain (*kilayim*) in a vineyard. The mishnah also discusses whether substances prohibited for different reasons, for instance *orlah* and Mixed Species, join together to exceed the ratio required to make the entire mixture permitted.

Leavening agents and spices are treated more strictly with regard to the laws of forbidden mixtures (2:4–12, 14–15).

Other rules regarding forbidden mixtures are also discussed: forbidden and permitted meat cooked in a dish (2:16–17); clothes dyed with *orlah* dye mixed with clothes dyed with permitted substances (3:1–3); dishes cooked with *orlah* fruit mixed with dishes cooked with permitted fruit (3:4); loaves of bread baked in an oven lit with the peels of *orlah* fruit mixed with other loaves of bread.

According to R. Meir, an item that is sold by number and not by weight is not nullified in a mixture even if the requisite ratio is reached. Other Sages limit this principle to particular items (3:7).

The prohibitions of *orlah* and *kilayim* in the vineyard, frequently treated together throughout the tractate, apply only in the Land of Israel (3:9).

Relationship to Scripture

The Mishnah develops a few notions hinted at in Leviticus 19:23, the only verse in the Torah to refer to the prohibition of *orlah*. The Torah prohibits the "fruit"—the Mishnah defines what is considered fruit. The Rabbis deduce from the verse that the fruit may neither be consumed nor provide any benefit whatever. Finally, the introduction to the verse clearly indicates that the rules of *orlah* apply only *when you come into the Land*. This leads to a determination of what exactly is, and is not, a tree planted in the Land of Israel.

Tractate Orlah

Chapter One

1:1–9 *Which Trees Are Subject to the Laws of Orlah*

1 One who plants [a fruit tree] as a fence or for wood beams—
[the tree] is exempt from *orlah*.
R. Yose says:
Even if he said, "The inward[-facing part of the tree] is for food,
and the outward[-facing part] is for a fence,"
the inward[-facing part] is liable [for *orlah*],
and the outward[-facing part] is exempt [from *orlah*].

2 When our ancestors came into the Land
and found [a fruit tree already] planted,
it was exempt [from *orlah*].
If they planted a tree,
even though they had not yet conquered [the Land],
it was liable [for *orlah*].
One who plants [a fruit tree] for the use of the many,
[the tree] is liable [for *orlah*];
but R. Judah declares it exempt [from *orlah*].
One who plants a tree in the public domain,
or a gentile planted it,
or a robber planted it,
or one who plants on a boat,
or a tree that has grown by itself—
[each of these trees] is liable for *orlah*.

3 A tree that was uprooted together with the hard soil,
[or] a stream swept it away together with the hard soil—
if it can [continue to] live, it is exempt [from *orlah*],

1:1 *exempt from orlah*: Since it was not planted for food. See Leviticus 19:23.

R. Yose adds that that even if some of the tree to be used as a fence was intended for food, the part not intended for food is exempt.

1:2 *When our ancestors came into the Land*: Based on Leviticus 19:23. The laws of *orlah* apply only to trees planted after the Israelites entered the Land.

1:3 *if it can [continue to] live*: From the soil that was uprooted with it.

but if not, it is liable [for *orlah*].
If the hard soil was detached¹ from its side,
or if a plowshare shook it,
or if one shook it and reset it with earth—
if it can [continue to] live, it is exempt [from *orlah*],
but if not, it is subject [to *orlah*].

4 A tree that was uprooted, but [one] root was left [in the ground]
is exempt [from *orlah*].
How [thick] must the root be?
Rabban Simeon b. Gamaliel said in the name of R. Eliezer b. Judah a man of Bartota:
As [thick as] a pin used for stretching.

5 A tree that was uprooted, and from it a shoot took root,
and [the tree] derives sustenance² from [the shoot]—
the old [tree] returns to the status of the shoot.
If one caused a shoot to take root year after year, and it became detached—
one counts [the three years of *orlah*] from the time it became detached.
A grafted shoot of vines,
and a grafted shoot [growing] on another grafted shoot,
even if he rooted them in the soil,
are permitted.
R. Meir says:
In a place where it is strongly [grafted], it is permitted,
but in a place where it is weakly [grafted], it is forbidden.
Likewise,³ a shoot that has become detached and is full of fruit—
if it increased one two-hundredth, it is forbidden.

---

¹ Lit. "uprooted."   ² Lit. "lives."   ³ Absent in **K**, **P**, and most manuscripts.

---

it is exempt: The tree is not considered replanted with regard to *orlah*.

but if not: If the farmer must add soil to the rootball to keep the tree viable, it is as if he is planting the tree anew and the three-year *orlah* clock restarts from the beginning.

If the hard soil was detached from its side…shook it: And the roots were exposed.

1:4 *a pin used for stretching*: A pin that weavers used for stretching cloth.

1:5 *the old [tree] returns to the status of the shoot*: And is exempt from *orlah*.

and it became detached: One of the new vines becomes detached from the original vine.

A grafted shoot of vines: A detached vine grafted onto an older vine.

are permitted: The count for the years of *orlah* follows the older vine.

in a place where it is strongly [grafted]: The grafted branch onto which the new one is being grafted has already taken firm hold.

weakly [grafted]…forbidden: Since the original branch's graft was weak, the new branch is likely to take root in the ground in order to survive, and therefore counts as newly planted for the purposes of *orlah*.

Likewise: Referring back to the earlier clause about a shoot that became detached.

if it increased one two-hundredth, it is prohibited: The fruit is prohibited as *orlah* if it grew $1/200$ in size after having been detached. This follows the standard rule that a mixture containing $1/200$ of *orlah* is prohibited. See 2:1 and *Kilayim* 5:6.

6 A planting of *orlah*
or of Mixed Species of the vineyard,
that became mixed with [other] plantings—
in this situation one may not gather [the fruit].
But if one gathered [it],
it is neutralized in one and two hundred,
provided that he did not gather [the fruit] deliberately.
R. Yose says:
He may even deliberately gather [the fruit],
and it will be neutralized in one and two hundred.

7 Leaves, sprouts, sap of vines, and vine-buds—
are permitted in [the three years of] *orlah*,
and in the fourth year,
and to a *nazir*,
but are forbidden if they come from an *asherah* [tree].
R. Yose says:
Vine-buds are forbidden, because they are fruit.
R. Eliezer says:
One who curdles [milk] with the resin of [a tree liable for] *orlah*,
[the cheese produced] is forbidden.
R. Joshua says:
I have received an explicit tradition that one who curdles [milk]
with the resin of the leaves,[4]
[or] with the resin of the roots,
[the cheese produced] is permitted;
[but one who curdles milk] with the resin of the unripe berries,
[the cheese produced] is forbidden,
because they are fruit.

[4] A marginal gloss in **K** inserts "[the cheese produced] is forbidden."

1:6 *Mixed Species of the vineyard*: Deuteronomy 22:9 (cf. Leviticus 19:19) and *Kilayim* 8:1.

became mixed with [other] plantings: Which were not *orlah* or Mixed Species of the vineyard.

one may not gather [the fruit]: While attached to the ground, the prohibited shoots are not neutralized by the permitted ones.

provided that he did not gather [the fruit] deliberately: It is prohibited to intentionally neutralize a prohibited substance; see *Terumot* 5:9.

He may even deliberately gather [the fruit]: In R. Yose's opinion, this is not a case of intentional neutralization of prohibited substances, since picking the produce does not neutralize the prohibited plants. They are, rather, only nullified when the produce has been entirely picked and it turns out that the permitted outnumbers the prohibited by a 200:1 ratio.

1:7 *fourth year*: When fruit must be brought to Jerusalem and consumed there (see Leviticus 19:24 and *Ma'aser Sheni* chapter five).

nazir: Who is otherwise prohibited from grapes and grape products (Numbers 6:3–4); cf. 1:8.

an asherah: A tree used in idol worship (Deuteronomy 7:5, 12:3; *Avodah Zarah* 3:7).

8 Defective grapes, grapeseeds, grape peels, and their *temed* extract,
the peel of a pomegranate and its sprout,
nutshells and [fruit] seeds[5]
are forbidden
in the [three years of] *orlah*,
and if they come from an *asherah* [tree],
and [are forbidden] to a *nazir*,
but are permitted in the fourth year.
Unripe fruit is forbidden in all of these.

9 R. Yose says:
One may plant a shoot of *orlah*,
but one may not plant a nut of *orlah*,
because it is fruit.
And one may not graft early date berries of *orlah*.

Chapter Two

2:1–17 *Mixtures of Permitted and Forbidden Substances*

2 Terumah,[6]
terumah from the tithe from *demai*,
dough offering,
and firstfruits
are neutralized in one and a hundred,

[5] K, P, and several other manuscripts: "pits."
[6] K, P, and most manuscripts insert "and *terumah* from the tithe."

1:8 *temed extract*: A wine made from soaked grapeseeds and skins.

but are permitted in the fourth year: The laws of second tithe and fourth-year produce apply only to the parts of the plant that are normally eaten (*Ma'aser Sheni* 2:1).

1:9 *One may plant a shoot of orlah*: The laws of *orlah* do not apply to the branches or shoots of a tree, only to the fruit.

And one may not graft early date berries of orlah: It was their practice to graft date berries from a male tree onto a female date tree.

2:1 *Terumah*: Numbers 18:11 and *Terumot*.

terumah from the tithe: Levites receive the tithe (Numbers 18:21–24; *Ma'aserot*) and, in turn give *terumah* to the priests (Numbers 18:25–32).

demai: Produce about which there is doubt whether tithes were separated; see *Demai*. Just as regular produce can be suspected of not having had tithes removed, tithe too can be subject to the same doubt as to whether the requisite *terumah* was separated or not. Similar lists appear in *Bava Metsi'a* 4:8 and *Me'ilah* 4:2.

are neutralized in one and one hundred: If *terumah* produce accidentally falls into a pile of regular, nonsacral produce at a ratio of 1:100, the mixture is permitted; at less than this ratio, the whole mixture must be treated as *terumah* and may only be consumed by a priest. See *Terumot* 4:7, 5:1; *Bikkurim* 2:1.

combine [to form the statutory minimum],
and one must remove [from the mixture an amount
equal to that of the forbidden produce contained in it].
Orlah and Mixed Species of the vineyard
are neutralized in one and two hundred
and combine [to form the statutory minimum],
but one need not remove [from the mixture an amount
equal to that of the forbidden produce contained in it].
R. Simeon says:
They do not combine.
R. Eliezer says:
They combine when they impart flavor, but not to forbid.
   2 *Terumah* can neutralize *orlah*,
and *orlah* can neutralize *terumah*.
How so?
If a *se'ah* of *terumah* fell into one hundred [*se'ah* of nonsacral produce],
and afterward three *qav* of *orlah*
or three *qav* of Mixed Species of the vineyard fell in—
this is [an instance] in which *terumah* neutralizes *orlah*,
and *orlah* [neutralizes] *terumah*.

combine: For instance, if half-part *terumah* is mixed in with another half-part firstfruits, there will need to be one hundred parts nonsacred produce for the mixture to be neutralized. Parallel at *Me'ilah* 4:2.

one must remove: Even if the forbidden substance is neutralized, an amount of produce equal to the amount that fell in to the mixture must be removed and treated as if it was holy. See *Terumot* 4:11, 5:8.

Orlah and Mixed Species of the vineyard…combine…R. Simeon: Parallel at *Me'ilah* 4:6.

but one need not remove: Since *orlah* and Mixed Species cannot be consumed by anyone, one need not remove anything to make restitution.

They do not combine: According to R. Simeon, distinct categories of forbidden produce never combine; see 2:10.

They combine when they impart flavor: When a forbidden item becomes mixed with permitted items of a different species, the mixture is prohibited only if the forbidden item imparts flavor (2:7; *Hallah* 3:10). If *orlah* and Mixed Species jointly impart their respective tastes to the entire mixture, they combine for purposes of neutralization. If not, then each is neutralized individually.

but not to forbid: This refers to mixtures of like species, which become prohibited if the forbidden substance mixes in at a ratio below neutralization. R. Eliezer concurs with R. Simeon that in such a case, each category of forbidden produce need only be neutralized individually. Cf. *Me'ilah* 4:2.

2:2 *Terumah can neutralize orlah*: *Terumah* combines with nonsacral produce in order to create the necessary 1:200 ratio so as to neutralize any *orlah* or Mixed Species in the mixture. Similarly, *orlah* combines with nonsacral produce to create the necessary 1:100 ratio to neutralize *terumah*.

a se'ah of terumah fell into one hundred: The mishnah must mean ninety-nine *se'ah* of nonsacred produce, since at a ratio of 1:100 the *terumah* would have already been neutralized.

three qav of orlah or three qav of Mixed Species of the vineyard fell in: Three *qav* is half of a *se'ah*. The one *terumah* *se'ah* combines with the ninety-nine nonsacral *se'ah*, producing a 200:1 ratio to neutralize the *orlah* or Mixed Species that fell in.

orlah [neutralizes] terumah: The scenario presented does not work mathematically in reverse, since there are only 99.5 *se'ah* of non-*terumah* produce, which does not reach the necessary threshold of 1:100 to neutralize the *terumah*. The Mishnah might simply expect the reader to construct a parallel scenario,

3 *Orlah* can neutralize Mixed Species [of the vineyard]
and Mixed Species [of the vineyard can neutralize] *orlah*,
and *orlah* [can neutralize] *orlah*.
How so?
If a *se'ah* of *orlah* fell into two hundred [*se'ah* of nonsacral produce]
and afterwards a *se'ah* and a bit more of *orlah* fell in,
or a *se'ah* and a bit more of Mixed Species of the vineyard [fell in]—
this is [an instance] in which *orlah* neutralizes Mixed Species [of the vineyard],
and Mixed Species [of the vineyard neutralizes] *orlah*,
and *orlah* [neutralizes] *orlah*.

4 Whatever causes [food] to ferment,
or seasons [food],
or makes a *terumah* mixture[7] with *orlah*
or with Mixed Species of the vineyard—
is forbidden.[8]
The House of Shammai say:
It also conveys impurity.
But the House of Hillel say:
It conveys impurity only if it contains an egg's bulk.

5 Dostai, a man of Kefar Yatmah,
was [one] of the disciples of the House of Shammai,
and he said:
I received a tradition from Shammai the Elder who said:[9]
It conveys impurity only if it contains an egg's bulk.

6 And when[10] did they say:
"Anything that causes [food to] ferment or seasons [food] or makes a *terumah* mixture"
is stringent? [11]

---

[7] Text and meaning uncertain. [8] **K, P**, and several manuscripts: "forbids."
[9] **K, P**, and most manuscripts: "I asked Shammai the Elder and he said."
[10] Lit. "why." The translation of the first half of this mishnah is uncertain.
[11] **K** lacks "is stringent."

---

such as: a *se'ah* of *orlah* is mixed with two hundred *se'ah* of nonsacral produce, and then *terumah* fell into the mixture. If the *orlah* and nonsacral produce are more than 100:1 of the *terumah*, the *terumah* is neutralized.

2:3 *a se'ah of orlah fell into two hundred*: Sufficient to neutralize the *orlah*.

afterwards a se'ah and a little bit more of orlah fell in: The 201 *se'ah* nullify the one *se'ah* and a little bit more (1/200 of a *se'ah*) of *orlah* or Mixed Species.

2:4 *Whatever causes [food] to ferment or seasons [food]*: Leaven and spices are not nullified in the 1:100 or 1:200 ratios.

or makes a terumah mixture: The text and meaning of these words is disputed by commentators. Some interpret this to means that if the leaven or seasoning is *terumah* it creates a *terumah* mixture which is prohibited to nonpriests even if there is more than a 100 or 200:1 ratio.

only if it contains an egg's bulk: The usual amount required for food to transmit impurity (see *Tohorot*).

2:6 *did they say*: In 2:4.

[In the case of] a species [mixed] with its [like] species.
[When did they say it is]
[sometimes] lenient and [sometimes] stringent?
[In the case of] a species [mixed] with a different species.
How so?
If leaven of wheat fell into a dough of wheat,
and there is in it enough to cause fermentation,
whether there is enough in it to be neutralized in one and a hundred,
or whether there is not enough in it to be neutralized in one and a hundred,
it is forbidden.
If there is not enough to become neutralized in one and a hundred,
whether there is enough to cause fermentation,
or whether there is not enough to cause fermentation,
it is forbidden.

7 "[Sometimes] lenient and [sometimes] stringent,
[in the case of] a species [mixed] with a different species":
how so?
For instance,[12] if crushed beans [of *terumah*] were boiled[13] together with [nonsacral] lentils,
and there is in them enough to impart flavor,
whether there is enough in them to be neutralized in one and a hundred,
or whether there is not enough in them to be neutralized in one and a hundred,
it is forbidden.
[But] if there is not enough in them to impart flavor,
whether there is enough in them to be neutralized in one and a hundred,
or whether there is not enough to be neutralized in one and a hundred,
it is permitted.

8 If leaven of nonsacral [grain] fell into [nonsacral] dough,[14]
and there is in it enough to cause fermentation,
and afterwards leaven of *terumah* fell in,
or leaven of Mixed Species of the vineyard,
and there is in it enough to cause fermentation,
it is forbidden.

[12] Absent in **K**, **P**, and the majority of manuscripts.   [13] Or "cooked."
[14] **K** and several manuscripts add "of nonsacral [grain]."

a species [mixed] with its [like] species: When like substances mix (for instance *terumah* wheat with nonsacral wheat) the law is always strict.

If leaven of wheat ... dough of wheat: These are examples of like with like.

2:7 *or whether there is not enough to be neutralized in one and a hundred, it is permitted*: Mathematical ratios are relevant only when a species is mixed with its own kind. When mixed with unlike species, the forbidden species prohibits only if it imparts taste. See *Hallah* 3:10.

2:8 *it is forbidden*: Even though the second piece of leaven was not needed.

9 If leaven of nonsacral [grain] fell into [nonsacral] dough
and caused it to ferment,
and afterwards leaven of *terumah* fell in,
or leaven of Mixed Species of the vineyard,
and there is in it enough to cause fermentation,
it is forbidden.
R. Simeon permits it.

10 Seasonings [consisting] of two or three categories of one species,
or [consisting] of three [species of one category],
are forbidden and combine.
R. Simeon says:
Two or three[15] categories of one species,
or two species of one category,
do not combine.

11 Leaven of nonsacral [grain] and [leaven] of *terumah* that fell into a dough,
and neither in this one is there enough to cause fermentation
nor in that one is there enough to cause fermentation,
[but] combined they caused [the dough] to ferment—
R. Eliezer says:
I go after the last.
But the Sages say:
Whether the forbidden [leaven] fell in first or last,
it never forbids [the dough]
unless there is enough in it [by itself] to cause fermentation.

12 Yoezer a man of the Birah,
was [one] of the disciples of the House of Shammai,
and he said:
I asked Rabban Gamaliel the elder
[as he was] standing at the eastern gate [of the Temple], and he said:
It never prohibits [the dough]
unless there is enough in it [by itself] to cause fermentation.

[15] **K**, **P**, and the majority of manuscripts lack "or three."

2:9 *and caused it to ferment*: This is the distinguishing factor from the previous mishnah.

R. Simeon permits it: Since the dough was fermented before the prohibited leaven fell in.

2:10 *categories*: i.e. legal categories, such as *terumah*, Mixed Species, or *orlah*.

species: For example, pepper.

three [species of one category]: For instance, pepper, onion, and garlic of *terumah*.

combine: See 2:1.

2:11 *I go after the last*: Since that is the leaven that causes the dough to ferment.

2:12 *Birah*: The commentators debate the meaning of this title; all agree that it has something to do with the Temple. See Nehemiah 7:2; *Pesahim* 3:8 and 7:8.

13 Clothing[16] which one oiled with impure oil,
and [then] went back and oiled with pure oil;
or which one [first] oiled with pure oil,
and [then] went back and oiled with impure oil—
R. Eliezer says:
I go after the first.
But the Sages say:
After the last.

14 Leaven of *terumah* and [leaven] of Mixed Species of the vineyard
which fell into [nonsacral] dough,
and neither in this one was there enough to cause fermentation,
nor in that one was there enough to cause fermentation,
but they combined and caused [the dough to] ferment—
it is forbidden to nonpriests and permitted to priests.
R. Simeon permits [it] to nonpriests and to priests.

15 Seasonings of *terumah* and of Mixed Species of the vineyard that fell into a pot:
neither in this one was there enough to season [the dish],
nor in that one was there enough to season [the dish],
but they combined and seasoned it—
it is prohibited to nonpriests but permitted to priests.
R. Simeon permits [it] to nonpriests and to priests.

16 A piece of [meat from] offerings of the highest sanctity
and [a piece] of [meat which is] *piggul*,
or [a piece] of [meat which is a] remnant,
which were cooked with pieces [of nonsacral meat]—

[16] Lit. "utensils" or "vessels."

2:13 *I go after the first*: When the clothing expels oil, it will expel the first oil it absorbed.

After the last: The first oil is absorbed by the clothing and when used the objects will expel the last oil used.

2:14 *it, the dough, is forbidden to nonpriests*: Since both *terumah* and Mixed Species of the vineyard are forbidden to nonpriests.

and permitted to priests: Since the Mixed Species, which is forbidden to priests, was not sufficient by itself to cause fermentation. This follows the position of the Sages in 2:11.

R. Simeon permits it to nonpriests and to priests: In accordance with his opinion in 2:10, that different categories of prohibited substances do not combine.

2:16 *offerings of the highest sanctity*: Such as the purgation offering or the guilt offering, which may be eaten only by priests (see *Zevahim* 5:1–5).

piggul: A sacrifice that was rendered unfit because the priest who offered it intended to eat it either at the wrong place or at the wrong time. See Leviticus 7:18, 19:7; *Zevahim* 2:2.

remnant: Sacrificial meat that was not consumed by the statutory deadline. See Leviticus 7:16–17, 8:32; *Zevahim* 4:5.

which was cooked with pieces [of nonsacral meat]: Similar to 2:14, there is not enough of any one of the prohibited meats individually to prohibit the entire dish, but they are present in sufficient quantity when combined with each other. While the Mishnah never gives a neutralization threshold for sacrificial meat cooked with nonsacrificial meat, the Tosefta sets the ratio at 100:1, just like *terumah*. Cf. *Hullin* 7:5.

it is forbidden to nonpriests but permitted to priests.
R. Simeon permits [it] to nonpriests and to priests.

17 Meat of offerings of the highest sanctity
or meat of offerings of lesser sanctity
that was cooked together with nonsacrificial meat[17]
is forbidden to the impure, but permitted to the pure.

Chapter Three

3:1–8 *Making Use of Orlah Produce*

3 A garment that one dyed with peels of *orlah* [fruit] must be burned.
If it became mixed up with other [garments], all of them must be burned—
the words of R. Meir.
But the Sages say:
It becomes neutralized in one and two hundred.

2 One who dyes [a thread] the whole [length] of a *sit* with *orlah* peels,
and wove it into a garment,
and it is not known which [thread] it is—

---

[17] Lit. "the meat of desire"; see Deuteronomy 12:20 and 14:26.

---

forbidden to nonpriests: Who cannot eat any of the meats that were mixed with the nonsacral meat.

permitted to priests: Who can eat meat from offerings of the highest sanctity, which combine with the rest of the nonsacral meat to neutralize the *piggul* or remnant.

R. Simeon...and to priests: Consistent with their dispute above, he considers these different categories of prohibited substances that do not combine, and are therefore neutralized by the nonsacral meat.

2:17 *Meat of offerings of the highest sanctity*: Permitted only to priests.

meat of offerings of lesser sanctity: Such as the thank offering, or well-being offering, which are permitted to pure nonpriests. See *Zevahim* 5:6–8.

with nonsacrificial meat: While there is sufficient nonsacrificial meat to nullify each piece of sanctified meat on its own, the amount is insufficient to nullify the combination of sanctified meats.

The dish *is forbidden to the impure*: In this case, R. Simeon agrees because the category of prohibition of most holy sacrifices and less holy sacrifices is the same—both are prohibited to the impure.

but permitted to the pure: The Sages agree that the dish is permitted to pure nonpriests, since only the offerings of the highest sanctity are prohibited to nonpriests, and they are neutralized by the combination of the other meats.

3:1 *with peels of orlah [fruit]*: The laws of *orlah* apply even to the inedible peels.

must be burned: It is forbidden to derive benefit from them.

all of them must be burned: Important objects are not nullified in any ratio, according to R. Meir. See 3:7 below.

R. Meir says:
The garment must be burned.
But the Sages say:
It becomes neutralized in one and two hundred.

3 One who weaves [a thread] the whole [length] of a *sit*
from the wool of a firstborn animal into a garment—
the garment must be burned.
[One who weaves a thread] from the hair of a *nazir*
or from the firstborn of a donkey into sackcloth,
the sackcloth must be burned.
And [wool or hair of] consecrated [animals],
consecrates in any amount.

4 A dish which one cooked with peels of *orlah* [fruit] must be burned.
If [the dish] became mixed with other [dishes],
it becomes neutralized in one and two hundred.

5 An oven which one lit with peels of *orlah* [fruit],
and [then] one baked bread in it—
the bread must be burned.
If [the bread] became mixed with other [loaves of bread],
it becomes neutralized in one and two hundred.

6 If one has bundles of fenugreek of Mixed Species of the vineyard,
they must be burned.
If they became mixed with other [bundles],
all of them must be burned—

It becomes neutralized in one and two hundred: See 2:1.

3:2 *the whole [length] of a sit*: A *sit* is a measure of distance, either the distance between the outstretched thumb and forefinger, or the distance between the outstretched forefinger and middle finger.

it becomes neutralized in one and two hundred: Two hundred threads in the garment neutralize the thread dyed with *orlah* peels.

3:3 *from the wool of a firstborn animal*: From which it is forbidden to derive any benefit (see Deuteronomy 15:19 and *Bekhorot* 3:4).

the hair of a nazir: Which must be burned (Numbers 6:18).

the firstborn of a donkey: Which must be redeemed with a sheep (Exodus 13:13, 34:20).

consecrates: That is, creates a prohibition to derive benefit from it. (On this use of consecrate, see Deuteronomy 22:9 and *Kilayim*.) It need not be burned, however, because consecrated things can be redeemed (see Leviticus 27).

in any amount: Even less than the whole length of a *sit*.

3:4 *cooked with peels of orlah*: The peels were used as kindling.

must be burned: Since it is prohibited to derive benefit from *orlah*.

it becomes neutralized in one and two hundred: In this case R. Meir agrees, for a cooked dish is not considered an "important item" as is an article of clothing (3:7).

3:6 *Mixed Species of the vineyard*: From which it is forbidden to derive benefit (Deuteronomy 22:9 and *Kilayim*).

the words of R. Meir.
But the Sages say:
They become neutralized in one and two hundred.

7 For R. Meir used to say:
Anything that is normally [sold] by counting consecrates.
But the Sages say:
Only six things consecrate
But[18] R. Aqiva says:
Seven [things].
And these are they:
(1) nuts with soft shells;
(2) *badan* pomegranates;
(3) stopped-up jars;
(4) beet shoots;
(5) cabbage-heads;
(6) Greek gourds.
R. Aqiva says:
(7) also loaves [baked by] a householder.
Those to which *orlah* applies
are *orlah*;
those to which the law of Mixed Species of the vineyard applies
are Mixed Species of the vineyard.

8 If the nuts cracked,
or if the pomegranates split open,
or the jars became unstopped,

---

[18] K, P and the majority of manuscripts lack the conjunction.

3:7 *is normally [sold] by counting*: Such as bundles of fenugreek or clothing. This excludes items sold by weight or volume.

consecrates: Forbids, in even the smallest amounts, anything with which they become mixed; see 3:3.

Only six things "consecrate": Due to their importance.

stopped-up casks: Containing *orlah* wine.

loaves [baked by] a householder: More valuable than bread baked by a professional baker, and identifiable as such (see *Bava Metsi'a* 2:2).

Those to which orlah applies: Pomegranates, nuts, and wine.

to which the law of Mixed Species of the vineyard applies: Beet shoots and cabbage-heads. Concerning Greek gourds, see *Kilayim* 2:11.

3:8 *they become neutralized in one and two hundred*: If one of the foods mentioned in 3:7 becomes in some way broken up, it loses its importance and it becomes neutralized like normal *orlah* or Mixed Species produce (2:1).

or the gourds were cut,
or the loaves were sliced up,
they become neutralized in one and two hundred.

3:9 The Status of Doubtful Orlah outside the Land of Israel

9 Doubtful *orlah*—
in the Land of Israel it is forbidden,
in Syria it is permitted,
and outside the Land [of Israel] one may go down and purchase,
provided that [the buyer] does not see him gathering it.
If a vineyard is planted with vegetables [which constitute Mixed Species],
and the vegetables are sold outside of it—
in the Land of Israel they are forbidden,
in Syria they are permitted,
and outside the Land [of Israel] one may go down and gather[19] them,
provided that he does not gather [them] by hand.
New [produce] is forbidden by the Torah in all places,
orlah is [forbidden outside the Land of Israel as] a *halakhah*,
and Mixed Species [of a vineyard is forbidden as] an enactment of the scribes.

[19] Some citations read "purchase."

3:9 *Doubtful orlah*: For instance, produce sold outside of the field in which it is grown.

in Syria: Where some of the agricultural laws apply and some do not (see *Demai* 6:11; *Shevi'it* 6:2).

provided that [the buyer] does not see him gathering it: For that would be "certain *orlah*."

and the vegetables are sold outside of it: This causes them to have the status of "doubtful Mixed Species."

New [produce]: Produce harvested before the *omer* (barley harvest) was offered on the second day of Passover (see Leviticus 23:9–14; *Hallah* 1:1).

forbidden by the Torah in all places: Cf. *Qiddushin* 1:9.

halakhah: There are two interpretations in the Talmud, either "custom" or "law."

Tractate Bikkurim

Naftali S. Cohn

Introduction

Overview

The word *bikkurim* means "firstfruits," the firstfruits of the harvest—specifically of grapes, figs, pomegranates, olives, dates, and perhaps wheat and barley (the seven species of the Land of Israel, Deuteronomy 8:8). The landowner must bring them to the Temple and give them to the priest. The term also refers to the public communal offerings of the first of the barley harvest and the first of the wheat harvest, discussed in tractate *Menahot* but not appearing in our tractate.

Structure and Organization of the Tractate

Cleverly framed in terms of the two variables of "bringing" the firstfruits and "reciting" the ritual declaration, chapter 1 opens the tractate with a series of laws specifying various circumstances in which a person would or would not perform the ritual and its components. Chapter 2 employs a different structure, making a detailed comparison between the firstfruits and the related obligations of *terumah*, the second tithe, and the *terumah* from the tithe. The extended comparison shows how the obligations are similar to, but different from, one another.

The centerpiece of the tractate (3:1–8) is the narrative description of how the firstfruits were brought to the Temple of Jerusalem. It forms a cohesive narrative, which begins with the farmer in the field collecting firstfruits. It then describes the pilgrims gathering in the central town of the district, traces the stages of the pilgrimage to Jerusalem and the Temple, and concludes with the ritual declaration and the final bow and the departure from the Temple. This narrative is part of a subgenre of passages in the Mishnah that purport to describe how various rituals used to be done in the Temple. While the narratives appear realistic, the evidence of nonrabbinic sources (e.g. Philo, Josephus) suggests strongly that the rabbis have shaped these accounts for their own ends and that the rituals were not performed exactly as described.

Chapter 4 provides various laws pertaining to the *androgynos* (intersex person with both male and female genitalia), whose existence challenges the binary gender system. This chapter is omitted from the Mishnah quoted in the Yerushalmi, from the commentary of Maimonides (twelfth century), and from many printed editions of the Mishnah. It does, however, appear in some printed editions and in all the early manuscripts of the Mishnah, including the important Parma and Kaufmann manuscripts. Some scholars suggest that it was not original to the Mishnah but migrated from the Tosefta, whose text, however, frequently differs from what is found in our Mishnah. The systematic exploration of the status of the *androgynos* is similar to the topics of chapter 2, especially the case of the *koy* (2:8–11), and it seems to follow naturally from that material (and from the mention in 1:5). The Hebrew text translated here is that of the standard printed edition of the Mishnah (Vilna: Romm, 1908–1909). Other sources preserve numerous variants.

Main Ideas

The Mishnah takes a number of details in the Torah's description of the ritual and turns them into legal obligations. The Mishnah regulates who may, or may not, fulfill these particular legal obligations and in which circumstances the requirements are, or are not, binding. The most basic legal obligation is to "bring" the firstfruits to the Temple and present them to the priest (see 1:1–11, 2:2, and 3:2–8). A second key requirement, also stemming from the biblical description, is to "recite the ritual declaration" of Deuteronomy 26:3 and 26:5–10.

A third legal obligation, a nonbiblical one, is the requirement to "separate" the firstfruits, namely to set them aside and mark them as sacred (1:7–8 and 3:1). This ritual action appears elsewhere in the Mishnah with respect to other types of sacred produce obligations. Additional legal obligations that must be fulfilled in making the firstfruits offering (some biblical and some not) include: an animal sacrifice, the singing of Psalms, "waving" the offering, and staying overnight in Jerusalem (see 2:4). Similarly, additional fruits that "supplement" and "wreathe" the firstfruits are brought together with them (see especially 3:10).

Neither the Torah nor the Mishnah specifies when the firstfruits are to be brought to the Temple. The Tosefta and the book of Tobit claim or hint that the firstfruits were brought on the pilgrimage festivals of *Atseret* (Festival of Weeks, seven weeks after Passover) and Sukkot (in the fall). However, the Mishnah's narrative (3:2–8) makes no connection with the pilgrimage festivals, and suggests that different districts would bring their firstfruits at different points during the summer, depending on the maturation of the fruit in each district. The fruits can be brought as early as *Atseret* (1:3, 1:6) and as late as Hanukkah (1:6; and see *Hallah* 4:10).

Relationship to Scripture

Deuteronomy 26:1–10 describes a ritual for taking *some of the best of every fruit* and bringing it *to the place in which the Lord your God will choose to place his name*, namely, the Temple in Jerusalem. This ritual involves placing these firstfruits in a basket, going to the temple, reciting a set of ritual declarations, giving the basket to the priest, placing the basket down, and finally, bowing (26:2–10). The Mishnah quotes from this passage in Deuteronomy several times, and the biblical description of the ritual serves as the basis for the Mishnah's own narrative description in chapter 3 and for the Mishnah's understanding of the ritual as a whole. As throughout the Mishnah, the rabbinic authors have developed the biblical material and made it their own.

Special Notes for the Reader

There is no Talmud Bavli to *Bikkurim*, however there is Talmud Yerushalmi. I have benefited from the standard commentaries, in particular that of Maimonides and Obadiah of Bertinoro (who largely follows Maimonides). Among modern commentaries I have regularly consulted those of Pinhas Kehati and Hanokh Albeck.

Tractate Bikkurim

Chapter One

1:1–3   *Those Who Do Not Bring the Firstfruits*

1   There are those who bring the firstfruits [to the Temple in Jerusalem] and recite [the declaration],
those who bring but do not recite,
and those who do not bring.
The following are those who do not bring:
the one who plants in his own property but sinks a shoot into the ground
so that it grows from the property of [another, whether] an individual or the public.
So too one who sinks a shoot from the property of [another, whether] an individual or the public
so that it grows from his own property.
The one who plants in his own property and sinks a shoot into the ground
so that it grows from his own property,
but there is a path of an individual or a path of the public in the middle—
this one does not bring.

1:1 *There are those who bring...recite*: The language translated here in the present indicative ("brings" and "recites") is ambiguous. While it could be descriptive—this is what people do in practice—it more likely indicates that one is obligated to "bring" and "recite." It is a commandment (Deuteronomy 26:1–10). The negative "does not bring/recite" is more ambiguous. Is this simply a statement of practice, or does it mean "need not bring/recite" or "should not bring/recite" or even "may not bring/recite"? The exact force may differ from case to case.

those who do not bring: This paragraph lists three situations in which replanting a shoot creates ambiguous ownership of the tree itself, with the tree both in the planter's property and on the property of another or on public property. The reason the person need not or ought not or may not bring such firstfruits is explained in 1:2.

sinks a shoot into the ground: On this agricultural practice, see also *Kilayim* 7:1–2, *Shevi'it* 2:6, *Orlah* 1:5, and *Sotah* 8:2.

So too one who sinks a shoot from the property of another...so that it grows from his own property: This is a further case of ambiguous ownership; alternatively, it is theft (see 1:2).

a path of the individual or a path of the public in the middle: The plant grows only in the person's property but traverses the ground under other property.

R. Judah says:
In a case like this, one brings.

2 For what reason does he not bring?
Because it says, *The best firstfruits of your land*—
[One does not bring] until all of the growth is from *your* land.
Sharecroppers, tenant farmers, those holding confiscated property, and a robber
do not bring for the same reason,
because it says, *The best firstfruits of your land.*

3 One does not bring firstfruits from other than the seven species.
Not from dates in the hills,
nor from fruits in the valleys,
nor from oil-olives that are not among the choicest.
One may not bring firstfruits before the Festival of Weeks.
The people of Har Tsevo'im brought their firstfruits before the Festival of Weeks,
but the [Temple authorities] did not accept them from them,
because of that which is written in the Torah,
And the festival of the harvest of the firstfruits of your work, of what you sow in the field.

1:2 *The best firstfruits of your land*: Exodus 23:19 and 34:26. The emphasis is on *your* land. Bringing the firstfruits is only required when the planter fully owns the land.

Sharecroppers, tenant farmers: Sharecroppers pay a percentage yield (see for instance, *Bava Metsi'a* 5:8 and *Bava Batra* 3:3), tenant farmers a fixed rent in kind (see *Demai* 6:1).

those holding confiscated property: See *Gittin* 5:6.

1:3 *the seven species*: Five fruits—dates and oil-olives (as indicated in this paragraph and in 1:10) and figs, grapes, and pomegranates (see 3:1)—and two grains—barley and wheat—derived elsewhere from Deuteronomy 8:8. Firstfruits are thus not exclusively fruits in the botanical sense. It is unclear whether one may bring other types of produce for the offering if one wishes or if this is forbidden.

Not from dates in the hills: According to most commentaries, dates in the hills and fruits in the valleys are, like the less-than-best quality oil-olives mentioned here, not the choicest types. The notion of the choicest firstfruits may derive from Exodus 23:19 and 34:26 and Deuteronomy 26:2.

oil-olives: As in Deuteronomy 8:8 and in 1:10 below (according to the manuscript reading), oil-olives are in fact the choicest. The commentaries thus interpret this as other nonchoice oil-producing olives, or simply those olives that have not grown under ideal conditions and do not produce good-quality oil.

before the Festival of Weeks: Heb. *Atseret*, literally, "assembly," the rabbinic name for what is now called Shavu'ot, or, the Festival of Weeks, celebrated seven weeks after Passover. See 1:6 for the latest time for bringing the firstfruits.

The people of Har Tsevo'im: See also *Hallah* 4:10.

did not accept: This indicates that in the case of calendrical timing, one may not bring the firstfruits outside of the specified time.

And the festival of the harvest: That is, the Festival of Weeks. Exodus 23:16 implies that the period of the firstfruits begins then.

1:4–9 *Those Who Bring the Firstfruits but Do Not Recite the Declaration*

4 The following bring [firstfruits] but do not recite the declaration:
The proselyte brings but does not recite
for he is unable to say *as the Lord swore to our forefathers to give us.*
But if his mother is of Israel,
he brings and recites.
And when he prays privately he says "The God of the forefathers of Israel."
But when he is in the synagogue, he says "The God of your forefathers."
But if his mother is of Israel, he says "the God of my forefathers."
   5 R. Eliezer b. Jacob says:
A woman who is the daughter of proselytes may not be married into the priesthood, unless her mother is of Israel.
The law is one and the same for proselytes and freed slaves,

1:4 *The proselyte*: A gentile who has converted to Judaism cannot truthfully make the declaration, which refers to the biblical ancestors as one's own ancestors. Nor can s/he truthfully refer to "my forefathers" in the daily prayers. In the case of the prayers, the language can be changed. The biblical language of the first-fruits declaration, however, cannot, and thus the proselyte cannot make the declaration. In his commentary to the Mishnah, Maimonides rules—following the Yerushalmi—that the convert can indeed recite both texts, since Abraham is the forefather of all.

as the Lord swore: Deuteronomy 26:3.

if his mother is of Israel: If a proselyte's mother is an Israelite, that is, a native-born Jew, then the original utterances about ancestors are true and can be recited. This passage seems to contradict the view found elsewhere in the Mishnah (*Qiddushin* 3:12 and *Yevamot* 7:5) and in later rabbinic law that holds that the child of a Jewish woman to be a Jew by birth. How then can a proselyte have a Jewish mother? One explanation is that this mishnah reflects the prerabbinic view that Jewishness, in the case of mixed union between Jew and gentile, is determined by the father. Since this person has a gentile father, s/he can become a proselyte. Alternatively, when the Mishnah says "proselyte," it means a second-generation proselyte, child of a proselyte father who is a Jew by birth through her/his mother and who can refer to her/his own *forefathers*.

when he is in the synagogue: Presumably the proselyte (of non-Israelite parents) is reciting the prayer aloud, and thus referring to the community at large.

1:5 *A woman who is the daughter of proselytes*: Priests (*kohanim*) may not marry proselytes; see *Qiddushin* 4:1. This view extends the concern for lineal purity to the child of proselytes.

Mother is of Israel: R. Eliezer b. Jacob may mean that only a Jewish mother is sufficient. Alternatively, perhaps a father (but not a mother) from Israel is sufficient. It is also possible he holds that both parents must be nonproselytes. Maimonides interprets him to mean that the restriction is only if the woman does not have a single nonproselyte ancestor.

freed slaves: A woman whose mother is a freed slave (or perhaps is the descendant of freed slaves in some other combination) may not be married to a priest.

proselytes and freed slaves: As parents or ancestors. See the annotation to 1:4.

even up to ten generations, unless their mother is of Israel.
A legal guardian, an agent, a slave, a woman, a *tumtum*, and an *androgynos*
bring but do not recite,
for they cannot say, Which you, O Lord, have given me.

6 One who acquires two trees within his fellow's field
brings but does not recite.
R. Meir[1] says:
He brings and recites.
If the spring dried up or the tree was cut down,
he brings but does not recite.
R. Judah says:
He brings and recites.
From the Festival of Weeks to the Festival,
one brings and recites.
From the Festival to Hanukkah,

---

[1] **K, P**: Judah (marginal correction, in later hands, to Meir).

---

ten generations: Maimonides, as noted, reads this as permissive—as long as any ancestor going back even ten generations is a native Israelite, she may be married to a priest. Alternatively, it might be meant restrictively—she must have all Israelite ancestors going back ten generations in order to be married to a priest. A third possibility is that there is only concern for the mother's purity (as the phrasing suggests), that her female line must be fully Israelite.

A legal guardian, an agent, a slave: All three act on behalf of another, and thus they cannot refer to the land or the firstfruits as their own.

a woman: It is possible that the woman is imagined here acting on behalf of her husband, as in the previous examples (and see *Ketubbot* 9:4 and perhaps *Shevu'ot* 7:8). Most commentators understand that it is a matter of gender status, however, as in the cases that follow. If so, she does not recite even when bringing fruit from land that she herself owns, because, according to the Mishnah, women were not given a share in the land when it was originally distributed by Moses and Joshua. The commentators explain that the daughters of Zelophehad (Numbers 27:1–7; 36:32), received a share in the land only through inheritance from their father, not in the initial allotment.

tumtum . . . androgynos: Two types of people of uncertain gender. A *tumtum* has genitalia that are covered up (*Yevamot* 8:6). An *androgynos* is a person with both male and female genitalia. Both the *tumtum* and *androgynos* are thus legally considered in part female. See more on the *androgynos* in 4:1–5 (and on the *tumtum* in 4:5).

Which you, O Lord, have given me: Deuteronomy 26:10.

1:6 *two trees*: See 1:11. According to 1:11, below, and *Bava Batra* 5:4, if purchase of the ground is not explicitly specified, only when purchasing three trees does one also buy the ground itself. Thus the requirement of the verse quoted in 1:2 (one's own ground) is not met.

R. Meir: See 1:11.

If the spring dried up or the tree was cut down: If there is no longer a natural water source or if there are no longer any trees, the field has become useless, and one can no longer properly speak of owning the land (Maimonides). R. Judah would argue that in spite of it all the person still owns the land. In the case of the cut tree, presumably the firstfruits were harvested beforehand.

Festival of Weeks: See also 1:3.

the Festival is the Mishnah's term for Sukkot (the fall harvest festival).

one brings but does not recite.
R. Judah b. Betera says:
One brings and recites.

7 One who separated his firstfruits and [then] sold his field
brings but does not recite.
And the other person—
[if the fruits are] of the same type,
he does not bring.
If of a different type,
he brings and recites.
R. Judah says:
Even if of the same type,
he brings and recites.

8 If [a person] separated his firstfruits
and they were plundered, or became rotten, or were stolen or lost, or became impure—
he brings other fruits in their stead but does not recite.
And as for the replacements—
he does not become liable to the added fifth on their account.
If the firstfruits became impure in the Temple Court,
he scatters them and does not recite.

9 And what is the scriptural source that one is accountable for them
until he brings them to the Temple Mount?
As it says, *The best firstfruits of your land you shall bring to the house of the Lord your God.*
This teaches that one is accountable for them until he brings them to the Temple Mount.
In the case of one who brought [firstfruits] of one type and recited the declaration,
and then returned to bring [firstfruits] of another type—
he does not recite.

1:7 *One who separated...does not recite*: Although the person did own the land when the fruit came into existence, he does not own it at the moment when the declaration would be made.

the other person: The new owner need not bring the offering again on the same type of fruits.

R. Judah...recites: For the new owner, these are the first of the harvest regardless of what the previous owner did.

1:8 *If [a person] separated...in their stead*: Once the fruits have been sacralized by "separating" them (see 3:1), they must be replaced if for any reason they cannot be brought to the Temple.

added fifth: This is the penalty for a nonpriest eating the sacred fruit (inadvertently). See 2:1 and *Terumot* 6:1–6.

impure in the Temple Court: Once the fruits have been brought into the Temple Court (see 1:9 and 3:4), the ritual obligation to "bring" them has been fulfilled, even if they have not been given to the priest.

scatters: Impure fruits cannot be given, as in the beginning of 1:8. It is unclear who would clean up this mess.

1:9 *Temple Mount*: This slightly contradicts the previous paragraph, which made reaching the Temple Court (see also 3:4) the key moment at which the obligation is fulfilled. The prooftext is interpreted to mean that the obligation of presenting firstfruits is satisfied upon reaching the Temple itself. This interpretation conflates the Temple with the Temple Mount.

The best firstfruits: Exodus 23:19.

one who brought [firstfruits] of one type...does not recite: One person does not make more than one declaration even if that person makes multiple trips to bring fruits with different harvest seasons.

1:10–11 Those Who Bring the Firstfruits and Recite

10 And the following bring [the firstfruits] and recite the declaration:
from the Festival of Weeks until the Festival,
from the seven species,
from the fruits of the hills,
from the dates of the valleys,
and from oil-olives of the Transjordan.[2]
R. Yose the Galilean says:
One does not bring firstfruits from the Transjordan
because it is not a *land flowing with milk and honey*.

11 One who acquires three trees within his fellow's field brings and recites.
R. Meir says:
Even two.
If one acquired a tree and its associated ground,
he brings and recites.
R. Judah says:
Even sharecroppers and tenant farmers bring and recite.

Chapter Two

2:1–5 Firstfruits, Terumah, and Second Tithe

2 *Terumah* and firstfruits—
one is liable to the death penalty and the added fifth on their account;
and they are forbidden to nonpriests;

---

[2] **K**, **P**, and most other manuscripts read "from oil-olives and from the Transjordan."

1:10 For the names of these festivals, see 1:6. The specified fruits (in terms of location) are considered the "best." Cf. the inverse types in 1:3. In most of the manuscripts (and in virtually all traditional commentaries) *oil-olives* and the fruits of the *Transjordan* are two separate cases (see n. 2). On oil-olives see 1:3.

R. Yose limits the obligation of firstfruits to the Land of Israel proper.

land flowing with milk and honey: Deuteronomy 26:9.

1:11 *three trees…R. Meir…two trees*: A sale of three trees implicitly includes the ground as well, and ownership of the ground is necessary to make the recitation. See 1:6. R. Meir believes that a sale of even two trees implicitly includes the ground as well.

R. Judah says: Against the anonymous opinion in 1:2.

2:1 *Terumah*: This is the portion of the crop that must be given to the priest. On *terumah* and on tithes, see especially *Terumot*, *Ma'aserot*, and *Ma'aser Sheni*.

liable to the death penalty and the added fifth: If a nonpriest intentionally eats these types of sacred produce, he or she is liable to the death penalty (at the hands of heaven). Inadvertent violation requires repaying the value of what was eaten plus a penalty of one-fifth. See 1:8 and *Terumot* 6:1–7:4; *Hallah* 1:9.

and they are the property of the priest;
and they become neutralized in a mixture of one hundred and one;
and they require the washing of hands
and the setting of the sun.
These [laws] apply to *terumah* and firstfruits, but not to the [second] tithe.

2 There are [laws] that apply to the [second] tithe and firstfruits but not to *terumah*.
For the [second] tithe and the firstfruits require bringing to the place;
require a declaration;
are forbidden to the *onen*—
but R. Simeon permits—
[their remains] must be destroyed—
but R. Simeon exempts—
even the smallest amount of them [mixed with regular produce] in Jerusalem
is forbidden to be eaten;
and the shoots [that grow from the mixture] in Jerusalem are forbidden to be eaten
even by nonpriests and domestic animals—
but R. Simeon permits.
These [laws] apply to the [second] tithe and firstfruits but not to *terumah*.

property of the priest: The priest can sell them and use the proceeds for any purpose. See 3:12. See also *Hallah* 1:9. The proceeds of selling the second tithe, in contrast, can only be used to purchase food, drink, and oil for lotion (*Ma'aser Sheni* 1:7).

neutralized in a mixture of one hundred and one: When there is a mixture of sacred produce and regular produce, if the sacred produce is diluted in a very small fraction—one part sacred produce to one hundred parts regular (total fraction $1/101$) —the sacred produce is considered neutralized and the mixture is nonsacred. If less dilute (for instance, $1/75$), the mixture is considered sacred and may be consumed only by a priest. See *Terumot* 4:7–5:9; and *Hallah* 1:9.

washing of hands: Before touching these types of sacred produce. Cf. *Hagigah* 2:5.

the setting of the sun: At the end of a period of impurity, the priest must immerse and wait for sunset before being able to consume the sacred produce. See Leviticus 22:7. See also *Hallah* 1:9.

the [second] tithe: An individual sets apart the second tithe and then eats it in Jerusalem (or redeems the value, using the money in Jerusalem). See Deuteronomy 14:22–26 and 12:17–18; and *Ma'aser Sheni*. The text throughout the chapter uses only the word "tithe" but refers to the second tithe.

2:2 *bringing to the place*: Firstfruits are to be given to the priest in the Temple (see 3:2–8); second tithe is to be brought to Jerusalem and consumed there (*Ma'aser Sheni*).

declaration: Firstfruits: Deuteronomy 26:5–10 (see *Bikkurim* 3:6–7). Second tithe: Deuteronomy 26:13–15 (see *Ma'aser Sheni* 5:10).

onen: See *Ma'aser Sheni* 5:12. An *onen* is a mourner before the burial. R. Simeon permits the *onen* priest to eat firstfruits.

[their remains] must be destroyed. See *Ma'aser Sheni* 5:6, based on Deuteronomy 26:12–15. R. Simeon does not require this for firstfruits.

even the smallest amount...shoots...nonpriests and domestic animals...R. Simeon: The commentaries debate how to make sense of these statements. The usual explanation is: if even the smallest amount of second tithe or firstfruits falls into nonsacred produce in Jerusalem, the mixture (or its *shoots*, namely, produce grown from the mixture) is forbidden to be eaten as nonsacred produce. The neutralization effected by a mixture of 1:100 described in 2:1, according to this explanation, applies only when the mixture was created outside Jerusalem. The first-fruits mixture is also forbidden to nonpriests, and the second tithe mixture must also not be fed to animals. R. Simeon's lenient position (on these clauses), according to the commentaries, extends only to produce grown from planting the mixture's seeds (the *shoots*), not to the mixture itself.

3 There are [laws] that apply to *terumah* and the [second] tithe but not to firstfruits. For *terumah* and the [second] tithe make the granary forbidden,
they have a statutory minimum,
and they apply to all types of produce,
when there is a Temple and when there is no Temple,
and to sharecroppers, tenant farmers, those holding confiscated property, and the robber.
In sum, these [laws] apply to *terumah* and the [second] tithe but not to firstfruits.

4 And there are [laws] that apply to the firstfruits but not to *terumah* and the [second] tithe.
For firstfruits acquire their status[3] when still attached to the ground,
and a person may make his entire field firstfruits,
and he is accountable for them,
and they require an offering and song and waving and staying overnight.

5 *Terumah* from the tithe is equivalent to firstfruits in two ways and to *terumah* in two ways.
(1) It is taken from the pure for the impure,
and (2) from produce that is not nearby,
like firstfruits.

[3] Lit. "are acquired."

2:3 *make the granary forbidden*: The grain that has been harvested, once brought to the granary, is forbidden for use until both *terumah* and second tithe have been designated.

statutory minimum: See *Terumot* 4:3 regarding *terumah*. Tithe by definition is one-tenth. Firstfruits have no required minimum; see *Pe'ah* 1:1.

all types of produce: Firstfruits are brought from the seven species; see 1:3.

Temple: Lit. "house." On this rule, see also *Sheqalim* 8:8.

sharecroppers, tenant farmers, those holding confiscated property: See 1:2 and 1:11.

2:4 *attached to the ground*: Still attached to the tree or plant on which they grew, which is still attached to the ground. See 3:1.

accountable: See 1:8–9.

an offering: See 3:3, 3:5.

song: See 3:4.

waving: See 3:6.

staying overnight in Jerusalem following the giving of the firstfruits. Or perhaps this may refer to sleeping in the main town of the district, as in 3:2.

2:5 *Terumah from the tithe*: The Levite must give *terumah* to the priest from the tithe he receives (the first tithe). See Numbers 18:25–32.

It is taken...not nearby: When separating *terumah*, the part designated as sacred must be near the larger body of produce for which it is fulfilling the obligation of *terumah*. An additional rule is that if the larger body of produce is impure, one may not designate other pure produce as *terumah* in order to fulfill the

And (1) it makes the granary forbidden
and (2) it has a statutory minimum,
like *terumah*.

2:6–7 Additional Comparisons of Categories

6 An *etrog* tree is equivalent to other [fruit] trees in three ways and to vegetables in one way.
It is like other [fruit] trees with respect to (1) *orlah*, (2) the fourth year, and (3) the Seventh Year.
And like vegetables in one way:
it becomes susceptible to tithing at the moment that it is picked—
the words of Rabban Gamaliel.
R. Eliezer says:
It is equivalent to other [fruit] trees in all matters.

7 The blood of those who walk on two is equivalent to the blood of domestic animals
in that it makes seeds susceptible to impurity.
And the blood of vermin—
one is not liable on its account.

obligation for the impure set. See *Terumot* 2:1 and *Hallah* 1:9. These rules do not apply to firstfruits or *terumah* from the tithe.

granary forbidden…minimum: See 2:3.

2:6 *Etrog*: Citron, the fruit used for the ritual of the four species on the festival of Sukkot.

orlah: See *Orlah*.

fourth year: See *Ma'aser Sheni*.

seventh year: See *Shevi'it*. Since the Seventh-Year rest applies to vegetables as well as tree fruit, commentators argue that what is meant here is how the age of the produce is reckoned. See next note.

like vegetables…picked: Lit. "Its tithing is at the same time it is picked." This would not seem to fit well with the rules in *Ma'aserot* 1:2 ff. The commentaries understand this rule, too, in relation to the reckoning of years, in this case, the years in which particular tithes (first tithe, second tithe, tithe for the poor) are brought. For vegetables, this is determined by when they are picked (not when the fruits are formed, as with trees). The first view is that the *etrog* follows the rule of vegetables in this case.

2:7 *walk on two*: Humans.

seeds susceptible to impurity: Blood (human and animal according to this passage) is one of the seven liquids that make food susceptible to becoming impure through contact with an impure agent. See *Makhshirin* 6:4 and Leviticus 11:34. The language of "seeds" stems from Leviticus 11:38. The blood of vermin, in contrast, does not make food susceptible to impurity; cf. *Makhshirin* 6:5.

And the blood…not liable: The commentaries interpret as follows: eating the blood of vermin does not fall under the prohibition of eating blood, but rather under the separate prohibition of eating vermin.

2:8–11　*The Koy*

8 The *koy*:
there are ways in which it is equivalent to a wild animal;
there are ways in which it is equivalent to a domestic animal;
there are ways in which it is equivalent to both a domestic and a wild animal;
and there are ways in which it is not equivalent to either a domestic or a wild animal.

9 How is it equivalent to a wild animal?
Its blood requires covering, like the blood of a wild animal.
And one may not slaughter it on a festival;
but if one slaughtered it [on a festival], one does not cover its blood.
And its abdominal fat transmits carcass-impurity, like a wild animal.
And its impurity is uncertain.
And one may not use it to redeem the firstborn of an ass.

10 How is it equivalent to a domestic animal?
Its abdominal fat is forbidden like the abdominal fat of a domestic animal,
but [if one eats it] one does not incur the punishment of *karet*.
And it may not be purchased with the redemption money of the [second] tithe
which is to be consumed in Jerusalem.
And one is required to give the shoulder, cheek, and stomach [as priestly gifts].

2:8 A *koy* is an animal that blurs the boundaries between the categories of wild and domestic animals (see also *Hullin* 6:1 and *Bekhorot* 1:5). In the Talmud, opinions differ as to whether the *koy* is a unique species or a cross between a deer (wild) and a goat (domestic). Plato and Aristotle are familiar with a similar creature (a *tragelaphos*).

wild animal...domestic animal: Particular species fall within one category or the other. Domestic animals include cows, sheep, and goats. Wild animals include deer.

2:9 *covering*: Upon slaughtering, one must cover the blood of a wild animal with earth. See Leviticus 17:13 and *Hullin* 6:1.

one may not slaughter it...one does not cover its blood: One does not cover the blood if slaughtered on a festival, because digging the dirt is an otherwise forbidden act. For the wild animal, this is allowed on a festival, but for the ambiguous *koy* it is not. Cf. the ruling for wild animals in *Betsah* 1:2.

carcass-impurity: The abdominal fat of a domestic animal is pure (even though it is prohibited to be eaten); see Leviticus 7:23–24 and *Uqtsin* 3:9. But the abdominal fat of a (kosher) wild animal is impure (even though it is permitted to be eaten).

uncertain: There is uncertainty whether the *koy* is to be classified as a wild animal or as a domestic one.

redeem the firstborn of an ass: Exodus 13:13 allows this redemption with a sheep. Since we are unsure whether the *koy* is a domestic animal, it may not be used. See also *Bekhorot* 1:5.

2:10 *forbidden...karet*: See also 2:9 regarding the abdominal fat. *Karet*, often translated "extirpation," is a punishment of uncertain meaning that appears frequently in the priestly portions of the Torah. See *Keritot* 1:1–2 (and 3:1–4).

redemption money from the [second] tithe: See *Ma'aser Sheni* 1:3–4; with the redemption money of the second tithe, a wild animal may be purchased for eating, but a domesticated animal may only be taken as a *shelamim* offering. The *koy* cannot be taken as a *shelamim* offering, but as a partially or potentially domesticated animal it cannot be taken simply for eating either.

shoulder, cheek, and stomach: Deuteronomy 18:3.

R. Eliezer exempts,
because one who would take from his fellow bears the burden of proof.

11 How is it not equivalent to either the wild or the domestic animal?
It is forbidden, on account of prohibited mixtures, [to yoke it or mate it]
with either wild or domestic animals.
One who writes [a deed gifting] his wild and domestic animals to his son
has not gifted him the *koy*.
If one said: "I am hereby a *nazir* on condition that this is a wild animal"
or[4] "[I am hereby a *nazir* on condition that this is a] domestic animal,"
he is a *nazir*.
And in all other ways it is equivalent to both a wild and a domestic animal.
[In order to be eaten] it requires slaughter like both,
and it causes impurity on account of the law of the carcass,
and on account of the law of the limb from a living animal,
like both.

Chapter Three

3:1–8 *Bringing the Firstfruits to the Temple*

3 How does one separate firstfruits?
When a person goes down into his field and sees
a fig that is first to ripen,
a cluster of grapes that is first to ripen,
or a pomegranate that is first to ripen,
he ties it with a reed and says:
"These are firstfruits."

[4] **K**, **P**, and other witnesses read "wild animal and domestic animal."

---

one who would take…burden of proof. A standard argument in mishnaic law. The one currently in possession retains possession when there is no clear evidence.

2:11 *prohibited mixtures*: See *Kil'ayim*, esp. 8:2, and Leviticus 19:19.

nazir: See *Nazir* 5:7. A vow formulation with any possible definition of the *koy* (including that it is both wild and domestic or that it is neither) renders the person a *nazir*.

carcass: See Leviticus 11:27–28, 39–40.

limb from a living animal: Torn from a living wild or domestic animal; it imparts impurity.

3:1 *fig…cluster of grapes…pomegranate*: For these specific fruits see Numbers 13:23. Mention of fruit specifically (here and in 3:3) suggests that individuals (in groups) brought fruits, not wheat and barley (cf. 1:3). As noted in the introduction to the tractate, the first yield of wheat and barley is brought as a special communal offering.

R. Simeon says:
Even so, he declares them "firstfruits" again after they have been plucked from the ground.

2 How does one bring the firstfruits up [to Jerusalem]?
All the towns in the *ma'amad* would gather in the main town of the *ma'amad*,
and sleep in the town square,
but would not enter the houses.
And to those who arose early, the one in charge would say:
Arise, and let us go up to Zion, to the house of[5] *the Lord our God.*

3 Those who were near [Jerusalem] would bring figs and grapes
and those who were far would bring dried figs and raisins.
And the ox would go before them,
and its horns were covered in gold, and an olive wreath was on its head.
The flute would play before them until they arrived near Jerusalem.
When they arrived near Jerusalem,
they would send out messengers ahead of them
and wreathe their firstfruits.
The officers, chiefs, and treasurers would go forth to greet them;
in accordance with the status of those entering they would go forth.
And all of the artisans of Jerusalem would stand before them and greet them:
"Our brothers from such-and-such place, welcome!"[6]

4 The flute would play before them until they reached the Temple Mount.
When they reached the Temple Mount,
even King Agrippa would take the basket on his shoulder and enter,

---

[5] **K, P**, as well as manuscripts of Jeremiah 31:5, lack "the house of."
[6] Lit. "You have come for [**K, P**: in] peace."

3:2 *would gather*: The tenses in the following narrative constantly shift between perfect, iterative past, and participle (which may be intended as kind of historical present or as modal or as iterative past, or as a combination of these aspects). The translation here aims for consistency, stressing that these events would take place regularly in the past.

ma'amad: Lit. "station." This refers to the groups of Israelites, corresponding to each of the twenty-four priestly watches (*mishmarot*), that would gather in the Temple for prayer and study while the daily *tamid* was being offered (*Ta'anit* 4:2–5). Here the meaning seems to extend to the district in Israel from which each group would come.

would not enter: Presumably to avoid possible impurity.

Arise...Lord our God: Jeremiah 31:5.

3:3 *ox*: As in Roman culture, this is presumably intended as a sacrifice (perhaps the one to which 2:4 refers).

wreathe their firstfruits: See 3:10. The pilgrims would place a different kind of fruit atop the basket as a wreath or crown.

officers, chiefs, and treasurers...in accordance with the status.: Temple officials would go out to greet the party of pilgrims. The status and perhaps size of the greeting party would depend on the status of those within the group of pilgrims.

3:4 *Agrippa*: Either Agrippa I, grandson of Herod and king in 41–44 CE, or his son Agrippa II, who lived during and after the Temple's destruction. He is also mentioned in *Sotah* 7:8.

enter: The Temple Mount, on which the Temple was situated, or, the Temple compound itself.

until he reached the Temple Court.
When he reached the Temple Court,
the Levites would sing,
I will exalt you, Lord, for you have raised me up and not allowed my enemies to rejoice over me.

5 They would offer the pigeons that were on top of the baskets as whole burnt offerings and give to the priests what was[7] in their hands.

6 While the basket was still on his shoulder,
he would recite from *I proclaim today to the Lord your God* until he completed the entire passage.
R. Judah says:
Until *My father was a wandering Aramaean.*
When he reached *My father was a wandering Aramaean,*
he would lower the basket from his shoulder,
grasp it by its lip—the priest would place his hands underneath it—
and he would wave it,
and recite from *My father was a wandering Aramaean* until he finished the entire passage.
And he would place it at the side of the altar,
and bow and exit.

7 At first, all who knew how to recite would recite
and [the priests] would dictate to all who did not know how to recite.

---

[7] **K** reads "those that were."

---

the Temple Court refers to any or all of the three courts of women, of Israelites, or of priests. See *Middot* 2:5–6, 5:1–4, and introduction to *Middot*.

I will exalt…rejoice over me: Psalms 30:2. Presumably they sang the entire psalm.

3:5 *in their hands*: This could refer to pigeons in their hands (as opposed to those on top of the baskets; the reading in **K**), or, to the baskets of firstfruits.

3:6 *I proclaim…Lord your God*: Deuteronomy 26:3.

R. Judah: The wording might suggest that only R. Judah holds that there is a waving ritual (and that the first, anonymous opinion does not know of such a ritual). This, however, would contradict the undisputed view in 2:4. The simplest reading, therefore, is that R. Judah holds that the declaration is interrupted for the waving ritual, while the first, anonymous view is that the waving takes place when it is *finished*.

My father…Aramaean: Deuteronomy 26:5.

grasp…place his hands…wave: There are two ways to interpret this succession of actions: (1) The priest puts his hands directly under the hands of the Israelite (who brings the firstfruits) and they wave the basket together (though the verb is in singular); the Israelite then continues with his recitation and lays down the basket, bows, and leaves. (2) The Israelite grasps the basket by its lip, the priest merely places his hands under the basket, and the Israelite waves the basket; the Israelite continues with the rest of his actions. Waving refers to ritually moving the object back, forth, up and down; see *Menahot* 5:6.

place it…altar…bow: See Deuteronomy 26:10 and 26:4.

[As a result] they refrained from bringing [the firstfruits];
they enacted that they would dictate to both those who know and those who do not know.

8 The wealthy bring their firstfruits in baskets of silver and gold,
and the poor bring them in wicker baskets of peeled willow.
And the baskets and the firstfruits would be given to the priests.

3:9–11 *Supplementary Fruits*

9 R. Simeon b. Nanas says:
One may wreathe the firstfruits with [fruits that are] not from the seven species.
R. Aqiva says:
One may wreathe the firstfruits only [with fruits] from the seven species.

10 R. Simeon says:
There are three components to the firstfruits:
(1) the firstfruits,
(2) the supplement to the firstfruits,
(3) the wreathing of the firstfruits.
The supplement to the firstfruits—from the same kind [of fruit];
the wreathing of the firstfruits—from a different kind [of fruit].
The supplement to the firstfruits is to be eaten in a state of purity
and is exempt from the laws of *demai*,
but the wreathing of the firstfruits is obligated in the laws of *demai*.

11 In what case did they say that the supplement to the firstfruits
is equivalent to the firstfruits?

3:7 *they refrained*: Out of embarrassment, perhaps, that they could not recite the Hebrew on their own. The change in practice would alleviate such embarrassment.

3:8 *bring*: Alternatively, "would bring," if these lines are part of the narrative.

3:9 *wreathe*: See 3:3 and 3:10. Each basket is wreathed on top with fruit different from the kind in the basket.

3:10 *same…different kind* as the firstfruits with which they are given.

purity: The supplement to the firstfruits, which are presumably additional fruits from the same harvest, take on the feature of the firstfruits that they must be eaten only in purity. This does not seem to apply to the "wreathing" of the firstfruits.

laws of demai: *Demai* is produce whose tithing status is not clear because it was acquired from someone who cannot be trusted to have tithed it properly. See *Demai*. Firstfruits are not subject to tithing, and consequently are not subject to the laws regulating *Demai*. The additions to the firstfruits partake of the quality of the firstfruits and therefore are also not subject to the laws of *Demai*.

3:11 *did* unnamed Sages *say that the supplement…equivalent*: This seems to refer to the final sentence in the previous paragraph, which does not contain this exact formulation; alternatively, it may refer to laws that preceded our Mishnah collection. The equivalencies include: they must be eaten only by priests, in a state of purity, and within the city of Jerusalem; they are not subject to tithing.

When it comes from the Land [of Israel].
But if it does not come from the Land, it is not equivalent to the firstfruits.

3:12   Firstfruits as Property

12 Why did they say that the firstfruits are equivalent to the priest's property?
For he can purchase slaves, property, and impure animals with them.
A creditor may take them [as payment] for a loan,
and a woman [may take them] as her *ketubbah* payment,
just like[8] a Torah scroll.
R. Judah says:
One may give them only as a favor, only to a Fellow.
But the Sages say:
One may give them to the men of the watch,
and they distribute them among themselves,
as[9] with the sacred offerings of the Temple.

[8] K: "and."   [9] K, and perhaps P, read only "with."

---

not…from the Land: This may refer to the firstfruits being brought from across the Jordan (1:10) or perhaps to a case of only the supplementary fruits being from outside of Israel (but the firstfruits from within the Land).

3:12 *Why did they say* in 2:1.

purchase…with them: Presumably this means that the priest may sell the fruit or dispose of it only to another priest, or that if a nonpriest gains possession of it, he or she must then sell it or give it to a priest to eat. It could, however, mean that once the priest sells or disposes of it in another way, it can be eaten by a nonpriest, perhaps not even in a state of purity, and outside of Jerusalem. R. Judah then appears to dispute this.

just like a Torah scroll: A creditor and a woman owed her *ketubbah* may take a Torah scroll as payment for the debt owed them. The alternative reading (in **K**) may be understood as indicating that the priest can also purchase a Torah scroll with the firstfruits.

R. Judah says…Fellow: The *haver* or "Fellow" can be trusted to observe properly the laws of tithing and purity, whereas someone who is not a *haver* is suspected of not observing these laws properly. See *Demai* 2:3. R. Judah may mean that, in contrast to the previously quoted view, the priest who has received the firstfruits can only give them to another priest (or perhaps to a nonpriest, as Maimonides seems to interpret) as a favor (and not sell them or use them in the other ways) and that this priest (or nonpriest) must be a Fellow. Alternatively, R. Judah's comment may be in contrast to the view of the Sages that follows, and he may be arguing that regular Jews (Israelites) must give their firstfruits in the first place only to a priest who has undertaken the stringencies of the tithing laws. *The Sages* hold that the firstfruits are distributed among the priests serving in the Temple, whether Fellows or not (presumably they observe the purity rules in the Temple). Perhaps they (also) mean to exclude the possibility of selling or giving them to a nonpriest.

men of the watch: The group of priests on duty in the Temple. According to the Mishnah, there were twenty-four watches that served in a regular rotation. See 3:2 above, *Ta'anit* 4:2, and especially Tosefta *Ta'anit* 2:1–3.

sacred offerings: This refers to the animal and grain offerings of which the priests partake. Firstfruits belong to the most sacred category of offerings, and must be eaten in the Temple.

Chapter Four

4:1–5   *The Androgynos*

4 The *androgynos*—
there are ways in which he is equivalent to men;
and there are ways in which he is equivalent to women;
and there are ways in which he is equivalent to men and women;
and there are ways in which he is equivalent to neither men nor women.
  2 How is he equivalent to men?
He becomes impure with white [discharge], like a man.
He is responsible to fulfill the levirate marriage, like a man.
And he dresses and styles his hair, like a man.
And he marries but is not married, like a man.
And he is obligated to perform all of the commandments of the Torah, like a man.
  3 How is he equivalent to women?
He becomes impure with red [discharge], like a woman.

4:1–5 See the introduction to this tractate for a discussion of chapter 4, which is included in some textual witnesses but omitted in others and has numerous textual variants.

4:1 *The androgynos*: The *androgynos* is an intersex person who has both male and female sex organs. The pronouns and verbs in this chapter are all in the masculine despite the gender ambiguity and boundary blurring and despite sometimes being "equivalent" to a woman.

4:2 *white*: A white genital emission (semen) causes a man to be impure in the category of *zav*, and he conveys impurity to others. A woman with a white genital emission does not enter this category of impurity. See *Zavim* 2:1. Such a flow is deemed to have come from the *androgynos*'s male sexual organs.

levirate marriage: The obligation to marry the widow of a brother who died childless (see *Yevamot*). Cf. Tosefta *Bikkurim* 2:5, which rules that the *androgynos* does not perform levirate marriage.

marries but is not married: Marries a woman (as a man, in the Mishnah's heteronormative framework); is not married by a man. See *Yevamot* 8:6. Though this passage speaks of marriage and not sexual relations, the commentaries in *Yevamot*, reading this rule together with R. Eliezer's position there, equate the two. Thus, this mishnah rules that an *androgynos* may have sex only with a woman and not with a man. In Tosefta *Yevamot* 10:2, however, R. Eliezer (Elazar) concedes that if a man has vaginal sex with the *androgynos*, he is exempt from the biblical punishment for male same-sex intercourse.

all of the commandments of the Torah: Women are exempt from certain commandments, or ritual obligations, as in *Qiddushin* 1:7–8 and *Berakhot* 3:3. Partly male, the *androgynos* is not exempt.

4:3 *red*: A flow of blood from the genital area puts a woman in the status of menstruant or *zavah*. This applies to an *androgynos*, who has female sexual organs.

alone with men: A woman may not be alone with a man for fear of improper or illicit sexual relations (see *Qiddushin* 4:12). This suggests a fear that a man, if left alone with an *androgynous*, may engage in sexual relations with him. For some reason, the passage does not seem to forbid the *androgynos* to be alone with a woman (despite allowing marriage with a woman). Cf. Tosefta *Bikkurim* 2:4, which prohibits the *androgynos* from being alone with women.

And he may not be alone with men, like a woman.
And the prohibitions of *rounding off, destroying*, and
becoming impure by contact with the dead
do not apply to him, as for a woman.
And he is disqualified from giving testimony, like a woman.
And he may not have intercourse[10] that is sinful, as for a woman.[11]
And he is disqualified from the priesthood, like a woman.

4 How is he equivalent to men and women?
One is culpable for striking or cursing him, as for a man or a woman.
And one who kills him: if accidentally, he is exiled; if intentionally, he is executed,
as for a man or a woman.
And a woman remains in the state of impure blood and blood purification on his account,

[10] The verb is passive, indicating the female position in sex (the male taking the active verb).
[11] One manuscript of the Tosefta reads (for this and the following clause) "If he has intercourse that is sinful, he is forbidden from [marrying into] the priesthood, like a woman."

rounding off, destroying: Rounding the hair on the corners of the head and "destroying" (that is, removing) the corners of the beard are forbidden according to Leviticus 19:27. These prohibitions are incumbent on men alone.

contact: Male priests may not come into contact with the dead (Leviticus 21:1). This does not apply to an *androgynos* priest, just as it does not apply to the wife or daughter of a priest, perhaps because, like priestly women, the *androgynos* may not serve in the Temple. Cf. Tosefta *Bikkurim* 2:4, which nevertheless rules that he follows the practice of male priests in this instance.

testimony: Women are ineligible to serve as witnesses (*Shevu'ot* 4:1).

intercourse that is sinful: The meaning here is ambiguous. The use of a passive construction for the verb (*niv'al*) suggests that the case is an *androgynos* having sex with a man. Tosefta *Yevamot* 10:2 (see annotation to 4:2) suggests that perhaps this refers to having vaginal sex with a man, which is forbidden but not punishable as male same-sex intercourse. Alternatively, perhaps this refers to sexual relationships forbidden only to a woman and not to a man, such as having multiple partners.

from the priesthood: Only men serve as priests, and the *androgynos* is excluded. Alternatively, this builds on the previous case (as in the version in one Tosefta manuscript): if the *androgynos* has a forbidden sexual relationship, he may not marry into the priesthood. Note that this cannot mean marrying a male priest, as the language might seem to imply, since the *androgynos* may never marry a male. Thus this would mean that the *androgynos* can not marry a woman from the priestly caste.

4:4 *striking or cursing*: The first three examples are mundane ones in which men, women, and the *androgynos* are equivalent, and therefore seem unnecessary. Perhaps they hint at the tendency toward violence against the gender-ambiguous and underscore the *androgynos*'s common humanity. The first two examples prohibit striking and cursing one's parents (the *androgynos* is the parent) (Exodus 21:15, 17). Alternatively, these refer to causing shame (see *Bava Qamma* 8:6), or injury (in the case of *striking*; *Bava Qamma* 8:1–5).

kills him: Killing an *androgynos* is no different than killing a man or woman. On the punishments, see *Sanhedrin*.

a woman... blood purification: After the birth of a boy or girl, a woman is initially impure as a menstruant, and then enters a state of blood purification (Leviticus 12:1–7). The mother who gives birth to an *androgynos* goes through these stages as well. Since the periods differ for a boy and girl, this statement is odd, as it does not take on the central ambiguity of the length of the blood purification. The similar-sounding ruling on the same case in *Niddah* 3:5 may suggest that the mother must observe the relevant periods for both male and female child, which may mean that she observes the overlap, de facto the longer time for the girl, or, following the commentaries to *Niddah* 3:5, perhaps that the impurity period follows that of the girl and the blood-purification period that of the boy.

as for a man or a woman.
And[12] he partakes of the offerings of highest sanctity, like a man or a woman.
And he inherits all forms of inheritance, like a man or a woman.
And if one said: "I am hereby a *nazir* on the condition that this one is a man and a woman,"
he is a *nazir*.

5 How is he equivalent to neither men nor women?
One is not culpable for striking or cursing him, unlike for a man or woman.
And he is not subject to a vow of valuation by others, unlike for a man or woman.
And if one said:
"I am hereby a *nazir* on the condition that this one is neither man nor woman,"
he is not a *nazir*.
R. Meir says:
An *androgynos* is its own type,[13]
and the Sages could not decide whether he is a man or a woman.
But this is not the case for a *tumtum*,
for sometimes he is considered a man and other times a woman.

---

[12] K adds "he takes part in offerings consumed outside the Temple, like a man or a woman, and…"
[13] Lit. "creation" or "creature."

---

offerings of highest sanctity: According to this version of the text, an *androgynos* (and a woman) may partake of this class of sacrifices (eaten in the Temple). *Zevahim* 12:1, however, states that anyone not fit for service in the Temple—which includes women and the *androgynos* (see 4:3 here)—does not partake. Cf. the opposite ruling, which makes more sense, in *Tosefta Bikkurim* 2:5. Cf. also the added clause in K, according to which the *androgynos*, if a priest, may eat the gifts normally eaten outside of the Temple, such as *terumah*.

all forms of inheritance: The simplest explanation is that any type of property can be inherited. This, however, seems obvious and does not resolve the ambiguity of whether and how an *androgynos* inherits when there are also brother(s) and/or sister(s). Cf. Tosefta *Bikkurim* 2:5, where the *androgynous* does not inherit if there are brothers.

a man and a woman: An *androgynos* is thus considered both male and female (cf. R. Meir in 4:5).

4:5 *not culpable for striking or cursing*. This contradicts the previous paragraph, is nonsensical (and obviously an error), and is omitted by the Tosefta.

vow of valuation by others: See *Arakhin* 1:1. Biblical law (Leviticus 27:2–8) allows for people to vow that they will donate a person's value to the Temple. Mishnaic law specifies that when vowing to donate the value of another person (as opposed to one's own value), that person must be unambiguously male or female (the precise amount is gender dependent). A vow to donate the value of an *androgynos* is invalid.

neither man nor woman: See 4:4, where the implication of the *nazir*-vow formulation is that the *androgynos* is both man and woman. This may be an extension of the same logic: the *androgynos* is not one or the other, but both. Cf. Tosefta *Bikkurim* 2:7, where this vow is indeed valid, and the *androgynos* is also neither man nor woman. Presumably, if the person vowed on condition that the *androgynos* were a man (similar to *Nazir* 2:7), or on the condition that the *androgynos* were a woman, the vow would also not be valid.

own type: The *androgynos* is its own gender, one partially male and partially female. Being both male and female, the *androgynos* is a third, hybrid category.

tumtum. See 1:5. Again, despite the ambiguity, the male pronoun is used. The implication of this statement is that *tumtum* is not a unique sex or gender, but a category that shifts between the categories of male and female. Tosefta *Bikkurim* 2:7 has a different formulation, with a different implication: "the *tumtum* is either a doubtful man or a doubtful woman."

ORDER OF MO'ED

Tractate Shabbat   367
Shaye J. D. Cohen

Tractate Eruvin   438
Charlotte Elisheva Fonrobert

Tractate Pesahim   494
Jonathan Klawans

Tractate Sheqalim   557
Miriam-Simma Walfish

Tractate Yoma   589
Yonatan S. Miller

Tractate Sukkah   628
Jeffrey L. Rubenstein

Tractate Betsah   658
Judith Hauptman

Tractate Rosh Hashanah   678
Steven D. Fraade

Tractate Ta'anit   697
David Levine

Tractate Megillah   720
Alyssa Gray

Tractate Mo'ed Qatan   741
Gail Labovitz

Tractate Hagigah   753
Michal Bar-Asher Siegal

Tractate Shabbat

Shaye J. D. Cohen

Introduction

Overview

Tractate *Shabbat* is devoted almost entirely to the numerous and diverse prohibitions associated with the Sabbath. What one does on the Sabbath is of no interest to the Mishnah, aside from lighting lamps on Friday afternoon (2:1–7), the study of Scripture on the Sabbath day (16:1, 18:1), and the consumption of three meals (16:2, 22:1). The theological or philosophical meaning of Sabbath is also of no interest to this tractate. The tractate has strong thematic connections with *Eruvin* and *Betsah*.

Structure and Organization of the Tractate

The organization and structure of the tractate have long puzzled commentators, medieval and modern alike. 1:1 stands by itself, implicitly announcing that the prohibition of transportation ("taking out") will be a major theme of the tractate. From 1:2 to the end of chapter 4 the Mishnah deals with actions undertaken on Friday afternoon in preparation for the Sabbath. Chapters 5–6 treat what one may and may not wear on the Sabbath. The "thirty-nine prohibited labors" follow (7:1–2). The last, the prohibition of transporting an object from one domain to another, is discussed and illustrated from 7:3 to the end of 11 (with a digression in 9:1–4). Chapters 12–15 treat in turn some of the other thirty-nine prohibited labors. From chapter 16 to the end of the tractate the thirty-nine labors no longer provide the organizational framework; these chapters tend to highlight what is permitted (or at least not culpable) as well as what is prohibited. Chapter 16 is about saving items from a fire; chapters 17–21 concern the permissibility of moving items on the Sabbath which have not been prepared in advance. Chapter 19 is a digression (which grows out of the end of 18) about the performance of a circumcision on the Sabbath. Each of the last three chapters (22–24) is a miscellany of Sabbath law.

Main Ideas

Tractate *Shabbat* assumes that the prohibition of labor on the Sabbath applies to precisely conceptualized and defined activities. Thirty-nine "primary labors" are listed in 7:2, but even this list is not exhaustive. Elsewhere in the tractate the Mishnah assumes that taking medicine (14:3), squeezing a wet sponge or fruit (22:1), and speaking of business (23:3) are all prohibited on the Sabbath, in spite of their absence from the list of thirty-nine. So while the Torah is content with the generalization *You shall not do any manner of work on the seventh day* (see below), the Mishnah is all about specifics. Part of the conceptualization and definition of these prohibited labors is the determination that a given act may be prohibited or permitted, culpable or not culpable, depending upon how, how much, under what circumstances, and with what intention, it is done. Thus if a labor is shared between two people, such that each does only half of the prohibited act, or if a person performs only half a labor at a time, there is no culpability (10:2). If a person does not perform an act "properly," that is, in the way that it is normally done, it too is not culpable (10:3). If a person intended to violate a prohibition one way, but unknowingly violated it some other way, the act is not culpable (10:4). Extenuating circumstances might render a prohibited act nonculpable (2:5). And many of these labors incur punishment only when a certain minimum threshold is met, which the Mishnah spells out in great detail. For example, weaving is culpable only if two meshes are woven (7:2 no. 18), writing is culpable only if two letters are written (7:2 no. 32), transporting straw is culpable only if an amount sufficient to fill a cow's mouth is transported (7:3). Tractate *Shabbat* is full of fine distinctions between the culpable and the nonculpable, the prohibited and the permitted (see e.g. chapter 11).

Why these labors should be prohibited on the Sabbath, and what is the source of their prohibition, the Mishnah seldom explains. The Mishnah contains motive clauses from time to time (e.g. 1:3, "A tailor may not go out with his needle [on Friday] near nightfall lest he forget and go out [on the Sabbath]") but they are not sufficiently numerous or detailed to explain the Mishnah's Sabbath prohibitions as a whole. The Talmuds suggest that the thirty-nine prohibited labors (7:2) are deduced from the Torah's account of the Tabernacle in the wilderness. Whatever activity was performed in order to erect and maintain the Tabernacle is "labor." The Sabbath is thus in concept a kind of mirror image of the Tabernacle: inside the Tabernacle on the Sabbath these labors are performed, while outside the Tabernacle on the Sabbath they are prohibited. Tractate *Shabbat* itself hints that it knows this explanation (10:3, 11:2), but given its predilection not to engage in theological or philosophical subjects, it does not pursue the matter. The Talmuds also advance explanations for many of the Mishnah's prohibitions: they are "weekday work," inappropriate for the Sabbath; they are designed to keep the Israelites far from sin (that is, the Mishnah prohibits *x* because it fears that behavior *x* will lead to *y*, and it is *y* that is the Mishnah's real concern). Later commentators will develop these and other explanations. The Mishnah itself is not interested in explanations.

Two prohibitions that recur frequently in the tractate merit comment here. The first is the prohibition of transporting an object from one domain to another, whose significance for the tractate can be gauged by its prominence (1:1) and its extensive coverage (7:3–11:6). In Jeremiah 17:21–27 the prophet tells the people in the name of God that they are not to take a burden out of their houses on the Sabbath (Jeremiah 17:22) and are not to bring it to or through the gates of Jerusalem (Jeremiah 17:21). The parallel passage in Nehemiah 13:15–21 strongly implies that "burden" means commerce, goods for sale. For the Mishnah, however, the legally determinative aspect of this prohibition is not whether the object that has been carried is a "burden" but rather whether it has been carried from one "domain" (*reshut*) to another. The Mishnah divides the landscape into "domains": the private domains of individual houses, the public domains of streets and markets, and shared areas like alleys and courtyards that are not quite public and not quite private. The prohibition of transporting is violated when one moves an object from one domain to another. The Mishnah goes even further in eliminating the literal notion of "burden" from this prohibition. It declares that the prohibition is violated only if the object that has been carried is an object that people in general, or at least its carrier, value or use or keep; if it has no value or if it is too small to be used or if it is not worth keeping, then it is does not qualify as an "object" for the purposes of this prohibition.

After investing enormous intellectual energy in defining domains and objects, the Mishnah invests even more intellectual energy in presenting a way to circumvent the whole prohibition. Through the process of *eruv*, lit. "mixing," all the residents of a given block of private domains can link their properties together so as to permit transporting on the Sabbath from one domain (e.g. a house) to another and across the semiprivate domain (e.g. a courtyard) in between. See tractate *Eruvin* (and *Shabbat* 2:7, 16:1–3).

The second prohibition worthy of note is the prohibition of moving certain objects even within one's own domain. The Talmuds call these objects *muqtseh* "set aside (from use)." Human intention is the key to the distinction between *muqtseh* and non-*muqtseh* objects. If an object has no permitted use on the Sabbath (e.g. a saw, a hammer); if on the eve of the Sabbath an object's owner could not have foreseen a use for it on the Sabbath and hence could have had no intention of using it; if an object did not yet exist or was not yet in one's possession on the eve of the Sabbath—any such object is said by the Talmud to be *muqtseh* "set aside (from use)" and may not be moved from one place to another, even within one's home. The Mishnah does not use the word *muqtseh* in this sense, but certainly has the concept (especially chapters 16–21). The Mishnah devotes substantial attention to the laws of *muqtseh* in particular to the question of the portability of an item whose primary function is not permitted on the Sabbath but whose secondary function is permitted (e.g. may a hammer be picked up in order to smash the shell of a nut? 17:2). The opposite of *muqtseh* is *mukhan*, "prepared," a category that is applied primarily, but not exclusively, to food (*Shabbat* 3:6, 17:1, and 24:4; *Betsah* 3:4). An item which was in one's possession on the eve of the Sabbath and which one intended to use on the Sabbath, or which, because of its very nature, is the sort of thing that a person might normally use on the Sabbath—such an object is *mukhan* and may be moved and used on the Sabbath. Food that is "prepared" before the Sabbath can be consumed on the Sabbath, provided that it meets the following two tests: first, at the moment that the Sabbath began the food was ready to be eaten; second, at the moment that the Sabbath began its owner intended—or can be assumed to have intended—to eat this food on the Sabbath. This focus on human intentionality as a determining factor in law is characteristic of Mishnaic law in many areas.

Relationship to Scripture

The Torah states *you shall not do any manner of work on the Sabbath day* (Exodus 20:10, 23:12, 34:21, 35:2, Deuteronomy 5:14). Which activities exactly are included in the prohibition the Torah does not explain, except to say that kindling a fire is prohibited (Exodus 35:3), and except to imply that gathering food (Exodus 16:26) and wood (Numbers 15:32–36), cooking (Exodus 16:23) and traveling (Exodus 16:29), plowing and harvesting (Exodus 34:21), are also prohibited. What is striking is that the Mishnah's list of thirty-nine prohibited labors omits three of the Torah's prohibitions: gathering food, gathering wood, and traveling. The Mishnah's relative independence of Scripture is evident too in the fact that tractate *Shabbat* seldom quotes Scripture (6:4; 8:7–9:4, 19:3) and never derives its legal rulings from verses of the Torah.

None of the main ideas of tractate *Shabbat* sketched above is attested in the Torah (or the Tanakh for that matter). The Mishnah is a totally new statement of the prohibitions of the Sabbath.

Special Notes for the Reader

I have benefited greatly from the edition and commentary of tractate *Shabbat* by Abraham Goldberg (Jerusalem: Jewish Theological Seminary, 1976). My translation and annotations were much improved through the comments of my friend Rabbi Leonard Gordon.

Tractate Shabbat

Chapter One

1:1 *Transporting from Inside to Outside and Outside to Inside on the Sabbath*

1 The different types of prohibited transport on the Sabbath are two which are four for one who is inside,
and two which are four for one who is outside.[1]
How?
If a beggar stands outside and a householder inside:
(1) If the beggar stretched his hand inside and put something into the householder's hand,
or if he picked up something from it and took it out,
the beggar is culpable and the householder is exempt.
(2) If the householder stretched his hand outside and put something into the beggar's hand,
or if he picked up something from it and brought it in,
the householder is culpable and the beggar is exempt.

---

[1] Lit. "The goings-out of the Sabbath are two which are four inside and two which are four outside."

1:1 This mishnah is placed at the beginning of the tractate to signal that the prohibition of "taking out" (or transporting) on the Sabbath (7:2 no. 39) will be a major theme of the entire tractate (see esp. chapters 5–11).

The different types of prohibited transport: Lit. "the goings-out," or "acts of going-out"; "going out" here means "taking out" or "transporting." The language is modeled on Exodus 16:29; cf. Jeremiah 17:22.

two which are four: The original version of this clause appears in *Shevu'ot* 1:1, "The different types of prohibited transport on the Sabbath are two which are four," which seems to refer to four prohibited acts of transporting on the Sabbath: (1) a person inside a house may not bring from the outside in; (2) a person inside may not take from the inside out; (3) a person outside may not take from the outside in; (4) a person outside may not bring from the inside out. Our mishnah, however, has added the phrase *for one who is inside, and two which are four for one who is outside*, the meaning of which is debated by the commentators.

inside...outside: Elsewhere, rather than contrast "inside" with "outside," this tractate contrasts "private domain" with "public domain." See below 7:2 no. 39.

culpable: Guilty of violating the prohibition of transporting on the Sabbath and liable to punishment.

exempt: from punishment. According to the Mishnah, willful violation of the prohibition of labor on the Sabbath (7:2) entails death by stoning, inadvertent violation a purgation offering. Neither of these punishments was practicable after the destruction of the Temple in 70 CE.

(3) If the beggar stretched his hand inside and the householder picked up something from it,
or if [the householder] put something into it and [the beggar] took it out,
both of them are exempt.
(4) If the householder stretched his hand outside and the beggar picked up something from it,
or if [the beggar] put something into it and [the householder] brought it in,
both of them are exempt.

1:2–11 Permitted and Prohibited Activities on Friday Near the Arrival of the Sabbath

2 A person may not sit down before the barber near the time of the afternoon prayer
unless he has already prayed.
Nor may a person enter a bath-house or a tannery, nor begin a meal or judge a suit.[2]
But if one has begun, he need not interrupt [the activity].
One must interrupt in order to recite the *Shema*,
but one need not interrupt for the *tefillah*.
3 A tailor may not go out with his needle [on a Friday] near nightfall
lest he forget and go out [on the Sabbath],
nor a clerk with his quill,
nor may one examine his clothes for vermin
or read by the light of a lamp.
Nevertheless[3] they have said:[4]

---

[2] Lit. "nor to eat nor to judge." [3] Lit. "in truth." [4] **K, P** lack "they have said."

---

both of them are exempt: Because each has done only half of the labor (see 10:2, 5).

1:2 *A person may not sit down*: This mishnah, which addresses the concern that a person may be too preoccupied to recite the afternoon prayers at the appropriate time, would seem to apply to every day of the week. The rulings in the rest of this chapter concern Friday afternoon specifically.

enter a bath-house: i.e. bathe.

But if one has begun the meal or the judging *he need not interrupt* it: If there is time for the Prayer to be recited afterwards.

One must interrupt in order to recite the Shema: This line seems to qualify the previous: one need not interrupt for the *tefillah*, but must interrupt for the *Shema*. The time limits for the recitation of the *Shema* are stricter than the time limits for the recitation of the *tefillah*. Some commentators, following the Talmud, argue that this line is unrelated to what comes before and means "one must interrupt Torah study in order to recite the *Shema*, but one need not interrupt Torah study for the *tefillah*."

Shema: The liturgical recitation of Deuteronomy 6:2–5 and 11:13–21 and Numbers 15:37–41; see *Berakhot* 1–2.

tefillah: The *Amidah* or *Shemoneh Esreh*, the Eighteen Benedictions that form the core of the rabbinic liturgy.

1:3 *read by the light of a lamp*: He may, forgetful of the Sabbath, tilt the lamp to make the oil flow into the wick more abundantly to give a brighter light. These prohibitions apply to Friday near nightfall and, all the more so, on the Sabbath itself.

A school-master[5] may look [by the light of a lamp] where the children are reading,
but he himself may not read.
Likewise, a *zav* may not eat with a *zavah*,
since this would be an opportunity[6] for sexual transgression.

4 And[7] these are among the legal rulings which they said
in the upper room of Hananiah b. Hezekiah b. Gorion[8]
when they went up to visit him.
They were counted,
and the House of Shammai outnumbered the House of Hillel;
and eighteen things did they decree on that very day.

1:5–8   *Debates between the Houses of Shammai and Hillel*

5 The House of Shammai say:
One may not soak ink, dyestuffs, or vetches [on a Friday]
unless there is time for them to be [wholly] soaked while it is still day.
But the House of Hillel permit it.

6 The House of Shammai say:
One may not put bundles of flax in an oven [on a Friday]
unless there is time for them to steam off while it is still day,
nor wool into a dyer's cauldron
unless there is time for it to absorb the color[9] [while it is still day].
But the House of Hillel permit it.
The House of Shammai say:
One may not spread nets for wild animals, birds, or fish [on a Friday]
unless there is time for them to be caught while it is still day.
But the House of Hillel permit it.

[5] Or "deacon," or "assistant."   [6] Lit. "habit" or "habituation."   [7] K, P lack "and."
[8] K, P: "Garon."   [9] Lit. "the eye," perhaps "appearance."

zav: Leviticus 15:1–15.

zavah: Leviticus 15:25–30.

Likewise... an occasion for transgression: He is impure and she is impure; nevertheless, they should not dine together. All of the rulings in 1:3 are governed by the same principle: to prevent the creation of situations which may be licit in themselves but provide an opportunity for transgression.

1:4 *And these*: The Talmud and all subsequent commentators debate whether this statement looks back to the rulings of 1:3 (not to examine clothes or read by the light of a lamp) or ahead to the debates of the Houses in 1:5–9.

eighteen things: The Talmuds have different versions of a list of "eighteen things." Some commentators have ingeniously tried to count eighteen teachings in the preceding three paragraphs.

1:5 *vetches*: Used for cattle fodder; repeated at 20:3.

7 The House of Shammai say:
One may not sell to a gentile or load [his beast] with him or raise [a burden] on to him [on a Friday]
unless there is time for him to reach a place nearby [before the onset of the Sabbath at sundown].
But the House of Hillel permit it.

8 The House of Shammai say:
One may not give hides to a gentile tanner
or clothes to a gentile launderer [on a Friday]
unless there is time for the work to be done while it is still day.
But all these the House of Hillel permit while the sun is up.[10]

1:9–11 *Agreement between the Houses*

9 Rabban Simeon b. Gamaliel said:
The members of my father's household were accustomed to give white clothes[11] to a gentile launderer
three days before the Sabbath.
Both these and those agree
that one may load the beams of the olive press or the rollers of the winepress [on a Friday].

10 One may not roast meat, onions, or eggs [on a Friday]
unless there is time for them to be roasted while it is still day.
One may not put bread into the oven at nightfall,
nor cakes upon the coals,
unless there is time for their top to form a crust while it is still day.
R. Eliezer[12] says:
[Unless there is] time for their bottom to form a crust.

---

[10] Lit. "with the sun."
[11] K, P: "their white clothes."
[12] K, P: "Eleazar."

1:7 *a gentile*: Gentiles make an appearance also in 1:8, 1:9, 16:6, 16:8, 23:4, 24:1.

1:8 *But all these*: The rulings in which the House of Shammai prohibit and the House of Hillel permit (1:5–8)—in all five cases the House of Hillel permit the commencement of the activity on Friday as long as the sun has not yet set. The House of Hillel agrees with the House of Shammai, however, in the matter of food preparation, for here even the Hillelites agree that food must be completely cooked before the onset of the Sabbath; see 1:10 and 3:1.

1:9 *three days before the Sabbath*: In accordance with the House of Shammai; according to the House of Hillel they could have given the clothing to the launderer even as late as Friday afternoon (1:8).

Both these and those: That is, the two Houses. An anonymous comment, not a continuation of the statement of R. Simeon b. Gamaliel.

1:10 This mishnah and the next (1:11) seem to be a continuation of 1:9, listing various rules on which there was consensus.

top…bottom: The commentators debate which surface forms a crust first, top or bottom, and therefore which of the two views is the more stringent.

11 One may let down the Passover sacrifice into the oven at nightfall [on a Friday].
And [at nightfall on a Friday] one may feed the fire in the fireplace of the Chamber of the Hearth,
but outside the Temple[13] [one may do so]
only if there is time [before the Sabbath]
for the fire to take hold of the greater part [of the wood].
R. Judah says:
When lighting charcoal,
any quantity whatsoever.

Chapter Two

2:1–4 *Lighting a Lamp for the Sabbath*

2 With what may one light [a lamp for the Sabbath],
and with what may one not light?
Not with cedar fiber or uncarded flax or raw silk or a wick of bast or a wick of the desert or duck-weed;

---

[13] Lit. "in the territories" or "in the border regions."

1:11 *One may let down* with ropes or chains *into the oven*: "At the Samaritan Passover at the present time the ovens are pits in the ground" (Danby). The Mishnaic ovens were made of clay and shaped like large bowls; see *Kelim* 5. For another reference to Passover ovens see *Ta'anit* 3:8.

at nightfall [on Friday]: When the 14th of Nisan, the day of the Paschal sacrifice, falls on Friday.

one may feed the fire: Inside the Temple the Sabbath prohibitions do not apply (see 7:2n.).

the Chamber of the Hearth: Or: *Bet Hamoqed*. A fire was kept burning continuously in this chamber in the Jerusalem temple; see *Tamid* 1:1 and *Middot* 1:1.

If one is lighting *charcoal* on Friday at nightfall, one may do so according to R. Judah if there is time for the fire to take hold of any quantity whatsoever before the Sabbath.

2:1 This chapter continues the subject of the previous: actions that may be performed before the arrival of the Sabbath even though their effects carry forward into the Sabbath itself. Lighting a lamp on the Sabbath itself is forbidden (9:2), but lighting a lamp before the onset of the Sabbath is permitted; in fact, it was a normal part of the preparation for the Sabbath (2:6–7).

With what: Wicks and oils.

Not with cedar fiber: Wicks. Some of these translations are not certain. These wicks are prohibited because they do not draw oil well, thus tempting the householder to adjust the lamp on the Sabbath.

wick of the desert: The fiber out of the "apples of Sodom" or "Dead-Sea fruit."

or pitch or wax or castor oil or oil that is to be burnt or [grease from] the fatty tail [of a sheep] or tallow.
Nahum the Mede says:
One may light with boiled tallow.
But the Sages say:
Boiled or not boiled is one and the same:
one may not light with it.

2 One may not light [a lamp] on a Festival day with oil that is to be burnt.
R. Ishmael says:
One may not light with tar
out of respect for the Sabbath.
But the Sages permit all kinds of oils:
sesame oil, nut oil, radish-seed oil, fish oil, colocynth oil, tar, and naphtha.
R. Tarfon says:
One may not light with any oil except olive oil.

3 Anything that derives from a tree—
except flax—
one may not light with it;
and anything that derives from a tree
does not contract the impurity of Tents
except flax.
A cloth wick that one folded but did not singe—
R. Eliezer says:

or pitch or wax: Oils. These oils are prohibited either because they do not burn well, thus tempting the householder to adjust the lamp on the Sabbath, or, as the commentators explain, because they emit an unpleasant odor.

oil that is to be burnt: Oil that is *terumah* that has become impure. (*Terumah* is produce given to a priest in consonance with Numbers 18; after it has been designated *terumah* the produce must not be allowed to become impure, and may be consumed only by a priest or his household.) This oil, like other Holy things that have become impure, must be burnt, since there is no way to purify it, but disposing of impure Holy things is prohibited on the Sabbath and on festivals (2:2).

2:2 *on a Festival day*: Igniting a fire is prohibited on a festival day (*Betsah* 4:7) but transferring a flame that is already lit is permitted if it is done for the sake of a labor permitted on a festival (e.g. cooking). The Talmud explains that this mishnah is speaking of lighting a lamp (that is, transferring an already existing flame from one lamp to another) on a festival day for the Sabbath (in a situation where the festival occurred on a Friday).

oil that is to be burnt: See note on 2:1.

out of respect for the Sabbath: Because burning tar is malodorous.

2:3 *Anything that derives from a tree*: A wick made of material that comes from a tree. The Mishnah regards flax as of arboreal origin because of Joshua 2:6.

impurity of Tents: This sentence has no connection with the laws of the Sabbath; it appears here solely because of its formal similarity ("except flax") with the previous sentence. *Impurity of Tents* is impurity that is transmitted to a person or object within an enclosed space ("Tent") that contains material from a human corpse (Numbers 19). See *Oholot*. The Tent itself does not become impure if it is made of material that derives from a tree, unless that material be flax, in which case the Tent becomes impure from the corpse within it. The Talmud bases this ruling on Numbers 19:18.

It is susceptible to impurity,
and one may not light with it;
R. Aqiva says:
It is not susceptible to impurity,
and one may light with it.
    4 A person may not pierce an eggshell and fill it with oil
and put it on the opening of a lamp
so that it should drip [oil into it].
[This is forbidden] even if [the device] be of earthenware.
But R. Judah permits.
But if the potter had attached it from the first,
it is permitted because it is a single utensil.
A person may not fill a dish with oil and put it beside a lamp and put the end of the wick in it
so that it should draw the oil.
But R. Judah permits.

2:5 *Extinguishing a Lamp on the Sabbath*

    5 One who extinguishes a lamp
because he is afraid of gentiles or thieves or an evil spirit,
or in order to allow a sick person to sleep—
he is exempt.

---

susceptible to impurity and one may not light with it: This mishnah seems to suggest that susceptibility to impurity renders a wick unfit for service in a Sabbath lamp. In a number of passages the Mishnah juxtaposes purity law to Sabbath law; see 6:1, 6:4, 6:8, 17:3, and 21:3. It is more likely, however, that the Mishnah has juxtaposed here two unrelated rulings and that susceptibility to impurity has no bearing on the possibility of serving as wicks for Sabbath lamps. According to R. Eliezer a twisted cloth wick is susceptible to impurity because (as long as it is of a minimum size; see below 24:5 and *Kelim* 27:1) it is still considered a piece of cloth, hence a Garment, hence susceptible to impurity. *One may not light with it* because it does not work well as a wick.

not susceptible to impurity: According to R. Aqiva the act of twisting (even without singeing) is sufficient to remove a piece of cloth from the category of Garment, hence from susceptibility to impurity.

and one may light with it: Apparently because R. Aqiva thinks that twisted cloth works well enough as a wick.

2:4 *A person may not pierce an eggshell*: On Friday before the Sabbath, and all the more so on the Sabbath itself.

so that it should drip [oil]: The point of this device was to replenish the contents of the lamp during the Sabbath, hence to prolong the hours of illumination. The Talmud explains that the fear is that the householder may be tempted to draw oil out of the reservoir, thus violating the prohibition of extinguishing a flame (9:2). If the device were a single piece, however, it would be more obvious that extracting oil contributes to extinguishing. In any case, R. Judah does not believe that this device, whether made of earthenware or of a separate dish, will tempt a householder to violate the Sabbath.

if the potter had attached it: That is, had attached the reservoir to the lamp.

2:5 *he is exempt*: Because he violated the Sabbath in order to save a life. According to the Talmud "exempt" here means not only "exempt from punishment" but "permitted."

[But if one does so] to spare the lamp, to spare the oil, or to spare the wick,[14]
he is culpable.
But R. Yose exempts him in all these cases except that of the wick,
since he thereby makes it charcoal.

2:6–7 Two Sayings about Three Things, One of Which is Lighting a Lamp for the Sabbath

6 For three transgressions women die when they give birth,
because they are not careful in [the observance of the laws of]:
(1) menstruation,
(2) the dough offering,
and (3) the lighting of the [Sabbath] lamp.

7 Three things must a person say within his house at nightfall on the eve of Sabbath:
(1) "Have you tithed?"
(2) "Have you prepared the *eruv*?"
(3) "Light the lamp!"

[14] Lit. "like one who spares the lamp, spares the oil, or spares the wick."

he is culpable: Because he intended to benefit from the act of extinguishing (which is prohibited, 7:2 no. 36). The intention of an actor determines the legal status of the act; this principle will recur regularly in this tractate and elsewhere. If a person willfully performs on the Sabbath one of the prohibited labors (7:2), and intends to benefit from the prohibited act itself, he is culpable for violating the Sabbath. If his violation was not entirely willful, or if he intended to benefit from a consequence of the prohibited act, and not from the prohibited act itself, he is not liable to punishment.

he thereby makes it charcoal: By extinguishing the lamp he intended to improve the wick, so that it would be easier to light the next time. Hence he intended to benefit from the act of extinguishing, and is culpable. However, according to R. Yose, when he extinguishes a lamp in order to spare the lamp or spare the oil, what he desires is not the act of extinguishing but a consequence of that act; hence he is not culpable.

exempts: Even according to R. Yose the action is prohibited, but does not entail punishment.

2:6 *women die*: Death in childbirth was relatively common in antiquity, and this text tries to explain it in theological terms (punishment for sin). Or perhaps the passage should be understood as a "text of terror," whose purpose is to frighten women into following the regimen that the rabbis expected of them.

menstruation: Leviticus 15:19–24; see *Niddah*.

the dough offering: Numbers 15:18–21; see *Hallah*.

2:7 *Three things must* a householder *say within his house* to his wife or servants.

"Have you tithed?" All food that is to be eaten on the Sabbath must be prepared before the Sabbath. Untithed produce may not be eaten and must be tithed before the Sabbath if it is to be eaten on the Sabbath (*Demai* 7:1). Tithing untithed food on the Sabbath is deemed to be food preparation, hence prohibited.

"Have you prepared the eruv?" The *eruv* is cooked food that is set aside before the Sabbath in order to create a legal mechanism by which to ease some Sabbath restrictions. One kind of *eruv* allows the transportation of items from one domicile to another within a common courtyard; another kind of *eruv* allows walking beyond the 2,000-cubit Sabbath limit. See *Eruvin*.

If there is doubt whether night has or has not fallen:
one may not tithe produce that is known to be untithed,
or immerse utensils,
or light the lamps;
but one may tithe produce of uncertain status,
and prepare the *eruv*,
and store hot food.

Chapter Three

3:1–2 *Keeping Cooked Food Hot in a Stove or Oven*

3 A double-stove which was lit with stubble or straw—
one may put upon it [a pot of] cooked food;
but if it was lit with peat or wood,
one may not put [upon it a pot of cooked food]
until he has scraped it or put on ashes.
The House of Shammai say:
Hot water but not cooked food.
But the House of Hillel say:
Either hot water or cooked food.
The House of Shammai say:
One may remove [the pot on the Sabbath from the double-stove],

---

immerse utensils: Certain utensils that became impure can be purified through immersion in water.

but one may tithe produce of uncertain status: In contrast with produce that is known to be untithed, and consequently that must be tithed before it may be eaten, produce of uncertain status (*demai*) may, or may not, have been tithed already. See *Demai*. At the eve of the Sabbath at twilight, *demai* may be tithed (*Demai* 1:4). Once the Sabbath has definitely begun even *demai* may not be tithed.

store hot food: In order to keep it hot. This is the subject of chapter 4.

3:1 Cooking food and boiling water are prohibited on the Sabbath, but keeping hot food hot is permitted as long as one does not increase the heat of the food. Hence certain sources of heat, which give off so much heat that we are sure that cooking will take place (3:1–2), may not be used. Chapter 4 discusses the prohibition of increasing the heat of food that is already hot. If one violates the prohibition and cooks on the Sabbath, or increases the heat of hot food, the affected food may not be consumed on the Sabbath (3:4).

one may put [upon it a pot of cooked food] before the onset of the Sabbath, thus keeping the food hot during the Sabbath, but one may not place the pot upon it during the Sabbath itself.

peat: Pressed olive peels, what remains in the olive press after the olive oil has been extracted.

scraped the double-stove *or put on ashes*: So as to lower the temperature.

Both the *House of Shammai* and the *House of Hillel* agree that hot water may be placed on a double-stove before the Sabbath; they disagree only regarding cooked food. The opening line of the mishnah follows the House of Hillel. In principle the Hillelites permit beginning an action on the eve of the Sabbath even if it carries forward onto the Sabbath itself (see above 1:5–8), but in the realm of cooking they are more stringent.

but one may not put it back.
But the House of Hillel say:
One may also put it back.

2 An oven which was lit with stubble or straw—
one may not put [a pot] either within it or upon it.
A single-stove which was lit with stubble or straw—
in this case, it is like the double-stove;
if it was lit with peat or wood—
in this case it is like the oven.

3:3 Lightly Cooking an Egg on the Sabbath

3 One may not put an egg beside a kettle
so that it should cook,[15]
nor may one wrap it[16] with [hot] cloths;
but R. Yose permits.
Nor may one stow it in [hot] sand
or in the dust of the road
so that it should be roasted.

3:4–5 Hot Water on the Sabbath

4 It once happened that the people of Tiberias passed[17] a tube of cold water through a channel of hot water.
The Sages said to them:
If [you did this] on the Sabbath,
[the water coming from the tube] has the status of water heated on the Sabbath:
forbidden for washing and for drinking.
If [you did this] on a Festival day,
[the water] has the status of water heated on a Festival day:

---

[15] Lit. "So that it should roll."   [16] Or "crack it."   [17] Lit. "brought."

3:2 *one may not put* a pot on it before the onset of the Sabbath.

single-stove…double-stove…oven: The heat of an oven is greater than that of a stove because its design retains heat more efficiently; hence leaving a pot on the former is prohibited, while leaving a pot on the latter is permitted. A single-stove is more closed than a double-stove; hence the rules governing use on the Sabbath depend on the fuel with which it was lit.

3:3 *One may not put an egg beside a kettle* on the Sabbath *so that it should cook*.

R. Yose permits, because to place an egg next to a kettle or to wrap it in hot cloths cannot be considered cooking.

3:4 *Tiberias…through a channel of hot water*: Perhaps through one of the hot springs just south of the city.

forbidden for washing, but permitted for drinking.
A *muliar* that was scraped—
one may drink from it on the Sabbath;
an *antikhi*, even though it was scraped—
one may not drink from it.
    5 A kettle [holding hot water] that was taken off [a stove]—
one may not put cold water into it
in order that [the cold water] become hot;
but one may put [cold water] into it
or into a cup
in order to make [the hot water] lukewarm.

3:5 cont.   *Hot Food*

A pan or pot that was taken off [a stove] while boiling—
one may not put seasonings into them.
But one may put seasonings into a plate or a dish.
R. Judah says:
One may put seasonings into any dish[18] except that which contains vinegar or fish-brine.

[18] Lit. "anything."

permitted for drinking: Because to heat water on a Festival day for drinking (or cooking) is permitted (*Betsah* 2:5).

muliar...antikhi: Water-heating utensils with fuel compartments, akin to a samovar.

scraped: If its hot coals were scraped out before the Sabbath. The *antikhi*, even when scraped, retains its heat more effectively than the *muliar*; hence water may not be drunk from the *antikhi*, out of a concern that water may have been heated on the Sabbath.

3:5 *taken off [a stove]*: The commentaries explain that the kettle has been removed from the fire just before the onset of the Sabbath, and the question is whether cold water can be added to it after the onset of the Sabbath. If the kettle is still on the stove on the Sabbath, one may not add cold water to it.

one may not put cold water into it... one may put [cold water] into it: Commentators, following the Talmud, explain that one may not add a lot of cold water (in order to heat the cold water) but one may add a little bit of cold water (in order to cool the hot water). The mishnah, however, distinguishes between the two cases not on the basis of the amount of water but on the basis of the intent of the actor alone.

into a cup: in which he has poured the hot water from the kettle.

A pan or pot containing hot food *that was taken off [a stove]*: Just before the onset of the Sabbath.

one may not put seasonings into them: After the onset of the Sabbath because the hot food will cook the seasonings.

plate or dish containing hot food: That is, one may put seasonings not into the original utensil in which the food was cooked but into a secondary utensil into which the food has been transferred.

any dish: Even a boiling hot pan or pot.

vinegar or fish-brine: Since these through their tartness cook the seasonings. R. Judah's statement appears verbatim at *Ma'aserot* 1:7.

3:6 *Preparing a Lamp and Its Appurtenances before the Sabbath*

6 One may not put a utensil under a lamp
by which to receive the [dripping] oil;
but if one put it there while still day,
it is permitted.
One may not derive any benefit from it
since it does not belong to [the category of] that which is already prepared.
One may move an unused[19] lamp from one place to another,
but not a used[20] lamp.
R. Simeon says:
All lamps may be moved on the Sabbath
except for a lamp that is already lit.
One may put a utensil under a lamp to catch the sparks
but one may not put water into it,
since it extinguishes [the sparks].

Chapter Four

4:1–2 *Keeping Cooked Food Hot by Covering*

4 In what may one store [a container of hot food],
and in what may one not store?

[19] Lit. "new."   [20] Lit. "old."

3:6 This mishnah would seem to be a continuation of 2:4.

One may not put a utensil under a lamp: On the Sabbath.

while still day: On Friday.

One may not derive any benefit from it the oil that collects in a utensil that was placed under a lamp before the onset of the Sabbath *since it does not belong to [the category of] that which is already prepared*: An item which was in one's possession on the eve of the Sabbath and which one intended to use on the Sabbath, or which, because of its very nature, is the sort of thing that a person might normally use on the Sabbath—such an object is *mukhan*, "prepared," and may be moved and used on the Sabbath. See 17:1, 24:4, and *Betsah* 3:4. An object that was not so prepared may not be moved or used on the Sabbath. The oil that has now collected in a utensil under a lamp was at the onset of the Sabbath in the lamp, and the owner intended for it to burn in the lamp. Hence, this oil may be used for no other purpose on the Sabbath, even though it was extracted licitly from the lamp.

All lamps: Whether used or unused.

extinguishes: See 7:2 no. 36.

4:1 See introductory note to chapter 3. Hot food may be kept hot on the Sabbath but its heat may not be increased. The Mishnah permits storing a container of hot food before the onset of the Sabbath if the covering material will merely preserve the heat; if the covering material will, in the Mishnah's estimation, add heat to the food, it may not be used.

One may not store in peat or dung or salt or lime or sand,
whether wet or dry;
or straw or grapeskins or soft-cloths, or herbs if they are wet—
but one may store in them when they are dry.
One may store in clothing or produce, pigeon feather or sawdust of carpenters, or fine bits of flax.[21]
R. Judah forbids the fine but permits the coarse.

2 One may store [a container of hot food] in hides and move them,
in wool-shearings but not move them.
What[22] does one do?
He takes the lid off and the wool-shearings fall away [of themselves].
R. Eleazar b. Azariah says:
A basket [containing a food container]—
one turns it over on its side and takes [the food out of the container].
[He must act thus], lest he take [the container]
and not be able to return it.
But the Sages say:
He takes [the container] and returns it.
If one did not cover it while it was still day,
he may not cover it after nightfall.

[21] K, P: "or bits of flax or sawdust of carpenters."   [22] Lit. "How."

peat: See 3:1.

grapeskins: What remains in the winepress after the juice has been extracted from the grapes.

bits of flax: What remains when flax is combed ("hackled" or "heckled").

R. Judah forbids the fine: See n. 21. In our text R. Judah dissents from the preceding opinion about the permissibility of stowing hot food before the onset of the Sabbath in fine bits of flax. In the manuscript reading, however, R. Judah merely qualifies the previous opinion about the permissibility of both sawdust and flax bits.

4:2 *One may store* hot food *in hides* on the eve of the Sabbath in order to keep it hot; the hides may be moved on the Sabbath because they have permissible uses on Sabbath (e.g. they may be used as cushions for sitting). See note on 3:6. In contrast, wool-shearings as a rule are used to provide thread for weaving, an activity prohibited on the Sabbath (7:2); hence they may not be moved on the Sabbath.

What does one do?: When he wishes to take food out of a container that has been stored in wool-shearings.

one turns it over on its side and takes the food out of the pot, not moving the pot from its place.

not be able to return it: If he removes the container from the basket, he might disturb the storage material; in that case, should he wish to return the container to its place, he would not be able to do so, because he would appear to be storing a food container pot on the Sabbath, which is prohibited.

R. Eleazar b. Azariah...: What is at issue in the debate between R. Eleazar b. Azariah and the Sages is not clear.

If one did not cover it...cover it...covered it...cover it: It is not clear whether *cover* is to be distinguished from *store*, or whether they are synonymous. If they are synonymous, it is not clear why one would be permitted to cover hot food on the Sabbath, since 2:7 clearly implies that this is prohibited.

while it was still day on Friday; *after nightfall* on the Sabbath.

If he covered it and it became uncovered,
it is permitted to cover it [afresh].
One may fill a jug and put it under a cushion or under a bolster.

Chapter Five

5:1–2 *What an Animal May "Wear" on the Sabbath*

5 With what items may an animal go out [from one domain to another on the Sabbath],
and with what may an animal[23] not go out?
A camel may go out[24] with its bit,
a female camel with its nose-ring,
a Libyan ass with its bridle,
a horse with its chain.
All[25] [animals] which wear a chain may go out with a chain
and may be led by a chain [on the Sabbath];
and [if the chains become impure] one may sprinkle them or immerse them [while they remain] in their place.

2 An ass may go out with its saddlecloth when it is tied on;
rams may go out strapped,
and ewes may go out exposed, chained, or clasped,

---

[23] Lit. "she" ("animal" is a feminine noun).
[24] K: "A camel may not go out," probably a scribal mistake.
[25] Lit. "and all."

One may fill a jug with cold water *and put it under a cushion* even on the Sabbath in order to keep the water cold.

5:1 Taking out an object from one domain to another is prohibited on the Sabbath (see 1:1 with note), but wearing shoes, clothes, or jewelry is not (see chapter 6). Israelites are commanded to see to it that their domestic animals rest on the Sabbath (Exodus 20:10 and Deuteronomy 5:14). This chapter attempts to establish conceptual parity between people and animals. People may wear clothes on the Sabbath; animals may "wear" items that correspond to clothes, that is, items that are necessary for an animal's well-being or security. All other items are prohibited; an Israelite may not attach prohibited items to an animal on the Sabbath or allow an animal transporting such items to cross from one domain to another on the Sabbath.

one may sprinkle the chains with waters of purification if the chains had contracted corpse impurity *or immerse them* in an immersion pool (a *miqveh*) if they contracted a milder form of impurity. The purification can be performed *while* the chains *remain in their place* on the animal. This ruling has nothing to do with the laws of the Sabbath.

5:2 *when it is tied on*: Before the Sabbath. See 5:4.

strapped: With a protective leather coat tied on. Alternative explanation: their genitals are strapped up to prevent intercourse. The commentators discuss various other possibilities too.

exposed: With their tails tied in a raised position.

chained: With their tails tied in a lowered position.

clasped: Wrapped in a protective cloth.

and goats may go out [with their udders] bound up.
R. Yose forbids all of these
except for ewes that are clasped.[26]
R. Judah says:
Goats may go out [with their udders] bound up in order to keep them dry,
but not in order to collect the milk.

5:3–4   *What an Animal May Not "Wear" on the Sabbath*

3 And with what may [an animal] not go out?
A camel may not go out with a rag, nor bound nor leg-tied.
And likewise all other animals.
One may not tie camels one to another and lead them,
but one may gather the ropes [of each one] into his hand and lead them[27]—
provided that he does not twist [the ropes] together.

4 An ass may not go out with its saddlecloth when it is not tied on,
or with a bell even though it be plugged,
or with a ladder on its neck,
or with a strap on its leg.
Chickens may not go out with bands or straps on their legs.
Rams may not go out with a wagon under their fat tail,
nor may ewes go out with a cap;[28]
nor may a calf go out with its training-yoke,[29]
nor a cow with hedgehog-skin [tied round its udder] or with a strap between its horns.
R. Eleazar b. Azariah's cow used to go out with a strap between its horns,
without the consent of the Sages.

[26] **P**: "chained."   [27] **K, P** lack "and lead them."   [28] Translation uncertain.
[29] Text and translation uncertain.

5:3 *with a rag*: The function of this rag is uncertain. The commentators offer various suggestions (identification mark, protective pad, ornament).

bound: With fore and hind legs bound together.

leg-tied: With the hoof of one leg tied to its thigh.

provided that he does not twist [the ropes] together: The origin of this prohibition is not clear. The Talmud explains that the prohibition derives not from Sabbath law but from the law of diverse kinds (see *Kilayim*). If one rope is made of wool and another is made of flax and they are twisted together and carried in the hand, they could constitute a Garment (akin to a glove); hence the prohibition of twisting them together. Perhaps the mishnah's concern is that twisting strands together will create a new rope.

5:4 *when it is not tied on*: It may fall off, and the owner may wind up transporting it. If it is tied on, the ass may wear it; see 5:2.

ladder: A device to prevent it from twisting its neck around to bite at its saddlesores.

bands...straps: Ownership tags.

wagon: A small cart supporting the heavy tail (a prized part of the sheep) and saving it from harm through contact with stones and rocks.

hedgehog-skin: To prevent animals from sucking its milk.

R. Eleazar b. Azariah's cow: See *Betsah* 2:8 and *Eduyot* 3:12. The strap was either for ornament or protection.

Chapter Six

6:1–4 *What a Person May Not Wear on the Sabbath*

6 With what [attire] may a woman go out,
and with what may she not go out?
A woman may not go out with bands of wool or bands of flax or with a strap on her head—
nor may she immerse while wearing any of them[30]
unless she has loosened them—
nor [may she go out] with a forehead-band or head-bangles
when they are not sewn on,
or with a hairnet into the public domain,
or with a city of gold, or a necklace, or nose-rings,
or a ring that does not have a seal upon it, or a needle without an eye.
But if she went out,
she is not liable to a purgation offering.

2 A man may not go out with studded sandals,[31]

---

[30] Lit. "with them."   [31] Or "sandals shod with nails."

6:1 *With what [attire] may a woman go out*: The Mishnah answers this question in 6:5. The prohibition of transporting or "taking out" something from one domain to another on the Sabbath does not apply to clothing. Ornaments (jewelry, for example) in principle are considered clothing except that some types of ornaments are prohibited by rabbinic ordinance.

with what may she not go out: If a person wears something that is neither clothing nor ornament and goes from one domain to another, he or she has violated the prohibition of transporting.

nor may she immerse herself: This clause does not concern Sabbath law but is placed here by association with the previous clause; see *Miqva'ot* 9:1.

when they are not sewn on to her headdress; if they are sewn on, wearing them is permissible. See 6:5.

public domain: See below 7:2 no. 39 and esp. chapter 11.

with a hairnet into the public domain: The commentators debate whether *into the public domain* refers to all the items in this paragraph or only to the hairnet. The parallelism with 6:5 suggests the latter.

city of gold: A tiara shaped like the city of Jerusalem; see *Eduyot* 2:7 and *Kelim* 11:8.

a ring that does not have a seal upon it, or a needle without an eye: If the ring has a seal, or if the needle has an eye, the prohibition of taking it out would be absolute; see 6:3.

But if she went out wearing any of these and inadvertently went from one domain to another, thereby violating the prohibition of "taking out," nevertheless *she is not liable to a purgation offering*, because wearing the items listed in this paragraph is prohibited on the Sabbath only by rabbinic ordinance. In principle they are ornaments and may be worn on the Sabbath, except that for some unstated cause the rabbis prohibited them. (The Talmud suggests that we fear that the wearer may remove the item and thus inadvertently transport it from one domain to another.) Consequently, the prohibition of wearing one of these items is relatively minor, and inadvertent taking out incurs no liability to a purgation offering.

6:2 *studded sandals*: Standard military sandals (see Josephus, *Jewish War* 6.85).

or with a single sandal
if he has no wound in his foot,
or with *tefillin*,
or with an amulet if it is not from an expert,
or with a breastplate, or with a helmet, or with greaves.
But if he went out,
he is not liable to a purgation offering.

3 A woman may not go out with a needle that has an eye,
or with a ring that has a seal upon it,
or with a cochlea brooch,
or with a spice box,
or with a perfume flask.
And if she went out she is liable to a purgation offering,
the words of R. Meir.
But the Sages exempt [her from a purgation offering]
in the case of a spice box or a perfume flask.

4 A man may not go out with a sword or a bow or a shield or a club or a spear,
and if he went out he is liable to a purgation offering.
R. Eliezer says:
These are adornments for him.
But the Sages say:
They are nothing but shame,[32]
as it is said, *And they shall beat their swords into plowshares, and their spears into pruning-hooks: nation shall not lift up sword against nation, neither shall they learn war any more.*
A garter is not susceptible to impurity,[33]

[32] **K, P** add "for him."   [33] Lit. "is pure."

---

with a single sandal if he has no wound in his foot: If he has no obvious wound on his foot, people will suspect him of transporting the other sandal under his cloak.

an amulet: An amulet prepared by an expert amulet-maker would be permitted for the sake of healing (6:10). An amulet prepared by a nonexpert amulet maker is neither an aid to healing nor an ornament.

breastplate...helmet...greaves: Military gear is not ornamental; cf. 6:4.

But if he went out: See note on 6:1, "but if she went out."

6:3 *needle...ring*: See 6:1.

And if she went out wearing any of these and inadvertently went from one domain to another, thereby violating the prohibition of "taking out," *she is liable to a purgation offering* because these objects are neither clothing nor ornament.

6:4 *liable to a purgation offering*: See note on 6:3, "And if she went out."

And they shall beat their swords: Isaiah 2:4.

A garter is not susceptible to impurity because for the purposes of purity law it is not considered a garment (see *Kelim* 12), but for the purposes of Sabbath law it is considered clothing, and therefore may be worn. Contrast the reading of **K** (see n. 34).

and one may go out with it on the Sabbath;[34]
ankle-chains are susceptible to impurity,[35]
and one may not go out with them on the Sabbath.[36]

6:5–10 *What a Person May Wear on the Sabbath*

5 A woman may go out with bands of hair,
whether her own or another woman's or from cattle;
or with a forehead-band or head-bangles,
when they are sewn on;
with a hairnet or with a wig[37] into the courtyard;
with a soft-cloth in her ear,
or with a soft-cloth in her sandal,
or with a soft-cloth
that she prepared for her menstruation;
with a peppercorn or piece of salt or anything that she may put in her mouth—
provided that she does not put it there for the first time on the Sabbath—
but if it falls out she may not put it back.
An artificial[38] tooth or a tooth of gold—
Rabbi permits,
but the Sages forbid.

6 She[39] may go out with the coin that is upon a bunion;
young[40] girls may go out with threads, or even wood chips, in their ears.
Arabian women may go out veiled and Median women looped.

---

[34] **K**: "A pure garter—one may go out with it on the Sabbath."   [35] Lit. "are impure."
[36] **K**: "but impure ankle-chains—one may not go out with them."
[37] Lit. "foreign hair," or "foreign curls."   [38] Lit. "inserted."   [39] **K, P**: "they."
[40] **K, P** lack.

---

ankle-chains: Apparently worn by young women to train themselves to walk daintily; they are not considered clothing. Contrast the reading of **K**. For the juxtaposition of purity law to Sabbath law, see 2:3.

6:5 *when they are sewn on* to her headdress; see 6:1.

into her own courtyard: But she may not wear them into the public domain, presumably because we fear that she may remove them and carry them. See 6:1.

provided that she does not put it there for the first time on the Sabbath: She may put it in her mouth during the Sabbath only if she was already habituated, even prior to the Sabbath, to carry it in her mouth. This is not a habit that she may institute on the Sabbath. See 6:7. Pepper and salt were common remedies for bad breath, toothache, and the like.

6:6 *upon a bunion*: As a cure.

in their ears: To keep open a hole pierced for earrings. Though the threads or wood fragments are not ornaments, nevertheless they are permissible.

Arabian women: Jewish women of Arabia who dress in the Arabian manner.

Median women: Jewish women of Media who dress in the Median manner.

looped: With their cloaks looped up over their shoulders. See 6:7.

[The same rule applies to] every person, but the Sages spoke of the usual.⁴¹

7 She may loop up [her cloak] with a stone or nut or coin,
provided that she does not loop it up [thus] for the first time on the Sabbath.⁴²

8 A leg-amputee may go out with his wooden stump—
the words of R. Meir,⁴³
but R. Yose⁴⁴ forbids it.
If it has a cavity for pads
it is susceptible to impurity.⁴⁵
His cushions are susceptible to *midras* impurity;
one may go out with them on the Sabbath,
and one may enter with them into the Temple Court.⁴⁶
His seat and⁴⁷ its cushions are susceptible to *midras* impurity;
one may not go out with them on the Sabbath,
and one may not enter with them into the Temple Court.

---

⁴¹ Lit. "of the present," "of that which is."
⁴² Or "provided that she does not loop it up initially on the Sabbath."   ⁴³ P: "Yose."
⁴⁴ P: "Meir."   ⁴⁵ Lit. "impure."
⁴⁶ K: "one may not go out…one may not enter." Probably a dittography, since K lacks the next paragraph (it is supplied in the margin).
⁴⁷ K, P lack "and."

---

every person: Any Jewish woman may go out on the Sabbath wearing a veil or a looped cloak, but since these modes of dress primarily characterize the Jewish women of Arabia and Media, the Sages of the Mishnah formulated the law as referring to them. The same phrase appears below 6:9.

6:7 *loop up [her cloak]*: One corner of the garment is wrapped around some object (in this case, a stone or nut or coin) to form a sort of button, and this is fastened to a loop or hole in another corner.

provided that she does not loop it up [thus] for the first time on the Sabbath: She may loop up her cloak with a stone or nut or coin on the Sabbath only if she had been accustomed to do so prior to the Sabbath. This is not a habit that she may institute on the Sabbath. See 6:5. The Talmud understands the passage in accordance with the alternative translation: if the cloak is looped up before the Sabbath, she may wear the cloak on the Sabbath, but she may not loop up the cloak on the Sabbath. The Talmud explains that this ruling applies only to a coin, since handling a coin on the Sabbath is prohibited. She may loop up her cloak on the Sabbath if she is using a stone or nut that she customarily uses for this purpose.

6:8 *cavity for pads*: Padding put in the concave top of the wooden leg to protect the end of the amputee's limb. The cavity in the stump is a receptacle, thus making the stump into a utensil and susceptible to impurity. See *Kelim* 15.

cushions that protect his extremities while he shuffles on the ground.

midras impurity: If a *zav* (a man with a nonseminal emission; see Leviticus 15:1–15) steps or sits or reclines or leans or rides upon an object upon which people customarily sit or recline or ride, the *zav* transfers his impurity to that object; this type of impurity is called *midras* impurity. In our case, if the amputee is a *zav*, his cushions contract *midras* impurity from him (and may transfer that impurity to other objects; see *Zavim* 2:4). Leg-amputees may *go out with them on the Sabbath* because the cushions are considered clothing, and *may enter with them into the Temple Court* because the pads are not considered shoes. It is prohibited to enter the Temple Court while wearing shoes (*Berakhot* 9:5).

In contrast, *his seat and its cushions* are considered shoes for purposes of entering the Temple (and therefore prohibited), but not shoes for purposes of the Sabbath (and therefore not to be worn from one domain to another). The commentators debate the precise distinction between the permitted and the prohibited cushions.

The wooden stumps [of arm-amputees] are not susceptible to impurity,[48]
and one may not go out with them [on the Sabbath].

9 Boys may go out with garlands,[49]
and the sons of kings with little bells.
[The same rule applies to] every person, but the Sages spoke of the usual.[50]

10 One may go out with a locust's egg or a fox's tooth
or a nail from one who was crucified,
for the sake of healing—
the words of R. Meir.[51]
But the Sages say:
Even on a weekday this is forbidden,[52]
because [of the prohibition] of the ways of the Amorite.

Chapter Seven

7:1–3 *General Rules: the Thirty-Nine Primary Labors*

7 A great general rule have the Sages[53] said concerning the Sabbath:
(a) one who forgets the principle of the Sabbath
and performs many acts of prohibited labor on many Sabbaths
is liable to only one purgation offering;

[48] Lit. "pure."   [49] Lit. "knots."   [50] Lit. "of the present," "of that which is."
[51] K, P: "the words of R. Yose."   [52] K, P: "But R. Meir forbids even on a weekday."
[53] Lit. "they."

---

wooden stumps [of arm-amputees] lack a receptacle, consequently are not deemed to be utensils, consequently *are not susceptible to impurity*. Arm-amputees *may not go out with them* in accordance with the view of R. Yose at the beginning of this paragraph. For the juxtaposition of purity law to Sabbath law, see 2:3.

6:9 *every person*: Any Jew may go out on the Sabbath wearing a garland or decorative bells, but since these modes of dress characterize boys (for the former) and princes (for the latter), the Sages of the Mishnah formulated the law as referring to them. The same phrase appears above 6:6.

6:10 A *locust's egg* was believed to be a cure for earache.

A *fox's tooth* was believed to be a cure for sleep disorders.

A *nail from one that was crucified* was believed to be a cure for wounds.

the ways of the Amorite: This phrase (which also appears in *Hullin* 4:7) designates "magical" practices that were deemed to be Amorite, hence "Canaanite," hence prohibited.

7:1 This mishnah concerns the unintentional violation of the Sabbath; each unintentional violation incurs a purgation offering (Leviticus 4:27–35).

(a) one who forgets the principle of the Sabbath: That is, he is completely unaware of the existence of a day called the Sabbath and its associated prohibitions.

only one purgation offering: Because he has only forgotten one thing, the principle of the Sabbath.

(b) one who knows the principle of the Sabbath
and performs many acts of prohibited labor on many Sabbaths
is liable [to a purgation offering] for each and every Sabbath;[54]
(c) one who knows that it is the Sabbath
and performs many acts of prohibited labor on many Sabbaths
is liable [to a purgation offering] for each and every primary labor;[55]
(d) one who performs many acts of prohibited labor that are of one type
is liable to only one purgation offering.

2 The primary prohibited labors[56] are forty minus one:
(1) sowing,[57] (2) plowing, (3) harvesting, (4) binding sheaves, (5) threshing, (6) winnowing, (7) selecting, (8) grinding, (9) sifting, (10) kneading, (11) baking;
(12) shearing wool, (13) bleaching it, (14) hackling it, (15) dyeing it, (16) spinning, (17) stretching the threads, (18) making two meshes, (19) weaving two threads, (20) dividing two threads, (21) tying, (22) untying, (23) sewing two stitches, (24) tearing in order to sew two stitches;
(25) trapping a deer, (26) slaughtering it, (27) flaying it, (28) salting it, (29) curing its hide, (30) scraping it, (31) slicing it, (32) writing two letters, (33) erasing in order to write two letters;
(34) building, (35) pulling down;
(36) extinguishing, (37) kindling;
(38) striking with a hammer;
(39) taking out from one domain to another.
These, then, are the primary prohibited labors: forty minus one.

[54] K, P: "each and every act of labor."   [55] K, P lack clause (c) but it is supplied in the margin.
[56] Lit. "labor-fathers"; Danby translates "main classes of work."
[57] Lit. "the sower, the plower," etc. K, P list "plowing" before "sowing."

(b) one who knows the principle of the Sabbath but forgets, or does not know, each time that the day is the Sabbath.

(c) one who knows that it is the Sabbath but does not know that these primary labors are prohibited on the Sabbath.

primary labor: See 7:2.

(d) one who knows the principle of the Sabbath, and knows that the day is the Sabbath, and knows that these labors are prohibited on the Sabbath, but inadvertently *performs many acts of prohibited labor* is liable to only one purgation offering if all the acts of labor are *of one type*, that is, if they all belong to one primary group (7:2). (d) restates (c).

7:2 *primary prohibited labors*: These labors are "primary" in the sense that secondary and tertiary labors unfold under each of them. Each, then, is an archetype (or "father"). So, for example, weeding, trimming, and pruning are included in the category of plowing, and gathering loose wood or grass is included in the category of harvesting (see 12:2). Labors 1–11 are the steps required to obtain wheat in order to bake bread; labors 12–24 are the steps required to obtain wool in order to sew a garment; labors 25–33 are the steps required to obtain leather in order to write something; the remaining six belong to diverse categories. The Mishnah elaborates on many of these labors in subsequent chapters (esp. chapters 12–16). The Talmud derives these labors from the acts performed by the Levites in the wilderness to transport and set up the Tabernacle, and those performed by the priests in the wilderness to run the Tabernacle. See 10:3 and 11:2.

(39) taking out from one domain to another: i.e. from the private domain to the public, or from the public to the private. See chapters 5–6 above, the remainder of this chapter, and chapters 8–11 below.

3 Another general rule have the Sages[58] said:
Whatever is fit to be stored,
or[59] is of an amount as is usually stored,[60]
and one takes it out [inadvertently] on the Sabbath [from one domain to another]—
he is liable thereby to a purgation offering.
But whatever is not fit to be stored,
or[61] is not of an amount as is usually stored,[62]
and one takes it out [inadvertently] on the Sabbath [from one domain to another]—
only the one who stores it is liable [to a purgation offering].

7:4 Taking Out Foodstuffs, Animal and Human

4 One who takes out:
straw—enough to fill a cow's mouth;
pea-stalks—enough to fill a camel's mouth;
ears of grain—enough to fill a lamb's mouth;
grass—enough to fill a kid's mouth;
leaves of garlic or leaves of onion:
if fresh—about a dried fig,
if dry—enough to fill a kid's mouth.
They cannot be combined with one another,
since they are not equal in their statutory amounts.
One who takes out a dried fig's volume of [human] foodstuffs is culpable;
and they can be combined with one another,

[58] Lit. "they."   [59] Or "and."   [60] Lit. "and they store akin to it."   [61] Or "and."
[62] Lit. "and they do not store akin to it."

7:3 This mishnah states the minimum quantity or size that one must carry from one domain to another on the Sabbath in order to incur a penalty for violating the prohibition of "taking out." The minimum is determined by what people commonly accept as valuable or useful.

Whatever is fit to be stored: Whatever is of sufficient quality that it is worth something to people.

only the one who stores it is liable: Because only he regards the item as something of value, and therefore when he carries it from one domain to another he has violated the prohibition of transporting. Others, who would not store something of such little quality or quantity, do not violate the prohibition by inadvertently transporting such an item. See 10:1.

7:4 This mishnah and the long series that follows exemplify the previous. In the present case, how much food, whether animal or human, is the minimum amount that people value and/or store? If someone takes an amount of food below that minimum and carries it from one domain to another on the Sabbath, that person is exempt from penalty for violating the prohibition of transporting. The minimum of each type of food will vary depending on its standard use.

*straw…pea-stalks…grain…grass…*dried *leaves of garlic or leaves of onion*: These are animal feed, and therefore the minimum amount is given in terms of animals.

grass—enough to fill a kid's mouth: See 12:2.

They cannot be combined with one another: Small amounts of the various animal feeds do not combine so as to produce the prescribed minimum for liability. See 9:5.

and diverse human foodstuffs *can be combined* so as to produce the requisite minimum…*except* the inedible parts like the husks, kernels, etc. These are not taken into account for this purpose.

since they are equal in their statutory amounts,
except their husks, kernels, stalks, coarse bran, or fine bran.
R. Judah says:
Except the husks of lentils,
because they are cooked together with them.

Chapter Eight

8:1 *Taking Out Liquids*

8 One who takes out:
wine—enough to mix the cup;
milk—enough for a gulp;
honey—enough to put on a sore;
oil—enough to anoint a small limb;
water—enough to rub off eye-cream;
all other liquids—in [the amount of] a quarter-*log*;
and liquid refuse—in [the amount of] a quarter-*log*.
R. Simeon says:
In all of these [the minimum] is a quarter-*log*;
and[63] the Sages[64] have stated all these statutory amounts[65]
only for those who store [such small amounts].

[63] **K, P** lack "and," suggesting that the following statement should be understood not as a continuation of R. Simeon's statement but as a new sentence, an anonymous statement of the Mishnah itself.
[64] Lit. "they."
[65] **K, P**: "all these statutory amounts have been stated."

R. Judah says: An exception to the exception. The husks of lentils are taken into account when calculating the minimum amount of foodstuff.

8:1 This entire chapter continues the subject of 7:3–4.

a small limb: The Talmud, perhaps translating this phrase as "the limb of a minor," explains that the reference is to the smallest limb of a day-old infant.

all other liquids: Makhshirin 6:4 lists seven liquids, the five of our mishnah plus blood and dew.

liquid refuse: Nonpotable water that is used for purposes other than drinking.

R. Simeon says: In all of these, wine, milk, honey, oil, water, *[the minimum] is a quarter-log* just as it is with other liquids; *and the Sages have stated all these statutory amounts* (enough to mix the cup, enough for a gulp, etc.) *only for those who store [such small amounts]* of these items], but for everyone else the minimum is much higher, a quarter-*log*. R. Simeon seems to reject the Mishnaic view in 7:3, according to which a person who stores a quantity of a substance, no matter how small, and transports that quantity from one domain to another on the Sabbath, is liable. In contrast, according to R. Simeon, there are absolute minimums, at least of liquids, for the violation of the prohibition of transporting.

8:2–7 *Taking Out Various Items, Neither Food nor Liquid*

2 One who takes out:
rope—enough to make a handle for a basket;
reed-grass—enough to make a hanger for a sifter or sieve.
R. Judah says:
Enough to take from it the measure of a child's shoe.
Paper—enough to write upon it a tax-collector's receipt;[66]
and he who takes out a tax-collector's receipt[67] is culpable.
Paper that has been erased[68]—enough to wrap around the mouth of a small perfume-flask.

3 Leather—enough to make an amulet;
parchment—enough to write on it the shortest passage in the *tefillin*,
which is *Hear O Israel*;
ink—enough to write two letters;
eye-paint—enough to paint one eye.

4 Glue[69]—enough to put on the tip of a branch;
pitch or sulfur—enough to mend[70] a hole;
wax—enough to put on the mouth of a small hole;
clay—enough to mend[71] the mouth of a goldsmith's furnace;
R. Judah says:
Enough to make a prop[72] [for the furnace].
Bran—enough to put on the mouth of a goldsmith's furnace;
lime—enough to lime the littlest of girls.
R. Judah says:

---

[66] Lit. "knot."   [67] Lit. "knot."
[68] **K, P**: "paper that is unfit," that is, a legal document that has expired or has been canceled.
[69] **K, P** put the clause about "glue" between "wax" and "clay."
[70] Lit. "make."   [71] Lit. "make."   [72] Or "peg" or "little leg."

8:2 *R. Judah says*: It is not clear whether R. Judah's comment applies only to reed-grass or also to rope.

And he who takes out a tax-collector's receipt: This is a parenthetical comment. If one takes a tax receipt on the Sabbath and carries it from one domain to another, presumably in order to show it to a tax-collector, he is liable for transporting.

8:3 *Hear O Israel*: Deuteronomy 6:2–5.

two letters: Cf. 7:2 no. 32.

8:4 *to put on the tip of a branch*: In order to catch birds.

to mend: To plug, close up.

to put on the mouth: In the case of wax, this means to stop up or close a hole; in the case of bran, this means (apparently) to stoke the fire by adding bran through the mouth of the furnace (the opening for the insertion of the bellows).

lime: Both a noun and a verb. Lime was used both as a depilatory (as here) and also as plaster for walls (see 8:5).

Enough to make *kilkul*;[73]
R. Nehemiah says:
Enough to make *andiphi*.[74]

5 Red clay—about [the size of] the seal on large sacks—
the words of R. Aqiva.
But the Sages say:
About [the size of] the seal on letters.
Manure or fine sand—enough to manure the stalk of a cabbage—
the words of R. Aqiva.
But the Sages say:
Enough to manure a leek.
Coarse sand—enough to put on a full trowel[75] of lime;
Reed—enough to make a pen;
But if it is thick or shattered—enough [to feed a fire sufficiently so as] to cook an egg: the easiest of eggs, beaten, and put in a pan.

6 Bone[76]—enough to make a spoon.
R. Judah says:
Enough to make of it a tooth-of-a-key.
Glass—enough to scrape with it the head of a shuttle;
a pebble or a stone[77]—[big] enough to throw at a bird.
R. Eliezer b. Jacob says:
[Big] enough to throw at an animal.

7 A potsherd—[big] enough to place between one board and another—
the words of R. Judah.
But R. Meir says:
[Big] enough to stoke a fire with it.

[73] **K, P**: "*kanbul*." [74] **K**: "*antophê*"; **P**: "*antuphê*." [75] Or "spoon." [76] **K, P**: "wood."
[77] **K, P**: "pebble."

---

kilkul: Text and meaning uncertain. The term is usually understood as referring to a woman's hairstyle that requires the depilation of the hair between the ear and the temple.

andiphi: A Greek term (*netôpion*) for a skin cream.

8:5 *seal on large sacks*: Cf. Oholot 17:5.

full trowel of lime: Plasterers would mix lime with sand.

thick or shattered: Since this reed cannot be made into a pen, it is treated as firewood.

the easiest of eggs: The egg that cooks the most quickly; according to the commentators this is the egg of a chicken. See 9:5.

8:6 *Bone*: Yadayim 4:6, which refers to spoons (same word as here) of bone, supports our text. But **K** and **P** read "wood" (the orthographic difference in the Hebrew between "bone" and "wood" is the addition of the smallest of letters); and the juxtaposition with 8:5, which ends with a discussion of reed as firewood, supports that reading. If the reading is indeed "wood," to avoid a contradiction with 9:5 below, we must explain that 8:6 deals with wood that is intended to be used as raw material, while 9:5 deals with wood that is intended to be used as firewood.

Glass: Cf. 17:5.

8:7 *[big] enough to place between one board and another*: As a shim or spacer.

R. Yose says:
[Big] enough to hold in it a quarter-*log* [of liquid].
R. Meir says:
Although there is no proof of the matter [in Scripture],
there is an indication of the matter:
So that no shard is left in its breakage to stoke a fire from a brazier.
R. Yose said to him:
From there [you bring] a proof?
[The verse concludes] *or to ladle water from a puddle.*

Chapter Nine

9:1–4 *Seven Laws for which Scripture Provides Not a Proof but an Indication*

9 R. Aqiva said:
Whence [in Scripture do we learn] concerning an idol
that it conveys impurity by being carried,
just like a menstruant?
As it is said, *You will cast them away like a menstruating woman. "Out!" you will call to them.*
Just as a menstruant conveys impurity by being carried,
so too an idol conveys impurity by being carried.

So that no shard: Isaiah 30:14. The verse begins *It is smashed as one smashes an earthen jug.*

From there, that biblical verse, *[you bring] a proof?* R. Meir said explicitly that he was not bringing a proof from the biblical verse. R. Yose means that the verse supports his position as much as it supports R. Meir's.

9:1–5 is a single block of material consisting of seven units, each one opening with "Whence [in Scripture] do we learn," presenting scriptural support for a given rabbinic law. The scriptural passage is not so much a "proof" as an "indication." Although only one of the seven laws, the fifth, bears on the Sabbath, the editor of the Mishnah inserted this block here because of its obvious affinity with 8:7. The phrase "although there is no proof of the matter [in Scripture], there is an indication of the matter," appears at the beginning of the ensemble (8:7) and at the end (9:5). The scriptural proof text in 9:1 comes from the same chapter of Isaiah as the proof text adduced in 8:7.

9:1 *just like a menstruant:* That is, if someone carries a menstruant, even without touching her, the carrier becomes impure. R. Aqiva extends this principle to an object of idolatry. Cf. *Avodah Zarah* 3:6.

You will cast them away: Isaiah 30:22. The beginning of the verse is *And you will treat as impure the silver overlay of your images and the golden plating of your idols. You will cast them away,* etc.

2 Whence [in Scripture do we learn] concerning a ship that it is not susceptible to impurity?[78]
As it is said, *The way of a ship in the heart of the sea.*
Whence [in Scripture do we learn] concerning a garden bed
six handbreadths square
that one may sow in it five [kinds of] seeds,
four on the four sides of the garden bed,
and one in the middle?
As it is said, *For as the earth brings forth her growth, and as a garden makes the seeds sown in it to shoot forth.*
Its seed is not said, but *the seeds sown in it.*

3 Whence [in Scripture do we learn] concerning a woman who emits semen on the third day [after intercourse]
that she is impure?[79]
As it is said, *be ready for the third day.*[80]
Whence [in Scripture do we learn] that one washes a circumcision[81] on the third day [even] if this falls on a Sabbath?
As it is said, *on the third day when they were in pain.*

[78] Lit. "that it is pure."   [79] K, P: "pure."   [80] K, P add "*do not go near a woman.*"
[81] K, P: "the child."

9:2 *The way of a ship*: Proverbs 30:19. How this verse supports the desired conclusion is not clear. The commentators explain that the verse is understood to imply that a ship resembles the sea in which it travels, in that neither is susceptible to impurity.

five [kinds of] seeds: And nonetheless not violate the prohibition of mixed seeds. See *Kilayim* 3:1.

For as the earth: Isaiah 61:11.

the seeds sown in it: Many seeds. The Talmud tries to detect in the verse a basis for the number five.

9:3 A person or garment that comes into contact with semen is rendered impure and becomes pure again only after nightfall of the day on which the person bathed or the garment was washed in water (Leviticus 15:16–18).

be ready on the third day: Exodus 19:15. From the whole verse, *And he [Moses] said to the people, "Be ready for the third day; do not go near a woman,"* the Sages deduced that the impurity of semen lapses three days after ejaculation; the point of Moses' instruction, at least according to an early rabbinic midrash on the verse, was to make sure that men and women alike could participate in the revelation at Mount Sinai. What was debated by the Sages, however, was the status of semen on the third day itself. According to R. Eleazar b. Azariah, the impurity lapses on the third day itself; according to others, however, it lapses only upon the conclusion of the third day (see *Miqva'ot* 8:3). This debate is reflected in the variant readings in our mishnah.

one washes: Meaning either "may wash" or " must wash."

a circumcision: The Talmud debates whether we override the Sabbath to wash only the actual circumcision wound, or the entire baby. That debate is reflected in the variant readings of our mishnah. Note that at 19:3 below, the standard printed edition and the manuscripts read "the child" (not "the circumcision").

on the third day: Genesis 34:25. Since the pain is intense on the third day, we fear for the life of the infant and therefore permit the violation of the Sabbath on his behalf.

Whence [in Scripture do we learn] that one ties a strip of crimson on the head of the scapegoat?
As it is said, *Though your sins be like crimson they shall be as white as snow.*
4 Whence [in Scripture do we learn] concerning anointing
that on the Day of Atonement it is [prohibited] just like drinking?
Although there is no proof of the matter [in Scripture],
there is an indication of the matter,
as it is said, *May it enter his body like water, his bones like oil.*

9:5–7 Taking Out Various Items

5 One who takes out:
wood—enough to cook an easy egg;
seasonings—enough to season an easy egg;
and they combine one with another.
Peels of walnuts, peels of pomegranates, woad, or madder—enough to dye thereby a small garment in a hairnet;[82]
urine, soda, soap, cimolian [earth], or *ashlag*—enough to launder thereby a small garment in a hairnet.
R. Judah says:
Enough to spread over a stain.

[82] Meaning not certain. **K**, **P**: "as small as a hairnet," here and in the next line.

a strip of crimson: Yoma 4:2 and 6:6.

Though your sins be like crimson: Isaiah 1:18.

9:4 *anointing* is among the actions prohibited on the Day of Atonement (*Yoma* 8:1).

May it enter his body: Psalms 109:18. The entire verse reads, *May he be clothed in a curse like a garment; may it enter his body like water, his bones like oil.* In the verse drinking water is parallel to anointing with oil.

9:5 This mishnah continues (from 8:7) the exposition of the minimum quantities that must be transported from one domain to another on the Sabbath if the act is to be deemed liable to punishment.

wood: See note on 8:6.

they the various seasonings *combine one with another* to make up the forbidden minimum (in this case, enough to season an easily cooked egg). See 7:4.

an easy egg: An egg that is easily cooked. See 8:5.

woad…madder: Plants that yield dyes. The minimum amount for violating the prohibition of dyeing differs from that stated here (see 13:4).

cimolian [earth]: Clay from the island of Cimolia that was used in cleaning clothes.

ashlag: Meaning uncertain; an alkaline substance used as soap. In modern Hebrew the word means "potash."

to spread over a stain: To determine whether it was caused by blood or not. See *Niddah* 9:6.

6 Sweet pepper—any amount whatever;
or tar— any amount whatever;
[all] types of fragrances and [all] types of metals[83]—any amount whatever;
of the stones of the altar or of the earth of the altar,[84]
decayed [bits of] scrolls, or the decayed [bits of] their wrappers—any amount whatever,
because one stores them in order to hide them away.
R. Judah says:
Even one who takes out any amount whatever of the appurtenances of idolatry [is culpable],
as it is said, *Let nothing that has been consigned to destruction stick to your hand.*

7 One who takes out a peddler's basket,
although there are in it many different kinds,
is liable to only one purgation offering.
Garden seeds—less than about [the volume of] a dried fig.
R. Judah b. Betera says:
Five [garden seeds].
The seed of cucumbers—two [seeds];
the seed of gourds—two [seeds];
the seed of Egyptian beans—two [seeds].
A pure[85] locust:
if live—any amount whatever,
if dead—about [the size of] a dried fig.
A bird of the vineyard,
whether alive or dead—

[83] **K**: "of their metals," apparently an error.
[84] **K, P**: "of the earth of the altar, [**P** adds: or] of the stones of the altar."
[85] **K, P** lack "pure."

9:6 *because one stores them in order to hide them away*: When these sacred items become unusable, even the smallest bits retain their sanctity, hence are hidden away. On hiding away *the altar* that had been desecrated during the Antiochan persecution, see 1 Macabees 4:44–46 and *Middot* 1:6. On hiding away used scrolls, see 16:1.

Let nothing: Deuteronomy 13:18, with reference to the destruction of the city that has worshiped other gods. The verse demonstrates that even the tiniest fragment of idolatry is forbidden as idolatry; hence, argues R. Judah, such a fragment is also to be considered consequential for the purposes of Sabbath law.

9:7 This mishnah continues the subject and syntax of 9:5–6, except for the first sentence which syntactically stands by itself.

One who inadvertently *takes out a peddler's basket* from one domain to another on the Sabbath, *although there are in it many different kinds* of spices, fragrances, etc., *is liable to only one purgation offering*, because he has committed only one act of inadvertent sinning; see 7:2.

less than about [the volume of] a dried fig: If the aggregate of the seeds amounts in volume to less than the volume of a dried fig. The volume of a dried fig is the normal minimum for violating the prohibition of transporting human foodstuffs; see 7:4. Garden seeds are apparently not considered to be standard human food, hence their minimum amount is less. How much less is not clear.

A pure locust: A locust that may be eaten (Leviticus 11:22).

any amount whatever: No matter how small the locust may be.

bird of the vineyard: The commentators debate whether this is a type of bird or a type of locust.

any amount whatever,
since one stores it for healing.
R. Judah says:
Even one who takes out a living impure locust—any amount whatever—
[is culpable]
since one stores it for a child to play with it.

Chapter Ten

10:1 *Culpability for Transporting an Amount Less Than the Statutory Minimum*

10 One who stores [a tiny amount of grain] for seed, or for a sample, or for healing, and took it out on the Sabbath
is culpable for any amount whatever;
but every [other] person is culpable only if [he took out] its [stated minimum] quantity.
If [the one who stored a tiny quantity] brought it in again [after taking it out],
he is culpable only if [he brought in] its [stated minimum] quantity.

10:2–5 *Culpability for Transportation is Incurred Only if an Object Is Carried in Its Usual Manner*

2 One who takes out foodstuffs and puts them on the threshold—
[no matter] whether he returned and took them out,[86]

---

[86] Or "whether he afterward took them out."

---

any amount whatever: No matter how small the bird of the vineyard may be.

for healing: Even the smallest amount of a substance that has medicinal value may not be carried from one domain to another; see 10:1.

a living impure locust: A locust that may not be eaten.

any amount whatever: No matter how small the impure locust may be.

10:1 This mishnah explicates the principle stated in 7:3.

is culpable for any amount whatever: Because his act of storage demonstrates that he values even minute quantities.

[stated minimum] quantity: Listed in 7:4, 8:1–7, and 9:5–7.

he is culpable only if [he brought in] its [stated minimum] quantity: Because the act of bringing in what had just been taken out is understood as a change of mind. Originally he valued even the most minute quantities of grain, but having changed his mind he no longer does so. Hence the universal statutory minimum applies.

10:2 Violating the prohibition of taking out from one domain to another incurs penalty only if the act is performed by one person at one time.

or whether another took them out,
he is exempt,
since he did not perform the [entire] prohibited labor at one time.
A basket that is full of produce and one puts it on the outer threshold—
even though the greater part of the produce was outside,
he is exempt,
unless he takes out the entire basket.

3 One who takes out [an object from one domain to another],
whether by his right hand or by his left hand, in his bosom or on his shoulder,
is culpable,
for thus was the manner of carrying by the sons of Kohath.
[One who does so] on the back of his hand,
or with his foot,
or with his mouth,
or with his elbow,
or in his ear,
or in his hair,
or in his wallet while its mouth is downwards,
or between his wallet and his shirt,
or in the hem[87] of his shirt,
or in his shoe, or in his sandal
is exempt,
since he has not taken it out in the normal manner.[88]

4 One who intends to take out [an object from one domain to another by placing it in his garment] in front of him
and it came around behind him
is exempt;
but if [he intended to take it out] behind him
and it came around in front of him
he is culpable.

[87] K: "border." [88] Lit. "in the manner of those that take out."

whether another took them out to another domain: Each of two persons did half the labor of taking out an object from one domain to another, hence neither is liable.

10:3 Transporting an object from one domain to another is culpable only if the carrier carries the object normally.

for thus carrying on the shoulder *was the manner of transporting* the Tabernacle *by the sons of Kohath*: Numbers 7:9. Hence carrying on the shoulder is deemed "transporting." See note on 11:2 below.

in the normal manner: That is, none of these is a "proper" act of carriage, hence none of these incurs liability for transporting from one domain to another.

10:4 The carrier is culpable for transporting an object from one domain to another only if they intend to carry the object normally or approve of the manner in which the object is actually carried.

is exempt: Even though he intended to carry it normally or properly (in front), it was carried abnormally or improperly (behind).

he is culpable: Even though he intended to carry it abnormally or improperly, in the end he followed the usual practice.

Nevertheless[89] they have said:[90]
A woman who is engirdled in a *sinar*[91] [and takes out an object from one domain to another by placing it in her *sinar*],
whether in front of her or behind her
is culpable,
since it [the *sinar*] is likely[92] to move around.
R. Judah says:
[The same law applies] even to those who accept notes [for delivery].

5 One who takes out a loaf into the public domain
is culpable;
if two took it out,
they are exempt.
If one could not take it out and two took it out,
they are culpable;
but R. Simeon exempts them.
One who takes out in a utensil foodstuffs less than the statutory amount
is exempt even for the utensil,
since the utensil is secondary to the food.
[One who takes out] a living person on a couch
is exempt even for the couch,
since the couch is secondary to the living person;
[but if one takes out] a corpse on a couch,
he is culpable.
And likewise, [if one takes out] as much as an olive's bulk of a corpse
or an olive's bulk of carrion,
or a lentil's bulk of dead vermin,
he is culpable,
but R. Simeon exempts him.

---

[89] Lit. "in truth."   [90] K, P lack "they have said."
[91] Danby translates "drawers." Perhaps "petticoat."   [92] Lit. "fit," "worthy."

---

is culpable because we may assume that she knew all along that her *sinar* was *likely to move around*.

those who accept notes [for delivery] know that the bags or pouches they carry are likely to move around.

10:5 *if two took it out, they are exempt*: Because each has done only half the labor.

If one could not take it out: Because of its size or weight.

the statutory amount: The minimums required for incurring culpability for the violation. These minimums are listed in 7:4, 8:1–7, and 9:5–7.

since the utensil is secondary to the food: He is transporting the utensil only because he wants the food—he has no interest in the utensil itself.

exempt even for the couch: The act is prohibited but the actor is not culpable for transporting the living person, since a living person could walk by himself. Cf. 18:2.

[if one takes out] a corpse on a couch, he is culpable for transporting the corpse and for transporting the bier.

an olive's bulk…a lentil's bulk: The minimum amounts that impart impurity; see *Tohorot* 3:4 and *Miqva'ot* 6:7. The householder wants to remove these sources of impurity from his house and therefore takes them out, thus violating the prohibition of transporting. Why R. Simeon exempts him is debated by the commentators.

dead vermin: One of the eight creeping creatures (see 14:1) listed in Leviticus 11:29–30.

10:6 *Other Acts that Incur No Penalty if Performed in an Unusual Manner*

6 One who pares his fingernails by his nails[93] or his teeth;
and likewise his hair, or his moustache or his beard;
and likewise a woman who braids [her hair] or paints [her eyelids] or reddens [her face]—
R. Eliezer declares them liable,[94]
but the Sages forbid [these acts, though only] on account of Sabbath rest.
One who plucks [a plant] from a plant pot with a hole in its bottom
is culpable;
but from a plant pot without a hole in its bottom,
he is exempt.
R. Simeon declares him exempt in either case.

Chapter Eleven

11:1–6 *Throwing from One Domain to Another*

11 One who throws [something] from a private domain to a public domain,
or from a public domain to a private domain
is culpable;
[but] from a private domain to another private domain
with a public domain in between—
R. Aqiva declares him culpable,
but the Sages declare him exempt.
2 How?
Two balconies, one opposite the other in the public domain:
one who passes something, and one who throws something, from one to the other

---

[93] Lit. "this one by that one."   [94] Or "culpable." **K**, **P** add "to a purgation offering."

10:6 *R. Eliezer declares them liable* to punishment because these acts come under one or more of the thirty-nine categories of prohibited labor (7:2). Hence, deliberate acts would be punished with the death penalty, accidental acts with a purgation offering. The Sages agree with R. Eliezer that these acts are prohibited, but disagree as to the nature of the prohibition. According to the Sages these acts violate not the prohibition of labor (Exodus 20:10) but the positive command to rest on the Sabbath (*Betsah* 5:2). There is no death penalty or purgation offering for violating a positive commandment.

a plant pot with a hole in its bottom and resting directly on the ground. The hole establishes a connection between the soil in the pot and the ground (*Demai* 5:10); hence plucking a plant from the pot is akin to harvesting, one of the thirty-nine prohibited labors (7:2). Without a hole in its bottom, however, a plant pot is not earth, and without earth there can be no legal act of harvesting. Such plucking would be prohibited only by the rabbinic extension of the injunction to rest on the Sabbath.

11:2 *How?* The mishnah illustrates the position of the Sages; R. Aqiva would disagree.

Two balconies: Each of which is a private domain, and each of which extends out over the public domain.

one opposite the other: So that a person needs to reach across the public domain to reach from one to the other.

is exempt.
If the two of them were in the same line—
one who passes something [from one to the other]
is culpable;
but one who throws something [from one to the other]
is exempt.
For such was the service of the Levites:
two wagons, one behind the other in the public domain:
they would pass beams from the one to the other but would not throw them.
A bank of earth around a cistern,[95] or a rock,
that is ten handbreadths high and four[96] wide—
one who picks up something from them, or puts something upon them
is culpable;
[but if they were] less than [these dimensions]
he is exempt.

3 One who throws something [a distance of] four cubits at a wall—
[if it sticks to the wall] higher than ten handbreadths,

[95] Or "pit." [96] K: "ten" (corrected in the margin to "four").

If the two of them the two balconies, each of which is a private domain, *were in the same line* on the same side of the street. Cf. *Eruvin* 8:11. The two balconies were not across the street from each other but adjacent to each other along the length of the street, as if lined up in a caravan.

the service of the Levites: See 10:3 and 12:3. The various acts that the Levites performed in the wilderness in order to transport and set up the Tabernacle, and, according to the Talmud, the various acts performed by the priests in order to keep the Tabernacle functioning, are the paradigms of the labors prohibited on the Sabbath (7:2). See the introduction to this tractate. Whatever they did is defined as labor and therefore prohibited on the Sabbath; whatever they did not do is not defined as labor and therefore not prohibited on the Sabbath, or at least it incurs no liability. In this case, the Merarites transported the beams of the Tabernacle (Numbers 4:31) via wagons (Numbers 7:8). The Mishnah imagines that the Merarites would park their *wagons*, each of which had the status of a private domain, *one behind the other*, in the Israelite encampment, which had the status of a *public domain*; the Mishnah further imagines that the Levites would *pass beams from one* wagon *to the other*, but would *not throw them*, either because they were too heavy or because throwing would have seemed to be disrespectful. Hence, if balconies are arrayed in a manner reminiscent of the Levites' wagons, one adjacent to the other along the length of the public domain, passing something from one balcony to another is prohibited on the Sabbath, but throwing something from one balcony to another is permissible (or at least not punishable). However, if the balconies are opposite each other (rather than "behind" each other), both passing and throwing from one balcony to another are permissible (or at least not punishable) since there is no Levitical precedent for either act. R. Aqiva, however, disagrees (11:1).

ten handbreadths high and four wide is the minimum size for a legally constituted private domain enclosed by a public domain. The digger of a pit in the public domain is responsible for damage that it causes (*Bava Qamma* 1). If it is ten handbreadths high/deep and four handbreadths wide, for the purposes of Sabbath law it is considered to be a private domain surrounded by a public domain. (On the height of ten handbreadths, see annotation to 11:3.) Hence, if one transfers something from the public domain to a private domain of this sort or transfers something to the public domain from a private domain of this sort, he is culpable; if the pit was less than this minimum size, he is not culpable, since he has not transferred an item from one domain to another.

11:3 *four cubits*: In addition to the prohibition of transporting an object from one domain to another on the Sabbath, according to the Mishnah the Torah also prohibits transportation of an object four cubits within a public domain.

ten handbreadths: The space of a public domain is deemed to be public domain up to the height of ten handbreadths; above that height the space is not considered public domain. See *Eruvin* 9:7–9.

it is as if he has thrown it into the air;
below ten handbreadths,
it is as if he has thrown it on to the ground.
One who throws something [a distance of] four cubits onto the ground
is culpable.
If one threw it within four cubits
and it rolled beyond the four cubits,
he is exempt;
beyond four cubits
and it rolled back within the four cubits
he is culpable.

4 One who throws something [a distance of] four cubits into the sea
is exempt.
If it was shallow water and a public domain passed through it—[97]
one who throws [something a distance of] four cubits into it
is culpable.
How much is shallow water?
Less than ten[98] handbreadths [deep].
If it was shallow water and a public domain passed through it,
one who throws [something a distance of] four cubits into it
is culpable.

5 One who throws [something] from the sea to the dry land,
or from the dry land to the sea,
or from the sea to a ship,
or from a ship to the sea,
or from one ship to another
is exempt.

[97] K lacks "through it" (but the word is added in the margin).
[98] K: "five" (corrected to "ten" in the margin).

it is as if he has thrown it into the air and therefore is not culpable. His throwing has not exceeded the four-cubit limit for carrying (or throwing) within a public domain, since at the four-cubit mark it landed and remained more than ten handbreadths above the ground, and therefore not in the public domain.

it is as if he has thrown it on to the ground: That is, below the height of ten handbreadths, the area deemed to be public domain. Throwing something more than four cubits within the public domain is akin to carrying it and therefore prohibited.

11:4 *sea...he is exempt*: Because the sea is deemed neither public domain nor private domain.

shallow water...is culpable: Since the shallow water is deemed to be public domain.

The Talmuds and the commentators debate why the fourth clause of this mishnah repeats the second.

11:5 *is exempt*: Because he has not transported an item from one domain to another, the sea not being considered a domain. Throwing an object from one ship (a private domain) to another (also a private domain) over an expanse of sea (which is neither private domain nor public domain) differs from the case discussed in 11:1–2.

If the ships were tied together
one may move [items] from one to the other;
if they were not tied together,
even though they were adjacent,
one may not move [items] from one to the other.

6 One who throws something
and remembers [that it is the Sabbath] after[99] it left his hand,
[or] if another caught it,
[or] if a dog caught it,
or if it was burnt,
he is exempt [from a purgation offering].
If he threw it intending to make a wound on either a person or an animal,
and before the wound was made he remembers [that it is the Sabbath],
he is exempt [from a purgation offering].
This is the general rule:
All those who [may be] liable to a purgation offering are liable
only if they acted inadvertently at both the beginning and end.
If at the beginning they acted inadvertently but at the end they acted deliberately,[100]
or if at the beginning they acted deliberately[101] but at the end they acted inadvertently—
they are exempt [from a purgation offering]
unless they act inadvertently at both the beginning and end.

[99] K, P: "before"   [100] Or "willfully."   [101] Or "willfully."

If the ships were tied together they are considered a single domain; hence it is permissible to move items from one to the other on Sabbath. *If they were not tied together*, we fear that they may separate at any moment, undoing the legal bond; hence it is not permissible to move items from one to the other on Sabbath.

11:6 *One who throws…he is exempt*: The commentators debate how to construe this paragraph: should the clauses "if another caught it, if a dog caught it, or if it was burnt" be understood (as translated here) as an alternative to the clause "and remembers that it is the Sabbath," or as a continuation of it (so the case is: one throws something on the Sabbath, immediately after which [or in some texts: immediately before which] he remembers that it is the Sabbath, and the object is caught by a person, or caught by a dog, or burnt)? How exactly does this paragraph relate to the "general rule" stated at the end of the mishnah, according to which an act, if it is to be liable to a purgation offering, must be inadvertent at both its inception and conclusion? The textual variant "before/after" shows that the tradents of this paragraph were not sure how to construe it. The text as translated here means the following: *One who throws something and remembers [that it is the Sabbath] after it left his hand…he is exempt [from a purgation offering]*. By the time the object landed the person remembered that it was the Sabbath, hence the condition for a purgation offering, as stated in the general rule, has not been met. The beginning of the act was inadvertent (when he threw the object he did not remember that it was the Sabbath), but the end of the act was intentional (because by the time the object landed the thrower knew that it was the Sabbath).

if another caught it: The thrower is exempt because the act of labor was divided between two people (10:5).

if a dog caught it, or if it was burnt before it landed: The thrower is exempt because the object never landed in the public domain.

purgation offering: The penalty for inadvertent sin (Leviticus 4:27–35). See 7:1.

Chapter Twelve

12:1 Building

12 One who builds—
how much must he build
so that he is culpable?
One who builds any amount whatever;
one who hews, or strikes with a hammer or a chisel, or bores, any amount whatever
is culpable.
This is the general rule:
Anyone who performs an act of labor on the Sabbath and his labor endures[102]
is culpable.
Rabban Simeon b. Gamaliel says:
Even one who strikes with a mallet on the anvil
during an act of labor
is culpable,
since he has the status of one who prepares the labor.

12:2 Labor in the Field

2 One who plows any amount whatever;
one who weeds or trims or prunes any amount whatever
is culpable.
One who gathers wood—
if to improve [the ground]—any amount whatever;
if to burn—enough to cook the easiest of eggs.
One who gathers grass—
if to improve [the ground]—any amount whatever;
if for the cattle—enough to fill a kid's mouth.

---

[102] Or "if anyone performs an act of labor and his labor endures on the Sabbath."

12:1 *builds*: See 7:2 no. 34.

how much: Through 13:4 the mishnah pursues this question in reference to various kinds of labor.

strikes with a hammer: See 7:2 no. 38

This is the general rule: This principle would seem to apply to many different kinds of labor, not just building (cf. 12:5, 15:2). The rule is brought here, it seems, to limit the previous statement: building "any amount" on the Sabbath is culpable provided that the act of building "endures," that is, has some measure of wholeness or permanence.

prepares the labor: By striking the anvil with the mallet, he prepares the mallet for use.

12:2 The primary labor of plowing (7:2 no. 2) includes weeding, trimming, and pruning; harvesting (7:2 no. 3) includes gathering loose wood or grass.

enough to cook the easiest of eggs: See 8:5.

enough to fill a kid's mouth: See 7:4.

12:3–6 *Writing*

3 One who writes two letters,[103]
whether with his right hand or with his left,
whether the same letter or different letters,[104]
whether in different inks,[105]
in any language—
is culpable.
R. Yose said:
The Sages[106] declared [the writer of] "two letters" culpable
only because they constitute a mark;
for so they used to write[107] on the boards of the Tabernacle
that they might know which paired with which.
Rabbi[108] said:
We find a short name formed from a longer name:
Shem from Shimeon or Shemuel,
Noah from Nahor,
Dan from Daniel,
Gad from Gadiel.

4 One who writes two letters in one period of forgetfulness
is liable [to bring a purgation offering].
If one wrote in ink or caustic or red dye or gum or copperas or anything that marks;
or on two walls forming an angle or on two tablets of an account book so that [the two letters] can be read together,
he is culpable.[109]
One who writes on his skin

---

[103] K, P lack "two letters."   [104] Lit. "whether of one category or two categories."
[105] K, P: "signs" or "markings."   [106] Lit. "they."   [107] K, P: "mark."
[108] K, P add "Judah."   [109] K lacks "he is culpable."

12:3 The opening statement explains that the prohibition of "writing two letters" should be understood broadly. R. Yose explains that the letters need not even be letters. Levites in the wilderness would mark the boards of the Tabernacle so that they would know, when disassembling and reassembling the Tabernacle, which board was to be paired with which. These pairs of marks—not necessarily letters—are the source of the prohibition of "writing two letters." The Tabernacle provides the archetype for the definition of "labor"; see 10:3 and 11:2.

writes two letters: See 7:2 no. 32.

with his right hand or with his left: See 10:3.

Rabbi Judah (see n. 108) seems to disagree with R. Yose and perhaps with the opening statement (this point is debated by the commentators). Rabbi [Judah] seems to limit culpability to the writing of two Hebrew letters, perhaps only two Hebrew letters that constitute a Hebrew name.

12:4 *in one period of forgetfulness*: See 7:1.

or on two walls…or on two tablets: Each of the two letters is written on a different surface. Contrast 12:5.

One who writes…one who scratches on his skin on the Sabbath. The issue here is not the prohibition of "tattooing" but the prohibition of writing on the Sabbath.

is culpable.
One who scratches[110] on his skin:[111]
R. Eliezer declares him liable to a purgation offering,
but R. Joshua declares him exempt.

5 If one wrote with liquids or with fruit juice or with dust from the roads or the dust of scribes or with anything that does not endure,
he is exempt.
[If] with the back of his hand or with his foot or with his mouth or with his elbow;
if one wrote one letter beside one already written, or if he wrote over what was already written;
if one intended to write a *het* but wrote two *zayin* instead;
[if one wrote] one letter on the ground and another on the roof;
if one wrote on two walls of a house or on two pages of an account book
so that [the two letters] cannot be read together—
[in all these cases] he is exempt.
If he wrote one letter as an abbreviation—
R. Joshua b. Betera declares him culpable,
but the Sages declare him exempt.

6 One who writes two letters during two periods of forgetfulness, one in the morning and one at twilight—
Rabban Gamaliel declares him liable [to bring a purgation offering],
but the Sages declare him exempt.

Chapter Thirteen

13:1–4 *Weaving, Sewing, Tearing, and Related Activities*

13 R. Eliezer says:
One who weaves three threads at the beginning [of the web],

---

[110] Or "incises" or "tattoos."
[111] K begins paragraph 5 at this point with the words "R. Eliezer declares him liable," an obvious scribal mistake.

liable to a purgation offering: If done inadvertently. See 6:2–3.

12:5 *anything that does not endure*: 12:1.

with the back of his hand or with his foot or with his mouth or with his elbow: 10:3.

if one intended to write a het but wrote two zayin instead: He is exempt because he intended to write only one letter. The letter *het* is formed by creating a small bridge between two adjacent *zayin*.

if one wrote on two walls: One letter on each of two walls. Contrast 12:4.

12:6 Cf. 12:4.

but the Sages declare him exempt from a purgation offering, because during each period of forgetfulness he wrote only one letter, one half of the minimum labor needed to incur the penalty. Cf. 7:1.

13:1 *two threads*: See 7:2 no. 19.

or a single thread on that which is already woven
is culpable.
But the Sages say:
Whether at the beginning or the end,
the [prohibited statutory] amount is two threads.

2 One who makes two meshes on the heddles or the sley [of a loom],
or in a sifter or sieve or basket,
is culpable;
likewise,[112] one who sews two stitches or one who tears in order to sew two stitches [is culpable].

3 One who tears [his clothing] in his anger or because of his dead,
and[113] all those who destroy
are exempt.
But one who destroys with the intention of making anew—
for him the [prohibited statutory] amount is the same as for him who makes anew.

4 The [prohibited] statutory amount for one who bleaches, hackles, dyes, or spins
is double the full breadth of a *sit*;
one who weaves two threads—
his [prohibited statutory] amount is the full breadth of a *sit*.

13:5–14:1 *Trapping*

5 R. Judah says:
One who traps[114] a bird in a tower trap,

---

[112] K, P lack "likewise" (lit. "and").
[113] K, P lack "and."
[114] K lacks "one who traps."

13:2 *two meshes*: See 7:2 no. 18.

the heddles or the sley: Thus Danby. For a full inventory of the parts of a loom, see *Kelim* 21:1.

sews two stitches or...tears in order to sew two stitches: 7:2 nos. 23–24.

13:3 *and all those who destroy* (lit. "ruin"): According to our text tearing clothing in anger or in grief illustrates the general principle that acts of destruction are not culpable. According to the text of the manuscripts, which omits "and," tearing clothing would seem to belong to the previous mishnah: sewing two stitches, tearing in order to sew two stitches, and tearing in anger or grief—all these are culpable.

the [prohibited] statutory amount is the same as for him who makes anew (lit. "sets in order," "fixes," or "repairs"): Tearing (= destroying) for the sake of repairing is culpable if the tear equals or exceeds the prohibited minimum dimension of repair, which equals the prohibited minimum dimension of making a new cloth. See 13:2.

13:4 *bleaches...spins*: See 7:2 nos. 13–16.

A *sit* is the distance from the tip of the outstretched thumb to the tip of the outstretched index (or middle) finger; see *Orlah* 3:2–3.

13:5 *traps*: See 7:2 no. 25.

or a deer in a house
is culpable.
But the Sages say:
[One who traps] a bird in a tower trap,
or a deer in a house,[115] a courtyard, or an animal pen—
[all these are culpable].
Rabban Simeon b. Gamaliel says:
Not all animal pens are alike.
This is the general rule:
[One who does] an act of trapping that is incomplete
is exempt;
but [one who does] an act of trapping that is not incomplete
is culpable.[116]

6 If a deer enters a house and one closed [the door] before it,
he is culpable;
but if two closed [the door],
they are exempt.
If one alone was not able to close [the door]
and two closed [the door],
both are culpable,
but R. Simeon declares them to be exempt.

7 If [after a deer enters a house] one sat in the entrance but did not fill it,
and [therefore] a second sat there and filled it [thus trapping the deer],
the second is culpable.
If the first sat in the entrance and filled it,
and then a second came and sat beside him,
even if the first stood up and went away,
the first is culpable and the second is exempt.
What does this case resemble?

[115] K, P have "garden" instead of "house."
[116] K, P read "This is the general rule: any act of trapping that is incomplete—he is culpable; but an act of trapping that is not incomplete—he is exempt."

the Sages have a more inclusive definition of "trapping" than R. Judah.

an act of trapping that is incomplete...exempt: For example, driving a bird into a house is an incomplete act of trapping according to both R. Judah and the Sages, since the bird can still fly about and is not yet under full human control.

exempt...culpable: The manuscripts read just the opposite (*culpable...exempt*) but probably mean the same thing. Our printed text refers to driving an animal into a trap; the manuscripts refer to removing an animal from the trap. If the trap was complete, the act of removing the animal is not culpable since the act of hunting had already taken place; if the trap was incomplete, removing the animal from the trap completes the act of hunting and is culpable. See *Betsah* 3:1.

13:6 *he is culpable* because shutting a deer into a house is deemed to be trapping; see 13:5.

if two closed the door, they are exempt because each has done only half of the act; see 10:5.

13:7 *the second is culpable*: The one who closes up the entrance, thus trapping a deer inside, is culpable for trapping. 13:7 restates and elaborates 13:6.

The case of one who closes up his house to guard it,
with the result that the deer is now guarded inside.

Chapter Fourteen

14 The eight vermin spoken of in the Torah—
if one traps or wounds any of them
he is culpable.
But[117] other abominable creatures or creeping things—
one who wounds any of them
is exempt;
one who traps any of them—
if for a purpose,
he is culpable,
but if not for a purpose,
he is exempt.
A wild animal or bird in his private domain—
one who traps them
is exempt,
but one who wounds them
is culpable.

14:2–4 *Compounding Medicines and Other Preparations*

2 One may not make pickling-brine on the Sabbath,
but one may make salt water and dip his bread in it
or put it into cooked food.
R. Yose said:

[117] K, P add "all."

14:1 *in the Torah*: Leviticus 11:29-30.

he is culpable: These eight creatures have skins that are useable (*Hullin* 9:2), hence they are regularly hunted (trapped) and trapping them is defined to be trapping for a purpose. In addition, wounding them is a subset of slaughtering (or, according to another interpretation, of dyeing, since the blood that emerges from the wound dyes the skin). *other abominable creatures* (Leviticus 11:41-42) *or creeping things*, however, do not have useable skins, hence wounding them is not a subset of slaughter, and trapping them is a violation of the Sabbath only if they are hunted for a purpose, e.g. for use in potions (*Eduyot* 2:5).

14:2 *One may not make pickling-brine on the Sabbath*: Apparently because of the prohibition of salting (7:2 no. 28). The difference between pickling-brine and salt water is that the former is commercial, made by artisans in large quantities, whereas the latter is domestic, made in the home at the table.

R. Yose apparently believes that there is no distinction between preparing pickling-brine and preparing salt water—both are prohibited.

But is this not pickling-brine,
whether much or little?
And which is the salt water that is permissible?
If one first puts oil into the water
or into the salt.

   3 One may not eat Greek hyssop on the Sabbath
since it is not the food of the healthy;
but one eats pennyroyal or drinks knotgrass.
A person may eat any food that [also] serves for healing,
or drink any liquid except the water of palm trees[118] or a cup of root water,
since these are for jaundice;
but he drinks the water of palm trees[119] to quench his thirst,
and he anoints himself with root oil if it is not for healing.

   4 One who suffers in his teeth may not suck vinegar through them
but he may dip [his bread in vinegar] in his usual manner,
and if he is healed, he is healed.
One who suffers in his loins may not anoint them with wine or vinegar,
but he may anoint them with oil—
but not rose oil.
The children of kings anoint their wounds with rose oil [on the Sabbath]
since it is their custom to anoint with it on ordinary days.
R. Simeon says:
All Israel are the children of kings.

[118] K, P: "except purgative water."   [119] K, P: "purgative water."

And which is the salt water that is permissible? This is either a continuation of R. Yose's statement or a third opinion.

14:3 This and the following mishnah assume that any activity that is exclusively for medicinal or therapeutic purposes is prohibited on the Sabbath. The source of the prohibition is not explained. (The medical conditions about which the Mishnah speaks are not life-threatening; if they are, then any action would be permitted on the Sabbath. See 9:3, 19:3.)

Greek hyssop was not normally eaten as food; it was eaten solely for its medicinal value.

pennyroyal…knotgrass: Thus Danby; precise identification uncertain. These herbs were eaten both as food and as medicine.

14:4 *in his usual manner, and if he is healed, he is healed*: See 22:6.

wine or vinegar were not normally used for anointing, hence if they are being so used, it must be for the sake of healing, which is prohibited on the Sabbath.

rose oil was so rare and precious that it would not normally be used for anointing. Hence if it is being so used, it must be for the sake of healing. Since *the children of kings* use rose oil regularly, for them it is not exclusively for healing, and therefore they may use it on the Sabbath.

All Israel: Cf. Bava Qamma 8:6, Bava Metsi'a 7:1.

Chapter Fifteen

15:1–3 *Tying and Untying, Folding and Spreading*

15 For which knots is one culpable?
The knot of camel drivers and the knot of sailors.
And[120] just as one is culpable for tying them,
so one is culpable for untying them.
R. Meir says:
Any knot which he can untie with one of his hands—
one is not culpable on its account.

2 You[121] have knots on whose account one is not culpable
[in contrast] with the knot of camel drivers and the knot of sailors.[122]
A woman may tie up the opening[123] of her shift,
or the strings of a hairnet or belt,
or the straps of a shoe or sandal,
or leather bottles of wine or oil,
or [a cover over] a pot of meat.
R. Eliezer b. Jacob says:
One may tie [a rope] before an animal
so that it should not go out.
One may tie a bucket to a belt
but not to a rope;
but R. Judah permits.
R. Judah stated a general rule:
Any knot that does not endure—
one is not culpable on its account.

3 One may fold garments even four or five times.
And one may spread beds[124] on the night of the Sabbath for the Sabbath,
but not on the Sabbath for the night following the Sabbath.

---

[120] **K, P** lack "and."   [121] **K, P:** "and you."
[122] Lit. "You have knots on whose account one is not culpable as [one is culpable] for the knot of camel drivers and the knot of sailors." Or "You have knots which are similar to [lit. like] the knot of camel drivers and the knot of sailors but for which [nevertheless] one is not culpable."
[123] **K, P:** "openings."   [124] Or "cushions" or "couches."

15:1 *tying…untying*: See 7:2 nos. 21–22.

15:2 *You*: This is the only example in the Mishnah of a legal ruling formulated in the second person.

not culpable: But apparently still prohibited. Since the next line indicates an activity that is completely permissible (*a woman may tie up the opening of her shift*), the Talmud deduces that the clause *You have knots* is the header for a missing list of prohibited but not culpable knots.

a bucket: To be let down into a well.

Any knot that does not endure: All the permitted knots of 15:2 are impermanent. Cf. 12:1.

15:3 *even four or five*: See 18:1.

R. Ishmael says:
One may fold garments and spread beds[125] on the Day of Atonement for the Sabbath; and[126] the fat pieces of the Sabbath [sacrifice] may be sacrificed on the Day of Atonement.
R. Aqiva says:
The Sabbath [sacrifices] may not be brought on the Day of Atonement,
nor may [the sacrifices] of the Day of Atonement be brought on the Sabbath.

Chapter Sixteen

16:1–7 *Saving from Fire*

16 Any of the Holy Scriptures
may be saved from a fire,[127]
whether they are read [on the Sabbath] or not.
And[128] even though they are written in any language,

---

[125] Or "cushions" or "couches."
[126] K, P lack "and."
[127] Lit. "one may save…"
[128] K, P lack "and."

Sabbath [sacrifices]: Numbers 28:9–10.

[the sacrifices] of the Day of Atonement: Leviticus 16; Numbers 29:7–11. For R. Ishmael the sanctity of the Sabbath exceeds that of the Day of Atonement, consequently leftover sacrifices from the Day of Atonement (when it falls on Friday) may not be offered on the Sabbath following it, but leftover sacrifices from the Sabbath may be offered on the Day of Atonement (when it falls on Sunday). According to R. Aqiva their sanctity is equal, consequently leftover sacrifices of neither may be offered on the other. (We may presume that R. Aqiva would also prohibit folding garments and spreading beds on the Day of Atonement for the Sabbath.) If the Day of Atonement falls on the Sabbath, the sacrifices of each are offered, according to both R. Ishmael and R. Aqiva.

16:1 *Any of the Holy Scriptures*: Whether the Torah, the Neviim (Prophets), or Ketuvim (Hagiographa or Sacred Writings). Selections from the Torah and Neviim are read publicly in synagogue on the Sabbath, but not selections from the Ketuvim.

may be saved: By removing them from the scene of the fire, even if this action involves a violation of the prohibition of transport on the Sabbath.

And even though they are written in any language, they must be hidden away: Heb. *genizah*, cf. 9:6. The commentators, ancient and modern, debate the relationship of this line to the previous. According to one approach, the first two lines constitute a unit. All scrolls of Holy Scripture, whether Torah or Prophets or Sacred Writings (Hagiographa), whether read publicly in synagogue on the Sabbath or not, whether written in Hebrew or not, may be saved from a fire on the Sabbath and are to be stored in a *genizah* when worn out. According to another approach, however, the first two lines are meant to contrast with each other. The only sacred scrolls that may be saved from a fire on the Sabbath are those written in Hebrew; non-Hebrew scrolls may not to be saved on the Sabbath. Within this approach to our mishnah there is a debate how to understand the reference to *genizah*. First interpretation: even though non-Hebrew scrolls may not be saved from a fire on the Sabbath, they are to be treated respectfully; they may be studied in private and if they wear out they are not to be tossed in the garbage but are to be treated like Hebrew scrolls: they are to be stored in a *genizah*. Second interpretation: the mishnah assumes that non-Hebrew scrolls are not to be read at all, whether publicly or privately, whether on the Sabbath or any other day; they are to be hidden away, not because they are venerated but because they are not. They are to be removed from circulation.

they must be hidden away.
And[129] why may one not read them [on the Sabbath]?
Because of the neglect of the house of study.
One may save the case of a scroll with the scroll,
and the case of *tefillin* with the *tefillin*,
even though there are coins in them.
To what place may one save them?
To an alleyway that is not open.
Ben Betera says:
Even to one that is open.

2 [In case of fire] one may save food for three meals;
for people, that which is suitable for people,
and for cattle, that which is suitable for cattle.
How?
If fire broke out in the night of the Sabbath,
one may save food for three meals;
if in the morning—
one may save food for two meals;
if in the afternoon,
food for one meal.
R. Yose says:
One may always save food for three meals.

3 One may save a basket full of loaves even though it contains a hundred meals,
or a cake of figs or a jar of wine.
He may say to others:
"Come and save for yourselves."
If they are prudent,

---

[129] K, P lack "and."

---

the neglect of the house of study: "The Hagiographa, owing to their seductive attractiveness, tend to distract the mind from the graver subject of Sabbath instruction in matters relating to the Law" (Danby). People might not attend the public Sabbath discourse if they are permitted to study Scripture at home. Cf. 18:1.

To what place may one save them? Any of the objects listed above (Holy Scriptures, scroll, *tefillin*) may be saved from a fire by removal to another location, though not by removal from a private domain to a public domain; that would be too great a violation of the prohibition of transport (see 1:1).

alleyway or entrance *that is not open*: An alleyway that is not open at both ends and consequently does not serve to connect a courtyard or a private domain with a public domain. Removal of an object (for example, a sacred scroll) from a private domain to a closed alleyway is a lesser violation of the prohibition of transport than removing an object to an open alley, which is functionally equivalent to a public domain. Even Ben Betera would not permit removal to an actual public domain. We may assume that both Ben Betera and his anonymous interlocutor would permit removal to a courtyard with or without an *eruv*. See the last line of 16:3.

16:2 *three meals*: See 22:1.

16:3 *He* the owner of the house on fire *may say to others* nearby *"Come and save* food *for yourselves."* See also 22:1.

they make a reckoning with him after the Sabbath.
To what place may one save them?
To a courtyard whose owners have joined together in an *eruv*.
Ben Betera says:
Even to one whose owners have not joined together in an *eruv*.

4 And to that place he may take out all the utensils that he needs,
and he may wear all that he is able to wear
and wrap himself in all that he is able to wrap.
R. Yose says:
[Only] eighteen garments.
And he may return and put on [other clothes] and take them out,
and he may say to others:
"Come and save [them] with me."

5 R. Simeon b. Nanos says:
One may spread the hide of a kid over a chest, a box, or a cupboard[130] that have caught fire,
because it will [only] scorch;
and one may make a barrier of any utensils,
whether filled [with water] or empty,
so that a fire should not pass.
R. Yose forbids new earthenware utensils filled with water
because, unable to withstand the fire,
they burst and extinguish the fire.

[130] Lit. "tower."

they make a reckoning with him after the Sabbath: See 23:1. "Too honest to profit by keeping his goods which they rescued, they can at least bargain for some return for their labor" (Danby).

To what place may one save them? The three meals' worth of food of 16:2 and the loaves, figs, and wine of 16:3.

eruv: By joining together via a common meal, all the householders whose property abuts on a common courtyard can treat that courtyard as an extension of their private domain, hence may carry items in it or across it on the Sabbath. This legal device is an *eruv*. See 2:7 and *Eruvin*.

To a courtyard whose owners have joined together in an eruv: No license is made at all for saving food from a fire; food can be removed only to an area to which transport is permitted Even according to *Ben Betera*, less license is given for the rescue of food than for the rescue of sacred objects. See 16:1.

16:4 *to that place*: The courtyard mentioned at the end of 16:3.

that he needs: For the Sabbath meals.

The *eighteen garments* are specified in the Talmud. They are the clothes normally worn by a man, even if normally he would not wear all eighteen at once.

And he may return to the burning house: This might be a continuation of R. Yose's statement (in which case *and* should be replaced by *but*) but it seems more natural to see it as a continuation of the opening statement.

16:5 *One may spread the hide of a kid*: In order to prevent the fire from spreading. This action is permissible *because it will [only] scorch*; that is, it will neither extinguish the fire (which is prohibited, see 7:2 no. 36) nor feed the fire (which is also prohibited, see 7:2 no. 37).

6 If a gentile comes to extinguish [the fire],
they may not say to him, "Extinguish!" or[131] "Do not extinguish!"
since his observance of the Sabbath is not their responsibility.[132]
But if a minor comes to extinguish [the fire],
they may not permit[133] him to do so,
since his observance of the Sabbath is their responsibility.[134]

7 One may turn a dish over a lamp
so that [the flame] should not take hold of the rafter,
and over the excrement of a child,
and over a scorpion so that it should not bite.
R. Judah said:
[Such] a case came before R. Yohanan b. Zakkai in Arav, and he said:
I suspect that he [is liable to] a purgation offering.

16:8 *The Labor of Gentiles*

8 If a gentile lit a lamp,
an Israelite may use its light,
but if [he lit it] for the Israelite,
it is forbidden.
If he filled [a trough] with water to give drink to his cattle,
an Israelite may give drink [to his own cattle] after him;
but if [he did it] for the Israelite,
it is forbidden.
If a gentile made a gangway by which to come down [from a ship],
an Israelite may come down after him,
but if [he did it] for the Israelite,
it is forbidden.
It once happened that Rabban Gamaliel and the elders were traveling in a ship,

[131] K, P lack "or."   [132] Lit. "upon them."   [133] Lit. "listen to."
[134] Lit. "upon them."

16:6 *they may not say to him "Extinguish!"*: A Jew may not ask a gentile to do something on the Sabbath that would be a violation of the Sabbath if done by the Jew himself. See 16:8 and contrast 24:1.

or "Do not extinguish!": If the gentile wishes to extinguish the fire on his own, we do not stop him. See 16:8.

16:7 *[Such] a case*: In which someone trapped a scorpion under a dish. Cf. 22:3.

Arav: The town of Garaba, mentioned by Josephus, in lower Galilee near Sepphoris.

purgation offering: For inadvertently violating the prohibition of trapping.

16:8 This mishnah is an appendix to 16:1–7, and attaches itself naturally to 16:6. The principle assumed here (and in 23:4) is that an Israelite can take advantage of an action performed by a gentile on the Sabbath, an action that would have been prohibited for the Israelite himself to perform, only if the gentile performed that action for his own benefit and not for the benefit of the Israelite.

traveling in a ship: Cf. *Ma'aser Sheni* 5:9; *Eruvin* 4:1–2.

and a gentile made a gangway by which to come down,
and Rabban Gamaliel and[135] the elders came down by it.

Chapter Seventeen

17:1–18:2 *Utensils and Foodstuffs That May Be Moved or Carried on the Sabbath*

17 All utensils may be moved[136] on the Sabbath,
and their doors with them,
even though they were detached on the Sabbath;
for they do not resemble the doors of a house,
which do[137] not belong to [the category of] that which is already prepared.

2 A person may take a mallet by which to crush walnuts,
or a hatchet to cut a cake of pressed figs,
or a saw by which to scrape cheese,
or a trowel by which to scrape up dried figs;
a winnowing shovel or fork on which to give something to a child;
a spindle or a shuttle-staff by which to insert something;
a hand-needle by which to take out a thorn,
or a sackmaker's [needle] by which to open a door.

3 A reed for olives—
if it has a knot at its end,[138]

[135] K, P lack "Rabban Gamaliel and." [136] Lit. "lifted," "carried," "taken."
[137] K, P: "which does." [138] Lit. "head."

17:1 *utensils*: In some contexts the same word means "garments" (e.g. 15:3, 22:4), in others it refers primarily to kitchenware (e.g. 16:4), and in others, as here, it means "any objects that are of use" (including furniture, tools, equipment).

All utensils: For two exceptions, see 17:4.

utensils that have *doors* or lids: For example a chest, a box, or a cupboard.

for they do not resemble the doors of a house: See 3:6, 24:4, and *Betsah* 3:4. Most people assume that the doors of a house will stay attached to a house; if the doors fall off on the Sabbath they are not to be moved on the Sabbath because they were not *already prepared* on Friday for being moved. However, furniture doors are different. If they fall off on the Sabbath they may be moved (that is, moved out of the way).

17:2 The manuscripts provide various spellings for the nouns and verbs of this mishnah. The point is that utensils whose chief use is prohibited on the Sabbath and which as a result may not normally be moved or carried on the Sabbath, may nonetheless be taken up and used on the Sabbath if they will be used for a permitted purpose.

17:3 In a series of passages the Mishnah coordinates the laws of purity/impurity with Sabbath law; see note on 2:3.

A reed: With which to probe maturing *olives* to see whether they are ready for pressing.

a knot at its end: Thus making the reed into a receptacle, which then becomes susceptible to impurity. See 6:8 and *Kelim* 17:15–17.

it is susceptible to impurity;
if not, it is not susceptible to impurity.
In either case it may be moved on the Sabbath.

4 R. Yose says:[139]
All utensils may be moved[140]
except for a large saw or the spike of a plow.
All utensils may be moved
[whether] for a purpose or not for a purpose.
R. Nehemiah says:
They may be moved only for a purpose.

5 All the utensils that may be moved on the Sabbath—
their fragments may be moved with them,[141]
provided that they are able to[142] perform some type of work:
fragments of a kneading trough by which to cover the mouth of a jar,
or fragments of glass by which to cover the mouth of a cruse.
R. Judah says:
[Fragments may be moved on the Sabbath] provided that they are able to[143] perform some type of their [previous] work:
fragments of a kneading trough into which to pour a thick stew,
or fragments of glass into which to pour oil.

6 The stone that is in a gourd—
if one draws water with it[144]
and the stone does not fall out,
one may draw water with it;
if not, one may not draw water with it.
If a branch is tied to a pitcher,
one may draw water with it on the Sabbath.

---

[139] **K, P** lack "R. Yose says." [140] **K, P** add "on the Sabbath."
[141] **P**: "All the utensils that may be moved on the Sabbath—their fragments too may be moved." **K**: "All utensils may be moved on the Sabbath [cf. 17:1, 4], and their fragments may be moved." A later hand corrected **K** to agree with **P**. Both **K, P** lack "with them," which probably entered the text from 17:1.
[142] Lit. "provided that they will." [143] Lit. "provided that they will."
[144] Lit. "fills with it."

17:4 *All utensils may be moved*: On the Sabbath, as in 17:1.

except for a large saw or the spike of a plow: That is, a plowshare. These have no permitted use on the Sabbath and consequently may not be moved on the Sabbath.

17:5 *their fragments*: That is, if they break on the Sabbath.

some type of work: Work permitted on the Sabbath.

glass: Cf. 8:6.

17:6 *The stone that is in a gourd*: To weigh it down so that the hollowed-out gourd can be used as a bucket for drawing up water from a well. If the stone is firmly attached to the gourd, the assembly is deemed to be a utensil and permissible for use. (The Mishnah does not prohibit drawing water from a well on the Sabbath.) If the stone falls out, the gourd and the stone are regarded as separate items, neither of which may be moved on the Sabbath.

7 A window stopper—
R. Eliezer says:
When [the stopper] is tied and hanging,
one may stop up a window with it;
if not, one may not stop up a window with it.
But the Sages say:
In either case one may stop up a window with it.
  8 All utensil lids that have handles may be moved on the Sabbath.
R. Yose says:
To what do these words refer?
To lids [over openings in] the ground;
but utensil lids may be moved on the Sabbath in either case.

Chapter Eighteen

18 One may clear away even four or five large baskets of straw or grain for the sake of guests
or for the sake of [avoiding] neglect of the house of study,
but not the storehouse.[145]
One may clear away *terumah* that is pure,
demai,

[145] K: "storehouses."

17:7 *A window* was an opening in a wall to admit light and air. To keep out rain and cold it would be closed up with a *stopper*.

When [the stopper] is tied and hanging on the wall, ready to be inserted into the opening.

one may not stop up a window with it: Because it was not prepared (see 17:1), or because such an act is deemed to be building (7:2 no. 34).

17:8 *in either case*: Whether they have handles or not.

18:1 *even four or five*: See 15:3.

large baskets: Sheqalim 3:3.

for the sake of guests to make room for guests *or for the sake of [avoiding] neglect of the house of study* to make room for people in the house of study (cf. 16:1).

One may not clear out *the storehouse* because the food there is not prepared for use on the Sabbath.

One may clear away food that has some use as food: pure *terumah* (see 2:1) may be eaten by a priest; produce of uncertain status (*demai*, see 2:7) may be given to the poor; first tithe from which *terumah* has been removed may be given to Levites; second tithe and consecrated produce that have been redeemed may be eaten by all. Second tithe is produce that is to be eaten in Jerusalem on pilgrimage (Deuteronomy 14:22–27); the produce can be redeemed, however, and then eaten anywhere by anyone. Produce and objects of all kinds can be consecrated, that is dedicated to the Temple, for use by the priests in the running of the Temple, but such produce or objects can be redeemed and then eaten/used by anyone anywhere. In contrast food that is not edible in its current state cannot be moved since it is not prepared for use on the Sabbath.

first tithe from which *terumah* has been removed,
second tithe and consecrated produce that have been redeemed,
and dried lupine, since it is food for the poor;[146]
but not produce that has not yet been tithed,
nor first tithe from which *terumah* has not been removed,
nor second tithe and consecrated produce that have not been redeemed,
nor arum or mustard.
Rabban Simeon b. Gamaliel permits [clearing away] arum,
since it is food for ravens.

2 Bundles of straw, bundles of wood, and bundles of young shoots—
if one prepared them as food for cattle,
one may move them;
but if not, one may not move them.
One may overturn a basket before chicks
so that they may ascend and descend.
If a hen escaped,
one may push it until it comes in.
One may pull along calves or young asses in a public domain.[147]
A woman may pull her child along.
R. Judah[148] said:
When [does this ruling apply]?
When the child raises one [foot] and lowers one;
but if he drags [his feet] it is forbidden.

18:3–19:6 *Birth and Circumcision on the Sabbath*

3 On a Festival day one may not [directly] assist cattle to give birth,
but one may provide [indirect] support.
But[149] on the Sabbath one may assist a woman to give birth,
summon a midwife for her from one place to another,
and profane the Sabbath on her account.
One may tie up the umbilical cord.
R. Yose says:
One may even cut it.

---

[146] **K, P:** "for goats."   [147] **K, P** lack "in a public domain."   [148] **K, P:** "R. Yose."
[149] Or "and"; absent in **K, P**.

18:2 *it is forbidden*: Because the mother is in effect carrying the child. Cf. 10:5 and 21:1.

18:3 *on a Festival day*: And all the more so on the Sabbath.

but one may provide [indirect] support: On a Festival day. On the Sabbath even indirect support is prohibited. The commentators suggest that direct assistance involves actively extracting the fetus from the mother's womb, while indirect support can involve waiting to catch the young as it emerges, pressing on the mother's body to hasten delivery, and the like.

summon a midwife: Even from a place beyond the Sabbath limit (*Rosh Hashanah* 2:5).

Whatever things are necessary for a circumcision,
one may do them on the Sabbath.

Chapter Nineteen

19 R. Eliezer says:
If one did not bring a knife[150] on the eve of Sabbath,
he may bring it openly on the Sabbath;
but in time of danger he covers it in the presence of witnesses.
Furthermore, R. Eliezer said:
One may cut wood in order to make charcoal
or in order to forge an iron knife.[151]
R. Aqiva stated a general rule:
Any labor that can be done on the eve of Sabbath
does not override the Sabbath;
but that[152] which cannot be done on the eve of Sabbath
overrides the Sabbath.

2 On the Sabbath one may do whatever is necessary for a circumcision:
circumcise, uncover, suck, and apply a bandage and cumin.
If one did not grind [the cumin] on the eve of the Sabbath,
one may chew it with his teeth and apply it.
If one did not beat [together] the wine and oil on the eve of the Sabbath,
each should be applied by itself.[153]
One may not make a wrap[154] for the circumcision[155] in anticipation,
but one may wrap a rag around it.

[150] Lit. "utensil." [151] Lit. "utensil." [152] K, P: "but circumcision."
[153] Lit. "let this one be applied by itself, and let that one be applied by itself."
[154] Lit. "shirt." [155] Lit. "it."

Whatever things are necessary…one may do them on the Sabbath: 19:2; cf. *Nedarim* 3:11 (R. Yose).

19:1–6 This is the only chapter in the Mishnah that is devoted to the ritual details of circumcision.

19:1 *If one did not bring* to the place of circumcision.

in time of danger: Persecution, when circumcision was prohibited by the Romans.

in the presence of witnesses: Who can attest to other Jews that he is carrying a circumcision knife.

R. Aqiva stated a general rule: *Pesahim* 6:2, *Menahot* 11:3. R. Aqiva disagrees with R. Eliezer.

19:2 *circumcise* the foreskin, *uncover* the corona by cutting off the membrane that adheres to it, *suck* blood from the wound, *and apply a bandage and cumin* to stop the bleeding.

wine and oil: To salve the wound.

in anticipation: Before the act of circumcision. If a special bandage was not prepared before the Sabbath, it is not prepared on the Sabbath (following the view of R. Aqiva in 19:1).

If one had not prepared the rag on the eve of the Sabbath,
one wraps it around his finger and brings it,
even from another courtyard.

3 One may wash the child,
whether before or after the circumcision,
and sprinkle him by hand,
but not by a utensil.
R. Eleazar b. Azariah says:
One may wash the child on the third day
if it falls on a Sabbath.
As it is said:
And it came to pass on the third day when they were in pain.
[If there is a child about whom there is] doubt,
or an *androgynos*,
one may not profane the Sabbath on its account.
But R. Judah permits [circumcision on the Sabbath] for the *androgynos*.

4 If one had two infants,
one to circumcise after the Sabbath and one to circumcise on the Sabbath,
and he forgot, and circumcised on the Sabbath the after-the-Sabbath-one,
he is culpable.
If [he had two infants,] one to circumcise on the eve of the Sabbath and one to circumcise on the Sabbath,
and he forgot and circumcised on the Sabbath the eve-of-the-Sabbath-one,
R. Eliezer declares him liable to a purgation offering,
but R. Joshua declares him exempt.[156]

---

[156] In **K, P** the two sets of cases are reversed.

---

one wraps it around his finger: In order to minimize violation of the prohibition of transporting from one courtyard to another.

19:3 The commentators debate whether the permission to *sprinkle* is meant to limit the permission *to wash* (that is, the washing that is permitted is sprinkling by hand), or whether these are separate rulings.

R. Eleazar b. Azariah says: See 9:3.

And it came to pass…: Genesis 34:25.

[*…a child about whom there is*] *doubt*: Doubt whether it was born on the Sabbath or not (see 19:5); or doubt whether the child is viable or not.

androgynos: Possessing sexual organs of both male and female.

19:4 *he is culpable*: He is required to bring a purgation offering (see 7:1) because he violated the Sabbath unintentionally by circumcising a seven-day-old boy; circumcision overrides the Sabbath only if the boy is eight days old (see 19:5).

R. Eliezer declares him liable to a purgation offering because he violated the Sabbath unintentionally by circumcising a nine-day-old boy, *but R. Joshua declares him exempt* because the commandment to circumcise, and consequently permission to override the Sabbath, applies even after the eighth day, at least after the fact. See n. 156 for a different reading.

5 A child is circumcised on the eighth, ninth, tenth, eleventh, or twelfth [day]: no less, no more.
How is this?[157]
[If born] in its regular way—on the eighth.
If born at twilight, he is circumcised on the ninth.
If at twilight on the eve of the Sabbath, he is circumcised on the tenth.
If a Festival day falls after the Sabbath, he is circumcised on the eleventh.
If the two Festival days of the New Year [fall on Sunday and Monday], he is circumcised on the twelfth.
If a child is sick, one may not circumcise him until he becomes healthy.

6 These shreds [of the foreskin, if not removed] invalidate the circumcision:
flesh[158] that covers the greater part of[159] the corona.
[A priest with such shreds] may not eat *terumah*.
If he is fat[160] [and the corona appears to be covered], he must fix it for appearance's sake.
If one circumcises but does not uncover the circumcision,
it is as though he has not circumcised.

Chapter Twenty

20:1–3 *Pouring on Water, Soaking in Water*

20 R. Eliezer says:
On a Festival day one may stretch out[161] a filter [over a utensil's mouth] and, on the Sabbath, put [wine] through it

---

[157] K, P lack "How is this." [158] K lacks "flesh." [159] K, P lack "the greater part of."
[160] Lit. "if he is an owner of flesh."
[161] Here and in what follows, "stretch(ed) out" is lit. "hang" or "hung."

19:5 *on the ninth*: If the earlier of the twilight days is reckoned as day one, the circumcision takes place on day nine (the eighth day after day two of the twilight days).

at twilight on the eve of the Sabbath: Late Friday afternoon.

on the tenth: Sunday.

on the eleventh: Monday.

on the twelfth: Tuesday.

19:6 This mishnah deals with circumcision in general, not circumcision on the Sabbath. It seems to be attached to 19:2.

may not eat terumah: Because he is deemed to have a foreskin, and a priest with a foreskin may not eat *terumah* (*Yevamot* 8:1). On *terumah* see 2:1.

uncover the circumcision: That is, remove the membrane under the foreskin that covers the corona; see 19:2.

if it has already been stretched out.
But the Sages say:
One may neither stretch out a filter on a Festival day
nor put [wine] through it on the Sabbath
[even if] it has already been stretched out;
but on a Festival day one may put [wine] through
it if it is already stretched out.

2 One may put water over wine dregs so that they may be clarified,
and[162] one may strain wine through a napkin or an Egyptian basket.
One may put an egg in a strainer of mustard leaves;
and one may prepare honeyed wine on the Sabbath.
R. Judah says:
On the Sabbath, in a cup;
on a Festival day, in a flask;
and during [the intermediate days of] a Festival, in a jar.
R. Zadok says:
It all depends on [the number of] the guests.

3 One may not soak asafetida in warm water,
but one may put it into vinegar.
One may neither soak vetches nor rub them;
but one may put them into a sieve or into a basket.

20:3 cont.–5 *Sifting and Moving Straw*

One may not sieve chopped straw through a sieve,
nor may one put it on a high place so that the chaff will fall out,

[162] K, P lack "and."

20:1 *a filter*: Akin to cheesecloth. The dispute between R. Eliezer and the Sages turns on three issues. Is stretching a filter over a vessel's mouth akin to the labor of building (7:2 no. 34)? Is pouring wine through a filter akin to the labor of selecting (7:2 no. 7)? Does the permission to prepare food on a Festival day include even those steps that could have been taken before the Festival day? R. Eliezer is more lenient than the Sages, just as he is more lenient than R. Aqiva in 19:1.

20:2 *so that they* the dregs *may be clarified*: So that the water will absorb wine-flavor from the dregs.

Egyptian basket: A cheap basket made of palm leaves; cf. *Sotah* 2:1, 3:1.

One may put an egg: In order to separate the white from the yolk. Or, some commentators suggest, to coat the mustard leaves. A strainer may be used on the Sabbath.

honeyed wine: A combination of wine, honey, and spices.

R. Judah says: Small quantities may be prepared on the Sabbath for individual use, but not larger amounts. Cf. 14:2.

[the intermediate days of] a Festival: In the Land of Israel days 2–6 of Passover and 2–7 of Sukkot. The status of these days, which are regarded in part as Festival days and in part as regular days, is the subject of *Moed Qatan*.

20:3 *vetches*: 1:5.

but one may put them into a sieve or into a basket: To separate out the shells.

but one may take it in a sieve and put it in the feeding trough.

4 One may scrape out [the trough] before a fatted ox
and move [fodder] to the sides
on account of excrement—
the words of R. Dosa.
But the Sages forbid it.
One may take [fodder] from before one animal
and put it before another on the Sabbath.

5 Straw that is on a bed—
one may not move it with his hand,
but one may move it with his body.
But if it was [intended to be] cattle fodder,
or if there was a cushion or sheet upon it,
one may move it with his hand.
A clothes press of householders—
one may loosen it but not tighten it;
and that of launderers—
one may not touch it.
R. Judah says:
If it was loosened on the eve of the Sabbath,
one may loosen all of it and pull it apart.[163]

[163] K, P: "one may recognize his garments and extract them."

one may take it in a sieve: To carry it, not to sift it.

20:4 *on account of excrement*: So that the ox should not soil the feed.

R. Dosa...the Sages: It is not clear whether the permission to scrape and the permission to move fodder are two separate rulings or one, and whether R. Dosa and the Sages are arguing only about the latter or about the former as well.

20:5 *Straw that is on a bed*: But its intended purpose is not clear. Does the owner intend to burn it (after the Sabbath)? To rest on it? To feed it to his cattle? *One may not move it with his hand* because it is not prepared for use on the Sabbath, *but one may move it with his body*, for example by resting on it, because this action causes movement only indirectly.

But if it was [intended to be] cattle fodder: See 18:2.

or if there was a cushion or sheet upon it: Thus establishing clearly that the straw was intended to be used as bedding.

one may loosen all of it and pull it apart: In consonance with the ruling of 17:1 and 17:4, the individual pieces of the launderers' press, which are utensils in themselves, may be moved on the Sabbath. And all the more would R. Judah permit the extraction of clothes from the press. According to the reading of the manuscripts (see n. 163), however, an individual may remove his garments from the loosened clothes press, but nothing is said about the dismantling the clothes press itself; we may presume that this would be prohibited.

Chapter Twenty-One

21:1–3 *Moving Items That Have No Permitted Use on the Sabbath*

21 **1** A person may carry[164] his child
even though there is a stone in its hand,
or[165] a basket
even though a stone is within it.
One may carry[166] impure *terumah* together with pure[167] or with common produce.
R. Judah says:
One may even remove the one [part of *terumah* that is] mixed with a hundred [parts of common produce].[168]

2 If a stone was on the mouth of a jar,
one may turn it on its side
and the stone falls off.
If it was among [other] jars,
one may lift it up and turn it on its side
and the stone falls off.
If there were coins on a cushion,
one may shake the cushion
and the coins fall off.
If there was filth[169] on it,

---

[164] Or "moves."   [165] K, P lack "or."   [166] Or "moves."
[167] K, P: "One may carry pure *terumah* together with impure."
[168] Translation uncertain; see annotation.
[169] Variously translated "nasal mucus" or "bird excrement."

21:1 *A person may carry his child*: This ruling seems to contradict 18:2 which permits pulling a child, but apparently not carrying it. In 18:2, R. Judah is explicit on this point: a child that cannot toddle on its own may not be carried. The commentaries offer various explanations (e.g. that our mishnah is speaking of a child inside a closed courtyard).

impure terumah: Which may not be eaten by anyone (see 2:1).

R. Judah says: The meaning of R. Judah's statement is not clear. The translation given here means the following. If a unit of *terumah* (e.g. an apple), which may be eaten only by priests, accidentally falls into a pile of common produce (e.g. a barrel of apples), which may be eaten by all, the resulting mixture cannot be eaten by nonpriests, out of fear that the unit of food (apple) being consumed is precisely the forbidden one. However, if the mixture contains at least 101 units of produce (e.g. 101 apples), namely, at least one hundred units of common produce plus the 1 unit of *terumah* that accidentally fell in, the mixture can be rendered edible by the removal of any one unit (apple) at random and declaring that it has the status of *terumah*. See *Terumot* 4:7-13. This removal can be done on the Sabbath according to R. Judah. Another possibility is that R. Judah is permitting the addition on the Sabbath of sufficient units of common produce to the mixture to reach a total of 101, although the Mishnah elsewhere prohibits such a procedure, Sabbath or no Sabbath (*Terumot* 5:9). Furthermore, both explanations suffer from the difficulty that they don't fit the context of 21:1–3 which is the permissibility of moving a prohibited object attached to a permitted object. The meaning of the text remains uncertain.

21:2 *on its side*: Cf. 4:2.

one may wipe it off with a rag.
If the cushion was made of hide,
one may put water on it until the filth is gone.

3 The House of Shammai say:
One may remove[170] bones and shells from the table.
But the House of Hillel say:[171]
One may take the entire tray and shake it out.
One may remove crumbs from the table
if they are less than [the bulk of] an olive, or pods of chickpeas, or pods of lentils,
since it is cattle fodder.
A sponge—
if it has a handle,[172] one may wipe with it;
but if not, one may not wipe with it.
But the Sages say:
In either case it may be moved on the Sabbath,[173] and it is not susceptible to impurity.

Chapter Twenty-Two

22:1–4 *Preparing Food on the Sabbath*

22 If a jar broke [on the Sabbath],
one may save food from it for three meals.
And he may say to others:

---

[170] Lit. "raise."
[171] **K, P:** "The House of Hillel say: One may remove shells and bones from the table. But the House of Shammai say…"
[172] **K, P:** "a handle of hide."
[173] **K, P:** "In either case one may wipe with it"; the words "it may be moved on the Sabbath" are added in the margin; the words "and it is not susceptible to impurity" are absent.

---

with a rag: But not with water, either because Sabbath law aside, one does not use water to clean a cushion or because washing a cushion is not an appropriate activity for the Sabbath.

21:3 *House of Shammai…House of Hillel*: See *Berakhot* 8 for further discussion between the Houses about proper procedure at table. As evidenced in the Talmud and in the manuscripts, later tradition was not sure which House was lenient and which stringent in the rules for disposing of food remains that no longer have any use on the Sabbath.

One may take the entire tray upon which the meal was served, but one may not touch the bones and shells directly.

cattle fodder: See 18:2, 20:5.

A sponge: The concern is that the user of a sponge will express water from it, which is prohibited (22:1).

it may be moved on the Sabbath: Following 17:1.

not susceptible to impurity: See annotation to 2:3. Apparently a sponge was not deemed a utensil for the purposes of purity law.

22:1 *one may save food…for three meals*: See 16:2.

he the owner *may say to the others "Come and save for yourselves"*: 16:3.

"Come and save for yourselves,"
provided that one does not sponge it.
One may not squeeze fruits to extract liquid from them;
even if it came out on its own, it is forbidden.
R. Judah says:
If [the fruits were intended] to be eaten,
that which comes out from them is permitted,
but if the fruits were [intended] for their liquid,
that which comes out from them is forbidden.
If one broke open honeycombs on the eve of the Sabbath
and the liquid came out on its own [on the Sabbath],
it is forbidden.
But R. Eliezer permits it.

2 Any [food] that was cooked in hot water[174] on the eve of the Sabbath,
one may soak it [again] in hot water on the Sabbath;
but any [food] that was not cooked in hot water[175] on the eve of the Sabbath,
one may rinse it in hot water on the Sabbath,
excepting old salted fish, small salted fish, and Spanish tunny-fish,
because rinsing them [in hot water] is the completion of their preparation.

3 A person may break a jar to eat dried figs from it,
provided that he does not intend to make a utensil.[176]
One may not pierce the stopper of a jar—
the words of R. Judah.
But the Sages permit it.[177]
One may not pierce it from its side;
and if it was pierced already
one may not put wax on it,
because this is an act of smoothing over.

---

[174] Lit. "that entered hot water."   [175] Lit. "that did not enter hot water."
[176] K, P: "to make it a utensil."
[177] Instead of "but the Sages permit it," K has "But R. Yose says" and P has "but R. Yose permits it."

---

provided that one does not sponge it: Should the broken jar have contained a liquid such as wine, one may not use a sponge to soak it up, lest he squeeze out the liquid from the sponge. The prohibition of squeezing out liquid, which is assumed here, is not listed in 7:2.

If [the fruits were intended] to be eaten, the juice *which comes out from them* on its own *is permitted*: Because the owner intended to eat the fruit, and drinking fruit juice is akin to eating fruit.

but if [the fruits were intended] for their liquid, he could not have intended to drink the liquid on the Sabbath, since extracting liquid by squeezing is prohibited; therefore any liquid that oozes out by itself is deemed to be not prepared for use on the Sabbath.

The honey *is forbidden* for use on the Sabbath: Because if it were permitted we fear that the owner would break the honeycombs on the Sabbath itself; or perhaps the honey is forbidden because, not yet available on the eve of the Sabbath, it is not regarded as "prepared" (annotations to 2:6, 3:6).

22:2 *one may rinse it in hot water*: But not soak it, lest the hot water cook the food.

22:3 *One may not pierce the stopper of a jar*: Rather, one should remove it outright.

smoothing over: Not listed in 7:2; the commentators explain that smoothing is a subset of scraping (7:2 no. 30) or erasing (7:2 no. 33).

R. Judah said:
[Such] a case came before Rabban Yohanan b. Zakkai in Arav,
and he said:
I suspect that he is liable to a purgation offering.

4 One may put [a pot of] cooked food inside a cistern
so that it should be preserved;
[a pot of] potable[178] water into foul
so that it should become cool;
[a pot of] cold water in the sun[179]
so that it should become warm.
One whose clothes fell off[180] into the water[181] while [he was] on the way
may walk in them and not worry;
when he has reached the outermost courtyard [of the town],
he spreads them out in the sun,
but not in the sight of people.

22:5–6 *In the Bath*

5 One who bathes in the waters of[182] a cave or in the waters of Tiberias
and sponges himself dry,[183]
even with ten towels—
he may not bring them away in his hand.
But ten people may sponge themselves dry with one towel,
[wiping] their faces, their hands, and their feet,
and[184] they may bring it[185] away in their hands.

---

[178] Lit. "beautiful, good." [179] K, P: "in hot water." [180] Or "were soaked."
[181] K, P lack "into the water." [182] K, P lack "the waters of."
[183] K, P: "may sponge himself dry."
[184] K lacks "and," implying the following translation: "But [if] ten people sponge themselves dry with one towel…they may bring it away in their hands."
[185] K: "them" (a mistake).

---

case came before Rabban Yohanan b. Zakkai: See 16:7.

22:4 *preserved*: By being kept cool.

not worry: That others will suspect him of having laundered his clothes on the Sabbath. Or: he need not worry that he may accidentally wring out his clothes while walking.

in the sight of the people: Who may suspect him of violating the Sabbath.

22:5 *of a cave*: Instead of "in the waters of a cave" the Talmud of the Land of Israel (Yerushalmi) has "in Be'erah," a place (near the Dead Sea) whose name, which means "fire, heat," refers to its hot springs. This variant differs from the standard text by only a single letter.

the waters of Tiberias: The hot springs just south of the town (3:4). Bathing in hot springs is permitted on the Sabbath.

even with ten towels: And the tenth one will be barely damp.

he may not bring them away in his hand: Lest he squeeze them dry.

they may bring the towel *away*: Even though it is soaked; the members of the group will see to it that none of their number wrings out the towel.

6 One may anoint [with oil] and rub[186] the belly,[187]
but not be kneaded[188] or scraped.
One may neither go down to the wrestling ground [to exercise] nor induce vomiting.[189]
One may not straighten a child or set[190] a fracture.
One whose hand or foot is dislocated may not stir them in cold water,
but he may wash in his usual manner,
and if he is healed, he is healed.

Chapter Twenty-Three

23:1–2 *Guests and Food*

23 A person may borrow from someone else jars of wine or jars of oil,
provided that he does not say to him, "Lend me";
so, too, a woman may borrow from someone else loaves of bread.
If he does not trust him,
he may leave his cloak with him
and make a reckoning with him after the Sabbath.
So, too, in Jerusalem—
if the eve of Passover[191] falls on a Sabbath,
one may leave his cloak with him,
take[192] his Passover lamb,
and make a reckoning with him after the Festival day.

[186] Or "massage." [187] K, P lack "the belly."
[188] Or "massaged." Alternative translation: "may not exercise."
[189] Lit. "make an emetic." K, P add "on the Sabbath."   [190] Lit. "return."
[191] K, P: "the eve of the Passover sacrifices."   [192] K, P: "eat."

22:6 *anoint…rub…kneaded…scraped*: Typical activities of the Roman bathhouse.

wrestling ground: Lit. a place of mud and clay, where wrestlers exercised. The manuscripts and printed editions provide numerous variants of this unusual word.

vomiting: Wrestlers would induce vomiting so as to control weight and cleanse the digestive system. The manuscripts and printed editions provide numerous variants of this unusual word.

One may not straighten: the limbs of a newborn, which was part of the normal post-partum process for the newborn.

in his usual manner, and if he is healed, he is healed: See 14:4.

23:1 *"Lend me"*: It should not be a formal transaction, which would be forbidden on the Sabbath, but an informal one.

If he the lender *does not trust him* the borrower, *he* the borrower *may leave his cloak with him* as surety.

make a reckoning: See 16:3.

if the eve of Passover falls on a Sabbath one who would like to purchase a Passover lamb *may leave his cloak as surety* with the seller. On the phrase "eve of Passover" see notes on *Pesahim* 4:1, 10:1.

2 A person may count his guests and his delicacies by word of mouth[193]
but not from what is written.
And he may cast lots with his children and the members of his household at table [for portions of food],
provided that he does not intentionally make one portion large and another portion small,[194]
[which is forbidden] because [this is deemed to be a form of] playing dice.
One may cast lots on a Festival day for sacred offerings
but not for portions.

23:3–5 *Preparing on the Sabbath for after the Sabbath*

3 A person may not hire[195] laborers on the Sabbath,
nor may a person ask[196] someone else to hire laborers for him.
One may not await nightfall at the Sabbath limit
to hire laborers or to bring back produce,
but one may await nightfall there
in order to safeguard produce,
and [after nightfall] he may bring back the produce himself.[197]
Abba Saul stated a general rule:

---

[193] Lit. "by his mouth."
[194] Lit. "provided that he does not intend to make a large portion against a small portion."
[195] K: "One may not hire for himself"; P: "One may not hire." [196] Lit. "say to."
[197] Lit. "in his hand."

23:2 *delicacies*: Appetizers before the meal (*Pesahim* 10:3) or desserts after it (*Berakhot* 6:5).

by word of mouth but not from what is written: The host is not to use a written list, apparently because this was felt to be inappropriate for the Sabbath.

the members of his household: His retainers, apparently not the same people as the *guests* in the first line.

provided that he does not intentionally make one portion large and another portion small, which would then turn the lottery into *playing dice*, which is forbidden every day of the week, not just on the Sabbath. Rather the householder should intend to make the portions the same size.

for sacred offerings (the festival sacrifices that were offered on the Festival day itself) *but not for portions* of the sacrifices that were offered the day before—these should have been distributed by lottery before the onset of the Festival.

23:3 *A person may not hire laborers*: on the Sabbath even though no money changes hands. Certain kinds of speech, including this, are prohibited on the Sabbath.

Sabbath limit: A distance of two thousand cubits from one's home or from the edge of one's settlement; it was forbidden to go beyond this on the Sabbath. See *Sotah* 5:3.

One may not on the Sabbath go to the edge of the Sabbath limit in order to *await nightfall* there so as *to hire laborers or to bring back produce* from beyond the Sabbath limit. Since hiring laborers on the Sabbath is prohibited, and since bringing back produce on the Sabbath from beyond the Sabbath limit is prohibited, this person has no permitted purpose to go to the edge of the Sabbath limit; hence he may not. But a person may go to the edge of the Sabbath limit in order to *safeguard produce*; and since he arrived there with a permitted purpose, *he may bring back produce* after the Sabbath.

Abba Saul either modifies the previous position or disagrees with it.

Anything I have the right to speak about,
I am [also] permitted to await nightfall [at the Sabbath limit] on its account.

4 One may await nightfall at the Sabbath limit
in order [after the Sabbath] to take care of matters concerning a bride or matters concerning a corpse,
[that is], to bring a coffin and shrouds for it.
If a gentile brought flutes on the Sabbath,
an Israelite may not lament with them unless they have come from a nearby place.
If they made a coffin [on the Sabbath] for one of their own[198]
or if they dug a grave for one of their own,[199]
an Israelite may be buried in it;
but if for an Israelite,
he may never be buried in it.

5 [On the Sabbath] one may do whatever things are necessary for a corpse—
anoint it, wash it—
provided that one does not move any limb;[200]
draw the cushion away from beneath it and place it on sand
so that it[s putrefaction] may be delayed;
bind the jaw—
not so that it go up but so that it not increase.
Likewise, if a rafter is broken,
one may support it with a bench or with the side-pieces of a bed,
not so that it go up but so that it not increase.
One may not close [the eyes] of a corpse on the Sabbath,

[198] Lit. "for him." [199] Lit. "for him." [200] K, P: "provided that no limb move."

Anything I have the right to speak about to others on the Sabbath, for example, matters concerning burial or concerning a wedding (23:4). For rulings formulated in the first person, cf. *Shevi'it* 2:3, *Bava Qamma* 1:2.

23:4 *matters concerning a bride*: Preparations for a marriage and a wedding.

gentile: An Israelite may not derive benefit from any work performed by a gentile on the Sabbath for the Israelite's benefit; he may derive benefit from work performed by the gentile for his own benefit; see 16:6 and 16:8. Contrast 24:1.

flutes were used as accompaniments to processions, whether joyous (*Sukkah* 5:1) or funereal (*Ketubbot* 4:4; see *Bava Metsi'a* 6:1).

lament with them: Recite a eulogy to their accompaniment.

unless they have come from a nearby place: In which case they may be used after the Sabbath. The Talmud and the commentaries debate the meaning and rationale of this ruling.

they gentiles *made a coffin for one of their own* a gentile.

23:5 It is not clear how to reconcile the prohibition of *moving any* of its *limbs* with the permission (command?) to remove the cushion from under the corpse and to *place* the corpse *on sand* on the floor.

not so that it go up: Not to close the mouth. *but so that it not increase*: That the mouth not open further.

not so that it go up: Not to raise the rafter to its previous position. *but so that it* the breakage *not increase*. The same phrase appears in *Shevi'it* 4:6.

One may not close [the eyes] of a corpse on the Sabbath: Because moving any of its limbs is prohibited.

nor on a weekday at the moment of the departure of the soul.
One who closes [the eyes] at the moment of the departure of the soul
is indeed a shedder of blood.

Chapter Twenty-Four

24:1–4 *Care of Animals*

24 If [on the eve of the Sabbath] one was on the road at nightfall,
he may give his purse to a gentile;
and if there is no gentile with him,
he may put it on the ass.
When he has reached the outermost courtyard [of the town],
he may take [from the ass] whatever utensils may be moved on the Sabbath;
but as for those utensils that may not be moved on the Sabbath,
he [may not move them but] loosens the cords and the sacks fall off of themselves.

2 One may loosen bundles of sheaves in front of cattle and spread branches,
but not tightly bound bundles.
One may not chop up unripe grain or carobs in front of cattle,
whether small or large.
R. Judah permits carobs for small cattle.

3 One may not stuff a camel [with food] or cram it,
but one may give it to swallow.
One may not stuff calves,

24:1 *gentile*: Contrast 16:8 and 23:4, which emphasize the prohibition of benefiting from gentile labor on the Sabbath. Perhaps this ruling is in agreement with House of Hillel in 1:7. Commentators explain that the traveler handed over his purse to the gentile before sundown.

he may give...may put: He may do so in spite of the prohibition of benefiting from the labor of a gentile or of livestock on the Sabbath. The prohibition of having one's livestock work on the Sabbath is of Torah origin (Exodus 20:9); hence it outranks the prohibition of deriving benefit from the labor of a gentile, a prohibition that derives from the Sages.

When he has reached: A separate case, which involves an ass but neither gentile nor purse.

the outermost courtyard: Same phrase as 22:4.

utensils that *may be moved*: Because they have a permitted use on the Sabbath. *utensils that may not be moved*: Because they have no permitted use on the Sabbath. See chapter 17.

24:2 *bundles of sheaves...branches...tightly bound bundles*: Text and precise meaning uncertain. The main point, however, is clear: fodder that requires only modest human preparation may be given to cattle on the Sabbath, but not fodder that requires substantial preparation.

small cattle: Goats and sheep. *large* cattle: cows and oxen.

24:3 *a camel*: May not be forcefed on the Sabbath as preparation for labor during the week.

one may give them to swallow: Encourage the animal to eat by putting food in its mouth.

but one may give them to swallow.
One may strew [food] for chickens.[201]
One may put water into fine bran,
but one may not knead it;
One may not put water before bees or before doves in the dovecotes,
but one may put it before geese and chickens and Herodian[202] doves.

4 One may slice gourds before cattle,
or a carcass before the dogs.
R. Judah says:
If it was not a carcass on the eve of the Sabbath it is forbidden,
since it does not belong to [the category of] that which is already prepared.

24:5 Annulling Vows, Plugging Holes, and Taking Measurements

5 One may annul vows on the Sabbath
and consult [a sage] concerning [vows that affect] matters that are necessary for the Sabbath.
One may stop up a window;
one may measure a strip of cloth or an immersion pool.
It once happened in the days of R. Zadok's father and in the days of Abba Saul b. Batnit

---

[201] Or "stuff chickens."
[202] P: "Rhodian." See *Hullin* 12:1.

One may put water into fine bran: To make chicken feed.

One may not put water before animals that can get water for themselves.

geese…chickens…Herodian (Rhodian) doves: These are domesticated species entirely dependent on humans.

24:4 *that which is already prepared*: See 3:6, 17:1.

24:5 *One may annul vows*: Husbands and fathers may annul the vows of wives and daughters even *on the Sabbath*: The Torah gives them the right of annulment only on the day of learning of the vow (Numbers 30:5–9; *Nedarim* 10).

A sage has the authority to release someone from a vow, if the sage determines that the vow was taken in error or without awareness of its consequences. The sage may conduct such an inquiry, and release a person from his/her vow on the Sabbath, if the vow affects matters *that are necessary for the Sabbath*, a category that is not explained.

a window: Cf. 17:7.

one may measure a strip of cloth: To determine if its size is at least three fingerbreadths by three fingerbreadths, in which case it is deemed to be a garment and susceptible to impurity. See annotations to 2:3.

immersion pool: Or *miqveh*, to see if it contains at least one cubit by one cubit by three cubits of water, in which case it is fit for use.

It once happened: The commentators explain the case as follows. Two houses were separated by a passage which was surmounted by a roof in which there was a crack (an *opening*). Windows in each house opened onto the passage. A person in one of the houses was at the point of death. If he died, corpse impurity would pass through the window of that house and would be conveyed (by means of the covered passageway) to the

that [on the Sabbath] they stopped up the window with a pitcher
and tied a fire-pot with reed-grass [to a stick]
in order to determine if there was an opening in the roof of one square handbreadth or not.
And from their words we learn that one may stop up, measure, and tie on the Sabbath.

opposite house and enter it by the window. To prevent this from happening they *stopped up* the window of the second house *with a pitcher* (a small pitcher used for drawing water, same word in 17:6), and, using *reed-grass* (cf. 8:2), *tied a fire-pot* (a small clay pot or a fragment of a clay pot, typically used to move a flame from one place to another) to a stick in order to measure thereby the crack in the roof, for if the crack were at least a handbreadth square (see *Oholot* 3:6) it would be sufficiently large to allow the impurity to escape upward and outward, thus sparing the neighboring building from any impurity.

from their words: From the words of this report.

tie: Cf. 7:2 no. 21; 15:1–2.

Tractate Eruvin

Charlotte Elisheva Fonrobert

Introduction

Overview

Tractate *Eruvin* deals with two kinds of *eruv* (pl. *eruvin*), the "*eruv* of courtyards," and the "*eruv* of Sabbath limits." Each addresses one of the two Sabbath prohibitions with which *Eruvin* is concerned: (1) the prohibition of carrying anything within the public domain, or across the boundary between domains, and (2) the prohibition of walking beyond two thousand cubits from the location where one happens to find oneself at the beginning of the Sabbath. Tractate *Shabbat* devotes a significant amount of attention to the first prohibition, though the laws of the Sabbath limits are only briefly mentioned toward the end of the tractate (23:4; 24:1). It is thus surprising to turn to *Eruvin* and realize that this tractate develops a set of procedures that enable a person to circumvent those prohibitions. Tractate *Eruvin* is dedicated to the development of a legal fiction allowing a person to do precisely that which tractate *Shabbat* prohibits, namely to carry something out of and into one's house or to enlarge the distance one is permitted to walk on the Sabbath.

The name of the tractate derives from a verb connoting "mixing," "merging," "mingling." An *eruv*, the noun derived from the verb, is the result of an act or a number of acts of merging, although the Mishnah nowhere spells out what precisely is merged.

Main Ideas

The "*eruv* of courtyards" addresses a situation in which a number of residents share one walled courtyard (see chapter 6). By rabbinic regulation, the residents are prohibited from carrying anything from their residence into the courtyard, even though that courtyard, an enclosed space, is considered only a semipublic area. Before the onset of the Sabbath the residents of the courtyard can collect contributions of food, preferably bread (7:10), from each of the households; these will form one collective meal that is deposited in one of the households in the courtyard. This symbolic meal, which is not consumed, allows the residents to carry out of their house into the shared courtyard, and it is this collected food that is referred to as an *eruv*. Here the possible targets of the act of "merging" are (a) the food from each individual household, (b) the individual households, or (c) the participating residents.

The tractate also envisions the larger setting of a walled alleyway into which a number of courtyard communities open. If the residents from these communities want to move objects into the alleyway on the Sabbath, that shared space will need to be unified as well, a procedure that the Mishnah refers to as forming a "partnership" or "partnership of alleyways." This is accomplished by another food ritual (7:6–9), in addition to which a marking of the entry to such an alleyway by supplemental structural elements (the subject of chapter 1) is required. This "partnership" also has to be established before the Sabbath begins. The tractate touches only briefly upon "merging" an entire town; see 5:6.

The "*eruv* of Sabbath limits," on the other hand, is relevant primarily to an individual who wishes to travel further than the permissible two thousand cubits. One can do so primarily by depositing a symbolic meal at the two-thousand-cubit limit before the onset of the Sabbath, either by oneself or through a proxy (3:2). Again it is this food that is referred to as an *eruv*. The particular place of an individual is normally imagined as her place of regular residence, but a traveler (chapter 4) may declare her current location (or any other location within two thousand cubits of there) as her Sabbath place (4:8) and measure the permissible distance from that place. Further, the Mishnah envisions the possibility of making such an *eruv* for one's entire town, in which case the preferred term again is forming a "partnership of limits" (see 8:1–2). Indeed, it imagines towns as drawing virtual Sabbath maps (chapter 5), measuring and marking a town's boundary from which the Sabbath distance is to be measured.

Relationship to Scripture

Tractate *Eruvin* remarkably creates from scratch a whole set of ritual acts designed to allow that which is theoretically forbidden. This has led some scholars to speculate that what is merged is the forbidden and the permitted. None of these acts (the food, the symbolic marking of the entry to the alleyway) has any basis in biblical law, but the prohibitions themselves are not based in biblical law either. The only indirect basis for the tractate in Mosaic law is one biblical verse, and even that verse is relevant only to the underlying concept of Sabbath limits: *Let every man stay in his place; a man should not go out from his place on the seventh day* (Exodus 16:29). In rabbinic exegesis, the first part of this verse confines a person to his personal space ("his place") of four cubits on the Sabbath, the space within which one can move oneself and things around when in the public domain, while the second part expands that limit to two thousand cubits. Both figures, four and two thousand cubits, are rabbinic in origin, though the Talmudic sages find some support for the distance of two thousand cubits in the biblical description of the levitical cities (Numbers 35:5). The verse in Exodus is also said by some exegetes to provide the source for the prohibition of moving anything from one's "place" or domain outside, by changing the Hebrew vocalization from "should not go out" to "should not bring out." However, in prophetic literature (see Jeremiah 17:22) the prohibition "to carry burdens from your houses" is noted as a divine prohibition. Second Temple literature widely refers to such a prohibition.

One quickly realizes that while this exegesis establishes the rabbinic Sabbath limits and the ban on transporting across domain boundaries, it does not help to support the concept of an "*eruv*" or justify circumventing that particular Sabbath limitation. Hence the tractate ends with one of the most remarkable statements in the Mishnah: *wherever the Sages permitted you something, they gave you what is yours already* (10:15; see annotations). *Eruvin* is perhaps the least biblical and the most rabbinic of all the tractates in the Mishnah, demonstrating the early rabbis' willingness to circumvent the law in the name of the law.

Special Notes for the Reader

The present translation and annotations have been greatly aided by Abraham Goldberg's immensely learned critical edition and commentary (*The Mishna Treatise Eruvin*, Jerusalem, 1986). I have consulted the classical interpretations and commentaries as well, but have referred to them only where the meaning of the mishnaic text remains completely obscure.

Tractate Eruvin

Chapter One

1:1–2 *Adjusting the Entry to an Alleyway for the Sabbath*

1 If an [entry to an] alleyway is higher than twenty cubits,
it should be reduced.
R. Judah says:
This is not necessary.
And [if it is] wider than ten cubits,
it should be reduced.
But if it has the shape of a doorway,
then even if it is wider than ten cubits,
it does not need to be reduced.
    2 The validation of [an entry to] an alleyway—
the House of Shammai say:
A sidebeam and a crossbeam.
The House of Hillel say:

1:1 The tractate opens with a discussion of the requirements for adjusting the entry into a residential alleyway. The Mishnah does not explain why this adjustment is to be made, but the implication is that such an adjustment allows the residents within to move things around on the Sabbath. In addition to manipulating the entry to the alleyway, the topic of the current chapter, its residents or their representatives have to perform a food ritual allowing them to form a "partnership," the topic of the seventh chapter below.

If an [entry to an] alleyway: The alleyway is imagined as turning off a larger street or thoroughfare or some other space representing a public domain. Such a walled alleyway is enclosed on three sides and connects a number of residential courtyard communities. The term "alleyway" can refer to the alleyway as a whole and not just its entry, but most medieval commentaries agree that this opening paragraph refers to the entry alone. The Mishnah rules that the entry has to follow certain specifications, and in the absence of these must be manipulated accordingly, as is spelled out in the subsequent paragraphs.

twenty cubits…ten cubits: Elsewhere the Mishnah lists these measurements as those of the entrance to the Sanctum of the Temple; see *Middot* 4:1. Twenty cubits is also cited as the maximum height for a *sukkah*; see *Sukkah* 1:1.

1:2 This paragraph appears to explicate the preceding one, describing the means by which to adjust (or "validate") the alleyway's entry by providing it with elements of a doorway. Alternatively, the "validation" discussed here can be read as an additional requirement, separate from adjusting the dimensions of the entryway as in 1:1. The question behind the explication in this paragraph would then be what kind of structural elements provide sufficient appearance of a doorway.

A sidebeam or a crossbeam.
R. Eliezer says:
Two sidebeams.
In the name of R. Ishmael,
a disciple said in front of R. Aqiva:
The House of Shammai and the House of Hillel did not disagree
with respect to [an entry to] an alleyway of less than four cubits
that it [can be validated]
with either a sidebeam or a crossbeam.
About what did they disagree?
Regarding [an entrance with] a width between four and ten cubits,
that the House of Shammai say:
A sidebeam and a crossbeam,
and the House of Hillel say:
Either a sidebeam or a crossbeam.
R. Aqiva said:
About both of these[1] they disagreed.

1:3–5 The Crossbeam for the Entry to the Alleyway

3 The crossbeam of which they spoke
[should be] wide enough to carry a lath,
and the lath is half a brick
[that is] three handbreadths wide.
It is sufficient for the crossbeam
that it should be one handbreadth wide,
in order to receive a lath along its length.[2]

4 Wide enough to receive a lath,
and strong[3] enough to receive a lath.
R. Judah says:
Wide enough even if it is not strong enough.

---

[1] Lit. "on this and on this."   [2] Var. "width."   [3] Lit. "healthy."

R. Eliezer says: It is not clear whether he requires two sidebeams in addition to the cross-beam or only two sidebeams.

In the name of R. Ishmael a disciple said in front of R. Aqiva: This is the only time in the Mishnah that a sage is identified in this way, but the phrase appears more often in other rabbinic texts.

1:3 The set of rules for the cross-beam specify minimal requirements.

The crossbeam of which they spoke: Referring back to 1:2.

along its length: The variant "width" envisions the same picture.

1:4 *R. Judah says…not strong enough*: In R. Judah's view the structural function of the cross-beam is not what matters.

5 If it was made from straw or reed,
one should regard it as if it were made from metal.
If curved,
one should regard it as if it were straight.
If round,
one should regard it as if it were square.
Anything three handbreadths in circumference
has one handbreadth in width.

1:6–7 *The Sidebeams for the Entry to the Alleyway*

6 The sidebeams of which they spoke
[must be at least] ten handbreadths high,
and [of] any width or thickness.
R. Yose says:
Their width [must be at least] three handbreadths.

7 One may make the sidebeams with anything,
even with an animate object,
but R. Yose[4] forbids [this].[5]
It conveys impurity if used as a seal for a grave,
but R. Meir deems it to be pure.[6]
And one may write upon it women's divorce bills,
but R. Yose the Galilean invalidates [these].

[4] P: "Meir."
[5] K lacks "forbids," which yields the sentence "R. Yose deems [it] impure if used as a seal for a grave…"
[6] That is, insusceptible to impurity.

1:5 It seems that this paragraph is a continuation of R. Judah's statement in 1:4. Note that the mathematics of the last clause is imprecise, and see 1 Kings 7:23.

1:6 *The sidebeams of which they spoke*: Referring back to 1:2.

1:7 *an animate object*: Lit. "something that has the spirit of life in it." Compare *Sukkah* 2:3, which considers the case of a *sukkah* being built on a camel.

It conveys impurity if used as a seal for a grave: "It" refers to the "animate object." This and the following subclause have nothing to do with *eruvin*, but make cross reference to other legal issues where an "animate object" is used for ritual-legal purposes. On the seals of graves see *Oholot* 15:9, where R. Meir's disagreement with the anonymous Mishnah is found. On bills of divorce see *Gittin* 2:3, where R. Yose the Galilean's disagreement with the anonymous Mishnah is found.

1:8–10 *Making Sabbath Boundaries for a Traveling Encampment*

8 If a caravan encamped in a valley
and they surrounded it with the animal trappings,
one may carry within it [on the Sabbath],
provided that the fence is ten handbreadths high
and the gaps do not exceed the constructed parts.
Any gap that is around ten cubits wide is permitted,
since it is like a doorway;
more than that is prohibited.

9 [The encampment] may be encircled with three ropes,
one above the other,[7]
provided that between one rope and the next
there not be [more than] three handbreadths.
The measure of the ropes and their thickness [should be]
more than a handbreadth,
so that the whole [amounts to] ten handbreadths.

10 [The encampment] may be encircled with reeds,
provided that between one reed and the next
there be not [more than] three handbreadths.
They spoke about a caravan [specifically]—
the words of R. Judah.

[7] Lit. "this above this and this above this."

1:8 The last three paragraphs of the chapter consider a different setting: a traveling caravan. The location in a valley is significant, since the rabbis regard the valley as only a semipublic rather than an entirely public domain. For that reason, some leniencies, such as those spelled out in these paragraphs, apply.

a caravan: A caravan is constituted minimally by three people.

in a valley: Although one should not carry in such a space without the provisions described here, one is also exempt from punishment if one has done so, since a valley is not a regular public domain.

ten cubits: As is the case with the entry to the alley in 1:1. See *Kilayim* 4:4 for the partition between fields sown with different species.

1:9 *may be encircled*: That is, if one wishes to carry objects within the space.

ten handbreadths: As long as the space between each rope and the next is less than three handbreadths, it may be considered "filled in" and solid. If the ropes are of the indicated thickness, then the whole structure will reach a height of ten handbreadths, which is the minimum size for a valid surrounding partition (1:8). The text is ambiguous, but the meaning is probably the total thickness of the three ropes, rather than the thickness of each.

1:10 The first anonymous clause continues the rulings about encampments from the previous paragraph. The disagreement between R. Judah and the Sages that follows concerns the application of those rulings. The chapter ends with further leniencies in the case of a military encampment.

about a caravan [specifically]: According to R. Judah, the leniencies laid out in 1:9 and here apply only to a caravan, but not in any other situation, even to persons encamped in a valley for any other reason.

But the Sages say:
They spoke of the caravan only as the usual.[8]
Any partition that does not have [both] warp and woof
is not a partition—
the words of R. Yose b. Judah.
But the Sages say:
One of the two [is sufficient].
They granted exemption for four things in a [military] encampment:
(1) Wood may be brought from anywhere;
and [those in the camp] are exempt
(2) from the washing of hands,
(3) and from *demai*,
(4) and from preparing an *eruv*.

Chapter Two

2:1–4 *Sabbath Enclosure for Public Wells*

2 One [may] set up boards around wells,
four corner-pieces that seem like eight—
the words of R. Judah.[9]
R. Meir says:
Eight that seem like twelve:
four corner-pieces,

---

[8] Lit. "of the present," "of that which is."

[9] K: "R. Aqiva," in all likelihood a mistake, since a disagreement of R. Meir with his teacher R. Aqiva is unlikely.

---

as the usual: Anyone can make boundaries like these, but since caravans are the most common users of this procedure, the Sages of the Mishnah formulated the law as referring to them. The same phrase appears in *Shabbat* 6:6, 6:9 and elsewhere.

warp and woof: A metaphor for a combination of vertical and horizontal elements in the partition. As opposed to the Sages, R. Yose requires both elements for the enclosure of an encampment, apparently even for a caravan.

Wood…from anywhere: And the wood will not be considered stolen.

the washing of hands: Before eating.

preparing an eruv: The entire encampment, once enclosed, is considered a single location and no further "mixing" of the individual tents is required (See Shabbat 2:7).

2:1 *One [may] set up boards around wells*: That are located within the public domain. For the animals to be able to drink on the Sabbath and their owner not be guilty of drawing water in the public domain, the well needs to be enclosed, thus creating a fictitious private domain.

corner-pieces: A unique word in the Mishnah, the meaning of which was no longer clear to later sages.

and four straight ones.
Their height [should be] ten handbreadths
and their width six,
and their thickness any measure,
and between them space
for two teams of three cattle each—
the words of R. Meir.
R. Judah says:
Of four each,
connected to each other and not apart,
[so that] one [team] enter and the other exit.
    2 It is permitted to move [the boards] close to the well,
provided that the head and the greater part of the cow
be within when it drinks.
It is permitted to move [the boards] back any distance,
provided that he [also] increases [the number of] boards.
    3 R. Judah says:
As much as a two-*se'ah*-sized plot.
They said to him:
They said two-*se'ah*-sized plot
only with regard to a garden or a *qarpaf*,
but regarding a cattle pen or fold,
or a backyard or courtyard,
even a five- or ten-*kor*-sized plot is permitted,
provided that he increases [the number of] boards:
and it is permitted to move [the boards] back any distance,
provided that he increases [the number of] boards.
    4 R. Judah says:
If a public path cuts through them,[10]

[10] K, P: "If a public path cuts through it..." This leaves the referent somewhat unclear.

connected to each other...: It is not clear whether these details continue R. Judah's opinion or pertain to R. Meir's as well.

2:3 *two-se'ah-sized plot*: R. Judah disagrees with the anonymous opinion in the previous paragraph, which is also quoted at the end of this mishnah. One *se'ah*-sized plot would be 2,500 square cubits.

They said two-se'ah-sized plot: The anonymous collective agrees with R. Judah on the limitation of a two-*se'ah*-sized plot under other circumstances, but holds that this does not apply to a public well.

qarpaf: An area outside a human settlement used for wood storage or the like. Cf. 5:2 and annotations.

five- or ten-kor-sized plot: One *kor* equals thirty *se'ah*.

it is permitted to move [the boards] back: This restatement of the end of the previous mishnah is puzzling, since the Mishnah usually employs a terse economy of language.

2:4 *If a public path cuts through them*: i.e. through the boards enclosing the public well. Such a road should be diverted, since otherwise the domain can no longer be considered a private domain.

he should divert it to the sides,
but the Sages say:
That is not necessary.
A public cistern, a public well, and a private well[11]
are [all] one:
one may put up boards around them.
But for a private cistern
one must put up a partition ten handbreadths high—
the words of R. Aqiva.
R. Judah b. Bava says:
One may put up boards only for a public well,[12]
but for the rest
one should make a belt[13] ten handbreadths high.

2:5 A Related Ruling by R. Judah b. Bava

5 And further, R. Judah b. Bava said:
If a garden or a *qarpaf* has an area of seventy and a fraction cubits square,[14]
surrounded by a fence ten handbreadths high,
one may move [things] around within it,
provided that it contains a guardhouse[15] or a dwelling place,
or that it is close to the town.
R. Judah says:
Even if it contains only a cistern or pit or cave,
one may move [things] around within it.
R. Aqiva says:
Even if it contains none of these,[16]
one may move [things] around within it,

---

[11] Text is uncertain; see annotations.   [12] **K**: "public cistern"; see annotations.
[13] See annotations.   [14] The word "cubit" is crossed out in **K**.
[15] "Guardhouse" is missing in **K**, but supplied in the margins, perhaps by a different scribe.
[16] **K, P**: "Even if it contains only one of these…"

A public cistern, a public well, and a private well: The translation here matches **P**, while **K** lacks the public well. The text of R. Judah b. Bava's dissent is also unclear: in **K** he disagrees with respect to the public well and in **P** with respect to the public cistern.

a belt ten handbreadths high: He requires ropes (alternatively, an unbroken partition) instead of boards for the public cistern and private well.

2:5 This paragraph is only tangentially related to wells, and spells out different lenient opinions in the case of the garden and *qarpaf* that was already mentioned in 2:3. R. Judah's opinion also mentions a cistern.

provided that it contains the space of seventy and a fraction cubits square.[17]
R. Eliezer says:
If its length exceeded its breadth by even a single[18] cubit,
one may not move [things] around within it.
R. Yose says:
Even if its length is twice the width,
one may move [things] around within it.

2:6   A Collection of R. Eliezer's Teachings

6 Said R. Ila'i:
I have heard from R. Eliezer:
Even if it is a *kor*-sized plot.
And likewise I heard from him:
The residents sharing a courtyard,
one of whom forgot to prepare the *eruv*—
it is forbidden for him
to bring anything into his house [on the Sabbath]
or take anything out from it,
but for [the others] it is permitted.
And likewise I heard from him
that one may fulfill the obligation [of eating bitter herbs] on Passover
with palm ivy.
And I went around all of his disciples
and sought a fellow for myself,
but could not find one.

[17] **K** lacks "cubit" here.
[18] The word "cubit" was deleted in **K** and replaced with "a hundred and one"; the two words differ by a single letter, but the emendation remains very strange.

provided that it contains a guardhouse: R. Judah b. Bava requires some sort of structure for human use in order to consider it an enclosure for Sabbath purposes.

2:6 The first of R. Eliezer's statements is a continuation of the preceding paragraph.

The residents sharing a courtyard: Lit. "the men of a courtyard." See esp. 6:3 below for the problem of joining the residents of a courtyard community into an *eruv* community for the Sabbath when one of them forgets to join the *eruv*. The rule there, however, differs from R. Eliezer's tradition here.

palm ivy: The botanical referent of this rare word was already unclear to the post-Mishnaic sages. In *Shevi'it* 7:2 it is listed as an example of plants that cannot be used as food for either human or animal consumption. The unfamiliarity with the term is also reflected in the varying orthography in the manuscripts.

fellow: Another disciple who had heard the same teachings.

Chapter Three

3:1–2 *Foods that Are Valid for Eruv*

3 One may prepare an *eruv* or a partnership with any [food],
except for water and for salt.
And[19] any [food] may be purchased with tithe money,
except for water and salt.
A person who takes an oath [to abstain] from food
is permitted water and salt.
One may prepare an *eruv* for a *nazir* with wine,
and for a layperson with *terumah*.
Symmachus says:
With unconsecrated food.[20]
And for a priest in a grave area.
R. Judah says:

---

[19] K, P lack "and."
[20] K: "even with unconsecrated food," although apparently some scribe tried to erase the word. See annotations.

3:1 This chapter shifts from the requirements for marking the boundary of the putative shared domain to the symbolic food required to prepare an *eruv*. The chapter is introduced with a collection of rules having to do with food, from all of which water and salt are excluded; most of these are unrelated to the topic of the tractate.

One may prepare an eruv or a partnership with any [food]: This ruling, presented anonymously here, is identified at 7:10 below as "the words of Rabbi Eliezer." The medieval commentaries differ as to whether "preparing an *eruv*" here refers only to the *eruv* of distance or also to the *eruv* of courtyards. This depends on whether one reads R. Eliezer's ruling in 7:10 and the anonymous parallel here as two separate rulings. However, a tradition in the Talmud insists that a residential *eruv* can be effected only by bread, leading some commentators to suggest that here the Mishnah must refer to the *eruv* of distance.

any [food] may be purchased with tithe money: See *Ma'aser Sheni* 1:5. Deuteronomy 14:26 provides a list of exemplary food items that may be purchased from tithe money, raising the question of what counts as food.

One may prepare an eruv for a nazir with wine, even though he is prohibited from enjoying it, *and for a layperson (Israel) with terumah*, even though he is prohibited from eating it. The *eruv* food is not to be consumed and has mostly symbolic value.

Symmachus says…: The text here is uncertain; the Palestinian manuscript tradition has "even," while the Babylonian one does not. The Babylonian version, translated here, presents two distinct statements: "Symmachus says: [A layperson] with unconsecrated food, [by implication not with *terumah*]," and then an anonymous voice says "and for a priest in a grave area." This reading is attested by Maimonides and other medieval commentaries. In the Palestinian version the text reads as one statement by Symmachus: "And for a priest even with unconsecrated food and in a grave area."

grave area: On the definition of "grave area" see *Oholot* chapter 17. Under certain conditions the priest is allowed to enter there and thus could theoretically have access to the *eruv* food.

Even in a graveyard,
since he can go outside and eat.

2 One may prepare an *eruv* with *demai*,
with first tithe from which its *terumah* was taken,
and with second tithe or consecrated food that were redeemed,
and[21] priests [may prepare an *eruv*] with dough offering and *terumah*.[22]
But not with untithed produce,
and not with first tithe from which its *terumah* was not taken,
and not with second tithe or consecrated food that were not redeemed.
If one sends his *eruv* with a deaf-mute, one who is not legally competent, or a minor,
or with someone who does not agree to [the principle of] *eruv*—
it is not a [valid] *eruv*.
But if he said to another to receive it from him,
in such a case it is a [valid] *eruv*.

3:3–4 *Places Where the Eruv Food May Be Deposited*

3 If he put [the *eruv*] in a tree—
above ten handbreadths,
his *eruv* is not a [valid] *eruv*;
below ten handbreadths,
his *eruv* is a [valid] *eruv*.

---

[21] K lacks "and."
[22] Some manuscripts lack this clause, but **K**, **P** have it.

---

graveyard: A place with known graves.

since he can go outside: That is, outside the graveyard. Alternatively he can put up a screen. See *Oholot* chapter 8 for what counts as a screen impermeable to impurity. The priest can put a separation between himself and the impurity of the graves.

3:2 The first part of this anonymous paragraph continues the question of the kind of food that is valid for making the *eruv*. It is the symbolic food that is called the *eruv*. The second part raises the question of who can deposit the *eruv* food at the distance of two thousand cubits outside of the residential area. This food deposit allows all participants to establish their "place" at this location and then to walk another two thousand cubits.

and priests [may prepare an eruv] with dough offering and terumah: Compare *Pesahim* 2:5 for the same list, there for establishing what kind of unleavened grain products can be eaten on Passover.

If one sends his eruv: To be deposited at the limit of two thousand cubits that he is allowed to walk on the Sabbath. This is done before the onset of the Sabbath.

someone who does not agree to [the principle of] eruv: See also 6:1 below.

it is not a [valid] eruv: Lit. "this is not an *eruv*." If deposited by inappropriate agents, the food cannot effectively serve as *eruv*. The reason may be that such persons cannot be trusted to carry out their task reliably; alternatively, they lack legal agency to "acquire a Sabbath place" at the intended location.

3:3 The food for an *eruv* must be deposited in such a way that it will not be consumed by animals.

If he put it in a cistern—
even if it were one hundred cubits deep,
his *eruv* is a [valid] *eruv*.
If he put it on top of a reed,
or on top of a pole—
if it was uprooted
and [then] thrust [back into the ground],
even if it was one hundred cubits high,
in this case it is a [valid] *eruv*.
If he put it in a cupboard[23]
and the key was lost,
in this case it is a [valid] *eruv*.
R. Eliezer[24] says:
If he does not know[25] that[26] the key is in its [proper] place,
it is not a [valid] *eruv*.

4 If [the *eruv*] rolled beyond the Sabbath limit,
or if a heap [of stones] fell upon it,
or if it burned,
or if [it was] *terumah* and it was rendered impure—
while it was still day [before the Sabbath],
it is not a [valid] *eruv*;
if after dark [on the Sabbath],
in this case it is a [valid] *eruv*.
If there is a doubt,
R. Meir and R. Judah say:
In this case this [person] is [in the position of] an ass and camel driver.
R. Yose and R. Simeon say:[27]
A doubtful *eruv* is fit.
Said R. Yose:
Avtolemos testified in the name of five elders
regarding a doubtful *eruv*,
that it is fit.

---

[23] Lit. "tower." K, P: "and locked it up."   [24] K: "R. Eleazar"; P: "R. Leazar".
[25] K, P: "if it is not known."   [26] Or "whether."   [27] K: "say that a doubtful *eruv* is fit."

---

and the key was lost: The food must be accessible. R. Eliezer does not accept alternative (destructive) means of access. If he knows that *the key is in its [proper] place*, but he does not remember where that place is, he will not break the cupboard.

3:4 *beyond the Sabbath limit*: Beyond the limit of two thousand cubits. The food has to be deposited within this limit; otherwise it would be unavailable on the Sabbath.

an ass and camel driver: This is a rhetorical image. A person who is guiding both a donkey and a camel cannot move forward or backward, because a camel needs to be pulled and a donkey pushed. So too the owner of a doubtfully deposited *eruv* cannot move on the Sabbath beyond his Torah-based four cubits. See also 4:10 below.

fit: This is the only time in this tractate that the Mishnah explicitly uses the word "fit" (*kasher*) for the preparation of an *eruv*. Usually the locution is merely that the deposit "is (or is not) an *eruv*." Compare 1:2: "validation of an alley."

3:5–7   Conditional Eruv

5 A person may make conditions concerning his *eruv* and say:
"If non-Jews come from the east,
my *eruv* [shall be] to the west;
from the west,
my *eruv* [shall be] to the east;
if they come from both sides,²⁸
I will walk to the place I wish;
if they come from neither direction,
in this case I [shall be] like the residents of my town.
If a sage comes from the east,
my *eruv* [shall be] to the east;
from the west,
my *eruv* [shall be] to the west;
if he comes from both sides,
I will walk toward the place I wish;
if from neither direction,
in this case I [shall be] like the residents of my town."
R. Judah says:
If one of them was his teacher,
he [should] go toward his teacher;
if both of them were his teachers,
he [may] walk toward the place that he wishes.

6 R. Eliezer says:
If a festival falls next to a Sabbath,
whether before or after it,
a person may make two *eruvin* and say:
"My *eruv* [for] the first [day shall be valid] toward the east
and [for] the second toward the west,
[or] the first toward the west
and the second toward the east;

---

²⁸ Lit. "from here and from here," and so throughout, in the negative clauses as well.

3:5 *A person*: The text has *adam*, which in this context includes women.

A person may make conditions…: That is, he may prepare two different sets of *eruv* food and deposit them at the Sabbath limit in opposite directions from his location, allowing him to choose in which direction to walk on the Sabbath.

like the residents of my town: Who can walk two thousand cubits in any direction even without an *eruv*.

if he comes from both sides: If one sage comes from one side and another comes from the other.

3:6 *If a festival falls next to a Sabbath*: If a holiday falls on a Friday or a Sunday. Walking beyond two thousand cubits outside the residential area is also prohibited on a holiday.

a person may make two eruvin: According to R. Eliezer, a person may prepare two separate *eruvin* for the two respective days, and deposit them in opposite directions, allowing him to walk in those directions on

[or] my *eruv* [shall be valid for] the first day,
and on the second [I shall be] like the [other] residents of my town;
[or] my *eruv* [shall be valid for] the second day,
and on the first [I shall be] like the [other] residents of my town."[29]
But[30] the Sages say:
He should make an *eruv* for one direction,
or he does not make an *eruv* at all;
either he makes an *eruv* for both days,
or he does not make an *eruv* at all.
How should he proceed?
On the first [day] he brings it [to the Sabbath limit],
and waits till darkness
and takes it and goes his way;
on the second [day] he waits till darkness
and eats it.
And thus he gains the benefit
both of his walking and of his *eruv*.
If it is eaten on the first [day],
his *eruv* [is valid] for the first day [only],
and it is not a [valid] *eruv* for the second.
Said R. Eliezer to them:
You do agree with me
that they are two [separate times of] holiness.

[29] This fourth scenario was missing in **K** and written by a later hand into the margin.
[30] Or "and."

the respective days. As per R. Eliezer's reasoning at the end of the paragraph, he considers each day to have its own distinct identity ("two holinesses"), so each day should be treated on its own.

my eruv [shall be valid] for the first day: A person can prepare an *eruv* for only one of those two holy days.

But the Sages say: R. Eliezer's anonymous interlocutors disagree and insist that one can only make a uniform *eruv* that is intended for both days simultaneously, and extends walking in one direction only.

How should he proceed? This question continues the scenario of the Sages, i.e. what should he do if he is allowed to make only one *eruv*?

On the first [day] he brings it [to the Sabbath limit]: An elaborate scheme: before the start of the holiday that falls on Thursday evening he (or she) walks to the Sabbath limit of two thousand cubits in the direction in which he intends to continue to walk on the holiday and waits till darkness, upon which he can carry the *eruv* food back with him, since the *eruv* (if in place) is effective at the moment the holiday starts, and he can carry on the holiday. He is justified to do so for fear that the *eruv* might get consumed by an animal. On the Friday evening before the onset of the Sabbath he carries the *eruv* food to the Sabbath limit in the other direction and sets up camp till darkness there, upon which the *eruv* is effective for the entire Sabbath. But he cannot carry it back, since it is the Sabbath, and he should eat it right there.

And thus he gains the benefit: i.e. he gets to walk the extra two thousand cubits in the desired direction and he gets to eat the *eruv* food too.

Said R. Eliezer to them: He points to the implicit logic of the Sages' dissent, which ends up being in agreement with his own concept. Should the *eruv* be consumed on the first evening, the Sages consider it to hold for that one day only; this means the Sages also consider there to be a separate "holiness" for the holiday and for the following Sabbath.

7 R. Judah says:
If one was worried on the New Year
that [the month] might be intercalated,
one may prepare two *eruvin* and say:
"My *eruv* for the first [day shall be valid] toward the east
and for the second toward the west,
[or] for the first [day] toward the west,
and for the second toward the east;
[or] my *eruv* [shall be valid] on the first [day],
and on the second [I shall be] like the [other] residents of my town;
[or] my *eruv* [shall be valid] on the second [day],
and on the first [I shall be] like the [other] residents of my town."
But the Sages did not agree with him.

3:8–9 *Other Rules for Two-Day Festivals*

8 And R. Judah said further:
A person may make conditions concerning a basket [of untithed produce]
on the first [day of a two-day] festival
and eat it on the second.
And similarly, an egg that was laid on the first [day of such a festival]
may be eaten on the second.
But the Sages did not agree with him.
9 R. Dosa b. Harqinas says:
He who goes before the Ark on the festival of the New Year says:
"Give us strength, O Lord, our God,
on the first day of this month,
whether today or tomorrow."
And on the following day he says:
"…whether today or yesterday."
But the Sages did not agree with him.

3:7 R. Judah's opinion is parallel to R. Eliezer's in the preceding paragraph.

If one was worried on the New Year that [the month] might be intercalated: On intercalation see *Rosh Hashanah* 3:1. If the court in charge of declaring the new moon does not do so in time, a day will be added to the last month of the outgoing year, making this and the first day of the New Year a two-day holiday.

3:8 This paragraph is unrelated to *eruvin* but connected to the preceding one by the name of R. Judah, and because of issues arising from a possible two-day New Year.

A person may make conditions: See 3:5.

an egg that was laid on the first [day…]: See *Betsah* 1:1, which records a disagreement between the Houses of Hillel and Shammai as to whether an egg laid on a holiday can be eaten that same day. R. Judah here seems to agree with the House of Hillel that it may be eaten on the second day, but not on the day it was laid.

3:9 Another independent paragraph that is not connected to the topic of the *eruv*.

He who goes before the Ark: To serve as a prayer leader.

4:1–3 *Permissible Movement When Outside the Sabbath Limit*

4 If non-Jews or an evil spirit took him out [outside the Sabbath limit],
he has only four cubits [around himself to move about].
And if they returned him,
it is as if he had never gone out.
If they took him to another town,
[or] put him into a shed or a stable—
Rabban Gamaliel and R. Eleazar b. Azariah say:
He may walk throughout its entirety.
R. Joshua and R. Aqiva say:
He has only four cubits.
It once happened
that they were coming from Brundisium,[31]
and [on the Sabbath] their ship was sailing on the sea:
Rabban Gamaliel and R. Eleazer b. Azariah walked throughout its entirety.
R. Joshua and R. Aqiva did not move beyond four cubits,
because they wanted to impose a more stringent ruling upon themselves.

2 One time they did not enter the harbor before nightfall [on Friday].
They said to Rabban Gamaliel:
May we disembark?

---

[31] Multiple spellings occur for this toponym.

4:1 *he has only four cubits*: This limit is based on the first part of Exodus 16:29, *remain every man in his place*. This was understood to mean that a person's freedom of movement is limited to his or her town plus two thousand cubits in every direction; once outside that area one cannot move about at all, other than within the four cubits in circumference around himself (*in his place*). The "Sabbath boundary" of two thousand cubits is first mentioned in 4:3 below.

as if he had never gone out: He has two thousand cubits in any direction, like the other residents of the town.

from Brundisium: Modern Brindisi. A journey by ship of Rabban Gamaliel and "the elders" is mentioned elsewhere in the Mishnah; see *Shabbat* 16:8 and *Ma'aser Sheni* 5:9. In the latter text the "elders" are identified as the other three Sages named here.

they wanted to impose a more stringent ruling upon themselves: This last clause indicates that R. Joshua and R. Aqiva differentiate between the moving ship and a shed or stable as enclosed spaces; for the ship they merely impose a stringency upon themselves, whereas in the case of the shed/stable, they prohibit movement beyond four cubits outright.

4:2 This mishnah is paired with the previous one.

did not enter the harbor before nightfall: They could only disembark from the ship if they had reached the Sabbath area of two thousand cubits measured from the coast by nightfall.

before nightfall [on Friday]: This timing is implied throughout this chapter, even when not mentioned explicitly.

He said to them:
It is permitted,
since I was already looking,
and we were within the [Sabbath] limit before nightfall.

3 One who went out [beyond the established Sabbath limit] with permission
and then was told,
"The deed has already been done,"
has two thousand cubits in every direction.
If he was within the [Sabbath] limit,
it is as if he had never gone out,
since all who go out to rescue,
may return to their place.

4:4–6 *Permissible Movement When Overtaken by the Sabbath While Traveling*

4 If one sat down while traveling[32] [before the Sabbath],
and got up [after the beginning of the Sabbath]
and saw that he was close to a town,
since it had not been his intention to [enter],
he may not enter—
the words of R. Meir.
R. Judah says:

[32] Lit. "on the way."

4:3 This mishnah continues the theme started in 4:1. This ruling considers leaving the Sabbath area deliberately but with good reason, whereas the previous rule applied to a person who was taken outside the area against his will.

with permission: e.g., in order to rescue someone, as in the final clause. See also *Rosh Hashanah* 2:5.

the deed has already been done: The rationale for the journey beyond the permitted two thousand cubits has been removed. Here the Mishnah goes beyond the ruling in *Rosh Hashanah* 2:5; in our text, one who leaves for a legitimate purpose can always journey back.

two thousand cubits: Like the four cubits in 4:1, this number is classified by medieval commentators as based on rabbinic tradition rather than biblical law.

since all who go out: The Babylonian Talmud's version of the Mishnah here lacks "since," turning this into an independent clause.

4:4 This group of cases considers various scenarios for determining one's formal Sabbath place, from which the area that one may travel on the Sabbath is measured. This is done by a verbal act before the beginning of the Sabbath, i.e. nightfall on Friday (see 3:5 above or 4:7 below), but can also occur by mistake as in the current case, or unconsciously, as in 4:5.

he may not enter: The medieval commentators differ as to whether he may not enter at all, or whether he may enter only as far as two thousand cubits measured from the Sabbath place he set by mistake.

He may enter.
Said R. Judah:
It once happened
that R. Tarfon did enter
without having had the intention.

5 If he fell asleep while traveling,[33]
and was not aware[34] that darkness had set in,
he has two thousand cubits in every direction—
the words of R. Yohanan b. Nuri.
But the Sages say:
He has only four cubits.
R. Eliezer[35] says:
And he is at the center of these.
R. Judah says:
He may walk in any direction he desires.
But R. Judah agrees[36]
that once he has made a choice,
he may not change his mind.

6 If there were two [people],
some of the cubits of this one
within the cubits of the other,[37]
they may bring [food] into the middle
and eat [together],
provided that this one does not bring [anything]
out of his [Sabbath space] into that of the other.
If there were three,
and the [Sabbath area] of the middle one
was enclosed by [the other two],
he is permitted [to eat] with them,

---

[33] Lit. "on the way." [34] Lit. "did not know." [35] K: "R. Eleazar" = P: "R. Leazar."
[36] Or "admits." [37] Lit. "within the cubits of this one."

---

without having had the intention: That is, the original intention to enter the town. Clearly he now wishes to enter intentionally.

4:5 This paragraph considers the case of an unconscious establishment of one's Sabbath place by falling asleep.

at the center of these: He may not choose to walk four cubits in any direction he likes, but can walk only two in one direction and then (if he wishes) two in the other from his original starting point. R. Judah disagrees.

4:6 This case builds on the previous one in that it presumes that two or three people fell asleep along the way and the Sabbath began while they slept. Now it is the Sabbath areas of these individuals that overlap, just as previously the Sabbath area of the traveler and that of the town. The ruling here is based on the preceding in that the individuals are surrounded by their respective areas of four cubits. These may intersect with each other to allow them to share a meal.

some of the cubits of this one: That is, his individual Sabbath area.

and they are permitted [to eat] with him,
but the two on either side[38]
are prohibited [from eating] with each other.
Said R. Simeon:
What does this resemble?
Three courtyards opening one into the other
and opening [as well] into the public domain.
If the two [outer ones] prepared an *eruv* with the middle one,
then that one is permitted to them
and they to it,
but the two on either side are prohibited to each other.

4:7–8 How to Determine One's Sabbath Place While Traveling

7 He who was traveling[39]
and it was becoming dark,
and he knew a tree or a hill[40] [in the area]
and said:
"My Sabbath place [shall be] under it"—
he has said nothing.
"My Sabbath place [shall be] by its root"—
he may walk from where he stands[41] to its root
[up to] two thousand cubits,
and from its root until his house
[up to another] two thousand cubits.
It turns out he may walk for four thousand cubits after dark.

8 If he does not recognize [any landmark],

[38] Lit. "the two outside ones."   [39] Lit. "coming along the way."   [40] Alt., "fence."
[41] Lit. "the place of his feet."

What does this resemble? R. Simeon's analogy is interesting and difficult insofar as it introduces the concept "*eruv* of courtyards" into a discussion of determining the Sabbath limit. The accidental overlapping of the Sabbath places of the individual travelers turns this case into an issue of shared place, rather than a question of permissible distance.

4:7 This mishnah returns to the situation of a person traveling on Friday evening but unable to reach town or home before nightfall; he must designate a place along the road as his Sabbath place and measure his two thousand cubits from there.

my Sabbath place: A technical term designating the place from which the area of permissible movement on the Sabbath is measured. When travelling, one's *Sabbath place* needs to be designated by a speech act.

he has said nothing: i.e. his speech act is invalid. He did not properly designate a Sabbath place, since his designation was not specific enough, as in the next clause.

four thousand cubits: Presumably this emphasis underlines the lenient ruling that he can walk the same distance merely by speaking as he can after having prepared an *eruv* meal at the boundary of two thousand cubits.

4:8 This paragraph still considers the scenario of a traveling person.

or he is not knowledgeable in matters of *halakhah*,
and he said:
"My Sabbath place [shall be] in my current location"[42]—
his place has acquired for him
two thousand cubits in every direction.
Circular—
the words of R. Hanina b. Antigonus.
But the Sages say:
Square, like a square tablet,
so that he gain the corners.[43]

4:9 The Essence of the Eruv of Distance

9 And it is [of] this that they said:
"The poor person makes an *eruv* with his feet."
Said R. Meir:
We are concerned only with the poor person.[44]
R. Judah says:
Whether poor or rich:
They[45] said one prepares an *eruv* with bread[46]
only to make it easier for the rich person,
that he not [need to] go out
and make an *eruv* with his feet.

---

[42] Lit. "in my place."
[43] A secondary hand in K erased something and filled in "benefits are gained"; the same happens in 5:1. The syntax in Hebrew is a bit awkward, which might explain an attempt to adjust, either by the original scribe or the secondary hand.
[44] Lit. "we only have the poor person," or "for us there is only the poor person."
[45] K, P: "because…," making this a continuation of R. Judah's statement.
[46] K lacks "bread."

---

not knowledgeable: Commentators take this to mean that the traveler is unaware that he can designate a Sabbath resting place at some distance from his present location. Strictly speaking he need not say anything to acquire a resting place where he is; the formulation echoes the other clauses in this mishnah.

so that he gain the corners: Compare *Oholot* 12:6 and the geometric comparison of circle and square there. See also 5:1 below.

4:9 The dispute in this paragraph is about which practice fundamentally establishes the *eruv* of distance, whether it depends on walking the distance, or the deposit of food at the limit.

And it is [of] this that they said: Referring back to the situation of the traveler in 4:7. The traveler can establish his *eruv* of distance "with his feet," i.e. by walking there, and does not need to deposit food.

We are concerned only with the poor person: R. Meir holds that this leniency applies to a poor person only, while a rich person would need to deposit food.

Whether poor or rich: R. Judah argues that both can establish their *eruv* of distance with their feet.

They said one prepares an eruv with bread: This is most likely an explanation of R. Judah's statement: the symbolic food is a concession to the rich person, allowing him to send a representative to deposit symbolic food at the limit of two thousand cubits, which otherwise he would have to do himself.

4:10–11 *Additional Rules for Returning to One's Original Sabbath Domain after Leaving*

10 He who leaves [his own town] to go toward [another] town
[with] which they [want to] make an *eruv*,
and his fellow made him turn around—
he [himself] is permitted to go,
but all the residents of the town are forbidden—
the words of R. Judah.
R. Meir says:
Whoever could prepare an *eruv*
and did not prepare one,
he is indeed [like] an ass and camel driver.
11 He who went outside the Sabbath limit,
[by] even only one cubit,
may not enter [again].
R. Eliezer[47] says:
[if] two—he may enter,
three—he may not enter.
He whom nightfall has overtaken
outside the Sabbath limit,
even [if by] only one cubit—
may not enter [again].[48]
R. Simeon says:

[47] K: R. Leazar (= R. Eleazar), as in 4:5 above.
[48] K lacked this entire clause, but it is scribbled in the margin.

4:10 *He who leaves [his own town]*: The wording is terse and unclear. Later commentaries suggest that before the Sabbath, one person goes in order to deposit the symbolic food at the limit of two thousand cubits, in order to allow the residents of his own town to walk on the Sabbath to a neighboring town which is less than four thousand cubits away. An *eruv* at the halfway point makes it possible to visit the other town on the Sabbath.

and his fellow made him turn around: So that he himself does not deposit the food. It is not clear why his fellow would do so, but perhaps to save him the trouble and do it for him.

he [himself] is permitted to go: The difference between him and the other townspeople remains unclear. R. Judah's opinion here is likely connected to his previous ruling: the person sent to make the *eruv* on behalf of his townspeople does not need to deposit the food in order for the *eruv* to take effect for himself, since he can make the *eruv* of distance "by foot." Indeed he does not even need to walk the whole way, since he can designate his Sabbath place from afar. However, the other townspeople cannot, since for them the *eruv* depended on the deposit of the food.

he is indeed [like] an ass and camel driver: On this figure of speech, see 3:4 above. R. Meir emphasizes that the scenario under consideration cannot be likened to the one in 4:7 about the person on the road, and therefore the principles discussed in 4:9 do not apply. Since he could have walked the whole way but did not, he cannot walk the additional two thousand cubits to the neighboring town, like the rest of his townspeople, nor can he walk the two thousand cubits from his own town in any direction, unlike the rest of his townspeople, since he was about to establish his Sabbath place in that one direction only.

4:11 *R. Eliezer says*: See his opinion in 4:5, where a person has two cubits in each direction when he is caught "outside" on a journey.

even [if] fifteen cubits—he may enter,
since the surveyors did not measure exactly,
because of those in error.

Chapter Five

5:1 *Mapping a Town's Sabbath Boundary*

5 How does one extend towns?
If a house [at the edge of town] recedes
and a house projects outward,
a part of the wall[49] recedes,
[or] part of it projects outward,
if there were ruins ten handbreadths high,
or bridges,
or tomb structures with rooms to dwell in,
one may extend the measurement [for the Sabbath boundary of the town]
outward in accordance with these.
And one may make it like a kind[50] of square tablet,
so that he gain the corners.

[49] Lit. "a turret."   [50] K, P lack "a kind of."

those in error: Referring either to those who accidentally walk too far, or to the surveyors whose measurement may not have been precise, as suggested in the Talmud.

5:1 This chapter details the rules of establishing the Sabbath area of towns. The first paragraph lays out the initial establishment of the boundaries of the town itself, from which the two thousand cubits of permissible walking on the Sabbath are measured in each direction from the town.

extend towns: "Extending" here means computing the town's Sabbath boundary expansively. The verb is the same as for intercalation of a month or a year (see 3:7 above). This Sabbath boundary is primarily virtual or mental, and may thus extend beyond the physical boundaries of the town for the purposes of more clearly measuring the two thousand cubits, as spelled out here.

a part of the wall recedes: The word evokes indentation or bulge, and could refer to the indentation of either the town's or the house's wall. In a parallel version of the text the spelling suggests the Greek architectural word for something like a trestle or turret.

tomb structures: Heb. *nefashot*, "souls." The point is that this tomb counts as enough of a residential structure to allow inclusion in the town's virtual boundary.

And one may make it like a kind of square tablet: Referring to the imaginary map of the town. See 4:8 above, there applying to an individual's space. Just as above, the square tablet is considered to add an "advantage" over the circle, namely, the possibility of added distance.

5:2–3 *The Additional Peripheral Area for Towns and Villages*

2 An [additional] peripheral area for a town may be provided—
the words of R. Meir.
But the Sages say:
They only mentioned a peripheral area
for [an area] between two towns.
If one of them has seventy cubits and a fragment,
and the other one has seventy cubits and a fragment,
one may establish a peripheral area for them to become like one.
  3 And likewise, three villages that form a grouping:
if between the two outer ones
there are 141 ⅓ [cubits],
the middle one makes all three become like one.

5:4–5 *The Measurement of Two Thousand Cubits*

  4 One only measures with a rope of fifty cubits,
no less and no more.
And he should measure only [by holding the rope] opposite his heart.
If he was measuring
and reached a valley or a hill,
he should calculate the beeline[51]
and return to his measuring.

[51] Lit. "absorb it," here and below.

5:2 *peripheral area*: In 2:3 and 2:5 the term *qarpaf* denotes an enclosed space, but here it refers to a peripheral area to be added to town boundaries before measuring the two thousand cubits of allowable distance; it does not imply actual fencing.

They only mentioned a peripheral area: The Sages refer back to earlier unidentified authorities who developed the teachings of the peripheral area.

seventy cubits and a fragment: Lit. "seventy and a remainder." From the following paragraph it is clear that the precise figure is 70⅔.

to become like one: The wording here is ambiguous as to whether a single peripheral area of 70⅔ between both towns is to be imagined, or one to each, so that the boundaries overlap and the towns become like one for the purpose of walking from one to the other on the Sabbath.

5:3 *And likewise*: The referent here is unclear; it could be either R. Meir's or the Sages' opinion in the previous paragraph, and the interpretation of this paragraph changes accordingly.

that form a grouping: The imagined arrangement here is a bit difficult to understand, because the Mishnah does not specify either the configuration of the three towns, whether a line of three or a triangle, or the distance of any from the others.

5:4 *calculate the beeline*: That is, he should not measure the actual length of the slope of such impediments, but should calculate the straight line across with the help of the fifty-cubit rope.

If he reached a mountain,
he should calculate the beeline
and return to his measuring,
provided that he not leave the Sabbath area.
If he cannot calculate the beeline,
in this matter,
R. Dostai b. R. Yannai said in the name of R. Meir:
I heard that one cuts through mountains.

5 Measuring should only be done by an expert.
If he increased [the limit] toward one place,
and[52] decreased [it] toward another,
one goes by[53] the one he increased.
If he increased toward[54] one,
and decreased toward another,
one goes by the one that was increased.
Even a slave,
even a female slave,
is believed to say, "The Sabbath limit [extends] till here,"
because the Sages did not pronounce the matter [of the Sabbath limit]
in order to be stringent,
but to be lenient.

5:6 *A Ruling about the Eruv of Courtyards*

6 If a town of an individual [owner] was made into one of many [owners]
one may prepare an *eruv* for all of it,

[52] Or "or."   [53] Lit. "hear" in the sense of "obey" or "observe," here and immediately below.
[54] K looks as if someone tried to erase the preposition. See annotations.

If he cannot calculate the beeline: Alternatively, the phrase "with this" belongs here and refers to the fifty-cubit rope. In that case a different method of calculating the straight distance applies.

cuts through mountains: i.e. imagine a straight line from one side of the mountain through to the other. The Mishnah remains unclear on this procedure.

5:5 *by an expert*: The phrasing is awkward (lit. "from an expert"). One commentator drops the preposition. Other traditions understand the phrase to mean "the beaten track," supported both by a manuscript variant and the punctuation in **K**.

if he increased…toward one place: The meaning of this statement, almost identical to the preceding one, is difficult to determine. **K** does not have the pronouns and reads more clearly: "if one increased, and another decreased, one goes by the one who increased," referring to two different experts. The Babylonian Talmud suggests precisely this answer, apparently without knowing the reading in **K**.

5:6 This paragraph seems out of place: the text abruptly turns to the issue of *eruv* of courtyards, when the rest of the chapter deals with the *eruv* of distance. This ruling probably fits here because this chapter deals with mapping the Sabbath areas for a town, the topic of this ruling as well. The topic of the *eruv* of courtyards will be taken up again in the next chapter.

but if [a town of] many owners was made into one of a single owner,
one may not prepare one *eruv* for all of it,
unless one provided an external section,[55]
like the Newtown that is in Judaea,
which has fifty residents—
the words of R. Judah.
R. Simeon says:
Three courtyards of two houses [each].

5:7 Arranging an Eruv of Distance While Still Outside the Town

7 One who was in the east
and said to his son:
"Prepare an *eruv* for me[56] in the west";
in the west
and said to his son:[57]
"Prepare an *eruv* for me in the east"—
if there were two thousand cubits
from him to his house,
and to his *eruv* more than this,
he is permitted [to walk] to his house,
but forbidden [to walk] to his *eruv*.
[If there were] two thousand cubits to his *eruv*
and to his house more than this,

---

[55] Lit. "unless one made 'an outside' for it." [56] K: "to prepare an *eruv* for him."
[57] "said to his son" missing in K but added in the margins.

---

one of a single owner: Or "a 'private' town." Another view insists that the defining factor is accessibility rather than ownership.

one may prepare an eruv for all of it: That is, with a single *eruv*, rather than having to prepare an *eruv* for every single alleyway. This arrangement is preferable because the separate alleyways are themselves joined into a single area, and only a town with one owner may do this; those with multiple owners must leave an "external" section somewhere that is excluded from the town *eruv*. The lenient ruling here means that the original status of the town can be preserved.

unless one provided an external section: As a reminder of its former status.

R. Simeon says: The disagreement here concerns the required size of the external section; the legal concept is not at issue.

5:7 One who was in the east: The case presumes that on the eve of the Sabbath one finds oneself outside of his town, to the east (or west) of it and approaching it. He has told his son, presumably before departing, to prepare an *eruv* at the opposite side of town, to allow him to walk on the Sabbath another two thousand cubits beyond the town's limits in that direction.

if there were two thousand cubits from him to his house…but forbidden [to walk] to his eruv: In this first scenario, he can walk to his house from his "Sabbath place" (see 4:7) within the two thousand cubits. Since the *eruv* that his son deposits is beyond the permissible distance of walking for him, he cannot proceed to it from his house. The second case scenario considers the opposite case.

he is forbidden [to walk] to his house,
but permitted [to walk] to his *eruv*.
One who puts his *eruv* in the expansion of the town
has done nothing.
If he put it outside the Sabbath limit,
even by one cubit,[58]
that which he gained he loses.

5:8–9 The Distance One May Walk When an Eruv Is Placed in a Town

8 The people of a large town may traverse an entire small town,
but[59] the people of a small town may not[60] traverse the entire large town.
How?
[If] someone was in[61] a large town
and put his *eruv* in a small town,
in a small town
and put his *eruv* in a large town,
he can traverse it entirely
and beyond it two thousand cubits.

---

[58] K, P lack "even by one cubit."
[59] K, P lack the conjunction here, but a second hand restored it in K.
[60] K, P lack the negative.
[61] K, P: "from," here and in the next clause.

One who puts his eruv in the expansion of the town: i.e. in the area of the additional 70⅔ cubits (see 5:2–3). Such an *eruv* deposit has no effect, since the expansion of the town is considered part of the town itself, and he does not gain any distance beyond the two thousand permissible cubits for the Sabbath.

If he put it outside the Sabbath limit: That is, beyond the two thousand cubits. The commentators and the Talmud are divided as to the meaning of "Sabbath limit" here, whether this refers to the "expansion of the town," as in the previous clause (thus the Babylonian Talmud), or the regular Sabbath limit of two thousand cubits.

that which he gained he loses: He gains in one direction, but loses in the opposite.

5:8 *The people of a large town may traverse...but the people of a small town may not traverse...*: The meaning of this clause depends on whether the second statement is negative. Some important manuscripts of the Mishnah do not contain the negative participle, hence equating both scenarios in the first clause. In this version, the first clause coheres better with its subsequent explication in the second clause, which seems to make small and large towns equal. The version with the negative participle in the first clause, reflected in the Talmud and some medieval commentaries, is more difficult since in this case there is a disjunction between the first and second clauses. In order to explain the disjunction, the Talmud and some commentators develop a complicated explanation. They distinguish between measuring the two thousand cubits of one's Sabbath limit and depositing an *eruv* there in order to gain another two thousand. By depositing an *eruv* a person gains the town's diameter in addition to the two thousand cubits, and this is not a difference between a small and large town with respect to depositing one's *eruv*. But for walking one's permissible distance the distinction does apply and he can walk only as far as his two

But R. Aqiva says:
He has two thousand cubits only
from the place of his *eruv*.[62]

9 R. Aqiva said to them:
Do you not agree with me
about someone who put his *eruv* inside a cave
that he has two thousand cubits
from the place of his *eruv*?
They said to him:
When [is this the case]?
When there are no residents in it;
but when there are residents,
he may traverse it entirely
and beyond it two thousand cubits.
It turns out that [if the *eruv* is] inside [the cave]
[the law] is more lenient than [if it is] on its top.
And to the measurer of whom they have spoken
they give two thousand [cubits],
even if his measurement finishes in the cave.

---

[62] R. Aqiva's statement was missing in **K**, and was restored in the margins by a secondary hand. Most likely the omission arose because both the previous clause and R. Aqiva's statement end with "two thousand cubits."

---

thousand permissible cubits and no more, regardless of where in the town he ends up. The last clause of 5:9 seems to confirm this distinction.

But R. Aqiva says: He has two thousand cubits only: R. Aqiva insists that even if a person deposited the *eruv* in the town, he can walk an additional two thousand cubits only, the actual permissible distance, rather than adding the diameter of the town.

5:9 *Do you not agree with me…from the place of his eruv?*: R. Aqiva tries to argue from the case of the cave, which is an enclosed space, in analogy to the town in the preceding paragraph.

When [is this the case]? R. Aqiva's interlocutors make a distinction for the case of the cave. The issue to them is not enclosed space but habitation: If the cave had inhabitants, like the town on the path of establishing one's permissible distance, then the person who deposited his *eruv* there gains the diameter of the cave/town in addition to his two thousand cubits.

[if the eruv is] inside [the cave][the law] is more lenient than [if it is] on its top: A summarizing comment on the case of the cave, in accordance with the anonymous interlocutors. When one deposits one's *eruv* food in a cave with residents, one gains the diameter of the cave. But if one deposits the food right above the same spot on the ground, where there are no residents, he has only the two thousand cubits.

And to the measurer of whom they have spoken they give two thousand cubits: This clause continues the previous one, so "they" seems to refer to R. Aqiva's anonymous interlocutors, who agree with R. Aqiva on the limit of two thousand actual cubits for the person who measures his permissible distance. Hence this last clause somewhat clarifies the positions.

6:1–2 When Living in a Mixed Neighborhood

6 If one lives with a gentile in a courtyard,
or with someone who does not agree with the [principle of] *eruv*,
that one imposes [the] prohibition [of carrying] upon him—
the words of R. Meir.[63]
R. Eliezer b. Jacob says:
He never imposes a prohibition[64]
unless there are two Israelites[65]
who impose a prohibition upon each other.
2 Said Rabban Gamaliel:
It once happened
that a certain Sadducee used to live with us
in an alleyway in Jerusalem,
and Father said to us:
"Hurry and bring out all the vessels into the alleyway,

---

[63] K, P lack "the words of R. Meir."
[64] K: "is forbidden" rather than "imposes a prohibition" as here.
[65] P: "two Israel (sing.)"; K has an ambiguous abbreviation.

6:1 This chapter switches from discussion of the *eruv* of distance to the *eruv* of courtyards. A shared courtyard creates a small local community, and this explains the turn to social concerns.

someone who does not agree with [the principle of] eruv: See also 3:2 above. Presumably, such a person would be a nonrabbinic Jew, potentially a traditionalist who finds the whole concept of *eruv* making too innovative with respect to traditional or biblical Sabbath law and therefore rejects it.

that one imposes [the] prohibition [of carrying] upon him: The non-Jew, who cannot join the *eruv*, renders carrying into the courtyard on the Sabbath forbidden to the Jew.

two Israelites: This is one of the rare occasions in the Mishnah where the common designation for the individual Jew—"Israel"—appears in the plural form. However, the manuscript attestation for the plural version is poor, and it is very likely that the correct version is "two 'Israel.'"

that impose a prohibition upon each other: In R. Eliezer's opinion, there need to be at least two Jews living in the courtyard in order for the prohibition of carrying to take effect, and only then the additional presence of a non-Jew would affect the ability to carry. In theory, the two Jews could circumvent that prohibition by making an *eruv*, but according to this ruling, the presence of a non-Jew in the joined courtyard community renders that impossible.

6:2 *a certain Sadducee*: Probably an example of "someone who does not agree to the principle of *eruv*," although the Talmudic discussions consider the possibility that Sadducees are equivalent to gentiles.

bring out all the vessels into the alleyway, before he brings out [his]: This paragraph is connected with 6:3–4 and the rules of symbolically giving away one's right of domain, but the exact situation is not clear. Did the rabbinic residents of the alley come to an agreement with the Saducean neighbor but fear he will back out, or was no such agreement even possible? The assumption here is that by placing their pots and pans in the alleyway before the neighbor has acted, Rabban Gamaliel and his family establish a (symbolic) domain, and so can use the alleyway on the Sabbath.

before he brings out [his],
and imposes a prohibition [of carrying] upon you."
R. Judah says in a different version:
"Hurry and do all your needs in the alleyway,
before he brings out [his vessels]
and imposes a prohibition upon you."

6:3–4 How to Merge the Neighborhood if Someone Forgot to Join the Eruv

3 If one of the people in the courtyard
forgot and did not contribute to the *eruv*,
his house is prohibited from the bringing of [items] in and out of it,
both to him and to the others.
But their [houses] are permitted,
both to him and to the others.
If they gave him their right of domain,
he is permitted,

in a different version: The difference between the two versions of the story is difficult to understand. Perhaps there is just a difference in the language by which the story reached R. Judah, or perhaps the first version implies that the alley becomes usable regardless of what the Sadducee does, as long as the family has already brought their vessels out of the house. Otherwise the implication in both versions would seem to be that Rabban Gamaliel and his family can make use of the alleyway by way of carrying only as long as the Sadducee has not yet brought out his pots, but as soon as the Sadducee does put his pots there, the alleyway is rendered forbidden for further use on the Sabbath.

6:3 *If one of the people in the courtyard forgot*: At 2:6 above, R. Ila'i teaches in the name of R. Eliezer that each of the other residents can still carry between his house and the shared courtyard, and that only he is prohibited from doing so.

and did not contribute to the eruv: "Making/preparing an *eruv*" in this context, where several people are involved, also can be understood in the sense of "joining the *eruv* (community)." The verb form is the same as for the *eruv* of distance, but here the sense of "integrating/mingling/mixing" applies also to the number of people involved. They are "merged" into an *eruv* community.

If they gave him their right of domain: The term for "right of domain" (*reshut*) also bears the sense of "permission." What the other residents give to their neighbor who forgot to join the *eruv* community is their right to carry between their houses and the shared courtyard, *their right of domain* in the sense of carrying into that space. If they give up that right to him, he becomes the fictive sole proprietor of the shared courtyard, and can now carry out of his house into the courtyard even though he had forgotten to join the *eruv*. By excluding themselves collectively from carrying into the courtyard, they allow him to do so. A parallel text expands on the actual act of transferring the right of domain and understands it to be a *verbal* act, so that someone simply says: "My right of domain is (symbolically) given to you, [or] is cancelled out for you," but does not have to perform a physical act of acquisition.

but they are prohibited.
If there were two,[66]
they [all] impose a prohibition [of carrying] onto each other;
since one may give and take the right of domain,
[but] two may give
but not take the right of domain.

4 From when on may one give the right of domain?
The House of Shammai say:
When it is still day [on Friday].
But the House of Hillel say:
After darkness sets in.[67]
If someone gave his right of domain,
and [then] brought out [something],
whether by accident or deliberately,
in such a case he imposes a prohibition—
the words of R. Meir.
R. Judah says:
If deliberately,
he imposes a prohibition,
but if by accident he does not impose a prohibition.

[66] K lacks these words, but this is clearly a scribal error, since the scribe continues midsentence with "they impose a prohibition onto each other…"

[67] Var. "even after…"

but they are prohibited: To carry from their houses into the courtyard and vice versa, and according to most commentators, also from his house.

If there were two: Presumably two Jews who forgot to join the *eruv*. According to this ruling, in such a scenario the fictive act of transferring the right of domain does not work: the other neighbors in the joined courtyard may not give their symbolic right of domain to those two neighbors because the fictive ownership would still be divided. According to the Babylonian Talmud a secondary transfer of symbolic right of domain (e.g., after the neighbors transfer their rights, one of these two then gives to the other) is not possible, though it is not clear that the Mishnah already knows this rule.

6:4 *When it is still day*: All the arrangements, even this symbolic one involving only a verbal act, have to be made before the Sabbath. The House of Hillel do not consider mere abandonment a transaction forbidden on the Sabbath.

If someone gave his right of domain to his neighbors in the shared courtyard.

brought out [something] into the courtyard.

he imposes a prohibition: As in 6:2, this is to be imagined as someone having made the verbal commitment not to make use of his right of domain who then does carry something out into the shared courtyard. He has thereby violated that commitment and made it impossible for the others to carry into the courtyard on the Sabbath.

6:5–7 *Whether Different Types of Preexisting Associations Need to Prepare an Eruv*

5 If a head of household was partnered with the neighbors,
with one through wine,
and with another with wine,
they do not have to prepare an *eruv*.
With one through wine
and with the other through oil,
they do have to prepare an *eruv*.
R. Simeon says:
In either case,
they do not have to prepare an *eruv*.
    6 If five associations were observing the Sabbath
in one banquet hall:
the House of Shammai say:
An *eruv* [is required] for each and every association.
But the House of Hillel say:
One *eruv* for all of them.
But they do agree
that if some of them occupy [separate] rooms
or upper chambers,
they need an *eruv*
for each and every association.

6:5 This and the following paragraphs explore types of social connection that preexist the formation of an *eruv* community. Since one of the goals of forming the *eruv* community is to establish a community of purpose, the Mishnah here explores which kinds of association are sufficient by themselves and render an *eruv* community superfluous.

was partnered with the neighbors: The head of household has a preexisting partnership with his neighbors through some sort of business. The Hebrew term is the same as the one employed for forming a symbolic "alleyway" community (e.g. 3:1), and this paragraph suggests that the business partnership can count for the residential amalgamation under certain conditions.

they do not have to prepare an eruv: Because they already have a preexisting partnership. According to this anonymous opinion, the business partnership among neighbors should involve a common stock in trade in order for it to count also as an *eruv* community on Sabbath.

R. Simeon says: According to his opinion, it does not matter if there is a diversity of merchandise. What matters is that there is a partnership beforehand.

6:6 Here the preexisting groups ("associations") have come together to share their meals; they are different from the business partnerships in 6:5.

five associations: Or: "groups." The number is generic and used in the sense of "several"; see also 6:8 below.

banquet hall: The shared banquet hall is similar to the shared courtyard.

the House of Shammai say: They consider each association as retaining a distinct character, even though they dine together in one large space, so that each must make their own contribution to the formation of the *eruv* community. The House of Hillel, however, consider them to be sufficiently unified for one *eruv* contribution to suffice.

if some of them occupy [separate] rooms: A parallel text suggests that in such a case the banquet hall is analogous to the shared courtyard in relation to the rooms.

7 Partnered[68] brothers who eat at their father's table
but sleep in their own houses
need an *eruv* for each and every one.
Therefore, if one of them forgot
and did not join the *eruv*,
he should nullify his right of domain.
When?
When they bring their *eruv* to another place;
but if the *eruv* came to them,
or if there were no [other] residents in the courtyard with them,
they do not need to prepare an *eruv*.

6:8–10 *The Relationship between Adjoining Courtyard Communities*

8 If five courtyards open one into the other
and [also][69] open into an alleyway—
if they prepared an *eruv* for the courtyards,

---

[68] Var. "brothers and partners." Other witnesses lack the word "partners" altogether.
[69] A well-attested variant lacks from "open" in the preceding line to here.

6:7 This paragraph is thematically connected to the two previous ones in that it considers the kinship connection as a type of preexisting social group. The family is a joined household in some respects—through eating—but not in others (sleeping).

Partnered brothers: Some versions do not have "partnered" here. The partnership in addition to the kinship relation does not seem to add anything to the question at stake here. The variant with "and" seems to combine two types of grouping—familial and commercial—under a single legal rubric.

sleep in their own houses: That adjoin the same courtyard. Even though they eat at one shared table, they are still to be considered as individual, distinct residents, who each need to make their own contribution to the formation of the *eruv* community in the courtyard, rather than being counted as members of the father's household (which would have made them exempt from such a contribution). Therefore even a brother who forgot to join the *eruv* has to forgo his (symbolic) right of domain. See further on 6:3 above.

When? The question refers back to the beginning of this mishnah.

When they bring their eruv to another place: If they deposit the symbolic *eruv* bread (or meal) in a house in the courtyard that belongs to someone who is not part of their family. In that case, the brothers' households are each to be considered as a distinct household, and each of them has to make a contribution.

but if the eruv came to them: If the symbolic bread was deposited in their father's house, they do not have to make a contribution, since they are part of the actual meal anyhow. The father's house in that case would be considered the residence to which the entire courtyard is joined. By virtue of the (symbolic) *eruv* bread the courtyard is integrated, and that house itself does not have to make a contribution.

6:8 The final three paragraphs of this chapter switch from a focus on the character of the *eruv* community to a focus on connected courtyards and how they can be integrated for the purpose of forming the *eruv* community. This first paragraph additionally considers the relationship between the courtyard community and the alleyway partnership, but also makes a connection to the last two paragraphs because it imagines five interconnected courtyards that are also connected to the alleyway.

five courtyards: As in 6:6, "five" here functions in the sense of "several."

but did not prepare a partnership for the alleyway,
they are permitted [to move things around] in the courtyards
but prohibited [from moving items] into the alleyway.
But if they prepared a partnership for the alleyway,
they are permitted [to move items into] both spaces.[70]
If they prepared an *eruv* for the courtyards
and a partnership for the alleyway,
but one of the courtyard residents forgot
and did not join the *eruv*,
they are permitted [to move things into] both spaces.
[But[71] if one] of the alleyway residents [forgot
and] did not join the partnership for the alleyway,
they are permitted [to move items] in the courtyards
but prohibited [from doing so] in the alleyway,
because the alleyway is to the courtyards
as the courtyard[72] is to the houses.

9 Two courtyards, one within the other:
if the inner [courtyard residents] prepared an *eruv*,
but the outer did not,
the inner one is permitted,
but the outer one is prohibited.
If the outer one [did so]
but not the inner one,
both are prohibited.
If each prepared an *eruv*,
this one by itself,
and this one by itself,
this one is permitted by itself
and this one is permitted by itself.
R. Aqiva forbids the outer one,
because the right of way [of the people from the inner courtyard] renders it prohibited,
but the Sages say:
The right of way does not render it prohibited.

[70] Lit. "here and here." The same phrase appears in the next rule as well.
[71] K adds "and so too" here, but almost all other versions lack this word. If the word is genuine, it may represent a scribal error for a very similar word meaning "but."
[72] K has the plural here: "as courtyards are to the houses."

But if they prepared a partnership for the alleyway: The symbolic integration of the larger space (the alleyway) is inclusive of the smaller adjoining one (the courtyards), but not vice versa. That contrast applies to the last two scenarios as well.

because the alleyway is to the courtyards: This sounds like a general statement and would thus apply to the whole paragraph, rather than just the immediately preceding clause.

6:9 *If the outer one prepared an eruv, but not the inner one*: Here one might have assumed that the outer one includes within it the inner courtyard, somewhat similar to the relation between alleyway and courtyard in the previous paragraph. But the Mishnah rules that the inner courtyard in fact renders the outer one invalid; since the inner residents must pass through the outer courtyard, they are *de facto* residents of both.

renders it prohibited: That is, to carry objects around. The right of free passage is not in question.

10 If one [resident] of the outer [courtyard] forgot
and did not join the *eruv*,
the inner courtyard is permitted,
but the outer one is prohibited.
[If one resident] of the inner [courtyard forgot]
and did not join the *eruv*,
both of them are prohibited.
If they put their *eruv* in one place,
and one [resident],
whether from the inner or from the outer,
forgot and did not join the *eruv*,
both of them are prohibited.
But if they were [courtyards] of individuals,
they do not need to prepare an *eruv*.

Chapter Seven

7:1–5 *When to Consider Two Adjacent Courtyards as One*

7 A window [in the wall] between two courtyards—
if it is four by four [handbreadths],
and within ten [handbreadths from the ground],
they may prepare an *eruv* as two
and if they want,
they may prepare a [joined] *eruv* as one.
[But] if [it is] less than four by four,
or above ten [handbreadths from the ground],
they must prepare an *eruv* [as] two,
and they may not prepare a [joined] *eruv* [as] one.

6:10 *If they put their eruv in one place*: In the same place for both courtyards, to join the two, presumably in the outer courtyard as suggested in the Talmud. If even one resident of the courtyards has not contributed, the project of joining the two has failed.

if they were [courtyards] of individuals: That is, a single owner occupies the entire courtyard. This case is in agreement with the Sages' opinion in the previous paragraph.

7:1 The first five paragraphs of this chapter roughly continue the topic of the end of the previous chapter: adjoining courtyards. The focus is slightly different though, namely, on the nature of the partitions between the two courtyards.

and within ten [handbreadths from the ground]: A ten-handbreadth barrier would constitute an indubitable separation between the two adjacent courtyards. The window disrupts that separation and the two courtyards are no longer clearly separated.

they may prepare a [joined] eruv as one: The barrier is not decisive and one *eruv* is sufficient, so that they would be able to move things from one space into the other.

they must prepare an eruv [as] two: Here and in the following paragraphs, this phrase indicates that the two adjacent spaces remain distinct; each must therefore prepare its own *eruv* and residents remain forbidden to move items from one courtyard to the other.

2 A wall between two courtyards—
if it is ten [handbreadths] high,
and four thick,
they must prepare an *eruv* [as] two;
and they may not prepare a [joined] *eruv* [as] one.
If there was fruit on top of it,
these [residents] may climb up from one side and eat,
and those [residents] may climb up from the other side and eat,
provided that they do not bring [the fruit] down.
If there was a breach in the wall—
fewer than ten [cubits wide] they may prepare an *eruv* [as] two;
and if they want,
they may prepare a [joined] *eruv* [as] one,
because [the breach] is like a door opening.
More than that,
they must prepare a [joined] *eruv*,
and they may not prepare an *eruv* [as] two.

3 A trench between two courtyards,
ten [handbreadths] deep and four wide—
they should prepare an *eruv* [as] two,
and they may not prepare a [joined] *eruv* [as] one,
even [if the trench] is full of stubble or straw.
If it is full of dirt or pebbles,
they should prepare a [joined] *eruv* [as] one,
and they may not prepare an *eruv* [as] two.

4 [If] one put a board across [the trench]
that is four handbreadths wide,
and likewise [between] two balconies facing each other,
they may prepare an *eruv* [as] two,
and if they want,
they may prepare a *eruv* [as] one.
Fewer than that,
they should prepare an *eruv* [as] two,
and they may not prepare a [joined] *eruv* [as] one.

5 A heap of straw that is between two courtyards,
ten [handbreadths] high—
they must prepare an *eruv* [as] two,
and they may not prepare an *eruv* [as] one.

7:2 *if it is ten [handbreadths] high, and four thick*: The thickness does not necessarily matter for this clause, but it matters in the following case of the fruit, which can only be consumed on top of the wall since something with these measurements constitutes a private domain, and the fruit cannot be brought across domain boundaries.

because [the breach] is like a door opening: See 1:1 and 1:8 above for the measurements and the concept of doorway.

7:5 *A heap of straw*: In 7:3 straw is not considered effective filling for a trench, but such a pile would separate the two courtyards like the wall in 7:2.

These feed from one side, and these feed from the other.
If the straw is reduced to fewer than ten [handbreadths high],
they must make an *eruv* [as] one,
and they may not make an *eruv* [as] two.

7:6–8 *How a Partnership for the Alleyway is Prepared*

6 How does one prepare a partnership for an alleyway?
One places a barrel [there] and says:
"This is hereby for all the residents of the alleyway."
And he may grant them possession [of the barrel]
through his adult son or daughter,
or through his Hebrew slave or female slave,
or through his wife.
But he may not grant possession [of the barrel]
through his minor son or daughter,
nor through his Canaanite slave or female slave,
because their hand is like his hand.

7 If the food [in the barrel] has been diminished [to less than the required amount],
one [of the residents] adds
and [again] grants possession,
but he does not have to announce [the partnership again].
If the residents [of the alley] increased [in number],
one [of the residents] adds [food]
and grants possession,
and he must announce [the partnership again].

These feed from one side, and these feed from the other: The cattle in each courtyard.

7:6 The text abruptly switches from discussing the structural boundaries between two adjacent courtyards to the food ritual that brings about the ritual integration of courtyard and alleyway. The food is in fact that which gives the tractate its name, as in 7:10 where R. Joshua says that "the loaf of bread is an *eruv*." This section of the chapter would have worked nicely as an introduction to the tractate as a whole.

How does one prepare a partnership for an alleyway? As opposed to the "partnership" of the Sabbath limits of towns that is discussed in 8:1–2 below.

One places a barrel [there]: Notably the Mishnah does not explicate what is supposed to be in the barrel; this is spelled out in the Talmud and other rabbinic texts: wine, produce, dried figs, or other kinds of food. See 7:10 where the text is specific as to the kind of food required for the *eruv* of courtyards, but there too the partnership food remains undefined.

he may grant them possession [of the barrel]: This ritual act of symbolic transfer to another person of a share in the barrel of food makes all the residents of the alleyway symbolic "partners" for the purposes of the Sabbath, and enables them to carry from the adjoining courtyards into the alleyway. The fictive recipient must be someone who can legally assume title of his or her share.

because their hand is like his hand: The indicated categories of person do not acquire possession for themselves but for their guardian or owner. If such a person is the fictive donor of the shares, no virtual transfer has taken place.

7:7 *If the food [in the barrel] has been diminished*: The required amount is spelled out in the following paragraph.

8 What is its [required] quantity?
When there are many residents,[73]
food for two meals,
for all of them.
When they are few,
[the amount] of a dried fig—
[the amount which constitutes violating the prohibition of] carrying out on the Sabbath,
for each of them.

7:9–10 *The Parallel between Eruv and Partnership Preparation*

9 Said R. Yose:
When does this apply?
For the starting amount of the *eruv*,
but for the remainder of the *eruv*
any amount [is sufficient].
And[74] they said to prepare an *eruv* for the courtyards
only so as not to let the children forget.

10 One may prepare an *eruv* or a partnership with anything,
except with water and salt—
the words of R. Eliezer.

[73] Lit. "When they are many."
[74] K, P do not have "and," thereby making it an independent statement.

7:8 *its [required] quantity*: This refers to the partnership of an alleyway and the *eruv* of courtyards. For the *eruv* of distance, see 8:2.

When there are many residents: In the Babylonian Talmud "many" is defined as eighteen and more, and in the Jerusalem Talmud as seventeen and more.

food for two meals: That is, as if for a single person. In 8:2 the rule is more demanding.

[the amount which constitutes violating the prohibition of] carrying out on the Sabbath: See *Shabbat* 7:4.

7:9 The statement attributed to R. Yose explicates the preceding paragraph, but it contradicts 7:7.

And they said: It is uncertain whether this statement is a continuation of R. Yose's opinion or an independent clause.

to prepare an eruv for the courtyards: In the case where a partnership of the alleyway already is in place. In such a case, the residents of the courtyards branching off the alleyway would theoretically not have to make their separate *eruv* for the courtyard. According to the ruling here, however, such an *eruv* is required anyhow, out of concern for children's perception of what is and is not permissible on the Sabbath.

7:10 This paragraph clarifies the kinds of food that can constitute a valid *eruv* of courtyards.

One may prepare an eruv or a partnership with anything: In 3:1 above this statement is anonymous and most likely refers to the *eruv* for the Sabbath limit of the town, or the *eruv* of distance; here the reference is clearly the *eruv* of courtyards. See also 8:1–2 for the food of a partnership of distance.

R. Joshua says:
A [whole] loaf [of bread] is an *eruv*.
If [an *eruv* contribution] is baked
[from] even a *se'ah* [of flour],
but it is broken,
one may not prepare an *eruv* with it.
If a loaf is [the size of] an *issar*,[75]
[as long as] it is whole,
one may prepare an *eruv* with it.

7:11 Whether Money May Count as a Contribution to the Joined Eruv

11 One [may] give a *ma'ah*[76]
to a shopkeeper or to a baker
so as to gain for himself [a share in] the *eruv*—
the words of R. Eliezer.
But the Sages say:
His money has not earned him [a share].
But they agree with regard to other people
that his money has earned him [a share],
since one may prepare an *eruv* for someone else
only with his consent.[77]

---

[75] K, P: "like/as an *issar*," rather than "with an *issar*" as in the printed edition. See the annotations.
[76] K, P have different general terms for "money" rather than naming a particular denomination as here.
[77] Lit. "his knowledge."

R. Joshua says: A [whole] loaf...is an eruv: He disagrees with R. Eliezer in that he limits the kinds of food for the *eruv* to bread, and emphasizes that the loaf, whatever its size, be whole.

se'ah...issar: The former is a large quantity (around two gallons), the latter is very small.

[the size of] an issar: Most manuscripts have "like/as an *issar*," suggesting the size of the coin as a reference rather than its monetary value; but an *issar* was also of limited value (twenty-four in a *dinar*), so the point is the same.

7:11 This last paragraph of the chapter is connected to the previous one by considering whether food can be replaced by money as a form of contribution to the *eruv*. Indeed, **K** and **P** do not start a new paragraph here.

to a shopkeeper or to a baker: A monetary transaction with these two professionals is ambiguous with regard to the *eruv* or partnership, since such a transaction might be considered a purchase. Contributions to the collection of *eruv* food, however, should be contributions and not purchases.

with regard to other people: The regular heads of household who are neighbors in the joined courtyard.

since one may prepare an eruv...only with his consent: This seems to be an independent teaching which the Sages cite here to explain why a person can commission someone else with money to secure his share in the *eruv*. By doing so he clearly indicates his intent to join the *eruv*.

R. Judah said:
When does this apply?
In the case of the *eruv* of distance,
but in the case of the *eruv* of courtyards
one may prepare an *eruv* with or without his consent,
since one may act to a man's advantage in his absence,
but not to a man's loss in his absence.

Chapter Eight

8:1–2 *The Requirements for an Eruv of Distance*

8 How does one prepare a partnership for Sabbath limits?
He places a barrel [at the Sabbath limit] and says:
"This is hereby for all the residents of my town,
for anyone who will go to a house of mourning
or to a house of feasting."
And anyone who accepted[78] upon himself [the benefit of this *eruv*]
while it was still day

---

[78] K originally had "who will accept" but the indication of the future tense is crossed out. Most versions have "who accepted."

R. Judah said: He restricts the application of the teaching that consent is needed to the *eruv* of distance, since that *eruv* can work to the disadvantage of a person in that the location of the *eruv* food will determine the direction in which he can walk away from the town, while he might have preferred to go in another direction. The *eruv* of courtyards however can only work to the advantage of a person: he will be enabled to carry into the courtyard. Thus, according to R. Judah, a person's consent is not needed to secure his share in the *eruv*.

8:1 The first paragraph of this chapter connects to the preceding paragraphs—and especially 7:6—by focusing on the food ritual itself that establishes the unification. But it switches from the *eruv* of courtyards to the partnership of Sabbath limits.

partnership: The Mishnah seems to be using "partnership" and *eruv* interchangeably here, but less so in the context of the *eruv* of courtyards. Thus the paragraph starts out with "partnership" but ends with reference to an *eruv*.

He places a barrel: That is, at a distance of two thousand cubits measured from his town, his permissible distance on the Sabbath. That *eruv* allows him to walk beyond the two thousand cubits (see 4:7 above), and his declaration extends this exemption to everyone in the town.

to a house of mourning or to a house of feasting, that is, a wedding. Both are matters of social and religious obligation, rather than mere pleasure, suggesting that the extension of the permissible distance to walk on the Sabbath by means of the *eruv* should be carried out specifically for the purpose of performing a religious obligation.

anyone who accepted upon himself: The past tense indicates that only those who are aware of their inclusion in the *eruv* can benefit from it, and the person affected by the *eruv* has to agree consciously to accept his inclusion (and see 7:11 above).

is permitted [to walk beyond the permissible two thousand cubits];
after nightfall,
he is prohibited [from doing so],
since one may not prepare an *eruv* after nightfall.

2 What is its [required] quantity?
Food for two meals for each:[79]
weekday meals[80] and not Sabbath [meals]—
the words of R. Meir.
R. Judah says:
Sabbath, and not weekday.
And both[81] intend to be lenient.
R. Yohanan b. Beroqa says:
[Minimally] one loaf of bread worth a *dupondius*
from wheat costing one *sela* for four *se'ah*.
R. Simeon says:
Two-thirds of a loaf,
when three [loaves are made] from a *qav* [of wheat].
Half of this loaf [is the quantity required in]
the case of a house afflicted by *tsara'at*,
and half of its half [is the quantity]
to disqualify one's body [from eating *terumah*].

8:3 *Allocating Structural Elements in the Shared Courtyard*

3 If the residents of a shared courtyard
and of an upper gallery [above it]

---

[79] K, P emphasize: "for each and every one."   [80] Lit. "his food for weekday."
[81] K, P: "and all these."

8:2 *What is its [required] quantity?* See 7:8 for the *eruv* of courtyards.

two meals for each: As opposed to the *eruv* of courtyards which requires two meals to be shared in theory by all the residents.

And both intend to be lenient: Each has a different understanding of the quantity of bread one consumes on the different days, but each intends to require the least amount considered valid for a meal.

one loaf of bread worth a dupondius: A Roman coin. Elsewhere in the Mishnah (*Pe'ah* 8:7) this is the amount of food a poor man passing through town should be given.

two-thirds of a loaf: R. Simeon's opinion requires a slightly smaller amount of bread.

Half of this loaf: If one stays in a stricken house for as long as it takes to eat half of such a loaf, he and the clothes on his body become impure; see *Nega'im* 13:9 and *Keritot* 3:3.

half of its half: If one ate this amount of impure food, one would be disqualified from eating the priestly offering.

8:3 The text returns to the topic of the *eruv* of courtyards.

an upper gallery: The residents of the upper gallery do not have their own access to the public sphere, but have to walk down into and through the courtyard in order to get there. The residents of each level have prepared an *eruv* among themselves, but not with one another.

forgot and did not prepare an *eruv* [together],
anything higher than ten handbreadths
[belongs] to the gallery,
less than that,
to the courtyard.
The bank of earth around a cistern
or a rock
that is ten handbreadths high
[belongs] to the upper gallery,
less than that,
to the courtyard.
When does this apply?
When it is close [to the upper gallery],
but if it is at a distance,[82]
even if it is ten handbreadths high,
it is part of the courtyard.
What is "close"?
Anything that is not four handbreadths away.

8:4 *The Kind of Courtyard Structures to Be Considered Proper Residences*

4 If he puts his *eruv* [food]
in a gatehouse, a portico, or an upper gallery,
his *eruv* is not valid,[83]
and anyone dwelling there
does not impose a prohibition [of carrying] on him;
in a straw shed, or a cattleshed, or a woodshed, or storehouse [in the courtyard],
in that case it is a valid *eruv*,

[82] Or "but at a distance…"   [83] Lit. "it is not an *eruv*."

[belongs] to the gallery: That is, the residents of the upper or lower level, as the case may be, may carry objects around in that space.

The bank of earth around a cistern: At *Shabbat* 11:2 the same structure is considered a distinct space onto which nothing can be deposited on the Sabbath.

8:4 *a gatehouse, a portico, or an upper gallery*: As opposed to the sheds in the second clause, none of these can be considered valid residential structures. For a courtyard gatehouse, see *Bava Batra* 1:5.

If the householder has any right of storage: In this opinion it is not just the structure itself that should be considered, but the question of who has access to it. If in addition to a tenant the owner has a continuing right to use shed for storage, that shed is to be considered as part of his household along with the tenant in it, and not a separate dwelling of the tenant, who would then have to make his own contribution to the *eruv*.

[the resident] does not impose a prohibition [of carrying] upon him: The tenant does not impose a prohibition of carrying upon the other residents of the courtyard if he did not join the *eruv*, since he is not considered an independent resident in the courtyard.

and anyone dwelling there
does impose a prohibition [of carrying] on him.
R. Judah says:
If the householder has any right of storage[84] there,
[the resident] does not impose a prohibition [of carrying] upon him.

8:5 Whether an Empty Residence Has to Be Considered for Eruv Purposes

5 One who has left his house
and gone to spend the Sabbath in another town,
whether [he is] gentile or Israelite,
imposes a prohibition [of carrying]—
the words of R. Meir.
R. Judah says:
He does not impose a prohibition.
R. Yose says:
A gentile does impose a prohibition,
[but] an Israelite does not,
since it is not the way of an Israelite
to come [back] on the Sabbath.
R. Simeon says:
Even if he left his house
and went to spend the Sabbath
with his daughter in the same town,
he does not impose a prohibition,
because he has already removed from his mind [the intention of returning].

[84] Lit. "grasp of hand."

8:5 The question raised in this paragraph is whether one has to join an *eruv* of courtyards only when one is actually present in the courtyard community on the Sabbath, or whether regular residence there establishes that obligation.

whether…gentile or Israelite: The difference between Jewish and gentile residence in the courtyard was introduced in 6:1. In R. Meir's opinion, the difference here does not matter, and both Jew and gentile have a share in the courtyard even in their absence. Resident Jews should therefore make a contribution to the *eruv* or in the case of a gentile rent out their share. To R. Judah, that difference does not matter either here, but he does consider absence a valid factor, and the absent resident does not have to make a contribution to the *eruv*.

A gentile does impose a prohibition: Both R. Yose and R. Simeon hold that the difference between Jewish and non-Jewish residents does matter because of likely differences in their behavior. Accordingly, a non-Jew's share in the courtyard needs to be considered even in his absence, since he might return on the Sabbath, as he is not concerned about travel restrictions on the Sabbath, while the Jew can apparently be counted on to stay away for the duration of the Sabbath. R. Simeon considers this to apply even when the Jew leaves to spend Sabbath elsewhere in the same town.

to spend the Sabbath with his daughter: Does the text specifically mean his daughter but not his son or some other relative? The Babylonian Talmud takes this to be the case.

8:6–8 *Drawing Water on the Sabbath in Courtyards*

6 If a cistern is between two courtyards,
one may not draw water from it on the Sabbath
unless one makes a partition ten handbreadths high,
whether from above or from below or from within its rim.
Rabban Simeon b. Gamaliel says:
The House of Shammai say:
[Only] from below,
and the House of Hillel say:
[Even] from above.
Said R. Judah:
The partition should not be more effective[85]
than the wall that is between them.

7 If a channel of water passes through a courtyard,
one may not draw[86] [water] from it on the Sabbath
unless he has made a partition ten handbreadths high
at the entrance and the exit.
R. Judah says:
The wall that is on top of it
may be regarded as a partition.
Said R. Judah:
It once happened with the water channel of Abel,
that they would draw water from it on the Sabbath
according to [the instruction of] the elders.
They said to him:
Because it was smaller than the [required] measurement.

8 If a balcony is above a body of water,
one may not draw [water] from it on the Sabbath
unless he has made a partition ten handbreadths high,

[85] Lit. "greater than."   [86] Lit. "fill."

8:6 The remainder of this chapter considers issues related to drawing and pouring water on the Sabbath.

partition: The purpose of the partition is to divide the cistern between the two courtyards, so that the residents of each *draw water for it*.

above…below: The partition can end above the surface of the water or extend below it. A third possibility (*within its rim*) is equivalent to the former, and some variants lack the words "whether above."

Said R. Judah: If there is already a wall that separates the courtyards and passes directly over the cistern, no further partition is needed.

8:7 *partition*: In this case, partitions where the channel enters and leaves the courtyard convert it from a separate domain to part of the courtyard.

the water channel of Abel: A place in the upper Galilee, close to Sepphoris.

They said: These are the anonymous Sages who disagree with R. Judah.

Because it was smaller than the [required] measurement: It was less than ten handbreadths deep and four wide and therefore did not constitute a separate domain. Accordingly, R. Judah cannot use the water channel of Abel as a precedent.

whether from above or from below.
And so too [for] two balconies,
one above the other.
If they had made [a partition] for the higher one
but not the lower one,
both of them are prohibited [from drawing water]
unless they join in an *eruv*.

8:9–11 *Rules for Pouring Out Water into Courtyards on the Sabbath*

9 If a courtyard is less than four cubits [square],
one may not pour water into it on the Sabbath,
unless they made a trough for it
that holds two *se'ah* from its hole and downward,
whether [the trough] is outside or inside,
except that [if it is] outside one needs to cover [it];
inside, one does not need to cover it.

10 R. Eliezer b. Jacob says:
If a drain is covered [for] four cubits in the public domain,
one may[87] pour water into it on the Sabbath.
But the Sages say:
Even if a roof or courtyard is one hundred cubits,
he may not pour water over the mouth of the drain,
but he may pour it from one roof to the next,
and the water flows into the drain.
The courtyard and the portico may be combined to [make up] four cubits.

[87] K: "one may not." See annotations.

8:8 *two balconies, one above the other*: This case parallels the one of two courtyards, one nested into the other (6:9 above), where the outer one grants right of passage to the inner one.

8:9 This paragraph is connected to the previous ones in its concern with the transport of water on the Sabbath, although here the water is poured out rather than drawn.

one may not pour water into it on the Sabbath: The courtyard is so small that it cannot absorb larger quantities of water, and overflow might flow out into the public domain.

a trough…that holds two se'ah: The Babylonian Talmud suggests that two *se'ah* is the amount of water a person uses daily, hence that particular amount.

from its hole and downward: The draining hole allows the water to flow out from the courtyard into the public domain. From the height of that draining hole downward to the bottom of the trough it must be able to hold the two *se'ah* of water.

whether [the trough] is outside or inside the courtyard.

[if it is] outside one needs to cover [it]: To mark it off as a continuation of the courtyard as a private domain.

8:10 *If a drain is covered [for] four cubits in the public domain*: The difference between the trough and the drain is that the drain continues further on into the public domain, beyond the four cubits, while the trough apparently can be covered in its entirety.

11 And likewise[88] two rows of buildings
one opposite the other:
if some of them made a trough,
and some of them did not make a trough,
those who made a trough are permitted [to pour water],
and those who did not make a trough are forbidden.

Chapter Nine

9:1–3 *Roofs as Sabbath Domain*

9 All the roofs of a town constitute one [single] domain,
provided that no roof is higher [by] ten [handbreadths]
nor lower [by] ten [than the others]—
the words of R. Meir.
But the Sages say:
Each constitutes a domain by itself.
R. Simeon says:
Whether roofs, courtyards, or *qarpaf*,
they constitute one [single] domain
with respect to objects

---

[88] K lacks "and likewise."

---

one may pour water into it on the Sabbath: There are two different manuscript versions of R. Eliezer b. Jacob's opinion. In the Babylonian manuscripts, followed here, R. Eliezer voices a permissive opinion: even though the water continues to flow into the public domain, he may pour water into the drain, as long as the first four cubits of the drain are covered. The Palestinian manuscript tradition, however, records a restrictive ruling; even if he covers the first four cubits of the drain, he may not pour water into the drain.

portico: See comments to 8:4.

8:11 *rows of buildings*: Or "upper compartments."

9:1 *one [single] domain*: Carrying an item from one roof to the next is therefore permitted on the Sabbath, even without an *eruv*, so long as the difference in height between roofs does not divide them into distinct domains.

qarpaf: See 2:3 above, but this is different from the town's *qarpaf* in 5:2–3.

one [single] domain with respect to objects that spent the Sabbath there: According to R. Simeon such objects may be carried from courtyard (roof) to courtyard (roof) without having to make an *eruv* between courtyards.

but not with respect to objects that began the Sabbath inside the house: Objects that were still in the house cannot be carried onto the roof and then to other roofs, unless the residents of the respective houses have joined in an *eruv*. R. Simeon thus takes a position between R. Meir's ruling and that of the Sages.

that spent the Sabbath there,
but not with respect to objects
that spent the Sabbath inside the house.

2 If a large roof is adjacent to a small one,
the larger one is permitted,
but the smaller one is prohibited.
If a large courtyard was breached into a smaller one,
the larger one is permitted,
but the smaller one is prohibited,
because it is like the doorway of the larger one.
If a courtyard was breached into the public domain,
one who carries [anything] from it into a private domain
or from a private domain into it,
is liable—
the words of R. Eliezer.
But the Sages say:
From it into the public domain
or from the public domain into it,
[he] is exempt,
since it is [considered] like a *karmelit*.

3 A courtyard that was breached into the public domain[89]
from two directions,
and likewise
a house that was breached
from two directions,
and likewise
an alleyway the beams[90] or sidebeams of which were taken away:

[89] K, P lack "into the public domain."   [90] K, P: "beam"; see 1:2–5.

9:2 The first clause of this paragraph is thematically connected to the preceding one, and also forms the bridge for shifting the discussing back to courtyards in the second clause by analogy.

but the smaller one is prohibited: The residents in that house cannot carry anything onto the roof, because it is entirely open to the larger roof and therefore does not constitute a distinct (private) domain. The larger roof still has recognizable partitions on the side that opens to the smaller roof.

breached into a smaller one: The sides of the larger courtyard, extending on both sides beyond the smaller one, still allow it to be considered as a distinct space. But the smaller courtyard is "open to" the larger one for one entire length, so it loses its status as distinct space.

breached into the public domain: The ruling does not spell out the size of the breach, but in any case the rupture opens the courtyard for potential public use, thereby turning the courtyard into a public space in R. Eliezer's view.

liable…exempt: From the penalty for violating the Sabbath by carrying.

like a karmelit: According to the Sages, the courtyard is not turned into a public space proper, but remains distinct enough from the public space to warrant a classification of *karmelit*. Carrying into it is still not permitted on principle, but in the case of transgression he is exempt from penalty.

9:3 As in the preceding paragraph the structures listed here lose their status as clearly marked private spaces. In these cases, moreover, the breach could not even be considered a doorway.

they are permitted on that same Sabbath,
but prohibited for the future—
the words of R. Judah.
R. Yose says:
If they are permitted for that same Sabbath
they are permitted for the future,
and if they are prohibited for the future,
they are prohibited for that same Sabbath.

9:4 *The Status of High Structures on the Sabbath*

4 If one builds an upper room on top of two houses,
and likewise [with respect to] overpasses open on both sides:
one may carry underneath them on the Sabbath—
the words of R. Judah.
But the Sages forbid [this].
Moreover, R. Judah said:
One may prepare an *eruv* for an open-ended alleyway.
But the Sages forbid [this].

on that same Sabbath: The disagreement is not about the permissibility of the breached structures, since both seem to agree that they have technically become prohibited. However, R. Judah still deems it permissible to carry into them for the remainder of the Sabbath on which the breaches occurred, though not future Sabbaths unless the breaches were fixed. In R. Yose's opinion, however, there cannot be a temporary extension of permissibility till the end of that Sabbath and the prohibition of carrying would apply the moment of the breaches.

9:4 The chapter concludes with a disagreement on the status of open-ended structures with regard to carrying on the Sabbath. It connects to the previous paragraph where courtyard and house were breached on two sides. Here the overpass (lit. "open-ended bridge") and alleyway are open on both ends.

an upper room on top of two houses: These are on opposite sides of a through street, or a public domain.

overpasses: Bridging a public domain.

the words of R. Judah: In R. Judah's opinion, the covering on top of the street allows the space underneath to lose its status as public domain, but the Sages disagree.

One may prepare an eruv for an open-ended alleyway: More commonly the Mishnah uses partnership for the alleyway and *eruv* for the courtyard. See 6:8 and 7:6–11.

open-ended alleyway: This is not the dead-end alleyway presumed in the first chapter. The residents can make a partnership for a simple alleyway once the entrance is symbolically marked, but the case of multiple entrances was not included in those discussions.

Chapter Ten

10:1–3 *Retrieving Valuable Objects from Beyond the Sabbath Limit*

10 If one finds[91] *tefillin* [on the Sabbath] one should bring them in
a pair at a time.
Rabban Gamaliel says:
Two [pairs] at a time.
When does this apply?
When they are old,
but if they are new,
one is exempt.[92]
If one found them in sets or bundles,
one should wait by them till nightfall,
and then bring them in.
And in [a time of] danger,
one should cover them up
and go on one's way.
2 R. Simeon says:
He gives them[93] to his fellow

[91] K: "one brings out," a mistake though the words are very similar.
[92] See annotations.
[93] K: "they give [them]."

10:1 This last chapter has to do with the general prohibition of carrying something across Sabbath boundaries, and would have fit better in Tractate *Shabbat*. Perhaps it was placed here deliberately so as to make this chapter serve as a conclusion to both tractates. A connection with *Eruvin* might however be detected in the various permitted circumventions of the prohibition.

If one finds tefillin: In an undefined place, though the next paragraph implies that they are found outside of a town, somewhere out in the open, where they were abandoned. Normally one would be prohibited from picking up items on the Sabbath, but rescue of the phylacteries warrants modification of Sabbath observance. Although the Sabbath is mentioned explicitly only sporadically in this chapter, it is obvious that the entire chapter deals with Sabbath rules.

old ones show signs that they were used as phylacteries.

one is exempt: From the obligation of bringing them "in," the reason being that new objects that resemble phylacteries may in fact be forbidden amulets. *Shabbat* 6:2 rules that a person cannot "go out" with phylacteries, so an alternative interpretation here might be that one who rescues phylacteries in this way is exempt from the penalty for Sabbath violation.

till nightfall: When the Sabbath will be over.

danger: That is, when he should not be seen wearing phylacteries identifying him as a Jew. See *Shabbat* 19:1.

10:2 *R. Simeon says*: He does not necessarily disagree with the paragraph above, but adds the human chain to it.

and his fellow to his fellow,
till [someone] reaches the outermost courtyard [of the town].
And likewise one's child:[94]
he can give him to his fellow,
and his fellow to his fellow,
even if [it takes] one hundred [people].
R. Judah says:
A person may give a barrel to his fellow
and his fellow to his fellow,
even beyond the Sabbath limit.
They said to him:
It should go no further than the feet of its owners.

10:3 Retrieving a Sacred Scroll That Slipped Out of One's Hands

3 If one was reading in a scroll on the threshold [of a doorway],
[and] the scroll rolled from his hand,
he [may] roll it [back] toward himself.
If one was reading on top of the roof
and the scroll rolled from his hand,
he [may] roll it [back] toward himself
if it has not reached ten handbreadths [above ground].
If it has reached ten handbreadths [above ground],
he should turn it around toward [its side of] writing.
R. Judah says:
Even if it is above ground
only by a needle's thickness,
he [may] roll it [back] toward himself.
R. Simeon says:
Even if [it touches] the ground itself,
he [may] roll it [back] toward himself,

[94] Lit. "his son."

one's child: If it is born somewhere outside of town.

R. Judah says: According to R. Judah the human chain is permitted not just for the sake of the rescue, but for the sake of someone's need, as the vessel contains food.

the feet of its owners: The barrel cannot be brought farther than its owner can walk. See also *Betsah* 5:3.

10:3 *on the threshold [of a doorway]*: The threshold is normally considered a *karmelit* or an in-between domain rather than a private domain, though some commentators consider it a private domain. In the present case he is still holding on to the other end of the scroll; if that were not the case, he might not be allowed to roll it back.

on top of the roof: The roof is considered a private domain. The anonymous opinion spells out what should be done once the other end of the scroll has reached the indicated height, namely turning around the scroll so the blank side faces outward. This will protect the writing from undue exposure as the day goes on.

since there is[95] nothing concerning the laws of Sabbath rest
[that] stands before the sacred writings.

10:4–7 Activities across the Boundary between Private and Public Domains

4 If a ledge is in front of the window,
one may put [something] onto it
and take [something] off it on the Sabbath.
A person may stand in the private domain[96]
and move [something] around in the public domain,
[or may stand] in the public domain
and move [something] around in the private domain,
provided that he does not move it out
beyond [the space] of four cubits.[97]
5 A person may not stand in the private domain
and urinate into the public domain,
or in the public domain
and urinate into the private domain.[98]
And likewise he may not spit [from one into the other].
R. Judah says:
Also, if his spittle is collected[99] in his mouth,
he should not walk [beyond] four cubits [in the public domain]
without spitting [it out].

[95] Lit. "you have…"
[96] K lacks the following words and continues with "and move something around in the private domain," which does not make sense. The missing words are supplied by another scribe in the margins.
[97] See annotations.
[98] K commits the same error as in the preceding paragraph ("he may not stand in the private realm and urinate into the private realm").
[99] Lit. "detached."

the sacred writings: The sacredness of the holy writing overrides the laws of the Sabbath. See *Shabbat* 16:1, 16:8, and 18:1.

10:4 *a ledge is in front of the window*: See *Oholot* 14:1–2 for various characteristics of a ledge. In the present context, it is a space ambiguous enough to require an explicit ruling: someone may put something onto it from either side.

move [something] around in the public domain: As long as he does not move it beyond the four cubits of restricted movement in the public domain, as per the final clause of the paragraph. Obviously, he cannot move it inside.

provided that he does not move it out: Although most versions attest to the word order as translated, the early medieval commentators were puzzled by it. The last clause presumably refers to the public domain, but syntactically it would seem to refer back to the immediately preceding clause.

10:5 There is nothing in the text that indicates humorous intent. One suspects this was a familiar situation.

if his spittle is collected in his mouth: i.e. it is no longer part of his body, and therefore considered an object carried around in the public domain.

6 A person may not stand in the private domain
and drink in the public domain;
[or stand] in the public domain
and drink in the private domain,
unless he has moved his head
and the major part of his body[100]
into the place where he drinks.
And likewise with a winepress.
A person may catch [water] from a gutter
[if it is] less than ten handbreadths from the ground,
and from a waterspout
he may drink in any case.

7 If a cistern is in the public domain,
and its surrounding embankment is ten handbreadths high:
if a window was above it—
one may draw water from it on the Sabbath.
If a garbage pile ten handbreadths high:
it is in the public domain:
if a window was above it—
one may pour water onto it on the Sabbath.

10:8–10 *Partitions, Stopgaps, and Doors*

8 A tree overshadows the ground—
if [the tips of its] branches are fewer than three handbreadths above the ground,
one can move things around underneath.
[If] its roots are three handbreadths above the ground,
one may not sit on them.
A door in the rear court,
or stopgaps [stuffed] into a breach [in the wall],
or matting—

[100] Lit. "most of him."

10:6 *his head and the major part of his body*: In which case he would be considered being in the same domain as the beverage even though his feet are in the other domain.

a winepress: Which is considered a private domain.

a gutter: Running along the roof. The person stands in the public realm, and up to ten handbreadths above ground is considered part of the public realm.

waterspout: Since it projects outward far enough from the roof, it is part of the public domain rather than the roof itself.

10:8 *A tree overshadows the ground*: This case is discussed in various contexts in the Mishnah, see *Oholot* 8:2, *Ma'aserot* 3:10, and *Makkot* 2:7. Here the tree stands in the public domain.

fewer than three handbreadths above the ground: See 1:9.

one may only stop up with them
if they are [suspended] above ground.

9 A person may not stand in the private domain
and open [a door] within the public domain,
[or] in the public domain
and open [a door] in the private domain,
unless he has made a partition ten handbreadths high—
the words of R. Meir.
They said to him:
It happened at the butchers'[101] market
that was in Jerusalem,
that they would lock up [their shops]
and leave the key in the window above the door opening.
R. Yose says:
That was the wool-traders' market.

10 A bolt with a lock at its top:
R. Eliezer[102] prohibits [its use on the Sabbath],
but R. Yose permits [it].
Said R. Eliezer:
It happened in the[103] synagogue in Tiberias
that [such a device] was treated as permitted,
until Rabban Gamaliel and the elders came
and prohibited [it] to them.
R. Yose says:
It used to be treated as prohibited;
Rabban Gamaliel and the elders came
and permitted [it] to them.

---

[101] Translation uncertain.   [102] K, P: "(E)leazar" here and below.
[103] Or perhaps "a."

---

one may not sit on them: Betsah 5:2 prohibits climbing on trees on the Sabbath.

if they are [suspended] above ground: Otherwise their use as temporary stopgaps would be considered "building" on the Sabbath, one of the thirty-nine prohibited labors (*Shabbat* 7:2).

10:9 *butchers' market*: Or poulterers' market, but in any case those who trade fattened stock.

wool-traders' market: He does not disagree with his anonymous interlocutors about their ruling, but on the detail of the case story.

10:10 The reason for the dispute is not made clear. According to the commentaries, the question turns on whether the device itself may be handled or used on the Sabbath.

10:11–15 *Rules Pertaining to the Temple; Concluding Homily*

11 A bolt which is dragged:
in the Temple one may lock with it [on the Sabbath],
but not elsewhere,[104]
but one that rests [on the ground]
is prohibited [for use] in both areas.[105]
R. Judah says:
The one that rests [on the ground]
is permitted [for use] in the Temple.
And the one that is dragged [is permitted] elsewhere.

12 One may reinsert[106] a lower pivot [into its socket] in the Temple,
but not elsewhere,
but the upper one is prohibited [from reinsertion] in both areas.
R. Judah says:
The upper one is permitted [for reinsertion] in the Temple,
and the lower one elsewhere.

13 One may renew[107] plaster on a wound in the Temple,
but not elsewhere;
if it was the first time,
it is forbidden in both areas.
One may tie a string [of a musical instrument] in the Temple,
but not elsewhere;
if it was the first time,
it is forbidden in both areas.
One may cut off a wart [of a sacrificial animal] in the Temple,
but not elsewhere.
But if [he needed to do so] with a tool,
it is forbidden in both areas.

14 If a priest is wounded in his finger,
he may wrap some reed-grass around it in the Temple,

---

[104] Lit. "in the province," here and below. See annotations on *Nazir* 6:8.
[105] Lit. "here and here," and so until the end of the chapter.
[106] Lit. "return."
[107] Lit. "return."

10:11 It is noteworthy that this chapter and therefore the tractate ends with rules concerning the Temple in Jerusalem; this either provides a messianic closure to the tractate or emphasizes the glorious past of Jewish Jerusalem. Note the present tense here and in the following paragraphs for permissions in the Temple.

A bolt which is dragged: Obscure ancient locking mechanism. According to the commentaries, this mishnah and 10:12 are concerned with whether using the device is tantamount to prohibited labor, or whether the prohibition is a secondary rabbinic one.

10:13 *a wart [of a sacrificial animal]*: See Leviticus 22:22, also *Pesahim* 6:1.

10:14 *he may wrap*: Even though he is dressing a wound, normally prohibited on the Sabbath. The priest is granted the exception in the Temple, presumably because he is performing services there.

reed-grass: Elsewhere used for making rope, see *Kilayim* 6:9 and *Shabbat* 8:2.

but not elsewhere.
If [he did so in order] to squeeze out blood,
it is forbidden in both areas.
One may scatter salt on the [Temple] altar's ramp,
so that they will not slip;
and one may draw water, by using the wheel,
from the cistern of the Exiled Community
and from the great cistern,
on the Sabbath,
and from the Hakar well
on a [regular] festival day.

15 If [dead] vermin was found in the Temple,
a priest may bring it out with his belt,
so as not to allow the impurity to remain [in the Temple]—
the words of R. Yohanan b. Beroqa.
R. Judah says:
With tongs of wood,
so as not to increase the impurity.
From where do they bring it out?
From the Sanctum and from the Porch and from between the Porch and the altar—
the words of R. Simeon b. Nanos.
R. Aqiva says:
The place where one would be liable for *karet* because of deliberate transgression,
and liable for a purgation offering because of accidental transgression—
from there they bring it out,

If [he did so in order] to squeeze out blood: He is prohibited from doing so, presumably because this resembles inflicting a wound.

so that they will not slip: Since the ramp was inclined, the priests could easily slip on it.

the cistern of the Exiled Community: This cistern and the wheel set above it are also mentioned in *Middot* 5:4. The "great cistern" is not mentioned there.

the Hakar well: Obscure reference. Hakar seems to be a proper noun, although the Babylonian Talmud relates the term to Jeremiah 6:7 and explains that it refers to a specific type of well in the vicinity of Jerusalem. Those on pilgrimage to the Temple would wash themselves there.

10:15 In more ways than one this last paragraph forms a nice conclusion to the tractate as a whole. First, as in the previous paragraphs it ends with discussing the Temple, the ultimate space. Second, it considers how to keep the space of the Temple free from impurities, when regular Sabbath rules pose an impediment. This in a way underwrites the tractate's sentiment as a whole, namely how to negotiate regular Sabbath prohibitions and their circumvention. And finally, the tractate offers R. Simeon's somewhat grand statement at the very end.

[dead] vermin: By rules of Sabbath one is to refrain from handling a dead "creeping thing."

"between the Porch and the altar": A standard designation for a certain area in the Temple. See Ezekiel 8:15, Joel 2:17, also *Middot* 3:6; *Kelim* 1:9.

deliberate transgression…accidental transgression: i.e. if someone deliberately entered in a state of ritual impurity. See *Kelim* 1:8.

but in all the other places they put a *psykter* on top of it.
R. Simeon says:
The place that the Sages permitted to you—
that which is yours they gave you,
since they permitted to you[108]
merely that which [they had prohibited] due to "Sabbath refraining."

[108] K lacked "since they permitted you," but it was restored in the margin.

psykter: A Greek word for what is essentially a large pot. *Tamid* 5:5 describes the *psykter* used in the Temple in great detail, including a reference to the dead creeping thing.

R. Simeon says: The place that the Sages permitted to you: The Babylonian Talmud attempts to relate the statement to specific rulings of R. Simeon, but one cannot help but read R. Simeon's statement here as a general conclusion: the leniencies pronounced in *Eruvin* (and *Shabbat*) are leniencies with regard to issues that are theoretically—which is to say, by Torah law—permitted. The affected actions are prohibited only because of rabbinic rulings, and therefore "whatever they permitted you was permitted to you to begin with." The sentiment here is similar to the one expressed in *Hagigah* 1:8, where the rabbinic laws of the Sabbath are famously described as "mountains hanging on a hair."

Tractate Pesahim

Jonathan Klawans

Introduction

Structure and Organization of the Tractate

Tractate *Pesahim* treats a number of topics relating to the observance of Passover, the festival held each spring in commemoration of the Israelites' Exodus from Egypt. In biblical and rabbinic parlance, "Pesah" (translated as Passover) refers in particular to the special sacrificial offerings of the day; these constitute a partial reenactment of the protective sacrifices performed by the people of Israel during the tenth plague (Exodus 12:1–51).

According to the biblical tradition, the tenth plague took place at midnight, on the night that followed the fourteenth day of the first month (12:29). Following this chronology, the Exodus itself took place the next day (12:51). In the Mishnah and other postbiblical Jewish traditions, this month is known by its Babylonian name, Nisan. So the Passover sacrifice is performed on the afternoon of the fourteenth of Nisan. The biblically mandated seven-day festival of unleavened bread (12:18–20) begins on the fifteenth of Nisan, which immediately follows the performance of the Passover on the afternoon of the fourteenth. The offering would then be consumed at a special meal held after sundown, when the fourteenth of Nisan has ended and the fifteenth has begun.

Although we are dealing with a seven-day festival, tractate *Pesahim* is decidedly focused on the rules pertaining to matters preceding and immediately following the Passover sacrifice. Indeed, the overall structure of the tractate follows this sequence, beginning with the prefestival preparations concerning the removal of leaven (chapters 1–3), proceeding through the various rules concerning the Passover sacrifice (chapters 5–9), and concluding with a detailed discussion of the festival meal that is to be held after the sun has set (chapter 10). The tractate's loose general structure unravels at times with major and minor digressions. In chapter 4, a discussion of local Passover customs veers off onto the topic of local customs, veering off even further from there. Chapter 9 includes comparisons and contrasts between different kinds of Passover celebrations. The final chapter of the tractate treats the rabbis' particular way of performing the special Passover meal (known today as the *seder*). This chapter of the Mishnah ranks among the best-known rabbinic passages in the Jewish tradition because of its overlaps with the traditional *Haggadah*—the Passover liturgy used in many Jewish homes on that night, to this day.

Main Ideas

The bulk of the early chapters of this tractate are devoted to rules concerning the searching for *hamets* (leaven) and its elimination. The Torah not only prohibits the consumption of *hamets* (Exodus 12:15), it also mandates that none should be found in Israelite homes (12:19) or even seen within Israel's borders (13:7). Accordingly, *hamets* must be searched for and eliminated, all before the Passover sacrifice is slaughtered. Because *hamets* cannot be duly owned by an Israelite during Passover, it is also forbidden for any Israelite to derive benefit from *hamets* during the holiday, or to derive such benefit even after the holiday from *hamets* that remained in the possession of Israelites during the holiday (*Pesahim* 2:1–3).

And what precisely constitutes *hamets*? Any leavened product of one or another of the following five grains constitutes *hamets*: wheat, barley, spelt, oats, and rye (2:5). These—and their derivatives (3:1)—must be removed, sold, or otherwise eliminated before Passover begins (preferably, according to the Sages, by burning: 2:1). Failure to remove leaven leaves one liable to "extirpation" (3:1; cf. Exodus 12:15, 19).

In addition to the requisite removal of leaven, the Passover sacrifice is in a number of ways distinct from other sacrifices offered during the year. The obligation to perform the sacrifice falls on all Israelites (Exodus 13:6), and includes not simply bringing an animal for offering, but consuming the roasted carcass, in its entirety, during that very night (13:9–11). In order to ensure that everyone has the opportunity to eat from a Passover—and in order to prevent any meat from being left over—the Mishnah mandates that each Passover offering be slaughtered explicitly for that purpose, for a designated group of suitable size, and then be duly shared among all members of that group. A good portion of this tractate addresses complications arising from these situations, such as when a Passover offering is slaughtered for some other purpose or for the wrong people (5:2–3).

Overview

The tractate's plural name—Passovers—is curious and multivalent. On the simplest level, the plural points to one of the key differences between Passover and other Temple rites: because the obligation to perform the Passover sacrifice falls on the entire people of Israel (Exodus 12:6), the sheer number of offerings must have been staggering. The tractate, accordingly, includes traditions that indicate various means of crowd control the rabbis remembered—or imagined—having been put in place (*Pesahim* 5:5–10). The crowded situation imagined by the rabbis no doubt also explains their concern with offerings that become confused: different families or groups might disagree over which of the many animals being slaughtered and burned properly belongs to them (9:8–11). Although the historical accuracy of these memories cannot be confirmed, various external sources attest to the vast crowds that assembled in Jerusalem at Passover during the late Second Temple period (e.g. Matthew 27:15; Josephus, *Antiquities* 17.213–214).

But the plurality of Passovers in our tractate extends beyond the sheer number of offerings brought by the crowd. The rabbis recall and reckon with the fact that the Passover sacrifice described in Exodus 12 is vastly different from the Temple service that concerns our tractate. The so-called "Passover of Egypt" was performed in haste, standing, with blood on the door. By contrast, the subsequent Passover—which the rabbis term the "Passover of the Generations," is performed in Jerusalem, at the Temple, and at the beginning of a seven-day festival (9:5).

Following biblical law (Numbers 9:6–12), the Mishnah discusses the so-called "Second Passover," offered precisely one month after the first Passover—in the second month, Iyar. This Second Passover is held especially for those on a journey or defiled by corpse impurity during Nisan; these will have a second chance to fulfill the obligation a month later. Like the First Passover, the Second is consumed roasted, on unleavened bread, with bitter herbs (9:3). Yet as the Mishnah explains, the Second Passover differs from the First in a number of respects, perhaps most significantly with regard to the prohibition of leaven: this pertains only to the First Passover, not the Second (9:3).

Scripture ordains that ritual defilement disqualifies one from performing the Passover at its proper time (Numbers 9:7, 10; *Pesahim* 9:1–3), but the rabbis of the Mishnah consider a scenario not addressed by the biblical rules: what happens when a great number of the priests and people are defiled? This is yet another one of the diverse kinds of Passovers discussed in our tractate: the (First) Passover that is performed in a state of defilement (7:4–6; 9:4). Students of ancient Judaism often assume that rules of ritual purity were consistently and stringently maintained at all costs by the Temple authorities, but tractate *Pesahim* reminds us that purity rules could, at times, be relaxed. Indeed, the ritual defilement of the sanctuary could later be ameliorated by means of sacrificial atonement (see *Shevu'ot* 1:4–7). Therefore, when necessary, the Temple's sanctity could withstand ritual defilement. The Passover that is performed in defilement is yet another distinct kind of Passover, one so-named for this very circumstance.

One final type of Passover is addressed by our tractate, though it is not labeled as such, and the eventuality is only explicitly acknowledged in chapter 10: this is the Passover that continued to be practiced after the destruction of the Temple in 70 CE even though the sacrifice could no longer be offered (cf. 10:3). As assumed in that chapter—and as practiced by many Jewish people today—numerous Passover practices pertain even after the destruction, from the elimination of leaven, to the consumption bitter herbs, and of course the telling of the Passover story to the child who asks (10:4; cf. Exodus 12:26–27).

So the plural in our tractate's title is warranted indeed, for tractate *Pesahim* discusses the First and Second Passovers, the Passovers of Egypt and of the Generations, the Passovers performed in defilement and those performed in purity, as well as Passover before and after the destruction of the Temple in 70 CE. And all this is to say nothing of the great many Paschal sacrifices offered on the evenings of all of these Passovers, when throngs of pilgrims came to Jerusalem to celebrate this festival.

Tractate Pesahim

Chapter One

1:1–3 *The Search for Leaven*

1   On the night of the fourteenth [of Nisan]
one searches for leaven by lamplight.
Any place where one does not bring in leaven
does not require searching.
If so, why did they say:
Two rows of the [wine] cellar?
[Concerning] a place into which they do put leaven.
The House of Shammai say:
Two rows covering the entire cellar.
The House of Hillel say:
The two outer rows,
which are the upper rows.
  2 One does not worry
that a weasel may have dragged [leaven]
from house to house
or from place to place;
if so,
from courtyard to courtyard
or from city to city:
there is no end to the matter.

1:1 *On the night*: Lit. "The light of the fourteenth…." This is an odd way to refer to nighttime, but there is little doubt about the phrase's meaning in the present context: the lamplit search for leaven takes place on the night preceding the day of the fourteenth of Nisan. Much of the rest of this chapter concerns what takes place the next day (the fourteenth of Nisan itself); the term in question appears below in 1:3, once again to denote the nighttime that precedes the morning of the fourteenth.

searches: For leaven, as explained in the introduction.

by lamplight: Because it is already dark.

If so, why did they say: This phrase appears to introduce the discussion of an earlier tradition, one that was later the subject of dispute between the Houses of Hillel and Shammai.

Two rows of the [wine] cellar? The early Sages mandated that two rows of the wine cellar must be searched, and this mishnah first clarifies that this ruling applies only to wine cellars into which some leaven may have been introduced. The Houses then dispute the meaning of "rows": the House of Shammai maintain that two entire layers of the cellar must be searched; the House of Hillel limit the search to outer and upper rows.

1:2 *there is no end to the matter*: For a similar application of this principle, see *Yoma* 1:1.

3 R. Judah says:
One searches the night of the fourteenth,
the morning of the fourteenth,
and at the hour of burning.
The Sages say:
If one did not search on the night of the fourteenth,
he should search on the fourteenth;
if he did not search on the fourteenth,
he should search during the holiday.
If he did not search during the holiday,
he should search after the holiday.
Whatever he leaves aside,
he should put it in a discreet place,
so that it will not become necessary
to search after it.

1:4–2:4 *The Elimination of Leaven (and Other Burnings)*

4 R. Meir says:
One may eat [*hamets*] throughout the fifth [hour],
and one should burn [the *hamets*] at the beginning of the sixth.
R. Judah says:
One may eat throughout the fourth,

1:3 *the morning of the fourteenth*: Granted that the search is supposed to take place that night, R. Judah permits searching through the day of the fourteenth, until the time of burning (see 1:4 below).

during the holiday: The search is not permitted on the Festival day, but is permitted, according to the Sages, on the intermediate days of Passover. The position attributed to R. Judah does not permit this.

after the holiday: The search for leaven has become a requirement in and of itself, and according to the Sages must still be done even after the holiday. Because it is prohibited to derive any benefit from leaven that was kept over Passover (see 2:1), there remains a reason to search for leaven, even after Passover, in order to identify that leaven which has become prohibited for consumption and any other use.

Whatever he leaves aside: It remains permitted to consume leaven after the search (see 1:4). Therefore, he sets aside carefully what he intends to consume so that it will not become necessary to search for it later.

1:4 *One may eat*: The leaven that has been discovered during the search must be eliminated. This passage considers the schedule for consuming any retained leaven (see 1:3) and then disposing of all that remains.

throughout the fifth [hour]: As elsewhere in the Mishnah, the hours of the day are counted from sunrise, with the first hour beginning at sunrise and the twelfth ending at evening; so if the sun rose at 6:00 a.m. by modern reckoning, then according to R. Meir, consumption of leaven is permitted until around 11:00 a.m.

burn: In 2:1 below it emerges that the leaven can also be eliminated by other means; this passage specifies burning as the preferred means of destruction.

at the beginning of the sixth: When counting hours from sunrise, the noontime would come at the end of the sixth hour. The beginning of the sixth hour is, therefore, an hour before noontime.

eat throughout the fourth: that is, until around 10:00 am by the modern reckoning.

wait during the entire fifth,
and burn at the beginning of the sixth.

5 And R. Judah also said:
Two loaves of the thanksgiving sacrifice
that are unfit for use
are placed on the roof of the portico.
For as long as they are set out,
all the people may eat.
When one has been removed,
they wait:
they do not eat [the *hamets*],
nor do they burn [the *hamets*].
When both have been removed,
all the people began to burn [the *hamets*].
Rabban Gamaliel says:
Hullin may be eaten throughout the fourth [hour]
and *terumah* throughout the fifth,
and they burn at the beginning of the sixth.

6 R. Hanina,[1] Prefect of the Priests says:

[1] **K**: "R. Hananiah."

---

wait during the entire fifth: R. Judah mandates a transition period of one hour between the time when leaven may no longer be consumed (at the end of the fourth hour) and the time when the burning of leaven should take place (at the beginning of the sixth hour).

1:5 Continuing from the last statement of the previous mishnah, another statement of R. Judah's describes how the three periods of time previously mentioned were marked. The alternation of tenses here is bewildering, but the translation has attempted to reflect the text as it stands.

Two loaves of the thanksgiving sacrifice: According to Leviticus 7:12–13, a sacrifice of thanksgiving is to be accompanied by both leavened and unleavened loaves.

that are unfit for use: For their original purpose as offerings, presumably because the time limit for eating them (Leviticus 7:15) has passed. It seems that leavened loaves were used for this purpose; and the staged removal corresponds to the stages of eliminating all leaven in the view of R. Judah.

on the roof of the portico: A raised platform within the Temple confines, from which they can be seen by all; cf. *Sheqalim* 8:4.

When one has been removed they wait: That is, the people neither eat leaven nor burn it. This would mark the fifth hour, in accordance with R. Judah's view.

When both have been removed, the burning of the leaven begins; this would take place at the beginning of the sixth hour.

Hullin: That is, food with no particular sanctity.

terumah: Priestly dues; see Numbers 18:8–11, and *Terumah*. Even though this *terumah* is *hamets*, on account of its sanctity it is better for it to be eaten than burned; therefore an extra hour is permitted for its consumption.

1:6 *R. Hanina, Prefect of the Priests*: According to Talmudic traditions, this sage was a first-century *tanna* who had served, before the destruction, as the deputy high priest on call should the high priest become defiled on the Day of Atonement. Here as elsewhere in rabbinic literature (e.g. *Sheqalim* 4:4), Hanina is

All their days,
the priests never refrained
from burning meat
defiled by derived source of impurity
together with meat
defiled from a primary impurity,
even though they thereby added impurity to impurity.
R. Aqiva added:
All their days,
the priests never refrained
from kindling oil
that was rendered unfit
by contact with a *tevul yom*
in a lamp
defiled by a person with corpse impurity,
even though they thereby added impurity to impurity.

7 R. Meir says:
From their words, we learn that one burns pure *terumah*
along with the impure on Passover.
R. Yose said to him:
That is not the right logic.

recalled as an eyewitness authority on Temple praxis. This mishnah relates to Passover only indirectly, through the practice of burning, in this case the burning of defiled sacrificial meat.

meat defiled by a derived source of impurity: As indicated in *Kelim* 1:1–4, there are degrees of ritual impurity. A derived source of impurity is something that has been rendered impure by a primary impurity, such as a defiling reptile or some other inherently impure substance.

added impurity to impurity: Something defiled by a primary impurity would in turn defile to a greater extent something previously defiled only by a lesser impurity. Even so, these variously defiled meats could be burned all together.

oil rendered unfit by contact with a tevul yom: the "day-bather" has already immersed during the same day, and will become completely pure at sundown (see *Tevul Yom*). Though he is pure enough so as not to defile the oil in question, any oil he touches would be rendered unfit for sacred use. To kindle such oil in a truly defiled oil lamp (such as that defiled by a corpse) would add impurity to impurity, yet this was done. R. Aqiva's tradition extends Hanina's logic, for in this case something unfit but not impure at all is rendered impure even as it is burned.

1:7 *From their words*: This mishnah builds on the previous passage, but returns to the laws of burning leaven prior to Passover. R. Meir argues that the Temple practices recalled in the previous mishnah attest that pure and impure *terumah* would be burned together on Passover.

That is not the right logic: In the traditions recalled in the previous mishnah, a defiled or unfit substance is defiled yet more in the act of burning, but according to R. Meir an entirely pure substance could be burned along with an impure one. R. Meir could justify his position in that even the pure *terumah* that is *hamets* becomes unfit at the time of burning. Nevertheless, R. Eliezer and R. Joshua agree with R. Yose against R. Meir that the two categories of *terumah* are burned separately. Even these two Sages disagree, however, regarding *terumah* that is doubtfully impure. R. Eliezer says that even these two types of *terumah* would have to be burned separately. R. Joshua allows these two categories to be burned together, following therefore to some degree the logic of the traditions in the prior mishnah.

And R. Eliezer and R. Joshua agree[2]
that one burns this by itself
and that by itself.
On what did they disagree?
With regard to doubtful [impure *terumah*]
and the [surely] impure.
For R. Eliezer says:
Let this be burnt by itself
and that by itself.
R. Joshua says:
The two as one.

Chapter Two

2 Any hour it is permitted to eat [*hamets*],
one may feed cattle, wild animals, and birds,
and he may sell it to a gentile,
and one is permitted to derive benefit from it.
When its time has lapsed,
one is prohibited from deriving benefit from it,
and one may not [even] light the oven or a stove with it.
R. Judah says:
There is no elimination of *hamets*
other than by burning;
and the Sages say:
One may even[3] grind and cast to the wind
or throw it to the sea.
   2 It is permissible to derive benefit
from *hamets* that belonged to a gentile

---

[2] In both **K** and **P**, the verb "agree" is in a singular form, suggesting perhaps that originally only one named sage agreed. In the printed editions, a plural form of "agree" matches the dual subject.

[3] **K, P** lack "even."

2:1 *one is permitted to derive benefit from it*: It is a standard rabbinic presumption that if one does not properly own something one cannot derive benefit from it, and *hamets* must not be owned during Passover. Therefore while one can do what one will with *hamets* before the holiday has begun, once the hour of elimination has arrived, one is prohibited from deriving benefit from it. Such benefit includes, but is not limited to, feeding it to animals and selling it.

one may not [even] light the oven or a stove with it: It is of course perfectly appropriate to burn *hamets*. But lighting an oven is an action that produces a benefit, and becomes prohibited with the hour of elimination.

2:2 *hamets that belonged to a gentile through Passover*: The prohibition of deriving benefit from *hamets* applies not only to one's own *hamets*, but to that belonging to any Israelite. This law is derived from the

through Passover;
it is not permissible to derive benefit
from that which belonged to an Israelite,
as it is written:
And no leaven shall be seen with you.

3 If a gentile lent to an Israelite on his *hamets*,
it is permissible[4] after Passover
to derive benefit from it.
If an Israelite lent to a gentile on his *hamets*,
it is prohibited[5] after Passover to derive benefit from it.
Hamets that is buried
under something that has collapsed:
in this case
it is as if it has been eliminated.
Rabban Simeon b. Gamaliel says:
Whatever a dog cannot search for.

[4] In both **K** and **P**, the main text reads "prohibited," but each was subsequently corrected; other manuscripts and the printed editions agree with the corrected reading.

[5] In both **K** and **P**, the main text reads "permitted," but each was subsequently corrected; other manuscripts and the printed editions agree with the corrected reading.

passage quoted (Exodus 13:7), which continues by commanding that *no leaven shall be seen with you, in all your borders*. Understanding these borders to run on ethnic lines, the rabbis permit deriving benefit from *hamets* that belonged to a gentile through Passover, meaning that once Passover has concluded it becomes permissible to acquire, use, and derive benefit from such *hamets*. But this does not apply to *hamets* that belonged to other Jews during the holiday. The modern custom of selling *hamets* to gentiles before Passover still rests on this principle.

2:3 *If a gentile lent to an Israelite on his hamets*: If one person lends money or an object to another and receives a deposit in return, that deposit is duly owned by the creditor during the course of the loan. If a gentile lends to an Israelite and the Israelite deposits his *hamets* with the gentile to secure the loan, then that *hamets* duly belongs to the gentile for the duration of the holiday. The manuscripts reverse this ruling, perhaps concerned that the borrower might default on the loan during the holiday; ownership would then have transferred at the time of the default.

it is permissible…to derive benefit from it: If the loan is repaid and the *hamets* returned after Passover, the Israelite is permitted to derive benefit from this *hamets*, for it was duly owned by the gentile throughout the holiday.

If an Israelite lent to a gentile on his hamets: In this scenario, *hamets* that originally belonged to a gentile is deposited with an Israelite to secure a loan over Passover. Such *hamets* is considered as if it had been owned by the Israelite during Passover, and it is indeed prohibited to consume or even derive benefit from it.

Hamets that is buried under something that has collapsed: And is therefore completely inaccessible for searching.

it is as if it has been eliminated, and one need not excavate simply for the purpose of eliminating *hamets*, even though it remains "with you, in all your borders" (Exodus 13:7); cf. 3:7 below for other circumstances regarding excavating something that has collapsed.

4 One who inadvertently[6] eats
terumah that is *hamets*
during Passover
pays the principal and one-fifth.
If he does so deliberately,
he is exempt from payment
and [even] from its value as kindling.

2:5–3:5   *Passover Foods: Obligatory and Permitted*

5 These are things by which a person fulfills one's obligation on Passover:
[*matsah* made from] wheat, barley, spelt, oats, and rye.
And one fulfills the obligation with *demai*,
and with first tithe

[6] K lacks "inadvertently."

2:4 *One who inadvertently eats terumah*: i.e., not knowing the food was *terumah*, even if knowing the food was *hamets*. When priestly dues (*terumah*) are inadvertently consumed by nonpriests, the punishment is to replace the amount of consumed food, adding one-fifth more (Leviticus 22:14; *Terumot* 6:1). Intentional consumption of priestly dues is expressly prohibited (Leviticus 22:10–13), and any violator must pay a monetary fine equal to the value of the consumed material, though without the added fifth (*Terumot* 7:1; *Bikkurim* 2:1).

terumah that is hamets during Passover: Any such priestly dues have no monetary value, since they are forbidden. Nevertheless, in the case of inadvertent consumption, *the principal* (the equivalent amount of food) and *one-fifth* can still be measured and repaid in kind.

If he does so deliberately: Knowing the food was *terumah*, whether or not he knows the food is *hamets*.

exempt from payment: Since *terumah* that is *hamets* has no monetary value, there can be no monetary fine.

kindling: Even inedible food, if stolen, could be considered to have a minimal value as fuel for a fire. But *hamets* has no value whatsoever during Passover.

2:5 From here until the end of this chapter additional laws concerning Passover food are delineated. While the prohibitions continue to mount, the text here and below begins to spend more time on those foods that can, and in some cases must, be consumed on Passover. According to Exodus 12:8, the meat of the Passover offering is to be consumed on *matsot* (unleavened loaves) and *merorim* (bitter herbs). This mishnah delineates rules concerning the production of *matsot* appropriate for fulfilling that command. The rules concerning *merorim* are discussed in the next mishnah.

wheat, barley, spelt, oats, and rye: These five grains, when mixed with water, leaven sufficiently to be considered *hamets*. These same grains are also liable to the dough offering (*hallah*; see *Hallah* 1:1–2), and are in these two important ways seen as the proper grains for baking bread, be it leavened or unleavened. Of course, general agricultural rules such as the requirement to tithe pertain as well.

demai: Or "uncertain produce"—grains which may or may not have been properly tithed. Such produce is generally considered prohibited until it has been properly tithed for certain, but because *demai* may be used to feed the poor (*Demai* 3:1), it may also be used for *matsah*, the "bread of affliction." See also *Eruvin* 3:2 and *Shabbat* 18:1.

first tithe from which terumah has been taken: Once the Levite has tithed his tithe (see Numbers 18:26), the rest can be eaten by anyone.

from which *terumah* has been taken,
and with second tithe,
and with consecrated offerings
that have been redeemed;
and priests [may do so] with *hallah* and *terumah*.
But not with *tevel*,
and not with first tithe
from which *terumah* has not been taken,
and not with second tithe
and consecrated offerings
that have not been redeemed.
Loaves for the Thanksgiving offering
and wafers for a *nazir*:
if he made them for himself,
one cannot fulfill the obligation with them;
if he made them for selling in the market,
one may fulfill the obligation with them.

6 And these are the vegetables by which a person fulfills one's obligation on Passover:
lettuce, chicory, pepperwort, snakeroot, and *maror*.
One fulfills the obligation with them whether fresh or dried,[7]
but not pickled, stewed, or boiled.

[7] **P** and printed editions agree here, "withered."

second tithe: this is normally produce set aside for use in Jerusalem (see Deuteronomy 14:22–26 and *Ma'aser Sheni*).

consecrated offerings: This is produce that has been dedicated for sacrifice or for some other use in the Temple.

that have been redeemed: Both second tithe and consecrated produce may be exchanged for money, which in turn can be brought to Jerusalem to purchase replacements. The produce that has been redeemed can be used for *matsah*.

priests [may do so] with hallah and terumah, since these are duly permitted to them.

But not with tevel: Grain that is known to be untithed is prohibited outright for any use, including as *matsah*. Simlarly, *tithe from which terumah has not been taken* is prohibited, even to the Levite, until *terumah* has been taken.

Loaves for the Thanksgiving offering: See Leviticus 7:12 and above, 1:5.

wafers for a nazir: See Numbers 6:15. Like the thanksgiving loaves, these wafers too were to be made as *matsot*. If a person produced such *matsot* with the definite intent of using them in the sacrificial ritual, they could not be used for Passover. If, however, they were made with the hope (but not the certainty) of their being used for this purpose by others who might purchase them, they could be used as *matsot* for Passover, for the seller's plans are insufficient to establish their ritual status.

2:6 As noted above, according to Exodus 12:8 the Passover sacrifice and its *matsot* are to be consumed with *merorim*—bitter herbs. This obligation can be fulfilled with the various bitter vegetables listed here.

maror: The Hebrew term is the generic designation for "bitter herbs"; most commentators see here a reference to some kind of dandelion.

whether fresh or dried, but not pickled, stewed, or boiled: The latter processes presumably involved too much liquid in preparation or altered the taste too much.

And they may be joined together
to constitute an olive's bulk.
And one fulfills the obligation with their stalks,
and with *demai*,
and with first tithe
from which *terumah* has been taken,
and with second tithe
and consecrated offerings that have been redeemed.

7 One may not soak bran for chickens,
but one may scald it.
A woman may not soak the bran
that she brings with her to the bathhouse,
but she may rub it dry on her skin.
A person may not chew grains of wheat
to put on his wound during Passover,
since they ferment.

8 One may not put flour into *haroset* or into mustard;
and if one did so
he must eat it immediately,
but R. Meir forbids [this].
One may not cook the Passover lamb in liquids
or in fruit juice,
but one may baste it
or dip it into them.
Water that has been used by a baker
must be poured out,
since it ferments.

And they may be joined together to constitute an olive's bulk: The obligation here—as in many places—is fulfilled provided the minimum measure of an olive's bulk is consumed. This olive's bulk can be met even by combining some or all of these vegetables together. Even the *stalks* of these vegetables may be used or combined into the minimum measure.

and with demai: As with the grain for *matsah* in the previous mishnah, the vegetables for bitter herbs must be tithed, though produce in the uncertain category of *demai* is once again permitted.

2:7 Having just mentioned some food-production methods (e.g. pickling) that use liquids, the present passage discusses other presumably common uses of grain products involving liquids.

soak bran: That was taken from any the five grains specified in 2:5 above. Doing so is forbidden, even to feed chickens or to use in the bathhouse, for soaked bran would become *hamets*, and it is forbidden to derive any benefit from it.

chew grains of wheat: Doing so long enough to produce a substance that could bind a wound would also produce *hamets*.

2:8 *One may not cook the Passover lamb in liquids or in fruit juice*: The Passover lamb is to be roasted and not cooked in liquids (Exodus 12:9, and see below, 7:1–2).

Water that has been used by a baker: Such water might itself ferment, and therefore cannot be used for another purpose on Passover.

Chapter Three

3 One removes these things on Passover:
Babylonian porridge, Median beer, Edomite vinegar, Egyptian barley beer, dyers' mixtures, cooks' starch flour, and scribes' paste.
R. Eliezer says:
Also women's cosmetics.
This is the general rule:
All that is made from [any kind of] grain
must be removed on Passover.
These are in the category of prohibition;
but these do not warrant extirpation.

2 Dough that is in the cracks of a trough—
if there is an olive's bulk in any one place,
one is obligated to eliminate it;
if not,
it is [considered] annulled by its smallness.
And so too in the matter of impurity:
if one would be particular about it,
it constitutes a partition;

3:1 This mishnah continues the discussion of the status of various grain–liquid mixtures on Passover.

One removes: It is not clear whether this term implies elimination or, as some interpreters prefer, a simpler process, perhaps involving removal from sight (cf. Exodus 13:7) by putting them away and not using them during the holiday. Some of the items listed, such as barley beer, would seem likely to become full-fledged *hamets*. Nevertheless, these items require only removal.

This is the general rule: All grain products must be removed, whether they constitute *hamets* or not.

but these do not warrant extirpation: This is the "cutting off" spoken of in Exodus 12:15, understood by the rabbis as a punishment carried out by God (see *Keritot*). The exemption from extirpation suggests indeed that this list is meant to include items that combine grain and liquid but are unlikely to become full-fledged *hamets*.

3:2 *Dough that is in the cracks of a trough*: Over the course of time the trough used by bakers for mixing dough with water develops cracks into which dough could seep.

olive's bulk: The same minimal amount that is sufficient for meeting various obligations (see 2:6 above) here constitutes the minimal amount that would require elimination.

annulled by its smallness: If less than an olive's bulk is caught in a crack, the *hamets* does not require elimination and is considered eliminated simply by its insignificance.

And so too in the matter of impurity: Where a similar ruling has been established.

if one would be particular about it, it constitutes a partition: This ruling appears in *Miqva'ot* 9:3–7 with regard to what may constitute a partition against the spread of impurity or an impediment to purification. Irrespective of minimum measures, any amount of dirt, dung, or other filth that one would wish to remove constitutes a "partition" against the spread of impurity or purification (cf. also *Oholot* 8:1ff.). By this logic, any amount of dough must be removed, even if it be less than an olive's amount, if the baker would be concerned to remove it from the trough.

and if one desires it to remain,
then it becomes like [part of] the trough.
Dough that is "mute"—
if what is similar has fermented,
it is forbidden.

   3 How does one separate *hallah*
in impurity[8]
on the Festival day?
R. Eliezer says:
She should not declare it [as *hallah*]
until it is baked.
R. Judah b. Betera says:[9]
She should toss it into cold water.
Said R. Joshua:
This is not the kind of leaven
about which we have been warned
against seeing and finding,
so she separates it and sets it aside until evening;
if it leavens it leavens.

[8] K, P: "impure *hallah*."   [9] K, P: "b. Betera says."

and if one desires it to remain: If the baker would have no interest in removing such amounts of dough from the cracks in any circumstance.

then it becomes like [part of] the trough: And therefore need not be removed. The comparison with the purity case suggests that the permission granted here applied only to what is below the minimum measure, but interpreters have also understood this ruling to permit the dough to remain, even if greater than an olive's amount.

"mute": Dough that has not yet showed signs of fermentation. If dough that was mixed with a similar amount of water at the same time has already fermented, this dough must be removed as well.

3:3 *How does one separate…on the Festival day?* Extending from the previous juxtaposition of Passover and purity, the text now addresses a somewhat convoluted yet intriguingly problematic scenario: the separation of *hallah* (the dough offering; Numbers 15:17–21, and see *Hallah*) from impure dough on the Festival day of Passover. Because the dough is impure, and a priest cannot consume defiled *hallah*, it is prohibited to separate *hallah* from the dough; the priestly portion would have to be burnt, and burning is prohibited on the Festival. Since the priest can never eat it, nor can anyone else eat the baked dough before *hallah* is taken, it cannot be baked and consumed by anyone at all, for it is not permitted to cook on the Festival day what cannot be consumed (see *Betsah* 5:2, also 6:1–2 below). How can this dough be saved from going to waste?

She should not declare it [as hallah] until it is baked: The baking will prevent the dough from becoming *hamets*, and since the *hallah* will be separated after the baking, the baking is permitted on the Festival day. The priestly portion can be burnt after the Festival day, while the rest can be eaten at once.

She should toss it into cold water: So as to prevent its becoming *hamets*.

This is not the kind of leaven: R. Joshua does not propose a solution, but suggests rather that the *hallah* imagined in this scenario is not included in the general category of *hamets* that must be removed from the house; it is the priest's property, not the homeowner's. The priestly portion can therefore simply be set aside, without worrying about it leavening, and destroyed later on if it in fact becomes leavened.

seeing and finding: See Exodus 13:7 ("seeing") and 12:19 ("finding").

4 Rabban Gamaliel says:
Three women may knead dough at one time
and bake it one after the other in a single oven;
and the Sages say:
Three women may work with the dough:
one kneads, one rolls, one bakes.
R. Aqiva says:
Not all women,
not all wood,
and not all ovens are equal.
This is the general rule:
If the dough swells,
she should wipe[10] it with cold water.

5 Partly leavened dough must be burned,
and one who eats it
is exempt.
Fully leavened dough must be burned,
and one who eats it
is liable to punishment by extirpation.[11]
What is partly leavened dough?
[Dough with streaks] like locust antennae.
Fully leavened dough?
Its cracks are jumbled together—
the words of R. Judah.
The Sages say:
This and that:
one who eats it is liable to extirpation.[12]
And what is partly leavened dough?
Any whose surface[13] has become pale,
like a person whose hair stands straight.

[10] Lit. "polish" or perhaps "sharpen." [11] K, P: "liable for capital punishment."
[12] K, P: "liable for capital punishment." [13] Lit. "face."

3:4 *one after the other*: Even though the three kneaded the dough simultaneously, they may bake it in sequence, without fear that the second or third woman's dough will leaven while she waits.

Three women may work with the dough: In order to prevent the possibility that the dough leavens, the Sages suggest a division of labor, so that each woman's dough is rolled and then baked immediately after it is kneaded.

wipe it with cold water: Cold water can be applied to prevent leavening.

3:5 *partly leavened dough*: Heb. *si'ur*.

exempt: According to R. Judah partly leavened dough (*si'ur*) may not be consumed, but it is not treated as absolute *hamets* so one who eats it is exempt. According to the printed editions, R. Judah exempts those who eat such from extirpation (see 3:1 above). According to the manuscripts, R. Judah exempts those who eat such from capital punishment.

fully leavened dough: Heb. *siduq*.

This and that: The two types of dough just mentioned.

3:6–8 The Elimination of Leaven: The Sabbath and Last-Minute Concerns

6 When the fourteenth falls on a Sabbath,
one eliminates all [*hamets*] before the Sabbath—
the words of R. Meir.
And the Sages say:
At their time.
R. Eleazar b. Zadok[14] says:
Terumah before Sabbath,
nonsacral food at its time.

7 One on his way to slaughter the Passover,
or to circumcise his son,
or to eat the betrothal meal at his in-laws' house,
who remembers that he [still] has *hamets* in his own house—
if he is able to turn back to eliminate it
and return to his commanded act,
he should turn back and eliminate it;
and if not,
he should annul it in his heart.

---

[14] **K:** "b. Rabbi Zadok."

3:6 Having completed the discussion concerning *hamets* and related grain–liquid mixtures, the Mishnah returns, albeit briefly, to its chronological review of the rituals of Passover, and resumes consideration of the hours of elimination that occur on the fourteenth of Nisan.

When the fourteenth falls on a Sabbath: Because burning anything is prohibited on the Sabbath, R. Meir proposed that the elimination of *hamets* take place on the previous day. R. Meir's position here may well be aligned with R. Judah's position in 2:1 above, that elimination can only be done by burning. The Sages, in agreement with their view on the matter of burning, propose that the elimination can take place on the fourteenth, even on a Sabbath, but presumably by means other than burning. The *hamets* can also be consumed or fed to animals at least during the morning of the Sabbath, thereby reducing the need for elimination by other means. The times referred to here are those delineated at 1:4 above.

Terumah before Sabbath: R. Eliezer points out that *terumah* that is *hamets* ought to be burned before the Sabbath starts, since it cannot be fed to animals or eaten by nonpriests over the Sabbath.

3:7 *slaughter the Passover…circumcise his son*: The Passover sacrifice and circumcision are the only two positive commandments which are punishable by extirpation upon failure to perform them (*Keritot* 1:1).

or to eat the betrothal meal: Although missing such a meal would not result in deadly divine punishment, the rabbis here clearly acknowledge the importance of such an event, and the dangers that could follow upon any perceived slight to the groom's in-laws.

if not, he should annul it in his heart: The commentators understand this to mean that a person who cannot return home for the reasons just listed should declare to himself that whatever *hamets* may remain is like the dust of the earth. The Jewish tradition now mandates that such a formula of annulment be recited at the time of searching for leaven (on the eve of the fourteenth), and at the time of its elimination (on the day of the fourteenth).

[One on his way] to save someone from invaders,
or from a flood,
or from brigands,
or from a fire,
or from a collapsed building—
he should annul it in his heart.
But [if he was on his way] to celebrate the Sabbath at a place of his choosing,
he must turn back at once.

8 And likewise, one who left Jerusalem
and remembered
that he still possesses sanctified meat—
if he passed Mount Scopus,
he burns it where he is;
and if not,
he turns back and burns it before the *birah*,
from the wood of the woodpile.
And for how much do they turn back?
R. Meir says:
[For] this and for that,
an egg's bulk.[15]
R. Judah says:
[For] this and that,
an olive's bulk.[16]
The Sages say:
Sanctified meat,
for an olive's bulk;
leaven,
for an egg's bulk.

---

[15] In both **K** and **P**, the main text reads "olive's bulk," but each was subsequently corrected; other manuscripts and the printed editions agree with the corrected reading.

[16] In both **K** and **P**, the main text reads "an egg's bulk," but each was subsequently corrected; other manuscripts and the printed editions agree with the corrected reading.

---

to save someone from invaders: The Mishnah continues to indicate a number of life-threatening situations when one should annul whatever *hamets* remains, instead of turning back. These cases represent various degrees of emergency, so the option of turning back is not even raised.

to celebrate Sabbath at a place of his choosing: There is no reason why the person cannot simply return home, eliminate the remaining *hamets*, and celebrate the Sabbath (and Passover) in or near his home. Some commentators understand "Sabbath" here as actually meaning the Festival itself; this is in keeping with the traditional rabbinic interpretation of Leviticus 23:15–16.

3:8 *one who left Jerusalem and remembered that he still possesses sanctified meat*: This rule has no connection to Passover, but was included because it deals with a situation resembling that in 3:7.

Mount Scopus: Quite possibly, the still so-named high mountain east of Jerusalem's Roman-era Old City is meant. But the expression here is likely figurative, referring to the approximate distance from the Temple one has traveled, in whatever direction. If one has traveled beyond the mountains around Jerusalem in any direction—so that one can no longer see the Temple—he need not turn back.

and burns it: Sacrificial meat that has been taken out of Jerusalem may no longer be eaten. See *Zevahim* 5:6-8.

before the birah, from the wood of the woodpile: Sages in the Talmud dispute whether *birah* refers to the entire Temple or to a place within it. See also Nehemiah 2:8 and Josephus, *Antiquities* 15.403.

this and that: Forgotten leaven and forgotten sanctified meat.

Chapter Four

4:1–9   *Local Customs*

4 [In a] place
where it has been customary
on Passover Eves[17]
to perform work
until midday,
one may do so.
[In a] place
where it has been customary
not to do so,
one may not do so.
One who goes
from a place
where they work
to a place
where they do not work,
or from a place
where they do not work
to a place where they do—
one places on himself
the stringencies of the place that he left
and the stringencies of the place where he went.
And a person should not differ,
because of conflict.[18]

[17] Lit. "Eves of Passovers."   [18] K, P: "conflicts."

4:1 *work*: In certain contexts this term designates the various forms of labor prohibited on Sabbaths and Festival days (see *Shabbat* 7:2 and 6:1–2 below), but here it probably refers to one's ordinary weekday activities. It was expected that one would cease from such work on the fourteenth of Nisan at noon in order to prepare for the impending festival, but there were locations where the custom was to spend the entire day in such preparation. Until noon it was permitted to do such work in places where this custom did not hold.

Passover Eves: On the plurals in this expression here and below—as well as in the title of this tractate—see the introduction.

One who goes from a place: Local customs are to be respected by visitors, but visitors do not necessarily get to take advantage of local leniencies. One should also not violate one's own local custom, even when traveling.

stringencies of the place: By requiring local stringencies as well as the stringencies of one's own place, the hope is to avoid any offense by doing something permitted where it is considered prohibited.

And a person should not differ, because of conflict: The precise meaning of this passage is unclear. The Talmud disputes whether this is understood to permit work for one who has arrived at place where work is customarily performed or rather to underscore the seriousness of following local stringencies if one arrived at a place where work is customarily not performed. The general sentiment, however, remains clear: differing from a local custom can lead to conflict, and in such situations, the local custom is to take precedence over one's own.

2 In the same way:
one who brings Seventh-Year produce
from a place
where it is finished
to a place
where it is not finished,
or from a place
where it is not finished
to a place where it is finished—
he is obligated to eliminate it.
R. Judah says:
One says to him:[19]
You too,
go and get for yourself.
    3 [In a] place
where it has been customary
to sell small cattle to gentiles,
one may sell;
[in a] place
where it has not been customary
to sell, one may not sell.
And in every place,
one may not sell them large cattle, calves, or foals,
whole or maimed.
R. Judah permits maimed.
Ben Betera permits a horse.

[19] K, P lack "One says to him."

4:2 *In the same way*: The Mishnah now stays with the theme of local customs; it will return to Passover customs below.

Seventh-Year produce: It is prohibited to farm or deal in farmed produce during the Seventh Year (see Leviticus 25:1–7, also *Shevi'it*). It is, however, permitted to consume what grows naturally without farming, such as fruit from trees.

where it is finished: Fruit will become "finished" (that is, none will be found on local trees or animals will have eaten what grew naturally in the fields) in some places sooner than in others.

eliminate it: Once no fruit is naturally available in the fields, one may not store at home any more than is needed for one's own needs. The rest must be "eliminated," that is, placed outside where anyone can take it.

One says to him: As noted, this phrase is missing in the manuscripts, and indeed it makes no sense. Without the phrase, the following words can be understood as the response of someone who has been told to "eliminate" the produce he has brought; he can tell his challengers that they can go and get their own from the place where he got his. It may be that the single word "he [can] say …" was lost as the duplicate of "R. Judah says."

4:3 This mishnah also appears, verbatim, in *Avodah Zarah* 1:6, and is further explained there.

sell small cattle to gentiles: The Mishnah applies various restrictions on selling items to gentiles, lest they be used for idolatry or, in the case of animals, lest they be used for work on Sabbath. Small cattle (chiefly sheep and goats) are typically not used for labor, so the Sabbath-related concerns (which are more fully explained in the annotations to *Avodah Zarah* 1:6) do not pertain.

4 [In a] place where it has been customary
to eat roasted [meat] on Passover night,[20]
one may eat it.
[In a] place where it has been customary
not to eat it,
one may not eat it.
[In a] place where it has been customary
to light the lamp
for the night[21] of the Day of Atonement,
one lights;
[in a] place where it has been customary not to light,
one does not light.
And one does light in synagogues and in houses of learning and in dark alleys and for[22] sick persons.

5 In a place where it has been customary
to do work on the ninth of Av,
one may do so;
in a place where it has been customary
not to do work,
one may not do so.
And in every place,
the scholars are idle.
Rabban Simeon b. Gamaliel says:
A man should always make himself out
to be a scholar.[23]

[20] Lit. "nights of Passovers." [21] Lit. "nights." [22] Lit. "over."
[23] K, P: "All men should make themselves out to be scholars."

4:4 *roasted [meat]*: The Passover sacrifice was consumed roasted (Exodus 12:9; below, 7:1–2), but customs differed regarding nonsacrificial meats consumed that evening. Some avoided roasted meats, to mark the roasted sacrifice as distinctive. Others roasted any and all meat consumed that night. One of the original three questions asked at the Passover feast presumes the custom of eating only roasted meat on Passover (10:4 below).

light the lamp: Doing so was customary on the Sabbath (*Shabbat* 2:1), and became customary on holidays as well. According to some commentators, one concern underlying the present rule is that the light would allow a husband to see his wife at night, and be thereby tempt him to violate the prohibition against sexual contact on the Day of Atonement (see *Yoma* 8:1).

And one does light in synagogues…sick persons: In places where light would be needed for communal use or for safety, it is always permitted to light.

4:5 *the ninth of Av*: The fast day observed in commemoration of the destructions of the two temples and other tragedies (*Ta'anit* 4:6). Although work is not technically prohibited on this day, it became customary in some locales to abstain.

scholars: Lit. "disciples of the Sages" or "wise students," but used at times, and here too, to refer to the students and Sages of the rabbinic academies.

And the Sages say:
In Judaea,
they would do work
on Passover Eves[24]
until midday,
and in the Galilee they would not do anything at all.
And the night:
the House of Shammai forbid
and the House of Hillel permit
until sunrise.

6 R. Meir says:
All work that he began
before the fourteenth
he may finish
on the fourteenth;
but he may not begin something
on the fourteenth,
even if he could finish it.
And the Sages say:
Three kinds of artisans do their work
on Passover Eves[25]
until midday,[26]
and these are they:
tailors, barbers, launderers.
R. Yose b. Judah says:
Even cobblers.

7 One may set up coops for chickens
on the fourteenth,
and one may return an escaped hen to her place;
and if she died
one may place another in her stead.

[24] Lit. "Eves of Passovers."   [25] Lit. "Eves of Passovers."   [26] K, P lack "until mid-day."

And the Sages say: The Mishnah now returns to the issue that began this series in 4:1 above, namely local customs regarding working on the fourteenth of Nisan. We are now told—apparently in disagreement with the information provided in 4:1 above—that there ought not to have been many variations in local customs at all: the general prohibition of work pertained in the Galilee all day, and in Judaea, work ceased at noon. The House of Shammai even go as far as prohibiting work in the Galilee during the previous night.

4:6 *And the Sages say*: Because the work done by these artisans would enhance the holiday for their customers, these sorts of work may be done.

4:7 *coops for chickens*: The word translated "coops" is elsewhere translated "dovecotes." The reference to "chickens" here is ambiguous, and therefore the meaning of this passage is disputed. According to some commentators, "chickens" means "hens," in which case the Mishnah permits setting unhatched eggs and nesting material under hens so that the chicks will emerge safely and properly. According to another interpretation, "chickens" means "chicks," and the Mishnah permits setting up nesting material for newly born chicks.

One may sweep under the legs of cattle
on the fourteenth,
and during the holiday
one may move [the dung] to the sides.
One may bring utensils to
or retrieve them
from the craftsman,
even if they are not for the purpose of the holiday.

8 The men of Jericho did six things:
for three they were rebuked,
and for three they were not.
And these are they
for which they were not rebuked:
they grafted palms the entire day,
they wrapped the *Shema*,
they reaped and stacked
before the *omer*—
and they did not rebuke them.
And these are they
for which they were rebuked:
they permitted caprifigs from consecrated [trees],
they would eat on the Sabbath fruit from under fallen leaves,
and they would give *pe'ah* from vegetables—
and the Sages rebuked them.

may sweep under the legs of cattle on the fourteenth: Although this is not permitted on the holiday, it may be done before, in order to enhance the holiday. During the middle days of the holiday one may move the droppings to the side but not remove them to the dungheap.

One may bring utensils: It is prohibited to bring such once the holiday begins (see *Mo'ed Qatan* 2:4), but this too may be done on the fourteenth.

4:8 Only the first custom listed here has anything to do with Passover.

they grafted palms the entire day, of the fourteenth of Nisan, even after midday, when it is otherwise agreed that work should cease (see 4.1).

wrapped the Shema: it is not clear which custom pertaining to the *Shema* is meant here. Perhaps they did not recite the traditional doxology—"blessed be the honored name…"—following the recitation of Deuteronomy 6:4 ("Hear, O Israel…").

reaped and stacked before the omer: It is forbidden to reap the new crop each spring until a ceremonial sheaf (*omer*) has been brought to the Temple (Leviticus 23:10–16), but the men of Jericho reaped and stacked what they reaped.

caprifigs from consecrated [trees]: The men of Jericho reasoned that because these fruits were not customarily eaten, the dedication of such trees to the Temple applied to the trees' trunks, and did not place any restriction on their fruits. Caprifigs are wild figs whose male flowers are used to pollinate cultivated trees.

fruit from under fallen leaves: It being unknown whether the fruit had fallen before or during the Sabbath, the men of Jericho ate such fruit nevertheless.

give pe'ah: That is, they left the corner of the fields for the poor, following Leviticus 19:9–10 (see *Pe'ah*).

from vegetables: The Sages considered vegetables exempt from *pe'ah* but liable to tithe (see *Pe'ah* 1:4, 6). The men of Jericho, however, left the corner of such fields to the poor, thereby wrongly exempting them from tithe.

9 King Hezekiah did six things;[27]
on three they agreed with him,
and on three they did not agree.
He dragged the bones of his father on a bier of ropes,
and they agreed;
he ground the bronze serpent,
and they agreed;
he hid the book of healing,
and they agreed.
On three they did not agree:
he cut down the doors of the Temple
and sent them to the King of Assyria,
and they did not agree;
he sealed the waters of the upper Gihon,
and they did not agree;
he intercalated Nisan in Nisan,
and they did not agree.

[27] This entire mishnah is lacking in both **K** and **P**. See annotations.

4:9 *Hezekiah*: This King of Judah was known for his cultic reforms as well as his celebration of Passover (on the latter see 2 Chronicles 30). This mishnah is lacking in the best manuscripts. Medieval commentators recognized that the passage derived originally from the Talmud, where it immediately follows the previous mishnah, albeit as the beginning of the *Gemara*. It was later mistaken for a continuation of the previous passage, making its way into the printed editions.

He dragged the bones of his father: According to 2 Chronicles 28:27 (compare 2 Kings 16:20), Hezekiah's father King Ahaz—who is numbered among Judah's sinful rulers—was not buried in the royal tomb, presumably an act of his son and successor.

he ground the bronze serpent: made by Moses at God's request (Numbers 21:8–9), to avert a plague of snakes. This was destroyed by Hezekiah during his cultic reform (2 Kings 18:4).

he hid the book of healing: The biblical accounts of Hezekiah's illness and recovery are extensive (2 Kings 20:1–11; Isaiah 38:1–22; 2 Chronicles 32:24), but nothing is said in the biblical record about such a book of healing.

he cut down the doors of the Temple: In an unsuccessful attempt to avert siege by Sennacherib (see 2 Kings 18:16).

he sealed the waters of the upper Gihon: Presumably in preparation for siege (see 2 Chronicles 32:3–8, 30). Many archaeologists and historians identify this account with what is known today as Hezekiah's tunnel in Jerusalem.

he intercalated Nisan in Nisan: According to 2 Chronicles 30:2–3, Hezekiah celebrated Passover in the second month, because the people and priests were insufficiently prepared for the holiday. This event—which sounds more like a Second Passover (see chapter 9 below)—was understood by the rabbis as the addition to the calendar of a second Nisan, instead of a second Adar, as is customary in the Jewish tradition to this day (see *Megillah* 1:4, *Eduyot* 7:7).

Chapter Five

5:1–10 *The Passover Sacrifice*

5 The continual offering is slaughtered
halfway into the eighth hour,
and it is offered
halfway into the ninth hour.
but on Passover Eves[28] it was slaughtered
halfway into the seventh hour,
and offered
halfway into the eighth hour,
whether it was a weekday or a Sabbath.
If Passover Eve
fell on the eve of Sabbath,
it was slaughtered
halfway into the sixth hour,
and offered
halfway into the seventh hour,
and the Passover [offering] after that.

2 The Passover [offering] that was slaughtered
not in its name,
or [whose blood] was collected, carried, and sprinkled
not in its name,
or in its name and not in its name,

---

[28] Lit. "Eves of Passovers." **K, P**: "Eve of Passovers." See annotations.

5:1 *The continual offering*: The afternoon daily sacrifice (see Numbers 28:3–5, and *Tamid*). It was generally customary for the afternoon daily sacrifice to be the last sacrifice of the day, but on the eve of Passover the continual offering was offered earlier, to allow plenty of time for slaughtering the numerous Passover sacrifices while it was still day.

eighth hour: On the reckoning of time, see 1:4 above.

but on Passover Eves: On the plural here and elsewhere, see the introduction. Presumably the ruling here would apply to the Second Passover as well. The reading in the manuscripts (lit. "Eve of Passovers") is strictly ungrammatical.

5:2 Each of four significant aspects of the Passover sacrificial ritual must be performed with the precise intention of doing so for the sake of Passover: the slaughter of the sacrifice, the collecting of the blood from the slaughtered animal, the carrying of the blood from the site of slaughter to the altar, and the sprinkling of the sacrificial blood on the altar.

not in its name: If during the sequence of necessary actions the person offering the sacrifice intended even one act for an offering other than the Passover (e.g. the offering of well-being), the sacrifice is rendered *invalid*: unfit from the moment of the incorrect intention for consumption as a Passover sacrifice or any other use. Sacrifices rendered invalid would be burned (see below, 8:2; 9:9). See *Zevahim* 1:1–4 for further laws concerning purposeful slaughter.

or not in its name and then in its name,
is invalid.
How in its name and not in its name?
[First] in the name of Passover
and [then] in the name of an offering of well-being;
How not in its name and then in its name?
[First] in the name of an offering of well-being
and [then] in the name of a Passover [offering].

3 If he slaughtered it for those who cannot eat of it
or for those not designated among those who should eat it,
or for uncircumcised men or impure people,
it is invalid.
For those that can eat of it and those who cannot eat of it,
for those designated for it and those not designated for it,
for the circumcised and uncircumcised,
for the impure and the pure,
it is valid.
If he slaughtered it before midday,
it is invalid,
for it is said,
between the evenings.
If he slaughtered it before the continual offering,
it is valid,
provided that someone stirs its blood
until the blood of the continual offering is sprinkled;
but if it was sprinkled before,
it is valid.

4 One who slaughters his Passover sacrifice over *hamets*
violates a negative commandment.

5:3 *for those who cannot eat of it*: Certain people such as the ill or elderly, may not be able to eat even an olive's bulk of the Passover sacrifice. If the sacrifice is offered for them alone, it is invalid. See further 8:6 below.

for those not designated: Exodus 12:4–5 imagines groups of families coming together in order to share the Passover feast, to ensure that the Passover sacrifice can be consumed in its entirety (12:10). The Mishnah presumes that such groups are to be established in advance, and that the Passover offering must be slaughtered for its designated group. If an animal is slaughtered only for those not designated, the sacrifice is invalid.

uncircumcised: Exodus 12:43 prohibits foreigners from eating the Passover, and 12:48 bans the uncircumcised; the latter obviously includes uncircumcised Israelites, since foreigners are already banned. See 8:8 below with respect to proselytes.

before midday: The Sages find a biblical mandate that the Passover sacrifice is to take place in the afternoon in the words *between the evenings* (Exodus 12:6).

someone stirs its blood: If the blood becomes congealed, it cannot be poured on the altar as required. This is also done in other similar situations (*Yoma* 4:3).

5:4 *over hamets*: Before he or those included within his group have eliminated *hamets* from their households (see 3:7–8 above).

a negative commandment: See Exodus 23:18 and 34:25.

R. Judah says:
The continual offering too.
R. Simeon says:
The Passover sacrifice on the fourteenth—
in its name,
he is liable;
and if not in its name,
he is exempt.
And all other sacrifices—
whether in their names
or not in their names,
he is exempt.
And during the holiday—
in its name,
he is exempt,
not in its name,
he is liable;
and all other sacrifices,
whether in their names
or not in their names,
he is liable,
except for the purgation offering
that he slaughtered not in its name.

5 The Passover sacrifice is slaughtered in three [successive] cohorts,
as it is said:
And they shall slaughter it, the entire assembly of the congregation of Israel:

R. Judah: In his opinion the afternoon continual offering of the fourteenth of Nisan is covered by the same prohibition. See 1:4–5 above for R. Judah's stringent view regarding the timing of the prohibition of leaven.

and if not in its name, he is exempt: Such a sacrifice is declared invalid in the previous mishnah. If he has not offered a valid Passover at all, he cannot have violated the prohibition of leaven connected with it.

And all other sacrifices: If offered on the fourteenth over *hamets*, sacrifices other than the Passover and daily offerings do not violate the prohibition of Exodus 34:25.

And during the holiday: Once the holiday has begun the situation is different. A Passover sacrifice offered at the wrong time is therefore invalid; as above, it cannot constitute a violation of the negative commandment in question.

not in its name, he is liable: A Passover sacrifice offered not in its name during the holiday is treated like an ordinary well-being sacrifice (*shelamim*), and is valid. As with almost any other sacrifices offered on *hamets* during the holiday, the negative command has been violated and he is liable to the appropriate penalty for his violation; see further on 6:5 below.

except for the purgation offering that he slaughtered not in its name: A sin-offering must always be offered "in its name"; see *Zevahim* 1:1.

5:5 *three [successive] cohorts*: The Mishnah describes the rabbis' memory (or imagination) of the requisite control of the large crowds that assembled for the festival. The division of the people into three groups is exegetically based, albeit loosely, on the quoted passage.

And they shall slaughter: Exodus 12:6.

"assembly," "congregation," and "Israel."
The first cohort entered:
when the courtyard was full,
they locked the doors to the court.
They blew [a *shofar*]:
sustained, staccato, sustained.
The priests stand in rows,
and in their hands are bowls of silver and gold;
one row entirely silver,
one row entirely gold.
They were not mixed together.
And the bowls did not have bases,
lest they put them down
and the blood congeal.

6 An Israelite slaughtered,
and the priest collected.
He [would] give it to his fellow,
and his fellow to his fellow;
he would receive the full
and pass back the empty.
The priest closest to the altar
sprinkles it in one throw
against the base [of the altar].

7 The first cohort departed,
and the second cohort entered.
The second departed,
and the third entered.
Like the process for the first,
such was the process
for the second and the third.
They recited *Hallel*;
if they completed it,
they repeated it.

bases: Bowls with bases, legs, or stands could be put down without spilling their contents; but if priests let blood rest in such bowls, the blood can more readily congeal.

5:6 *An Israelite slaughtered*: The Passover may be slaughtered by an Israelite, as is the case for sacrifices in general (*Zevahim* 3:1). In this case a representative from each group slaughtered the Passover for the group.

the priest collected the blood; this must be done by a priest (*Zevahim* 2:1).

He [would] give it to his fellow: To prevent too many priests from running back and forth with bowls full of blood, the Mishnah records the practice of passing bowls by lines of priests from the places of slaughter to the altar.

5:7 *They recited*: It was customary for the Levites to sing in the Temple (see *Tamid* 7:4).

Hallel: The rabbinic name for a section of the book of Psalms (113–118) that was customarily recited on holidays. It took its name from the frequency with which terms of praise (e.g. Hallelujah) appear. The collection pertains to Passover in particular, as Psalm 114 begins with a reference to the Exodus from Egypt.

And if they had repeated it,
they recited it a third time,
even though they never recited it a third time.
R. Judah says:
Never during the time of the third cohort
did they reach *I loved the Lord because he heard my voice*,
because its people were few.

8 Like the process on a weekday,
such was the process on the Sabbath,
except that the priests washed out the Court,
against the Sages' wishes.
R. Judah says:
[A priest] would fill a cup
with the blood from the mixture;
he sprinkled it with one throw
against the altar;
but the Sages did not agree with him.

9 How [would] they hang up and flay?
Iron hooks were fastened to the walls and columns,
from which they would hang and flay.
And [for] anyone who did not have a place to hang and flay,
there were thin, smooth staves there,
and he could place [one] on his [own] shoulder
and on his fellow's shoulder,
and hang and flay.
R. Eliezer says:
If the fourteenth fell on a Sabbath,
he would rest his hand on his fellow's shoulder,
and his fellow's hand on his shoulder,
and hang and flay.

I loved the Lord: Psalm 116:1. The recitation of Hallel for the third group never made it more than halfway through even the first reading.

5:8 *on the Sabbath*: Various Temple practices override the Sabbath (see *Temurah* 2:1), and the Passover was one of these (see 6:1 below).

except that the priests washed out the Court: The Sages would have preferred that they not do what could have waited until after the Sabbath.

[A priest] would fill a cup with the blood from the mixture: Collected from the floor of the Court, when cleaning it, whether on Sabbath or weekday.

he sprinkled it: If by chance all of the blood of a single sacrifice had been spilled on the ground, this cup would include at least a drop of that blood, thereby validating this sacrifice. The Sages, however, reject R. Judah's report.

5:9 *hang up*: The carcass of the Passover sacrifice. Cf. *Middot* 3:5; *Tamid* 3:5.

he would rest his hand: If the two placed their arms on each other's shoulders, they could create a human frame on which to hang the carcass. Doing so would prevent having to use the staves on the Sabbath.

10 He tore it open and took out the indicated portions,
he put them²⁹ on a tray
and [a priest] burned them on the altar.
The first cohort departed
and sat on the Temple Mount;
the second on the ledge and the third stood³⁰ in its place.
When it became dark,
they went out
and roasted their Passovers.

Chapter Six

6:1–6 *The Passover on Sabbath*

6 These are the aspects of Passover
that override the Sabbath:
its slaughter,
and the sprinkling of its blood,
and the cleaning of its entrails,
and the burning of its fat;
but its roasting
and the rinsing of the entrails
do not override the Sabbath.

---

²⁹ Lit. "it."   ³⁰ **K, P** lack "stood."

5:10 *indicated portions*: The innards, organs, and fats that would be burned on the altar (*Yoma* 6:7). The Hebrew term for these is *emurim*, lit. "spoken for."

first cohort: Of the three mentioned in 5:5 above.

departed: From the Temple Court. Upon completing the slaughter of the sacrifice, the first group was directed outside the Temple structure to the Temple Mount. As implied in the last sentence of this mishnah, the rules specified here speak still of a fourteenth of Nisan that is also a Sabbath, when it would be necessary for all three groups to remain until it is dark and the Sabbath has ended. Otherwise each person could take his offering at once and return to his group and begin roasting.

ledge: Heb. *heyl*. A space ten cubits wide, between the Temple structure and the Temple Mount. See *Middot* 2:3.

in its place: In the Temple Court, where their Passovers are slaughtered.

When it became dark: Upon the conclusion of the Sabbath, those aspects of Passover that do not override the Sabbath—such as its roasting, as explained in the next mishnah—can take place.

6:1 The Passover sacrifice itself overrides the Sabbath because it must be performed "at its time" (Numbers 9:3; that is, on the fourteenth). But those aspects of the Passover service that can safely wait until the Sabbath has ended or that can be performed before the Sabbath has begun do not override the Sabbath, and are to be performed afterwards or in advance. See also *Shabbat* 19:1.

Carrying it
and bringing it beyond the boundary limit
and cutting off its wart
do not override the Sabbath.
R. Eliezer says:
They do override.

2 [31]Said R. Eliezer:
And is it not a matter of logic?[32]
If slaughter,
which is in the category of forbidden work,
overrides the Sabbath,
shall these matters,
which are in the category of *shevut*,
not override the Sabbath?
R. Joshua said to him:
Let the Festival day prove the case,
for they permitted
what is in the category of forbidden work
but prohibited
what is in the category of *shevut*.
R. Eliezer said to him:
What is this, Joshua?

---

[31] This very lengthy passage is subdivided into five numbered passages in **K** and into four in **P**.

[32] **K, P** lack "And is it not a matter of logic?"

Carrying it: This can easily be done beforehand.

cutting off its wart: Warts invalidate sacrifices (Leviticus 22:22). If these can be removed then the sacrifice can proceed, but this must be done before the Sabbath.

6:2 In a dialectical-exegetical style more typical of midrash, R. Eliezer defends his opinion at the end of 6:1, arguing first with R. Joshua and then with R. Aqiva. The latter successfully defends (and, in turn, clarifies) the Sages' position articulated in 6:1.

And is it not a matter of logic? R. Eliezer argues *a fortiori*.

of forbidden work: Slaughter is included among the thirty-nine major categories of work normally expressly prohibited on the Sabbath (*Shabbat* 7:2); yet sacrificial slaughter is permitted on the Sabbath.

these matters: The ones prohibited by the Sages in the previous mishnah.

the category of shevut: Labors in this category are technically permitted on Sabbath according to the Torah, but prohibited by the rabbis in order to protect the integrity of Sabbath rest (see *Shabbat* 10:6). R. Eliezer argues: if what is prohibited in general by the Torah itself is permitted for Passover on Sabbath, should not those acts prohibited only by the rabbis be permitted for Passover on Sabbath?

Festival day: R. Joshua offers a comparison with the Festival day, attempting to show that R. Eliezer's logic does not work. Cooking is a form of work that is prohibited on Sabbath (*Shabbat* 7:2); yet it is permitted on holidays, even though activities in the category of *shevut* remain prohibited (*Betsah* 5:2). Therefore, R. Joshua argues, the permission to slaughter the Passover on the Sabbath does not logically entail permission to perform other Passover-related activities in the category of *shevut*: these would remain prohibited on the Sabbath, just as they remain prohibited even on a Festival day when cooking is nevertheless allowed.

What proof does a voluntary act
hold for a commanded act?
R. Aqiva answered and said:
Sprinkling shall prove it,
for it is commanded,
in the category of *shevut*,
and it does not override the Sabbath.
Even you should not be surprised about these,
that even though they are commanded
and under the category of *shevut*,
that they do not override the Sabbath.
R. Eliezer said to him:
And I could argue on this too:
if slaughter,
which is in the category of forbidden work,
overrides the Sabbath,
[with] sprinkling,
which is in the category of *shevut*,
is it not logical
that it should override the Sabbath?
R. Aqiva said to him:
Or the opposite!
If sprinkling,
which is in the category of *shevut*,
does not override the Sabbath,
slaughter,
which is in the category of forbidden work,
is it not logical
that it should not override the Sabbath?
R. Eliezer said to him:

What proof does a voluntary act hold for a commanded act? While cooking on a holiday is permitted, it is not commanded (one may eat cold food, or food cooked before the holiday). R. Eliezer here counters R. Joshua's logic by observing that the slaughter of the Passover overrides the Sabbath precisely because it is a commanded act that must be done at its time; so too, therefore, the other acts relating to Passover, even those in the category of *shevut* delineated in 6:1 above, should be permitted, for they relate to the commanded performance of the Passover sacrifice.

Sprinkling: Of the potion made from the ashes of the red heifer (Numbers 19:1–13). This is to be done for all those defiled by contact with a corpse, on the third and seventh days after their defilement (19:12). R. Aqiva points out, in argument with R. Eliezer, that this too is a commanded act, yet it is one that the rabbis prohibited on the Sabbath, even though the actions involved are in the category of *shevut*. Therefore, if a person's mandated seventh-day sprinkling fell on the fourteenth of Nisan that was also a Sabbath, the sprinkling would nevertheless not be performed, even though the sprinkling is commanded. Such a person would remain impure until after the start of the holiday, and would perform Second Passover (see below).

on this too: In response to R. Aqiva, R. Eliezer attempts to prove, by his logic, that the sprinkling on the seventh day, which is normally prohibited by virtue of being in the category of *shevut*, should be performed on the Sabbath of the fourteenth of Nisan, just as the slaughtering of Passover is permitted.

slaughter…that it should not override the Sabbath? R. Aqiva argues rhetorically, demonstrating that R. Eliezer's logic could be used to prohibit slaughtering the Passover on the fourteenth of Nisan if it fell on the Sabbath.

Aqiva!
You have overturned what is written in the Torah:
between the evenings...at its time:
whether on a weekday
or on the Sabbath!
He said to him:
Rabbi,[33] bring me a fixed time for these
like the fixed time for the slaughtering.
R. Aqiva stated the general rule:
All forbidden work that can be done on the eve of the Sabbath
does not override the Sabbath;
slaughter,
which is impossible to do on the eve of the Sabbath,
overrides the Sabbath.
   3 When does someone bring a festival offering with it?
When it comes on a weekday,
in purity,
and is insufficient.
And when it comes on the Sabbath,
in abundance,
or in defilement,
one does not bring a festival offering with it.

[33] **K, P** lack "Rabbi."

overturned what is written in the Torah: Quoting from Numbers 9:3, R. Eliezer points out what R. Aqiva already knows, that his argument leads to a ruling that would violate what the rabbis all agree is a biblical mandate: to perform the Passover at its proper time, even on the Sabbath.

like the fixed time for the slaughtering: In response, R. Aqiva points out that the slaughtering of the Passover sacrifice is an activity that has a biblically mandated narrow timeframe: the afternoon of the fourteenth (Numbers 9:3). But the actions spoken of in the prior mishnah can all safely be done earlier. Therefore, these actions do not override the Sabbath, even on the fourteenth of Nisan, as explained in the general principle stated at the end of this mishnah. This rule also appears in *Shabbat* 19:1.

6:3 *festival offering*: Deuteronomy 16:16 mandates pilgrimage on certain festivals. The rabbis understand this obligation to entail bringing a special festival offering called *hagigah* (see *Hagigah* 1:1–2). On Passover, therefore, pilgrims would offer two sacrifices: the Passover and a festival offering.

on a weekday: Discretionary sacrifices may not be offered on the Sabbath. The *hagigah* could be offered before or (more likely) after the Sabbath.

in purity: As long as most of the people and priests are pure, the Passover is performed in its normal way, and festival offerings would accompany Passover sacrifices.

insufficient: For providing a full meal. Passover sacrifices can be shared among a large group of worshippers, each fulfilling the obligation with an olive's bulk. However, the Passover offering is supposed to leave those who consumed with a feeling of satiety. The meat of the festival offering can be used to ensure that all will have enough to eat for a full meal. According to the Talmud, the Passover offering is consumed afterward, to create the sense of fullness.

in abundance: If there will be enough meat from the Passover to satisfy the members of the group, a festival offering is not brought.

in defilement: If too many of the people or priests are defiled, the Passover is nevertheless performed, in a state of ritual defilement; see 7:6 below.

4 The festival offering comes from the flock or the herd,
from sheep or from goats,
from males or females,
and may be consumed for two days and one night.[34]

5 The Passover that was slaughtered
not in its name
on the Sabbath—
one is liable to offer a purgation offering for it;
and all the other sacrifices that are offered
in the name of the Passover—
if they are not appropriate [for Passover],
he is liable;
but if they are appropriate—
R. Eliezer holds him liable for a purgation offering,
but R. Joshua exempts.
Said R. Eliezer:
If the Passover,
which is permitted when offered in its name,
when he changes its name,
he becomes liable,
the sacrifices which are prohibited in their own names,
when he changes their names,
is it not logical that he should be liable?
R. Joshua said to him:
No.
If you said so with regard to the Passover,
which he changed into a prohibited thing,
would you say so for the other sacrifices,

[34] K, P lack "and one night."

6:4 *the flock or the herd*: The Passover, however, comes only from the flock.

males or females: The Passover, however, comes only from yearling males.

for two days and one night: The Passover must be consumed in its entirety that very night. Therefore, the less restricted festival offering was better suited to ensure that the worshippers had enough to eat, as explained in the previous mishnah. It has already been noted, however, that the festival offering was eaten before the Passover in order that the latter might produce satiety. If the festival offering was larger than required for this purpose, the rest might be left over.

6:5 *slaughtered not in its name*: See 5:2 above; such an offering is invalid.

on the Sabbath: The Passover overrides the Sabbath, but this offering is invalid, so the Sabbath has been violated.

purgation offering: This is the standard reparation for unintentional performance of forbidden labor on the Sabbath (see *Shabbat* 7:1). The presumption here is that the violation was inadvertent. Defiant violation cannot be expiated with a sacrifice.

not appropriate [for Passover]: If, on the Sabbath, one sacrificed for the sake of the Passover an animal that could not be a proper Passover sacrifice (such as a female, or an ox—see 6:4 above), the offering is invalid and Sabbath has been violated.

which he changed into a permitted thing?
R. Eliezer said to him:
Public sacrifices will prove the matter:
for they are permitted in their names,
and the one who slaughters [other offerings]
in their names
is obligated.
R. Joshua said to him:
No.
If you said so with regard to the public offerings,
which have a fixed number,
would you say the same for the Passover,
which has no number?
R. Meir says:
Even one who slaughters
in the name of the public offerings
is exempt.

but if they are appropriate: If one intended to offer a yearling male goat as a Festival offering, but erred and offered it as a Passover instead, the offering falls under the category of a sacrifice offered in the wrong name (see *Zevahim* 1:1). The particular obligation has not been fulfilled, even though the offering itself is valid.

R. Eliezer holds him liable: Because by offering a sacrifice not specifically mandated on the Sabbath, the Sabbath has been violated.

R. Joshua exempts: Since the sacrifice inadvertently offered remains valid, the Sabbath has not been violated.

the sacrifices which are prohibited in their own names: R. Eliezer points out here that, from the outset, while Passover overrides the Sabbath, other offerings do not. Therefore one who intended to offer on the Sabbath that which should not be offered on the Sabbath ought not be absolved from penalty by virtue of the mistaken misnaming of the prohibited sacrifice as a permitted Passover.

which he changed into a permitted thing: R. Joshua argues, against R. Eliezer, that indeed, the misnaming has turned what would have been a prohibited sacrifice on the Sabbath into a permitted Passover, so that the offerer has not violated the Sabbath by this sacrifice.

Public sacrifices: Such as the daily sacrifices and the additional Sabbath offerings; these similarly override the Sabbath. R. Eliezer argues that if someone offered other sacrifices in the name of these on the Sabbath, the Sabbath would be violated, and the person would be liable. Therefore, in the case of the sacrifice offered on the Sabbath and misnamed as a Passover, so too the one who brings the offering should be liable.

which have a fixed number: Only two daily sacrifices are offered each morning and afternoon; similarly, only two additional sacrifices are offered. But a great number of Passovers are offered. According to R. Joshua, public offerings and Passovers are not comparable, and therefore logical deductions cannot be drawn. The commanded public offerings are so few that any additional offerings are noticeably extraneous. But there is no limit to the number of valid Passovers offered, even on the Sabbath.

Even one who slaughters in the name of the public offerings: R. Meir goes further even than R. Joshua, rejecting the premise (let alone the conclusion) of R. Eliezer's argument regarding public sacrifices. According to R. Meir, even one who slaughters on the Sabbath some other sacrifice as an extraneous continual offering is exempt from the purgation offerings mandated when truly invalid offerings are offered on Sabbath.

6 If he slaughtered it for those who cannot eat of it,
or for those not designated among those who should eat it,
or for uncircumcised men
or impure people,
he is liable.
For those that can eat of it and those who cannot eat of it,
for those designated for it and those not designated for it,
for the circumcised and uncircumcised,
for the impure and the pure,
he is exempt.
If he slaughtered it,
and it was found to be blemished,
he is liable.
If he slaughtered it,
and it was found to be torn internally,
he is exempt.
If he slaughtered it,
and it became known
that the owners had withdrawn their hands from it,
or that they had died,
or that they had become impure,
he is exempt,
since he slaughtered it with permission.

6:6 *If he slaughtered*: A Passover, on the fourteenth of Nisan that is also a Sabbath.

for those not designated: The cases listed here are explained in 5:3 above. A Passover offered for such people exclusively is invalid.

he is liable: To offer a purgation offering, for inadvertently violating the Sabbath by offering an invalid Passover.

For those that can eat of it and those who cannot eat of it: If, as explained in 5:3 above, one slaughters a Passover on the fourteenth of Nisan that is also a Sabbath for a group that includes those who may not eat of it along with others who can and may consume it, then the sacrifice is valid, and he is therefore not guilty of violating the Sabbath.

found to be blemished, he is liable: A blemished Passover is invalid. Because the offerer should have examined the animal for blemishes before slaughtering, this discovery renders the act of slaughter a violation of the Sabbath.

torn internally: Although internal or hidden blemishes also render the sacrifice invalid, in this case it was not possible for the one bringing the offering to know what was hidden from him. Therefore he is considered as someone who violated under duress, and he is exempt.

it became known: Similarly, since the one who slaughtered the Passover on Sabbath in this instance did so with proper intention and with permission, the Sabbath violation resulting from these scenarios does not render him liable for the purgation offering.

Chapter Seven

7:1–3 *Roasting the Passover*

7 How is the Passover roasted?[35]
They bring a stake made of pomegranate wood,
and he skewers it from its mouth through its buttocks,
and he places its legs and entrails inside it—
the words of R. Yose the Galilean.
R. Aqiva says:
This would be a kind of boiling;
rather he hangs them outside of it.

2 The Passover is not roasted on a [metal] skewer
nor on a grill.
R. Zadok said:
It once happened
that Rabban Gamaliel said to his slave Tabi:
Go and roast the Passover offering for us on a grill.
If it touched the earthenware of the oven,
he should pare down that place.
If some of its juice dripped onto the earthenware
and bounced back onto it,

---

[35] In **P**, the main text reads "flayed" (cf. 5:9) but this is corrected so that it agrees with **K** and the printed editions.

7:1 Following Exodus 12:9, the rabbis believed that the Passover sacrifice was to be roasted (cf. Deuteronomy 16:7 and 2 Chronicles 35:13 for alternative biblical traditions). The Mishnah goes to some extent to ensure that the meat of the Passover is cooked entirely by the flames of the fire.

pomegranate wood: The spit could not be made of metal, for metal would conduct heat and cook the meat from within, whereas the Passover had to be cooked entirely from the fire, and not by heat conducted by the spit. Pomegranate wood was favored because it was completely dry, even within; the concern was that moisture within the spit would conduct heat from the spit to the meat, thus cooking it.

This would be a kind of boiling: According to R. Aqiva, if the legs and entrails were placed inside the carcass, they would boil in the juices of the meat; therefore they were to hang on the spit, outside of the carcass, where they would be cooked entirely by the flames of the fire.

7:2 *[metal] Skewer*: A spit made of metal would conduct heat into the center of the carcass, thus cooking the meat from within.

Rabban Gamaliel: Probably Rabban Gamaliel the Younger, who is elsewhere remembered as having a slave named Tabi (see *Sukkah* 2:1).

on a grill: Rabban Gamaliel maintained that the heat of the grill touching the meat from the outside would not interfere or compete with the heat of the flames, and thus the Passover cooked on a grill could be properly roasted.

that place: Any part of the surface meat that may have been cooked by heat conducted by the wall of the oven must be pared down.

he should trim away that place.
If some of its juice dripped into the flour,
he must remove a handful from its place.

3 If he basted it with oil that is *terumah*,
if it is a group of priests,
they may eat it.
If a group of Israelites—
if it is raw,
he may rinse it off;
if it is cooked,
he must pare the outer part.
If he basted it with oil that is second tithe,
he may not charge the members of the group,
for second tithe may not be redeemed in Jerusalem.

7:4–12 Defiled Passovers

4 Five things may be brought in impurity
but may not be consumed in impurity:
the *omer*,
the two loaves,

If some of its juice: From the meat itself. If some of this liquid dripped into the fire and bounced back onto the meat, that part must be cut off, so that any part of the meat heated by this liquid would be removed.

If this liquid *dripped into flour*, a handful of flour around the spill must be removed and destroyed, while the rest, unheated by the spilled juice, can still be eaten.

7:3 Although liquids should not be placed on the meat while it is being cooked, it was permitted to baste the meat before or even after it was cooked.

oil that is terumah: This is permitted only for priests, and a Passover so basted cannot be consumed by Israelites.

group: See on 5:3 above; the Passover is shared by a group organized in advance for that purpose. See further 8:3–4 below.

if it is raw: The raw meat would not absorb the oil, so that that it could be washed off.

if it is cooked: This can refer either to the basting of a cooked Passover, or a cooked Passover that was basted when raw. In either case, the solution provided mandates paring off the outer layer of the cooked meat all around, because the nonpriestly members of the group may not consume the *terumah* oil.

second tithe: See 2:5 above. Second tithe must be consumed in Jerusalem, but it may be "redeemed" (that is, sold) as long as the proceeds are used to purchase produce for consumption upon arrival in Jerusalem. This process, however, must be carried out away from Jerusalem. If the second tithe is brought into the city, it must be consumed as such. Therefore, the owner of this oil cannot ask the other members of his group to share the cost of the oil, since this would constitute selling ("redeeming") it.

7:4 *brought in impurity*: The sacrificial contributions listed here must be brought in any event—even if no pure specimens are available. If offered while defiled, however, they cannot be consumed by the priests. They must rather be burned (see 1:6–7 above).

omer: The sheaf of the first crops that is brought after Passover; see Leviticus 23:6–10 and 5:8 above.

two loaves: That are brought on the Festival of Weeks (Leviticus 23:17).

the bread of presence,
public offerings of well-being,
and the goats for the new months.
The Passover that is brought in impurity
is consumed in impurity,
for from the start it is only brought for consumption.

5 If the meat is defiled
but the fat is preserved,
he does not sprinkle the blood.
If the fat is defiled
and the meat is preserved,
he sprinkles the blood.
And with [other] sacred things it is not so;
rather even if the meat is defiled
and the fat is preserved,
he sprinkles the blood.

6 If the [entire] assembly,
or the greater part of it,
is impure,
or if the priests are impure
and the assembly pure,
it should be done in impurity.
If a minority of the assembly is defiled,
the pure do the First [Passover]
and the impure do the Second.

the bread of presence: These twelve loaves are placed in two rows of six on the table in the Temple (Leviticus 24:5–6).

public offerings of well-being: Two such are brought along with the loaves on the Festival of Weeks (Leviticus 23:19).

goats for the new months: One goat is offered each new month (Numbers 28:15).

The Passover that is brought in impurity: Under certain circumstances the Passover can be offered in impurity (below, 7:6; 9:4). Unlike the items previously listed it may also be consumed in impurity, the reason being that the main purpose for bringing a Passover is to consume it (Exodus 12:8).

7:5 *If the meat is defiled*: The subject is a Passover that was brought in purity whose meat was defiled after the separation of the "said portions" (5:10 above); the latter remained pure.

he does not sprinkle the blood: Even though the sacred parts have been preserved as pure, the defilement of the meat means the Passover cannot be eaten. Since the purpose of the Passover is to be consumed, there is no purpose in sprinkling its blood.

it is not so: The Passover offering is distinctive in being rendered pointless if it cannot be consumed. For all other sacrifices, the consumption is secondary to the act of offering.

7:6 Normally, a defiled person would observe the Second Passover, held on the fifteenth of the second month (see 9:1–3 below).

If the [entire] assembly: If everyone, or most of the people, or most of the priests, are defiled, then the First Passover is done at its time, and *in impurity*: further qualifications will be introduced below. According to rabbinic memory, various communal concerns (such as the requirement to celebrate Passover at its proper time) could override concerns with ritual purity, even where the Temple itself was concerned.

7 If the blood of a Passover was sprinkled,
and subsequently it became known that it was impure,
the high priest's frontlet effects acceptance.
If the [owner's] body became impure,
the frontlet does not effect acceptance.
For they have said:
The *nazir* and one who performs the Passover—
the frontlet effects acceptance for[36] impurity of the blood,
but the frontlet does not effect acceptance for impurity of the body.
If he became impure
by the impurity of the deep,
the frontlet effects acceptance.

8 If its entirety or the greater part of it became impure,
it is burned before the *birah*,
from the wood of the woodpile.

[36] K initially lacked "For they have said…effects acceptance for," but this was added in the margin.

7:7 *If the blood of a Passover*: As explained in 7:5 above, a defiled Passover's blood is not sprinkled on the altar. In the case addressed here, it becomes known that the Passover has been defiled only after the blood has been sprinkled. Even so, the Passover cannot be consumed, and any person defiled (or defiled by the defiled Passover) must now wait and perform Second Passover.

high priest's frontlet: According to Exodus 28:36–38, an engraved frontlet was to be placed on the mitre of the high priest.

effects acceptance: Following the implications of Exodus 28:38, the rabbis determined that the high priest's frontlet could absolve the people from certain sins relating to defiled sacrifices (see *Zevahim* 8:12, *Menahot* 3:3). Inadvertent sprinkling of blood from a defiled Passover is among those transgressions.

If the [owner's] body: The Hebrew word used here for "body" can also refer to the carcass of the sacrifice (cf. 10:3 below), and this is indeed the subject of the next mishnah.

the frontlet does not effect acceptance: A defiled person cannot offer the Passover at all, and must wait until Second Passover. The frontlet's atonement powers do not pertain to this instance.

For they have said: As in 1:1 above, this phrase apparently introduces what the Mishnah considers to be a very early tradition.

The nazir: See Numbers 6:1–21 and *Nazir*. A *nazir* who has contracted corpse impurity must bring special sacrifices and then restart fulfilling his or her vow all over again.

impurity of the blood: That is, the blood of the defiled sacrifice, which has been inadvertently sprinkled on the altar.

impurity of the body: Of the person offering the sacrifice.

the impurity of the deep: See *Nazir* 9:2. The priest's frontlet effects atonement in the case of a person who was, at the time of sacrifice, unknowingly defiled by corpse impurity.

7:8 *If its entirety*: Meaning the whole Passover sacrifice, now rendered useless by ritual impurity.

greater part: Any unconsumed flesh left over from the Passover is to be burned, following Exodus 12:10; see further 10:9 below.

it is burned before the birah: See 3:8 above.

If a small portion of it became impure,
or its remainder,
it is burned in their courtyards or on their roofs
from their own wood.[37]
Stingy people burn it before the *birah*,
in order to make use of the wood of the woodpile.

9 The Passover that was taken out
or that was defiled
is to be burned immediately.
If the owners became impure,
or they died,
it is set aside to rot
and it is burned on the sixteenth.[38]
R. Yohanan b. Beroqa says:
Even this should be burned immediately,
since it has no one eating it.

10 The bones, the sinews, and the remainder
shall be burned on the sixteenth.
If the sixteenth falls on a Sabbath,
they must be burned on the seventeenth,
for these do not override the Sabbath
or the Festival day.

---

[37] **K** has been corrected to read "from the wood of the woodpile," though a marginal notation refers also to "their own" [wood].

[38] **K** adds: "and goes to the house of burning."

If a small portion: If the defilement of the Passover occurred only to a small portion of the meat, once outside the Temple Court. This meat cannot be consumed, but it may be burned privately.

Stingy people: Those reluctant (or unable) to burn this unusable meat with their own wood could bring it back to the Temple area and burn it along with other invalidated sacrifices.

7:9 *that was taken out*: Beyond the area of Jerusalem, and is therefore invalidated (cf. *Zevahim* 14:8).

burned immediately: On the fourteenth of Nisan, even before other Passovers are consumed.

If the owners of the Passover sacrifice.

became impure, or they died: These circumstances render the Passover unusable, even though it is not otherwise defiled or invalidated.

on the sixteenth: As no forbidden work may be done on the fifteenth, the Passover rendered unusable as described here is burned on the sixteenth, just like the unconsumed remainder left over from any other Passover offerings.

since it has no one eating it: R. Yohanan b. Beroqa here argues that a Passover rendered entirely unusable is not like remainder, for what will later become remainder could be eaten in its proper time, but the invalidated Passover has no one to eat it even at its proper time. Therefore, it is like invalidated offerings, and ought to be burned immediately, on the fourteenth of Nisan.

7:10 *The bones, the sinews*: These inedible portions of the Passover, along with any remainder (as noted above) are burned.

11 All that can be consumed of a grown ox
must be eaten of a small kid,
[even] the ends of the shoulder blades and the gristles.
One who breaks the bone of a pure Passover
incurs forty stripes.
But the one who leaves remainder of pure Passover
and one who breaks [the bones of an] impure [Passover]
does not incur forty stripes.

12 If a limb partially went out,
he cuts it until he reaches the bone,
and then he pares it until he reaches the joint,
and cuts.
And for [other] sacrifices
he may chop it with a cleaver,
since the rule concerning breaking the bone does not apply.
From the doorjamb inward
is as inside;
from the doorjamb outside,
as outside.
The windows and the thickness of the walls
count as inside.

7:13–8:8   *Consuming the Passover*

13 If two groups were eating the Passover in one house,
these face one way and eat;

7:11 *grown ox*: Whatever may be eaten of fully grown animals, whose tissues have toughened through growth and work, must be eaten of a smaller Passover in order to fulfill the command of eating the entire animal. What is not normally eaten of larger animals need not be eaten of the smaller, younger Passover.

breaks the bone: This is forbidden, following Exodus 12:46 and Numbers 9:12, and violations of this statute are punished by stripes. This rule is repeated at *Makkot* 3:3.

pure Passover: A defiled Passover is invalid and therefore not a Passover at all. Breaking the bones of defiled Passover does not violate the biblical commandment, and does not incur punishment.

7:12 *a limb*: Of a pure Passover.

went out: Beyond the city walls of Jerusalem (see 7:9 above) or outside the house in which the Passover was to be eaten.

he cuts it: The flesh. One may use a knife to cut the meat until one reaches the bone of the limb that extended out. Then one cleans the flesh off the rest of that bone, and then slices that bone off at the joint. All this is to prevent breaking a bone of the Passover. These procedures apply only to the Passover, following Exodus and Numbers as explained before.

as inside: The walls of the city or the house.

7:13 *two groups*: As explained at 5:3 above, the Passover is consumed in groups which must be designated for this purpose in advance. This mishnah imagines two groups consuming different Passovers in the same house. See also 8:4 below, which depicts a scenario of two separate groups that divide a single Passover.

those face the other way[39] and eat,
with the kettle between them.
And when the servant stands to mix [the wine],
he should close his mouth
and turn his face away
until he reaches his [own] company again,
and continues eating.
And the bride may turn her face away while she eats.

Chapter Eight

8 When a woman is at her husband's house—
if her husband slaughtered for her
and her father slaughtered for her,
she should eat of her husband's.
If she went on the first Festival to celebrate at her father's house,
and if her father slaughtered for her
and her husband slaughtered for her,
she may eat at the place of her choosing.
An orphan for whom guardians slaughtered

[39] Lit. "this way…this way."

the kettle: The two groups can share a kettle, which serves also as a physical divider between them.

the servant: The two groups can even share a servant, who will have joined himself to one group but can serve the other provided precautions are taken. He must be careful to avoid any action, even swallowing food already in his mouth, while serving the group to which he does not belong, for he must not give the impression that he is also eating with them.

And the bride: Her turning away from the group is understood to be an expression of modesty, not a symbol of self-exclusion from the group.

8:1 In principle, as explained above (5:3), each Israelite will be included in a single group, designated in advance, for the purpose of consuming the Passover offering. This mishnah addresses a number of cases when one person could be presumed to be included in more than one group.

When a woman is at her husband's house: A married woman, living with her husband, should consume the Passover consumed also by her husband, even if her father included her in his group as well. The father's offering would then be one that is slaughtered for those included and not included in the group, and remains valid (as also explained in 5:3 above).

on the first Festival: If, on the first Passover after her marriage, a woman returned to celebrate Passover at her father's house, then the father would have good reason to assume she might do so again. In this case, since both the father and the husband have an equally good reason to presume the woman's participation within their respective groups, the woman in question can choose which group to join.

An orphan: Similarly, an orphan being cared for my multiple guardians, each of whom included the orphan in his group, can choose which group to join.

may eat at the place he chooses.
A slave belonging to two partners
may not eat of [the Passover] of either.
He who is half-slave and half-free
may not eat of his master's.

   2 One who says to his slave,
"Go and slaughter the Passover for me"—
if he slaughtered a kid
he may eat it;
if he slaughtered a lamb
he may eat it.
If he slaughtered a kid and a lamb,
he should eat from the first.
If he forgot what his master told him,
how shall he act?
He should slaughter a lamb and a kid,
and say:
"If my master told me 'kid,'
the kid is his
and the lamb is mine;
if my master told me 'lamb,'
the lamb is his
and the kid is mine."
If his master forgot what he told him,
the two of them go to the house of burning,
and they are exempt from doing Second Passover.

A slave belonging to two partners: This case differs from the rest, in that neither owner independently has full authority to include the shared slave in his group. The slave, therefore, has not been appropriately included in either group, and cannot eat of either Passover.

half-slave and half-free: A slave once owned by two partners could find himself half-free: released by one partner, but still (half-)owned by the other. In such a case, the slave cannot eat from his (half-)master's offering, since the (half-)owner does not have the necessary full authority to include him in his group.

8:2 *if he slaughtered a kid*: The Passover sacrifice is to be taken "from the sheep or the goats" (Exodus 12:5). The slave in this scenario is not given specific instructions, and thus whichever is chosen may be consumed by the master who gave these instructions.

he should eat from the first: If the slave slaughtered one of each—a kid and a lamb—then the master should consume as a sacrifice whichever of the two animals was slaughtered first. The second, as a Passover rendered invalid, would be burned (see 5:2–3 above).

If he forgot: The slave who forgot his master's instruction can slaughter one of each, and then designate the one his master intended for his master and the other for himself, thereby designating each person to a different Passover, and rendering both valid.

If his master forgot: But if then the master too forgot his instruction, then neither animal can be duly designated to either of them, and both must be burned as invalid offerings.

they are exempt from doing Second Passover: They cannot consume a Passover now because they do not know which Passover was slaughtered for which person. Yet, each one did have a valid sacrifice offered on his behalf; hence the exemption from Second Passover (see 8:6 and 9:9 below for similar exemptions in certain circumstances).

3 One who says to his sons:
"I am slaughtering the Passover
for whomever among you
comes first to Jerusalem."
As soon as the first brings in his head
and the greater part of his body,
he acquires his portion
and acquires for his brothers along with him.
[Others] may always be counted in on it
as long as each and every one can have of it an olive's bulk.
They may be counted in
and they may withdraw their hands from it
until it is slaughtered.
R. Simeon says:
Until its blood is sprinkled.
 4 If one includes others into his own portion,
the members of the group[40] are entitled to give him his [portion].
He eats from his [portion],
and they eat from theirs.
 5 A *zav* who experienced two issues—
one may slaughter for him
on his seventh day.

[40] K, P lack "the members of the group," and read "they are entitled…"

8:3 *for whoever among you comes first to Jerusalem*: Apparently in order to encourage his sons to hasten their pilgrimage, the father announces a race, to be won by the fastest of his sons.

he acquires his portion…along with him: The winner of the race is then required to invite his brothers to share his portion with him. Commentators assume this is the father's intent all along, though this is not made explicit in the text.

[Others] may always be counted in on it: Generalizing from this case, the Mishnah points out that a person may include as many others as he wishes from his own share of a Passover offering, as long as everyone so included will have at least an olive's bulk.

until it is slaughtered: Persons may be included this way until the Passover is slaughtered, and they may also withdraw from the group—presumably to be included in another—until this same point. R. Simeon's position apparently permits joining and withdrawing until the completion of the processes (see 5:2–3 above), but the Talmud limits R. Simeon's position so that he permits only withdrawal after the slaughter, not joining.

8:4 *If one includes others*: An individual duly included in a group has decided to include others into his own share, as just explained in 8:3. The initial group could choose to share more equally, but they are only required to give this person his own original share of the total, irrespective of how many he has chosen to share that portion with him. Compare 7:13 above, which could also pertain to this case as the original group has now in effect split into two.

8:5 *two issues*: Of defiling genital fluid, on the same day or consecutive days. He is now impure rendering him until sunset of his seventh day (see *Zavim*).

on his seventh day: The Passover is slaughtered for him while he remains impure (before sunset on his seventh day), because he will be able to eat of it by the time the holiday begins (after sunset when he will be pure).

If he experienced three,
one may slaughter for him
on his eighth day.
A woman who is watching for a day matching a day—
one may slaughter for her on her second day.
If she saw for two days,
one may slaughter for her on her third day.
And the *zavah*—
one may slaughter for her on her eighth day.
  6 [41]A mourner,
one who clears away a ruin,
and likewise he whom they promised to release from captivity,
and the sick and the elderly
who can eat an olive's bulk—
one may slaughter for them.
For all of these, one may not slaughter for them[42] exclusively,

[41] K places 8:7 before 8:6.
[42] K lacks "For all these, one may not slaughter for them," though this is then added in the margin.

on his eighth day: The third incident obliges him to bring a sacrifice on the eighth day, when he is pure. The Passover can only be slaughtered for him after he has brought that sacrifice.

A woman who is watching for a day matching a day: Because this flow occurs when her menstrual period is not expected, she is not immediately deemed defiled for a full week, but must wait to see whether more blood flows (*Niddah* 4:7; *Zavim* 1:1). In the hope that she will be pure and able to eat after sunset of this second day, the Passover may be slaughtered for her on that day. This same logic pertains to all the cases considered here: the Passover may be slaughtered in the afternoon, with the expectation that these will be pure, and permitted to eat of it, after sunset. In all these cases, the Passover would be slaughtered not just for these people, but also for those who will certainly be able to consume it, in line with 5:3 above and 8:6 that now follows.

8:6 Building on the cases discussed in the previous passages, the Mishnah here lists a number of categories of person who may or may not in fact be able to consume the Passover, or who would be unable to eat it at the time of slaughter. Even so, the Passover is slaughtered for all of these in the expectation that it will turn out that they will be permitted to consume of the Passover come sundown.

A mourner: The term used here applies to one who has suffered the death of a close relative on that very day. According to biblical law this status ends at sundown; see 8:8 below.

one who clears away a ruin: He who has helped excavate a collapsed building—looking for survivors trapped within—will not know what lies beneath until the search is completed. As long as the search is ongoing, the person in question knows he is at risk of becoming defiled by corpse impurity.

they promised to release from captivity: But it is not known for certain whether in fact he will be released on time.

and the sick and the elderly: Even if these can eat an olive's bulk at the time of the slaughter, their capacity to eat this amount could diminish at any time.

For all of these, one may not slaughter for them exclusively: Because all of these may turn out to be incapacitated or otherwise excluded from the group, they must be included in a mixed group, ensuring insofar as is possible that at least some of the group will in fact be able and permitted to consume the Passover. This will prevent the entire offering from being rendered invalid, which would indeed happen if the entire group were unable or forbidden to consume the Passover.

lest they render the Passover invalid.
Therefore, if it should happen
that one among them is disqualified,
they are exempt from Second Passover,
except for the one who clears away a ruin,
since he is impure from the outset.

7 One may not slaughter the Passover for an individual—
the words of R. Judah.
And R. Yose permits [this].
For a group of even one hundred
who cannot eat an olive's bulk,
one may not slaughter.
And one does not form a group of women, slaves, and minors.

8 The mourner immerses
and eats his Passover at evening,
but not [other] sacrifices.

exempt from Second Passover: As in the case considered in 8:2 above, those who are for these reasons excluded from the Passover offered for them on the fourteenth of Nisan are exempt from the Second Passover, for they were duly included in a properly constituted group, and the blood from their offering was sprinkled on the altar.

except for the one who clears away a ruin: In this case, the person in question learns later that he was defiled by corpse impurity even on the fourteenth of Nisan, so he is obligated to perform the Second Passover along with all others so defiled at that time.

8:7 *for an individual*: According to R. Judah, a Passover cannot be slaughtered for one person. If we understand his ruling in light of what precedes, the concern is that the person could become defiled or otherwise incapacitated, rendering the Passover invalid. If we understand Judah's ruling in light of what follows here, then the concern is whether an individual can in fact consume an entire Passover. R. Yose permits doing so, presumably under the assumption that the individual in question could eat the entire Passover in question.

who cannot eat an olive's bulk: The concern now is with those who can hardly eat at all. The Passover cannot be offered exclusively for such people, even if there are one hundred of them, for none of them on their own can render the offering valid.

a group of women, slaves, and minors: All of these are properly included within groups for the purpose of consuming Passover offerings as we have seen above. The Mishnah appears to prohibit forming groups consisting exclusively of women, exclusively of slaves, or exclusively of minors. The Talmud, however, explicitly permits this and prohibits only combinations of two or three of these types of members—fearing frivolity or impropriety among mixed groups not properly supervised by an adult, free male. The ruling here may mean to suggest that a proper group must include at least one free male who has reached adulthood—such that each group can have some semblance of being a household, following Exodus 12:4.

8:8 *The mourner*: As before (8:6), one who has suffered the death of a close relative on that very day. Such a person is not necessarily ritually defiled in any way: the status of mourner pertains to any person who has suffered the death of a close relative, irrespective of any corpse impurity. The mourner is nevertheless obligated to immerse before consuming sacred things (*Hagigah* 3:3.). Any mourner who actually contracted corpse impurity would have to wait until Second Passover.

but not [other] sacrifices: By rabbinic decree the status of mourner extends into the night, but an exception is made for eating the Passover as this is a biblical command.

One who has heard of a death
and one who gathers bones
immerses and eats sacrifices.
A convert who converts on Passover Eve:
the House of Shammai say:
He immerses and eats his Passover in the evening.
The House of Hillel say:
One who separates from his foreskin
is like one who separates from a grave.

Chapter Nine

9:1–3　*First and Second Passover*

9 One who was impure,
or on a distant journey—
if he did not do the first [Passover],
he must do the second.
Whether inadvertently,
or coerced,

One who has heard of a death: Of a close relative that has died at an earlier time.

one who gathers bones: This refers to the widespread practice of gathering bones for reburial.

immerses and eats sacrifices: The rabbis extended the prohibitions of the mourner to these as well, but in their case all prohibitions end at sundown so that such persons may immerse and eat all sacrifices, including of course the Passover.

A convert who converts on Passover Eve: So that his circumcision is performed on the fourteenth of Nisan.

He immerses and eats his Passover in the evening: The House of Shammai compare the Passover-day proselyte to the mourner. Although such a person cannot perform the Passover slaughter himself, the Passover slaughter may be performed for him by others, and following his immersion before sundown, he may join his group just like an Israelite whose day of mourning has ended. As in the case of the mourner, the immersion required does not imply prior defilement.

like one who separates from a grave: The House of Hillel here take a stricter view, though the precise meaning and logic are notoriously obscure. One possibility is that they deem the recently circumcised proselyte to be ritually impure in the category of corpse impurity. By this reasoning, the proselyte would be banned from celebrating this Passover, and would also require sprinkling on the third and seventh days (see 6:2 above) in order to become ritually pure. Another possibility is that they deem the recent proselyte to be *like one who separates from a grave* in this one respect only: banned from the (First) Passover. By either reasoning, the House of Hillel would presumably obligate the recent proselyte to participate in the Second Passover.

9:1 A Second Passover was mandated by Numbers 9:6–12 for those defiled by a corpse or on a distant journey (9:10).

Whether inadvertently, or coerced: That is, the Second Passover should also be performed by others who failed to do the first, whether it is was by mistake or force.

if he did not do the first,
he must do the second.
If so,
why does Scripture say,
impure or on a distant journey?
Because these are exempt from extirpation,
while the others are liable to extirpation.

2 And what constitutes a distant journey?
From Modi'im and further,
and that measure in all directions—
the words of R. Aqiva.
R. Eliezer says:
From the threshold of the Court and further.
Said R. Yose:
Therefore there is a point over the letter *heh*,
to say not because it is really so far,
rather from the threshold of the Court and further.

3 What differentiates[43] First Passover from Second Passover?
The first:
the prohibitions against seeing and possessing pertain;
but the second:
matsah and *hamets* are with him in the house.

---

[43] Lit. "What is between…and…"

If so, why does Scripture say: Because the Mishnah understands Scripture's provision for a Second Passover also to apply to others who miss the first, the question arises why those categories explicitly identified in Numbers 9:10 are mentioned at all.

extirpation: This punishment is imposed on those who fail to participate in a Passover offering (*Keritot* 1:1, and see comments on 3:7 above). However, those who are explicitly exempted from the first Passover—because of defilement or distance—are also exempted from this punishment, even if they fail to perform the Second Passover. For the rest, they are liable to extirpation unless they perform the Second Passover.

9:2 *And what constitutes a distant journey?* Such that the exemption from the first Passover and the obligation for the Second Passover is triggered.

Modi'im: The traditional birthplace of the Maccabees, a town located on the Judaean foothills, approximately halfway from Jerusalem to Jaffa. Its precise location has not been conclusively identified, though the likeliest locations are all close to the modern Israeli city bearing the same name.

from the threshold of the Court: R. Eliezer suggests that any distance outside of the Temple is considered to be sufficiently far away.

a point over the letter heh: Torah scrolls, as well as Hebrew Bibles pointed according to the Masoretic tradition, place a dot over the final letter of the word for "distant." According to R. Yose, the dot is there precisely to indicate that the word is not to be understood in accordance to its plain meaning. See Numbers 9:10.

9:3 *the prohibition against seeing and possessing*: As explained above (1:1), *hamets* is not to be found in one's home during Passover in accordance with Exodus 12:19; it must not even be seen (13:7). These prohibitions apply only to the (First) Passover that falls on the fourteenth of Nisan.

The first requires *Hallel*
during its consumption;
the second does not require *Hallel*
during its consumption.
This and that require *Hallel*
during the preparation,
and are consumed roasted,
on *matsah*[44] and bitter vegetables,
and override the Sabbath.

9:4–5   *Other Passovers*

4 The Passover that is brought in impurity—
zavim and *zavot*, menstruants and parturients may not eat it.
And if they ate of it,
they are exempt from extirpation.
R. Eliezer exempts them
even from [any penalty for] approaching the sanctuary.

---

[44] P: "on *matsot*" (plural); see annotations.

Hallel: See on 5:7 above and 10:6 below.

roasted: See Exodus 12:9; Numbers 9:11.

on matsah and bitter vegetables: See Exodus 12:8. Echoing this verse, some manuscripts and printed editions read *matsot* (plural).

override the Sabbath: See especially 5:7 and 6:1 above.

9:4 The Second Passover directly addresses the situation of those individuals who cannot participate in Passover because of defilement by corpse impurity. However, the rabbis also consider (see 7:4–6 above) what should be done when most of the people (or most of the priests) are so defiled. In this case the Passover is offered and consumed in a state of defilement.

zavim and zavot, menstruants and parturients may not eat it: The contingency of the Passover brought in impurity applies only to those defiled by corpse impurity, just as with Second Passover. These others, defiled by flows, menstrual blood, or birth (see especially *Zavim* and *Niddah*) may not eat even of the Passover brought in impurity.

exempt from extirpation: Those defiled by impurities other than corpse impurity who wrongly eat of the Passover brought in impurity are nevertheless exempt from extirpation, since these offerings are already being consumed by others who are impure.

exempts them ... approaching the sanctuary: All those so defiled are normally prohibited even from entering the sanctuary (see *Kelim* 1:5), and they are liable to extirpation (see *Keritot* 1:1). But once again, because the Passover brought in impurity is already degraded by its nature, R. Eliezer exempts those impure in other ways from punishment for these violations.

5 What differentiates[45] the Passover of Egypt
from the Passover of the Generations?
The Passover of Egypt:
it was taken on the tenth,
required sprinkling with a hyssop bunch on the lintel and doorposts,
and it was consumed in haste,
during one night.
The Passover of the Generations
is observed all seven days.

9:6–11 *Passovers That Cannot Be Offered*

6 R. Joshua said:
I have heard
that a substitute for the Passover
is offered,
and that a substitute
for the Passover
is not offered,

[45] Lit. "What is between…and…"

9:5 The Mishnah now leaves matters of defilement behind, following the theme of distinctions among Passovers.

The Passover of Egypt: This is the Passover that was offered by the Israelites in Egypt on the evening before their departure, as described in Exodus 12–13.

taken on the tenth: See Exodus 12:3.

required sprinkling: Of blood on the lintel and doorposts; see Exodus 12:7.

consumed in haste, during one night: See Exodus 12:10–11.

The Passover of the Generations: This is the Passover that is to be observed in perpetuity, in memory of the Passover in Egypt; see Exodus 12:14–20.

is observed all seven days: Following Exodus 12:15–16, 18. The seven-day observance concerns the elimination of *hamets*, not the Passover sacrifice.

9:6 *I have heard*: This phrase is used a number of times in the Mishnah, particularly when one sage testifies to a tradition learned from earlier authorities (see *Orlah* 2:5; *Eruvin* 2:6).

a substitute: According to Leviticus 27:10, if someone declares one animal to be a substitute for another that has already been designated for a sacrificial offering, the status of holiness pertains to both the animal and its substitute. Such substitutions are prohibited, but the transfer of sanctity is nevertheless effective, and therefore the Mishnah records a variety of laws concerning such situations (see *Temurah*).

a substitute for the Passover: An animal that has been declared to be a substitute for another animal already designated as a Passover.

is offered…is not offered: R. Joshua claims to have heard that such a substitute Passover would be offered in some situations but not offered in others, but he cannot explain what the different cases would be.

and I cannot explain this.
R. Aqiva said:
I will explain this:
if the [original] Passover is found
before the Passover is slaughtered,
it shall graze until it becomes blemished,
then it should be sold,
and he should purchase[46] an offering of well-being with the money,
and so too its substitute.
[If it is found] after the Passover is slaughtered,[47]
it should be offered as a well-being offering,
and so too its substitute.

7 If one sets aside a female for his Passover,
or a male that is two years old,
it shall graze until it becomes blemished,
then it shall be sold,
and its value transferred into a voluntary offering.

[46] K, P: "and he brings."   [47] K, P: "after the Passover."

if the [original] Passover is found before the Passover is slaughtered: If an animal designated as a Passover goes missing, a replacement must be designated (see 9:9 below). If the original Passover is then discovered before the time for slaughter, the new Passover is offered, and the first is left to *graze until it becomes blemished*, at which point it is no longer suitable for sacrifice (see 6:6 above). This one can now be sold, and with the proceeds the owner purchases an animal to offer as an offering of well-being.

and so too its substitute: If one were then to designate a substitute for this unusable Passover, the substitute also would not be offered, but would be left to graze. Some interpreters understand "substitute" as if it refers the replacement for the lost Passover mentioned earlier. But finding a replacement for a lost Passover is necessary. The technical term here denotes the form of substitution prohibited in Leviticus. The substitute here must be a stand-in for the Passover that is left to pasture. For similar scenarios—lost and found offerings, replacements, and even substitutes for replacements—see *Temurah* 4:1–4.

[If it is found] after the Passover is slaughtered: In this case the original Passover is only discovered after the replacement Passover has been slaughtered. The original Passover animal must then be offered as a well-being sacrifice.

and so too its substitute: If one were now to designate a substitute for this offering—originally intended as a Passover, but now to be offered as a well-being sacrifice—the substitute would indeed be offered, as a well-being sacrifice. Although the scenarios conjured by Aqiva are complicated, they resemble other rabbinic traditions concerning sacrificial substitutions for replacement offerings (esp. *Temurah* 4:1–4). The two scenarios also provide an answer to R. Joshua's challenge: the substitute of a Passover left to graze is also left to graze, while the substitute of a replaced Passover that is offered as a well-being sacrifice is also offered as a well-being sacrifice.

9:7 *female … or a male that is two years old*: The Passover must be a year-old male; see Exodus 12:5. In both of these cases, as in 9:6, the incorrect designation leaves the animal in a sacred state nevertheless.

it shall graze: The animal is left to pasture until a blemish emerges, which renders the animal unfit for sacrifice; then it may be sold, and the proceeds (which are themselves sacred) can be used to purchase a donative offering. By following these procedures, no improper sacrifices are offered, and yet no sacred animals or funds are used for nonsacred purposes.

If one sets aside his Passover
and then dies,
his son may not bring it thereafter in the name of Passover,
but in the name of an offering of well-being.

8 If a Passover gets confused with [other] offerings,
they must all graze until blemished,
then they are sold,
and he shall bring,
at the value of the best of them,
for this type,
and he shall bring,
at the value of the best of them,
for the other[48] type,
and he must lose the added value
from his own household [funds].
If it was confused with firstlings—
R. Simeon says:
If they were a group of priests,
they [may] eat [them].

[48] Lit., again, "this type."

If one sets aside his Passover and then dies: The Passover of the deceased now has no one registered in its group.

his son: The man's heir inherits the animal in its sacred state, but he does not inherit inclusion in the father's group (the Mishnah assumes that the son was not already included in that group). Therefore he may not bring it as a Passover; rather he must bring the animal to the Temple as an offering of well-being.

9:8 *with [other] offerings*: With other types of offerings, which would by nature include offerings that differ with regard to their slaughter, sprinkling of blood, and consumption (for a comparative review of such differences, see *Zevahim* chapter 5, with the Passover procedures included at 5:8).

they must all graze: The mingled animals cannot be offered, since it cannot be known which process to follow for which animal. As above, therefore, they must be left to pasture, so that once blemished they can be sold, and new offerings purchased with the proceeds.

at the value of the best of them: Naturally, not all animals will sell at the same price. But because it is not known which animals were designated for which offerings, the price received for the best of the sold animals is taken to be the standard value for all of the replacement sacrifices this person must offer, one for each type of those confused in the first place.

firstlings: These are by nature young male offerings, just like proper Passovers. What is more, Firstlings are offered in ways similar to the Passover, with the slaughter taking place anywhere in the Court, and the blood sprinkled once toward the base of the altar (see *Zevahim* 5:8).

If they were a group of priests: The Passover is to be eaten by all Israelites, but Firstlings only by priests. According to R. Simeon, therefore, if a group of priests confused Firstlings with their Passover, they may still consume the offerings, since priests are entitled to consume both. Presumably, all must be consumed that night, as if they were all Passovers.

9 A group that lost its Passover,
and they said to one of them:
"Go and seek [it]
and slaughter [it] for us,"
and he found and slaughtered [it],
but they [meanwhile] took [another] and slaughtered [it]—
if his was slaughtered first,
he eats from his,
and they eat with him from his.[49]
If theirs was slaughtered first,
they eat from theirs
and he eats from his.
And if it is not known
which of them was slaughtered first,
or if they slaughtered the two of them at once,
he eats from his,
and they do not eat with him,
and theirs must go to the house of burning,
and they are exempt from doing Second Passover.
If he said to them:
"If I am late,
go and slaughter for me";

[49] K, P lack "from his."

9:9 *A group that lost its Passover*: A living animal can of course run off. So now the group must find another proper animal to designate for slaughter.

"Go and seek [it] and slaughter [it] for us": Because the evening time is approaching, the selected one is empowered not only to find the missing animal but also to go ahead and slaughter it. And indeed he succeeds in doing so.

but they [meanwhile] took [another] and slaughtered: While awaiting word on the missing Passover, the group in the meantime purchases and slaughters a new Passover.

"if his was slaughtered first": Their second offering is rendered invalid in that they were included in the first. Therefore all eat from his; the second is to be burned.

If theirs was slaughtered first: Their first offering is rendered fully valid for all those included in it.

he eats from his: Because he had no knowledge of, and could not therefore be included in, their subsequent decision to offer a different Passover.

if it is not known: In the event of any confusion regarding the relative timing of the two Passovers, the individual may nevertheless eat from his own, since he may do so regardless of which was slaughtered first. The others, however, may not eat with him lest theirs was offered first, and they may not eat their own lest theirs was offered second.

theirs must go to the house of burning: As an invalid offering.

they are exempt from doing Second Passover: Although the confused Passovers cannot be consumed, it remains the case that a valid Passover was offered on their behalf.

he said to them: If I am late, go and slaughter for me: By saying this, the man sent to look for the lost Passover also includes himself in their group, should they decide to offer another. In this case, however, they do not ask him to slaughter for them. Once again, both missions are successful.

if he found [the original] and slaughtered [it],
and they found and slaughtered [another]—
if theirs was slaughtered first,
they eat from theirs,
and he eats with them;
and if his was slaughtered first
he eats from his
and they eat from theirs;
if it is not known
which of them was slaughtered first,
or if they slaughtered the two of them at one time,
they eat theirs,
and he does not eat with them,
and his goes out to the house of burning,
and he is exempt from the Second Passover.
If he said to them [as above]
and they said to him [as above]—
they all eat from the first,
and if it is unknown which was slaughtered first,
the two go out to the house of burning.
If he said nothing to them
and they said nothing to him,
they are not responsible for one another.

10 Two groups whose Passovers were confused—
these take one for themselves
and those take one for themselves.

if theirs was slaughtered first: This sacrifice is then valid for all of them, so all of them eat of it, and his is sent to the house of burning.

if his was slaughtered first: He then eats of his own, since he obviously included himself in this offering, and was not yet included in the second. They may still eat theirs: he was not asked to include them, so theirs is the only animal offered on their behalf.

if it is not known: In the event of confusion, he is now the individual whose status is unclear, since he requested inclusion in their decision, but still slaughtered his own. So they may eat from theirs nevertheless, since theirs was valid for them irrespective of timing. He may not eat of his, and it goes to be burned, yet he is exempt from Second Passover as above.

he said to them…and they said to him: Both parties provisionally included the other in their sacrifice, as explained above.

they all eat from the first: Either sequence of slaughter includes everyone in the first. But everyone is excluded in the case of a confusion, so both are burned, and presumably all are exempt from Second Passover.

If he said nothing to them and they said nothing to him: By separating without instructions, the individual becomes his own group, and all are covered by any eventuality.

9:10 *these take one*: Of the two confused Passovers, so that each group has one.

One from these comes to those,
and one from those comes to these,
and so do they say:
"If this Passover is ours,
your hands are withdrawn from yours
and will be counted in on ours;
if this Passover is yours,
our hands are withdrawn from ours
and we will be counted in on yours."
And so too for five groups of five people
and ten groups of ten people.
They select for themselves one for each group,
and thus do they say.

11 Two whose Passovers were confused—
this one takes one
and that one takes one,
and this one counts in with him one from the market
and that one counts in with him one from the market,
and this one goes to that one
and that one goes to this one,
and so do they say:
"If this Passover is mine,
your hands are withdrawn from yours
and counted in on mine;
if this Passover is yours,
my hands are withdrawn from mine
and counted in on yours."

One from these comes to those: One member from each group approaches the other group, to speak with them on behalf of his own companions.

"If this Passover is ours": Each group addresses the representative from the other with a set of conditional statements that effect withdrawal from the Passover of the other group and registration for the Passover that each group currently possesses. This complicated procedure is made necessary by the need to ensure that neither Passover be left ownerless at any time.

9:11 *Two whose Passovers were confused*: Individuals by themselves cannot follow quite the same procedure for resolving the confusion of two Passovers. But each may choose one of the two offerings.

this one counts in with him one from the market: Then each one must find a partner, someone who happens to be nearby. With two groups so constituted, the rest of the procedure as mandated in the previous mishnah can be followed.

Chapter Ten

10:1–7 *The Passover Meal*

10 On Passover Eves,[50] close to *minhah*,
a person may not eat
until it gets dark.
And even the poorest that is among Israel
shall not eat until he reclines.
And they may not give him less than four cups of wine,
and even if [it must come] from the collection plate.
  2 They mixed for him a first cup:
the House of Shammai say:

---

[50] Lit. "Eves of Passovers." **K, P**: "Eve of Passovers."

10:1 Up until now, the Mishnah's focus on the Passover sacrifice in the Jerusalem Temple serves both to recall the practice of the past and to anticipate the practice of the future when, the rabbis believed, the Temple would be restored. Now the focus turns to the Passover meal at which, before the destruction of the Temple, the sacrifice was consumed. But here the rabbis also have in mind the nonsacrificial meal practices that would be taking place in their own postdestruction era.

Passover Eves: on the plurals in this expression, see the introduction.

close to minhah: The term literally means "grain offering," but it had long served as well to designate the late-afternoon daily sacrifice (1 Kings 18:29, Daniel 9:21). This phrase elsewhere refers to the beginning of what the Talmud calls the "larger afternoon"—the full range of time when it was permissible to offer the afternoon daily sacrifice or recite the afternoon prayer, beginning about a half-hour after noon (*Berakhot* 4:1, *Shabbat* 1:2). The expression, however, is imprecise. Many commentators understand that here it refers only to the midafternoon time when the afternoon sacrifice was offered on ordinary days, but there was conceivably a practice of abstaining from food from around the time the *hamets* was burned until it was time to consume the Passover.

eat until it gets dark: According to Exodus 12:8, the Passover is eaten at nighttime. Commentators say that the reason for abstaining from food for this time is to ensure that the Passover is consumed with an appetite.

until he reclines: As a wealthy person would eat.

four cups of wine: Each cup accompanies a particular stage of the Passover meal, and the timing of each cup in relation to other Passover rituals is noted below. The Palestinian Talmud already suggests symbolic explanations for the four cups, such that they correspond to the four references to Pharaoh's cup in Genesis 40:11–13, or to God's four promises of redemption in Exodus 6:6–7.

the collection plate: A public fund to supply food to those in need (*Pe'ah* 8:7).

10:2 *They mixed*: Wine was customarily mixed with water before drinking.

a first cup: For the recitation of the "sanctification" blessing (*qiddush*).

He blesses over the day,
and afterwards he blesses over the wine;
and the House of Hillel say:
He blesses over the wine,
and afterwards he blesses over the day.

3 They brought before him,
he dips in the lettuce,
until he reaches the breaking of bread.
[Then] they brought before him
matsah, lettuce, *haroset*, and two cooked foods,[51]
even though *haroset* is not a commandment.
R. Eliezer b. R. Zadok says:
It is a commandment.

[51] K, P lack "and two cooked foods."

He blesses over the day: The *qiddush*, for both Sabbaths and Holidays, includes two elements, the longer blessing sanctifying the holy day, and the briefer standard formula blessing God as the creator of the fruit of the vine. This dispute, along with others between the houses concerning festival meal practices, also appears at *Berakhot* 8:1–5.

10:3 *they brought before him*: Clearly some food is intended, as part of an appetizer course consisting of vegetables and sauces for dipping, but the phrase lacks a grammatical direct object.

the lettuce: In 2:6 above, lettuce is listed first among the vegetables that may be used to fulfill the commandment of consuming the Passover "with bitter herbs" (Exodus 12:8). Here, however, the lettuce is part of the appetizer course involving dipping, accompanying the first cup of wine and presaging other diversions from standard meal practice, as will be elaborated in the next mishnah.

the breaking of bread: The phrase here is obscure, and conjoins two terms ("breaking" and "bread") used in *Berakhot* 6:5 to refer to two different courses of a standard meal (an appetizer course and a bread course). Because appetizers are already being served, many commentators understand the phrase here to refer to the point at which the *matsah* will be consumed, with the appropriate blessing.

matsah: As commanded in Exodus 12:8, and as prepared according to 2:5 above.

Haroset: A sauce traditionally sweetened to soften the taste of the bitter vegetables dipped into it. See 2:6 above.

and two cooked foods: This phrase is lacking in the best manuscripts. Moreover the brief dispute that immediately follows—concerning whether eating the *haroset* is a commandment—flows directly from what precedes it, suggesting indeed that "and two cooked foods" is a later gloss. The Talmud understands these cooked foods as substitutes for the Passover sacrifice and the festival offering typically offered along with the Passover (see 6:3–4 above).

haroset is not a commandment: When the *haroset* is understood—as implied throughout this passage thus far—as a sauce for softening the taste of the bitter vegetables, its importance can be seen as secondary to the command of eating bitter vegetables.

It is a commandment: Already by the time of the Talmud a tradition emerged associating the *haroset* with the mortar used by the Israelite slaves. The food symbolism serves to underscore the independent significance of this food.

And in the Temple,
they would bring before him
the carcass of the Passover.

4 They mixed for him a second cup,
and here the son asks his father.
And if the son does not have knowledge,
his father teaches him:
What differentiates this night from all other nights—[52]
that on all other nights
we eat *hamets* and *matsah*;
this night
is all *matsah*;
that on all other nights
we eat all other vegetables,
this night,
a bitter vegetable;
that on all other nights
we eat meat roasted, cooked, or boiled,

[52] In **K, P**, this night is differentiated from all others only in three ways, and these are presented in a slightly different order: dipping, *hamets*, roasted meat.

And in the Temple: Along with the problematic phrase "two cooked foods" above, this phrase provides a clear indication that, in this chapter, the Mishnah is not only recalling the predestruction Passover practice but also prescribing how Passover meal practices would continue after the destruction of the Temple in 70 CE, in the absence of a proper sacrificial meal.

10:4 *a second cup*: At a standard festival meal, a second cup would be used only upon the conclusion of the meal (compare the third cup below).

and here the son asks his father: Triggered by the change in practice regarding the pouring of the second cup, the son is to question his father about Passover practices, in accordance with Exodus 12:26; 13:14, and elsewhere.

his father teaches him: Tradition has taken what follows here to be the questions that the child is supposed to ask the parent, though the child could instead be taught to ask the very questions that appear in Scripture (see e.g. Exodus 13:8). Despite the widespread current custom of having young children ask these questions, there is something strange about having children spontaneously ask about differences that haven't yet been observed, and a straightforward reading of this mishnah allows the alternative possibility that the father himself raises a single rhetorical question, pointing out to his son the ways in which Passover is different. The translation reproduces the four "questions" as they appear in the printed editions, though only three of these appear in the manuscripts, as noted below. The traditional Passover Haggadah, like the printed editions, also includes four "questions," though the one concerning the requirement to recline has not made its way into editions of the Mishnah. The manuscripts likely preserve the earliest text, reflecting the customs of Palestinian Jews, while the printed editions preserve a four-question tradition from a later period, perhaps incorporating Babylonian customs. The custom eventually canonized in the Haggadah is later still.

that on all other nights: At the time of this formulation, the Passover meal was still celebrated only once, not twice as is the present Diaspora custom.

a bitter vegetable: Certainly the consumption of bitter herbs (as broadly understood, see 2:6 above) would take place on many other nights, just as the consumption of various other vegetables would continue on Passover. But it is distinctive to Passover that the consumption of a bitter vegetable is not only customary, but required.

this night is all roasted;
that on all other nights
we dip only once,
this night
twice?
And according to the knowledge of the son,
his father teaches him.
He begins with disgrace
and ends with praise.
And he expounds
from *My father was a wandering Aramaean*
until he completes the whole portion in its entirety.[53]
    5 Rabban Gamaliel used to say:[54]
Whoever does not mention these three things on Passover
has not fulfilled his obligation.

[53] K, P lack "in its entirety."   [54] K: "Rabban Gamaliel says."

---

this night is all roasted: There was a custom of eating only roasted meat on Passover, presumably as a remembrance of Temple practice (see 4:4 above). The custom of eating only roasted meat eventually fell out of fashion, and so this "question" eventually fell out of use, to be replaced by the "reclining" question noted above.

this night twice: It was apparently customary to have a dipping course preceding all formal meals, so the "question" as phrased remarks on the mandated second dipping. When dipping became less customary, the question was rephrased to the form in current Haggadot: "That on all other nights we do not even dip once, but on this night we dip twice…"

And according to the knowledge of the son: The father's elaboration of these differences, and any explanations offered, should be commensurate with the child's knowledge and capacity for learning.

He begins with disgrace: The Talmud offers two understandings of "disgrace," as slavery or as idolatry; passages beginning with each "disgrace" are included in traditional Passover Haggadot. In any case the Mishnah mandates that the story must have a happy ending.

And he expounds: Offering an expansive interpretation (*midrash*) of the biblical passage specified here.

My father was a wandering Aramaean: Deuteronomy 26:5 and following. This is a curious choice in some respects, since this declaration in its Deuteronomic context is associated not with Passover but with the bringing of first fruits on the Festival of Weeks (Deuteronomy 26:2). Nevertheless, the passage does concisely retell the Exodus, beginning with its own kind of disgrace, reaching an uplifting conclusion.

until he completes the whole portion: The requisite endpoint is left unspecified. The recitation accompanying first fruits ends in Deuteronomy 26:10. Traditional Haggadot finish the exegesis earlier, at the end of 26:8, with the reference to the plagues, omitting any reference to the Temple or the land (see 26:9). Masoretic Bibles mandate a paragraph break after 26:11, which is therefore another possible intended endpoint.

10:5 Rabban Gamaliel: There were two Sages named Rabban Gamaliel (see 7:2 above). The elder lived before the destruction of Jerusalem (see Acts 22:3), while the younger is remembered as a leader of the Yavneh generation (e.g. *Rosh Hashanah* 2:8). The bulk of the named Sages in this chapter are postdestruction figures, and therefore most scholars believe that the Mishnah intends to attribute this saying to the younger.

not fulfilled his obligation: Because Gamaliel's ruling speaks of the requirement to *say* three things, the obligation in question must be the obligation to tell the Passover story on the day of Passover, following Exodus 13:8: *You shall tell your son on that day*…Even if the child's capacity for learning is minimal (see 10:4 above), these three things must be explained nevertheless.

And these are they:
Passover, *matsah*, and bitter vegetable.
Passover:
because the Omnipresent passed over the houses of our ancestors in Egypt.
Matsah:
because our ancestors were redeemed from Egypt.
Bitter vegetable:[55]
because the Egyptians embittered the lives of our ancestors in Egypt.
In every generation[56]
a person is obligated to see himself
as if he left Egypt,
as it is said:
And you shall tell your son on that day saying,
Because of what the Lord did for me when I left Egypt.
Therefore we are obligated
to give thanks, to praise, to worship, to glorify, to honor, to adore, to bless, exalt, and extol[57]
the one who did for our ancestors and[58] for us
all these miracles:

[55] K, P: "bitter vegetables"; in K and P the *matsah* is explained after the bitter vegetables.
[56] K, P lack from "In every generation…" and continue with "Therefore…"
[57] In K, P, the first five words of praise are as above; in K these are followed by "magnify," for a total of six; in P the first five are followed by "to magnify and to laud."
[58] P lacks "for our ancestors and."

Passover: Gamaliel's requirement to speak about the Passover offering is consistent with a postdestruction setting, which would be bereft of a real Passover to consume. The explanation summarized here—with its "Passover" wordplay—comes from Exodus 12:27, which is itself a script for answering a child's question.

matsah, and bitter vegetable: These two food items could still be consumed after the destruction, even though the original command to eat them presents them as an accompaniment to the Passover sacrifice (Exodus 12:8). For the bitter vegetable, the tradition here also supplies a wordplay-related symbolic explanation, connecting the bitter vegetable of Exodus 12:8 with the Egyptians embittering the lives of the Israelites (Exodus 1:14). Curiously, the meaning of *matsah* in relation to the Israelites' redemption is presented as self-evident. Greatly expanded versions of Rabban Gamaliel's dictum, with fuller explanations of each item, have been included in the traditional Passover Haggadah.

In every generation: This sentence, along with this concluding quotation of Exodus 13:8, is lacking in the manuscripts, and modern scholars believe it came into the Mishnah from early Passover Haggadot. The traditional Haggadah, in turn, preserves an expanded form of this tradition.

And you shall tell your son: Exodus 13:8.

Therefore we are obligated: Unlike the previous sentence, a version of this passage is found in the manuscripts. Nevertheless, scholars deem this sentence to be a liturgical gloss added to the Mishnah at a later date, quite possibly from early Passover liturgies. The shift to the first person plural ("we") is one sign of non-Mishnaic style. The inclusion within the passage of a complete liturgical hymn without truncation or alternative versions (compare 10:6 below) is another. Hymns of praise utilizing (and expanding upon) the formula preserved here appear in traditional Passover Haggadot. Even if the hymnic passage is a post-Mishnaic gloss, modern scholars have identified this as a very early Jewish hymn from the Tannaitic and possibly even the late Second Temple period. For other examples of liturgical passages appearing as glosses to the Mishnah, see *Ta'anit* 4:8 and *Tamid* 7:3.

he brought us from servitude to freedom,
from sadness to happiness,
and from mourning to Festival day,
and from darkness to a great light,
and from slavery to redemption.[59]
And let us say before him,
"Hallelujah!"

6 Until what point does he say?
The House of Shammai say:
Until *The mother of the children will rejoice*,
and the House of Hillel say:
Until *the flint into a pool of waters*;
and he seals with "redemption."
R. Tarfon says:
"…who redeemed us and redeemed our ancestors from Egypt,"
and he does not seal it.
R. Aqiva says:
"So shall the Lord our God and the God of our ancestors
bring us to other sacred times and festivals that are coming for us in peace,
joyful in your built city,
and delighted in your service,[60]
and we will eat there from the sacrifices and from the Passovers, etc.,"[61]
until "Blessed are you, Lord, who redeemed Israel."

[59] K, P lack "from sadness…to redemption." [60] K lacks "delighted in your service."
[61] In place of "etc.," K, P add: "the blood of which reaches the wall of your altar for acceptance, and we will give thanks [P: with a new song] to you for our redemption. Blessed are…"

And let us say before him, "Hallelujah!": This fitting conclusion to the hymnic passage serves to introduce the recitation of Hallel (see 5:7 above). The liturgical phrase in its present context also provides a smooth transition to the very next passage; perhaps some very truncated version of the hymnic passage here is indeed integral to the Mishnah.

10:6 *Until what point does he say?* This question continues the topic of "saying" to God "Hallelujah"; that is, Hallel (see above, 5:7; 9:3). Hallel was to be recited both during the offering of the sacrifice (5:7) and during the meal. The rabbinic custom of dividing the Hallel into two parts possibly reflects the situation in Temple days, when the entire Hallel was recited twice, once over the sacrifice and once over the meal; see 10:7 below.

The mother of the children will rejoice: Psalm 113:9, which is the conclusion of the first Psalm of Hallel.

the flint into a pool of waters: Psalm 114:8, which is concludes the second Psalm of Hallel.

and he seals with "redemption": To "seal" a blessing is to conclude it with the standard blessing formula ("Blessed are you, O Lord…"); see *Berakhot* 1:4. Here the requisite blessing to conclude Hallel is to praise God as the redeemer of Israel.

R. Tarfon says…and he does not seal it: R. Tarfon presumably agrees with all authorities that one must conclude Hallel with a blessing, but the formulation of the blessing attributed to Tarfon here is a "short" blessing: one that begins with the "blessing" formula but does not include a signature at the end (again see *Berakhot* 1:4). So Hallel is still "sealed" with a blessing, but the blessing itself lacks a signature.

R. Aqiva says…and we will eat there from the sacrifices…: The version of the prayer attributed to Aqiva here is longer and also "long" in the technical rabbinic sense, by beginning and ending with the blessing formula. Aqiva's blessing also, notably, looks forward to the time when the Temple will be rebuilt and the Passover performed again. Traditional Haggadot follow the tradition attributed here to Aqiva.

7 They mixed for him a third cup.
He blesses over his meal.
A fourth:
he finishes *Hallel* over it,
and says the Blessing of the Song over it.
Between those [earlier] cups
if he wants to drink,
he may drink;
between the third and the fourth
he may not drink.

10:8–9 *After the Passover*

8 One may not conclude after the Passover with *afiqoman*.
If some of them fell asleep,
they may eat;
if all fell asleep,
they may not eat.
R. Yose says:
If they dozed off,
they may eat;
if they fell into a deep sleep,
they may not eat.

10:7 *Blessing of the Song*: Possibly this obscure term refers to a blessing formula used to conclude the recitation of Hallel; alternatively this refers to some other independent liturgical hymn of praise that is to be recited following the Hallel. Customs that would satisfy both understandings have developed and are included in traditional Jewish Passover celebrations.

Between those [earlier] cups: One may drink additional wine between the first and second cup and between the second and the third, but not between the third and the fourth.

10:8 *One may not conclude after the Passover with afiqoman*: The precise meaning of *afiqoman* here is unknown, though its later meaning that one should conclude the Passover meal with the consumption of *matsah* set aside earlier is surely not intended. The Greek term is commonly understood to refer to some dessert course, accompanied perhaps by musical merriment, or by going to other homes to celebrate anew in larger groups. Whatever the precise prohibition may be, the general concern is clear: just as the rabbis limit the drinking in the previous passage, here too the ruling is meant to prevent the celebration from degenerating.

If some of them fell asleep: Lacking revelry as a tool to keep people awake, now the rabbis address the opposite problem: that some of a group may fall asleep. As long as some of the group have remained awake and on task, the Passover may still be consumed—even by those who awaken after nodding off to sleep. If everyone has fallen asleep, none may eat of whatever remains. The reasoning is not entirely clear, but various explanations have been offered. If everyone has fallen asleep, then perhaps they have also lost track of the time (see next mishnah). Alternatively, everyone falling asleep establishes a clear break in the ritual action, thus ending the meal. This situation also leaves whatever remains of the Passover unattended, and subject to some unknown invalidating event. By any measure, an entire group asleep constitutes a problematic irony for what was supposed to be "a night of watching" (Exodus 12:42).

9 The Passover after midnight
renders the hands impure.
Piggul and remainder
render the hands impure.
If he recited the blessing of Passover,
he is exempt from the blessing over the sacrifice.
If he recited the blessing of the sacrifice,
he is not exempt from that of the Passover—
the words of R. Ishmael.
R. Aqiva says:
This does not exempt from that,
and that does not exempt from this.

10:9 *The Passover after midnight*: According to Exodus 12:10, the Passover is not be left until morning, and any that remains must be burned. It is not clear whether the rabbis interpreted "until morning" as "until midnight," or whether they moved up the deadline only as a precaution; see *Berakhot* 1:1.

renders the hands impure: A low-grade defilement, which can be ameliorated by washing the hands. See *Yadayim*.

Piggul: A special category of invalidated sacrifices, referring to those sacrifices that are potentially valid and properly prepared, but which the bringer intended to consume at an improper time (see *Zevahim* 2:2–3).

remainder: Time ranges are specified for the proper consumption of all edible sacrifices (see *Zevahim* 5:3–8). Any meat that remains after this allotted time is considered to be "remainder." Like the Passover (Exodus 12:10), all "remainder" is to be burned.

the blessing of Passover: The reference here is to a blessing sanctifying the consumption of the Passover, thus marking the act as the fulfillment of a commandment.

blessing over the sacrifice: The festival offering, offered alongside the Passover (see 6:3 above); a blessing was mandated to mark the fulfillment of this commandment as well.

he is exempt from the blessing over the sacrifice: As elsewhere in the Mishnah, blessings over some items can serve to exempt one from other blessings over related foods or actions (see, e.g., *Berakhot* 6:5). According to this view, because the festival sacrifice is secondary to the Passover, the blessing for the Passover takes precedence over, and exempts one from, the blessing over the festival offering, but not the other way around.

This does not exempt from that: According to the view attributed here to R. Aqiva, the two sacrifices fulfill separate commandments, each worthy of its own blessing, and neither can be subsumed by the other.

Tractate Sheqalim

Miriam-Simma Walfish

Introduction

Overview

Tractate *Sheqalim*, "*sheqel* coins" or "*sheqel* weights," deals with the obligation of every Jewish male (see 1:3) above the age of twenty, except perhaps priests (see 1:3–4), to donate every year to the Temple the monetary equivalent of the biblical "half-*sheqel*." The main biblical passage standing behind this tractate is Exodus 30:11–16. The accumulated funds are to be used by the Temple authorities to purchase the animals (and other supplies) for communal sacrifices and other Temple necessities.

Structure and Organization of the Tractate

The tractate is organized into two major units: the first (1:1–4:2) addresses the collection and allocation of the *sheqel* payment, while the second (4:3–8:8) addresses other Temple procedures, primarily but not exclusively related to the collection and allocation of other types of donations. Within each larger unit, however, related topics are introduced, clouding the overarching structure.

Chapters 1–2 primarily present the rabbinic understanding of the procedures for collecting the *sheqel* offering. Chapter 1 details different classes of people in rabbinic society such as women and slaves and states how to treat the *sheqel* offering of each. It then describes the money-changing fee called the *qolbon*. Chapter 2 treats donations from the Diaspora, as well as procedures for treating excessive offerings of all types (2:3–5), a topic treated again in 4:3–5.

Chapters 3 and 4:1–5 deal with the practice of "collecting [from] the chamber," which was the procedure for gathering coins that had been stored in a special chamber and using them to purchase various Temple goods. The rules regarding the dedication of personal possessions to the Temple are treated in 4:6–8 and completed in 4:9 with an account explaining how the authorities set the price of goods purchased for the Temple.

Chapter 5 shifts the discussion to other Temple procedures, beginning with a list of Temple functionaries and continuing to the way individuals procured the required libations for their offerings. The chapter concludes with a description of the Temple chambers. Chapter 6 delineates thirteen prostrations, thirteen tables, and thirteen *shofar* chests for the collection of various donations that were in the Temple. Chapter 7 deals with cases of uncertainty—uncertainty regarding the allocation of coins found between collection chests (7:1), coins found outside the Temple (7:2), and meat found inside and outside the Temple (7:3–5). It closes with a list of seven ordinances governing the use of communal funds to support Temple activities (7:6–7).

Chapter 8 discusses certain aspects of purity. In chapter 8:1–3 the tractate addresses the purity status of objects found in Jerusalem and how this status changes based on an object's physical or temporal location. Chapter 8:4 treats the manner of dealing with impurity of the Temple curtains, and 8:6–7 the disposal of impure meat found in the Temple.

The tractate concludes with two miscellaneous laws relating to the Temple—the placement of various offerings on the ramp of the altar and the applicability of laws regarding Temple donations once the Temple is no longer in existence.

In sum, only about one half of the tractate deals with the annual half-*sheqel* tax, prompting many commentators, both medieval and modern, to speculate why this tractate was placed in the Order of *Mo'ed*, which deals overwhelmingly with festivals and sacred times, and not in the Order of *Qodashim*, which deals overwhelmingly with the Temple, its layout, procedures, and offerings. Indeed, many passages in our tractate are paralleled by passages in *Zevahim*, *Tamid*, and *Middot*. The question remains open.

Main Ideas

Perhaps the most profound idea developed by the Mishnah is the establishment of a linkage between the people of Israel and the sacrifices that were brought in their name at the Temple. In Exodus 30:11–16 the purpose of the half-*sheqel* payment is to protect from plague the participants in a military census; the half-*sheqel* is a ransom payment, an expiation of the soul. (For a plague caused by divine wrath on the occasion of a census, see 2 Samuel 24.) By the time we get to tractate *Sheqalim*, however, the military census, the plague, and expiation are completely forgotten. The purpose of the half-*sheqel* payment, as chapter 4 makes clear, is to provide funds for the communal sacrifices. Communal offerings must be purchased from communal funds (see 4:1).

A related idea is developed in chapter four of *Ta'anit*. The *Tamid* sacrifice is offered every morning and every evening on behalf of the welfare of Israel (see tractate *Tamid*.) But how can the sacrifice be offered on behalf of the people of Israel when they are not standing nearby? The early prophets, says the mishnah, enacted that representative groups of the people should coordinate the time of their prayers with the times of the sacrifice (see *Ta'anit* 4:2). The facticity of these traditions is unknown. But what is important is the Mishnah's assumption that there must be an intimate link between the people and the sacrifices offered in the Temple. The half-*sheqel* was contributed to the Temple not just by the Jews of the Land of Israel but also by the Jews of the Diaspora (see 3:4), as is attested in many Greek and Roman sources.

Relationship to Scripture

Exodus 30:11–16 commands every Israelite male over the age of twenty to offer a half-*sheqel* of silver when the people are being counted (apparently a military census) in order to ward off a plague (30:11). The collected money was to be used to support Tabernacle worship (30:16). In the Second Temple period, this offering served as a tax. Nehemiah 10 describes a rededication to the covenant, including renewed *sheqel* offerings to the Temple. One of the Dead Sea Scrolls instructs its adherents to donate the half-*sheqel* once in their lifetime, while the rabbis understood it to be an annual offering.

One should note the shift in the size of the donation. Nehemiah 10:33 records a third of a *sheqel* as the required donation, while Exodus 30:11–16 speaks of a half-*sheqel* of silver. Commentators attribute the disparity to the fact that the *sheqel* had grown by the time of Nehemiah. The rabbinic *sheqel*, in contrast, seems to have shrunk; the weight, in silver, of one rabbinic *sheqel* was equivalent to half a biblical *sheqel* and was thus understood to be the required amount.

Special Notes for the Reader

Eliezer Pinczower collected significant manuscript variants in his dissertation on tractate *Sheqalim* (Hebrew University, 1998, in Hebrew). Especially noteworthy is his collection of manuscripts of the Yerushalmi Talmud that reflect a different tradition from that of manuscripts **K** and **P**. These are noted with the letter **Y** (for Yerushalmi). There is no Babylonian Talmud on *Sheqalim*.

Tractate Sheqalim

Chapter One

1:1–2 *Public Maintenance during the Month of Adar*

1 On the first of Adar,
one makes a public announcement regarding *sheqalim* and forbidden mixtures.
On the fifteenth,
one recites the scroll of Esther in the cities
and fixes thoroughfares, roads, and ritual baths.
One takes care of all the needs of the community,
marks the graves,
and also one goes forth on account of forbidden mixtures.
   2 R. Judah said:
At first they would uproot [the forbidden agricultural mixtures]
and discard them before [their owners].
When the number of sinners increased,

1:1 *one makes*: The referent of many of the verbs in this chapter is unclear, but here it is perhaps the priests or a judicial authority making the announcement.

announcement regarding sheqalim: Reminding everyone that the Temple's fiscal year was about to begin and that they should prepare to pay their half-*sheqel* tax in a timely manner.

forbidden mixtures: Leviticus 19:19 and Deuteronomy 22:9. See also *Kilayim* 8:1.

ritual baths: Among other uses these were used for purification before entering the Temple precincts. See *Miqva'ot*.

all the needs of the community: Apparently those activities necessitated by the wear and tear of winter weather. Alternatively, the Jerusalem Talmud explains this phrase as referring to the same needs as those listed in *Mo'ed Qatan* 1:2.

marks the graves: Graves were marked with white paint so that people would not accidentally walk over them and become impure. See Matthew 23:27 and Luke 11:44. Winter rains would erase these markings.

one goes forth: Apparently messengers of the court or Temple. See 1:2.

go forth: To verify that farmers had in fact uprooted the forbidden agricultural mixtures.

1:2 *the number…increased*: The practice of uprooting forbidden mixtures set up incentives for noncompliance. Owners of fields were letting the court do their weeding and then they were feeding the uprooted plants to their livestock.

they would uproot and[1] discard them onto the thoroughfares.
They [ultimately] decreed that they would declare the entire field ownerless.

1:3–5   Collection of the Sheqel Offering

3 On the fifteenth [of Adar],
money changers would sit at tables outside of the Temple.
On the twenty-fifth,
they would sit in the Temple.
From then on,
one began exacting collateral.
From whom does one exact collateral?
From Levites and Israelites, converts and freed slaves,
but not from women, slaves, or minors.
Any minor whose father started donating a *sheqel* on his behalf—
[his father] may not stop [donating].
One does not exact collateral from the priests
for the sake of peace.

4 R. Judah said:
Ben Bukhri[2] testified in Yavneh:
Any priest who brings a *sheqel*
does not sin.
R. Yohanan b. Zakkai said to him:
Not so!
Rather, any priest who does not bring a *sheqel* sins,
but the priests expound the following verse to their own advantage:

---

[1] K, P lack "uproot and."
[2] K: "ben Kubari." P: "ben Kovari." There is no other tannaitic attestation of this person.

They…ownerless: Even throwing the forbidden mixtures into the streets did not reverse the incentives. The Mishnah thus reports that finally the court annulled the ownership of fields whose owners did not weed out the forbidden mixtures; now anyone could reap produce grown there.

1:3 *outside of the Temple*: Lit. "in the province." The term can indicate: country dwellers as opposed to city dwellers (*Terumot* 2:5); areas outside of Jerusalem (*Ma'aser Sheni* 3:4); and areas outside of the Temple (*Eruvin* 10:11–14, *Tamid* 7:2).

collateral: Temple agents would exact collateral from those who had not yet brought their *sheqel* offering.

freed slaves: The slaves referred to in this mishnah are freed Canaanite (i.e. gentile) slaves, who, after immersing ritually, had all ritual obligations of full Jews.

women, slaves, or minors: A common grouping in the Mishnah (e.g. *Berakhot* 3:3; *Sukkah* 2:8).

for the sake of peace: Lit. "because of the ways of peace." It is not clear whether the "ways of peace" would be threatened because such a demand would show a disregard for the priests' alternative exegesis as reported below in 1:4, or simply because the Temple was the priestly domain so it would be disrespectful to demand a donation from them to support their own work. *Gittin* 5:8–9 contains a list of other actions prescribed because of the "ways of peace." See also *Shevi'it* 4:3 and 5:9.

1:4 *does not sin*: This statement implies that the priests are exempt or perhaps discouraged from bringing the *sheqel*; this contrasts with the previous clause which implies that they are obligated.

…any meal offering of the priest will be completely burnt,
it will not be eaten.
Since the *omer*, the two breads, and the showbreads are ours,
how may they be eaten?
  5 Although they said:
One does not exact collateral
from women, slaves, and children,
if[3] they bring a *sheqel*
one accepts it from them.
The gentile or the Samaritan who brought a *sheqel*,
one does not accept it from them.
One also does not accept from them:
bird offerings[4] of *zavim*,
bird offerings of *zavot*,
bird offerings of women who have recently given birth,
purgation[5] offerings and guilt offerings.[6]
But one accepts from them
vow and free-will offerings.
This is the rule:
One accepts anything
that is [consecrated] through a vow or a free-will offering,
but one does not accept anything from them
that is not [consecrated] through a vow or a free-will offering.
This is also made explicit by Ezra:
You shall have no part with us in building a house to our God.

[3] P adds "but." [4] Lit. "nests" here and below.
[5] P: "one does accept from them purgation offerings and guilt offerings."
[6] K adds "one does not accept from them."

---

any meal offering…will not be eaten: Leviticus 6:16.

omer: sheaf offering. Leviticus 23:10–14.

two breads: A special offering of two loaves, later associated with the Festival of Weeks, that was brought seven weeks after the *omer* offering: see Leviticus 23:15-20.

showbreads: Exodus 25:30; *Menahot* chapter 10.

ours: All three of these offerings were eaten by the priests and purchased with public funds.

how may they be eaten? The priests understand Leviticus 6:16 to prohibit the consumption of any grain offering supplied, even if only partially, by a priest. If priests were to donate a *sheqel*, any grain offering purchased with that *sheqel* would have to be burnt and not consumed. According to the priests, this would cause a problem for communal offerings such as the sheaf offering or the offering of the two breads, which priests were, in fact, meant to consume.

1:5 *they said*: In 1:3 above.

the Samaritan: According to 2 Kings 17, the Samaritans worshipped the God of Israel without giving up their former gods and practices. Because of some shared practices, Samaritans are mentioned in a number of laws in the Mishnah (e.g. *Demai* 5:9, *Shevi'it* 8:10, *Niddah* 4:1 and 7:4).

zavim…zavot: the male *zav* or the female *zav*. See Leviticus 15.

women who have recently given birth: Leviticus 12:1–8.

You shall have no part…to our God: Ezra 4:3. Ezra 4:1–4 describes a group of non-Israelites who wished to aid in the building of the Temple. They were told that they might not participate in this endeavor.

1:6–7   Assessment of a Fee for the Exchange of Currency

6 These are the people obligated [to pay] the fee:
⁷Levites, Israelites, converts, and freed slaves,
but not priests,⁸ women, slaves, or minors.
One who brings a *sheqel*
on behalf of a priest, woman, slave, or minor is exempt [from the fee].
If he brought one on his own behalf
or on behalf of his fellow,
he is obligated [to pay] one fee.⁹
R. Meir says:
Two fees.
If he exchanged a *sela* for a *sheqel*¹⁰
he is obligated [to pay] two fees.

7 One who brings a *sheqel*
on behalf of a poor person,
or on behalf of his neighbor,
or on behalf of a resident of his city
is exempt [from the fee].
But if he loaned it to them,
he is obligated.
Brothers and partners¹¹
who are obligated [to pay] the fee
are exempt from tithes of livestock,
and when they owe tithes of livestock
they are exempt from the fee.

---

⁷ Y adds "priests" here.   ⁸ K, P lack "priests."
⁹ Y lacks "is obligated to pay one fee. R. Meir says." It thus reads: "If he brought one on his own behalf or on behalf of his fellow, he is obligated [to pay] two fees."
¹⁰ Alt. "If he gave a *sela* in order to receive a [rabbinic] *sheqel* in return," one rabbinic *sheqel* having remained in the hands of the Temple. In this case, a fee is levied for each rabbinic *sheqel*.
¹¹ The word "and" is missing from many manuscripts. This would mean that the brothers themselves are partners rather than all partners being exempt from the fee.

1:6 *fee*: In the original, *qolbon*: For the precise value of this payment see 1:7 below. The gospels use the same Greek word to refer to the moneychangers in the Jerusalem Temple (John 2:15, Mark 11:15, Matthew 21:12). This fee may have been the moneychangers' commission or may have been used to ensure that each donor was bringing the full required amount despite the use of a foreign currency. It is thus unclear whether this fee was given to the moneychanger or to the Temple.

sela: The *sela* is a coin equal in value to the full biblical *sheqel*. The rabbinic *sheqel* was worth half of a biblical *sheqel*, and therefore was accepted as payment of the required half-*sheqel*.

1:7 *tithes of livestock*: The owner of a herd of animals was obligated each year to consecrate a tenth of all newborns and bring them to Jerusalem to be sacrificed (see Leviticus 27:32–33). See 3:1.

Brothers and partners: Or "brothers who are partners," perhaps brothers who have inherited their father's estate but not yet divided it into their respective portions. In general, partners are liable for the fee but exempt from the tithe of livestock because the rabbis understood Numbers 18:15 to limit the tithe to animals in the sole possession of an individual. See also *Bekhorot* 9:3.

How much is the fee?
One silver *ma'ah*—
the words of R. Meir.
But the Sages say:
A half.

Chapter Two

2:1–2 *Exceptional Circumstances of Collection*

2 One combines *sheqalim* into *darkonot*
because of the travel burden.
Just as there were *shofar* chests in the Temple,
so too, there were *shofar* chests[12] outside of the Temple.
Residents of a town who sent their *sheqalim*
but they were stolen or lost—
if collection had already taken place
they swear to the treasurer,
but if not they swear to the [other] town members
who donate *sheqalim* in their place.
If they are found or the thieves return them,
both sets of *sheqalim* are considered *sheqalim*
and do not count towards the following year.

  2 One who gives his *sheqel* to his fellow to donate on his behalf
but [the fellow] donates it on his own behalf
If collection had taken place—
he has committed sacrilege.

[12] K, P lack "*shofar* chests."

One silver ma'ah: About a twelfth of a rabbinic *sheqel*.

2:1 *darkonot*: Gold *darics*—a Persian coin worth sixteen *sheqel*. While the coin went out of circulation with Alexander's conquest, the term may have come to be used for any gold coin. Perhaps related to the *adarkhonim* of Ezra 8:27 and 1 Chronicles 29:7, where it is also associated with the Temple. See *Bava Batra* 10:2.

travel burden: Darics were worth more, thus lessening the burden for messengers coming into Jerusalem from the Diaspora.

shofar chests: Collection boxes in the shape of a *shofar*. See also chapter 6 below.

Residents of a town: See *Eruvin* 4:10, *Betsah* 5:6, and *Megillah* 3:1.

collection: See 3:1 below.

they swear: The messengers.

2:2 *sacrilege*: Illicit use of sacred property.

One who gives his *sheqel*
from funds[13] designated for Temple use—
if collection had taken place and the animal sacrificed—
he has committed sacrilege.
[If] from funds[14] of second tithes or from Seventh-Year funds,
he consumes a corresponding amount.

2:3–5 Allocation of Funds from Excessive Offerings

3 One who gathers coins and says,
"These are for my *sheqel* donation"—
the House of Shammai say:
Their surplus is a free-will offering,
while the House of Hillel say:
Their surplus remains unconsecrated.
"I will bring of these for my *sheqel* donation":
Both agree that their surplus remains unconsecrated.
"These are for a[15] purgation offering":
Both agree that the surplus is a free-will offering.
"I will bring of these for a purgation offering":
Both agree that the surplus is unconsecrated.
4 R. Simeon said:
What is the difference between *sheqalim* and the purgation offering?
[16]*Sheqalim* have a limit,

[13] P lacks "funds."   [14] P lacks "funds of."
[15] K, P: "my purgation offering," here and in the next clause.   [16] P adds "rather."

---

second tithes: These tithes were set aside in the first, second, fourth, and fifth years of the Sabbatical cycle. The owners were to consume these tithes in Jerusalem. However, if the owner was concerned that the food would rot or become impure on the journey, he could redeem the produce for money that would be used to purchase food in Jerusalem. See Deuteronomy 14:22–26; *Ma'aser Sheni* esp. 1:1, 1:7.

Seventh-Year funds: Fruit gathered during the Sabbatical (Seventh) Year may only be eaten until its counterparts left on the tree would rot. Seventh-Year fruit may be sold, but the funds may only be used by the seller to purchase edible goods which will be consumed by the end of the consumption time of the initial fruit. See *Shevi'it* chapter 7–9, especially 8:2; *Pesahim* 4:2.

consume a corresponding amount: If one sells second-tithe or Seventh-Year produce and then uses this money for the *sheqel* donation, one must then purchase a corresponding amount of food with other funds and consume it according to the rules of second-tithe or Seventh-Year produce respectively.

2:3 *surplus*: The amount remaining after the *sheqel* donation has been removed.

2:4 R. Simeon is explaining the view of the House of Hillel (2:3) who require that the excess of funds gathered for purgation offerings be given to the Temple as a free-will offering, while excess of funds gathered for *sheqel* donations remain unconsecrated.

have a limit: Exodus 30:15 states that a poor person may not give less nor a rich person more than the half-*sheqel*.

and the purgation offering has no limit.
R. Yehudah says:
Even *sheqalim* have no limit.[17]
When Israel immigrated[18] from the Diaspora
they would donate *darkonot* as a *sheqel* offering.
They then donated *sela'im*;
they then donated *teva'in*.
They desired to donate *dinarim*.[19]
R. Simeon said:
Even so the hand of each is equal.
But regarding the purgation offering,
one person may offer[20] a *sela*,
while another offers two,
and a third offers[21] three.

5 The surplus [of funds gathered] for a *sheqalim* donation
is unconsecrated.
The surplus of funds of the tenth of an *efah* offering,[22]
bird offerings of *zavim*,
bird offerings of *zavot*,
bird offerings of women who have recently given birth,
as well as purgation and guilt offerings—
their surplus is a free-will offering.
This is the rule:
The surplus of anything offered for[23] the purpose of purgation or guilt
is a free-will offering.
The surplus [of funds] of a burnt offering
[is reserved] for a burnt offering,
the surplus of a grain offering
for a grain offering.

[17] K: "have a limit."   [18] Lit. "came up."
[19] Y adds "and they did not accept them from them."
[20] Lit. "bring," here and throughout.   [21] K lacks "offers."
[22] Y reads "…remain unconsecrated."   [23] P has "from" rather than "for."

has no limit: Since there is no fixed price for a purgation offering, a person collecting coins for its purpose intends to give all the collected coins to the Temple.

darkonot: Worth two *sheqel*. See 2:1 above.

sela'im: Equivalent to two half-*sheqel*.

teva'in: Coins equaling half a *sela*, which are thus equivalent to a half-*sheqel*.

dinarim: A *dinar* (or *denar*) was worth half of a half-*sheqel*.

the hand of each is equal: Rich and poor all donated the same amount.

2:5 *the tenth of an efah offering*: This grain offering was brought by those who could not afford an animal for the guilt offering. Leviticus 5:11; *Keritot* 6:8.

bird offerings of zavim…zavot: See above, 1:5.

bird offerings of women who have recently given birth: See above, 1:5.

The surplus of an offering of well-being
for an offering of well-being,
the surplus of Passover offerings
for an offering of well-being.
The surplus of *nazir* offerings for *nezirim*,
the surplus [of the offering of a particular] *nazir* for a free-will offering.
The surplus of poor people for poor people,
the surplus [of the offering of a particular] poor person for that poor person.
The surplus [for the redemption of] captives for captives,
the surplus [for the redemption of a particular] captive for that captive.[24]
The surplus [for burial of] the dead for the dead,
the surplus [for a particular] deceased person for his inheritors.
R. Meir says:
The surplus [for a particular] deceased person
must remain untouched until the coming of Elijah.
R. Nathan says:[25]
The surplus [for a particular] deceased person
must be used to build a monument on his grave.

Chapter Three

3:1–4 *Removal of the Collected Sheqalim*

3 At three points of the year
one collects [from] the chamber:
half a month before Passover,
half a month before the Festival of Weeks,
and half a month before the Festival of Sukkot,

---

[24] **K, P** have "captives" before "poor people."
[25] R. Nathan's statement is missing from **Y** and from genizah fragments.

---

offering of well-being: A celebratory offering; see Leviticus 19:5, Deuteronomy 27:7.

for an offering of well-being: Since it is not possible to bring a second Passover offering, an additional offering of well-being is brought instead; see *Pesahim* 9:6–7.

surplus of nazir offerings for nezirim: Funds were collected for poor *nezirim* to help them afford the necessary sacrifices at the end of their period of abstention. Leftover funds from these offerings were reserved for other poor *nezirim*.

surplus of poor people for poor people: i.e. money collected for charity.

3:1 *collects [from] the chamber*: The *sheqalim* have been placed in a special chamber for storage until this point. Now they are removed in order to purchase sacrifices and meet other Temple needs.

half a month: Commentators understand this to be half of the month of preparation time for each holiday mentioned. See *Bekhorot* 7:9.

and these are the same points as the gathering of tithes of livestock—
the words of R. Aqiva.
Ben Azzai says:
On the twenty-ninth of Adar,
on the first of Sivan,
and on the twenty-ninth of Av.[26]
R. Eleazar and R. Simeon say:
On the first of Nisan,
on the first of Sivan,
and on the twenty-ninth of Elul.[27]
Why did they say "on the twenty-ninth of Elul"
and not "on the first of Tishre"?
Because [the first of Tishre] is a holiday
and it is impossible to tithe on a holiday.
Therefore, they pushed it back to the twenty-ninth of Elul.

2 One collects [from] the chamber
using three baskets of three *se'ah* each.
Aleph, bet, gimel are written on them.
R. Ishmael says:
Greek is written on them—*alpha, beta, gamla*.[28]
The one who collects may not enter [the chamber]
with a bordered cloak,[29] shoe, or sandal,
or with *tefillin* or an amulet,
lest he become impoverished and people say:
"He became poor because of the sin of [stealing from] the chamber,"
or lest he become rich and people say:

[26] K: "twenty-ninth of Elul."
[27] K: "the first of Tishre."
[28] MSS, correctly, *gamma*.
[29] Lit. "covered"; see annotations.

gathering of tithes of livestock: Animals could not be consumed until they were tithed. At each of these periods, owners were obligated to designate a tithe from the animals born since the previous tithing period. See Leviticus 27:32; above 1:7, also tractate *Bekhorot*.

twenty-ninth of Adar: R. Aqiva and Ben Azzai apparently agree on this date, but R. Aqiva thinks that Adar sometimes has twenty-nine and sometimes thirty days, so that it is more precise to speak in terms of the amount of time before Passover. Ben Azzai thinks that Adar always contains twenty-nine days.

twenty-ninth of Av: See *Bekhorot* 9:5–6 for more on this dispute.

twenty-ninth of Elul: The Talmud in *Bekhorot* explains that since the first of Tishre is the New Year for tithing of livestock (*Rosh Hashanah* 1:1), one must tithe the animals of the previous year before this date.

3:2 The *three baskets* correspond to the three times of year discussed above in 3:1.

Aleph, bet, gimmel: The Hebrew equivalent of A, B, C. The baskets would be filled in the order in which the *sheqalim* had been originally donated, and were labeled so that the *sheqalim* donated first would be used first.

bordered cloak: Commentators explain that the cloak has a breastpocket or a folded border such that coins could have been hidden in it.

"He became rich from chamber funds."[30]
A person must discharge [the suspicion] of people
in the same way as that of God,
as it is written: *...you shall be clear before the Lord and before Israel,*
and it says: *And you will find favor and approbation in the eyes of God and man.*

3 [A member] of the house of Rabban Gamaliel used to enter
and his *sheqel* was between his fingers.
And he would throw it in front of the one collecting.
The one collecting would take care to push it into the basket.
The one collecting may not collect until he says to [the Temple treasurers]:
"Shall I collect?"
and they say to him:
"Collect, collect, collect!" three times.

4 After he collected [from] the first [basket],
he covered it with hides.
After he collected [from] the second,
he covered it with hides.
He would not cover the third,[31]
lest he forget and collect from what he had already collected.
He collected [from] the first one in the name of the Land of Israel,
[from] the second in the name of the surrounding towns,
and [from] the third in the name of Babylonia, Media, and the distant provinces.

---

[30] Alt. "collecting from the chamber."
[31] **K** adds "and why would he not cover [the third]?"; **P** adds "and why would he cover?"

---

discharge [the suspicion] of people: The rules laid out in this mishnah are to prevent not theft but rather the suspicion of theft.

you shall be clear...before Israel: Numbers 32:22.

And you will find favor...God and man: Proverbs 3:4.

3:3 *A member...before the one collecting*: Rabban Gamaliel's motivation would be that the last *sheqalim* donated would have been on the top of the pile and would thus have been used right away for the purchasing of sacrifices.

three times: See also *Parah* 3:10.

3:4 *hides*: See *Kelim* 16:4. The one removing funds from a basket would cover it with hides as a reminder that funds had already been taken from it.

He collected...distant provinces: Thus, the basket gets emptied at the time when it could be expected that the donations from the designated area had come in.

Chapter Four

4:1–2 *What Was Done with the Collected Funds?*

4 What would they do with the collected funds?
They would purchase with them continual offerings and additional offerings along with their libations,
the *omer* and the two loaves and the showbread and all communal offerings.
Those who guard the aftergrowths in the Seventh Year
receive their wage from the collection of the chamber.
R. Yose says:
Though one who desires may volunteer as an unpaid guard.
They said to him:
Even you say that they come only from communal funds!
  2 The heifer and the scapegoat and the red thread
come from the collection of the chamber.
The ramp of the heifer
and the ramp of the scapegoat

4:1 *continual offerings*: The daily offering of lambs in the morning and afternoon (the *Tamid*). See Numbers 28:1–8.

additional offerings: Numbers 28:9ff.

omer: See 1:4 above.

two loaves: See 1:4 above.

aftergrowths: During the Seventh (Sabbatical) Year growing new produce is prohibited. However, new sheaves were necessary for the *omer* offering. Thus, Temple functionaries would find sprouts growing spontaneously and guard them until they were ready for harvesting.

may volunteer: The statement that they are paid from the funds in the chamber does not mean that they must work for a wage, only that if they do expect payment their wages come from that source.

they: The *omer* and the two loaves and the showbread.

from communal funds: If the guards of the produce were not paid for their services, it would be as if they had individually donated these offerings.

4:2 *The heifer*: See Numbers 19.

the scapegoat: Leviticus 16:7–10, *Yoma* chapters 4 and 6.

the red thread: Four red threads are mentioned in the Bible and Mishnah. The first is the red thread used in the purification ceremony of one recovered from skin affliction (Leviticus 14:4) and in the burning of the red heifer (Numbers 19:6). There are also red threads associated with the scapegoat ceremony in *Yoma* 4:2. Finally, a red thread, attached to the door of the Temple, would, it was said, turn white when the scapegoat reached the wilderness (*Yoma* 6:8). The thread mentioned here could refer to any or all of these threads.

ramp of the heifer: *Parah* 3:6 describes the building of a ramp to lead the heifer from the Temple Mount to the Mount of Olives.

ramp of the scapegoat: *Yoma* 6:4 describes the ramp that would take the scapegoat to the wilderness.

and the thread between its horns
and the water channel
and the city wall and its towers
and all the needs of the city
come from what remained in the chamber.[32]
Abba Saul says:
The high priests make the ramp of the heifer
using their own funds.

4:3–5   Use of Surplus Funds

3 The surplus of funds from what remained in the chamber—
what would one do with them?
One would purchase with them wine, oil, and fine flour.
And the profit is consecrated—
the words of R. Ishmael.
R. Aqiva says:
One may not earn money from consecrated goods
nor from money for the poor.
   4 Surplus from the collected funds—
what would one do with it?
One would make with it golden plates
as a covering for the Holy of Holies.
R. Ishmael says:
Surplus from the profits[33]
for the awakening of the altar,[34]
and the surplus from the collection
for the Temple vessels.

[32] P: "from the collection of the chamber."
[33] Alt. "surplus from the fruit."   [34] Alt. "summer [fruits] of the altar." See 2 Samuel 16:2.

thread between its horns: Yoma 6:8.

water channel: Yoma 5:6.

city walls: Of Jerusalem.

what remained in the chamber: After the three removals of 3:1 above.

4:3 *surplus of funds*: After the expenses listed in the previous mishnah have been met.

wine, oil, and fine flour: These goods would then be sold at a profit to worshippers who needed them for their offerings.

R. Aqiva…the poor: R. Aqiva seems to think that Temple funds may not be used to make a profit even if it is a profit for the Temple.

4:4 *Surplus from the collected funds*: Money left over in the baskets. See 3:2 above.

awakening of the altar: Keeping the altar active when it would otherwise lie dormant. Based on 2 Samuel 16:2, many commentators interpret the phrase to mean "summer [fruits, that is, refreshment] of the altar."

R. Aqiva says:
Surplus from the collection
for the awakening of the altar,
and the surplus from the libations
for the Temple vessels.
R. Hanina, Prefect of the Priests says:
Surplus from the libations
for the awakening of the altar,
and the surplus from the collection
for the Temple vessels.
And neither would concede regarding the profits.[35]

5 Surplus from the incense—
what would one do with it?
One would separate from it
the wage of the craftsmen,
and one would redeem[36] it
with the wage of the craftsmen,
and then one would give it to the craftsmen
as their wage,
and then one would purchase it
[with *sheqalim*] from the new collection.
If the new one[37] came on time,
one would purchase it
with the new donation,[38]
but if not—from the old one.

[35] Or "fruits." [36] Or "desanctify."
[37] Alt. "the month" (i.e. that the year is not a leap year such that the first of Nisan comes a bit later). The difference involves only the vowels, and the manuscripts vary.
[38] P: "from the new donation."

surplus from the libations: See below, 4:9.

neither would concede: Neither R. Aqiva nor R. Hanina would concede to R. Yishmael. See R. Aqiva's view in 4:3 above.

4:5 *Surplus from the incense*: After the first of Nisan the priests were required to use incense purchased with the *sheqalim* for that year. The question here is how they deal with incense left over from the previous year so that it would not go to waste.

one would redeem it: In order to turn goods designated for Temple use into goods that could be used by others, one had to exchange them for other goods of equivalent value which would then themselves become sacred. Here the priests are drawing on funds set aside for the craftsmen and are turning them into sacred goods by "purchasing" the leftover incense with them. The incense thereby loses its sanctified status.

one would purchase it: This repurchasing is the reversal of the previous process. One would take the sacred *sheqalim* and exchange them for now ordinary incense, which thereby takes on the sanctified status of the new year rather than that of the year which had passed.

4:6–8 *Use of Sanctified Personal Belongings*

6 One who consecrates his possessions
and they contained objects appropriate for communal sacrifices—
let them be given to the craftsmen as their wage—
the words of R. Aqiva.
Ben Azzai said to him:
This is not the rule.[39]
Rather, one ought to separate the wages of the craftsmen from them
and desacralize them using the coins of the craftsmen.
One is then able to give them to the craftsmen as their wage
and then purchase them back from newly collected funds.

7 One who consecrates his possessions
and they contained an animal appropriate for the altar,
both male and female animals—
R. Eliezer says:
Let the males be sold to those who need whole burnt offerings
and let the females be sold to those who need sacrifices of well-being[40]
and let their funds accrue[41] with the rest of the possessions
to the upkeep of the Temple.
R. Joshua says:
Let the males themselves be brought
as whole burnt offerings
and let the females be sold to those who need offerings of well-being,
and he should bring out of their proceeds whole burnt offerings.
Let the rest of the possessions accrue to the upkeep of the Temple.
R. Aqiva says:
I understand the opinion of R. Eliezer more than that of R. Joshua,
for R. Eliezer applied his rule equally
while R. Joshua made a distinction.

[39] Or "this is not consistent with what is" the rule in 4:5.
[40] K adds: "and he should bring whole burnt offerings using their funds." This seems to be an error.
[41] Lit. "fall."

4:6 *One who consecrates his possessions*: This must be a case in which the donor did not designate a particular use for the consecrated goods. If the person had done so they could only be used for that purpose. See *Temurah* 7:3.

given to the craftsmen as their wage: See *Temurah* 7:1.

4:7 *females*: Since these could not be whole burnt offerings. See Leviticus 1:3 and *Sheqalim* 7:4 below.

and let their funds accrue…upkeep of the Temple: R. Eliezer thinks that sanctified goods whose use is unspecified automatically accrue to the upkeep of the Temple, but money procured through the sale of anything which could be offered on the altar may only be used for the sake of the altar. See *Temurah* 7:1.

Let the males themselves be brought: R. Joshua presumes that people consecrating their goods intend to have the animals sacrificed on the altar in their name.

applied his rule equally: All of the possessions end up going towards Temple upkeep.

R. Joshua made a distinction: He said that the animals go toward the altar, while other possessions go toward Temple upkeep. He also distinguished between male and female animals.

R. Papias said:
I have heard in accord with both their opinions,
that when one consecrates on explicit terms,[42]
[the ruling] follows R. Eliezer's opinion,
but when one consecrates without specifying,
[the ruling] follows R. Joshua's opinion.

8 One who consecrates his possessions:
if there were among them things fit for the altar,
wine, oil, or birds—
R. Eleazar says:
Let them be sold to those who need that kind,
and with their price
he offers whole burnt offerings,
and let the rest of the possessions
accrue to the upkeep of the Temple.

4:9 Setting Prices for Temple Goods

9 Once in thirty days
one sets the chamber's prices.
Anyone who had agreed to provide fine flour at four,
and the price stood at three,
he must still provide it[43] at four;
if at three,
and the price stood at four,

[42] K, P: "I understand [or agree with] both of them: when one consecrates …"
[43] K lacks "he must still supply it."

on explicit terms: i.e. he stated that all of his possessions should go towards Temple upkeep. Some commentators suggest alternatively that the deceased stated explicitly that all of his animals, wine, oil, and flour be consecrated after his death. Since this is still a general pronouncement and does not specify which offerings his possessions should purchase, the assumption is that they all have the same type of consecration—that of the upkeep of the Temple.

4:8 *birds*: turtle doves or pigeons. See below, 5:1.

whole burnt offerings: R. Eleazar seems to accord with R. Joshua's view in 4:7 above, that items fit for the altar belong to the altar. Thus if they are sold, the money received must be used to purchase goods for the altar.

4:9 *one sets the chamber's prices*: One sets the price of wine, oil, and flour for the libations and grain offerings. The Temple needed to pay these prices to the suppliers of these goods. During each thirty-day period, the market value could not be raised, nor could the suppliers retract their offers.

Anyone who had agreed to provide flour at four: Suppliers who agreed to supply four *se'ah* of flour for the price of one *sela*.

and the price stood at three: Because flour became more expensive.

he must provide it at four,
since the Temple[44] has the upper hand.
If the flour grew worms—
he must bear the loss;
if the wine turned sour—
he must bear the loss.
He does not receive payment
until after the altar has atoned.

Chapter Five

5:1–2 *List of Temple Appointments*

5 These are the officers who were in the Temple:
Yohanan b. Phineas over the seals,
Ahiah over the libations,[45]
Matitiah b. Samuel over the lots,
Petahiah over the bird offerings;
Petahiah was Mordechai.[46]
Why was he called Petahiah?
Because he would open matters and expound them,
and he knew seventy languages.
Ben Ahiah over those with bowel sickness,

[44] P: "sanctified goods."
[45] K, P: "grain offerings." Along with libations grain offerings accompanied each sacrificial offering (Numbers 15).
[46] K, P lack "Petahyah was Mordechai."

until after the altar has atoned: Until the libation has been offered on the altar. The merchant remains answerable for the quality of his wares. *Zevahim* 8:12.

5:1 *over the seals*: See below, 5:3–5.

Matitiah b. Samuel is also mentioned in *Yoma* 3:1 and *Tamid* 3:2.

the lots: *Yoma* 2:2–4 describes the lots as being used to determine which priest would carry out which part of the Temple service.

over the bird offerings: Petahiah would sell turtle doves and pigeons for bird offerings. For a discussion of bird offerings, see *Qinnim* chapters 2–3.

he would open: The literal meaning of "Petahiah" is "The Lord has opened."

over those with bowel sickness: The Jerusalem Talmud understands this to be an officer who provides priests with remedies for stomach problems resulting from walking barefoot, drinking lots of water, and following a heavy meat diet.

Nehunyah [was] the digger of pits,
Gevini was the herald,
Ben Gever over the locking of the gates,
Ben Bevai over the wicks [of the *menorah*],
Ben Arzah over the cymbal,
Hugras b. Levi over the song,
the House of Garmu over the preparation of the showbread,
the House of Avtinas over the preparation of the incense,
Eleazar over the curtains,
and Phineas over the [priestly] garments.

2 One may not [appoint]
fewer than three treasurers and seven supervisors,
and one may not appoint
fewer than two
to hold financial office over the community,
except for Ben Ahiah who oversaw those with bowel sickness
and Eleazar who oversaw the curtains,
because most of the community[47] agreed to accept them.

5:3–5 Temple Procedures for Procuring Libations

3 There were four seals in the Temple
and on them was inscribed "Calf," "Male," "Kid," "Sinner."
Ben Azzai says:
There were five and Aramaic was inscribed on them:
"Calf," "Male," "Kid," "Poor Sinner," and "Rich Sinner."

---

[47] **K**: lacks "most of."

---

digger of pits: He would supervise the digging of wells and cisterns to supply the pilgrims to Jerusalem with water.

herald: He would herald the beginning of the Temple work day each morning. According to *Tamid* 3:8, his voice could be heard as far as Jericho.

Ben Arzah over the cymbal: *Tamid* 7:3 describes how Ben Arzah would lead the Levites in song using the cymbal.

Hugras b. Levi…preparation of the incense: *Yoma* 3:11 reports that Hugras b. Levi, the House of Garmu, and the House of Avtinas were not generous with their knowledge.

5:2 *three treasurers*: The treasurers were responsible for administering the Temple treasury.

supervisors: According to the Tosefta these supervisors possessed the keys to the Temple courtyard.

5:3 *four seals*: Such a seal served as confirmation that the worshipper had purchased the libations for the offering inscribed upon it.

"Calf," "Male," "Kid": Numbers 15 lists the different libations and grain offerings that were required for each type of animal being sacrificed.

Aramaic: While Ben Azzai says that they are written in Aramaic, the language of these labels is reported in Hebrew. Contrast with 6:5 below, where "new sheqels" and "old sheqels" are actually reported in Aramaic.

"Calf" signifies the libations of cattle [offerings],
large or small, male or female;
"Kid" signifies the libations of [offerings from the] flock,
large or small, male or female, except rams.
"Male"[48] signifies the libations of ram offerings alone.
"Sinner" signifies the libations accompanying the three animals
offered by those with *tsara'at*.
    4 One who seeks libations
goes to Yohanan who is appointed over the seals.
He gives him money and receives a seal from him;
he then goes to Ahiah who is appointed over the libations,
gives him the seal,
and receives libations from him.
And in the evening the two come together,
and Ahiah brings out the seals
and receives the corresponding funds.
If there was a surplus,
the surplus was consecrated
and if there was any deficit,
Yohanan paid it from his own means,
since consecrated goods have the upper hand.
    5 One who lost his seal—
they had him wait until evening;
if they found [money left over] enough for his seal,
they gave him a seal,
but if not, he did not have [libations or money].
And the name of the day was inscribed on the seals
because of defrauders.

5:6 *Temple Chambers*

    6 There were two chambers in the Temple:
one the Chamber of Discretion
and the other the Chamber of Vessels.
Into the Chamber of Discretion,

[48] K, P: "ram."

except rams: See *Parah* 1:3. Rams had to be older than thirteen months old.

"Sinner"…those with tsara'at: It was widely believed that skin affliction strikes those who have sinned. Leviticus 14 distinguishes between the offerings to be brought by a wealthy person who has recovered from *tsara'at* and a poor person.

5:4 *appointed over the libations*: He would procure libations from contractors (see above 4:9) and would hand them over to worshippers in exchange for their seal.

the surplus was consecrated: R. Aqiva (4:4 above) suggests that this surplus goes to purchase vessels of ministry.

5:6 *Chamber of Vessels*: Also mentioned in *Tamid* 3:4.

the pious would deposit [gifts] in secret,
and the poor of good family
would receive support from there in secret.
The Chamber of Vessels—
whoever donated a vessel would cast it in,
and once every thirty days
the treasurers would open it;
any article which they found useful for the Temple-upkeep fund
they would leave;
and the rest were sold
and their funds accrue to the chamber[49] of the Temple-upkeep fund.

Chapter Six

6:1–4   *The Number Thirteen in the Temple*

6 There were thirteen *shofar* chests,
thirteen tables,
and thirteen prostrations in the Temple.
Those of the House of Rabban Gamaliel
and of the House of R. Hanina, the Prefect of the Priests,
used to make fourteen prostrations.
And where was the extra one?
Opposite the woodstore,
because they had a tradition from their ancestors
that the Ark was hidden there.
   2 It once happened that a priest who was occupied [with his work]
saw a block of pavement that was different from the rest.

---

[49] Y lacks "chamber of the."

---

in secret: So that they are not embarrassed.

they would leave: See above, 4:7.

6:1 *shofar chests*: See 2:1 above and 6:5 below.

thirteen tables: See 6:4 below.

thirteen prostrations: Listed in 6:3.

woodstore: *Middot* 2:5 describes the woodstore as the place where blemished priests would work, checking the wood for worms before it was used on the altar.

the Ark was hidden there: During the period of the Second Temple the Holy of Holies was an empty room. The whereabouts of the Ark of the Covenant was a mystery.

6:2 *his Temple work*: The implication may be that he was a blemished priest working in the woodstore. See above, 6:1.

He came and reported to his fellow,
but did not manage to finish the story[50] before his soul departed.[51]
So they knew with certainty that the Ark was hidden there.

3 And where did they bow?
Four in the north, and four in the south, three in the east, and two in the west, opposite the thirteen gates.[52]
The southern gates, counting from the west, were:
the Upper Gate, the Kindling Gate, the Gate of the Firstborn, and the Water Gate.
And why was it called the Water Gate?
Because through it one brings in the flask of water for the libation at the Festival [of Sukkot].
R. Eliezer b. Jacob says:
Through it *the waters trickle forth*
and will in the future *issue out from under the threshold of the House*.
And opposite them, on the north, counting from the west:
the Gate of Jeconiah, the Gate of Offering, the Gate of Women, and the Gate of the Song.
And why was it called the Gate of Jeconiah?
Because through it Jeconiah went out in[53] his exile.
In the east was the Gate of Nicanor,
and it had two wickets,
one at its right and one at its left.
And there were two to the west which had no name.

4 There were thirteen tables in the Temple:
in the butchery were eight of marble[54]
on which they rinsed the innards,
and there were two to the west of the ramp,
one of marble and one of silver.
On that of marble they would lay the limbs [of the offerings],

[50] Lit. "thing," "word," "matter." [51] K: "departed in the north." [52] K, P lack "thirteen."
[53] K, P: "and his exile." [54] Y has "silver" in place of "marble" here and below.

6:3 *opposite the thirteen gates*: Ezekiel 46:2 also reports bowing at the gates of the future Temple. *Middot* 2:5 parallels much of this mishnah.

festival [of Sukkot]: Sometimes translated as Festival of Booths. See *Sukkah* 4:9.

the waters trickle forth: Ezekiel 47:2.

issue out from under the threshold of the House: Ezekiel 47:1.

his exile: See 2 Kings 24:10–16.

wickets: *Middot* 2:5 also contains this information about Nicanor's gate.

6:4 *they rinsed the innards*: See *Tamid* 3:5.

to the west of the ramp: See *Middot* 3:3.

they would lay the limbs: The marble absorbed less heat than the precious metals and may have helped prevent spoilage. *Avot* 5:5 refers to the lack of spoilage as one of ten Temple miracles.

and on that of silver the service vessels.
There were two in the inner hall at the entrance of the House,
one of marble and the other of gold.
On the table of marble they would lay the showbread when it came in,
and on that of gold [they would lay it] when it went out,
since one elevates [the level of] holiness and one does not lower it.
And inside was a table of gold
on which the showbread lay continually.

5 There were thirteen *shofar* chests in the Temple,
On them was inscribed:
(1) "new *sheqels*," (2) "old *sheqels*," (3) "bird offerings," (4) "chicks of the burnt offering,"
(5) "wood," (6) "frankincense," (7) "gold for the *kapporet*,"
and on six of them (8–13), "voluntary offerings."
"New *sheqels*" are those for the current year;
"old"—someone who had not paid his *sheqel* the past year pays it the following year.
"bird offerings"—these are the turtle doves;
and "chicks for the whole burnt offering"—these are the young pigeons;
and both are whole burnt offerings—
the words of R. Judah.
But the Sages say:
"Bird offerings"—regardless of whether they are purgation or whole burnt offerings,
but the "chicks for the whole burnt offering" are all whole burnt offerings.

6 One who says "I pledge wood"
must bring not less than two pieces;
"frankincense"—not less than a handful;
"gold"—not less than a golden *dinar*.
"Six for free-will offerings"—

the House: The inner sanctuary. See *Middot* 4:1 and a parallel in *Menahot* 11:7.

when it came in: See Leviticus 24:8. The bread was baked on Friday and then brought inside the sanctuary on Saturday.

one elevates [the level of] holiness: The bread sat on a table of gold inside the sanctuary and therefore it would be improper for it to sit on a lesser material when it leaves the sanctuary.

continually: See Exodus 25:23–30.

6:5 *"new sheqels," "old sheqels"*: Both of these phrases are in Aramaic.

bird offerings: One might vow to offer a bird, chick, wood, or frankincense to the Temple. These chests were there to collect the funds for each.

kapporet: Often translated as "place of atonement" (King James Version, "Mercy Seat"), it is mentioned in Exodus 25, where it is a gold slab placed on top of the Ark of the Covenant containing the tablets of the covenant, both found in the inner sanctum of the Tabernacle.

whole burnt offerings: See *Qinnim* 1:1.

6:6 *two pieces*: Such as those that go into the pile of wood on the altar. See the parallel in *Menahot* 13:3.

"Six for free-will offerings": Surpluses from six types of sacrifices (see 2:5) are stored here for use.

what did they do with the free-will offerings?
They bought whole burnt offerings with them;
the flesh for God and the hides for the priests.
Yehoyada the High Priest expounded the following:
It is a guilt offering: he is certainly guilty before the Lord—
this is the general rule:
Anything that comes from [the surplus] of a purgation or guilt offering
must be used to purchase whole burnt offerings—
the flesh for God and the hides for the priests.[55]
Thus both scriptures are fulfilled:
A guilt offering to the Lord
and *a guilt offering to the priests*.
It says also: *Money for the guilt offerings and the money for the purgation offerings was not brought into the house of the Lord: it was the priests'*.

Chapter Seven

7:1–2   *Proper Allocation of Found Coins*

7 Coins which were found between the *sheqels* and the voluntary offerings—
those near the *sheqels* fall to the *sheqels*,
those near the voluntary donations fall to the voluntary donations.
Halfway—they fall to the voluntary donations.
[Coins found] between the wood and the frankincense—
if they were near the wood they fall to the wood,
near the frankincense they fall to the frankincense.

---

[55] P: "priest."

It is a guilt offering…before the Lord: Leviticus 5:19. Yehoyada seems to be trying to resolve an internal contradiction. A guilt offering can generally be eaten by the priests, but the verse says that it is completely for the Lord.

whole burnt offerings: Hence "to the Lord."

guilt offering to the Lord: Leviticus 5:15.

guilt offering to the priest: Leviticus 5:18.

Money for the guilt offerings…it was the priests': 2 Kings 12:16.

7:1 *coins…and the voluntary offerings*: Most of this mishnah describes what to do with coins that have fallen between different types of *shofar* chests so that it is not readily apparent which chest was intended.

Halfway—they fall to the voluntary donations: This ruling follows the general rule stated at the end of the mishnah: if coins are found halfway between two chests they are allocated in a stringent way. Voluntary donations were allocated to pay for whole burnt offerings, while *sheqel* donations were used for a variety of purposes. See above, 4:1–2.

Halfway—they fall to the frankincense.
[Coins found] found between the bird offerings and the chicks for whole burnt offerings—
if they were near the bird offerings they fall to the bird offerings,
near the chicks for whole burnt offerings they fall to the chicks for whole burnt offerings.
Halfway—they fall to the chicks for whole burnt offerings.
[Coins found] between common money and second-tithe money—
if they were near the common money, they fall to the common money,
near the second-tithe money, they fall to the second tithe.
Halfway—they fall to the second tithe.
This is the general rule: One follows the near [even] to be lenient,[56]
but [when coins are found] halfway [they are allocated] stringently.
  2 Coins found in front of livestock dealers are always tithe money,
[coins found] on the Temple Mount—common money.
[coins found] in Jerusalem—
during a festival [they are deemed to be] tithe money,
and on all other days of the year—common money.[57]

7:3–5 *Found Meat and Livestock*

  3 Meat found in the Temple Court—
[whole] limbs are [assumed to be from] whole burnt offerings,
cut-up pieces from a purgation offering.

---

[56] K and P lack "to be lenient."
[57] K and P start with the rule for the year and continue with the ruling for the festival season. P also adds "all" before "tithe money."

Halfway—they fall to the frankincense: Frankincense is the more stringent because it is its own independent offering, while the wood serves as prerequisite for a variety of offerings, namely those that must be burnt.

Halfway—they fall to the chicks for whole burnt offerings: This is more stringent because, according the Sages in 6:5, bird offerings could be purgation or whole burnt offerings.

Coins found…second tithe: The discussion has shifted to coins found in one's own home. See 2:2 above for a discussion of second tithes.

lenient…stringently: In this context the "lenient" is that which allows freer use of the found coin, while the "stringent" is more restrictive.

7:2 *livestock dealers*: In Jerusalem.

always: Even during the nonfestival season.

Coins…second-tithe money: Any coins found in Jerusalem were likely going to be used to purchase animals for offerings of well-being (see Deuteronomy 14:22–26).

on the Temple Mount: Coins here have fallen after animals were purchased and thus they revert to common use.

in Jerusalem: But not in front of livestock dealers.

other days of the year: During the holiday season more coins were likely intended for use as part of the second tithe, while at other times of year this was not the case.

[Meat found] in Jerusalem—
from sacrifices of well-being.
In both cases its appearance must be altered
and it must be taken away to the place of burning.
[Meat] found within the borders [of the Land of Israel]—
whole limbs [are assumed to be] carrion,
but if [found] in cut-up pieces it is permitted.
But at the time of a festival,
when there is much meat,
even entire limbs are permitted.

4 Livestock found between Jerusalem and Migdal Eder,
or within a similar distance in any direction—
males are [assumed to be] whole burnt offerings
and females are [assumed to be] sacrifices of well-being.
R. Judah says:
Those[58] which are fit to be a Passover offering
are [assumed to be] Passover offerings
within the thirty days prior to the festival.

5 At first, they used to exact pledges
from one who found livestock
until he offered the accompanying libations.
Those who found livestock began to leave it[59] and flee.

[58] P: "even those."   [59] P lacks "it."

7:3 *are assumed…whole burnt offerings*: Whole burnt offerings were cut up into individual limbs before being offered. See *Yoma* 2:3 and *Tamid* 4:2–3.

cut-up pieces: Purgation offerings (and guilt offerings) were eaten by priests and thus were cut up into cuts of meat appropriate for consumption. Thus, cut-up meat was assumed to have been cut for this purpose.

sacrifices of well-being: Unlike other sacrifices, sacrifices of well-being might be consumed anywhere in Jerusalem.

its appearance must be altered: It could not be eaten or burnt at the moment of discovery, rather it sat until after an acceptable sacrificial time (a day and a night for purgation and guilt offerings or two days for offerings of well-being). This interval was understood to be enough time for the meat to have rotted sufficiently such that its appearance would have changed. It was then burnt.

the place of burning: A place in the Temple Court for burning marred or otherwise invalid sacrifices.

[are assumed to be] carrion: See Deuteronomy 14:21. The meat in this case might have been discarded as food for an animal.

in cut-up pieces: One does not go to the trouble of preparing meat in well-proportioned cuts for one's animal.

entire limbs are permitted: At festival-time, people would not skimp on meat and therefore would often cook large pieces and not just small ones.

7:4 *Migdal Eder*: This town is mentioned in Genesis 35:21 and Micah 4:8.

females are…sacrifices of well-being: According to Leviticus 1:3 female animals are not valid as whole burnt offerings.

fit to be a Passover offering: Male sheep or goats less than one year old.

7:5 *the accompanying libations*: See above, 5:3.

7:6–7 Seven Court Ordinances Regarding Sacrifices

6 R. Simeon said:
The Court ordained seven things
and this was (1) one of them.
(2) If a gentile sent his whole burnt offering from[60] a region beyond the sea
and sent libations with it,
his libations are offered;
but if he did not,
the libations are brought at the expense of the community.
(3) So too, a convert who died and left sacrifices:
if he has libations they are offered,
but if not, they are offered at the expense of the community.
(4) It was a stipulation of the court regarding a high priest who died,
that his grain offering should be brought at the expense of the community.
R. Judah says:
From the property of his heirs.
It was offered undivided.

7 (5) [The court ordained] regarding [consecrated] salt and wood
that the priests may make use of them,
(6) and regarding the [red] heifer
that deriving benefit from its ashes was not considered a sacrilege.
(7) and regarding invalid bird offerings,[61]
that [others] should be offered at the expense of the community.
R. Yose says:
The one who provides the bird offerings
provides [others in place of] the invalid ones.[62]

---

[60] P: "to" or "for" a region.   [61] Y: "regarding bird offerings and regarding invalid offerings."
[62] K: "as if he provides," rather than simply "provides."

7:6 *this*: That is, the rule in the preceding mishnah *was one of* the Court's enactments.

at the expense of the community: From the fact that non-Jews are specified here, it seems that if a Jew neglected to send libation funds they were nonetheless exacted from him and would not be provided by the community.

a convert who died and left sacrifices: A convert to Judaism is presumed not to have Jewish heirs from whom to demand funds for the libations.

grain offering: See Leviticus 6:14–18.

undivided: During the high priest's life, he would bring half of the offering in the morning and half in the afternoon. After his death, the whole offering would be brought at once. See *Menahot* 4:5.

7:7 *may make use of them*: They could use consecrated salt to flavor their food and wood to warm themselves.

heifer: See Numbers 19.

one who provides: This seems to refer to a supplier like those in 4:9 above.

Chapter Eight

8:1–3 Purity Status of Objects Found in Jerusalem

8 Any spit found in Jerusalem is pure,
except what is found in the upper market—
the words of R. Meir.
R. Yose says:
At other times of the year,
spit found in the middle [of a street in Jerusalem] is impure,
but that found on the sides is pure;
during a festival,
spit in the middle of the street is pure
but that found at the sides is impure,
for because they are few they withdraw to the sides.
   2 All vessels found in Jerusalem:
on the path down to the place of immersion are impure,
but on the path back they are pure;
for the path by which they are taken down
is not the same as that by which they are brought back—
the words of R. Meir.
R. Yose says:
All are pure except the special basket, shovel, and pick
used specifically for graves.
   3 A knife found on the fourteenth [of Nisan]
may be used for slaughter immediately;
but if found on the thirteenth,
it must be immersed again;
a butcher's cleaver in either case must be immersed again.

8:1 *Any spit*: In *Tohorot* 4:5, spit of doubtful origin triggers such a severe assumption of impurity that *terumah* coming in contact with it must be burnt. Here, however, the assumption is reversed. We assume that in Jerusalem impure individuals are careful not to transmit their impurity to others.

the upper market was in the southwest of Jerusalem. *Menahot* 10:5 describes events happening in the market of Jerusalem that went against the desires of the Sages.

during a festival: At the time of a festival there was incentive for those with impurity to purify themselves to visit the Temple.

because they are few: Those with impurity.

8:2 *All are pure*: See *Tohorot* 4:5 for the contrast with vessels found outside of Jerusalem.

8:3 *immediately*: Without immersion. It can be assumed that such a knife was immersed on the thirteenth in preparation for slaughtering the Passover offering on the fourteenth.

a butcher's cleaver: It could slice through bone. See for example *Pesahim* 7:12.

must be immersed again: Since it was not used for the Passover offering, it is possible that its owners intended to immerse it on the fourteenth.

If the fourteenth fell on the Sabbath,
one may use it for slaughter immediately.
If [it was found] on the fifteenth,
one may use it for slaughter immediately.
If [a cleaver] was found tied to a knife,
it may be treated in such a case like a knife.

8:4–5 *Temple Curtains*

4 A Temple curtain that contracted impurity from a secondary impurity
may be immersed within [the Temple Court] and be brought back in immediately.
But that which contracts impurity from a primary impurity
must be immersed outside and spread out on the rampart.[63]
If it is new, one spreads it out on the roof of the portico
so that the people see that its craftsmanship is fine.

5 Rabban Simeon b. Gamaliel says
in the name of R.[64] Simeon, son of the Prefect:
The curtain was one handbreadth thick
and was woven on [a loom having] seventy-two strands,[65]
and over each strand were twenty-four threads.[66]

---

[63] P adds "because it requires the setting of the sun."
[64] K lacks the title "Rabbi."
[65] Y: "woven on seventy-two strands." K, P here only: "cross-rods."
[66] Or: "each strand was of twenty-four threads."

---

one may use it for slaughter immediately: Since it is not permissible to immerse vessels on the Sabbath, it is assumed that the cleaver was immersed the day before.

8:4: *A Temple curtain*: This curtain separated between the central Temple hall and the Holy of Holies (see Exodus 26:33).

secondary impurity: Impurity that results from contact with a primary source of impurity. See *Pesahim* 1:6.

immediately: Since the source of impurity is a secondary source, it is only rabbinic. Therefore, unlike something that came into contact with biblically impure substances it does not need to wait until sundown before being purified.

contracts impurity from a primary impurity: Comes in direct contact with a primary impurity such as a corpse of one of the eight creeping things of Leviticus 11:29–30 or carrion.

rampart: Leviticus 11:31–32 describes how certain animals transmit impurity and how items that contract impurity can be purified. Since these items had to sit unused until sundown following immersion, the curtain, too, could not be used until sundown. It therefore stayed on the rampart, which marked the boundary of the outer court, until then. For more on the rampart see *Middot* 2:3 (where it is translated "ledge") and *Kelim* 1:8.

portico: See *Pesahim* 1:5, *Sukkah* 4:4.

8:5 *twenty-four threads*: Exodus 26 provides instructions for weaving the curtains. The curtain was to be made with four different colors of thread: blue, red, purple, and twisted linen. Perhaps the twenty-four threads were six threads of each type mentioned there.

Its length was forty cubits and its width twenty cubits.
It was made from⁶⁷ eighty-two myriads,⁶⁸
and they make two each year,
and three hundred priests immerse it.

8:6–7 Disposal of Impure Temple Meat

6 Meat of offerings of the highest sanctity that contracted impurity,
whether through a primary or secondary source of impurity,
whether inside [the Temple Court] or outside it:
the House of Shammai say:
Any of these should be burnt inside,
unless it has contracted impurity outside through a primary source of impurity.
But the House of Hillel say:
Any of these should be burnt outside,
unless it has contracted impurity inside through a secondary source of impurity.
  7 R. Eliezer says:
That which has contracted impurity through a primary source of impurity,
whether inside or outside [the Temple Court],
must be burnt outside,
and that which has contracted impurity through a secondary source of impurity,
whether inside or outside,
must be burnt inside.
R. Aqiva says:
The place where it contracted impurity is where it should be burnt.

---

⁶⁷ **K, P**: "With" or "in": see annotation.
⁶⁸ One manuscript of **Y**: "by eighty-two maidens." See annotation.

---

myriads: The meaning of this phrase is unclear. Perhaps it means that it cost eighty-two myriad *dinar*s to make it. One manuscript's reading of "maidens" perhaps reflects the tradition that maidens labored in the Temple.

they make two each year: Yoma 5:1 describes a dispute regarding whether or not two curtains separated the hall and the Holy of Holies.

immerse it: When it becomes impure. The number of priests given here is hyperbolic to illustrate how large the curtain was.

8:6 *offerings of the highest sanctity*: See *Zevahim* 5:1–5.

8:8 *Placement of Sacrificial Limbs*

8 The limbs of the continual offering
are placed on the lower half of the ramp on its east[69] side;
those of the additional offerings
on the lower half of the ramp on its west[70] side;
those of the New Moon offerings
are placed between the horns of the altar above.[71]

8:8 cont. *Sanctifying Goods without a Temple*

Sheqel dues and firstfruits
apply only when the Temple stands;
but the tithe of grain, the tithe of livestock, and the offering of the firstborn
apply both when the Temple stands
and when it does not.
If one consecrates the *sheqel* dues or firstfruits,
they are thereby consecrated.
R. Simeon says:
If one declares firstfruits [to be] sanctified,
they are not sanctified.

---

[69] K, P: "west." See *Tamid* 4:3.   [70] The versions with "west" above have "east" here.
[71] Y: "beneath the rim of the altar below."

8:8 Limbs from whole burnt offerings would be temporarily placed on the ramp leading up to the altar. The limbs from each type of sacrifice would have their own place on the ramp so that they would not be confused.

limbs of the continual offering: *Yoma* 2:3 lists these limbs and *Tamid* 4:1–5 the sacrificial procedure involving these limbs.

ramp: The inclined plane at the south of the altar which was used instead of steps. *Middot* 3:3 lists its length as thirty-two by sixteen cubits.

west: See *Tamid* 4:3.

New Moon offerings: See Numbers 28:11.

between the horns of the altar above: *Middot* 3:1 describes this area as the place on which the feet of the priests trod, outside the twenty-four square cubits of the altar fire.

firstfruits: Exodus 23:19, Deuteronomy 26:1–11.

tithe of grain: This includes *terumah*, not strictly a tithe. See Numbers 18:12, Deuteronomy 12:17.

tithe of livestock: Leviticus 27:32.

firstborn: Exodus 13:12, Numbers 18:15–18.

If one consecrates: At a time when there is no Temple.

Tractate Yoma

Yonatan S. Miller

Introduction

Overview

In an elaborate rite observed one day each year, on the tenth day of the month later known as Tishre, the People of Israel and the innermost sanctum of the Tabernacle (and subsequently that of the two Temples) were to be purged through animal sacrifice, blood manipulation, and incense offerings, of any accidental defilement incurred during the previous year. The Torah twice calls this day *Yom ha-Kippurim* (Leviticus 23:26, 25:9), which is loosely translated as the Day of Atonement (*kippurim* is plural, but it is thought to be a "plural of intensification" [Milgrom]). Literally meaning "The Day" in Aramaic, *Yoma* is the name passed down for the tractate in manuscripts of the Babylonian Talmud that deal with this day. It is likely that the tractate's name was once *Kippurim*, the name reflected in manuscripts of parallel texts.

Tractate *Yoma* presents itself as a manual for the Day of Atonement rituals as observed in the Second Temple, and employs vivid narrative form to instruct the high priest in the finest points of the rite as if the Temple were still standing. That the Temple was destroyed in 70 CE, over a century before the compilation of the Mishnah, is of no consequence. Indeed, the tractate's temporal consciousness solely concerns the Ark of the Covenant, which was present only in the First Temple (5:1–2; but cf. 7:5). Only a small fraction of its laws, which are detailed near the end of the tractate (8:1–5), can be construed as applicable to post-Temple times. (A similar arrangement can be found at the end of tractate *Pesahim*.)

Structure and Organization of the Tractate

By and large *Yoma* has a cohesive structure that follows a clear chronological trajectory. Chapter 1 narrates the preparations of the high priest for his multifaceted service on the Day of Atonement. These preparations transition into a chapter-length tangent (1:8–3:2) on the service of the *Tamid*, the continual offering brought in the Temple each morning and afternoon—including the Day of Atonement. The bulk of the tractate (3:2–7:4) narrates the high priest's Day of Atonement service. Two minor digressions relate to some of the extraordinary donations of Temple furnishings, a number of infamous Temple personnel, and the priestly garb (3:10–11, 7:5). Ritual laws relevant to post-Temple times, largely centering on fasting, though also digressing into Sabbath law, are presented in the final chapter (8).

Relationship to Scripture

The most concentrated and detailed scriptural treatment of the Day of Atonement is in Leviticus 16, and *Yoma*'s ritual narrative (3:2–7:4) evinces a profound, if unspoken, connection with that text. With few exceptions, *Yoma* tracks the sequence of the rituals in Leviticus 16. And in a style evoking Leviticus 16, a pivot from provisions exclusively concerning the high priest to the whole community occurs suddenly at the end of the tractate (see the transition at verse 29).

This is not to say that *Yoma* is constrained by Leviticus 16. Numerous extrabiblical traditions punctuate the tractate, e.g. the preparations of the high priest, the killing of the scapegoat, and the Torah-reading service. Moreover, Leviticus 16 is not the only biblical text that relates to the Day of Atonement. It is evident, for example, that the Mishnah works to integrate Numbers 29 (see 7:3). Finally, although the text is rife with biblicisms (e.g. 3:2, 7:3, 8:6), Scripture is nevertheless rarely invoked as a proof-text (cf. 1:1).

Main Ideas and Assumptions

Beyond a close adherence to Leviticus 16, *Yoma* situates the Day of Atonement firmly in the rabbinic world of ritual law. The sacrificial rites are practiced and coordinated with (rabbinic) elders sent from the Court; the service takes place in a prescribed order, and the text articulates the consequences of deviation from that order. In addition, ambiguous measures are quantified, and long dormant sectarian concerns are seemingly resuscitated. Sadducean cultic practices, although not mentioned explicitly, seem to be lurking behind *Yoma*'s concerns about the high priest deviating from his training, particularly with regard to the incense offering. The assumption that the high priest is ignorant and requires supervision and training likewise indicates the political intrigues of the Second Temple period, which, starting in the early second century BCE, saw the commoditization and politicization of the office.

The Day of Atonement in *Yoma* scarcely resembles the Day of Atonement of later rabbinic sources. While the day has gravitas, there is little that presages a somber observance (cf. Jubilees 34:18). Moreover, *Yoma* does not spell out what one is to *do* on the Day of Atonement; the tractate does not contain any positive commandments or liturgical prescriptions for the post-Temple observance of the day (cf. *Rosh Hashanah* chapter 4). If anything, *Yoma* preserves vestiges of the festive nature of the day (7:4, *Ta'anit* 4:8; Philo, *Spec. Leg.* II:193), which may be viewed as on a continuum with the composite traditions that underlie the extant biblical text in Leviticus 16.

Yoma stands largely on its own in ancient Jewish literature. As in other tractates with substantial blocks of ritual narrative, disagreements are rare, as are named rabbis. Prior to its elucidation in the Palestinian and Babylonian Talmuds, *Yoma* is by far the lengthiest and most comprehensive single treatment of the Day of Atonement in ancient Jewish literature. Notably several of the extrabiblical traditions attested in *Yoma* find explicit parallels in the writings of a number of early Christian authors, some of whom predate the Mishnah.

Special Notes for the Reader

I have consulted and benefited much from the translation of Herbert Danby and from the commentaries of Hanoch Albeck, Pinhas Kehati, and Shmuel and Ze'ev Safrai. I was helped in assessing some of the finer points of the *Yoma* manuscript tradition by consulting Yehoshua Rosenberg, "Mishna 'Kipurim' (Yoma)—A Critical Edition with Introduction" (PhD diss., The Hebrew University of Jerusalem, 1995). I have likewise made use of Jacob Milgrom, *Leviticus 1–16*, Anchor Bible v. 3 (New York: Doubleday, 1991); Joseph Tabory, *Jewish Festivals in the Time of the Mishnah and the Talmud*, 3rd ed. (Jerusalem: Magnes Press, 2000 [Hebrew]); and Daniel Stökl Ben-Ezra, *The Impact of Yom Kippur on Early Christianity* (Tübingen: Mohr Siebeck, 2003).

Tractate Yoma

Chapter One

1:1–7 *The High Priest Is Prepared for the Day of Atonement*

I Seven days before the Day of Atonement,
they remove¹ the high priest
from his house to the Chamber of the Palhedrin,²
and they designate³ for him another priest in his place,
lest a disqualification⁴ befall him.
R. Judah says:
They also designate⁵ for him another wife
lest his wife die,
as it is written,
And he shall effect atonement for himself and for his household.
His household—this is his wife.
They⁶ said to him:
If so,⁷ the matter is without end.

---

¹ Or "separate." ² K, P: "Parhedrin." See annotations. ³ Or "prepare."
⁴ Or "unfitness." ⁵ Or "prepare." ⁶ K, P: "The Sages." ⁷ K, P lack "if so."

1:1 *Seven days*: Perhaps inspired by Leviticus 8:33. See also *Parah* 3:1.

they remove: The authorities performing the activities in this mishnah are not identified. But see below, 1:3ff.

his house: Not elsewhere identified, but perhaps a reference to the "Chamber of the High Priest" in *Middot* 5:4.

Chamber of the Palhedrin: Text and meaning are uncertain. Perhaps a chamber for governing officials or those alternate priests who had been called upon to serve as high priest.

lest a disqualification befall him, that is, by becoming ritually impure. See 1:7 below.

And he shall effect atonement…for his household: Leviticus 16:6, 11, 17.

His household—this is his wife: R. Judah interprets this biblical phrase as mandating that the high priest be married when performing the Day of Atonement service; a high priest cannot effect atonement for his "household" if he does not have a wife. Having an additional wife at the ready would thus ensure the high priest's ability to serve if his first wife were to die.

the matter is without end: Following R. Judah's logic, an unlimited number of potential wives should be at the ready lest the second wife die as well.

2 All seven days he sprinkles the blood,
offers the incense,
tends[8] to the lamps,
and offers the head and [right hind]leg.
On all other days,
if he wished to offer,
he may offer—
for the high priest offers the first portion
and takes the first portion.

3 They delivered to him elders from the elders of the Court,
and they recite[9] before him the order of the day,
and they say to him:
"My lord, High Priest,
recite the order yourself[10]
lest you have forgotten,
or lest you did not learn it."
[On] the morning of the eve of the Day of Atonement
they stand[11] him at the eastern gate
and pass before him bulls, rams, and lambs
in order that he be aware of and familiar with the service.

[8] Lit. "improves."   [9] The verbs in this extended narrative appear in a disorderly pattern of tenses.
[10] Lit. "with your mouth."   [11] Or "place him."

1:2 This mishnah refers to the daily rituals associated with the continual offering, all of which will be performed by the high priest on the Day of Atonement. See Exodus 29:38–42 and the introduction to *Tamid*; and see below 1:8–3:2.

All seven days of the preparatory period. See 1:1.

he sprinkles the blood: *Tamid* 4:1.

offers the incense: Exodus 30:1–8; *Tamid* 5:4–6, 6:2–3.

tends to the lamps of the Lampstand. See Exodus 30:7; also *Tamid* 3:9, 6:1.

offers the head and [right hind]leg: See below 2:3 and *Tamid* 3:1, 7:3.

On all other days: Even when he is not under sequestration in preparation for the Day of Atonement.

for the high priest offers the first portion and takes the first portion: The high priest is allowed to bypass the lottery system employed by the rotating course of priests officiating during any specific week. See below 2:2–4, *Tamid* 7:3, *Ta'anit* 4:2.

1:3 *the Court*: The Mishnah does not name the court from which the elders were dispatched, though the Great Sanhedrin is said to have met in a chamber on the Temple Mount (*Middot* 5:4, *Sanhedrin* 11:2). As portrayed here and elsewhere in the Mishnah, this court exercises control not only over capital punishment but also over the finest details of ritual law in the Temple. See e.g. *Parah* 3, *Menahot* 10:3–5.

order of the day: This may refer to the three excerpts from the Torah relating to Yom Kippur, the Day of Atonement, that the high priest reads at the conclusion of his service; see below 7:1. Alternatively, a compilation of instructions for the service not unlike our mishnah.

recite…lest you did not learn it: The assumption of the high priest's ignorance is made explicit in the Talmud, which ascribes the presumption of his poor ritual knowledge to the commoditization of the high priest's office.

they stand him: The verb employed here presents the high priest as if he had no personal agency. See also below, note to 1:5.

4 All seven days they would not withhold from him food and drink.
Toward dusk on the eve of the Day of Atonement,
they would not allow him to eat much,
for food brings on sleep.

5 The elders of the Court handed him over to the elders of the Priesthood,
and they brought him up to the upper chamber of the House of Avtinas,
administered his oath,
took leave of him,
and went on their way.
[This is what] they said to him:
"My lord, High Priest,
we are agents of the Court
and you are our agent
and an agent of the Court.
We adjure you by Him Who made His name dwell in this house
not to change anything from all we have said to you."
He steps away and weeps,
and they step away and weep.

6 If he was learned,
he expounds [Scripture];
and if not,
learned disciples[12] expound [Scripture] before him.
And if he is accustomed to reading,
he reads;
and if not,
they read before him.

---

[12] K: "If he was a student, scholars lecture before him."

1:4 *for food brings on sleep*: As 1:7 clarifies, the high priest was kept awake all night. Commentators interpret this mishnah as referring to the high priest's last meal before the fast, taken just before dark.

1:5 *handed him over*: Again portraying the high priest as lacking personal agency. See annotations to 1:3.

House of Avtinas: Few details about this household and eponymous house are known. See below 3:11, also *Sheqalim* 5:1 and *Tamid* 1:1.

We adjure you … not to change anything: Left unclear is whether the oath refers solely to the incense service or to the entire rite; and whether the need for an oath was driven by the high priest's presumed ignorance (see 1:3, 1:6) or to possible sectarian concerns (cf. *Sukkah* 4:9). Especially as the high priest performed the incense service in private (see below, 4:3–5:1), deviation in the manner of the offering of the incense may have been of particular concern.

Him Who made His name dwell: A biblicism echoing the oft-repeated locution in Deuteronomy, which refers to the centralized sanctuary as "the place chosen by God to make His name dwell there" (e.g. Deuteronomy 12:11, 14:23, 16:2).

He steps away and weeps…: According to various traditions, the very need for an oath caused the elders to weep, and the suspicion that he was a sectarian who would intentionally deviate in the service caused the high priest to weep.

1:6 *they read before him*: Again underscoring the lack of confidence in the high priest's cultic training, if not his basic literacy.

And from what do they read before him?
From [the books of] Job, Ezra, and Chronicles.
Zechariah b. Qabutal says:
Many times I read before him from [the book of] Daniel.

7 If he was about to doze off,
young[13] priests[14] snap at him with their middle finger,
and say to him:
"My lord, High Priest,
stand up and cool down for a moment on the floor."
And they keep him occupied until the time of the slaughter arrives.

1:8–2:1 The Clearing of the Ashes

8 Each day they clear the ashes from the altar at cockcrow,
or near it, whether before or after.
On the Day of Atonement [they do so] from midnight
and on festivals from the first watch.
And by the time the cock crowed[15]
the Court was [already] filled with Israelites.

---

[13] Lit. "blossoms." [14] K, P: "Levites."
[15] Lit. "and cockcrow would not arrive before…"

Job, Ezra, and Chronicles: The Yerushalmi suggests that the interesting contents of these books made them suitable for keeping the high priest awake, but these are among the less riveting books in the Hebrew Bible. There may be a nod here to Esther 6:1, where the sleepless King Ahasuerus asks that his "book of records, the annals [or: chronicles]" be brought and read to him. Perhaps it seemed that Chronicles is a work to be read in the middle of the night.

Daniel: In contrast with the three recommended books, a good portion of Daniel is written in Aramaic. An uneducated high priest would likely be fluent in Aramaic but not Hebrew.

1:7 *If he was about to doze off*: The Mishnah implies that the high priest was forbidden from sleeping on Yom Kippur night, but never states this outright or why that might have been the case. *Avot* 5:5 states that the high priest miraculously never had a seminal emission on Yom Kippur, presumably as a result of a nocturnal occurrence. Other rabbinic texts record the custom of many residents of Jerusalem to stay awake through the night of Yom Kippur.

young priests: Cf. *Sukkah* 5:2, *Sanhedrin* 9:6, and *Middot* 3:8.

stand up and cool down for a moment on the floor: By standing barefoot on the cold marble floor the high priest would avoid drowsiness.

until the time of the slaughter of the morning continual offering.

1:8 *Each day they clear the ashes from the altar*: Leviticus 6:3, *Tamid* 1:2–2:2.

from the first watch: The night is divided into thirds; the end of the first watch is thus earlier than midnight. See also *Berakhot* 1:1.

by the time…Israelites: A substantial crowd would have already gathered in the Temple Courtyard before dawn. Whether this statement relates solely to the Day of Atonement service or to all holidays is left unclear.

Chapter Two

2 At first, whoever wanted to clear the ashes from the altar did so.
When they were many [priests who wished to do this],
they would run and ascend the ramp,
and whoever reached within four cubits [of the altar] ahead of his fellow
won [the privilege].
If they were tied,
the Appointed One says to them:
"Extend your fingers!"
And how many[16] do they put out?
One or two;
but[17] one does not put out a thumb in the Temple.

2:2–4 *The Four Lots*

2 It once happened that two [priests] were tied
while running and ascending the ramp,
and one pushed his fellow,
and he fell and his leg was broken.
As soon as the Court recognized
that they were coming to danger,
they ordained that the clearing of the ashes from the altar
be [assigned] solely by lot.[18]
There were four lots in the Temple,
and this is the first lot.

---

[16] Lit. "what."   [17] Or "and."   [18] Lit. "That one not clear the ashes from the altar except by lot."

2:1 *whoever wanted* from among the course of priests that was officiating in the Temple at the time.

the ramp: See *Middot* 3:3. The ramp was almost fifty feet long.

within four cubits [of the altar]: The "finish-line" was four cubits before the ramp met the altar.

the Appointed One: An officer in charge of administering the Temple lots. See *Sheqalim* 5:1.

One or two: The process of the selection is not detailed here. According to tradition the Appointed One would choose a random number and a priest from whom he would begin counting. He then counted the extended fingers, and the priest whose finger was selected for the final number would win the privilege of clearing the ashes.

one does not put out a thumb in the Temple: Perhaps because of the possibility of cheating: a priest who had extended a distant finger could also discreetly extend his thumb in the hope of influencing the final result.

2:2 *one pushed his fellow and he fell and his leg was broken*: Another rendition of this story has one priest pull out a knife and stab the other in the heart.

lot: Commentators disagree as to whether these lots employed the same finger-counting system as above (2:1) or a different scheme. *Shabbat* 23:2 suggests that there is a fine line between casting lots and forbidden gambling, which might indicate a scheme that involves dice or some licit form of gaming. See also *Sukkah* 5:6; Luke 1:8–9. In the sectarian community at Qumran, lots were employed in a wide variety of applications, from membership in the sect to legal decisions.

3 The second lot [determines] who slaughters,
who sprinkles the blood,
who clears the ashes from the inner altar,
and who clears the ashes from the Lampstand,
and who lifts the limbs—
the head and [hind]leg, the two forelegs, the rump and the [other hind]leg, the breast and the neck, the two flanks, the innards, the fine flour, the cakes, and the wine—
onto the ramp.
Thirteen priests won this [lot].
Ben Azzai said before R. Aqiva
in the name of R. Joshua:
It was offered [according to] the way it walked.

4 The third lot—
[priests] new to the incense rite—
"Come and cast[19] lots!"
And the fourth—
[for] novices and veterans alike—[20]
who lift limbs from the ramp onto the altar.

2:5–7 *How Many Priests Are Required for the Temple Sacrifices?*

5 The continual offering is offered
with nine, ten, eleven, or twelve[21] [priests]—
no fewer and no more.

---

[19] Or "draw."   [20] Lit. "novices with veterans."   [21] K lacks "twelve."

2:3 Much of this mishnah is paralleled in *Tamid* 3:1. As in that text, the mishnah here lists *the fine flour, the cakes, and the wine* as though they are sacrificial limbs.

who lifts the limbs…onto the ramp: After being butchered, the parts of the continual offering were placed (by the priests who had won the privilege) halfway up the altar ramp and salted; see *Tamid* 4:2–3. See also *Sheqalim* 8:8.

the fine flour, the cakes, and the wine: In addition to the sacrificial limbs, the continual offering service also includes a grain offering and wine libation (Exodus 29:40, Numbers 28:5, 7). On these offerings, see *Menahot* introduction; chapters 5 and 6; 8:6–7.

the cakes: See Leviticus 6:13–14, *Menahot* 4:5.

the way it walked: In contrast to the untidy order in which the first opinion lists the butchered limbs, Ben Azzai contends that the parts should be offered in the same sequence with which the animal walks: from the head to the hindlegs.

2:4 Largely parallel to *Tamid* 5:2.

[Priests] new to the incense rite: Priests who had never before offered the incense; these were summoned with the call to *"come and cast lots."* The Talmud notes that priests would offer the incense only once in their lifetime. Cf. Luke 1:8–9.

[for] novices and veterans alike: Echoing Song of Songs 7:14.

onto the altar: Where they are incinerated in the fire.

How so?
It itself is with nine.
On the Festival [of Sukkot]—
in the hand of one is a flask of water;
there are thus ten.[22]
The afternoon [continual offering] is with eleven—
it itself is with nine,
and two in whose hands are two wooden logs.[23]
And on the Sabbath with eleven—
it itself is with nine,
and two in whose hands are two censers of frankincense
for the showbread.
And on the Sabbath that is during the Festival [of Sukkot]—
in the hand of one is a flask of water.[24]

6 A ram is offered with eleven—
the flesh with five,
and the innards, fine flour, and wine
with two each.[25]

---

[22] Lit. "here are ten."   [23] K, P add "to make the wood more plentiful."
[24] K: "spices," which differs by a single letter; perhaps a scribal error.   [25] Lit. "two two."

2:5 *it itself*: i.e. the continual offering.

nine: (1–6) Who bring the six butchered limbs (or sets of limbs) of the continual offering (see above, 2:3), (7) the fine flour, (8) cakes, and (9) wine along the altar ramp. See 2:3 above, and *Tamid* 4:3 for a more elaborate description.

Festival [of Sukkot]: Keeping with the biblical style of referring to *Sukkot* occasionally as "the Festival." See Introduction to *Sukkah*.

a flask of water for the water libation, an extrabiblical ritual performed on all seven days of Sukkot. See *Sukkah* 4:9–10.

The afternoon [continual offering]: The continual offering was repeated every afternoon, per Exodus 29:41 and Numbers 28:8. The Mishnah offers few details about the specifics of the afternoon service; see introduction to *Tamid*, and *Tamid* 4:1, 6:1.

two wooden logs: According to K and P (see variant), these served the purpose of sustaining the fire on the altar.

the Sabbath…showbread: Per Leviticus 24:7–8. See also *Menahot* chapter 11.

the Sabbath that is during the Festival [of Sukkot] has the continual offering offered by twelve priests.

in the hand of one: In addition to the eleven priests who offered the continual offering on a regular Sabbath.

2:6 *A ram*: Such as the guilt offering; see Leviticus 5:14–26; *Zevahim* 5:5.

two each: Perhaps additional hands are required as the amount of flour and wine offered together with the burnt offering of a ram—two-tenths of an *ephah* of flour and one-third *hin* of wine (Numbers 15:6–7)—is greater than that offered with the continual offering—one-tenth an *ephah* of flour and one-quarter *hin* of wine. Being one year older than the yearling lamb of the continual offering, the ram's innards were likely heavier as well.

7 A bull is offered with twenty-four—
the head and hindleg—
the head with one and the hindleg with two;
the rump and the [other] hindleg—
the rump with two and the [other] hindleg with two;
the breast and the neck—
the breast with one and the neck with three;[26]
the two forelegs—with two;
the two flanks—with two;
the innards, the fine flour, and the wine—with three each.[27]
When does this apply?
For communal offerings.
But for an individual offering,
if [a single priest] wishes to make the offering,
he [may] make the offering.
The flaying and butchering of both[28] are equal.

Chapter Three

3:1–3 *Final Preparations before the Continual Offering Service*

3 The Appointed One said to them:
"Go out and see if the time for slaughtering has arrived."

---

[26] K: "two," with a faint strikethrough and "three" in the margin. [27] Lit. "three three."
[28] Lit. "these and these."

2:7 *A bull*: Such as the bull for the communal purgation offering; see Leviticus 4:13–21, *Horayot* 1:4–5.

twenty-four: Fifteen of whom are required for the butchered parts alone, surely a function of their weight.

three each: The flour and wine offerings are incrementally more substantial than those brought with the rams and continual offerings: three-tenths an *ephah* of flour and a half *hin* of wine (Numbers 15:9–10).

When does this apply? That the designated number of priests ("no fewer and no more") is required for each of the above offerings.

if [a single priest] wishes to make the offering on his own and without assistance.

The flaying and butchering of both: Communal and private offerings *are equal* in that the same (unspecified) number of priests flays and butchers the animal, regardless of its size. According to the Talmud, however, these functions might be performed by nonpriests so they *are equal* in that no headcount or lottery was necessary. Further distinctions between communal and individual offerings are made in *Temurah* 1:6, 2:1.

3:1 Parallel to *Tamid* 3:2. While this and the following mishnah commence the narration of the Day of Atonement service, their language is borrowed from that of the everyday service.

The Appointed One: Presumably the priest in charge of the lots that govern the continual offering (see above 2:2–4); indeed *Sheqalim* 5:1 names Matitiah b. Samuel as holding this office. On this individual see also *Tamid* 3:2.

the time for slaughtering the morning continual offering.

If it has arrived,
the one who sees it says:
"Barqai!"[29]
Matitiah[30] b. Samuel [would] ask:[31]
"Has the entire face of the east until Hebron been illuminated?"[32]
And he would respond:
"Yes."

2 And why was there a need for this?
For on one occasion the moonlight arose,
and they reckoned that the east was illuminated
and slaughtered the continual offering
and [had to] take it away to the Place of Burning.
They led the high priest down to the Place of Immersion.
This was the general rule in the Temple:
One who moves his bowels[33]
requires immersion,
and one who urinates[34]
requires the sanctification of his hands and feet.

3 One may not enter the [Temple] Court for[35] service,
even if he is pure,

---

[29] Meaning uncertain; **K**, **P**: "Burqi" (though **K** is clearly written in a different hand over an erasure).
[30] **K**, **P**: "Matia." [31] Lit. "says." [32] **K** lacks "been illuminated."
[33] Lit. "covers his feet"; see annotations. [34] Lit. "deposits water."
[35] **K**: "or for"; see annotations.

Barqai: Perhaps "shining" (light).

the entire face of the east until Hebron: Hebron is to the south of Jerusalem, rather than to its east; the question is thus whether the light from the east has reached a distant point of reference.

And he: Presumably the person who announced "Barqai" would respond "Yes."

3:2 *they reckoned that the east was illuminated*: Moonrise takes place during the dawn hours in the week leading up to a new moon, so this incident did not occur on the Day of Atonement, which takes place ten days after the new moon.

Place of Burning: Located outside the Temple precinct. This is the treatment accorded to an invalid sacrifice. See *Sheqalim* 7:3.

They led…to the Place of Immersion: Description of the Day of Atonement resumes. This was his first immersion, ahead of the morning continual offering service.

moves his bowels: See Judges 3:24.

immersion: In a full ritual bath.

sanctification: Washing, with water from the laver. On the distinction between bathing and sanctification, see the next mishnah.

3:3 *One may not enter*: Though phrased generally, the printed text of the Mishnah appears to be referring only to priests. The variant in **K** opens the possibility, mentioned in the Talmud, that there is also a prohibition for pure nonpriests to enter the Courtyard without immersion.

until he has immersed.
The high priest undergoes five immersions and ten sanctifications[36] on that day,
and all of them
in the Holy [Precinct] on[37] [the roof of] the Parvah House
save for this one.

3:4–5 The High Priest Performs the Morning Continual Offering

4 They spread a linen sheet between him and the people.[38]
He stripped, descended, and immersed,
he ascended and dried himself.
They brought him [the] gold vestments,
and he put [them] on
and sanctified his hands and feet.
They brought the [lamb for] the continual offering to him.
He made an incision into it,
and another [priest] finished the slaughter on his behalf.
He received the blood and tossed it.
He entered to offer the morning incense,
tend to the lamps,
and offer the head, innards, cakes, and wine.
   5 The morning incense was offered
between the blood and the innards.

[36] Lit. "immerses five immersions and sanctifies ten sanctifications." K, P lack "and ten sanctifications."
[37] K, P: "in."
[38] K adds "he sanctified his hands and feet."

five immersions: Leviticus 16 prescribes two immersions for the high priest; one before he dons the special linen garments (v. 4) and again at the end of the service (v. 24) after he takes them off. The Mishnah additionally requires that the high priest undergo three more immersions in the course of the day.

ten sanctifications: According to Exodus 30:19–21, priests were required to wash their hands and feet before entering the Tent of Meeting or officiating at the altar. This process—which is not mentioned in Leviticus 16—is called "sanctification of the hands and feet." The mishnaic rite has the high priest sanctify his hands and feet both after he gets dressed and before he strips his vestments either for the next immersion, or for the completion of the service.

all of them: The initial immersion (see 3:4) took place at the Water Gate, but the rest took place *on [the roof of] the Parvah House*, a chamber in the Temple complex (3:6 below, *Middot* 5:3). According to the variant in **K** and **P** the interpolated mention of the roof is unnecessary.

3:4 *gold vestments*: Which the high priest wore throughout the year; see Exodus 28 and below 7:5. They were either woven with gold yarn or accented with gold.

tossed: See *Tamid* 4:1.

He entered the Sanctum.

morning incense…wine: See above 1:2, *Tamid* 7:3.

3:5 *between the blood and the innards*: After the sprinkling of the blood and before the offering of the innards.

The afternoon [incense was offered]
between the innards and the libations.
If the high priest was elderly or infirm,
they would heat water for him
and pour it into the cold waters
so as to reduce their chill.

3:6–9 *Preparing the Purgation Offerings*

6 They brought him to the Parvah House;
it was in the Holy [Precinct].
They spread a linen sheet between him and the people.
He sanctified his hands and feet,
and he stripped.
R. Meir says:
He stripped;
he sanctified his hands and feet.[39]
He descended and immersed,
he ascended and dried himself.
They brought him [the] white vestments;
he put [them] on
and sanctified his hands and feet.
7 In the morning he would wear Pelusine [fabric]
worth twelve *maneh*,
and in the afternoon [he would wear] Indian fabric
worth eight hundred *zuz*,
the words of R. Meir.
But the Sages say:
In the morning he would wear [clothing] worth eighteen *maneh*,
and in the afternoon [he would wear clothing] worth twelve *maneh*;
thirty *maneh* in all.
These were from the public;[40]

[39] K lacks "and he stripped...feet."   [40] K, P: "sacred funds."

libations: The fine flour and wine.

cold waters of the immersion pool.

3:6 *in the Holy [Precinct]*: As opposed to the place of the first immersion, which took place just outside. See above 3:2.

white vestments: According to Leviticus 16:4 the Day of Atonement service begins with the high priest bathing himself before donning special linen vestments, which the Mishnah presumes to be white. On the priestly vestments, see below 7:5.

3:7 *Pelusine*. Pelusium, a city on the Nile Delta, was known in antiquity for its manufacture of fine linen.

These were from the public: The funds with which these vestments were purchased for the high priest came from public donations to the Temple.

if he wished to supplement,
he would supplement from his own [funds].

8 He came to his bull,
and his bull[41] would be standing between the Porch and the Altar,
its head toward the south
and its face toward the west.
And the priest stands on the eastern side,
his face toward the west,
and he lays his two hands upon [the bull]
and confesses.
And this is what he would say:
"O Lord,[42]
I have committed iniquity, I have transgressed, I have sinned before you—
I and my household.
O Lord,
Please forgive the iniquities, transgressions, and sins
that I have committed, that I have transgressed, and that I have sinned before you—
I and my household.
As it is written in the Torah of Moses your servant,
For on this day He will effect atonement for you, etc."[43]
And they respond after him:
"Blessed be the name of the glory of His kingdom forever and ever."

9 He came to the east of the Court,
to the north of the altar,
the Temple Prefect to his right
and the Chief of the paternal house to his left.

---

[41] K, P: "a bull."   [42] Lit. "the Name" here and immediately below.
[43] K lacks "He will effect atonement for you."

3:8 *his bull*: The purgation offering for the high priest and his household (Leviticus 16:6).

between the Porch and the Altar: A twenty-two-cubit-wide area spanning the north–south axis of the Temple; this area contains the laver. See Ezekiel 8:16, Joel 2:17, *Middot* 3:6.

he lays his two hands: An extrabiblical addition; in Scripture the laying on of hands is prescribed only for the he-goat that is sent to the wilderness (Leviticus 16:21). See *Menahot* 9:7.

confesses: As with the laying on of hands, confession is prescribed in the biblical account only for the scapegoat (Leviticus 16:21).

"Lord": Lit. "the Name"—perhaps a circumlocution for the Tetragrammaton, which the high priest invokes explicitly later in the service; see below, 6:2. The phrase evokes Psalm 118:25. See also *Tamid* 7:2.

"For on this day…": Leviticus 16:30.

they respond: Presumably priests were present at the service as well as observers in the Israelite Courtyard; see *Middot* 2:6.

3:9 *Temple Prefect*: See *Tamid* 7:3.

Chief of the paternal house: That is, the head of the priestly household that happened to be on service that day. See *Ta'anit* 2:6, 4:2; *Tamid* 1:1.

There were two he-goats present,
and an urn[44] was there
and two lots were inside.
They were [made] of boxwood,
though Ben Gamla made them of gold,
and they would recall[45] him favorably.

3:10–11   *Famous and Infamous Temple Personnel*

10 Ben Qatin made twelve spigots for the laver,
for previously there were only two.
He also made a mechanism for the laver
so that its water not be invalidated
by remaining overnight.
King Monobaz fashioned all of the handles
of the vessels for the Day of Atonement
from gold.
Helena his mother fashioned a gold lamp
[to be affixed] over the entrance to the Sanctum.
She also fashioned a gold tablet
on which the portion of the suspected adulteress was written.
Nicanor—his doors underwent miracles,
and they would recall him favorably.

11 And these [they recalled] to their shame:
those of the House of Garmu,
for they did not want to teach

---

[44] Or "box."   [45] Or "mention."

---

boxwood: A fine-grained wood ideal for ornate carving.

3:10 *invalidated…overnight*: Water left in the laver overnight was deemed invalid for the sanctification of hands and feet on the following day. The indicated *mechanism* presumably drained the laver at night and refilled it the following day from an underground cistern.

King Monobaz II, of Adiabene, a Parthian satellite located between modern-day Mosul and Kirkuk, who ruled in the mid-first century CE. Both Monobaz, and his mother *Helena*, who reigned as Queen of Adiabene in the previous generation, are said to have converted to Judaism. From the text it is not clear whether Monobaz financed the production of all these handles or actually fashioned them himself. The former is more likely. The same uncertainty attaches to the report about Queen Helena immediately below.

tablet: The tablet would have included Numbers 5:11–31. See Introduction to *Sotah*.

Nicanor: Identity unknown.

miracles: According to tradition, one of the Temple doors, brought by Nicanor from Alexandria, was lost to stormy seas, but miraculously bobbed out of the water as the boat arrived in Joppa with the remaining door.

3:11 *to their shame*: That is, to the shame of those so remembered. The first three names in this mishnah are mentioned in *Sheqalim* 5:1.

about the making of the showbread;
those of the House of Avtinas,
for they did not want to teach
about the making of the incense;
Hugras[46] b. Levi knew [the] break[s] in the songs,[47]
but did not want to teach [them];
Ben Qamtsar did not want
to teach about scribal practices.
With regard to the former it is said:
The memory of the righteous is a blessing;
and with regard to these it is said:
The name of the wicked will rot.

Chapter Four

4:1–3 *Further Preparations for the Purgation Offering*

4 He shook the urn and removed the two lots.
One was inscribed: "For the Name";
The other was inscribed: "For Azazel."
The Prefect was to his right
and the Chief of the paternal house to his left.[48]
If "For the Name" came up in his right hand,
the Prefect says to him:
"My lord, High Priest, raise your right hand!"
If "For the Name" came up in his left hand,
the Chief of the paternal house says to him:
"My lord, High Priest, raise your left hand!"

---

[46] **K**: "Hogdam"; **P**: "Hogdas."   [47] Singular in original. Meaning unknown.
[48] **K, P** lack "The Prefect…to his left."

---

break[s] in the songs: Precise meaning unknown, but see *Tamid* 7:3.

the former: Those recalled favorably in 3:10.

The memory…The name…: Proverbs 10:7.

4:1 The Mishnah resumes the narration of the Day of Atonement service. See Leviticus 16:8–9.

removed the two lots: One in each hand.

Prefect…Chief: See above, 3:9.

"For the Name": Heb. *la-Shem*. It is unclear whether this is employed in the Mishnah as a circumlocution for the Tetragrammaton (as above, 3:8), which was inscribed on the lot, or whether *la-Shem* was itself inscribed on the lot.

He placed [the lots] on the two goats,
and says:
"For the Lord[49]—a purgation offering."
R. Ishmael says:
He did not need to say "purgation offering,"
rather "For the Lord."
And they respond after him:
"Blessed be the name of the glory of His kingdom forever and ever."
  2 He tied a strap of crimson to the head of the scapegoat,[50]
and he stood it
opposite the place of its dispatch;
and for the [he-goat] to be slaughtered,
[he tied a strap] alongside the place of its slaughter.
He came to his bull a second time,
and he lays his two hands upon the bull and confesses.
And this is what he would say:
"O Lord,[51]
I have committed iniquity, I have transgressed, I have sinned before you—
I and my household and the sons of Aaron, your holy people.
O Lord,
Please forgive[52] the iniquities, transgressions, and sins[53]
that I have committed, that I have transgressed, and that I have sinned before you—
I and my household and the sons of Aaron, your holy people.
As it is written in the Torah of Moses your servant,
For on this day He will effect atonement for you
to purify you from all of your sins;
before the Lord you shall be purified."
And they respond after him:
"Blessed be the name of the glory of His kingdom forever and ever."

[49] K, P represent the name of God with two *yod*s, here and immediately below.
[50] Lit. "the he-goat to be sent away."   [51] Lit. "the Name," here and immediately below.
[52] K lacks "the iniquities…forever and ever."
[53] P lacks "that I have committed…forever and ever."

He placed…: Leviticus 16:8 prescribes that the lots be "placed" on the he-goats. This may mean physical placement, or perhaps only assignment.

4:2 a strap of crimson: See below 6:6, 8; *Shabbat* 9:3.

scapegoat: The he-goat that received the lot "For Azazel."

place of its dispatch: The gate through which it was later led out of the Temple. See below, 6:2ff.

to be slaughtered, viz., the purgation offering "For the Lord." The scapegoat was not slaughtered; see below, 6:6.

alongside the place of its slaughter on its neck.

a second time: Per Leviticus 16:11. The high priest's first confession on the bull is recorded above, 3:8.

For on this day…: Leviticus 16:30.

3 He slaughtered [the bull],
received its blood in a bowl,
and he gave it to the one who would stir it
—on the fourth landing in the Sanctum—
so that it would not coagulate.
He took the fire-pan,
ascended to the top of the altar,
swept the coals to and fro,[54]
scooped out some of the inner embers,[55]
descended,
and placed the fire-pan on the fourth[56] step in the Temple Court.

4:4–6 Distinctions between the Day of Atonement and the Rest of the Year

4 Every [other] day he would scoop with the silver [fire-pan]
and pour into the golden [fire-pan];
on this day he scoops with the golden [fire-pan]
and with it he would bring [the incense] in.
Every [other] day he scoops with a [fire-pan] of four *qav*
and pours into [a fire-pan] of three *qav*;
on this day he scoops with [a fire-pan] of three *qav*
and with it he would bring [the incense] in.
R. Yose says:
Every [other] day he scoops with a [fire-pan] of a *se'ah*
and pours into [a fire-pan] of three *qav*;
on this day he scoops with [a fire-pan] of three *qav*
and with it he would bring [the incense] in.
Every [other] day it was heavy;
on this day [it was] light.
Every [other] day its handle was short;

[54] K, P lack "swept...to and fro." [55] K, P lack "some of the embers." [56] K, P lack "fourth."

4:3 *He slaughtered [the bull]*: Per Leviticus 16:11.

who would stir it: In order to follow the order of the service prescribed in Leviticus 16, the high priest would need to slaughter the bull, then offer the incense, and only thereafter sprinkle the bull's blood.

fourth landing: There were twelve steps, in four groups of three, from the floor of the Temple Court (adjacent to the altar) up to the Porch—the "entrance hall" to the Holy Precinct and the Holy of Holies. Every third step was a landing; the top step was thus the fourth landing. See *Middot* 3:6.

fire-pan: A shovel-like censer.

scooped...embers: See Leviticus 16:12.

4:4 *scoop with the silver*: See *Tamid* 5:4–6.

on this day [it was] light...on this day [it was] long: Easing the rite for the high priest, who performed the entire incense service on his own. See below, 5:1.

on this day it was long.
Every [other] day its gold was yellow;
on this day it was red,
the words of R. Menahem.
Every [other] day he offers half [a *maneh*] in the morning
and half in the afternoon;
on this day he adds two handfuls.
Every [other] day [the incense] was finely ground;
on this day it was the finest of the fine.

5 Every [other] day the priests ascend the ramp on the eastern side
and descend on the western side;
on this day,
the high priest ascends in the middle
and descends in the middle.[57]
R. Judah says:
At all times the high priest ascends in the middle
and descends in the middle.
Every [other] day the high priest sanctifies his hands and feet
from the laver;
on this day, from the golden pitcher.
R. Judah says:
At all times the high priest sanctifies his hands and feet from the golden pitcher.

6 Every [other] day there were four woodpiles there;
on this day, five—
the words of R. Meir.
R. Yose says:
Every [other] day three;
on this day, four.
R. Judah says:
Every [other] day two;
on this day, three.

[57] **K, P**: "On this day they (= the priests) ascend in the middle and descend in the middle."

red: Gold alloys with a high copper content take on a reddish hue.

adds two handfuls on top of the incense offered twice each day as a part of the continual offering.

two handfuls: Leviticus 16:12.

finely ground: See Exodus 30:36.

finest of the fine: See Leviticus 16:12.

4:5 *golden pitcher*: See *Tamid* 3:6.

4:6 *four woodpiles there* on the altar.

Every [other] day two; on this day, three: All agree, at minimum, that there were two woodpiles for daily use and that on the Day of Atonement there was an additional woodpile. The first was said to be for the continual offering and the second was for embers to be used in the daily incense offering; the additional pile was for embers used in the special incense offering on the Day of Atonement. R. Yose posits that a third pile was used on a daily basis to maintain the various fires; R. Meir agrees, and argues that there was yet another woodpile for incinerating the remnants of the previous day's afternoon continual offering.

Chapter Five

5:1–2 *The Incense Offering*

5 They brought out to him the ladle and the pan,
and he took two handfuls [of incense],
and put [it] into the ladle—
a large [priest] according to [the] largeness [of his hand],
and a small [priest] according to [the] smallness [of his hand]—
such was its measure.
He took the fire-pan in his right hand
and the ladle in his left.
He would walk through the Sanctum
until he arrived between the two curtains
separating the Holy and the Holy of Holies—
between them was one cubit.
R. Yose says:
There was only one curtain there,
as it is written:
The curtain shall separate for you between the Holy and the Holy of Holies.
The outer [curtain] was held back[58] on the southern side,
and the inner [curtain] on the northern side.
He walks between them
until he reaches the northern side.
[When] he reaches the northern side,[59]
he turns to face the south,
and he walks with the curtain to his left

---

[58] Or "clasped."   [59] K lacks "When…side."

5:1 *a large [priest] according to [the] largeness…*: For other areas of ritual law lacking statutory amounts, see *Pe'ah* 1:1. For similar phrasing, see *Jubilees* 5:15.

He would walk through the Sanctum to the west.

two curtains: See Exodus 26:31–33, 36:35–36. See also *Tamid* 7:1.

The curtain shall separate…: Exodus 26:33.

He walks…northern side: He has already entered on the southern side, coming from the east; he turns to the right, and walks between the curtains until he reaches the northern wall.

he turns around 180 degrees *to face the south*, steps past the inner curtain to his right, and enters into the Holy of Holies.

walks with the curtain to his left: A logistical necessity, as the Ark's two poles are said to have been so long that they protruded through the inner curtain. To reach between the two poles the high priest would have to push the inner curtain aside with his hip.

until he reaches the Ark.
When he reaches the Ark,
he places the fire-pan between the [Ark's] two poles.
He piled the incense onto the coals,
and the entire[60] chamber was filled with smoke.
He exited,
taking the path through which he entered,
and he prays a short prayer in the outer chamber,
but he would not prolong his prayer[61]
so as to not alarm the people.[62]

2 After the Ark was taken away:
there was a rock there
from the time of the early prophets,
called "Shetiyyah,"
three fingerbreadths higher than the ground,
and upon it he would place [the fire-pan].

5:3–6   *Blood Manipulations*

3 He took the blood from the one who was stirring it,
entered where he had entered,

[60] K, P lack "entire."   [61] K, P lack "his prayer."   [62] Lit. "Israel."

---

the Ark of the Covenant (Exodus 26:33, Deuteronomy 10:1–8). The Ark was not present in the Second Temple (see introduction and below, 5:2).

the [Ark's] two poles: Described in Exodus 25:13–15.

chamber: Lit. "house." A reference to the Holy of Holies.

filled with smoke: The mark of a successful offering; see Leviticus 16:13. The high priest leaves the ladle and fire-pan in the Holy of Holies, and he retrieves them only toward the end of the day's service. See below, 7:4.

prays a short prayer: Perhaps because according to Leviticus 16:13 an unsuccessful incense service will result in the death of the high priest. A medieval folk-tradition speaks of a rope that was tied to the high priest in order to pull him out of the Holy of Holies in the event of his death, but this tradition is without basis in classical rabbinic literature.

outer chamber: The Sanctum.

so as not to alarm the people who presumably feared for the life of the high priest.

5:2 *After the Ark was taken away*: There are various traditions concerning the disappearance of the Ark. See 2 Maccabees 2:1–8; *Sheqalim* 6:1–2.

early prophets: Perhaps referring to David and Solomon. See 1 Chronicles 9:22; *Ta'anit* 4:2.

Shetiyyah: Meaning uncertain. The Talmud offers two explanations: the rock upon which the world was founded; the rock from which the world was woven. Both involve plays on the name.

upon it he would place [the fire-pan] when performing the incense service on the Day of Atonement.

5:3 *He took the blood* of the slaughtered bull. See above, 4:3.

entered where he had entered: Into the Holy of Holies.

stood where he had stood,
and sprinkled from it
once upward and seven [times] downward.
He would not intend to sprinkle upward or downward;
rather he made a whipping motion.
And this is how he would count:
One,
one and one,
one and two,
one and three,
one and four,
one and five,
one and six,
one and seven.
He exited and placed the [bowl of blood]
on the golden⁶³ stand in the Sanctum.

4 They brought him the he-goat.
He slaughtered it
and received its blood in a bowl.⁶⁴
He entered where he had entered,⁶⁵
stood where he had stood,
and sprinkled from it
once upward and seven [times] downward.
He would not intend to sprinkle upward or downward;
rather he made a whipping motion.
And this is how he would count:
One,
one and one,

---

⁶³ K lacked "golden" but it was restored in the margin.
⁶⁴ K lacks "received…bowl" but substitutes "and he tossed its blood." Likely a scribal error.
⁶⁵ K lacks "He entered where he had entered."

---

stood where he had stood: Before the place of the Ark.

sprinkled from it once upward and seven [times] downward: Leviticus 16:14 appears to prescribe two sets of sprinkling; a single sprinkling followed by seven.

He would not intend…: Meaning uncertain. Perhaps the high priest was not to flick his wrist either upward or downward.

a whipping motion: Meaning uncertain. Perhaps the high priest is to lock his wrist and, as if he were whipping, make a full up-and-down motion of the arm, regardless of whether he is tossing upward or downward.

One: For the first, upward sprinkling.

one and one: One upward and one downward; and so on.

5:4 *the he-goat* that had been designated "For the Lord." See above, 4:1. The Mishnah is keeping with the sequence of Leviticus 16; here tracking with v. 15.

He entered…: Leviticus 16:15 prescribes that the blood of the he-goat be tossed in an identical manner to that of the bull. See above, 5:3.

one and two, etc.⁶⁶
He exited and placed the [bowl of blood]
on the second⁶⁷ stand that was in the Sanctum.
R. Judah says:
There was only one stand.
He took the blood of the bull
and set down the blood of the he-goat,
and he sprinkled from it
on the curtain opposite the Ark
from the outside
once upward and seven [times] downward.
He would not intend, etc.⁶⁸
And this is how he would count, etc.
He took the blood of the he-goat
and set down the blood of the bull,
and he sprinkled from it
on the curtain opposite the Ark
from the outside
once upward and seven [times] downward, etc.⁶⁹
He poured the blood of the bull
into the blood of the he-goat
and placed the full [bowl] in the empty one.
   5 *And he shall go out to the altar that is before the Lord:*⁷⁰
this [refers to] the Golden Altar.
He began to purge [the altar] in a downward [direction].

⁶⁶ K, P lack "one…etc."
⁶⁷ K lacks "second" (added in margin).
⁶⁸ K, P complete the formula: "…to toss upward or downward; rather he made a whipping motion."
⁶⁹ K, P complete the formula "He did not intend a whipping motion."
⁷⁰ K, P add the continuation of the verse: "*and purge it.*"

---

the second stand: The blood of the bull was presumably resting on the other stand; see above, 5:3.

He took the blood of the bull: Apparently understanding Leviticus 16:16 as prescribing a separate purgation ritual for the Sanctum.

He took the blood of the he-goat: Leviticus 16:16 does not specify how the purgation is to be effected. The Mishnah requires the separate sprinkling of blood from both the bull and he-goat, perhaps to cover all possibilities.

He poured the blood: Leviticus 16:18 calls for the priest to take from the blood of the bull and the he-goat, and the next verse prescribes that the blood be "put" on the horns of the inner altar (see below, 5:5). The Mishnah understands this as referring to a mixture of both types of blood.

5:5 *And he shall go out…*: Leviticus 16:18.

this [refers to] the Golden Altar: Our mishnah identifies the unnamed altar in Leviticus 16:18 with the incense altar in the Holy Precinct, which was overlaid with gold (Exodus 30:3; cf. Hebrews 9:3–4, which locates the Golden Altar in the Holy of Holies). Exodus 30:10 prescribes that Aaron perform a purgation rite on this altar once each year with the blood of the purgation offering.

purge [the altar] by daubing blood on its "horns," per Leviticus 16:18. See also Exodus 29:36, Leviticus 8:15.

From where does he begin?
From the northeastern corner,
[to the] northwest,
[to the] southwest,
[to the] southeast.[71]
The place where he begins
[to sprinkle the blood] of the purgation offering on the outer altar,
from there he would finish[72] on the inner altar.
R. Eliezer says:
He would stand in his place and purge.
And on all of the [corners]
he would apply [the blood with an] upward[73] [motion],
except for the [corner] in front of him,
upon which[74] he would apply [the blood with a] downward[75] [motion].
  6 He sprinkled [the blood]
on the surface of the altar
seven times,
and he would spill the remaining blood
onto the western base of the outer altar.
[The remaining blood] from the outer altar
he would spill onto the southern base.
[The blood from] both [sides of the altar] mixes in the channel,
goes out to the Kidron Valley,
and is sold to gardeners for fertilizer,
for [otherwise] [its use constitutes] misuse of sacred property.

[71] **K**: "south"; east added in margin.
[72] **K, P** lack "from"; they read "that [same corner is where] he finishes."
[73] Lit. "down-to-up."   [74] **K, P** lack "upon which."   [75] Lit. "up-to-down."

From where does he begin to daub the blood.

The place where he begins: The blood of the purgation offering is first sprinkled on the southeastern corner (*Zevahim* 5:3).

from there the southeastern corner *he finishes* daubing the blood *on the inner altar*.

on all…downward [motion]: Only for R. Eliezer, according to whom the high priest would have to reach out to apply the blood on three out of the four corners of the altar. For those corners, the blood is to be applied in an upward motion; for the remaining corner, at which the high priest stood, the application was downward.

5:6 In addition to being daubed with blood (per Leviticus 16:18), the incense altar is also to be sprinkled with blood seven times (Leviticus 16:19).

he would spill: For the drainage of the blood from the outer altar, see *Middot* 3:2.

the channel: This was a water conduit that led into (or out of) the Temple Coutryard; see *Sheqalim* 4:2, *Middot* 3:2.

fertilizer: Because of its high nitrogen content, dried blood is regarded, even nowadays, as an excellent organic fertilizer.

misuse of sacred property: *Me'ilah*, often translated "sacrilege." The dried blood could not be used without paying for it. See introduction to *Me'ilah*.

7 Every stated act on the Day of Atonement
[must be performed] in order.[76]
If he performed an act before another,
he has done nothing.
If he [sprinkled] the blood of the he-goat
before the blood of the bull,
he must go back
and sprinkle from the blood of the he-goat
after[77] the blood of the bull.
And if before he completed the interior sprinkling
the blood spilled,
he must bring other blood
and sprinkle anew in the inside [chamber]
from the start.[78]
And so too with the Sanctum,
and so too with the Golden Altar,
since they each effect atonement[79] separately.
R. Eleazar and R. Simeon say:
From the place he stopped—
from there he begins.

Chapter Six

6:1–8   *The He-Goat Offerings*

6 The two he-goats of the Day of Atonement—
it is commanded that they both[80] be equal

[76] Lit. "the order"; K lacks the definite article.
[77] K: "and after."
[78] K, P: "and sprinkle as before from the inside."
[79] K, P: "atonement and atonement."
[80] K, P lack "both."

5:7 *interior*: That is, the Holy of Holies. The sprinklings are described above, 5:3–4.

so too with the Sanctum…the Golden Altar: In the event that the blood has spilled out before he has completed sprinkling on the outer curtain or the incense altar, the high priest must bring other blood, go back, and sprinkle anew.

since they each effect atonement separately: The high priest need not go back and restart the entire service in the event that blood has spilled out. Those parts of the service that were completed correctly are regarded as having successfully effected atonement. Only the specific service during which the blood spills must be repeated.

From the place he stopped: The high priest need not even repeat the sprinklings he performed before the blood spilled out.

6:1 *it is commanded…*: Scripture refers to the animals as "two he-goats," when "he-goats" alone would have sufficed, given that the minimum number of plural "he-goats" is two. Rather than regarding the "two" as superfluous, the rabbis derived that the two must be uniform. See also *Nega'im* 14:5 for a similar formula.

in appearance,
and in height,
and in price,[81]
and that they be purchased together.
But even if they are not equal,
they are valid.
If he purchased one on one day
and one on the next day,
they are valid.
If one of them died—
if it died before he drew the lots,
he purchases another to pair with the second.
And if it died after he drew the lots,
he brings another pair[82]
and casts lots anew.
If [the one] "For the Lord" died, he says:
"This one designated by lot as 'For the Lord'
will be in its stead."
If [the one] "For Azazel" died, [he says:]
"This one designated by lot as 'For Azazel'
will be in its stead."
And the second grazes
until it becomes unfit for sacrifice[83]
and should be sold;
its proceeds are put toward[84] a voluntary offering,
for a communal purgation offering is not left to die.[85]
R. Judah says:
It should be left to die.
R. Judah further said:
If the blood had spilled out,
the scapegoat should die.
If the scapegoat dies,
the blood should be spilled out.

[81] Lit. "money."   [82] K, P: "he brings two."   [83] Lit. "soiled."   [84] Lit. "fall."
[85] Lit. "does not die."

If [the one] "For the Lord" died after the lots were drawn, and consequently, a new pair of he-goats has been brought forward and lots cast anew.

And the second: Whether this "second" animal is the surviving he-goat from the original pair or the "second" he-goat of the new pair is left unclear. A dispute in the Talmud centers on these two possibilities.

grazes until it becomes unfit for sacrifice: The hope is that the animal, while grazing, will become blemished in such a way that it becomes unfit for sacrifice.

If the blood of the he-goat slaughtered "For the Lord" *spilled out* before the high priest completed sprinkling the blood in the Holy of Holies. According to R. Judah the animal cannot be used, and must be left to die. Cf. above 5:7.

If the scapegoat dies before the completion of the blood rites for the he-goat "For the Lord."

the blood of the he-goat "For the Lord" *should be spilled out*, and presumably, a new pair drawn and the service started again.

2 He comes to the scapegoat,
and he lays his two hands upon it
and confesses.
And this is what he would say:
"O Lord,[86]
They have committed iniquity,
they have transgressed,
and they have sinned—
your nation, the House of Israel.
O Lord,[87]
please forgive the iniquities, transgressions, and sins
that they have committed,
that they have transgressed,
and that they have sinned before you—
your nation, the House of Israel,
as it is written in the Torah of Moses your servant,
For on this day He will effect atonement for you to purify you from all of your sins;
before the Lord you shall be purified."
And the priests and the people who were standing in the Court,
when they heard the explicit Name
coming out of the mouth of the high priest,
would bend at the knee, bow, fall on their faces and say,
"Blessed be the name of His glorious kingdom forever and ever."[88]

3 He handed [the scapegoat] over
to the one who would walk it away.
All are fit to walk it away,
but the high priests established a fixed [practice],
and they would not allow an [ordinary] Israelite to walk it away.
R. Yose said:
It once happened that Arsela[89] walked it away,
and he was an Israelite.

[86] Lit. "the name."   [87] Lit. "by the name"; **K**: "the name."
[88] **K** lacks "Please forgive…forever and ever"; **P** lacks "the iniquities…forever and ever." See annotation.
[89] **K**: "Ad Shala"; **P**: "Arsala from Sepphoris."

6:2 The Mishnah resumes the Day of Atonement service.

he lays his two hands upon it and confesses: According to Leviticus 16:21. The confession formula is extrabiblical, but the tripartite listing of iniquities, transgressions, and sins is attested in this verse.

For on this day…: Leviticus 16:30. See further on 8:9 below.

And the priests…"forever and ever": Most manuscripts do not attest this paragraph, which appears to have originated in the synagogue liturgy for the Day of Atonement.

6:3 *walk it away*: As commanded in Leviticus 16:21, the scapegoat was to be sent off to the wilderness.

All are fit to walk it away: Scripture specifies that the scapegoat is sent off by what translators render as a "man in waiting"; the exact meaning of this unique Hebrew phrase is unknown.

Israelite: A non-priest.

4 They made a ramp for it
because of the Babylonians,
who would pluck its hair
and say to him:
"Take and go! Take and go!"
Some of the[90] eminent Jerusalemites would escort him[91] until the first booth.
There were ten booths from Jerusalem to [the] precipice,
[a distance of] ninety *ris*;
there are seven and a half [*ris*] per *mil*.

5 At each and every booth they say to him
"Here is food and here is water."
And they escort him from booth to booth,
save for the last of them,
for he does not reach the precipice with him;
rather he stands from afar
and watches his actions.

6 What would he do?
He splits the strap of crimson;
half of it he tied to the rock,
and half of it he tied between [the he-goat's] two horns.
He shoved its posterior,[92]
and it tumbled and fell,
and it would not [even] reach halfway down the mountain
before it was dismembered.[93]
He came and sat under the final booth

[90] K, P lack "Some of the." [91] Or "it," viz., the he-goat. [92] Or "he shoved it backward."
[93] Lit. "was made into [separate] limbs."

6:4 *Babylonians*: A seemingly pejorative depiction of Babylonians is likewise found in *Menahot* 11:7, where Babylonian priests are said to have eaten raw sacrificial meat.

who would pluck its hair: Whether the Babylonians plucked the hair of the he-goat or of the priest accompanying it is left unclear. Early Christian sources also reflect a tradition concerning abuse of the scapegoat.

"Take and go!" Presumably the people were anxious for the scapegoat, which bore their collective sins, to be dispatched—they wanted atonement to be effected as soon as possible.

precipice: Either a toponym or a generic descriptor for a precipice suitable for the fatal dispatching of the scapegoat.

mil: Slightly more than a kilometer. The *ris* was evidently already an unfamiliar measure.

6:5 *At each and every booth they say to him*: Each booth was manned by an attendant.

"Here is food and here is water.": While the Talmuds assert that the priest never actually partook of the food, in general it is unclear whether the afflictions described below in 8:1 were binding for the priesthood.

save for the attendant in *the last* booth, who does not accompany the priest to the precipice.

6:6 *What would* the one leading the goat *do* once he reached the end of the route?

He splits the strap of crimson that had been tied to the head of the scapegoat; above, 4:2.

He shoved…: An extrabiblical ritual. Cf. Leviticus 16:22.

until it became dark.
And from when does he[94] render [his] garments unclean?
From when he goes outside[95] the wall of Jerusalem.
R. Simeon says:
From the time he pushes [the he-goat] from the precipice.

7 [The high priest] came to the bull and he-goat
which were [to be] incinerated.
He tore them open
and removed their altar portions;
he placed them on a tray
and burned them on the altar.
He slung [the carcasses] into slings[96]
and removed them to the Place of Burning.
And from when do they render [their] garments unclean?
When they go outside[97] the wall of the Court.
R. Simeon says:
When fire has ignited around the greater part [of the two carcasses].

8 They said to the high priest:
"The he-goat has reached the desert."
And whence would they know
that the he-goat reached the desert?
They would station[98] relays[99]
and wave flags,

[94] Or "it." [95] K, P lack "outside." [96] K, P: "he slung [the carcasses] onto poles."
[97] Lit. "exit outside." K, P lack "outside." [98] Lit. "make."
[99] Meaning of word uncertain; spelling varies.

And from when…? According to Leviticus 16:26, the person responsible for sending the scapegoat off into the wilderness must launder his clothing before re-entering the camp. That his clothes require laundering presupposes that they are rendered impure at some juncture, and our mishnah interrogates this point.

6:7 *the bull and he-goat* which had previously been slaughtered (4:3; 5:4) and their blood sprinkled are now *[to be] incinerated*, with the exception of their suet, as commanded in Leviticus 16:27. Here the Mishnah departs from the sequence of Leviticus 16, which at this point in the service would prescribe the bringing of the whole burnt offerings—recorded in our mishnah only in 7:3.

altar portions: The abdominal fats; see Leviticus 16:25.

removed them…: The Torah instructs that the carcasses be incinerated outside the Israelite "camp" (Leviticus 16:27). See *Zevahim* 12:5–6.

And from when…? As above, the persons responsible for incinerating the carcasses are commanded to launder their clothing and undergo ritual immersion before re-entering the camp (Leviticus 16:28). See also *Parah* 8:3.

6:8 *"The he-goat has reached the desert"*: The criterion for resuming the service.

flags: Cf. *Rosh Hashanah* 2:2–4.

and they [thus] knew that the he-goat had reached the desert.
R. Judah said:
But did they not have an ample indicator?[100]
From Jerusalem to Bet Hiddudo[101] is three *mil*;
they can walk one *mil*,
walk back one *mil*,
wait one *mil*,
and know that the he-goat had reached the desert.
R. Ishmael said:
But did they not have a different indicator?
A strap of crimson was tied
to the entrance to the Sanctum,
and when the he-goat reached the desert,
the strap would whiten,
as it is written:
Though your sins are like crimson,
they shall turn white like snow.[102]

Chapter Seven

7:1–2 *The Reading of the Torah*

7 The high priest came to read.
If he wished to read in linen vestments,
he may do so.[103]
If not,
he reads in a white vestment of his own.
The minister of the assembly takes a Torah scroll

---

[100] Lit. "great sign."
[101] K, P: "Haroro."
[102] K, P lack "R. Ishmael...white like snow." See annotations.
[103] Lit. "he reads."

Bet Hiddudo: Text and meaning uncertain, perhaps a place name. This place marks the beginning of the desert according to R. Judah.

wait the time that it would have taken to walk a distance of *one mil*.

R. Ishmael said...: Absent from numerous manuscripts. This is likely an addition to the Mishnah influenced by the Babylonian Talmud and its presentation of various practices relating to the display of the crimson strap (see above 4:2, 6:6, and *Shabbat* 9:3).

Though your sins...: Isaiah 1:18.

7:1 Largely parallel to *Sotah* 7:7.

The high priest came to read from the Torah; a further extrabiblical tradition.

minister of the assembly: Portrayed elsewhere as engaged in some of the logistical aspects of Temple rituals.

and gives it to the head of the assembly,[104]
and the head of the assembly gives it to the Prefect,
and the Prefect gives it to the high priest,
and the high priest stands,
and receives it,
and reads[105] [the portions of] *After the death*
and *Now on the tenth day*.
And he rolls the Torah,
and rests it in his bosom,
and says:
"More than what I have read before you is written here."[106]
And [the portion of] *On the tenth day* from the Book of Numbers
he recites from memory,[107]
and he blesses upon it eight benedictions:
For the Torah,
for the [Temple-]Service,
for the Thanksgiving,
for the Forgiveness of Sin,
for the Temple—a separate [blessing],[108]
for Israel—a separate [blessing],
(for Jerusalem—a separate [blessing])[109]
for the priests—a separate [blessing],
and for the remainder of the prayer.

2 The one who sees the high priest when he is reading
does not see the bull and he-goat being burnt.
And the one who sees the bull and he-goat being burnt
does not see the high priest when he is reading.
And not because it is not permitted,
rather it was a long distance [between them],
and the two services were done simultaneously.[110]

---

[104] "Head of the assembly" lacking in **K**, but added in a different hand in the margin.
[105] **K, P** add "He stands and reads."   [106] **K, P** lack "here."   [107] Lit. "by mouth."
[108] **K, P** lack "a separate [blessing]," here and throughout the paragraph.   [109] **K, P** lack this item.
[110] Lit. "equal as one"; **K, P** lack "equal."

After the death and Now on the tenth day: Respectively, Leviticus 16 (in its entirety) and Leviticus 23 (presumably verses 26–32). These are the two most extensive scriptural treatments of the Day of Atonement.

"More than what I have read before you is written here." Read simply, the high priest is declaring to the masses that he has read only a small portion of the Torah. The purpose of this declaration is unclear.

on the tenth day: Numbers 29:7–11. This passage offers a very concise list of the Day of Atonement offerings.

he recites from memory: In order to save time and spare the crowd's patience, he abstains from rolling the scroll.

eight benedictions: Whether these benedictions had a precise formula or whether they were thematic "modules" to be filled with the high priest's own wording is left ambiguous. See *Berakhot* 4:3, *Rosh Hashanah* 4:5, *Tamid* 5:1.

7:2 *the one who sees the bull and he-goat being burnt*: This was apparently a public spectacle, to the extent that officers are said to have been stationed to prevent onlookers from falling into the flames.

a long distance: The Place of Burning was outside of Jerusalem, to the north. The precise location of the Torah reading within the Temple is not specified.

7:3–4 *Completing the Service*

3 If he read[111] in linen vestments,
he sanctified his hands and feet,
stripped,
descended and immersed,
ascended and dried himself off.
They brought to him [the] golden vestments,
and he got dressed
and sanctified his hands and feet.
And[112] *he went out and offered*[113]
his ram and the people's ram,
as well as the *seven unblemished yearling*[114] *lambs*—
the words of R. Eliezer.
R. Aqiva says:
They would be offered together with the morning continual offering.
And[115] the bull for the whole burnt offering
and the he-goat offered[116] outside
were offered[117] together with the afternoon continual offering.

4 He sanctified his hands and feet
and stripped
and descended and immersed;
and ascended and dried himself off.
They brought to him [the] white vestments,
and he got dressed
and sanctified his hands and feet.
He entered to remove the ladle and fire-pan.

[111] Lit. "reads." [112] K, P lack "and." [113] Lit. "made." [114] K, P lack "yearling."
[115] K: "but." [116] Lit. "done." [117] P lacks "were offered."

7:3 *If he read in linen vestments*: See above 7:1.

And he went out and offered: The Mishnah here integrates this quotation from Leviticus 16:24 to continue its narration of the service.

his ram and the people's ram: These are the whole burnt offerings mentioned in Leviticus 16:24. That the offerings consist of the high priest's ram and the people's ram is gleaned from the opening verses of Leviticus 16 (vv. 3, 5).

seven unblemished yearling lambs: Part of the supplementary offerings specified in Numbers 29:7–11.

They would be offered: The disagreement here stems from the need to interpolate the supplementary offerings of Numbers 29 into the Day of Atonement service, as Leviticus 16 does not mention these offerings.

outside: This is in contrast with the other purgation offerings sacrificed on the Day of Atonement, whose blood was sprinkled inside the Holy of Holies.

were offered together with the afternoon continual offering: Both R. Eliezer and R. Aqiva appear to regard the people's ram of Leviticus 16:24 as fulfilling the requirement of the supplementary ram that is stated in Numbers 29:8, but they disagree as to the timing of the offering of the seven yearling lambs.

7:4 *white vestments*: Necessary for entering the Holy of Holies to retrieve the incense implements.

He entered to remove the ladle and fire-pan: See above, 5:1.

He sanctified his hands and feet,
and stripped,
and descended and immersed;
he ascended and dried himself off.
They brought to him [the] golden vestments,
and he got dressed
and sanctified his hands and feet,
and entered to offer the afternoon incense
and tend to the lamps;
and he sanctified his hands and feet
and stripped.
They brought to him his own clothing,
and he got dressed.
And they accompany him to his house.
And he would make a celebration for[118] his friends
when he exited the Holy [Precinct] in peace.[119]

7:5 The Priestly Vestments

5 The high priest serves with eight vestments,
and the common [priest] with four:
in (1) a tunic, and in (2) breeches, and in (3) a turban, and in (4) a girdle.
The high priest adds to this:
(5) a breastplate, (6) an *ephod*, (7) a robe, and (8) a frontlet.
[While he is wearing] these, the Urim and Thummim are consulted.
And they are consulted[120] only for a king,
for the Court,
or for someone whom the community needs.

---

[118] K adds "all of his."   [119] K, P: "for exiting in peace."
[120] K, P: "And they are not consulted for a commoner, but only for..."

And entered to offer...: See note to 2:5.

a celebration: Underscoring the festive nature of the Day of Atonement service in the Temple, also alluded to in *Ta'anit* 4:8; see introduction to *Yoma*.

7:5 *four* vestments; these are described in Exodus 28:40–42 as the vestments for Aaron's sons, who here represent the common or ordinary priests.

The high priest adds to this four more garments or implements, described in detail in Exodus 28:1–39 and Exodus 39:1–31.

Urim and Thummim: The breastplate inlaid with twelve precious stones (Exodus 28:15–30) served an oracular function (e.g. Numbers 27:21, 1 Samuel 23:9–12). Elsewhere in the Mishnah (*Sotah* 9:12) it is said that the Urim and Thummim ceased to function with the death of the First/Early Prophets. See also introduction and above 5:2.

Chapter Eight

8:1–5 *Observance of the Day of Atonement: Restrictions and Exceptions*

8 [On] the Day of Atonement
eating, drinking, washing, anointing, wearing shoes,[121] and sexual relations[122] are forbidden.
A king and a bride may wash their faces,
and a woman in childbirth may wear shoes,
the words of R. Eliezer,
but the Sages forbid it.
  2 One who eats[123] the volume of a large date,
itself and its pit,
and one who drinks a cheekful
is liable.
All foods join to [constitute] the volume of a date,
and all drinks join to [constitute] a cheekful.
One who eats and drinks—
these do not join.

---

[121] Lit. "a sandal." See annotation.   [122] Lit. "using the bed."
[123] K, P add "on the Day of Atonement."

8:1 The Mishnah here turns from the narrative that described the Temple ritual to provisions that govern the day's observance in the lives of ordinary people.

wearing shoes: The Talmud interprets this prohibition as an injunction against wearing specifically leather shoes, but the Mishnah possibly demands that the day be observed barefoot.

are forbidden: Scripture does not attest any of these prohibitions. The main prohibition associated with the Day of Atonement is an injunction against performing prohibited labor (Leviticus 16:29, 23:28; Numbers 29:7). These other prohibitions presumably stem from a strong reading of the prescription—repeated five times—to practice "self-denial" on the Day of Atonement (Leviticus 16:29, 31; 23:27, 32; Numbers 29:7). Isaiah 58:3–5 seems to associate the expression with fasting, and this connection is made explicit in other ancient sources.

A king: Kings are accorded numerous privileges in rabbinic law; see e.g. *Sanhedrin* 2:2.

8:2 See also *Me'ilah* 4:5.

liable: While the penalty is not specified here, Scripture (Leviticus 23:29) speaks of *karet* ("extirpation"), an unspecified divine punishment for not practicing "self-denial." Rabbinic law restricts this penalty to intentional violation; inadvertent violation could be cleansed with a purgation offering (see below).

All foods join: Regardless of whether one eats a date's worth of a single food, or minute amounts of various foods that add up to the volume of a date, the prohibited volume is cumulative. The same goes for drinking.

One who eats and drinks: Eating and drinking are regarded as two distinct prohibitions. Consequently, there is no violation if one eats less than the prohibited amount and then drinks enough such that the combined volume adds up to the volume of a date.

3 If one ate and drank in a single act of forgetfulness,
he is liable for only one purgation offering.
If one ate and performed [prohibited] labor,
he is liable for two purgation offerings.
If one ate foods that are not suitable for eating,
or drank drinks that are not suitable for drinking,
or drank brine or *muries*—
he is exempt.

4 One does not compel children to fast on the Day of Atonement,
but one trains[124] them
one year before or two years before [they come of age]
in order that they be habituated with the commandments.

5 If a pregnant woman smelled [food],
one may feed her
until she regains her energy.[125]
If someone is ill,

---

[124] Or "educates."   [125] Or "until she is full"; lit. "until her life returns." See annotations.

8:3 *a single act of forgetfulness*: By forgetting either that it was the Day of Atonement or that the acts of eating and drinking were prohibited. See *Shabbat* 12:4.

he is liable for only one purgation offering: With respect to unintentional violations the Mishnah considers eating and drinking as one act; both fall under the rubric of the biblical imperative to practice "self-denial." The purgation offering designated for unintentional violations of ritual law is described in Leviticus 4:27–35. See also *Shabbat* 7:1, 9:7; *Keritot* 3:2.

If one ate and performed [prohibited] labor in a single act of forgetfulness.

he is liable for two purgation offerings, as eating and performing prohibited labor constitute two separate acts; eating violates the imperative to practice "self-denial" and labor is prohibited in a separate injunction (Leviticus 16:29, 23:28; Numbers 29:7).

muries: A fish brine to which other ingredients may be added to make a dipping sauce. See *Terumot* 11:1.

he is exempt from any type of punishment. In the rabbinic mind, a violation of the prohibition against eating and drinking requires sufficient quality, volume, and intention.

8:4 *compel children*: The rule may be limited to fasting, or may refer to other prohibitions as well.

but one trains them by having the child abstain from eating for a number of hours during the fast (Talmud).

one…or two years before [they come of age]: Thirteen years and one day old for a boy, and twelve years and one day old for a girl. See *Niddah* 5:6, *Avot* 5:21.

in order that they be habituated with the commandments: A turn of phrase reminiscent of the training of the high priest in the week leading up to the service (1:3).

8:5 *If a pregnant woman smelled [food]* and, presumably, felt a very strong craving for that food or some other.

energy: Heb. *nefesh*. The Mishnah appears to be playing on the semantic range of this noun, which usually denotes life or soul, but here may mean "the gullet." The statement may therefore mean "until she is full."

one feeds him according to specialists,[126]
and if there are no specialists available[127]
he is fed according to his wishes
until he says "Enough!"

8:6–7 *Extenuating Circumstances That Allow for Violation of the Law*

6 If someone is overtaken[128] by ravenous hunger,
one may feed him even impure[129] foods
until his eyes brighten.
If someone is bitten by a mad dog,
one may not feed him
from the lobe of its liver,
but R. Matia[130] b. Heresh permits it.
R. Matia b. Heresh further said:
If someone has a pain in his throat,[131]
one administers[132] medicine into his mouth[133]
on the Sabbath
because there is uncertainty as to whether life [is endangered],
and any uncertainty as to whether life [is endangered]
overrides[134] the Sabbath.

7 If rubble fell on someone,
and there is uncertainty
as to whether he is there or not there,
[or] there is uncertainty

---

[126] Or "experts," here and immediately below.   [127] Lit. "there."
[128] Or "seized."   [129] Or "forbidden."
[130] K: "R. Matatyah b. Harash," here and immediately below.   [131] K, P: "mouth."
[132] Lit. "drops" or "pours."   [133] K, P lack "into his mouth."   [134] Lit. "pushes off."

---

according to specialists: While it is unclear what training, medical or otherwise, these "specialists" are meant to have, the Talmud and later commentators gloss the term as "physician."

8:6 *eyes brighten*: A biblical idiom found, appropriately enough, after Jonathan has eaten forbidden food. See 1 Samuel 14:27.

lobe of its liver: A widespread remedy known from other ancient sources.

R. Matia b. Heresh permits it: Dogs are forbidden for consumption under Jewish dietary laws, but according to Matia b. Heresh, those laws may be suspended when there is possible danger to life.

any uncertainty as to whether life [is endangered] overrides the Sabbath: Rabbinic Sabbath law generally prohibits any medicinal or therapeutic activity: see *Shabbat* 14:3–4, 22:6. Here is perhaps the earliest surviving formulation of the principle that the Sabbath is suspended when there is possible danger to life. Earlier Jewish sources indicate that some preferred to die rather than violate the Sabbath, even under extenuating circumstances (see e.g. 1 Maccabees 2:29–37).

8:7 *If rubble fell on someone* on the Sabbath or Day of Atonement.

as to whether he is alive or dead,
[or] there is uncertainty
as to whether he is a gentile or Israelite,
one clears the pile of stones for him.[135]
If he they found him alive,
they [continue to] clear for him.
And if [he was] dead,
they leave him.

8:8–9 *Repentance and Atonement*

8 A purgation offering and an offering for definite guilt
effect atonement.
One's death and the Day of Atonement
effect atonement
with repentance.
Repentance effects atonement
for minor transgressions
of positive and negative commandments.

[135] **K, P:** "they watch over him," here and immediately below. See annotation.

---

one clears the pile of stones for him: Sabbath law ordinarily prohibits digging, but even the most remote possibility of saving an endangered life allows for overriding the prohibition. Other ancient Jewish sources place restrictions on which implements (if any) might be used to rescue someone who had fallen. But see the variant in **K, P**, and also *Rosh Hashanah* 4:8.

they leave him: Sabbath law does permit a limited number of activities for tending to a corpse and preparing it for burial (see *Shabbat* 23:5), but activities that would require manual labor (e.g. digging a grave, bringing a coffin) are forbidden (*Shabbat* 23:4).

8:8 *A purgation offering* is brought in the event of an unintentional transgression of a sin for which intentional violation would be punishable by *karet*; see *Keritot* 1:1–2 for those thirty-six sins that require a purgation offering.

an offering for definite guilt is brought in the event of transgressing five specific sins; see *Zevahim* 5:5.

effect atonement without any need for supplemental offerings or activities.

One's death …: See 2 Maccabees 12:45. Cf. the Christian view in Romans 6:7, where death is considered as atoning in and of itself.

repentance: Supplemented with repentance, one's death and/or the Day of Atonement also effect atonement. While axiomatic in later Judaism, the notion of repentance as a part of the process of the absolution of sin is not present in the Hebrew Bible and is systematized only in rabbinic literature.

Repentance alone suffices to effect *atonement for minor transgressions of positive* commandments, e.g. failure to don *tefillin*. The Talmud limits the scope of *negative commandments* for which repentance alone suffices to those sins which can be rectified through a positive commandment; the classic example is that of theft (a negative commandment) which can be remedied through the return of the stolen object (a positive commandment; see Leviticus 5:23).

For grave transgressions
[repentance] suspends [punishment]
until the Day of Atonement comes
and effects atonement.
   9 If one says
"I will sin and then I will repent,
I will sin and then I will repent,"
he is not furnished with [the possibility of] repentance.
[If one says:] "I will sin and the Day of Atonement [will] effect atonement"—
the Day of Atonement does not effect atonement.
Transgressions between man and God—[136]
the Day of Atonement effects atonement.
Transgressions between man and his fellow—
the Day of Atonement does not effect atonement
until he appeases his fellow.

Closing Homily

This [teaching] was expounded by R. Eleazar b. Azariah:
From all of your sins you shall become pure before the Lord.
Transgressions between a person and God—
the Day of Atonement effects atonement.
Transgressions between one person and another—
the Day of Atonement does not effect atonement
until he appeases his fellow.
R. Aqiva said:
Happy are you, O Israel!
Before whom are you purified?
Who purifies you?
Your father in the heavens,
as it is written:

[136] Lit. "the Place," here and below.

grave transgressions, e.g. violations of negative commandments (see previous note) and sins punishable by execution or *karet*.

8:9 *he is not furnished with [the possibility of] repentance*: Repentance requires sincere remorse after the sin has been committed. Remorse cannot be cynically planned. See also *Avot* 5:18.

Transgressions between a person and God: The rabbis distinguish between laws governing the relationship of humans and God (e.g. idolatry, Sabbath) and laws governing interpersonal relations (e.g. theft, torts).

This [teaching] was expounded: i.e. the above teaching was given scriptural support.

From all of your sins: Leviticus 16:30. The previous distinction between transgressions against God and those against other humans suggests a different parsing of this verse: "from all your sins against the Lord you shall become pure."

Happy are you, O Israel! See Deuteronomy 33:29.

I will sprinkle clean water upon you, and you shall be pure.
And it says:
The hope of Israel is the Lord.
Just as the immersion pool purifies the impure,
so too the Holy One blessed is He purifies Israel.

I will sprinkle…: Ezekiel 36:25.

The hope…: Jeremiah 17:13.

Just as the immersion pool purifies the impure: A nice example of midrashic wordplay. Generally speaking, *miqveh* in biblical Hebrew denotes "hope." In a few instances, however, *miqveh* refers to a body of water (Genesis 1:10, Exodus 7:19, Leviticus 11:36), and so in rabbinic Hebrew *miqveh* comes to refer exclusively to a pool for ritual immersion. The exegetical move here reads the rabbinic meaning of *miqveh* into the biblical verse, thus making God into Israel's "ritual bath."

purifies Israel: This homily is a stark departure from the tannaitic position that views purification and atonement as pertaining to two separate different areas of ritual law, namely impurity and sin (cf. Mark 1:4). But it is also a biblically grounded teaching, in that Leviticus 16:30 also employs the language of purification from sin.

Tractate Sukkah

Jeffrey L. Rubenstein

Introduction

Overview

Tractate *Sukkah* is devoted to the commandments and rituals of the Festival of Sukkot ("Booths"). One of the three pilgrimage festivals, this was celebrated for seven days from the fifteenth to the twenty-first of the Hebrew month of Tishre (Leviticus 23:33–36; Numbers 29:12). In rabbinic times the main festival rituals were the festal booth (*sukkah*; Leviticus 23:42–43) and the *lulav*, a bouquet comprised of four species (Leviticus 23:40). The tractate also describes many other rituals that were performed at the Jerusalem Temple during the Second Temple period but no longer practiced after the destruction in 70 CE.

Organization and Structure of the Tractate

The tractate consists of five chapters. Chapter 1 deals with the construction of the festal booth. Some attention is given to the dimensions and the walls, but the primary interest of the tractate is the roofing which provides the shade, and which the rabbis considered to be the essential characteristic of the festal booth. Chapter 2 continues with some rules governing the structure and roofing of the festal booth, but primarily attends to how the commandment of dwelling in the festal booth is fulfilled. The festal booth becomes one's "regular dwelling" throughout the festival week (2:9), and one must eat all meals and sleep there, although various circumstances exempt one from the obligation (2:5, 8–9). Chapter 3 is devoted to the commandment of the four species of the *lulav*, providing rules for distinguishing fit from unfit palm fronds, willows, myrtles, and citrons (*etrogim*), the four species the rabbis understood to fulfill the prescription of Leviticus 23:42. There are also directions as to how the ritual should be performed, namely when the *lulav* is to be shaken during the liturgy. Chapters 4 and 5 describe the rituals of the Festival of Sukkot as practiced in Temple times, and contain a number of "ritual narratives" akin to those of tractates *Yoma*, *Pesahim*, and *Tamid*. Besides the *lulav* (4:4), we have descriptions of: (1) the "willow ritual" (4:5–7), a procession with willows from a nearby town up to Jerusalem and ultimately to the altar, which was circumambulated and then adorned with the willows; (2) the water libation (4:9–10), a procession accompanied by trumpet blasts from the Siloam pool, from which water was drawn, to the altar, where it was poured together with the daily wine libation; (3) the "Rejoicing at the Place of Water Drawing" (5:1–4), an all-night festival celebrated in the Temple courtyards involving singing, dancing, and music, which culminated at dawn with the libation procession. The tractate concludes with an appendix about various Temple practices, not all of which are connected to the Festival of Sukkot (5:5–8).

Relationship to Scripture

Apart from the name "Festival of Sukkot," the Hebrew Bible refers to the fall pilgrimage festival as "the Festival of the Lord" (Leviticus 23:39, Judges 21:19), or simply as "the Festival," i.e. the festival *par excellence* (1 Kings 8:2, 12:32; Ezekiel 45:25), an indication that throughout biblical and Second Temple times the Festival of Sukkot was the most important festival of the Israelite year. Despite the Bible's repeated injunction to appear in the Temple thrice annually (Exodus 23:14–17; Deuteronomy 16:16), it seems that in practice many Israelites made the journey but once, only after the autumnal harvest closed the agricultural year, when all remaining crops, including fruits, olives, and grapes were gathered in before the onset of winter and the rainy season. Another biblical name for this festival is accordingly "the Festival of Ingathering" (Exodus 23:16, 34:22; cf. Deuteronomy 16:13).

The name "Festival of Sukkot" derives from the booths (*sukkot*) which provided shade and shelter for agricultural workers throughout the hot summer months (Isaiah 1:8. 4:6; Job 27:18), and which may also have served as the site of popular harvest festivals immediately after the conclusion of the harvest. However, as with Passover, the Hebrew Bible adds to the agricultural dimension a historical link between the Festival of Sukkot and the exodus from Egypt. Leviticus 23:42–43 commands the Israelites to dwell in *sukkot* for seven days "in order that future generations may know that I made the Israelite people live in booths when I brought them out of the land of Egypt." Dwelling in the ritual booth thus commemorates or reenacts the booths in which the Israelites dwelled during their sojourn in the desert.

The *lulav* ritual derives from Leviticus 23:40, "On the first day you shall take the fruit of *hadar* trees, branches of palm trees, boughs of leafy trees, and willows of the brook, and you shall rejoice before the Lord your God seven days." The rabbis interpreted the directive to "take" as holding and shaking the four species mentioned above. This interpretation probably antedates the rabbis, but it is by no means the only possible understanding of the verse, and other groups in the Second Temple period interpreted it differently (cf. Nehemiah 8:14–18).

We know from the title "*the* festival" and scattered hints in the Prophets and Writings that the Temple celebrations of the Festival of Sukkot were the most festive and joyous of the entire year, and yet also among the most sober. Tremendous joy and gratitude for the bounty of the harvest combined with anxiety over the winter rains, which would determine whether the people prospered or suffered during the next year. Thus the eschatological vision of Zechariah threatens that nations which fail to make a pilgrimage to the Temple to observe the Festival of Sukkot will not receive rain (Zechariah 14:16–17). The diverse Temple rituals seem primarily to have been directed toward tapping into the Temple's mythic powers of fertility to attain sufficient rainfall in the coming months. But what were those rituals? Here the Bible is almost completely silent, and we know of them primarily from our tractate, as described above (some information can also be gleaned from sources in the Apocrypha, Pseudepigrapha, and Dead Sea Scrolls). This is a fascinating case of the rabbis preserving detailed information about earlier practices that otherwise would have been unknown, and thereby shedding much light on the Bible itself.

The tractate has very little to say about the concluding "Eighth Day Assembly" mentioned in Leviticus 23:36 and Numbers 29:38.

Main Ideas

In rabbinic midrashim (though not in our tractate), the rabbis understand the festal booth as a symbol of the mythical "clouds of glory" that protected the Israelites during their desert sojourn, and more generally the sheltering "shade of God" associated with the divine presence (Psalms 91:1–4, 121:5–7). Tractate *Sukkah* therefore takes great pains to regulate the roofing so as to ensure that it casts shade and that the occupant experiences its shade by dwelling in the booth throughout the festival week, in particular by eating all meals and sleeping there. Few laws deal with the walls or structure of the booth itself, as the rabbis required the roofing (and not the booth's walls, or even nearby trees) to produce the shade by which the commandment was fulfilled.

The *lulav* was originally one of the diverse rituals performed in the Temple celebrations, as indicated by the directive to "rejoice before the Lord" in Leviticus 23:40. It was just about the only Temple-based ritual distinctive to the festival that the rabbis preserved in post-Temple times, presumably because it is commanded explicitly in the Torah. Like the water libation and the other Temple rituals, the primary function of the *lulav*—to the extent we can speak of rituals in this way—was to petition God for rain, or even ritually to induce the rain to fall. The ritual consisted of reciting a blessing and shaking the *lulav*, and also holding and shaking the *lulav* during the recitation of certain verses of the *Hallel* liturgy of the morning service (Psalms 113–118), a practice that probably originated in the Temple liturgy.

Tractate Sukkah

Chapter One

1:1 *Minimum and Maximum Dimensions of the Sukkah*

1 A *sukkah* higher than twenty cubits is not valid.
R. Judah deems it valid.
And one not ten handbreadths high,
or one lacking three walls,
or one with more sun than shade
is not valid.
An old *sukkah*:
the House of Shammai deem it invalid,
and the House of Hillel deem it valid.
What is [considered an] old *sukkah*?
Any that was made thirty days prior to the Festival [of Sukkot].
But if it was made for the sake of the Festival,
even from the beginning of the year—
it is valid.

1:2–4 *The Sukkah's Roof and Walls*

2 One who makes his *sukkah* under a tree—
it is as if he made it inside the house.
A *sukkah* on top of a *sukkah*—

1:1 *more sun than shade*: Provided by the *sukkah* roofing.

old sukkah: *Sukkot* were used for various agricultural purposes, especially to provide shade for workers in the fields; see *Ma'aserot* 3:7. The House of Shammai require the *sukkah* for the festival to be made specifically for that purpose.

thirty days prior to the Festival: Or more. But if made within thirty days of the festival, we assume it was specifically made for the sake of the festival, as in the final clause.

beginning of the year: Even if built anytime in the previous year.

1:2 This and the subsequent mishnayot deal primarily with the proper construction of the *sukkah* roofing, which the Sages considered to be the essence of the *sukkah*. The walls are subject to a few rules too, though the limitations are not as extensive as those of the roofing.

inside the house: And it is not valid, as the *sukkah* roofing does not produce shade. Branches of the tree are not a permitted source of shade; cf. 1:4.

the upper one is valid and the lower one is not valid.
R. Judah says:
If there are no occupants in the upper one,
the lower one is valid.

3 If one spread a sheet over [the *sukkah* roofing] because of the sun,
or below it because of falling [leaves],
or if he spread it upon a canopy bed—
it is not valid.
But one may spread it upon the posts of the bed.

4 If he trained a grapevine or a gourd[-vine] or ivy over [the *sukkah*]
and placed [valid] *sukkah* roofing upon them—
it is not valid.
But if the [quantity of valid] *sukkah* roofing was greater than they,
or if he severed them—
it is valid.
This is the general rule:
Anything susceptible to impurity,
or that does not grow from the earth—
one may not use it for *sukkah* roofing.
And anything that is not susceptible to impurity
and that grows from the earth—
one may use it for *sukkah* roofing.[1]

1:5–8 The Use of Bundles, Boards, and Beams for the Sukkah Roofing

5 Bundles of straw and bundles of twigs and bundles of shoots—
one does not use them for *sukkah* roofing.

[1] **K, P** lack the final line ("And anything…*sukkah* roofing").

lower one is not valid: Because the upper *sukkah* interposes between the lower *sukkah* and the sky.

1:3 *over…or below*: In both cases the sheet prevents the occupant from experiencing the shade of the *sukkah* roofing.

canopy bed: With four bedposts, thus interposing between the sleeper and the *sukkah* roofing so that the occupant does not experience the shade.

posts of the bed: A bed with two posts such that the sheet forms a tent-like covering, which is not considered an interposition.

1:4 *trained*: Sukkah roofing may not be live vegetation, that is, may not be "attached" to the earth (Talmud).

This is the general rule: This is the reading of most printings. The manuscripts formulate the principle slightly differently.

susceptible to impurity: Such as utensils (though made of wood) and clothing (though made of flax).

does not grow from the earth: Animal or mineral material.

1:5 Mishnayot 1:5–8 offer exceptions to the principle offered in 1:4 governing valid *sukkah* roofing. Although straw and twigs are permitted, bundles of straw and twigs are forbidden, as they make the sukkah look like

And all of them, if one untied them, are valid.
And all of them are valid for the walls.

6 One may use boards for *sukkah* roofing—
the words of R. Judah.
But R. Meir forbids [it].
If one placed upon [the *sukkah*] a board four handbreadths wide—
[the *sukkah*] is valid,
provided that he does not sleep under [the board].

7 A [timber] ceiling that had no plastering—
R. Judah says:
the House of Shammai say:
One must loosen [the beams]
and remove one from between each two.
But the House of Hillel say:
One must either loosen [the beams]
or remove one from between each two.[2]
R. Meir says:
One removes one from between each two and need not loosen.

[2] K, P: "R. Judah says in the name of the House of Hillel: One must either loosen [the beams] or remove one from between each two. The House of Shammai says: One loosens [the beams] and removes one from between each two."

a shed for storing or drying out such materials, rather than a habitation. Some types of wooden boards and beams likewise should be permitted according to a strict application of the principle, but they create the type of roof characteristic of a house, not the shade required of a *sukkah*.

all of them: This rule probably refers to the items prohibited in 1:3–4 too.

valid for the walls: The essence of the *sukkah* is the roofing, not the walls, hence the laws governing the production of shade (as required in 1:1) pertain only to the roofing.

1:6 *boards*: Even though flat boards resemble the roof of a house, R. Judah permits their use for *sukkah* roofing. The Talmud limits R. Judah's ruling to boards less than three handbreadths in width. This limitation may be implied by the end of this mishnah, assuming it reflects the view of R. Judah too.

R. Meir forbids [it]: Even though flat wood boards should be permitted according to the principle provided in 1:4, they make a solid roof and do not create the shade characteristic of a *sukkah*.

1:7 *must loosen [the beams] and remove…loosen [the beams] or remove*: R. Judah in 1:6 rules that one may use boards for *sukkah* roofing. Nevertheless, the *sukkah* roofing must not be the same as a normal roof, as the roof of a house does not really create an experience of shade, that is, the sense of comparative darkness and shelter from direct sunlight. He claims that, according to the House of Hillel, this house roof may be converted to *sukkah* roofing either by loosening the beams, which displaces them slightly, or by removing every other beam and placing acceptable roofing in its place, such that more than half of the area contains fit roofing. The House of Shammai require both acts.

R. Meir says…need not loosen: Because in 1:6 R. Meir prohibits the use of boards, loosening will make no difference, and the only way to render the roof fit for a *sukkah* is to remove every other board and replace it with acceptable *sukkah* roofing.

8 One who uses spits or bed-boards for the roof of his *sukkah*,
if there is space between them equal to their width—
it is valid.
One who hollows out a stack to make himself a *sukkah*—
it is no *sukkah*.

1:9–11 Walls That Do Not Touch the Ground or the Roof

9 If one lets down walls from the top [of the *sukkah*]:
if [the walls] are three handbreadths above the ground—
it is not valid.
From the bottom upward:
if they are ten handbreadths higher than the ground—
it is valid.
R. Yose says:
Just as from the bottom upward ten handbreadths [is valid],
so from the top downward ten handbreadths [is valid].
If one placed the *sukkah* roofing three handbreadths distant from the walls—
it is not valid.

10 A house [with a roof] that caved in and one placed *sukkah* roofing upon it,
if there are four cubits between the wall and the *sukkah* roofing—

1:8 *spits…bed-boards*: These are vessels susceptible to impurity that 1:4 rules are not valid for *sukkah* roofing. The space between them must be covered with valid *sukkah* roofing so that there is a majority of fit *sukkah* roofing, as per 1:1.

stack: Of grain or straw.

it is no sukkah: Since he did not place the *sukkah* roofing there for the purpose of the ritual; it was already part of the stack beforehand. See 1:1 above.

1:9 *three handbreadths above the ground*: The *sukkah* consists of corner posts with partitions or walls that do not quite reach the ground. If these are three handbreadths or more from the ground, they do not count as walls; see 1:1.

From the bottom upward…ten handbreadths: This mishnah adds to 1:1 that, even if the *sukkah* roofing rests on a frame of corner posts and the partitions do not reach the *sukkah* roofing, the partitions count as valid walls.

R. Yose…ten handbreadths: For R. Yose the walls need not be near the ground, provided they are ten handbreadths in length.

three handbreadths distant from the walls: Along the entire width or length of the *sukkah*. A small interior space invalidates the *sukkah*, as opposed to the standard for unfit *sukkah* roofing provided in the next mishnah.

1:10 *house*: Or room.

four cubits between the wall and the sukkah roofing: Here the walls of the house may count as the walls of the *sukkah* despite the separation of up to four cubits of the plaster from the original roof of the house. This measure differs from the maximum separation of empty space between the *sukkah* roofing and the walls, which 1:9 sets at three handbreadths. One is not permitted to eat or sleep under the roofing that separates the walls from the *sukkah* roofing.

it is not valid.
Similarly, a courtyard surrounded by a peristyle.
A large *sukkah* that was surrounded with material
that may not be used for *sukkah* roofing,
if there are four cubits under [the invalid material]—
it is not valid.

11 If one made his *sukkah* in the shape of a cone,
or if one leaned it against a wall,
R. Eliezer deems it invalid because it has no roof.
But the Sages deem it valid.
A large reed mat—
if one made it for lying upon,
it is susceptible to impurity
and may not be used for *sukkah* roofing;
for *sukkah* roofing,
then it may be used for *sukkah* roofing
and is not susceptible to impurity.
R. Eliezer says:
whether large or small—
if one made it for lying upon,
it is susceptible to impurity
and may not be used for *sukkah* roofing;
for *sukkah* roofing,
then it may be used for *sukkah* roofing
and is not susceptible to impurity.

peristyle: The *sukkah* roofing is placed across the open space surrounded by the columns of the peristyle. In this case the columns serve as walls, but due to the thickness of the columns, the *sukkah* roofing will be at some distance from the outside of the columns, and that distance is limited to four cubits.

large sukkah: A *sukkah* larger than that of the minimum size, such that there is a minimum area of valid *sukkah* roofing in the center of its roof, and then unfit material surrounding it. For the minimum size, see 2:7.

four cubits: Here too the area in the middle constitutes a valid *sukkah*, and the unfit material does not render the *sukkah* invalid or prevent the walls from counting for the *sukkah*.

1:11 *cone*: In a triangular shape, with the walls meeting at the top.

leaned it against a wall: Leaned the wall of the *sukkah* against a house wall like a lean-to.

reed mat: See *Kelim* 17:17, 20:7. If the mat is considered a utensil, as per 1:4 above, then it is susceptible to impurity and may not be used for *sukkah* roofing.

Chapter Two

2:1 *Sleeping in the Sukkah*

2 One who sleeps under a bed in the *sukkah* has not fulfilled his obligation.
R. Judah says:
It was our custom to sleep under beds in the presence of the elders,
and they said nothing to us.[3]
R. Simon said:
It once happened that Tavi the slave of Rabban Gamaliel
was sleeping under the bed,
and Rabban Gamaliel said to the elders:
Have you seen my slave Tavi,
who is a learned disciple,
and knows that slaves are exempt from [the commandment] of the *sukkah*;
therefore he sleeps under the bed.
In this way we learn
that one who sleeps under the bed has not fulfilled his obligation.

2:2–4 *Sukkot That Are Propped Up or Rest on Other Objects*

2 One who leans his *sukkah* against the legs of the bed—
it is valid.
R. Judah says:
If it cannot stand by itself—
it is not valid.
A *sukkah* that is dilapidated and [yet][4] has more shade than sun—

---

[3] K, P lack "and they said nothing to us."
[4] This line could be translated "A *sukkah* that is dilapidated or one with more shade than sun—it is valid," referring to two different cases, though if so the second case appears to repeat the ruling in 1:1. P reads "A dilapidated *sukkah* that has more shade than sun—it is valid."

2:1 The second chapter deals with the commandment of dwelling in the *sukkah*, which is expressed primarily by sleeping and eating therein (2:1, 5–9). Mishnayot 2:2–4 and 2:7 continue the topic of the previous chapter with additional rules for constructing the *sukkah* itself and ensuring its stability.

under a bed: The bed interposes between the sleeper and the *sukkah* roofing.

Tavi: See too *Berakhot* 2:7, *Pesahim* 7:2.

2:2 *cannot stand by itself*: In the opinion of R. Judah, this structure does not have the status of a *sukkah*, as removal of the bed entails its collapse.

dilapidated: Opinions in the Talmud disagree whether this means that the *sukkah* roofing is thin or that it is in disarray. The contrast with the next line perhaps suggests the former.

more shade than sun: Provided by the *sukkah* roofing, as per 1:1.

it is valid.
If [the *sukkah* roofing] is thick like that of a house,
even though the stars cannot be seen from within it,
it is valid.

3 One who makes his *sukkah* on top of a wagon or on top of a boat—
it is valid,
and one may go up into it on the Festival day.
If on top of a tree or upon a camel—
it is valid,
but one may not go up into it on the Festival day.
If two [*walls*] were in a tree,
and one was manmade [and on the ground],
or if two were manmade
and one was in a tree—
it is valid,
but one may not go up into it on the Festival day.
If three were manmade
and one was in a tree—
it is valid,
and one may go up into it on the Festival day.
This is the general rule:
Any [*sukkah*] that can stand on its own if the tree is removed—
it is valid
and[5] one may go up into it on the Festival day.

[5] **K**, **P** lack "it is valid and."

thick: Even though thick *sukkah* roofing resembles the roof of a house and does not really cast shade.

stars: The Yerushalmi understands "stars" to refer to the sun.

2:3 *wagon…boat…valid*: Even though the *sukkah* rests on a surface that moves and is not completely stable.

one may go up into it: One may go into this *sukkah* on the Festival day, in contrast to the tree, below.

tree…camel…not go up into it: Climbing trees and riding animals are forbidden on Sabbaths and Festivals. This *sukkah* may be used on the intermediate days of Sukkot.

If two [walls] were in a tree…one was in a tree: If one or two of three walls or of three beams that support the *sukkah* roofing rest on trees. Some commentaries, however, understand this mishnah to deal with supports for the floor of the *sukkah*.

may not go up into it: Because a tree provides support for one of the walls or beams necessary for the *sukkah* to stand, going into the *sukkah* is tantamount to making use of the tree, which, like climbing, is forbidden on Sabbaths and Festival days.

go up into it: Enter it. The mishnah uses "go up" for "enter," as *sukkot* were typically made on the roofs of houses.

4 One who makes his *sukkah* between the trees,
and the trees are its[6] walls—
it is valid.

2:4 cont.–5 *Men Exempt from the Commandment of Dwelling in the Sukkah, and Food Exempt from Being Eaten in the Sukkah*

Emissaries sent to perform a commandment
are exempt from [the commandment of] the *sukkah*.
The sick and their attendants are exempt from [the commandment of] the *sukkah*.
One eats and drinks occasional [snacks] outside of the *sukkah*.
  5 It once happened
that they brought a cooked dish to R. Yohanan b. Zakkai to taste,
and two dates and a pail of water to Rabban Gamaliel.
They said:
Take them up to the *sukkah*.
And when they gave R. Zadok a quantity of food less than an egg's bulk,
he took it in a napkin and ate it outside the *sukkah*,
and did not say the blessing after [eating] it.

2:6 *The Number of Meals That Must Be Eaten in the Sukkah*

  6 R. Eliezer says:
A person is obligated to eat fourteen meals in the *sukkah*,
one [each] day and one [each] night.
But the Sages say:
There is no prescribed number for this matter,

[6] **K, P** lack "its."

2:4 *trees are its walls*: In contrast to the previous mishnah, here the *sukkah* roofing does not rest on walls or beams in trees, but on posts stuck in the ground or the like, and trees serve as walls. The rules for the walls are much more lenient than the rules for the *sukkah* roofing, as noted in 1:4.

Emissaries: They are occupied with the performance of another commandment and may not have access to a *sukkah* on their travels. This is one example of a general principle formulated by the Talmud: "one engaged with a commandment is exempt from the [other] commandments."

sick and their attendants: They may suffer discomfort if required to eat and sleep in the *sukkah*.

occasional [snacks]: But not regular meals.

2:5 *take them up to the sukkah*: Apparently disagreeing with the rule of the previous clause, or possibly just to adopt a strict practice for themselves.

napkin: Because it may have been wet, and the liquid in turn may have rendered his hands impure: see Leviticus 11:34; *Makhshirin* 6:4.

blessing: It was less than the minimum quantity of food that requires a blessing after eating; cf. *Berakhot* 7:2.

except for the night[7] of the first Festival day alone.
R. Eliezer also said:
Whoever did not eat [in the *sukkah*] on the night[8] of the first Festival day
should compensate on the night[9] of the last Festival day.
But the Sages say:
There can be no compensation for this matter.
About this it is said:
A twisted thing cannot be made straight, a lack that cannot be made good.

2:7 The Minimum Size of a Sukkah

7 If one's head and the greater part of his body were in the *sukkah*
and his table was within the house—
the House of Shammai deem it invalid
but the House of Hillel deem it valid.
The House of Hillel said to the House of Shammai:
Did it not once happen[10]
that the elders of the House of Shammai and the elders of the House of Hillel
went to visit Yohanan, son of the Horonite,
and found him sitting[11] with his head and the greater part of his body in the *sukkah*,
and his table within the house,
and they did not say anything to him?
The House of Shammai said to them:
[You bring] proof from that case?
In fact they said to him:
If such has been your custom,
you have never fulfilled the commandment of the *sukkah* in [all] your days.

---

[7] Lit. "nights."   [8] Lit. "nights."   [9] Lit. "nights."
[10] **K, P**: "It once happened that."   [11] **K, P** lack "sitting."

2:6 *the night of the first Festival day alone*: And not the intermediate days of the festival. On these days if one wishes to fast or to suffice with snacks and not to eat a proper meal, one need not eat in the *sukkah*. If one wishes to eat a meal, he must do so in the *sukkah*, but there is no specific commandment to eat a meal in the *sukkah* on these days.

compensate on the night of the last Festival day: On the "Eighth Day Assembly," when eating in the *sukkah* is not required, as it is technically an independent festival. The Talmud, however, understands this to mean that he eat additional food at his Eighth Day Assembly meal, but not eat it in the *sukkah*. See too *Hagigah* 1:6.

A twisted thing…: Ecclesiastes 1:15.

2:7 *House of Shammai deem it invalid*: They forbid the use of such a small *sukkah*, and require that the table also fit inside. The concern is that the occupant inadvertently will shift towards the table so that he is no longer eating in the *sukkah*. In fact this mishnah does not read smoothly and seems to have been altered from its original formulation. It is possible that the mishnah deals with the position of the occupant and not the size of the *sukkah*. If a *sukkah* (of any size) is built adjacent to the house, may one "recline" (i.e. eat in Roman style while reclining on a couch), such that the greater part of his body is in the *sukkah* but the table is in the house? Or will he inadvertently come to eat inside the house?

they said: The elders of the House of Shammai said to Yohanan, son of the Horonite.

2.8–9 *Other Grounds for Exemption from the Commandment*

8 Women, slaves, and children are exempt from the [commandment] of the *sukkah*.
Any child who no longer needs his mother
is obligated [to fulfill] the [commandment] of the *sukkah*.
It once happened
that the daughter-in-law of Shammai the elder gave birth,
and he removed some of the roof plaster
and placed *sukkah* roofing above the bed for the child.

9 All seven days [of the Festival] one makes his *sukkah* his regular [dwelling]
and his house his occasional [dwelling].
If rain fell,
from when is he permitted to empty out [the *sukkah*]?
From when the dish spoils.
They made a parable:
to what is this matter similar?
To a slave who comes to mix a cup [of wine] for his master,[12]
and he poured out the flagon on his head.

Chapter Three

3:1–8 *The Four Species of the Lulav*

3 A palm frond that was stolen or is dried out is not valid.
[If it was] from an *asherah* or from a proscribed city, it is not valid.

---

[12] **K, P:** "to mix for his owner."

2:8 *women…are exempt*. The *sukkah* is a time-bound positive commandment, from which women are generally exempt. See *Qiddushin* 1:7.

for the child: He adopted a stricter standard than that set forth in the previous clause.

2:9 *regular [dwelling]*: He treats the *sukkah* as if it were his house.

to empty out: To remove the food and utensils so that they not spoil, and to go into the house. Cf. 4:8.

poured out the flagon: By making it rain God "rejects" the proffered service of sitting in a *sukkah*.

3:1 This chapter is devoted to the commandment of the *lulav*, the four species of Leviticus 23:40. The Mishnah describes the species and lists imperfections that render each invalid for ritual use.

palm frond: Heb. *lulav*. This term refers both to the palm frond individually and as *pars pro toto* for the palm frond, willows, and myrtles taken together, and sometimes for all four species. The rabbis understand *branches of palm trees* of Leviticus 23:40 to refer to the palm frond, the immature palm branch.

asherah: A tree worshipped by idolators. See Deuteronomy 12:3, *Avodah Zarah* 3:5.

proscribed city: A city that has worshipped idols and must be destroyed. Deuteronomy 13:12–18; *Sanhedrin* 10:4.

If its tip was severed or its leaves were split, it is not valid.
But if its leaves were spread, it is valid.
R. Judah says:
He must bind it at the top.
The stone palms of the Iron Mountain are valid.
A palm frond of at least three handbreadths' length,
sufficient to shake,
is valid.

2 A myrtle that was stolen or is dried out is not valid.
[If it was] from an *asherah* or from the proscribed city, it is not valid.
If its tip was severed or its leaves were split,
or if its berries outnumbered its leaves,
it is not valid.
But if he reduced the [berries],
it is valid.
One may not reduce on the Festival day.

3 A willow that was stolen or is dried out is not valid.
[If it was] from an *asherah* or from a proscribed city, it is not valid.
If its tip was severed or its leaves were split,
[or it was a] mountain willow,
it is not valid.
If it was withered, or it had lost some of its leaves, or it was from a field, it is valid.

4 R. Ishmael says:
Three myrtles, two willows, one palm frond, and one citron
[are required for the *lulav*],
even if two [myrtles] are severed and one is not severed.
R. Tarfon says:
Even if all three are severed.
R. Aqiva says:
Just as one palm frond and one citron [are required],
so one myrtle and one willow.

5 A citron that was stolen or is dried out is not valid.
[If it is] from an *asherah* or from a proscribed city, it is not valid.

---

stone palms of the Iron Mountain: The identity of the "Iron Mountain" is uncertain.

3:2 *myrtle*: The "boughs of leafy trees" of Leviticus 23:40.

3:3 *mountain willow*: Evidently a different species. A parallel text explains that the leaves of the mountain willow resemble a saw, i.e. have saw-like teeth.

field: Although Leviticus 23:40 states "willows of the brook," the willows may grow elsewhere.

3:4 *two [myrtles] are severed and one is not severed*: Their tips are severed. See 3:3.

3:5 Rabbinic tradition interpreted *the product of hadar trees* (Leviticus 23:40), which can also be translated "the fruit of goodly trees," as the citron. As opposed to the other three species, the citron is a fruit, hence subject to the agricultural laws that confer various legal statuses. This mishnah includes rulings on whether a citron of these statuses may be used in the ritual.

If it is *orlah*, it is not valid.
If it is impure *terumah*, it is not valid.
If it is pure *terumah*, he may not take it [for the commandment],
but if he took it, it is valid.
If it is *demai*:
the House of Shammai deem it invalid,
and the House of Hillel deem it valid.
If it is of second tithe in Jerusalem,
he may not take it [for the commandment],
but if he took it, it is valid.

6 If the greater part was afflicted with fungus,
if its nipple was removed,
if it was peeled, slit, or perforated and missing any of its substance,
it is not valid.
If the lesser part of it was afflicted by a fungus,
if its stalk was removed,
if it was perforated but not missing any of its substance,
it is valid.
A black citron is not valid.
One green like a leek:
R. Meir deems it valid
and R. Judah deems it invalid.

7 The minimum size of a citron—
R. Meir says:
Like a walnut.
R. Judah says:
Like an egg.
And the maximum—
such that he can hold two in one hand[13]—
the words of R. Judah.
R. Yose says:
Even one in his two hands.

[13] **P, K**: "Both of them," i.e. the *lulav* and citron.

orlah: One may neither eat nor benefit from fruit of the first three years of a tree's production; Leviticus 19:23–25. See *Orlah*, introduction.

impure terumah: *Terumah* is roduce which must be given to priests, and which must be burned if it becomes impure. An impure *terumah* citron therefore cannot be used for the ritual.

pure terumah: The Talmud explains that the citron may be rendered impure in the course of performing the ritual.

demai: Produce of Jews who are suspect of not tithing. See the introduction to *Demai*.

second tithe in Jerusalem: Produce of second tithe must be eaten in Jerusalem. Outside of Jerusalem, where the citron cannot be eaten, it may not be used in the ritual.

He may not take it: Like the pure *terumah*, the concern is that it be rendered impure.

3:6 *nipple*: The small protuberance at the top.

black: Lit. "Ethiopian."

3:7 *two in one hand*: Two citrons.

8 One may only bind the *lulav* with something of its own substance—
the words of R. Judah.
R. Meir says:
Even with a cord.
R. Meir said:
It once happened
that the men of Jerusalem bound their *lulav* with golden bands.
They said to him:
Underneath they bound it with something of its own substance.[14]

3:9–11   *The Lulav and the Hallel*

9 And where did they shake [the *lulav*]?
At *Praise the Lord, for He is good*
at the beginning and at the end.
And at *O Lord, deliver us*—
the words of the House of Hillel.
But the House of Shammai say:
Also at *O Lord let us prosper*.
R. Aqiva said:
I was watching Rabban Gamaliel and R. Joshua;
the entire people were shaking[15] their *lulav*,
but they shook only at *O Lord, deliver us*.
If one arrived from a journey
and had no *lulav* with him,[16]

---

[14] This final response is missing in K. P reads "They said to him: You bring proof from there? Underneath…"
[15] K, P "thrusting", i.e. continuously shaking them vigorously, as opposed to the Sages who were "shaking" at the appropriate time, and not "thrusting."
[16] Lit. "in his hand."

3:8 *bind* the palm, myrtle, and willows together so that they can be easily held.

own substance: i.e. leaves of palm, myrtle, or willows. Otherwise one will appear to be waving a cluster of five species as opposed to the four specified in Leviticus 23:40.

3:9 The rabbinic *lulav* ritual has two components. First, one recites the standard blessing for the commandments ("Blessed are you…who has sanctified us with your commandments and commanded us on the taking of the *lulav*") and shakes it. Second, the *lulav* is shaken during the recitation of certain verses of the *Hallel* liturgy (Psalms 113–118), which is recited on the festivals. This mishnah debates which verses were accompanied by the shaking of the *lulav*.

where: At what point in the service?

at the beginning and at the end of Psalm 118 (vv. 1, 29).

O Lord, deliver us…let us prosper: Psalm 118:25.

the entire people were shaking: Apparently the people shook their *lulav* throughout the *Hallel*, as opposed to the practice of Rabban Gamaliel and R. Joshua. But see n. 15.

when he enters his home,
he must take it up at his table.
If he did not take it up in the morning,
he must take it up at twilight,
as the whole day is fit for the [commandment of the] *lulav*.

10 He who has a slave or woman or minor recite [the *Hallel* liturgy] to him,
he answers them with what they have said—
and let him be cursed.
If an adult recites to him,
he answers him with "*Hallelujah*."

11 A locale where it is the custom to double [the verses of the *Hallel*]—
let him double;
to say one time—
let him say one time;
to say a blessing afterwards—
let him say a blessing afterwards.
Everything accords with the local custom.
One who buys a *lulav* from his fellow during the Seventh Year,
let him give him a citron as a gift,
for he is not allowed to buy it during the Seventh Year.

take it up for the ritual *at his table*: If he did not perform the ritual immediately upon returning home when he gained access to the *lulav*, he should even interrupt his meal to do so.

whole day is fit: See *Megillah* 2:5.

3:10 This and the next mishnah deal with the recitation of the *Hallel* liturgy, which was mentioned in 3:9 in connection with the performance of the *lulav* ritual. *Hallel* was also recited on the other pilgrimage festivals, on Hanukkah, and on New Moons.

woman or minor recite: Because he does not know how to recite it himself.

answers them with what they have said: He repeats their words, as they are not obligated in the recitation, and cannot fulfill a man's obligation.

cursed: For being dependent on social inferiors and for not having learned the liturgy himself.

adult: An adult man is also obligated to recite the *Hallel*, and can fulfill another's obligation, so he need not repeat the words.

3:11 *double*: To repeat the verses of the *Hallel*. Some interpreters believe this applies only to the last nine verses of Psalm 118.

afterwards: A blessing after the *Hallel* liturgy, as is the current practice.

let him give him a citron as a gift: Albeck explains that the buyer should insist that the citron be given as a gift and that the payment be for the palm frond (or the palm frond and the other two species) alone. The prohibition against selling produce of the Seventh Year applies only to the citron, as the palm had grown in the previous year, whereas the citron came to maturity only after the beginning of the Seventh Year.

Seventh Year: See Leviticus 25:1–7 and the introduction to *Shevi'it*.

3:12 The Lulav after the Destruction of the Temple

12 Originally the *lulav* was taken up seven days in the Temple
and one day in the countryside.
After the Temple was destroyed,
Rabban Yohanan b. Zakkai ordained
that the *lulav* be taken up seven days in the countryside,
as a remembrance of the Temple,
and that new grain is forbidden on the entire day of waving.

3:13–15 The Lulav on the Sabbath

13 When the first Festival day falls on the Sabbath,
the entire people take their *lulav* to the synagogue [before the Sabbath].
On the next day they arise early and come [to the synagogue].[17]
Each one recognizes his own [*lulav*] and takes it up,
since the Sages[18] have said:
One may not fulfill his obligation on the first Festival day with his fellow's *lulav*.
But on the rest of the days of the Festival,
one may fulfill his obligation with his fellow's *lulav*.
14 R. Yose says:
If one forgot and carried his *lulav* out into the public domain

---

[17] K lacks "On the next day they arise early and come." P lacks "they arise early and come."
[18] K, P: "Since they have said."

3:12 *seven days…in the countryside*: Leviticus 23:40 commands that one take the four species and "rejoice before the Lord," i.e. in the Temple. In all likelihood the *lulav* ritual originally was associated with the other Sukkot Temple rituals, which probably functioned primarily to bring rain; these are described in 4:5–14. The mention of the *first day* in Leviticus 23:40 probably resulted in a popular custom of taking up the *lulav* on the first day even outside the Temple.

countryside: Outside of the Temple.

Rabban Yohanan b. Zakkai ordained…as a remembrance: This mishnah also appears in *Rosh Hashanah* 4:3 among a list of other ordinances of Rabban Yohanan b. Zakkai in "remembrance of the Temple."

new grain is forbidden…day of waving: This ordinance is also mentioned in *Menahot* 10:5. Leviticus 23:11–14 permits new produce to be eaten after the offering of the sheaf of barley on the "day of waving," which the rabbis understood as the second day of Passover, the sixteenth of Nisan. Rabban Yohanan b. Zakkai forbade eating it until the next day, the seventeenth, as the destruction of the Temple entailed that no offerings could be brought on the sixteenth.

3:13 *to the synagogue [before the Sabbath]*: Because carrying in a public domain, or from private to public domains, is forbidden on the Sabbath. See the following mishnah.

not fulfill his obligation…his fellow's lulav: This rule derives from an exegesis of Leviticus 23:40, which was understood by the Sages to require that one own his *lulav* on the first day.

3:14 *into the public domain*: Carrying from a private to a public domain is forbidden on the Sabbath; see *Shabbat* 1:1, 7:2.

on the first Festival day that fell on the Sabbath—
he is exempt,
because he carried it out with permission.

15 A woman may receive [a *lulav*] from her son or from her husband
and return it to water on the Sabbath.
R. Judah says:
On the Sabbath, one returns it [to its water].
On the Festival day one adds [water],
and during the Festival [week]
one replaces [the water].
A minor[19] who knows how to shake
is obligated [to fulfill] the [commandment of] *lulav*.

Chapter Four

4:1–3 The Sukkot Rituals As Practiced during the Temple Period

4 The [commandments of the] *lulav* and the willow
[are performed] [either] six or seven [days],
the *Hallel* and rejoicing eight [days],
the [commandment of the] *sukkah* and the water libation seven [days],
and the flute five or six [days].

---

[19] K, P: "every minor."

---

exempt: From bringing a purgation offering, the standard punishment for unintentional violations of the Sabbath.

carried it out with permission: He was involved in performing the commandment (though carrying it out into the public domain is not permitted).

3:15 *woman*: Even though a woman is not obligated to fulfill the commandment of the *lulav*, as it is a time-bound positive commandment; see *Qiddushin* 1:7. In 2:8 above, a woman is exempted from the commandment of the *sukkah*.

return it to water: Replace it in a container containing water to prevent it from drying out. Placing it in water does not violate the Sabbath.

Festival [week]: The intermediate days of the festival.

minor: Cf. 2:8.

4:1 *willow…Hallel…rejoicing…water libation*: Details of the rituals are provided in the following mishnayot.

six or seven: Depending on whether the first or seventh day of Sukkot falls on the Sabbath, as spelled out in the following mishnayot.

seven [days]: The *lulav* is taken on the Sabbath only on the first Festival day, because Leviticus 23:40 specifically states, *You shall take on the first day*. See 3:12–13.

2 The *lulav* seven [days]—how so?
If the first Festival day fell on a Sabbath,
the *lulav* [is taken] seven [days].
And [if on] all other days,
six [days].

3 The willow seven days—how so?
If the seventh day of the willow fell on the Sabbath,
the [commandment of the] willow is performed seven [days],
and [if on] all other days [of the week],
six [days].

4:4 *The Lulav Commandment As Performed at the Temple on the Sabbath*

4 The commandment of the *lulav*—how [was it done]?
If the first Festival day fell on the Sabbath,[20]
they[21] would bring their *lulav* to the Temple Mount,
and the attendants would receive them
and set them on the roof of the stoa.
The elders would place their [*lulav*] in a chamber [of the Temple],
and they would instruct them to say:
"Whoever winds up with my *lulav* in his hand,
it is hereby given to him as a gift."
On the next day they would arrive early,
and the attendants would throw [the *lulav*] before them,

[20] K, P lack "On the first…Sabbath."   [21] K, P: "The entire people."

4:2 *other days*: As is suggested by 3:14–15, the concern is that one will forget that it is the Sabbath and carry his *lulav* from a private to a public domain, or four cubits within the public domain, violating the Sabbath.

4:3 *willow*: As described in 4:5–7.

fell on the Sabbath: The ritual came to a climax on the seventh and final day of Sukkot, later known as Hoshana Rabbah, the "Great Hosanna Day." On this day they circled the altar seven times, even on the Sabbath. On the other days of Sukkot, they circled the altar but once, and not at all on the Sabbath.

4:4 This mishnah describes the *lulav* ritual as practiced in the Temple when the first day of Sukkot fell on a Sabbath. See 3:12 for the ritual as practiced in the synagogue.

commandment of the lulav—how [was it done]?: When the first day of Sukkot fell on the Sabbath.

bring their lulav: On Friday.

stoa: See *Pesahim* 1:5, the roofed colonnade.

The elders: To avoid the stampede described below.

they would instruct: The attendants instructed the people.

to say "Whoever…as a gift.": Since one must own his *lulav* on the first day of Sukkot (see above, 3:14), this declaration confers ownership on whoever winds up with the *lulav*.

and they would grab and hit each other.
And when the court saw that they were in danger,
they ordained that everyone should take [the *lulav*] in his own house.

4:5–7 *The Willow Commandment*

5 The commandment of the willow—how [was it done]?
There was a place below Jerusalem called Motsa.
They would go down to there and collect branches of willows from there.
And they would come and erect them at the sides of the altar
[such that] their tops were bending over the altar.
They sounded a sustained blast, a quavering blast, a sustained blast.
Each day they would circle the altar once saying:
O Lord, deliver us! O Lord, let us prosper.[22]
R. Judah says:
[They would say]: "*ani vaho*[23] deliver us."[24]
And that day they circled the altar seven times.
When they departed what did they say?
"Beauty is yours, O Altar. Beauty is yours, O Altar."
R. Eliezer says:
[They would say:] "To Yah and to you, O Altar. To Yah and to you, O Altar."[25]

[22] K: "*O Lord, deliver us! O deliver us!*" P: "*O deliver us! O deliver us!*"
[23] Meaning uncertain. If translated literally perhaps "I and He." See annotation.
[24] K, P repeat this line.
[25] K, P, and other manuscripts lack "When they departed…To *Yah* and to you, O Altar." These lines were taken from another source and added to the Mishnah later.

grab and hit: In their eagerness to get a *lulav*.

in danger of injury.

take…in his own house: On the Sabbath they perform the ritual at home, before going to the Temple, rather than bringing their *lulav* to the Temple on Friday.

4:5 The next three mishnayot describe the Temple willow ritual, one not mentioned in the Torah. Willows were brought in procession to the Temple, and each day the priests would carry them around the altar and then erect them beside the altar. These willows are also called "Hoshannot" because of the liturgy recited during the circling: *hosha na* ("deliver us").

branches: The Talmuds explain that they were eleven cubits (16.5 feet) long, such that they leaned over the altar.

blast: On trumpets.

O Lord, deliver us! O Lord, let us prosper: Psalm 118:25.

deliver us! By providing rain. The primary purpose of the ritual was probably to petition God for rain. The willows around the altar are perhaps symbolic of the verdant earth.

ani vaho: It is not clear whether R. Judah is explaining how they pronounced the first words of Psalm 118:25 or providing an alternative tradition of what they said.

that day: The seventh day.

6 As it was done on a weekday so it was done on the Sabbath,
except that [if the seventh day fell on the Sabbath]
they would collect the willows[26] on the eve of the Sabbath
and set them in golden vessels
so that they not wither.
R. Yohanan b. Beroqa says:
They would bring branches of palm,
and beat them upon the ground beside the altar.[27]
And that day was called, "The Day of Beating Branches."

7 Immediately the children would loosen their *lulav* and eat their citrons.

4:8 *The Eighth Day Assembly*

8 The *Hallel* and the Rejoicing eight [days]—how so?
This[28] teaches that a person is obligated [to recite] *Hallel*, and in Rejoicing,

[26] Lit. "them."   [27] K, P: "beat them upon the altar."   [28] See annotations.

4:6 *As it was done on a weekday…Sabbath*: They performed the ritual of the willow on a weekday just as they did when the seventh day of Sukkot fell on the Sabbath. If the Sabbath fell on the other days of Sukkot, the willow ritual was not performed; see 4:3.

eve of the Sabbath: It was forbidden to collect the willows or travel from Motsa to Jerusalem on the Sabbath.

R. Yohanan b. Beroqa…"Day of Beating Branches.": And not "The willow" or "The Great Hosanna [Day]." He seems to reject the previous description and claims that the ritual involved palm branches, not willows. In all likelihood many and diverse rituals took place at the Temple, and both willows and palm branches may have been used in various ways.

4:7 *Immediately*: After they concluded the willow ritual on the seventh day.

loosen: The band holding the palm frond, willows, and myrtle together.

eat their citrons: This entire line is ambiguous and can also be translated "They would grab the *lulav* from the hands of children and eat their citrons," i.e. as a type of celebration or play adults would grab the ritual items from children.

4:8 There is an incongruity in this mishnah, as the continuation of the "How so?" should be a description of the ritual, as in the other mishnayot in this chapter. The editor of the Mishnah seems to have integrated a different source here, although he retained the framing structure of 4:1–3.

Hallel: As described in 3:9. *Hallel* was originally recited as part of the Temple liturgy, and later became part of the synagogue liturgy.

This teaches: The obligation to recite *Hallel* and to rejoice for eight days, and not just on the seven days of Sukkot. According to the variant found in the manuscripts, the subject of "This teaches" is the practice of reciting *Hallel* and Rejoicing all eight days. That is, the fact that *Hallel* and Rejoicing are practiced for eight days "teaches" that one "honors" the last day of the Festival equally.

Rejoicing: Leviticus 23:40 commands *You shall rejoice before the Lord your God seven days*. The rabbis understand this to refer to eating the offerings of well-being brought on the festival; see too Deuteronomy 16:13–16; *Hagigah* 1:5.

and[29] in the honor of the last Festival day of Sukkot,[30]
in the same manner as all the other days of Sukkot.[31]
The *sukkah* seven [days]—how so?
When he has finished eating he does not take apart his *sukkah*,
but from the [time of the] afternoon prayer on
he takes down the utensils [into the house] from the [time of the] afternoon prayer and onwards
for the honor of the last Festival day.

4:9–10 The Water Libation

9 The water libation—how so?
He would fill a golden flask that held three *log* from the Siloam.
When they reached the Water Gate,
they sounded a sustained blast and a quavering blast and a sustained blast.
He went up the ramp and turned to his left,
where there were two silver bowls.
R. Judah says:
They were of plaster,
but they had a blackened appearance because of the wine.
They were perforated like two narrow nostrils,
one wide and one narrower,
so that they would empty at the same time;
the western one was for water,
and the eastern one for wine.
If he poured the water into the bowl for the wine
or the wine into the bowl for the water,

---

[29] P, K lack "[to recite] *Hallel*, and in Rejoicing, and." See annotations.
[30] Lit. "of the Festival."   [31] Lit. "of the Festival."

---

in the honor of the last Festival day: The Eighth Day Assembly, although it is in some respects an independent festival.

finished eating: On the seventh day of the festival.

takes down the utensils [into the house] for the honor of the last Festival day: Ritual *sukkot* were often built on the roofs of houses, so the utensils were brought down into the house for the Eighth Day Assembly, when eating in the *sukkah* is not obligatory.

4:9 *water libation*: One of the Temple rituals not mentioned in Scripture (see the introduction). The purpose of the ritual was probably to produce rain.

He: A priest.

Siloam: The pool in the City of David into which the Gihon spring emptied through the water tunnel famously dug by King Hezekiah; 2 Kings 20:20.

Water Gate: See *Middot* 2:6.

one wide and one narrower: The wide for the wine libation, the narrower for the water libation, as wine flows more slowly.

he fulfilled the obligation.
R. Judah says:
He would pour a libation of a *log* for all eight days.
And they would say to the one pouring the libation,
"Lift up your hand,"
since once someone poured the libation on his feet,
and the entire people stoned him with their citrons.

10 As it was done on the weekday,
so it was done on the Sabbath,
except that on Friday he would fill [with water] from the Siloam
a golden jug that had not been sanctified
and leave it in a Temple chamber.
If it spilled or was left uncovered
he would fill it from the laver,
for water and wine that have been left uncovered
are unfit for the altar.

Chapter Five

5:1–4 *Rejoicing at the Place of Water-Drawing*

5 The flute five or six [days].
This is the flute of the Place of Water-Drawing

---

eight days: Including the "Eighth Day Assembly," and not just on the seven days of Sukkot.

"Lift up your hand": The Sadducees apparently did not accept the extra-scriptural tradition of the water libation, so the priest attempted to spill the water on the ground rather than pouring it upon the altar, to the consternation of the people. Josephus attributes a similar case of citron pelting to the time of the Hasmonaean High Priest Alexander Jannaeus.

4:10 *Friday*: Since they could not carry the water from the Siloam to the Temple on the Sabbath.

laver: That provided water for the priests; see Exodus 30:18–21; *Yoma* 10:3.

had not been sanctified: Had not been formally dedicated to the Temple. Liquids remaining in sanctified vessels overnight were unfit for ritual use; see *Menahot* 7:4.

uncovered: Water and wine that that remained uncovered overnight were prohibited to drink; see *Terumot* 8:4. The Talmud explains that such liquids are dangerous because a snake may have drunk from them and released venom into them.

5:1 The "Rejoicing at the Place of Water-Drawing" was another of the Sukkot Temple rituals not mentioned in Scripture (see the introduction). This seems to have been a popular all-night festival held in the Temple courtyards that led up to the water libation in the morning.

The flute five or six days: As mentioned in 4:1.

flute of the Place of Water-Drawing: To distinguish this flute from the flute that was one of the instruments of the Levites that accompanied the sacrifices; see *Arakhin* 2:3, and cf. *Bikkurim* 3:2–3.

that does not take precedence over either the Sabbath or the Festival day.
They said:
He who never saw the Rejoicing at the Place of Water-Drawing
never saw [true] rejoicing in his life.

2 On the night following the first Festival day
they would go down to the Court of Women
and make a great arrangement there.
There were golden candelabra there,
and golden bowls atop them;
four ladders were around each and every [candelabrum],
and four boys from among the young priests
[had] in their hands pitchers of oil that held 120 *log*,
from which they would fill each and every bowl.

3 They would make wicks from the worn-out garments and belts of the priests,
and they would light [the lamps] with them.
And there was no courtyard in Jerusalem
that was not illuminated from the light of the Place of Water-Drawing.

4 Pious men and men of deeds would dance before the people[32]
with blazing[33] torches in their hands
and would recite songs[34] and praises before them.
The Levites [played] lutes and lyres and cymbals and trumpets[35]
and innumerable musical instruments
on the fifteen stairs that descend from the Court of Israelites to the Court of Women,
corresponding to the fifteen "Songs of Ascent" in the Book of Psalms,

[32] Lit. "them."   [33] P, K lack "blazing."   [34] P, K lack "songs and."
[35] P, K lack "and trumpets."

does not take precedence: Therefore if the first day of Sukkot fell on the Sabbath, the ritual of the "Rejoicing of the Place of Water-Drawing" would take place on the remaining six days of Sukkot. If the Sabbath fell on an intermediate day, this ritual would not take place on either the first day of Sukkot or the intermediate Sabbath; hence it would take place five days.

5:2 *Court of Women*: Of the Temple; see *Middot* 2:5.

arrangement: The Talmuds explain that the women assembled above on the balconies that overlooked the courtyards (*Middot* 2:5), and the men below. Others explain that they constructed special extensions of the balconies for the women.

5:3 *garments and belts*: The priestly garments are listed in *Yoma* 7:5.

5:4 *Pious men and men of deeds*: Efforts to identify these terms with social groups have been unsuccessful. Apparently the mishnah simply refers to those who were particularly devout.

fifteen stairs: See *Middot* 2:5.

Court of Israelites…Court of Women: See *Middot* 2:5–6.

Songs of Ascent: Psalms 120–134, which all begin *A Song of Ascents*.

Levites were standing with instruments and reciting songs: The Levites played music and chanted songs each day when sacrifices were offered (*Arakhin* 2:3). According to *Arakhin* 2:6, they typically stood on a "platform" near the altar (see *Middot* 2:6), but here they stand on the fifteen stairs.

and on which the Levites were standing with instruments[36] and reciting songs.
And two priests stood in the Upper Gate
that led down from the Court of Israelites to the Court of Women
with two trumpets in their hands.
When the cock crowed,
they sounded a sustained blast, a quavering blast, a sustained blast.
When they reached the tenth step,
they sounded a sustained blast, a quavering blast, a sustained blast.
When they reached the Court [of Women],
they sounded a sustained blast, a quavering blast, a sustained blast.
They would sound the trumpets while walking
until they reached the gate that leads out to the east.
When they reached the gate that leads out to the east,
they turned to face the west and said:
"Our forefathers who were in this place—
their backs were to the Sanctuary of the Lord,
and their faces were to the east,
and they were bowing to the sun in the east.
But we—our eyes are to Yah."[37]
R. Judah says:
They would repeat it and say [twice]:
"But we are for Yah and our eyes are to Yah."

5:5 *The Number of Trumpet Blasts Sounded in the Temple*

5 One does not sound fewer than twenty-one blasts in the Temple,
and one does not exceed forty-eight.
Each day there were twenty-one blasts:
three for the opening of the gates,
nine for the morning continual offering
and nine for the twilight continual offering.

[36] P, K lack "with instruments."   [37] K "We are for Yah, and our eyes are to Yah."

the gate that leads out to the east: From which they would proceed to the Siloam pool to draw the water for the libation.

backs to the Sanctuary…to the sun: A slightly modified quotation from Ezekiel 8:16. The purpose of this disavowal of the sun worship practiced in earlier times is not completely clear.

5:5 Trumpet blasts that accompanied the Sukkot Temple rituals were mentioned in 4:5, 4:9, and 5:4. This mishnah specifies the number of trumpet blasts sounded each day throughout the year.

opening of the gates: When they opened the Temple gates each morning.

regular offering: Exodus 29:38–42 and Numbers 23:3–8, described in *Tamid*. The blasts are mentioned in *Tamid* 7:1.

With the additional offerings they would add another nine.
And on the eve of the Sabbath they would add another six:
three so that the people cease work,
and three to separate between sacred and ordinary [time].
On the Sabbath eve of the intermediate days of the Festival [of Sukkot]
there were forty-eight:
three for the opening of the gates,
three at the Upper Gate
and three at the Lower Gate,
and three when they filled [the libation flask] with water,
and three upon the altar.
Nine for the morning continual offering,
and nine for the twilight continual offering,
and nine for the additional offerings.
Three so that the people cease work,
and three to separate between sacred and ordinary [time].

5:6–7 *Dividing the Sacrifices among the Priestly Watches*

6 The first Festival day of Sukkot[38]—
there were thirteen bulls there, and two rams, and one he-goat [to be sacrificed].
Fourteen sheep remained there for the [other] eight priestly watches.
On the first day [of Sukkot] six priests offer two [sheep] each,
and the rest offer one each.

[38] Lit. "The Festival."

---

additional offerings: On Sabbaths and festivals.

Upper Gate…Lower Gate: These blasts are mentioned in 5:4. However, the three blasts on the tenth step mentioned there are not reckoned in this mishnah, which evidently reflects a different tradition.

three when they filled [the libation flask] with water: As above, 4:9.

three upon the altar: When they poured the libation upon the altar. Some explain these three "upon the altar" are the blasts mentioned in 4:5 when the willows were erected beside the altar.

5:6 Priests were divided into twenty-four watches (*mishmarot*, sing. *mishmar*), which served in the Temple on a rotational basis during ordinary weeks, but all came to participate on the festivals (see 1 Chronicles 24–26; *Ta'anit* 4:2). This mishnah deals with how the many sacrifices prescribed for Sukkot in Numbers 29:12–13 were distributed among the watches.

thirteen bulls…rams…he-goat: See Numbers 29:12–13.

Fourteen sheep…eight priestly watches: Sixteen of the twenty-four watches each offer one bull, ram, or he-goat, leaving fourteen sheep for the remaining eight watches.

six priests…two [sheep]…one each…five…one each: Thirteen bulls are offered on the first day, and each day the number of bulls decreases by one, as prescribed by Numbers 29:12–34, while the two rams and he-goat are offered each day. Therefore on the first day six of the remaining eight watches offer two sheep each and the remaining two watches offer one sheep each. The number of bulls sacrificed on the second day decreases to twelve, freeing up one more watch from the bulls, thus leaving nine watches for the sheep. On this day five watches offer two sheep each, leaving one sheep apiece for the other four watches. And so forth.

On the second day five offer two each and the rest one each.
On the third day four offer two each and the rest one each.
On the fourth day three offer two each and the rest one each.
On the fifth day two offer two each and the rest one each.
On the sixth day one offers two and the rest offer one each.
On the seventh they are all equal.
On the Eighth [Day Assembly] they returned to casting lots [for the privileges] as on the [other] festivals.
They said:
Whoever offers bulls one day does not offer on the morrow,
but returns to the back.[39]

5:7–8   *The Priestly Watches and the Three Pilgrimage Festivals*

7 At three seasons during the year all the priestly watches were equal in the Festival sacrifices and in the division of the showbread.
On the Festival of Weeks they say to him:
Here is unleavened bread. Here is leavened bread.[40]

---

[39] Lit. "goes back to their turn."
[40] P, K repeat "Here is unleavened bread. Here is leavened bread."

---

all equal: With the seven bulls prescribed for the seventh day, the total number of animals sacrificed is twenty-four (seven bulls, two rams, one he-goat, fourteen sheep), one for each watch.

casting lots: As detailed in *Yoma* 2:1–4.

Whoever: Whichever watch.

returns to the back: Of the cycle. The first thirteen watches offer the thirteen bulls on the first day of Sukkot, and the other watches offer the sheep, rams, and he-goat. The second day watches fourteen through twenty-four offer eleven of the twelve bulls, and the first watch offers the twelfth bull. The third day watches two through twelve offer the eleven bulls. And so forth.

5:7 Having mentioned the priestly watches in the previous mishnah, in this and the following mishnayot the text provides general rules concerning the distribution of responsibilities for various Festival sacrifices and the division of the showbread.

three seasons: On the three pilgrimage festivals: Passover, Booths (Sukkot), and Weeks (*Atseret* in the Mishnah, *Shavu'ot* in post-Mishnaic texts).

equal: In performing the sacrifices and receiving a portion of the showbread.

showbread: Leviticus 24:5–9. The twelve loaves of showbread were typically divided among the incoming and outgoing watch on duty that Sabbath. But on the Festivals all the watches served in the Temple, hence if a Festival fell on or adjacent to the Sabbath, all watches shared equally in the showbread.

On the Festival of Weeks: Called *Atseret* in the Mishnah. Two loaves of bread were offered (Leviticus 23:15–17), and these too were distributed among the priests. If the festival fell on or consecutive with the Sabbath these loaves would be distributed along with the showbread.

Here is unleavened bread. Here is leavened bread: The showbread was unleavened bread, while the two loaves were leavened (*Menahot* 5.1). They distribute both equally among the watches, and do not give some the unleavened bread and others the leavened.

The priestly watch for which it is the set time offers the continual offerings, vow offerings, free-will offerings, and the other communal offerings. And it offers all.[41]
If the Festival day[42] fell next to the Sabbath, whether before or after, all the priestly watches were equal in the division of the showbread.

8 If one day separates between [a Festival and the Sabbath], the priestly watch whose set time it is [to serve that week] takes ten loaves, and those[43] which remain [in the Temple] take two. On all other days of the year, the incoming priestly watch takes six and the outgoing priestly watch takes six. R. Judah says: The incoming takes seven and the outgoing takes five.

[41] P lacks "And it offers all."
[42] K: "First Festival day." K formulates this rule for Sukkot, but the same rule would apply to Passover and Shavuot.
[43] Lit. "The one which remains."

set time: To serve in the Temple according to the weekly rotation.

regular offerings: The regular offerings for each morning and evening; see above 5:4.

vow offerings…communal offerings: These offerings are not specifically for the festival, hence the watch which was due to serve has the rights to them.

And it offers all: Other types of offerings not specifically for the festival.

whether before or after: If the first day of a festival fell on Sunday, or if the last day fell on Friday, all the priests would have been at the Temple, in the former case because the festival had just ended on a Sabbath, in the latter to prepare for the festival starting on the next day.

watches were equal: As is the rule when the festival fell on the Sabbath, as all the watches had to remain at the Temple, though they were not actually serving on that Friday or Sunday.

5:8 This mishnah continues to rule on the impact of the pilgrimage festivals on the division of the showbread, and then discusses the division of the showbread on normal weeks.

one day separates: The festival ended on Thursday or began on Monday.

set time: To serve that week, according to the weekly rotation of priests.

ten loaves: Of the twelve loaves of showbread.

remain: Priests of the other watches who did not return home on Friday even though the festival ended on Thursday.

take two: Even though their presence is not absolutely necessary, as travel is permitted on the Friday following a festival that ends on Thursday. But they chose to spend the proximate Sabbath at the Temple.

The incoming [priests] distribute [the showbread]
in the north [of the Temple Court],
and the outgoing in the south
[The priestly watch of] Bilgah always shares in the south,
and its ring is fixed,
and its wall niche is sealed.

incoming … outgoing: The weekly rotation of watches changed on the Sabbath.

Bilgah: One of the twenty-four watches named in 1 Chronicles 24:14. According to other rabbinic texts they were penalized, either because Miriam, daughter of Bilgah, apostatized, or because they neglected their duties such that another watch had to serve for them.

shares in the south: That they must share the showbread in a specific location is a stigma.

fixed: The rings were used in the slaughtering process; *Middot* 3:5. This ring was fixed in place so that they could not use it.

wall niche: Where priests kept their vestments; *Tamid* 5:3.

Tractate Betsah

Judith Hauptman

Introduction

Overview

This tractate has two names, either *Betsah*, meaning "egg," because its opening words are "If an *egg* is laid on a festival," or *Yom Tov*, meaning festival. This usage of *yom tov* derives from several verses in Esther (8:17; 9:19, 22) which describe the holiday of Purim as a *yom tov*, a day of feasting and rejoicing. In rabbinic literature, *yom tov* denotes not all festivals, but only those that are *holy convocations* (the phrase comes from Leviticus 23:2), days on which one may not perform ordinary labor.

Structure and Organization of the Tractate

Chapter 1 speaks of preparations for the festival, such as the need to designate before the onset of the festival the food one will eat on the festival (1:3–4). It also rules that food preparation on a festival should be done differently from an ordinary day (1:7–8). Chapter 2 discusses preparing food on a Friday festival for the Sabbath that immediately follows (2:1) and the rules of immersion for ritual purity when a festival immediately follows a Sabbath (2:2–3). It presents food-preparation rules on a festival that differ from those on ordinary days (2:5–8). Chapter 3 focuses on capturing and slaughtering animals on a festival (3:1–7). It discusses procuring food from a merchant without violating the ban on buying and selling on a festival (3:8). Chapter 4 surveys auxiliary food-preparation activities, such as chopping wood and making a fire on a festival (4:1–4, 7). Chapter 5 makes a general statement about the difference between the Sabbath and festivals (5:2). The tractate ends with some miscellaneous rules about transporting food on a festival from one town to another (5:3–6).

Main Ideas

Betsah can with good reason be viewed as a spin-off of tractate *Shabbat*. From the outset, *Betsah* assumes that the Sabbath labor restrictions listed in *Shabbat* 7:2 apply to festivals as well, and so do not need further attention. Neither does *Betsah* address festival prayers or any practice specific to one festival only, such as building booths for the festival of Booths (Sukkot). Its focus is food. Why so? For all their similarity to the Sabbath, festivals differ in one key way: food-preparation activities, which are forbidden on the Sabbath, are permitted on festivals (Exodus 12:16; *Betsah* 5:2). Among other permitted activities one may slaughter animals (3:6), roast their flesh (3:3), cook stews (2:1), bake bread (2:6), and give gifts of prepared food to friends and relatives (1:9).

Even as the Sages of the Mishnah relaxed cooking restrictions on festivals, they left some limits on food preparation in place. All foodstuffs to be cooked and consumed on a festival had to be in existence and ready to be used at the onset of the festival. That very point underlies the debate of the Houses of Shammai and Hillel in the opening mishnah as to whether or not an egg laid on a festival—and hence not yet in existence at the onset of the festival—may be eaten that same day (1:1). The Sages also stipulate that food preparation on a festival has to differ from that on an ordinary day. According to the House of Shammai, spices have to be ground with different implements (1:7). Wine jugs have to be transported on one's shoulder and not in a basket (4:1). In short, one may prepare meals on a festival as long as one accepts certain limitations.

Complicating the situation further, the Mishnah sometimes presents a rule but then suggests how to circumvent it. Buying and selling are forbidden on a festival, but the Mishnah provides a way to procure foodstuffs from a merchant without technically violating the ban on business transactions on a festival (3:8). Preparing food on a festival for consumption the next day is not allowed, but one may slaughter an animal on the verge of death if there is still time in the day to consume an olive's bulk of roasted flesh (3:3). The Mishnah also extended a leniency, allowing one to make a fire not just for heating water but also for warmth (2:5).

A contemporary parallel text (*Tosefta*) provides some insight into this patchwork of leniencies and stringencies. It states that at first all but three kitchen utensils were prohibited for Sabbath use, but over time the Sages allowed any utensil with a permitted Sabbath function to be handled and used on the Sabbath. The same text reports that to be used on the Sabbath a utensil had to be available and ready for use at the onset of the Sabbath, and one Sage stipulates that food for animals had to be in existence at the onset of the Sabbath in order to be fed to them on the Sabbath (*Shabbat* 24:4). It appears that the Sages applied this set of Sabbath rules to festival food preparation.

Although pronouns in the singular always appear as masculine, such as "he prepares a cooked dish" (2:1) or "he separates pods from peas" (1:8), domestic cooking and baking activities in the rabbinic world were generally performed by women. If so, men needed to inform the women of their household of any new rules developed in the (male) study house so that the food these women served them at home would comply with these rules. Moreover, it was the wife, or some other female in the household, who set the *eruv tavshilin* (2:1) that allowed her to cook on a Friday festival for the Sabbath and who separated the dough offering when baking bread (see tractate *Hallah*). As for the many verbs that appear in the plural, they are often best translated in the passive voice; the subject can then be understood as referring to both men and women.

Relationship to Scripture

The rules of this tractate flow from just one verse in the Bible. In reference to Passover, Exodus 12:16 states *You shall celebrate a sacred occasion on the first day, and a sacred occasion on the seventh day; no work at all shall be done on them; only what every person is to eat, that alone may be prepared for you.* This verse was understood to mean that unlike the Sabbath, when cooking is not allowed, food preparation is permitted on a festival (not just Passover), but only for consumption that same day. Perhaps there is a connection between the scriptural commandment to rejoice on the festivals (see Deuteronomy 16:15) and the rabbinic elaboration of the permission to cook on the festivals. Surely freshly cooked meals would enhance festival joy.

Tractate Betsah

Chapter One

1:1–4 *Designating Festival Food in Advance of the Festival*

1 If an egg was laid¹ on a festival—
the House of Shammai say:
It may be eaten [on the festival].
But the House of Hillel say:
It may not be eaten.
The House of Shammai say:
[One violates the Passover ban on] leaven by [owning] an olive's bulk,
And the ban on leavened products by [owning] a date's bulk.
But the House of Hillel say:
Both by [owning] an olive's bulk.
  2 If one slaughters a wild beast or fowl on a festival—
the House of Shammai say:
He must dig up [earth] with a mattock and cover.
But the House of Hillel say:
A person may not slaughter [a wild beast or a fowl] on the festival
unless he prepared earth before the onset of the festival.
But they concede that if he did slaughter on the festival
he may dig with a mattock and cover [the blood],
because stove ash is considered as [having been] prepared [to cover blood].
  3 The House of Shammai say:
One may not move a ladder [on a festival] from one dovecote to another,

---

¹ Lit. "if an egg was 'born' on a Festival."

1:1 *It may not be eaten*: Because the egg was not in existence before the onset of the holiday and hence not available for holiday use.

leaven...leavened products: Exodus 13:7 forbids the possession on Passover of either leaven itself or leavened products.

1:2 *and cover* the blood of the slaughtered animal. Leviticus 17:13 requires one who slaughters a wild animal or fowl to cover its blood with dirt. The rule does not apply to domestic cattle.

1:3 *One may not move a ladder [on a festival]*: The apparent reason is that either the act itself is work or it gives the appearance of work.

from one dovecote to another: To take doves for a festival meal.

but one may incline it from one opening to another opening]in the same dovecote].
But the House of Hillel permit [both actions].
The House of Shammai say:
One may only take [a dove on the festival]
if he shook [the dove] while it was still day.
But the House of Hillel say:
One may stand and declare,
I am taking this one and that one [for a festival meal tomorrow].

4 If a person designated black [doves before the festival]
and [on the festival] found [only] white doves [at the dovecote],
or [designated] white [doves]
and found [only] black ones,
or [designated] two and found three—
[in all these cases the doves are] forbidden.
[But if he designated] three and found [only] two, they are permitted.
If [he designated them before the festival] inside a nest
and [then] found [them on the festival]
in front of a nest [with other doves],
they are [all] forbidden.
But if they are the only ones there,
In such a case they are permitted.

1:5–6   *Food-Related Festival Restrictions*

5 The House of Shammai say:
One may not remove shutters on a festival.
But the House of Hillel permit [not only to remove them]
but even to return them [to their place].
The House of Shammai say:
One may not take a pestle to carve meat on it,
but the House of Hillel permit.
The House of Shammai say:

while it was still day: Before the festival, thereby designating it for festival use.

One may stand near the dovecote before the onset of the festival.

1:4 *and found three*: And does not know which two doves he designated.

they are [all] forbidden: Because he does not know which doves he designated the day before.

1:5 *One may not remove shutters on a festival* to take items for festival meals. Removing shutters gives the appearance of razing a building, which is forbidden on a festival. See *Shabbat* 7:2.

One may not take a pestle to carve meat on it. Since it generally functions in a way forbidden on a festival, it is considered off limits on the festival.

One may not place a hide to be trodden upon [in order to tan it],[2]
nor may one lift it up
unless an olive's bulk[3] of flesh remains on it,
but the House of Hillel permit.
The House of Shammai say:
One may not carry out a child, a *lulav*, or a Torah scroll
to the public domain [on the festival],
but the House of Hillel permit.

6   The House of Shammai say:
One may not take dough offering or [priestly] gifts to a priest on a festival,
whether they were set aside for the priest the night before or on the festival day itself.
But the House of Hillel permit.
The House of Shammai said to them:
It is an analogy.
Dough offerings and gifts are both gifts to the priest;
just as one may not take *terumah* to a priest on a festival,
so too may one not take [other] gifts to a priest on a festival.
The House of Hillel replied:
Not so! Can you say that the [rule] that applies to *terumah*,
which one may not designate [on a festival],
similarly applies to [priestly] gifts,
which one may designate [on a festival]?

---

[2] K, P: "house of tanning."
[3] K, P lack "olive's bulk," which means they rule more leniently. Any amount of flesh permits the hide to be handled on a festival.

---

remains on it: Which permits the hide to be handled on the festival.

but the House of Hillel permit: So that one does not refrain from slaughtering an animal on the festival.

One may not carry out a child, a lulav, or a Torah scroll: Because these items are not food. Carrying items from domain to domain is prohibited on the Sabbath and festivals. See *Shabbat* 7:2.

a lulav: A palm branch and its attendant bouquet of plants, waved during prayers on the festival of Booths (Sukkot). See Leviticus 23:40 and *Sukkah* 3:9.

but the House of Hillel permit: Since transporting items from domain to domain is often a necessary aspect of food preparation, the House of Hillel hold that one may do so for other purposes too.

1:6 *One may not take dough offering (hallah)*: According to Numbers 15:17–21, one is required to set aside a loaf for God from the "the first yield of your baking." This became known as setting aside *hallah*. The Sages mandated that the dough (or baked bread) be given to a priest.

or [priestly] gifts: The shoulders, cheeks, and stomach of an animal offering are to be designated for the priests. See Deuteronomy 18:3.

similarly applies to [priestly] gifts: According to the House of Hillel, if one is permitted to designate a priestly gift on a festival, it follows that one may take it to the priest on a festival.

1:7–8 Festival Food Preparation Must Differ from Normal Preparation

7 The House of Shammai say:
Spices may be pounded [on a festival] with a wooden pestle[4]
and salt in a [clay] jar with a wooden pot ladle.
But the House of Hillel say:
Spices may be crushed in their usual manner
but salt with a wooden pestle.

8 If one separates legumes on a festival,
the House of Shammai say:
One must pick out what is edible and eat it.
But the House of Hillel say:
One may pick out what is edible, as is the custom,
and collect it in one's lap or a basket[5] or a plate
but not on a board or in a small or large sieve.
Rabban Gamaliel says:
One may also pour water [over the legumes]
and pick out [pods and skins that rise to the surface].

1:9–10 Sending Gifts on a Festival

9 The House of Shammai say:
One may send gifts only of prepared food [to a friend or relative] on a festival.
But the House of Hillel say:
One may send cattle, or a beast, or a fowl, whether alive or already slaughtered.
One may send wine, oil, fine flour, legumes, but not grain.
But R. Simeon permits grain [as well].

---

[4] K: "with a stone pestle."   [5] K, P lack "basket."

1:7 *Spices may be pounded…with a wooden pestle*: One normally used a stone pestle, but this was forbidden on the festival. Although cooking is permitted on a festival, the Sages stipulated that certain food preparation activities be performed differently from usual. See next mishnah.

1:8 *If one separates legumes*: Such as peas or beans from their pods or skins on a festival.

One must pick out what is edible and eat it: One must eat the legumes right away and not collect them in a vessel because that gives the appearance of preparing food on the festival for the next day, which is prohibited. See *Shabbat* 15:3 which does not allow one to fold up bed linens on the Sabbath for use after the Sabbath.

but not on a board or in a small or large sieve: As one would do on an ordinary day. A parallel text bans the standard manner of operation for this very act of separation.

and pick out: This is a lenient position because the separation occurs on its own and could be viewed as removing the inedible from the edible, which is not permitted on a Sabbath or festival. See *Shabbat* 7:2.

1:9 *prepared food*: So that they can be eaten that same day.

but not grain: Because it is not ready to be used.

R. Simeon permits grain [as well]: Grain can be used for food as is, without being ground into flour.

10 One may send garments
whether sewn [and ready to wear] or not sewn,
even if they contain a forbidden mixture,
as long as they fill a festival need.
But one may not [send] a sandal [decorated] with nails,
nor a shoe that is not [yet] stitched.
R Judah says:
Also not a white shoe because it needs an expert [to dye it].
This is the general rule:
Anything which one may use on the festival,
one may send it [on a festival to someone else].

Chapter Two

2:1 Preparing Food on a Festival for Immediately Following Sabbath

2 If a festival falls on the eve of the Sabbath,
a person may not cook from the outset[6] on the festival for the Sabbath,
but he may cook for the festival,
and if he prepared more than needed,
he may leave it over for the Sabbath.
And he may prepare a cooked dish on the eve of the festival
and rely on it [to prepare food] for the Sabbath.
The House of Shammai say:
[A person must prepare] two cooked dishes.
But the House of Hillel say:
One cooked dish [is sufficient].

[6] Or "from the first," "intentionally." So too below.

1:10 *One may send garments*: To a friend or relative on a festival.

forbidden mixture: Linen mixed with wool. See Leviticus 19:19.

a sandal [decorated] with nails: Because such sandals are forbidden on the Sabbath or a festival. See *Shabbat* 6:2.

an expert [to dye it]: Dyeing is not allowed on a Sabbath. See *Shabbat* 7:2.

2:1 *rely on it [to prepare food] for the Sabbath*: The Talmuds call this act *eruvei tavshilin*, a "mixture of cooked dishes," which means that Sabbath and festival food preparation are commingled.

two cooked dishes: On the eve of the festival for the Sabbath.

And they agree[7] that a fish with egg on it is [considered] two cooked dishes.
If a person consumed it or if it spoiled,
he may not [rely on it] from the outset [to cook for the Sabbath].
But if even a morsel remains,
he may rely on it [to cook] for the Sabbath.

2:2–3 *Immersion before a Festival That Immediately Follows a Sabbath*

2 If a festival falls right after the Sabbath—
the House of Shammai say:
Everything that needs immersion must be immersed before the Sabbath,[8]
but the House of Hillel say:
Utensils must be immersed before the Sabbath,
but a person [may immerse himself] on the Sabbath.

3 But they agree that one may effect surface contact for [impure] water in a stone vessel
in order to make [the water] pure,[9]
but may not immerse the water [with its container].
One may immerse [a utensil to change it]
from serving a lower purpose to serving a higher one.
And one may immerse [utensils on a festival if leaving one] *havurah* to eat with another.

2:4 *Animal Offerings and Laying On of Hands on a Festival*

4 The House of Shammai say:
One may bring offerings of well-being [on a festival]

---

[7] **K, P:** "they concede." See annotations.

[8] Lit. "One must immerse everything before the Sabbath."

[9] **K, P:** "for purification."

And they agree: The variant in the manuscripts does not indicate who "conceded" to whom, but possibly the "concession" produced the agreement reported in the standard text.

If a person consumed it: The cooked dish he prepared on the eve of a festival.

2:2 *Utensils must be immersed before the Sabbath*: To make them pure for the festival. See *Hagigah* 3:6–8.

a person [may immerse himself] on the Sabbath: Sabbath immersion is permitted because people also immerse themselves on the Sabbath for pleasure. See *Shabbat* 22:5.

2:3 *but may not immerse the water*: In an impure utensil that will itself become pure upon immersion.

to serving a higher one: Such as from holding ordinary food to holding ritually pure food.

havurah: Lit. "fellowship." This was a group that consumed its meals together at a certain agreed level of purity. The term often specifically designates a company that has been assembled to eat a paschal lamb.

to eat with another: *Havurah* that will eat food of a greater degree of sanctity. Since such an immersion does not change the purity status of the immersed item, it is permitted on a festival.

and one does not lay hands on them
but not whole burnt offerings.
But one may not perform laying on of hands.
But the House of Hillel say:
One may bring both offerings of well-being and whole burnt offerings [on a festival] and perform laying on of hands.

2:5–8 *Leniencies and Stringencies regarding Food Preparation on a Festival*

5 The House of Shammai say:
A person may not warm water for his feet [on a festival]
unless the water is also fit for drinking.
But the House of Hillel permit.
A person may make a fire [on a festival] and warm oneself at it.
6 Rabban Gamaliel issued three stringencies in accordance with the House of Shammai:
(1) one may not store water warmed on a festival for the Sabbath;
(2) one may not right a [fallen] candlestick on a festival;
(3) one may not bake thick loaves [on a festival] but only thin ones.
Said Rabban Gamaliel:
In the days of Father they did not bake thick loaves but only thin ones.
[His colleagues] responded:
What can we do about your father's family,
for even though they would deal stringently with themselves
they would rule leniently for all Israel,
permitting them to bake thick loaves and loaves baked on coals!

2:4 *laying on of hands*: On the head of the animal. According to Leviticus 1:4 and 3:2, 8, 13, when bringing an animal as a whole burnt offering or an offering of well-being, the owner must lay hand(s) on the head of the animal prior to slaughtering it. See parallel at *Hagigah* 2:3.

2:5 *But the House of Hillel permit* warming water for one's feet even if not fit for drinking. The House of Hillel holds that if one is permitted to warm water to cook food, one may similarly warm water for other purposes.

A person may make a fire [on a festival] and warm oneself at it: Since one may light a fire to heat water, one may also light a fire for warmth. This statement appears to be the view of the House of Hillel alone.

2:6 *one may not store water warmed on a festival for the Sabbath*: It is not clear why Rabban Gamaliel prohibits such storing. If no *eruv* was set to permit cooking food on a festival for the Sabbath, as prescribed at 2:1 above, there is no need to separately ban storing hot water for the Sabbath. If an *eruv* was set, why the stringency? See parallel at *Eduyot* 3:10–12.

one may not bake thick loaves [on a festival] but only thin ones: It is not clear why thin loaves are permitted and thick ones prohibited. The Talmud suggests that since thick loaves are easier to bake, one would be tempted to bake more than one could reasonably consume on a festival.

7 He also issued three leniencies:
(1) one may sweep among the couches [on a festival],
(2) and one may set incense [to burn] on a festival,
(3) and one may prepare a goat in *mequlas* [fashion] on Passover nights.
But the Sages forbid [all three].

8 There are three things that R. Eleazar b. Azariah permits but the Sages forbid.
(1) His cow would go out [on the Sabbath]
with a band tied between its horns,
(2) one may curry cattle on a festival,
(3) and one may grind peppercorns in pepper mills.
R Judah says:
One may not curry cattle on a festival because it may break their skin,
but one may comb [their hair].
But the Sages say:
One may not curry or even comb.

2:9–10 *Impurity of Objects*

9 Pepper mills are susceptible to impurity
as three [separate] utensils:
(1) as a receptacle [for ground pepper],
(2) as a metal utensil,
(3) and as a sieve.

10 A child's wagon is susceptible to *midras* impurity
and may be handled on the Sabbath,

2:7 *in mequlas [fashion] on Passover nights*: Roasting it whole with entrails and legs on the head, like a helmet. The word *mequlas* seems to mean "helmeted."

But the Sages forbid [all three]: They apparently regarded sweeping and incense burning as work and not necessary for festival meals. As for a helmeted goat, they probably thought it was too similar to the preparation of a paschal lamb in Temple times.

2:8 *His cow would go out*: Into public space on the Sabbath. One is not permitted to transport items from private to public space on the Sabbath.

a band tied between its horns: The ban on transporting items applies to the head of household, members of his household, and even his cattle. See *Shabbat* 5:4.

and one may grind peppercorns in pepper mills: R. Eleazar b. Azariah needed to articulate this last leniency because one can grind pepper in advance of the festival, although the pepper might lose its potency.

2:9 *as three [separate] utensils*: One might think that if one part of a pepper mill contracted impurity, the other two parts would become impure too. This mishnah rules otherwise.

2:10 *midras impurity*: Lit. "impurity caused by treading." Should a *zav* sit or stand or lie or lean against an object, it becomes impure with *midras* impurity. See Leviticus 15:1–12.

may be handled on the Sabbath: Because it serves a permitted purpose.

but it may be dragged only on fabric.[10]
R. Judah says:
No utensil may be dragged [along the ground] other than a wagon
because it presses down.

Chapter Three

3:1–2 *Trapping Fish and Animals before the Onset of a Festival*

3 One may not catch fish from a vivarium on a festival,
nor may one give them food.
But one may capture beasts and fowl from a vivarium [on a festival]
and also give them food.
Rabban Simeon b. Gamaliel says:
Not all vivaria are alike.
This is the rule:
If an animal is not yet captured,
it is forbidden.
But if an animal is already captured
one may [slaughter it on a festival].
  2 If a person set traps for beast, fowl, or fish on the eve of a festival,
he may not remove the catch from them [on a festival]
unless he knows that they were [already] caught
before the onset of the festival.
It once happened that a certain non-Jew brought fish to Rabban Gamaliel [on a festival]
and he said:
The fish are permitted [to be eaten]
but I do not wish to accept [them] from him.

[10] Lit. "utensils."

but it may be dragged only on fabric: The reason for not dragging it on a dirt floor is to avoid making a rut in the floor, which, because it is like plowing, is forbidden on the Sabbath. See *Shabbat* 7:2.

because it presses down: According to R. Judah, a wagon merely presses down the earth, which is permitted on the Sabbath, but does not make a rut or furrow, which is forbidden.

3:1 *From a vivarium*: An enclosed fishpond. Partial parallel at *Shabbat* 13:5.

nor may one give them food: Possibly because feeding fish may lead one to catch fish on a festival, which is forbidden.

it is forbidden: To chase and capture it on a festival.

already captured: If one need not chase it.

3:2 *before the onset of a festival*: One may not eat food on a festival that did not already exist as food before the onset of the festival.

to accept [them] from him: It is not clear whether the non-Jew caught the fish before or on the festival.

3:3–5 *Slaughtering Animals on a Festival*

3 An animal that is about to die may not be slaughtered [on a festival]
unless there is enough time left in the day
to eat an olive's bulk of roasted [flesh].[11]
R. Aqiva says:
Even an olive's bulk of raw meat from the place of slaughter.
If he slaughtered it in the field,
he may not bring in the [carcass] on a pole or in a small wheelbarrow[12]
but limb by limb in his hand.

4 If an [unblemished] firstborn animal falls into a pit,
R. Judah says:
Let an expert go down and examine [it] to see [if it is now blemished].
If it is, he may bring up the animal and slaughter it.
If not [blemished], he may not slaughter it.
R. Simeon says:
Any animal whose blemish was not observed before the onset [of a festival],[13]
is not considered available.[14]

5 If an animal died [on a festival],
one may not move it from its place.
They once asked R. Tarfon about such an animal
and about dough offering that had become impure [in the course of the festival].
He entered the study house and asked [for a ruling].
And they told him not to move them from their place.

---

[11] K, P: "unless it is certain that he can eat of it an olive's bulk of roast meat while still daytime."
[12] K, P: "on a couch (or plank)."   [13] K, P: "from the eve of the festival," a better locution.
[14] Or "prepared."

3:3 *an olive's bulk of roasted [flesh]*: One may not slaughter an animal on a festival for consumption after the festival. The text seems to imply that he need not actually consume the meat as long as there is enough time that he could.

the place of slaughter: The neck. An olive's bulk of raw meat is sufficient.

3:4 *to see*: Firstborn animals, if unblemished, must be given to a priest. If they are blemished, the owner may slaughter and eat them. See Deuteronomy 15:19–22.

not slaughter it: But must leave it there.

not considered available: Not ready to slaughter and eat on the festival.

3:5 *If an animal died*: Of natural causes.

one may not move it from its place: Since it is no longer available for festival use, it may not be handled or moved.

dough offering (hallah) that had become impure in the course of the festival. *Pesahim* 3:3 states that impure hallah may not be eaten or burnt.

And they told him not to move them from their place: The question was whether these items, which had been ready for use at the onset of the festival, could be handled and moved now that they had become impure.

3:6–8 Circumventing the Rule of Not Purchasing Food on a Festival

6 One may not, from the outset, register on a festival
[to take a share of] an animal [slaughtered on a festival],
but one may register on the eve of a festival.
They may slaughter an animal [on a festival]
and divide it up amongst themselves.
R. Judah says:
A person may weigh out meat [on a festival]
corresponding to a utensil or a butcher's knife.
But the Sages say:
One may not pay attention to the pan of a scale at all.

7 One may not sharpen a knife on a festival,
but one may draw it over another [knife to sharpen it].
A person may not say to a butcher,
"Weigh out for me[15] a *dinar*'s worth of flesh,"
but the butcher slaughters [the animal]
and they may [then] divide it among themselves.

8 One person may say to another,[16] "Fill this vessel for me,"
but he may not specify a measure.
R. Judah says:
If the vessel were itself a measure, he may not fill it.
It was reported that Abba Saul b. Botnit
would fill his measures [with produce]
on the eve of a festival and [then]
hand them to [his] customers on the festival.
Abba Saul says:
He also[17] used to do so on the intermediary days of the festival

---

[15] K, P: "sell me." If so, the manuscripts would allow someone to say "weigh out for me," because that is not the same as saying "sell me."

[16] K, P: "to a shopkeeper." See the end of this mishnah. The manuscript readings seem smoother than the printed text.

[17] No "also" in the manuscripts. Accordingly Abba Saul disagrees with the report about Abba Saul b. Botnit.

3:6 *One may not, from the outset, register on a festival*: Business transactions are forbidden on a festival, as on the Sabbath. See *Shabbat* 23:1.

They may slaughter: The registered members of the group may proceed to consume the animal on the festival.

to a utensil: Of known weight.

3:7 *One may not sharpen a knife on a festival*: With a sharpener.

among themselves: Without discussing price.

3:8 *not fill it*: With produce on a festival.

because of the clarity of measures: So that his many customers would receive the full amount.

because of the clarity of measures.[18]
But the Sages say:
He would do so even on ordinary days
because of the draining of measures.
A person may approach his regular shopkeeper [on a festival] and say,[19]
"Give me such-and-such number of eggs or nuts,"
For it is standard for a person to count eggs and nuts in this way in his own home.

Chapter Four

4:1–3 *Gathering and Chopping Wood on a Festival*

4 When a person transports jugs of wine from place to place [on a festival],
he may not bring them in a small or large basket,
but carries them on his shoulder or in front of him.[20]
And similarly,[21] one who transports straw may not cast the basket over his shoulder
and have it hang down his back,
but rather brings it in his hand.
And one may begin [to take straw] from a pile of straw,
but one may not [take wood] from the [supply of] stored wood.
  2 One may not take wood on [a festival] from a shed,
but only from wood that is near a shed.
One may bring in wood from a field if it was gathered together,
and from an enclosure even if it is scattered.
What is an enclosure?
Any [fenced-in] area adjoining the town—

[18] The manuscripts lack "because of the clarity of measures."
[19] K, P read "A person may say to another."
[20] K, P read "on his shoulder in front of him," as one continuous descriptive statement.
[21] K, P lack "similarly." The text reads better without this word.

because of the draining of measures: He would invert his measure over the customer's vessel to make sure that every drop transferred from his measure to theirs.

eggs or nuts: On credit.

to count eggs and nuts in this way in his own home: And the transaction, therefore, is not considered a purchase.

4:1 *he should not bring them in a small or large basket*: As he does on an ordinary day.

And one may begin [to take straw] from a pile of straw: Even if not designated in advance for use on a festival.

from the [supply of] stored wood: Because the stored wood is not ready and available for use.

4:2 *from a shed*: By breaking down the shed.

near a shed: But not part of a shed.

the words of R. Judah.
R. Yose says:
Any area that one needs a key to enter,
even [if it is] within the Sabbath boundary.

3 One may not chop wood [taken] from [a stack of] beams
or from a beam that broke on a festival.
And one may not chop with an ax or a saw or a scythe,
but only with a butcher's knife.
If a sealed shed was full of produce and an opening appeared,
one may remove [produce] via the opening.
R. Meir says:
He may even make an opening from the outset and remove [produce].

4:4–6 Ban on Fashioning a Utensil on a Festival

4 One may not make a depression [in a ball of clay] for a lamp,
because he thereby fashions a utensil [on a festival],
and one may not make charcoal on a festival,
and one may not cut a wick into two parts.
R. Judah says:
One may cut a wick into two parts with a flame.

5 One may not smash earthenware [on a festival],
and one may not cut paper to roast a salt-fish in it,
and one may not rake out an oven or a stove
but may press down,

Any area: That is fenced in or locked.

even [if it is] within the Sabbath boundary: By implication, if a person finds wood in an enclosure within the Sabbath boundary but needs no key to enter, he may still not take wood from there on a festival.

the Sabbath boundary: A person may walk outside town on the Sabbath a distance of two thousand cubits, and no more. If one prepares an *eruv* at the edge of the town's Sabbath boundary, he may walk another two thousand cubits from there. See *Eruvin* chapter 3.

4:3 *or from a beam that broke on a festival*: Because such a beam was not available for use at the onset of the festival.

not chop with an ax or a saw or a scythe: As he does on an ordinary day.

one may remove [produce] via the opening: Even though he had not considered using this produce at the onset of the festival. Food is normally considered ready and available for use on a festival.

4:4 *because he thereby fashions a utensil [on a festival]*: On the Sabbath, it is prohibited to fashion a utensil. See *Shabbat* 22:3.

4:5 *rake out an oven or a stove* of coal and ashes.

but may press down the sediment for better baking.

and one may not place two jugs side by side
in order to set down a pot on them,
and one may not prop up a pot with a wood chip,
and likewise for a door,[22]
and one may not drive an animal with a stick on a festival.
But R. Eleazar b. R. Simeon permits [it].[23]

6 R. Eliezer says:
A person may take a chip [of wood] from [that which is] before him[24]
in order to pick his teeth,
and he may collect [kindling from anywhere] in the yard
and set it on fire,
for everything in the yard is considered available[25] for use.
But the Sages say:
He may collect [kindling] and set it on fire,
[but only] from [that which is] before him.

4:7 *Making a Fire on a Festival*

7 One may not make a fire [on a festival] from wood, or stones, or earth, or water.
And one may not heat tiles until white hot in order to roast in them.[26]
R. Eliezer also said:
A person may stand near his store of produce
on the eve of the Sabbath in the Seventh Year and say,
"From here I will eat tomorrow."
But the Sages say:
[The produce is not properly tithed] until one marks it and says,
"From here and until there."

---

[22] K, P: "and likewise a door"; the printed text does not make sense.
[23] K, P lack this line.
[24] K, P lack "from that which is before him," but the idea is implicit.
[25] Or "prepared."
[26] K, P: "on them," a superior reading.

---

and one may not prop up a pot with a wood chip: The Talmud comments that wood chips may only be used on a festival as kindling. They are not ready for other purposes.

4:6 *before him*: In his home but not from his yard.

4:7 *But the Sages say* the produce is not tithe-free.

I will eat tomorrow From here and until there: He thereby designates tithe-free Seventh-Year produce for himself to eat on the Sabbath. See Leviticus 25:1–7. During a Sabbatical (Seventh) Year, when no planting is allowed, the naturally occurring produce of a field or orchard is free for all to eat, even the owner. Tithes need not be designated.

Chapter Five

5:1 Avoiding Loss of Produce on Sabbaths and Festivals

5 One may send produce down[27] the garret window on a festival but not on the Sabbath,
and one may cover produce with utensils [to protect it] from a water leak,
and similarly jugs of wine and oil,
and one may put a vessel under a leak on the Sabbath.

5:2 Difference between Sabbath- and Festival-Restricted Activities

2 Any [act] which makes one liable on the Sabbath
such as *shevut*,
such as an optional act,[28]
or such as a religious act,[29]
[similarly] makes one liable on a festival.
And these are [the acts] forbidden on account of *shevut*:
one may not climb a tree,
nor ride on an animal,
nor swim in water,
nor slap one's thighs,
nor clap [one's hands],[30]
nor jump up and down.[31]
And these are [the acts] that are forbidden on account of being an optional act:[32]
one may not judge,[33]
nor betroth,
nor perform *halitsah*,
nor enter into levirate marriage.
And these are [the acts] that are forbidden on account of being religious acts:[34]
one may not consecrate [property to the Temple],

---

[27] K, P: "pass through," presumably referring to the window. [28] Or "an act of authority."
[29] Or "a commandment." [30] K, P: "One may not clap hands or slap thighs."
[31] Or "dance." [32] Or "an act of authority."
[33] K lacks "one may not betroth, nor perform *halitsah*, nor enter into levirate marriage. And these are the acts that are forbidden as religious acts: one may not dedicate property to the Temple." These phrases appear in a marginal note.
[34] Or "commandments."

5:1 *One may send produce down the garret window*: To protect the produce from rain or other threats.

wine and oil may be covered on a festival.

one may put a vessel under a leak on the Sabbath to catch the water. Similar to *Eruvin* 10:6.

5:2 *liable*: For punishment.

shevut: An act rabbinically forbidden on the Sabbath because it is inconsistent with the spirit of the Sabbath.

a halitsah…levirate marriage: See Deuteronomy 25:5–10 and *Yevamot*.

nor make a vow of personal value,
nor renounce private use [of an object],
nor designate *terumah* or a tithe.
For all of these acts the Sages made a person liable on a festival,
and how much the more so on the Sabbath.
The only difference between a festival and a Sabbath
is that on a festival one may cook food to be consumed that same day.

5:3–7 *Transporting on a Festival*

3 Animals and utensils are as the feet of their owners.
If a person turns over his animal to his child or a shepherd,
[the animal] is as the feet of the owner.
Utensils that are designated for the use of just one of the brothers in a house
are as his feet.
Those that are not designated for the use of just one brother
may only [be taken to] the place where all walk.
4 If one borrows a utensil from his fellow on the eve of a festival,
[the utensil is] as the feet of the borrower.
[If one borrows a utensil] on a festival,
it is as the feet of the lender.
If one woman borrows from another woman
spices or water or salt for her dough,
these are as the feet of both.
R. Judah exempts water because it has no substance.
5 A glowing coal is as the feet of its owner,
but a flame [may be transported] anywhere.
A glowing coal that belongs to the Temple
is subject to [the rules of] sacrilege.

a vow of personal value: See Leviticus 27:1–9. See also *Arakhin* chapter 1.

renounce private use [of an object]: See Leviticus 27:28 and Numbers 18:14.

one may cook food to be consumed that same day: See Exodus 12:16 and introduction.

5:3 *Animals and utensils are* subject to the same restrictions as the feet of their owners. They may go, or be taken, on the Sabbath or a festival, only to where their owners may go, i.e. to the end of the Sabbath boundary of 2,000 cubits beyond the town boundary. See above 4:2, and *Eruvin* 4:1.

The animal is subject to the same restrictions.

where all of the brothers are permitted to *walk*.

5:4 *the utensil is* subject on the festival to the same restrictions.

as the feet of the borrower: And may only be transported to places where the borrower is permitted to go.

exempts water from these restrictions.

5:5 *sacrilege*: See Leviticus 5:15–16. See also *Me'ilah*. The Sages define sacrilege as benefiting inadvertently from property belonging to the Temple.

But as for a flame,
although it is not subject to sacrilege,
one may not derive benefit from it.
One who takes out a glowing coal to the public way is liable,
[but one who takes out] a flame [by fanning it] is exempt.[35]
[Water from] a cistern[36] that has an owner is
as the feet of its owner.
But water from a cistern that belongs to the people of the town is
as the feet of the people of that town.
And [water from a cistern] that belongs to those who returned from Babylon
is as the feet of the one who draws [water from it].

6   If a person had [stored] produce in another town,
and the people of that town established an *eruv*
so that they could bring him his produce [on a Sabbath or a festival],
[even so] they may not bring him [his produce].[37]
But if he [himself] established an *eruv* [in his town],
then his produce is like him.

7   If one invited guests,
they may not take away any portions with their own hands,
unless he transferred ownership of their portions[38] on the eve of the festival.
One may not give drink to, or slaughter, pasture animals [on a festival],
but one may give drink to, and also slaughter, household animals.
Household animals are ones that lodge overnight in town;
pasture animals are ones that lodge overnight in the pasture.

[35] K, P lack this statement.   [36] K, P: "a well."   [37] K, P explicitly add "his produce."
[38] K, P: "unless he transferred ownership of their portions to them through another person."

for a flame that belongs to the Temple.

[Water from] a cistern that has an owner is subject to the same restrictions.

as the feet of its owner: And may only be taken to places he is permitted to go on the Sabbath or a festival.

those who returned from Babylon: In the time of Ezra. According to a passage in the Talmud they dug wells and opened them to the public. See also *Nedarim* 5:4–5.

5:6 *eruv*: See 5:3 above. If the Sabbath boundaries of two towns overlap, the townspeople can prepare a joint *eruv* which will allow them to go on the Sabbath from one town to the other.

may not bring him [his produce]: Because it is subject to the same restrictions as its owner.

then his produce is like him: Thanks to his *eruv* the owner may now go from town to town, and therefore the produce, which is subject to the same restrictions to which he is subject, may be brought to him on a Sabbath or festival.

5:7 *If one invited guests*: From another town to dine with him on a festival.

any portions: That he gives them.

transferred ownership: Because otherwise the portions are subject to the same restrictions as the host.

household animals: They are considered ready for slaughter at any time. Pasture animals are not.

in the pasture: Outside town limits.

Tractate Rosh Hashanah

Steven D. Fraade

Introduction

Overview

Rosh Hashanah, the eighth tractate in the order *Mo'ed*, comprises four chapters. Its name literally means "head of the year," and denotes the Jewish New Year; this falls on the first day of the month of Tishre, the seventh month according to the biblical practice of counting the months from Nisan in the spring (Exodus 12:2; Leviticus 23:24–25; Numbers 29:1–6; Nehemiah 8:2). However, as the Mishnah immediately specifies, there are not one but four New Years in the Jewish calendar, that is, four dates with which annual reckonings begin for different purposes.

That being said, it is the New Year beginning in Tishre with which the remainder of the tractate deals, with particular attention to the intercalation of the preceding month of Elul, which could be twenty-nine or thirty days in length. The tractate also deals with the festival's significance as a day of divine judgment, the rules for blowing the *shofar* (ram's horn), which is uniquely associated with this festival, and other liturgical aspects of the festival.

In Mishnaic times, the determination of which day commenced the month of Tishre was based on the testimony of witnesses who had directly seen the new moon on the thirtieth or thirty-first day of the preceding month; this determined whether that month would last twenty-nine or thirty days (a full lunar month lasts about 29.5 days). This determination of the length of the month of Elul would, in turn, determine not only the day on which Rosh Hashanah would be celebrated, but also that of Yom Kippur (the Day of Atonement), with even greater consequences due to the supreme sanctity of that day and its attendant practices of fasting and other forms of self-denial.

Structure and Organization of the Tractate

It is this procedure, especially with respect to the validation of witnesses and their testimony, and the manner of publicly announcing and disseminating via messengers the correct day of Rosh Hashanah, that occupies most of the laws and narratives of the first two chapters of the tractate. The second chapter concludes with a dramatic story of a confrontation between Rabban Gamaliel and R. Joshua over the correct determination one year of the beginning of the month of Tishre; this bore more importantly on the relation between patriarchal authority and rabbinic autonomy, reflecting the idea that patriarchal (and judicial) authority is divinely vested (Leviticus 23:2) in the rabbinic courts, especially those which determine the calendar.

The third chapter continues with courts and witnesses, but turns to rules for the blowing of the ram's horn (*shofar*: Numbers 29:1; Psalms 81:4), and the importance of proper intention in doing so. The fourth chapter continues with matters regarding the *shofar*, especially innovative enactments by Rabban Yohanan b. Zakkai regarding the blowing of the *shofar*, as well as other festival observances, in response to the loss of the Temple. In this regard this tractate is particularly expressive of the differences between the time when the Temple existed and the time after its destruction: see 1:4; 4:1, 3, 4. The remainder of the fourth chapter deals with the order of blessings and special readings of verses from Scripture appropriate to the themes of Rosh Hashanah: (Divine) Sovereignty, Divine Remembrance, and *Shofar*. The chapter concludes with additional rules for the proper procedures for blowing the *shofar* on Rosh Hashanah.

Tractate Rosh Hashanah

Chapter One

1:1–3 *New Years, New Moons, and Festivals*

I There are four New Years:
on the first of Nisan is the New Year for kings and for festivals.
On the first of Elul is the New Year for the tithe of cattle.
R. Eleazar and R. Simeon say:
On the first of Tishre.
On the first of Tishre is the New Year for years,
for Years of Release,
for Jubilees,
for planting,
and for vegetables.
On the first of Shevat is the New Year for trees,
according to the words of the House of Shammai.
The House of Hillel say:
On the fifteenth thereof.

1:1 *Nisan*: The first month, the spring month.

New Year for kings: That is, for the count of regnal years.

festivals: The annual cycle of festivals is held to begin with Passover in Nisan; see Exodus 12:1.

Elul: The sixth month.

tithe of cattle: Each year's crop of newborn cattle must be tithed separately.

Tishre: The seventh month, in the fall, on the first day of which is Rosh Hashanah.

for years: Commentators vary as to what this means; perhaps the reference is to the regnal years of gentile kings or to the start of year-long contracts.

Years of Release...Jubilees: See Leviticus 25 and *Shevi'it*.

planting: That is, of trees, to count off the first three and then the fourth year of their production; see Leviticus 19:23–25.

vegetables...trees: To determine liability to tithes.

Shevat: The eleventh month.

2 At four times of the year
the world is judged:
at Passover with respect to grain;
at the Festival of Weeks with respect to the fruits of trees;
at Rosh Hashanah all that enter the world pass before him like legions of soldiers,[1]
as it is said: *He who fashions the hearts of them all, who discerns all their doings*;
and at the Festival [of Sukkot] they are judged with respect to water.

3 With respect to six New Moons messengers go forth:
with respect to Nisan because of Passover;
with respect to Av because of the Fast;
with respect to Elul because of Rosh Hashanah;
with respect to Tishre because of regulating the Festivals;
with respect to Kislev because of Hanukkah;
and with respect to Adar because of Purim.
And when the Temple existed,
one would go forth also with respect to Iyyar
because of [the need to set] the Second Passover.

1:4–9 *Witnesses to the New Moon*

4 With respect to two New Moons
one may profane the Sabbath:
with respect to Nisan and with respect to Tishre.
Because on them messengers go forth to Syria
and on them the festivals were regulated.
And when the Temple existed,

---

[1] Alt. "like flocks of sheep."

1:2 *Festival of Weeks*: *Shavu'ot* in post-Mishnaic texts, *atseret* ("Assembly") in the Mishnah.

He who fashions the hearts of them all…: Psalms 33:15.

with respect to water: Rainfall.

1:3 *messengers go forth*: To proclaim the New Moon. In these particular months an important holiday would fall, and it was necessary to inform distant communities of its proper date.

Passover: Commencing on the afternoon of the fourteenth of Nisan.

the Fast: The ninth day of Av, the fifth month.

Rosh Hashanah: The first of Tishre.

regulating the Festivals: Establishing the proper dates for the Day of Atonement and Sukkot; see 1:4 below.

Hanukkah: The twenty-fifth day of Kislev, the ninth month.

Purim: The fourteenth and fifteenth days of Adar, the twelfth month.

Second Passover: The fifteenth day of Iyyar, the second month. See Numbers 9:6–13.

1:4 *profane the Sabbath*: To bring testimony regarding the New Moon, since major festivals occurred in those months.

one would profane [the Sabbath] with respect to all of them,
because of regulating the sacrifice.

5 Whether [the New Moon] was seen clearly or not seen clearly,
one may profane the Sabbath for its sake.
R. Yose says:
If it was seen clearly,
one does not profane the Sabbath for its sake.

6 It once happened
that more than forty pairs [of witnesses] passed through [on the Sabbath],
but R. Aqiva detained them in Lod.
Rabban Gamaliel sent to him:
If you detain the multitude,
you will put a stumbling block before them for the future.

7 A father and son who saw the New Moon
[may] go [to bear witness],
not because they can join together [as two witnesses],
but rather,
if one of them is disqualified,
the other can join with another [witness].
R. Simeon says:
A father and his son,
or all [other] relatives,
are fit to bear witness about the New Moon.
R. Yose said:
It once happened
that Tobiah the Physician saw the New Moon in Jerusalem,
he and his son and his freed slave,
and the priests accepted him and his son [as witnesses],
but disqualified his slave.[2]
But when they came before the court,

---

[2] From here to the end of this mishnah missing in **K** and inserted in the margin.

---

all of them: All twelve months, since the special sacrifice for the New Moon (Numbers 28:11–15) had to be offered ("regulated") on the proper day.

1:5 *R. Yose says*: The court would expect a greater number of witnesses, some of whom could arrive without violating the Sabbath.

1:6 *put a stumbling block before them for the future*: They will not bother to bring forth testimony lest they be blocked from doing so.

1:7 *join together [as two witnesses]*: Being close relatives, their testimonies cannot be presumed to be independent of one another.

join with another [witness]: To constitute a valid pair of witnesses.

fit to bear witness about the New Moon: In contrast to other kinds of legal testimony, where close relatives would be disqualified.

But when they came before the court: The Mishnah distinguishes between "the priests" and "the court" as two distinct authoritative bodies for judging such calendrical matters. Earlier sources generally presume more

they accepted him and his slave,
but disqualified his son.

8 These are disqualified [from bearing witness]:
a dice player, and those who loan on interest, and pigeon flyers,
and those who sell Seventh-Year produce, and slaves.
This is the general rule:
[With respect to] any evidence which a woman is disqualified [from bringing],
these too are disqualified.

9 If one saw the New Moon but cannot walk,
they [may] bring him [on the Sabbath] on a donkey,
even on a bed.
If any lie in ambush for them,
they [may] carry staves.
And if it was a long way, they [may] carry food.
For with respect to a journey of a night and a day
one [may] profane the Sabbath
and go forth to bring evidence of the New Moon,
as it is said:
These are the set times of the Lord…which you shall declare each at its appointed time.

Chapter Two

2:1–4   *Interference of Heretics and the Lighting of Flares*

2 If [the judges] do not recognize [the witness],
one sends another [witness] with him
to testify regarding him.
In former times,
they accepted testimony regarding the New Moon from anyone.

---

overlap between priests and the courts. Here the two bodies disagree whether a close relative or a slave is preferable as a second witness.

1:8 *These are disqualified*: At *Sanhedrin* 3:3 a similar list of disqualified witnesses in property cases does not disqualify slaves.

1:9 *a night and a day*: If the trip is any longer than that, there would be no gain from profaning the Sabbath since they would arrive after the New Moon had been declared.

which you shall declare …: Leviticus 23:4. Since the preceding verse proscribes work on the Sabbath, this verse may be understood to say that the setting of the proper time for the festivals, through the setting of the length of the month, may override the Sabbath restrictions.

2:1 *do not recognize [the witness]*: And cannot be certain of his fitness.

they: Presumably a court or officials of his own town.

When the sectarians became corrupt,
they enacted
that they would only accept [testimony]
from those whom they recognized.

2 In former times,
they kindled flares.
When the Samaritans became corrupt,
they enacted that messengers would go forth.

3 How did[3] they kindle flares?
They bring long sticks of cedar and reeds and oleaster wood and flax yarn,
and [someone] ties them together with rope
and ascends to the top of the hill
and sets them aflame.
And he moves [them] back and forth
and up and down
until he sees his fellow doing likewise on the second hilltop,
and likewise on the third hilltop.

4 And whence did they kindle flares?
From the Mount of Olives to Sarteba,
and from Sarteba to Agrippina,
and from Agrippina to Hauran,
and from Hauran to Beth Baltin.
They did not go beyond Beth Baltin,
but he would move [the flare] back and forth
and up and down
until he would see all of the Exile before him
like an expanse of fire.

2:5–6 *Assembling and Examining the Witnesses*

5 There was a large courtyard in Jerusalem
that was called Beth Ya'azeq,

[3] K: "do."

---

sectarians: Also translated "heretics," Heb. *minim*, whose exact identity is often difficult to discern. For other mishnaic passages that allude to polemical calendrical disputes, perhaps with Sadducees or related groups, and specifically with respect to the dating of the Feast of Weeks (cf. Leviticus 23:11, 15), see *Hagigah* 2:4 and *Menahot* 10:3.

2:2 *flares*: To announce the New Moon. See 2:3 below.

Samaritans: The Samaritans rejected rabbinic calendrical authority.

corrupt: Lighting misleading flares of their own to announce the New Moon, even if not sighted.

messengers would go forth: To announce the New Moon, without relying on flares.

2:3 *oleaster wood*: Lit. "oil-wood."

2:4 *all of the Exile*: That is so say, Babylonia.

at which all of the witnesses were assembled,
and the court examined them there.
And they prepared large meals for them
so that they would be accustomed to coming.
In former times,
they did not move from there the whole [Sabbath] day.
Rabban Gamaliel the Elder enacted
that they might move two thousand cubits in any direction.
And not these alone,
but also the midwife that comes to deliver a child,
and one who comes to rescue from a burning [building],
or from an [enemy] army,
or from a [flooding] river,
or from a fallen house.
These are considered to be like the people of the city,
being able to move[4] two thousand cubits in any direction.

6 How do they examine the witnesses?
They first examine the first pair [that arrives],
and they bring in the elder of them and say to him:
Tell, how did you see the moon,
ahead of the sun or behind the sun?
To its north or to its south?
How high was it and to which side[5] was it leaning?
And how wide was it?
If he said:
"Ahead of the sun,"
he has said nothing.
Afterward they would bring in the second [witness]
and examine him.
If their words are found to be in agreement,
their testimony is valid.
They inquire of all the remaining pairs [of witnesses]
only regarding the major points.
Not because they needed them,
but in order that they not depart in disappointment,
so that they would be accustomed to coming.

[4] Lit. "they have."   [5] Lit. "where."

2:5 *Rabban Gamaliel the Elder*: Early first century CE. Unless "the Elder" is specified, "Rabban Gamaliel" is his grandson.

in any direction: For Sabbath limit, see *Eruvin* 4:1–3; 8:1.

2:6 *examine the witnesses*: See *Sanhedrin* 3:6.

he has said nothing: It would have been the old moon or not the moon at all. He cannot be relied upon as a witness.

2:7 *Proclaiming the New Moon*

7 The head of the court says:
"It is sanctified!"
And all of the people respond after him:
"It is sanctified! It is sanctified!"
Whether it appeared at its proper time
or did not appear at its proper time,
they sanctify it.
R Eleazar b. Zadok says:
If it did not appear at its proper time
they do not sanctify it,
for Heaven has already sanctified it.

2:8–9 *False Witnesses and a Story of Judicial Authority*

8 Rabban Gamaliel had a likeness of the shapes of the moon on a tablet
and on the wall of his upper room,
which he would show nonexpert [witnesses], saying:
Did you see it like this or like that?
It once happened that two [witnesses] came and said:
We saw it at dawn in the east and at evening in the west.
Said R. Yohanan b. Nuri:
They are false witnesses!
When they came to Yavneh,
Rabban Gamaliel accepted them.
Another two came and said:
We saw it at its proper time,

2:7 *at its proper time*: On the eve of the thirtieth day of the concluding month, meaning that the concluding month had twenty-nine days.

did not appear at its proper time: If the moon is not seen on the eve of the thirtieth day, it can be presumed that the concluding month had thirty days; this is the maximum length of a lunar month. There is no need to wait for it to be seen on what would be the thirty-first day of the concluding month.

for Heaven has already sanctified it: It is only humanly sanctified on the testimony of witnesses, in the absence of which the new month is presumed to begin on the thirty-first day of the concluding month, without the need for the court to declare it sanctified.

2:8 *We saw it at dawn*: On the morning of the twenty-ninth day of the concluding month.

They are false witnesses: For the moon to appear like this twice in the same day is impossible.

When they came to Yavneh: Having previously testified before another court.

accepted them: Their testimony. Even if they erred in what they saw in the morning, their sighting of the moon the following evening could be accepted as valid in its own right.

at its proper time: On the eve of the thirtieth day of the concluding month, rendering it a month of twenty-nine days, with the thirtieth day being declared the first day of the new month.

but on the night of the added day
it did not appear,
and Rabban Gamaliel accepted them.
Said R. Dosa b. Harqinas:
They are false witnesses.
How can they testify that a woman has given birth,
when on the very next day
her stomach is between her teeth?
R. Joshua said to him:
I see your point.[6]

9 Rabban Gamaliel sent to [R. Joshua]:
I decree upon you that you come to me with your staff and your purse
on the Day of Atonement as determined by your calculation.
R. Aqiva went and found [R. Joshua] troubled.
He said to him:
I can infer [from Scripture]
that whatever Rabban Gamaliel has done is [validly] done,
as it is said:
These are the appointed times of the Lord, the sacred occasions, which you shall proclaim.
Whether they are in their proper time
or not in their proper time
I have no other appointed times but these.
[Rabbi Joshua] came to R. Dosa b. Harqinas.
He said to him:
If we come to take issue with the court of Rabban Gamaliel,
we need to take issue with every single court

[6] Lit. "your words."

the night of the added day: The night following the thirtieth day of the concluding month, being the eve of the thirty-first day.

accepted them: And declared the thirtieth day of the concluding month to be the first day of the new month, with the preceding month having been one of twenty-nine days.

between her teeth: That is, their first sighting of the moon was false and the concluding month would have to have been one of thirty days, delaying the new month by one day from the determination of Rabban Gamaliel.

I see your point: That is, I endorse your words, contrary to the position of Rabban Gamaliel, and consider the concluding month to have been one of thirty days.

2:9 *by your calculation*: A day *later* than by Rabban Gamaliel's reckoning, that is, a sacred day (no work or travel) for R. Joshua, but not for Rabban Gamaliel. R. Joshua must violate the sanctity of the most solemn day of the year.

These are the appointed times…: Leviticus 23:4.

no other appointed times but these: Whose times you, through your human courts and witnesses, shall determine, and with which I will comply.

He said to him: In the first appearance of this phrase, R. Aqiva to R. Joshua; in the second, R. Dosa to R. Joshua.

that has served[7] from the days of Moses until now,
as it is said:
Then Moses and Aaron, Nadab and Abihu, and seventy elders of Israel ascended.
And why were the names of the elders not specified?
To teach that every group of three [elders] who have served[8] as a court of Israel,
indeed they are as the court of Moses.
[R. Joshua] took his staff and his purse in his hand
and went to Yavneh,
to Rabban Gamaliel,
on the Day of Atonement
as determined by [R. Joshua's] calculation.
Rabban Gamaliel stood up and kissed him on his head
and said to him:
Come in peace,
my master and my disciple!—
My master in wisdom
and my disciple for having accepted my words.

Chapter Three

3:1 *More on Court Procedures*

3 If the court and all of Israel had seen [the New Moon],
and the witnesses had been examined,
but they did not have sufficient time to declare
"It is sanctified!"
before nightfall,
in such a case it is intercalated.
If the court alone saw it,

[7] Lit. "stood."   [8] Lit. "stood."

Then Moses and Aaron, Nadab and Abihu…: Exodus 24:9.

as the court of Moses: Even if their names (and qualifications) have not been transmitted, their legitimacy and authority is the same as that of those named.

3:1 Thematically, this should follow after 2:7.

had seen [the New Moon]: On the thirtieth day of the concluding month, which would normally render that day the first day of the new month.

before nightfall: All court proceedings, including sanctification of the month, must take place by day.

in such a case it is intercalated: The concluding month contains thirty days and the next day is the first day of the new month, even though the concluding month should have contained twenty-nine days.

two [of its members] should stand
and testify before them,
and then they [the court] say
"It is sanctified! It is sanctified!"
If three [judges] saw it,
and they constitute a court [for such purposes],
two of them stand,
appoint two of their colleagues to join the remaining one,
and [the witnesses] testify before them,
and they say
"It is sanctified! It is sanctified!"
For no individual is [considered] trustworthy in himself.

3:2–7 Valid Shofar and Proper Intention

2 All [kinds of] *shofar* are valid
except for that of a cow,
since it is a "horn."
R. Yose said:
Are not all [kinds of] *shofar* called "horn,"
as it is said:
When a long blast is sounded on the horn.

3 The *shofar* [blown in the Temple] on Rosh Hashanah is of a wild goat,
straight,
with its mouthpiece overlaid with gold.
And two trumpets [are blown] at either side.
The *shofar* blows long
and the trumpets blow short,
for the obligation of the day
is [fulfilled] through the *shofar*.

4 On [public] fast days [the *shofar*] are of rams,
rounded,
with their mouthpieces overlaid with silver.

---

trustworthy in himself: A minimum of two witnesses is required to give testimony before a court consisting of a minimum of three judges. The sole remaining judge of the original panel cannot sanctify the New Moon on his own.

3:2 *shofar*: Ram's horns.

it is a "horn" and is not considered a *shofar*. According to rabbinic teaching a cow's horn cannot be used because it is reminiscent of the Golden Calf.

When a long blast is sounded on the horn: Joshua 6:5. Elsewhere in this same verse the "horn" is called a *shofar*.

3:3 *The shofar [blown in the Temple]*: While the commentaries place this mishnah in the Temple, in fact the text does not specify this.

And two trumpets [are blown] in the middle.
The *shofar* blows short.
and the trumpets blow long,
for the obligation of the day
is [fulfilled] through the trumpets.

5 The Jubilee is like Rosh Hashanah
with respect to the blowing [of the *shofar*]
and the Blessings.
R. Judah says:
On Rosh Hashanah they blow [*shofar* of] rams,
while on the Jubilee they blow [*shofar* of] of wild goats.

6 A *shofar* which was split and stuck together
is not valid.
If its shattered pieces were stuck together,
it is not valid.
If it had developed a hole and was stopped up,
if it hinders the blowing,
it is not valid;
and if not,
it is valid.

7 One who blows [the *shofar*] into a cistern
or into a cellar,
or into a large jar:
if he hears the sound of the *shofar*,
he has fulfilled [his obligation];
if he hears a muffled sound,
he has not fulfilled [his obligation].
Similarly,
one who passes behind a synagogue,
or whose house is next to a synagogue,
and he heard the sound of the *shofar*
or the sound of the Scroll [of Esther being read on Purim],
if he directed his heart,
he has fulfilled [his obligation];
if not,
he has not fulfilled [his obligation].
Even though this one heard
and that one heard,
this one directed his heart
and that one did not direct his heart.

3:4 *in the middle*: That is, two *shofars* are blown at either side, and between them are blown two trumpets.

3:5 *and the Blessings*: See 4:5–6.

3:7 *has not fulfilled [his obligation]*: To hear the "voice of the *shofar*."

directed his heart: Listened with the intent of fulfilling thereby the commandment to hear the sound of the *shofar* or the reading of the Scroll of Esther.

3:8 Interpretive Narratives on Proper Intention

8 *Then, whenever Moses held up his hand, Israel prevailed,* etc.
Can it be
that the hands of Moses
could advance a battle
or hinder a battle?
Rather [it comes to] say to you:
So long as Israel looked upward
and subjected[9] their hearts
to their Father in heaven,
they would be victorious.
But if not,
they would fall.
Similarly you might say:
Make a serpent figure and mount it on a standard.
And if anyone who is bitten look at it, he shall recover.
Can it be that a serpent kills
or that a serpent gives life?
Rather,
whenever Israel looks upward
and subjects[10] their hearts
to their Father in heaven,
they are healed.
But if not,
they are squashed.
A deaf-mute, one who is legally incompetent, and a minor
cannot enable the public[11] to fulfill their obligation.
This is the general rule:
Whoever is not obligated in a matter,
cannot enable the public[12] to fulfill their obligation.

[9] **K:** "directed."   [10] **P:** "directs."   [11] Lit. "many."   [12] Lit. "many."

3:8 This mishnah continues the theme of proper intention.

Then, whenever Moses held up his hand…: Exodus 17:11. The verse continues: "but whenever he let down his hand, Amalek prevailed."

Make a serpent figure…: Numbers 21:8.

Can it be that a serpent kills…: The reference is to the bronze serpent that Moses prepared.

their Father in heaven: For a similar understanding, see Wisdom of Solomon 16:7.

A deaf-mute, one who is legally incompetent, and a minor: These three are often considered together in the Mishnah.

to fulfill their obligation: e.g. to hear the *shofar*. The first two cannot do so with the proper intent due to their inability either to hear the *shofar* or to understand the obligation, while the minor, not being obligated himself, cannot enable those who are obligated to fulfill their obligation.

Chapter Four

4:1–3 *Festival Rituals and the Memory of the Temple*

4 When the festival day of Rosh Hashanah fell on the Sabbath,
they would blow the *shofar* in the Temple,
but not in the provinces.
When the Temple was destroyed,
Rabban Yohanan b. Zakkai enacted
that they would blow the *shofar*
in every locale in which there was a court.
Said R. Eleazar:
Rabban Yohanan b. Zakkai enacted only with respect to Yavneh alone.
They said to him:
Both Yavneh and every locale in which there is a court.
  2 And in this regard also did Jerusalem exceed Yavneh:
In every town within sight and sound [of Jerusalem] and nearby,
and able to come up [by foot] to Jerusalem,
they blow the *shofar*.
But as to Yavneh,
they blow the *shofar* in the court alone.
  3 In former times,
the *lulav* was taken up in the Temple for seven days,
and in the provinces for one day.
When the Temple was destroyed,
Rabban Yohanan b. Zakkai enacted
that in the provinces the *lulav* be taken up for seven days,

---

4:1 *in the Temple*: According to some, in the whole city of Jerusalem.

Yavneh alone: Yavneh (Jamnia in Greek) is a town west by northwest of Jerusalem near the Mediterranean coast, where the first two generations of rabbinic Sages are said to have gathered following the destruction of the Second Temple in 70 CE. Other texts express the view that such prerogatives will again be restricted to the Temple (and Jerusalem) upon its being rebuilt.

4:2 *they blow the shofar*: Jerusalem's status exceeds that of Yavneh in that its status, at least in this regard, extends to its surrounding areas, and is not limited to its court. It is not clear whether all of the stated conditions must apply to areas outside of Jerusalem, or any of them.

4:3 *lulav*: palm branch and accompanying species (citron fruit, myrtle branches, and willow branches) used in the Festival of Sukkot; see Leviticus 23:40. This mishnah is also found in *Sukkah* 3:12.

for one day: The first day of the festival.

in memory of the Temple: The *lulav* is frequently depicted with other objects associated with the Temple (*menorah*, *shofar*, and incense shovel) in late antique and Byzantine Jewish iconography, especially in synagogue remains, often in close proximity to the depiction of the Holy Ark.

the day of waving: That is, waving of the *omer* or ceremonial sheaf on the sixteenth of Nisan according to rabbinic practice. See Leviticus 23:10–11.

in memory of the Temple;
and that the day of waving should be wholly prohibited.

4:4 *Before and After the Destruction of the Temple*

4 In former times,
they would receive testimony to the New Moon throughout the day.
Once the witnesses were so delayed in coming
that the Levites were disordered in the song.
They enacted
that testimony could only be brought
until the time of the afternoon daily sacrifice.
And if witnesses came from the afternoon sacrifice and onward,
they would treat that day as holy
and the following day as holy.
When the Temple was destroyed,
Rabban Yohanan b. Zakkai enacted
that they would accept testimony to the New Moon
throughout the day.
R. Joshua b. Qorhah said:
And Rabban Ben Zakkai enacted this too:
Regardless of where the head of the court might be,
the witnesses [to the New Moon] come only
to the place of assembly.

---

wholly prohibited: With regard to the eating of new produce. That is, new produce could only be eaten after nightfall, whereas previously it could be immediately eaten after the waving of the *omer*. See Leviticus 23:14.

4:4 *throughout the day*: Most commentators interpret this mishnah with respect to the last day of Elul, the day before Rosh Hashanah. The reference to the day being "holy" supports this reading, but the same difficulty might have arisen at the end of any other month as well. According to the dominant interpretation, if witnesses came and their testimony was accepted by the court, that day would then become the first of Tishre, Rosh Hashanah.

the song: The Levites would sing a different psalm, depending on whether or not a New Moon was declared on that day. Since the decision had to be made by midafternoon so as to know with which song to accompany the late-day whole burnt offering, it would be impossible to wait beyond that for the arrival of witnesses.

that day as holy: That is, what remained of it, being retroactively considered the first of the new month of Tishre.

the following day: Now understood to be the second day of Tishre, but the first full day observed as Rosh Hashanah.

When the Temple was destroyed: And sacrifices ceased, there no longer being a risk of confusing the Levite singers.

the place of assembly: That is, of the court; if necessary, they would hear testimony and decide without the head of the court.

4:5–6 *The Order of Blessings*

5 The order of blessings:
[The prayer leader] recites the "Fathers," "Powers," and the "Sanctifying of the Name,"
incorporating the Sovereignty verses with them,
but he does not blow [the *shofar*];
the "Sanctifying of the Day"
and blows;
the Remembrance [verses]
and blows;
the *Shofar* [verses]
and blows;
and he recites the "[Temple] Service," and the "Thanksgiving," and the "Priestly Blessing"—
the words of R. Yohanan b. Nuri.
R. Aqiva said to him:
If he doesn't blow for the Sovereignty [verses],
why does he mention [them]?
Rather, he recites the "Fathers," "Powers," and the "Sanctifying of the Name,"
and combines the Sovereignty [verses] with the "Sanctifying of the Day"
and blows;
the Remembrance [verses] and blows;
the *Shofar* verses and blows;
and he recites the "[Temple] Service," and the "Thanksgiving," and the "Priestly Blessing."

6 One does not recite fewer than ten Sovereignty [verses],
ten Remembrance [verses],
or ten *Shofar* [verses].
R. Yohanan b. Nuri says:
If one said three from each
he has fulfilled [his obligation].
One does not recite [a verse of] Remembrance, Sovereignty, or *Shofar*
that makes mention of [divine] punishment.
One begins with the Torah
and finishes with the Prophets.
R. Yose says:
If he finished with the Torah,
he has fulfilled [his obligation].

4:5 *order of blessings*: By tradition, the additional prayer on Rosh Hashanah must include series of biblical passages on the themes of God's sovereignty, God's recollection, and the sound of the *shofar*. The present mishnah specifies how these verses are to be included in the normal blessings of the festival prayer.

"Fathers," etc.: These are standard designations for the seven blessings that constitute the usual festival prayer.

mention [them]: What is their purpose if not to introduce the blowing of the *shofar*?

4:6 *fewer than ten ... [verses]*: It would appear that the specific verses to be recited for each of these had not yet been set.

One begins ... and finishes: That is, one chooses verses in this order from the indicated divisions of Scripture and includes verses from the Writings between those of the Torah and the Prophets.

4:7–9 *Additional Rules for Blowing the Shofar*

7 The one who passes before the Ark
on the festival day of Rosh Hashanah [does not blow the *shofar*],
[but] the second one does so.
But when it is time to recite *Hallel*,
the first one leads the recitation of the *Hallel*.

8 One may not pass beyond the [Sabbath] limit
for the sake of a *shofar* of Rosh Hashanah,
nor clear away a pile [of stones] for its sake.
One may not climb a tree,
nor ride on the back of cattle,
nor swim on the surface of water,
nor cut [the *shofar*],
whether by a means that [transgresses the rabbinic rules of] Sabbath rest
or that [transgresses] an [explicit] negative commandment [of the Torah].
But if he wanted to put into it water or wine,
he may do so.
One does not hinder children from blowing [the *shofar*],
but [may] engage[13] with them until they learn [how to do so].
And one who is engaged
does not fulfill [his obligation].
And one who hears from one who is engaged
does not fulfill [his obligation].

9 The order of blowing [the *shofar*]
is three [blasts] of three apiece.
The length of the sustained blast
is three times that of a quavering blast.
If one blew the first blast,
and extended the second blast as long as two,

---

[13] Or "practice."

4:7 *passes before the Ark*: To lead the first part of the service.

[blow the shofar]: Or, prompt the one who does so.

the second one: Probably the prayer leader for the Additional service.

Hallel: Psalms 113–118.

4:8 *[Sabbath] limit*: Two thousand cubits beyond the city or town limit.

for the sake of a shofar: One may engage in these acts neither to deliver a *shofar* to a distant location nor to travel there in order to hear it.

Sabbath rest: Heb. *shevut*; see *Betsah* 5:2.

engaged: In teaching or practicing.

4:9 *three [blasts] of three*: These are the blasts he should properly have attached to the three sets of verses (Sovereignty, Remembrance, and *Shofar*) during the prayer when he had no *shofar*.

[the second] is only accounted to him as one.
One who recited the blessings
and afterward was provided with a *shofar*,
must blow sustained, quavering, and sustained three times.
Just as the public agent is obligated,
so too is each and every individual obligated.
Rabban Gamaliel says:
The public agent [in prayer]
enables the many to fulfill their obligation.

is only accounted to him as one: The lengthened blast was intended to serve as the third note of one set of sounds and also the first note of the next, but the mishnah rules that this is unacceptable.

recited the blessings: That is, recited the additional New Year prayer without having a *shofar* at his disposal.

and afterward: After reciting the prayer he obtained a *shofar*.

and sustained three times: Each set consists of three blasts (long, quavering, long), one set each for Sovereignty, Remembrance, and *Shofar*.

public agent, or prayer leader, *is obligated* to say the designated prayers on behalf of the congregation.

each and every individual…: Individuals who are capable of praying are not freed from their obligation to pray by the prayer leader, who prays on behalf of those incapable of doing so. The same is true for hearing the *shofar* blasts. Rabban Gamaliel disagrees.

Tractate Ta'anit

David Levine

Introduction

Overview

Tractate *Ta'anit* (lit. "affliction" or "fasting") describes the norms and practices that were prescribed by the Rabbis as communal responses to public distress, most especially drought.

Structure and Organization of the Tractate

The community responds to public catastrophe with rituals of mourning and penance: fasting, cessation of commerce and productive labor and minimizing occasions of pleasure and rejoicing (chapter 1). The tractate describes the sermons and prayers that were offered in these public assemblies (2:1–3). The fast-day liturgy has a unique structure and is described in detail (2:3–5, 3:9). The blowing of the *shofar* (ram's horn) figures prominently in these public rituals (1:6, 2:5), and "sounding the *shofar*" is one of the terms that designates communal fasts (chapter 3 *passim*).

Chapter 4 is devoted mostly to the institution of the *ma'amadot*, lit. "stations," groups of lay people who would assemble, some in their towns and villages, and some at the Temple in Jerusalem, at the same time that the priests in the Temple would be offering the continual offering (the *Tamid*) and the additional sacrifices of Sabbath and festivals. The tractate then gives, in a chronological aside, a listing of five disasters that befell "our ancestors" on the seventeenth of Tamuz and five on the ninth of Av (4:6), which is why these are fast days. The tractate closes with some law and lore about the ninth and fifteenth of Av (4:7–8).

Relationship to Scripture

The Bible speaks of a clear correlation between human disloyalty and divine wrath (e.g. Deuteronomy 11:16–17); communal distress is seen as conveying, either as punishment or as warning, divine displeasure with unacceptable human acts. Introspection, atonement, and a commitment to modify behavior are the means by which to resolve the crisis. This perception informs postbiblical Jewish religion and was shared by almost all ancient civilizations.

Ancient Jewish literature, from the Bible on, provides ample precedent for communal responses of gatherings, fasting, and prayer in times of trouble (e.g. Numbers 10:9, Joel 2:15–17, Judith 4:9–15; 1 Maccabees 3:44–54).

Main Ideas

Mediterranean cultures, past and present, diligently monitor their rainfall. Drought and irregular rains are the prevailing illustrations of public distress throughout *Ta'anit*. The first chapter of the tractate is devoted entirely to concern over rainfall. The chapter progresses chronologically from prayers for rain in early autumn, through initial anxiety over tarrying rain later in the season, to intensifying public response as the drought continues through the winter months. Insufficient and inappropriate rainfall engages much of the third chapter, which is devoted to listing different types of communal crises and the appropriate response to each.

The commemorative fast of the ninth of Av is of a different nature as it serves to mark the destruction of the Jerusalem temple as a fixed annual event. However, only two paragraphs deal with the ninth of Av (4:6–7), out of a total of thirty-four in the tractate. This marginality of the ninth of Av in the tractate corresponds to the Mishnah's lack of sustained interest in this commemorative fast. The editor of the Mishnah, Rabbi Judah the Patriarch, distinguished himself by promoting a policy of reconciliation and rehabilitation between the Jewish community in the Land of Israel and the Roman Empire. There is congruence between the diminished attention to the ninth of Av here and other traditions describing Rabbi Judah's attempts to abolish, or modify, public fasts that commemorate the Roman destruction of the Jerusalem temple.

The tractate mentions different groups and individuals who assisted in maintaining Temple activities, namely the rotation of priests responsible for the sacrificial routine and the groups of laymen that accompanied these priests (2:6–7, 4:2). These lay groups had an elaborate schedule of prayer, Torah reading, and other rituals during their week-long duty (4:3–4). There were also specific families who provided wood for the Temple altar and celebrated their contribution on designated days of the year (4:5). The idea that the people of Israel need to be connected with the Temple priests at the very moment that the priests are tending to their duties, is a quintessential rabbinic idea.

Two images of pre-70 Jerusalem present themselves at the beginning and end of tractate *Ta'anit*. The tractate opens with the manner in which concern for rain is included in the *Amidah* prayer. One opinion delays the request for rain for two weeks after the festival of Sukkot "so that the last person of Israel will have reached the Euphrates" after making pilgrimage for the festival (1:3). The last paragraph of the tractate speaks of young people of Jerusalem who "would go out and dance in the vineyards" as a courting custom on appointed days (4:8). The rhetoric seems to present this image of Jerusalem not only as reminiscence but also as an aspiration for the future.

Tractate Ta'anit

Chapter One

1:1–3 *Prayer for Rain in the Daily Prayer*

1 From when does one mention the "power of rain"?
R. Eliezer says:
From the initial holiday of the Festival.
R. Joshua says:
From the final holiday of the Festival.
R. Joshua said to him:
Since rains during the Festival are a sign of a curse,[1]
why should he mention them?

[1] **K, P:** "are not a sign of blessing."

There are two distinct sections in chapter 1. The first, 1:1–3, deals with prayers for rain and the rules for their insertion in the daily *Amidah* prayer; the second, 1:4–7, describes the developing communal response to a rainless autumn and beyond.

1:1 *the "power of rain"*: The "power of rain" is the sentence, "You cause wind to blow and rain to fall," that is added in the second blessing of the daily *Amidah* prayer (*Berakhot* 5:2). As a result the second blessing is called *Gevurot*, "powers" (*Rosh Hashanah* 4:5). Mentioning the "power of rain" will contrast below with "requesting rain" which is a season-appropriate addition to the ninth blessing of the *Amidah* directly requesting rain as part of God's sustenance.

from the initial/final holiday: A work-prohibited day during the course of Passover or Sukkot is called a *yom tov* (lit. "good day"), here translated as "holiday." The Mishnah is referring to the first day and eighth days of the autumn Sukkot festival.

the Festival: In talmudic usage the word "Festival" otherwise unmodified denotes the Sukkot festival.

a sign of a curse: Rainfall during the festival of Sukkot is considered a bad omen, indicating divine displeasure. Elsewhere, the Mishnah likens this to a servant handing his master a cup of wine and the master throwing the contents in the servant's face (*Sukkah* 2:9). During the festival people dwell in temporary booths outside their homes, and falling rain would make this duty uncomfortable or impossible. Another reason may be that rainfall during a time of pilgrimage will cause hardship, as is implied in Gamaliel's opinion, below 1:3.

why should he mention them? All agree that the mention of rain is season-dependent, as it is not said during the summer months. R. Joshua questions the need for this "mentioning" if rainfall is not wanted during the festival.

R. Eliezer said to him:
Indeed I did not say "to request" but only "to mention"—
"who causes the wind to blow and the rain to fall" in their due time.
[R. Joshua] said to him:
If so, let him always mention it!

2 One requests rains only in [immediate] anticipation[2] of the rains.
R. Judah says:
The prayer leader[3] on the final holiday of the Festival—
the last one mentions [rain], the first one does not;
On the first holiday of Passover—
the first [prayer leader] mentions [rain], the last does not.
Until when does one request rains?
R. Judah says:
Until Passover passes;
R. Meir says:
Until Nisan ends,
as it is said:
He has made the rain fall, the early rain and the late, as before.

[2] Lit. "adjacent to."   [3] Lit. "one passing before the ark."

I did not say: R. Eliezer makes the distinction between the mentioning of rain which lists rainfall as one of the divine attributes sustaining the world, and the request for rain which petitions God for rainfall in the present. The one is a praise of God, the other an explicit request.

in their due time: Listing God's actions that hail him as provider and sustainer of human life does not necessarily mean that every power mentioned is manifested always. Each divine action will occur in its own good time.

1:2 *One requests rain*: See 1:3.

R. Judah says: R. Judah's specification is based on R. Joshua's opinion in the previous mishnah that the "final" day of Sukkot is when one commences mentioning rain.

prayer leader: In anticipation of the communal *Amidah* prayer, the intended prayer leader would rise and "pass before" the Torah ark. This ark, or movable chest (see below 2:1), was at the front of the prayer hall. Hence, the idiom "*passing* before the ark" for the prayer leader.

last one…first one: On the morning of a holiday two *Amidah* prayers are recited, the first is the *Shaharit* (morning) service, and the second is the *Musaf* (additional) service. The "first one" is the *Shaharit* leader and the "last one" is the *Musaf* leader. The final holiday of Sukkot is the eighth day, called *Shemini Atseret* in post-talmudic tradition.

On the first holiday of Passover: The mentioning of rain in the *Amidah* prayer lasts for half a year, from the end of Sukkot until the first day of Passover.

Until when does one request the rains? As described here, requesting rain in the weekday *Amidah* continues even after mentioning rain has stopped. R. Judah says that the request for rain continues through the end of the Passover festival, however R. Meir prolongs this until the end of the month.

as it is said: Joel 2:23. The final word in this verse means "as before," but it can more literally be rendered as "in the first." It is therefore understood in this context as "during the first month," Nisan.

3 On the third of Marheshvan one requests rains;
Rabban Gamaliel says:
On the seventh of the month,
fifteen days after the Festival,
so that the last person of Israel will have reached the Euphrates.

1:4–7 *Communal Responses to Drought during Autumn and Winter*

4 If the seventeenth of Marheshvan came and rains had not fallen—
the individuals began fasting for three fast days;
one may eat and drink after dark,
and one is permitted to engage in labor,
in bathing, anointing, wearing sandals,
and sexual intercourse.[4]

5 If the first of Kislev has come and rains have not fallen—
the court decrees three fasts upon the public;

---

[4] Lit. "using the bed."

1:3 *on the third of Marheshvan*: According to the first opinion the request for rain in the weekday *Amidah* prayer commences on the tenth or eleventh day after Sukkot.

On the seventh: Rabban Gamaliel's dissenting opinion requires fifteen days to pass after the end of the festival to ensure that all pilgrims have made their way home.

last person of Israel: That is, those who had just been in Jerusalem on pilgrimage.

Euphrates: Any rainfall in the Land of Israel and its environs would not affect people beyond the perimeter signified by this river.

1:4 *if the seventeenth of Marheshvan*: In early autumn, the lack of rainfall is not yet construed as a serious problem, therefore the initial response is minor and does not involve the community as a whole.

individuals: The Mishnah is not clear about the people intended. The Yerushalmi explains that they are communal leaders; the Bavli explains that they are sages.

three fast days: All sequences of fast days referred to here are not on consecutive days, but rather occur on Mondays and Thursdays only: See below 1:6, 2:9.

eat and drink…bathing, anointing, wearing sandals, and sexual intercourse: This list parallels the activities that are associated with the Day of Atonement abstentions (*Yoma* 8:1), though not yet as severe (see below 1:6).

and one is permitted to engage in…: At this stage, the prohibitions include only eating and drinking, and do not extend to the nighttime.

1:5 *if the first of Kislev*: The ongoing lack of rainfall, although not yet late in the season, is perceived as a communal affair and the appropriate response encompasses the public as a whole.

the court is not identified.

three fasts: As before, Mondays and Thursdays only.

one may eat and drink after dark,
and one is permitted to engage in labor,
in bathing, anointing, wearing sandals,
and sexual intercourse.

6 If these [fasts] have passed and have not been answered—
the court decrees another three fasts upon the public;
one eats and drinks [only] while it is still day,
and one is prohibited from engaging in labor, in bathing, anointing, wearing sandals,
and sexual intercourse;
and the bathhouses are locked.
If these [fasts] have passed and have not been answered—
the court decrees another seven fasts,
totaling thirteen fasts upon the public.
These [fasts] go beyond the former ones,
for on these one sounds the *shofar* and the shops are locked.
On Mondays they partially open (the shops) with [the arrival of] darkness,
and on Thursdays they are permitted (to open) because of the honor due to the Sabbath.

7 If these [fasts] have passed and have not been answered—

one may eat and drink after dark and one is permitted: The normative framework laid out in the previous mishnah applies in this case as well. The duration of the fast is sunrise to sunset and the prohibitions include only eating and drinking.

1:6 *three fasts upon the public*: The number of public fasts has remained the same, and the intensification will be in the duration of the fast and in the abstentions mandated.

one eats and drinks [only] while it is still day: Only while it is still afternoon of the previous day is food consumption permitted, but once the sun has set the fast day and its prohibitions are in full effect. This fast day lasts for over twenty-four hours, from sundown to sundown.

and one is prohibited from engaging: Not only is eating prohibited, but also labor and the additional four actions of bathing, anointing in oil, wearing leather shoes, and having sexual intercourse. At this point the communal fast has the same halakhic-behavioral framework as the Day of Atonement (see *Yoma* 8:1).

the bathhouses are locked: This is not only to enforce the ban on bathing, but also to make a public display of the disruption of routine activities caused by the ongoing crisis.

the court decrees another seven fasts: This set of seven fasts, observed on Mondays and Thursdays, would span almost four weeks. Extending the number of fasts in the set to seven is an expression of the growing intensity of the situation.

These [fasts] go beyond the former ones: Even though the basic Day of Atonement-like character is common to both the previous set of three fasts and this set of seven, the latter set has additional observances associated with it.

one sounds: The ritual context for the blowing of the *shofar* is not spelled out here, and only alluded to in parallel texts (below, 2:5).

On Mondays…on Thursdays…: Dispensation is provided for acquiring necessities and preparing for the Sabbath.

the honor due to the Sabbath: See below 2:7, 4:3, 4:7.

1:7 *If these [fasts] have passed and have not been answered*: Three sets of communal fasts have not been effective in alleviating the drought. The communal fasting is discontinued because "one does not cause the public too much hardship." However, the usual routine cannot be resumed.

one lessens commerce, construction and planting,
betrothal and marriage, and greetings between people,
as [is fitting to] people who are rebuked by God.
The individuals resume their fasting until Nisan ends.
If Nisan has ended and then rains fall,
it a sign of a curse, as it is said:
It is the season of the wheat-harvest etc.

Chapter Two

2:1–2 *The Fast-Day Ritual in the Town Square*

2 How is the order of fast days [performed]?
They carry the [Torah] ark out to the town square,
and place burnt ash on the ark
and on the heads of the *Nasi* and *Av Bet Din*,
and every person places it on his head.
The elder among them speaks words of admonition to them:

---

one lessens: Regular social and economic activities are brought to a minimum. This behavior combines that of a mourner with that of one who is excommunicated.

people who are rebuked by God: The ongoing distress and the failure of the communal responses clearly indicates to the Mishnah that the members of the community have incurred divine anger.

individuals resume their fasting: See above, 1:4.

If Nisan has ended: Rain as the harvest ripens is harmful and therefore an ominous sign.

as it is said: In this biblical narrative (1 Samuel 12:17) Samuel wishes to mortify the people by causing rainfall at an unusual and destructive time.

2:1 *carry the [Torah] ark*: The chest containing the Torah scrolls was transportable, and was usually carried into the main hall of the synagogue from a side room. Ancient Galilean-type synagogues reflect this practice and have no apse or niche that might indicate a fixed location of the scrolls.

town square: Convening in a central location serves both to enable mass participation and to underscore the severity of the occasion by interrupting regular practice. On the role and status of the town square, see *Sanhedrin* 10:6, *Nedarim* 5:5, *Megillah* 3:1.

burnt ash: Both ark and participants are visibly implicated in this act, which both expresses mourning and marks disgrace.

Nasi and Av Bet Din: The active participation of communal leaders—"patriarch" and "head of the court"—conveys a sense of urgency. These titles were used on both the local and national levels.

and every person: Social solidarity and cohesion are underscored when there is a leveling of all participants who don the ashes together.

The elder: The Mishnah's description of the public ritual turns to a second component—the fast-day sermon. The person delivering the sermon is distinct from the two communal leaders mentioned above. This elder is identified in later talmudic tradition as a rabbinic sage advanced in wisdom and years.

"Our brethren,
it is not said of the people of Nineveh
that 'God saw their sackcloth and their fasting,'
rather *God saw their deeds, how they turned away from their evil way.*"
And in tradition it says:
Rend your hearts, rather than your garments, and return to the Lord your God.

2 [When] they have stood[5] in prayer,
they assign a prayer leader,
an elder and competent man,
who has children but whose house is empty,
so that he may be wholehearted in prayer.
He recites before them twenty-four blessings,
eighteen daily ones, to which he adds an additional six.

2:3–5 *Fast-Day Prayer*

3 And these [six additions] are:
(1) Remembrance [verses],
(2) and *Shofar* [verses],
(3) *In my distress I called to the Lord and he answered me,*
(4) *I turn my eyes to the mountains,*
(5) *Out of the depths I call You, O Lord,*
(6) *A prayer of a lowly man when he is faint.*

---

[5] K adds "before them."

"*Our brethren*": This salutation expresses the solidarity and "leveling" of the community in times of crisis.

"*God saw their deeds…*": Jonah 3:10.

tradition: The reference here is to the prophetic books of the biblical canon.

Rend your hearts…: Joel 2:13.

2:2 *stood in prayer*: The Mishnah continues its description of the fast-day ritual, with the communal prayer as a third component.

they assign a prayer leader: The literal meaning of the idiom "they lower (cause to descend) before the ark" is similar to the designation of the prayer leader as one who "passes before the ark" (above 1:1).

an elder: The "elder" here seems distinct from the previous "elder" who has delivered the sermon.

competent man…empty: The person leading prayer should have the knowledge and ability to lead the community in prayer, but also be experiencing distress himself.

eighteen daily ones: Different components of the daily *Amidah*, also referred to as the "Prayer of Eighteen" or "the Prayer," are alluded to throughout the Mishnah (e.g. *Berakhot* 4:3, 5:2, *Rosh Hashanah* 4:5).

2:3 *and these [six additions] are*: This mishnah enumerates the text of the six additional blessings. The Remembrances blessing collates verses that mention God remembering his covenant with the forefathers. The verses of the *Shofar* (ram's horn) blessing articulate the themes of the praise of God and the heralding of redemption (compare *Rosh Hashanah* 4:5–6). The next four blessings are comprised of texts of Psalms beseeching God for deliverance (the first verses of Psalms 120, 121, 130, and 102).

R. Judah says:
He did not have to say Remembrance [verses] and *Shofar* [verses],
but instead of them he says:
If there is a famine in the land, a pestilence,
The word of the Lord which came to Jeremiah concerning the droughts.
And he says their endings.[6]

4 For the first he says:
"May he who answered Abraham on Mount Moriah
answer you and listen to the voice of your outcry this day.
Praised are you, who redeems Israel."
For the second he says:
"May he who answered your ancestors at the Sea of Reeds
answer you and listen to the voice of your outcry this day.
Praised are you, who remembers things forgotten."
For the third he says:
"May he who answered Joshua at Gilgal
answer you and listen to the voice of your outcry this day.
Praised are you, who hears the sound of the *shofar*."
For the fourth he says:
"May he who answered Samuel at Mitzpah
answer you and listen to the voice of your outcry this day.
Praised are you, who hears outcry."
For the fifth he says:
"May he who answered Elijah on Mount Carmel
answer you and listen to the voice of your outcry this day.
Praised are you, who hears prayer."
For the sixth he says:
"May he who answered Jonah in the belly of the fish
answer you and listen to the voice of your outcry this day.
Praised are you, who answers in times of distress."
For the seventh he says:
"May he who answered David and Solomon his son in Jerusalem,
answer you and listen to the voice of your outcry this day.
Praised are you, who has mercy on the Land."

[6] Lit. "their seals."

R. Judah says: This opinion seems uncomfortable with including blessings that are strongly associated with the Rosh Hashanah liturgy and offers two alternative biblical texts that fit the current setting. The first blessing speaks of calamity, supplication, and God's response (1 Kings 8:37). In the other blessing the prophet beseeches God for relief from drought (Jeremiah 14:1).

2:3-4 *their endings*: What follows in 2:4 is a list of similarly constructed endings for the additional blessings. Each ending includes a supplication referring to a biblical figure whose distress was alleviated by divine response. The glaring issue is the numeric discrepancy between the six additional blessings of the previous mishnah and the seven conclusions laid out in this latter mishnah. The simplest answer is to view the first "conclusion" as appended to the regular Redemption (*Ge'ulah*) blessing of the weekday *Amidah*, which has an identical ending ("Praised are you, O God, who redeems of Israel"). This can also imply that the special fast-day blessings were added to the daily *Amidah* after the seventh, "Redemption" blessing.

5 It once happened
in the days of R. Halafta and R. Hananiah b. Teradion,
that a person led public prayer[7]
and concluded the blessing in its entirety.
And [the congregation] responded[8] "Amen."
"Blow [the *shofar*], priests, blow!
May he who answered Abraham on Mount Moriah
answer you and listen to the voice of your outcry this day";
"Sound [the *shofar*], sons of Aaron, sound!
May he who answered your ancestors at the Sea of Reeds
answer you and listen to the voice of your outcry this day."
And when the matter came before the Sages they said:
Such was not our practice
except at the eastern gates (of the Temple) and on the Temple Mount.

2:6–7 *Priests and Fast Days*

6 On the first three fast days,
members of the [priestly] watch [serving that week] fast

[7] Lit. "passed before the ark." [8] Medieval emendation yielded "they did not respond."

2:5 *It once happened*: For other such anecdotes in this tractate, see 3:6, 8, 9.

concluded the blessing in its entirety: The reference is to each of the seven special fast-day blessings.

[the congregation] responded "Amen": The original text indicates that the blessing and communal response concluded before the *shofar* blowing and before the recitation of the "may he who answered" sentences. A medieval emendation renders the text as "they did not respond 'Amen,'" so identifying an error in the congregation's response to the blessing (see below).

"Blow"…"Sound"…: Two alternating types of a *shofar* blast are indicated. Other contexts identify the "blow" as one simple blast and the "sound" as several shorter blasts (*Rosh Hashanah* 4:9).

"priests"…"sons of Aaron": The prominence of the priests reflects the temple-oriented nature of what was done in this liturgical anecdote.

"may he who answered": The sequence described is as follows: (1) The prayer leader completes a blessing; (2) the congregation responds; (3) the *shofar* blowing is announced; (4) the "He who answered" sentence is recited. The actual blowing of the *shofar* is not mentioned; see below.

the matter came before the Sages…: The disapproval of "the Sages" stems from Temple practice being observed outside of Jerusalem and after its destruction. What precisely was at issue in this case? Talmudic commentators offer three answers: (1) The response to the blessing was not "Amen," but the more elaborate Temple response to blessings. This interpretation is dependent on emending the text here (see above). (2) Proper practice outside the Temple did not include sounding the *shofar* after each blessing; the instrumental response was reserved for Temple precincts. This interpretation bases itself on there being no mention of *shofar* blasts in the previous mishnayot describing the fast day prayer. (3) The Temple blessings had the "He who answered" sentence recited (repeated?) after the blessing with the *shofar* being blasted as a response. This interpretation is sensitive to the different placement of the "He who answered" sentence in 2:4 and in 2:5 and uses material in other rabbinic texts for elucidation.

2:6 *first three…second three…final seven*: These refer to the three stages of communal fasting that are described above 1:5–6, where each stage is more severe than the previous one.

priestly watch: The priests were divided into twenty-four lineage-based duty groups (1 Chronicles 24:7–18, see below 4:2), with every group or "watch" officiating in turn for a week, from Sabbath to Sabbath.

but do not complete [the day of fasting],
and members of the paternal house [serving that day] do not fast at all;
On the second three [fast days],
members of the [priestly] watch fast and complete,
and members of the paternal house fast but do not complete;
On the final seven [fast days],
both fast and complete—
the words of R. Joshua.
The Sages say:
On the first three fast days,
neither fast at all;
on the second three [fast days],
members of the [priestly] watch fast but do not complete,
and members of the paternal house do not fast at all;
On the final seven [fast days],
members of the [priestly] watch fast and complete,
and members of the paternal house fast but do not complete.

7 Members of the [priestly] watch [on duty]
are permitted to drink wine
at night but not during the day;
members of the paternal house [are permitted]
neither during the day nor during the night.
Members of the [priestly] watch and members of the *ma'amad*
are forbidden from cutting hair and washing clothes.
On Thursdays they are permitted
because of the honor due to the Sabbath.

paternal house: Each priestly watch was comprised of several "paternal houses" who were responsible for specific days of the "watch's" week.

fast and complete: A completed fast is one observed until nightfall.

2:7 *Members of the priestly watch*: Those who were not on duty that day (but some other day of the order's week) could drink wine at night. This mishnah digresses and speaks of Temple routine beyond the issue of fast days.

members of the paternal house: The family officiating that day could not drink wine from the previous night and throughout the day.

ma'amad: These were groups of laypeople corresponding to the watches of the priests; they symbolically represented the people of Israel on whose behalf the Temple sacrifices were executed. On the *ma'amad*, its composition, and liturgy, see below 4:2–4.

forbidden from cutting hair and washing clothes: This is usually explained as means of ensuring that haircutting and laundry be done prior to the week of the *ma'amad*.

the honor due to the Sabbath: See 1:6, 4:3, 4:7.

2:8–10 Days on Which Fasts Cannot be Decreed

8 Any [day of which it is] written in the Scroll of Fasts,
"Not to eulogize"—
[the day] before is [also] forbidden, but [the day] after is permitted.
R. Yose says:
[The day] before and [the day] after are forbidden.
"Not to fast"—
[both the day] before and [the day] after are permitted.
R. Yose says:
[The day] before is forbidden, [but the day] after is permitted.

9 One may not decree a fast day upon the public beginning on a Thursday,
so as not to increase the [market] prices.
Rather, the first three fast days are Monday–Thursday–Monday,
and the second three are Thursday–Monday–Thursday.
R. Yose says:
Just as the first [set] do not [begin] on a Thursday,
similarly the second [set] and the final [set of seven].

10 One may not decree a fast day upon the public
on a New Moon or during Hanukkah or Purim,
but if they had begun [a set of fast days] they do not stop [the sequence],
the words of Rabban Gamaliel.
R. Meir said:
Even though Rabban Gamaliel said "they do not stop,"

2:8 *Scroll of Fasts*: The Mishnah recognizes the authority of a Second Temple list of celebratory days on which fasting and eulogizing are prohibited. This list is in Aramaic and in a brief sentence identifies the reason for each celebration. The eight days of Hanukkah and the two days of Purim are the best-known and most enduring of these celebrations. The importance of this scroll is underscored by the fact that, besides the Bible, it is the only book quoted in the Mishnah.

"Not to eulogize"…"Not to fast": The "Scroll of Fasts" indicates two levels of prohibition to be observed on these days. The stricter level permits neither eulogies nor fasts on the day of celebration; the other level prohibits only fasting.

2:9 *so as not to increase the [market] prices*: Thursdays are days of higher market demand in anticipation of Sabbath, so if a set of fasts is declared to begin on a Thursday prices might spike because of increased demand. If the sequence of fasts begins on a Monday the more usual and moderate demand will control prices and avert a price boost.

the first three…second three…: This opinion applies the above guideline only to the first set of communal fasts (see above 1:5–6), the logic being that the subsequent sets of fasts (if necessary) directly continue the former.

R. Yose says: It is unclear whether this opinion is concerned with market prices, creating a similar sequence as before, or a desire to create a lull between the sets of communal fasts.

2:10 *if they had begun…they do not stop*: If a set of fasts has already commenced and the listed festivals fall on one of the following Mondays or Thursdays, then the fasting proceeds.

R. Meir said: R. Meir claims that the above opinion should be modified. If communal fasts coincide with the New Moon, Hanukkah, or Purim they are not to be observed to their conclusion (nightfall).

he conceded that they do not complete [the whole day of fasting].
The same applies if the ninth of Av falls on a Friday.

Chapter Three

3:1–2 *Irregular Rainfall*

3 The aforementioned order of these fast days
is [applied] during [the time of] the first rainfall.[9]
However, if the crops change,
one sounds the *shofar* for them immediately.
Similarly, if there was a lapse of forty days between rainfalls,
one sounds the *shofar* for them immediately,
because it is a calamity of drought.
  2 If [the rains] fall [appropriately] for crops but not for trees,
for the trees but not for the crops,
for both of these but not for cisterns, pits, and caves—
one sounds the *shofar* for them immediately.

[9] Lit. "first fructification."

The same applies: That the fast is not completed.

the ninth of Av falls on a Friday: In anticipation of the Sabbath the commemorative fast (see below 4:4–6) is terminated early.

3:1 *The aforementioned order*: The gradual response of the community, building up in intensity as detailed in 1:5–6, applies only in mid-autumn when the early rains are expected.

However, if the crops change: Change color, show signs of failing. If crops or plants need immediate irrigation, a gradual response is not sufficient. The urgency calls for timely action.

one sounds the shofar for them immediately: The context here indicates that in this and subsequent instances of distress, the communal response ("one sounds the *shofar* immediately") is similar to the final stage of the gradual framework described in chapter 1. The unique characteristic of this final stage of seven fasts is the sounding of the *shofar*.

sounds the shofar: Throughout chapter 3, the term "one sounds the *shofar* for them" signifies the communal response that in previous chapters is alluded to as "a fast upon the public." These two different phrases are used for the creation and observance of communal responses to distress: "sounding the *shofar*" in chapter 3 and "decreeing a fast (upon the public)" in chapters 1 and 2. "Decreeing a fast" occurs in chapter 3 only within a secondary literary level, in the anecdotes.

forty days: Intermittent rainfall is also a cause for communal response.

3:2 *crops…trees…cisterns…*: When seeds are sown in a field or garden they need light rain to take root and sprout. Heavy rains will wash them away. Trees require heavier rains to penetrate the top soil and reach their roots. Too light a rain will not provide them with water. Sufficient quantity of water, stored for subsequent use, depends on absolute amounts of rain. If even one of these needs is not met, there is reason to "sound the *shofar*."

cisterns, pits, and caves: Different facilities for storing water, manmade and natural.

3:3–4 *A Town and its Surroundings*

3 Similarly, a town on which rains did not fall—
as it is written: *I will make it rain on one town, and not on another, one field received rain, etc.*[10]—
that town fasts and sounds the *shofar*,
and all its surroundings fast but do not sound the *shofar*.
R. Aqiva says:
They sound the *shofar* but do not fast.
  4 Similarly, a town that suffers from pestilence or collapse (of structures)—
that town fasts and sounds the *shofar*,
and all its surroundings fast but do not sound the *shofar*.
R. Aqiva says:
They sound the *shofar* but do not fast.
What is pestilence?
A town that sends out five hundred adult men[11]
in which three dead have gone out during three consecutive days:[12]
that is pestilence.
Less than this is not pestilence.

3:5–7 *Other Threats*

5 For these one sounds the *shofar* everywhere:
for blight and for mildew,

[10] K quotes more of this verse. [11] Lit. "infantry."
[12] Lit. "one after the other"; P: "three people have died one after the other, one after the other."

3:3 *I will make it rain on one town…*: Amos 4:7. The verse is quoted to illustrate the significance of uneven rainfall in a given region. The plight is to be understood as general divine displeasure, which is not limited to the town experiencing the drought (see ibid. 4:6–11). The Talmud states that "both cities are being cursed."

that town…its surrounding…: The differentiation between fasting and sounding the *shofar* is necessary in anticipation of the partial participation of the affected town's neighbors who only observe one element. The afflicted town observes both.

fast but do not sound the shofar: The participation of the surrounding, unaffected areas is not merely to express solidarity, but to acknowledge common responsibility for the crisis.

3:4 *Similarly*: The differentiated communal response to unevenly distributed distress extends to situations besides lack of rain.

pestilence: The epidemic spread of a lethal disease.

collapse: Unexplained or uncontrolled structural collapse.

What is pestilence? The definition of the mortality rate that would define a plague is three dead in three days in a town of five hundred military-aged male adults (the total population would amount to between three and four times that number).

that sends out: For military service.

3:5 *everywhere…a roaming calamity*: All areas are considered equally affected when the crisis is of an uncontained, spreading nature. Therefore the response is the same all over the region. "Everywhere" does not mean the world over, but in the region (other sources speak of the "province").

blight…mildew…locusts…caterpillars: These are crop hazards. For similar lists see Leviticus 26:6, 1 Kings 8:37, Amos 4:9–10.

for locusts and for caterpillars,
for wild beasts and for war—
one sounds the *shofar*
because it is a roaming calamity.

6 It once happened that
elders descended from Jerusalem to their towns
and decreed a fast
because blight [the size of] an oven's opening
had been seen in Ashkelon;
and further decreed a fast[13]
because wolves had eaten two children in Transjordan.
R. Yose says:
Not because they had eaten,
but because they had been seen.

7 For these they sound the *shofar* on the Sabbath:
for a town encircled by gentiles[14] or [flooded by] a river,
or a ship sinking at sea.
R. Yose says:
[The *shofar* is sounded] for help
but not for pleading.[15]
Simeon of Timnah says:
Also for pestilence,
but the Sages did not agree with him.

3:8 Abundant Rain

8 For any distress that befalls[16] the public they sound the *shofar*,
except for abundant rains.

[13] K, P add "on the next day." [14] P: "an army." [15] Lit. "shouting."
[16] Lit. "that might not befall" (euphemistically).

3:6 *It once happened*: This anecdote illustrates a sweeping response to a local occurrence. The arrival of "elders" indicates that this is a countrywide crisis, thus illustrating the preceding mishnah. For R. Yose, the mere sighting is warrant for fasting and concern.

3:7 *on the Sabbath*: The urgency of the problem does not allow for any delay in response.

help...pleading: A crucial distinction is introduced between a functional blowing of the *shofar* intended to communicate the distress and summon help, and a ritual "sounding of the *shofar*." Yose's dissenting opinion permits only the former and rules out the latter. There are two ways this opinion can be understood. (1) Yose prohibits a ritual blowing of the *shofar* (pleading) on the Sabbath, but has no argument with its permissibility on a weekday. (2) Yose does not allow any ritual response at all when dealing with this kind of distress. The urgency is such that any available person must engage in rescue, not ritual. The *shofar* is only to be used when summoning help.

pestilence: Simeon of Timnah wanted to add pestilence to this list of urgent, non-delayable woes.

3:8 *for any distress*: The survey of the range of predicaments and their assorted responses culminates with this generalization.

except for abundant rains: In the dry climate of the Land of Israel, one is hard put to perceive too much rain as a problem.

It once happened that
they said to Honi the *Me'agel*:
Pray that rains may fall.
He said to them:
Go and bring in your Passover ovens so they will not become moldy.
He prayed, but rains did not fall.
What did he do?[17]
He drew a circle, stood inside it, and said:
Master of the world,
your children have depended on me,[18]
for I am as a household member before you;
I swear by your great name
that I will not move from this place
until you have mercy on your children.
Rain began drizzling.
He said:
This is not what I requested, rather rains of cisterns, pits, and caves.
[The rains] fell harshly.
He said:
This is not what I requested, rather rains of good will, blessing, and generosity.
[The rains] fell appropriately,

---

[17] **K, P** lack this line.   [18] Lit. "have set their faces upon me."

It once happened: The text presents this story as illustrating the previous sentence. However, the story is exceptional in many ways. Its length and detail are unequalled in the Mishnah. Its protagonist Honi is not mentioned in any other context in rabbinic literature, nor does his behavior conform to accepted rabbinic norms and sensibilities. Onias the rainmaker is mentioned by Josephus (*Antiquities* 14:22–4).

Honi the Me'agel: The appellation is usually understood as "circle drawer" and therefore a reference to the circle Honi drew. Another possible interpretation is a person who seals roofs by compressing the mortar with a roller (see *Makkot* 2:1, *Mo'ed Qatan* 1:10). The same word also denotes pressing figs into storage jars at *Ma'aserot* 1:8.

Passover ovens: The drought continued into late winter/early spring, when preparations for the *Passover* sacrifice would have started. Honi exhibits extreme self-assurance when he counsels protection from the yet-to-be-realized promise of rainfall.

He drew a circle: Drawing a circle can be viewed either as a means of protection when attempting to manipulate (super)natural forces, or as expressing an ultimatum.

I am as a household member: This self-perception is echoed by Simeon b. Shatah later on in the story.

I swear by your great name: The power and efficacy of God's name are utilized to force God into providing rain. This irony adds to the picture of Honi's insolence.

this place: The circle he drew.

This is not what I requested: The ensuing audacious negotiation between Honi and God confirms Honi as unique in maneuvering the forces of nature.

until [the people of] Israel climbed from Jerusalem to the Temple Mount
on account of the rains.
They came and said to him,
Just as you prayed for them to fall, pray they depart.
He said to them,
Go and see if the Stone of the Seekers is dissolved.
Simeon b. Shatah sent [a message] to him [saying],
Were you not Honi, I would decree your excommunication,[19]
but what can I do to you?
For you act familiarly before God
and he fulfills your wish,
like a son who acts familiarly before his father,
and [his father] fulfils his wishes.
Of you Scripture says:
Your father and mother will rejoice, and she who bore you will exult.

3:9 *Rain during a Fast*

9 If they had been fasting
and rains fell before sunrise,
they do not complete [the fast];

---

[19] K, P: "you are worthy of excommunication."

---

to the Temple Mount: A high point in the city, to avoid the rising waters.

pray they depart: This is the rather tenuous connection to the stated ruling that abundant rains are no cause for communal response. The problem is that the story is not about communal response, but rather the intercession of an endowed individual.

Stone of the Seekers: This was a well-known high point on the Temple Mount. The Talmud explains its name as a place where lost objects might be retrieved from those who had found them.

Simeon b. Shatah: In contradistinction to Honi, Simeon b. Shatah is part of the world of the rabbis, a link in the chain of tradition (*Avot* 1:8) who represents established, mainstream religiosity in the story.

I would decree your excommunication: This potential censure serves to set Honi and his behavior apart from routine expectation.

familiarly: Another meaning of this Hebrew root is "to sin." The choice of language conveys both the intimacy and the problematic nature of Honi's behavior as a religious paradigm.

a son: Perhaps the family metaphor suggests that not everything accepted and contained within the family is similarly regarded as legitimate outside.

Your mother and father…: Proverbs 23:25.

3:9 *they had been fasting*: During a communal fast for rainfall it actually rains, presumably rendering the fast unnecessary. However, the obligation to observe the fast-day prohibitions is perceived as independent of its (realized) purpose and may still be incumbent upon the community.

sunrise: The sunrise-to-sunset time unit can be a fast period in and of itself. This may be the reason a fast can be unexpectedly terminated before sunrise, since the core period has not begun.

if after sunrise,
they complete [the fast].
R. Eliezer says:
Before midday,
they do not complete [the fast];
after midday,
they complete [the fast].
It once happened that
they decreed a fast in Lod
and it rained for them before midday.
R. Tarfon said to them:
Go out and eat and drink and celebrate a holiday.
They went out and ate and drank and celebrated a holiday,
and came together at dusk and recited the Great *Hallel*.
[What is the Great *Hallel*?
Praise the God of gods, His grace is eternal.
Praise the Lord of lords, His grace is eternal.][20]

Chapter Four

4:1 *Priestly Blessing*

4 On three occasions throughout the year—
on fast days, *ma'amadot*, and the Day of Atonement—
the priests raise their hands four times during the day—

[20] **K** and **P** add this sentence.

---

complete the fast: A full, completed fast concludes at nightfall (compare above 2:6, 2:9).

midday: Halfway through the core period of the fast. When the bigger part of the day has been spent in observance of the fast-day prohibitions, it must be completed.

It once happened: This legal anecdote mirrors R. Eliezer's opinion that the cut-off point, after which a fast must be completed, is midday. The anecdote is situated in Lod, R. Eliezer and R. Tarfon's city of residence.

Great Hallel: Psalm 136 is called the "Great *Hallel*". It repeats the refrain "His benevolence is eternal" twenty-six times. The liturgical recitation of Psalms 113 to 118 is known as the "Egyptian *Hallel*" (an allusion to Psalm 114:1) or simply as "the *Hallel*"; see below 4:4.

4:1 *three occasions…four times*: On each of these occasions there would be four instances of the priestly blessing. As noted in the Talmud, there is in fact no additional service on fast days or (necessarily) during the *ma'amadot*. The Talmud emends the text and harmonizes it with this liturgical practice.

raise their hands: The priestly blessing is called "raising of hands." The priests stand facing the congregation while raising their hands and reciting the biblical blessing of Aaron and his sons (Numbers 6:22–27; *Sotah* 7:6, *Tamid* 7:2).

at the morning service, the additional service, the afternoon service, and at the closing of the gates.

4:2–4 Ma'amadot

2 What are the *ma'amadot*?
Since it is written:
Command the children of Israel and say to them, My offering, My food…—
and how can a person's sacrifice be offered when he is not standing over it?—
the early prophets established twenty-four watches,
and on each watch there was a *ma'amad* in Jerusalem
of priests, Levites, and Israelites.
When the time came for a watch to ascend [to Jerusalem],
its priests and Levites would go to Jerusalem
and the Israelites of that watch would gather in their towns
and read the story of creation.

3 [The members of the *ma'amad* would fast four days a week,
from Monday to Thursday.
They would not fast on Friday because of the honor due to the Sabbath.
nor on Sunday so that they would not emerge from rest and pleasure
to hardship and fast, and die.][21]
On Sunday [they would read]: *In the beginning* and *Let there be firmament*;
on Monday: *Let there be firmament* and *Let the waters be gathered*;
on Tuesday: *Let the waters be gathered* and *Let there be lights*;
on Wednesday: *Let there be lights* and *Let the waters be filled*;
on Thursday: *Let the waters be filled*; *Let the earth bring forth*;
on Friday: *Let the earth bring forth* and *The heavens and earth were finished*.

---

[21] These two sentences are lacking in all medieval manuscripts and were erroneously added to the text of the Mishnah in the *editio princeps* of Naples 1492.

---

closing of the gates: This can be a reference to the Temple gates that close with the conclusion of the day's service at dusk, or to the heavenly gates that remain open throughout the solemn day that is now at its end. It is also the name given to the extra liturgy that ends such a day.

4:2 *ma'amadot*: Lit. "stations." See above 2:7. The daily sacrifices are portrayed in this verse as an obligation of the entire people—*Command the children of Israel* (Numbers 28:2). The actual execution is, of course, the priests' duty. However, a symbolic representation of the nation was to be present. This is presented as an ancient practice instituted by "early prophets."

watches: See above, 2:7.

in Jerusalem…in their towns: The description indicates that members of the *ma'amad* on duty could be found either in Jerusalem or gathered in the central towns of their districts.

read the story of creation: Genesis 1:1–2:3 as detailed below.

4:3 *on Sunday*: The portion of the day included the corresponding day of creation and its morrow. *In the beginning*—Genesis 1:1–5; *Let there be firmament*—Genesis 1:6–8; *Let the waters be gathered*—Genesis 1:9–13; *Let there be lights*—Genesis 1:14–19; *Let the waters be filled*—Genesis 1:20–23; *Let the earth bring forth*—Genesis 1:24–28; *The heavens and earth were finished*—Genesis 2:1–3.

A long paragraph is read by two people,
and a short one by one person,
for the morning service and the additional service.
In the afternoon they convene and recite orally, as the *Shema* is recited.
On Friday in the afternoon service they would not convene
because of the honor due to the Sabbath.

4 Any day that has *Hallel* does not have a *ma'amad* during the morning;
an additional sacrifice, does not have [a *ma'amad*] during the closing of the gates;
a wood offering, does not have [a *ma'amad*] during the afternoon—
the words of R. Aqiva.
Ben Azzai said to him,
This is how R. Joshua would teach:
[Any day that has] an additional sacrifice does not have [a *ma'amad*] during the afternoon;
a wood offering, does not have [a *ma'amad*] during the closing of the gates.
R. Aqiva retracted [his former opinion] and taught as Ben Azzai.

4:5 *The Wood Offering*

5 The times for the wood [offering] of the priests and people were nine:[22]
(1) on the first of Nisan,
[the offering of] the family[23] of Arah from [the tribe of][24] Judah.
(2) on the twentieth of Tammuz,
[the offering of] the family of David from [the tribe of] Judah.
(3) on the fifth of Av,
[the offering of] the family of Par'osh from [the tribe of] Judah.
(4) on the seventh [of Av],
[the offering of] the family of Yonadav b. Rekhav.

---

[22] K, P: "The time...on the ninth." [23] Lit. "sons," and so throughout.
[24] Lit. "son," and so throughout.

---

long paragraph...short one: A long paragraph had six or more verses, so that each reader would have at least three verses in his segment.

recite orally, as the Shema is recited: Not as a liturgical reading from a Torah scroll.

because of the honor due to the Sabbath: See 1:6, 2:7, 4:7.

4:4 *Hallel*: Psalms 113–118 are recited on the three pilgrimage festivals, Hanukkah, and in later talmudic tradition, on the New Moon. It is sometimes called the "Egyptian *Hallel*" (because of the reference to the exodus from Egypt in 114:1) and is distinct from from the "Great *Hallel*" (above 3:9).

does not have [a ma'amad]: These days do not have the Torah-reading service described above.

additional sacrifice: Offered after the morning sacrifice on Sabbaths, New Moons, and festivals (Numbers 28).

wood offering: See Nehemiah 10:35, and the next mishnah.

4:5 *The times...were nine*: Manuscripts read: "The time...was on the ninth," making this an independent sentence providing a truncated date.

(5) on the tenth [of Av],
[the offering of] the family of Sena'ah from [the tribe of] Benjamin.
(6) on the fifteenth [of Av],
[the offering of] the family of Zattu from [the tribe of] Judah.
Together with them
priests and Levites
and all who were unsure of their tribe,
and [the family of] pestle smugglers and [the family of] fig pressers.
(7) on the twentieth [of Av],
[the offering of] the family of Pahat Moab from [the tribe of] Judah.
(8) on the twentieth of Elul,
[the offering of] the family of Adin from [the tribe of] Judah.
(9) on the first of Tevet,
the family of Par'osh returned for a second time.
On the first of Tevet there was no *ma'amad*,
because it had *Hallel* and an additional sacrifice and a wood offering.

4:6–7 *Seventeenth of Tammuz and Ninth of Av*

6 Five things happened to our ancestors on the seventeenth of Tammuz,
and five things on the ninth of Av.
On the seventeenth of Tammuz:
(1) the tablets were broken;
(2) the continual offering was abolished;
(3) the city was breached;
(4) Apostemos burned the Torah; and
(5) erected a statue in the Temple.

from [the tribe of] Judah…Benjamin: The families listed are among those returning from the Babylonian exile (Ezra 2, Nehemiah 7), except for the Rekhavite clan who are mentioned as tent dwellers who eschewed agriculture and refrained from drinking wine (Jeremiah 35). The returnees were descendants of those exiled from the destroyed kingdom of Judah, hence the ubiquity of that tribe in the list.

and all who were unsure: This is probably a general invitation to all of uncertain lineage to join the celebration on this date, although we find reference to priests who could not establish their ancestry (Nehemiah 7:64). The courting event on the fifteenth of Av is similarly inclusive (2:8).

pestle smugglers and…fig pressers: Parallel sources relate the story of people who smuggled wood and first fruits for the Temple in defiance of royal persecution. The figs and pestles were part of their ruse.

first of Tevet: This day had *Hallel* because of Hanukkah, an additional sacrifice because of the New Moon, and a wood offering of the Par'osh family. The *ma'amad* Torah-reading could not take place that day.

4:6 *tablets were broken*: Exodus 32:19.

continual offering the Tamid was abolished: Perhaps during the Seleucid decrees of 167–164 BCE, perhaps later in besieged Jerusalem during the final stages of the War of Destruction, 69–70 CE. See Josephus, *Jewish War* 6.94.

the city was breached: In the summer of 70 CE. Jeremiah 52:6–7 speaks of ninth of Tammuz for the events in 586 BCE.

Apostemos: Unidentified person and event.

erected a statue in the Temple: Perhaps a reference to Gaius Caligula's order to place his statue in the Temple in 39 or 40 CE (Josephus, *Antiquities*, 18:263; *Jewish War* 2:184).

On the ninth of Av:
(1) it was decreed upon our ancestors not to enter the Land;
(2) the Temple was destroyed for the first and
(3) second time;
(4) Beitar was captured; and
(5) the city was plowed over.
When Av begins, one reduces celebration.

7 [During] the week in which the ninth of Av occurs,
it is forbidden to cut hair and wash clothes,
but on Thursdays it is permitted because of the honor due to the Sabbath.
On the day before the ninth of Av,
a person may not eat two cooked preparations
nor eat meat nor drink wine.
Rabban Simeon b. Gamaliel says:
Let him change [his eating habit].
R. Judah requires overturning the bed,
but the Sages did not agree.

4:8 *Fifteenth of Av*

8 Rabban Simeon b. Gamaliel said:
There were no happier days for Israel than the fifteenth of Av and the Day of Atonement.
On them, the maidens[25] of Jerusalem would go out with white clothing—

[25] Lit. "daughters." **K**: "sons."

not to enter the Land: Numbers 14:29.

for the first and second time: First Temple, 586 BCE—Jeremiah 52:12–13; Second Temple, 70 CE—Josephus, *Jewish War* 6:249.

Beitar was captured: This town southwest of Jerusalem saw the last stand of the Bar Kokhba rebels in 135 CE.

the city was plowed over: Hadrian established the city of Aelia Capitolina on the ruins of Jerusalem, probably one of the causes of the Bar Kokhba revolt in 132 CE (Cassius Dio, *Roman History* 69.12.1). For Romans, plowing a furrow symbolized the founding of a city and establishing its *pomerium* (boundary).

When Av begins: As the manuscripts indicate, this statement is the beginning of the next mishnah and is the first stage in anticipation of the fast of the ninth of Av.

4:7 *the week*: See also *Pesahim* 4:5. The Mishnah has no further discussion of this fast.

forbidden to cut hair and wash clothes: These customs parallel the seven days of mourning following a relative's death and burial.

the honor due to the Sabbath: See above 1:6, 2:7, 4:3.

overturning the bed: A mourning custom.

4:8 *fifteenth of Av and the Day of Atonement*: In medieval commentary the courtship event was limited to the fifteenth of Av. The fifteenth of Av links the previous material and this final mishnah, either because it was mentioned as a central date of the wood-offering sacrifices (4:5), or as a chronological progression after the observance of the ninth of Av.

that was borrowed so as not to embarrass those who do not own [white clothing]—
all the clothing required immersion.
And the maidens of Jerusalem would go out and dance in the vineyards.
And what would they say?
Young man, lift up your eyes and look,
What do you choose for yourself?
Do not gaze upon beauty,
gaze upon family:
Grace is deceptive and beauty is an illusion,
a woman who fears the Lord is to be praised.
And it says: *Give her from the fruit of her hands*
and let her deeds praise her in the gates.
Likewise it says: *Go forth and gaze, maidens of Zion, upon King Solomon, upon the crown with which his mother crowned him on his wedding day, and on the day of the gladness of his heart.*
"On his wedding day," this is the giving of the Torah;
"On the day of the gladness of his heart," this is the building of the Temple.
May it be rebuilt speedily in our days, Amen.

the maidens of Jerusalem: This courting custom is set in Jerusalem, before the destruction of the Temple. **K** reads "sons" instead of "maidens."

borrowed…required immersion: The event seeks to be socially egalitarian and inclusive, so no one owned the clothing they wore and all the garments were immersed to ensure ritual purity.

Grace is deceptive…Give her from the fruit: Proverbs 31:30–31.

Likewise: This might indicate an addition to the end of the tractate.

Go forth and gaze: Song of Songs 3:11.

Solomon…his wedding day: Although allegorical interpretation of the Song of Songs is almost universal in rabbinic literature, this verse is quoted right after depicting the courting event, and its plain description is of the king's wedding day.

Temple: This final interpretation continues the chapter's concern with Temple-related activities of groups and individuals and closes on an optimistic note.

Tractate Megillah

Alyssa Gray

Introduction

Overview

This tractate's name is *Megillah* ("scroll"), as befits its focus in chapters 1 and 2 (and 4:1) on the reading of *Megillat Esther* (the Esther Scroll) on Purim. The word *megillah* is also the very first word of the tractate. In chapters 3 and 4 the tractate treats the subject of public readings from the Torah and the prophets. Those readings were done from scrolls as well (as is the public Torah reading even today).

Structure and Organization of the Tractate

Megillah consists of four chapters. Chapter 1 falls into two unequal parts. The first three paragraphs (and the first line of the fourth) determine when the Esther Scroll must be read and establish that cities walled from the days of the biblical Joshua bin Nun read it on the fifteenth of Adar and large towns on the fourteenth of Adar, while villages may move up their reading to the "day of assembly," provided that is not earlier than the eleventh of Adar. The fourth through eleventh paragraphs—the balance of the chapter—form a distinct unit distinguished by the refrain "There is no difference between X and Y except…" The first item in the unit pertains to the months Adar I and Adar II (an additional leap month) apropos of Purim, and then the list moves on to deal with an eclectic range of topics including the Sabbath, vows, purities, scrolls, priests, public and private "high places" in the biblical period, and the respective sanctities of Shiloh and Jerusalem.

Chapter 2 resumes a focus on the reading of the Esther Scroll. The first two paragraphs deal with technical aspects of the reading that determine whether or not a reading fulfills the religious obligation to read the Scroll. The third paragraph is an odd blend of two topics: how a townsperson or walled city-dweller should behave if each finds himself in the other type of urban settlement on Purim, and how much of the Esther Scroll must be read in fulfillment of the religious obligation. The fourth paragraph opens with a discussion of who is religiously "fit" (*kasher*) to read the Scroll for others; the text then presents a list of religious acts—reading the Esther Scroll first among them—that must be done during the day. The fifth paragraph continues with a long list of other rituals that may be performed all day, and then the chapter closes with the sixth paragraph, which, by contrast, discusses rituals that may be performed all night.

Chapter 3 falls into two equal parts. The first three paragraphs deal broadly with the sanctity of the synagogue and of the objects within it. The second three paragraphs deal with the Torah readings for the four Sabbaths preceding Passover, and then for the various holidays. In the Babylonian Talmud this is chapter 4; other rabbinic collections have this as chapter 3, as in the Mishnah itself.

Chapter 4 deals with Torah and *haftarah* (prophetic) readings as well as other synagogue issues: which synagogue liturgies require the presence of ten men, who is fit to be a prayer leader, and qualities that may render a person unfit to serve as the prayer leader. The first paragraph opens with the rule that the reader of the Esther Scroll—unlike the Torah reader—may choose whether to stand or sit as he reads. This and the second paragraph largely deal with the number of men reading the Torah on particular days. The discernible pattern is that the holier the day, the more Torah readers are assigned for that day. The third paragraph lists the rituals that require the presence of ten, and the fourth establishes minimum numbers of verses to be read in the Torah and prophets and maximum numbers of verses to be conveyed at a time to the public translator. The fifth and sixth paragraphs deal broadly with persons—minors, those with exposed body parts, and the blind—who may or may not read from the Torah or prophets publicly, or be a prayer leader. The seventh paragraph continues this treatment of "who may not" publicly perform a ritual with reference to priests who may not publicly bless the people on account of physical blemishes or discolorations on their hands. Paragraphs eight and nine shift the chapter's focus to possible indicia of heresy on the part of prayer leaders, and the chapter concludes with a paragraph about biblical passages that are neither read nor translated.

Relationship to Scripture

Remarkably, the biblical book of Esther itself does not explicitly mandate that it be publicly and annually read. A passage in the Yerushalmi even demonstrates discomfort with establishing this new holiday not commanded by Moses. Ultimately, both Talmuds claim divine approval for the human initiative to establish the holiday, and rabbinic exegesis locates a specific mandate to read the Scroll in Esther 9:28: *Consequently, these days are recalled and observed in every generation.* For the rabbis, the public reading of the Esther Scroll is the ritual enactment of "remembering."

Tractate Megillah

Chapter One

1:1–3 When to Read the Esther Scroll

1 The Scroll is read on the eleventh, the twelfth, the thirteenth, the fourteenth, or the fifteenth [of Adar]—
not earlier and not later.[1]
Cities surrounded by a wall from the days of Joshua bin Nun
read on the fifteenth.
Villages and large towns read on the fourteenth,
except that villages move up [the reading] to the day of assembly.

2 How? If the fourteenth[2] [of Adar] falls on Monday,[3]
villages and large towns read on that day,
and [cities] surrounded by walls on the morrow.
If it falls on Tuesday or Wednesday,
villages move up [the reading] to the day of assembly,
and large towns read on that day,
and [cities] surrounded by walls on the morrow.

---

[1] Lit. "not less and not more." [2] K, P lack "the fourteenth."
[3] Lit. "the second [day of the week]," and so in the next paragraphs as well.

1:1 *the eleventh, the twelfth, the thirteenth, the fourteenth, or the fifteenth*: The Sages instituted the eleventh, twelfth, and thirteenth as possible alternative dates on which village dwellers could read the Scroll, for reasons that will shortly be explained.

Cities surrounded by a wall…read on the fifteenth: Shushan is referred to in the Esther Scroll as a *fortress* (9:6), and Shushan is expressly distinguished from *unwalled towns* (9:19). One might have thought that other walled cities (like Shushan) whose enclosure dates back to the time of Mordechai and Esther would also read on the fifteenth. The Yerushalmi explains that out of respect for the Land of Israel—whose towns and walled cities were in ruins at the time of Mordechai and Esther—the Sages considered its currently unwalled cities as "walled" for purposes of reading the Scroll if they had been walled at the time Israel entered the Land.

except that villages move up [the reading] to the day of assembly: This accommodation is due to the fact that villagers assemble in the large towns on days of assembly (Mondays and Thursdays) to go to market and bring cases before the courts. For years when the fourteenth of Adar does not fall on a day of assembly, the Sages allowed the villagers to avoid an extra trip to the towns by hearing the reading of the Scroll on the day of assembly closest to the fourteenth. Based on the rabbinic interpretation of Esther 9:27 (*it shall not pass*), that day of assembly has to be prior to the fourteenth and the fifteenth: in rabbinic interpretation, *it* refers to the reading of the Esther Scroll.

1:2 *Sabbath eve*: Friday.

after the Sabbath: Sunday.

If it falls on Thursday,
villages and large towns read on that day,
and [cities] surrounded by walls on the morrow.
If it falls on Sabbath eve,
villages move up [the reading] to the day of assembly,
and large towns and [cities] surrounded by walls read on that day.
If it falls on the Sabbath,
villages and large towns move up [the reading] and read[4] on the day of assembly,
and [cities] surrounded by walls on the morrow.
If it falls after the Sabbath,
villages move up [the reading] to the day of assembly,
and large towns read on that day, and [cities] surrounded by walls on the morrow.

3 What is a "large town"?
Every [town] within which there are ten idle persons.
Less than this, it is a village.
As to these [dates for reading the Scroll] they said:
One moves [them] up and does not postpone [them].
But the time of the priests' wood [offerings],
the ninth of Av, the Festival sacrifice, and the Gathering—
one postpones and does not move [them] up.
Even though they said:[5]
One moves [them] up and does not postpone,
eulogies, fasts, and gifts to the poor are permitted

[4] **K, P** lack "and read."   [5] **K**: "because they said."

1:3 *Every [town] within which there are ten idle persons*: These are persons supported by the community so that they are ready at any time to constitute a prayer quorum in the synagogue.

But the times of the priests' wood [offerings]: These were nine fixed times of year at which designated priestly families provided wood for the altar in the Jerusalem Temple. This is referred to as the *wood offering* (Nehemiah 10:35). See also *Ta'anit* 4:5. If these times fall on the Sabbath, the offering is delayed until later.

the ninth of Av: If this or other fast days (except for the Day of Atonement) fall on the Sabbath, they are delayed until afterwards.

the Festival sacrifice: This is the Festival offering of well-being offered by pilgrims in the Jerusalem Temple on the three pilgrimage Festivals (the Festival of Passover, the Festival of Weeks [*Atseret*], and the Festival of Booths [*Sukkot*]). The meat of this offering is shared by the pilgrims and the priests. If the Festival falls on the Sabbath, this sacrifice is offered afterwards.

the Gathering: This is the national gathering during the Seventh (Sabbatical) Year at the time of the Festival of Sukkot, when the king would read to the people from the Torah (Deuteronomy 31:10–13; *Sotah* 7:8). If the date for this reading falls on the Sabbath, the Gathering is held afterwards.

eulogies, fasts, and gifts to the poor are permitted: Eulogies and fasts would ordinarily be prohibited on Purim, so the Mishnah must provide the counterintuitive direction that they are permitted on the eleventh, twelfth, or thirteenth of Adar if the Scroll is read on those days. What "permitted" means in connection with "gifts to the poor" is unclear. As noted in n. 6, "gifts to the poor" is missing from a quotation of this mishnah that is found in the Talmud.

[on those days to which the reading of the Scroll was moved up].⁶
R. Judah said:
When [do villages move the reading up to the day of assembly]?
In a place [where the population] assembles on Monday and Thursday.
But a place [where the population] assembles neither on Monday nor Thursday—
they read [the Scroll] only at its [proper] time.⁷

1:4–11 *The Only Difference*

4 If they read the Scroll in Adar I and the year was intercalated,
they read it in Adar II.
The only difference between Adar I and Adar II
is the reading of the Scroll and gifts to the poor.
5 The only difference between a Festival and the Sabbath
is [the preparation of] a person's food.
The only difference between the Sabbath and the Day of Atonement
is that intentional violation [of the Sabbath] [is punishable] by human hands,
and intentional violation [of the Day of Atonement] [is punishable] by *karet*.
6 The only differences between
a person prohibited by vow from deriving any benefit from his peer

⁶ Elsewhere in the Talmud (*Ta'anit* 18a–b) "gifts to the poor" is absent.
⁷ K, P: "they read it in its proper time."

1:4 *If they read the Scroll in Adar I and the year was intercalated*: The Court determined after Purim had passed that it was necessary to have a leap year and add a thirteenth month. The additional thirteenth month is always a second Adar.

they read it in Adar II: The Esther scroll is publicly read again in Adar II.

The only difference…gifts to the poor: With this phrase, the chapter begins a set of paragraphs distinguished by the refrain "The only difference between X and Y is…" This refrain is a mnemonic device meant to assist in the memorization of the list. In this case, the reading of the Scroll and the giving of gifts to the poor must be done in Adar II, not Adar I. Eulogies and fast days may not take place on the fourteenth and fifteenth of both Adar I and Adar II.

1:5 *The only difference between a Festival and the Sabbath is [the preparation of] a person's food*: Food preparation for a Festival may be done on the Festival itself (Exodus 12:16), whereas cooking is prohibited on the Sabbath as a forbidden primary labor. This line appears as well at *Betsah* 5:2.

the Sabbath and the Day of Atonement: A person who deliberately violates the Sabbath is punished by stoning. A person who deliberately violates the Day of Atonement is punishable by *karet*. The precise nature of *karet* is uncertain, but it is not a punishment administered by human beings. *Karet* may mean dying before one's time, dying without children, or some other form of divinely administered punishment.

1:6 *The only differences between a person prohibited by vow…and one prohibited food from him by vow*: In the first case, X imposes a prohibition by vow on Y that the latter may derive absolutely no benefit from him at all, or Y vows not to accept any benefit from X. In the second case, X imposes a prohibition by vow on Y that the latter may not get food from X, but X does not impose a general prohibition on Y against deriving any and all benefit from him. (Or Y takes a vow imposing on *himself* a prohibition against accepting food from X, but the vow does not impose a general prohibition against any deriving any and all benefit from X.) These sorts of vow are the principal focus of *Nedarim*. For this rule in particular see *Nedarim* 4:1.

and one prohibited food from him by vow
are the treading of the foot
and utensils in which a person's food is not prepared.
The only difference between
[sacrificial obligations undertaken as] vows
and free-will offerings
is that [in the case of] vows,
he is obligated[8] to replace them [should the animals be lost or stolen],
but [in the case of] free-will offerings
he is not obligated to replace them.

7 The only difference between
a man experiencing a genital discharge twice
and one who experiences three
is a sacrifice.
The only differences between a quarantined person with possible *tsara'at*
and one definitively declared to have *tsara'at*
are the disheveling [of the latter's hair]
and the tearing [of the latter's clothes].

[8] **K, P**: "they" [the vows] are liable..." here and (in **K** only) in the following clause as well.

the treading of the foot and utensils in which a person's food is not prepared: The person prohibited by his own or another person's vow to derive any sort of benefit from that other person may not even enter the latter's property or borrow any sort of utensil from him. If the vow only prohibits the acceptance of food, then the person so prohibited may enter the latter's property and borrow from him utensils not used in the preparation of food.

vows and free-will offerings: A vow to bring a sacrifice is in the form "There is upon me [the obligation] to bring a sacrifice." A commitment to bring a free-will offering is more specific: "Behold this [animal] is to be a sacrifice."

vows: If the animal designated as the offering is unavailable or unfit for sacrifice for any reason, then the taker of the vow must designate another. The vow being general, the absence or unfitness of the designated animal does not vitiate the obligation.

but [in the case of] free-will offerings: Since the undertaking to bring a free-will offering was expressed in specific terms, the obligation is vitiated should the designated animal be unavailable or unfit for sacrifice.

1:7 *twice...three...a sacrifice*: A man who experiences two episodes of genital discharge—whether on the same day or on two consecutive days—need not bring a sacrifice. He will count seven days of cleanness, after which he bathes and is again ritually fit. A man who experiences three episodes of discharge—whether on the same day, or over two or three consecutive days—must bring the required sacrifice in addition to counting clean days and immersing (Leviticus 15:14). See Leviticus 15:1–15 and *Kelim* 1:5.

a quarantined person with possible tsara'at: A person who develops a rash or discoloration of the skin must show it to the priests (Leviticus 13:2). Under certain circumstances the priest must quarantine the person for seven days to see whether the affliction spreads or changes. If the affliction remains unchanged, the priest must quarantine the individual for an additional seven days (Leviticus 13:1–5). See *Nega'im* for more detail.

one definitively declared to have tsara'at: One who has been declared impure by a priest.

disheveling [of the latter's hair] and tearing [of the latter's clothes]: These acts are required of the person who has been declared impure because of *tsara'at* by a priest (Leviticus 13:45).

The only differences between one declared pure after quarantine
and one declared pure after a definitive declaration
are [the latter's] shaving and [offering of] birds.⁹

8 The only difference between books
and phylacteries and *mezuzah*
is that books may be written in any language,
and phylacteries and *mezuzah* may be written only in the Hebrew language and script.¹⁰
Rabban Simeon b. Gamaliel says:
Even as to books, they permitted them to be written only in Greek.

9 The only difference between a [high] priest anointed with the oil of anointing
and [the high priest] of many garments
is the bull that comes [to atone] for [an inadvertent violation of] *all the commandments*.
The only difference between the serving [high] priest
and the [high] priest who has passed [out of office]

⁹ K, P add "shaving and birds" to the end of the previous clause after "loosening and tearing." They lack the second "there is no difference" clause.

¹⁰ Lit. "Assyrian."

one declared pure after a definitive declaration…[the latter's] shaving and [offering of] birds: A person who is declared pure after a period of quarantine may simply wash his clothes (Leviticus 13:6). The person who is declared pure after having been definitively declared impure must also shave his entire body and undergo a purification ritual (a bird offering). See Leviticus 14:1–9 and *Nega'im* 8:8.

1:8 *books*: Pentateuch, Prophets, and Writings.

Greek: The Talmud explains that Greek, which is the "beauty" of Noah's middle son Japheth, should dwell in the tents of Noah's older son Shem (the ancestor of Israel) (see Genesis 9:27). Therefore Greek is more acceptable than other foreign languages. This of course also reflects the overwhelming importance of Greek language and culture in the eastern Mediterranean world, where the Mishnah was produced.

1:9 *[the high priest] of many garments*: High priests were originally anointed with oil, regular priests were not (Leviticus 4:3, 6:15; cf. 7:36). After the oil of anointment disappeared (hidden, it was said, by King Josiah), high priests were distinguished from ordinary priests by the wearing of eight, rather than four, priestly garments; see Exodus 28. The high priests who served without having been anointed with oil are referred to as being "of many garments." See *Yoma* 7:5; *Horayot* 3:4.

the bull that comes [to atone] for [an inadvertent violation of] all the commandments: Leviticus 4:3 directs that if the *anointed priest* (understood by the Sages to be the high priest) sins so as to cast guilt upon the people, he atones by offering a bull. Rabbinic interpretation of the verse is that if the anointed priest makes a legal ruling permitting himself a violation of a law—the advertent violation of which is punishable by *karet*—and he acts on his own ruling, he must offer the bull. In the same circumstances, the high priest of many garments instead offers the same sacrifice required of an ordinary Israelite. See *Horayot* 2:1–3.

the serving [high] priest: Should the high priest become temporarily unfit for service, another will be appointed. The priest currently serving as high priest is referred to as "the serving [high] priest." This rule may also reflect the situation under Herodian and Roman rule when the authorities dismissed and replaced high priests at will.

the [high] priest who has passed [out of office]: This refers to a [high] priest removed from service, either an anointed priest who was (perhaps temporarily) removed or his replacement who was removed so that the anointed priest could resume his service.

is the bull of the Day of Atonement and the tenth of an *ephah*.

10 The only difference between a large "high place" and a small "high place" is the paschal sacrifice.
This is the general rule:
All which is vowed or pledged may be offered on a [small] "high place,"
and all which is neither vowed nor pledged may not be offered on a [small] "high place."

11 The only difference between Shiloh and Jerusalem
is that in Shiloh one ate sacrifices of lesser holiness and second tithe
in all [areas] that see [Shiloh],
and in Jerusalem, [only] within the [city] wall.
And in both,
sacrifices of greater holiness are eaten within the enclosures [of the sanctuary].
The sanctity of Shiloh was followed by permission [to sacrifice at "high places"],
but the sanctity of Jerusalem was not.

---

the bull of the Day of Atonement and the tenth of an ephah: A tenth of an *ephah* of fine flour was first offered during the dedication of Aaron and his sons as priests during Israel's wandering in the desert, and was thereafter to be offered by the high priest every day; see Leviticus 6:13–15. Both the priest's bull of the Day of Atonement (Leviticus 16:6) and the tenth of an *ephah* might be offered only by the serving high priest.

1:10 *a large "high place"*: The communal altars in the biblical towns Gilgal, Gibeon, and Nob. See e.g. Joshua 5:10, 1 Samuel 11:15 (Gilgal); 1 Kings 3:4, 1 Chronicles 21:29 (Gibeon); 1 Samuel 22:19 (Nob).

a small "high place": Private altars built by individuals.

the paschal sacrifice: These can only be offered at the large altars. The Talmud points out that the reference to paschal sacrifice is only an example; all obligatory offerings that must be offered at a fixed time may be offered only at large "high places."

All which is vowed or pledged…may not be offered on a [small] "high place": Sacrifices brought pursuant to individual vows or free-will donations—and these alone—may be offered by individuals at small "high places." (Obligatory sacrifices that must be offered at fixed times can only be offered at large "high places.")

1:11 *Shiloh and Jerusalem*: "Shiloh" refers to the tabernacle that stood there (e.g. 1 Samuel 1), and Jerusalem to the Temple.

sacrifices of lesser holiness and second tithe: Sacrifices of lesser holiness are listed at *Zevahim* 5:6–8.

second tithe: This was separated out by farmers from their harvested produce in all except years three, six, and seven of the seven-year Sabbatical-year cycle (see Deuteronomy 14:22–26). This produce, or other food bought with the proceeds of its sale, had to be eaten in the indicated places. See *Ma'aser Sheni*.

sacrifices of greater holiness: Purgation offerings and guilt offerings (*Zevahim* chapter 5).

within the enclosures [of the sanctuary]: The same term refers to the curtains surrounding the tabernacle in the Shiloh sanctuary and the walls around the courtyard of the Jerusalem Temple.

The sanctity of Shiloh…but the sanctity of Jerusalem was not: When Shiloh was destroyed, "high places" were again permitted (*Zevahim* 14:7), but this was not the case when the first Jerusalem Temple was destroyed.

Chapter Two

2:1–4 *Fulfilling One's Obligation to Read the Esther Scroll*

2 One who reads the Scroll out of order has not fulfilled his obligation.
If he recited it by heart,
read it in [Aramaic] translation,
or read it in any language [other than Hebrew]
he has not fulfilled his obligation.
But one may read it to foreign language speakers in a foreign language.
And the foreign language speaker who heard [the Scroll read in] Hebrew[11]
has fulfilled his obligation.

2 If he read it with interruptions, or while dozing,
he has fulfilled his obligation.
If he [read aloud as he] was copying it, expounding it, or correcting it—
if he directed his heart, he has fulfilled his obligation;
and if not, he has not fulfilled his obligation.
If it was written with caustic, red dye, gum, or copperas,
on paper or on an incompletely prepared skin,
he has not fulfilled his obligation.
[He has not fulfilled his obligation] unless it is written in Hebrew[12]
on a book[13] and in ink.

---

[11] Lit. "Assyrian."   [12] Lit. "Assyrian."   [13] **P**: "hide."

2:1 *he has not fulfilled his obligation*: One who understands Hebrew does not fulfill his obligation by reading the Scroll in Aramaic or any other language, even if he is reading from a written text.

in a foreign language: The text does not say so, but presumably this means in a language that the foreign-language speaker does understand.

And the foreign-language speaker…has fulfilled his obligation: This is so even if he does not understand Hebrew.

2:2 *If he read it with interruptions*: One who reads and pauses between the passages still fulfills his obligation.

dozing, he has fulfilled his obligation: "Dozing" means awake and not quite awake: one who can respond if addressed, but who is incapable of giving a thoughtful, reasoned response.

If he [read aloud as he] was copying it: Reading each verse aloud before copying it from one scroll to the one he is writing.

expounding it: He was interpreting the Scroll aloud, interrupting his reading of the text with his interpretations.

correcting it: He was reading the Scroll aloud only in order to spot errors requiring correction.

if he directed his heart: See *Berakhot* 2:1 and *Rosh Hashanah* 3:7.

on a book and in ink: This phrase is found in Jeremiah 36:18.

3 A townsperson who went to a [walled] city
or the resident of a [walled] city who went to a town:
If in future he will return to his place,
he reads [the Scroll] like [the other residents of] his place;
and if not, he reads with them [the residents of the place to which he has come].
From where does a person read the Scroll in order to fulfill his obligation?
R. Meir says:
[A person must read] all of it.
R. Judah says:
[From] *A Jewish man.*
R. Yose says:
[From] *After these things.*

4 All are fit to read the Scroll,
except for the deaf, the legally incompetent, and the minor.
R. Judah declares the minor fit.
One [may] neither read the Scroll, nor circumcise, nor immerse, nor sprinkle[14]—
and likewise a woman who watches [for blood]
for a day corresponding to a day may not immerse—
until the sun has risen.
And all of these, if they did so once the morning star rose—
[the act] is fit.

[14] P: "one neither reads the Scroll, nor circumcises, nor sprinkles, nor immerses, except during the day."

2:3 *A townsperson who went to a [walled] city*: Townspeople read the Scroll on the fourteenth of Adar, and the residents of walled cities on the fifteenth of Adar. See 1:1.

If in future he will return to his place: If the traveler has the intention of eventually returning to his own place, then he reads the Scroll according to the custom of his own place even though he is temporarily residing in a place with a different custom.

A Jewish man…After these things: See Esther 2:5 and 3:1.

2:4 *All are fit to read the Scroll*: And to enable others to fulfill their obligation.

except for the deaf, the legally incompetent, and the minor: Terumot 1:2. Normally the first of these terms refers to a deaf-mute. But since the mishnah here discusses reading the Scroll, it must refer to a deaf person who can speak. In all these cases the general rule of *Rosh Hashanah* 3:8 applies: whoever is not obligated as to a matter cannot fulfill others' obligation as to that matter.

immerse, nor sprinkle: To be cleansed of any sort of impurity.

sprinkle: A person who has contracted impurity through contact with the dead must be sprinkled with water mixed with ashes of the red heifer on the third and seventh days following the contact (Numbers 19:19).

a woman who watches [for blood] for a day corresponding to a day: A woman is to count at least seven days for her menstruation (more if she menstruates beyond seven days), and these days are followed by an eleven-day period understood as separating one menstruation from the other. If she sees blood during one of these eleven days, she immerses in the morning of the following day. If she does not see blood again that day, she is pure in the evening.

And all of these, if they did so once the morning star rose—[the act] is fit: The listed rituals should be performed after the sun has risen. Nevertheless, if they were performed earlier—after the dawning of the morning star—the acts are valid.

2:5–6 *Rituals That May Be Performed All Day or All Night*

5 The entire day is fit for:
the reading of the Scroll,
the recitation of *Hallel*,
the sounding of the *shofar*,
the taking of the *lulav*,
the additional prayer,
the additional offerings,
the confession over the bulls,
the declaration over the tithe,
the confession of the Day of Atonement,
leaning [on the head of a sacrificial animal],
[sacrificial] slaughter,
the waving,
the presentation,
the taking of a fistful,
the burning [of it],
the pinching off [a bird's head],
the receiving [of blood],
the sprinkling [of blood],
giving the *sotah* to drink,
the breaking of the neck of the heifer,

2:5 This mishnah builds on 2:4 and provides a more complete list of rituals that may be performed at any point during the day.

taking of the lulav: This is the waving of the palm branch on the Festival of Sukkot (Leviticus 23:40; *Sukkah* 3:8–9).

additional prayer…additional offerings: Additional prayers are offered on Sabbaths, festivals, and New Moons, corresponding to the additional sacrificial offerings on such days. See Numbers 28–29; *Berakhot* 4:1.

confession over the bulls: If the high priest rules erroneously about a matter of law, or if the Great Court errs as to a matter of law and all or most of the people of Israel transgress inadvertently in accordance with the ruling, the Great Court must bring an expiatory bull on its own and the people's behalf (cf. Leviticus 4:3; 4:13). Those who offer the bull recite a confession of sin over it.

declaration over the tithe: In the fourth and seventh years of the Sabbatical cycle, the Israelite farmer was to distribute all his tithes and make a declaration. See Deuteronomy 26:13–15.

waving: This is the annual waving of a harvested sheaf; see Leviticus 23:12 and 2:6 immediately below.

presentation…taking of a fistful…burning [of it]: All these pertain to the flour offering in the Jerusalem Temple.

pinching off [a bird's head]: See Leviticus 1:15; 5:8.

receiving [of blood]…sprinkling [of blood]: "Receiving" refers to the collection of the sacrificial animal's blood so that it can be sprinkled on the altar. See *Zevahim* 5:1–2.

giving the sotah to drink: The *sotah* is a woman whose husband suspects her of adultery; see Numbers 5:11–31 and *Sotah*. Her trial by ordeal involves the drinking of a potion.

breaking of the neck of the heifer: This is the ceremony described in Deuteronomy 21 for expiation in the event a corpse is found outside a city.

and the purification of the one with *tsara'at*.
   6 The entire night is fit for the harvesting of the *omer*,
and for burning the fat pieces and limbs.
This is the general rule:
Something that is commanded to be done by day
may be performed all day;
something that is commanded to be done by night
may be performed all night.

Chapter Three

3:1–2 *Sale of Sacred Spaces and Objects*

3 Townspeople who sold the town's open space
may purchase a synagogue with the proceeds.
[If they sold] a synagogue, they may purchase an ark;
an ark, they may purchase [Torah-scroll] coverings;
[Torah-scroll] coverings, they may purchase [biblical] books;
[biblical] books, they may purchase a Torah [scroll].
But if they sold a Torah [scroll], they may not purchase [biblical] books;
[biblical] books, they may not purchase [Torah-scroll] coverings;
[Torah-scroll] coverings, they may not purchase an ark;
an ark, they may not purchase a synagogue;
A synagogue, they may not purchase an open space.
And likewise with leftover [monies].
One may not sell public property to an individual,

---

and the purification of the one with tsara'at: See 1:7 above and *Nega'im*.

2:6 *The entire night is fit for the harvesting of the omer*: The *omer* is the first sheaf of the harvest, which is ceremonially "waved" each spring. See Leviticus 23:10 and *Menahot* chapter 10.

and for burning the fat pieces and limbs: These fat pieces and limbs come from sacrificial animals the blood of which was sprinkled on the altar during the day. Had the limbs and fat pieces not been burned on the altar during daylight, this might be done all night until dawn. See Leviticus 6:2 and *Berakhot* 1:1.

3:1 *Townspeople who sold the town's open space*: The town's open space has some holiness, since the people gather in it for prayer on public fast days. See *Ta'anit* 2:1.

may purchase a synagogue with the proceeds: A synagogue has greater holiness than a town's open space. The monies earned through selling the latter must be put toward purchasing something of greater holiness than what was sold. This is the principle at work throughout this mishnah.

[biblical] books: Scrolls of the Prophets and Writings.

And likewise with leftover [monies]: If a holy object was sold and monies were left over after an object of greater holiness was purchased, the leftover monies may not be used to buy an object of lesser holiness.

public property: This applies to a Torah scroll that belongs to the public (Yerushalmi).

because one thus reduces its sanctity—
the words of R. Judah.[15]
They said to him:
If so,
then one may not even [sell property] from a large town to a small town.

2 One may sell a synagogue only on the condition
that if [the sellers] wish,[16] [the buyers] will return it—
the words of R. Meir.
And the Sages say:
One may sell it permanently,
except for four purposes:
(1) to be a bathhouse;
(2) to be a tannery;
(3) for immersion;
(4) or to be a privy.
R. Judah says:
One may sell it to serve as a courtyard,
and the buyer may do as he wishes.

3:3 Proper Treatment of a Destroyed Synagogue

3 And R. Judah said further:
One may not eulogize in a synagogue that has been destroyed,
nor twist ropes within it,
nor spread out nets within it,
nor spread out fruits on its roof,
nor use it as a shortcut,
as it is said:

---

[15] K, P: "R. Meir."   [16] K, P: "when they wish…"

---

from a large town to a small town: If a holy object belonging to the public cannot be sold to an individual because that will result in a loss of sanctity, then objects may not even be sold by large towns—where they are used by a greater number of people, and hence there is greater sanctity—to small towns. As there is no such prohibition, there is no prohibition against selling public property to an individual.

3:2 *One may sell a synagogue*: In R. Meir's view the unconditional sale of a synagogue is disrespectful. Such a sale makes it appear as if the community does not value the synagogue.

the buyer may do as he wishes: R. Judah's view is that the sale of the synagogue should be for an undefined purpose, after which the buyer may use the site however he wishes. This would include the four uses prohibited by the Sages.

3:3 *One may not eulogize in a synagogue that has been destroyed*: The implication seems to be that one may eulogize in a functional synagogue. The Yerushalmi, however, distinguishes between a synagogue owned by an individual and one owned by a community. In the latter, eulogies are never permitted.

nor twist ropes within it, nor spread out nets within it, nor spread out fruits on its roof: Although no mundane tasks are permitted within a synagogue, these three are singled out because they require a lot of room, and one might be especially tempted to make use of the synagogue for these purposes.

I will make your sanctuaries desolate.
Their holiness [persists] even when they are desolate.
If grass grows up in it one may not pluck it,
because of grief.

3:4–6 *Torah Readings on Special Occasions*

4 If the New Moon of Adar falls on the Sabbath,
One reads the [Torah] portion of *sheqalim*.
If it falls during the week,
one moves up [the reading] to the preceding [Sabbath]
and interrupts [the cycle of seasonal readings] on the following Sabbath.
On the second [Sabbath in Adar], *Remember*,
on the third, *The Red Heifer*,
on the fourth, *This month shall be for you*,
[and] on the fifth one resumes the [customary] order [of readings].
One interrupts [the regular sequence of readings] for all [other sacred times]:
for New Moons,
for Hanukkah,
for Purim,
for fast days,

I will make your sanctuaries desolate: Leviticus 26:31. Synagogues retain their status as *sanctuaries* even when they are destroyed.

If grass grew up in it one may not pluck it, because of grief: The grass should be allowed to grow so that people will remember the days when the synagogue stood, and be moved either to rebuild it or to pray for the opportunity to do so. Grass that is plucked from the site should be left there for the purpose of provoking grief, and not removed or used to feed animals.

3:4 *One reads the [Torah] portion of sheqalim*: This is the first of four special readings done on the Sabbaths leading up to Passover. The reading is Exodus 30:11–16, which discusses the collection of the half-*sheqel* from the biblical Israelites. In Temple times an announcement was made at the beginning of Adar to bring *sheqel* offerings to the Temple. See *Sheqalim* 1:1.

and interrupts [the cycle of seasonal readings]: In the event the New Moon of Adar falls on a weekday and Exodus 30:11–16 is read on the preceding Sabbath, the second special section (*Remember*, Deuteronomy 25:17–19) cannot be read on the Sabbath immediately following the New Moon, but must be deferred one more week so that it will be read on the Sabbath immediately preceding Purim.

On the second [Sabbath in Adar], Remember: This reading from Deuteronomy 25:17–19 is about Amalek's surprise attack on the Israelites in the wilderness, and is a suitable preparation for the reading of the Scroll of Esther and its account of Haman, the descendant of Amalek. See also 3:6 below.

on the third, The Red Heifer: Numbers 19 describes the ritual of preparing the ashes of a red cow, which were used to purify Israelites who contracted impurity through contact with a corpse. Only Israelites in a state of purity could participate in the Temple cult. This reading is meant to motivate Israelites to purify themselves in the weeks leading up to Passover, at the start of which the Passover sacrifice was performed.

on the fourth, This month shall be for you: This reading (Exodus 12:1–20) is about Passover.

[and] on the fifth one resumes the [customary] order [of readings]: The mishnah's assumption is that on those four Sabbaths, only those four special readings were read from the Torah. On the fifth Sabbath, therefore, the normal cycle of weekly Torah lections would resume.

for *ma'amadot*,
and for the Day of Atonement.

5 On Passover, one reads the section on the Festivals in Leviticus.[17]
On the Assembly, *Seven weeks*.
On Rosh Hashanah, *In the seventh month, on the first day of the month*.
On the Day of Atonement, *After the death*.
On the first day of the Festival,
one reads the section on the Festivals in Leviticus.
And on the other days of the Festival,[18] the sacrifices of the Festival.

6 On Hanukkah, the princes.
On Purim, *And Amalek came*.
On New Moons, *On your new moons*.
On *ma'amadot*, the work of Creation.
On fast days, blessings and curses.
One may not interrupt [the reading of] the curses;
rather one [person] reads them all.
On Mondays, Thursdays, and Sabbath afternoons one reads [the Torah portions] according to their [weekly] order.
[What was read at those times] is not taken into account

---

[17] Lit. "the Torah of the Priests," the rabbinic name for Leviticus.
[18] K, P add "[one] reads."

---

for ma'amadot: See *Ta'anit* 4:2–3.

and for the Day of Atonement: There really is no need to include the Day of Atonement here, as it is mentioned in the next mishnah. But the Day of Atonement is listed together with "fast days and *ma'amadot*" elsewhere in the Mishnah (see *Ta'anit* 4:1), which likely explains its appearance here.

3:5 *the section on the Festivals in Leviticus*: Leviticus 23.

On the Assembly: the biblical and mishnaic name for the Festival of Weeks, later known as *Shavu'ot*.

Seven weeks: Deuteronomy 16:9.

On Rosh Hashanah, In the seventh month, on the first day of the month: Leviticus 23:23.

On the Day of Atonement, After the death: Leviticus 16:1.

the Festival: In rabbinic parlance the Festival of Sukkot, the Festival par excellence.

3:6 *On Hanukkah, the princes*: Numbers 7 deals with the dedication of the desert Tabernacle, which corresponds to Hanukkah's celebration of the rededication of the Jerusalem Temple after its defilement by Antiochus Epiphanes.

On Purim, And Amalek came: Exodus 17:8. The link to Purim is the alleged Amalekite descent of Haman, the villain of the Esther Scroll. See also 3:4 above.

On New Moons, On your new moons: Numbers 28:11.

On ma'amadot, the work of Creation: Genesis 1:1–2:3. See *Ta'anit* 4:2–3.

On fast days, blessings and curses: Leviticus 26; Deuteronomy 28.

One may not interrupt [the reading of] the curses; rather one [person] reads them all: One reason for this is that dividing them up makes it seem as if one reader is having difficulty reading them all, which violates Proverbs 3:11: *Do not reject the discipline of the Lord…Do not abhor His rebuke*.

[in determining what is read the following Sabbath]
as it is said:
So Moses declared to the Israelites the set times of the Lord—
the commandment is to read [the relevant Torah portion for] each and every one at its [proper] time.

Chapter Four

4:1–2   *Rules Governing Public Readings of Scripture*

4 The reader of the [Esther] Scroll [may] stand or sit.
[Whether] one or two read it, they have fulfilled their obligation.
[In] a place in which they are accustomed to bless, [the reader] blesses;
if not to bless, he does not bless.
Three read on Monday, Thursday, and during the afternoon prayer on the Sabbath.
One neither reduces nor adds to them,
and one may not complete [the Torah reading with a reading] from the prophets.
The one who opens and closes the Torah [reading] blesses before and after it.
  2 On New Moons and on the intermediate days of the Festivals, four read.
One neither reduces nor adds to them,
and one does not complete [the Torah reading with a reading] from the prophets.
The one who opens and closes in the Torah blesses before and after it.
This is the general rule:
On any [day] that has an additional prayer but is not a Festival, four read.

So Moses declared to the Israelites the set times of the Lord: Leviticus 23:44. An abrupt return to the issue of the Torah readings on Festivals. In its scriptural context Leviticus 23:44 seems redundant, so this verse is understood to teach that Torah lections pertaining to particular Festivals must be read on those Festivals.

4:1 *The reader of the [Esther] Scroll [may] stand or sit*: Either the one or the other, as the reader wishes.

[Whether] one or two read it: If two readers read the Scroll, they—both readers and listeners—have fulfilled their obligation.

[the reader] blesses: According to both Talmuds this refers to a blessing after the reading. It is understood that the reading is preceded by a blessing.

one may not complete [the Torah reading with a reading] from the prophets: This is the *haftarah* from the prophetic books that follows the Torah reading on Sabbaths and festivals.

the one who opens and closes the Torah [reading] blesses before and after it: This statement contemplates that the first Torah reader recites a blessing before the reading, the last Torah reader recites a blessing after the reading, and the intermediate reader(s) do not recite blessings at all.

4:2 *On New Moons and on the intermediate days of the Festivals, four read*: "Intermediate days" are the days between the first and last days of Passover and Sukkot. As these intermediate days are bookended by Festival days they have some sanctity, expressed in part through the offering of the additional sacrifice, the additional prayer, and an additional Torah reading.

On a Festival: five.
On the Day of Atonement: six.
On the Sabbath: seven.
One does not reduce them, but one may add to them,
and one completes [the Torah reading with a reading] from the prophets.
The one who opens and closes in the Torah, blesses before it and after it.

4:3 Rituals Requiring the Presence of Ten

3 One may not apportion the *Shema*,[19]
nor may [anyone] pass before the ark,
nor [may priests] raise their palms [for their priestly blessing],
nor may [anyone] read from the Torah,
nor complete [the Torah reading with a reading from] the prophets,
nor perform a *ma'amad u-moshav*,
nor recite the mourners' blessing,
the mourners' consolations,[20]
or the bridegrooms' blessing,
nor invite[21] [others to recite Grace after Meals] with the Name—

[19] Meaning uncertain.   [20] K, P lack "the mourners' consolations."
[21] K, P insert "over food."

On a Festival: five. On the Day of Atonement: six. On the Sabbath: seven: The hierarchy of holy days is expressed through the assigned number of Torah readers.

4:3 *One may not apportion the Shema*: Meaning and translation uncertain. One traditional understanding of what "apportion" means is that ten men who entered the synagogue after the worshipers had recited the *Shema* and its blessings, and who thus had missed some essential parts of the service, would gather together, and one would recite for all of them the parts that they had missed, including the first blessing prior to the *Shema*. A modern scholarly understanding is that it refers to an ancient practice whereby one member of a praying group would recite the opening passage of the *Shema* ("Hear O Israel...") and the others would silently respond "Blessed be the name of His glorious kingdom forever and ever" after which everyone would continue reciting the remaining sections of the *Shema* together.

nor may [anyone] pass before the ark: The prayer leader would stand before the ark to lead the *Amidah* prayer (see also *Berakhot* 5:3–4; *Ta'anit* 2:5).

nor [may priests] raise the palms [for their priestly blessing]: See Numbers 6:24–26.

nor perform a ma'amad u-moshav: On their way back from burying the deceased—and possibly on the way to the burial as well—the mourners would stop seven times to mourn. Each time they would stop, one of the mourners would call out "Stand, dear ones, stand" (this is referred to as *ma'amad*; literally, a "standing") and "sit, dear ones, sit" (*moshav*; a "sitting").

nor recite the mourners' blessing...consolations: When the mourners returned from burying the deceased, they would stand together in the street and someone would recite a blessing for them while others stood in a line to offer their condolences.

or the bridegrooms' blessing: The seven blessings recited during a wedding and the following week of celebration.

nor invite [others to recite Grace after Meals] with the Name: If at least ten dined together, one diner may invite the company to recite the Grace after Meals using God's Name. See *Berakhot* 7:2.

[one may not do any of these things]
with fewer than ten [people].
And as to real properties—
nine and a priest,
and likewise a person.

4:4 Rules Governing Public Readings of Scripture

4 The one who reads the Torah must not read fewer than three verses.
He must not read more than one verse [at a time] to the translator,
or three in the prophets.
If the three [prophetic verses] were three sections,
one must read them [to the translator] one at a time.
One may skip in the prophets,
but not skip in the Torah.
And up to how much may he skip?
Enough so that the translator does not [have to] stop
[while the reader finds the new place].

4:5–9 Who May and May Not Perform Various Rituals in Public

5 The one who completes [the Torah reading with a reading from] the prophets, apportions the *Shema*,[22]
passes before the ark,

[22] Meaning uncertain. See 4:3.

---

with fewer than ten [people]: Each of these activities requires the presence of ten, who are understood to be males.

And as to real properties—nine and a priest, and likewise a person: The evaluation of real estate or of a person's market value donated to the Jerusalem Temple treasury must be done by ten people. One of the ten must be a priest, presumably to represent the Temple's interests. See also *Sanhedrin* 1:3.

4:4 *the translator*: In addition to the Torah reader, there was an Aramaic translator. The translator was to be given one Torah verse at a time to avoid the possibility of confusion and error. But the translator could be given as many as three verses at one time of the prophetic reading since the content of that reading was more important than conveying its precise wording.

If the three [prophetic verses] were three sections: If each of the three verses constitutes a marked-off section by itself, then the reader must give the verses to the translator one at a time. The Babylonian Talmud gives the example of Isaiah 52:3–5.

skip in the prophets, but not skip in the Torah: The reader from the prophets may skip from one section to another, but not the reader from the Torah.

Enough so that the translator does not [have to] stop [while the reader finds the new place]: If the prophetic scroll can be rolled to the new section before the translator has finished translating the last-read verse(s), then the reader may skip to that new section. If not, then the reader may not skip that far. The concern is not to impose on the congregation by having them wait for the scroll to be rolled to the new place.

and raises his palms [for the priestly blessing].
And if he is a minor,
his father or teacher pass [before the ark] on his behalf.

6 A minor may read from the Torah and translate,
but not apportion the *Shema*,[23]
nor pass before the ark,
nor raise his palms [for the priestly blessing].
One [with] exposed [body parts]
may apportion the *Shema* and translate,
but not read from the Torah,
nor pass before the ark,
nor raise his palms [for the priestly blessing].
A blind person apportions the *Shema* and translates.
R. Judah says:
Anyone who has never seen lights in his life does not apportion the *Shema*.

7 A priest with blemishes on his hands may not raise his palms.
R. Judah says:
Even one whose hands were stained with woad or madder
may not raise his palms,
because the people will stare at him.

[23] Meaning uncertain here and below. See 4:3.

4:5 *raises his palms [for the priestly blessing]*: Perhaps the mishnah is emphasizing that the reader from the prophetic books can do these things in order to distinguish him from the people described below in 4:6. Alternatively, the emphasis may imply that reading from the prophets ranks below these other liturgical activities in importance, so that the one who does that reading should fulfill some other more honored role as well.

and if he is a minor: A minor can read from the prophets but can neither apportion the *Shema*, nor pass before the ark, nor raise his palms to recite the priestly blessing if he is a priest. Instead, his father or master must do these other activities for him. "Passing before the ark" is singled out as a representative example.

4:6 *A minor may...not apportion the Shema, nor pass before the ark*: The minor is not (yet) obligated in the twice-daily recitation of the *Shema* or in prayer, and thus cannot be the means through which other people who are so obligated fulfill their obligation. See *Rosh Hashanah* 3:8.

nor raise his palms [for the priestly blessing]: It is inconsistent with the dignity of the congregation for them to be blessed by a minor.

One [with] exposed [body parts]: He may apportion the *Shema* because he does so from his place and does not pass before the ark. He may also translate because this activity lacks importance.

A blind person: One might think that a blind person should not apportion the *Shema* because the first blessing preceding it mentions God's creation of lights. The Talmud explains that a blind person may nevertheless benefit from light at night; other people may see him and offer him assistance. The blind person can translate the Torah and prophetic readings because that is done by heart.

4:7 *A priest with blemishes*: People may then be inclined to look at him and become distracted from the priestly blessing.

woad or madder: Woad is a plant that leaves a bluish tinge, and madder is one that leaves a reddish tinge. These were used by dyers.

4:8–9 Indicia of Possible Heresy

8 One who says,
"I will not pass before the ark in colored garments"
may not pass even in white garments.
"I will not pass in sandals,"
may not pass even barefoot.
One who makes his phylactery circular—
this is a danger
and there is in it no [fulfillment of the] commandment.
If he placed it on his forehead or the palm of his hand—
this is the way of heresy.
If he covered them in gold or placed them on his sleeve—
this is the way of outsiders.
9 One who says:
"May good ones bless you":
This is the way of heresy.
[One who says] "May your mercies extend to the nest of the bird"
or "May your name be mentioned over good"
or "Thank, thank"—
one silences him.
One who substitutes [phrases] in [reading] the forbidden sexual relations [in the Torah]— one silences him.
One who renders:

4:8 *One who makes his phylactery circular*: The reference is to the phylactery worn on the head. The Talmud declares that it is a "commandment to Moses at Sinai" that the phylacteries be rectangular. The "danger" posed by a circular phylactery is unclear.

If he placed it on his forehead or the palm of his hand: By placing the head phylactery on the forehead and the arm phylactery on the palm of the hand, the wearer is demonstrating that he takes literally the scriptural direction to *Bind them as a sign on your hand and let them serve as a symbol on your forehead* (Deuteronomy 6:8). The wearer thus brazenly rejects the rabbinic exegesis according to which the phylacteries are placed on the hairline and the upper arm. This rejection of rabbinic exegesis points to a commonality between the wearer and the rabbis' opponents.

this is the way of outsiders: Those who follow their own path and do not adhere to the rabbis' path. The precise difference between "the way of heresy" and "the way of outsiders" is unclear.

4:9 "*May good ones bless You*": One who expresses the wish that good people (alone) bless God implies that God is not also God of evildoers.

"*May your mercies extend to the nest of the bird*" *or* "*May your name be mentioned over good*" *or* "*Thank, thank*": The first phrase may mean "Just as your mercies extend to the bird's nest (see Deuteronomy 22:6), have mercy and compassion upon us." According to the Talmud this is problematic either because the person is introducing jealousy and competition into creation (by singling out the case of the bird's nest), or else because this formulation implies that God's laws are principally about mercy when in fact they are to be understood as Divine decrees. The second phrase implies that God's Name is to be associated with good and not with evil (implying dualism), and the third phrase, a doubling of "thank," even more clearly implies that there are two heavenly powers.

One who substitutes [phrases]: One who says that a biblical phrase such as *Your father's nakedness* (Leviticus 18:7) should not be understood literally, but as "your father's disgrace," is to be silenced.

And do not give of your seed to cause to pass over to Molekh
As "And do not give of your seed to pass over to gentileness"—
one silences him sharply.[24]

4:10 Scriptural Passages Not to Be Read or Translated in Public

10 The story of Reuben is read but not translated.
The story of Tamar is read and translated.
The first [golden] calf story is read and translated,
and the second is read but not translated.
The priests' blessing and the story of David and Amnon are neither read nor translated.[25]
One may not complete the reading with [a reading from] the Chariot,
but R. Judah permits.
R. Eliezer says:
One may not complete the reading with *Proclaim Jerusalem's abominations*.

[24] P reverses the order of "One who substitutes…" and "One who renders…"
[25] The Babylonian Talmud has "read but not translated."

Molekh: The Molekh verse is Leviticus 18:21. The unacceptable interpretation is that the verse interdicts raising one's child according to the laws and customs of the gentiles.

4:10 *The story of Reuben is read but not translated*: Genesis 35:22.

The story of Tamar is read and translated: Genesis 38.

The first [golden] calf story: Exodus 32:1-20 is both read in Hebrew and translated because the people were permitted to atone for their sin. The second golden calf story (Exodus 32:21-24) is Aaron's brief recapitulation of the event to Moses. This account is read but not translated out of respect for Aaron.

The priests' blessing and the story of David and Amnon are neither read nor translated: The priests' blessing (Numbers 6:24-26) is neither read nor translated because only the priests should recite that blessing with upraised hands. The reference to the "story of David and Amnon" is unclear. This might refer to the story of David and Bathsheba (2 Samuel 11:2-27) and to the subsequent story of Amnon's rape of his sister Tamar and its aftermath (2 Samuel 13), or just to the verse in which David and Amnon are mentioned together (2 Samuel 13:1).

the Chariot: Ezekiel 1 and *Hagigah* 2:1.

R. Eliezer says: One may not complete the reading with Proclaim Jerusalem's abominations: Ezekiel 16, an exceedingly harsh indictment of the people of Israel.

Tractate Mo'ed Qatan

Gail Labovitz

Introduction

Overview

This tractate is known as *Mo'ed Qatan*, which may be literally translated as "Minor Festival." Its topic is the intermediary days of the festivals of Passover and Sukkot (Shavu'ot being only a single day and thus having no intermediary days), though these holidays are not mentioned explicitly in the tractate. Because the intermediary days of the festival are part of the special time but are not celebrated as full-fledged festivals with the corresponding prohibition on work activities (see below, Relationship to Scripture), it should not be surprising that the Sages pondered how these days are or should be distinguished from other ordinary days of the year. Nowhere else in rabbinic literature, however, are these days referred to by the name *mo'ed qatan*; the common term which appears consistently in most strata of rabbinic writings is *holo* [or *hulo*] *shel mo'ed*, "the ordinary [period] of the festival." In later sources and today these days are typically known by the slight variant *hol hamo'ed*. The tractate is also sometimes known as *Mashkin* ("One waters"), after its first word.

Structure and Organization of the Tractate

The tractate begins by addressing agricultural tasks and most particularly irrigation and other maintenance of fields and crops (1:1–4). In these cases, a connection is drawn between the restrictions of the midfestival and those of the seventh year, as both involve restrictions on agricultural work. A miscellany of other tasks—examinations for skin disease, preparing graves and coffins for the dead, marriage, women's application of cosmetics and depilatories, sewing, building, and setting up various domestic items—round out the first chapter. Chapter 2 addresses time-sensitive tasks such as the processing of olive oil and wine, and preparing flax for use; also mentioned are commercial transactions and workers whose products are likely to be used during the festival. Chapter 3 takes up persons who were unable to perform tasks that typically should be done prior to the festival due to unavoidable circumstances; writing; and finally what is to be done when bereavement and mourning coincide with the festival.

Main Ideas

As noted above, the term *mo'ed qatan* does not actually appear in the tractate itself or anywhere else in rabbinic literature. Nor, intriguingly, does *holo shel mo'ed*, a term which appears only once in the Mishnah (*Megillah* 4:2), but which is frequent in the other main classical rabbinic texts. The key technical term in the tractate, then, is simply *mo'ed*, which most commonly means the midfestival (and has been translated as such), but also occasionally means the days at the beginning and end of the festival that are celebrated as sacred days.

The general thrust of the tractate is to limit work and strenuous activities during the midfestival while not banning them outright. Several broad principles, therefore, may be said to guide the deliberations regarding permitted and forbidden activities. The first of these, while not explicitly named as such in the Mishnah, does appear with a technical term in parallel materials and clearly underlies a number of the Mishnah's rulings (such as 2:1–2): *davar ha'aveid*, something that will be lost in some way if not done in due time. Such tasks are commonly permitted so long as there was no deliberate attempt to leave the work for the midfestival. In a similar vein, tasks from which the benefit or use accrues during the midfestival—for example, pickling foods that will be eaten later during the festival (1:10), or preparing ritual objects for personal use during the festival (3:4)—may be allowed. Another distinction may be made between work done for personal use in a nonprofessional (or nonskilled) manner and that which is done professionally for the purpose of financial benefit. Even professional work may be allowed, however, if the person who thereby benefits would not otherwise have sufficient means of sustenance during the midfestival.

Also, a general spirit of happiness and enjoyment is to be maintained during the festival. Tasks that would impede a person's happiness are thus prohibited; hence, for example, the ban on examining and diagnosing skin disease (1:5), which might lead to the quarantine and isolation of the sufferer, or women's use of lime because it (temporarily) mars their appearance and/or is uncomfortable to them. This is also the reason why the latter part of chapter 3 provides the most extended discussion of mourning in the Mishnah, as the text works out the conflicting obligations of tending to the dead and mourning versus celebrating on the festival.

Relationship to Scripture

While biblical law notes multiple times that both Passover and Sukkot are to be celebrated for seven days (with an eighth day of Assembly attached to Sukkot), the focus there remains on the restrictions on labor during the first and last days. The days of the midfestival are addressed obliquely in regard to ritual practices performed (such as refraining from leavened products during Passover or taking the ritual items of Sukkot) and sacrifices brought throughout all days of the festivals. These biblical concerns, however, are addressed by the Mishnah in the tractates specifically dedicated to these festivals (*Pesahim* and *Sukkah*). The question of whether there should be restrictions on day-to-day activities during the midfestival, on the other hand, which is the subject of *Mo'ed Qatan*, has no clear basis in scriptural sources other than the general injunction to be happy during the festival, as found in Leviticus 23:40 and Deuteronomy 16:11, 14–15.

Tractate Mo'ed Qatan

Chapter One

1:1–4 *Agricultural Work during Midfestival and the Seventh Year*

1   One may water a field dependent on irrigation during the midfestival and during the Seventh Year,
whether from a newly emerged spring
or from a spring that is not newly emerged.
But one does not water from [collected] rainwater
or from water [drawn from a well with a] swipe and bucket;
and one does not make trenches for vines.
  2 R. Eleazar b. Azariah says:
One does not newly make a [water] channel during the midfestival and during the Seventh Year.
And the Sages say:
One may newly make a [water] channel during the Seventh Year,
and one may repair damaged ones during the midfestival.[1]
And one may repair damaged waterways[2] that are in the public domain, and clean[3] them out.
And one may repair roads and open spaces and pools of water,
and perform all public needs,
and mark graves,

[1] K lacks "and one may repair…"   [2] K, P: "all water vessels."   [3] Or "rake."

1:1 *a field dependent on irrigation*: More literally, a field of irrigation ditches.

from a newly emerged spring: Even though some labor may be needed to guide the water to the field.

swipe and bucket: An apparatus by which a long rod was used to lower a bucket into a deep well to draw water.

trenches: Cavities to hold water that are dug around the roots of a tree or vine.

1:2 *And one may repair roads…*: See *Sheqalim* 1:1.

open spaces: i.e. an open plaza within a town or city, used for public gatherings.

mark graves: i.e. mark their locations so they are recognizable as gravesites.

and also go out regarding prohibited mixtures.

3 R. Eliezer b. Jacob says:
One may draw water from tree to tree,
but only so long as one does not water the entire field.
[As for] seeds which had not been watered[4] before the midfestival,
one may not water them during the midfestival.
But the Sages[5] permit [both] this and that.

4 One may trap moles and mice from a field of trees
and from a sown field,
[though] not[6] in his [usual] manner,
during the midfestival and during the Seventh Year.
But the Sages say:
From a field of trees in his [usual] manner,
and from a sown field not in his [usual] manner.
And one may close up a breach during the midfestival,
and during the Seventh Year one may build in his [usual] manner.

5 R. Meir says:
One may view skin blemishes to begin[7] with to be lenient,
but not to be strict,
but the Sages say:
Neither to be lenient nor to be strict.
And R. Meir further said:
A person may gather the bones of his father and his mother,[8]
because it is happiness for him.
R. Yose says:
It is mourning for him.
A person should not stir up mourning over his dead
and should not make lamentation for him
for thirty days before the festival.

[4] Lit. "which had not drunk."
[5] Missing from **K**, and restored in the margin.
[6] **K**, **P**, and certain printed editions lack "not."
[7] **K** adds "during the midfestival" in the margin.
[8] Alt. "a person may gather (for him) the bones of his father and mother."

go out also regarding prohibited mixtures: Emissaries may be sent out to check that no mixed species are growing in fields and vineyards. See *Kilayim*.

1:4 *a sown field*: more literally, a "white field," that is, a bright, unshaded field, planted with grain or vegetables.

close up in a rough, basic way.

a breach in a fence or a wall.

1:5 *to begin with*: As distinct from reinspection after the stipulated seven-day quarantine; see Leviticus 13.

it is happiness for him to have brought his parents' bones to rest in the family grave.

make lamentation: Understood in later texts to mean hiring a professional lamenter/eulogizer.

6 One does not dig burial niches and tombs during the midfestival, but one may finish off burial niches during the midfestival.[9]
And one may make a wash-pond during the midfestival,
and a coffin with the dead [body] in the courtyard.
R. Judah forbids [this],
unless he has boards with him.

7 One does not marry women during the midfestival,
neither virgins nor widows;
and one does not enact levirate marriage,
because it is happiness for him;[10]
but he may remarry[11] his divorcee.[12]
A woman may apply her adornments during the midfestival.
R. Judah says:
She should not apply lime
because it is disfiguring to her.

8 A common[13] person may sew in his [usual] manner,
and an artisan makes irregular stitches.
And one may interlace [the straps of] a bed.
R. Yose says:
One may even tighten [them].

9 One may set up an oven, stoves, or millstones during the midfestival.
R. Judah says:
One may not[14] initially put the millstones in working order.

[9] K, P lack "during the midfestival."
[10] K, P lack "because it is happiness for him" in this location; see below.
[11] Lit. "return."
[12] K, P each include slightly different variants here that both may be translated: "because it is happiness for him."
[13] Or "untrained."
[14] K: "one may even…"

1:6 *finish off*: i.e. one may complete, repair, or adjust a niche that has already been dug.

wash-pond: This is the common translation/explanation; see *Bava Batra* 2:1, where this interpretation makes sense. Here, however, the term is more likely to mean some form of temporary grave or a sarcophagus. The latter suggestion obviously fits the context much more closely.

boards: That is, boards that were already prepared, i.e. sawn, prior to the festival.

1:7 *it is happiness for him*: It is noteworthy that in connection with burial this argument is used to permit a certain behavior, while here it serves to justify a prohibition. The motive here seems to be that one's personal celebration should not coincide with, and overshadow, a public festival.

apply lime as a depilatory.

1:8 *a common person*: The term indicates a person who does not perform the indicated task for a living and/or distinguishes between a trained artisan and a person with no special training or expertise in the task.

interlace [the straps of] a bed: Onto the bedframe, to create support for the mattress. See also *Kelim* 19:1–6.

1:9 *put the millstones in working order*: The Babylonian Talmud suggests this may include roughening the stones for grinding, and/or making and adjusting the eyehole.

10 ¹⁵One may make a parapet for a roof and for a balcony
as the handiwork of a common person,
but not the handiwork of an artisan.
One may plaster over cracks
and roll them with a roller
by hand or by foot,
but not with a windlass.¹⁶
The hinge or the socket or the beam or the lock or the key which broke—
one may repair them during the midfestival,
but only so long as one does not intend [to do] his work during the midfestival.
And all preserved foods that he can eat during the midfestival—
he may preserve them.

Chapter Two

2:1–3 *Time-Sensitive Labor During the Midfestival*

2 One who turned over his olives,
and mourning or¹⁷ unavoidable interference befell him,
or workers¹⁸ deceived him:
he may load the first beam [on the olives]
and leave it until after the festival—
the words of R. Judah.

---

¹⁵ In **K** this is not a separate mishnah, but rather the continuation of 1:9.
¹⁶ Or "a trowel."
¹⁷ Initially absent in **K** but restored above the line.
¹⁸ This word is missing from **P**.

1:10 *parapet*: See Deuteronomy 22:8.

cracks in the roof of a house or building.

intend: i.e. intentionally leave his repair work from before the festival to be done during the midfestival.

that he can eat: If the process will be finished in time to enjoy the product during the festival, he may put them up for preserving during the midfestival.

2:1 *turned over his olives* before the onset of the festival. The olives were placed in a vat or pit to soften before pressing, and must be turned to prevent rotting.

mourning: During the first seven days of mourning, the mourner is not supposed to engage in labor.

unavoidable interference: Anything that prevented him from completing the processing of the olives.

workers deceived him: Perhaps by failing to appear at the scheduled time. All of these circumstances occur before the festival, and hence the work is not done at the start of the festival and the olives are at risk of spoiling.

load the first beam: He may place the beam of the press on the first load of olives so that its weight will begin to extract the oil from the fruit. But he must not move the beam or replace the first load of fruit.

R. Yose says:
He may pour out and finish [the work]
and seal[19] [the containers] in his [usual] manner.

2 And so too [for] one whose wine was in the cistern,
and mourning or unavoidable interference befell him,
or workers[20] deceived him:
He may pour out and finish [the work]
and seal [the containers] in his [usual] manner—
the words of R. Yose.[21]
R. Judah says:
He makes a covering of shingles for it,
so that it does not turn sour.

3 A person may bring in his produce because of thieves,
and draw out his flax from the steeping pond
in order that it not be spoiled,
but only so long as he not intend [to do] his work during the midfestival.
And [regarding] all of [these cases],
if one intended [to do] one's work during the midfestival,
it must [be left to] perish.

4 One does not purchase houses,[22] slaves, or livestock
except for the need of the festival
or for the need of the seller who does not have anything to eat.
One does not remove [items] from [one] house to [another] house,
but he may remove [them] to his courtyard.[23]
One does not bring utensils from the house of the artisan;

---

[19] This word is absent in **K** and **P** manuscripts, but appears in **K** to be written in above the line in small letters.
[20] This word is missing from **K, P**.
[21] "R. Yose" is missing from **P** but restored above the line.
[22] **P** adds "stones."   [23] **K, P** add "because it is a happiness for him."

---

pour out: That is, pour out the olives from the vat into the press. Alternatively, squeeze out the oil from the olives. Either way, the implication is that R. Yose allows for the complete pressing of the olives to be done during the (mid)festival.

2:2 *pour out* the wine into containers.

covering of pieces of wood.

2:3 *bring in his produce*: Move it to a protected location.

steeping pond: Flax stalks must be steeped in water to soften before they can be further processed into usable fibers; if oversteeped, however, they will rot. Removing flax from the steeping pond is thus a prime example of a time-sensitive task.

it must [be left to] perish: i.e. the material that a person deliberately intended to process during the midfestival.

2:4 *for the need of the festival*: i.e. for use during the festival, here uncharacteristically including the first and last days.

if he is concerned about them, he may move them to another courtyard.

5 One may cover packed figs with straw.
R. Judah says:
One may even pile them up.
Sellers of fruit, clothing, and utensils
may sell privately[24]
for the need of the festival.
Hunters, groats-makers, and grits-makers
may do [their work] privately
for the need of the festival.
R. Yose says:
They were strict upon themselves.

Chapter Three

3:1–2 *Those Unable to Cut Their Hair or Launder before the Festival*

3 And these [may] cut [their] hair[25] during the midfestival:
one who comes from overseas,
and from captivity,[26]
and one who leaves prison,
and the excommunicated person whom the Sages have released;
and so too one who inquired of a Sage and was released,
and the *nazir*
and the one with *tsara'at* who rises[27] from his impurity to his purity.

2 And these [may] launder during the midfestival:
one who comes from overseas,
and from captivity,
and one who leaves prison,
and the excommunicated person whom the Sages have released,
and similarly one who inquired of a Sage and was released;

---

[24] Or "discreetly."   [25] Or "shave."   [26] Lit. "the house of capitivity."
[27] This word is missing from both **K** and **P**, but is restored in smaller letters above the line in **K**.

if he is concerned about them: For their safety, for example that they might be stolen.

2:5 *pile them up*: In this manner the upper layers protect the lower.

They were strict upon themselves and did not work during the midfestival at all.

3:1 *And these [may]...*: The obvious implication being that all others may not; see 3:2.

released from excommunication.

inquired of a Sage regarding a vow that prevented the maker of the vow from haircutting.

was released from the vow. See *Nedarim* chapter 9.

hand towels and barbers' towels[28] and drying towels;
zavim and *zavot*
and menstruants and women who have given birth;[29]
and all who rise from impurity to purity—
these are permitted,
and all other persons are forbidden.

3:3–4   *Writing during the Midfestival*

3   And one may write these during the midfestival:
[documents relating to] women's betrothals, divorce documents, and receipts,
wills, [documents attesting to] a gift, and *prozbul* documents,
letters of evaluation and letters guaranteeing maintenance,
documents of *halitsah* and of refusal,
and documents of selection,
and decrees of the court and

---

[28] Or, with a slight change in vocalization, "wraps for scrolls."
[29] This entire section (from "*zavim*..." to "given birth") is absent from **K** and **P**.

3:2   *hand towels*, etc.: i.e. these items may be washed during the midfestival. The phrase "these are permitted" is transferred from the agent of the action to its object.

3:3   *receipts* for debts that have been repaid.

prozbul documents: A mechanism allowing loans to be collected after the Seventh Year. See Deuteronomy 15:1–11 and *Shevi'it* 10:4.

letters of evaluation: That is, documentation of an official valuation of property mortgaged for collateral on a debt.

letters guaranteeing maintenance: At least three (not necessary mutually exclusive) interpretations of this phrase are possible: (1) The Yerushalmi defines it as "food support of widows"—that is, the letter documents the claim and right of a particular widow to collect the support due her from her deceased husband's assets and/or from his heirs. (2) Wives are entitled to maintenance throughout the course of a marriage (*Ketubbot* 4:4) and unmarried daughters at least from the time of the father's death until they become married (*Ketubbot* 4:11). Hence, "letters of food support" might document a wife's right to collect food support when the husband is not meeting his obligation to provide it for some reason, or a daughter's right to collect out of her deceased father's estate. (3) A later commentary suggests that the document attests to a commitment that a man has made to support his wife's daughter(s) from a prior marriage (see *Ketubbot* 12:1).

refusals: If a girl's father has died, other family members, notably the girl's mother and/or brothers, may arrange a marriage for her with her consent while she is a minor, but this marriage is not fully legally binding until she reaches legal adulthood, at which time she has the right to revoke her consent and reject the marriage. See *Yevamot* 13:1–5.

documents of selection: A document recording litigants' agreement on the selection of judges to hear their case; see *Sanhedrin* 3:1. Alternatively, a document recording a court decision on the apportionment of an estate or disputed property.

letters of a voluntary nature.

4 One should not write debt documents during the midfestival,
but if [the lender] did not trust [the borrower]
or he does not have anything to eat,
then this [person] may write [the document].
One does not write [sacred] scrolls, *tefillin*, or *mezuzot* during the midfestival,
and one does not correct one letter,
even in the scroll of the Temple Court.
R. Judah says:
A man may write *tefillin* and *mezuzot* for himself,
and he spins *tekhelet* on his thigh for his fringes.

3:5–8 *Mourning during the Festival*

5 If one buries his dead three days before the festival,
the restriction of seven is cancelled for him;
eight,[30]
the restriction of thirty is cancelled for him.
For they said:[31]
The Sabbath counts and does not interrupt; the festivals interrupt and do not count.
6 R. Eliezer says:
Since the Temple was destroyed, the Festival of Weeks is like the Sabbath.
Rabban Gamaliel says:
The New Year and the Day of Atonement are like the festivals.

---

[30] **K, P** add "days before the festival." [31] **K** adds "[For/Regarding] 'thirty.'"

---

letters of a voluntary nature: The word used here has a particularly wide semantic field, encompassing implications of governmental authority, permission and optional acts, ownership, that which is secular, and debt and similar claims. There are thus multiple possibilities for the meaning of this phrase, including: official letters, letters of authority (that is, either correspondence with secular governmental authority, or communicating decrees and decisions and appointments from Jewish governmental authorities), secular documents, optional (that is, personal/social) correspondence, and perhaps documents related to a loan (though loan documents themselves are discussed in the next mishnah). Many of these suggestions are debated in commentaries and adopted by different translators; there is no clear consensus on which understanding is to be preferred. The translation follows Yerushalmi.

3:4 *he does not have anything to eat*: i.e. the borrower. Alternatively, the scribe needs the fee.

for himself: For his own use, but not for sale.

3:5 *seven*: The restrictions of the first seven days of mourning after burial.

thirty: The restrictions of the first thirty days after burial.

counts as one of the seven days of mourning.

interrupt: To end the mourning period.

3:6 *the Festival of Weeks*: Which is a single-day festival.

like the Sabbath and does not end the seven-day mourning period.

like the festivals and cut off either the seven or thirty day mourning periods.

And the Sages say:
Not like the words of this one and not like the words of this one;
rather, the Festival of Weeks is like the [other] festivals,
the New Year and the Day of Atonement are like the Sabbath.

7 One does not tear [clothing],
and one does not bare [the shoulder],
and one does not partake of the mourner's meal,
except for the relatives of the deceased.
And one does not partake of the mourner's meal
except on an upright couch.
One does not take [food] to the house of the mourner
either on a platter or on a salver,
and not in a reed basket,
[but] rather in wicker baskets.
And one does not say the mourners' blessing during the midfestival,
but [the others do] stand in a line and comfort,
and [the mourners do] dismiss the public.

8 One does not set down the bier in the open space [of the town],
so as not to cause lamentation.[32]
And that of a woman not ever, out of respect.
Women during the festival may say dirges,
but may not clap.
R. Ishmael says:
The ones who are close to the bier may clap.

9 On New Moons, on Hanukkah, and on Purim,
they may say dirges and clap.[33]

---

[32] Or "eulogizing."   [33] K: "but not clap."

3:7 *One does not...except for the relatives*: During the midfestival.

tear [clothing]...bare the shoulder: Ancient mourning customs.

relatives: One's parents, siblings, spouse, and children.

couch on which a person reclined to eat. During mourning, these couches are to be "overturned," except in this instance when burial took place during the midfestival, in which case couches are not to be overturned until the conclusion of the festival.

platter: i.e. a large board or tray. These rules about the delivery of food pertain to the mourners' first meal after the funeral and were designed to avoid embarrassing poor mourners who lacked elaborate serving implements; they applied at all times, and not just during the festival.

salver: That is, probably a small platter of metal or glass.

the mourners' blessing: See *Megillah* 4:3.

3:8 *And that of a woman*: i.e. the bier carrying a deceased woman.

3:9 *they may say dirges*: All verbs in this mishnah appear in the feminine form, either plural or singular; that is, the mishnah continues to discuss women's mourning practices at funerals.

In this [case] and that,
they may not lament.³⁴
[Once] the dead is buried,
they may not say dirges and may not clap.
What is "saying dirges"?
That all respond as one.
[What is] "lamenting"?
That one speaks,
and all of them respond after her.
As it was said:
Teach your daughters wailing, and a woman to her neighbor lamentation.
But regarding the time to come,
it says:³⁵
He will swallow up death forever, and the Lord God will wipe away tears off all faces, etc.

³⁴ K: "and they may not..." See the annotations.
³⁵ K, P: "what does it say?"

In this [case] and that they may not lament: Generally understood to mean neither during the midfestival (discussed in the previous mishnah) nor on the days listed in this mishnah. The variant in **K** suggests a different punctuation: "On New Moons...they may say dirges but not clap, [whether] in this [case or in] that. And they do not lament." The likely implication would be "whether on the New Moon or on the minor festivals of Hanukkah and Purim."

Teach your daughters…: Jeremiah 9:19.

He will swallow up…: Isaiah 25:8. **P** adds the continuation of the verse: *and the insult of His people He shall take away from off all the earth; for the Lord has spoken.*

Tractate Hagigah

Michal Bar-Asher Siegal

Introduction

Overview

The word *hagigah*, as the title of the tractate, refers to the festal offering (1:2, 8) made during the celebration of the three pilgrimage festivals: Passover, the Festival of Weeks, and the festival of Booths (Sukkot). The obligation to celebrate thrice yearly before God is repeatedly mentioned in the Torah (Exodus 23:14–18; 34:23–24; Deuteronomy 16:14–17).

Structure and Organization of the Tractate

Hagigah is the last tractate in the Order of *Mo'ed* and includes three chapters. These divide into two major sections. The first (1:1–7; 2:2–4) covers laws governing the celebration of the three festivals in Jerusalem, such as the scope of the obligation to go to Jerusalem, and the details of the offerings to be made during the festival. The second part of the tractate (2:5–3:8) deals with laws of purity and impurity. Among other things, it constructs a hierarchy of purity from the consumption of unconsecrated produce to participation in the red heifer ritual, it identifies differences between consecrated produce and *terumah* in the realm of impurity, and records laws concerning the trustworthiness of various types of person when testifying to a degree of purity.

The connection between the two parts of the tractate is unclear. Some scholars have suggested that because the laws of purity during festivals encompass a wider population, more people are considered trustworthy during those seasons. Both here in the Mishnah and in Second Temple period writers such as Philo and Josephus, the laws of purity are outlined together with the laws of the festival.

In the middle of the first section a few pericopes address broad topics with theological repercussions: in 1:6–7, interpretation of the verse *That which is crooked which cannot be straightened* (Ecclesiastes 1:15); various categories of laws and their dependence, or lack thereof, on biblical verses (1:8); and restrictions on the topics that one may expound (2:1). The treatment of the creation story and of Ezekiel's chariot (see Ezekiel chapter 1) in 2:1 inspires discussion in the Talmud of mystical traditions that have preoccupied scholars ancient and modern.

Various laws are divided into three categories with respect to their relation to Scripture: (1) those that "fly in the air and have nothing to lean on," (2) those that resemble "mountains hanging by a strand, since they are little Scripture and many laws," and (3) those which "have upon what to lean, and it is they that are the bodies of the Torah" (1:8). As a rare metatheoretical statement, this mishnah displays the Sages' reflection on the nature of their halakhic system and the relation between its primary components (the laws) and their ostensible source (Scripture). Even if one cannot deduce the precise nature of the law collections that stood in front of the author, this mishnah does give insight into the topics discussed prior to the redaction of our own mishnah.

Main Ideas

Scholars have pointed out a few passages from *Hagigah* that appear to come from an earlier period than other parts of the Mishnah. Their archaic character is suggested by their language; scant reference to later tannaitic sages; numerous references to disagreements between the Houses of Hillel and Shammai; reference to an early disagreement regarding the laying of hands (2:2); the construction of purity rules as conditions of admittance to a social circle, as in Qumran writings; and use of the term Pharisees (2:7) instead of the more common Fellow or Associate. While not all of these proofs are of equal value in evaluating the antiquity of the rabbinic material preserved in *Hagigah*, the quantity and variety of the evidence suggest the archaic character of at least parts of the tractate.

Special Notes for the Reader

The tractate employs three different terms, with different shades of meaning, to denote festivals. I have translated *yom tov* as "the festival"; *hag* as "the Feast"; and *regel* as "pilgrimage." In the footnotes to the translation I compare the printed text to manuscripts **P** and **K**. Occasionally, I add relevant information about other textual variants attested, for example, MS. Cambridge Add 470.1, published by W. H. Lowe in 1883 as *The Mishnah on Which the Palestinian Talmud Rests* and designated here as **L**, also the Mishnah of the Babylonian Talmud or as found in Geniza fragments.

The annotations make use of Chanoch Albeck's commentary in his edition of the Mishnah, *Shishah Sidre Mishnah* (Jerusalem: Bialik, 1952–9), Herbert Danby's notes (Oxford: Clarendon Press, 1933), and other medieval and modern scholarship. Two recent works proved especially useful: David Henshke's *Festival Joy in Tannaitic Discourse* (Jerusalem: Magnes, 2007) and Yair Furstenberg's "Eating in a State of Purity during the Tannaitic Period" (PhD thesis, Jerusalem 2010).

Tractate Hagigah

Chapter One

1:1–6; 2:2–4 *Laws concerning the Celebration of the Festival in Jerusalem*

I All are obligated to [make an] appearance except:
one who is deaf, one who is not legally competent, or a minor,
and a *tumtum*, and an *androgynos*, and women, and slaves that have not been freed,
one who is lame, and one who is blind, and one who is sick, and one who is aged,
and one who is unable to go up on foot.
Who is [deemed] a minor?
One who is unable to ride on his father's shoulders[1]
and go up from Jerusalem to the Temple Mount,
the words of the House of Shammai;
the House of Hillel say:
One who is unable to hold his father's hand
and go up from Jerusalem to the Temple Mount,
as it is written *three regalim*.
  2 The House of Shammai say:
The pilgrimage offering[2] [must be worth] two [*ma'ah*] of silver,
and the festal offering[3] one *ma'ah* of silver.

---

[1] K, P: "shoulder."   [2] Lit. "appearance."   [3] Lit. "Festival."

1:1 *to [make an] appearance*: At the Temple three times a year; see Exodus 23:14–17; Deuteronomy 16:16.

A *deaf* person may refer to a deaf person who is also mute (see *Terumot* 1:2), but not necessarily (see *Megillah* 2:4).

tumtum: One of indeterminate sex.

androgynos : Androgyne, one having both male and female sexual characteristics and organs.

unable to go up to the Temple Mount.

tree regalim: Exodus 23:14. The Hebrew term *regalim*, usually translated "pilgrimages," is understood here as the plural form of the Hebrew *regel*, "leg."

1:2 *The pilgrimage offering*: a whole burnt offering brought during the pilgrimage (see Leviticus 1).

ma'ah: The smallest silver coin in circulation; a loaf of bread might cost a *pundion*, which was half a *ma'ah* (*Eruvin* 8:2).

festal offering: An offering of well-being, mostly eaten by the pilgrim (see Leviticus 3).

And the House of Hillel say:
The pilgrimage offering [must be worth] one *ma'ah* of silver,
and the festal offering two [*ma'ah*] of silver.

3 Whole burnt offerings during [the intermediate days of] a festival
are brought from unconsecrated [money].
Offerings of well-being
are brought from tithe [money].
On the first Festival day of Passover,[4]
the House of Shammai say from unconsecrated [money]
and the House of Hillel say from tithe [money].

4 Israelites may fulfill their obligation
with vow and free-will offerings and cattle tithe.
And the priests with purgation and guilt offerings,[5] and firstlings, and the breast and thigh,
but not by bringing birds or meal offerings.

5 One who has many eaters but few possessions
brings many offerings of well-being and few whole burnt offerings;
if many possessions but few mouths,[6]

---

[4] K before correction and P, as well as L and other manuscripts have "on the first festival day of the Feast," a term used in rabbinic literature for Sukkot (Booths). It seems that **BT** had "Passover," while **JT** had "Feast."

[5] K, P: "offering."   [6] K, P: "few mouths but many possessions."

1:3 *[the intermediate days of] a festival*: The period between the first and last days of Passover and the Festival of Sukkot.

brought from unconsecrated money: See *Menahot* 7:6.

from tithe [money]: The second tithe (Deuteronomy 14:22–26) or the cattle tithe (Leviticus 27:32–33).

1:4 *Israelites* who are not priests.

their obligation to bring offerings of well-being on the Festival.

vow and free-will offerings: Voluntary offerings to which one has obligated oneself during the year. They may be sacrificed and eaten during the pilgrimage to Jerusalem to satisfy the obligation of rejoicing on the festival.

cattle tithe: See Leviticus 27:32–33; this too had to be eaten in Jerusalem.

purgation and guilt offerings: Brought by pilgrims and eaten by the priests; see Numbers 18:9.

firstborn of a pure animal, given to the priests; see Numbers 18:17–18.

breast and thigh from Israelites' offerings of well-being, given to the priests as their portion; see Leviticus 7:31–39.

birds or meal offerings: Though priests receive gifts from these offerings, they are not meat, see *Qinnim* and Leviticus 2:1–10.

1:5 *eaters*: i.e. mouths to feed, people from one's household who eat at one's table.

brings many offerings of well-being and few whole burnt offerings so as to have more meat to supply one's household.

one brings many whole burnt offerings and few offerings of well-being.
If few of both, about this it was said:[7]
"[one] *ma'ah* of silver," and "two of silver."
If many of both,
about this it was said:
Each [shall bring a gift][8] according to the blessing of the Lord your God that he has given you.

6 One who did not bring a festal offering[9] on the first Festival day of the Feast[10]
may offer it[11] during the whole pilgrimage,
including the last Festival day of the Feast.
If the pilgrimage ended and one did not bring a festal offering[12]
one is not liable to make restitution.
About this it was said:
That which is crooked cannot be straightened,
and that which is lacking cannot be counted.

1:7–2:1 *Biblical Passages and Their Interpretation or Application*

7 R. Simeon b. Menasya says:
What is *that which is crooked* which *cannot be straightened*?[13]
One who has intercourse with one of his forbidden relations
and fathered a *mamzer* by her.[14]
If you will say
[the verse] applies to the one who steals or robs—

[7] **K, P**: "about this they said," which fits better since this is not a biblical quotation but rather a reference to a rabbinic text, namely 1:2 above.
[8] First part of the verse missing from **P**.   [9] Lit. "One who did not make festival."
[10] Most manuscripts lack "of the Feast."   [11] Lit. "may feast."   [12] Lit. "one did not feast."
[13] **K, P** have a different grammatical form of the same verb, probably since the form in Scripture does not appear in Mishnaic Hebrew.
[14] **K, P** lack "by her."

many whole burnt offerings and few offerings of well-being since one must finish all the meat and not leave any leftovers (Leviticus 7:17).

"[one] ma'ah of silver": The reference is to the minimum measures mentioned in 1:2 above.

Each shall bring…has given you: Deuteronomy 16:17.

1:6 *Of the Feast*: In rabbinic literature this term usually designates the Festival of *Sukkot*. These words do not appear in the manuscripts.

one is not liable to make restitution: One does not have to bring festal offerings. This lack of obligation also means lack of opportunity: the chance to celebrate is gone.

That which is crooked…cannot be counted: Ecclesiastes 1:15.

1:7 *forbidden relations*: Women with whom one may not have intercourse according to Leviticus 18:6–18.

mamzer : A child born of a forbidden sexual relationship who therefore "may not enter the assembly of the Lord" (Deuteronomy 23:3).

one can make restitution[15]
and make it straight.[16]
R. Simeon b. Yokhai says:
You only call *crooked*
one who was first straight
and afterward became crooked;
and who is this?[17]
A disciple of a Sage[18]
who separated himself from the Torah.

8 The [laws concerning] dissolution of vows fly in the air
and have nothing to lean on.
The laws of the Sabbath, festal offerings, and sacrilege
are as mountains[19] hanging by a strand,
since they are little Scripture and many laws.
[Laws of] civil cases, temple services, purities and impurities, and the forbidden relations
have upon what to lean,
and it is they that are the bodies of the Torah.

[15] Lit. "bring it back." **K, P**: "return."
[16] **K, P** display the same variation as in the preceding question.
[17] **K, P** add: "it is." [18] **K** has "Sages."
[19] The plural form for mountains here is unique in all the Mishnah. **P** differs by one letter; see annotations.

make restitution by bringing back what he has stolen.

1:8 *The [laws concerning] dissolution of vows* by a Sage. It is not clear whether the list in this mishnah refers to existing collections of laws known to the composer or to the actual laws we now have in the Mishnah, or if the list simply names topics. Laws relating to the dissolution of vows can now be found for example in *Nedarim* chapters 9 and 10.

have nothing to lean on: Have no basis in biblical verses. Numbers 30 discusses the annulment of a woman's vows by her father or husband, but the Mishnah here seems to distinguish this from the action of dissolution of vows by a Sage.

The laws of the Sabbath: Exodus 20:7–10, 31:12–17, 35:1–3; Leviticus 23:3; Numbers 15:32–36; Deuteronomy 5:11–14. See also *Shabbat* and *Eruvin*.

festal offerings: These are treated in the current tractate.

sacrilege: See Leviticus 5:14–16 and *Me'ilah*.

mountains hanging by a strand: This is the version in most manuscripts, but this imagery is difficult to understand, and the word used for mountains (pl.) is unparalleled in mishnaic Hebrew. The text in **P** (ḥararim instead of the more widely attested hararim) suggests an image in Jeremiah 17:6, as understood in *Avot* 3:17, to mean a tree with many branches and few roots that the wind can easily uproot. The Mishnah here likens the laws in this list to a plant hanging by a thread, i.e. with few roots, since they are based on little Scripture but are very numerous.

civil cases: Laws relating to civil cases can now be found in the Mishnaic Order of *Neziqin*.

temple services: Laws relating to temple services can now be found in the Mishnaic Order of *Qodashim*.

purities and impurities: Laws relating to purities and impurities can now be found the Mishnaic Order of *Tohorot*.

forbidden relations: Laws relating to forbidden relations can now be found the mishnaic order of Nashim.

bodies of the Torah: The term "body of" in mishnaic Hebrew can mean the principal or essential part; see for example *Horayot* 1:3.

Chapter Two

2 One may not expound the forbidden relations
among three [people],
nor the creation account
among two,
nor the chariot [account]
by oneself
unless one is a sage
and understands[20] with his own intellect.
Anyone who looks into four things:
it were better for him[21]
as if he had not come into the world:
(1) what is upward?
(2) what is downward?
(3) what is forward?
(4) And what is backward?[22]
And anyone who does not spare his creator's[23] honor:
it were better for him[24]
if he had not come into the world.

2:2–3 *The Laying On of Hands*

2 Yose b. Yoezer says:
One may not perform the laying on of hands.[25]

---

[20] K: "understood."
[21] K, P, here and at the end of the mishnah, have a word that differs by one letter which may mean either "better" or "pity" or "mercy," as in: "it would have been a mercy to him not to have been born."
[22] See annotations.
[23] The word can also mean "master."   [24] K, P add here "as if."
[25] Lit. "says not to lay on…says to lay on," and so throughout.

2:1 *may not expound*: The Hebrew *darash* (whence "midrash") generally refers to the exposition of Scripture. Inquiry into the meaning of these biblical passages is restricted.

forbidden relations: See Leviticus 18:6–18.

creation account: Genesis chapters 1 and 2.

chariot account: Ezekiel chapter 1.

oneself: The Mishnah is setting the maximum size of the group (Tosefta): the *chariot account* may only be studied alone and by select people. Alternatively, the concern is the size of the audience to whom the master expounds (Babylonian Talmud), but the disciple must be appropriate.

upward…downward…forward…backward: A formula signifying the intellectual search in all places. The translation "forward" and "backward" keeps all four adverbs as describing space, but some have understood the last two adverbs as describing time: "beforetime" and "hereafter."

2:2 *the laying of hands* on a beast that is to be sacrificed (see Leviticus 1:4; 3:2 etc.). In this case it is the laying of hands on festal and pilgrimage offerings that is being debated. The laying of the hands, because it involves

Yose b. Yohanan[26] says:
One may.
Joshua b. Perakhiah says:
One may not;
Nittai[27] of Arbela says:
One may.
Judah b. Tabbai says:
One may not;
Simeon b. Shetakh says:
One may.
Shemaiah says:
One may;
Avtalyon says:
One may not.
Hillel and Menahem did not disagree.
Menahem exited,
Shammai entered.
Shammai says:
One may not;
Hillel says:
One may.[28]
The former [of each pair] were Presiding Officers
and the latter [of each pair] Heads of the Court.

3 The House of Shammai say:
One may bring offerings of well-being
and not perform the laying on of hands,
but not whole burnt offerings.
The House of Hillel say:
One may bring both offerings of well-being and whole burnt offerings
and perform the laying on of hands.

---

[26] A Genizah fragment as well as a few Talmudic variants of this mishnah add here: "man of Jerusalem."
[27] K, P, L, and other witnesses have "Mattai," here and in *Avot* 1:6.
[28] K, P, L, and almost all other witnesses have the order reversed: "Hillel says one may…Shammai says one may not."

---

leaning, is considered making use of an animal, hence forbidden on the Sabbath. While the Mishnah argues in a few places that all laws apply equally for the Sabbath and festival days (excluding the preparing of one's food, see *Megillah* 1:5 and *Betsah* 5:2), in this case the laying of hands on the festival is debated.

Menahem exited: The Talmudim offer a few traditions according to which Menahem left to be employed in the king's service, or went into evil ways. Josephus reports that a certain Menahem was an Essene and had a close relationship with King Herod (*Antiquities* 15, 10:5).

2:3 This mishnah also appears in *Betsah* 2:4.

One may bring offerings of well-being on the festival day, since they supplied meat for the festival feast.

not perform the laying of hands on the festival day, but rather on the eve of the festival.

but not whole burnt offerings which were wholly consumed on the altar.

One may bring both offerings of well-being and whole burnt offerings: Since they are part of the festival offerings they can all be brought during the festival.

2:4 The Day of Slaughter after the Festival of Weeks

4 When the Festival of Weeks coincides with the Eve of the Sabbath,
the House of Shammai say:
The day for slaughter [should be] after the Sabbath.
The House of Hillel say:
There is no day for slaughter after the Sabbath.[29]
But they concede
that if it coincides with the Sabbath,
that the day for slaughter
[should be] after the Sabbath.
The high priest should not put on his garments,
and mourning and fasting are permitted,
so as not to uphold the words of those who say
the Festival of Weeks follows the Sabbath.

2:5–7 Degrees of Purity

5 One must wash one's hands
for unconsecrated food, tithe, and *terumah*;

---

[29] K, P, L, and other witnesses lack "after the Sabbath."

2:4 *Eve of the Sabbath*: Friday during the day.

The day for slaughter: The day on which the pilgrimage offerings can be slaughtered in celebration of the feast. The text now resumes the topic of 1:6 above; making up for not having offered the pilgrimage offerings on the first day. During the Festival of Sukkot and Passover there are several days of festival when this can be done, but the Festival of Weeks lasts only one day.

[should be] after the Sabbath: On Sunday, since whole burnt offerings according to the house of Shammai are offered neither on the Festival day nor on the Sabbath.

There is no day for slaughter after the Sabbath: According to the house of Hillel, whole burnt offerings can be made on the Festival day, so there is no need for a make-up day afterwards.

[should be] after the Sabbath: They both agree that whole burnt offerings are not made on the Sabbath.

The high priest … are permitted: On the day of slaughter that occurs on a Sunday, to make it clear it is not a festival day.

his garments: The high priest's eight special garments, see Exodus 28 and *Yoma* 7:5.

those who say the Festival of Weeks follows the Sabbath: According to Leviticus 23:11, 15, one counts fifty days starting "from the day after the Sabbath" to reach the Festival of Weeks. Different sources (e.g. *Menahot* 10:3) preserve echoes of a Second Temple era dispute on the interpretation of the word "Sabbath." Later rabbinic sources follow the view that "the day after the Sabbath" is the day after the first festival day of Passover, while others (identified as Sadducees or Boethusians) understand "the day after the Sabbath" to mean Sunday, and in particular, the first Sunday after Passover. According to this latter view, the Festival of Weeks will always occur on the very Sunday of which the Mishnah here speaks, and precautions are therefore prescribed to clarify that this Sunday is not celebrated as a festival. Scholars debate whether this sectarian dispute affected historical practice or remained a matter for exegetes.

2:5 *One must wash* before eating the indicated categories of food, according to the Babylonian Talmud. The Palestinian Talmud interprets this rule to refer to touching rather than eating.

tithe: Second tithe; see *Ma'aser Sheni*.

one must immerse them
for consecrated food;
and as for purgation,
if one's hands are impure
his body is impure.

6 One who immerses for [the purpose of eating] unconsecrated produce,
and is presumed fit[30] [to eat] unconsecrated food,
is prohibited from [eating] tithe.
One who immersed[31] for tithe,
and is presumed fit for tithe,
is prohibited from *terumah*.
One who immersed for *terumah*,
and is presumed fit for *terumah*,
is prohibited from consecrated food.
One who immersed for consecrated food,
and is presumed fit for consecrated food,
is prohibited from purgation.
One who immersed for the more stringent
is permitted[32] for the less stringent.
One who immersed
but was not presumed fit,
it is as if he did not immerse.

7 The garments of an *am ha'arets*
convey *midras* impurity for *Perushim*.
The garments of *Perushim*

[30] See annotations.
[31] K, P have the participle in all the verbs—"immerses" rather than the past tense "immersed."
[32] K, P: "became permitted."

one must immerse in a full immersion pool containing forty *se'ah* of undrawn water; see *Miqva'ot*.

purgation: Here and throughout this chapter this term designates preparation or use of the water needed to remove corpse impurity (Numbers 19; see *Parah*).

his body is impure and requires a full-body immersion.

2:6 *presumed fit*: Commentators, following the Talmudim, have understood this to mean that one's intentions during the immersion were directed at a certain level of purity, but this seems merely to repeat the first condition—"immersion for the purpose of…." Therefore, as in other occurrences of this verb in mishnaic Hebrew, the reference seems to be to one who is considered by others to maintain a certain level of purity.

tithe: Second tithe.

2:7 *midras impurity*: An impurity similar to that of objects with which a *zav* came into contact by sitting, lying, standing, or leaning on them (Leviticus 15:1–15, *Zavim* chapter 5). The garments of each group mentioned are understood to convey this impurity to members of more rigorous groups via direct contact.

Perushim: Lit. "those who separate themselves." In this context it is clear they contrast with the *am ha'arets*. In other rabbinic sources it is usually the *Haver* or "Fellow" (*Demai* 2:3) who separates himself from the *am ha'arets* in order to eat unconsecrated food in purity. The epithet is used elsewhere in rabbinic literature to signify members of the Pharisaic sect, in contrast with members of the Saducean sect, but it is debatable whether the epithet signifies a sectarian group in this context.

convey *midras* impurity for eaters of *terumah*.
The garments of eaters of *terumah*
convey *midras* impurity for consecrated food.
The garments of [eaters of]³³ consecrated food
convey *midras* impurity for purgation.³⁴
Joseph³⁵ b. Yo'ezer was a *Hasid* among the priesthood
and yet his apron conveyed *midras* impurity for consecrated food.
Yohanan b. Gudgada used to eat
in accordance with the purity of consecrated food all his days,
and yet his apron conveyed *midras* impurity for purgation.

Chapter Three

3:1–3 *Consecrated Food Is a More Stringent Case Than Terumah*

3 Greater stringency applies to consecrated food than to *terumah*,³⁶
for one may immerse utensils within utensils for *terumah*
but not for consecrated food,
the exterior and interior [sections of utensils]
and the area by which they are held
[are considered distinct] for *terumah*
but not for consecrated food;

---

[33] The bracketed word is missing in most witnesses but does appear in a marginal note in **K**.
[34] This entire line is missing in **P** and in **K** is only added in the margin.   [35] **K, P:** "Yose."
[36] **K** has a marginal note adding: "and greater stringency [applies to] *terumah* than to consecrated food; greater stringency [applies to] consecrated food than to *terumah*."

---

eaters of terumah: Priests and members of their household.

for consecrated food: That is, those who may eat consecrated food.

Hasid: Lit. "pious." Joseph was the most pious among the priesthood. Elsewhere the term can mean a person belonging to a certain faction (*Berakhot* 5:1; *Sukkah* 5:4).

apron: A piece of cloth or leather tied from the waist and hanging on the front of one's clothes. It is mentioned in rabbinic literature as being used to wrap food, among other objects.

3:1 *utensils* that are impure.

but not for consecrated food: Utensils to be used for consecrated produce must be immersed separately.

the exterior…held: If one of these parts becomes impure it does not affect any other part of the utensil. See also *Kelim* 25:7, 9.

but not for consecrated food: In this case, if one of these parts becomes impure the whole utensil is considered impure.

one who carries an object that is *midras* impure[37]
may [also] carry *terumah*
but not consecrated food;
the garments of eaters of *terumah*
convey *midras* impurity for consecrated food.
The rule[38] for consecrated food
is not the same as the rule for *terumah*,
since in the case of consecrated food
one should untie [the knot of a utensil],
dry [it],
immerse,
and after that [re]tie it,
but in the case of *terumah* one [may first] tie [the knot]
and then immerse.

2 Utensils that have been completed in purity
require immersion for consecrated food
but not for *terumah*.
A utensil unites all its contents
in the case of consecrated food,
but not in the case of *terumah*.
Consecrated food can become invalid
at the fourth remove,

---

[37] Lit. "One who carries a *midras*."   [38] Lit. "measure of."

---

an object that is midras impure: An object with which a *zav* came into direct contact.

may [also] carry terumah at the same time (while not actually touching the *terumah*).

the garments of…for consecrated food: See above, 2:7.

untie [the knot of a utensil] that is about to be immersed.

dry [it]: The place of the (now open) knot.

[re]tie it only after the immersion, so that the knot does not interfere with complete immersion of the utensil.

one [may first] tie [the knot]: In the case of *terumah* there is no such concern for complete immersion, so one may immerse the utensil with the knot intact.

3:2 *have been completed in purity*: Utensils protected from defilement since their completion, the moment from which defilement becomes possible.

A utensil unites all its contents: If there are noncontiguous portions of consecrated food in a utensil, and one becomes impure, all of the food in the utensil becomes impure as well.

but not in the case of terumah: Where portions that were not in contact with the impure portions are still considered pure.

at the fourth remove: The Mishnah defines certain objects, such as dead creeping things or semen as "primary sources of impurity" (*Kelim* 1:1). When these objects come into contact with other objects, the latter become "derived sources of impurity," with a lesser degree of impurity. Thus an object touched by a "primary source of impurity" becomes a "first," which can in turn make a "second," which can in turn make a "third." If the third is *terumah* it is considered invalid; it is impure but cannot make another object impure (as a "fourth"). However, if the third is consecrated food, it can still make a "fourth," though the "fourth" cannot make a "fifth."

but *terumah*
only at the third remove.
In the case of *terumah*,
if one of one's hands becomes impure
the other remains pure,
but in the case of consecrated food
one should immerse both hands,
for[39] one hand renders the other impure
in the case of consecrated food
but not in the case of *terumah*.

3 One may eat dry foodstuff with unclean[40] hands
in the case of *terumah*
but not in the case of consecrated food.
The *onen* and one whose atonement is incomplete
require immersion in the case of consecrated food
but not in the case of *terumah*.

3:4–8   *Laws concerning Trustworthiness of an Am Ha'arets*

4 Greater stringency applies to *terumah*:
for in Judaea [all] are considered trustworthy
concerning the purity of wine and oil
all days of the year,
and during the season of wine and oil presses
even concerning *terumah*.

[39] K, P, L: "and."   [40] Lit. "dirty."

the other hand *remains pure* and can be used to touch *terumah*.

for one hand renders the other impure: See *Yadayim* 3:2. According to the manuscripts, which have "and" rather than "for," this sentence is not an explanation for why one should immerse both hands, but rather an additional difference between consecrated produce and *terumah*.

3:3 *dry foodstuff* that, not having come into contact with water, is not susceptible to impurity.

unclean hands: Impure.

onen: A mourner, whose dead is not yet buried, and who has not become corpse impure.

one whose atonement is incomplete such as a woman who had given birth, or a man with an abnormal sexual discharge (*Keritot* 2:1) whose purification process is not yet complete, because they must still bring sacrifices the next day.

require immersion in the case of consecrated food but not in the case of terumah: These liminal cases allow for eating *terumah* but not consecrated food, which requires immersion first.

3:4 *the purity of wine and oil*: Consecrated wine and oil.

during the season of wine and oil presses: During this time, all are considered trustworthy to purify their utensils for the purpose of setting aside consecrated foodstuffs, and therefore *even concerning terumah*, but not during the rest of the year.

If the season of wine and oil presses has passed
and they brought [the priest] a jar of *terumah* wine,
he may not accept it of him,
but [the owner] may set it aside
until the next [season of] winepress.
And if he said to him
"I have put inside[41] it
a quarter[-log] of consecrated [wine],"
he is [considered] trustworthy.
They are [considered] trustworthy
concerning jars of wine and jars of oil
that are intended for the use of *terumah*[42]
during the season of wine and oil presses,
and seventy days before [the season of] winepresses.
  5 From Modi'it and inward
they are [considered] trustworthy
in the case of earthenware utensils;
from Modi'it outward
they are not considered trustworthy.
How?[43]
The potter who sells the pots—
if he entered inward of Modi'it,
the very same potter, and the very same pots, and the very same buyers,
are [considered] trustworthy.
If he left,

---

[41] Lit. "set apart therein." [42] Translation uncertain. See annotations.
[43] Certain witnesses to **BT** lack this one-word question.

---

they brought [to the priest]: An *am ha'arets* brought to the priest, who eats his *terumah* in purity.

he may not accept it of him since he is no longer considered trustworthy, but the *am ha'arets* can retain this very same jar until the next winepress season, when he is again considered trustworthy.

I have put inside it a quarter[-log] of consecrated [wine]: If one puts consecrated foodstuffs, concerning which one is considered trustworthy all year long, inside the jar, he is considered trustworthy over the entire jar, including the *terumah*. A *log* is a measurement equal to six eggs.

They are [considered] trustworthy: The *am ha'arets*.

intended for the use of terumah: This translation takes the sentence to be dealing with empty jars intended to store *terumah*, but the same Hebrew word can also refer to a mixture of common produce with either consecrated produce or *terumah*. These different possibilities can already be seen in differences between the Talmuds.

seventy days before [the season of] winepresses: the time period in which the jars are being prepared for storage of *terumah*.

3:5 *Modi'it*: Possibly Modi'in, a city northwest of Jerusalem (*Pesahim* 9:2).

and inward: Toward Jerusalem.

they are [considered] trustworthy: Potters who have the status of *am ha'arets*.

the very same…: The only factor that determines his trustworthiness is the geographical location: inward or outward of Modi'it.

If he left: Went outward.

he is not [considered] trustworthy.

6 [Tax] collectors who entered the house,
and likewise thieves who returned [stolen] utensils,
are [considered] trustworthy when they say "we did not touch."
And in Jerusalem
they are [considered] trustworthy
concerning consecrated food
and during the pilgrimage even concerning *terumah*.

7 One who opened his jar [of wine],
or one who started his dough
due to the pilgrimage,
R. Judah says:
He may finish,
but the Sages say:
He may not finish.
As soon as the pilgrimage was over
they used to disregard[44] the purity of the Temple Court.
If the pilgrimage ended on a Friday,[45]

---

[44] Translation obscure; see annotations.
[45] K, P have "Thursday," but K was corrected to "Friday."

3:6 *[Tax] collectors…and likewise thieves…* But compare *Tohorot* 7:6.

we did not touch utensils and make them impure.

they though they have the status of *am ha'arets*.

3:7 *One who opened his jar…started his dough* to sell them during the festival. During this period even an *am ha'arets* was considered trustworthy to preserve the purity of the merchandise.

R. Judah says: He may finish selling the remainder of the jar's contents or the dough, even to those who do not eat food touched by an *am ha'arets*. The wine and dough may be considered pure even after the festival has passed.

the Sages say: He may not finish selling the remainder after the festival has passed. One now returns to the presumption that contact with an *am ha'arets* during the festival may have retroactively rendered the wine and dough impure.

they used to disregard the purity of the Temple Court: The term so translated was understood by some to refer to a public announcement, or to removal of the temple utensils. But in light of other occurrences of the verb in mishnaic Hebrew, the verb seems to indicate "disregard" or "override." That is, we disregard the assumed purity of the Temple Court according to the more lenient standard of the festival, and a return to the regular, more stringent, standard of purity.

If the pilgrimage ended on a Friday: When the last day of the festival was Thursday, the purity of the Temple Court was presumed on Friday as well, so as not to disturb preparations for the Sabbath. R. Judah maintains that even if the festival had ended on Wednesday the purity of the Temple Court was still maintained on the day after the festival, in this case Thursday, since the priests were too preoccupied (e.g. with clearing the altar of ashes, per the Bavli) to engage in clearing out the courts.

they did not disregard,
on account of the honor of the Sabbath.
R. Judah says:
Not even on a Thursday
since the priests are not available.

8 How should one disregard the purity of the Temple Court?
One immerses the utensils that were in the Temple,
while saying to them
"Beware not[46] to touch the table and the lampstand[47]
and render it impure."[48]
All utensils that were in the Temple
have[49] second and third [replacements]:
so if the first [set of utensils] became impure,
they might bring a second set in their stead.
All utensils in the temple require immersion,
except the gold altar and the bronze altar
since they are as ground—
the words of R. Eliezer.
The Sages say:
Because they are coated.

[46] K, P have "lest" instead of "not."
[47] The Mishnah of the **BT** does not have the words "and the lampstand."
[48] K, P lack "and render it impure."   [49] K, P: "used to have."

3:8 *How should one disregard the* previously assumed *purity of the Temple Court?*

while saying to them "Beware not to touch...": Some have taken the addressees of this warning to be ignorant priests who could have rendered the table impure during the festival. Alternatively, the table was brought outside to be shown to the people, who were warned not to render it impure (a problematic historical hypothesis). Most likely, however, the warning is addressed to the priests who were immersing the impure utensils. They are told to be careful not to touch the table and lampstand with those utensils, lest they be defiled by those utensils.

the table of showbread (Exodus 25:23-30). The bread rested continually on it, hence the emphasis on the need to be careful not to render the table impure.

the lampstand: Exodus 25: 31-40.

require immersion: After the festival or if they ever become impure at some other time.

the gold altar: Exodus 30:1-10.

the bronze altar: Exodus 27:1-8.

are as ground: And therefore not susceptible to impurity.

Because they are coated: With gold and bronze, and the coating does not become impure (*Kelim* 11:4, 6).